# THE NOVEL:
# A BIOGRAPHY

# THE NOVEL:
# A BIOGRAPHY

MICHAEL SCHMIDT

The Belknap Press of Harvard University Press

*Cambridge, Massachusetts, and London, England*

*2014*

Library of Congress Cataloging-in-Publication Data

Schmidt, Michael, 1947–
    The novel : a biography / Michael Schmidt.
        pages   cm
    Includes index.
    ISBN 978-0-674-72473-0 (alk. paper)
    1. Fiction—History and criticism.   I.  Title.
    PN3491.S36    2014
    809.3—dc23
                                                2013026938

For John Coyle, John Kerrigan, and David Ward,
gratefully; and for Angel García-Gómez

# ACKNOWLEDGMENTS

I am grateful to the Institute for Advanced Study in Princeton, New Jersey, for hospitality during the writing of this book, and to St. John's College, Cambridge, which hosted me as a fellow commoner and later as a Writer in Residence. Much of *The Novel: A Biography* was written while I was teaching at Manchester Metropolitan University and the University of Glasgow, where I owe students and colleagues thanks. I am especially grateful to Evelyn Schlag, for many years my first reader, who followed the book chapter by chapter; to the poet Gerry McGrath, who offered insights and patiently and severely helped me cut it back from 660,000 words to its current extent; and to my agent, Maggie McKernan, who restored my belief in the project in 2008; and to my editor, John Kulka, who sharpened its focus and suggested crucial excisions and additions. I am also grateful to Paul Abbott, Iain Bamforth, Andrew Biswell, Amy Burns, Dan Burt, John Coyle, Matthew Frost, Chris Gair, Kate Gavron, Katie Grant, Mary Griffiths, Stella Halkyard, Sophie Hannah, Edward Hirsch, Evan Jones, Stuart Kelly, John Kinsella, Nigel Leask, Christopher Maclehose, Micaela Maftei, Robyn Marsack, Cameron Maynard, Joan McAllister, John McAuliffe, Kei Miller, Sinéad Morrissey, Eric Percak, Frederic Raphael, Charles Schmidt, Alan Trotter, Jeffrey Wainwright, and David Ward for suggestions and encouragement along the way. I would also like to record my thanks for the editorial overview of Maria Ascher, Kimberly Giambattisto, and Wendy Nelson.

This book has been informed by discussions stemming from articles, editorials, and lectures I have given, and in a few places touches on my *Lives of the Poets* (1999).

# CONTENTS

# THE NOVEL:
# A BIOGRAPHY

# Prologue

Ford Madox Ford chose as his guide through the vast, haunted house of fiction not critics, experts, or theorists but "artist-practitioners." He describes them as "men and women who love their arts as they practice them." These people feel "hot love" for the books they advocate, unlike what Cyril Connolly in *Enemies of Promise* describes as "literary die-hards, old cats that sit purring over the mouse-holes of talent in wait for what comes out." The forms their advocacy takes also illuminate their own lives and times.

Martin Amis in this respect is of Ford's party, going with what he calls "artist-critics," whose "authority has never seemed more natural and welcome" than today. They are like members of an eccentric family in an ancestral mansion— *Bleak House,* say, with its looming portraits on the stairs. Each makes a different kind of accommodation (in both senses) with the heavy furniture, the figured carpets, the china, crystal, and silver, the spoils. Some are full of respect, some reserved, others bend double with laughter; the rebellious and impatient slash the canvases, twist the cutlery, raise a toast, and throw the crystal in the grate. Their damage is another chapter in the story.

The most penetrating insights into Cervantes are those of Fielding, Smollett, and Sterne, of Stendhal and Flaubert and Turgenev, Dickens and Faulkner and Hunter S. Thompson: not only what they say about *Don Quixote,* but how they incorporate the sad knight and his sidekick into their own imaginations. This buffeted figure of chivalry, his ideals resisted or thrown back in his teeth, inspired women writers, too, the American Talitha Gilman Tenney, who wrote *Female Quixotism: Exhibited in the Romantic Opinions and Extravagant Adventures of Dorcasina Sheldon* in 1801. Half a century before, Charlotte Lennox, who spent several years in America, published *The Female Quixote* (1751). In 1983 the Finnish novelist Leena Krohn published *Doña Quixote,* a contemporary refiguring of the types and tensions of the original.

This book, *The Novel: A Biography,* is told mainly by novelists and through novels. Virginia Woolf reminds us that "to go from one great novelist to another— from Jane Austen to Hardy, from Peacock to Trollope, from Scott to Meredith— is to be wrenched and uprooted; to be thrown this way and then that." Pleasure is to be had, but stamina and creative effort are required: "To read a novel is a difficult and complex art. You must be capable not only of great fineness of perception, but of great boldness of imagination if you are going to make use of all that the novelist—the great artist—gives you." Between the lofty trunks of the great novels and novelists is the lower growth of the good and not so good, a forest that feeds and sustains; and among that lesser vegetation there is much that rewards attention.

In this book, the aspects of novelists' lives that matter are those that cast light on their work and on that of other writers. What tips a novelist into writing? How does she or he take root in that forest at all? "The Childhoods of writers are thought to have something to do with their vocations," says Margaret Atwood. What these different childhoods tend to have in common is "books and solitude."

A sense of canon, though not a stable one, governs my approach. It allows me some anachronisms, when modern writers are read in a historical context, especially when their own age misvalued their work. In its first half this book follows an approximate timeline. After that there are too many geographies, too many genres and genealogies, complex, overlapping, to maintain chronology. But because the novelists are themselves the narrators and critics, by the time we do reach the chapter including Scott, for example, or James or Cather or Woolf or Martin Amis, they are already familiar companions.

Some theorists reject the idea of canons as repressive constructs. The emancipation they propose can lead to a much narrower place than the one from which it delivers us. It makes dialogue hard, depriving us of agreed-upon terms and points of formal reference. This book proposes a canon that expands and is never stable or closed, its very instability precluding the idea of "evolution" that bedevils conventional canonical commentary. Development is not invariably progressive, assimilative, or linear. And the novel form is not singular, even in its earliest stages. Its manifestations alter in relation to language, histories, and geography.

In writing what sets out to be a brief life of the novel in English, it makes sense as in any biography to concentrate on things that shape, distort, and reconfigure it. What are its origins? What made the novel, after its severely moral beginnings, so promiscuous? We pass lightly over longueurs that can last for decades. Then it sets out on new adventures. It has been declared dead more than once, so we attend its funerals and chronicle its afterlives.

There is for this *Biography* as for novels themselves the problem of beginning. I start in earnest with Sir John Mandeville, the first invented English narrator (even though his book was written in French). Some centuries later, there is the problem of ending. A line was drawn at 2000 A.D. Some younger novelists who straddle the millennium are included, tentatively. Others are present as readers. Writers like Jonathan Lethem (b. 1964) proved especially troublesome. I love his *aperçus,* his enthusiastic contrariness. "The reason postmodernism doesn't die," he writes, "is that postmodernism isn't the figure in the black hat standing out in the street squaring off against the earnest and law-abiding 'realist' novel . . . postmodernism is the street." His boyish engagement with he-man Norman Mailer remains illuminating comedy. But in this book his novels are the future.

He had something like the same experience himself, as a young man. When he got to Bennington College in Vermont, that veritable factory of modern literature, he recalls, "I found that Richard Brautigan and Thomas Berger and Kurt Vonnegut and Donald Barthelme were not 'the contemporary,' but were in fact awkward and embarrassing and had been overthrown by something else." What a change was here: "No one read Henry Miller and Lawrence Durrell, the Beats were regarded with embarrassment. When all that was swept away, I stopped knowing what contemporary literature was. I didn't replace it; I just stopped knowing."

With the twenty-first century ticking in my ear, I stopped.

The organization of the chapters in the second half of this book is hard to explain from the outside, as it were. The writers came together in configurations that seemed to me expressive: there was a dialogue between them or their works. Salman Rushdie and Anita Desai have more to say to Michael Ondaatje and Margaret Atwood, for example, and to Peter Carey and David Malouf, than they do to R. K. Narayan and Mulk Raj Anand. More conventional dialogues might have been pursued. But I tried to avoid, where it made sense to do so, the kinds of ordering that insist on geographical, ideological, cultural, or sexual zoning. Other things can prove more interesting to the writers, and to readers. One might have combined Chapters 23 and 27, or 27 and 29, 37, 38 and 43. The modern core of the book runs insistently from Chapters 30 through 36. Even there the succession and juxtaposition of modernists, their beneficiaries and detractors, in an academic account might have taken other forms.

I set out to write this book without an overarching theory of the novel. I had no point to prove. I read in a spirit of committed curiosity, the spirit of essay in the old sense of the term, exploratory, not demonstrating and proving something I already knew. I did have an instinct: that the relationships between novels, and between writers, would illuminate the properties and values of this diverse literary form, in which English-language writers in different ages and societies have excelled. If a theory were to emerge, it would be that the achieved novel belongs to an unsubornable family, that whatever use a novel is put to in its own age, it survives not because of its themes or its intentions but because of something else, to do with form, language, invention, and an enduring resistance to cliché, an irreducible *quality*. A *something*.

# Introduction

"It is all true. A French student, his name was Gastoscha . . . with a trim black goatee, with patent leather shoes . . . Let lightning strike me if it isn't true! How he loved me . . . Oh, how he did love me." In Maxim Gorky's 1902 play *The Lower Depths,* Nastiah is always reading. Threadbare, hungry, twenty-four, her nose (red and running) buried in a romance, she carries a mop, she heats the frugal meal. She tends the samovar, and she is used and abused. The baron fallen on hard times lives in her "like a maggot in an apple." "Some apple!" says the Baron. Nastiah believes what she reads, reciting love scenes, disappointments and suicides, lamenting the well-heeled heartbreaks of fiction.

No wonder the Reverend Oliver Goldsmith instructed his brother that his young nephew "never touch a romance or a novel; these paint beauty in colors more charming than nature; and describe happiness that man never tastes. How delusive, how destructive are those pictures of consummate bliss." Many readers live in an expectation of love and passion learned from books and mis-value "the little good which fortune has mixed in our cup, by expecting more than she ever gave." It is a truth universally acknowledged, even in novels themselves. Consider Don Quixote, a prototype for Catherine Morland, Julian Sorel, Lucien de Rubempré, Madame Bovary, Dorian Gray. He proves Goldsmith's point. Why should it be so?

"The novel was born in Christendom," John Updike reminds us, "and the possibilities of good and evil, heroism and villainy are crucial to it." Evil and villainy are multiple, dramatic: so many more bad than good motives and deeds occur to the imagination. "Without souls to save, are mundane lives worth writing about?" asks Updike.

Early in the lives of most readers there is a period in which stories possess an enchanting *presence.* "When we are young," says the Argentinean writer Alberto Manguel with a sleight of tense, "stories never seemed to conclude on the book's last page." Innocent reading is an instinct we never entirely lose. From an early age we surrender to stories and resent interruptions even for meals and bedtime; we recline in improbable positions for hours without getting cramps. Willa Cather says: "We have all known the time when Porthos, Athos and d'Artagnan were vastly more real and important to us than the folks who lived next door." Growing up, "we have all dwelt in that country where Anna Karenina and the Levins were the only people who mattered much." The Scottish writer and collector of folktales Andrew Lang writes to an Eton schoolboy in the late 1880s, reliving his own reading history, "But you have read [Haggard's] *She,* and you have read all Cooper's, and Marryat's, and Mr. Stevenson's books, and *Tom Sawyer,* and *Huckleberry Finn,* several times. So have I, and am quite ready to begin again. But, to my mind, books about 'Red Indians' have always seemed much the most interesting."

Among my contemporaries, as soon as we finished one book by Franklin W. Dixon, the pseudonymous author of the Hardy Boys series, or Lucy Maud Montgomery, who wrote *Anne of Green Gables* and other books for girls, or C. S. Forester (see Chapter 9), H. Rider Haggard (see chapter 22), or Arthur Ransome of the Swallows and Amazons series, we pestered our parents for another: we wanted to stay in those adventures with their smells, colors, and voices, the stories with more shape and purpose than our own experience, and we didn't want a book to end even as we rushed to the climax. Edgar Allan Poe: "How fondly do we recur, in memory, to those enchanted days of our boyhood when we first learned to grow serious over Robinson Crusoe!—when we first found the spirit of wild adventure enkindling within us, as, by the dim fire light, we labored out, line by line, the marvellous import of those pages, and hung breathless and trembling with eagerness over their absorbing—over their enchaining interest!"

"'Welcome, white men from the stars,' he said; '. . . Kisses and the tender words of women are sweet, but the sound of the clashing of men's spears, and the smell of men's blood, are sweeter far! Would ye have wives from among our people, white men? If so, choose the fairest here, and ye shall have them, as many as ye will'; and he paused for an answer." We hold our breath for the reply. Such voices clear a space for an insufficiently ironic grown-up as they did for the child, despite posturings that are no greater than those we encounter, as children or adults, in the turmoil of J. R. R. Tolkien's *The Lord of the Rings* with its bizarre names and creatures. C. S. Lewis's loose Narnia sequence, Terry Pratchett's infectious Discworld fantasies, the nostalgic world of J. K. Rowling's Harry Potter series, in debt to T. H. White's *The Once and Future King,* are all palpably anxious about growing up. Philip Pullman's resourceful, synthetic *Dark Materials* has its own varieties of suspense.

Until my brother and I were eleven or twelve, each night at bedtime my parents took it in turns to read to us. I grew up in Mexico, and every few months a brown parcel tied up with string arrived from a bookshop in London called Foyle's. (Doris Lessing remembered a similar experience, growing up in Southern Rhodesia. Her mother with difficulty ordered the books. "The parcels came back by boat and then up by train. These parcels were the great joy of my childhood.") My father ordered books he had loved as a boy, in particular those of

G. A. (George Alfred) Henty (1832–1902). Henty, a journalist like Kipling, was with the British army in the Crimea, a witness to Garibaldi's struggle in Italy, to the effects of the Franco-Prussian war in Paris; he was in Spain with the Carlists, and he was present when the Suez Canal was declared open. As a member of the Prince of Wales's party he toured India, and he visited the California gold fields. He outlived Queen Victoria by a year. He was a spellbinding storyteller, dictating his later books (there are said to be 144 books in total) to a secretary as he paced back and forth, his abundant white beard pressed into his chest.

At the heart of his best books is an unexceptional boy who gets mixed up in momentous events that test him. Henty teaches sound, conservative history, drawing battle scenes, places, and events. He does not question Christian or imperial values. He is today a book collector's enthusiasm. Early bindings are bright, embossed, gilded, each book aspiring to the condition of furnishing. Once read, it remains decorative.

*In the Reign of Terror: The Adventures of a Westminster Boy* (1888) Henty prefaced with a letter to "My Dear Lads": "My object has been rather to tell you a tale of interest than to impart historical knowledge, for the facts of the dreadful time when 'the terror' reigned supreme in France are well known to all educated lads." He promises his account is factually correct "except that the Noyades at Nantes did not take place until a somewhat later period than is here assigned to them." After this caution, we plunge in. The book was published first in the United States and a year later in Britain: by the end of the nineteenth century the American market was calling the shots.

*In the Reign of Terror* does what many novels do. It is not *just* fiction but lays claim to broad historical accuracy. It foregrounds an everyboy figure and addresses a specific readership. The social class of the author and of his target reader are aspects of design, production, and marketing. It was tailored to a market, and it achieved its goal at home and abroad. Dorothy L. Sayers's languorous detective Lord Peter Wimsey declares he "never read much except Henty and Fenimore Cooper at school." He was not alone. In 1900 the *Library Journal* said that when boys discovered Henty, they lost interest in all other authors.

A novel is a kind of rabbit hole. It led Gorky's Nastiah into all-absorbing emotion, the Victorian schoolboy into adventure, and a young Mexican into an imaginary, heroic Europe. Novel reading begins in a paradoxical double action of escape and engagement; reading conventional novels takes readers from where they are to realms that are shaped, with beginnings, middles, and ends. Taste changes over time: Our developing habit requires increasingly subtle stimuli and satisfactions—a hunger for experience trans*formed,* that transformation being the writer's aim. Climaxes, epiphanies, metamorphoses are in the nature of storytelling, from fairy tale and ballad to *Finnegans Wake*.

———•———

"There is nothing more disenchanting to man," Robert Louis Stevenson says, "than to be shown the springs and mechanism of an art." Once we know where and how the magic happens, chances are we will not return to a book, not before time changes us and the demands we make are different from those of a first-time reader. Readers grow, and authors like Jane Austen and Charles Dickens grow with them. We used to measure ourselves against Dickens, moving on from Scrooge, Pip, and Mr. Pickwick through *Bleak House* and the more complex novels: the first books grow in complexity and suggestion. We seldom experience in adult reading, so jaded, so exacting do we become, the exhilaration of early encounters, how they dissolved time and space and we emerged reluctantly as from a dream. A few novels ask to be re-read and become living parts of memory that affect how we hear, speak, see, feel, and act. Those novels and their authors are this book's quarry, and those that provide sources and contexts for them, or that imitate and cannibalize them.

Every novelist has a culture that shapes the imagination. A personal chronology describes the order of a novelist's own reading—Kipling before Defoe, Emily Brontë before Jane Austen, Faulkner before Cervantes. That chronology maps the order of a writer's acquisition of resources and formal understanding, what was chanced upon and what was urgently sought out. Also, what gaps exist. Canon, on the other hand, entails the historical order of publication of the principal works. It is in that respect objective, with authors, titles, and dates of publication, histories of reception, the fever charts of sales marking success and failure over time. Jonathan Franzen reminds us that the writer's relationship with this objective canon is mysterious. "When I write, I don't feel like a craftsman influenced by earlier craftsmen who were themselves influenced by earlier craftsmen. I feel like a member of a single, large virtual community in which I have dynamic relationships with other members of the community, most of whom are no longer living."

Without a sense of this community, readers too lose their bearings: the "new" is everywhere, there is little pressure to hear antecedents, the works out of which the new arises. If we miss the play of echoes on which many powerful effects of fiction depend, we lose essential qualities in the novel itself. Dickens was steeped in the King James Bible, and phrases, images, and cadences call to memory pertinent scriptural passages. If we do not hear them, we miss part of the meaning, whether an irony or a resonance. Melville's *Moby-Dick* can hardly be *read* without a sense of the Bible, and a vital memory of Shakespeare, who informs the rhythm of the prose. Critics speak of intertextuality, the harmonies and dissonances that exist between books and passages. Joyce's *Ulysses* is enriched and more accessible for readers who know the *Odyssey* and are not entirely unfamiliar with English prose from Middle English to Bloomsday, June 16, 1904. In a more obvious sense, it is hard to understand Jean Rhys's *The Wide Sargasso Sea* without a knowledge of Charlotte Brontë's *Jane Eyre,* Julian Barnes's *Flaubert's Parrot* without *Madame Bovary* and the story "A Simple Heart," or J. M. Coetzee's *Foe* in the absence of *Robinson Crusoe.* The connections are important; those who regard them as expendable, a zone reserved for highbrow critics and specialists, impoverish their reading.

In Norman Douglas's *South Wind* (1917) Mr. Heard declares: "We are rearing up a brood of crafty egoists, a generation whose earliest recollections are those of getting something for nothing from the state." Theirs was, and is, a widening culture of contempt for things that require effort to create and make demands on those who read them. This culture impatiently dismisses hard books and long books, declaring Dickens a caricaturist whose political vision serves the status quo, Kipling a mere imperialist, Hardy a mere pessimist. Joyce's *Ulysses* is "grossly overrated," declare some Irish novelists weary of the critical insistence on Joyce and the inevitable yardstick he represents. "*Ulysses* could have done with a good editor," Roddy Doyle told a pre-Bloomsday audience in New York in 2004. "You know people are always putting *Ulysses* in the top ten books ever written but I doubt that any of those people were really moved by it." Discredit not only the work, but also those who purport to enjoy it. The best Irish writer, according to Doyle, is not Joyce but Jennifer Johnston, author of *The Captains and the Kings* (1972).

One can understand impatience with the Joyce industry in Dublin. On the centenary of Bloomsday the Irish government supported half a year of festivities, contributing to a culminating celebration, "Bloom's breakfast." Ten thousand people were to convene in O'Connell Street to consume "fried offal and mutton kidneys washed down with Guinness." Another sponsor of the feast was Denny Sausages, advertised by Joyce in his book. Leopold Bloom was certainly partial to kidneys, and to offal. But such celebrations tend to stick in the craw of Dubliners weary of their national writer. "I declare to god, if I hear that name Joyce one more time I will surely froth at the gob," an exasperated Flann O'Brien exclaimed, at a time when the Industry was much less vigorous than it is today. O'Brien was shaped and distorted by Joyce. In his novel *The Dalkey Archive* he depicts an aging Joyce who never *actually* wrote any of his books. Yet O'Brien never emancipated himself from the master who defined comprehensively the matter of Ireland. He thought Joyce was a kind of devil and could not quite desist from devil worship. O'Brien's resistance is ironic and informed. Roddy Doyle's is commercial, spoken by a modern market leader with macho hubris. The newspaper article reporting Doyle's New York lecture concludes with statistics: "Online bookseller Amazon.co.uk has sold 97,107 copies of Roddy Doyle's *Paddy Clarke Ha Ha Ha* and 2,374 copies of James Joyce's *Ulysses*." What more proof does the crafty egoist need? (Between 2002 and 2012, *Paddy Clarke Ha Ha Ha* sold 26,824, *Ulysses* 190,694.)

A culture of contempt cannot be answered with contempt: There is much to be said, if the king is naked, for children to point and say so. But when the king is brilliantly attired and children point, it is best to reason with them. They should be assured that a reader actually gets pleasure from Joyce's *Ulysses*. We learn to read with our ears as well as our eyes and gradually draw sense in all its diversity from the book. The word Doyle would balk at is "gradually": he has better things to do with his time. Those who enjoy fiction are not obsessed with denouements and ever-afters. They are less eager to finish a book than to prolong it. "The thing—a privilege—a miracle—what you will—is not quite hidden from the meanest of us who run as we read. To those who have the grace to stay their feet it is manifest," says Joseph Conrad with reference to Henry James, a writer who taxes fast readers but rewards those for whom reading is about understanding the medium and the subject as well as being entertained. Conrad's style stutters toward sense. Mimesis.

In his *Dictionary of Accepted Ideas* Flaubert says drily, "One should 'know the great authors'; no need to know their names." Readers, book by book, build up for themselves, the way a novelist does, a chronology. Reading is a cumulative act, adding skills, increasingly creative as it goes. To become a "good reader" one must give oneself over to a regime of concentrated pleasure. One does not set out to read a book a day (there is no necessary pleasure in that) but may spend two or three years on one book (as I did on Thomas Mann's *The Magic Mountain*), read only portions of another, devour a third at a single sitting. Reading for school is different from reading we do for ourselves: geared to "course outcomes," the former entails *reading about,* the novel stunned like a creature in an abattoir while a class crawls over it, prodding, appraising, slicing.

In premodernist times, new writing, the kind that made a difference and effected changes in taste and reading habits, rose like a tide and covered older landmarks, then ebbed and the older emerged again, enhanced. Now it can seem that the waves burst like tsunamis over what was there before and wash it away. Demands for "originality," not of form but of story and teller; the personalization of the product so that what we know about the writer stands in the way of the book; the violence of accolades and scrutinies; and the speed with which new readers are empowered or compelled to forget informing traditions (as if ignorant originality were possible) are features of an economy of "disposables" with built-in obsolescence in the arts quite as much as in kitchen appliances. The fiction industry is an industry like any other.

———•———

In 1911 the San Francisco writer and adventurer Ambrose Bierce published *The Devil's Dictionary*. With the exasperation of a busy journalist he defined the word:

> Novel, *n*. A short story padded. A species of composition bearing the same relation to literature that the panorama bears to art. As it is too long to be read at a sitting the impressions made by its successive parts are successively effaced, as in the panorama. Unity, totality of effect, is impossible; for besides the few pages last read all that is carried in mind is the mere plot of what has gone before. To the romance the novel is what photography is to painting. Its distinguishing principle, probability, corresponds to the literal actuality of the photograph and puts it distinctly into the category of reporting; whereas the free wing of the romancer enables him to mount to such altitudes as he may be fitted to attain; and the first three essentials of the literary art are imagination, imagination and imagination. The art of writing novels, such as it was, is long dead everywhere except in Russia, where it is new. Peace to its ashes—some of which have a large sale.

His account is peremptory and comprehensive. It is more useful, in what it says about the problems of narrative and in response to the Russian novels that took Europe and America by storm, than the current *Oxford English Dictionary (OED)*. Here the novel is "a genre." It is also "a fictitious prose narrative or tale of considerable length (now usu. one long enough to fill one or more volumes), esp. & orig. (frequently contrasted with romance) representing character and action with some degree of realism; a volume containing such a narrative."

As soon as the lexicographer commits his definition to paper, we begin, in defense of the form, to cross-question him. Can the novel be so readily encompassed? We cannot proceed unless we share, at least for this book's duration, a few terms. Our sense of "rules" will rest on the common-law principle. Actual novels, from Lyly's *Euphues* to B. S. Johnson's *Christie Malry's Own Double-Entry*, create the expanding space in which fiction exists and is read. No statutory laws stemming from Aristotle hold. "Should" and "must" knock the life out of imagination. "The only thing which can tell us about the novel is the novel"—Edwin Muir's is a serviceable tautology.

The word *novelist* has survived a variety of meanings, some of them contradictory. In the late sixteenth century it meant "an innovator," and it retained this meaning even in the mid-seventeenth century when it also came to mean "a novice," someone without experience. Novelist: innovator and innocent. (The word *original* underwent its transformation at roughly this period: from meaning something rooted in the past, attesting to its origins, to something self-originating, unprecedented.) *Novelist* came to mean (with a pejorative inflection) "newsmonger." In the late eighteenth century it acquired the meaning "a writer of novels," retaining some of the historical nuances.

Newness and renewal are included in the word *novel,* which derives from the Latin *nŏvus,* "new," in diminutive form. In late Middle English and up to the eighteenth century it meant something new, and also a piece of news. Its literary application derives from the Italian *novella,* diminutive still, the short tales or fictional stories comprised in a larger work, the chapters of Boccaccio's *Decameron,* for example (early attestation, 1566). By 1643 one of the senses given by the *OED* was established: "A fictitious prose narrative or tale" and so on. A century later it stood proud with a definite article as *the* novel: the eighteenth century turned it lapidary and categorical.

The *OED* alerts us to the fact that *novel* is not the same thing as *romance.* The French word for *novel* is *roman* (the French *nouvelle* is a novelette or novella, closer to the original Italian meaning). *Roman* attests to the genre's source (in France), less in news reports, more in medieval and Renaissance verse and prose romances, with distinct patterns and readerships. The difference between *novel* and *roman* signals a cultural distance between English pragmatism and an abstracting approach. When English novels began to be composed in earnest, they were different from Continental novels and soon became popular there.

In German, too, a novel is a *Roman,* and there are various genres in German and French, some of which entered our critical language: the psychological novel dealing with a character's formative years is *der Bildungsroman* or *development novel;* a novel with an ulterior motive is a *Tendenzroman;* a *roman à clef* (novel with a key) includes "real" characters concealed behind fictional names and fictionalized incidents.

The distinction between *novel* and *romance* is useful but hard to sustain, especially when the novel is taking shape. The English romance is for the most part pure fiction in terms of story, and most romances are rooted in earlier romances. Literature out of literature: Ford Madox Ford distinguishes between writers who display artistry and those who show virtuosity. The latter generally derive their work from earlier books. In crucial respects virtuosos are performers playing music not of their own invention. For Ford it is the artist, in his terms the novelist, not the virtuoso, that matters in the long term.

The best-selling book of Elizabethan times and through the first half of the reign of James I was Sir Philip Sidney's romance *Arcadia,* a mixture of romantic stories, poetic interludes, allegory, and moral edification. It is considered here among the prototypes for the English novel, Continental though it is in allegiance and tone, and though it hardly gets off the ground for more than a few pages at a time. The Puritans had little time for Sidney; the great Puritan romance, categorized as a novel, is *The Pilgrim's Progress,* allegorical and formally anomalous in its day, deriving its method and form from earlier centuries yet able to serve Puritan interests. *Arcadia* and *The Pilgrim's Progress* are opposite poles of fictional prose that portray social and moral types whose trials are "everyman's" and whose foes embody the moral forces ranged against "us." Most novels are about trials; they use the rhetoric and the form of gathering and presenting evidence, inviting judgment.

The *OED* insists that a novel is "a fictitious prose narrative or tale." Are we happy with any of these terms? Why "fictitious," in the first place? Did Defoe not go out of his way to insist upon the *factuality* of his stories, from *A Journal of the Plague Year,* an apparent piece of firsthand journalism that is in fact a novel, to *Robinson Crusoe,* loosely based on the life of a real castaway? His readers required facts, and he supplied convincing simulacra. Through the eighteenth century it was conventional to affirm the factuality of a story, and this insistence was a starting point for parody for Swift, Fielding, Sterne, Smollett, and others. In the twentieth century Saul Bellow speaks of the "poetry of fact" in American fiction, rooted in the real, answerable to history: the novel as, or of, *information,* with what he chooses to call inevitable *journalistic* elements. "Does the challenge of journalism in our time carry us higher than that of art?"

In modern times novelizations of true stories are commonplace. In *Oswald's Tale: An American Mystery* Norman Mailer creates Lee Harvey Oswald, and Don DeLillo's *Libra* tackles the same subject. Truman Capote described *In Cold Blood: A True Account of a Multiple Murder and Its Consequences* as a "nonfiction novel." Thomas Keneally's *Schindler's Ark,* with its elaborate attempt at verisimilitude, is in this category. Books that fuse fiction and borrowed biography, such as D. M. Thomas's *The White Hotel,* blur the line between history and novel. When historical elements combine with invention, readers are inclined to judge in moral rather than artistic terms, demanding a specific kind of accountability. Capote's book is a controversial experiment in an impossible genre.

Do we accept the *OED* condition that a novel must be written in prose? What of Robert Browning's *The Ring and the Book,* which left its mark on the genre of detective fiction even as late as *The Name of the Rose* by Umberto Eco? Arthur Hugh Clough's *Amours de Voyage* belongs in the zone of the epistolary novel: It is complex in all the ways that a novel should be, with an added dimension in the form the language takes—thrift of effect, unmediated voices, a wit that inheres in the characters, their languid moods and flickering passions. Alexander Pushkin's *Eugene Onegin: A Novel in Verse* (1833) shunned prose, and the Indian poet and novelist Vikram Seth in his verse novel *The Golden Gate* (1986) responded to Pushkin's example and form. Les Murray, the Australian poet, produced a remarkable picaresque verse novel entitled *Fredy Neptune* (1998). More recently the American Brad Leithauser published *Darlington's Fall* (2002). The Canadian poet Anne Carson calls her *Autobiography of Red* (1998) a novel in verse, and the English poet Craig Raine describes his long sequence of poems *History: The Home Movie* (1994) in similar terms.

The dictionary says a novel must be a "narrative or tale," a story with beginning, middle, and end (not necessarily in that order). This is the least contestable of its terms, yet even here we might cavil. In what useful sense can we say that *Arcadia* or *Tristram Shandy* or *Finnegans Wake* are narrative? Christine Brooke-Rose's *Amalgamemnon,* in which the tenses are unrealized and nothing happens, defers narrative. Samuel Beckett's novels cannot usefully be said to tell stories.

And what is meant by "considerable length"? Bruce Chatwin's *Utz* weighs in at a mere ninety-six generously spaced pages, while Marcel Proust's *À la recherche du temps perdu* exceeds a million words. Joseph Conrad's *Heart of Darkness* and Henry James's *The Turn of the Screw* count as novels, though they are tiny compared with these writers' larger works. Julian Barnes won the Booker Prize with *The Sense of an Ending,* inflated to 150 pages by typography. And what does "characters and actions representative of real life" mean? Lexicographers must be aware, assuming they researched "c" as well as "n," that the word "character" has reversed its meaning. In ancient times, when Theophrastus (ca. 371–ca. 287 B.C.) wrote his book of ethical *Characters,* and in the heyday of the English "characters" of Joseph Hall, Sir Thomas Overbury, and Nicolas Breton, culminating in Bishop Earle's *Microcosmographie; or, A Peece of the World Discovered: Essays and Characters* (1628), "character" referred to a type, not to an individual. These characters people the early drama and appear in Bunyan and even in Fielding representing virtues and vices, their being compassed in their moral and ethical nature and their names. But "character" has come to refer preeminently to defined and differentiated individuals.

And *actions?* Can aftermath count as action? Can the refusal to act? What of the fragmented narratives of William Burroughs, for example, or the nonconsecutive narratives of Donald Barthelme? What is meant by *representative:* typical? If so, many novel genres (fantasy, science fiction, crime fiction) are excluded from the definition. *Real life* is a vexed term, too, begging questions.

James Baldwin says, "One's own experience is not necessarily one's twenty-four-hour reality. Everything happens to you, which is what Whitman means when he says in his poem 'Heroes,' 'I am the man, I suffered, I was there.' It depends on what you mean by experience." And "portrayed in a plot": are no other forms of portrayal permissible?

With misgivings, we translate the dictionary definition into terms that include the sprung reality of the novel today. A novel is a narrative, *generally* in prose, certainly longer than a short story, probably (though not invariably) more than 25,000 words in extent, often combining a number of stories, incorporating elements of invention, in which characters, individuals, or voices are presented in relation to one another and their worlds in appropriate language. Is this definition *too* open-ended? Does it leave sufficient space for radical imagination? The novel takes in and takes on invention like no other literary form. The generic space between Defoe's *Robinson Crusoe,* Fielding's *Tom Jones,* and Richardson's *Clarissa* is wide, though the writers were contemporaries and Fielding's fiction grew strong on predatory parody. Agatha Christie, Ivy Compton-Burnett, and Muriel Spark, or Stephen King, William Burroughs, and James Baldwin play equally diverse variations. The distance between them can be measured in each writer's sense of character and sequence, how the language relates to the things and actions it expresses, the style, structure, and voice.

In the twentieth century something profound happened to the novel. The Hungarian critic Georg Lukács foresaw what was afoot in *The Theory of the Novel* (1920), after the Great War and before he became a committed Marxist. The project of modernism was under way. Old forms no longer held; a writer alive to his time could not presume upon common worldviews, common values, or the kinds of stability that make the fiction of the nineteenth century at once various and universal, so that the great Russian, French, Portuguese, Italian, and German writers existed in English with almost native valence, and English and American writers survived crossing the Channel or the Atlantic. Lukács says, "A totality that can be simply accepted is no longer given to the forms of art: therefore they must either narrow down and volatilize whatever has to be given form to the point where they can encompass it, or else they must show polemically the impossibility of achieving their necessary object and the inner nullity of their own means. And in this case they carry the fragmentary nature of the world's structure into the world of forms."

Early in the day Lukács recognizes the causes and formal consequences of modernism. His modern storyteller is "self-conscious," not "natural," to use Woolf's distinction. It is impossible for a modern storyteller to be "natural": the authoritative voice that spoke to the reader is no longer tenable, and if novelists need such narrators, they must contrive them. Writers and readers fell from grace long ago.

E. M. Forster appreciated what that fall from grace entailed. Lukács had defined it as a kind of imperative, the compulsory ironic stance, the distance the writer creates between the saying and the thing said. "The writer's irony is a negative mysticism to be found in times without a god. It is an attitude of *docta ignorantia* [informed ignorance] towards meaning, a portrayal of the kindly and malicious workings of the demons, a refusal to comprehend more than the mere fact of these workings; and in it there is the deep certainty, expressible only by form-giving, that through not-desiring-to-know and not-being-able-to-know he has truly encountered, glimpsed and grasped the ultimate, true substance, the present, non-existent God. This is why irony is the objectivity of the novel." The phrase "a refusal to comprehend" describes the unreliable and the absent narrator; it is deliberate and artful. When Lukács speaks of irony as "the objectivity of the novel," he is saying two things. Irony gives authors a purchase on subject and subject matter; they are able to hold them at a distance, or to push them back to a distance when the novel threatens to become too serious, too sincere, too conclusive in effect; in other words, to unbalance the structure of the narrative. It is also an author's way of keeping outside the narrative, manipulating without being engulfed in the process of the story. In a different sense from, for example, Tolstoy or Thackeray with their habit of directly addressing readers and their understanding of what they have created, authors who stand outside occupy a place like that of the reader. They are beside us, not above: *mon semblable, mon frère.*

Forster describes "the ingredients of fiction" as "human beings, time, and space." He omits a chief ingredient in the modern novel, this curious, ironic perspective, a development of Henry James's narratorial "point of view," a key to understanding most novels. Here in particular the *art* of the novel can be explored. Ford's distinction between artistry and virtuosity again: primary art creates and sustains a consistent, credible, and living perspective. It need not use a voice or a single point of view: it can entail orchestrating elements appropriate to the story being told (arranging the plot, contriving the proportions and pace of the telling, and the singleness of final effect). In a novel, "unity, totality of effect, is impossible," says Bierce. This "impossible" the ambitious novel sets out to achieve. When it works, it is impossible for a reader not to observe and appraise: the changing rhythms of the prose; the development of images, symbols, and structures of recurrence; where and how chapters break, and paragraphs.

And plot? Edwin Muir speaks of it as "the chain of events in a story and the principle which knits them together." He identifies an "internal principle" but cannot be more specific. Story is the sequence of events in time, plot the reordering of those events for effective telling, to bring out of the subject matter the true subject. If, in the absence of Julian Barnes, we were straightforwardly to tell the story of *Flaubert's Parrot,* we might say that it is about a man who is doing his best to distract himself from his wife's infidelity and death. The novel tells the story in that form. Plot evades story, and that evasion is the novel's subject. In T. S. Eliot's "Burnt Norton" man flits about between tasks and pleasures, "distracted from distraction by distraction." Readers can be distracted from story by plot. They are caught between two forms of narrative, two patterns of notation. We can imagine it as lines of music that create harmonies and dissonances. Some novels are *about* the distance between telling and what is told.

Once a story is chosen, a novelist makes formal calculations. They may not present themselves in this deliberate form, but whether consciously or instinctively made, they are choices whose rightness, more than the detail of the story, engages a reader. Readers aware of what the choices are and why they have been made are likely to read with *formal* understanding, one of fiction's intensest pleasures. Good novels take calculated and uncalculated risks.

# | 1 |

# *"Literature Is Invention"*

*Mandeville's Travels,* Ranulf Higden's *Polychronicon, De Proprietatibus Rerum*

One of the first popular English authors of fiction is Sir John Mandeville. *Mandeville's Travels,* originally known as *The Voiage and Travaile of Sir John Maundevile,* is not a novel as such, but it has a consistent narrator who combines personal memoir and travel book. It pretends to be true but is in fact woven from half-truths and lies. For a century and more after it was written, readers believed it. They believed in Sir John. Gradually his book has found its place in the realm of fantasy, but fantasy based less in romance than invention. Most of the invention was not Mandeville's own: it was borrowed from "authorities." The author may himself have believed what he pretended to have seen: lands where men's heads grew under their arms, for example; gryphons, hippocentaurs, men with dogs' heads, dames with breasts like basilisks, banana trees figuring the Cross, lambs that grew on plants.

The narrator is English. The book was composed in French around 1356 or 1357 and disseminated in manuscript between 1357 and 1371. It was so popular that more than 250 manuscripts survive, among them translations into Latin and most of the vernaculars of Europe. In English it soon existed in at least five different versions, one of them in galumphing rhyming couplets. None is authoritative: scribal copies seldom are. Copyists making cheap scripts truncated the text, or worked from defective sources with sheets missing, or had deadlines to meet. If the copyist knew something the "original" omitted, he had no compunction in adding it. We talk with caution about "form" in early works. The process of transmission distorted whatever the original forms might have been.

First printed in English in 1496, *Mandeville's Travels* has stayed in print ever since, often in illustrated editions. Wynkyn de Worde, Caxton's successor in the printing business, published an edition in 1499 with bold woodcuts, following in the manuscript tradition that included illustrations, some pious, some bizarre. The Duc de Berry had the *Travels* illuminated. There is a Czech manuscript of the first half of the book, the journey to the Holy Land, in which the travels are told entirely in clear grisaille images, a proto–comic book.

The first part of the *Travels* is a pilgrim's guide, not a pious Fodor or Guide Bleu but a "personal" account tracing the routes a traveler might take to get to Rome and the Holy Land, and a description of the holy places. Mandeville's

Rome is recognizable, but once off the beaten track things get brighter, more allegorical, fantastic, and yet more orderly than the actual places ever were. A traveler trusting him as sole guide would never get home. After Jerusalem, he ventures south and east. He becomes embroiled in Egyptian politics, Chinese conflicts; he works as a consultant, even a mercenary, before making his way back to Europe suffering from a rheumatic gout ("gowtes artetykes that me distreyen": that much is quite believable), and stopping in Liège to convalesce is attended by Bearded John, a physician he had vaguely known in Cairo, who urges him to write down his story, to combat boredom. This the earliest Latin translation tells us. The earliest surviving French version is mute on the subject.

So plausible is the narrator's courtesy, his unemphatic, persuasive manner, his firsthand witness, his amazement at the things he sees and does, and his backing evidence of other witnesses, from Roman Pliny to sources nearer to his own day, that it is no wonder he was believed. He is also steeped in scripture that underwrites his truthfulness. He invites readers into complicity, challenging them to supply further wonders from their own travels. Given the variations from text to text, it would seem that some scribes did just that. In one version Sir John remembers a story he heard as a boy, about a man who traveled east and east until one day he arrived at an island where a ploughman called to his oxen in words he understood. He had gone around the world. For Mandeville the world was round, even if not quite in the way that our world is. But round enough to inspire a reader a century later, Christopher Columbus. Chaucer, the Gawain poet, the mathematical magician John Dee, and (more skeptically) Shakespeare read him too, and Donne, and Milton; his enchantment (by then celebrated as mere enchantment) affected Keats and the Romantics.

"A writer's country is a territory within his own brain," writes Virginia Woolf in her first contribution to the *Times Literary Supplement* in 1905, "and we run the risk of disillusionment if we try to turn such phantom cities into tangible brick and mortar." More emphatically: "Literature is invention," Vladimir Nabokov tells us. "Fiction is fiction." This is most true when (as it so often does, from Mandeville to Defoe, from Flaubert to Atwood) it either claims to be fact or seems to imitate "the real world" in detail. Fiction not only requires the reader to suspend disbelief, as poetry does; it also requires the reader for the duration of reading to *believe,* not with the skeptical, critical kind of belief we reserve for history, but with the unironic belief we reserve for dreams. Plausibility, the connection of fact and fact, the sequence of cause and effect, movement from place to place as on a map (credible space) we expect from most fiction. And yet we expect fiction. "To call a story a true story is an insult to both art and truth." Nabokov's insistence on the fictionality of fiction is important in our pursuit of the lives of the novel. We know lives in a retrospect that finds shapes, narrative pattern, consistencies. Biography, though not fiction, shares crucial elements with it. "The good reader is aware that the quest for real life, real people, and so forth is a meaningless process when speaking of books," Nabokov says. "In a book, the reality of a person, or object, or a circumstance depends exclusively on the world of that particular book." Even a history book.

Sir John Mandeville is a knight, born and bred in St. Albans, Hertfordshire. At Michaelmas (September 29) 1322 he left his country suddenly, for reasons variously explained (perhaps he slew another nobleman and fled), and went on a pilgrimage; but pilgrimage turned to obsessive travels that were to last for thirty-four years. The things he saw! In Turkey, in little and big Armenia, in Chaldea and Ethiopia and Libya, in Syria, in little and middle and larger India and Tibet, in Java and Sumatra . . . He traveled to Russia and Poland and to places so wonderful and remote that they do not appear on maps. He even managed, on the Malabar Coast, to drink from the reviving Well of Youth, which explains why he was able to travel so far and long. He watched the stars right side up and upside-down and recorded his bearings. When gout got the better of him, he went home—not all the way home to St. Albans, but to Liège—and wrote his book. We know rather too much about Mandeville. And this is because he, too, like his travels, is fictional. A real medieval author would not go out of his way to tell about himself and his circumstances. Mandeville is explicit; and he has consistency of tone unusual in medieval prose. We cannot say for certain that the author was English or, more likely, Belgian or French. Was he a cleric masquerading as a layman? His piety, especially in the epilogue, is priestly, his learning broad, but his attitude to the papacy and church at large sometimes sounds a dissenting note, at least in the English versions we have. Why do we assume *him*? One scholar, Linda Lomperis, argues that the author was a woman living in male disguise.

The Mandeville we come to know in "his" narrative makes sense as a voice. Much of what he says, and the ways in which he speaks, his tolerant, curious manner, more like a modern anthropologist than a devout pilgrim, would have exposed a monk to censure. Some of the incidents in the book, too, are inappropriate for one who had tied the knot of celibacy. There is little exceptionable in the pilgrimage to Jerusalem, a common enough type of travel book, but the journey onward is marked by unorthodox matter and manner.

Mandeville draws on various writings. His travels attempt a synthesis. His prevailing tone is that of witness. Coming from one end of the world to its center (Jerusalem), he travels away from the center to the far end, then returns exhausted by age and ill health, being much wiser. In some versions he comes home via Rome and shows his manuscript to the pope, who approves it. Such an interpolation, giving the book papal sanction and exonerating the author of heresy, adds authority.

He almost reaches the Earthly Paradise in Asia, a reward for his tolerance and persistence. In a sense, for a man of his temperament, the various world is itself paradise, so full of wonders, what with the diamond growing or diamond breeding; and the monopods of Ethiopia, who, when they rest, raise a giant foot like an umbrella to shade themselves from the sun; and the barnacle geese, who are hatched from barnacles attached to floating driftwood; and the grape clusters so large that a strong man could hardly bear a single one on his shoulder; and the massive ipotaynes (hippopotamuses), phoenixes, crying crocodiles, and goat-men; bearded women; snails with shells huge as houses; the isle where each inhabitant enjoyed the sexual organs of both sexes; and the grains of paradise out of which grew the trees used to make the Cross.

The *Travels* ends with a blessing and a prayer, and beautiful they are, spoken by a man who abruptly casts off the dusty trappings of the traveling knight and becomes an aging priest, soliciting our prayers for his soul, and offering his work and himself to God, invoked in a traditional series of paradoxes. Here is how, before his spirit takes flight, he solicits us, in a form whose unmodernized grace is remote in time and intimate in tone and effect: "And alle tho that seyn for me a *Paternoster,* with an *Ave Maria,* that God forgeve me my synnes, I make hem parteneres and graunte hem part of all the gode pilgrymages, and of all the gode dedes that I haue don, if ony ben to his plesance; and noght only of tho, but of all that euere I schall do unto my lyfes ende."

Thus Sir John Mandeville, the first almost consistent and coherent English voice in prose, the first fictional narrator, almost the first novelist, bids adieu. Prose was functional, used in church, in education, the courts, and public administration, in keeping records, chronicles, and histories. Here it fulfilled a different purpose, telling lies as artfully as if they had been truths. Prose could make characters, invent lands and creatures. Conditions for fiction were not yet right: Mandeville is a prophet in the wilderness before printing and the standardization of a national English (or any other national language of northern Europe). Something new is promised.

The Scottish writer Andrew Lang addressed one of his *Letters to Dead Authors* to Mandeville, imitating the unstable English of his correspondent. Confessing him a liar, "nevertheless, Sir John, for the frailty of Mankynde, ye are held a good fellow, and a merry; so now, come, I shall tell you of the new ways into Ynde." How strange is the Victorian India he depicts, the routes there, the imperial conquests that opened them, then jealously guarded them, the whole colonial enterprise. Mandeville would never have believed such tosh, yet Lang tells him history in a parody of his own form.

—————•—————

The English prose tradition from which the novel emerges began in the Middle English period. Latin and French were the languages of administration and the church. Old English had been outlawed but a hybrid vernacular evolved, differently in different parts of the country. Common folk did not understand the languages of spiritual and secular power and required translations. The Latin used in accountancy and clerical work was full of English words. The French used in government was similarly corrupted by the vernacular, but the vernacular itself was submerged.

Then, in 1362–1364, three successive parliaments were opened with speeches in English. It was an English remote from King Harold's eleventh-century Old English. But the Norman tide was receding. Pleading in English courts of law began to be conducted in the vernacular. After the black death (1347–1350), the language of teaching was English rather than French. John Cornwall, abetted by his follower Richard Pencrich, helped to effect this change: "In all the grammar schools of England children leaveth French and construeth and learneth in English." The key speeches during Richard II's deposition (1399) were conducted in English (and his Master Cooke set down his *Forme of Cury* in English).

Three books, all taken to heart not only as "wisdom" but as "fact" in fourteenth- and fifteenth-century Britain, had virtually the authority of scripture and helped establish English prose as a narrative and reflective medium. All three were translations. Mandeville we have considered. John de Trevisa's version of Ranulf Higden's *Polychronicon* (1387) and of *De proprietatibus rerum* (*On the Right Order of Things,* written between 1240 and 1250, translated from the Latin in 1398) were the other two. This latter was by Bartholomeus Anglicus, who, his name indicates, was English. He was not, as far as we can tell, a fiction: so little is known about him, he must have been real. He may have been nobly born and studied at Oxford, and his original surname may have been Glanville. In 1231 he traveled to Saxony to teach, and there in a school for friars he composed *De proprietatibus rerum.*

These books, along with the Bible, which was being seriously translated by John Wycliffe and his comrades, describe a European Christendom and an emerging English consciousness. They complement one another: religion, geography, history, and the material world. The three nonscriptural books are underpinned by scripture. Mandeville's geography and anthropology are the most suggestive: spiritually restive if not insubordinate, radical in entertaining without censure customs and beliefs remote from his declared faith. Higden's

*Polychronicon* is universal history, so revered a century after its first publication that William Caxton revised and updated it to 1467, printing it in 1482, the most important partly original work by Caxton that we possess. Bartholomeus's *De Propietatibus,* an encyclopedia in nineteen volumes, includes the natural sciences, astrology, and theology, as understood by one of the great synthesizing minds of the mid-thirteenth century, touched by the Arabic scholarship of the time, yet rooted (sometimes incongruously) in the orthodoxies of his received faith. He includes bees among the birds, and his bestiary is celebrated.

The emergence of a coherent intellectual culture in the vernacular was delayed by the variations in English spoken and written in the British Isles. The south was more deeply infected with French, the north remained in a loose Scandinavian orbit, as regards diction and accent. John de Trevisa in his translation of *Polychronicon* comments: "It seemeth a great wonder how English, that is the birth-tongue of Englishmen, and their own language and tongue, is so diverse of sound in this land," while Norman French, a foreign idiom, was the lingua franca. Trevisa's language makes sense when read aloud: "For men of the est with men of the west, as hyt were vnder the same party of heuene, acordeth more in sounyng of speche than men of the north with men of the south. Therefore hyt ys that Mercii, that buth men of myddel Engelond, as hyt were parteners if the endes, vnderstondeth betre the syde longages, Northeron and Southeron, than Northeron and Southeron vnderstondeth eyther other." But it is the Southeron idiom that prevails and becomes the written form, even for Northeron writers. The Northeron, Higden says, is *scharp, slyttyng, and frotyng*— harsh, piercing, and grating (early evidence of an abiding prejudice).

The emergence of prose, especially with the translation of the Bible, so long resisted by the Roman Catholic Church, coincided with a period of ferment and spiritual revolt. The black death gave new power to the laboring classes, whose value rose steeply. An urban middle class was shaping. Schooling spread, and with it instruction in English. If the medieval period was marked by a strong sense of Christendom, and Europe was an entity that, whatever its secular variations, was united by allegiance to Rome, in the fourteenth century questioning began, first within the church itself; the Reformation contributed to the growth of distinct vernacular cultures. A gathering protestant spirit of individual witness and salvation affected the sense of "self" and community. These selves, from Mandeville to Gibreel Farishta, are at the heart of this book.

A century after Richard II was deposed, Caxton took up Trevisa's argument about language, but he was in a position to do something about it. He wrote in his preface to *Eneydos* (his version of part of Virgil's *Aeneid,* 1490) of the diversity of English spoken in the British Isles. What advantages might accrue to a nation from a language all could understand! As a printer, translator, and publisher, he established norms unthinkable in a scribal culture, and developed some of the conventions of writing that, in evolved forms, enable the communication represented by this book. Because he could reproduce several hundred copies of the same text in more or less identical form, the peril of scribal error vanished (there was now a new problem, the universal misprint). Texts became stable in transmission. Lost was the flexibility of the scribe, who could add modern fact to out-of-date history, correct mistakes, elaborate style, doodle in the margins (the one "portrait" we have of Chaucer is such a doodle). And how stable did English become? In the middle of the eighteenth century Jonathan Swift impatiently inquired, "How then shall any man, who hath a genius for history equal to the best of the ancients, be able to undertake such a work with spirit and cheerfulness, when he considers that he will be read with pleasure but a very few years, and in an age or two shall hardly be understood without an interpreter? The fame of our writers is usually confined to these two islands [Britain and Ireland], and it is hard it should be limited in time as much as place by the perpetual variations of our speech." With the emergence of so many Englishes in the Norman colonial and postcolonial periods, Caxton's dream of possible stability in the language, which men like Doctor Johnson worked for, has faded. There is less difference, thanks to the mediums of radio, film, television, and to the World Wide Web, than might have been the case if printing alone had been the guarantor.

But printing made the production of books cheaper, and their number and circulation grew. The relatively small readership for scribal books expanded. There was a call, no longer confined to the church and the law, for writers to provide material so that the printer could feed a growing hunger. As the language of writing stabilized, book production grew, and it was only a matter of time before a publisher's notion of a limited, known readership was displaced by the sense of a market, the vocation of "writer" became tenable, and the book became a commodity in the wider marketplace.

The profile of new readers was different from the old. Chaucer and Gower entertained the nobility and the prosperous bourgeoisie as well as those churchmen who wanted humor and beauty to leaven their more somber pursuits. The new reader was not necessarily brought up on Latin or French, was not necessarily conversant with narrative beyond ballads and Bible stories. Rather slow of understanding, he had to be addressed by the writer in prolix terms; things had to be repeated two or three times to get them across. This verbosity made for a slow, accruing prose, cadential, repetitive.

In the age of translation, what mattered was meaning, not style; obscurities in the original had to be explained or ironed out. A translator needed broad learning, not meticulous scholarship. The economy of an original was dissipated, translation overinterpreted and sometimes misread in its zeal to make clear. When Trevisa finds a bit he can't understand, he makes a bold attempt and then declares, "God wot what this is to mean." In its origins modern English prose is marked not by lucidity but by wordy earnestness. The doublets intended to make things understandable (saying things in two ways, using synonyms and approximate repetitions) became features of style in Sir Philip Sidney, John Lyly, and at purple moments in John Bunyan, keen to add to the sonority of the prose. With assonance and alliteration they brought aesthetic corpulence into writing.

Mandeville's translators were an exception. For them, the original needed little enhancement. Its brisk pace, from incident to incident, place to place, is maintained; there are few protracted digressions into moral or theological zones, but a continuous voice shapes the disparate matter into a single-seeming whole. The illusion of form sets it in a category of its own, alongside the work of the English poets. Mandeville has Homer's skill in bringing what is remote and strange close up, using a simile that even a rustic reader will understand. When a crocodile moves through a gravelly place, it "seemeth as though men had drawn a great tree through." The beast leaves a besom mark. The Mandeville who tells us his adventures is not a hero but a curious, commonsensical Christian who has gone traveling, like John Bunyan's Christian and Daniel Defoe's Robinson Crusoe, and who has come home.

# True Stories

William Caxton, Thomas Malory, Foxe's *Book of Martyrs*

"The next day came thither an old Bishop, who had a pearl in his eye, and he brought with him to my Lord a dish of apples, and a bottle of wine. For he had lost his living, because he had a wife. Then the Bishop called me again to the orchard, and said to the old Bishop: this young man hath a child, and will not have it christened." This is from John Foxe's *Actes and Monuments,* published in London in 1588, concerning "Queene Mary, the examination of Thomas Haukes Martyr." He was martyred.

Some historians of the novel seek its origins deep in the past, in Babylon and further east and south, buried in history so deep that it feels like geology. Others fix the genesis firmly in the seventeenth and eighteenth centuries. Without returning to Babylon, the English novel has relevant English and European antecedents. What would develop into a core readership for the novel was shaping in the late fourteenth and the fifteenth century. In the sixteenth it developed and grew.

The novel, a form that grows with protestant individualism, education, technology, and capitalism, is rooted in medieval soil. In structure, in intended effect, it has more in common with medieval than Renaissance concerns. Its audience is not, to begin with, aristocratic or learned; nor is it limited to the new middle class. The illusion of factuality that fiction tried and often still tries to create, lying to entertain and at the same time morally to instruct and exhort, means that it has much in common with allegory. Concentrating on trial, on testing character, with evidence presented and examined, it relates also to medieval verse debates and dialogues and early theater, the mystery and miracle plays. It is more serious in its intentions than romance, which supplied pleasure but only a specialized kind of *moral* uplift. In formal terms it owes little, in its early phases, to the classics or to humanism.

Caxton, agent of irreversible change, was temperamentally conservative. His version of *The Golden Legend* is full of stories, a cache of sacred and traditional tales including saints' lives, homilies, explanations (often in narrative form) of church services, and a chronicle and calendar outlining the use of the book in weekly worship. Jacobus de Voragine compiled it as a lectionary for priests to use, reading it out in church according to the calendar of saints' and feast days. The stories are reassuring: the saints hover nearby and intercede in the lives of the faithful. Caxton's *The Golden Legend* was in part translation, in part his own redaction. It proved popular, combining lore and moral entertainment, and had a life outside the church: readers acquired it for home use. It went through many editions, and the literary hunger to be entertained and instructed is the kind the early purveyors of narrative set out to feed.

Then, for contrast, Caxton edited (clumsily, it is said) Sir Thomas Malory's *Le Morte d'Arthur* and published it with less immediate success, though it has outlived *The Golden Legend* by centuries. Close to romance, it assembled translated material from various sources. Given coherent form and unified tone, it charmed English readers. *Le Morte d'Arthur* explores the theme of justice and "the matter of England." It spawned a literature of legend and a subgenre, the Arthurian romance.

Little is known of Malory (ca. 1416–1471) except that he was a soldier and a man of learning justly imprisoned for some years. He entertained himself by writing a book about shadowy figures with virtues he certainly did not possess. Born in Newbold Revel in Warwickshire into the established gentry, he enjoyed advantages as a young man. His father was a justice of the peace and member of Parliament, and Thomas followed in his footsteps. In 1450 things began to go wrong: he was part of a gang that set an ambush for the Duke of Buckingham; four months later he was charged with the rape of a married woman. Later that month he attempted extortion and was detained. Bailed, he reoffended. He served the Yorkist and then the Lancastrian cause in the Wars of the Roses. When he died, he was buried in Grayfriars, Newgate. Despite this last address, near one of the prisons where he did time, he was given a marble tombstone appropriate to his rank and his achievement as chronicler.

The principal characters in *Le Morte d'Arthur* are consistent in speech and plausible in motive. They manifest, as well as character, something like a cast of mind if not a psychology: a sense of motive, in romances of deep love, in tragedies of real perturbation. It is misleading to refer to *Le Morte d'Arthur* as a "prose epic," though it is set in the past and shares with epic heroic and elegiac coloring. It has in its cumulative strategies as much, if not more, in common with Sidney's *Arcadia* and Lyly's *Euphues,* both regarded as early examples of the novel, as it does with Spenser's Christian, allegorical epic, *The Faerie Queene.*

———•———

In April 1579 *The Golden Hind* with its allegorical name and figurehead put in at the port of Huatulco in Oaxaca, Mexico. It was laden with booty, having recently taken one of its principal prizes, a Spanish treasure ship nicknamed *Cacafuego* (Shitfire), intercepted on its way from Peru to Panama with a huge cargo of bullion. Sir Francis Drake, a privateer licensed by Queen Elizabeth I, took a few of the town's citizens hostage on board and reprovisioned his ship. One hostage, the local priest Simon de Miranda, later told the authorities of the Inquisition that every day the English captain came ashore and read from a large book. It was not the Bible. It was illustrated with images of the first martyrs and, nearer in time, of Protestants burned in Spain. With this volume, which he read aloud from daily, he rekindled the anti-papist zeal of his comrades.

The book Drake showed his captive hosts was *Actes and Monuments of These Latter Perilous Times Touching Matters of the Church,* better known as *Foxe's Book of Martyrs,* published in English for the first time only fifteen years before and already enjoying the status of holy writ. It is a compendious history of Protestant martyrdoms, an answer to the long-popular lives of saints that the Roman Catholic Church had been producing for centuries. John Foxe lays emphasis on Bloody Mary's martyrs. They are evoked in plain style, with dialogue between persecutors and victims.

The author John Foxe was born in Lincolnshire in 1516. He went to Magdalen College, Oxford, where he mastered Greek and Latin, read the fathers of the Church, learned Hebrew, and became a fellow. He wandered about a good deal, in his solitude venting deep emotions, praying, enjoining God's mercy. He became a martyr to his own sincerity: questioned, he told the authorities what he thought and was expelled from his fellowship. He was employed to tutor the children of Sir Thomas Lucy in nearby Warwickshire, the estate where not long afterward the boy Shakespeare was accused of poaching. Foxe married a woman of Coventry and, to escape persecution, went to his father-in-law's house for protection. Late in Henry VIII's reign he went to London, where he nearly starved to death, but God kept an eye on him. A stranger found him "fasting" at St. Paul's, gave him money, and promised him his luck would change. Three days later the Duchess of Richmond invited him to tutor the children of the Earl of Surrey, he being imprisoned in the Tower with his father, the Duke of Norfolk. Foxe was safe until Queen Mary ascended the throne, when he was targeted by emerging factions. Stephen Gardiner (ca. 1497–1555), the bishop of Winchester, made it his business to persecute the young Foxe and drive him and his pregnant wife out of England. Gardiner became a target of Foxe's anger.

Imprisoned in the Tower under Edward VI, Gardiner was promptly released in 1553 and scaled spiritual heights under Mary. He set the crown upon her head, becoming her lord chancellor and, in a sense, her inquisitor. With Bishop Edmund ("Bloody") Bonner he made martyrs and sought out and burned Tyndale Bibles. He replaced Thomas Cranmer and saw to it that Ridley, Latimer, Ferrar, and others were burned. Here, says John Foxe, is the fox, here is the wolf, here the false priest who feeds upon his flock. Other clerics, too, allies of

Gardiner, felt the brunt of Foxe's anger. He takes his text from Ezekiel 34:2–3: "Woe be unto the idolatrous shepherds of England, that feed themselves. Should not the shepherds feed the flock? But ye have eaten the fat, ye have clothed you with the wool, the best fed have ye slain, but the flock have ye not nourished." He translates the Roman Catholic clergy into beasts, and his ridicule has something of a comic-book effect. Man and beast merge, as in Jeff Noon's *Automated Alice.* When the authorities condemn a Protestant as willful, Foxe quips, "Willful because he will not put himself willfully into the wolf's mouth." And elsewhere, "O my good master Philpot, which art a principal pot indeed, filled with most precious liquor . . . O pot most happy, of thy high potter [the creator God] ordained to honor, which do'st contain such heavenly treasure in thy earthen vessel: O pot thrice happy, in whom Christ hath wrought a great miracle, altering thy nature, and turning water into wine.—When martyrdom shall break thee, O vessel of honor, I know the fragrant savour of thy precious nard will much rejoice the heavy hearts of Christ's true members." This is the wordplay of Shakespeare's early comedies.

In 1554, from Strasbourg, he began his publications. First came the *Commentarii,* an early Latin version of the *Actes and Monuments.* The next year he made his way to Basel, Switzerland, knowing that there he would find a community of English people who, like him, were biding their time until Mary's reign was over. He completed the extended English version of his book. He stayed in Basel for four years, working as a reader—editing, advising, and proofing—for the powerful Protestant publishing house of Johann (Herbst) Oporinus (1507–1568). Herbst had published key work by Martin Luther and, at Luther's behest, the monumental Toledo Latin translation of the Quran (1543). He was responsible, too, for the illustrated edition of Andreas Vesalius's *De humani corporis fabrica.* Foxe was regarded as a man of intellectual stature, whose knowledge of Latin, Greek, and Hebrew was of value to the firm. Of Foxe's books, Herbst published the five-act "apocalyptic comedy" *Christus triumphans,* dramatizing the Marian persecutions as part of the revelation of the true church, in 1556, and the *Commentarii* in 1559. It was the English printer John Day who issued the *Acts and Monuments* in England, in 1563. Foxe had returned in 1559. Elizabeth ascended the throne the year before. She rewarded him with a prebendary in Salisbury—he was made a canon of the cathedral—which he accepted with reluctance and managed to get out of in due course thanks to his delicate conscience. Again he found himself at odds with an establishment that had not thoroughly reformed.

His *Actes and Monuments* is more than an anthology of harrowing and heartening stories, some of them still familiar (Latimer, Ridley, Cranmer among them). It includes theological debates, digressions, and sermonizing. To it clings the reek of the smoke of burning witnesses. Many types of writing figure in the impure mix of Foxe's encyclopedia of bigotry and cruelty. Elements that became common concerns of the novel are contained here and the novel prefigured.

The exemplary story, Foxe insists, is the core of his project. In his life of Thomas Hawks his procedure is exemplified. He begins by evoking a character, instancing his conversation, telling of his origins and vocation and then how he entered into conflict with the Roman Church "and other adversaries," in the detail and proportion the telling requires. It is not formulaic; it refuses (by its own account) to go further than recorded fact. In modernized English we read:

> Thomas Hawks, with six others, was condemned on the ninth of February 1555. In education he was erudite; in person, comely, and of good stature; in manners, a gentleman, and a sincere Christian. A little before death, several of Mr. Hawks's friends, terrified by the sharpness of the punishment he was going to suffer, privately desired that in the midst of the flames he should show them some token, whether the pains of burning were so great that a man might not collectedly endure it. This he promised to do; and it was agreed that if the rage of the pain might be suffered, then he should lift up his hands above his head towards heaven, before he gave up the ghost.
>
> Not long after, Mr. Hawks was led away to the place appointed for slaughter by Lord Rich, and being come to the stake, mildly and patiently prepared himself for the fire, having a strong chain cast about his middle, with a multitude of people on every side compassing him about, unto whom after he had spoken many things, and poured out his soul unto God, the fire was kindled.
>
> When he had continued long in it, and his speech was taken away by violence of the flame, his skin drawn together, and his fingers consumed with the fire, so that it was thought that he was gone, suddenly and contrary to all expectation, this good man being mindful of his promise, reached up his hands burning in flames over his head to the living God, and with great rejoicings as it seemed, struck or clapped them three times together. A great shout followed this wonderful circumstance, and then this blessed martyr of Christ, sinking down in the fire, gave up his spirit, June 10, 1555.

Foxe is a truth teller, as against false fabulists and historians. If he reports something he does not believe, he declares, "Mark here a fable." The Marian martyrs were near in time; some were friends or acquaintances. Unlike Catholic books of martyrs, Foxe's is a collection of "histories" in a specific sense. He does away with painted ceilings crawling with angels and saints reaching down to intercede and assist afflicted souls. Such tales cannot "abide the touch of history," misshapen by dogma and invention. His saints go through flames aided only by the pure intensity of faith; their deeds are, therefore, imitable by those with faith; there is choice, and virtue is made manifest in that choice.

Truth and falsehood do not correlate as conveniently with fact and fiction as writers sometimes ask them to do today. Foxe chides the Catholic Sir Thomas More for "juggling with the truth" in *Utopia,* a deliberate fiction and just one aspect of his treachery to his Protestant country and countrymen. *The Golden Legend* he despises because it stains faith with fable, mixes legend with history, so that fact becomes unstable and unfixed. But he had time for Dante, the poet of damnation and grace in the *Divine Comedy,* who equated the pope with the whore of Babylon and said that civil power might take priority over the pope's authority. He is an honorary member of Foxe's party. So too are other great Roman Catholic writers, like Petrarch, similarly harsh on the papacy. They are among those who helped open a way for the mighty reformer, Martin Luther. Foxe regarded Chaucer and Gower as comrades in spirit: How is it that the bishops never understood their force or forbade the reading of their tales? Foxe has referred to archives, documents, and letters; he has used comparative techniques. But he has also understood the poets and dramatists. A natural alliance can exist between "preachers, players and printers" against "the Pope's three-storeyed crown." The traditional language to which Foxe commonly resorts for actual quotation, metaphor, or oblique allusion is that of the Bible. His book is an adjunct to it, a continuing enactment and vindication.

He records histories in order to affect readers. This instrumentality on occasion licenses deviations from verifiable fact. Hawks "clapped" his burning hands together, not once but three times: this hideous reflex Foxe has us read as affirmation. A Roman Catholic witness might have read the sizzling applause quite differently.

Some of his men are larger than the mortals in his audience can ever be; they are halfway between the human and the legend realm. Sometimes he writes with a grim humor of tone and incident, closer to comedy than tragedy, especially when dealing with recent martyrs whose circumstances were too well known to be idealized, and who were able to quip and argue with the flames. Some whom we habitually regard as martyrs he mocks. Hilary Mantel would applaud his Thomas à Beckett ("that olde Romish traitor"), his death rather less than martyrdom. Foxe dramatizes the rise and fall of great men in the manner of a wheel of fortune. Earthly downfall is for the Protestant counterbalanced by spiritual ascent; for the Catholic it leads to the justice without end of hellfire.

---

The humanist Roger Ascham in *The Schoolmaster* associates *Le Morte d'Arthur* with the discredited medieval and monastic texts: it taught nothing but "lewd manslaughter and bold bawdry." But Foxe took this legendary history of Britain as writ: it gave the English church a genealogy of its own and effectively unplugged it from Rome. John Bale and Foxe declared that Joseph of Arimathea came as a missionary and founded the true faith among the British. The Tudor dynasty descended from King Arthur. With Bale, Foxe took medieval English works, regarded as quaint and archaic by the Roman Church, and turned them to Protestant use. *Actes and Monuments* is a repository of such works; in Foxe and Bale begins that prejudice against humanist learning, subtlety, and wit, the belief in downright Anglo-Saxon common sense that enriches the early novel and in the long term impoverishes the intellectual spirit of England.

Though his cause is clear, Foxe's rhetorical objectives are never single or simple. He addresses a mixed audience, combining complicated materials. Readers are surprised at the lapses from solemnity, the admission of laughter into the stern courts of the spirit. In this sense his narratives, like much else in the informing tradition of the novel, are based in impure or indecorous medieval customs of speech. Spiritual foes are debased. Beast fables play a part. The spoof letter that Lucifer, writing from his "dolorous consistory," dispatched to the prelates of the Roman Church, plays its role; Foxe generates mock speeches and sermons by selective quotations—from papal bulls, for instance—as a modern satirist might cobble together phrases from a politician's speeches. The use of wordplay (the bishop is a "bite-sheep"), of parody, and hyperbole in somber settings unsettles the tone. His design, not overarching, is at least local and deliberate. It would have been hard for a Catholic in his company to find a space in which to answer back.

A taste for fiction develops when readers and writers grow uncomfortable in a posture of subordination to ecclesiastical or political power. Writing can serve and support; it can also subvert. The resistances of Luther point toward the resistances of Foxe, of Nashe and Bunyan, and the more refined strategies of Sidney. Writers need not be radical for their writing to have a radical impact; corrupt or ineffective institutions lay themselves open; they are probed and tested by language that becomes a capable instrument when it finds appropriate forms. It is a way of telling the truth, in part because it wears the mask of truth and marshals facts and seeming facts into plausible narratives.

Foxe spent his remaining years improving his book, completing what he thought would be the definitive version in just over a decade. An obsessive writer, he refused to share responsibility with an amanuensis even for note taking, copying out the whole text himself. He pushed himself relentlessly, by daylight, candlelight, and rushlight. He shriveled and altered beyond recognition, "consumed by an inner fire." If we believe the hagiographies (he has himself been the subject of edifying "lives"), we can say that despite his heroic labors on *Actes and Monuments* he fulfilled his parish duties and remained pious. He stayed at his post when the plague of 1563 broke, pursuing pastoral duties and administering alms on behalf of the rich, who kept a safe distance. His reputation was large. In 1570 he preached his famous sermon on Christ Crucified at Paul's Cross. The Queen referred to him as "Our Father Foxe" and recognized that, though he loathed the Catholic Church, his was a spirit much more generous and conciliatory than some who vexed her.

His book went through four editions in his lifetime. He died at seventy and was buried at St. Giles, Cripplegate, where he was vicar after leaving Salisbury. His account of the Marian persecution was rooted in fact, not legend. It told a truth. *A* truth, not *the* truth: by the middle of the sixteenth century, truth was no longer unitary. The age of "point of view" was on the way, and his book, regularly updated, was taken over by the foe and filled with Roman Catholic martyrs as well.

# | 3 |

## *Three Springs*

Sir Philip Sidney, Fray Antonio de Guevara, John Lyly, Thomas Nashe

When Anthony Trollope set out to write an account of English fiction (he never finished it), he began "with works much earlier than *Robinson Crusoe*." He labored "through a variety of novels which were necessary for my purpose," but without pleasure. "I never worked harder than at the *Arcadia,* or read more detestable trash than the stories written by Mrs. Aphra Behn; but these two were necessary to my purpose," to discover where novels had come from and got to, and "to inquire whether their great popularity has on the whole done good or evil to the people who read them." He is unjust to Aphra Behn, and his impatience does Sidney a disservice.

Sir Philip Sidney, the cynosure and patron of Elizabethan literature, died at the age of thirty-two, in 1586, of wounds received at Zutphen in the Netherlands campaign against Roman Catholic forces. He had ridden recklessly into "a hail of lead" from the enemies' harquebuses. Protestant Europe mourned him: The Dutch proposed to erect a monument, and his memory was draped in more than thirty elegies in Holland alone. His body, ceremonially shipped home, was spectacularly disposed of with volumes of elegies by more than 140 English mourners. Tributes continued accruing for years. And yet in 1586 his main literary works had not been published. He was mourned as a hero and a patron, not an author.

He was not a great reader of Foxe's best-selling *Actes and Monuments.* Though firmly Protestant, his family was too close to Rome and Spain to feel comfortable in Foxe's slaughterhouse of the righteous. But Sidney, too, produced a best seller, though he did not intend publication, see it through press, or profit from its success. *The Countess of Pembroke's Arcadia,* an enormous, unfinished "trifle," as he called it, hangs in the gallery of ancestors of the novel, but in a different alcove from *Acts and Monuments.* In his dedicatory letter to his sister he called it "this idle work of mine: which I fear (like the Spiders web) will be thought fitter to be swept away, than worn to any other purpose." The version authorized by his sister, first published in 1593, went through ten editions in the next century and was pirated in Scotland. Other writers "continued," imitated, and embroidered it. In 1616 the unfinished third book was completed by Sir William Alexander. Sir Richard Beling composed a sixth book. James Johnstoun added to book 3. It was translated into the major languages of the Continent and exerted influence there.

Judged by his refinement of diction, formal conventionality, and elevated sentiment, Sidney is pure spirit. "Reason, look to thyself! I serve a goddess," he exclaims in a sonnet. There may be rosy mists, painted clouds, shipwrecks, pirates, and storms, but these are not to be confused with the smokes of burning martyrs or of the battles in which he impetuously distinguished himself. The world of imagination is precisely that. Foxe's spiritual—or is it political—journalism, his purposeful polemic, falls well short of literature in Sidney's eyes.

Sidney, the first major English poet-critic, is a model of correctness, clarity, and measure, but not a man with a "point of view" like Mandeville's or Foxe's. Born with a set of silver spoons in his mouth, he excelled in all he did, but each advantage was discrete from the other: he is a figure of complementarities. There are few literal exchanges between his day-to-day world and his *Arcadia*: experience feeds into imagination through filters; it is translated, encoded. When his niece, Lady Mary Wroth, composed *The Countesse of Montgomery's Urania* in 1621—the first published work of fiction by an Englishwoman—she created a *romance à clef,* a political allegory that entailed (for those in the know) actual people and incidents. Sidney had no truck with shadow play. He encodes themes, some delicate and even dangerous (for example, the sexual ambiguities that emerge from his tales and proved of use to Shakespeare and others): his interest is in ideas and universals.

He compared the mastery of the art of writing to the mastery of horsemanship, but this conceit he pursues more for its elegance than as a serious analogy. He was a moralist in the highest sense, not dogmatic but pragmatic. Fulke Greville in his *Life of Sidney* declared: "His end was not writing, even while he wrote . . . both his wit and understanding bent upon his heart, to make himself and others, not in words or opinion, but in life and action, good and great." Legend says that Charles I, before his execution, read Pamela's prayer, from the episode of her captivity, to give himself a clear mind and heart. (Milton poured scorn on the king, and on *Arcadia,* as a result.)

Portrayed by his contemporaries as a complex, generally attractive Englishman, Sidney appears a Renaissance *uomo universale,* universal man, without the Earl of Surrey's political ambition or Sir Walter Ralegh's overweening libido and hubris. Brittle, buffed, noble in word, thought, and deed, his figure steps out of romance. Greville called him "the wonder of our age" in his "Epitaph," which concludes:

> Now rhyme, the son of rage, which art no kin to skill,
> And endless grief, which deads my life, yet knows not how to kill,

Go, seek that hapless tomb, which if ye hap to find,
Salute the stones, that keep the limbs, that held so good a mind.

Ralegh in an elegy recounts the life:

A king gave thee thy name; a kingly mind,
That God thee gave, who found it now too dear
For this base world, and hath resumed it near,
To sit in skies, and sort with powers divine.

Kent thy birth-days, Oxford held thy youth;
The heavens made haste, and stay'd nor years nor time,
The fruits of age grew ripe in thy first prime;
Thy will, thy words; thy words the seals of truth.

Great gifts and wisdom rare employ'd thee thence,
To treat from kings with those more great than kings.

On Greville's tombstone appear the words "Servant to Queen Elizabeth, Counceller to King James, Frend to Sir Philip Sidney, Trophaeum Peccati [Monument of a sinner]." Such friendship was equivalent to royal service, a distinction when the final trumpet sounds. In every page of his life Sidney lived up to the prescriptions of Castiglione's influential textbook *The Courtier,* down to the matter of writing verse and prose—not to "be a writer" but so that "by that exercise he shall be able to give his judgment on other men's doings." So too he familiarized himself with the arts of music and painting.

There was more, and less, to Sidney than memorialists recount. He was born, the eldest son, in 1554 at the estate that Ben Jonson celebrated in "To Penshurst," in Kent. The king who gave him a name was Philip of Spain, his godfather. He grew up in the presence of well-educated, independent-minded women. They shaped his sense of specific readers and were a readership to whom polite address was due (first his mother, then his sister). His mother was Lady Jane Grey's sister-in-law. A minor writer, she fell victim to smallpox, caught while nursing the Queen through the disease in 1562. She remained a presence at court into the 1570s, by then estranged from her husband. A confidant of Edward VI, he went on to serve Elizabeth.

From an early age Philip was solemn and cool to social and intellectual inferiors. He attacked even his friends with ungrounded suspicions. He could be overzealous in religion. His father reminded him, "Nature hath rampiered up (as it were) the tongue, with lips, yea, and hair without the lips, and all betokening reins, or bridles, for the loose use of this member." Perhaps from his father he derived a fondness for similes and the pathetic fallacy. No tree in Arcadia is without a tongue.

He entered Shrewsbury School, Shropshire, on the same day as Greville. From there he went up to Christ Church, Oxford, but left due to the plague. He spent time at court, writing a masque in the Queen's honor in 1578 to mark her visit to Wanstead, with modest music, recorders, and cornets; and going on missions to the Continent. He spent time as well with his beloved younger sister, Mary, later Countess of Pembroke. His travels began early. At eighteen, in Paris, he witnessed the St. Bartholomew Day Massacre (August 24, 1572); the officially orchestrated mob slaughter of Protestants triggered a rash of massacres across France that lasted for several weeks. England's revulsion ended the unhappy alliance with France; Sidney's Protestant conscience was appalled and fortified. He traveled on to Germany and to Italy, where at Padua his portrait was painted by Veronese. His letters show him generally indifferent to local culture, custom, and architecture. He traveled to meet and make connections.

He returned to Britain in 1575, refined. The following year he visited Ireland and Wales with his father, then deputy of Ireland and president of Wales, and ably defended his conduct of Irish policy. He received from Spenser the dedication of *The Shepherds Calendar,* and from Richard Hakluyt the dedication of the *Voyages.* He served as a member of Parliament, was knighted in 1582, and in 1583 married the daughter of Sir Francis Walsingham, the Queen's powerful secretary and spymaster. He made preparations to accompany Ralegh and Drake to the West Indies in 1585, but he was dispatched instead to the Netherlands, where in 1586 he died. As he lay wounded he called for music, "especially that song which himself had entitled *La cuisse rompue.*" His was a musical family.

A century after Sidney's death John Aubrey, who "nothing affirms" but is a consummate gossip and detractor, apostrophizes him thus: "He was not only an excellent wit, but extremely beautiful: he much resembled his sister, but his hair was not red, but a little inclining, viz. a darke amber color. If I were to find a fault in it, methinkes 'tis not masculine enough." That "not masculine enough" gives pause. As John Lyly said in quite another context, "Appion, raising Homer from Hell, demanded only who was his father; we, calling Alexander from his grave, seek only who was his love." Who *was* his love? Today Sidney draws readers not only to what his prose and poetry say, but to what they do not say, what they imply and withhold even as they twitch the curtain over it.

His sister, Mary Herbert, Countess of Pembroke (1561–1621), loved learning and learned people. Philip was her constant companion in her early years. It was she who urged him to compose *Old Arcadia.* He revised and added to it, and it became the incomplete *The Countess of Pembroke's Arcadia.* He instructed that on his death his friends should not publish it but enjoy it privately. His fame and the proliferation of unauthorized copies made piracy inevitable.

In dedicating the book to Mary, he recalls how he wrote it at her house in Wilton, "in loose sheets of paper, most of it in your presence, and the rest by sheets sent unto you as fast as they were done." Not collaboration, but creative intimacy as close as that between Dorothy and William Wordsworth. There is in *Old Arcadia* an epistolary charm that gives the work more warmth than his poetry possesses. Sidney divided *Arcadia* into books or "Acts," and the work had an impact on the principal Elizabethan dramatists, but certainly not on their dialogue: his characters are undifferentiated in speech, his writing decidedly *written*. Weaving a contentious subject in was a less compromising task for writers of the "newer" writing classes than for those who breathed the air of court. A knight, accustomed to convention and aspiring to preferment, would shy away even from an oblique exploration of the libidinal margins. Sidney's place in the public scheme of things, while it did not check his pen, dictated that his musings should remain among friends.

In 1577 Sidney, rather out of favor in London, first visited his sister at Wilton, which after her marriage had become her "court"; it was here that two years later, after a quarrel with the Earl of Oxford in which the Queen took Oxford's part, he withdrew and wrote *Old Arcadia*. The "rustic" surroundings and the society of articulate and lively women stimulated his sense of the pastoral. He may have possessed a copy of Jacopo Sannazaro's famous, affected pastoral, mixing verse and prose, *Arcadia* (1504), from one of his visits to Venice. Along the way he acquired Jorge de Montemayor's *Los siete libros de la Diana* (*The Seven Books of Diana,* 1559), an early pastoral novel in slow, conventional, moralizing prose, with verse passages and a baffling plot. Sidney's plot is also complicated, and though *Arcadia* isn't rich in advertent humor, some of the disguises and convolutions of narrative raise a smile. *Old Arcadia* was completed in 1581.

Sidney's marriage, an elaborate political and financial arrangement to ease him out of debt, occurred in 1583. Walsingham had no male heir; he agreed to underwrite up to £1,500 of debt and changed his will to include the recently knighted Philip, and the sixteen-year-old Frances became his wife. By marriage he acquired two new seats, both comfortably removed from court but less inaccessible than Wilton House in Wiltshire. In this new situation, Sidney began revising *Arcadia*.

The massive, unfinished revision and expansion known as the *New Arcadia,* begun in 1583, represents a departure and is less a "toy" than the *Old*. More than twice its length, it was intended for a different kind of reader. Sidney adds characters—more than 130 throng the later version—and expands the plot, providing more philosophy and moralizing. The unfolding prose is spacious, its structure classical. Readers move from one crafted sentence to the next as though through the bounteous rooms of a cool, well-lit mansion. The vestibule prepares us for the style of the whole building: "Arcadia among all the provinces of Greece was ever had in singular reputation, partly for the sweetness of the air and other natural benefits: but, principally, for the moderate and well tempered minds of the people, who, (finding how true a contentation is gotten by following the course of nature, and how the shining title of glory so much affected by other nations, doth indeed help little to the happiness of life) were the only people, which as by their justice and providence, gave neither cause nor hope to their neighbors to annoy them, so were they not stirred with false praise, to trouble their quiet." Even the shepherds, living in the neighborhood of such a sentence, are favored by the Muses and speak with an indecorous (because too refined) clarity.

Arcadia, with its classical toponymy, oracles, and pastoral trappings, is not England; nor are its characters veiled allusions to actual men and women of the day. Sidney is creating a moral, not a parallel, social world. Had the Queen recognized herself in the foolish, irresolute, and driven Basilius, for virtue's sake taking his female household into Arcadia to keep it morally safe, and there succumbing himself to moral temptation, or had she sensed herself satirized in any of the other figures of aging power, she would have been displeased.

*Old* and *New Arcadia* say no more than they mean. Here is writing whose primary intention is to give pleasure. The governing plot, presented obliquely and frequently digressed from, centers on the aging "Paphlagonian king" Basilius, troubled by the passing of time, who ignores good counsel to pursue his "baser" desires. Basilius is the father of two highly eligible daughters, Pamela and Philoclea. He visits an oracle for advice, but gets sounder counsel (Sidney being hostile to superstition) from his old friend Philanax, who says the best thing he can do to ensure the future of his stable, prospering realm is to go home and govern it. Basilius is reluctant to return.

Pyrocles and Musidorus, seemingly respectable princes but bent on pleasure, woo the princesses. Pyrocles has his way with Philoclea. Meanwhile the king falls for the tall, blonde eighteen-year-old Amazonian girl called Cleophila, who is actually Pyrocles in drag. His queen, Gynecia, seeing through the disguise, is equally beguiled. Basilius is racked with guilt and would kill himself, but is dissuaded by Philoclea who, though she has lost her maidenhead to the overheated prince, emerges stronger and wiser than before, a pleasant change from the usual punishments meted out to misled virgins. Things (complicatedly) sort themselves out; in the end the princes are spared and marry the princesses.

This work is quite without misogyny, which reflects on Sidney's attitude to women and his sense of audience. Women's perspectives are significant. Heroines upstage the male leads. Philoclea counsels despairing Pyrocles against suicide. Gynecia, the mature, sexually alert queen, could have been made a grotesque. She is presented as an educated woman with passions neither unseemly nor comical. Male characters when they err, as Basilius does, get shorter shrift. In the subplots, there is no sympathy for the Don Juanesque Pamphilus, whereas Argalus's continued love for Parthenia, despite injuries sustained in an acid-throwing incident, is celebrated. Critics keen to find contemporary reference see in virtuous Pamela a shadow of Lady Jane Grey, in the aging Andromana a veiled, unflattering reference to the "Fortress of Perfect Beauty," the Queen.

Though *Arcadia* is not allegory but figurative narrative, like all works initially transmitted in manuscript form, it is a notoriously unstable text. *Old Arcadia* went through four or more substantial revisions, the *New Arcadia* was similarly revised, and when the composite version was finally published in 1593, it had no authorial sanction but was an attempt to knock faultier versions out of circulation. The 1593 printed version, which we owe in all likelihood to Mary, splices the concluding three acts of *Old Arcadia* to the *New,* which concludes midsentence in book 3, inviting later writers to fill in a substantial blank.

The volume includes verse, dialogue that falls short of dramatic, moral reflection, and description. Excitement is to be found not in the unfolding of plot but in the development of argument and production of unexpected ideas. Some readers find a latent "psychology" behind the shepherds' masks. Here Samuel Richardson finds not only the character of Pamela but also plot elements explored, with less philosophical mercy, in *Clarissa*. The simple figurative language eloquently but not ostentatiously disposed is a model of good moral writing, with firm categories and sufficient visual reality:

> The fair Pamela whose noble heart had long disdained to find the trust of her virtue reposed in the hands of a shepherd, had, yet (to show an obedience) taken on a shepherdish apparel, which was of russet velvet, cut after their fashion with a straight body open breasted the nether part full of pleats with wide open sleeves hanging down very low, her hair at the full length wound about with gold lace: By the comparison, to show, how far her hair did excel in color, betwixt her breasts, which sweetly rise up like two faire mountainettes in the pleasant vale of Tempe, there hanging down a jewel which she had devised as an Impresa, of her own estate, it was a perfect white Lamb tied at a stake, with a great number of chains, as

if it had been feared lest the silly creature should do some great harm, neither had she added any word unto it, (which is as it were the life of an Impresa) but even took silence as the word of the poor lamb, showing such humbleness, as not to use her own voice for complaint of her misery. But, when the ornament of the earth, young Philoclea appeared in her nymphelike apparel, so near nakedness, as one might well discern part of her perfections: And yet so apparelled as did show, she kept the best store of her beauties to her self, her excellent faire hair drawn up into a net, made only of it self, a net in deed to have caught the wildest disposition, her body covered with a light taffeta garment, so cut, as the wrought smock came through it in many places, enough, to have made a very restrained imagination have thought what was under it: with the sweet cast of her black eye, which seemed to make a contention whether that in perfect blackness, or her skin in perfect whiteness were the most excellent.

---

Samuel Richardson was almost two centuries away, but Sidney had like-minded contemporaries whose work shared qualities with his. Robert Greene (1560?–1592) was a writer of promise and a controversialist. His performance fell short because he directed his wit against himself. He led a proto-Bohemian existence, in the end preferring life to art, abandoning his child and wife after spending her dowry, and dying of an overdose of pickled herring and Rhine wine in the house of a poor shoemaker. Among his earliest prose works is a pamphlet sequel to Lyly's *Euphues,* but his prose was to shed much of the affectation in which it began, thanks perhaps to the disciplines of the drama. His plays (and his contribution to other dramatists' work, including Shakespeare's) are his chief legacy. He also wrote memorably, though in journalistic vein, about low life in his autobiographical work and in *Conny-catching* (1591, 1592). His most deliberate compositions were romances, hortatory and moral, chaste, remote from the accidents of his own short life. *Menaphon* (1589), described by Gabriel Harvey as "an acrid review of recent literature," reprinted ten year's later as *Greene's Arcadia,* mixes prose and verse and creates credible female voices. Princess Sephestia, shipwrecked on the Arcadian coast, is found by the shepherd Menaphon. He falls in love with her, and in due course she finds her way back to her husband and son. Greene also composed *Pandosto, or Dorastus and Fawnia* (1588), from which Shakespeare drew plot elements for *The Winter's Tale;* also *Perimedes the Blacksmith* (1588) and *Philomela* (1592).

One of Sidney's immediate, unsubtle heirs was his niece. In publishing *Urania*, Mary Wroth (1587?–1651 / 1653) stressed her kinship with Sidney, standing on his dignity so to speak. Her work at first seems to resemble his in tone and manner but could not be more different in form. The enormous narrative, with a cast of dozens, is episodic with no thematic or structural dynamic. Her theme, she says, is "spider love," the kind that snares its quarry in a web, and which she had experienced in her miserable first marriage and then in her long incestuous relationship with her cousin William, the Earl of Pembroke, who fathered her surviving children. She is concerned with women who have been abandoned, deceived, maltreated. Unlike her uncle's, the characters in her imaginary country are based upon people and events whose reality is blurred but not effaced, courtiers and members of their families. Among her subjects was the Denny family, and Sir Edmund Denny, a harsh paterfamilias, was not pleased, referring to her as a "hermaphrodite in show, indeed a monster." After spiritedly defending herself, finding no support, she withdrew her book from circulation. There is something anachronistic about the dreadful fates that lie in store both for the sincere woman and for the lascivious, scheming kind: virtuous women's suffering reverses that of the disdained knights in courtly love romances, while the vicious suffer cruel executions more appropriate to men or, in more recent memory, to Scottish queens.

Was Sidney in *Arcadia* trying to provide an antidote to the fashionable example of John Lyly? *Euphues*—a rare work of literature whose title has become a noun and an adjective, *euphuism, euphuistic*—had a powerful impact on the fictional writing of its age, just as his courtly plays affected the drama. Lyly was socially far below Sidney's notice, and he does not allude directly to him. But Sidney's style and manner, which are formal and contrived, by contrast with Lyly's, come to seem subtle, direct, and nuanced in terms of character and tone.

John Lyly was born around in 1554, probably in Canterbury, into a locally noted family. His father, Peter, was city registrar, his grandfather the renowned grammarian William Lyly, a colleague of Thomas More. A scholar of King's School, the boy received a strict education. Christopher Marlowe may have been a fellow pupil. From King's, he went to Magdalen College, Oxford. There is no record that he suffered hardship or compromised his studies to earn bread and board. "More wit than scholar," he developed a preference for poetry and the classics over the logical and philosophical disciplines. He received his BA in 1573 and set about finding a patron. He applied, at first unsuccessfully, to Lord Burghley, who eventually relented.

At the age of twenty-four he completed the first part of the book for which he is principally remembered, *Euphues: The Anatomy of Wit* (published in 1579, it was immediately successful and went through five editions before the end of 1586). Lyly called this precocious work "my first counterfaite," meaning by that word not something factitious but something fictional, made against the grain of expectation. An *anatomy* is "a detailed examination," taking apart in order to understand, identifying all the constituents. Anatomists say that, having dissected a body, it is hard to stuff all the bits back inside and sew it up again. The sum of the parts in the end much exceeds the whole.

The sequel to *The Anatomy of Wit* is *Euphues and His England* (1580, four printings before the end of 1586), almost equally successful. Taken together, they consolidated a genre that, even when it passed out of fashion, continued to influence writing. Shakespeare, Jonson, and many others of the late sixteenth and early seventeenth centuries were affected (in both senses) by Lyly. The book remained in print until 1636, after which its neglect began. Lyly never quite replicated the early success, turning his refined energies to the stage instead.

Euphues is a young man from Athens, displaced to Naples. Here we can read for a figurative sense—Athens can mean Oxford, Naples can mean London—without doing violence to Lyly's intentions. In Naples he meets another youth, Philautus, who will balance out both books with him, and for whom he contrives an intimate affection: "Assure yourself that Damon to his Pythias, Pylades to his Orestes, Titus to his Gysippus, Theseus to his Pyrothus, Scipio to his Laelius, was never found more faithful than Euphues will be to his Philautus." At least, to start with. Philautus's fiancée is called Lucilla, and Euphues falls in love with her, only to be rejected. That is what happens, and fails to happen, in *Euphues: The Anatomy of Wit*. It is enough to keep the moral mills grinding, awfully fine. Old Eubulus has a lot to say about the silliness of youth and stands godfather to a number of pompous counselors and old men in the drama: Polonius and Ulysses have their Eubulian monologues, and Adriano de Armado in *Love's Labors Lost* embodies Shakespeare's exasperation with Euphuism.

*Euphues and His England* abandons Naples for England. Euphues and Philautus have patched up their differences. They go to Lyly's own Canterbury, and Fidus, a figure for generous faith rather than a character, entertains them. Here Philautus falls in love and it is Euphues's turn generously and garrulously to look on. First Philautus loses his heart to a woman already betrothed, echoing Euphues's misjudgment in the first volume; then he chooses less unwisely and fares better. Finally Euphues leaves England with much praise for it and its women and repairs to a hermitage in Silexedra, where he can be quietly miserable. The symmetries between the two books are mechanical. Both volumes are assembled from various sources and tend toward the anthology. The books appeared as "compilations" in the Stationers' Register.

The name Euphues means "well-grown, shapely, goodly" in Greek. As an adjective, "euphuistic" has come to mean "overworked, fussy, ornate" in English. Lyly's "counterfaite" was less original than it seems to us in retrospect: we have lost sight of the precious, overelaborated work that surrounded it and of the writings it is sourced in, but he "hatched the eggs that his elder friends laid." Just as Sidney took his bearings in *Arcadia* from Sannazaro and Montemayor, so Lyly's work is grounded in the Spanish writer Guevara and his *alto estilo* or "elevated style." Lord Berners's *Froissart* (1524) already employed such a style, and the leading teachers of the day did not discourage it in the schools. Pettie's *Petite Pallace of Pettie His Pleasure* (1576) is an absurd, earnest storehouse of proto-euphuistic rhetoric.

About *Euphues,* as about Lyly's plays, there is a classicizing, if not a classical enthusiasm, in continual retreat from the real world and its contingencies. Sir Thomas North's *Diall of Princes,* his translation—from a French version, not from the original Spanish—of Fray Antonio de Guevara's *Relox de principes* or *Libro aureo del Emperador Marco Aurelio* (The *Golden Book of the Emperor Marcus Aurelius*) is Lyly's most ample source text, and his two books closely parallel many features of the Spanish original.

Fray Antonio de Guevara (1480?–1545) spent his youth at a Spanish court that, with the marriage of Isabel of Castille to Ferdinand of Aragon, had begun a golden age of art, exploration, and science. At this court Guevara distinguished himself in eloquence and scholarship and became orator, and then chronicler, to Carlos V, and eventually—having entered the Franciscan order—Bishop of Gaudix and Inquisitor. His writings are those of a moralist, and his style was regarded either as "delicious" or (less enthusiastically) "loquacious" by his contemporaries: mouthfuls of sound, exquisite feats of clausal balance, antitheses, parallelisms, similes, repetitions, wordplay. It is said that he wrote as he spoke, and this seems as likely of him as of Lyly, an exquisite delighting in his exquisiteness: Wildean vanity without barbs. Where Guevara's formalities are genuinely courtly, Lyly's are academic: he was never at home at court, a place to which the language of Sidney was appropriate. In a sense, Lyly is inventing a courtly language from a subordinate position.

Guevara's *Relox* (1529) is fiction drawing on the life and legend of the philosophical emperor Marcus Aurelius and includes imaginary letters. It opens with a genealogy, the date of his birth calculated according to several different calendars to make it clear from the outset that our author knows everything and, what is worse, intends to share. His aim is to set out the duties of a Christian prince, but his argument, narrative, and meditation are so full of recondite divagations whose only purpose is to add specious seriousness to the enterprise, displaying the author's wit, that we content ourselves with the surface, magnificent and absurd. He also published *Epistolas familiares* (1539–1541), a variety of imaginary romantic letters that propose templates for formal letters. Richardson's specimen letter-book is foreshadowed here.

Like Guevara, Lyly was ostensibly engaged in writing a moral treatise, not without debts to Erasmus, when he stumbled upon the novel form. For him, too, it mixed modes: narrative, epistle, essay, dialogue, verse. In *Euphues* begins the novel of manners and the reflective romantic novel. It helped to shape Richardson's enterprise but not his style. Lyly develops logical and rhetorical architectures rather than narrative structure: we find here no engaging characters, no room for chance, no dailiness, no integration. Paradox is at home, preening paradox that flatters writer and reader. "The sun shineth upon the dunghill, and is not corrupted." Lyly controlled only the surface of his art. Part two of *Euphues* is more accomplished than part one, but not as fiction. A brief, aphorizing extract from Cassander's letter to Callimachus shows Lyly's high sentence:

> Enter not into bands, no not for thy best friends: he that payeth another man's debt seeketh his own decay, it is as rare to see a rich surety as a black swan, and he that lendeth to all that will borrow, showeth great good will, but little wit. Lend not a penny without pawn, for that will be a good gage to borrow. Be not hasty to marry, it is better to have one plough going, then two cradles: and more profit to have a barn filled then a bed. But if thou can'st not live chastely, choose such an one, as may be more commended for humility, then beauty. A good housewife, is a great patrimony: and she is most honorable, that is most honest. If thou desire to be old, beware of too much wine: if to be healthy, take heede of many women: if too be rich, shun playing at all games. Long quaffing, maketh a short life: fond lust, causeth dry bones: and lewd pastimes, naked purses.

This is a deliberated, protracted miscalculation, by turns ridiculous, tedious, and then, inexplicably and as it were accidentally, familiar and moving. ("Night has a thousand eyes.") Education damaged Lyly, unfitting him for the rough and tumble of the Elizabethan world. "Far more seemly to have thy study full of books, than thy purse full of money" is a charming, even compelling sentiment, but not a recipe for living, unless—as Lyly did not—one stayed within the confines of an old university. Study damaged his language, beautified it formulaically, destroyed natural proportion, and raised grace to a pitch of gracelessness. How he would labor for an assonance ("Many strokes overthrow the tallest oak"), how readily he rides from his primary sense on a sententious conceit ("Time draweth wrinkles in a fair face," he says, a beautiful metaphor, but then he erases it with a long sequel, "but addeth fresh colors to a fast friend, which neither heat, nor cold, nor misery, nor place, nor destiny, can alter or diminish.")

The short-phrased briskness of Lyly's best prose tends toward stasis and is proof against dramatic development. We read sentence by sentence, paragraph by paragraph: it is series rather than sequence, an anthology of effects drawn from the pastoral and classical rubble. Such a style calls attention to the author. Philautus means "self-love," a kind of narcissistic self-regard. Lyly has more in common, we might think, with Euphues's friend than with retiring Euphues himself. Sidney's *Arcadia* does not insist on the author's presence. Its investment in the classical world is genuine, by contrast with Lyly's self-affirming project. As a writer of fiction, Lyly after *Euphues* is of little interest.

———•———

Thomas Lodge (1558?–1625) was Lyly's most direct heir. He studied law, then turned to literature, then medicine. Though he traveled adventurously, as far as South America, his writings are lashed to Lyly's mast, and even though every line of *Rosalynde: or, Euphues' Golden Legacy* (1590) was (literally, we are supposed to assume) "wet with the surge" of his journey to the Canaries, there is no evidence of that journey in the writing. As the seas burst and the winds roared, Lodge's imagination moved among swains and milkmaids, roved in woods and daisied dells. *Rosalynd*'s abiding distinction is that Shakespeare drew *As You Like It* out of it. *Margarite of America* (written 1592, published 1596) he claimed to have written on his longer journey. The greatest exoticism is in the title.

Sidney noted—with Lyly in mind—how some of his contemporaries who concentrate on expression "often run from the matter." A stylized pastoral landscape is no closer to "nature" than an allegorical landscape is. Lyly did not listen to himself when he prettily declared: "Beauty—a deceitful bait with a deadly hook." To aim at beauty line by line is to forfeit that deeper beauty that issues from integration. After the stylistic novelty wore off, didactic narratives lacked urgency—and relevance. Prose readers wanted either solid information or brisk entertainment, full of sensation and surprise. Periphrastic politeness and the once-fashionable refinements of refinements that constituted euphuism became obsolete.

———•———

From the *politesse* of Euphues to the stentorian company of Thomas Nashe's Jack Wilton: it is like stepping from a cloister into a teeming marketplace. Lyly's purities and paradoxes stifle, his perfumes cloy; but Nashe's stenches, stridencies, and heartlessness are almost intolerable. Thomas Dekker, dramatist and pamphleteer, a champion of the underdog who revered and imitated Nashe, called his pen a "deadly stockado." "The Choice of Valentines," dedicated to Lord Strange, was a bawdy poem on a theme that led to its being dubbed "Nashe's Dildo." This was probably not his only foray into the world of "Gomorrah's filth." Gabriel Harvey hated him as a stirrer-up, a failed scholar, "this mud born bubble, this bile on the brow of the University, this bladder of pride new blown," and elsewhere, implicating him in an extended attack on Greene, "this Gogmagog Iewish Thalmud of absurdities." In *Love's Labors Lost* we encounter a different Nashe. Shakespeare created Moth in *A Midsummer Night's Dream* in Nashe's image, it is said. He addresses Moth as "dear imp" and "my tender juvenal." Nashe had admirers, loving contemporaries, and powerful foes. Marlowe he met at Cambridge, and they kept in touch until Marlowe's murder. He co-wrote Ben Jonson's first performed play, *The Isle of Dogs* (1597). In London his inner circle included Lyly, the poet Thomas Watson, and Greene.

Nashe's life was short, only two years longer than Sidney's. As a writer he rose, shone, and fell in the space of a single decade. He was pursued by destitution, lived hand to mouth, and died out of grace and out of town, avoiding the not quite long enough arm of the law. But his life was rich in incident, and he wrote on every subject and in almost every mode: satire, poetry, philosophy, theology, drama, political pieces, classical translations, and pornography. Poverty he turned, as Greene had done, to literary advantage, drawing characters and scenes both from his East Anglian childhood and from the slums of the city. He captured the character of a Tudor England from which his more decorous contemporaries averted their eyes. His candor tended toward satire. *The Unfortunate Traveller* qualifies as the first full-blown English novel, if we take that term, as we have done so far, to denote a work with a generally coherent narrator or narrative tone, a story line or lines, and one or more characters who carry the burden of the action and endure the *agons,* adventures, or trials of the book.

Nashe was born late in 1567 in the coastal town of Lowestoft, Suffolk, the easternmost town in England, one of seven children. Just one brother, Israel, survived childhood with him. His father was a parson, modestly well off. Nashe grew up around fishermen and developed a respect for all "seaborderers." He was probably home-tutored by his father.

At Cambridge he comes more sharply into view. He made his first literary friends and wrote his first serious work, published later when he got to London. He remembered fondly the effect university had upon him, despite want and the stifling new ideas then in vogue. He went up at the age of fourteen to St. John's College. In common with poorer undergraduates, he began student life as a sizar scholar, paying his way by performing menial tasks for the better off. Even so, he depended on his father's allowance to survive.

At Cambridge he contracted the enmity of the Harveys. The Harveys, Gabriel in particular, were university luminaries, but Gabriel was past his prime and had failed to become public orator in 1581. He then failed to become master of Trinity Hall. His brother Richard was a bitter, temperamental praelector of philosophy at Pembroke Hall, and John Harvey was an astrologer with medical responsibilities at Queen's College. None of the three could handle the invective in which Nashe's circle specialized, though in time they learned to dish it. Nashe became attached to the anti-Harvey party before the Harveys knew who he was. For one offense Nashe was put in the stocks.

In 1586 he took his BA, intending to follow on with a master's the next year. Instead, he left suddenly and mysteriously. It may be as well that he left: his talents were too eclectic for scholarship. His father's death in January 1587 cut off that stream of support. But his talents had been noted and his contemporaries were making their names. Nashe arrived in London in 1588, twenty and unknown. It was the year of the Armada, when "mice-eyed decipherers and calculators upon characters," as he called the censors, were busy sniffing out sedition. Poverty fueled his frenzied creativity. He fought for patronage, lived like a transient, flitted between patrons, friends, inns, lodging houses, and at least one jail cell. Beyond London's old city wall were acres of land that formerly belonged to the church. New arrivals escaping rural hardship crowded in; by the 1580s a huge, unsavory favela sprawled north of Bishopsgate. Here, and not among the spires, markets, and palaces of the city and Westminster, Nashe experienced the social disparities of the Tudor city. Marlowe and Shakespeare, both like Nashe newcomers to the city in the late 1580s, lived there as well. Anger, daily deprivation, and amazement turned Nashe into a satirist. Saintsbury despised him as "one of the not quite best class of 'newspaper men'—Thackeray's Bohemians." He is as much a begetter of journalism as of the novel.

In the pamphlet wars he was a pen for hire. By day he visited the Inns of Court or St. Paul's, which, despite the Church's efforts to quell it, had the character of a huge market for books, among other things. Jobbing authors sought out employment there. Best was "penny-a-line" work that theater companies sometimes offered. Money had to be more actively sought, too: Nashe grew accustomed to "following a gouty patron by the smell." The work he got sold him short. Manual workers, he said, were better paid and had more dependable incomes than writers. He fell into debt and did time for it, though generally he stayed on the right side of the law.

In 1589 it seemed that Nashe might begin to prosper. Robert Greene invited him to add a preface for *Menaphon*, published in the summer. Greene's work was popular, *Menaphon* was an ambitious effort, and the association of his name with Nashe's would enhance the younger author's chances of attracting patrons. Nashe was genuinely grateful. He later defended Greene (to his own cost) against attacks from the Harveys after Greene abandoned his wife.

In pamphleteering, in the pay of the government, Nashe found his feet. He worked alongside others, Lyly included, against an anonymous Puritan source, "Martin Marprelate." The exchanges lasted well into 1590: the controversy was a good earner and brought writers into contact with influential men, among them Archbishop Whitgift. It also exposed them to censure. Richard Harvey, though not a "Martinist," felt obliged to write against the hacks. The controversy tailed off in 1590, but pamphleteering remained Nashe's métier between more lucrative jobs. A few of the pamphlets survive. The discipline served Nashe, honing a style direct and emphatic, prying him free of university wit. The satirist sailed close to the wind in an age when political discourse was monitored. Secret presses were vulnerable, and it was hard to distribute prohibited texts. England's and Protestantism's enemies were strong. Nashe's conscience, like his style, was mercurial. His paymasters spanned a spectrum from Puritan printer to recusant gentry. In his independent writing, dwelling on the social minutiae that secure his modern appeal, Nashe avoided politics, neither supporting nor challenging the establishment unless for pay. No confusing him with a simmering urban radical: his gift was for impetuous, destructive criticism. He did not set himself against the squalor and fragmentation of sixteenth-century city life. Charitable even in poverty, he was cynical too. Satirizing the rich and powerful never stopped him from accepting their money. On the other hand, he saw no value in the "mungrel Democratia, in which one is all & all is one."

Ferdinando Stanley, Lord Strange, scion of an old, powerful, and sometimes recusant northern family, became for a time Nashe's regular patron. Lord Strange was a poet and a patron of the arts: Greene, Lyly, Spenser, Marlowe, and others took his shilling before his premature and suspect death in 1594 at the age of thirty-five. As one of "Strange's Men" Nashe made his name with *Pierce Penniless*. Three editions appeared in 1592 alone, two more followed later in the decade. Nashe refers to a French edition and considered writing a sequel. The book's influence extended directly into the next generation: it energized a genre, and it can be read today. Primarily a work of satire and semi-autobiography, it portrays common London folk and the servants of the rich. *Pierce* was pronounced *Purse:* the title's double entendre declares the theme. After the pamphlet's success, Nashe's nickname was Pierce.

"Pierce" is young, destitute, energetic, and angry, a vehicle for Nashe's own character and a legitimate way to bemoan his predicament and deal with sensitive issues at one remove. Pierce sets off to find the Devil in the hope of persuading him to carry off some misers and usurers and get money flowing again.

Pierce sells his own soul to the devil, as Marlowe's Dr. Faustus did at roughly the same time. Like Faustus's, Pierce's conjuration of the Devil brought charges of diabolism against the author. Here the energies of satire ceased to belong to the Puritan cause. Indeed, *Pierce Penniless,* though it anatomizes poverty and identifies foes, has no coherent "cause" as such, and no plot, simply that abundant linguistic verve seeking an appropriate form. Nashe excelled in the drama, but this was not dramatic material.

Greene died, and Nashe defended his memory; then the plague carried off 10,000 Londoners, and in 1593 Marlowe was murdered at a Deptford tavern. Nashe reflected, "It was but a word and a blow, Lord have mercy upon us, and he was gone." He and "the diviner Muse" may have drifted apart, but his lament was heartfelt.

Late in 1593 Nashe landed a relatively stable patron in Sir George Carey, a magnate who held court at Carisbrooke Castle on the Isle of Wight. Carey was son of a Lord Chamberlain and the Queen's first cousin via Anne Boleyn. Nashe traveled there before Christmas. He came to love the place: peaceful, bountiful, and far even from London. He stopped there two months. In the castle, exposed to "the image of the ancient hospitality," he thrived. Back in London he enjoyed the Carey connection well into 1594, the year in which he published *The Unfortunate Traveller.*

His later life remained one of conflict: a lighthearted exchange turned into a vitriolic battle of pamphlets, essays, and letters. He stayed close to Lyly and others in his circle, found new patrons, and wrote at the same astonishing rate, but his main work was done. The short golden age of ill-censored printing, of satire and pamphleteering, accelerated the gestation of new forms, but Puritanism, and with it the "pinchfarts" and "pennyfathers" that Nashe despised, grew stronger: for the iconoclast freelance it had been a false dawn. When he and Jonson wrote *The Isle of Dogs* (1597), it was instantly condemned as a "lewd play" and seditious. Arrests were made, Jonson was sent to the Marshalsea. Nashe removed himself from London. Then on July 28, 1597, London's theaters were closed. On June 1, 1599, Whitgift himself commanded that all "unseemly Satires & Epigrams," including scores of individual pieces by dozens of authors but also "all Nashes' books"—and all those of Dr. Harvey besides—be "taken wheresoever they may be found." No new printings of any of the impounded works were to be authorized. Some were ritually burned at Stationers' Hall.

*The Unfortunate Traveller* appeared when Nashe had made his name. *Pierce Penniless* was selling. He dedicated the first edition of *Traveller* to the recusant Earl of Southampton, a prolific patron known to us from Shakespeare's dedication of the *Sonnets.* He referred to the book as a "fantastical Treatise" combining "history, and variety of mirth." In the induction he calls it a "pamphlet," but it was at once longer than a pamphlet and served no particular party except the anti-papists. Its form is unusual: it creates a single narrator whose adventures are the subject of the book. This is not a framing device for a clutch of classical tales but a continuous picaresque "run."

The *picaresque* is important in the formation of the novel and is still alive and well. Ford Madox Ford defines it succinctly: "the strung-together life of a *picaro* or professional thief," a series of stories with a rogue for protagonist. It had its origin in Spain, where the novel first became a literary "commodity," and translations of picaresque novels gained popularity in England in the 1580s. The first and greatest of them, *Lazarillo de Tormes* (1554, of uncertain authorship), tells the story of a miller's son, beginning his adventures near Salamanca, where his widowed mother, fallen on hard times and with a new baby to feed, reluctantly sells Lazarillo into bondage. He becomes guide and helper to a cantankerous, evil old blind beggar, levels the score by stealing his food and money (much to readers' delight, so harsh was the boy's bondage), and then works his way through several low-life employers and patrons, each emblematic of some aspect of Spanish society (the false priest, the parasitic hidalgo, and so forth), until he becomes in the end the town crier of Toledo. David Rowland published a translation of *Lazarillo* in 1576, basing his version on the French, but also referring to the latest (1573) Spanish edition. The book in English was reprinted ten times in the next century. In the twentieth century, the Colombian novelist Gabriel García Márquez detects the original use of "interior monologue" later perfected by Joyce and Woolf in this striking, unsubtle book. Readers familiar with the early chapters of Defoe's *Colonel Jack* have read a softened English transposition of the classic Spanish work; and the cruel early scenes in *Oliver Twist* continue the tradition. The young V. S. Naipaul stumbled upon it, translating it and finding his way, thanks to it, to *Miguel Street* (his first novel, written in six weeks in 1955, published in 1959).

The episodic nature of the picaresque, Ford suggests, answered its original use: the adventures were read aloud at court, at home, at inns, at gatherings, night after night; Lazarillo's adventures with different masters are contrived to fill an early evening with half an hour's or a chapter's ribaldry. A Muslim tradition may be at the root of the picaresque, the one that produced the *1001 Nights* (not translated into English in full until the nineteenth century). But the picaresque concentrates on a single narrator's singular life. The ghost of the picaresque haunts European fiction (with the exception of Richardson) until, Ford says, Flaubert's *Madame Bovary* (1857) delivers the novel from it. After that the novel became a "complete work of art, having at once *progression d'effet, charpente, façade, cadences, mots justes*—and all the other attributes of a work of art in its glory, for which the English language has no name."

*The Unfortunate Traveller* is told by Jack Wilton, an unruly court page, a rowdy chap and a chancer, not unlike Nashe himself though younger, handsomer, and better born, but equally impecunious. Nashe sets the action in the past to avoid imputations of political or religious topicality. Jack succeeds in ways that Nashe never managed to do: he outwits, outlives, and outloves his foes. Jack addresses fellow court pages. The invocation ends, "Hey-pass, come aloft! Every man of you take your places, and hear Jack Wilton tell his own tale."

We are outside the French town of Therouanne ("Turwin"), newly under English control in the aftermath of Henry VIII's razzia of 1513. Nashe describes a large and messy place inhabited by the dregs of the late campaign: camp followers, drunkards, thieves, and the easily gulled. He deceives the Lord of Misrule in the English camp, dupes the cider merchant and the spendthrift bully captain, and cross-dresses to delude the fastidious fops. Suffering from the sweating sickness, he returns home. Soon he is back on the Continent, witnessing battles, the slaughter of Anabaptists, and much else.

When he meets the Earl of Surrey and enters his service, there is a change of tone and manner. He becomes less a lad, more a man. Jack traces Surrey's romance with Geraldine. Surrey is endowed with an appropriate voice. They meet Erasmus in Rotterdam, and Sir Thomas More. Surrey is greeted pompously at Wittenberg: "The heads of their university (they were great heads, of certainty) met him in their hooded hypocrisy and doctorly accoutrements." A "burstenbelly inkhorn orator" orates: "Why should I go gadding and fizgigging after firking flantado amphibologies?" We encounter Martin Luther.

The earl and his man exchange identities and proceed to Italy; Jack cozens a courtesan out of counterfeit gold, then gets accused for passing it on. He finds the irresistible Diamante, confined due to the jealousy of her husband, the Magnifico Castaldo. After further adventures Surrey recovers his identity, gains his beloved, and departs. Jack is left masterless in a Rome ravaged by the plague. He is entranced by beautiful Heraclida, who is raped by a villainous Spaniard, Esdras de Granado, in a mercilessly circumstantial passage. "On the hard boards he threw her, and used his knee as an iron ram to beat ope the two-leaved gate of her chastity." Her husband's murdered corpse provides the pillow "to his abomination." Heraclida commits suicide and Jack is falsely accused of her rape and once more imprisoned. Reflecting in his cell, he characterizes the nations of Europe and sends up the ritual of the Grand Tour.

Zadock the Jew enslaves him, then sells him to Doctor Zacharie for anatomical exploration. "Oh, the cold sweating cares which I conceived after I knew I should be cut like a French summer doublet!" The Jew, a cousin of Christopher Marlowe's Barabas in *The Jew of Malta*, foreshadows the intransigent Shylock; and Juliana, who tries to redeem Jack from captivity, is not unlike

Portia in her wit and wiles. Justice of a sort is in the end brutally done. Nashe delivers, with a kind of relishing, some of the most appalling accounts of protracted torture in our literature. Not until Bret Easton Ellis in *American Psycho* does he find his equal. Nashe knew what the public wanted and supplied it. Well in advance of the Jacobean dramatists, he deploys lewdness and violence, gory battles and close-up executions. He invents an almost convincing female lead in exotic Diamante. Then Jack decides he's had enough, gets married, does alms, and departs. He ends up at the Field of the Cloth of Gold.

The tale visits much of Western Europe, playing fast and loose with historical chronology. There is no evidence that Nashe traveled much beyond the Isle of Wight: his invention is Mandevillian. His depictive skills can make whole tableaux come alive through deft, earthy metaphor—for example, an aftermath of battle: "Here unwieldy Switzers wallowing in their gore like an ox in his dung; there the sprightly French sprawling and turning on the stained grass like a roach new taken out of the stream. All the ground was strewn as thick with battle-axes as the carpenter's yard with chips: the plain appeared like a quagmire, overspread as it was with trampled dead bodies. In one place you might behold a heap of dead murdered men overwhelmed with a falling steed instead of a tombstone; in another place a bundle of bodies fettered together in their own bowels."

As in other picaresque novels, there is narrative and progression but no overarching structure. It is more a novel than anything else Nashe wrote, indeed than almost anything else yet written in English. It doesn't wander lost in the corridors between philosophy, theology, and romance; it is not a protracted exercise in rhetorical styles. There is a narrator, and from time to time the story remembers where it has been and builds on an earlier character or effect.

Commercially, *The Unfortunate Traveller* did well; not as well as *Pierce Penniless* but well enough to require further printings. If there is no direct line from Nashe to Defoe, say, or Dickens, his achievement is not diminished. He wrote in a time before the broad readership that made the successes of Bunyan and Defoe possible; he wrote in the teeth of a censorship unevenly applied; many of his works were destroyed. But he wrote from and of the cities of Europe, he created characters; in place of classical draperies and marble bodies he supplied real voices, flesh and blood, rags and robes, the streets and alleys of cities his readers might walk through. He understood the negative emotions in a way and to a degree that only Jonathan Swift, among later writers, would do. He is inventive and fantastical; his figures exist on the verge of caricature, of melodrama.

Not only in the sixteenth but in later centuries too the Protestant spirit was not always sympathetic to the wider culture in which it moved; we find no tolerance or charity in Nashe. Like all believers, the Protestant writing for himself or his cause despises what he opposes, whether the Puritan or the Roman Catholic. He does not set out to comprehend or encompass. *The Unfortunate Traveller* is brutal. An Englishman displaced from his own country reveals his nature. His, and that of his readers who share some of his fears and disgust with alien ideas and people. In creating a "them," he creates an "us" around the morally obnoxious but humanly beguiling *picaro* Jack Wilton. Nashe is intuitive, not intellectual; imaginative rather than analytical. His bad taste is manifest in the failure of proportion, in the heartless prurience of the story, in over-elaboration. Dickens has the same rich abundance of matter, the sense of words and events pressing for admission. But Dickens's sense of form forces the disparate elements into shape; form limits his excesses.

# | 4 |

# Before Irony

John Bunyan

"Outwardly the extreme puritan appears narrow, crabbed, fanatical, gloomy and dull," writes V. S. Pritchett, "but from the inside—what a series of dramatic climaxes his life is, what a fascinating casuistry beguiles him, how he is be-mused by the comedies of duplicity, sharpened by the ingenious puzzles of the conscience, and carried away by the eloquence of hypocrisy." From the inside he is a spiritual *picaro*. "He lives like a soldier, now in the flash of battle, now in the wangling of camp and billet. However much he may bore others, he never suffers from boredom himself."

In *The Pilgrim's Progress* we get inside the puritan. "If you will go with us you must go against wind and tide," says John Bunyan, and because he is such a kindly guide we *will* go with him. He is, or seems to be, a man of dogged sincer-ity, integrity, and meticulous accuracy. If he describes the engines of war, each detail is correct. Factual correctness gives weight to the allegorical and moral truths he tells. "I have used similitudes," says the epigraph on the title page, taken from the Old Testament book of Hosea (12:10).

*"The Father of the Novel / Salvation's first Defoe,"* Rudyard Kipling called him. We believe Bunyan more readily than we do Defoe, despite Defoe's realism. Bunyan at his best is not only telling a story but building a marvelous structure in which all the parts relate to one another. Defoe tells a series of stories while Bunyan has a plot. Defoe describes others while Bunyan confronts us figura-tively with ourselves. His great literary beneficiary Melville, alluding to his re-peated imprisonment for his religious beliefs, invokes him: "Bear me out in it, thou great democratic God! who didst not refuse to the swart convict, Bunyan, the pale, poetic pearl." Ford Madox Ford says, "The difference between Bunyan and his predecessors is one more than anything of whole-heartedness." A more real difference, separating him from many of his successors as well, is his for-mal instinct. Bunyan is at once more medieval (allegorical) and more modern (synthetic) than most. And he has a gentle and generous sense of humor.

It is customary to condescend to him. Henry James deals with him obliquely, applauding Edgar Allan Poe for having the "courage to remark" that *The Pilgrim's Progress* is a "ludicrously overrated book." Even Ford: "So let us say that it was to the homespun illustrations, the simple imagery and the stern diction of the Bible that we owe Bunyan—for obviously Bunyan read the scriptures, year in and year out, during a lifetime of Bedford Gaol, of persecution and turmoil." Yet Bunyan is less homespun than Defoe, his imagery more complex and resonant than Richardson's. And C. S. Lewis showed that we can overplay the scriptural card where Bunyan is concerned. "His prose comes to him not from the Authorized Version [of the Bible] but from the fireside, the shop, and the lane. He is as native as Malory or Defoe." The Authorized Version had come to seem remote and archaic; it did not come back into literary fashion until the latter part of the eighteenth century with the recovery of "anciency." In the century before that it was not admired as a pattern for literary style or structure, and there was a gap between literary and spiritual language. The very familiarity of scripture limited the subtle uses to which it could be put.

It is Bunyan's didactic purpose that seems out of place in the world of fiction. Novels exist to test ideas, not affirm them. But here is an exception: *The Pilgrim's Progress*, or to give it its full title, *The Pilgrim's Progress from This World to That Which is to Come: Delivered under the Similitude of a Dream, Wherein Is Discovered the Manner of His Setting Out, His Dangerous Journey, and Safe Arrival at the Desired Country*, is for use, the characters are figures. Ford who condescended ends up marveling: "He just told on in simple language, using such simple images that the reader, astonished and charmed to find *the circumstances of his own life typified* [my italics] in word and glorified by print, is seized by the homely narrative and carried clean out of himself into the world of that singular and glorious tinker."

"Tinker" because his father Thomas was a tinsmith and brazier. In *Grace Abounding*, or *Grace Abounding to the Chief of Sinners, or a Brief and Faithful Relation of the Exceeding Mercy of God in Christ, to His Poor Servant John Bunyan. Namely, In His Taking of Him Out of the Dunghill, and Converting of Him to the Faith of His Blessed Son, Jesus Christ*, Bunyan declared: "My descent . . . was, as is well known by many, of a low and unconsiderable generation; my Father's house being of that rank that is meanest and most despised of all the families in the land." This overstates the case: his father owned land, his own house and workshop, and was by later accounts a royalist and an Anglican. Bunyan exaggerates in order to embrace as many readers as possible. "Wherefore I have not here, as others, to boast of noble Blood, or of a high-born State according to the Flesh; though, all things considered, I magnify the heavenly Majesty, for that by the door he brought me into the world, to partake of the Grace and Life that is in Christ by the Gospel."

And why is his style so simple? The reasons are moral, even though the aesthetic demands might have elicited a different mode of address, as he says in the preface to *Grace Abounding*: "I could have enlarged much in this my Discourse of my Temptations and Troubles for Sin; as also, of the merciful Kindness, and Working of God with my Soul: I could also have stepped into a Style much higher than this, in which I have here discoursed, and could have adorned all things more than here I have seemed to do; but I dare not: God did not play in tempting of me; neither did I play, when I sunk as into a bottomless Pit, when *the Pangs of Hell caught hold upon me;* wherefore I may not play in relating of them, but be plain and simple, and lay down the thing as it was: He that liketh it, let him receive it; and he that does not, let him produce a better. *Farewell."* Take it or leave it: in such Puritan writing we gape at the spiritual hubris implied in excessive humility, and in the believer's confidence that God cares so directly and *so much.*

Bunyan identifies his patron in the preface of *Grace Abounding.* The author's dedication is "to those whom God hath counted him worthy to beget to Faith, by his Ministry in the Word." In other words, the book is dedicated to those he has converted or brought back to church, and through their witness to God himself. Imprisoned ("I being taken from you in presence, and so tied up, that I cannot perform that duty, that from God doth lie upon me, to you-ward, for your further edifying and building up"), he provides an alternative presence, a witness. Clauses follow one another unaffectedly, building unambiguous and reassuring sentences.

John Bunyan was born in 1628 to his father's second wife in Harrowden, near Elstow, Bedfordshire. The cottage where he was born vanished long ago, but the spot is marked by a commemorative stone placed there during the Festival of Britain. He attended the thirteenth-century abbey church of St. Helena and St. Mary, where he was baptized in the font still in use today; the communion table, too, is from his time. The church overlooks the Green and the Moot Hall. His parents and sisters are buried in the churchyard. This is the village where he spent his youth, rang bells, and played tip-cat on the green, nine-holes, and perhaps stoolball (an early form of cricket). He was reportedly a strong, lusty lad with a commanding voice. The commanding voice of God spoke to him as a boy playing tip-cat on the Sabbath: "Wilt thou leave thy sins, and go to heaven? Or have thy sins and go to hell?" Some years later he took heed.

He went on to Bedford's Grammar School, or the Free School in Houghton Conquest. But he was, he said, unmarked by formal education, picking up at best a few words of Latin and Greek. He was apprenticed in the smithy with his father, soon learned the trade and traveled the countryside with his father or on his behalf. Later he laid claim to a blasphemous, wayward childhood and a troubled adolescence, racked with terrible, involuntary thoughts, visions, and dreams that drove him close to suicide. This may have been dramatic exaggeration, intended to emphasize how great an effort of divine Grace was required to heave him out of the mire.

He was in his teens when the First Civil War began (1642–1646). It is uncertain why he joined, whether he actually fought, whether he joined for Parliament, and if he did, whether he stayed on that side throughout the war. Bedford was broadly Parliamentarian, though Charles I recruited there as he passed through en route to his climactic defeat at Naseby in 1645. Did Bunyan see action? In *Grace Abounding* he relates, "When I was a soldier, I, with others, were drawn out to go to such a place to besiege it; but when I was just ready to go, one of the company desired to go in my room; to which, when I had consented, he took my place; and coming to the siege, as he stood sentinel, he was shot into the head with a musket bullet, and died."

In 1647 he entered his father's business, working in Bedford and elsewhere as an itinerant. Though not yet directly involved or even deeply interested in political or religious controversies, the roots of his spiritual reformation are here. He began attending church, reading scripture. He gave up swearing, gaming, and dancing. In 1648 he married his first wife, an orphan: "I changed my condition into a married state, and my mercy was to light upon a wife whose father was counted godly. This woman and I, though we came together as poor as poor might be, not having so much household stuff as a dish or spoon betwixt us both, yet this she had for her part, *The Plain Man's Pathway to Heaven,* and *The Practice of Piety,* which her father had left her when he died." He married a woman and two edifying books to add to his Bible. The next year, Charles I was executed.

Bunyan was soon a family man. His daughter Mary was born in 1650, blind from birth and the apple of his eye. Two sons followed, and another daughter. It was Mary who brought him a jug of soup each evening during his imprisonment. He made a violin out of tin and a flute from a chair leg. Music was integral to his Puritanism.

The year 1653 was his spiritual turning point. He befriended the Puritan pastor of St. John's Church, Bedford, Mr. Gifford, who became his mentor, baptizing him a second time in the Ouse, somewhere between what is now Duck Mill Lane carpark and the weir bridge. In the same year he fell from a boat into the Ouse and was narrowly saved from drowning. "I fell out of a boat into Bedford river, but mercy yet preserved me alive," he reports in *Grace Abounding.* He moved permanently to Bedford and became deacon at St. John's. He was invited to begin preaching, at first privately, then in public. He was good at it, quickly gained a following, and became insistently devout, a "soldier of Christ" in the words of Ebenezer Chandler. Then his wife died, followed shortly by Mr. Gifford.

In 1656 he began his attack on the Quaker preacher Edward Burrough, and on Quakerism generally, in *A Vindication of Gospel Truths Opened,* his first published pamphlet. He joined the tradition of "Martin Marprelate," Nashe, and Greene, a controversialist, but a consistent fighter, not a pen for hire. The next year *Vindication of Gospel Truths* followed. Formally recognized as a preacher, he was soon in trouble with the law for preaching outside his area. In 1658 he published *A Few Sighs from Hell.*

His concerns deepened as his life settled into a more coherent routine. He married a second time and published *The Doctrine of the Law and Grace Unfolded.* The larger, visible structure of his faith was taking shape. Then in 1660 came the Restoration. Charles II may have undertaken to tolerate religious dissenters with the Declaration of Breda, but politic intention and political will were at odds. The wind no longer blew the Puritan way. In October Bedfordshire magistrates ordered the reinstatement of Anglican liturgy. On November 12 Bunyan was scheduled to preach at Lower Samsell. Upon arrival he was advised that a warrant had been issued for his arrest by judge Francis Wingate. Wingate and his brother-in-law William Foster urged Bunyan to offer certain concessions in exchange for his freedom. He insisted he had broken no new law. He was imprisoned at Bedford, in a gaol on the old bridge over the Ouse. He spent a third of his adult life in jail, and it is in part to these restraints that we owe his writings.

In January he appeared before Sir John Keeling ("Lord Hate-Good" in *The Pilgrim's Progress*) at the Assizes, charged with "devilishly and perniciously abstaining from coming to Church to hear Divine Service, and for being a common upholder of several unlawful meetings and conventicles, to the great disturbance and distraction of the good subjects of this kingdom, contrary to the laws of our sovereign lord and king." When Bunyan tried to outline his objections to Anglican ritual, a voice exclaims, "Let him speak no further; he will do harm!" Keeling replied: "No, no, never fear him . . . he can do no harm; we know the Common Prayer Book hath been ever since the Apostles' time." He was sentenced to three months with the added threat of banishment if no recantation was forthcoming. Bunyan retorted: "If I were out of prison today, I would preach the gospel again tomorrow, by the help of God."

After twelve weeks Bunyan was visited in prison by Cobb, a clerk of the peace. Cobb urged that a loyal subject of the king was bound by St. Paul to obey the king's laws. Although St. Paul respected the authorities, Bunyan said, he spent time in prison nonetheless. His own loyalty to Charles II did not override what his conscience told him was his duty. Bunyan stayed in prison despite the amnesty marking the coronation.

The Act of Uniformity of 1662 institutionalized the episcopal character of the English church, depriving thousands of pastors of their right to preach while restoring others to their parishes. Bunyan's hitherto relaxed regime was tightened; the conditions of his imprisonment remained poor until 1668, though he was allowed a "library," "the least and yet the best that ever I saw": his Bible. "I was never out of the Bible either by reading or meditation." To support his family he spent his days making shoelaces, reading, writing, and preaching to and counseling fellow inmates. As Parliament passed more acts hostile to the Puritan cause, Bunyan's polemical and reflective work continued. In 1666 he published his autobiography, *Grace Abounding*. After a period of freedom he was rearrested for unauthorized preaching. Then he was allowed limited access to visit his congregations outside jail, and four years later, in 1672, he was elected pastor. Charles II's Declaration of Indulgence led to his release from Bedford Prison after twelve years. As pastor of the Independent Congregation, composed largely of burghers and tradesmen, he was now a famous man. He began to preach widely, as far afield as Reading and London. One account says that in London he drew a crowd of 1,200 even though he preached at seven in the morning on a working winter's day. On Sundays he drew 3,000 and more. Enemies dubbed him "Bishop Bunyan." Libels alleged immorality, Jesuitism, witchcraft.

It was too good to last. The Declaration of Indulgence was overturned in 1673: elements in Parliament thought it favored the Catholics. In 1674 Bunyan was accused of keeping Agnes Beaumont (herself accused of poisoning her father because of his disapproval) as his mistress. In 1675 Bunyan's license to preach was revoked and he went back to prison. He began work on *The Pilgrim's Progress*. He was briefly released, then rearrested.

In 1678 *The Pilgrim's Progress* was published, the first of an unprecedented twelve editions within Bunyan's remaining lifetime. By 1792 it had gone through 160 editions and was regarded, by most polite authors, with derision. Whatever the English intellectual classes thought, the book was translated into French and Dutch within a decade and popular all through the Protestant world. His prolific output quickened, but apart from the cautionary tale *The Life and Death of Mr. Badman* (1680), nothing lived up to *Grace Abounding* and *The Pilgrim's Progress*. *Mr. Badman* is an allegory in dialogue: Mr. Wiseman recounts the life of Mr. Badman, recently deceased, and Mr. Attentive comments. Mr. Badman drank too much, duped a maid, married for money, and, upon his wife's death, married a wicked woman. He died of a cocktail of diseases. Morally uplifting, the story is also funny.

In 1687, acknowledging his influence and power, James II offered him a "place of public trust"; Bunyan declined, but gained concessions for his friends. His health was in decline, and the next year he caught a fever from having traveled to London in bad weather to try to settle a conflict between a young man and his father. He preached a final sermon. August 31 brought "the Death of deare Brother Bunyan." He was buried at Bunhill Fields, where Defoe, Blake, and other radical spirits would join him. Due to Victorian restoration, his is by far the most elaborate tomb there, with an imposing marble effigy and bas-relief depicting scenes from *The Pilgrim's Progress*. In Bedford he stands nine feet tall and green with corrosion at the top of High Street.

In *The Pilgrim's Progress* the narrator, weary from walking "through the Wilderness of this World," finds a den, falls asleep, and starts to dream, all within the opening sentence. We are immediately in a world of allegory. *"The Pilgrim's Progress,"* writes Coleridge with respect, because from Bunyan he learned lessons that went into the making of *The Rime of the Ancient Mariner,* "is composed in the lowest style of English, without slang or false grammar. If you were to polish it, you would at once destroy the reality of the vision. For works of imagination should be written in very plain language; the more purely imaginative they are the more necessary it is to be plain." His success also has to do with consistency. The unfolding of the allegory, David Lodge reminds us, is controlled completely by correspondences, usually specific, to the qualities implied or declared in the given names. Lodge is wrong when he declares that Bunyan lacks what Henry James called "the sense of felt life." Here we find fear, friendship, tenderness, doubt, joy, grief. There are feelings, textures, scents, and savors. All that is lacking are literal contingencies, which, Bunyan might have remarked, are rather overvalued in the fictions of this world.

The sleeper spots Christian, bearing a burden on his back and reading from a book in which he learns that the city in which he and his family dwell will be burned. Advised by the Evangelist, Christian flees the City of Destruction, a kind of Gomorrah, having failed to persuade his wife and children to accompany him. Salvation is a lonely exercise, and the path leads through perils, temptations, and places of recuperation. In part one the ten chief stopping places are familiar, some from the Psalms, others from Blake, Thackeray, or elsewhere:

The Slough of Despond
The Interpreter's House
The Palace Beautiful
The Valley of Humiliation
The Valley of the Shadow of Death
Vanity Fair
Doubting Castle
The Delectable Mountains
The Country of Beulah
The Celestial City

On the way he encounters many faces and voices: Mr. Worldly Wise-man, Faithful (who goes with him but is killed in Vanity Fair), Hopeful (who also joins him), Giant Despair, the foul fiend Apollyon, and others. This world in its lineaments reminds us now of Spenser's *Faerie Queene,* except there is little decoration; now of Dante's *Inferno,* but there is more hope and forgiveness at hand, and Christian is supported from within and urges his way forward with hope rather than fear.

Bunyan in imaging the places of trial and temptation had specific places in mind: the wicket gate at Elstow church, Squitch Fen, St. John's Rectory, the Chilterns, and so on. Some of the allegorical figures are based on human models. Evangelist is John Gifford. These personal occasions are lost on us: they were part of his process of visualizing and composing, making the action real to the author and therefore to us.

In part two the family comes along. Christian's wife Christiana and the children set out on the same hard pilgrimage, accompanied by neighbor Mercy (Christiana's gossip) and overruling the objections of Mrs. Timorous. Their escort Great Heart overwhelms Giant Despair, and they too come to their destination. First man, then woman, first husband, then wife, make their way to salvation.

What makes Bunyan's predictable story, passage by passage derivative of the Bible, so compelling and *durable* is the reality of its allegorical figuration and its good humor. It is seen as well as visualized, and it is told in a human voice: close at hand, a man speaking to men, not a priest from a pulpit or a moralist wagging a finger. It is the best fruits of Puritan culture. "I could not have believed beforehand that Calvinism could be painted in such exquisitely delightful colors," said Coleridge.

Bunyan is a most uncommon common man, a man of the people and of a demanding, democratic, accountable faith. Into his novel of practical faith he works dramatic dialogue or interrogation, as when the Porter cross-examines Christian, or Greatheart elicits from Valiant, like an attorney, an account of his adventures and heroisms. He weaves in verse, including his famous hymn "Who would true valor see," and runs of homespun couplets for invocations and conclusions. He adds marginal rubrics, as in published sermons, summarizing action or speech, indicating biblical sources. These and other formal features create a rich impurity and variety of effect. Writing in the provinces, he rejects the new urban and the pastoral mode; he knows what literature is and avoids it because it falsifies. No university infected him with a wit. His book does not address a scholarly or cultured class. Yet it is figurative, it plays constantly between the Bible, allegory, and the living world, it is more complex in conception and consistent in execution than any English prose work that precedes it. It is original without meaning to be; it entertains even the pagan and atheist heart. Bunyan's direct legacy is to his faith; his oblique legacy is to writers including Defoe, Swift, and Smollett; Blake and Thackeray *(Vanity Fair)* and Coleridge; Hawthorne *(The Celestial Railroad,* 1843), Louisa May Alcott (in *Little Women* he inspires and sustains the March sisters and provides the author with chapter titles) and Harriet Beecher Stowe; James Joyce and Wyndham Lewis and Gore Vidal *(Burr* abundantly alludes to him); to all the makers and remakers both of plain and of figurative styles. Perhaps his chief heir is Kurt Vonnegut, whose Billy Pilgrim in *Slaughterhouse-Five* emerges intact but bleakly transformed from the Valley of the Shadow of Death.

# | 5 |

## *Enter America*

Aphra Behn, Zora Neale Hurston

"Anyone who has looked into the works of the Duchess of Newcastle and Mrs. Behn," declared Virginia Woolf in 1916, "knows how easily the rich prose style of the Restoration tends to fall languid and suffocate even writers of considerable force and originality." Few readers were then familiar with the writings of Aphra Behn. The claims made today for her plays, poetry, and fiction have much to do with the feminist enterprise, and with selective quotation, time after time, of the endorsement of her pluck (if not of her work) by Woolf in *A Room of One's Own*. For Woolf, Behn the phenomenon is significant. "Jane Austen should have laid a wreath upon the grave of Fanny Burney, and George Eliot done homage to the robust shade of Eliza Carter—the valiant old woman who tied a bell to her bedstead in order that she might wake early and learn Greek. All women together ought to let flowers fall upon the tomb of Aphra Behn, which is, most scandalously but rather appropriately, in Westminster Abbey, for it was she who earned them the right to speak their minds. It is she—shady and amorous as she was—who makes it not quite fantastic for me to say to you tonight: Earn five hundred a year by your wits."

Woolf then values the oeuvre: "She made, by working very hard, enough to live on. The importance of that fact outweighs anything that she actually wrote." She is a totemic figure. Unlike aristocratic Mary Wroth, withdrawing *Urania* in the wake of hostile gossip, Aphra Behn persisted. The twentieth-century attempt to establish a credible, readable canon of women's writing rooted in the seventeenth century, to identify and celebrate substantial foremothers, looks to Mrs. Behn because there are few other places to look for competent prose fiction and drama.

Behn possesses an unusually exciting biography, if we believe her own testimony (our chief source) and allow ourselves to speculate within those gaps and silences that brim with rumor. Some of her recent biographers speculate, and Behn has become not only a writer of fiction but a fiction in her own right.

She was not an aristocrat, this we know; she was widowed, this we think; she needed to make a living, and she had wit, energy, and an instinct for acceptable themes and styles. Events of her early years, including the famous sojourn in Surinam, are open to doubt. It is widely assumed that Aphra Behn was born

Aphra Johnson. It has been suggested that she was adopted. The record is complicated by rumor: for example, that she was James II's mistress (she certainly celebrated his coronation with poetic verve, three times, twice with hectic and high-spirited Pindaric odes). It may be that she fabricated her 1664 marriage to a London merchant of Dutch extraction, and his demise, in the plague of 1665, in the interests of respectability.

Her reputation was at low ebb when Virginia Woolf remembered her. Posterity had reduced her to little more than a smut peddler: she exemplified what a female writer should *not* be. We are not allowed to forget the inappropriate company she kept. In 1687 one of her ex-lovers, John Hoyle, was tried for sodomy. He was stabbed to death in a tavern brawl three years after her death. Why this information survives while more important facts are wanting must have to do in part with male phobia: not only had a woman written for the stage and the general reader; she had touched on themes that were indecorous for a woman to discourse upon, breaking the rules twice over. She was unnatural, surrounding herself with unnatural men. Positive speculation now flourishes, about her social attitudes, her sexuality, her integrity, and she is stretched in another direction. At least her work is again in print; literary judgment can be made.

To start at what may be the beginning: in 1640 Aphra Johnson, the second daughter of Bartholomew Johnson (possibly a high-class barber) and Elizabeth Denham, was born at Harbledown, by Canterbury. Alternative identities have been argued, in Kent, Herefordshire, and elsewhere. The name "Aphra" was not uncommon at the time, and those who doubt her marriage suggest her maiden name was Behn, a variant on Bean or Beane.

When she was sixteen her father took the family to Surinam in the West Indies. She says he was appointed lieutenant governor, but this is unlikely given his social station. Was she involved in a slave uprising? Was she the first European woman the natives ever saw? Or was this embroidery, to make her books more exotic? Her father is said to have died, and his wife and children returned to London no later than 1664, when Aphra is assumed to have married Mr. Behn, who the very next year died.

More verifiable are the intrigues and adventures that now began. As Astrea or Agent 160, she went to Antwerp as a spy against the Dutch for Charles II, returning the next year from a job well done, for which she was never properly paid. Indeed, her erstwhile employers did not even cover her expenses. Broke, she was confined in a debtors' prison. The trauma of jail and financial betrayal led to her decision to become, though a woman, a writer. She turned her attention first to the stage, and in 1670 her first play, *The Forc'd Marriage,* was performed, running for six nights, an exceptional achievement at the time, and lucrative because all the income from both "third days" went to the author. She was the first and for a time the only female playwright, suffering "the Author's unhappiness, forced to write for Bread and not ashamed to own it," as she declares in the preface to a later play, *Sir Patient Fancy.*

Her looks and native charm were asset and liability in this male world, leading to tensions, rebuffs, and gossip. The issues she raised, such as, in her first play, the iniquity of forced marriages, were not taken seriously. She became, after Dryden, the most prolific writer of plays during the Restoration and had some cause for bitterness, reflected in the preface to her late play *The Lucky Chance* (1686): "Had the Plays I have writ come forth under any Man's Name, and never known to have been mine; I appeal to all unbyast Judges of Sense, if they had not said that Person had made as many good Comedies, as any one Man that has writ in our Age; but a Devil on't the Woman damns the poet . . . All I ask, is the Priviledge for my Masculine Part the Poet in me."

Her most significant play, *The Rover* (1677), was a major success. The protagonist may have been based on John Wilmot, Earl of Rochester, her libertine patron and friend. The legendary actress Nell Gwyn may have been the "Miss Gwin" who played the courtesan Angelica Bianca: though she had retired by this date, she may have found the role irresistible. Gwyn is also rumored to have emerged from retirement to play in later works, and in 1679 Behn dedicated to her, without irony we must presume, *The Feign'd Curtezans.*

She continued writing for the stage, though income from this source dwindled. She extended her career as poet (she had already proven herself to Rochester, the salacious Sir Charles Sedley, and others) and began writing fiction.

She was a keen reader of French romances, which profited her efforts. She made translations from the French. In 1685 she translated, effectively it is said, Balthasar Bonnecorse's *La montre* as *The Lover's Watch,* followed by J. B. de Brilhac's story *Agnes de Castro* (1688). Her original works that have a place in the early history of the novel include *Love-Letters between a Nobleman and His Sister* (1684), the first substantial epistolary novel in English, in which Sylvia, seduced by her brother-in-law Philander, is first fulfilled and finally ruined (the nobleman remains a nobleman); *The Fair Jilt; or, Tarquin and Miranda* (1688), a novella usually grouped with her shorter fictions and translations; and, best and best known, *Oroonoko; or, The Royal Slave* (1688), a sensational brief novel set in Surinam, eloquent in its opposition to slavery, combining "memoir" and invention, travelogue and biography. The next year she died—"in pain and poverty," some accounts declare with moral satisfaction.

*Oroonoko* has unusual structural features. It also touches on issues of imperialism, colonialism, class, and race, central to modern academic discourse. A slave raid, an uprising of slaves, and all this by a seventeenth-century woman who may actually have been there: in terms of subject and subject matter it could hardly be better tailored for a modern seminar, despite the paternalism of its tone, the transformation (colonization?) of the "gallant" chief protagonist into a "Moor" and a virtual European.

The climate of *Oroonoko* is immediately exotic after Arcadia and England: sultry, African, Caribbean, American. There is not much description, but small details emit pungency and warmth: "the grove of the otan, which was all of oranges and citrons," for example. The world is more literal than the island Shakespeare created for *The Tempest,* and the subject not Caliban but a figure so noble that he comes to seem a superior European, with dark skin.

Behn anticipates Alex Hayley's Pulitzer Prize–winning *Roots: The Saga of an American Family* (1976). His book begins in 1750, however, while Behn is writing about the slave trade a century earlier. The methods of collecting slaves did not change much in the interim: there was collusion between slavers and native chiefs, the slaves were harvested and then handed over to the slavers for money or goods. Behn's narrative proper begins with Prince Oroonoko's passionate, ill-fated love for the handsome captured Imoinda. Hayley's Kunta Kinte and his rather different ill-starred love for Fanta is similarly conceived.

Like Defoe, Behn wants us to believe her testimony. She is writing history, she insists, not fiction; she has the authority to do so because she knew the protagonist and the place where he died. She has access to his articulate account of himself, and she is herself articulate. From the first paragraph we are promised a kind of duet.

> I do not pretend, in giving you the history of this Royal Slave, to entertain my reader with adventures of a feigned hero, whose life and fortunes fancy may manage at the poet's pleasure; nor in relating the truth, design to adorn it with any accidents but such as arrived in earnest to him: and it shall come simply into the world, recommended by its own proper merits and natural intrigues; there being enough of reality to support it, and to render it diverting, without the addition of invention. I was myself an eye-witness to a great part of what you will find here set down; and what I could not be witness of, I received from the mouth of the chief actor in this history, the hero himself, who gave us the whole transactions of his youth: and though I shall omit, for brevity's sake, a thousand little accidents of his life, which, however pleasant to us, where history was scarce and adventures very rare, yet might prove tedious and heavy to my reader, in a world where he finds diversions for every minute, new and strange. But we who were perfectly charmed with the character of this great man were curious to gather every cir-

cumstance of his life. The scene of the last part of his adventures lies
in a colony in America, called Surinam, in the West Indies.

The narrator starts with an account of the innocence and peaceable beauty
of the native people of Coromantee. The Rousseauian notion of the noble savage
is rumored, not least in the author's wonderment at their nakedness and chastity.
She then, by contrast with the natives, recounts how slaves were collected and
delivered to customers in Africa for transport to America, a cool, circumstantial telling. We meet the grandson of the king of Coramantee, and Behn is
careful to distinguish him and the nature of his beauty from that of his fellow
Africans: "He was adorned with a native beauty, so transcending all those of his
gloomy race that he struck an awe and reverence even into those that knew not
his quality; as he did into me, who beheld him with surprise and wonder, when
afterwards he arrived in our world." She has dwelt upon bodily adornment: *he*
is adorned with beauty, a word that genders the speaker, for, used of a man,
"beauty" implies a level of desire: "the most famous statuary could not form
the figure of a man more admirably turned from head to foot. His face was not
of that brown rusty black which most of that nation are, but of perfect ebony, or
polished jet. His eyes were the most awful that could be seen, and very piercing; the white of 'em being like snow, as were his teeth. His nose was rising and
Roman, instead of African and flat. His mouth the finest shaped that could be
seen; far from those great turned lips which are so natural to the rest of the
negroes. The whole proportion and air of his face was so nobly and exactly
formed that, bating his color, there could be nothing in nature more beautiful,
agreeable, and handsome."

Oroonoko is set apart also, beyond his hereditary leadership and beauty, by
the fact that he has been tutored by a French religious exile, has admired the
English and been drawn too to a friendly Spanish slave trader, learning their
languages. He himself trades slaves with the Europeans, and Behn does not
find this unnatural. When Oroonoko is tricked into slavery himself, he brings a
colonial culture with him to Surinam. What greater praise can there be than to
describe him in such a way as to appropriate him? "I have often seen and conversed with this great man, and been a witness to many of his mighty actions;
and do assure my reader, the most illustrious courts could not have produced a
braver man, both for greatness of courage and mind, a judgment more solid, a
wit more quick, and a conversation more sweet and diverting. He knew almost
as much as if he had read much: he had heard of and admired the Romans: he
had heard of the late Civil Wars in England, and the deplorable death of our
great monarch; and would discourse of it with all the sense and abhorrence of
the injustice imaginable . . . He had nothing of barbarity in his nature, but in all

points addressed himself as if his education had been in some European court." No man Friday, this.

He tells the ladies about his romance, his grandfather's exercise of *droit de seigneur,* his plan to escape, Imoinda's betrayal, and his dreadful fate. It is a tale of sincere love thwarted, of a cruel culture and its displacements, of English treachery under the guise of culture and courtesy, with consequences not only for one man but for a whole people. When the slaves are sold, no two men from the same tribe are sold together: they might conspire. The solitary confinement of slavery, even in open fields, was intolerable and irreversible. As Oroonoko leaves the slave ship, he says in magisterial English to the treacherous captain: "Farewell, Sir, 'tis worth my sufferings to gain so true a knowledge both of you and of your gods by whom you swear." Then he leaps down from the ship, a leader though in chains. A Cornishman called Trefry, educated and civil, becomes Oroonoko's immediate master and patron. Admiring his forceful beauty and strength, Trefry dubs Oroonoko Caesar. And he might have become a man of great fame, but "his misfortune was to fall in an obscure world, that afforded only a female pen to celebrate his fame." She follows Trefry and henceforth calls Oroonoko Caesar: "By that name he was received on shore at Parham-House, where he was destined a slave." There all the young male slaves were pining for a beautiful newcomer, dubbed Clemene but in fact the exiled Imoinda.

They are together, and the narrator is delegated to keep Oroonoko tame, to avoid the bloodletting of an uprising against the treacherous English. But she is soon to leave the island, "because my father died at sea, and never arrived to possess the honor designed him (which was Lieutenant-General of six and thirty islands, besides the Continent of Surinam) nor the advantages he hoped to reap by them." She is reluctant to go because she has a vision of what South America might be. It is a description wonderful for its materiality rather than its materialism:

> 'Tis a continent whose vast extent was never yet known, and may contain more noble earth than all the universe beside; for, they say, it reaches from east to west one way as far as China, and another to Peru: it affords all things both for beauty and use; 'tis there eternal spring, always the very months of April, May, and June; the shades are perpetual, the trees bearing at once all degrees of leaves and fruit, from blooming buds to ripe autumn: groves of oranges, lemons, citrons, figs, nutmegs, and noble aromatics continually bearing their fragrancies. The trees appearing all like nosegays adorned with flowers of different kinds; some are all white, some purple, some scarlet, some blue, some yellow; bearing at the same time ripe

fruit, and blooming young, or producing every day new. The very wood of all these trees has an intrinsic value above common timber; for they are, when cut, of different colors, glorious to behold, and bear a price considerable, to inlay withal. Besides this, they yield rich balm and gums; so that we make our candles of such an aromatic substance as does not only give a sufficient light, but, as they burn, they cast their perfumes all about. Cedar is the common firing, and all the houses are built with it. The very meat we eat, when set on the table, if it be native, I mean of the country, perfumes the whole room; especially a little beast called an armadillo, a thing which I can liken to nothing so well as a rhinoceros; 'tis all in white armor, so jointed that it moves as well in it as if it had nothing on: this beast is about the bigness of a pig of six weeks old. But it were endless to give an account of all the divers wonderful and strange things that country affords, and which we took a very great delight to go in search of; though those adventures are oftentimes fatal, and at least dangerous: but while we had Caesar in our company on these designs, we feared no harm, nor suffered any.

The narrator as Oroonoko's guardian characterizes him as peacemaker between the natives and the English. Then he leads the native revolt, not slaughtering English plantation managers but departing by night to establish a black community elsewhere on the island. The uprising fails, the English again break their word, and Oroonoko is whipped at the stake until his life is in the balance. "When they thought they were sufficiently revenged on him, they untied him, almost fainting with loss of blood, from a thousand wounds all over his body; from which they had rent his clothes, and led him bleeding and naked as he was, and loaded him all over with irons, and them rubbed his wounds, to complete their cruelty, with Indian pepper, which had like to have made him raving mad; and, in this condition made him so fast to the ground that he could not stir, if his pains and wounds would have given him leave." In the end, it is Oroonoko's love that proves his great heroism and heart and brings about his downfall, just as it had in Africa where his grandfather's jealousy cost his people dear. Love makes his life worth living and his death inevitable. The tale gathers force as Behn grasps it with understanding: a white woman tells it from an infatuated and astonished heart. Thus in romantic narrative Africa, America, the slave trade, brutal oppression, colonialism, and imperialism make their way into English fiction, displacing Arcadia and Utopia; the first female narrator of a novel speaks. New World adventure brings a consciousness of alternative cultures and reveals the vigor and frailty of English values in an unfamiliar world.

The Surinam that V. S. Naipaul visits in the 1960s is a place in which the moral bankruptcies told and foretold in *Oroonoko* have become endemic. In *The Middle Passage* (1962) the inhabitants of Coronie are typified: "A derelict man in a derelict land; a man discovering himself, with surprise and resignation, lost in a landscape which had never ceased to be unreal because the scene of an enforced and always temporary residence; the slaves kidnapped from one continent and abandoned on the unprofitable plantations of another, from which there could never more be escape: I was glad to leave Coronie, for, more than lazy Negroes, it held the full desolation that came to those who made the middle passage." Naipaul delivers a sentence that Caribbean writers have protested ever since: "The history of the islands can never be satisfactorily told. Brutality is not the only difficulty. History is built around achievement and creation; and nothing was created in the West Indies." The *not* nothing that emerges from displacement and repression, enforced in generations of slavery and then segregation, part of the experience of being black in a place whose culture has been made by others, and where black life and history have been formulated by white writers, however well or well-intentioned, imprisons the spirit. More than anger and music are required to make an escape.

Stereotypes lie in wait of the black writer. Zora Neale Hurston (1891–1960) issues a challenge not to the culture of reception but to the black imagination itself: "Roll your eyes in ecstasy and ape his every move, but until we have placed something upon his street that is our own, we are right back where we were when they filed our iron collar off." The "he" in her formulation is male and white; the "we" collective and ungendered. When she begins to place something that belongs to the "other" on the shared thoroughfare of language and literature, she insists on using a common language, elevating it into the "literary zone" because it expresses something larger than the individual or regional imagination. "Words walking without masters; walking altogether like harmony in a song." Much of her language has an aphoristic quality, common saws made uncommon by new contexts, repeated like refrains, giving her prose a balladic spareness. "An envious heart makes a treacherous ear." "If you kin see de light at daybreak, you don't keer if you die at dusk." "A man is up against a hard game when he must die to beat it." "She was too busy feeling grief to dress like grief."

She roots her language not only in speech but in specific speech. Her works in dramatic format can be read as sketch novels, novellas, and chapters (some, *The Mule Bone*, for example, she wrote with Langston Hughes). The voices are of black people, starting with the grownups she heard as a girl, eavesdropping outside Joe Clarke's store in her native Eatonville, Florida, the first black town in America to be incorporated, with a black mayor. The store comes alive in her comedy *De Turkey and de Law*. Children play and we encounter village characters from Joe Clarke himself, postmaster and storekeeper, to the town bully, the town hunter, the town vamp, the marshal, Methodist and Baptist villagers and reverends, all expressed in the living languages of the place. Hurston listened to the differing speech of Georgia, Alabama, New Orleans. She entrusts the fiction to the voices, children's, old people's, women's. The Haiti-born novelist Edwidge Danticat (b. 1969) notes in her introduction to *Their Eyes Were Watching God* that Hurston "was accused of stereotyping the people she loved when she perhaps simply listened to them much more closely than others, and sought to reclaim and reclassify their voices." *Speak that I may see thee,* says Ben Jonson, whose plays preserve the voices of his age; and the South African writer Olive Schreiner liked to quote Alexis de Tocqueville: "We must see the first images which the external world casts upon the dark mirror of his mind; or must hear the first words which awaken the sleeping powers of thought, and stand by his earliest efforts, if we would understand the prejudices, the habits, and the passions that will rule his life. The entire man is, so to speak, to be found in the cradle of the child." Hurston was at the differentiating cradle.

Her father, moderator of the South Florida Baptist Association, was a storyteller and the source of the religious themes that recur in her work: her last, unfinished project is a novel about King Herod. An unrealistic overreacher, she planned a study of world religions. Her weakness as an anthropologist was that she sometimes bent or doctored evidence to make it interesting and conclusive. She is dependable only in the area of imagination. Field anthropology took her deep into the imaginations of people that literature had left untouched. She stayed in lumber camps, among the rural and tropical poor. She learned about hoodoo (New Orleans voodoo) and subjected herself to its rituals. Her autobiographical *Mules and Men* (1935) had an introduction by her teacher Franz Boas: "It is the great merit of Miss Hurston's work that she entered into the homely life of the southern Negro as one of them and was fully accepted as such by the companions of her childhood." No white interlocutor could have got in so close. "Miss Hurston has been equally successful in gaining the confidence of the voodoo doctors and she gives us much that throws a new light upon the much discussed voodoo beliefs and practices."

Her best known, the second, of her four novels, *Their Eyes Were Watching God* (1937), was written in under two months. The author was in Haiti doing fieldwork. Perhaps she missed home and, needing to hear them, conjured up its voices. Though the book is conventional in structure, setting, and connecting scenes with prose and defining a narrative and symbolic framework, it is woven out of varieties of speech, each appropriate to the uttering body of the speaker. Hurston resisted the pressure of black critics to be radical in a prescribed way, to contribute to "motive fiction and social document fiction." For Richard Wright,

Hurston's novel played to white people and the language as set down, phonetically representing the voices as she heard them, might make white readers laugh. The negative issue of black speech and dialect transliterated by white writers making subordinate black characters was so entrenched in black criticism that what the *black* reader might hear and think hardly weighed at all in the struggle for redefinition. Yet redefinition itself masked the resources that were actually there. The censors were the very *men* who were affirming a franchise for the black imagination.

*Their Eyes Were Watching God* starts with an aphorism: "Ships at a distance have every man's wish on board." Here man does not include woman. Man waits for the ship to dock. For some men it comes in, others watch it far off until they know, too late, that it will never land. "Now, women forget all those things they don't want to remember, and remember everything they don't want to forget. The dream is the truth. Then they act and do things accordingly." Soon we realize that the sun is "he," and the bossman is "he," and when the sun goes down and the bossman goes home, the dark is free and freeing. The inhabitants on their verandas start to talk. "They became lords of sounds and lesser things. They passed nations through their mouths. They sat in judgment." Janie has come home, her hair plum-dark and full-bodied; she who has left one husband, two husbands, and who ran away with wild and sensual Tea Cake, has come back without him. They sit in judgment on her, but she gives them no evidence. She tells her story to a friend, to Pheoby.

Janie narrates without censoring details. Her lover was a rough man, he beat her. Janie makes no apology: this is how he was, this is how it was, the novel resists the temptation to correct, idealize, or moralize. The hurricane, the dog bite, the struggle to survive are rendered with rapid care, alive for writer and reader. Hurston knows that Tea Cake will give his life for Janie. She knows too that in his rabid love he would kill her. At the trial, Janie, clearly articulate, is not seen to speak in her own voice. Hurston takes over the narrative, and some readers are disappointed: they want Janie to speak out in her own defense. Alice Walker asks, Why should she? Why should we expect her to speak just because men call upon her to do so? Why do we demand obedience from fictional characters that we might censure in a living witness? This is the difficult area that Faulkner too explored in the character of Lucas Beauchamp in *Intruder in the Dust* (1948).

Hurston wrote without embarrassment or condescension, which is why her novel has a feeling of lived language, lived life, that much documentary fiction of the time lacks. The people's houses, their food, the texture of their clothes and furnishings, their frank sensuality, are neither romanticized nor apologized for. At its crisis the story possesses Brontësque intensity, as at the climax when the title detonates with all its force. "The wind came back with triple fury, and put out the light for the last time. They sat in company with the others in other shanties, their eyes straining against crude walls and their souls asking if He meant to measure their puny might against His. They seemed to be staring at the dark, but their eyes were watching God."

In this book, more than in Richard Wright's or Ralph Ellison's, Toni Morrison and Alice Walker (who found and approximately marked Hurston's grave, and in 1979 edited a Hurston *Reader*) are foreshadowed. Danticat notes how Janie in *Their Eyes Were Watching God* is like Celie in Walker's *The Color Purple;* she also finds a comparison with Janie's Nanny, who longs to preach a sermon but knows there is no pulpit for her, and Toni Morrison's Baby Suggs in *Beloved*, who gets the women to cry together. Nadine Gordimer assigns to the South African activist and writer Ellen Kuzwayo (1914–2006), author of the autobiography *Call Me Woman* (1985), a role in the South African context comparable to Hurston's in the American: she is "history in the person of one woman." Something starts with Behn, something starts with Hurston, both women brave against the fast-flowing currents of a given literature and politics, against sexual and racial prejudice.

Hurston invented herself in *Dust Tracks on a Road* (1942), billed as autobiography but embellished with fiction. She wants to elude here, as in her fiction, "the negro problem" conceived by the black critics. She sidesteps it. Her book is a dialogue between two dictions, the formal diction of a writer and the informing diction of her speech, an uneasy bilingualism that many modern writers practice as a result of ethnicity, class, location, intimacy. The sometimes excessive richness of her language may put us in mind of Thomas Wolfe, but having tried excess, she checks it.

For years Hurston was the only black woman in the United States who made a living as a writer. Then she couldn't make a living as a writer any more. She had burned herself out much as the great black musical entertainers did; she finished early, in a death that might have been avoided. She was proud and would rather be a domestic than lean on friends. Yet she was, in poet and novelist Jean Toomer's memorial phrase, "a genius of the South," not only an iconic figure but a considerable writer. Her great book ends with Janie's epiphany, as grand and eternal in its way as Molly Bloom's *yes:* "Here was peace. She pulled in her horizon like a great fish-net. Pulled it from around the waist of the world and draped it over her shoulder. So much of life in its meshes! She called in her soul to come and see."

# | 6 |

## *Impersonation*

Daniel Defoe, Truman Capote, J. M. Coetzee

More plausible than Prince Oroonoko is Robinson Crusoe's man Friday. Zora
Neale Hurston, Langston Hughes, and the writers of the Harlem Renaissance
were up against Friday quite as much as they were up against Uncle Tom. Crusoe names Friday after the day of the week on which he delivered him from his
pursuers, commanding the obliging native to call him Master. For two centuries and more this picture of subordination in one of the most popular novels
ever written seemed to reflect a natural order. Defoe described the aborigines
from whom he rescued Friday as "cannibals." His book, written in a first person
so matter-of-fact we forget it has an author, presents itself as a ballad or legend
might do, establishing stereotypes through which whole cultures and peoples
were viewed. Originally intended for adults, *Robinson Crusoe* became a popular
children's book. The stereotypes were imprinted on the Anglophone reader
from childhood.

Behn turned her Negro into a black-skinned European. She made him familiar. Defoe perceived a set of physical and qualitative differences that set Friday
apart. Behn wanted to include Oroonoko among "us." For Defoe, Friday was
intrinsically one of "them," could not aspire to be one of "us," and existed nearly
beyond divine grace. Defoe's book embodies, then formalizes, a division.

What Defoe has and Behn lacks is a developed dissenting conscience. This
gives his novels, in a first person that is dogmatically rooted, focus and direction.
Like her he writes for effect, but the effects he strives for are moral, a morality
anachronistic and problematic, not only in *Robinson Crusoe* but in *Moll Flanders*,
*Colonel Jack*, and *Roxana*. Behn writes of many people and incidents, Defoe focuses on the unfolding of a single destiny to which all others are subordinate.
He is close to Bunyan in this insistence on the developing spiritual diligence of
his protagonists, their progress toward salvation. Unlike Bunyan's, his characters move in a world close to his own: their adventures have unprecedented particularity of setting rather than allegorical universality. Defoe is not consistent,
but he is aware of spatial and causal imperatives that also constrain and shape
his moral realism. We want to trust him even when he contradicts himself.

Virginia Woolf describes Defoe's moralistic formula: "In the first pages of
each of his great novels he reduces his hero or heroine to such a state of un-

branded misery that their existence must be a continued struggle, and their survival at all the result of luck and their own exertions." Moll Flanders's mother is a criminal and Moll herself is born in Newgate Prison. Colonel Jack, born a gentleman, is apprenticed like Oliver Twist to a pickpocket. As a little boy Captain Singleton is kidnapped and sold to gypsies. Roxana, married off at fifteen, witnesses the bankruptcy of her husband and is left with a nest full of impoverished chicks. And Robinson Crusoe's venture begins in insubordination. "I would be satisfied with nothing but going to sea; and my inclination to this led me so strongly against the will, nay, the commands, of my father, and against all the entreaties and persuasions of my mother and other friends, that there seemed to be something fatal in that propension of nature tending directly to the life of misery which was to befall me." His father, as a minister might do to a wayward soul, cross-examines him, gives him every chance to see his error, thus making his decision wholly conscious and its consequences wholly his own responsibility. The man was responsible for his own undoing, and redoing.

The pattern is scriptural: temptation, counsel, wrong action, recognition, acceptance of punishment, repentance, and restitution expressed in worldly terms. Having got their just deserts, and then some (the book of Job is never far away), his protagonists reap material rewards. From the outset Defoe limits the sphere of his concern in order to tell a truth, deliver an insight beyond the story, beyond the physical world it generates. Like Foxe with his martyrs, or Bunyan with his moral figures, Defoe creates types, but in his case types of situations: emblematic conflicts rather than exemplary protagonists. Bad motives battle with good in his characters. We do not confuse this internalized conflict with a psychology. "He leaves out the whole of vegetable nature, and a large part of human nature," Woolf reminds us. The visible world exists, but only those parts of it that contribute to our sharp focusing in on his characters and their trials. Being among the first writers of novels as such, Defoe had no name for the form. He believed he had to honor readers' expectations of a true and edifying story. An untrue story had to seem true; if it visited morally dubious areas of experience, it had to bring back instructive mementos.

*Robinson Crusoe,* or to give it its full title, which includes a blurb and plot summary, as early titles tended to do because there was no striking book jacket or cover to attract the reader, *The Life and Strange Surprising Adventures of Robinson Crusoe, of York, Mariner: Who lived Eight and Twenty Years, All Alone in an Uninhabited Island on the Coast of America, near the Mouth of the Great River of Oroonoque; Having Been Cast on Shore by Shipwreck, wherein All the Men Perished but Himself. with an Account of How He Was at Last as Strangely Deliver'd by Pirates,* was Defoe's first extended piece of fiction. It is far more concentrated than his earlier writings. J. M. Coetzee says, "For page after page—for the first time in the history of fiction—we see a minute, ordered description of how things are done. It is a matter of pure writerly attentiveness, pure submission to the exigencies of a world which, by being submitted to in a state so close to spiritual absorption, becomes transfigured, real." The phrase "spiritual absorption" defines the virtue and limitation of the writing. Building of a shelter, gathering food, collecting, breeding, and tending goats, fashioning a canoe, making pots, the laborious designing of the umbrella, all assiduously observed, pursued with an intent focus, as though the tasks rose before him one at a time: this is not realism but a progressive *agon,* gaining control of self and of a harsh physical and *moral* environment, culminating in the acquisition of a companion whom he confesses he loves and who is also a slave.

The "one by one" progression of the story, its linear movement, the lack of subtle plotting, errors in "continuity" (as when the hitherto naked Crusoe fills his pockets with biscuits), and the disintegration of the narrative when Crusoe and Friday arrive back in Europe, tell us something not only about Defoe's moral aesthetic but also about his method of composition. When he wrote his first novel, he was nearing sixty. His output to that date included not one work that would have secured him a place much above a footnote in the history of the essay and pamphlet. In 1718, and in 1719 when *Robinson Crusoe* was published, he contributed regularly to Mist's *Weekly Journal* and the *Wednesday Journal* and to John Applebee's sensational magazines, and he was writing for the monthly *Mercurius Politicus,* for the *Whitehall Evening Post,* the *Daily Post,* the *Manufacturer,* and other periodicals. In 1718 he wrote no fewer than eight substantial prose works: biographies, polemics, journalism. In the year of *Crusoe*'s publication he perpetrated a sequel and also a vindication of dissenters. He did not linger over his work. There is no reason to think he lavished more preplanning, reflection, and revision on his novels than on his other works. Dickens marveled at how *Robinson Crusoe* "has nothing in it to make anyone laugh or cry": "In particular," he says, "I took Friday's death as one of the least tender and (in the true sense) least sentimental things ever written."

Defoe was a man of business. He was paid by the line or page, and he was paid on both sides; he was not a poet or dramatist with the dignity those vocations can confer. He was a liar, a forger of lives, a pretender to truth; he sold words and was paid by weight. He responded to what he sensed were the interests of his readership. A new kind of writer, he had a large progeny. Few of his successors equal him for clarity of purpose or moral consistency in his fiction. "As a thinker he may not be original, but his mind is acute and curious about life in all its aspects," Coetzee says. This sets him apart also: he was interested in characters who shared qualities with Everyman but transcended him either because of the demands of their fates, or because of their ambition or failure.

He was a common chronicler of more than common man and woman. Given the speed with which he wrote, we can be sure that Defoe did not regard himself as an *artist*.

His originality is clear, but it does not do to read back into him a greater originality than his work possesses. He may be "the first English or foreign writer to strive after some sort of satisfactory convention for the novel," as Ford says. His moral purpose required him to establish verisimilitude but not "realism." His novels, apart from *A Journal of the Plague Year*, are pseudobiographies, of a piece with the actual biographies he wrote or ghosted for money. They come near to being "historic forgeries." Robinson and Moll speak a language similar to one another's: it is not their voice, but Defoe's, that speaks. A whole dramatic dimension is missing. "Defoe was the first great journalist," says Ford. He was not only a successful truth-teller, but a successful liar too. Coetzee calls him a ventriloquist, an impersonator, a forger, though later ventriloquists find a distinctive voice for their dummies. Woolf says, "Had he possessed a little more power of projection or a little more subtlety in presenting his figures and had his writing been a little less pedestrian his works might have gained and held the power to arouse a great deal more enthusiasm than they actually do."

The waning popularity of *Robinson Crusoe* in the last century, and the rise of *Moll Flanders*, illustrate changes in reading habits and the politics of sensibility. Some basic aesthetic and political assumptions have shifted. So have readers' expectations. Adventure now is a matter of rapid development, change, and suspense, no longer the dogged history of spiritual clarification or physical survival. Virginia Woolf in 1919, writing to mark the two-hundredth anniversary of *Crusoe*'s first publication, is able to say without demur, and as a woman: "The book resembles one of the anonymous productions of the race rather than the effort of a single mind." Is this true? The word "race," in part thanks to Friday himself, has taken on a different resonance from what Woolf intended. She is thinking of an English race (Kipling's understanding of the word is not far away), and implicit in this a system of values with which we less readily acquiesce than Woolf did. For one thing, Crusoe was a Scot.

In her experience, "We have all had *Robinson Crusoe* read aloud to us as children." Ford agrees: "We have all of us read it in our first childhoods." The last two or three generations may have had an abridgment read to them, may have skimmed the book at school, but it is less part of the dependable, permanent furniture of our minds now than it was of Dickens's, or Stevenson's, or Joyce's, Woolf's, or Coetzee's, all of whom allude to it familiarly. And Joyce: at Dignam's funeral Leopold Bloom meditates upon a stranger who arrives and puts him in mind of Crusoe. "Always someone turns up you never dreamt of. A fellow could live on his lonesome all his life. Yes, he could. Still he'd have to get someone to sod him after he died though he could dig his own grave. We all do. Only man buries. No, ants too." Who will put Crusoe out of the light? "Say Robinson Crusoe was true to life. Well then Friday buried him. Every Friday buries a Thursday if you come to look at it."

*Robinson Crusoe* is a fruit of Defoe's maturity, and in an age of xenophobia and prejudice his was a relatively liberal spirit. Certain issues rose clear before him, but others, to do with race, slavery, and exploitation, did not rise at all. A year after Indian printed calicoes were banned because they were "too popular," the novelist-to-be wrote his one famous poem, *The True-Born Englishman* (1701), ridiculing national prejudices that threatened to impoverish English political and cultural life. (He also wanted to ingratiate himself for patronage: the king of England was not English-born and had himself become a catalyst of xenophobia.)

> The Romans first with Julius Caesar came,
> Including all the Nations of that Name,
> Gauls, Greeks, and Lombards; and by Computation,
> Auxiliaries or Slaves of ev'ry Nation.
> With Hengist, Saxons; Danes with Sueno came,
> In search of Plunder, not in search of Fame.
> Scots, Picts, and Irish from th' Hibernian Shore:
> And Conqu'ring William brought the Normans o'er.
>     All these their Barb'rous Offspring left behind,
> The Dregs of Armies, they of all mankind;
> Blended with Britons who before were here,
> Of whom the Welsh ha' blest the Character.
>     From this Amphibious Ill-born Mob began
> The vain ill-natur'd thing, an Englishman.
> The Customs, Surnames, Languages, and Manners,
> Of all those Nations are their own Explainers:
> Whose Relics are so lasting and so strong,
> They ha' left a Shibboleth upon our Tongue;
> By which with easy search you may distinguish
> Your Roman-Saxon-Danish-Norman English.

The next year Defoe, a Dissenter, was put in the pillory and imprisoned for six months because of a satirical prose pamphlet, *The Shortest Way with Dissenters.* The day of explosive prose pamphlets was not over.

Where did this industrious and contradictory writer come from, a Whig-Tory, a fully fleshed ghostwriter, a sensationalizing moralist? He was born in

1660, the year of the Restoration. He wrote all his novels in the last twelve years of his life in order to restore his reputation and his estate after bankruptcy. When we read him, we feel in the presence of a person from an earlier period. "It is . . . not in the pomposity of the eighteenth century that Captain Singleton or Colonel Jack or Moll Flanders seem to be clothed. They were rather mobile, swaggering, piratical creatures seated on barrels and smoking their yards of clay than strutters in brocades and ruffles," says Ford.

Until recently the earliest documentary proof of Defoe's existence was his marriage record. His first years remain obscure, though he provides an account we may choose to believe. Daniel was the third child of Presbyterian James Foe (spelled variously), a self-made tradesman, butcher, tallow-chandler, and Free-man of the City, and of Alice Foe. They were first-generation Londoners, out of Northamptonshire. During the plague of 1665, Mrs. Foe took young Daniel to the country. His father and elder brother Henry stayed in town. When he came to write *A Journal of the Plague Year,* he called his narrator "H.F.," as though put-ting the account in his brother's mouth.

The Great Fire followed the plague, and James Foe's livery company put money toward the £10,000,000 reconstruction. The family, who became com-mitted nonconformists under the influence of the Reverend Samuel Annesley, intended Daniel for the ministry: he was educated at great expense when educa-tion was in an experimental phase. At the time of the Act of Uniformity, requir-ing all clergy to use the Book of Common Prayer, and the Five Mile Act (1665) to prevent clergy expelled due to the Act of Uniformity from living within five miles of their old parishes—effectively exiling dissenting clergy from the conurbations—some of these displaced, articulate, vigorous, no-nonsense men of the cloth became teachers or set up schools. In Newington Green outside London, until the late eighteenth century a relatively rural area, two such acad-emies were created, the second by the distinguished Oxford mathematician Charles Morton. Here the young Defoe studied, as did Samuel Wesley, father of John and Charles and thus grandfather of Methodism. Wesley wrote: "This academy were indeed the most considerable, having annext a fine Garden, Bowl-ing Green, Fish Pond, and within a laboratory and some not inconsiderable rari-ties with air-pump, thermometer and all sorts of mathematical instruments."

Defoe recalled how, in addition to classical languages, pupils came up against French, Italian, Spanish, mathematics, natural sciences, history, geography, logic, and politics: an education more broad than that of the public and than many of the grammar schools. This far-sighted education left him with deep religious convictions, but it did not lead him to the ministry. He became one of the new Englishmen, a self-starting, responsible, hardworking, independent, and reflec-tively moral individual. His conscientiousness lasted a lifetime, and neither the shifting political sands nor personal reversals—bankruptcy, imprisonment, and the rest—deflected him.

When he left school in 1679, he showed signs of wanderlust, portending Robinson Crusoe's rebelliousness. He was restrained from travel not by his father's appeals but by love. He started writing and courting. Courtship, to lead to matrimony, required him to find a career, and in 1683 he entered the hosiery trade, establishing residence and warehouse at Freeman's Yard, Cornhill. He married Mary Tuffley and her irresistible dowry (£3,700) in 1684. They had seven children.

Defoe despised James II, participating briefly in an abortive insurgency in support of Monmouth. Legend has it that he happened upon the name "Robinson Crusoe" on a tombstone while hiding in a graveyard, the authorities in armed pursuit. Though pardons were issued, dissenters and rebels remained under suspicion and a sporadic threat of attack and dispossession. Defoe's association with the losing side was not a secret. Now he did travel abroad and saw much of the Continent, with forays into France, Holland, Italy, and Spain. He remained active in business, with the help of his father-in-law diversifying into imported goods, including wine and tobacco.

In 1692 he decided to go into the perfume business and bought seventy civet cats in an abortive musk-trading scheme. He tried for a £200 stake in a diving bell intended to retrieve sunken goods. He continued to support his family in a manner befitting their social standing. He retained two servants right up until liquidation. After legal procrastination and moral brinkmanship—drawing loans from friends in the knowledge he would be unable to repay them, using his mother-in-law's funds without her consent—his creditors pushed him to his first bankruptcy. He turned himself in to the Fleet Prison over a sum owed to John Selby, was transferred to King's Bench to answer charges, made undertakings and was discharged. The process began again. He went bankrupt with total debts of £17,000, a considerable sum at the time, despite the dowry and his once-substantial personal savings. Eventually he repaid all but £5,000; he was never again free of debt or properly solvent. He was helped by friends into various temporary jobs to keep body, soul, and family together.

He set up a brickworks and tileworks on land he retained in Chadwell and Tilbury. At first this seemed the answer to his problems, earning roughly £600 every year off the back of London's swift expansion, and winning several major contracts. Payment was slow and sometimes never came. Defoe paid most of his receipts to his old creditors.

He had always written. Now writing became a chief source of income. Though known today for his novels, he was responsible for more than 500 publications, a celebrated pamphleteer on politics, geography, religion, psychology, and metaphysical themes. He may have translated picaresque literature. He acted as agent for William III in England and Scotland to 1701, the peak of his civic career. *The True-Born Englishman* earned him favor and was the best-selling poem of its day. His hopes of preferment were short-lived. William III died in 1702, a moment Defoe had chosen to satirize the High Church attitude to Dissenters, an ill-timed intervention that made him enemies. The next year, having formally changed his name from Foe to Defoe, he was arrested for seditious libel and clapped in the pillory for three days at Charing Cross. There he ad-libbed the "Hymn to the Pillory," and when released he was carted off to prison at Newgate. He considered the possibility of suicide and endured a second bankruptcy: there seemed no escape from bad luck. "No man has tasted differing fortunes more, / And thirteen times I have been rich and poor."

Entrepreneurial even in despair, he began preparing his most durable journalistic project, *The Review (A Review of the Affairs of France, and of All Europe)*, which he wrote and edited singlehanded, "anonymously" (he argued later that anonymous authorship should be made an offense and would have been arraigned in his own court), at first weekly then thrice weekly, to 1713 when it was priced off the newsstands by the Stamp Act. A "one-essay journal," it featured a substantial piece of several thousand words printed on both sides of a broadside half-sheet. A 1938 edition of *The Review* runs to twenty-two volumes.

The intervention of the Tory statesman Robert Harley, later Earl of Oxford, brought him back into circulation in both senses. He became a hired pen, working as Harley's political agent and journalistic apologist—taking, indeed, the same course that Thomas Nashe had done a couple of centuries before. Though the age of the patronless writer had dawned, Defoe had yet to find a readership; and without it he needed a paymaster. Harley had come into his own in the 1690s, reaching the height of his career under Queen Anne, dominating politics by his presence and absence. Defoe was not entirely comfortable among Tories, but his willingness to work for either faction (to write for money) brought accusations upon him despite his frequent use of pseudonyms ("Heliostrapolis," "Eye Witness," "T. Taylor," "Andrew Morton, Merchant," and so on). At a political level Defoe was the Vicar of Bray, though in matters of religion he remained true to his Presbyterian roots.

In 1705 the first murmurings of fiction issued from him. He composed *A True Relation of the Apparition of One Mrs. Veal* and *The Consolidator; or, Memoirs of Sundry Transactions from the World in the Moon*. The one created out of scattered facts a "true" fiction, the other was an act of fantastic, satirical invention, going as far afield as Moscow, China, and the Moon, where the library was singularly well stocked with European writings. Better realized was the first. Keeping his eye on the market, he wrote, in the wake of the Act of Union, his *History of the*

*Union of Great Britain* (1709). Despite further brushes with the law in 1713, when he was twice arrested for debt and charged with sedition after publishing three pamphlets, he continued to write commercially, moving between allegiances. In 1715 the highly successful *The Family Instructor* appeared; and as a personal vindication *An Appeal to Honor and Justice,* his one overtly autobiographical work. Those who needed writing done knew Defoe to be a malleable wordsmith, trying to maintain his family at Stoke Newington.

How many millions of words Defoe wrote, in service of causes! He was fifty-nine when he published not only the pamphlet that most endeared him to Virginia Woolf, *On the Education of Women,* and his "true" biography of the Cornishman *Dickory Cronke, the Dumb Philosopher,* but also *Robinson Crusoe.* In the last twelve years of his life, the pamphleteer became the author of substantial books, clearing his debts, and providing for his daughter Hannah, who was well on her way to spinsterhood.

*Robinson Crusoe* was offered to several publishers before William Taylor acquired it. It was an immediate success: released on April 25, it was reprinted seventeen days later, again after twenty-five more days, then again on August 8. One contemporary declared contemptuously: "There's not an old woman that can go to the price of it, but buys *Robinson Crusoe.*" The first edition cost five shillings a copy, at the time as much as a quarter of a week's wages. Taylor acquired the copyright outright and benefited: he died with a fortune of £45,000 to £50,000. Defoe was merely the author. His name did not appear on early editions: the book belonged to its narrator. Defoe initially got £10 for the manuscript, what Milton received for the first and second printings of *Paradise Lost.* He may have written the first "true novel" in English, even (some claim) a "fantasy autobiography"; credit went to a publisher who brought it to market.

Defoe "seems to have taken his characters so deeply into his mind," says Virginia Woolf, with reference to Crusoe and Moll Flanders, "that he lived them without exactly knowing how; and, like all unconscious artists, he leaves more gold in his work than his own generation was able to bring to the surface." The most suggestive, if elliptical, reader of Defoe is Edgar Allan Poe. He notes "the potent magic of verisimilitude" that one experiences in *Crusoe,* "the faculty of *identification*—that dominion exercised by volition over imagination which enables the mind to lose its own, in a fictitious, individuality." Poe is right to insist that "Defoe is largely indebted to his subject." The art has a solid foundation to build on, a subject familiar to readers of popular journalism, a story they believe without question. Franz Kafka felt at one with Crusoe, writing to Milena Jesenská that he was even "more Robinson than he."

During 1720 Defoe published two readable books: *Memoirs of a Cavalier,* with its credible accounts of wars in England and Germany; and a month later *The*

*Life, Adventures and Piracies of the Famous Captain Singleton.* In this year, too, he began to work more closely in publishing with John Applebee, who specialized in true-life stories of the bad and condemned, preferably those with a noose already about their necks. Defoe was familiar with both sides of a prison gate. "In the School of Affliction I have learnt more Philosophy than at the Academy, and more Divinity than from the Pulpit: In Prison I have learnt to know that Liberty does not consist in open Doors, and the free Egress and Regress of Locomotion. I have seen the rough side of the World as well as the smooth, and have in less than half a Year tasted the difference between the Closet of a King, and the Dungeon of Newgate."

He had to seek out jail stories that he could adapt to the market (knitted into homilies). An old man delighted with a new form, he maintained an astonishing output. In 1722 he published no fewer than six substantial books, including *A Journal of the Plague Year* (not historical fiction so much as historical imagination), and his best child character in the first part of *The History and Remarkable Life of the Truly Honorable Colonel Jacque, Commonly Call'd Col. Jack.* It was the year of *Moll Flanders*, too, another picaresque "memoir." It incorporated the memory of his own rapid fall in the 1690s and the horrors of Newgate. Originally it sold under the title *The Fortunes and Misfortunes of the Famous Moll Flanders &c Who Was Born at Newgate, and during a Life of Continued Variety for Threescore Years, besides Her Childhood, Was Twelve Year a Whore, Five Time a Wife (whereof Once to Her Own Brother), Twelve Year a Thief, Eight Year a Transported Felon in Virginia, at Last Grew Rich, Liv'd Honest, and Died a Penitent,* his outstanding novel of character.

In 1724 he wrote his last important novel, now known as *Roxana: The Fortunate Mistress,* moving toward a subtly structured, complex plot, not simply following a linear development. He set the novel back in time, during the reign of Charles II. This distance made it possible to shape events and defer judgment. Roxana's decline, from middling propriety to prostitution, is told with a financial, rather than an erotic, relishing that rather coarsens the moral tone.

Defoe did not stop writing, but after this formal Indian summer no novels, only "true histories," followed. In 1725, for example, the notorious criminal Jonathan Wild was hanged, and in his gallery of rogues Defoe hung, that same year, *The True and Genuine Account of the Life and Actions of the Late Jonathan Wild,* upon which eighteen years later Henry Fielding based his mock biography *The Life of Mr. Jonathan Wild the Great.* In 1731, at lodgings in Ropemaker's Alley, Moorfields, Defoe died of what was described as "lethargy." He was buried near Bunyan in Bunhill Fields, where he enjoys a marble obelisk.

Despite setbacks, he had achieved his three-score years and ten. "On any monument worthy of the name of monument," wrote Virginia Woolf, "the names of *Moll Flanders* and *Roxana,* at least, should be carved as deeply as the name of Defoe. They stand among the few English novels which we can call indisputably great." They are absent from the obelisk, but it is to these women that modern readers turn to discover, among so many novels about men, the lives of women, and to understand Defoe's readerships, consisting as they did of women with leisure, income enough to acquire or borrow books, literacy, dreams of romance and independence.

Moll Flanders is believable, though her life is so full of incident, and she scatters so many children in her wake, that at times we doubt her. Still, it is not only the material world she inhabits or the adventures she is put through but her sensibility that Defoe "genders" by the tones and drives he gives it. The material insecurity into which she is born justifies her obsession with money; her own neglect as a child explains her neglect of her own children. Prostitution, bigamy, incest, and theft take on a different meaning when encountered in Moll's troubled life story. Both she and Roxana (also a great producer of offspring who tries to make a tally and is responsible for the death of one of her daughters) want security. Both are susceptible to love. They are beautiful, they trade upon that for a time. Roxana retains her beauty for over three decades. Both lapse into lives of crime to survive.

In these novels Defoe gives us details, says Woolf, that mean more to his characters than to him; for him they are observations, matters of mere fact, yet they animate the story, as if in excess, or even in contradiction, of the author's intent and tenor. Characters seem to insist on some elements that Defoe permits them without quite knowing why. His tolerance, entertaining their foibles, makes the books more theirs. Unlike his characters who are "not so much dead, as unalive," says Woolf, Moll lives fully. As a woman, she (like Roxana) is continually attentive to those about her. While Crusoe or Colonel Jack are intent on their own feelings and fates, Moll and Roxana read the faces and hearts of those upon whom they prey and depend. Moll's life reaches a contented ending. All her crimes have, as it were, expired. Roxana's closing sentences are like the dreadful opening of a haunted sequel: an unhappy ending, a feel-bad story: "Here [in Holland, where she had retired], after some few years of flourishing and outwardly happy circumstances, I fell into a dreadful course of calamities, and Amy [her co-conspirator] also; the very reverse of our former good days. The blast of Heaven seemed to follow the injury done the poor girl by us both, and I was brought so low again that my repentance seemed to be only the consequence of my misery, as my misery was of my crime."

These reflections lack the subtlety and style of Richardson, but the moral concerns are like his, and the voice that speaks is not a man's, even if it is not quite a woman's either. With less plot and more sensibility, less geography and more actual place, less "type" and more "character," with stronger moral categories and consciences, with narrative techniques that escape the first person, this strange prose form that gains in definitions will achieve truer romance, comedy, and tragedy. Defoe's is "a tongue that naked goes," as Wyndham Lewis says, whoever his speaker is. Such efficient, unaffected, and formally plain narrative represents a default position for the novel. V. S. Pritchett holds a contrary view: "The English novel was not a development from the reporting of Defoe, a way of writing which, of its nature, is prevented from imaginative development." He forgets the rich invention, or appropriation, of *A Journal of the Plague Year,* his inwardness with his female characters, and his ability to grasp, as an old man, the ways of seeing of a child.

———————

Defoe's heirs in the twentieth century are of three kinds: those who try for his sort of verisimilitude and thematic relevance in journalistic terms, those who revisit his themes from modern points of view, and those who build on the moral force of his single-mindedness with a refining artistry.

Thomas (Michael) Keneally (b. 1935) takes historical subjects and uses the biographical form to dramatize and moralize. The Holocaust narrative *Schindler's Ark* (1982) was awarded a Booker Prize and filmed by Stephen Spielberg as *Schindler's List* (1993). Based on interviews, documentary, and historical accounts, it reconstructs the development of a character, a human bridge between cynical Nazism and capitalist-Christian self-sacrifice. In Defoe, words even in dreams purport to address a reality that is material and consistent, in order to tell inescapably true things. Imitation of the real is crucial, and the word *real* is not undermined by semantic or philosophical anxiety. He "invents" a true story. Factual fiction, or "faction" as it was called after several controversial instances of fictional appropriation of real-life stories, tells of extreme experience and details the material reality of a place and a period. Good is pitted against evil, the actual geography of the labor camp is an allegorical figuration. "That's how it was," the author might argue, and perhaps so: but the literal never sufficiently underwrites the fictional or validates the moral lesson.

A far more significant heir to Defoe is the irresistibly talented, self-immolating Truman Capote (1924–1984). Harper Lee, a friend from childhood who was slowly piecing together her novel *To Kill a Mockingbird* (1960), declared, "There's probably no better writer in this country today than Truman Capote. He is growing all the time. The next thing coming from Capote is not a novel—it's a long piece of reportage, and I think it is going to make him bust loose as a novelist." He invented the term "nonfiction novel" for this "next thing coming," *In Cold Blood: A True Account of a Multiple Murder and Its Consequences* (1966), a book that, by means of thorough preparation and investigative style, seeks to erase the boundary between fact and fiction. The whodunit is traced back to motive, the relationship of the narrator to his subjects is eroticized. The word "True" in the subtitle put paid to Capote's career as a novelist: when the book appeared and had its enormous success, its truth was challenged by several witnesses and, like Harriet Beecher Stowe, he had to reply. In such circumstances the accused who keeps his counsel is assumed to be guilty.

Capote, having finished a brilliant novella, was looking for a project and, one account tells us, saw a brief report of the murder in the newspaper, the catalyst he needed. Another version says that his editor at the *New Yorker* gave him a choice of two stories and he chose this one, imagining it would be more sensational and easier to dramatize. Herbert Clutter, a Kansas farmer, Mrs. Clutter, and two of their children had been brutally killed. Before the murderers were caught, he decided to visit the scene and explore the story. He and Harper Lee went to Holcomb, Kansas, where they started digging and taking hundreds of pages of notes. The suspects were apprehended. Capote finessed his way into interviewing them.

Capote was born Truman Streckfus Persons in New Orleans. His parents divorced when he was a boy, and he was reared by relatives in several parts of the South. He was not an easy child. He completed high school in Connecticut, having taken his stepfather's surname Capote as his own. An early story published in *Mademoiselle* received an award. *Other Voices, Other Rooms* (1948), quietly homosexual, was published in the same year as Gore Vidal's forceful and controversial *The City and the Pillar*. "Capote I truly loathed," declared Vidal, "the way you might loathe an animal. A filthy animal that has found its way into the house." He loathed him because he was a liar, "the one thing I hate most on this earth."

Capote's stories proved a minor success. Further stories in *A Tree of Night* (1949) and the semi-autobiographical novel *The Grass Harp* (1951) brought him notice. Then came the novella *Breakfast at Tiffany's* (1958), a brilliant evocation of the threadbare, irresistible protagonist Holly Golightly, first cousin of Christopher Isherwood's Sally Bowles. While Capote was becoming better known, his mother killed herself; his father, caught embezzling, went to Sing Sing. This contributed to his fascination with prisons and detention. *In Cold Blood* was a big project slow to take shape. In writing it he proved himself the Flaubert of fact, believing style would follow naturally from the precision with which events and characters were observed.

Control, Capote said, consisted in "maintaining a stylistic and emotional upper hand over your material. Call it precious and go to hell, but I believe a story can be wrecked by a faulty rhythm in a sentence . . . or a mistake in paragraphing, even punctuation." He dubbed Henry James "the maestro of the semicolon," Hemingway "a first-rate paragrapher," and said Virginia Woolf "never wrote a bad sentence." His transformative subtlety is profound and his *obiter dicta* precise and enabling to good writers. "Finding the right form for your story is simply to realize the most *natural* way of telling the story." When it is written, a writer must imagine whether it might have been written in a different form and work as effectively. Is it "absolute and final" in the way that "an orange is final," he asks. The orange is a metaphor of effect, not of process, because the book does not grow, it is made. The writer must have ceased to be emotionally involved before being in a state "clinical enough" to analyze, and then to project it. Even if the narrator is entailed in the story, his presence must be as considered and "objective" as that of the characters whose experiences he tells. "I seem to remember reading that Dickens, as he wrote, choked with laughter over his own humor and dripped tears all over the page when one of his characters died. My own theory is that the writer should have considered his wit and dried his tears long, long before setting out to evoke similar reactions in the reader." He insists that "the greatest intensity in art in all its shapes is achieved with a deliberate, hard, and cool head." Techniques of cinema are integrated into his fiction, a fact he acknowledges in expressing his debt, and that of his generation, to the screen writing and criticism of fellow southerner James Agee. Tom Wolfe admired this "instinctive" quality in Capote's work, citing as "a wonderful example" the opening of *In Cold Blood,* "a very long shot of a Kansas wheat field, gradually focusing in on a solitary farmhouse on the horizon."

No doubt he was eccentric, first playfully and then deliberately impersonating himself. At eighteen he became a copy boy in the offices of the *New Yorker* and remained a contriver of his life, everything in it deliberated and carried through. When he realized he was losing control, he turned, as Agee had done, to drink. He could no longer write as he wished, because writing as he wished entailed telling the truth about experience, telling about his friends and acquaintances in ways they didn't like. Capote went to pieces. He published chapters from his long-gestating "Answered Prayers" in *Esquire.* Old friends saw themselves included and broke with him. "I'm a writer," he said plaintively, angrily, "I use everything." Not any more he didn't: the exposure of those chapters put an end to it.

Charles Henri Ford observed him at the opera in Paris, ascending the stairs "like a short caterpillar"; he said to a friend of the young Capote, "Sa voix n'est pas faite!" His voice never "broke," he remained shrill, ingratiating, self-absorbed. He thought lying down, and he needed copious coffee and cigarettes to function. He wrote in pencil, revised in longhand, and only when everything was satisfactory did he type. A meticulous, pedantic stylist, he weighed every punctuation mark on a jeweler's scales. Writers who do not take care with style are "sweaty typists blacking up pounds of bond paper with formless, eyeless, earless messages."

———•———

The South African novelist and 2003 Nobel Prize winner J. M. (John Maxwell) Coetzee (b. 1940) declares, "The nineteenth-century realist novel flourished on the basis of a web of tacit contracts between writer and reader about how 'the real' might be represented." Defoe precedes such contracts. He occupies the same kind of space as the modern writer for whom those contracts are null and void, though many popular writers fail to notice the situation. Defoe's realism is limited to an empirical take on the word. In 1986 Coetzee published *Foe,* a novel that depends on *Robinson Crusoe* for resonance but brings into play the long conflictive afterlife of that novel.

*Foe* is written from the point of Susan Barton, a woman who ended up on Crusoe's (or Cruso's) island and got to know him and Friday, already established there. It would have been easier for Coetzee to tell the story from Friday's perspective, but Friday has no tongue and cannot speak, which is part of Defoe's theme but also key to modern readings of this most European narrative. A female narrator, cut adrift due to a mutiny from the ship in which she was traveling, speaking from another culturally muted point of view, like his lecturer-character *Elizabeth Costello* (2003), the protagonist of *The Lives of Animals* (1999), is the inventive risk he took.

Like *Robinson Crusoe,* the story is one of aftermath. Susan has returned to England and wants a writer to ghost her tale. She goes to Daniel Foe in the hope that he can write her book in a popular form. He has the language, the skill, and as a man the power to carry out her task. But *she* has the story. She sets out to find her daughter, kidnapped and spirited away to America. Cruso she discovers resigned to his fate. He is looked after by Friday, a onetime slave whose tongue was removed and whose story is lost even though he is still alive and must contain and prolong it. After a year with these men, rescue comes, Cruso dies on the homeward journey, and Susan and Friday land in the old country. She tries to write and fails. Foe disagrees with her on which portions of her story will entertain a readership. They marry, Foe is in debt and cannot bend his mind to the task. Then her daughter, or is it her daughter, reappears.

Susan's inability to tell her own story, her failure of language, is a failure of authority. Language is power, the person with the skill to tell and interpret a story truly is also in a position to choose and to lie. The man she elects as her writer and lover appropriates and falsifies her witness. In a sense he writes over her story, as Defoe, with his singular concern for Robinson, writes over the story of Friday, making it not secondary but tributary. Barton wants to speak for herself and for Friday also. When Friday might tell his story he releases a froth of bubbles, his dead body heavy with water. The noises the body makes are without meaning, except that his story is lost. The political sense of his silence is clear in the South African context, but by introducing a woman Coetzee calls into question themes and stereotypes more modern in tenor. His book is in dialogue less with literature than with its aftermaths and legacies, what it contributed to ideologies of racial and cultural as well as political imperialism. He makes his story real in other terms. Coetzee's and Barton's voices merge.

When Magda at the end of Coetzee's 1977 novel *In the Heart of the Country* asks, "Am I at last going to yield to the spectre of reason and explain myself to myself in the only confession we protestants know?" she affiliates herself with Defoe's protagonists, whose stories explain them, an explanation that discloses a process and results in understanding but not expiation. The Karoo is a real place; it is also a large vacancy in which a soul can contend with every spiritual challenge that history and psychology propose.

Coetzee's and Defoe's single-mindedness are of a kind. Neither is programmatic: "Only those who can do no better submit to a given theme or carry out a programme," Coetzee says. In an essay on Kafka, commenting on the Muirs' translations, he notes how they heighten diction against the grain of Kafka's language, which is "restrained, even neutral," and which repeats rather than insisting on variation. Defoe is like that, too. South African writers from the seventeenth to the twentieth century seem to Coetzee to be suspended in a space that is free but vertiginous: they are "no longer European, yet not African," and being African in any significant way may well always elude them. His retirement from South Africa to Australia, where he is now a citizen, may be an attempt to choose a culture in which he might less ambiguously belong.

Caryl Phillips wrote a valuable essay on Coetzee in 1998. Coetzee had written seven works of fiction at that time. Phillips praises the ways he avoided the political predictabilities of Nadine Gordimer's novels, how he eludes the category of "political writer." Like the black writer James Baldwin composing *Giovanni's Room* (1956) without touching directly on issues of race, Coetzee composes outside the compulsory themes of the Republic of South Africa, though his books touch on them in ways more telling than a direct approach might have done. He spent most of the 1960s, when South Africa was politically at its darkest, in London, in Texas, in Buffalo, studying and teaching. In 1971 he returned to an academic career in South Africa. His first work, *Dusklands* (1974), is two novels, one centered on Vietnam, one a meditation, in the appalled and curious moral spirit of the Hawthorne of *The House of the Seven Gables,* on his own ancestor Jacobus Coetzee and the cruel legacies in South Africa. *In the Heart of the Country* is a severe Protestant allegory in avant-garde form. The novel is not just a novel but an *agon,* adding to an argument that develops book by book, each time finding an appropriate form. "It takes generations of life in the cities to drive the nostalgia for country ways from the heart. I will never live it down, nor do I want to. I am corrupted to the bone with the beauty of this forsaken world. If the truth be told I never wanted to fly away with the sky-gods."

Nadine Gordimer, once she decided Coetzee was a significant and original writer not avoiding but obliquely confronting the political realities that so single-mindedly exercise her, said that his mode, "from the beginning, is soon seen to have arisen solely out of the needs of content." His account of South Africa and his evocation of himself in it, is glum. His childhood with overly attentive parents was privileged: he sees it as a time of trial and deprivation, which perhaps it seemed, though in context a fortunate deprivation. He struggled to find his own resistances, to affirm himself within the tolerant and generous love he experienced. He took a master's degree in absentia from the University of Cape Town. His subject was Ford Madox Ford. Beckett's novels touched him; he abandoned the Romantic writers for the Augustans, then abandoned Alexander Pope for Jonathan Swift, whose vigorous candor and negativity appealed to him.

In his writing he avoids specific geographies, not tying his narrative to particulars irrelevant to the story. In *The Master of Petersburg* (1994), the city is undescribed, taken for granted. What matters is not the detail of place but the drama of relationship and incident. With this freedom he can explore a moral environment rather than follow the surface street to street. He is also able to parley with Dostoyevsky.

*Waiting for the Barbarians* (1980) and *Life and Times of Michael K* (1983, his first Booker Prize–winning novel) are crucial clauses in his argument. His subject is often a vulnerable person relocated to, or abandoned in, a hostile environment. Characters are marginal to the heartless cultures in which they live. They do not make a mark but are marked. A veritable outsider, like Kafka he creates plausible societies, landscapes, and situations, isolating and investigating his subjects with clinical *sang froid.* In a different way Defoe isolated and experimented on single protagonists.

*Life and Times of Michael K* marks a development in his approach. Cynthia Ozick notes its formal flaw as "the density of its own interior interpretations." The simple, harelipped protagonist tries to return his mother to her place of birth to die. When she dies, he continues on with her ashes. He is detained for not having the right papers, forced to labor, and then proceeds, reaching his destination and settling on an abandoned farm. When a relation of the owners arrives and treats him as the lowest of servants, he makes off into the mountains and a period of hunger. He begins to understand the world around him.

Coming back to civilization, he is detained once more and assigned to a work camp where he is politicized. After further unrest Michael bolts again, returns to the farm, and tries to become independent. The rebels persecute him. He escapes into captivity once more and is sent back to Cape Town to be rehabilitated. A doctor takes an interest in him, and the narrative is conducted through the doctor's notes. Ozick regards the use of the prison doctor's diary as marring the coherence of the novel's point of view. The doctor tells us how to read the story, tying symbols down, limiting their resonance, and the allegory becomes rigid. Michael eludes this overly articulate confinement too and meets with a nomadic group who feed him and where he finds sex for the first time. Back in Cape Town he returns to his mother's flat and reflects on the life he made at the farm in Prince Albert, where for a while he was free and self-sufficient.

Nadine Gordimer, like the doctor in the story, reads as allegory any narrative capable of symbolic interpretation, no matter how unstable the symbols. She habitually overreads. "For is there an idea of survival that can be realized entirely outside a political doctrine? Is there a space that lies between camps?" she asks, expecting a no. For Michael K the answer is yes, brief, hard won.

In *Age of Iron* (1990) Gordimer would be forgiven for reading allegorically. A very European professor of classics writes to her daughter about her illness and the end of apartheid in South Africa, the connections between the human and social organism being rather too obvious. Coetzee experiments with documentary techniques but violates them by interjection, as the doctor in *Michael K* mars his account. Here, even if the intention was to parody Gordimer, miscalculation mars the book. *The Master of Petersburg* is problematic, set in Russia in 1869 and not quite plausibly filling in a gap in Dostoyevsky's biography. It is in fact autobiographical, vulnerable but oblique, identifying Coetzee's own anxieties, without specific South African content. Contrived, the effects are worked for. But Coetzee is experimenting, finding things rather than just making them. The essayist in him balances the novelist, each novel driving at once into fictional and essayistic terrains, bringing them into convergence. Part of his technique is to make protagonists we do not warm to. He is not interested in a conventional relationship with the reader. There is more of Vladimir Nabokov in Coetzee than might at first appear, a severe Nabokov who plays with bones and broken things, but who plays; and for whom convention and realism are treacherous. The writer constructs, there is no question of words coming naturally as leaves to a tree, unless it is a blighted tree and the words that come sparse, creating little shade.

*Disgrace* (1999, which won his second Booker Prize) is Coetzee's most Defoe-like novel. His protagonist is an academic discredited for sexual misconduct who prefers not to defend himself. Language has become treacherous. "Only the monosyllables can still be relied on, and not even all of them." He goes finally, reluctantly, to his daughter, who lives a basic existence in the country, isolated and resigned, well on her way to becoming a post-apartheid Magda. He cannot shift his disgrace, his failure, and like earlier characters he occupies that in-between situation of the white South African, in suspension. "Is it enough for God, do you think, that I live my disgrace without term?" This book's moral and physical violence and irresolution are harsh, the action and characters credible. It is a parable and an argument about where things are, making sense but not proposing a direction. For the sake of his art and his sanity, and because he fell in love with a new country and the city of Adelaide, he left South Africa, almost abandoning the metaphors Calvinism proposed in the context of apartheid and its aftermaths. But those metaphors still have a hold on him.

# *Proportion*

François Rabelais, Sir Thomas Urquhart, Jonathan Swift,
Samuel Johnson, Voltaire, Oliver Goldsmith, Alasdair Gray

Jonathan Swift is a brilliant savage who understands, though he cannot control, the spiritual, political, and literary jungle in which he exists. Ford Madox Ford notes his unique power to inspire disgust. He inspires it because he feels it, so intense that it outweighs desire. Even pastoral irony cannot mask his revulsion from the manuriness of human being:

> So things which must not be exprest,
> When plumpt into the reeking chest,
> Send up an excremental smell
> To taint the parts from whence they fell,
> The petticoats and gown perfume,
> Which waft a stink round every room.
> Thus finishing his grand survey,
> Disgusted Strephon stole away
> Repeating in his amorous fits,
> *Oh! Celia, Celia, Celia shits!*

Portions of *Gulliver's Travels* (or, to give it its full title, *Travels into Several Remote Nations of the World: In Four Parts, by Lemuel Gulliver, First a Surgeon, and Then a Captain of Several Ships*) were to become, in expurgated and abbreviated forms, favorite children's stories, but as Thackeray declared, Swift "enters the nursery with the tread and gaiety of an ogre." He defines Swift's mission: "The humorous writer professes to awaken and direct your love, your pity, your kindness—your scorn for untruth, pretension, imposture—your tenderness for the weak, the poor, the oppressed, the unhappy . . . [Swift] takes upon himself to be the week-day preacher," for whom "yesterday's preacher becomes the text for today's sermon." But he also grants to Swift a peculiarly English eighteenth-century quality: "He does not speak above his voice, as it were, and the tone of society."

Doctor Johnson pays tribute to Swift's notion of good style, "proper words in proper places," and adds: "Perhaps no writer can be found who borrowed so little, or that in all his excellences and all his defects has so well maintained his claim to be considered as original." He is original in part because he is compact in his prose. "When I am reading a book," Swift remarks, "whether wise or silly, it seemeth to be alive and talking to me." His thoughts were "never subtilized by nice disquisitions, decorated by sparkling conceits, elevated by ambitious sentences, or variegated by far-sought learning," unless in a spirit of parody. His economy of style "suggests an acute summary rather than a full report of what it describes."

Born in Dublin in 1667, Swift was not comfortably Irish. Thackeray proclaims him "no more an Irishman than a man born of English parents in Calcutta is a Hindoo," unlike Goldsmith and Steele. "Swift's heart was English and in England, his habits English, his logic eminently English"; by which he means, "His statement is elaborately simple; he shuns tropes and metaphors, and uses his ideas and words with a wise thrift and economy, as he used his money . . . He never indulges in needless extravagance of rhetoric, lavish epithets, profuse imagery. He lays his opinion before you with a grave simplicity and a perfect neatness."

His father, a lawyer from Yorkshire, went to Dublin after the Restoration in search of opportunities and died before his son was delivered. Anticipating the Duke of Wellington, Swift declared, "I am not of this vile country; I am an Englishman." He would deny that he was born there, claiming he was taken there shortly after birth. Ireland, beyond its intractable spiritual challenge, represented his thwarted pride and hopes. At odds with the exploitative influence of England over Ireland, later in life he earned the respect of the Irish and a reputation for patriotism.

His widowed mother returned to her family in Leicestershire, leaving Jonathan to a possessive wet nurse and then to the guardianship of Godwin Swift, a well-to-do uncle who provided him with a good education. Swift, resenting his status as dependent and "outsider," loathed this uncle, later accusing him of "giving him the education of a dog." The dramatist William Congreve was among his younger contemporaries at Kilkenny College, then one of the best schools in Ireland, and later at Trinity College, Dublin, which Swift entered at the age of fourteen as a pensioner (a part-scholarship boy). Swift had hoped to study at Oxford. He was routinely called to account for misbehavior or for going absent in the city. His lifelong dislike for the prevailing rationalist fashion dates from this period. In his final year, he vaguely refers to "difficulties." His final results were poor and he graduated in 1686 *speciali gratia* (by special dispensation) by the skin of his teeth. As well as conventional learning, he had accumulated grievances, disappointment, bitterness, essential compost for his hectic, merciless imagination. Thackeray reveals a complementary face: "If you had been a lord with a blue riband, who flattered his vanity, or could help his ambition, he would have been the most delightful company in the world . . . His servility was so boisterous that it looked like independence."

Free of Trinity, Swift traveled to England and became secretary to Sir William Temple. He wrote poetry, mastered and began to break through the literary conventions of the age toward what Thomas De Quincey called his "vernacularity," a quality that marks his prose. At Temple's he was made tutor to Esther Johnson, the intermittently sickly and paradoxical "Stella," a lifelong attachment and subject of much of his feeling and some of his best writing. She was the daughter of a companion to Lady Giffard, Temple's sister; her father had died. She was eight years old at their first encounter. She had the effrontery to grow, stage by stage, into a woman.

He undertook missions for Temple, one to the king himself. In 1692, thanks perhaps to Temple's intercession, he took an MA from Hart Hall (later Hartford College), Oxford, fulfilling an early ambition, and was set for a career in the church. Though devout, Swift resisted organized religion, less because of its structures than because of those who exploited them. He entered the church because it seemed to offer the best chance of preferment for one in his circumstances. Ordained deacon in 1694, he took leave of Temple's service and the next year became a priest of the Church of Ireland, crossing the water once more. He courted an Ulster woman, Jane Waring, who disappointed him. Again Temple came to the rescue, organizing his return to England and helping him to his first living, his first release and sinecure, and later promotions.

Swift's prose career had begun in 1693 when he published *An Answer to a Scurrilous Pamphlet*. Retorting from the start, he set himself against, and this became his posture in writing; it entailed sometimes grudging advocacy of the "other" side. At Temple's estate at Moor Park in 1696, Swift's prose increased in volume and distinction. *The Battle of the Books,* his attack on academic pedantry, and *A Tale of a Tub,* satirizing current religious disputes and sectarian fanaticism, did not make friends but gained readers.

In 1699 Temple died, and Swift, no longer protected, began a life sentence in Ireland, earning infrequent furloughs. He returned to Ireland first as chaplain to the Earl of Berkeley, a post from which he was ousted by private intrigue. He became vicar of Laracor, by Trim, with Agher and Rathbeggan. His congregation numbered fifteen, and he found himself with time to plant willow trees and rebuild the vicarage. He frequently visited Dublin twenty miles away. Time passed. Embroiled in religious and political affairs, he ascended the hierarchy, returning to London from time to time. In 1708 he met Addison and Steele. He contributed to the *Tatler* and later to the *Spectator,* but fell out with the Whigs when, under the patronage of the Earl of Oxford, leader of a new Tory-dominated administration, he began to edit the *Examiner.* Queen Anne contrived a personal dislike for him, which did not help his cause, though it may have earned her a place in Lilliput. Swift continued unofficially as "ministerial *chef de propagande*" and befriended Alexander Pope, John Gay, Doctor John Arbuthnot, and Henry St. John Viscount Bolingbroke. He had become a parodist, useful for when he began work on *Gulliver's Travels,* mixing parody and oblique polemic, and in which foes might find themselves embedded.

In 1713 Swift was inaugurated as dean of St. Patrick's Cathedral, Dublin. He climbed no higher, though he harbored hopes. He had friends—correspondents with whom to exchange ideas and rancors, and to visit when he went to London. In the waning months of Queen Anne's reign they founded the Scriblerus Club with the express purpose of sending up the idiocies of learning and scholarship that then, as before and after, were in fashion. The third part of *Gulliver's Travels,* "A Voyage to Laputa, Balnibarbi, Luggnagg, Glubbdubdrib, and Japan," builds on these miasmic madnesses.

The eponymous Martin Scriblerus, a bungler more than a little based on John Gay, was Swift's first candidate as potential narrator of *Gulliver's Travels.* The book was conceived out of the intimacy of the group, and Swift imagined them as his first readers, an enabling fantasy because he developed the consistent, deadpan tone that governed their exchanges. Swift craved sharp company and friendly conflict and was happy in the company of Pope and his circle. But the Tory government of Robert Harley, first Earl of Oxford, fell, Queen Anne died, and the Whigs, his foes, came to power. He refused to bite his tongue. There was no further preferment. He returned to Dublin resigned "to die like a poisoned rat in a hole." For the next twelve years he remained in the hole, writing against the Whigs and their policies toward Ireland.

Around 1720 Swift began work on *Gulliver's Travels.* Like Defoe embarking on *Robinson Crusoe,* he was a man in his sixth decade. Unlike Defoe, he was not in a hurry. His intention, he explained to Pope, was "to vex the world, not to divert it." What vexed the world first was his anonymous 1724 intervention, *The Drapier's Letters,* his most explicitly political work. "Wood's ha'pence," a proposal that would have allowed the unscrupulous Wood to impose debased currency from England on Ireland, was defeated partly thanks to Swift's pamphlets. All religious parties celebrated the anonymous Drapier as an Irish patriot on the strength of his defense of Irish rights. Despite growing misanthropy, exacerbated by a dark, unhappy heart, Swift reserved about a third of his income for charitable causes, remaining a strict miser to himself.

In 1725 he completed *Gulliver's Travels* and the next year took the manuscript to England. He was staying with Gay at his Whitehall lodgings when he devised his scheme to get the book anonymously to the printer. Lemuel Gulliver's cousin, one "Richard Sympson," sent a single book of the four to the publisher Benjamin Motte, with a note requiring "a bank bill"—a guaranteed payment— "of two hundred pounds" to be placed in the hand of the delivery man "who will come in the same manner exactly at 9 o'clock on Thursday." Motte demurred: how could he raise such a sum in so short a time? "Sympson," not a skilled negotiator, agreed to accept payment in six months' time, and in due course, at night, Motte received the bulk of the work "he knew not from whence, or from whom, dropped at his house in the dark, from a hackney coach." Swift returned to Ireland in October, before the book was published. Motte made a few adjustments to avoid legal action. And he paid the agreed-upon sum, the only substantial money Swift ever earned from his writing.

*Gulliver* appeared in November and the first printing sold out in a week. Arbuthnot predicted for it "as great a run as John Bunyan," and John Gay wrote, "From the highest to the lowest it is universally read, from the cabinet-council to the nursery." An Irish bishop found it full of fiction and refused to believe it was true. Voltaire in London in 1727 found for Swift a French relation, but then corrected himself:

> I wonder why we so seldom hear in France of the books of the ingenious Doctor Swift, whom we might dub the English Rabelais. He has the honor of being a priest, like Rabelais, and to make fun of everything, like him; and yet one does him a great disservice, I modestly suggest, in calling him Rabelaisian. Rabelais, in his extravagant and unintelligible book, has scattered an excessive gaiety and an enormous impertinence; he has been prodigal with learning, excrement and boredom; a good story that ought to take up two pages is stretched out over volumes of tomfoolery . . . Monsieur Swift is Rabelais in his hours of sobriety, and living in good company.

Coleridge calls Swift "Anima Rabelaisii habitans in sicco" (the soul of Rabelais dwelling in a dry place).

François Rabelais (1494?–1553), whose name became an adjective early in the nineteenth century, found his way into English in the mid-seventeenth and was fortunate to have been translated by the inventive, spirited, if not always accurate Scot Sir Thomas Urquhart. The first two books appeared in 1653; Urquhart's work was continued by the Protestant French exile Peter Motteux, a man whose English is marked by its proto-Swiftean vernacularity, and who completed the task forty years later. Rabelais appealed to English writers because of his indecorous iconoclasm, his ability to address any subject, high or low, and his satirical excess. The Urquhart translation is a miracle of English, more abundant than the French because the translator was so excited by the original with its wide vocabulary and neologisms that he used it as a pretext and riffed on the numerous catalogs and series. If Rabelais has ten words for something, Urquhart will find twenty. Gargantua as a boy researches, to his father's delight, the best way to wipe one's bottom.

> Afterwards I wiped my bum, said Gargantua, with a kerchief, with a pillow, with a pantoufle, with a pouch, with a pannier, but that was a wicked and unpleasant torchecul; then with a hat. Of hats, note that some are shorn, and others shaggy, some velveted, others covered with taffeties, and others with satin. The best of all these is the shaggy hat, for it makes a very neat abstersion of the fecal matter.
>
> Afterwards I wiped my tail with a hen, with a cock, with a pullet, with a calf's skin, with a hare, with a pigeon, with a cormorant, with an attorney's bag, with a montero, with a coif, with a falconer's lure. But, to conclude, I say and maintain, that of all torcheculs, arsewisps, bumfodders, tail-napkins, bunghole cleansers, and wipe-breeches, there is none in the world comparable to the neck of a goose, that is well downed, if you hold her head betwixt your legs. And believe me therein upon mine honor, for you will thereby feel in your nockhole a most wonderful pleasure, both in regard of the softness of the said down and of the temporate heat of the goose, which is easily communicated to the bum-gut and the rest of the inwards, in so far as to come even to the regions of the heart and brains. And think not that the felicity of the heroes and demigods in the Elysian fields consisteth either in their asphodel, ambrosia, or nectar, as our old women here used to say; but in this, according to my judgment, that they wipe their tails with the neck of a goose, holding her head betwixt their legs, and such is the opinion of Master John of Scotland, alias Scotus.

To the eighteenth century he represented emancipation from rules of probability, scale, decorum, and "good taste." He was dangerous and, as an "antique," licensed. Coleridge, beyond laughter, revered him: "Rabelais is a most wonderful writer. Pantagruel is the Reason; Panurge the Understanding,—the pollarded man, the man with every faculty except reason . . . He every now and then flashes you a glimpse of a real face from his magic lantern, and then buries the whole scene in mist."

He was born in Chinon de Touraine, his father a man of law with large properties. The language and patterns of the law, the examination and cross-examination of characters, the imputations and inferences, the provision of evidence, the drama of refutation, are central to his writing. A priest, he started among reactionary Franciscans, then found his way among the more tolerant Benedictines, eventually leaving them to become a physician. His satire of spiritual and secular intellectuals is rooted in an informed knowledge of, bordering on an obsession with, the human body and its functions. Between 1532 and his death, *Gargantua and Pantagruel* grew into something like a final shape. The fifth book may be apocryphal, and when the work was published as a whole in 1564, it was ballasted with unreliable material.

In the city of Lyons he lectured and set up a practice. He corresponded with Erasmus. Toward the end of his life he was denounced by the Church and by the Sorbonne because of his satire on intellectual and spiritual obscurantism. He exchanged blows with Calvin. Few writers have roused such universal displeasure, or given such pleasure. Gargantua is a huge prince, his education described under the scholastic regime that Rabelais endured under the Franciscans, then under a demanding but liberal regime he favored. Personal material feeds into the work. Rabelais uncovers the small, trivial causes of great wars, the impoverishment that follows on bad education, the instability of moral categories. Gargantua gormandizes; he is also a good sort, a real scholar, an athlete, and deeply pacific.

*Pantagruel* was written first but belongs second in the sequence. Pantagruel is the name given by authors of fifteenth-century mystery plays to a demon whose effect was to cause thirst and who may have been a suffocator. For Rabelais he is "the all thirsty one," son of Gargantua and of Badebec, daughter of the king of the Amaurotes of Utopia (this being Thomas More's despised Utopia). The book of *Pantagruel* recounts his birth and education, mixing spiritual and temporal counsel with passages of burlesque. There is a dispute of signs between the English philosopher Thaumaste (More?) and Panurge (wily, loquacious, entertaining, and cowardly, full of vice, Falstaffian). The Thaumaste-Panurge debate is conducted with gestures, fingers in anuses and mouths, noises, pops, and farts. Language becomes *de trop*. We visit Utopia (around the Cape of Good Hope) and the underworld. Panurge comes to dominate while Pantagruel recedes into a kind of Henry V character performing justly but some way off. Shall Panurge marry? This elicits some riotous dialogue. There is much travel, much drinking.

Rabelais's characters grow out of what they say and how they speak and are never stable. They flicker and alter before our eyes. We read the work for characters not in our sense, but in his: as variations on a theme, changing humors in a single body. He loved his unconstraining, abundant medium; it was a mode of discovery: not a predetermined strategy for tacking meanings or people down to the page but a way of listening with laughter. He is, however, even at his most rumbustious, a scholar: the sources of his work are in books, folklore, and tradition. He is less a storyteller than a gamester. As a rhetorician, the motif that dominates most fictional structure dominates his: the *agon,* the debate, the trial. J. M. Cohen, a modern translator, says of the celebrated storm scene: "Rabelais had taken the trouble to find out the name for everything." Cohen cautions us not to see too much of Swift in Rabelais. Swift never lets his language carry him away, his misanthropy is remote from the carnivalesque anarchy of Rabelais's world, where people, to be sure, shit, but where there is pleasure as well as feces to be got from the human body.

The paradox of Swift's writing is that it retains Augustan formality but does not practice the emollient politeness of a middle style. He is cool and dry in relation to the reader. A unique irony is at work, not normative like Dryden's, but radical: an aspect of theme rather than style. This is why his prose, *Gulliver* in particular, retains force today. Bolingbroke was not quite right when he wrote to his friend, "If you despised the world as much as you pretend, and perhaps believe, you would not be so angry with it." Swift is certainly a vigorous hater, but his hatred is rooted in disappointed expectation. He is merciless not to those below him on the social ladder but to those above, the empowered, and to the vain who persist in self-deception. Self-deception is anything that has to do with categories and generalities. He wrote to Pope, "I have ever hated all nations, professions, and communities, and all my love is towards individuals." That phrase "all my love" is luminous. "But principally I hate and detest that animal called man, although I heartily love John, Peter, Thomas, and so forth." He adds, "Upon this great foundation of misanthropy . . . the whole building of my Travels is erected." Is this true misanthropy? His love of the individual is proof against his hatred of generalities and categories. He is a particularist, like Christ. Beside Swift's archaic passion, set the blithe modern optimism of Defoe: they seem to belong to different eras, and Gulliver, eight years Crusoe's junior, appears old enough to be his grandfather. Certainly the lands he travels through are rich in allegorical coloring; Crusoe's are insistently literal.

For a dozen years after *Gulliver* was published, Swift deployed the dark clouds and bright lightning of his personal weather. There were no more major books, but he was busy and effective as dean. His last major prose work was *A Modest Proposal* (1729), quintessence of the anonymous pamphlet: consistent, coherent, toneless, devastating. In 1738 he suffered a paralytic stroke followed by aphasia: a period of extreme pain succeeded by apathy. The last seven years of his life were marked by dementia. He was found "of unsound mind and memory" by the commission of lunacy. Guardians were appointed to manage his affairs. Thackeray records, "Sometimes, during his mental affliction, he continued walking about the house for many consecutive hours; sometimes he remained in a kind of torpor. At times, he would seem to struggle to bring into distinct consciousness, and shape into expression, the intellect that lay smothering under a gloomy obstruction in him." In such moments he said he was resigned to dying. It came in October 1745. His body was interred at St. Patrick's, beside that of Stella. They were both dug up in 1835 during repairs to St. Patrick's and the skulls went the rounds of curious houses. Phrenologists held a low opinion of Swift's cranium, Thackeray says. His larynx went missing at the time and was never recovered. He was re-interred, and his epitaph remains intact. William Butler Yeats translated it:

> Swift has sailed into his rest;
> Savage indignation there
> Cannot lacerate his breast.
> Imitate him if you dare,
> World-besotted traveller; he
> Served human liberty.

His substantial estate and savings he left to the founding of "an hospital . . . for idiots and lunatics," which survives, though it describes itself in different terms.

From his chair and table at St. Patrick's Cathedral Swift was a traveler, but not a world-besotted one. In 1721 he promised his friend Charles Ford "a large volume" with an account of travels to "countries hitherto unknown." Travel writing was in vogue: he was contributing to two popular genres: the adventure and survival book, and the travelogue. Vanessa knew about the giants in 1722. By 1724 the land of horses was complete and he was off to the Flying Island. In the final version the horses and the Flying Island change places: better to end with the unambiguous horses and apes. The satire of the Flying Island is specialized.

What makes each land credible is Swift's neutral style, Gulliver's way of imparting things, then taking them in his stride. He is a man apart, and each of *Gulliver's* four books sets him further apart from other men, and us with him. He seeks to convert "all honest men" to his "opinion," that anti-generalizing "misanthropy" that might be called Tory particularism, a universe of exceptions to arbitrary, tyrannical, reductive rules and categories. Arbuthnot was right to describe *Gulliver* as a "merry work": properly read, it loosens our shackles.

Swift's precision, first of all, is striking. When he scales up or scales down, for Lilliput or Brobdingnag, he observes a ratio: a foot is an inch, an inch is a foot, depending on the direction of the projection. He is generally consistent, though a few distortions are inevitable. When he writes about specific trades or disciplines, he usually gets the detail and the technical terms right, using a handbook. Fantasy is more plausible when underpinned with fact and made consistent by a scrupulous geometry. Samuel Butler, a beneficiary of Swift's example, says he does not mind lies but hates inaccuracy: the elements in a lie must be exact and in proportion if it is to be credible (which is not to say that we *believe* it, but we accept it as "true" in its terms, "suspending disbelief," in Coleridge's phrase).

In the different worlds Gulliver visits, there is a socially credible pattern to his reception, acculturation, and departure. In Lilliput terror, astonishment, then cordiality, followed by rejection; in Brobdingnag wonder, amusement, and revulsion. Wherever he goes he passes through a phase in which he is trusted and learns the crucial secrets of the place: the silliness and small-mindedness of the little people, the nobility and wisdom of the large, and so on. Observing them and their customs, the issue of scale becomes emblematic. The cause in Lilliput that leads to the war with Blefuscu—from which end should one crack an egg?—is part of the scale of the narrative. Small is trivial. The political parties divide between those who wear heels on their shoes and those who don't. Among the capering ministers in the Lilliputian court, we think we recognize the figure of Walpole, or the Earl of Nottingham. The more we know of Swift's world, the more we appreciate his revenges.

The narrator's change from Lilliput to Brobdingnag, from large to little, is, as Doctor Johnson says, on the face of it facile. "When once you have thought of big men and little men, it is very easy to do all the rest." The turning of the tables, however, for the reader, makes the first world and its fears more real, we feel anxiety for little Gulliver, more than we felt for the big one. Our concern for him is also a concern for ourselves, as he begins his disquisitions with the king and we start to realize just how remote our society is from justice. The people of Brobdingnag lack one faculty: they cannot grasp notions of "entities, abstractions, and transcendentals." As a result, they do not fall into the errors that follow from the falsifications and distortions implicit in all categorizations. Lilliput has much in common with England; Brobdingnag is, in satirical terms, the other side of the coin, a sane, wise, and just society. Swift creates a sufficient distance from his narrator to allow an ironic perspective.

"A Voyage to Laputa, Balnibarbi, Luggnagg, Glubbdubdrib, and Japan" is the least disguised of the four journeys. Swift ridicules here without a stable formula, and as a result the book is out of key with the other three, the lands visited more diverse and the beings caricatures of the human. This is the angry, satirical world of Alexander Pope's *Dunciad* (composed at this time also). Like Pope's verse satire, we sense in Swift's third book a lost topicality, a personal investment in the pique and ridicule. Here the sensible people are "John, Peter, Thomas, and so forth," tradesmen, practical folk, women, children. The philosophers, academicians, inventors, and scientific magicians are absurd to a man. In each of the lands he visits, Gulliver sheds illusions. When Gulliver escapes, he only just retains his sanity.

Swift put the Houyhnhnms last so Gulliver would end with as clear a delineation of right values as we experienced in Brobdingnag. Lilliput and Laputa are directly satirical, Brobdingnag and the land of the Houyhnhnms are visionary in a civic way, the triumph of common law and common sense over the hankerings for Utopia and the pettifying struggles of party and ideology. The land of the Houyhnhnms is rather like Sparta before its conquests made it cruel; the Yahoos, among whom Gulliver in the end must number himself and us, make him keen to avoid his kind. *Gulliver's Travels* could be a cold and heartless book. It is warmed by an anger that flows from disappointed love.

———•———

Doctor Samuel Johnson: lexicographer, biographer, critic, editor, pamphleteer, conversationalist, moral and critical center of his age, point of reference and illumination for later ages . . . and novelist? He represents with broad wisdom and authority of style a radical English intelligence, its power of generality and of discrimination. An account of his literary manner does not reflect the turbulent mind that his prayers, letters, and actions suggest. Literature was not a place in which to explore subjective impulse and distress; precise fact, discrimination, imaginative and moral insight were called for, it was a place of self-effacement, or as T. S. Eliot was to call it, "an escape from personality."

In condemning "the cant of those who judge by principle rather than perception," in a way Johnson is condemning himself. "The language used by the eighteenth century—and Samuel Johnson—was a translation," says Ford. "The eighteenth century retired from life that was coarse into a remoter region where individuals always became types and language more and more rarefied itself." Writers came obsessively to use the definite article. He itemizes stock phrases: "the poet," not "a poet"; "the hill," not "a hill"; and so on. A thing becomes the thing, a perception becomes a category or principle. Yet this is not quite right: an idea can be a perception, and if we allow ourselves to "listen with credulity to the whispers of fancy," as Johnson puts it at the beginning of his novel *The History of Rasselas, Prince of Abissinia* (1759), we are released from the falsifying constraints of principle and can range freely, as Sidney says we can do.

We may tire of the definite article, but as in all the best Augustan writing the power of the *verbs*, active and passive, is notable. For Johnson, wit (which Donald Davie defines as "the constant presence of critical intelligence") fuses idea and image to convey truth. Wit is seeing what is not obvious but what is acknowledged as just when first produced. In his *Life of Cowley* Johnson writes,

"Words being arbitrary must owe their power to association, and have the influence, and that only, which custom has given them. Language is the dress of thought." The dress must fit not only the thought but the dignity of the speaker or occasion. This is what decorum means. The complex association of words with thoughts, images, and speakers we call form, intrinsic form; we can appraise it in terms of its appositeness and proportion. Hazlitt had mixed feelings about Johnson's style: "The structure of his sentences, which was his own invention, and which has been generally imitated since his time, is a species of rhyming in prose, where one clause answers to another in measure and quantity, like the tagging of syllables at the end of a verse; the close of the period follows as mechanically as the oscillation of a pendulum, the sense is balanced with the sound; each sentence, revolving round its center of gravity, is contained with itself like a couplet, and each paragraph forms itself into a stanza." This may be thought especially true of *Rasselas,* the speed of whose composition required the prosodies that Hazlitt here describes.

What was Johnson doing with *Rasselas?* A phlegmatic man, if moved by need or passion he was capable of heroic labors. His first literary hack work was a translation of Father Lobo's *Voyage to Abyssinia* (published in 1735). His mind was so orderly and retentive that it must have come back to him twenty-three years later when the challenge of *Rasselas* was proposed.

Though Johnson was forty-two years Swift's junior, he was like him at heart a pamphleteer and essayist; his "Eastern Tale" *Rasselas* is fueled by disappointment at the disparity between youthful expectation and how the world actually wags. "Ye who listen with credulity to the whispers of fancy, and pursue with eagerness the phantoms of hope; who expect that age will perform the promises of youth and that the deficiencies of the present day will be supplied by the morrow; attend to the history of Rasselas, Prince of Abissinia." It is as pure an invention as *Gulliver's Travels.* In its one hundred pages, its forty-nine little chapters, it is more controlled, on a different scale of complexity and with a different occasion from *Gulliver.* Though a philosophical dialogue, it belongs in the company of Swift due to its intensity. Donald Davie insists, "It is the mind which knows the power of its own potentially disruptive propensities that needs and demands to be disciplined." Both men suffered, and their writing was in spite of that suffering, yet colored by it.

*Rasselas* was composed sentence by sentence, and within strict constraints. Johnson wrote fast to get money to cover the cost of his mother's impending funeral in Lichfield. The publisher Robert Dodsley, a man of sober good sense and a relatively modest wig, gave him £100, £70 in hand, such was his need. Had he been a better businessman, he might have got four times the amount, but Dodsley became his friend and a mainstay.

The story of *Rasselas* is remote from Johnson's bereavement. Some readers suggest that he was agitated by guilt for having spent twenty years away without revisiting his home, and that Imlac, who sometimes speaks with the author's voice as Gulliver sometimes speaks with Swift's, alludes to this, especially in chapter 12 when he reflects on the disappointment of his homecoming. At the end of the book, "The Conclusion, in which Nothing is Concluded," Imlac, the Prince, and the Princess resolve, despite their fantasies, to return to Abissinia. The reflections of the characters (who are barely characters) are philosophical. The confessional and personal hardly obtrude even at the level of symbol.

As luck would have it, *Rasselas* was published just a few weeks before its more famous cousin, with which it is often compared, Voltaire's *Candide; ou, l'optimisme*, with its fall from grace, protracted travels, sincere false philosopher-optimist Pangloss, and exposure of youth and inexperience to the real world that lies in wait of idealism. Calm, skeptical realism triumphs over the fashionable intellectual habits of the day. The book concludes with the famous dismissal of the philosopher who has an answer for everything: " 'Cela est bien dit,' répondit Candide, 'mais il faut cultiver notre jardin.' " (" 'That's all very well,' Candide replied, 'but let us cultivate our garden.' ") A decade later Johnson's younger, clubbable friend Oliver Goldsmith was reading Voltaire with keen, appropriative interest, different though their temperaments were.

"When he had a little money," says Ford, Goldsmith "bought a scarlet velvet coat trimmed with gold lace; when he had none he starved naked and wigless in a garret." In 1762, living near Doctor Johnson's, at 6 Wine Office Court, he owed heavy arrears in rent and his landlady stole and hid his clothes so he could not "flit." He sent word to Johnson, who took the manuscript of *The Vicar of Wakefield* (1766) and sold it for him for £60. Thus he avoided debtors' prison. The book was delayed, but when published four years later it was a success. In the attic of Johnson's house at Gough Square, the room where he assembled the *Dictionary*, hangs a painting of the Doctor reading *The Vicar* with Goldsmith watching his large implacable face; under Johnson's chair the painter Landseer added to the lackluster original a huge dozing hound.

"All the motion of Goldsmith's nature," writes Thomas De Quincey, "moved in the direction of the true, the natural, the sweet, the gentle." He had an "unpretending mind." This rather softens the lines of a writer who was much condescended to by Johnson's circle and did not always take happily to being infantilized. He was not a great conversationalist. Johnson made no bones about it: "Goldsmith had no settled notions upon any subject; so he talked always at random. It seemed to be his intention to blurt out whatever was in his mind, to see what would become of it." Yet he was a remarkable Anglo-Irishmen, like his friend Edmund Burke, the statesman whose roots remained in Ireland yet who flourished in England. He was as versatile a writer, though not so copious, as Johnson: poet, novelist, dramatist, journalist, nature writer, essayist, correspondent. Like Johnson's, his reputation as a novelist rests on a single work.

In 1728 or 1730 (biographers disagree), Oliver, fifth child and second son of the Reverend Charles Goldsmith, who might in unworldliness seem to resemble the Reverend Doctor Primrose, the Vicar of *The Vicar of Wakefield,* was born in Elphin, Roscommon, or in Pallas, near Ballymahon, County Longford, Ireland. The boy spent his childhood in Lissoy. At fifteen he went to Trinity College, Dublin, as a sizar. Two years later his father died. Oliver, who did not distinguish himself academically, was reprimanded for participating in a student riot. In 1750 he managed to take a degree. When he failed to get ordained, he became a tutor, toyed with emigrating to America, and at last settled into medical studies, at Edinburgh and then at Leyden. He traveled widely in Europe, paying his way by playing his flute, like George, the eldest Primrose boy in *The Vicar.*

In 1756 he was in London practicing medicine as an apothecary and physician. He worked too as a school usher and undermaster. He considered sailing to India as a physician with the East India Company at Coromandel. He may have served as a proofreader in Samuel Richardson's printing house and was familiar with Richardson's novels. He certainly worked for the publisher John Newbery, for whose journal *The Public Ledger* he wrote his *Chinese Letters,* serialized over eighteen months and later published as *The Citizen of the World.* These letters are Goldsmith's first serious work of fiction: he creates a philosophical Eastern narrator, innocent and wide-eyed, called Lien Chi Altangi, who has come to live in London, observing the place, its people, and their customs and writing candid letters. It was a tried and tested formula that Goldsmith practiced with insouciance. There is just enough action to reveal the foibles of the English. Altangi has a point of view, voice, and ceremonious manner suited to his needs.

Writing began to feed Goldsmith. He translated, he wrote essays. He was now known as Doctor Goldsmith and consorted with Tobias Smollett and other writers, including Edmund Burke and Johnson. He was a founding member of "The Club" and contributed to periodicals, including Smollett's *British Magazine.* For a short time he ran his own, the *Bee* (1759).

*The Vicar of Wakefield* is a modern Job story, the man of many blessings who loses them one by one but retains his faith and even his simplicity. Like Job, like Moll Flanders and Pamela, his trials are material, as are his rewards. This is an age of husbandry in which virtue and vice can be banked. Mrs. Primrose prides herself on her accountability, and on the happy symmetries of her family. Her daughters Olivia (handsome, ambitious in love) and Sophia (a subtle charmer) are well differentiated. Her son George is like Goldsmith, though his rewards are greater than any Goldsmith saw in his lifetime. The son Moses is a few pence short of a shilling: sent to the fair to sell the horse, he brings back a gross of green spectacles.

The fates that overtake the Primroses are familiar from the novels of the time. The vicar loses his income and security. In a new living, the patron, a roguish squire, seduces and abandons Olivia, who is reported dead. George is thrown into prison for trying to avenge the family honor. Sophia is kidnapped and carted off in a post chaise. But the vicar, whose innocence Stendhal admired, endures: eventually the tide turns, the evil are rebuked by time's justice, the good prosper exceedingly. Three narrative poems find their place in the novel, "The Hermit," "Edwin and Angelina," and "Elegy on the Death of a Mad Dog," along with Olivia's beautiful lyric "When lovely woman stoops to folly."

E. M. Forster loved the first half of *The Vicar,* but the fact that convention required Goldsmith to tie up loose ends, resolve all the dramatic and moral plots he had set in motion, spoiled it. Freshness of invention and a lively sense of fun give way to a movement that is "wooden and imbecile." Because Forster rejects chronology in appraising the novel, he sets Goldsmith alongside Meredith, Hardy, and Gide, which violates the integrity and culture of each writer, inviting anachronistic judgments that always diminish what is least familiar, what is farthest from his present. The essayistic and categorical delights of Goldsmith are misvalued.

Goldsmith was loved abroad. In his autobiographical *Life of Henry Brulard* Stendhal tried out a series of subtitles, most of them including the words "imitated from *The Vicar of Wakefield,*" as if to excuse to the police any political indiscretions and to the moral authorities any inappropriate divagations: "The hero, Henry Brulard, writes his life, at the age of fifty-two, after the death of his wife, the celebrated Charlotte Corday." He recounts how he planned to learn by heart the first four pages of *The Vicar of Wakefield* (he transliterates it "Ouaike-filde"), to help him master English.

His *Essays* (1765) and *The Vicar of Wakefield* the following year set Goldsmith in the first rank among his contemporaries. The unpedantic *readability* of his prose, which lacks the gravity of Johnson's and the orotundity of Burke's, is marked by the virtues of character that De Quincey and, incidentally, Goethe, who knew the book in Herder's translation into German, admired. His themes are always serious, his tone light. George Moore spoke of his "almost anonymous prose, a still reflection of the writer's mind, altogether free from that pleasure and pride in writing which began with Carlyle and was continued by Meredith and Stevenson."

———·———

Rabelais has taken us to France, Ireland, and England. But his birthplace in English is Scotland and his legacy to twentieth-century Scottish fiction is considerable. Sir Thomas Urquhart of Cromarty (1611–ca. 1660), writer and translator, appears as the protagonist of "Sir Thomas's Logopandocy," subtitled "The Secret and Apocryphal Diurnal of Sir Thomas Urquhart of Cromarty Knight" (in *Unlikely Stories, Mostly,* 1983). Alasdair Gray (b. 1934), Urquhart's spiritual scion, borrows the title from Urquhart's *Logopandecteision,* an elaborate plan for a universal language of considerable symmetry and subtlety, with twelve parts of speech, eleven declensions, four numbers, eleven genders (to include gods, goddesses, animals), eleven tenses, four voices, seven moods. The English subjunctive has never looked easier. Gray's "Diurnal" is a kind of dialogue between Urquhart and Cromwell's Latin secretary, who are working out a way "to repair the divided Nature of Man by rationally reintegering God's Gift of Tongues to Adam by a verboradical appliancing of Neper's logarithms to the grammar of an Asiatick people, thought to be the lost tribe of Israel, whose language predates the Babylonian cataclysm." It is a jest, in part. Urquhart had, after all, if not invented, then at least brought into literary use in his Rabelais (a fact Gray's Urquhart notes in passing), a goodly portion of modern English. Gray loves drawing this exuberant pedant, the maker of catalogs, with whom he identifies. No wonder Will Self judges him to be "a great writer, perhaps the greatest living in this archipelago today." This is not a universal opinion, but others share it.

Gray's origins were in East Glasgow. His father was a veteran wounded in the First World War who became a factory worker; his mother worked in a shop. Urquhart came of an old landed family in northern Scotland. At age eleven he started at Aberdeen University. Gray made his own education from a state school, from listening to the BBC, which had an educational mission all through his early years, and finally from the Glasgow School of Art, where he studied and later taught. He was from an early age a vivid caricaturist and illustrator who has been stretched by well-wishers into a cheerful decorative muralist.

Urquhart toured the Continent, participated in a royalist uprising, and was knighted by Charles I. Gray did not enjoy travel and advocated an independent Scotland. Urquhart's father died leaving huge estates and huger debts. The heir was pursued by creditors for the rest of his days. He escaped to the Continent, continued as a royalist, and was denounced as a traitor by Parliament. Gray has had his hardships, on a more conventional scale. Urquhart fought for the king at the Battle of Worcester and was captured, lost the manuscripts he always carried with him "for safekeeping," and forfeited his property, though not his debts, which had become his inescapable shadow. His time in prison in the Tower of London and then at Windsor was relaxed: he studied, and he wrote. Gray never had that kind of leisure, and it took him almost three decades to write his first novel. Paroled in 1652, Urquhart went back to Cromarty. He published his Rabelais and died no later than 1660. Legend says he died in a fit of laughter on receiving news of Charles II's Restoration. Gray lives and prospers at least in his reputation: he is regarded as Scotland's major novelist.

Despite different periods and lives, Urquhart was irresistible to Gray, most of all for his language, his crazy bagatelles. In 1652 he published the *Pantochronachanon*, a genealogy of the Urquhart family, unbroken from Adam and Eve all the way up to himself, through 153 generations. A joke? *The Jewel (Ekskybalauron)* (1652 also), a miscellany, contains his universal language prospectus. Most of the book, the title page says, is "a vindication of the honor of Scotland," including anecdotes of Scottish soldiers and scholars, among them his fictionalized life of James ("the honorable") Crichton (1560–1582), his most celebrated work after the Rabelais. Gray is also a patriot. Among his books we find *Why Scots Should Rule Scotland* (1992, then revised in 1997) and *How We Should Rule Ourselves* (2005). Gray *is* the modern Urquhart.

Gray admires the fact that Urquhart's Rabelais, steeped in medieval allegory, represents a decisive break with its constraints. Urquhart's Rabelais declares, "Do you believe, upon your conscience, that Homer, whilst he was a-couching his Iliad's and Odysseys, had any thought upon those allegories, which Plutarch, Heraclites Ponticus, Eustathius, Cornutus squeezed out of him, and which Politian filched again from them?" He scorns such believers, for the allegories "have been as little dreamed of by Homer, as the Gospel sacraments were by Ovid in his Metamorphoses." Urquhart achieves the sonorities of the French and then some. We can hear Scottish timbres in the short and protracted catalogs (for example, of animal noises) or in this battle scene when the monk throws off his habit and acts the part of a soldier. When he pauses to examine the inside of a skull, it is with a scientific curiosity. We remember that Rabelais's father was a physician.

> He hurried, therefore, upon them so rudely, without crying gare or beware, that he overthrew them like hogs, tumbled them over like swine, striking athwart and alongst, and by one means or other laid so about him, after the old fashion of fencing, that to some he beat out their brains, to others he crushed their arms, battered their legs, and bethwacked their sides till their ribs cracked with it. To others again he unjointed the spondyles or knuckles of the neck, disfigured

their chaps, gashed their faces, made their cheeks hang flapping on their chin, and so swinged and balammed them that they fell down before him like hay before a mower. To some others he spoiled the frame of their kidneys, marred their backs, broke their thigh-bones, pashed in their noses, poached out their eyes, cleft their mandibles, tore their jaws, dung in their teeth into their throat, shook asunder their omoplates or shoulder-blades, sphacelated their shins, morti-fied their shanks, inflamed their ankles, heaved off of the hinges their ishies, their sciatica or hip-gout, dislocated the joints of their knees, squattered into pieces the boughts or pestles of their thighs, and so thumped, mauled and belabored them everywhere, that never was corn so thick and threefold threshed upon by ploughmen's flails as were the pitifully disjointed members of their mangled bodies un-der the merciless baton of the cross. If any offered to hide himself amongst the thickest of the vines, he laid him squat as a flounder, bruised the ridge of his back, and dashed his reins like a dog. If any thought by flight to escape, he made his head to fly in pieces by the lamboidal commissure, which is a seam in the hinder part of the skull. If anyone did scramble up into a tree, thinking there to be safe, he rent up his perinee, and impaled him in at the fundament.

Here was a resource for the modern writer with a disposition for laughter, poli-tics, and experiment and not immediately comfortable with the new writing around him.

It took Gray twenty-five years to write *Lanark: A Life in Four Books* (1981), his first and most famous work. One reason it took him so long is its structure. The protagonist is two people in one, or one person in two; generically it hovers between science fiction (it was unsuccessfully promoted as such in the United States) and *Bildungsroman,* a coming of age for the author as well as the protago-nist. There is a burden of symbolism. The first two volumes are more accessible and seem to have been written more naturally than the later two. The protago-nist is keen to produce great art. The book is in part about the effort, in part the fruits of it. The process is the product, as it were, and it reaches a place of greater light than the place it set out from.

"If a city hasn't been used by an artist not even the inhabitants live there imaginatively," he says. His book inserted Glasgow into the atlas of the Anglo-phone imagination, though in the United States it bombed and Gray's reputa-tion has grown rather more slowly there. Anthony Burgess welcomed it. "A big and original novel has at last come out of Scotland." In the city of Unthank, Lanark is a citizen who rises to provost. He is allowed to look in on the life of

Duncan Thaw, a young Glaswegian aspiring artist—autobiography near at hand—who also wants to be a "normal" person. He remarks, "Imaginatively, Glasgow exists as a music-hall song and a few bad novels." Burgess is unsure whether the book is intended as satirical or not. This is part of its generic indeterminacy, its unprogrammed, deprogramming purpose. In letting Duncan say that Glasgow has been fictionalized in "a few bad novels," he neglects, on purpose, a number of novels quite successful in their day and still regarded as significant. He provides with his book an "Index of Plagiarisms" that makes it clear that he knew what he was up to. He is an assimilative writer, a realist at times, a fantasist, active in the neighborhoods of the Gothic and science fiction. And his books carry his decorations and illustrations. They also wear the indelible mark of James Joyce.

Just as his friends crop up in his murals, so they inhabit his books, some the better to settle scores, some because their presence is crucial, some simply because he wants them in the book with him. He invents, always with one foot in the real. One gets the feeling that he reverse-networks, less to ingratiate himself with others than to watch them, and when they ask him in, he expresses a tonic joy and gratitude. It is from such people and from books that he devises his nine novels. *1982, Janine* (1984) was an unsettling sequel to *Lanark,* bordering on obscenity. Among his books it is the one he likes best because he has created a protagonist remote from himself. He lost some readers with it, and more with *Something Leather* (1990) with its sadomasochistic content, flagellation, erotic tattoos, and lesbian characters. With *Poor Things* (1992), which won the Whitbread Prize, he was experimenting with form and making the larger picture once more, though this time less emblematically and on a smaller scale. It is the best point of entry into Gray, the chronology of whose work seems reversed: we get our *Ulysses* first and then *Portrait of the Artist.* Gray's is not an orderly mind; it trusts inspirations and tangents. It has more in common with the thundering twilight of Mervyn Peake and the postapocalyptic locations of Russell Hoban than with Joyce. His linguistic verve and abundance he shares with his direct fictional ancestor, Sir Thomas.

# | 8 |

## *Sex and Sensibility*

Samuel Richardson, Eliza Haywood, Anna Laetitia Barbauld, John Cleland

"Up until now we have understood the word 'novel' to entail a weave of fantastic and inconsequential events which affronted the taste and morals of its readers," says the French philosopher Denis Diderot in his elegy to Samuel Richardson (1689–1761). "I would like another word to be found to describe Richardson's works: they inspire, they stir the heart, they are infused with a love for the good, and they too are called novels."

Yet how tedious Samuel Richardson can be! Dickens was not fond of him: he never took off his top boots. Thackeray evokes him as "the puny cockney bookseller, pouring out endless volumes of sentimental twaddle," "a moll-coddle and a milksop." A century before: "Why, Sir," Doctor Johnson says, "if you were to read Richardson for the story, your impatience would be so much fretted that you would hang yourself. But you must read him for the sentiment, and consider the story as only giving occasion to the sentiment." Sentiment, and the fashions it fed, made Richardson a best seller in his century, with a huge general readership. His books should speak even to a charwoman, he said, and they did. In the century following, his appeal became more specialized: other novelists relished his work, the general reader lost patience. He became a "writer's writer." In the twenty-first century he is read by literary historians, critics, and occasional students. It is not that his language has become archaic: he is more direct and accessibly colloquial even than Defoe. Nor have his themes become less relevant, or his characters—Pamela and Clarissa in particular play well to a modern gallery. His tone and his pace are no longer tolerable.

Sir Walter Scott, whose work suffers a like fate, reflects on how changes in literary fashion throw out some works and revalue others, on grounds unrelated to literary merit. "If Clarissa should appear before a modern party in her lace ruffles and head-dress, or Lovelace in his wig, however genteelly powdered, I am afraid they would make no conquests." But more than this it is Richardson's geologically slow pace, the massive dimensions of his second and third novels, his moralism, the very *refinement* of environment and character, and the narrow bands of class and space in which he works, that leave modern readers, for the most part, cold. We are not like Jonathan Edwards, a rare spirit "conspicuous among the saints," who read *Sir Charles Grandison* "with such interest that he resolved to correct his own hitherto neglected style upon the example of Richardson"—a style of writing and of being. Nor are we like Benjamin Franklin, who pirated *Pamela* in Philadelphia in 1744, the year it appeared in New York and Boston as well. It was forty years before Richardson's later novels were published in America, and when they did appear they were abridged (as in France). Arnold Bennett, more interested in time and motion (and money) than his predecessors, doubted that any writer had ever composed such abundance at a faster rate than Richardson: going fast to go slow.

Without Richardson, in whom a European realist tradition is rooted, much would be different in literature. Jane Austen, George Eliot, even William Blake (who said of *Sir Charles Grandison:* "Richardson has won my heart") would have spoken otherwise. All admired and learned from him. Like Edmund Spenser's *The Faerie Queene, Clarissa* is a kind of acid test for the reader. It is not merely a stage in the evolution of the European novel: it is one of the great novels, and a reader who develops the taste to appreciate it will understand on the pulse what the novel form can be and do.

"The smug, juicy, pedestrian little printer from Derbyshire," says V. S. Pritchett, "more or less unlettered, sits down at the age of fifty and instructs young girls in the art of managing their virtue to the best advantage." An ungenerous characterization of an author revered on the Continent from the moment *Pamela* crossed the Channel. His characters became terms of daily discourse. Stendhal, Chateaubriand, and Flaubert were "all avowed followers of the author of *Clarissa.*" The French revolutionary and orator Mirabeau in 1789 dubbed the great Lafayette "Cromwell-Grandison": he possessed Oliver Cromwell's ambition, yet wore before the world the face of Sir Charles Grandison, a model Christian gentleman—Richardson inspired Rousseau's *La nouvelle Héloïse* and Choderlos de Laclos's *Les liaisons dangereuses* (which Stendhal calls "that imitation of *Clarissa* which has become the provincials' breviary"). He had the good fortune of being translated (rather freely, as was the custom at that time) by the novelist and stylist the abbé Prévost, a lover of English culture who contributed to the *Anglomanie,* English madness, of the French at the time. The rise of a culture of *sensibilité* coincided with the softening of spirit that led, in France, toward the Revolution. The virtue and goodness of heart such writing celebrates are rooted in secular values. In the place of Christian charity emerges a kind of altruism, an *acte de bienfaisance,* and such acts can be falsified: new forms of deception become possible in fiction and drama. As a boy Stendhal read *Clarissa* "in floods of tears" in the attic, having purloined it from his father's library.

In Germany Richardson's presence became like Shakespeare's and Milton's: he was so thoroughly assimilated as to become an honorary German writer.

Goethe saluted the shy English printer: here was the celebration of sensibility in all its manifestations, the pattern for compassionate men and women, sentiment subtilizing the moral sense; a rumor of the soon-to-be-swelling chords of the passions. As Pritchett says, the "first shoots of the Romantic movement . . . spring from the pool of Richardson's pious tears like the grateful and delicate trees of an oasis."

Of all his Continental readers, Diderot was the most articulate. His obituary essay, "Éloge de Richardson," appeared in the *Journal étranger* in January 1762, only six months after Richardson died in London of a stroke. Diderot's response reveals what the experience of reading Richardson felt like at the time. The characters were so real that readers felt they had met them, their fates were like those of friends dearly loved. The poet Colly Cibber declared that he would rather kill Richardson than permit him to convey Clarissa to the end she reaches. Klopstock longed to meet Clarissa and linger in her company; Diderot feels as though he has been as close to her as the pieces of paper on which she rained tears and rested her panting hand. "I still recall my first encounter with Richardson's work: I was in the country. How delightfully moved I was! With each moment I saw my happiness shrinking by a page. I had the feeling of a man who, having been very close to another, is about to say farewell. When the book was finished, I felt abandoned." Earlier he considers the universality of Richardson's impact. "Who has read of Lovelace or Tomlinson without a deep shudder? Who has not been horrified at the moving sincerity of tone, the seeming candor and dignity, the rhetorical mastery, with which such men hollowly perform all the virtues? Who has not in his heart resolved to abandon the society of men and hide deep in the forests, if there are many men capable of such deceptions?" And the apostrophe: "Oh, Richardson! Willy-nilly we are included in your work, we interject into the conversation, we approve or condemn, admire or recoil in anger. How often I have caught myself shouting out, like a child taken to theatre for the first time, *Don't believe him, he is betraying you!*"

The impact on such a reader is immediate and enduring: "In a matter of hours I had experienced a variety of circumstances which even a long life is unlikely to provide in its trajectory. I had witnessed the secret springs of selfish love and self interest manifesting themselves in multitude of ways . . . I felt I had added to my living experience . . . This writer does not show walls bathed in blood, he does not carry us off to distant lands, expose us to cannibals, he does not explore the secret sites of debauchery or stray into fantastic realms. The world we inhabit with him is rooted in truth, his characters are as real as characters can be, taken from the social world, his events are plausibly those of all civilised cultures, the passions he draws are ones which I myself feel." And a crucial question at the dawn of the age of sentiment: "What is virtue? It is, however one considers it, a sacrifice of oneself." With each page, Diderot insists, Richardson encourages us to prefer virtue. No one would wish to be in Lovelace's shoes. "Who would not prefer to be Clarissa, in spite of her misfortunes? As I read, I have often exclaimed, *I'd willingly give my life to be like this woman; I'd rather die than be that man.*" Death waits on both fates, but one is death in virtue.

Diderot was himself a great letter writer. His Richardson obituary reads like a love letter. It encourages Richardson's admirers to be spontaneous, to take the letters of the novels at face value, as though they were real in occasion and immediacy. To read is to engage not in aftermath but in the very process of living and experiencing moral challenges and tests. In the intensity of our engagement we are ourselves judged. Thanks to Richardson, Diderot was able to write his own little "novel" *Le neveu de Rameau (Rameau's Nephew)* (1760–1761, revised 1771–1772), rendered the shorter perhaps as a reaction to the vastness of *Clarissa* and because it aspires to be an essay as well as a story. With aphoristic clarity, Diderot portrays the great composer Rameau's nephew and sour dependent, a young man who is unstable, unfulfilled, unresolved, whose life does not issue in moral climaxes and yet is a moral process of painful, ironic intensity. The encounter is presented as a dialogue between *Moi* the philosopher and *Lui* the nephew. It opens out into essay, a surprising production, given the tenor of Diderot's civilizing and moralizing discourse. It visits a darkness that the eighteenth century preferred to veil or satirize. The nephew has the last word: "Rira bien qui rira le dernier" (He who laughs last laughs best). Readers heard this laughter first in 1804 when the essay was published in Goethe's German. The "original" French, printed soon after was, in fact, a *re*translation by Goethe. The actual French original was rediscovered at the end of the nineteenth century and published then for the first time. Thus, Diderot's parasitic, clever, amoral, and decadent character, psychologically questing, made his "original" appearance long after his progeny had become familiars of fiction and art. Lionel Trilling describes the "entrancing power" of the piece, which suggests "that moral judgement is not ultimate, that man's nature and destiny are not wholly comprehended within the narrow space between virtue and vice." Edith Wharton locates the beginning of the novel in this "appalling" (she uses the term as a compliment) work, "that one amazing accident of Diderot's."

The letter was very much "in practice" when Richardson wrote his novels. Lord Chesterfield was already composing regular doses of advice to his natural son, Lady Mary Wortley Montagu was writing her celebrated *Turkish Letters,* and Horace Walpole was busy corresponding (all published after Richardson's novels appeared). The letter form occupies a kind of halfway house between private and public utterance. It combines formality and intimacy. In fiction it allows an author to employ one or more first persons, to stand well apart as narrator, and to let characters conduct themselves seemingly unmediated before the reader's very eyes. What is the etymology of the term *correspondence?* Richardson supplies a false one that answers his purpose: "It is a word of Latin origin: a compound word; and the two elements here brought together are *respondeo,* I answer, and *cor,* the heart: *i.e.,* I answer feelingly, I reply not so much to the head as to the heart." (The *cor-* prefix is a form of *cum-*, "to answer with," though *correspondere* is already a medieval Latin verb.)

Richardson did not invent the epistolary novel. Aphra Behn was the first Anglophone writer to compose one. Richardson did, however, write the first dramatic novels in this form, books in which the action is primarily moral and psychological and is conducted before our eyes by the protagonists themselves. *"Much more* lively and affecting," he says, "must be the style of those who write in the height of a *present* distress, the mind tortured by the pangs of uncertainty . . . than the dry, narrative unanimated style of a person relating difficulties and danger surmounted can be." The letter creates immediacy; also, the novelist abdicates direct responsibility for any- and everything done. Readers are left to judge and engage. In letters action is confession and minute interpretation.

A letter has an addressee; it can also have date and place, "metadata" that themselves become part of a novelist's shorthand. A letter is generally addressed to one interlocutor and implies relationship, a history on which to build, a source for its shorthand intimacy. From a letter we infer a narrative and tone. A business letter, a letter to a priest, a parent, a lover, all penned by the same hand, are different in style, emphasis, and content, even if they relate identical facts. Pamela wails to her parents, weeping as she writes, "O how my eyes run! Don't wonder to see the paper so blotted." The letter is actually visualized. A dramatic analogy is appropriate: in an epistolary novel, whoever speaks, whoever is addressed, the fourth wall of the room is missing, the correspondent is exposed. To seem as natural as possible the process is artificialized. Most awkward, context and information must be imparted beyond the immediate sentimental content of the letter.

The successful letter integrates contextual and narrative matter without disrupting the drama of motive and moral development. Tone and economy of delivery are key. Pamela is naive and expansive, her feelings well up in her eyes, her biblical and cultural allusions predictably delivered. Sir Charles Grandison moves with marmoreal propriety, heart carapaced in correctness. The calculating, ironic, and self-assured style of Lovelace, rich in metaphor, heightens the delicate, correct, and vulnerable manner of Clarissa. Though in *Clarissa* the characters are drawn from a particular class, their language belonging to that class and period, the prose is varied in pace and diction. Its evenness can look flat, but like good manners it conceals and reveals variation. The letter writers' styles change: Clarissa becomes clearer, more focused; Lovelace loses his brilliance and wit and falls into the dark. "Sir," Doctor Johnson declares, "there is more knowledge in a letter of Richardson's, than in all *Tom Jones*." This story of rape incidentally provides a manual of epistolary propriety.

Richardson's novels began in a commission to compose a book of letter templates. His fellow printer-booksellers Charles Rivington and John Osborne knew him to be accomplished in the art of writing letters for all, even awkward, occasions. He produced "a little volume of letters, in a common style, on such subjects as might be of use to country readers who are unable to indite [write] for themselves." *Letters Written to and for Particular Friends, on the Most Important Occasions* (1741) included specimen letters and instructions on "how to think and act justly and prudently in the common Concerns of Human Life." The humbler classes would learn not only to express themselves but also lessons in moral action and nuance. "The misfortune of Richardson," says Isaac Disraeli, and by extension the misfortune of those who learn from him, "was, that he was unskilful in the art of writing, and that he could never lay the pen down while his inkhorn supplied it." He took expansive pleasure in his own work. A regular visitor at Richardson's house could not recall a single occasion on which she was not "taxed by our author reading one of his voluminous letters, or two or three, if his auditor was quiet and friendly." He suffered from what Disraeli unkindly called "a violent literary vanity."

One template letter, about a pretty serving girl under assault from a scheming master, reminded him of a story he had heard—*Pamela* was conceived, and she appeared in print in four volumes, two in the year before his book of letter templates, two in the same year, under the full title *Pamela; or, Virtue Rewarded*. The American novelist William Gass describes it as "the edifying history of a prick tease—a book bluer than any movie," which, if we read between the lines, it is. Richardson did not expect much from the book and sold two-thirds of the copyright for £20. He was wiser with his later novels; they contributed to his prosperity. *Clarissa* (1747–1748) was tremendously successful in England and abroad, and *The History of Sir Charles Grandison* (1753–1754) was too.

"That tranquil person," as Ford called him, Richardson was born in Derbyshire in 1689, a year after Bunyan died. He was twenty-seven years Defoe's junior, of a different generation, vocation, and sensibility, at once more modern and more domestic. His sensibility belongs wholly to the eighteenth century. There is no residue of the court about him: he exists within the commercial and social world of modern London. His mother was well born and his father a not unprosperous joiner from Surrey. The family moved to London when Samuel was ten and settled near Tower Hill. Soon he was writing, first a letter to chide a widow woman for censoriousness, written in a mature style but in a child's hand, so he was found out and disciplined. Taciturn and biddable, he became a favorite among young women; he tells how they had him read to them as they plied their needles, daughters and mothers together, and later girls confided their loves to him and appointed him their libidinal secretaries: he wrote their letters, the sentiments dictated for him to order and translate into text.

He was modestly educated (perhaps at Merchant Taylor's School). In 1706 he entered into a seven-year apprenticeship with the printer John Wilde and married his daughter. A printer at the time was also a manufacturer of books, their publisher (selecting, editing, and publishing them as sheets, quires, or bound volumes) and seller. The functions were becoming differentiated, but in Richardson's period differentiation was incomplete.

He spent his spare time reading; he tells a correspondent later in life how he bought his own farthing dips (candles) to read by. (Like Pamela, he is not backward in coming forward, describing his "Assiduity that, perhaps, has few Examples.") At twenty-six he was becoming successful: a freeman of the Stationer's Company, a citizen of London. He set up a printing business, first in Fleet Street, then at Salisbury Court. Among the books he published was Defoe's *Tour thro' the Whole Island of Great Britain* (1738). He won a lucrative contract, becoming printer to the House of Commons. In the 1750s he owned three printing houses and employed more than forty workers. His life was not entirely happy. His first wife died, their six children died as well; his second wife survived, and four of their six children outlived him.

Other printers sought his editorial advice when books were submitted. He was an early "slush-pile" editor, though in his day there was less slush, fewer writers sure their work merited publication. As his printing developed, he became an early commissioning editor. He published his first book, *The Apprentice's Vade Mecum,* in 1734. It grew out of a letter he had written to his own nephew, giving moral counsel and condemning the vices of the age: taverns, gaming, and theaters. His last book, which due to failing health, periods of paralysis, and lethargy was partly dictated to his daughters and culled from his three novels, was published in 1755: *Moral and Instructive Sentiments, Maxims, Cautions and Reflections.* It underlined his unease at the moral controversy his novels aroused. He always intended to "promote the cause of religion and virtue."

There is about Richardson, as about his characters, a moral hubris that marks writers with a stake in Puritanism. "Richardson had little conversation," Boswell says, "except about his own works, of which Sir Joshua Reynolds said he was always willing to talk, and glad to have them introduced." Men enjoyed his company less than women did. Ford says he was "a favorite correspondent and companion of innumerable young ladies who consulted him as to their amatory predicaments and because of that he is not only the first novelist in the modern sense of the word but also the first literary feminist. You might call him an eighteenth-century Henry James and not go so far wrong."

No wonder Jane Austen owes so much to Richardson. "The supreme of art is the supreme of common sense . . . and surely," says Ford, "the world cannot ever have produced two human beings more common-sensible than Richardson and Jane." *The History of Sir Charles Grandison* was Jane Austen's favorite of Richardson's novels; she even attempted to dramatize select scenes from it, her only surviving dramatic exercise. It may at first seem odd that she should choose so undramatic a book to adapt, yet for her it was his most dramatic, for in it Richardson's largest scale and socially most "worthy" character is put to the trials of propriety and moral delicacy. There is a parodic spirit at work when she reduces so vast a work, over a million words, to fifty-two little pages of manuscript, like Harold Pinter's reduction of Proust's *À la recherche du temps perdu* to *The Proust Screenplay* (1978). But there is earnestness in Austen (as in Pinter); tribute is intended. Her nephew James Edward Austen-Leigh wrote in his *Memoir* that his aunt's "knowledge of Richardson's works was such as no one is likely again to acquire, now that the multitude and the merits of our light literature have called off the attention of readers from that great master. Every circumstance narrated in *Sir Charles Grandison,* all that was said or done in the cedar parlor, was familiar to her; and the wedding days of Lady L. and Lady G. were as well remembered as if they had been living friends."

Austen liked his focus on individuals, the inherence (as in her own writing) of the informing historical and moral contexts. Mr. B is not entirely unrelated to Mr. Darcy and all those seeming-caddish masters who are overwhelmed by love for social inferiors. When Sir Charles wanders about Grandison Hall, the tenants are as respectful to him as Darcy's are. "Indeed, madam," says Mrs. Curzon, "we all adore him." Pamela is a prototype for Fanny in *Mansfield Park* and for other heroines who rise to the station that their nature, if not their nurture, intended for them.

*Pamela; or, Virtue Rewarded:* the rewards are social and material, and such rewards prefigure the pale, transcendent rewards of salvation. Pamela Andrews is a young, attractive servant, settled into her job when her mistress dies, leaving her to her son Mr. B. As her employer, he falls for her, resists, tries to force himself on her, repents, while she heroically preserves herself with feints and flights. Her reward is matrimony and a considerable improvement in class and wealth. Richardson was compelled to compose a sequel because the success of *Pamela* led to other writers jumping on the bandwagon, not only the parodists but opportunists like Hugh Kelly, whose *Pamela's Conduct in High Life* (1741) rankled not only because it was coarse but because it appropriated Richardson's characters. In his own sequel, Pamela is married and endures a profligate husband. The heroine was designed for what must have been a chief market for the book, and the plot was a protracted wish fulfillment for thousands of serving girls squinting at the text by rushlight. Women walking in Vauxhall Gardens carried copies of *Pamela* to indicate their quality, and she was merchandized: a "Pamela fan" existed, an emblem of flirtatious virtue to peer out from behind on hot days and nights.

Mrs. Eliza Haywood (1693?–1756), or Mrs. Novel as Henry Fielding called her, found *Pamela* silly and published her satire *Anti-Pamela; or, Feign'd Innocence Detected* in 1741 and *The Virtuous Villager; or, Virgin's Victory* the next year. She was not enthusiastic about Richardson's sense of female psychology. He did not understand women's work or virtue. Her Syrena Tricksy is another sort of heroine, a prototype for Thackeray's seductive cynic Becky Sharp, canny and feigning, reared by a clever mother to make the most of her assets. Haywood had a reputation for outspokenness but not for virtue, having written plays and libelous memoirs, and she was shortly to found women's magazines entitled the *Female Spectator* (1744–1746) and then the *Parrot* (1747). When she died, she was working on another magazine, the *Young Lady*. Two of her "racy" novels (she started writing such books in 1719) are not entirely forgotten and are certainly not negligible. *The History of Betsy Thoughtless* (1751) takes unambiguous aim at Fielding the magistrate and his fear of and hostility to the poor of London; and *The History of Jemmy and Jenny Jetsam* (1753) is equally forthright. She wrote more than sixty books on a variety of subjects and in a variety of genres in a career of forty years.

Pamela's first letter announces to her parents the death of "my good lady," her dowager employer, who in dying commends "my poor Pamela" (note the symmetries of address) to Mr. B, "My dear son!" The possessive pronoun is everywhere, because the novel is about possession and possessions, just as much as *Moll Flanders* is about money. Here is a heroine in the material world, and though Moll has a larger world and more fun and freedom than Pamela, the measure of everything, moral and religious, is property. Pamela, a cautious, vulnerable virgin, devoted and dutiful to her parents, is awed by the wealth of her employer and affected by the patronage of her dying mistress; she believes in providence and is a model of industry, piety, and obedience. The first reply she receives from her father is about her not getting above herself and not being "ruined." Her father has not seen her for six months, but his concern is her sexual purity, partly as a jealous father, more as a man who knows what gives a property value. The father is a ditch digger, but a moral saint: "for we had rather see you all covered with rags, and even follow you to the churchyard, than *have it said* [my italics], a child of our's preferred any worldly convenience to her virtue." Here is the humble Christian man's hubris, his concern with propriety and property, a concern so profound that it misvalues everything around it, projecting its vision like a death ray. The sexual scenes fall short, because they are about not sex but power, the balance of relationship, property, and class.

"There is no love in Puritanism. There is a struggle for power." D. H. Lawrence is clear about this: "As soon as there is sex excitement with a desire to spite the sexual feeling, to humiliate it and degrade it, the element of pornography enters." That "element of pornography" affects *Clarissa,* with its extended foreplay leading up to the drugged rape of the heroine. No wonder Lawrence speaks of Richardson's "calico purity and his underclothing excitements." Calico is apposite. Fabric and clothing are leitmotifs in *Pamela,* important in the degradation and elevation of her character. Pamela is working the "ugly waistcoat" for her master. The gift in letter 6 of her dead mistress's clothes brings out the paradoxes in her spirit. She wishes she could sell them and send money home. But when she puts them on, she is transformed, a sensual metamorphosis. "As soon as I have dined, I will put on my new clothes. I long to have them on. I know I shall surprise Mrs. Jervis with them." Her motives are clear. Pamela is too articulate to be an *ingénue.* Indeed, she is extremely articulate for her station, her discourse rich in allusions and pleased with itself when it rises to a flourish. Her humble father and Mrs. Jervis are also articulate. Richardson does not roughen style or fit language to the writer. Had Andrews *père* benefited from Richardson's manual of templates? Mr. B declares: "I have seen more of your letters than you imagine; (this surprised me!) and am quite overcome with your charming manner of writing; so free, so easy, and many of your sentiments so much above your years." And station. She is not outraged at his snooping; she may indeed be pleased, given the propriety of her comportment.

We see almost everything from her point of view, "a poor creature, that knows nothing of her duty, but how to cherish her virtue and good name," and (with modest sententiousness), "I have always been taught to value honesty above my life." She reports the views of others with syrupy modesty: Mrs. Jervis calls her "pretty *innocent* and *artless*" (Richardson's italics). Just occasionally we glimpse in her a hint of anger or resistance: Mrs. Jewkes is "this wretch. She is a broad, squat, pursy, *fat thing,* quite ugly, if any human being can be so called." We applaud, but resistance subsides into resignation. We believe in her except when the novelist breaks the epistolary convention. The form becomes mixed: the author moves into journal form, or into a list of moral outcomes. Richardson breaks in when the writing and dispatch of letters becomes impossible, or to impart information (for example, about how Pamela's letters are intercepted) and to number additional dangers of which she is unaware. Mr. B writes his letter of cruel deception to Pamela's father to undermine her, claiming she is fantasizing, intriguing with a clergyman, and the rest. Modern readers find it hard to accept that she can forgive him so many offenses and deliver herself up to him: evidence of a credulous, or a scheming, nature?

Mr. B says, "Take the little witch from me; I can neither bear nor forbear her!" His confusion in the continual self-contradiction of "go, no, stay" makes his character riveting. Mrs. Jervis's reported speech provides a vision of Mr. B's other side and affirms, without demonstrating, his sincerity. He actually *loves* Pamela. He is a catch: courted by "half a dozen ladies"; he loves only Pamela. "He has a noble estate; and yet I believe he loves you, though his servant, better than all the ladies in the land; he has tried to overcome it, because you are so much his inferior; and it is my opinion he finds he can't; and that vexes his proud heart, and makes him resolve you shan't stay: and so he speaks so cross to you when he sees you by accident." Mrs. Jervis speaks without tone, edge, or character. Indeed, is she *speaking* at all? Her sentence is elaborate: three major syntactical runs, each balanced with the one before: statement, contrast, conclusion. Forensic in reasoning, crescendo, and resolution, it belongs to a social and literary register remote from Mrs. Jervis's. *Clarissa* is more interesting and diverse than *Pamela* because of the variety of writers, their stylistic differentiation, and the developing tone and pace as the story unfolds. *Clarissa* is tragedy to *Pamela's* tendentious comedy, but what distinguishes them beyond genre is Richardson's development in assurance and diversity. *Clarissa* tests our moral engagement with each posting.

The plot of *Clarissa; or, The History of a Young Lady* (1747–1748) is complex. Clarissa's family want her to marry the egregious Mr. Soles. Desperate to avoid this fate, she turns trustingly to charming, rakish Mr. Lovelace, who first counsels, then courts (with dishonorable intentions), kidnaps, drugs, and rapes her. She wilts and withers over acres of correspondence, growing physically weak and morally strong, and returning home in a box. Lovelace is slain in a duel with Clarissa's cousin Colonel Morden. The whole of Europe is reduced to tears.

Lovelace is enthralling, a villain who charms. The language of his letters is tailored to his character. His coolly sadistic, crisp description of the caged bird, for example: he calls her an "ensnared volatile" (by the mid-eighteenth century, "volatile" for "bird" was archaic; Lovelace intends to combine two senses in one), he evokes its struggle, its scatter of feathers, pressing head through the wires but held at the "shoulders," its gasps for breath (becoming a woman as he writes); how it draws erect and looks up and tries the roof. It "bites the wires, and pecks at the fingers of its delighted tamer." At last it becomes acclimatized to captivity and pleases itself and its "keeper" with a song. "By my soul, Jack, there is more of the savage in human nature than we are commonly aware of." A few letters earlier he compares himself to a miner undermining, and to an "artful fowler," "spreading my snares."

The image of snaring the bird remains on his lips. He reflects with satisfaction how everything has, as if as a result of his own planning, fallen into place: her brother's, her uncle's, her father's actions: "Her father stormed as I directed him to storm; Mrs. Howe was acted by the springs I set at work; her daughter was moving for me, and yet imagined herself plumb against me; and the dear creature herself had already run her stubborn neck into my gin, and knew not that she was caught; for I had not drawn my sprindges close about her." And at so auspicious a moment, in a flush of madness, he proposed marriage to her! He reflects on the motives of his "black angel" in driving him so far. Angels and birds fuse, her white and his black. Why the fowler? Why did he snare her? "She was soaring upward to her native skies. She was got above earth." He would keep her "with us sublunaries."

Things that worked in *Pamela* are further developed here. Mrs. Sinclair replaces Mrs. Jewkes as gruesome bawd. Her lurid death counterpoints Clarissa's saintly passing. In the end the moral world is only black and white; shades of grey vanish as the action advances. Clarissa's letters to the charming Miss Howe are balanced by the letters of Richard Lovelace to his intimate, John Belford. Such nuance and prevarication as there are come from the correspondents who watch with growing alarm, comment, and caution. The pace is inexorable. "It is a novel written through a microscope," says Pritchett; "it is a monstrosity, a minute and inordinate act of prolonged procrastination. And the author himself is a monster."

*Clarissa* was initially published in seven, then eight little duodecimo volumes. Such books were generally priced at three shillings bound and two shillings and six pence as sheets. A reader would be hooked on the first installment, then feel compelled to buy the rest. This form of serialization imposes on the author a rhythm of narrative: each little volume has to end on a point of unresolved tension so a reader will buy the next. Characters have to be absorbing, and the story has to be talked about: a sensational element, seduction or rape, slow and deliberate, the novel as protracted foreplay ending in a consummation of sorts, marriage or tragedy.

Attention shifts from the artifice to the victim, and Clarissa makes virtue more compelling than vice, a remarkable achievement. Virginity is not attractive and virtue in fiction is usually chilling, expressed in scruple and denial. Here the assault on virtue is so violent, its effects so fatal, that the moral intention of the novel is fulfilled, even in an age in which the values that govern Clarissa's actions are stiff and remote. Richardson provides no subplot, no distraction from the matter. He is monomaniacal. Imagine him rising day after day to add further twists to the undoing of his heroine, his little tongue running along his upper lip with a leer, not of malice but of satisfaction. Lovelace is not Richardson. His intelligence, like his form, is entirely invented. The author may admire him, may live through him, but he does not live in him, he is genuine *fiction*. In this achievement Richardson is superior to any novelist of his age, or ours. He masters oblique narrative, reported incident. And though the book runs to a million words or more, Richardson is an economical writer. Each word counts. The moral and dramatic arguments are congruent.

If only the same could be said of *The History of Sir Charles Grandison*. After *Pamela,* Richardson entered into extensive correspondences, often with ladies, and these left their mark on the conception of his last novel. He had submitted drafts of *Clarissa* to various correspondents, inviting their comments and acting on them. Reader response was part of the creative process, workshop combined with market research. *Sir Charles Grandison* was a success on publication. Richardson had been reluctant to write another novel after the controversy of *Clarissa* and the success of Fielding's *Tom Jones*. He felt impelled to create an unambiguously good hero; Mr. B and Lovelace were bad examples of their class and sex.

We remain in the postman's debt. Beautiful Harriet Byron of Northampton comes to London. She is much sought after, especially by the snooty, affected, and persistent Sir Hargrave Pollexfen, who gets her kidnapped from a masked ball and tries to force a secret marriage on her. His coach is stopped by Sir Charles, who rescues her, they fall in love, but he is already betrothed to an aristocratic Italian, Clementina Porretta. After protracted complications, she releases him and he weds Harriet.

Richardson was concerned that Clarissa was too ideal a character; he ought to have been anxious about Grandison. Though he passes through complications, he never moves above or below propriety. He is something of a stuffed shirt. Lovelace makes us laugh, makes us angry, makes us care. Grandison is not capable of making us do anything except doze and wake to the nuanced endlessness of the narrative. A wholly admirable protagonist is, like God, static. We are back with allegory, a world of stable figures and moral categories.

The admirable and industrious Anna Laetitia Barbauld (1743–1825) edited six volumes of Richardson's (nonfictional) correspondence (1804). He is indeed "the most middling of middling men," guarding himself by careful control of information, creating a character even within the letters he writes. He is capable of humor, but not of inadvertent humor. His control is everywhere evident. For Barbauld, as a novelist herself, he was an exacting model. He was also her model as an editor. In 1810 she produced the fifty volumes of *The British Novelists,* a kind of complement to Johnson's *The Works of the English Poets* (1779–1781), comprising twenty-eight novels printed in full, a major introduction "On the Origin and Progress of Novel-Writing," and individual essays on each novelist. Unlike

Johnson, she included women writers—a dozen, just under half. For the first time the novel was seen as a form worthy of such major investment, and it was the first time women were properly included in a canonical collection. Barbauld is a just, measured critic, understanding the novel form better than most novelists of her period. "There is not in any of Richardson's works, one of those detached episodes, thrown in like make-weights, to increase the bulk of the volume, which are so common in other works: such as the story the Man of the Hill tells in *Tom Jones*. If his works are labored into length, at least his prolixity is all bestowed upon the subject, and increases the effect of the story. Flashes of humor, and transient touches of sensibility, shew, indeed, genius; but patient and persevering labor alone can finish a plan, and make every part bear properly on the main subject." This engages its subject, the critic so bent upon her task that she does not stand even for a moment in the subject's light.

Proportion attracts Ford Madox Ford to Richardson, who is "as little overdrawn as are his characters, whereas the besetting sin of almost all other English novelists from Henry Fielding to George Meredith is that they seem to cut their characters out with hatchets and to color them with the brushes of house-painters and, never, even at that, being able to let them alone, they are perpetually pushing their own faces and winking at you over the shoulders of Young Blifil, Uncle Toby, the Widow Wadman, Dick Swiveller, the Marchioness, Becky Sharp, Evan Harrington, and the rest."

Well before Jane Austen developed a taste for Richardson, he was popular with women writers. In the United States his moral concerns touched Susannah Rowson, whose *Charlotte Temple: A Tale of Truth* appeared in Philadelphia in 1794 (having been published in England three years before). It is a third-person seduction tale, one of her nine novels and by far the most successful and titillatingly virtuous. Here begins the American tradition of female sentimental writers, including, notably, Hannah Webster Foster, whose *The Coquette; or, The History of Eliza Wharton* (1797), actually based on a "true" story, traveled widely and survived in print for a couple of generations. These women's protagonists, however, were after independence: seduction, abandonment, struggle were formative rather than tragic; and the women they created, while nowhere as real or complex as Richardson's, certainly breathe a more credible air *as* women than those we meet in Fenimore Cooper's books.

This puritanical, heady fascination with sex, channeled into the celebration of chastity and dramatized in the rituals of courtship and the perverted rituals of seduction, provided a moral basis for much popular fiction. There was, as well, ample room for the pornographer who, playing with the rhetoric of chastity and purity, undressed the women and men and showed sexual functions in detail. The pornographer from Richardson's day whose work is still read is John

Cleland (1709–1789), a journalist and novelist who was employed by the East India Company and was British consul at Smyrna. When he returned without much to show for his time in Turkey, he decided to write for the market and calculated that sex would sell. He wrote *Memoirs of a Coxcomb* (1751) and similar erotic fiction and had plays and other writings to his credit. Not much credit, however: he died in poverty. His erotic classic *Fanny Hill: Memoirs of a Woman of Pleasure* he composed in debtors' prison; it was published in two volumes (1748, 1749) and was promptly censored as pornographic in 1749.

> Hating, as I mortally do, all long unnecessary preface, I shall give you good quarter in this, and use no farther apology, than to prepare you for seeing the loose part of my life, wrote with the same liberty that I led it. Truth! stark, naked truth, is the word; and I will not so much as take the pains to bestow the strip of a gauze wrapper on it, but paint situations such as they actually rose to me in nature, careless of violating those laws of decency that were never made for such unreserved intimacies as ours; and you have too much sense, too much knowledge of the ORIGINALS themselves, to sniff prudishly and out of character at the PICTURES of them. The greatest men, those of the first and most leading taste, will not scruple adorning their private closets with nudities, though, in compliance with vulgar prejudices, they may not think them decent decorations of the staircase, or salon.

When Cleland was arraigned before the Privy Council, he pleaded poverty and was awarded a £100 pension on condition that he not repeat the offense. He took the money, then repeated the offense, though his other books are less readable. In 1821 *Fanny Hill* was banned in Boston in the first known obscenity trial in the United States. As late is 1963 an unexpurgated version was seized by the police. The high courts of New Jersey and Massachusetts condemned it, a verdict the U.S. Supreme Court reversed in 1966. As it began to circulate more widely, it was burned in Berlin, Manchester, and Tokyo.

It is a saucy and lubricious book, and judging from my own adolescence it can temporarily debauch the male imagination. Like *Pamela* and *Clarissa*, the protagonist has a true love. She is also aware of the value of her chastity. Unlike her fictional cousins, she finds pleasure, first in a phase of preparatory lesbianism, then in voyeurism, watching through keyholes and gaps in the wall the activities of ladies and gents (and in one instance, gents and gents), and then pleasuring and taking pleasure herself, describing not only the loss of her own virginity, but numerous acts of love and lust. Like Pamela, she is fifteen when the story begins. Unlike Pamela's, her parents die and she sets off for London with a friend who abandons her. Mother Brown runs a brothel and takes her in. She falls in love with Charles and he keeps her for a time. She is shunted about, is kept then by a rich old man who dies and leaves her a fortune; she refinds Charles and they marry.

The two letters she addresses to her confessor owe little to Richardson's practice. They are retrospective, rich in circumstantial detail. She recreates intrigue and intercourse so the textures, sounds, and smells fill the imaginations. But only briefly. In her life there is little to linger over. Here is another woman imagined into sexual being by a male author, in all her whims, in all her ages, experiencing the range of human sexuality. Some argue that in fact the female voice disguises a male *eros,* male fascination, and Cleland addresses other men. But the book has had an impact on women writers, including modern writers who set work in a candlelit or gaslit past. The physicality of Fanny's observations, the particularity of setting and character, and the sensations and sentiments she experiences, have no parallel among other surviving novels of the time. Fanny may not be a bona fide woman, but she is certainly not a man in drag. Her last letter ends where her prosperous and, we assume, at last virtuous life begins: "Thus, at length, I got snug into port, where, in the bosom of virtue, I gathered the only uncorrupt sweets: where, looking back on the course of vice I had run, and comparing its infamous blandishments with the infinitely superior joys of innocence," and so on. She does not write of her marriage.

# *"Nuvvles"*

Miguel de Cervantes, Alain-René Lesage, Henry Fielding, Tobias Smollett,

Frederick Marryat, Richard Dana, C. S. Forester, Patrick O'Brian

After his mother died, little Marie-Henri Beyle, who would become the French novelist Stendhal, led a grim life with his weak-willed father and tyrannous aunt Séraphie. One day in the dark library of his house he stumbled upon *Don Quixote.* "Imagine the effect . . . in the midst of such horrible gloom! The discovery of this book, which I read sitting under the second lime-tree along the path on that side of the flower-bed where the ground was sunk a foot deep, was perhaps the greatest moment of my life." His father chided him for laughing and took the book away more than once, but he stole back to it, found a private arbor and read on. Cervantes's ironies played into the imagination of the author of *The Red and the Black* and *The Charterhouse of Parma.*

"What is prodigious about *Don Quixote* is the absence of art," the grown-up Gustave Flaubert writes to Louise Colet half a century later, "and that perpetual fusion of illusion and reality which makes the book so comic and so poetic. All others are such dwarfs beside it! How small one feels, oh Lord, how small one feels!" Later he says the great writers of old carved their works out of huge monoliths, while the moderns pile pebbles one upon another. Jorge Luis Borges speaks of Cervantes's prose as "spoken and not declaimed," and he puts it in a peculiar lineage with Dostoyevsky, Montaigne, and Samuel Butler. It is not tied into the Spanish language in the way that, for example, Fielding is into English. It can travel because, however rooted the story (or *stories*—the narrative consists of an anthology of smaller narratives told to or overheard and misunderstood by the gaunt knight), the manner of telling is generous, pliable. It is the great pattern book of fiction. "*Don Quixote*—I read that every year, as some do the Bible," William Faulkner declared. Lionel Trilling saw all prose fiction as "a variation on the theme of *Don Quixote.*" He uses "theme" in the singular to indicate the wholeness from which later partial visions derive. Trilling's hyperbole is not absurd. The Knight of the Sad Countenance is destined to act, regardless of success or failure. His deeds have consequences, he has no control over their outcome, but what matters is his moral consistency in service, and the intractability of the world that he seeks to serve. Don Quixote is buffeted, broken, but never in himself humiliated. Resilience is his triumph, not the triumph of the causes he seeks to serve. In this the book honors the Catholicism it displaces and at times satirizes, for Don Quixote is a man of faith. When given the opportunity to peek out from the blindfold, he recognizes his friend the barber behind a mask. He shields his eyes from doubt and retains his belief as belief, not theory. From others he expects a like trust, which they are unable to provide.

Don Quixote ventured from La Mancha across the whole of Europe and America. Nor is he confined to any particular period. His author is at home in the English eighteenth and later centuries quite as much as our native writers are. Miguel de Cervantes Saavedra (1547–1616) became British, just as Richardson became French, German, Dutch. Indeed, Cervantes's down-at-heel hidalgo, the gaunt Knight of the Sad Countenance, setting the fabled helm of Mambrino—surely not a vulgar barber's basin!—on his head, with his tubby friend Sancho Panza and his skeletal horse Rocinante, his bumpkin damsel Dulcinea del Toboso fragrant only to his nostrils, his windmill giants with their flailing arms, the bleeding wineskins, the kingdoms and dungeons are, with the excessive figures of Rabelais, inhabitants of the English imagination just as they are of all the imaginations of Europe and its colonies. Tom Jones and Partridge, Mr. Pickwick and Sam Weller are shadows cast by Don Quixote and Sancho Panza.

One tradition says Cervantes wrote *Don Quixote* in prison in Argamasilla in La Mancha. The story is not implausible. He was bankrupted once and saw the inside of a Spanish jail because of misdemeanors associated with tax evasion. Prison can be a nursery for writers. Instead of giving grants for them to *buy* time, let them *do* time. It worked for Malory, Sir Walter Ralegh, Bunyan, and others: poets, playwrights, novelists. Ten years later, the sequel appeared. English fiction is in debt to his novel.

What sort of debt? At a basic level, it is a debt of style. Cervantes subverts the rules of decorum and writes in a mixture of languages: the literary idiom of courtly romance and tales of knights, the aristocratic language of the "better people" of his day, and the vulgar, expressive idioms of common folk, rural and urban. Elements of dialect define the provenance of characters in accent or inflection. This variety characterizes works written for theater. In fiction, the effect was to differentiate and heighten character, to "stage" incidents, to mark off and define scenes and arrest the rapid flow of the prose. Such deliberate harmonies and dissonances make the language of *Don Quixote* an expressive instrument quite apart from anything it says: the ironies and paradoxes, the parody, the pathos, are in the play of sounds and in the dislocations of sense. The effects are poetic, dramatic: here the art of fiction is defined, and when it is later redefined, by Flaubert, Dickens, Conrad, and Dostoyevsky, by Proust, by Kafka, by Joyce and Faulkner, it is in how the language is reinvented that the novel gains new life without relinquishing the old.

There is another debt to *Don Quixote,* formal and conceptual but also philosophical. Georg Lukács evokes it in these terms: *"Don Quixote* is the first great battle of interiority against the prosaic vulgarity of outward life, and the only battle in which interiority succeeded, not only to emerge unblemished from the fray, but even to transmit some of the radiance of its triumphant, though admittedly self-ironizing, poetry to its victorious opponent." As the century progressed and darkened, the novel gained other resonances. Walter Benjamin reflects, "It teaches how the spiritual greatness, the boldness, the helpfulness, of one of the noblest of men . . . are completely devoid of counsel and do not contain the slightest scintilla of wisdom."

*Don Quixote* begins as burlesque of chivalric romance and its conventions. Cervantes was already known as a satirist. Here, because the characters became credible, he entered new terrain. Don Quixote is, for the most part, profoundly sane. His armor may be rusty, he has known better days (like Cervantes and his family, fallen on hard times in a new age), but he is almost normal, a kind of everyknight. *Reading* has led him astray. "The most illustrious example of a convert," Conrad calls him: "The delectable Knight of Spain became converted . . . from the ways of a small country squire to an imperative faith in a tender and sublime mission. Forthwith he was beaten with sticks and in due course shut up in a wooden cage by the Barber and the Priest, the fit ministers of a justly shocked social order."

Parts one and two were translated into English in 1612 and 1620 by Thomas Shelton. Don Quixote himself might have withheld his blessing from this enterprise. He declares, "Translation from one language into another, if it be not from the queens of languages, the Greek and the Latin, is like looking at Flemish tapestries on the wrong side; for though the figures are visible, they are full of threads that make them indistinct, and they do not show with the smoothness and brightness of the right side; and translation from easy languages argues neither ingenuity nor command of words, any more than transcribing or copying out one document from another. But I do not mean by this to draw the inference that no credit is to be allowed for the work of translating, for a man may employ himself in ways worse and less profitable to himself." Shelton's prose has a lively, Jacobean feel. It is worth noting with what speed a book successful in one language could find its way into another: in only seven years Quixote rode into London. Richardson was exported with even greater celerity. Reading a later version, William Dean Howells prophesied in 1895: "I cannot help thinking that if we ever have a great American novel it must be built upon some such large and noble lines." His prophecy had already been fulfilled in Cooper, Melville, and others.

Cervantes's best known, if not the best, translator was the Scottish novelist Tobias Smollett. At least thirty complete editions were published before 1839; thereafter, before the twentieth century, there was but one. It was first published in 1755. The romanticized Don Quixote of later centuries has nothing to do with Smollett's sense of the writer. He reads him as comic, careful, and cruel. He tries "to maintain that ludicrous solemnity and self-importance by which the inimitable Cervantes has distinguished the character of Don Quixote without raising him to the insipid rank of a dry philosopher, or debasing him to the melancholy circumstances and unentertaining caprice of an ordinary madman." This clear verdict stands against the sentimentalism of later approaches; Fielding and other novelists of the eighteenth century see Cervantes as Smollett does, and learn clarity and unsentimental compassion from him. Smollett devised an austere language for the gangling knight. Like many a translator working from a language he does not command as a native, he misses a deliberate anachronism or a clash of social registers, but much, even most, does come through, and his instinct for pace and tone is sound. Martin Amis, unenthusiastic about the original, declares Smollett's version as "astonishingly vigorous, a work of genuine symbiosis," and draws energy from its abrasiveness.

Cervantes is at the heart of our comic tradition, having, Smollett said, "reformed the taste of mankind." He infected Fielding, Sterne, Scott, Byron (poets too were susceptible), Dickens, Melville, Lewis Carroll, Joyce. Nabokov enters a sour note, dismissing Don Quixote as "a cruel and crude old book," but he lectured on it with conviction. When Martin Amis speaks of Don Quixote's "outright unreadability," he has just read the book, all 846 pages, having grasped its episodic nature. How different the expectations readers and listeners had in Cervantes's day! "The question 'What happens next?' has no meaning, because there is no next in Don Quixote's world: there is only more," Amis says.

This Iberian legacy was compounded by a Frenchman, Alain-René Lesage (1668–1747). He was famous for his plays and satires, but it was his picaresque romance L'histoire de Gil Blas de Santillane, published in three parts between 1715 and 1735, that became talismanic for eighteenth- and nineteenth-century novelists. Again, Smollett is responsible for the English: he translated it himself or revised a literal translation in 1749. In this imaginary autobiography, written over a period of twenty years, the style and character age and alter. In the later parts the manner becomes more reflective; the book ends, modern readers agree, with unsatisfactory, sentimental moralizing.

Gil Blas's autobiography, like Don Quixote, is broken into by other narratives, which it frames and contextualizes. It plays variations on linear narrative, and until it draws its conventional conclusions its manner is innocent, amoral. Gil is not a hero but a representative figure to whom extraordinary things occur. As in Defoe and Richardson, money is the measure of value. Indeed, he starts with a parable in which a skeptical student realizes that the soul of man can be a useful leather purse if it has a hundred ducats in it. The author aims to honor Horace's precept and instruct through pleasing us; and then he says, "I have set myself the task of showing the life of men as it actually is."

Lesage sets his novel in Spain. His characters are Spaniards. There is no evidence that he was familiar with the Spanish landscape or people. His grasp of his subject is derived from reading, and he creates a credible world in language out of language. There were many books about Spanish themes and characters in French to draw on, and he was a translator in at least two senses. Here and throughout his work he took material from every room in the Imaginary Museum: Turkish, Italian, but most particularly Spanish. It is not possible to distinguish between translated and appropriated material.

He does not provide much specific detail of character and setting. Highwaymen and dukes, insinuating sluts and alluring Laure, brigand cave and drawing room: there is an abundance of types and settings that, although they exist in specific-seeming spaces, possess a "transferability" that makes *Gil Blas* a suggestive resource for later writers. Dickens remembers the king's love letter: "Madam, there is a high wind. I have shot six wolves." The rich invention compares to Fielding's, but Fielding is more interested than Lesage in narrative architecture.

Gil, the son of a poor family, leaves home, as Tom Jones does, at the age of seventeen to make his way in the world. He has a handful of ducats and few moral inhibitions. En route to Salamanca, where he hopes to study, he is waylaid by robbers and his adventures begin. Gil feeds into Fielding, and through Fielding into English fiction down through Thackeray. Smollett in the preface to *Roderick Random* acknowledges the impact of Lesage, contrasting the Frenchman's with his own approach. Lesage is too rapid in transitions, too merely entertaining, to allow the pathos and anger of his social criticism to affect the reader (and narrator).

———•———

A year after *Pamela,* Henry Fielding published what started as a parodic life of Pamela's virtuous brother, *The History of the Adventures of Joseph Andrews (and of His Friend Mr. Abraham Adams, Written in Imitation of the Manner of Cervantes).* He sold it for £183.11s. Like *Don Quixote* it outgrew its parodic impulse. It was in the end, in the manner of *Gil Blas,* what he called in his preface a "comic epic poem in prose," a "picaresque tale" of innocents abroad. It is told by an omniscient narrator: we have escaped the epistolary and first-person convention. Certain freedoms are gained, certain constraints arise: Fielding as author interjects, ironizes, and buttonholes the reader, though he never quite occupies, as Sterne's narrator does in *Tristram Shandy,* the center of the novel. The story is straightforward: Joseph is dismissed from service because he resists Lady Booby's overtures, as his sister resisted Mr. B's in Richardson's book, and also the advances of Lady Booby's companion Mrs. Slipslop. The names suggest low comedy. Joseph is in love with Fanny, who lives in the village. He is mugged, borne to an inn, and found there by good Parson Adams. After this they travel, discourse, have adventures, and experience a hilarious climax. Mrs. Towwouse the inn hostess, Peter Pounce the steward, Trulliber, and others burst into life.

Fielding had a more conventional education than Richardson. He was conscious of literary antecedents, including fairy tales, that feed his fiction; he was playful and parodic by temperament and liberal in sentiment. Where the female sensibility fascinated Richardson, Fielding's is a world of male concerns and values. *Tom Jones* might be thought to prefigure "lad lit," were it not so ballasted with delightful learning. Richardson did not find it delightful. He told Johnson that, had he not known better, he would have assumed from the writing that Fielding was "an ostler." Johnson's friend Doctor Charles Burney, the novelist Fanny Burney's father, declared that Fielding wrote for men, Richardson for everyone. Without the implausible epistolary conventions refined by Richardson, without the moral ambivalence of maidenly-monstrous *Pamela,* Fielding would not have come to life as he did: disarming, ironic, and hilarious. Stendhal also loved Fielding, whose true characters he praises at the expense of the false characters in most novels.

By the time he found the novel form, Fielding was a man of advancing years, an experienced writer. He had engaged in all sorts of public affairs. Richardson knew how the spirit works in relative isolation; Fielding understood men and women in a social environment. Richardson understood the written record, Fielding understood speech, dialogue, and dramatic form. There was, too, a difference of class. Richardson overvalued refinement. Fielding could take or leave it.

He was born in 1707, the year of the Act of Union between England and Scotland, at Sharpham Park, near Glastonbury, Somerset, seat of his maternal grandparents, the Goulds. His father was Lieutenant-Colonel Edmund Fielding. They were not rich but they had fine connections. By the time Fielding was five, his father had run down the fortune, left the army; and the family, which kept growing, was hungry and clamorous. When Henry was eleven his mother died, and the next year the Colonel married an Italian Catholic widow, Anna Rapha. Henry's maternal grandmother, Lady Gould, contested his father for custody with legal allegations, sequestrations, and ill will. In the end Lady Gould prevailed and the children, along with what little was left of their fortune, went to her. By the time Colonel Fielding was brigadier in 1727, he was defrauded by a broker of his third, or fourth, fortune.

Henry was rather disorderly, like his father; restless and amorous, at Lyme he attempted to elope with, or abduct, an heiress, failed, and was beaten by her guardian's henchmen. He was charged with assault in London the next year and saw the inside of a courtroom. His father's financial distress in 1727 turned the young man loose on the world, where, having begun writing and selling poetry, he found his way into the theater, where his family had connections. In 1728 his first known play, *Love in Several Masques,* was well received at Drury Lane, ran for four nights, and was published.

He had enrolled to study law at Leiden but arrived late for term due to the play. He pursued legal studies less than single-mindedly. He kept writing plays and getting into debt and was evicted. In the end he turned out twenty-five not remarkable but not unsuccessful comedies and burlesques between 1730 and 1737. He adapted the plays of Molière. One play, notably, was performed and published in 1731, *Tragedy of Tragedies; or, The Life and Death of Tom Thumb the Great,* with a frontispiece by William Hogarth, through whose imagination we tend to see Fielding's world. In 1734, along with his virulent attacks on Walpole, appeared a play in which he began to repay his debts to Cervantes, *Don Quixote in England.* In the same year he married a longtime Salisbury friend with an ample dowry, who became a substantial heiress. It seemed they were out of the woods, but like his father, Henry had a talent for failure. He became a theater manager, his plays prospered, but the accounts wouldn't balance. The most decisive blow of fate affected theater in Britain at large. Despite protests, the Stage Licensing Act was passed by Parliament, placing all playwrights at the mercy of the Lord Chancellor's censors. The Act remained on the statute books until 1968. Fielding's was not the only career in theater that ended overnight. Later he challenged the Act with a puppet play, little more than a two-finger gesture. He had no option but to enter the legal profession.

There was another false dawn: an inheritance from an uncle, the proceeds contested and delayed for over a decade. His financial situation became desperate. In 1739 he was issuing "promissory notes" with giddy abandon. He moved his family close by the law courts in London. Then, with James Ralph, he edited the *Champion,* or the *British Mercury* (later the *Evening Advertiser*) under the pseudonym Captain Hercules Vinegar. He steadily attacked Walpole but included nonpolitical material. Debt overwhelmed the family in the winter of 1740: there wasn't money enough to buy coal, his daughter Penelope died. He was resilient. In the irrepressible person of Captain Vinegar, he issued a summons to the poet laureate Colley Cibber for the murder of the English language (Cibber had rewritten *Richard III*). At last, in 1741 he was called to the Bar and began to work as a Western Circuit lawyer. Late in the year Richardson published the first two volumes of *Pamela*.

Henry's father had died in debtors' prison and Henry seemed to be following his footsteps. He ran a short-lived periodical, *A History of Our Own Times*. In February 1742 the third and fourth volumes of *Pamela* appeared. Fielding was under arrest for debt. As his publisher and his wife were bailing him out, he, still standing on the moral high ground that detention by the bailiffs provided, derided high-minded *Pamela* and (though it has never been conclusively laid at his door) composed *An Apology for the Life of Mrs. Shamela Andrews*. Richardson wrote his own sequel to prevent others from capitalizing on his creation; he was not prepared for Fielding's or the other parodies that appeared. *Shamela* was an instant success and for a time eclipsed the original.

The paragon of "Vartue" becomes in his hands an unscrupulous, cunning hussy who exploits her neighbors, marries above her station, and smugly parades. *Shamela* launched Fielding's career as a novelist. Beside his predecessors he was an early starter at thirty-five. Sequels being all the rage, Fielding planned a sequel to *Shamela*, writing the picaresque story of her brother *Joseph Andrews*. But Joseph began to interest him. So did his friend Parson Adams, whose cheerful good nature, not unlike that of the Vicar of Wakefield, carries him through a series of adventures. It was 1742, Swift and Pope were only a step from the grave. Verse drama was nearly over. Satire, the genre of the day, was finding new forms, though at its best it still entailed parody and avoided the tenderizers of sentiment. *Joseph Andrews* earned Fielding, to his astonishment, almost ten times what Richardson received for two-thirds of the copyright in *Pamela*, but the sum was large only because the success of *Pamela* preceded it. He decided to turn his hand to more works of fiction.

In 1749 he produced three *Miscellanies*, including the satirical fragment *A Journey from this World to the Next*, his oddest production. It opens with the discovery of fragments of a manuscript, used by his stationer to wrap pens in. As the narrator starts to decipher the writing, a story emerges. The narrator is being met by Mercury, who as psychopomp is to bear him to the other world by a long route. The dying man contemplates spirits and the spirit world, narrates "The Adventures We Met With in the City of Diseases," describes the Palace of Death, travels on and meets "several spirits who are coming into the flesh," and evokes the wheel of fortune; he recounts Judge Minos's procedures at the Gates of Elysium, and the adventures upon entering Elysium. He meets Julian the Apostate who tells stories, and then he becomes a fop, a monk, a fiddler, a king, a fool, a beggar, a poet, and so on. The narrative stabilizes briefly when his spirit guide assumes a coherent physical form. This original fiction is carried by a narrative voice; by modern lights it is a novel, in the spirit of Ronald Firbank or Nathanael West. In its own day it might have stood beside Smollett's more baldly satirical *The History and Adventures of an Atom* (1769), in which an atom describes to Nathaniel Peacock how, transmigrating, it has lived in the body of a Japanese, and what adventures it has had. Japan is England and the various people are Smollett's contemporaries.

The third volume of the *Miscellanies* includes what is incontestably a novel, *The Life of Jonathan Wild the Great,* the crooked "Thief Taker" (what we would recognize as a bounty hunter) earlier celebrated by Defoe. V. S. Pritchett declares this "the diamond" of the *Miscellanies,* "the most dazzling piece of sustained satirical writing in our language." Fielding as a magistrate was "trained in the rogue's tale": untidy stories, low life, but also in the theater with its necessary efficiency and relative succinctness. He embellishes this rogue's story to show that no necessary connection exists between goodness and greatness. The assumption that it does is sentimental and literary. For fifty-six chapters, in the most abject of places, Wild is held up for our admiration in a heroic style full of moral epithets and ironic endorsements. "In that strange apologue," writes Thackeray, "the author takes for a hero the greatest rascal, coward, traitor, tyrant, hypocrite, that his wit and experience, both large in the matter, could enable him to depict; he accompanies this villain through all the actions of his life, with a grinning deference and a wonderful mock respect: and doesn't leave him, until he is dangling at the gallows, when the satirist makes him a low bow and wishes the scoundrel good day." Fielding shows the ways in which language can say the opposite of what it means, and language used without reflection and irony can discolor moral categories and misvalue deeds.

Merry and merciless as his writing was, his life continued its appalling course. In February his daughter Catharine was born, and buried. His exuberant habits began to undermine his health: gout took hold. His wife was ill at Bath, her situation worsening, and he was back and forth between the spa and the capital until her death. He had, well beyond her dowry and inheritance, loved her as a wife. She lives on in Sophia Western and again in the softer, more Richardsonian figure of Amelia, his last and least-read heroine.

Richardson enjoyed a figurative last laugh at Fielding's expense when, in 1747, his rival married his late wife's maid Mary Daniel. Mary had proven less resistant to her master than Pamela and was quite pregnant when the ceremony took place. She was to bear him five children. Fielding became justice of the peace and chief magistrate for Westminster; his reach later extended to include all Middlesex. In the late summer he began writing *Tom Jones,* setting it in the Jacobite year of 1745. A real Tom Jones is said to have appeared before Fielding the magistrate at Bow Street and, whatever the offense and verdict, his name went down in literature. Fielding was careful with facts, using an almanac to check phases of the moon and journey times, respecting *objective* time, making his story conform to the "time-table of the Jacobite rebellion of 1745, the supposed year of the action," as Ian Watt says. He is *literal* in locating characters in time and space: time includes history, and space can be mapped. These parameters are less aspects of "realism," more to do with the unalterable elements of form that he attempts to reconcile. For the American novelist and poet Allen Tate, this "putting man wholly into his physical setting" is what constitutes "the distinctive capacity of the novel form." Fielding himself thought the book ought to be regarded as "an epic prose poem," Hazlitt tells us.

In 1748 the first three volumes of *Tom Jones* were printed. Fielding, now a chief magistrate, found his head filled with narratives: constant contact with London's underworld gave him voices and incidents. It also devoured his time. A rigorous and unsentimental administrator and magistrate, he appears to have remained free of corruption and during his time more criminals were caught, justly tried, and detained in improved jails than ever before. Dealing with street crime in Holborn, he laid the foundations for what became the full-time police force of the nineteenth century.

By February 1749 all six little duodecimo volumes of *The History of Tom Jones: A Foundling* had been published, priced around three shillings, or two shillings sixpence unbound. The historian Gibbon called it "that exquisite picture of human manners [that] will outlive the palace of the Escurial and the Imperial Eagle of Austria." Its success was immediate, two reprints in three months; revised, it was republished in December. The publisher received 2,000 advance orders, and the sale in the first year is estimated at 3,500. When it appeared in the *General Advertiser,* a note was appended: "It being impossible to get Sets bound fast enough to answer Demand for them, such Gentlemen and Ladies as please, may have them sew'd in Blue Paper and Boards, at the Price of 16s. a Set, of A. Millar over against Catharine-street in the Strand." The author received £100 per volume. Despite its success, Richardson outsold it.

Fielding believed himself "founder of a new province of writing," though there are precedents in Cervantes, Lesage, and Swift, among others, and Richardson's style influenced his later work, especially *Amelia.* But for the first time in English the picaresque was raised to the level of high art, an art more complete than Nashe's, or Defoe's "mere reporting" in which we judge vivid detail, not coherent structure.

"When we admire Tom Jones as being the first portrait of 'a whole man' (a description which perhaps fits only Bloom in later fiction), it is Fielding's seriousness to which we are paying tribute, his power of discriminating between immorality and vice." This moral Graham Greene records, not taking into account Fielding's narrow moral scale, his lack of a sense of what T. S. Eliot called "supernatural evil and supernatural good." These categories are not real for him, the chief conflicts of good and bad attaching to sexual confusion and material cupidity. Fielding's real innovation in the English "province" of fiction was his discovery that the novel could be a serious art form if the artist understood (as Cervantes had done) the harmonies not only of narrative but also of levels of language, the coherence of metaphor, the sheer architecture that can enhance and extend an expressive form. Not that Fielding's form in *Tom Jones* is above reproach: to the "story within a story" of the Man of the Hill, the most excessive of several interpolations, Scott, Trollope, and Dickens all objected.

Scott commends the challenge he set himself, which no successor had the gumption to follow: "Fielding had high notions of the dignity of an art, which he may be considered as having founded. He challenges a comparison between the Novel and the Epic." His followers (Smollett in particular) allow themselves more leeway than he did. David Lodge dwells on the deliberate symmetries of *Tom Jones:* the book has "a hundred and ninety eight Chapters, divided into eighteen Books, the first six of which are set in the country, the second six on the road, and the final six in London." Such symmetries force proportions on the story itself, making it almost stanzaic, and give it a shape in language that counterpoints its shape in time; "it was Fielding who for the first time since the Elizabethan age directed the poetic imagination into prose fiction." Graham Greene too stresses the architecture of Fielding: moralizing he confines to his introductory chapter, not burdening his characters as Defoe does; he uses parody in the spirit Joyce was to do in *Ulysses.* He moves back and forward in time with ease, à la Conrad. And he is gratifyingly "modern" in coming clean with his readers: his novel is a fiction.

Fielding understood how a narrator's voice could become a positive presence in a novel, and the abdications permitted by the epistolary mode were precisely that, abdications. Pritchett overstates the effect of the theater on Fielding's fiction: dramatic and fictional dialogue are different in construction and effect, they flow in different rhythms and create distinct spaces about them. But the fictional character conceived as a figure always observed from the outside, as an actor, brings into play elements of dramatic differentiation, and that far Pritchett's argument holds. "The English novel started in *Tom Jones,* because the stage taught Fielding how to break the monotony of flat, continuous narrative. The methods of the theater are abstract and summary; there is an idea before there is a scene; and one of the fascinating things in *Tom Jones* is the use of the summary method to set the scene, explain the types of character, cover the preparatory ground quickly by a few oblique moralizings and antics so that all the realism is reserved for the main action."

Scenes are discrete and have each its own beginning, middle, and end. And scenes are juxtaposed, for contrast, irony, balance, or pathos. Yet dialogue is more expansive, scenes much more extended, than we would tolerate on stage. It may be, as Pritchett suggests, that Ben Jonson as dramatist affected Fielding. When we read his *Bartholomew Fair* or *Volpone* today, we read them almost as we would novels: they are generally too rich, too packed (not least with semantic challenges) for the modern stage. Greene comes close to the truth of the matter: "What puts us so supremely in [Fielding's] debt is this: that he had gathered up in his novels the two divided strands of Restoration fiction: he had combined on his own lower level the flippant prose fictions of the dramatists and the heroic drama of the poets."

In *Middlemarch,* just as she prepares to go deep into the character of Dr. Lydgate, George Eliot invokes Fielding as a kind of muse—a muse of history, one of the "colossi whose huge legs our living pettiness is observed to walk under" and remembers how he "glories in his copious remarks and digressions as the least imitable part of his work." She likes how, in the opening chapters to the different books of his novels, "he seems to bring his armchair to the proscenium and chat with us in all the lusty ease of his fine English." She follows, as does Thackeray and, on a smaller scale, Trollope; and on a larger scale, Tolstoy.

The new readership liked to laugh; it also liked to weep. It was intrigued by intimacy, by private zones into which it could peer, as well as by voices written or spoken out from different classes, provinces, and walks of life. Fielding's legacy is his clear perception of the readership he is addressing, and at the same time his refusal to write down or simplify his plan in the light of his readership. He knew readership as a journalist does. Writing with a sense of it encouraged directness; and when a journalist of Fielding's character turns his hand to fiction, he retains his habit of address; he does not set aside the essay style but brings it into play. Modern readers resist this aspect of *Tom Jones*. Ford's praise is damning: "Although *Tom Jones* contains an immense amount of rather nauseous special-pleading, the author does pack most of it away into solid wads of hypocrisy at the headings of Parts or Chapters." Modern readers enjoy the acknowledgment at the end of the book (Thackeray makes similar gestures) that the novel is a fiction, the shades disperse as the magic is withdrawn. Ford sees this as further evidence of "mismanagement" and self-projection. "But the truth is that both Thackeray all his life and Fielding in *Tom Jones* were intent first of all on impressing on their readers that they were not real novelists . . . but gentlemen." They cut themselves out, as it were. Writers of modern metafiction insist on artifice to indicate that they *are* real novelists, cutting themselves into the medium by structural and formal features. Ford, coming where he does in the story of the novel, does not quite appreciate what Fielding means to Thackeray and others of that generation, the one novelist who was "permitted to depict to his utmost power a man"; after Fielding, the spirit of Richardson and the market for fiction conspired to feminize the novel and make it polite. Richardson attacked *Tom Jones* and its author. The book was "too prescribing, too impetuous, too immoral, I will venture to say, to take any other Byass than that a perverse and crooked Nature has given him; or Evil Habits, at least, have confirm'd in him." In the *Rambler,* Johnson compared the "libertine" Fielding unfavorably with Richardson, though elsewhere he records a liking for *Amelia.* It was less rank than the other writings.

Fielding informs the main stream of English fiction through to the early Victorian period; he comes alive again in those novelists who rebel and resist the *politesse* and conservatism of the mid-Victorians, but then recedes once more, and the twentieth century is more indebted (obliquely, unconsciously) to the Richardsonian strand. Ford is Richardsonian in this context: Fielding is, he says, "at once a dreadful example of how not to do things" and "the begetter of Thackeray and the product that it is convenient to call the nuvvle as opposed to the novel." The nuvvle is that kind of "commercial product which Mamma selected for your reading." He adds, "I dislike Tom Jones, the character, because he is a lewd, stupid, and treacherous phenomenon; I dislike Fielding, his chronicler, because he is a bad sort of hypocrite. Had Fielding been in the least genuine in his moral aspirations it is Blifil that he would have painted attractively and Jones who would have come to the electric chair, as would have been the case had Jones lived to-day." Blifil for hero!

Fielding's last creative period was a time of personal grief: his sister and three of his children died in 1750. His civic writings were having their effect, however. He examined the causes of crime and proposed strategies for prevention. In 1751 his celebrated brother John, blind from youth, was appointed Commission of the Peace for Westminster. That was the year of Henry's last novel, subdued and elegiac *Amelia,* telling of a troubled marriage between the eponymous heroine and Tom-Jones-like William Booth. It was published in four volumes in an overly ambitious initial run of 5,000 copies. Fielding received £800 for the work.

Fielding was in decline. Month by month he grew weaker; he resorted to crutches, concentrated on social issues, and wrote *A Proposal for Making an Effectual Provision for the Poor, for Amending Their Morals, and for Rendering Them Useful Members of the Society* (1753). He made a difference to Society as to the literary world. A profligate spender even now, he borrowed £1,872 from his printer in

1753, a sum he never repaid. In 1754 he resigned the magistracy and all legal functions in favor of his brother John, made his will, and booked passage on the *Queen of Portugal* for Lisbon, taking his family and servants. His death was mistakenly reported. There was a final book in him, the witty *Journal of a Voyage to Lisbon*, published in 1755. But he died in Lisbon before it appeared, having settled at Junqueira and started planning a history of the country. In London his house and property were auctioned in December and raised £800. The next year his library fetched £365.

So much life, so much writing, he squeezed into forty-seven hectic years. Kingsley Amis's character Bowen in *I Like It Here* visits Fielding's tomb. "Perhaps it was worth dying in your forties if two hundred years later you were the only non-contemporary novelist who could be read with unaffected and whole-hearted interest, the only one who never had to be apologised for or excused on the grounds of changing taste." But there was more than reputation and readability in Amis / Bowen's mind: a nostalgia, a jealousy, for an age of moral certainties: "And how enviable to live in the world of his novels, where duty was plain, evil arose out of malevolence and a starving wayfarer could be invited indoors without fear." Here was "a moral seriousness that could be made apparent without the aid of evangelical puffing and blowing." George Eliot—or rather, the narrator of *Middlemarch*—reminds us how, "Fielding lived when the days were longer (for time, like money, is measured by our needs), when summer afternoons were spacious, and the clock ticked slowly in the winter evenings. We belated historians must not linger after his example."

Fielding's friend Lady Mary Wortley Montagu lamented his death, good manners keeping her eyes dry: she would have no more new works by him to read, and she adds, "His happy constitution (even when he had, with great pains, half demolished it) made him forget everything when he was before a venison pasty, or over a flask of champagne, and I am persuaded he has known more happy moments than any prince upon the earth." This despite bereavements, the financial and political upsets. Whatever the course of his life, in the present tense body and spirit always found gratification, in sensation, passion, or a brilliant phrase. Graham Greene reveres the richness of his life: "Fielding the rake, Fielding the country gentleman, Fielding the hack dramatist, and finally Fielding the Westminster magistrate who knew all the outcast side of life, from the thief and the cut-throat to the seedy genteel and the half-pay officer in the debtor's court, as no other man of his time." In Fielding the seventeenth century culminates and concludes.

Tobias Smollett attacked Fielding in his later years: Smollett whose way had been cleared by Fielding (though Smollett might have claimed that his translations had cleared a way for Fielding). Ford loves Smollett, and sensing that he is on unpopular ground, he declares that "it is hopeless to expect Anglo-Saxon readers to appreciate or to consume" him. And he is right. However wonderful the best of the novels, they are remote in language and, after Fielding's and Richardson's, old-fashioned in form. They retain a little of the "air and cadence" of the seventeenth century, and the writing is "sober and good enough." How good is it in fact? Pritchett finds a deep fault in Smollett: "Something is arrested in the growth of his robust mind; as a novelist he remains the portrayer of the outside, rarely able to get away from physical externals or to develop from that starting-point into anything but physical caricature." His is an art of retribution: the cheater is cheated, the bully in the end is bullied. Old Testament justice is at work. Thackeray said of him, not without admiration, "I fancy he did not invent much." The starkness of his drawing of character and the detailed externality of his approach recommended him to the early modernists.

Smollett sets out like Defoe, Richardson, and Fielding to be a moralist, to improve his readers and to reform the navy. He is a young man, in his twenties when he starts, with all the expectation and rancor of youth. Born a Scot, he stands at an oblique angle to the English, whose ambitions and institutions he regarded with a sometimes-hostile skepticism. Their brutal reprisals against the Jacobite rebels after the Battle of Culloden, conducted by the Duke of Cumberland in 1746, confirmed his Hanoverian sympathies and elicited his most powerful poem, "The Tears of Scotland":

> While the warm blood bedews my veins,
> And unimpair'd remembrance reigns,
> Resentment of my country's fate
> Within my filial breast shall beat . . .

The literary world, too, had its corruptions. Smollett's detractors later accused him of some of the sleights of hand (especially in the area of translation) that he exposed in *Peregrine Pickle:*

> He had, in his affluence, heard of several authors, who, without any pretensions to genius or human literature, earned a very genteel subsistence by undertaking work for booksellers, in which reputation was not at all concerned. One, for example, professed all manner of translation, at so much per sheet, and actually kept five or six amanuenses continually employed, like so many clerks in a counting-house, by which means he was enabled to live at his ease, and enjoy his friend and his bottle, ambitious of no other character than that

of an honest man and a good neighbor. Another projected a variety of plans for new dictionaries, which were executed under his eye by day-laborers; and the province of a third was history and voyages, collected or abridged by understrappers of the same class.

His first literary work was journalistic, and he burrowed deep into the review and magazine culture of his time. He was a key figure in the growth of book *reviewing,* following Ralph Griffiths (the *Monthly Review,* 1756 onward) with the *Critical Review* (also 1756 onward) in describing and appraising new books. A pioneer, he did not only describe in a marketing spirit but assessed critically the volumes submitted for consideration. He played a role in developing novel serialization. This practice dated from the end of the seventeenth century; in the last three decades or so of the eighteenth, it became a primary mode of publication. The first significant serialized novel is Smollett's own *Sir Lancelot Greaves,* published in the *British Magazine* over twenty-five issues from January 1760 through December 1761. It opened the way for later novelists (and their publishers), including Dickens and Dostoyevsky, to secure two bites of the publication cherry: periodical and volume.

Smollett was born in Dunbartonshire and always regarded himself as a Scot. His grandfather, Sir James Smollett, helped to negotiate the terms of the Act of Union. Though the son of a younger son, Tobias felt himself entitled to give himself airs. He began studies at Glasgow University but left without "means of support" and became a surgeon's mate on the *Chichester* in the brutal and insolent Sir Chaloner Ogle's West India squadron. He was present at the disastrous defeat at Cartagena in what is now Colombia, at the hands of the Spanish, an experience to which he referred often, even obsessively, going to prison much later in life for his "libels" of Admiral Knowles, one of the commanders. He remained for a time in Jamaica, where he married. When he returned to London in 1744, he practiced as a surgeon. He stayed in the medical profession even after literary success came his way, maintaining a practice in Downing Street and publishing also in the field of medicine. His first publication, when he was twenty, addressed the Siege of Cartagena; it also features in *Roderick Random* (1748), his first major novel. Later significant novels include *Peregrine Pickle* (1751, revised 1758), *Ferdinand Count Fathom* (1753, memorable for a few ur-Gothic episodes prefiguring the terror novel), followed by his version of *Don Quixote* (1755), *The Cervantic Adventures of Sir Launcelot Greaves* (1760–2), the amusing, grumpy *Travels in France and Italy* (not unrelated to Sterne's *Sentimental Journey*), the satire *The History and Adventures of an Atom* (1769), and what Thackeray calls "the most laughable story that has ever been written since the goodly art of novel-writing began," *The Expedition of Humphry Clinker* (1771). It was completed two years after he left England for good, for Leghorn (Livorno) in Italy, where he died. Both *Roderick Random* and *Peregrine Pickle* were attacked in the *Covent Garden Journal*, published twice a week during 1752 by Fielding; Smollett responded with *A Faithful Narrative of . . . Habbakuk Hilding, Justice: Dealer, and Chapman* (1752). Each had met his match: the two man on the face of it might have seemed natural allies, but between them was the bitterness that divides generations and, it may be, nations.

*The Adventures of Roderick Random,* described by the American novelist John Barth as "a healthy, hard-nosed counteragent to the cult of love," a kind of deliberate affront to Richardson and his followers, appeared in full the year before *Tom Jones,* and Smollett believed Fielding had stolen some of his thunder. In *Peregrine Pickle* he sends Fielding up in the figure of Mr. Spondy, and other real-life characters make thinly veiled appearances: David Garrick, for example, and the doctor-poet Mark Akenside. *Roderick Random* follows the example of *Gil Blas.* It is episodic, fast-paced, full of incident and argument, with interpolated narratives that enrich the fun but impoverish the form of the novel. It also expresses the bitterness of Smollett's frustrations, his failure to achieve success as poet and dramatist, his sense of being *outside* and utterly self-reliant. He wanted to "point out the follies of ordinary life" and provoke, in his words, "that generous indignation, which ought to animate the reader against the sordid and vicious disposition of the world."

Roderick is a protagonist selfish and without scruple. He tells the story, evoking the naval situation of the time. Much corresponds with the specifics of Smollett's own experience, though he was not press-ganged as a common sailor, nor did he do service on *Thunder,* a man-of-war. Being a journalist, he realized that he had to "scale up" his stories to draw and hold a readership. Love interest was provided: Roderick falls for Narcissa, is carried to France by smugglers, rescues his devoted naval uncle, works with his man Strap to snare a rich wife, but fails both with Miss Melinda Goosetrap and her mother. He loses what money he has in gambling, joins a ship commanded by his uncle, and discovers Don Roderigo, a rich merchant, who, it transpires, is his father. The book ends with Roderick marrying Narcissa and Strap marrying Miss Williams, her maid. Smollett includes an early, comic defense of homosexuality; *Peregrine Pickle* contains the first instance in fiction of a blackmailing homosexual.

*Roderick Random* and *The Adventures of Peregrine Pickle* are genuinely picaresque. Smollett, a brilliant craftsman, plots subtly and humorously, but those elements of higher architecture that Fielding achieves are not consistently found in his books. There is adventure, satire, rage, but limited interiority and a modest artistic instinct. *Peregrine Pickle,* a third-person narrative more protracted if not more sustained than his first effort, introduces us to a rogue like one out of

Nashe, possessed of a monstrous mother, witty and brave but with few other virtues. Propelled by a cheerful avarice, he gets involved in a series of love encounters and affairs intended to make his fortune through marriage; he sets out on a grand tour, a favorite subject for satire; he duels in Paris, meets artists, including the painter Pallet, who, in drag, is imprisoned in and then sprung from the Bastille. He has adventures in Holland, tricks the quacks in Bath, becomes physician, magician, politician; he is imprisoned in the Fleet, inherits his father's property, and finally becomes a husband, achieving his quarry (pursued throughout the book, on and off, by various devices, including drugs— reminiscent of *Clarissa*), the beguiling Emilia Gauntlet. Call no man happy until he is married.

The climax of the novel recalls *Tom Jones,* though Smollett's book falls short of its range or force. His characters exist at the level of caricature: Gamaliel, Peregrine's father; Grizzle, his aunt; the boatswain Tom Pipes, who becomes his man; and Commodore Hawser Trunnion, a fine nautical creation with his naval disciplines and his fantastic, almost fatal stormy journey on horseback to his own wedding. The most *Gil Blas* element in the book is the piling up of cultural satire and commentary at the end, reminding us of Gil's debates with his obscure poet friend. The dinner in the manner of the ancients, recalling classical symposia, is charmingly profligate. The narrative is disrupted by the interpolation of extraneous material (there is so much interpolation it might be described as a structural feature), notably in chapter 81, the protracted "Memoirs of a Lady of Quality" based on the actual amours of the scandalous Frances Anne Hawes, Viscountess Vane (1713–1788), whom Smollett seems to admire. The book is too long, though not for Dickens, a firm admirer disposed to forgive Smollett almost everything. He relished the detail and comedy page by page and shared something of Smollett's radical conservatism of outlook. To a friend Dickens wrote in 1854: "I am rather divided between *Peregrine Pickle* and *Roderick Random,* both extraordinarily good in their way, which is a way without tenderness," a phrase defining the proximity and distance between two writers and two Britains divided by a little under a century, the one harsh and unflinching, the other softened by sentiment now forgiving, now heartbreaking, now cloying.

Of his later novels, "certainly Smollett's best" (in Dickens's view) and his best loved is the last, *The Expedition of Humphry Clinker.* The author has mellowed. He adopts an epistolary form (having deployed every type of narrative current at the time: first person, omniscient narrator, now this). Mr. Matthew Bramble's party journeys through England and Scotland. There is Old Bramble, gruff and misanthropic but really a kindhearted bachelor; his sister Tabitha, who is in aggressive quest of a husband; the jolly young nephew Jery and niece Lydia;

Winifred Jenkins, the maid; and the eponymous Humphrey, whom the Brambles have picked up on their travels, needing a postilion, and who becomes their devoted servant. He is the Sancho Panza of the book, and Don Quixote has vanished, as he generally does in English fiction in this strand of the tradition. Also in keeping with this mutation of the form, Humphrey turns out to be old Bramble's son and marries; and Tabitha, as is proper, finds in Durham a Scottish soldier, Obadiah Lismahago, and marries him. *Humphry Clinker,* the book of his retirement, his Leghorn novel, is a cheerful note on which to end a life. After the pale and shadowy women of his earlier books, here are some credible figures whose wiles and attractions persuade. He was only fifty, but like Fielding he had packed his years and his books so full of character, incident, and the life of his times that the impression he leaves is of a man encyclopedically blessed.

The reward reserved for Smollett's heroes is a well-managed country estate, acquired through an advantageous marriage. His conservatism in an age of Whiggish change and social instability is not unlike Coleridge's love for the principles of permanence, though in Smollett's case there are no metaphysics, only a hankering after the stability that comes with a strict hierarchy that is permeable to the Scot. He was by temperament a man of reason and the Enlightenment, this imbued with less-orderly energies of an earlier century. Fielding's junior by a long way, in some respects he seems older, or earlier, retaining a sense of politics and values that were part of his Scottish character. On the other hand, he read Voltaire and was, in his history writing, a kind of encyclopedist; but his satire, in the *Atom* for example, has much in common with the manner, age, and anger of Swift. Thus, when the Brambles find Humphry Clinker and Tabitha assaults the bedraggled man with his unworthiness, Matthew Bramble declares, "Hark ye, Clinker, you are a most notorious offender. You stand convicted of sickness, hunger, wretchedness, and want."

The tradition of Fielding and Smollett survives the impact of Scott; it thrives in the writing of Captain Frederick Marryat (1792–1848). Ford declares, "Smollett begat Captain Marryat, who was one of the greatest of English novelists and is therefore regarded as a writer for boys." He was a man with less rancor than Smollett and possessed a less-developed sense of the art of fiction and satire; but he was skilled in telling a plain story and in creating believable male characters, and had a full and accurate appreciation of the sea and life upon it. *Peter Simple* (1834) is his most accomplished seagoing novel, while *Japhet in Search of a Father* (1836) may feel a little like an ancestor of Oliver Twist. He was, after all, a close friend of Dickens and his circle.

Marryat's grasp of detail is literal, like Defoe's, and one can understand why a writer of Conrad's severe temper found him inspiring if artistically inadequate. "To the artist his work is interesting as a completely successful expression of an unartistic nature. It is absolutely amazing to us, as the disclosure of the spirit animating the stirring time when the nineteenth century was young. There is an air of fable about it. Its loss would be irreparable, like the curtailment of national story or the loss of a historical document. It is the beginning and the embodiment of an inspiring tradition." Conrad notes, "He wrote before the great American language was born, and he wrote as well as any novelist of his time." He showed the way, in terms of genre, for Melville's *Redburn* and *White Jacket,* and Richard Dana's *Two Years before the Mast.* "It is in the dispassionate statement of plain material facts that Dana achieves his greatness," D. H. Lawrence writes. "Dana writes from the remoter, non-emotional centres of being—not from the passional emotional self." He adds, "Dana's small book is a very great book: contains a great extreme of knowledge, knowledge of the great element."

With Marryat more than with Dana, it is not a sense of form that keeps the reader attentive: plot hardly matters except to string together adventures related by a humane, humorous-toned narrator. "Marryat is the most good-humored of novelists, possessed of an exuberance that is rarely overplayed," writes Walter Allen; "there is a largeness of mind about him; a natural gallantry informs his work." *Peter Simple* is about navy life at the start of the nineteenth century, from the point of view of Peter, a young midshipman who regards himself as the simpleton of his family. After Defoe's *Colonel Jack,* Peter is one of the most convincing boys in English fiction. He is not Marryat's only original figure. *Snarleyyow; or, The Dog Fiend* (1837), about an indestructible hound, includes the figure of Nancy, a reformed prostitute and prototype for characters in Dickens and Gissing, and the cadaverous Smallbones, to whom Oliver Twist bears some resemblance.

He had important heirs in the twentieth century. C. S. (Cecil Scott) Forester (1899–1966) is in his more or less direct debt for his series of novels about the life and career of Horatio Hornblower, written between 1950 and Forester's death. Beyond Hornblower he wrote other novels of the sea and land. In a signal service to young readers, he encouraged the young Roald Dahl to begin writing in 1942.

Then there is Patrick O'Brian (Richard Patrick Russ, 1914–2000), who wrote twenty novels about the strangely ill-matched friends Captain Jack Aubrey and Stephen Maturin, the naval surgeon, the series starting in 1970. In O'Brian's work the maritime tradition of English fiction under sail reaches another, perhaps a final, climax. His novels follow a rather elastic historical sequence of events from 1800 to the years after the Battle of Waterloo, 1815. O'Brian's characters are intelligent, curious beyond the frame of their vocations and the plots of their novels, and the books move with compelling continuity, the installments impatiently anticipated by readers primed and conditioned, like soap-opera addicts or readers of Proust. O'Brian made himself into a scholar of the world that Smollett, Marryat, and Melville knew firsthand; he masters the technical language and the spoken registers of a wide range of men, so that, as in Melville but with less intense concentration, each novel carries a representative crew. It is tempting to hear in the awkward relationship between Captain Aubrey and Maturin an echo of Don Quixote and Sancho Panza, without caricature and hilarity but with some of the wisdom that comes from well-defined contrast.

# | 10 |

## *"A Cock and a Bull"*

### Laurence Sterne

"Nothing odd will do long. *Tristram Shandy* did not last," Doctor Johnson told Boswell. Sir Joshua Reynolds's portrait of the Reverend Laurence Sterne was painted in 1760, the year in which the first two volumes of what Richardson called the "execrable" novel *The Life and Opinions of Tristram Shandy, Gentleman* swept London. Reynolds makes the author look tall, skinny, ferret-faced under an abundant wig. His right hand rests against his cheek, his right elbow is propped on the disorderly manuscript of his disorderly masterpiece. An anonymous portrait, painted in the same year, shows him more at ease, with an insinuating smile, one hand hanging at his side, the other on the verge of emphasizing a point in conversation. His clerical bands could do with a wash and starch; but there is never much *starch* about Sterne. Back in his parish, "so slovenly was his dress and strange his gait, that the little boys used to flock around him and walk by his side," says a biographer. Slovenly, but not unclean: he changed his undergarments regularly.

Six years later, Joseph Nollekens made a life-size marble bust in which, viewed face-on, the author is anxious. If he judges us kindly, he will invite us into his confidence. In all three portraits, he watches us. This is in keeping with his style in *Tristram Shandy*. Earlier novelists address the reader directly, but not personally. They conceive of readers collectively as readership. Sterne particularizes us. There is intimacy in his address, complicity and the illusion of trust. This manner repelled his captious contemporaries and irritates some modern readers, too. "The man Sterne is unbearable," says Graham Greene, "even the emotions he displayed with such amazing mastery were cheap emotions." But he cannot resist the book.

Most readers accept his invitation and humor him. He mumbles and changes tack, he corrects and forgets himself. At one point he identifies a reader who is not paying sufficient attention and sends her back to the previous chapter. While she is gone, he chats to us, killing time until she rejoins us. The novel becomes a space through which we move, in which we go backward and forward, and time that mercilessly governs Defoe and Smollett, Fielding and Richardson, becomes inconsequential. Swift might prepare us for this world, or saintly Bunyan. It is a novel with its roots in unconventional holy ground. "It is impossible not to feel a faint disgust at this man, officially a man of God," Greene declares. Ford resists him, too: Sterne is "that dissolute, brandified and atheistic parson." But it is hard not to laugh, and hard too not to sigh, to succumb to the moments of sentiment in *Tristram Shandy*. For example, when Uncle Toby frees the irksome fly. Tristram's "uncle Toby had scarce a heart to retaliate upon a fly." And so, "—Go—says he, one day at dinner, to an over-grown one which had buzzed about his nose, and tormented him cruelly all dinner-time,—and which after infinite attempts, he had caught at last, as it flew by him;—I'll not hurt thee, says my uncle Toby, rising from his chair, and going across the room, with the fly in his hand,—I'll not hurt a hair of thy head:—Go, says he, lifting up the sash, and opening his hand as he spoke, to let it escape;—go, poor devil, get thee gone, why should I hurt thee?—This world surely is wide enough to hold both thee and me." This is a "tobyesque parable": "how it taught the lad philanthropy." He enjoins us to recognize the importance, to the whole, of the little creature and the small detail: "Oh, my countrymen, be nice; be cautious of your language; and never, oh never let it be forgotten upon what small particles your eloquence and your fame depend."

Sterne needs us on his side if he is to achieve his ends. "He is a writer claiming fictional freedom—freedom to have his chapters in the wrong order, the preface in the middle, the freedom to digress, upturn, change narrators, go back," says Malcolm Bradbury. He has to know we are with him ("Oh, my countrymen"), all of us in our differences of culture, class, and sex. We will be made curious in new ways, not with bated breath awaiting the next turn of plot, but with deferred expectations, curious, anticipating promised surprises in every fold of the garment, in every turn of syntax. "Digressions, incontestably, are the sunshine;—they are the life," Sterne says, with his characteristic drizzle of dashes, "the soul of reading;—take them out of this book for instance,—you might as well take the book along with them." He makes us obedient, rebuilds our habits of expectation away from action toward tone and sentiment, and in his teasing there is undeniably a kind of arousal, not least because what he promises is often naughty. George Eliot was amused and impatient: "The objections to Sterne's wild way of telling *Tristram Shandy* lie more solidly in the quality of the interrupting matter than in the fact of interruption."

Much of our aroused curiosity is sexual or scatological. Sterne provides chaotically choreographed striptease. The book *A Sentimental Journey* concludes just when the narrator's elaborate delicacy of intention can no longer avoid explicit sex. The whole novel of sensibility is a kind of charmed foreplay that resists consummation. That is the joke; it is also the fact. Gabriel Josipovici draws attention to what he calls "the collage elements" in *Tristram Shandy*, the mock-marbling of the paper, the pointing hands, the expressive asterisks, squiggles, dingbats, the black page and the tombstone, the varying lengths of dashes that, when the book was first published, were specified by the author to indicate the length of pauses and hesitations.

Josipovici sees the book as engaging us and affecting us *in our bodies.* He sees us, he looks back, directs us. We do not read an unfolding narrative but are gathered into an intimate and tangential series of dialogues with and through him; they are about curiosity, our curiosity too, our desire to know, our arousal. Interruption, the wink, the beckoning forward. Earlier novels, as narrative, attempt to be continuous; much of the humor of *Shamela* and *Joseph Andrews* is in the inexorability of story. Not so *Tristram Shandy.* An inexorable story creates distance; we stand outside it, as we stand outside the action of a play. But think of a play in which there are problems of continuity in the production, the lighting malfunctions, a flat falls in the second scene, actors forget or extemporize lines, jumble up the scenes: we are drawn into the drama that underlies the drama— the process area, not the product area. This is what Sterne brings us: not a failure of orchestration but rather a fascination with the process of annotation. The Argentinean writer Jorge Luis Borges declared, "Laurence Sterne unravelled the novel by making merry with the reader's expectations, and those oblique digressions are now the source of his multitudinous fame."

When we have read *Tristram Shandy* and look back on it, what do we remember? I think of gaps, of long sentences fitted together with dashes, sentences a paragraph long in which a single thing is left—unsaid: dashes, the places where the words have been lost or left out or groped for, where the speaker has paused in a world of approximations to try to find the least approximate word. I remember the notes, chords and key signatures, as it were, of a progression of indirections, elements of style, not story. There is too the sexual interest and scatology, elements in a wakening of the reader. The tone is, as Josipovici says, "by turns sentimental and prurient." Sir Walter Scott levels against Sterne a charge of indecency. Virginia Woolf has no moral qualms: "Even his indecency impresses one as an odd kind of honesty. In comparison other novels seem intolerably portly and platitudinous and remote from life." There is portliness about Sterne's writing, too, if not about the man, a portliness in the chosen style. And the style *is* chosen: Sterne was quite able to write more conventional, continuous narrative when he had a mind to. The autobiographical sketch he left for his daughter Lydia proves as much. He tells a story in sequence with beginning, middle, and a gap for the inevitable end. For his novel he chose not to write like Defoe or Smollett, to avoid the mode of Richardson. He cut a new furrow.

The autobiographical sketch recalls a peripatetic childhood. His father was an army ensign; his regiment was moved about, a pawn on a busy chessboard, and his wife, their children hanging off her skirts, followed in his wake. Four of the children "left us behind in this weary journey," the brothers little Jorum, then beautiful Devijeher, a bittersweet memory. But we must respect the sequence of events. To begin well before the beginning: the Sterne family had ecclesiastical roots in Yorkshire. Great grandfather Dr. Richard Sterne was archbishop of York. Uncle Ja(c)ques, his patron and then his bitter foe, was part of York Minster's hierarchy. But Laurence was born, because of his father's posting after the peace of Utrecht, in Clonmel, County Tipperary, in 1713, the year in which Swift was installed as dean at St. Patrick's.

As little Laurence followed from camp to camp, perhaps a dozen in a decade, always a few weeks or months behind his father, hurried on by an agitated, unstable mother who would become a burden to him in later life, he was an onlooker. He listened to men who had seen action in Flanders under William and Marlborough. He heard a dozen dialects, different registers. He listened rather than saw. Describing his experiences to Lydia, he writes pell-mell. We see where corporal Trim began, and how uncle Toby took shape in his mind. As he approached his teens, his father sent him to Yorkshire, where he might settle into school. Near Halifax he studied and received "more whippings than lessons," but he remembers one incident with pride. A classroom had been newly whitewashed and the ladder left behind. Little Laurence climbed the ladder and wrote LAU. STERNE boldly, in large letters, on the ceiling. The usher beat him, but the master insisted that the name should stay because he "was a boy of genius, and he was sure I should come to preferment."

Sterne had tender memories of his father, a "little smart man" who patiently sustained his disappointments. He was quick-tempered "but of a kindly, sweet disposition, void of all design; and so innocent in his own intentions that he suspected no one, so that you might have cheated him ten times in a day, if nine had not been sufficient for your purpose." He died in 1731, having been run through in Gibraltar in an argument over a goose, and having survived as far as a posting to Jamaica where one day, without warning or complaint, he "sat down in an arm-chair, and breathed his last, which was at Port Antonio, on the north of the island." This figure is familiar: we have met someone like him in *Tristram Shandy*.

The boy remained in school and read widely in French classical literature and then—following family tradition—went to Jesus College, Cambridge, as a sizar, supported by his cousin, described by Thackeray as "the Squire of Elvington." There he "read a little, laugh'd a great deal, and sometimes took the diversion of puzzling his tutors." His distant relation and dear friend, the louche and lively John Hall-Stevenson (who appears as Eugenius, the cautionary and directive voice in *Tristram Shandy*) started him on Rabelais, a determining influence when over two decades later he came to write. Thackeray sees him as "the occupier of Rabelais's easy chair, only fresh stuffed and more elegant than when in possession of the cynical old curate of Meudon." Virginia Woolf pictures Sterne and his friend reading Rochester and Aphra Behn "under a great walnut tree in the court of Jesus College." After a serious tubercular hemorrhage at College he realized how frail life was and resolved (it cannot have been too difficult a decision) to live for pleasure. He died at fifty-three, seven years younger than Defoe was when he started his career as a novelist.

He was impatient with most philosophers and their moral imperatives but came to love "the sagacious Locke": in his "doctrine of ideas" he recognized himself. Of *Tristram Shandy* he declared, "What it did arise from, I have hinted above, and a fertile source of obscurity it is,—and ever will be,—and that is the unsteady uses of words which have perplexed the clearest and most exalted understandings." Then there is a specific Locke-in-practice moment: "The thing is this," he says. "That of all the several ways of beginning a book which are now in practice throughout the known world, I am confident my own way of doing it is the best—I am sure it is the most religious—for I begin with writing the first sentence—and trusting to Almighty God for the second."

He took religious orders and was installed as vicar of Sutton-in-the-Forest, within his uncle's archdeaconry, in 1738 and stayed in post until 1759. He also saw preferment at the Minster and spent much time in York, the bustling, rather brilliant capital of the north of England. It is as well not to question his faith too closely. He taught the catechism and spoke of God as the "great sensorium of the world," a materialist and physiological conception in which it is hard to imagine the Trinity fitting comfortably. Whatever his beliefs, in 1744 he got the living of Stillington, near Sutton, and farmed it out to an assistant. By then he had married (1741) a sweetheart who turned sour, Elizabeth Lumley, "a homely woman" possessing much sentiment and a small fortune. The week after his marriage, legend has it, he preached a sermon on the text from the gospel of Luke 5:5, "We have toiled all night, and have taken nothing." He and Elizabeth "did not *gee* well together." She had phases of madness when she thought she was, for example, the Queen of Bohemia. The best thing she brought him was their daughter Lydia, whom she then took away with her.

The conflict with Uncle Jacques, precentor of York and archdeacon of Cleveland, may have been straightforward: he wanted his nephew to apply his writing skills to his own political campaigns; Laurence was not a pen for hire and may not have shared his uncle's principles. Another explanation is that Laurence got one of his uncle's women pregnant, or made inroads on his uncle's mistress. In any event, the bitterness of their relations grew, and when Laurence's mother and sister heard he had married a fortune they turned up on his doorstep expecting support. The fortune was not sufficient to meet their aspirations, nor was Laurence keen to have two demanding relations so close by. They turned to uncle Jacques, who had them put into something like a debtors' prison or workhouse, damaging Sterne's reputation. The damage survived their release, and Sterne's social and pecuniary reconciliation with his mother.

Because of his uncle, Sterne started spending more time away from York. John Hall-Stevenson eased his exile. He kept a disordered house at Skelton Castle, with a library full of dubious books. There he entertained the Brotherhood of the Demoniacs, pretend monks who were in fact local gentlemen and squires who drank, hunted, and told lewd stories, a congenial unholy order that delighted Sterne. Hall-Stevenson was an accomplished purveyor of salacious verse and wrote what Scott calls "the witty and indecent collection entitled *Crazy Tales.*" The word "Shandy" in local dialect meant "odd," "unpredictable," even "crazy."

Up until 1759, all that he had certainly written (or borrowed) was sermons. Then, as part of the politicking that went on in the Minster close, he published *A Political Romance,* a thinly veiled satire on the issues dividing the hierarchy. It defeated his foes and was suppressed. But Sterne was writing and being read. *Tristram Shandy* began. The first two volumes he wrote at speed and published in York at his own expense. He sent the volumes to the publisher Robert Dodsley in London, who at first resisted. Half the York printing was sent to Dodsley (at Sterne's risk) and the venture was successful. When Dodsley took on *Tristram Shandy* in earnest in 1760, printing it himself, Sterne added the famous footnotes, part of the work's madness and charm. Dodsley gave him £250 for the copyright to the first two volumes and a further £250 for the first two volumes of *The Sermons of Mr. Yorick.* The sermons advance was repeated for the third and fourth volumes. Sterne used part of the money to rent a house in Coxwold (where he had been awarded the perpetual curacy by Lord Fauconberg, who loved *Tristram Shandy,* though there was no rectory). He called it Shandy Hall (£12 per annum) and refurbished it.

Dodsley had published Johnson's *Rasselas.* He had also published Goldsmith and Pope. It cannot have pleased his established authors that he added the monstrous provincial Sterne to his catalog. Sterne's books were scandalous and well received, their authorship acknowledged, and in 1760 Sterne went to London to be lionized. Scott says, "He was engaged fourteen dinners deep." He returned home in his own carriage and pair later in the year. So famous was he, his friends claimed that a letter addressed to "Tristram Shandy, Europe" would reach him: his work crossed the Channel as well.

He planned to publish two volumes of *Tristram Shandy* each year. In London in 1761 he met Johnson at Reynolds's house, and Johnson took great offense. Sterne insisted on reading aloud and handed around "a drawing too indecently gross." Goldsmith and Richardson and Walpole joined the chorus of disapproval and established the moral tone that prevailed in some quarters for over a century. Thackeray, two and a half generations later, called him a "wretched worn-out old scamp." He *was* something of a scamp. His flirtations and, perhaps, adulteries had contributed to his wife's madness. In 1760 he entered into an intimate correspondence with Catherine de Fourmantelle at York (a young French woman residing there with her mother), and she is referred to in the novel as "dear, dear Jenny." The other major sentimental attachment of his later years was Mrs. Elizabeth Draper, for whom he kept a journal after she returned to her husband, Daniel Draper Esq., Counsellor of Bombay, and chief of the factory of Seurat. This was in 1767, the year in which the ninth and final volume of *Tristram Shandy* was published, and he arranged a final separation from his wife, who stayed on the Continent with Lydia.

Celebrity and seasons of heady living in London, combined with the cold and wet of Yorkshire, did nothing for Sterne's lungs, and in 1762 he was forced to go abroad for his health. From that time forward he had entered into his famous race with Death. When volumes seven and eight of *Tristram Shandy* appeared (the excitement surrounding his work having begun to die down), he started his seven-month tour of France and Italy, the crucial matter for his only other venture into fiction, *A Sentimental Journey,* published shortly before his death in 1768.

He died of pleurisy in an Old Bond Street lodging house, and he was reportedly penniless. His body was snatched from the graveyard of St. George's, Hanover Square, and sent for dissection by a Cambridge anatomist. The skull was trepanned, and then one witness recognized Sterne's face and fainted. Under cover of darkness the body was returned to London and reinterred. His skull and maybe a few bones, gathered up at the time of the deconsecration of St. George's graveyard and its rededication to property developers, were identified thanks to Nollekens's bust, removed from London, and now lie in the damp of the Coxwold churchyard.

His wife and daughter at the time of his death benefited from a collection organized by Eliza Draper, and by the income from three further volumes of sermons (1769). Mr. Yorick's conversation with Eliza was published, and further forgeries followed. A number of imitations and sequels litter the Sterne bibliography. As early as 1760 John Carr wrote a volume of *Tristram Shandy,* and John Hall-Stevenson composed a continuation of *A Sentimental Journey.* Sterne had intended it to be four volumes and only two were completed, so Hall-Stevenson might have said he was fulfilling a sacred duty. In Sterne's book, humor gives way to sentiment. We do laugh, it is impossible not to, at the strangely quixotic progress of the hero to Calais, Rouen, Paris, the Bourbonnais (where he finds

Maria from volume seven of *Tristram Shandy*), and almost to Lyons. Then the book stops, on the very brink of overstepping the propriety Sterne has vowed not to breach again, after all the charges against his big book. Yorick is sentimentally engaged by everything, in contrast to the bilious Smelfungus, a cruel caricature of Smollett, with whom Sterne coincided in Montpellier in the winter of 1763–1764, and Mundungus, caricaturing Dr. S. Shar, a grumpy and ungenerous traveler.

The 1780 *Collected Works* included letters, and plates by William Hogarth. Sterne had admired Hogarth and even ventured to imitate him. He was, after all, an amateur painter and musician as well as a writer. He recommended Hogarth's *Analysis of Beauty* to readers of *Tristram Shandy*. Rowlandson and Cruickshank later illustrated his works. The painter Gainsborough named one of his two dogs, a perky collie, Tristram.

It took eight years for *The Life and Opinions of Tristram Shandy, Gentleman* to emerge. In the end there was little of his life and few of his opinions. The epigraph from Epictetus appended to the second edition, translated from the Greek, says, "Not actions, but opinions about actions, unsettle men." The hero is not born until volume four and not "breeched" (put into trousers) until volume six. We do, however, learn many of the opinions of other characters, and we gather a sense of their past lives, even if the present they occupy seems remote from the times of action they enjoyed. First there is Walter Shandy of Shandy Hall, irritable, candid, giving, a man of contradictions, like Sterne's father in tetchy innocence and generosity. Uncle Toby bears no relation to Sterne's uncle Jacques; Toby's groin wound from the siege of Namur becomes an indecent focus of tension, speculation, and fascination: just what and how much did he lose? Uncle Toby's hobby is to recreate the scene and circumstances of his trauma: he devises in miniature on his bowling green the battlefield. He is a man "of unparalleled modesty" and benignity. Beside him stands his devoted man Corporal Trim, wounded in the knee at Linden, willing to play Sancho to Toby's Quixote and to share his enthusiasms. Yorick the parson is said to encompass Sterne's sense of himself. Of the remaining cast, some are drawn from the purlieus of York Minster, some from the townspeople of York. Dr. Slop, Mrs. Shandy, the eager Widow Wadman have taproots in a real world.

The book is in deliberate disorder. The preface starts in volume four. Slawkenbergius's treatise on noses and how they take shape against the hardness or softness of the nurse's breast during feeding (lifted more or less wholesale from Rabelais) disrupts the narrative, but so does almost everything else, such as Corporal Trim on Morality in volume five, or in volume six the "affecting episode of Le Fevre" and the dialogue at Tristram's breeching. Volumes seven and eight forget the preceding volumes and follow the author's travels in France, including the story of the king of Bohemia (in response, perhaps, to his wife's royal fantasy). In volume nine we pursue the affair between Uncle Toby and the widow Wadman.

In *Tristram Shandy* Sterne has gone more for consistency than structure, a consistency that is temporal (he gets the time sequences right even though he does not pursue chronology: the dates work, there is a consistent temporal infrastructure we can tease out if we wish to) and tonal, as though the book were a rambling commentary on foreknown actions. The language exceeds its occasions.

Though there is limited consecutive narrative, there are coherent settings and stable architectural spaces in which the characters move. Malcolm Bradbury shows how Shandy Hall becomes "part of the imaginative topography of the novel." It is one of those writers' houses that adds to an understanding of the work, the way Strawberry Hill, Chawton, Abbotsford, the Parsonage at Haworth, and Lamb House do. Sterne went to live at Coxwold just after he became famous. Shandy Hall is near the church and on a scale appropriate to the parson-author. He named it after the Shandy family. A little room at the front became his study, and there he composed in a drizzle of ink the subsequent volumes of *Tristram Shandy* and much of *A Sentimental Journey*. He was continually caught short with new ideas and having to run home to write them down while they were fresh. In earlier days he had stopped on his way to preach and gone back for his gun if one of his hounds flushed out some game; now it was language that interrupted him.

Sterne was never healthy at Shandy Hall, but he loved the security and stability of his "philosophical hut" with its homely irregularities of line and incline, twenty rooms to which he added features: paneling, Adam fireplaces, alcoves. He built Eliza Draper a choice apartment. Though his "wife elect" would never in fact visit, he could enter her space and be with her. He liked to solidify in stone and mortar the loose associations his imagination made, creating atmospheres into which voices could be summoned. Uncle Toby followed the same impulse, through maps and construction, recreating the place where he received the wound that provided so much of his identity.

The fault from which Sterne himself suffers, the sin he committed again and again, is far more insidious than an old war wound. His daughter included in a posthumous collection of his letters and fragments an "Extract in the Manner of Rabelais" in which a clergyman called Homenas takes down a book and is "transcribing it away like a little devil." He works "without any felonious intent," though he is committing an act of intellectual theft. As a priest, he was in good company as a plagiarist: it is unlikely that every Sunday in the eighteenth (or any other) century, in the thousands of parishes of the English-speaking world, vicars were writing original sermons. There were sermon collections in print and Homenas, or Sterne, or Mr. Yorick, weary after a Saturday carousal or barren of theological resource, reached for the anthologies. Once started, Sterne found it hard to break the habit of plagiarism. He has enthusiasms, sentiments, but his originality is formal, not intellectual, and the form he chooses and develops is hungry and commodious enough to contain anything. This make him a modernist *avant la lettre,* an anthologist, a shuffler of other men's ideas and images. We discover gobbets, scarcely digested, of Rabelais and Cervantes, of Montaigne and Erasmus, Horace and Bacon, Swift and Hall, of dozens of minor French and English writers, and most particularly, of Robert Burton's *The Anatomy of Melancholy.*

In 1812 Dr. John Ferriar of Manchester anatomized Sterne's plagiarisms in *Illustrations of Sterne.* Sterne steals not only in the novels but in the sermons, blatantly, even from famous writers like Bishop Hall, and then allows his sermons to be printed. It is one thing to use another writer to kick-start your own sermon or novel machine, quite another to borrow the machine. For Sterne, even the language love generates is interchangeable between relationships. In 1740 he wrote feelingly to and for Elizabeth, his wife to be. Twenty-seven years later he used the same writing to express his sentiments for Eliza. Both were, when the heat was on, the real thing; time had passed, but the language still said what it said, and he plagiarized himself. Self-plagiarism is a form of husbandry: why go to the expense of bespoke phrases when there is adequate accoutrement for feeling in the "off the peg" range?

Scott was inclined to forgive "the most unhesitating plagiarist who ever cribbed from his predecessors in order to garnish his own pages" on the grounds of his tact in appropriation. Scott quotes from Ferriar an amusing example: Sterne borrowed from Burton Burton's own diatribe against plagiarism. Scott is only *inclined* to forgive: Sterne possessed a genius that did not need to resort to fishing with so large a net in other men's waters.

It was not Sterne's freedom with other people's writing that made Goethe declare him the freest spirit of his century, or Nietzsche the freest writer of all time, though that spirit of "making free" is part of the genius of this devourer and regurgitator. "He is a writer claiming fictional freedom—freedom to have his chapters in the wrong order," says Malcolm Bradbury, "the preface in the middle, the freedom to digress, upturn, change narrators, go back." Sterne claims descent from Rabelais, but Rabelais's rambling and tangents are part of a narrative and discursive structure; they are not the principle and dynamic of the style. Rabelais's rambling was shrewd contrivance to contravene the censor, among other things. Sterne's is different in kind, putting himself, or his narrator, always in the frame, displacing the ostensible subject until we realize *he* is the subject. "For in this long digression which I was accidentally led into, as in all my digressions (one only excepted) there is a masterstroke of digressive skill, the merit of which has all along, I fear, been overlooked by the reader,—not for want of penetration in him,—but because 'tis an excellence seldom looked for, or expected indeed, in a digression;—and it is this: That tho' my digressions are all fair, as you observe,—and that I fly off from what I am about, as far and as often as any writer in *Great-Britain;* yet I constantly take care to order affairs so, that my main business does not stand still in my absence."

He works in from the periphery to create a center. A stuttering progression. Paragraphs like mattresses stuffed with a hay of dashes consist of a single intermittent sentence. The incongruity between desire, intention, plan, and the reality that misdelivers everything, is deliberate, and at every stage epistemological issues arise, but as conceits, not actual problems. Greene reflected on the tiny scale of Sterne when we compare him to Rabelais, the absence of real risk. "There is nothing he can tell us about anyone, we feel, but himself, and that self has been so tidied and idealized that it would be unrecognisable, one imagines, to his wife."

The Italian novelist Italo Calvino described the impact of *Tristram Shandy* on Diderot's *Jacques the Fatalist.* For Diderot, Richardson's votary, Sterne was an opposite talisman. His freedom contrasted with the relentless decorums of eighteenth-century French taste. Sterne met Diderot in France and later sent him English books; in return Diderot plagiarized Sterne, but without apology (indeed, announcing it before a concluding scene, something Sterne did not have the courtesy to do with Burton, for example). Calvino describes the core theme of *Tristram Shandy* as the Lockean one, "the concatenation of causes, the inextricable linkage of circumstances which determines every event, even the most insignificant, and which has taken the place of Fate for modern writers and readers." The irony is that the sentences of Sterne's text seem themselves to be parts of this concatenation, and once begun they have an insidious and irresistible logic. "The great gift bequeathed by Sterne . . . to world literature as a whole, which would subsequently affect a fashion for romantic irony," says Calvino, "was his unbuttoned attitude, his giving vent to his humors, the acrobatics of his writing." These humors, the gravity-defying acrobatics, in Diderot and Sterne owe a primary debt to Cervantes. Scott calls Sterne's style "vigorous and masculine," which is entirely wrong: it is deliberately enervated and, despite what Calvino calls his "misogyny," genderless.

Some readers find *Tristram Shandy* too discontinuous. Although Coleridge admired the first two books (the later parts about the widow Wadman he found "stupid and disgusting" and *A Sentimental Journey* "poor sickly stuff"), he conceded, "There is a great deal of affectation in Sterne . . . but still the characters of Trim and the two Shandys are most individual and delightful. Sterne's morals are bad, but I don't think they can do much harm to anyone whom they would not find bad enough before. Besides, the oddity and erudite grimaces under which much of his dirt is hidden, take away the effect for the most part; although, to be sure, the book is scarcely readable by women." Thackeray declares (though he much admires him), "There is not a page of Sterne's writing but has something that were better away, a latent corruption—a hint, as of an impure presence . . . The foul satyr's eyes leer out of the leaves constantly." Greene is repelled by the schoolboy cutenesses and humor and offended by the durable success of Sterne as against the gathering neglect of Fielding. We undervalue Fielding's technical innovations while Sterne, "who contributed nothing, can still give more pleasure because of what we call his genius, his skill at self-portraiture." For Greene even Uncle Toby is part of the author's egotism, his only "other" in the narcissistic pool, and even reflected in him he preens himself. Yet he concedes reluctantly, "No, one must surrender to Sterne most of the graces. What Fielding possessed, and Sterne did not, was something quite as new to the novel as Sterne's lightness and sensibility, moral seriousness." Even the mention of such a thing may send a chill through the modern reader.

As against Fielding's architecture, we have "this rhapsodical work," as he calls it. Early in the process of composition, which later writers imitate to loosen the shackles of causality or produce stream of consciousness, he discovers what he is about. "These unforeseen stoppages, which I own I had no conception of when I first set out; — but which, I am convinced now, will rather increase than diminish as I advance, — have struck out a hint which I am resolved to follow; — and that is, — not to be in a hurry; — but to go on leisurely, writing and publishing two volumes of my life every year; — which, if I am suffered to go on quietly, and can make a tolerable bargain with my bookseller, I shall continue to do as long as I live." But elsewhere he puts it differently: "It is a history-book, Sir, . . . of what passes in a man's own mind." One must close numerous ellipses to bring Sterne to direct sense, but direct sense is always there. When he compares writers with painters, he says that both err in the same way: "Where an exact copying makes our pictures less striking, we choose the less evil; deeming it even more pardonable to trespass against truth, than beauty."

*Tristram Shandy* is less a parody of the novel form as it was, more an appraisal by example of the limitations and shortcomings of the art of factual or fictional biography, the approach familiar to us from Mandeville to Foxe, Defoe to Smollett. Sterne asks in his roundabout way: Where does life start? What can it mean? What can we really know?

Another Yorkshire writer, but one who had an answer for everything, J. B. Priestley, insists, "Modern literature begins with Sterne . . . He seems to jump clean out of the ponderous eighteenth century, testing our patience, into our own time, impatient of inessentials. Scores of European novelists, hundreds of able journalists, owe a gigantic debt to Sterne's exquisite literary sensibility, his feeling for the very rhythm of intimate speech, his courage and audacity." Why is that gayest and most social century, the eighteenth, described as ponderous? Because the books are too long for a lazy twenty-first century? Ponderousness and shadow belong to the tubercular nineteenth century and to Priestley's own Marxizing twentieth. Greene cannot resist but cannot endorse *Tristram Shandy:* he places it in a kind of quarantine where we can visit so long as we wash our hands when we come away. The book "exists, a lovely sterile eccentricity, the last word in literary egotism."

# The Eerie

Horace Walpole, Clara Reeve, William Beckford, Ann Radcliffe,
Matthew Gregory Lewis, Charles Brockden Brown, Charles Robert Maturin

In the history of the novel, the Gothic (Edith Wharton prefers to call it "the eerie" because Gothic is too European and architectural) has a specific, dark and stormy birthday, and we can clearly describe its nightmare characteristics, especially in its early manifestations. It archaizes. It seeks its matter and its properties in the past. The Roman Catholic past and the age of superstition are favored, Italy and Spain provide many haunts, heroes, heroines, and villains. There is also the Muslim East, mysterious and alien. Virginia Woolf sees the Gothic as "a parasite, an artificial commodity, produced half in joke in reaction against the current style, or in relief from it."

There are similarities between the excesses of the Gothic and the steaming gore of Jacobean drama. In the plays of John Webster and John Ford, for example, the legacy of the Italian *novelle* is clear in the plots, which, however alien, are well made. Characters speak, their dialogue full of surprise and novelty. There is less mystery than passion in the plays. What the Jacobean dramatists learned from their predecessors and the romances of Italy and Spain, the English Gothic writers learned from their nightmares and anxieties and the stereotypes that informed their prejudices. They abandoned the credible material worlds of Defoe, Richardson, and Fielding for a spectral zone. The Gothic is an unusual English invention: it plays with types, and it is not content with the world of contingencies. It goes to sleep to get its plots, rather than staying awake to the world. Its theatrical analogies are with Romantic opera, the interminable death arias, statues that come alive, sudden lightning, rather than with the verse drama of earlier centuries.

Characters in the Gothic novels have much in common with characters in allegory. They embody properties and qualities: virgin innocence, chivalry, evil. Physically they are clearly defined as types. There are antique elements of diction and structural features, especially contrived spookiness, generating anxiety in the reader. Of all fictional forms, the Gothic most deliberately manipulates readers: writing for effect, for very *similar* effects.

Horace Walpole went to bed one night in June 1764 in the Great North Bedchamber at Strawberry Hill, Twickenham. He awoke from a tremendous nightmare: he was in a castle where, "on the uppermost banister of a great staircase I saw a gigantic hand in armor." On his own staircase in his pseudo-Gothic castle, which he had been enhancing since he moved into it in 1747, he had hung armor, but the dream dramatically increased the scale and brought with it a thrilling terror. The very next evening, after tea, he began writing, partly out of eagerness to find out what happened next, and partly because, he says, he wanted to stop thinking about matters that were troubling him. Adventure—and escape. He wrote from teatime until half past one in the morning. His hand was too cramped to continue, and he "left Matilda and Isabella talking in the middle of a paragraph." He generally claimed to have written the book in eight days. It certainly has about it a sense of haste, but according to a letter, it took him longer, though "less than two months." This was *The Castle of Otranto,* later subtitled *A Gothic Story* to indicate its historical period. But the term *Gothic* stuck.

Walpole had his own printing press, but nervous of what critics might say, he entrusted this romance to a London printer and issued it under a pseud-onym. Not only a pseudonym: he claimed that the book was a translation, by "William Marshall," of an Italian original by Onuphrio [Humphrey] Muralto [*Mur,* Wall; *alto,* high], "Canon of the Church of St. Nicholas, at Otranto." The original "was found in the library of an ancient Catholic family in the north of England. It was printed at Naples, in the black letter, in the year 1529 . . . The principal incidents are such as were believed in the darkest ages of Christianity; but the language and conduct have nothing that savors of barbarism. The style is the purest Italian." And the most formal English. In his preface Walpole wreathed his anonymous brow with laurel: he remarks the "beauty of the diction, and the zeal of the author (moderated, however, by singular judgment)."

*The Castle of Otranto* was a forgery when first published, a deliberate imposi-tion upon readers, the author keeping a distance from the work to create, much more than a suspension of disbelief in the reader, actual belief. Forgery was a way of eluding the conventions that checked his genius and that of his contem-poraries, like the poet Thomas Gray. James Macpherson's Ossianic forgeries and Thomas Chatterton's medievalizing Rowley poems and plays arrogate ancient authority. The author of *Otranto* might have been more generous to young Chatterton, who, inspired by his example, came to London from Bristol in 1769 seeking his patronage, and was rebuffed. This rebuff stands against Walpole. Had he helped the "marvellous boy," Chatterton might have survived to be a marvelous man. Instead, starving and in despair, he poisoned himself with ar-senic in a rented room in Holborn in his eighteenth year.

*The Castle of Otranto* was published on Christmas Eve 1764, official birthday of the Gothic, and "enjoyed an instant and surprising success. Quite a considerable number of distinguished persons were afraid to go to bed after reading it," Edmund Gosse records. The book was not just a local phenomenon. It went through twenty-one editions before 1800, appearing in Dublin, Amsterdam, Berlin, Parma, and Paris. The modern reader must remember that what Walpole wrote in the wake of nightmare was unprecedented and had a striking freshness. The solid eighteenth century sinisterly wavered in the taper light. He set out, Walpole said in his second preface, owning up to authorship after the book's success, "to blend two kinds of romance, the ancient and the modern."

To old Madame du Deffand in Paris, who sent him 840 surviving letters in her own hand and was almost blind and in love with him, though he could not accommodate her in his overfurnished heart, Walpole confided that *The Castle of Otranto* was his favorite among his works, for there "j'ai laissé courir mon imagination." Sir Walter Scott translates: "I have given rein to my imagination till I became on fire with the visions and feelings which it excited. I have composed it in defiance of rules, of critics, and of philosophers." It was a kind of possession, fire and feeling not being habitual to him. "He was indeed a garrulous *old* man nearly all his days," Hazlitt declares, and also "the very prince of Gossips," meaning it as a compliment and imbuing the author with Wildean attributes. "His mind, as well as his house, was piled up with Dresden china, and illuminated through painted glass; and we look upon his heart to have been little better than a case full of enamels, painted eggs, ambers, lapis-lazuli, cameos, vases and rock-crystals." Hazlitt notes Walpole's "utter poverty of feeling": feeling has been displaced by material enthusiasms. He wears the penitential horsehair as an "outer garment," the undergarments being of silk.

A Miss Hawkins described young Harry, excruciatingly affected in his approach, on tiptoe, knees bent, a ridiculous *politesse:* "His dress in visiting was most usually, in summer, when I most saw him, a lavender suit, the waistcoat embroidered with a little silver, or of white silk worked in the tambour, partridge silk stockings, and gold buckles, ruffles and frill generally lace." He never maintained an identity for long: impresario, grandee, gentleman host, author, collector, member of Parliament (for three different constituencies between 1741 and 1767), traveler, patron. Recalling Chatterton, Wordsworth dubbed him "that cold and false-hearted Frenchified coxcomb."

Horace Walpole, who came into the title of Fourth Earl of Orford after his most notable work was done, was the son of Sir Robert Walpole, the Whig leader, prime minister, and chancellor of the exchequer from 1715 to 1717 (the year Horace was born) and then from 1721 to 1742. The boy, like his father, enjoyed every privilege of access. He went to Eton, of course. There one of his best friends was Thomas Gray. They created an elaborate fictional life for themselves. Horry became Celadon, Gray Orozmades, and they were joined by

Favonius or Zephyrus (Richard West) and Almanzor (Thomas Ashton). These four established the Quadruple Alliance, coming together in mutual hatred of the sporting fraternity and sharing a love for classical poetry. In 1739 Celadon and Orozmades embarked on a tour of France and Italy. They fell out and remained estranged for four years, then reconciled. Walpole commissioned a portrait of Gray at thirty-one. When Walpole's cat drowned in a goldfish bowl, the accident elicited from Gray the great comic elegy "Ode on the Death of a Favorite Cat," satirizing the character of Woman, of which neither had much experience. Walpole superintended Gray's publications from his Strawberry Hill Press, whose chief activity was to publish his own writing on painting and history.

His misgivings about *Otranto* had to do with the preposterous story. Manfred, wicked prince of Otranto, is grandson of the usurper who poisoned Alfonso, the rightful Duke. His frail son Conrad and lovely Isabella are to be married, and he is keen to speed up the process though the boy is only fifteen. He wants the line, and the lie, to continue. Before the marriage can take place his son is crushed by an enormous helmet. Manfred determines to possess Isabella himself, though he is already provided with a devoted wife, the patient Hippolita. Isabella flees (this is the central action in much Gothic fiction, the fleeing beautiful innocent) and he follows. She is helped by Theodore, a peasant who looks suspiciously like the murdered Alfonso. Theodore is imprisoned but Manfred's daughter Matilda frees him and he falls in love with her. Sensing that Theodore is in love with Isabella, Manfred, at Alfonso's tomb, in error slays his daughter Matilda where she is praying with Theodore. Theodore is revealed to be the rightful heir (Manfred has delivered him inadvertently from incest, another perennial Gothic theme) and in a lugubrious spirit marries Isabella instead. Manfred is forced to confess and perishes. With the Gothic, says Peter Ackroyd, who has himself strayed into that zone, English writers can "depict horror with a certain theatricality, and garnish evil with a touch of humorous relish."

Writing in 1821, Byron celebrated Walpole as "author of the first romance and of the last tragedy in our language, and surely worthy of a higher place than any living writer, be he who he may." *Otranto* was the romance, distinguished more for its progeny than in itself. The verse tragedy to which Byron refers is *The Mysterious Mother* (1768), described by Scott as "horribly impressive but disgusting." It explores the remorse of a mother (the Countess of Narbonne) for an act of incest she committed years before with her son. He, in turn, has married their daughter, his sister. The Countess kills herself. The play, bad as it is, gave even more to the Gothic than *Otranto*. "What is this secret sin; this untold tale, / That art cannot extract, nor penance cleanse?" Mrs. Radcliffe quotes these lines in her Gothic excursion, *The Italian*. A revival in 2001 at the Citizens Theatre, Glasgow, revealed the inertia of Walpole's dramatic masterpiece, the revelation of incest coming less as dramatic climax than sensational effect.

The most glaring formal fault in *Otranto* has to do with continuity and plotting. Gosse is astonished at how *artless* the book is. The huge falling helmet is not like the chandelier in *Phantom of the Opera:* it crashes down, it eliminates the (innocently usurping) heir to the dukedom, but its provenance and size are not explained, its remains are not removed. Does it stay there in the courtyard, breeze fretting its sable plumes? It is conceived for effect, and once the effect is delivered it dissolves. Walpole is flash of lightning and thunderclap, never clouds and steady rain. Later we have the arm and armor, the portrait that comes to life and steps out of its frame, the statue with the bloody nose. Whatever they did for the eighteenth-century reader, in the twenty-first they keep no one awake.

Scott, close in time to Walpole, believed in him as a writer and an artist. He was simply "the best letter-writer in the English language." *Otranto* is "one of the standard works in our lighter literature." He admires qualities he aspires to in his own writing. More than the excitation of surprise and horror, Walpole attempts through particular detail, "the costume of the period in which the scene was laid," and a harmonizing of means and ends, to impart a sense of the world in which the events might have occurred. It seems to Scott less an act of creation than of conjuration, so that for the duration of the spell, we believe, in the way that superstitious, twelfth-century Catholics believed; he creates such a sense of context, says Scott, that he disarms our resisting skepticism. It undoubtedly worked for Scott.

Walpole's effects proceed, he suggests, from the same source as his architectural and other enthusiasms: "It was his object to unite the marvellous turn of incident and imposing tone of chivalry, exhibited in the ancient romance, with that accurate display of human character and contrast of feelings and passions which is, or ought to be, delineated in the modern novel." Scott's sense of a connection between Walpole's writing, building, and collecting is astute. *Otranto* was written the same year that the Gallery at Strawberry Hill, with its mock fan vaulting and gothic traceries, was being completed. How fabulous, by candlelight, the shadow play must have been. It was an opera set, like so much else at Strawberry Hill, requiring the master of the house to invent plots and arias, to find a history for so curious a collection of deliberate accidents and follies, and to dress for various parts. Thomas Gray calls it "all Gothicism, and gold, and crimson, and looking glass." The Norwich damask, bright crimson, must have seized the eyes in both hands, contrasting with what he called "the gloomth of abbeys and cathedrals." Strawberry Hill was not a place to die in: that was reserved for his London house at 11 Berkeley Square in 1797.

In reading Scott on Walpole, in setting Strawberry Hill alongside Scott's Abbotsford as expressions of character and personality, we realize to what extent the Gothic caught the imagination of the writer who was to mean more to the early nineteenth century than any other. Scott likes Walpole's *style,* so ultimate, so remote from the style of *Rasselas,* so little adorned, so unencumbered, so classical in "the best" sense; and so (we might argue) inappropriate for the period and themes evoked. Its thrift makes us think of it more as a sketch for a longer tale than a tale in itself. It is brief, long-winded only when it should be succinct, as in the death scenes with the big duets and arias, and the syrupy Matilda blessing and re-blessing her father, heaping coals of love on his already flaming head. It is a relief when her spirit exits the body through the holes he made, even if it is not seen to soar straight up to heaven. " 'I would say something more,' said Matilda, struggling, 'but it cannot be—Isabella—Theodore— for my sake—Oh!—' she expired." Hippolita is prized free of the corpse, "but Theodore threatened destruction to all who attempted to remove him from it. He printed a thousand kisses on her clay-cold hands, and uttered every expression that despairing love could dictate." "—Oh!—" Outside opera, has ever a final gasp been so hard-earned, so welcome when at last it was expired?

In Walpole's wake follows an inexhaustible fleet of Gothic novelists, a few of whom can be conjured here. They entertain their different ages; some of their works survive and retain a numerous, if specialized, readership. First among them is the lavish eccentric William Beckford (1759–1844), described by Hazlitt as "an industrious *bijoutier,*" like Walpole a child of privilege. His father was Lord Mayor of London during Wilkes's premiership, and his fortune—the largest in England—was based on Jamaican sugar and the things that went with it: estates, slavery. His mother was descended from Mary Stuart. Lady Hamilton was an aunt. Scandal—and untold wealth. When he was five, he was "tutored" in music by the nine-year-old Mozart and remained a delightful harpsichordist. Painting he learned from Alexander Cozens, and Sir William Chambers instructed him in architecture. He finished his education in Geneva and "did" the Continent, especially Portugal, and in 1778 (he was nineteen) he returned to England. He came into a fortune worth a million pounds, with income of £100,000 per annum. He longed to become a peer but his scandals interposed. In 1783 he married Lady Margaret Gordon who bore him two daughters. In the autumn of the first year of his marriage, rumors of a relationship with sixteen-year-old William "Kitty" Courtenay, son of Viscount Courtenay, during a visit to Powderham Castle, spread into the press. He was ostracized to such an extent that he went into exile on the Continent with his family. There two years later his young wife died. Byron, who was familiar with irregular passions, evoked "Unhappy Vathek" in *Childe Harold,* though the passage was suppressed until

1833: "How wondrous bright thy blooming morn arose! / But thou wert smitten with unhallowed thirst / Of nameless crime, and thy sad day must close / To scorn, and Solitude unsought—the worst of woes." Echoes of Milton: the fallen Lucifer.

From 1785 to 1798 Beckford lived abroad, traveling widely, returning to England only to visit. On one stay in 1790 he acquired Fonthill Abbey, possibly because of its association with Mervyn Touchet, an ancestor of his and Earl of Castlehaven, executed in 1631 after conviction in the first recorded trial for sodomy. He began to reconstruct the Wiltshire abbey as a Gothic extravagance, which he filled with not always choice pieces by choice artists, spending his inheritance at speed.

It was in the wake of a three-day Christmas party thrown in "Kitty's" honor in 1782 that *Vathek* was conceived, and Beckford claims that he wrote the book in outline at one long sitting, three days and two nights. Other reports suggest that he took a year over it. He wrote it in French, and it was later translated into English by an obliging clergyman and published in 1786. Byron at one time regarded *Vathek* as his "gospel." In *The Giaour* he acknowledged the "sublime tale," comparing the "Halls of Eblis" favorably with the exquisite "Happy Valley" in *Rasselas*.

Unlike Strawberry Hill, which rose piecemeal out of the excited imagination of Walpole, and which Beckford dubbed a "gothic mousetrap," there was in Fonthill a grand consistency of proportion. Walpole was jealous of his ostentatious disciple. Absent from Fonthill was the unpredictability of a building growing in response to need and change that makes the Gothic compelling. There was no *necessity* to the architecture, which was grandiloquent rather than eloquent. In order that it should be completed quickly and economically, Fonthill was erected out of inferior materials. The 275-foot tower (reminiscent less of Salisbury Cathedral's, more of Orthanc, Saruman's tower in *The Lord of the Rings*) collapsed in 1807; it was immediately rebuilt. Hazlitt memorialized Fonthill as "a desert of magnificence, a glittering waste of laborious idleness, a cathedral turned into a toy-shop," a monument to what is costly, and worthless. The only evidence of good taste in Beckford, Hazlitt said, was his getting rid of Fonthill. By the time the tower collapsed a second time Beckford had sold the estate and withdrawn to another, smaller but still grand pile near Bath. Lansdown Tower was neoclassical: clearly Beckford had had a bellyful of Gothic. When he died in 1844, well into his eighties, it is said that he preserved nearly to the end the rather pert good looks and smooth face he had worn in the previous century. Dorian Gray may have been a godson of his life story.

Beckford's two best-remembered creations are Gothic: Fonthill and *Vathek*. Beckford had already seen into print his accounts of travel in *Dreams, Waking*

*Thoughts, and Incidents* (1783, suppressed; republished 1834). *Vathek: an Arabian Tale* was quite different. It has been called the 1002nd Arabian Night. Caliph Vathek, grandson of Haroun-al-Raschid, the articulate and effective Abbasid caliph of the Arab Empire, has fallen under the evil influence of Carathis, his bewitching (in both senses) mother. He is insatiably curious and megalomaniacal. To achieve his ends he becomes the devil's servant, sacrificing fifty handsome youths in a scene of sexual suggestiveness and tension. He sets off from Samarah to Istakar, a ruined city beneath which he, a collector like Beckford with a desire to see the ultimate of everything, hopes to discover the treasures of the sultans of pre-Adamite times. In his travels he falls in love with Nouronihar, the beautiful daughter of an emir, and she joins his caravan, as keen as he is to know the unknowable and to experience the forbidden. The caliph has also succumbed to the charms of her cousin Gulchenrouz, a juicy lad. After various adventures in which his curiosity and power are tested, he is permitted to descend to the "subterranean halls of Eblis" and suddenly realizes the vanity of his ambitions and wealth. Here commences the eternal torture his cruelty and his irreversible pact with the devil have secured him and those who follow him. Chief punishment is the loss of hope. Beckford writes best of Vathek's desires, of young beauty on the point of puberty, and of the hell into which he and his fellow-damned descend. Part of the punishment is being condemned to be one with the "accursed multitude." Borges claims that the Palace of Subterranean Fire is "Beckford's greatest achievement" and "the first truly atrocious hell in literature." Horrible things happen to people in Dante's *Inferno*, but Beckford's Palace is horrible in itself.

Beckford, like Walpole, writes a clear style, but the clarity opens onto a more subtle and consistent world than Manfred's. Vathek is a larger monster than Manfred. He is not confined to a little Duchy but ranges across his world, and his cruelties and evil deeds are rooted in a theatrical metaphysics actually informed by a familiarity with some Eastern customs, though Beckford's grasp of Islam is fanciful. He tends to eroticize everything, from the beauty of youth to the pains of victims. Characters have a certain reality, but the world they move in is dreamlike. The reality of the novel merges with the stage paste of romantic masque.

After "Kitty," Beckford remained in the social doghouse for the rest of his life, but he made his mark on others outside the aristocracy, including the young Benjamin Disraeli. He was less concerned with the politics of the future prime minister, more with his writing, which he encouraged, especially praising *The Wondrous Tale of Alroy* with its debts to *Vathek*. George Meredith's *The Shaving of Shagpat* is out of *Vathek's* stable as well, and Joris-Karl Huysmans's *À rebours* (*Against Nature*) has it at heart. In 1876 the French symbolist poet Stéphane

Mallarmé wrote an introduction to a translation of *Vathek* (Beckford was to him what Poe was to Baudelaire), and the poetry of Algernon Charles Swinburne was brushed by Beckford's wing. How could he have resisted a symbolism so much more rounded and bold than Walpole's, or dialogue so excruciatingly mannered? "Gulchenrouz, alarmed at the agitation of his cousin, said to her with a supplicating accent: 'Let us be gone; the sky looks portentous, the tamarisks tremble more than common, and the raw wind chills my very heart; come! let us be gone; 'tis a melancholy night!'" Later that same evening there is a delicious silliness about the scene. A eunuch "who excelled in dressing a salad, having filled large bowls of porcelain with eggs of small birds, curds turned with citron juice, slices of cucumber, and the inmost leaves of delicate herbs, handed it round from one to another, and gave each their shares in a large spoon of Cocknos. Gulchenrouz, nestling as usual in the bosom of Nouronihar, pouted out his vermilion little lips against the offer of Sutlememe, and would take it only from the hand of his cousin, on whose mouth he hung like a bee inebriated with the quintessence of flowers."

Ronald Firbank is prefigured here, but Beckford's earnest manner suggests he took it all rather seriously, as in a dream from which there was no ironic waking. All are damned: "Thus the Caliph Vathek, who, for the sake of empty pomp and forbidden power, had sullied himself with a thousand crimes, became a prey to grief without end, and remorse without mitigation." But there is a happy ending for "the humble and despised Gulchenrouz" who, released, could now pass "whole ages in undisturbed tranquillity, and the pure happiness of childhood."

Dreams enjoy privileges in the Gothic that they do not earn in other fiction: there is prophecy in dreams, there are legends and prophecies implicit in narrated fact. The supernatural, the inexplicable, are tolerated as part of the "nature" within which the story unfolds. The figure of the wicked father, and by extension of the empowered male villain, preying off vulnerable (usually female) adolescents, with strong sexual overtones in the writing, is another commonplace. Is it a convention established by Walpole and persisted in, or does it answer to a need in the different authors? Is *The Castle of Otranto,* more than a dream, about the violence and virulence of fathers? Is *Vathek* a kind of confession and exorcism? Along with Gothic conventions comes something else, something not found in Defoe, Richardson, or Fielding, a miasmic sense that the rules of nature, human and otherwise, are in abeyance. An exotic setting, a remote historical moment, privilege a story to break rules of causality, plausibility, morality. Troubled spirits rise and walk again, the past is, terrifyingly, never past, while the future can lean into the frame and disclose itself in a chilling note of terror.

Certainly young Matthew Gregory Lewis (1775–1818), at the age of twenty trying to provide for his mother who had been abandoned by his father, seems to be settling scores in *The Monk* (1796), where, H. P. Lovecraft says, he displays "a new malignity." He wrote it—all 400 pages, it much exceeds the extent of *Otranto* and *Vathek* together—in three weeks, he said. Why this insistence on speed, from Walpole on, as though authors wish to affirm the urgency and spontaneity of the work, and to be taken in their own right as prodigious? Lewis was certainly in Walpole's debt, and he intended his book to shock. Why should readers be given a happy ending when all the material of the novel pointed in the other direction? So there is murder, indecency, and affront, the reader is shocked. Even Byron blanched when he first read it. Lewis became for posterity "Monk" Lewis, just as for Byron Beckford became Vathek, despite the character of their fictional characters.

Lewis based his novel on German models, and the form of the original published version was chaotic. The author revised and reshaped it for subsequent printings, but it remains a scramble, careless and (like *Otranto*) keener on effect than on coherence. The book so troubled Mrs. Radcliffe that some argue she stopped publishing fiction in the face of the travesty her own work had somehow spawned. Lewis's Matilda de Villanegas (we are in Italy, of course, and the tainting atmosphere of Catholicism is inescapable) is comparable as a villain to Radcliffe's "the Italian" himself, evil Father Schedoni in *The Italian*. And well might she have been shocked: Matilda (initially disguised as a boy) brings down the idolized, corrupted hero, sexually hungry Ambrosio, with great force. He rapes, commits incest, kills his mother. He dies in a mess of gore and is damned as eternally as Vathek, only more painfully.

———•———

Clara Reeve (1729–1807), a disciple of the master of Strawberry Hill, called *The Old English Baron* (1778) a "literary offspring of *The Castle of Otranto*." Mr. Dilly of the Poultry gave her £10 for the copyright. She dedicated the book to Mrs. Bridgen, Samuel Richardson's daughter, who helped in revising and correcting it. Reeve does not worship Walpole: she takes issue with his absurd sense of scale and with the violent excesses of the animated portrait and the cowled hermit. Ghosts, to be credible, should be sober and conform to convention. But as Scott says, if we have ghosts, let's give them liberties and make them do exciting things. Scott strongly objects to the anachronism of Reeve's society, speech, and dress, contrasting her unfavorably with Walpole's historical "veracity." He also objects to the Defoe-like particularity in description, not least because much of the detail strikes him as inaccurate. And she was keen on accuracy, writing in her critical dialogue *The Progress of Romance* (1785): "The Romance is an heroic fable, which treats of fabulous persons and things.—The Novel is a picture of real life and manners, and of the time in which it is written. The Romance in lofty and elevated language describes what never happened nor is likely to happen.—The Novel gives a familiar relation of such things, as pass every day before our eyes, such as may happen to our friend, or to ourselves." The novelist aims for probability, sustained "at least while we are reading": an early formulation of Coleridge's "suspension of disbelief," a suspension which in Scott she did not induce.

Reeve has in Mrs. Ann Radcliffe (1764–1823) a writer of fellow feeling who seeks obedience and answerability from the supernatural. Scott seriously admired her. Mrs. Radcliffe makes a distinction between her kind of fiction and that of Monk Lewis. In a semi-Socratic dialogue entitled "On the Supernatural in Poetry," left unfinished at the time of her death and published first in 1826, she contrasts the ghost scenes in *Hamlet* with the ghost scenes in *Macbeth*. "Who ever suffered for the ghost of Banquo, the gloomy and sublime kind of terror, which that of Hamlet calls forth?" The difference is one between "terror," which leads to the sublime, and "horror, which does not. 'Terror and horror are so far opposite, that the first expands the soul, and awakens the faculties to a high degree of life; the other contracts, freezes, and nearly annihilates them.'" In horror the sublime is never to be found. The gothic works produced by women like Radcliffe herself, by Clara Reeve before her and by many after, including the Brontës, Mary Shelley, and Daphne du Maurier, are terror- rather than horror-based. The horror-Gothic writer is keen on local effect, surprise, a series of impacts, where the terror-Gothic writer sustains and cranks up a single passion toward a resolution and, in the case of Mrs. Radcliffe, explanation.

Mrs. Radcliffe (née Ward) was born in London the year *The Castle of Otranto* was published. In her youth she was beautiful. She was also sharply intelligent, fascinated by the sound and precise sense of Greek and Latin words and passages. She was keen on verse and, like Lewis, was not against introducing it into her narratives. Shy in new company, she was lively and engaged among friends. At twenty-two she married an Oxford law graduate, William Radcliffe, who went into journalism and acquired the *English Chronicle,* which he then edited.

Mrs. Radcliffe was seriously successful as a writer. Her first book, published in 1789 when she was twenty-four, the romance *The Castles of Athlin and Dunbayne,* was meager and unpromising. *A Sicilian Romance,* published a year later, was much better, but still disconnected, the characters predictable, the approach picturesque, but with a difference she learned in part from the painters she admired. Salvatore Rosa taught her the use of darkness, not chiaroscuro but oscuroscuro. Elements take form in and from shadow, a suggestive half- or quarter-light is more eloquent than highlight. There is pleasure in the anxiety the reader feels, a teased desire for clarity, the teasing exquisite, the urgency of the desire overridden by the pleasure of it. If in Burke's words we can "accustom our eyes" to the light, we lose at the same time both the anxiety and its pleasure. We also lose interest, the suspense that keeps us reading. H. P. Lovecraft disliked the irruption of little poems into her fiction, but he loved her strong "visual imagination," which "appears as much in her delightful landscape touches—always in broad, glamorously pictorial outline, and never in close detail—as in her weird phantasies."

Such broad description is of a piece with the narrative technique, which imparts the plot withholdingly, in what must have been a deliciously agonizing and protracted fictional foreplay, creating, sustaining, and augmenting anxiety, until the release in a daylight of explanation that lets the reader gratefully down. Scott insists that Radcliffe is the first *poetess* of romantic fiction, different in kind from Richardson, Fielding, and "even Walpole."

An efficient writer, she published her third novel, *The Romance of the Forest,* in 1791. Her readership was growing, and for her next book, *The Mysteries of Udolpho,* she received the enormous sum of £500 from her publisher (1794). This was the first of her two enduringly interesting works and may, Lovecraft affirms, be taken as "a type of the early Gothic tale at its best." For *The Italian* (1797) she received £800. Such prices confirm the popularity of the Gothic, and of her brand of Gothic, at the time. She published no further novels in the twenty-six years that remained of her life. Some declare that she went mad out of fright at her own creations. She is almost as anonymous as Shakespeare: when Christina Rossetti considered writing her life, she could not begin: there was not enough known. Her husband published *Gaston de Blondeville,* which she had completed or abandoned in 1801, after her death, along with her poems and other writings.

Her plots terrified her age. They involve a heroine fleeing through a forest of Walpolean properties: tumbling ruins, dungeons, seeming ghosts. The heroine is always getting caught and escaping again, the tension building to a final climax after which she is delivered, ideally into the arms of a tested and handsome betrothed, and we are delivered back to the world of rational order; she marries, and we put the book back on the shelf. The manner is out of Walpole, the libidinal and moral struggles out of Richardson. Though *The Mysteries of Udolpho,* written after a trip along the Rhine, which Scott believes affected her sense of the book's landscapes, is her most famous novel, *The Italian* is her most successful, a romance of the Inquisition, with a compelling villain. On the whole, her villains are more memorable than her sometimes bland-seeming innocents, but her moral purpose and her aesthetic purpose are one: virtue, she says, is "little more than active taste," and her books are written in the service of bringing her readers to both taste and virtue. Her objections to the excesses of Monk

Lewis were clear on these and other grounds. Terror teaches, horror, a litera-ture of mere effect, degrades.

There is a tombstone in Dorchester Abbey near Oxford that commemorates a young woman who died of "an excess of sensibility." Many of the Radcliffe heroine's distresses arise from an acute sensibility, particularly a sensibility that yields to imagination. The moral of each novel is that sensibility must learn to reason and be guided by reason. Emily's dying father in *The Mysteries of Udolpho* makes no bones about it in his parting sermonic aria: "Those who really pos-sess sensibility ought early to be taught that it is a dangerous quality, which is continually extracting the excess of misery or delight from every surrounding circumstance. And since, in our passage through this world, painful circum-stances occur more frequently than pleasing ones, and since our sense of evil is, I fear, more acute than our sense of good, we become the victims of our feelings, unless we can in some degree command them."

The first professional American novelist explored the Gothic and gave it Ameri-can features. He was among Lovecraft's early examples of the horror writer; like Radcliffe, he "injured his creations by natural explanations; but also like her, he had an uncanny atmospheric power which gives his horrors a frightful vitality as long as they remain unexplained." Charles Brockden Brown (1771–1810) was born and died in Philadelphia. He trained as a lawyer. His novels appeared in 1798–1801, and the four Gothic specimens occupied the first two years. *Wieland* (1798) was the most successful, foreshadowing as it does (as the Gothic mode does) the psychological novel. The three that appeared in 1799, *Arthur Mervyn, Ormond,* and *Edgar Huntly,* reveal how indebted he was to Mrs. Radcliffe, but also to William Godwin. His novels are terror-driven but issue-based, with discussions of women's rights and other civic themes. He had English readers, but his main impact was in the United States. How different from his the pure, streamlined Gothic of Poe was to be.

The Gothic impulse survives in fiction, poetry, and the cinema. Elements of it were adapted, though the "classic" form found one of its last (and, in Love-craft's estimation, one of its best) expressions in the work of the Irish-born writer Charles Maturin (1780–1824), whose *Melmoth the Wanderer* was published in 1820. Scott admired and encouraged Maturin, whose double life as a clergyman overly imbued with Calvinism and a writer of controversial novels was hard. Maturin did not make it as a novelist or a dramatist, and he published *Melmoth* because he was terribly poor. In *Blackwood's Magazine Melmoth* was welcomed: "Mr. Maturin is, without question, one of the most genuine masters of the dark romance. He can make the most practiced reader tremble as effectually as Mrs.

Radcliffe, and what is better, he can make him think as deeply as Mr. Godwin." There is Godwin again, the Gothic now going hand in hand with radical social reform.

Like Vathek, Melmoth has sold his soul to the devil in exchange for an extra 150 years of life; but there is a surprising twist to the convention: he can get out of the contract if he finds someone to take his place. Of the older Gothic novels, this remains the most gripping. We lose sight of structural flaws in the speed and intensity of the narrative. Maturin set his cap against Lewis and the German dark-romancers, confessing to Scott in 1813 that he was setting out to write "a poetic Romance, a wild thing." "Tales of superstition were always my favorites, I have in fact been always more conversant with the visions of another world, than the realities of this." He intended "to display all my *diabolical* resources, out-Herod all the Herods of the German school, and get possession of the magic lamp with all its slaves from the conjuror Lewis himself." The book is less messy than *The Monk,* less grandiloquent than *Vathek,* the characters credibly drawn within their incredible circumstances, and the tension of love and contrast between Melmoth and Immalee might have fueled a nineteenth-century opera. There are moments of beautiful clarity: "We shall be told why we suffered, and for what; but a bright and blessed lustre shall follow the storm, and all shall yet be light."

By the time *Melmoth* was published, the tide was turning against the Gothic. Jane Austen had already parodied the mode in *Northanger Abbey,* sold in 1803 to Richard Crosby for £10 but not published until 1818. Mrs. Radcliffe was still alive, but probably not in a state in which she could enjoy seeing *The Mysteries of Udolpho* parodied. She had laboriously enchanted and then reliteralized the imagination in her novels, but it was the enchantment that stayed in people's minds. Austen enjoyed illusion as much as the next reader, but it ought to know its place, and in fiction its place was limited by plausibility. Virginia Woolf voiced a universal impatience when she wrote, "It is unlikely that a lady confronted by a male body stark naked, wreathed in worms, where she had looked, maybe, for a pleasant landscape in oils, should do more than give a loud cry and drop senseless. And women who give loud cries and drop senseless do it in much the same way." Hence, tales of terror are hard to sustain, they become "insipid and later ridiculous." For her, the Gothic is a degradation of romance, reducing it to gesture and stereotype: imagination becomes moonshine.

Still, in a rational age, strategies are devised to exercise the irrational faculties and to stimulate and purge irrational feelings. The "Sublime" is antirational in one direction, the Gothic in another. Edmund Burke in his *Philosophical Enquiry into the Origin of Our Ideas of the Sublime and Beautiful* stresses how what we cannot understand, what we do not know, is the foundation for the terror at the root of great art. The Gothic novel disregards the borders imposed by memory and rationality. It contributes to the *celebration* of the irrational and is instrumental in unleashing the Romantic spirit with its insatiable hunger for "further." Such may not have been the aims to Walpole or Mrs. Radcliffe; but Beckford and Lewis and Maturin, estranged as they were from the social world, enduring different spiritual, material, and psychological punishments, were pushing the limits, though held back by an unmalleable theology and a morality as unforgiving as that which carried Faustus, howling, down to Hell.

# | 12 |

# *Listening*

Maria Edgeworth, John McGahern, James Hogg, Sir Walter Scott, John Galt, Susan Ferrier

Over a century before Rose Macaulay patronized E. M. Forster for his success in making "even these brown men live" in *A Passage to India,* Maria Edgeworth was bringing the humble Irish into focus, creating (as Forster does for the Muslim and the Hindu characters in his book) something like their voices in their own exotic landscapes. "If I could but hit it," Sir Walter Scott wrote to a friend well before his first novel was published, "Miss Edgeworth's wonderful power of vivifying all her persons, and making them live as beings in your mind, I should not be afraid." The fact that Maria Edgeworth (1768–1849) was a woman did not affect his enthusiasm for her work. Or for the work of a still greater contemporary, Jane Austen. He contrasted her style with its "exquisite touch which renders ordinary commonplace things and characters interesting, from the truth of the description and the sentiment," with his "bow-wow" manner. He coveted Austen's and Edgeworth's *kind* of genius. He is a clear, prescient critic, most at home, it can seem, with work least like his own.

Virginia Woolf's take on Edgeworth is less generous than Scott's, more gendered. "She was diminutive in figure, plain in feature, and wrote demurely at her desk in the family living-room." Why mention the plain features, and why the adverb "demurely," with its suggestion of affected female seriousness? Scott read for the writing, Woolf for the writer whose work she did not enjoy. Yet the fiction of the new century owed a substantial debt to *Castle Rackrent* (1800).

Maria Edgeworth's father was an Anglo-Irish man of property much interested in education. On his successive wives he fathered twenty-one children. His favorite daughter, Maria, was the second child of his first wife. Bright and devoted, Maria was reared by him and stepmothers. When she was fourteen, her father took her to the family estate of Edgeworthstown in Ireland. Her first book, *Letters for Literary Ladies* (1795), might remind us of Richardson's beginnings. Then, in her thirtieth year, she collaborated with her father on a book entitled *Practical Education* (1798), inspired in part by Rousseau, who advocated forms (not a system) of education in which the pupil was led forward by curiosity rather than pursued by rote and the cane. She put some of the ideas into practice, as the education of the little Edgeworths fell largely to her.

While working on books of a moral and philosophical nature, Edgeworth wrote for the family's amusement little sketches based on the speech, manners, and dialect of the Irish steward of the estate, monologues with a specific accent and subject matter. These were maquettes for the large ensemble of *Castle Rackrent*. Parody and jest are at the heart of what becomes a serious enterprise. Parody leads, as with Cervantes and Fielding, into character, in Edgeworth's case by way of dialect cadence. In an age of decorum, writing so indecorous was a risk initially confined to the family circle. Her novels took shape, she was a traditional moralist, an advocate of marriage and motherhood and conventional roles for women. She excepted herself, remaining a spinster with an increasingly subtle intelligence. Her sense of the difference between her culture and the Irish steward's, her language and his, was heightened too by her awareness of the implications of sexual difference for character and language. She was not led astray by fame (her own or anyone else's) or by libido. Byron met her in London and found her unremarkable; for her part, she remarked on how unremarkable he looked.

In *Castle Rackrent* Thady Rackrent narrates the story of his family, creating a series of sketches of the menfolk. The themes are property and its transmission from hand to hand, with the jealousies, small irregularities, and changes entailed for a variety of characters, high and low. It is an early saga of generations, sharpened by the author's awareness of how Irish landlords exploited their land and tenants. The book works by demonstration; criticism (rather than satire) is best conveyed in action rather than rhetorical afterthought. This realism in language and detail was unusual. The age of Augustan satire did not touch Maria Edgeworth in the new age of accountable prose. *The Absentee* (1812) develops the themes of *Castle Rackrent,* in particular that of responsible stewardship.

*Belinda* appeared in 1801. It is this novel that Jane Austen commends, along with Fanny Burney's *Camilla* and *Cecilia,* in her defense of the novel in *Northanger Abbey* (1817). If Scott takes his bearings from *Castle Rackrent*, Austen relished the creation of the lovely Belinda, young, coming out in London under the aegis of blatant, affected Lady Delacour. Mrs. Freke cross-dresses and duels (with pistols, not rapiers); Lord Delacour does not wear the trousers in his household and (as a result?) enjoys his liquor too much. Seeming and being are at odds, the theme of race and cross-racial marriage tactfully develops, and in Belinda a not unworthy predecessor of Elizabeth Bennett and Emma Woodhouse is conceived.

In 1813 Maria and her father and stepmother went to London. Her fame was at its height. "The town ran mad to see her; at parties the crowd turned and twisted to discover her, and, as she was very small, almost closed above her head," writes Woolf, who finds her almost a figure of fun. Maria's seriousness had about it something of George Eliot's. When she gave up fiction after the death of her father, her first and best reader to whom all her intellectual striving was dedicated, she had learned the moral, if not the sexual, lessons she had espoused. Her later years she devoted to others, in 1847, for example, helping those who suffered in the potato famine.

But there were more books to come before she desisted. *Ormond* (1817) goes farther afield than *Castle Rackrent,* though it is rooted in Ireland. It visits Paris and the fashionable world she evoked in *Belinda.* The captivating, morally unsound guardian of the eponymous protagonist is Sir Ulick O'Shane, and Cornelius of that ilk, "king of the Black Islands." The history invested in this book proved exemplary to Scott.

How do Edgeworth's Irish rustics look a century and a half later, independent, writing in their own persons and no longer subject to English landlords or diminished by English norms? The real thing is far from comedy and cliché. John McGahern (1934–2006), a distinctive modern voice of rural Ireland, grew up in County Leitrim, the primary landscape of his imagination. His mother was a schoolmistress and kept a small farm, raising him and his six siblings until her death from cancer in 1944. His father was Garda sergeant in the village of Cootehall, County Roscommon, twenty miles away, where he lived in the police barracks, a place McGahern made real in his first novel, having moved with his siblings to Cootehall on his mother's death. He studied at University College, Dublin, and began adult life as a primary school teacher. As he became a well-known writer, he occupied various academic posts in Ireland, the United Kingdom, and the United States.

His writing featured in 1961 in the short-lived, visionary magazine *X* (1959–1962), edited by the South African poet David Wright and the Irish painter Patrick Swift, which set the common agenda for a generation of European painters, writers, and dramatists. Faber and Faber noticed McGahern's style—dispassionate, worldly—and invited the young writer to send work. The first of his six novels, *The Barracks,* appeared two years later. Told from the point of view of a sergeant's second wife (who in the novel dies of cancer: McGahern reunited his parents in fiction and relived his mother's death from different perspectives), it sets the harsh scene for what is to come. He built steadily, the later novels widely spaced, each adding to an exemplary body of work that influenced other writers, not least in its resistance to clichés of community and nation. *The Dark* (1965), *The Leavetaking* (1975), *The Pornographer* (1980), his best-known novel *Amongst Women* (1990), and *That They May Face the Rising Sun* (2001), published a year later in the United States as *By the Lake,* disclose an unsentimentalized Ireland.

Inevitably he fell foul of the Irish censor. *The Dark* was banned for its sexual content, and for the father's violence. The controversy the book caused precipitated McGahern's departure from teaching. He went to England, work-ing where he could, then returned to Ireland and became a small farmer in County Leitrim. His novels continued to explore and exploit his autobiography, and his actual autobiography *All Will Be Well* shows how close he stays, and the transformations he effects. *The Leavetaking* by means of flashbacks revisits his mother's death, his marriage, his dismissal from teaching. *The Pornographer* (with another death by cancer, this time an aunt's) is the harshest of the novels, confronting issues of sex and its consequences in a Church-heavy world.

Michael Moran, the protagonist of *The Leavetaking*, reappears in *Amongst Women*, an IRA veteran of the two Irish wars, a harsh old man with his ideals intact, disenchanted with the small-scale, small-minded leaders of the indepen-dent Ireland. His example empowers his children to succeed. The novelist has come full circle, with a new perspective on the world of *The Barracks* and on the figure of the father. *Memoir* (2005), published as *All Will Be Well: A Memoir* in the United States, is softened in the same way, returning to the trauma of his mother's death, driven there again and again by the incurable homesickness of bereavement. The landscape of his later years keeps calling her back, and an ide-alizing tendency absent from the fiction is given rein. The tensions are like those D. H. Lawrence confronts, but Lawrence did not suffer the additional compli-cations of Church, broken vows to the dead, and return to a haunted landscape. "When I reflect on those rare moments when I stumble without warning into that extraordinary sense of security, that deep peace, I know that consciously and unconsciously she has been with me all my life." What has been with him, giving his fiction its bite, is her death. The *Memoir* ends piously, cloyingly: "I would want no shadow to fall on her joy and deep trust in God. She would face no false reproaches. As we retraced our steps, I would pick for her the wild or-chid and the windflower." The distance from Edgeworth can best be measured in the self-abandon of this passage.

———————

Walter Scott began writing fiction early. Dissatisfied with the results, he locked them away. He was a poet: to dabble in the vulgar zone of fiction and jeopar-dize his reputation would be injudicious. Years later he searched for the draft of what was to become *Waverley* (1814), stimulated by "the extended and well-merited fame of Miss Edgeworth, whose Irish characters have gone so far to make the English familiar with the character of their gay and kind-hearted neighbors of Ireland, that she may be truly said to have done more towards com-pleting the Union than perhaps all the legislative enactments by which it has been followed up." He commends "the rich humor, pathetic tenderness, and admirable tact which pervade the works of my accomplished friend" and sets out to accomplish something similar for Scotland, "to introduce her natives to those of the sister kingdom in a more favorable light than they had been placed hitherto, and tend to procure sympathy for their virtues and indulgence for their foibles. I thought also, that much of what I wanted in talent might be made up by the intimate acquaintance with the subject which I could lay claim to possess, as having travelled through most parts of Scotland, both Highland and Lowland, having been familiar with the elder as well as more modern race, and having had from my infancy free and unrestrained communication with all ranks of my countrymen, from the Scottish peer to the Scottish plough-man. Such ideas often occurred to me, and constituted an ambitious branch of my theory, however far short I may have fallen of it in practice." In one respect he did not fall short. "Who shall tell us a story? Sir Walter Scott, of course," says E. M. Forster with derision.

Scott was stimulated, too, by the enormous success of the Gothic. It freed fiction to explore alien worlds and, more to his liking, historical ones. Walpole released not only ghosts and specters when he opened the Pandora's box of *The Castle of Otranto,* but geographies and periods. Scott uses the term *Gothic* usu-ally with reference to architecture. In *Waverley,* where it occurs a dozen times, it is in this connection. The five occurrences of the word in *The Heart of Midlo-thian* (1816) are adjectival and go with "entrance," "projections," "tower," "parish churches," and "cathedral." Yet beyond architecture there are Gothic features in his plots: the hidden identity, durable clannish hatreds, revenge at clannish rather than Jacobean levels, heroines (not many of them credible) in distress, settings remote in time. He can do "mystery," too; but he has no sense of tran-scendence or metaphysics. Gothic details, then, not a Gothic sensibility.

For Scott the novelist, already an experienced collector of ballads and a cele-brated author of enormous verse romances, the present vanishes altogether. He composed twenty-seven historical novels, a whole literature, in Jacobite settings half a century earlier than the world in which he grew up, or in Britain, France, and elsewhere, in earlier periods. The first modern best-selling author, the first to make a fortune from his writing (the loss of that fortune being his tragedy), he *invented* the historical novel. The otherness of the past, its "culture, ideology, manners and morals," its "whole 'way of life,'" says David Lodge, is as much his subject as the plot and characters are. In some cases plot and character seem secondary to the massive undertaking of making a past world real. Scott wrote history in ways that would affect artists, thinkers, and historians. He "revolu-tionised the writing of history" without being a trained historian.

The place of unremarked men and women in history, the similarity between the lives, ambitions, passions, and emotions of a remote then and an immediate now, became his themes. Accuracy of the surface and tonal authority were part of a new approach. Art was constrained not only by aesthetic rules but by facts (regarding costume, demography, architecture, dance) that before might have been invented or approximated, while the moral and dramatic elements of a story unfolded. "In literature," Robert Louis Stevenson says, "the great change of the past century has been effected by the admission of detail. It was inaugurated by the romantic Scott; and at length, by the semi-romantic Balzac and his more or less wholly unromantic followers, bound like a duty on the novelist." Stevenson knows the force of extensive detail, but also in his own day recognizes that what starts original becomes conventional. "For some time it signified and expressed a more ample contemplation of the conditions of man's life; but it [detail] has recently (at least in France) fallen into a merely technical and decorative stage, which it is, perhaps, still too harsh to call survival."

Occasionally Scott gets detail quite wrong. He would nod, even nod off: in *The Antiquary,* Stevenson remarks, the sun is seen to set in the east. When Flaubert's delightful, laboriously pedantic dodderers Bouvard and Pécuchet tired of reading straight history and turned to reading historical fiction instead, they were first beguiled and then repelled by Scott: "The heroine usually lived in the country with her father, and the suitor, a stolen infant, was restored to his rightful heritage and triumphed over his rivals." In addition you had "a philosophical beggar, a surly squire, virtuous young ladies"—among the chief problems, as well as "wisecracking servants, endless dialogues, pointless modesty, and an utter lack of depth." The stylizations of the Gothic and the morality of the time had a lot to answer for. Flaubert's duo particularly wearied of the historical errors in *Quentin Durward:* wrong dates, wrong identities, wrong killers and victims. "And the figure of Charles the Bold, when they found his corpse, could not have looked threatening, since wolves had half-devoured it." Pécuchet gave up in frustration. Bouvard read on until he "finally tired of having the same conceits repeated over and over" (Flaubert enumerates them) until the history drained away.

Scott left a mark on all the literatures of Europe, especially on French (Alexandre Dumas and others) and Russian (Alexander Pushkin being a special debtor). In Italy he was almost immediately a success. The great Sicilian novelist Giuseppe Tomasi di Lampedusa (1896–1957), author of *The Leopard,* says: "I have an edition of *Ivanhoe* published in Palermo in 1832." Without Scott's example, James Fenimore Cooper would have been a different kind of author. James Kirke Paulding, with Washington Irving and William Cullen Bryant a member of the lively Knickerbocker Group, set out to spoof Scott in *Koningsmarke: the Long Finne,* but found the reality of the world he was creating so engrossing that his book became a real novel with strong characters, including a convincing old black woman and rather soft-focus native Americans: another case of intended parody maturing into original fiction.

Scott cannot draw a heroine, critics say; heroines are rare in the early fiction of most countries. Another critic directs us to *The Heart of Midlothian:* he cannot draw a hero, either. But this, too, is part of the design: there is no pure hero, no pure villain. Plots demand happy endings, but those whom we last see bending together at the altar have their real, unobserved, and uncelebrated social lives ahead of them. Still, the charge against his female characters stands. Edith Wharton speaks for many writers who learned important lessons from him, including Balzac: "In deference to the wave of prudery which overswept England after the vulgar excesses of the Hanoverian court he substituted sentimentality for passion, and reduced his heroines to 'Keepsake' insipidities." He was indeed, like Dickens, Thackeray, Trollope, and George Eliot later on, "cramped by the hazard of a social convention."

Walter Scott was born at College Wynd in Edinburgh in 1771. His father, also Walter, was a Writer to the Signet, a judicial officer with the responsibility to issue warrants, writs, and the like, and a clerk in the office of the Secretary of State under Scottish law. To call him a "solicitor" is to sell him short. Scott followed his father into the law. His mother, Anne Rutherford, was the daughter of a professor of medicine.

As a boy Scott contracted polio, and he remained lame in the right leg. This stimulated his desire to be out and about in the Borders and elsewhere, exploring, gathering ballads, meeting countrymen. He grew tall—to over six feet—and was a man of vigor. Early portraits show him as plump and vacant, but fame brought more focused portraiture, the handsome adornment to Scottish currency. The age of the wig was over, and his own hair, combed forward, gives him a mature youthfulness. His death mask, preserved at Princeton University Library, is by contrast alarming, the domed forehead almost as high as the rest of the face is deep.

He spent his early years in Sandy-Know, in the house of his paternal grandparents, and got to know and love the Borders. His ancestors, Scotts and Rutherfords, were part of the history of the area. His grandmother had tales to tell, and she told them. She may have planted in him the ambition to become a laird, to take his place in the genealogy as it were: he was a witness who wanted to be a player. In the end the part he played was that of recorder, chronicler. Varnisher.

He attended Edinburgh High School (1779–1783) and then the university, where he studied arts and law (1783–1786, 1789–1792). Apprenticed to his father in 1786, he was called to the bar in 1792. By then he was a writer. Affected by the border ballads, he knew by heart much of Percy's *Reliques,* that anthology of real, literary, and fake balladry. He did not like Macpherson's Ossianic forger-ies, knowing on instinct that they were false, the wrong Celtic, the wrong ro-mance for him. He had developed an interest in German Romantic writing and anything to do with folktales and traditions. His interest in literature was an interest in living or surviving traditions: he collected ballads (starting at the age of seventeen) and explored the countryside.

He was a serious scholar with a sense of his culture's place in European tra-ditions. He learned Italian especially to read Ariosto and Boiardo, studied Old Norse to read the sagas and German to read and translate *Sturm und Drang*. He never learned Scots Gaelic. His first literary efforts were "cross cultural." In 1796 he anonymously published a translation of Gottfried Bürger's *Lenore* and *Der wilde Jäger (The Wild Hunter)*. He did not like novels, on the whole. The form seemed too capacious, too vulgar, the motive for writing less glory than gain.

He fell in love with Williamina Belshes of Fettercairn and then married (in 1797) Margaret Charlotte Charpentier of Lyon, producing five children. In 1799 he was appointed sheriff-depute of Selkirkshire. In the years that followed, his success as a poet began. During 1802 and 1803 the three volumes of his *Min-strelsy of the Scottish Border*, including collected ballads of all sorts as well as imi-tations, was published. His first big poem, *The Lay of the Last Minstrel*, in six cantos, appeared in 1805. The tale was told by an ancient minstrel and based on the Border legend of Gilpin Horner the goblin, set in the mid-sixteenth century. Canto 6 opens with the celebrated lines: "Breathes there the man, with soul so dead, / Who never to himself hath said, / This is my own, my native land!"

It was ten years before his first novel appeared. Having a reputation for poetry, he preferred not to "risk the loss of it by attempting a new style of com-position." Meanwhile, he was a committed editor, not only of ballads and antiq-uities. In 1808 he assembled in eighteen volumes the *Life and Works of John Dryden*. In 1814, the year of *Waverley*, he published the *Works of Jonathan Swift* in nineteen volumes. He helped establish the Tory-oriented *Quarterly Review* in 1809, after years of contributing to the *Edinburgh Review*: he had become disappointed with its Whiggery.

It was also in 1809 that he entered fatefully into a publishing partnership with James Ballantyne, an act that sealed his fate in 1826 when the company was drawn into the bankruptcy of Constable & Co. and as a partner Scott was liable. Once the assessment was made, he owed between £114,000 and £130,000, a fortune in the currency of the day. His friends offered to help. "My own right hand shall pay my debt," he declared. He worked for the rest of his life to dis-charge it. The creditors were paid in full after his death, but he had been forced to become, he confided to his diary, "a sort of writing automaton, and truly the joints of my knees, especially the left, are so stiff and painful in rising and sit-

ting down, that I can hardly help screaming—I that was so robust and active."
He kept two large work surfaces and labored at two projects, swiveling back
and forth between them. His books generally sold at 31 shillings sixpence (one
and a half guineas), mainly to the numerous middle class of readers. Popular
books cost between sixpence and 5 shillings, so Scott was unavailable to the
masses.

When in 1851 Dickens made a pilgrimage to Abbotsford, he felt in Scott's
disaster a warning to himself. "I saw in a vile glass case the last clothes Scott
wore. Among them an old white hat, which seemed to be tumbled and bent
and broken by the uneasy, purposeless wandering, hither and thither, of his
heavy head. It so embodied Lockhart's pathetic description of him when he
tried to write, and laid down his pen and cried, that it associated itself in my
mind with broken powers and mental weakness from that hour." His rise had
been steep and glorious. His poetry was acclaimed and sold well. Ballads and
long narratives came from his hand. Such was his reputation and poetic success
that he was offered the post of poet laureate in 1813. He refused, urging the appointment of Robert Southey.

His unrivaled ascendancy as Scottish poet was sharply challenged by Byron,
whose reputation was growing fast and whose new tones and styles were urbane,
gaslit, wry, and remote from Scott's fireside manner. But by 1813 Scott had resolved to court a different muse, no longer those of epic (Calliope), lyric (Erato)
and ballad (Melpomene, Terpsichore, Thalia). He had Clio, the Muse of History,
in his sights. "Walter Scott has no business to write novels, especially good
ones," Jane Austen complained in a letter to her niece. "It is not fair. He has
fame and profit enough as a poet, and should not be taking the bread out of the
mouths of other people. I do not like him and do not mean to like *Waverley* if
I can help it, but I fear I must."

While Clio cast her spell, she induced Scott to invest materially in his own
baronial seat. In 1811, after the lease on his favorite country dwelling at Athes-
tiel expired, he acquired a farm called Clarty Hole and adjacent land on the
River Tweed and began to develop it. The name "Clarty Hole" did not resonate
for Mrs. Scott. She rechristened the place Abbotsford because it was in the neighborhood of ancient Melrose Abbey. Abbotsford became a house that, taken in
conjunction with Scott's novels, affected Victorian style and culture in Britain
and throughout the Commonwealth. Beside the fantasy of Walpole's Strawberry Hill and the nightmare of Beckford's Fonthill, here was a building solidly
rooted not in wild or troubled fancy but in history: it suggested a style, a way of
life, and a vision of the world.

The beginning of building coincided with the composition of *Waverley*, and
*Waverley* is a novel deeply aware of architecture. There are chapters called

"Castle-Building," "The Chief and his Mansion," "Dulce Domum." Here the hero approaches "A Scottish Manor-House Sixty Years Since": "It had been built at a period when castles were no longer necessary, and when the Scottish architects had not yet acquired the art of designing a domestic residence. The windows were numberless, but very small; the roof had some nondescript kind of projections, called bartizans, and displayed at each frequent angle a small turret, rather resembling a pepper-box than a Gothic watchtower. Neither did the front indicate absolute security from danger. There were loop-holes for musketry, and iron stanchions on the lower windows, probably to repel any roving band of gypsies, or resist a predatory visit from the caternas of the neighboring Highlands." Those *bartizans* are there because the term was new to Scott (Waverley himself is clearly unfamiliar with it, and it contributes nothing to the narrative). The faults with the architecture are those Scott seeks to avoid in his own growing castle. Abbotsford became a mistress, Delilah, obsessing him, consuming his time, imagination, and money, fulfilling and shortening his life. As with many amours, he began with modest plans, but as he prospered his ambitions grew. In *Lives of the Novelists* Scott sends up Walpole's excesses at Strawberry Hill without realizing that Abbotsford also errs in taste and judgment. He employed English architects: the house lacks Scotch-Baronial heaviness. The windows drink a great deal of light and the eighteenth century contributes coherence and proportion.

When John Ruskin visited, Ruskin who with his father revered Scott, who had wept when he finished the Waverley novels because there were no more to come, felt betrayed by Abbotsford. It was Gothic trappings and effects, Gothic features, but at heart it was a late Georgian house disfigured by irrelevant invention. It *was* one of the first houses in Europe to be lighted by gas. Lockhart remembers it as overly bright. There is irony in a distinguished antiquary surrounding himself with all modern conveniences.

The contents of the house are also diverse in style and association. As in a holy place, there are history-hallowed relics: Flora Macdonald's pocketbook, Archbishop Sharp's basket-grate, a host of weapons, Robert the Bruce's skull, and so forth. The library catches the imagination, like the handsome library in *Waverley* itself. Scott designed it, and it is so complete and beautiful that one rather wishes he had not trusted English architects but followed his own instincts.

Scott was Queen Victoria and Prince Albert's favorite author and the impact of the style of Abbotsford spread. Town halls, pubs, houses, churches, all partook of the decorative, rational "revivalism," and as the urban environment was modernized and antiquated at the same time, Scott's material and literary taste had its ineradicable impact on the aesthetics of his time. That rudderless eclecticism, that mix of the legitimized antique with the modern, the imperial atavism that invented a past worthy of the present: in succeeding generations literature, art, architecture, and politics struggled to break free.

For more than a century critical fashion has condescended to Scott because he was so popular and is now "unreadable." But he isn't. The challenge, declares Lampedusa, is getting into one of his books. After a hundred pages of boredom a novel catches fire, characters are fleshed out more fully than those of Scott's French contemporaries. Lampedusa loved Stendhal, and Stendhal admired Scott, though one takes his point that Scott tended to paint elaborate armor and period dress when he should have depicted the hearts inside them. "The start of every novel is truly unbearable," Lampedusa says. To make Scott readable, remove the first hundred pages.

What makes Scott exciting for patient modern readers is his sense of the nature of character, deriving from his medieval enthusiasms and the legacy of his verse romancing. Scott was made a baronet in 1820; he bore it graciously. It transformed him, as such changes advanced the characters in his books. The old-fashioned Johnsonian in Scott regarded character as derived, not given. Individuals acquire not only their opinions, prejudices, and customs, but their nature, from external factors. His characters exist in the light of their personal histories (they all have contexts that entail the past); they have families, neighborhoods, communities, religions, and landscapes that determine who they are and how they act, and against which they are sometimes compelled by circumstance, or conscience, to act. They are involved by, and sometimes in, politics. Each has a social role, and that is the first given. We read characters for what they do and are and also for what makes them as they are. This is not to say they are merely representative: each is individual because of particular experiences. Character is inseparable from its history, just as in Jane Austen character is inseparable from the social hierarchy in which it is both snared and carried.

The material reality of Scott's novels is inseparable in his mind from their historical reality. Events, qualities, cultures, or their effects inhere in places and institutions and inform and determine characters, even when they are not consciously aware of the effect. His fiction entails a wholeness of vision more complex than what Forster calls "story-telling." We encounter characters' cultures in all their forms of expression. We are left, as in the world at large, to infer their "inner nature." Forster denies they have one; Pritchett insists the inner lives are wanting because something is lacking in Scott himself. "He has the power to present the outside of a character and to work from the outside to the inside. But once inside, he discovers only what is generic. There is the fault. He has, I would say, no power to work from the inside to the outer man." Maybe he has no desire to. He was the editor of Swift, after all.

Often peripheral characters, those who reflect upon the action and are only marginally touched by it, are most real because least causally trammeled, traced rather than drawn. Around what can feel like a deadwood center flourish ivies and small boughs, leafy, suggestive. If in *Old Mortality* there is a central plot and a social vision, there are also unintegrated bits, straying in from a more vital fictional world—Cuddie Headrigg and his mother, for instance.

In *Lives of the Novelists* Scott contrasted Richardson's "characters of nature" with Fielding's "characters of manners" and reflects on the different kinds of fiction that issue from these distinct constructions of character—in fiction, in life. Richardson assumes we can have access to and indeed "dive into the recesses of the human heart." Fielding, less invasive, less presumptuous, allows us to infer what is passing behind faces, under ribs, but respects his characters sufficiently not to violate them. In Scott we identify a third type of characterization. It entails the provision of contexts—histories, places, families—from which readers are invited to color in the character of the protagonists and villains. The result is complex relationships to and between the underlying contexts and their distinct languages, their clocks that tick at different speeds, their prides and purposes. What Scott provides is more comprehensive than a comedy of manners, yet characters never stand apart in their worlds. We see Moll Flanders or Lovelace or Tom Jones in our mind's eye, almost sculptural; Edward Waverley and Ivanhoe and Francis Osbaldistone and Jeanie and Effie Deane come to mind always trailing their worlds.

In the "Introductory Epistle" to *The Fortunes of Nigel* (1822), Scott's "author" says a demon sits on his quill and distracts him into excessive characterization and development of incident until "my regular mansion turns out a Gothic anomaly." This was an abiding impulse: "how much Scott owes to a sincere pleasure, even a joy, in the accoutrement of life," says Pritchett, comparing him to the Russians who drew so much sustenance and pleasure from him. A "paternal affection" means that when Scott finds a character he likes, "my imagination brightens, and my conception becomes clearer at every step which I take in his company, although it leads me many a weary mile away from the regular road." Were he to resist temptation, *he* would lose interest, his style weary of its task. He distinguishes between a dog compelled to go doggedly round and round in a wheel and a dog merrily chasing its own tail. He is with the latter. The merry dog is "possessed" and this possession is a kind of sorcery.

Thomas Love Peacock found Scott's dog more dogged and parodied him in *Crotchet Castle*. When Mr. Chainmail at last traces the mysterious Miss Susan to her rustic Welsh abode, Peacock asks, "Shall we describe the spacious apartment . . . the large dark rafters, the pendant bacon and onions, the strong old oaken furniture, the bright and trimly arranged utensils? Shall we describe the cut of Ap-Llymry's coat, the color and tie of his neckcloth, the number of buttons at his knees,—the structure of Mrs. Ap-Llymry's cap, having lappets over the ears . . . ?" He resolves, no, "We shall leave this tempting field of interesting expatiation to those whose brains are high-pressure steam engines for spinning prose by the furlong." What repelled him in this age of "venal panegyric" was the custom of selling fiction by the yard, by word count. His own novels rarely exceed a hundred pages.

*Waverley; or, 'Tis Sixty Years Since,* started, discarded for a decade, then retrieved, was a success as soon as it was published. It appeared anonymously, and Scott maintained his anonymity in fiction for a time, being regarded in Edinburgh as an energetic antiquary, poet, *bon vivant,* and lawyer, and in the country as a laird and sheriff. Writing novels was an activity for the merchant classes, and Scott felt himself above that level, at least until his bankruptcy. His novels, after the success of the first, were presented as "by the author of *Waverley.*" He used pseudonyms: Jebediah Cleisbotham, Crystal Croftangry, Malachi Malagrowther, Lawrence Templeton, Captain Clutterbuck.

*Waverley*'s two titles are eloquent. The first names a protagonist, the surname invented because Scott wanted readers to approach him, suspended between two ideologies, without preconceptions, and the new name is neutral (though Scott described him later as "a sneaking piece of imbecility"). On the other hand, a specific pastness is invoked: this is not Udolpho. It is November 1, 1805, and sixty years before takes us to 1745 and the momentous arrival of the Young Pretender, the Jacobite standard raised at Glenfinnan, the capture of Edinburgh, the march south to Derby where the cause fizzled out.

Edward Waverley was a romantic youth torn between loyalties, to the existing king and to the pretender, and therefore between his father and his uncle. He becomes an officer in the military, falls in love, and is compromised. The Hanoverians distrust him and the Jacobites use him. He is cashiered, imprisoned, and rescued by Rose Bradwardine, the daughter of a pedantic old Jacobite, his uncle's friend. He changes sides, becomes a Jacobite, and saves the Hanoverian Colonel Talbot, an old family friend, at the decisive Battle of Prestonpans, where General Cope's dragoons were routed. Talbot then saves him and old Bradwardine. Rebuffed by his first love, Flora, he marries Rose. Fergus Mac-Ivor, Flora's highland chief brother, is tried for high treason and heroically executed.

The novel is by turns exhilarating and enervating. The manner and matter are new, but in formal terms Scott is in thrall to the traditional novel with paced climaxes and a wedding-bell ending. Continually he celebrates *life in time;* how absurd, then, the formulaic conclusions, indeed any conclusive conclusion. Conventionality constrains his originality. A keen storyteller, he is less good at plotting; there are loose ends, characters intrigue him and then vanish, and hints of what's to come are too loud and clear. Tension does not build. The faults become acute as he proceeds, writing novel after novel at speed. Forster says, "To make one thing happen after another is his only serious aim." He is doing something new without considering the larger loom of his art. His misjudgment, repeated book after book, is to plant the romantic hero and heroine at the heart of things; his unreflecting obedience to this tired formal axiom added an extra half century to its life; indeed, Forster was still kicking against it a century later. The formal problem for Scott was complicated by the fact that he was embarrassed to write about sexual love; or perhaps he did not quite register libidinally, so happy were his personal circumstances, its force. As a novelist he, like his characters, is a construct and suffers the limitations they do. He respects the irrational in other zones, but in the sexual zone it has no force. There are hauntings and Gothic frissons but no tumescences, witches and mad folk but never a convincing clinch.

Scott's great readable novels include *Guy Mannering* (1815), in which we encounter the incomparable Meg Merrilies and Dandie Dinmont, and where the comeuppance of the evil lawyer Glossin provides a definite climax; *The Antiquary* (1816), Scott's own favorite among his novels, the antiquary himself based on George Constable, a friend of Scott's early days, and as in *Guy Mannering* there is a resolution of clouded identities and an unexpected inheritance; *Old Mortality* (1816), the sobriquet of Robert Paterson who in the late eighteenth century walked from place to place cleaning the graves of the old Cameronians, members of one of the severest of the Covenanter sects in the reign of Charles II, and the story of Henry Morton of Milnwood, bright, young, calmly Presbyterian who, though close to the Covenanters, is in love with Edith Bellenden, granddaughter of Margaret of Tillietudlem Castle, a royalist; *Rob Roy* (1817); my own favorite *The Heart of Midlothian,* taking its title from the old Edinburgh Tolbooth or prison, recounting the Porteous riot of 1736 and including the tale of Jeanie and Effie Deane; *The Bride of Lammermoor* (1819), which provided Donizetti with the story of one of his best operas; *Ivanhoe* (1819), in which Scott risked a wholly English subject and invested in English legends, including that of Robin Hood (Thackeray's *Rebecca and Rowena* is a sequel to *Ivanhoe* and a sort of critical interpretation of it); *Kenilworth* (1821), where the matter of England is closely investigated by means of the tragic Elizabethan legend of Amy Robsart; *Peveril of the Peak* (1823), which paints a cast of historical figures in credible detail; the satirical foray into contemporary life that is *St. Ronan's Well* (1823); and *Redgauntlet* (1824), which is more famous than it is good, and is the last novel Scott wrote during his years of prosperity. The later novels, written to dig his way out of a debt he had done little directly to incur, have about them a different air of urgency, written to sell. He decided to reveal his identity to affirm and protect his rights over the earlier books. Of the later novels, *Woodstock; or, The Cavalier: A Tale of the Year 1651* (1826) must have been the hardest to write, during the year of his financial ruin, his wife's death, and the serious illness of his favorite grandson. He wrote on, until even the gaslight failed, his eldest son drew down the lids on his eyes and kissed them shut.

David Lodge sees Scott as "the single Shakespearean talent of the English novel." He is paying an uncommon tribute to the range of the writing, the skill with which Scott differentiates dialects and registers, the firmness with which he portrays historical figures and incidents. Pritchett (Ford could hardly be more vehement in disagreeing) regards Scott as singularly "grown up," a writer mature in his art like Fielding and Austen. Yet, echoing Hazlitt, Pritchett stresses how Scott invests too copiously in the past of life, not in its potential.

Readers a century after Scott divide between those who love and accept the artistic and political impulse behind his work and those who don't. Forster in *Aspects of the Novel* doesn't. He stigmatizes Scott for lack of passion and, while conceding his importance in the development of the novel, sees him as much diminished if we divide him from his role in time and juxtapose him with later writers. His is "a trivial mind and a heavy style." The sum of his qualities is "a temperate heart and gentlemanly feelings, and an intelligent affection for the countryside." The trump: his is a "purely moral and commercial integrity." Beethoven chucked away a Scott novel, exclaiming, "Why, the man writes for money."

Balzac picks up the courage and vision to create *La comédie humaine* from Scott; and Zola owes him both direct and oblique debts. Tolstoy and Stendhal and Mérimée, too, revered him. Through his example they came to understand the nature of past time, and therefore of the present, to devise ways of holding the present or near present at a sufficient distance to "walk round it," to register its dimensions. They learned too that dialects and vulgar registers were a resource for drawing character, location, even landscape.

There is an anarchic element in Scott. He delights in odd protagonists, men and women whose integrity is not quite intact, whose mettle is truly tested; and he prefers the Borderer, the robber with a heart, the buccaneer with attitude, to more predictable folk: people whose identities are complicated by an off-beam relationship with the given order or orders: not outsiders, exactly, but men and women set apart or forced out by circumstances that have a historical resonance. His history is happiest when it includes living memory, as when in his legal chambers his own usher knew well a man who had seen Cromwell when he entered Edinburgh. The word of an eyewitness, even at second hand, has the smell of battle smoke about it in a way that chronicles do not. History and memory become one.

———•———

The French novelist André Gide in the 1940s advocated *The Private Memoirs and Confessions of a Justified Sinner* in a lecture at Oxford, first forgetting and then speaking aloud the name of "M. 'Ogg," better known as James Hogg, the Ettrick Shepherd.

"Gee me an unce o' opium, Mr. De Quinshy," says the Shepherd in one of the seventy-odd *Noctes Ambrosianae* (Nights at Ambrose's Tavern), the "imaginary conversations" that enhanced the popularity of *Blackwood's Magazine*. Hogg himself contributed from time to time to the collaborative *Noctes,* but the Ettrick Shepherd, a regular voice from 1822 to 1835, was Hogg's *semblable,* with his dialect, quick earthiness, gluttony, sexual appetite, and downrightness, but lacking his vulnerable side. Scott wrote to Lord Montagu, "I have heard of men born under a sixpenny planet and doomed never to be worth a groat. I fear something of this vile sixpenny influence gleaned at the cottage window when poor Hogg first came squeaking into the world." His financial ups and downs were dramatic, accompanied by moments of great independence followed by craven, desperate periods when he abased himself even before his foes in order to feed his family.

More than one member of the *Noctes* group could work the Ettrick Shepherd puppet in prose and verse. We witness our Esau-fleeced shepherd swimming nude off Portobello, deep in conversation. The discussion continues even when drowning seems possible. Nude, too, riding a beast, he rushes past a carriage and is glancingly recognized by a startled lady of his acquaintance. With the bailiffs virtually at the door, he and another debtor set off in a balloon to the moon. The exaggerations of fiction don't lie, they clarify truth, though Hogg and his family grew uncomfortable with the Rabelaisian monster his friends fathered on him.

Hogg was a real shepherd. His account of castrating sheep is marked by tender brutality: a love of the creature undeflected by the harsh necessities of rural custom. But what makes him unusual is that he was, at the same time, and without having to make many allowances, part of the thriving world of early nineteenth-century Edinburgh journalism. For a time Hogg edited a magazine, the *Spy.* It was accused of "indecency"; it had no compunction about borrowing published material. Any known writer could be parodied, plagiarized, or imitated; every successful writer was a public character, like a politician. Journalism was ad hominem, whether its purpose was to analyze or merely to entertain. In the end Hogg gave up the *Spy* and threw in his cap with *Blackwood's*

*Magazine,* though like most freelances he was not averse to occasional, often contentious, infidelities; as he grew famous, his hubris grew.

The Ettrick Shepherd caught the literary bug when he first heard Burns's "Tam o' Shanter" recited. The freedom of expression that Burns's Scots permitted, the way it broke the rules of decorum and moved in an instant from deep feeling to satirical verve showed Hogg how he might be in verse and prose. He regarded himself as Burns's heir. His mother was a strong-willed singer of ballads and tales, and he retained the burr and the manner of a countryman; however well-dressed he was, city clothes never convincingly fit him. Scott and Byron, Murray and Lockwood, put up with him because, volatile though he was, unpredictable, moody, undependable, he was *authentic.* Custom and class never reduced him to easy obedience.

*The Private Memoirs and Confessions of a Justified Sinner* (1824), set a hundred years before the time of publication, engages forms of religious fanaticism specifically Scottish in inflection, with unparalleled vehemence. Robert Wringhim, perhaps a relation of one of Scott's Calvinistic moral monsters, is the sinner in question. He shares his name with his teacher, who is probably also his father, though his assumed father (he being a second son) is the laird. This laird has married and had two children. The elder, George, is his, but the younger's paternity is doubtful. The estranged parents live separately in the same mansion. The old laird gets intimate with his "housekeeper" Miss Arabella Logan, and she is crucial in unraveling the murder. George and Robert meet in Edinburgh, fight, and Robert stalks and terrifies George. George dies in an unwitnessed "duel," murdered in fact, and the old laird dies heartbroken, so Robert inherits the estate.

Because he is in the Calvinist sense chosen and "justified" (he remembers the joy of being admitted by his teacher into the company of God's elect), there can be no doubt of his unconditional salvation, he is free of daily moral constraints. He has been urged on by a strange young man called Gil-Martin, who beguiles him with the notion that the saved can do as they like, can kill God's enemies. Robert does not enjoy his inheritance; he grows wary of Gil-Martin, now his persecutor. He ends up taking his own life.

Gil-Martin is a Mephistopheles, the more compelling, as Gide points out, because he is not a theological but a psychological figure, his "reality" is in relation to Robert rather than to an accepted structure of "objective" belief. The unbeliever believes in the reality of the devil in relation to the character. Wringhim's memoir is found when his body is exhumed a second time by Lockhart and other actual journalists and writers, Hogg himself having refused to act as guide. The real world, or rather, the literary world of Edinburgh, breaks in.

Robert Wringhim is not all bad; the crimes he is supposed to have committed—seduction, murder, matricide—he cannot remember. Hogg's structure is interesting: it tells the story twice. The first half works almost as a mystery story, though the genre had not yet been defined, with the death of the laird, the Justified Sinner taking over what is "rightly" his and then disappearing when he was on the point of arrest for murder. Miss Logan and a prostitute witnessed the crime, cornered him, tied him up, and rushed off to Edinburgh for the police. He is never seen again, except by us, who in the second half of the book are treated to his confession, in which the fanatical extremity of his faith and what it does to the brain are laid bare. Wringhim's servant tells him the story of the devil-priest who turns the people of Auchtermuchty. Gide thought this book of greater subtlety and penetration than Robert Louis Stevenson's *Dr. Jekyll and Mr. Hyde.* There is greater sexual tension, a tension not normative but perverse and Gothic. Binding, whipping, strange aversions: this is not Scott's world at all (though it is Stevenson's to a greater degree than Gide allows). Hogg does not indulge in these elements, there is more Bunyan than Rabelais in Hogg the novelist. It is much better than his other attempts at sustained fiction. He may have had help, from Lockhart perhaps. On the other hand, he was a man of talent.

Hogg responded to the "simplicity and extraordinary resemblances to truth" he found in reading *The Annals of the Parish* (1821) by John Galt (1779–1839), a lively spirit in the orbit of the influential, undependable editor and publisher William Blackwood. As one of his reluctant dependents and wits, he was required at times to cajole and bully, at times to befriend, the awkward Hogg. Galt dubbed Edinburgh, where by turns he almost prospered and almost starved, "the metropolis of Mind," a city in which the eighteenth century survived well beyond its term. Hogg admired Galt working in the Greenock customs-house, dressing as much as he could like a dandy, cutting what must have seemed a figure: "this most original and most careless writer," Hogg said. A late work of Galt's, the novella *Tribulations,* resembles the *Justified Sinner,* a work of suggestive indeterminacy. But in general in the case of Galt we cannot speak of demons. A sharp and charming writer, he knew his formal limitations and worked within them. He had little aptitude for plot and contented himself with exploring manners, displacing Scottish characters into England and vice versa, and bringing Scottish idioms into play. He traveled widely on the Continent, met Byron and wrote a life of the poet (1830), and knew Carlyle, who praised his work.

Three of his books retain their interest. *The Ayrshire Legatee* (1820) is an epistolary novel in which a minister from Scotland travels to London with his family to receive a legacy. The juxtaposition of cultures, idioms, and values satirizes both guest and host. This was followed in 1821 by a book written eight years earlier, but before *Waverley* had opened the way for novels of specifically

Scottish pitch. Constable told Galt it would not sell, but in due course it did. *The Annals of the Parish* takes its bearings (as to some extent *The Ayrshire Legatee* had done) from Goldsmith's *The Vicar of Wakefield*. There is, too, something of *Castle Rackrent* in the conception of the book. The vicar of Dalmailing, the Reverend Micah Balwhidder, is no Dr. Primrose and no Thady Rackrent, but he is a defined recorder of the events of the parish, from his installation in 1760 to his retirement half a century later. It is Mr. Balwhidder who first uses the word *utilitarian:* John Stuart Mill picked the term up from him. Where Scott focuses on dramatic events of the past, Galt is interested in process, growth, and continuity. The central theme, even the central *character,* is the parish itself, developing from a rural backwater into an industrial metropolis. The transformation is emblematic of the enormous change in British life, especially in the northern parts of the island, at the time. Micah Balwhidder writes simply, with increasingly old-fashioned views and misgivings. His humor is more pungent for being inadvertent.

His account of the death of the seemingly unrepentant and monstrous American millionaire Mr. Cayenne is Galt at his best, having created a credible narrator in a spiritually and socially trying situation.

> Mr. Cayenne of Wheatrig having for several years been in a declining way, partly brought on by the consuming fire of his furious passion, and partly by the decay of old age, sent for me on the evening of the first Sabbath of March in this year. I was surprised at the message, and went to the Wheatrig House directly, where, by the lights in the windows as I gaed up through the policy to the door, I saw something extraordinary was going on. Sambo, the blackamoor servant, opened the door, and, without speaking, shook his head; for it was an affectionate creature, and as fond of his master as if he had been his own father. By this sign I guessed that the old gentleman was thought to be drawing near his latter end; so I walked softly after Sambo up the stair, and was shown into the chamber where Mr. Cayenne, since he had been confined to the house, usually sat. His wife had been dead some years before.

This direct tone of narration, honoring a spoken Scots idiom, observes and characterizes in every sentence. The dialogue with Mr. Cayenne. in which Micah has no power or privilege except his implausible metaphysics, proceeds with dramatic vigor. "When I had been seated some time, the power was given him to raise his head as it were a-jee; and he looked at me with the tail of his eye, which I saw was glittering and glassy. 'Doctor,' for he always called me doctor, though I am not of that degree, 'I am glad to see you,' were his words, uttered with some difficulty." A strained conversation begins, Micah full of God and consolation, Mr. Cayenne approaching his impenitent end. " 'The devil take such love!" was his awful answer, which was to me as a blow on the forehead with a mell. . . . However, I was resolved to do my duty to the miserable sinner, let him say what he would." He presses on: "but the goodness of God is without bound." And here is a final blasphemy, and a corrective prayer: " 'Curse me if I think so, doctor!' replied the dying uncircumcised Philistine. But he added at whiles, his breathlessness being grievous, and often broken by a sore hiccup, 'I am, however, no saint, as you know, doctor; so I wish you to put in a word for me, doctor; for you know that in these times, doctor, it is the duty of every good subject to die a Christian.' " That moment when Micah loses his temper ("the dying uncircumcised Philistine") is more eloquent because he soon regains it. The chapter ends on an elegiac, seasonal note: "On Christmas-day the wind broke off the main arm of our Adam and Eve pear-tree; and I grieved for it more as a type and sign of the threatened partition, than on account of the damage, though the fruit was the juiciest in all the country side."

———•———

Scott described Susan Ferrier (1782–1854) as, "simple, full of humor and exceedingly ready at repartee, and all this without the least affectation of the bluestocking." Animated at first by a spirit not unlike Galt's, she has a gaiety in her language and sardonic charity in her social vision. Though she is sometimes linked with Austen, her roots go farther back, just as her art falls well short of that of her English contemporary. At first she seems like a lesser Smollett without, quite, his sting. Her main theme is displacement, and her plots are formulaic. The city-bred, aristocratic English lass is swept off her feet by romance and transplanted by marriage to the unforgiving highlands, with their dour, rheumy eyes and wagging chins. She might have been a tedious moralist, but her would-be severity is sugared, the pill so sweet that whatever medicine it carries is quite denatured.

Like Scott's, her father was a Writer to the Signet, and she devoted herself to him (as Edgeworth had done to hers); she traveled with him when, as manager of the highland estates of the Duke of Argyll, he performed his duties, and there she gathered material for her writing. Her satire depends on "crossing cultural boundaries" and national borders with the wrong luggage. There is irony in her juxtapositions: of nations, landscapes, classes, sexes. Her first novel, *Marriage* (1818), published anonymously by Blackwood, began as a collaboration with her friend the Duke of Argyll's niece, and was intended to warn girls against inappropriate eloping. She had finished it in 1811, but it was only when

*Waverley,* in the wake of *Castle Rackrent,* opened up the provincial thematic market that her book (like Galt's) could be published.

Lady Juliana is an earl's daughter (Ferrier's heroines are always upper-class) who elopes with Henry Douglas, a handsome, young, and impecunious officer, a second son and disinherited to boot. He carts her off to the Highlands, to an unfashionable house and neighborhood. It is not as though she had not been warned. In the first scene her father summons her to discuss marriage. She enters with her three dogs and he orders that they be removed. "Lady Juliana rang for the footman to take Venus; bade Pluto be quiet, like a darling, under the sofa; and, taking Cupid in her arms, assured her lordship he need fear no disturbance from the sweet creatures, and that she would be all attention to his commands—kissing her cherished pug as she spoke." The properties of classical irony are there, especially Cupid, from whom his lordship receives, in the end, great disturbance.

Juliana regards herself as a figure in fiction, indulging her romantic martyrdom. She "felt she was now in the true position of a heroine: a handsome lover—and ambitious father—cruel fortune—unshaken constancy. She sighed deeply—even dropped a tear, and preserved a mournful silence." The clichés fall over one another, as Ferrier intends. These are the instruments with which Juliana "thinks." When she arrives at Glenfern Castle, with her yapping pets, reality and romantic expectation collide. "At the entrance of the strangers, a flock of females rushed forward to meet them. Douglas good-humoredly submitted to be hugged by three long-chinned spinsters, whom he recognised as his aunts,"—they are duly fleshed out as the Misses Jackie, Grizzie, and Nicky—"and warmly saluted five awkward purple girls"—because of the color of their hair—"he guessed to be his sisters; while Lady Juliana stood the image of despair, and scarcely conscious, admitted in silence the civilities of her new relations; till, at length, sinking into a chair, she endeavored to conceal her agitation by calling to the dogs, and caressing her macaw." The humor is broad, the types predictable, coarsely realized, formulaic.

Ferrier's chapter epigraphs add a further dimension of sentiment and irony. Chapter 4 wears this badge from Doctor Johnson's *Journey to the Western Isles:* "Such solace as the bagpipe can give, they have long enjoyed." The first chapter's epigraph is more earnest, taken from *Alexander and Campaspe* by Lyly: "Love!—A word by superstition thought a god; by use turned to an humor; by self-will made a flattering madness." But the accumulation of epigraphs turns the book into a kind of anthology, the author at every stage demonstrating her culture and playing upon ours.

Juliana gives birth to two daughters. One of them grows up in Scotland appallingly virtuous, austere, rather plain; one grows up a mirror of her mother in London, coldhearted and beautiful (Douglas has been packed off to India and Juliana is thus released from the Highlands). Marriage is the end for each girl, one happy (virtue in this instance implausibly rewarded), one not. The evangelical strain is already present in *Marriage.* Ferrier repented of her art and became a committed member of the Free Church.

But not before *The Inheritance* (1824) and *Destiny; or, The Chief's Daughter* (1831), which Elizabeth Stevenson (who would become Mrs. Gaskell) read with enthusiasm three times over when it first appeared. The opening of *The Inheritance* echoes *Pride and Prejudice,* and the derivative quality of Ferrier's work proves a serious flaw, evidence of poor formal imagination and an intermittent connection with her social concerns. Gertrude St. Clair is regarded as the heiress of an earl; in fact we (and eventually she) discover her actual father, a low-born American; it turns out she was adopted and is in fact a servant's daughter. She loses her inheritance and her fiancé, the dashing, scheming Colonel Dolour, who is also her cousin. In the background, pining, is Edward Lyndsay, who picks up the pieces. The chin-wagging spinster Miss Pratt animates an occasionally somber scene.

*The Inheritance,* too, appeared anonymously in *Blackwood's Magazine.* But *Destiny* appeared under her name. Cadell the publisher paid her £1,700 for it, an enormous sum that proved the popularity of her earlier books. In this family or clan novel, Glenroy, the chief of the Malcolms, widowed, marries Lady Elizabeth Waldegrave from London. She finds the Highlands as intolerable as Juliana had done and separates from Glenroy. This most profitable was also the least entertaining of her books. We have to concede that unlike Galt's, unlike Edgeworth's, Ferrier's world is not real. It borrows energy from other writers. Her characters represent attitudes and are thin as figures of allegory. Juliana, on the verge of reciting, says: "My sentiments are all at second hand." The novel form is sufficiently developed for there to be a second, a third, and fourth hand.

# 13

# *Manners*

Fanny Burney, Jane Austen

In 1893 Henry James sent a set of the volumes of *Evelina* (1778), Fanny Burney's first novel, to the American expatriate Henrietta Reuball, who hosted a salon in Paris and whom Wilde described as "very ugly and very amusing." James was pleased when she acknowledged the gift. He said little about the novel itself, except to remember that he had once enjoyed it; but because he was addressing a woman, he added, "the little volumes *are* pretty & *font bien* on little shelves." Fanny Burney's novels can be decorative.

*Evelina* tells of a bright, innocent girl who eventually gets her rights and her man after social misunderstandings, counterplots, and detours. The key to the technique is an exquisite deferral of gratification for the protagonist and therefore the reader, a kind of forensic foreplay that leads to the life sentence of the marriage vows and stops there. In her preface Burney warns us of what we will not find here: there will be no fantastic settings, no Gothic properties; we will not visit that world of Imagination "where Reason is an outcast, and where the sublimity of the marvellous, rejects all aid from sober Probability." Her Probability is sober, but sobriety is not joyless. "The heroine of these memoirs, young, artless, and inexperienced, is 'No faultless Monster, that the world ne'er saw,' but the offspring of Nature, and of Nature in her simplest attire." This sentence concludes the preface and is not quite true, or it is true in a revisionist Rousseauian sense only, for Nature in Burney is topiaried and trellised, and if it runs wild, it does so only up to the hedge.

The frame of Burney's novel is larger than the picture it holds. Had she followed the male characters, she might have explored a world as various as Fielding's. But her concern is with her heroine, and she is, when she writes *Evelina,* herself a girl in her mid-twenties. All the same, she has an uncanny understanding of motive, male and female. Sir John Belmont marries, expecting a fortune; when it fails to materialize, he abandons his wife and small daughter. The daughter is raised in a secluded place (this much is Rousseauian) by a guardian, Mr. Villars. She becomes a beautiful young woman, visits London and Mrs. Mirvan, and falls in love with Lord Orville. He is as far above her station as Pamela's young master is above hers, and poor Evelina, for it is the eponymous heroine, suffers mortification whenever her coarse, vulgar relations appear.

What is more, she is pursued by indefatigable, unattractive Sir Clement Willoughby.

In time she gets her errant father to recognize her (he believed he was supporting her all along, whereas in fact he was supporting the daughter of Evelina's nurse, the clever old crone having provided for her own out of Sir John's desertion) and eventually all ends happily: she inherits a fortune and marries Lord Orville. The hurdles and pitfalls are social, psychological, and sentimental, and the sentimental ones are the hardest to negotiate and yet are the most important in teasing out the narrative. *Evelina* is vast. In Fielding the lines are boldly drawn, the moral categories paradoxically explored, but in Burney, a favorite of Doctor Johnson and Mrs. Thrale, there are precise niceties to resolve, understanding requires exactness that the bold, eighteenth-century spirit of Fielding would have found risible. Burney is newfangled in some respects.

On the site of the house where, in an upper room, Fanny Burney, aged twenty-five, completed *Evelina; or, The History of a Young Lady's Entrance into the World,* today stands Westminster Library. Some vestiges of her world survive in the neighborhood: facades, street names, a bustling atmosphere, an abundance of foreign voices and faces giving it a metropolitan aspect. In Fanny's time strict proprieties attached to class and sex, and she ran afoul of some of them. She had begun a book a decade earlier, in her mid-teens, but her stepmother discovered she was writing. Fanny burned her papers, persuaded that literary endeavor might devalue her in the marriage bourse. Her twelve-year-old sister, Susan, sobbed at her side during the bonfire, and Fanny had to practice lonely needlework for penance. How unlike Jane Austen, cheerfully quilting with her mother! Young Fanny herself was unsure whether writing novels was quite a proper activity, for there was a kind of "degradation" that went with the form, whether the author was male or female. She was, however, sure that needlework was not her vocation.

Frances Burney (1752–1840), later Madame d'Arblay, was the daughter of Dr. Charles Burney, the organist, composer, music historian, and travel writer. Her elder brother became an admiral and sailed with Captain Cook; her younger brother was the classical scholar Charles Burney, whose library of 13,000 volumes was acquired by the British Museum.

She was born in Norfolk but the family moved to London when she was eight. Her mother died when she was nine and was soon replaced. Dr. Burney's circle included Johnson and his friends Edmund Burke and Sir Joshua Reynolds. Fanny's sisters went to Paris for their education, but Fanny was kept at home where she had the run of her father's library, in which there was, Macaulay claims, but one novel, Fielding's *Amelia.* There she educated herself and socialized with her family's acquaintances. Despite the initial *contretemps* with her stepmother, it seems she was encouraged and her talents fostered by her father (who championed her work behind the scenes with the same assiduity he devoted to his own) and his friends. *Evelina,* published anonymously by Thomas Lowndes in January 1778, could not stay anonymous for long: it was more than her father could do to contain his pride, and the revelation of her identity elicited some powerful compliments, not least from Johnson, who confided to Mrs. Thrale, who confided to Dr. Burney himself, that "there were passages in it which might do *honor* to Richardson."

*Evelina* does indeed recall Richardson. The 1782 sequel, *Cecilia; or, Memoirs of an Heiress,* for which she was paid £250 by Payne and Cadell, was rather less compelling. Cecilia Beverley inherits a fortune on the condition that her husband assumes her surname. We are in the world of property, conditions, contracts, and trials, an eighteenth-century place but without that generous glow of wit with which Fielding illuminated its earlier decades. Cecilia comes through various travails and reaps her rewards. Among the secondary characters, Lady Honoria Pemberton is a voluble, engaging prankster. *Cecilia* was admired for its construction, but its style was too immediately in Johnson's debt. Burney courted his approval, and how better to get it than to ventriloquize.

When her identity was discovered, celebrity followed, and she accepted it graciously after a period of extreme excitement. She was appointed Second Keeper of the Robes to Queen Charlotte in 1786, a post that honored but did not suit her, given the demeaning nature of some of her tasks. She cried off in due course and, reduced from £200, was pensioned off with £100 per annum from the royal purse. In 1793 she married General d'Arblay, a French refugee of wide connections among the expatriate community.

In 1796 Jane Austen's father allowed the future novelist to invest a guinea and become a subscriber to Burney's next novel, *Camilla.* The Austen rectory was full of Burney; the concerns of the novel—young people and matrimony— interested the Austen girls. Burney imported elements from the drama into *Camilla,* and they did not travel well. Her fops and figures of ridicule are foursquare and unsubtle, lacking the reality of her earlier secondary characters. The lessons of economy of characterization that she teaches here, however, and the creation of "types," affected Austen and later George Eliot. A sentimental, Richardsonian story, it is told in Fielding's manner: the omniscient narrator keeps the love between Camilla and Edgar uncertain, a finally tedious, repetitive art of deferral through distance, misunderstanding, or error, the postponed climax. Misunderstanding is the chief protagonist. Tedious is the described rather than lived "interiority," a continual nuancing from without. It is puppetry.

Madame d'Arblay went abroad with her general and lived on the Continent, pursued some of the time by French government agents because of the English connection. A decade of wandering included a mastectomy conducted without anesthetic, which she survived. In 1812 she returned to England and stayed there for most of her twenty-eight remaining years. Her final novel was *The Wanderer* (1814). After that she edited her father's *Memoirs* (1832) and continued to write the *Diaries* that began appearing in 1889. They include illuminating recollections of Johnson and Goldsmith and are more valuable than her later fiction, and than her plays, of which eight were written and one produced. Readers who are keen to discover the pulse of the artist rather than the artistic form find in letters and diaries a rewarding quarry.

Much is said against Burney's late style, especially in *The Wanderer*. For modern readers it is difficult. But it is unclear to what extent this was "an affectation," any more than Henry James's late style is affected, or Johnson's: "How very like Dr. Johnson is to his writing; and how much the same thing it was to hear him or to read him . . . his language was generally imagined to be labored and studied, instead of the mere common flow of his thoughts." It is possible that Burney was similarly ceremonious, though her concerns were remote from his. Her abiding virtue is not in her late style but in the type she creates in her early writing of the inexperienced girl, well-bred and virtuous, entering challenged and amused, making her way in the world. And her abiding vice? Edmund Gosse declares that her "novels grow too bulky," and it is not until Meredith that the novel becomes portable once more.

———•———

In the case of Jane Austen, there was also a bonfire. Cassandra, guardian of the posthumous privacy of her sister Jane, whom she called Jenny, burned the letters she thought compromising, or informative, all those that might identify Jane's mysterious lovers (if they existed) and—who knows what else she suppressed. What Cassandra left was a carapace, the shell of the beetle without Gregor Samsa inside, a volume of crabby, gossipy, sometimes pedestrian letters through which we catch glimmers of the novelist, that wit and consummate formalist whose intimacy should be as sharp and tonic as, say, Elizabeth Bennett's. The surviving letters, E. M. Forster writes, "were temporary and local in their appeal, and their essential meaning went down with her into the grave." He dislikes the person Cassandra's winnowing leaves behind: "She faces the facts, but they are not her facts, and her lapses of taste over carnality can be deplorable, no doubt because they arise from lack of feeling."

That judgment is harsh, but Cassandra's protective love makes it unarguable if we base a judgment of Jane Austen on the epistolary residue. The "poverty of material," says Forster, which is a positive condition of the novels themselves, is a negative condition for the *literary* value of the letters. They seem to prove that "the supreme thing in life to her was the family. She knew no other allegiance." That family was "hard" and "humorous." Virginia Woolf evokes her with greater affection: "Charming but perpendicular, loved at home but feared by strangers, biting of tongue but tender of heart." And the novels show the same paradoxical complexities. Was Austen "tender of heart"? Or is Woolf, out of affection, sweetening a writer who had more severity and Old Testament justice about her than most, however gentled by manners?

How different the worlds of Burney and Austen! Though Burney is senior by twenty-three years and outlived Austen by another twenty-three, how much more "modern" and varied Burney's life seems than that of the eighteenth-century spinster who died in Winchester a young old lady of forty-one. Burney was a new type of citizen, urban, a "working woman" in the gradually thawing winter of English social division. And Austen? A vicar's daughter, rural, unpretentious, in youth a parodist, whose parodies propelled her into the heart of rhetoric, understanding how with language people restrict, maim, and deceive themselves. The fairy tales she tells are of narrow escape and rescue as well as of romance.

In chapter 5 of *Northanger Abbey,* the first novel she sold (to Richard Crosby in 1798, for £10), and the last published (1818), she defends the novel form against all comers. Credulous Catherine and charming, scheming Isabella have become friends, so close that they actually "read novels together." The author preempts our sense that it is an unworthy and slightly indecent pastime:

> Yes, novels;—for I will not adopt that ungenerous and impolitic custom so common with novel-writers, of degrading by their contemptuous censure the very performances, to the number of which they are themselves adding—joining with their greatest enemies in bestowing the harshest epithets on such works, and scarcely ever permitting them to be read by their own heroine, who, if she accidentally take up a novel, is sure to turn over its insipid pages with disgust. Alas! If the heroine of one novel be not patronized by the heroine of another, from whom can she expect protection and regard? I cannot approve of it. Let us leave it to the reviewers to abuse such effusions of fancy at their leisure, and over every new novel to talk in threadbare strains of the trash with which the press now groans. Let us not desert one another; we are an injured body. Although our productions have afforded more extensive and unaffected pleasure than those of any other literary corporation in the world, no species of composition has been so much decried. From pride, ignorance, or fashion, our foes are almost as many as our

readers . . . "I am no novel-reader—I seldom look into novels—Do not imagine that I often read novels—It is really very well for a novel." Such is the common cant. "And what are you reading, Miss—?" "Oh! It is only a novel!" replies the young lady, while she lays down her book with affected indifference, or momentary shame. "It is only *Cecilia,* or *Camilla,* or *Belinda*"; or, in short, only some work in which the greatest powers of the mind are displayed, in which the most thorough knowledge of human nature, the happiest delineation of its varieties, the liveliest effusions of wit and humor, are conveyed to the world in the best-chosen language.

Humorous, this is also impassioned, the tone and manner of the eighteenth century, the argument of the nineteenth, demanding for a new form, properly handled, the same respect that critics and snobs accord to poetry and the essay. She is sending up the tradition epitomized by Mrs. Radcliffe's sensational Gothic romances and pointing toward a morally more answerable, a truer aesthetic, a naturalism we associate with Burney, Edgeworth, and other heirs of Richardson. In *Northanger Abbey* on the very first page she declares what her novel is *not.* The father does not lock up his daughters, the heroine is only almost pretty, Mrs. Allen's footwear is serviceable and comical rather than decorous. This is an ordinary world and we are not to anticipate unnatural or metaphysical surprises, whatever the heroine might hope for.

Underpinning the vulnerable romance in Austen are the material energies that animated Defoe, that defined the social worlds of Richardson and Burney, Fielding and Edgeworth. The social tones of Austen's characters and the voice and manner of her narrator tell the reader about their place in society quite as much as they tell us about their nature. Throughout *Pride and Prejudice,* for example, in conversation and in the author's ironies, the word *money* is frequently coupled with a potential spouse, for in the eyes of society and in the sober eyes of time, fortune is first of all material. "Emma Woodhouse, handsome, clever, and rich"; "a single man in possession of a good fortune"; "Miss Maria Ward of Huntingdon, with only seven thousand pounds": at the entrance to each novel there is a summary balance. The principles of permanence are pitted against the principles of change, and the heroine must negotiate the difficult straits between sensibility and sense. Against the ephemeralities of uniforms, plumes, bosoms, the handsome flesh, the whispers of love, and the darkened carriage of misjudgment, stand bricks and mortar that time's fell hand defaces less briskly than it does body and heart. Jane Austen was aware of these realities, being a vicar's daughter, a spinster, a woman made frugal by circumstance and dependent on the goodwill of her relations. Waste not, want not: she did not paragraph her letters, she crammed as much as she could onto a single sheet, writing between the lines, in order to save her correspondent and herself the extra cost of transmission for a second sheet.

Why is it, asks Patricia Beer, the wryest Austenite, that so many male and some female critics believe that "no spinster can be wholly admirable"? Virginia Woolf's approach is different. She infers from *Persuasion* some missing facts. "There is an expressed emotion in the scene at the concert and in the famous talk about woman's constancy which proves not merely the biographical fact that Jane Austen had loved, but the aesthetic fact that she was no longer afraid to say so. Experience, when it was of a serious kind, had to sink very deep, and to be thoroughly disinfected by the passage of time, before she allowed herself to deal with it in fiction." Can we confuse Jane with Emma? Woolf concludes that had Austen lived, she would have become less a comic writer, a mistress of dialogue, more serious, more reflective, "the forerunner of Henry James and of Proust." Yet what is it that James, always respectful of Austen but always tetchy in her company, finally allows himself to say in 1914, in an essay later entitled "The New Novel"? "Why shouldn't it be argued against her that where her testimony complacently ends the pressure of appetite within us presumes exactly to begin?" It was after all the most Austenesque of her successors, E. M. Forster, who suggested that novels should begin rather than end with marriages: it was surviving in that situation, rather than reaching that end, that required attention.

Jane Austen was born in Steventon, Hampshire, in 1775, the sixth of eight children and the second of two daughters. Her father, George Austen, was the rector, a man of intellectual quality but limited fortune who married Cassandra Leigh, a woman above his station, with titled relations. John, the eldest son, followed his father into the church and succeeded him as rector at Steventon, a displacement that unsettled Jane Austen in her early adult life. George, the second child, was handicapped and remains a shadow in her biography. A wealthy relation, married and childless, adopted Edward, the third son, and he inherited their estates in Hampshire and Kent and helped provide for his mother and sisters when his father died. Then there was Henry, a lively banker and bankrupt, then clergyman, with whom Jane Austen stayed in London, liking his worldliness. After Henry came Cassandra and Jane, then two younger brothers, Francis and Charles, who rose to the top in the navy. Jane Austen is, Woolf suggests, overly sedulous in describing clergymen and sailors. Her humor becomes more reticent, unless the clergyman is a figure of fun, or a grotesque like Mr. Collins.

It was a large, cheerful family with a wide acquaintance, and Jane and Cassandra were on easy terms with neighbors of their own, and of slightly better, class. Among their closest friends were the three Bigg sisters, whose brother Harris Bigg-Wither proposed to Jane, was accepted one evening, and rejected the following morning. Had Jane Austen accepted him, she might have come before the world as Mrs. Bigg-Wither. She imagined marrying, not emotionally frail William Cowper, her favorite poet, or Doctor Johnson, for whom she felt filial devotion, but the clergyman-poet George Crabbe, author of verse narratives, a severe moralist of the provincial world. Her affection for the man behind *The Village* and *The Parish Register* was not a one-off joke but a running gag in the family. When Austen learned that Mrs. Crabbe had died, she had hardly realized he was married. "Poor woman! I will comfort *him* as well as I can, but I do not undertake to be good to her children. She had better not leave any." He did father a fictional child on Austen: her Fanny Price is born of his Fanny Price in part two of "Marriages" from *The Parish Register*. Crabbe's Fanny, like Austen's, is pursued by "an amorous knight" and is "meekly firm" with him. She knows her heart, and her heart is deeply complicit with her station. She can rise, but not to the very top.

It was at Steventon that Austen spent her first twenty-five years, and there she wrote in a spirit of parody and satire, sending up the literature of sentiment in all its forms. She composed *Love and Freindship* [*sic*] when she was seventeen. Woolf says, "And taking up her pen again she wrote, it is clear, as fast as she could write, and faster than she could spell, for the incredible adventures of Laura and Sophia popped into her head as quick as lightning." A sense of humor drove her, modulating now into hilarity, now into tenderness or sorrow; and an almost libidinal drive, bringing her characters by stages closer to one another and to their (at this stage inconsequential) destinies. From parody it was a short step—the step Cervantes took, and Fielding—to genuine interest in character and in the manners, affectations, and sincerities that gave rise to it.

*Pride and Prejudice,* originally entitled *First Impressions,* was drafted at similar speed in 1796. She read it aloud to her family (reading aloud was a regular pastime with the Austens), and her father undertook to get it published, sending it off to his university acquaintance Thomas Cadell in 1797, proposing to pay for its production. The novel, he wrote, was "comprised of three Vols. about the length of Miss Burney's *Evelina*." Cadell rejected it by return of post, after which Austen "lop't and crop't" it, so that when it was published, sixteen years later, it was considerably shorter than *Evelina*. She had changed the title, as well: in 1800 a novel called *First Impressions* was published by the Minerva Press. She may have taken her replacement title from the last chapter of Burney's *Cecilia*: "If to PRIDE and PREJUDICE you owe your miseries . . . to PRIDE and PREJUDICE you will also owe their termination." There were probably 1,500 copies in the first printing of *Pride and Prejudice*. But it was not to be her first published novel either.

The first three to be published—*Sense and Sensibility* (1811), *Pride and Prejudice* (1813), and *Mansfield Park* (1814)—were produced at the Military Library, Whitehall, by Thomas Egerton. He had misgivings about the love scenes in *Pride and Prejudice* and suggested immodesty on the author's part. "But Sir in the depiction of love, modesty is the fullness of *truth;* and decency frankness." All the same, sensing it was not quite nice, she chose to have her name removed from the title pages of her Egerton novels. The books were "By a Lady." In 1816 she changed publishers, with initial relief, though judging from the correspondence it was short-lived. Her letters to John Murray are tense and gently hectoring. Murray added to his list *Emma,* the last novel published in her lifetime. He was a great publisher, well connected, and he made certain that *Emma* was well received; this may have been why Sir Walter Scott reviewed it at length. The move to Murray was wise, whatever tone the author adopted. The distinction of the imprint set her above her earlier station. The book was a success, though not a substantial one. Her three Egerton novels and *Emma* together earned her no more than £700 profit, not enough to transform her life or reduce her dependence on her brothers' kindness.

Murray published *Northanger Abbey* and *Persuasion* in 1818, the year after Austen's death, as a single book in four volumes. Other work, incomplete, appeared later, notably *Sanditon,* the twelve chapters of her last project, which was originally entitled *The Brothers*. It appeared in 1925. Her earlier epistolary novel *Lady Susan* (1805), about a scheming widow with charm and appetite, and *The Watsons* of the same year, which J. E. Austen Leigh added to the second edition of his *Memoir of Jane Austen* (1871), were notable torsos. Elements in *The Watsons* recall *Mansfield Park*. Young Emma Watson returns to her modest home after her wealthy aunt, with whom she was living, remarries. She reenters a world of people less refined and cultivated than those to whom she had grown accustomed. Other characters seem like sketches for familiar figures. Lord Osborne is not unlike Darcy; the courteous man of the cloth Mr. Howard might suggest a matured Edmund; the confirmed trifler Tom Musgrave has much in common with Austen's other bounders. This earlier Emma would ultimately have married Mr. Howard, but the story did not prosper. This work, drafted when her life was unsettled and relatively peripatetic, is provisional, preparatory.

At Steventon she had started drafting *Sense and Sensibility* in 1797, basing it on a sketch she had read aloud to her family two years earlier. To begin with, that book too was in epistolary form—writing parodies of letters of sentiment was a favorite pastime with her. *Northanger Abbey* was also begun at Steventon in 1797 or 1798. Much was begun but little achieved there: it was a stable, happy home. When in 1801, without consulting his daughters, George Austen handed the living on to his son James and removed to Bath, Jane and Cassandra were shocked. Bath did not agree with Jane Austen, it was too strident and bright; Anne Elliott in *Persuasion* resembles her in her sense of the city's tedious depravity. When George died in 1805, leaving his widow and daughters too modestly provided for, the move to Southampton was hardly agreeable. There they stayed until 1809, living with young brother Frank. They made occasional forays to London, but—Cassandra's fiancé having died, and Jane not having acquired one—they had entered into spinsterhood and a dependence manifest to them every day.

In 1809 Edward, who had inherited his properties, offered Mrs. Austen and his sisters Chawton, a handsome little house on his estate near Alton in Hampshire. Together with a friend they moved in on July 7. Their situation was not unlike that of the Dashwoods in *Sense and Sensibility,* arriving to a mingled sense of relief and disappointment, because though the house was pleasant, it was more modest and less commodious than they expected. Chawton became home, "a household without men," as P. D. James called it, with Cassandra as devoted homemaker, and here Jane Austen spent eight years in an orderly, sympathetic environment where her time was more her own than it had ever been before. The original house had a large garden with an orchard, a shrubbery for exercise, a vegetable patch, and a field for the donkeys that pulled Jane Austen's trap, which is now parked in the bakehouse. Other mementos survive. Hanging on the wall in the bedroom she occupied is the patchwork quilt she and her mother worked; P. D. James speculates on which patches might have been from Jane's own gowns.

Austen wrote in the second drawing room, the one with the piano; the shrill of hinges alerted her to the approach of interruptions and gave her a chance to hide her writing under a blotting pad. The house has regained, after restoration, a sense of cool intimacy. The nomadic years were over; she resolved to bring her various drafts and beginnings to completion.

There was one last move for her, to Winchester, where she went for treatment to Mr. Lyford, the renowned physician, and where she was buried in 1817. She had seemed to be in good health when she went to London for the publication of *Emma* (1815), but by 1816 a wasting illness left her slow and exhausted. She finished the first draft of *Persuasion* in July 1816 and then wrestled with the penultimate chapter, exhausting herself. After she died, her illness was identified as Addison's disease, "a failure of the adrenal cortex . . . which results in increasing weakness and weight loss, severe gastrointestinal disturbances and often pain in the back," P. D. James records. "Jane complained of all these symptoms, together with the brown and black pigmentation of the skin typical of the disease."

Jane Austen's novels are set in English heartland, far from where ancient British and Celtic spirits trouble memory, an England that hears the pummeling of industrial development and the drumbeats of empire as thunder so remote it hardly seems to be thunder at all. Charlotte Brontë complained to G. H. Lewes about the lack of poetry in Austen's novels. "An accurate daguerreotyped portrait of a commonplace face; a carefully fenced, highly cultivated garden, with neat borders and delicate flowers; but no glance of a bright, vivid physiognomy, no open country, no fresh air, no blue hill, no bonny beck." As in a photograph (how up-to-date the image is) there is no main verb in the sentence to release the action. "I should hardly like to live with her ladies and gentlemen, in their elegant but confined houses." Her geography looks narrow, but given the distances and discomforts of eighteenth- and nineteenth-century travel, it must have seemed a large enough world to her and her early readers, who included the Prince Regent ("the Royal Adonis himself," J. C. Squire dubs him: with Burney and Austen in favor, it might have seemed that the court was reacquiring a sense of literary value), Sir Walter Scott, Archbishop Whatley, and the clergyman wit Sydney Smith, whose aphorisms might have dropped off the back of Jane Austen's trap, and who some like to imagine was the prototype for Henry Tilney.

Jane Austen writes of a known world, wholly familiar to her and to her readers. ("Have the courage to be ignorant of a great number of things, in order to avoid the calamity of being ignorant of everything," Sydney Smith counsels.) Henry James lumps Austen and Anthony Trollope together, the Trollope of the Barchester and English provincial novels, employing them as a pair of rhetorical tweezers with which to lift out the characters of inferior novelists, examine them, and leave them dead upon the table. He does not demonstrate but assumes the similarity in subject matter: provincial, at home in particular social registers, conservative or normative in intent.

In Austen, however, something new and remarkable begins to happen. In *Mansfield Park* Fanny walks alone in the shrubbery and, inspirited by the greenery and a kind of calm, reflects to herself in ways that do not advance the narrative but reveal the character. She is *coming into being;* she gathers into herself her own reality. Jane Austen is didactic quite as much as Burney, but at a different level, a level at which the nature of being human more than the rules of being good are explored. Fanny is among Austen's protagonists whose worlds become so real that they can step outside the frame of their particular novel and companion us. "There should be a clinical word for those who cannot leave Jane Austen alone," says Patricia Beer, referring here not only to the biographical obsessives but to those Janeites who build their own fictions on her characters and themes or out of her life. In *Changing Places,* David Lodge bears her out, creating an academic protagonist whose career is based entirely on the study of Austen: Morris Zapp of Euphoria State University describes her as "a pain in the ass," but then an academic's got to live. This is what licensed parasites do. Helen Fielding's *Bridget Jones's Diary* reduces and reprocesses Elizabeth Bennett and her difficult choices; *Mansfield Revisited* by Joan Aiken chews away at the old book with period teeth; *Antipodes Jane* by Barbara Ker Wilson takes her down under; there are also continuations and would-be authoritative completions of *Sanditon* and *The Watsons,* unfinished works "fulfilled" by another "lady."

In his essay "Force of Love" Martin Amis muses on how Jane Austen makes us so keen to see Elizabeth marry Darcy, how she creates in us that anxiety about Jane and Bingley, drawing us into a kind of complicity with monstrous Mrs. Bennett in our eagerness, prurience, and concern. We do not reserve judgment like Mr. Bennett, safe with a pipe behind the library door. We are lured out into the garden, into the heart. As Amis says, it works over and over. How can a story be so inexhaustible? It is not the story that remains fresh but the characters, and the sharp wit of the language in which they travel.

Is Woolf right to condemn her male characters as inadequate? The comic ones work, but the main protagonists, apart from Darcy (whose dark mystery seems more opaque than profound), are less able to step beyond the frame. Perhaps this is because Austen tends to characterize them by negatives, as a gossip might; male characters are first misperceived and then brought into true, while the heroines' transformations are triggered by plot (as in the case of Emma) but amply anticipated by their development and growth of conscience and consciousness. "More than any other novelist," says Woolf, "she fills every inch of her canvas with observations, fashions every sentence into meaning, stuffs up every chink and cranny of the fabric until each novel is a little living world, from which you cannot break off a scene or even a sentence without bleeding it of some of its life." The "little living world" (the word "little" condescends: there is nothing "little" about Emma's, or Elizabeth's, worlds) is less that of the story or plot, more that of the character.

This is new, but also in terms of its moral and psychological priorities more in debt to the eighteenth than the nineteenth century. Ian Watt contrasts the "feminine and youthful attitudes" of the writer with the Augustan values that she foregrounds: "Her young heroines finally marry older men—comprehensive epitomes of the Augustan norms such as Mr. Darcy and Mr. Knightley. Her novels in fact dramatize the process whereby feminine and adolescent values" (note the juxtaposition and the conjunction used) "are painfully educated in the norms of the mature, rational, and educated male world." As against the fashionable norms of the nineteenth-century society that is their element, there are the abiding norms, the "principles of permanence," represented by an older order. The satisfactions of her heroines can seem meager to modern readers.

What makes them abide in memory is their unclosed complexity; they are remote from the good and bad characters of Smollett, Fielding, even of Burney. When they marry, they will not cease to change and grow, they elude the commonplace moral polarities of a dramatic tradition that affected and even conditioned readers' expectations. Austen's characters are redeemable and corruptible, capable of change and subject to change. They feel anger, they are hurt, they internalize aggression and find ways of channeling it in action. They will experiment with other people, living vicariously, projecting until they realize that the roles they have invented are their own (Emma through Harriet, for example). In mature Austen, especially *Pride and Prejudice, Emma,* and *Persuasion,* it is not external events so much as internal changes that provide the drama.

Part of the successful creation of her characters' reality has to do with the ways in which they misunderstand dialogue, bringing to bear their own expectations. Dialogue becomes a means of oblique disclosure and characterization. *Emma* is a tissue of such eloquent misunderstandings. In *Sense and Sensibility,* "Marianne Dashwood was born to an extraordinary fate. She was born to discover the falsehood of her own opinions, and to counteract, by her conduct, her most favorite maxims." Mrs. Jennings is a purveyor of misunderstanding. In *Pride and Prejudice* Wickham and Willoughby, in *Persuasion* Anna and Captain Wentworth, are discovered for what they are by indirection. This is Jane Austen's hallmark, two subjectivities mishearing, misunderstanding; establishing understanding is required for marriage bells and the denouement. In Burney's *Evelina,* misunderstanding is mechanical, foreplay. In Austen it becomes proportionate, and its function relates not only to plot but to the larger realities of the book's world.

Yet what brings us closest to her characters is a trick of technique that other novelists (notably Burney) had used but that Austen perfected. Defoe in first-person narratives and Richardson in epistolary novels provide "realism of presentation," a sense of lived or living immediacy, a vision through the very eye sockets of Crusoe or Clarissa. Austen began as an epistolary novelist. *Love and Freindship* and *Lady Susan* were in letter form, and *Elinor and Marianne* was epistolary, though transformed into *Sense and Sensibility* the dynamic altered. The change of title itself indicates the nature of that alteration, from the names of two first-person correspondents to two abstract nouns describing dispositions. In Fielding's third-person narrator we experience "realism of assessment," action portrayed in the past and moral and satirical conclusions drawn. Austen enjoyed the satirical freedom such a style afforded, its deliberate distance from the plot. But she devised a technique that gave her the best of both worlds, a technique we associate with the innovations of Gustave Flaubert, the *style indirect libre,* or free indirect style, a way of narrating that integrates both reported thought and speech and direct speech.

Nabokov discriminates four levels of characterization in Austen. There is, first, external description, then reported speech, then quoted speech, and then the presentation of "speech" and thought when the author's "free indirect style" enters into a character and for a spell rides the rhythms and to some extent the diction of its discriminated consciousness. There is only the briefest preamble to indicate the shifting of focus—"he reflected" or "she felt." The writer is freed to move, without being seen, as it were, between "omniscient" objective narration and the subjectivities of the characters. This allows *their* sincerity or candor and the *author's* irony. There is no clear boundary, but there is clear differentiation. The narrative stays in third person but has the changing energies of first. Realism of presentation, then, and realism of assessment coexist. In the following passage from *Persuasion,* Anne Elliott's initial thoughts are generic, but as we get closer and closer to her, "while her fingers were mechanically at work," we enter into her reality, which includes her sense of herself past and present, alone and in relation. The pathos is intense, she is aware of her physicality and her age; we experience her discomfort, her embarrassment, her disappointment.

> It was a merry, joyous party, and no one seemed in higher spirits than Captain Wentworth. She felt that he had every thing to elevate him which general attention and deference, and especially the attention of all the young women, could do. The Miss Hayters, the females of the family of cousins already mentioned, were apparently admitted to the honor of being in love with him; and as for Henrietta and Louisa, they both seemed so entirely occupied by him, that nothing but the continued appearance of the most perfect good-will between themselves could have made it credible that they were not decided rivals. If he were a little spoilt by such universal, such eager admiration, who could wonder?

Then there is a change of key. From the social register, we move into the personal register, from looking out we begin to look in.

> These were some of the thoughts which occupied Anne, while her fingers were mechanically at work, proceeding for half an hour together, equally without error, and without consciousness. Once she felt that he was looking at herself, observing her altered features,

perhaps, trying to trace in them the ruins of the face which had once charmed him; and once she knew that he must have spoken of her; she was hardly aware of it, till she heard the answer; but then she was sure of his having asked his partner whether Miss Elliott never danced? The answer was, "Oh, no; never; she has quite given up dancing. She had rather play. She is never tired of playing." Once, too, he spoke to her. She had left the instrument on the dancing being over, and he had sat down to try to make out an air which he wished to give the Miss Musgroves an idea of. Unintentionally she returned to that part of the room; he saw her, and, instantly rising, said, with studied politeness–

Having overheard, having watched and trembled, she is suddenly directly addressed, she is *identified,* and we are outside once more, with the narrator, but we remain closer to Anne than we were, reluctant to leave her alone in such circumstances.

"I beg your pardon, madam, this is your seat"; and though she immediately drew back with a decided negative, he was not to be induced to sit down again.
  Anne did not wish for more of such looks and speeches. His cold politeness, his ceremonious grace, were worse than anything.

The free indirect style ceases to be free and becomes artistically treacherous at the point at which the narrator and one character or another are too closely identified. This, Kingsley Amis suggests, is what is wrong with *Mansfield Park:* Fanny becomes indistinguishable from the narrator, or rather, the narrator is so keen a cheerleader for her Cinderella that her focus unfocuses or biases the presentation of other characters and themes. In *Emma,* on the other hand, Austen keeps close to Emma and her points of view yet retains authorial irony; it is the magic of this intimate distance that makes Emma's transformation credible. We have seen Emma, but we have also seen around and through her. Suddenly she finds her own moral seriousness, she earns the attention we have invested in her charm and equivocation. We have seen the delusion and the actuality, and when *she* sees the actuality, she proves herself. The drama is less of incident than of transformation. Edith Wharton calls *Emma* "the most perfect example in English fiction of a novel in which character shapes events quietly but irresistibly, as a stream nibbles away at its banks."
  The Johnsonian titles *Sense and Sensibility* and *Pride and Prejudice* alert us to Jane Austen's starting points, in qualities rather than characters; but soon the

novelist in her overwhelms the moralist and goes to work not illustrating those qualities but embodying them. Elinor Dashwood in *Sense and Sensibility* is reasonable, high-principled, while her sister Marianne (how often sisters in the novels throw one another into relief, Maria and Julia, or Lady Bertram, Mrs. Price and Mrs. Norris in *Mansfield Park,* and Elizabeth and Anne in *Persuasion*) is impulsive and easily passionate. Jane is too partial to Elinor, and the book does bend in her direction. Her sense comes to incorporate enough sensibility for her resistant and ironic heart to start beating fast enough for love. Marianne recovers from her passion for Willoughby and marries old (well, thirty-five-year-old) Colonel Brandon, quiet, devoted, and serious, if not entirely credible.

There should be more red-letter days in the literary calendar, like saints' days in the church calendar, when important events occurred: we have Bloom Day and Shakespeare's birthday. We might observe other key days, such as the publication day of *Robinson Crusoe* (April 25) and *Pride and Prejudice* day (January 29). On January 29, 1813, Mr. and Mrs. Bennett and their five daughters came into circulation, and the obsequious, snobbish Reverend William Collins and monstrous Lady Catherine de Bourgh. Charles Bingley, taking up residence near Longbourn, where the Bennetts live, and inviting his sisters and Fitzwilliam Darcy, Lady Catherine's nephew, to stay, provides the fuse and fuel for the narrative. Love, a love that resists the rules of class and money but that ultimately affirms them, is in the air: Bingley and Jane Bennett, Darcy and Elizabeth, snare us in their web. This most Shakespearean of Austen's novels shares features of structure and plot with *Much Ado About Nothing,* not least the at first improbable and then inevitable romance of Darcy and Elizabeth, which puts us in mind of the richly ironic love of Beatrice and Benedick. There is some of the comic cruelty of Shakespeare in Austen's disposal of characters: Charlotte Lucas, Elizabeth's best friend, chooses to marry William Collins because he is not her best but her only hope, which marks the end of her intimacy with Elizabeth.

*Mansfield Park* was Austen's own least favorite among her novels, finished soon after the move to Chawton. Its "good sense" extends to its structure: there is something too rational about it, a geometry, a completeness of motive, an inevitability of outcome that make it appeal to formal zealots like Nabokov but that leave writers less dazzled by lucidity dissatisfied. What is wanting is mystery, and the absence of mystery is due to the character of Fanny Price, in whose fate the entire novel is invested. Austen introduces us to Fanny as a child, and whatever her feelings about children, she makes the young Fanny credible, drawing her vulnerability with tact. It is as she grows up and is drawn into the duplicities of the world that some at least of her actions appear to collude in duplicity; she becomes a little too good, a little unbearable.

When Nabokov was preparing his course on great novels at Cornell University, Edmund Wilson urged him to consider Jane Austen, with whose work Nabokov was then unfamiliar. He settled on *Mansfield Park,* reading it with forensic thoroughness. Austen feared taking risks of the wrong sort, so if a detail was doubtful (hedges in Northamptonshire, for instance), she erased it rather than risk the *literal* error. The refusal to tamper with the physical world reflects her kind of integrity: the liberties a novelist can take are in the creation, development, and reward of characters, but their world must remain close to the actual. Nabokov would have tolerated greater inventiveness, but he did not require it.

He returns to the theme of *speculation,* the distractions it brings when Sir Thomas travels abroad, and what it means in romance, landscaping, husbandry. Speculation entails the breaking of old patterns and the risk of establishing new; it can effect changes in order and structure that are economic, social, and therefore cultural. He notes a kind of holistic quality in the novel, where (as it were) a butterfly flapping its wings in Thornton Lacy will cause a flood of tears in Mansfield Park. Speculation goes hand in hand with economy in all its senses. Grotesque, broadly comic characters (Lady Bertram, Mrs. Norris) are given a specific tick or property (pugs, apricots, obsessions with money) to mark them out, the way Homer uses epithets. Austen's imagery is subdued, her range of colors and their intensity restrained. Few metaphors are used, comparisons are conventional. Thus, the descriptions that do occur can electrify with their precise economy: there are moments of beautifully staged description: "A young woman, pretty, lively, with a harp as elegant as herself; and both placed near a window, cut down to the ground, and opening on a little lawn, surrounded by shrubs in the rich foliage of summer, was enough to catch any man's heart." (In *Emma* we read a more generalized, moral landscape that nonetheless has a smell of mown hay about it: "It was a sweet view—sweet to the eye and the mind. English verdure, English culture, English comfort, seen under a sun bright, without being oppressive.") Some vivid descriptions are assigned to characters and have the double effect of characterizing them and evoking from a specific point of view that we are prepared to color with irony, given our knowledge of the character. There is a sense in which the present participles are elements of thrift, there as stage directions, not as part of the description itself.

In *Emma* the protagonist is a woman of fortune, with looks as well. Her possessions and accomplishments and her faults are summarized in the novel's opening pages. She is too free, too powerful; she needs a subordinate companion, and the marriage of her friend and instructor Miss Taylor to Mr. Weston must soon be made good with the acquisition of another biddable bosom friend. Emma considers Miss Taylor and Mr. Weston's marriage to be her own special achievement, and sets up as a kind of matchmaker. She "adopts" Harriet Smith, "parlor-boarder" working at Mrs. Goddard's school in nearby Highbury. Harriet is pretty, naive, and seventeen, a canny contrast to wise, morally wily little Fanny Price. Emma seeks to advance Harriet on the road of romance and prosperity, not considering that Harriet's heart might run in contrary directions. Harriet is not to accept Robert Martin, an eligible mere farmer who asks for her hand. Mr. Elton, the young vicar, is a better catch, though well above her station. (Mr. Elton wants Emma, well above *his* station.) Mr. Knightley, owner of Donwell Abbey and unmarried himself, finds Emma's conduct reprehensible. Into this knot of plotting and misunderstanding comes the handsome, self-absorbed catalyst Frank Churchill, son of Mr. Weston by an earlier marriage. Emma toys with being in love. She "continued to entertain no doubt of her being in love. Her ideas only varied as to how much."

Harriet misunderstands Emma's intentions: her heart rises like a helium balloon to the dizzying heights of Mr. Knightley. Emma does not know it, but *she* is in love with him. Frank Churchill is secretly engaged elsewhere, and suddenly Emma loses him and finds Harriet out.

> Emma's eyes were instantly withdrawn; and she sat silently meditating, in a fixed attitude, for a few minutes. A few minutes were sufficient for making her acquainted with her own heart. A mind like hers, once opening to suspicion, made rapid progress. She touched— she admitted—she acknowledged the whole truth. Why was it so much worse that Harriet should be in love with Mr. Knightley, than with Frank Churchill? Why was the evil so dreadfully increased by Harriet's having some hope of a return? It darted through her, with the speed of an arrow, that Mr. Knightley must marry no one but herself!

Her repentance when it comes is abject and total. "Seldom, very seldom, does complete truth belong to any human disclosure; seldom can it happen that something is not a little disguised, or a little mistaken." What does Austen mean by the phrase "Emma's eyes were instantly withdrawn"? They look suddenly inward, she is suddenly blind or blinded like St. Paul on the road to Damascus. Religious imagery underlies this remarkable paragraph: St. Paul, meditation, heart, truth, evil, hope, and then the thrilling image of the physical sensation that understanding brings with it, the dart/arrow suggesting Saint Sebastian. Emma is Austen's most complete and delightful, if not her most complex, creation. Of all the novels *Emma* is formally the most satisfactory.

"Think away the surface animation," says Virginia Woolf, "the likeness to life, and there remains, to provide a deeper pleasure, an exquisite discrimination of human values. Dismiss this too from the mind and one can dwell with extreme satisfaction upon the more abstract art which, in the ball-room scene [*Emma*], so varies the emotions and proportions the parts that it is possible to enjoy it, as one enjoys poetry, for itself, and not as a link which carries the story this way and that." In her essay "On Not Knowing Greek" Woolf returns to the ballroom scene. "There comes a moment—'I will dance with you,' says Emma—which rises higher than the rest, which, though not eloquent in itself, or violent, or made striking by beauty of language, has the whole weight of the book behind it. In Jane Austen . . . we have the . . . sense . . . that her figures are bound, and restricted to a few definite movements."

In July 1816 Jane Austen finished *Persuasion*. She died a year later. Her heroine Anne Elliott is older than the earlier protagonists, and wiser, or at least more resigned. Her story is austere, less humorous, close up in a different way from *Emma,* the irony tempered by a new tone. What an unpromising character she is, observed from a distance. "Anne's object was, not to be in the way of any body," out walking, in the drawing room. "Her *pleasure* in the walk must arise from the exercise and the day, from the view of the last smiles of the year upon the tawny leaves and withered hedges." How eighteenth-century those last smiles, and the gilding of "tawny leaves" is about as close as Austen gets to natural description of the newfangled sort. Anne has passed the first and the second flush of youth and is on the cusp of spinsterhood. She is smart but not witty, certainly not Elizabeth Bennett; she lacks Emma's infuriating attractiveness. She was the most difficult of all Austen's protagonists to draw, and to make the drawing attractive to readers.

Yet in this novel Austen experiments more ambitiously than ever with style, she is in love with her medium. In the poetry passage, there is a wonderful enormous sentence, enactive. Anne and Captain Benwick, he poetry-besotted, she keen to divert him on to the sensibilities of prose, produce the famous aphorism: "It was the misfortune of poetry, to be seldom safely enjoyed by those who enjoyed it completely; and that the strong feelings which alone could estimate it truly, were the very feelings which ought to taste it but sparingly." Her play goes further, into "intertextuality," with *Emma:* "She endeavored to be composed, and to be just. Without emulating the feelings of an Emma towards her Henry, she would have . . ." and so on. The monstrousness of Sir Walter Elliot, Anne's widowed father, is captured in his absurdly narrow reading, his vanity founded on lineage. His profligacy is in the end his daughter's fortune, for he must rent out the family seat, and the tenants of Kellynch Hall bring with them Anne's erstwhile beau. It is not, in the end, too late, though it takes some time for the couple to return to the necessary sincerity of expression to declare themselves. At last they come together in what has been thought a version of one of Austen's own courtships.

Austen's novels, Forster says, "live their own wonderful internal life." Each is a world that relates to the other worlds she creates. The novels are not deliberately calibrated, but they work together, different cuts from the same bolt of cloth. Woolf diminishes Austen when she says, "Never did any novelist make more use of an impeccable sense of human values. It is against the disc of an unerring heart, an unfailing good taste, an almost stern morality, that she shows up those deviations from kindness, truth, and sincerity which are among the most delightful things in English literature." Forster's sense of aesthetic integrity is closer to the truth.

Austen has been translated into other languages, but she has never been very popular outside English. Lampedusa suggests why: She is a writer who must "be read slowly: a moment's inattention can make one overlook a crucial phrase, for her art is one of nuances and ambiguities under an apparent simplicity. Her novels are the *Maximes* of La Rochefoucauld set in motion." Her unsuccess in Italy, he says, is due to the fact that she is *"l'anti-melodramma,* the antithesis to opera." Woolf declares, as if it were a deficiency, that "she has too little of the rebel in her composition, too little discontent, and of the vision which is the cause and the reward of discontent." This is like saying that William Cowper did not write about his breakdowns and is deficient for that reason. Yet there is a divided sense in Jane Austen that she at once accepts as given the order of things in her world, in social and class terms, and manages to find it silly, as though possessing inbuilt ironies. Her conservatism is not affirmative but unindignant, passive. What matters to her (as, on a different scale, to Scott, the impact of whose work seems so contrary to its intentions) is the survival, and where necessary the revival, of Augustan terms and categories as aesthetic and moral "verities," as against the disintegrative elements that were already unpaving the way for Romanticism.

# 14

# Roman à Thèse

Thomas Love Peacock, William Godwin, Edward Bulwer-Lytton, Mary Shelley, Thomas Carlyle

"Very true, sir," says Mr. Flosky in Thomas Love Peacock's *Nightmare Abbey*. "Modern literature is a north-east wind—a blight of the human soul. I take credit to myself for having helped to make it so. The way to produce fine fruit is to blight the flower. You call this a paradox. Marry, so be it. Ponder thereon."

Close behind the success of Richardson came the corrective Fielding; after the excesses of the Gothic came bright and brittle Thomas Love Peacock, cocking a snook at Walpole and Monk and the rest, building his novels out of conversations, caricatures, parody, and satire. But Peacock came in the wake of another writer whose success eclipses his as surely as Shakespeare's eclipses Ben Jonson's. John Fowles calls him "Austen-drowned Peacock." Unfortunate: they are different in kind. *Northanger Abbey* relates to *Nightmare Abbey* only in that both were published in 1818 and made fun of the Gothic. Peacock was unaware of the shadow; he never mentions her in his letters and may not have read her.

He is occasionally a lively letter writer. On April 9, 1811, he sent his publisher and friend Edward Hookham one of the most joyful letters ever written, a description of his walk home from Merionethshire to London. He was in love with Jane Gryffydh, "the most innocent, the most amiable, the most beautiful girl in existence," whom he had left behind knowing that she reciprocated his feelings. He was young and vigorous, it was spring, and he was in amazing landscapes, glad to be alive:

> Yesterday morning, walked through a succession of most sublime scenery to the pretty little lake, Tal-y-llyn, where is a small public house, kept by a most original character, who in the triple capacity of publican, schoolmaster, and guide to Cadair Idris, manages to keep the particles of his carcase in contact. I ascended the mountain with him, seated myself on the Giant's Chair, and "looked from my throne of clouds o'er half the world." The view from the summit of this mountain baffles description. It is the very sublimity of Nature's wildest magnificence. Beneath, the whole extent of Cardigan Bay: to the right, the immense chain of the Snowdonian mountains, partly smiling in sunshine, partly mantled in flying storm: to the

> left, the wide expanse of the southern principality, with all its
> mountain-summits below us.—This excursion occupied five hours.
> I then returned to Minffordd Inn, as he calls it, took some tea, and
> walked hither through a romantic and beautiful vale.—The full
> moon in a cloudless sky illumined the latter part of my march . . . I
> have a clean shirt with me, and Luath [Peacock's dog], and Tacitus.
> I am in high health and spirits . . . On the top of Cadair Idris, I felt
> how happy a man may be with a little money and a sane intellect,
> and reflected with astonishment and pity on the madness of the
> multitude.

Here is a generous self-confidence, a sense not of superiority to others but of enjoying better fortune than "the multitude." Born with modest advantages, he multiplied them at no one else's expense; he created the conditions in which he could live pleasantly and study and write as he wished. Some regard the character of Mr. Hilary in *Nightmare Abbey,* "a very cheerful and elastic gentleman," as being a self-portrait of sorts. Peacock invests fragments of himself in many of his protagonists, even the satirized ones, and though some critics of a tidy frame of mind assume that his novels are romans à clef with exact equivalences between characters and real people, he is seldom so easily resolved. As an anti-realist in terms of narrative, he builds characters out of arguments. Rarely can we say that fleeting figures, mentioned but not met—Richard Southey as Mr. Roderick Sackbut, a journalist who reviews his own books, and as Mr. Rumble-sack Shantsee, paired with Mr. Wilful Wontsee (Wordsworth), both turners-away from the integrity of their early visions—can be entirely identified.

A contrary sweetness of temper marks Peacock. As a satirist he ridicules rather than scourges, and though everyone receives deserts, they are not always harsh enough to seem just. We might anticipate that some of his more monstrous characters will fare worse than they do, until we reflect that their monstrosity is intellectual, and that the action of the novels is primarily dialogue, the kind of dialogue in which characters conduct tangential monologues and through parallelisms harmonize moments of irony and paradox. "We are always being brought into touch, not with Peacock himself, as with Trollope himself, . . . but all the time," says Virginia Woolf, "our thought is taking the color of his thought, we are insensibly thinking in his measure." This is true too of E. F. Benson and of Evelyn Waugh, comic writers who tease us into their company. Mary McCarthy calls the books "conversation novels," and Gore Vidal "symposium novels" and "dialogue novels"; this is not quite right, because there is a single coloring applied to the various voices, there is a deliberate puppeteer, though the word "symposium" well describes the breakfasts and suppers that frame so many of Peacock's best sequences of intercut monologue.

How to characterize his style? It is always elaborated; every sentence has, it seems, been worked out with precision and laughter. The extended similes are beautiful and absurd in equal measure. In *Nightmare Abbey* Scythorp, torn by love for two women, is likened to a shuttlecock, the similarities unpacked one by one, the way a priest unpacks the meanings folded into his scriptural text: "Passing and repassing several times a day from the company of the one to that of the other, he was like a shuttlecock between two battledores, changing its direction as rapidly as the oscillations of a pendulum, receiving many a hard knock on the cork of a sensitive heart, and flying from point to point on the feathers of a super-sublimated head." Attempting to dupe his father and conceal beloved Stella, Scythorp pretends he has been writing a play and reads it out in a loud voice to his father, to conceal the incriminating noises. This gives Peacock the occasion for comedy, but also for satire on the kind of exaggerated drama of his day. The stage directions show the emotional exchange between the Great Mogul, living in exile in Kensington, and his daughter the Princess Rantrorina: "*A pause, during which they look at each other expressively. The princess changes color several times. The Mogul takes snuff in great agitation. Several grains are heard to fall on the stage. His heart is seen to beat through his upper benjamin.*"

Peacock was born in Dorset in 1785. His father was a London glass merchant about whom little is known. Peacock mentions him (only once) in a letter to his mother written in 1792 when he was seven years old, instructing her to instruct him "to send home some Sweet meats, for your dutiful son." In that year his father died "in poor circumstances," leaving his widow and son each a small annuity. His mother, a Presbyterian, was the daughter of a retired Royal Navy master who had lost a leg in the triumphant struggle of Rodney with de Grasse in the West Indies. This grandfather played an important part in the boy's upbringing. Thomas was sent to board at a school in Englefield Green, where he composed his first poem at the age of ten. His master was inspiring, if not erudite, and found him full of promise. In 1798 Thomas was removed from school for financial reasons and thereafter schooled himself. He started work as a clerk at fifteen.

A beautiful, biddable boy, he possessed a lavish crop of curls, "flaxen" of course. Queen Charlotte was so taken with him that she stopped her carriage to kiss him. As he grew older, he developed a passion for walking: to Scotland and, fatefully, to Wales, where he found his favorite landscapes and his love, Jane, whom he married eight years later, "the white Snowdonian antelope" mentioned in Shelley's "Letter to Maria Gisborne."

He developed, too, a passion for reading, even as he acquired a certain scorn for the universities that circumstance had placed beyond his reach. He was often to be found in the British Museum Reading Room gathering a classical education, becoming, indeed, a leading classicist of his day. Tacitus was his *vade mecum:* he relished his condensed style. Thomas also mastered French and Italian. He had no taste for Spanish or German, languages he associated with religious and political vehemence. "His own strongest predilections," says Richard Garnett, "were naturally for the humorists, and rather for the genial extravagance of Aristophanes and Rabelais, or the polished wit of Voltaire and Petronius, than the moody bitterness of writers like Swift." He kept a distance from the Christian God, and in particular from Christ himself: "I came not to send peace, but a sword," an intolerable Messiah.

Peacock started as a poet but failed. There is much that is romantic about his early work, though his is not a romantic temperament. The spirit of the age spoke in the vapid rhyming of an anemic Muse, plangent, occasionally banal. Some of the verse embedded in his novels is pleasing, but his force and originality are in his prose, including his prose about poetry. His friend Percy Bysshe Shelley said his poems belonged to the "exact and superficial school."

In 1820, the year of his marriage, Peacock wrote his most famous essay, "Four Ages of Poetry" (*iron* of panegyric; *gold* of power and growth, of expansion; *silver,* "the poetry of civilized life"; and contemporary *brass*). This lightly learned but coat-trailing product of his own disappointment as a poet—the books he published at his own expense generated limited enthusiasm—elicited from Shelley his celebrated *A Defense of Poetry,* though all references to Peacock have been edited out of modern editions. Shelley wrote to his friend, "Your anathemas against poetry itself excited me to a sacred rage . . . of vindicating the insulted Muses." Shelley presented his *Defense* as an antidote; Peacock never completed the attack that should have accompanied it.

Peacock also tried to write for the stage. In 1808 he became private secretary to Sir Home Popham, Commander of the Fleet, and sailed on the *Venerable,* working on comedies and light pieces for public entertainment. The humor was forced, the plotting elaborated to no real end. The post itself was not congenial and he quit a year later, making a pedestrian excursion to the source of the Thames.

Hookham organized Peacock's introduction to Shelley in 1812 and they became friends, Shelley expressing more admiration for Peacock than Peacock reciprocated during the poet's lifetime. Peacock became executor for Shelley's literary estate when the poet died. He got to know Shelley well, first with Harriet, Shelley's ill-fated first wife, and then with Mary Godwin. They lived near him in Marlowe, where Peacock loved to take them boating. He traveled widely with the Shelleys, walking to London with Percy Bysshe, enjoying uninterrupted discussion. For a time Shelley paid Peacock an annuity of £50. When he went to Italy, it was to Peacock that he wrote some of the fine letters describing his sojourn there; Peacock in return confided to him his motives in writing. A key letter of 1818 describes *Nightmare Abbey:* "I think it necessary to take a stance against the encroachments of black bile (the melancholy humor)."

Shelley praised *Nightmare Abbey:* "the lightness, chastity and strength of the language of the whole." He liked "the catastrophe," because the series of surprises and the resolution were dramatic and delightful. But Peacock was *too* amusing, there was a lack of moral rigor in his satires. Shelley liked the figure of Scythorp Glowry, based loosely upon himself. A lad "of sad or gloomy countenance," he is the occasion for satire on the educational system and the Gothic mode. Scythorp in a typical evening at Nightmare Abbey, indulging a Gothic attitude, is observed. "He was a burnt child, and dreaded the fire of female eyes. He wandered about the ample pile, or along the garden-terrace, with 'his cogitative faculties immersed in cogibundity of cogitation.' The terrace terminated at the south-western tower, which . . . was ruinous and full of owls. Here would Scythorp take his evening seat, on a fallen fragment of mossy stone, with his back resting against the ruined wall,—a thick canopy of ivy, with an owl in it, over his head,—and the Sorrows of Werter in his hand." Turbulent, melancholy Scythorp, with his nightcap and his striped calico dressing gown, in the end takes the Madeira in place of the bullet in the brow. This, even though his beloved Marionetta, so pretty and sensual and nonsensical, has married the Honorable Mr. Listless and fiery, intellectual Stella (actually Celinda, daughter of Mr. Toobad) has married the philosophical and laxly mystical Mr. Flosky, an unsympathetic shadow of Coleridge. For Scythorp (like Shelley) has been passionately, sincerely in love at the same time with two women, one representing sentiment and sensuality, the other a romantic passion. They have found one another out and abandoned the irresolute young man.

As with his first novel, *Headlong Hall* (1815), Peacock published anonymously. He had given up the drama but retained script elements in the disposition of his dialogue. There is something effortful about his first venture into fiction, but it set the pattern for his later, more assured works that hardly digress from the Peacockian template. A range of people converge on a dwelling where there is good food, hierarchy, and accommodation. Each male person represents a philosophy, prejudice, or point of view. The women are rather more nuanced, though the pretty ones—and they are generally pretty, one way or another, Peacock having a sharp eye for female beauty and being susceptible to romantic entanglements, leading a not wholly regular but probably an inventive private life—are rendered in conventional hues. This is an art of surfaces, attitudes, and manners of speech

rather than voices. His second novel, *Melincourt* (1817), has as one of its protagonists an amiable, in the end quite aristocratic, orangutan.

Peacock wrote Jane a beautiful proposal of marriage eight years after he met
her in Wales, without having troubled her with communication in the intervening period. She accepted, and the next year, 1820, they were married. She may
have lost a little of her charm. "Mrs. Peacock seems to be a very good-natured,
simple, unaffected, untaught, prettyish Welsh girl," said his and Shelley's friend
Mrs. Gisborne in a letter. Marriage lasted thirty-two years, some happy, but many
disturbed by her mental illness. Peacock learned of her death on Christmas Day
1851. He did not attend her funeral. He did not attend the funeral in 1861 of his
beloved elder daughter, either.

A provident man, Peacock got a job the year before he married. He entered
the East India Company as an examiner of Indian correspondence, a demanding, pleasurable job, and well paid. By 1822 he was earning over £1,000 a year.
In 1836 he was appointed chief examiner (a post in which John Stuart Mill succeeded him), providing well for his family. In 1837 he supervised the design,
construction, and outward voyages of the *Atalanta* and *Berenice,* the first vessels
to steam the entire distance to India. Later he was involved in commissioning
iron ships.

Prosperity did not bring happiness. His second daughter died in infancy in
1826, and this contributed to Mrs. Peacock's madness; his first, Mary Ellen, an
intelligent and talented woman, became, after being widowed by her first husband, George Meredith's wife and, despite her desertion of him for the painter
Henry Wallis, his abiding Muse. Meredith originally dedicated "Love in the
Valley" (1851) to Peacock. The poem may build on the vivid description of the
sleeping woman in *Crotchet Castle,* where Mr. Chainmail sees his mysterious
soon-to-be-beloved asleep on a perilous bough above a chasm.

Peacock's writing had been in abeyance, but when his wife died he began
again, more fluently, even as he became reclusive and spent the remaining
fourteen years of his life among his books and flowers at his spacious house at
Lower Halliford. He wrote his three major essays on Shelley and his final novel,
*Gryll Grange,* which was serialized in *Fraser's Magazine* in 1860 and published the
following year. There had been thirty years between this final, stiff fictional
production (Gore Vidal regards it as "the most satisfying of his works") and his
masterpiece, *Crotchet Castle* (1831). He died at home.

*Crotchet Castle* Garnett calls "the most mature and thoroughly characterized
of all his works." It is marred by a strain of anti-Semitism that runs through the
literature of the time, complemented by a vexing hostility to the Scots and their
Caledonian hubris. Propaganda about the "Athens of the North" repelled him,
and in *Crotchet Castle* he creates the cocksure materialist Mr. Mac Quedy (Q.E.D.)

who riles the metaphysical Mr. Skionar (another Coleridge figure), and the Reverend Doctor Folliott, a man with an enormous but discriminating appetite and classical learning.

He was not Augustan, lacking moral acerbity and intellectual rigor; at the same time he distrusted romantic release. Laureate of the Middle Way and the Middle Register: his is measured conscience, enemy of excess. Here is the reductio ad absurdum, the triumph of logic over thought, of design over natural growth. In the congeries of different ideologies and faiths that are represented at his well-catered symposia, he retains a stance of seeming neutrality.

Peacock is memorable for the brightness of the entertainment, the leavening and sweetening of the verses breaking the dialogue, changing the key of a description. How various are Peacock's poetic registers: he can do the voices of the Romantics (Byron in particular), and he can do his own voice. In *Crotchet Castle* the dramatic form survives not only in the dialogue but in seeming stage directions: it is comic, it is operatic. It also employs, when it needs to, epistolary convention, allowing remote satire from as far away as the backwoods of the United States, and tonal candor in a different key from the main rumbustious narrative.

Gore Vidal notes a distinct mixing of genres. In *Gryll Grange,* for instance, "the characters are composing a comedy in the Aristophanic manner while the book itself is a variation on Old Comedy." This makes Peacock unusual, unassimilable and inimitable. His writing is classical, impersonal; it lacks those manifests of feeling and sentiment that reassure the reader. Indeed, there is little reassurance in Peacock, just as in his characters there is little interiority; instead, clarity and even cruelty of definition mark his writing. Forster reminds us how parody serves well those with abundant ideas to express, "who do not see the world in terms of individual men and women—who do not, in other words, take easily to creating characters."

Mary Shelley (1797–1851) regretted the support Shelley gave Peacock: even when she and the poet were in dire straits they supported him, until he got his India House appointment. Shelley settled £120 out of his father's annuity of £1,000 on Peacock, more than a tithe, between 1815 and 1819. His will was also generous, and eventually Peacock received £2,000 and £500 in legacies. Mary's resentment was not justified, for Shelley had *used* Peacock. In 1814 he consulted him about his love life before eloping with Mary and Claire Clairmont, and he left Peacock in charge of his money (what there was of it) and affairs until he returned in the autumn and Peacock met Mary for the first time. Shelley treated him as a kind of agent, and appointed him (with Byron) as an executor of his will. Byron fell out with Mary and retired, but Peacock took his duties seriously and looked after the interests of Percy Junior and his family—not that he got thanks; on the contrary.

There may have been literary resentments at work as well in Mary Shelley's mind. Peacock disliked the excesses of the Gothic. Paradoxically, what has proved its most durable excess, Mary's *Frankenstein; or, The Modern Prometheus*, was published in the same year as *Nightmare Abbey*, 1818. Peacock reported to Shelley on the review reception of the book but passed no judgment of his own. William Beckford, on the other hand, loathed the book, writing on the flyleaf of his copy, "This is, perhaps, the foulest toadstool that has yet sprung up, from the reeking dunghill of the present times," a dunghill to which he contributed some choice ordure himself. Scott reviewed *Frankenstein* in *Blackwood's Magazine* in 1818 under the mistaken impression (it appeared anonymously) that it *might* be by "Godwin's son-in-law" Shelley. Like many reviewers under pressure and obligation, he did not read the book through but depended on a summary of it from a friend. He reviewed it as a favor, favorably.

Half a century ago in *The English Novel*, Walter Allen did not mention Mary Shelley. Her book, a phenomenon in its own time, remained a feature of children's horror literature. It was not taken seriously. The reasons are not far to seek. Its abstracting wordiness and its deliberate quest for effect, the designs it has on readers more than on its subject, a pursuit of sensation over truth, put it beyond the pale. That pale has altered. Semiotics, feminism, and an increasingly craven respect for what is "popular" have brought it into the canon, and then the curriculum, so that students are required to read it because of the issues of gender and science it raises. It is less a novel than a "text" to talk about and around.

Mary Shelley has passionate advocates, none more so than Muriel Spark, who, even as Walter Allen ignored her, had begun her defense. "Her novels *Frankenstein* and *The Last Man* . . . are almost entirely without counterpart in feminine literature," she writes, and moving out of the merely feminine, she calls them "prototypes of the scientific extravaganzas popularized by H. G. Wells, . . . Aldous Huxley and George Orwell." *Frankenstein* was "the first English novel in which a scientific theme had been combined with the Gothic horror convention." And *The Last Man* (1826), despite its moralizing solemnity, Spark calls "an amazingly powerful story," characteristic of an age in which poets and painters explored the theme in "a general pessimistic reaction to the progressive time-spirit." Spark describes Shelley as the author of "prophetic fiction" who in *The Last Man* lays humanism to rest.

Mary was the daughter of Mary Wollstonecraft, campaigner for women's rights and author of the *A Vindication of the Rights of Woman*, who died of a fever just after her daughter was born, and of William Godwin (1756–1836), the philosopher whose severe rationalism affected Wordsworth and his generation in their formative years and whose novel *Things as They Are; or, Adventures of Caleb*

*Williams* (1794) can detain us for a moment, both for itself and for its stiffening legacy. Its impact, for example, on *Falkland* (1827), an early novel by Edward Bulwer-Lytton (1803–1873), was detrimental.

Godwin began as a dissenting minister, then became atheist, anarchist, and advocate of the positive power of reason and rational action. He believed novels could be used to explore and propagate philosophical ideas. Hostile to the powerful and the ill effects of their exploitation of the rest of us, he tried to illustrate his thesis through the story of a crime and its detection. The first half of *Caleb Williams* explores the causes of the sudden irrational outbursts of the generally calm, wealthy, and just Ferdinando Falkland, provoked by Tyrrel, an arrogant, irresponsible neighboring squire. When Tyrrel is murdered, Falkland is blamed, then two humble people are condemned and executed. Caleb Williams becomes Falkland's secretary and proves Falkland was the murderer. Caleb is pursued and persecuted, but at last elicits Falkland's confession. He is then persecuted by Falkland for his knowledge, escapes, joins a band of thieves, and survives numerous adventures, in the published end bringing out the best in Falkland and an ambiguous kind of justice is done. There is another ending in which, though Falkland dies, Caleb goes mad in prison.

Godwin's language is more stiflingly literary, anachronistic, and artificialized than his daughter's in *Frankenstein*. The book fascinated younger writers. Dickens wrote to Edgar Allan Poe in 1842: "Apropos of the 'construction' of *Caleb Williams,* do you know that Godwin wrote it backwards,—the last volume first,— and that when he had produced the hunting down of Caleb, and the catastrophe, he waited for months, casting about for a means of accounting for what he had done?" Perhaps backward composition is why the novel lies still on the modern page. It took Scott to bring period and idiom into sync, to make language and sense occupy the same time frame again. Yet before Scott identified himself as the author of his novels, they were assumed to be by Godwin.

The impact on Bulwer-Lytton was paralyzing: on the style, the wafer-thin psychology, and characters as wooden as those in Walpole. Thackeray says Lytton's later novel *Aram* was composed to show that the protagonist, "though a thief, a liar, and a murderer, yet being intellectual was amongst the noblest of mankind." Trollope was "offended by devious conversations" of a kind that please the author but not the reader, because they do not advance the story. Godwin's novels and their progeny (including plays like Wordsworth's *The Borderers*) were "exercises in rhetoric, attempts at heightened narrative, at a bastard poetry, in fact. They seem grotesquely inflated now."

To Dickens, Godwin was a reckonable writer and a trusted critic of his own fiction, and Godwin has never lacked advocates, though he continues to lack readers. Dickens also valued Lytton as writer and friend. He may even have had time for *The Caxtons* (1849), Lytton's labored imitation of *Tristram Shandy*. It contains a few passages of effective mimicry, but this parody of parody is ill-judged, deliberate, and artful set against the irrationalist Sterne. Lytton declared, "Nearly all criticism at this day is the public effect of private acquaintance." He enjoyed the benefits of this corruption and even today retains a few devoted readers.

Trollope found Lytton a figure at once of genius and of fun, sublime and ridiculous. *Pelham; or, The Adventures of a Gentleman* (1828) he takes as "another instance of the sublime, though there is so much in it that is of the world worldly, though an intentional fall to the ludicrous is often made in it. The personages talk in glittering dialogues, throwing about philosophy, science, and the classics, in a manner which is always suggestive and often amusing. The book is brilliant with intellect. But no word is ever spoken as it would have been spoken;—no detail is ever narrated as it would have occurred." His aesthetic and his miscalculations are a world away from Peacock. And Edgar Allan Poe, who had a sneaking respect for what he, from the safe distance of America, took to be Lytton's "taste and comprehension," if not his penetration, agreed with the harshest critics in one respect, "in condemning by wholesale Bulwer-Lytton's absurd pretence to metaphysical knowledge. The parade he always makes of this arises from a consciousness of his total ignorance and deficiency. He has warm passions and a flowing imagination—but nothing can be more perplexed and indistinct than his reasoning powers, and nothing possibly worse than his style." His social peer was Disraeli, a novelist more accomplished by far, and yet lacking Bulwer-Lytton's warmth.

Mary Godwin grew up encouraged, but not closely attended, by her father, and neglected by her stepmother. The house in which she lived was frequented by Coleridge, Lamb, and Hazlitt, and there she heard Coleridge recite *The Rime of the Ancient Mariner*. Much of her early life she spent in Scotland, "on the blank and dreary northern shores of the Tay, near Dundee," she remembered without nostalgia. She eloped at the age of seventeen with Shelley. They revealed their love for one another over her mother's grave, a scene worthy of Peacock at his most mischievously Gothic. A precocious, strong-minded individual, even in the company of Shelley (who tended to treat her as a disciple or tutee some of the time) and of his circle, she wrote *Frankenstein* at nineteen or twenty, and it was published in her twenty-first year.

By her account, Byron catalyzed the story. One day, in the unusually rainy Swiss summer of 1816, the Shelleys, Byron, and Byron's physician, the sinisterly attractive William Polidori, were entertaining one another with ghost stories, having found volumes of Gothic translations from German. Byron ordered each to write a ghost story. The first to finish was Polidori with "The Vampire," a narrative of middle length and of some literary and historical value, though Mary could not quite recall its plot when she described it years later. She was slow to get started, but as with Walpole, so with Mary a nightmare (what Joyce Carol Oates prefers to call "a hypnagogic fantasy in her bed") showed her the way to her "pale student of unhallowed arts" and his monstrous creation that "stands at his bedside, opening his curtains," the whole spookiness of the situation contained in that hesitant comma, the monster's fear, and the pale student's, and ours as readers congealed in that tiny curled pause. She tried to contrive something that would frighten her reader as much as the nightmare had frightened her. In her celebrated 1831 introduction she recalls her excitement in a vivid reenactment of the successive moments of conception: the intellectual seed of the nightmare, the nightmare itself witnessed (she was not its subject), and so forth. Thus she began: "It was on a dreary night of November . . ." Shelley kept her at it, made her develop it: not an extended story but a proper novel.

She takes her epigraph from Milton's *Paradise Lost:* "Did I request thee, Maker, from my clay / To mould me man? Did I solicit thee / From darkness to promote me?" Her monster learns to read, reads Milton, and likens his situation to Adam's, though, as he mournfully reflects, the first man was made in the image of God, and the first man-made man was a perversion of that image. If we were to assign to the novel an *intellectual* purpose, we would say that it is a meditation on creating life against the designs of nature and of God. Victor usurps the role of woman as the nurturing womb for new life, and of God in designing a form that necessarily warps the form of man. Some critics, taking into account the gender of the author, see the monster himself as a paradigm for the situation of woman, marginal, debarred from education. This attributes a weight to the author's purposes, and to the book itself, that they cannot sustain. The novel teems with ideas and half-ideas, proposed less for fictional or philosophical reasons, more for effect. And the ideas, if not their development in the story, are those debated between Byron and Shelley that wet summer, while she listened and, being young, was reluctant to interrupt. Galvanism in particular fascinated her: how electrical currents might animate plant life and animal tissue.

The book opens with a brief, breathless preface, of which, she conceded in her 1831 introduction, Shelley composed every word. It affirmed the literal possibility of the tale, the writer adducing Dr. Darwin (Erasmus, Charles's grandfather, whose *Zoonomia; or, The Laws of Organic Life* of 1796 considers the properties of electricity in relation to tissue and to life itself) and "some of the physiological writers of Germany." Shelley insists that the story is in some fundamental way *true,* that it is not wasting time by "merely weaving a series of supernatural terrors."

Then Mary begins with a formal clearing of the throat. Captain Walton, an explorer and romantic protagonist on a less grand scale than Victor Frankenstein, writes four letters to his sister, reassuring her that he is in fine shape on his trip to the Arctic, and then describing the circumstances in which he encounters the worn and wandering doctor, who tells his story. The captain sets it down for his sister's entertainment. There follow the twenty-four chapters of the book itself. Twenty-four: the number of books in the *Iliad* and the *Odyssey*. Shelley apostrophizes Homer, alongside Shakespeare and Milton, in the original preface. Taken with the reference to Prometheus, we can see Mary intended to write a modern epic, to transcend the social form of the conventional novel with its contingencies ("the enervating effects of the novels of the present day") and to let a larger imagination loose.

The story is universally familiar. What still focuses attention (the mechanical elements of the tale having rusted along with the science that suggested them) is the emergence into consciousness of the monster, his potential humanity warped and deflected by human alarm at his monstrous features. Man, formed in God's image, fell from grace; the monster, made in man's image, cannot rise no matter how hard he tries. There is a beauty in the monster, the humanity of his desire is touching, but no Disney magically transmutes him into a sentimental, affirmative form. The parable of human presumption unfolds, an irreversible logic worthy of the daughter of William Godwin.

Mary Shelley survived her husband, who drowned in 1822, by almost three decades and wrote prolifically, considering the market with a degree of calculation and giving it what she thought it required, following the model of Scott, whom Carlyle stigmatized for turning writing into a trade. For a brief time her name was linked to that of the American writer Washington Irving, though this unlikely romance had no issue, Irving being a confirmed bachelor or, modern biographers suggest, "a confirmed bachelor." She humbly sought Scott's advice on her historical fiction (referring to him privately as "a hypochondriacal Dandy," but reading and rereading his work with attention). Shelley's *The Fortunes of Perkin Warbeck: A Romance* (1830) is a pale offspring of *Ivanhoe*. Her medievalizing fiction, sometimes derivative of unacknowledged texts and sources, in Scott's manner without his assurance, is no longer entertaining. Only *The Last Man* keeps a formal claim on our attention, and a frail claim it is.

Percy Shelley was fascinated by modern science, but Mary's concern with its darker sides, its treachery when pursued too far or in the wrong ways, beyond understanding into the realm of instrumentality, manifested Romantic hostility to its pretensions, a hostility that became more virulent as the century advanced. Writers as persuasive as Thomas Carlyle took up the theme, alarmed by a mechanistic perspective that trammeled the imagination and misled the "dynamic" quest for larger truths, universal rules. "Practically considered," he declared in "Signs of the Times" (1829), "our creed is Fatalism; and, free in hand and foot, we are shackled in heart and soul with far straiter than feudal chains."

———·———

In 1869 in the offices of the publishers Chapman and Hall, an old man was pointed out to a young man negotiating with his publisher-to-be. "[Thomas] Hardy turned and saw leaning on one elbow at the clerk's desk an aged figure in an inverness cape and slouched hat. 'Have a good look at him,' continued [Frederick] Chapman. 'You'll be glad I pointed him out to you one day.'" Hardy was astonished that a man of Carlyle's distinction was dealt with by a mere clerk. In later years Hardy lost patience with the Scottish sage. "Carlyle was a poet with the reputation of a philosopher," he reflected, not really a "thinker."

Whatever Carlyle became in response to his rigorous political analysis and growing pessimism in the Age of Machinery, in his beginnings he could be an irrepressibly funny writer. Born in 1795 in Dumfries and Galloway, in the south of Scotland, Carlyle attended the University of Edinburgh and became a school-teacher. At the age of twenty-nine he first went to London and on to Paris. He was, though new, a learned traveler. Translations from the German were among his first publications when he returned to Scotland.

With his wife, Jane, he removed from Edinburgh to her family home, a social and intellectual rural hermitage in Craigenputtock, sixteen miles from Dumfries, in order to get a clearer perspective on the world, free of the pressure of urban life. Jane Carlyle (née Welsh) crucially complemented Carlyle. For Virginia Woolf she was a would-have-been novelist turned letter writer. "Letters of the 'inner woman' sort, 'all about feelings,' anything that savored of self-analysis or introspection she checked ruthlessly. But in spite of this reserve, which drove her to make her letters out of facts, they were facts which did more to illuminate herself than most people's feelings." There was at once deep sympathy in her nature and ruthless justice. "Someone declared her to be a 'cross between John Knox and a gypsy.'" Thomas Carlyle always wrote for his biographer and posterity, even (or especially) his letters to her.

Carlyle was introduced to Jane Welsh in 1821. Theirs was a close, unromantic relationship, described by one biographer as comradely. He lent her books, they had earnest conversations: he treated her initially rather as Pygmalion does his statue, but her stone was proof against him and she was irreducibly herself. She far exceeded his initial expectations, resisting, shaping him back. A crucial moment, early in their unimpassioned intimacy, came when she told him not to underline words in the books he lent her. She could detect the sense and provide the emphases herself.

At Craigenputtock he composed *Sartor Resartus* (The Tailor Re-tailored), subtitled *The Life and Opinions of Herr Teufelsdröckh,* a "questionable little Book" in which he not only satirizes his own cultural preferences and point of view but also, disarming us with laughter, vindicates his speculative radicalism. He entertains unexpected ideas and is intolerant of mere respectability. Jorge Luis Borges remembers his "first encounter with *Sartor Resartus* by the maniacal Thomas Carlyle" as "passionate—a book now huddled in some corner, which has been reading itself for years in my library." A young man's book, clearly, in every sense. To his brother Carlyle wrote, "I do think it will be a *queer* Book; one of the *queerest* published in this century." A "Treatise on Things in General," it is disguised as an essay on Dress. Orwell was struck by "the ill-humor, the queer, wounding adjectives ('O seagreen Prophet,' and so forth), the instinctive sneer." And for him it is those "adjectives which, living a strange life of their own, give an air of profundity—but no real depth of thought." George Moore quotes Carlyle's satire on Coleridge, "snuffling: Subjectivity! Objectivity! as he comes across the lawn," and comments: "How dare this impotent Scot speak contemptuously of the author of 'Christabel'!"

But *Sartor Resartus* was not a young man's two-finger gesture at the establishment. His mix of compound terms, German and French words, Cockney, extended metaphors, neologisms, and strange adjectives indicates no failure of style. He could write eloquent, controlled, conventional English when he wished to, but as he explained to a friend, the novelty of his thoughts and of his subject matter demanded a new idiom; new words must be *made,* though not excessively, for comprehensibility must always be an aspect of the expanding language. Steeped in German literature and philosophy, he was sensible to its excesses and its compound ponderousness. His fictional protagonists are decidedly Teutonic in complexion and expression. This was an aspect of the book's radical spirit, "the whole structure of our Johnsonian English breaking up from its foundations." For Hogg (and Carlyle's writing here often, in its excess, reminds readers of the Hogg of the *Noctes Ambrosianae*) such affronts to received style were a comic tool, producing effects. For Carlyle the necessity runs deeper, into the artistic intention itself. Robert Louis Stevenson remarks, "The words in Carlyle seem electrified into an energy of lineament, like the faces of men furiously moved." We are in the zone of stylistic Galvanism.

V. S. Pritchett relished the book's radicalism, calling it "a masterpiece of the grotesque; the strain of sanity, like the strain of simple religion and pure poetry, never dried up in him, and they worked together to make him a wonderful comic writer, one of the great clowns who are subtle with self-irony and who are untainted (on the whole, in a book like *Sartor*) by the poison of satire." Writing to a friend in 1835, responding to criticisms of *Sartor Resartus,* Carlyle speaks of his protagonist as "the hardened, kiln-burnt, altogether contradictory Professor Teufelsdröckh." Diogenes (after the cynic) Teufelsdröckh: it is his emblematic "life" we follow; we meet Counsellor Heuschrecke (Grasshopper), the not-fair Blumine (Flower Goddess), and other figures who inhabit the imaginary Germanic landscape of Ichweissnichtwo (I Know Not Where) and the allegory of manners that this book reveals. (Late in life Carlyle was referred to and caricatured as Diogenes without his tub, or his onions.)

In a passage entitled "Reminiscences," the environment in which Professor Teufelsdröckh composed his great treatise on clothes is evoked by "the editor" of the papers that constitute it: "Here, perched-up in his high Wahngasse watch-tower, and often, in solitude, outwatching the Bear, it was that the indomitable Inquirer fought all his battles with Dullness and Darkness; here, in all probability, that he wrote this surprising Volume on *Clothes.*" The editor declines to describe his "wide sort-out" or "the color of his trousers, fashion of his broad-brimmed steeple-hat." These things he leaves to our imagination, allowing us to invest in the Professor, who is, indeed, rather a monster in the manner of Dr. Frankenstein's, only not sinister, a monster-visionary and pedant, a creature of the age, great-uncle of the book-demented Edward Casaubon, great nephew of the book-demented Don Quixote. How dreadfully serious the Professor is, how bizarre when his earnestness gives way: "Here, however, we gladly call to mind that once we saw him *laugh;* once only, perhaps it was the first and last time in his life; but then such a peal of laughter, enough to have awakened the Seven Sleepers!"

Carlyle finished his book in 1831 and went to London to sell it. He failed. Serialized eventually in *Fraser's Magazine* (1833–1834), it was not published in book form until 1836, in the United States, with an introduction by Ralph Waldo Emerson, who had visited the author in Craigenputtock two years earlier. "I found the house amid the desolate, heathery hills, where the lonely scholar nourished his mighty heart." Emerson and Carlyle stayed in close touch for years. Henry James dubbed Carlyle Emerson's "lurid correspondent."

Two years later *Sartor Resartus* appeared in Britain. By that time the author had moved south, to 5 Great Cheyne Row, Chelsea. Though his later years were devoid of fiction, Carlyle learned from Scott's practice important lessons about historical narrative. David Lodge reflects on how Carlyle read everything he could find about the French Revolution, behaving like a historian, but then "synthesized and dramatized this mass of data like a moralizing novelist." He had a marked impact on Dickens: "No wonder Dickens was enraptured by [*The French Revolution,* 1837], and carried it about with him everywhere on its first publication. Not only *A Tale of Two Cities,* but also Dickens's panoramic novels of English society were indebted to its example," Lodge says. From Scott's novels through Carlyle's histories to Dickens's novels: as always, the commerce between literal and figurative worlds was busy and productive.

James contrasts Emerson and Carlyle, the one with little concept of evil, the other with only a frail concept of good. They were complementary. They made different use, each in his way, of Puritan antecedents. And Carlyle is unique, says James. "No man of equal genius was probably ever less of a man of the world at large—more exclusively a product of his locality, his clan, his family." James quotes Taine, who said that Carlyle "would limit the human heart to the English sentiment of duty, and the human imagination to the English sentiment of respect." Taine was not considering *Sartor Resartus,* and he did not discriminate the resistant Scottish elements in Carlyle's manner. Perhaps they became so mainstream in their time that they subsumed the English, rather as Scott became English fiction by sheer force of invention.

# 15

# Declarations of Independence

Washington Irving, James Fenimore Cooper, Edgar Allan Poe

Washington Irving (1783–1859) was the last of his parents' eight surviving children. The week of his birth the British declared the ceasefire that ended the American War of Independence, and Mr. and Mrs. Irving, he a Scot who had emigrated from Orkney to Manhattan, she English-born but a patriotic American, named their baby after the victorious general. True to his namesake, Irving was to extend that independence into the realms of literature: the essay, history, biography (even a vast life of Washington, completed a few months before his own death), and narrative. Among his stories, "The Legend of Sleepy Hollow" and "Rip Van Winkle," both first collected in *The Sketch Book of Geoffrey Crayon, Gent.* (1819), represent a new strand of Gothic and haunt the American imagination. Rip Van Winkle dozes off and wakes up twenty years later: "I was myself last night; but I fell asleep on the mountain–and they've changed my gun–and every thing's changed–and I'm changed–and I can't tell what's my name, or who I am!" There in the Kaatskills was Henry Hudson with his Dutch crew bowling loudly. Irving left the United States for seventeen years and returned to his own puzzled awakening. Perhaps like Ichabod Crane in "The Legend" he felt himself driven from the Dutch settlement by the headless horseman, another Gothic dream from which he was to wake a richer and a wiser man.

These are the first two great American short stories. Like much classic early American literature, they were written while the author was in Europe: Irving both remembered and imagined his country while sketching, for the same book, the English world with a sense of alienated belonging. The landscapes his imagination most relished were those around the Hudson. Henry James had no very high opinion of him, except as a distant relation, and when he visited Irving's house Sunnyside in Tarrytown, New York, on the Hudson, he felt in it "the quite indefinable air of the little American literary past."

Along with James Fenimore Cooper, Irving was among the earliest American writers to sell well in Europe. He was befriended by leading British contemporaries. Scott warmed to his work, got it reviewed by, among others, his friend Lockhart, and helped him to secure a British publisher in John Murray. They met in Paris and became friends. Byron admired him. Dickens's first letter to Irving expresses a debt not uncommon among his British followers. "Diedrich Knickerbocker"—another of Irving's pseudonyms, elaborately heralded in anticipation of "his" work being published, so that he had a fictional existence before he had readers—"Diedrich Knickerbocker," says Dickens, "I have worn to death in my pocket, and yet I should show you his mutilated carcass with a joy past all expression." It is from Irving's Christmas stories that Dickens drew some of the energy of *A Christmas Carol* and his other festive stories, and of the *Pickwick* Christmas. When Dickens visited America, he stayed with Irving at Sunnyside.

*Knickerbocker's History of New York* has a long title:

A History of New York
from the Beginning of the World
to the End of the Dutch Dynasty

Containing

Among Many Surprising and Curious Matters, the Unutterable
Ponderings of WALTER THE DOUBTER, the Disastrous Projects
of WILLIAM THE TESTY, and the Chivalric Achievements of
PETER THE HEADSTRONG, the Three Dutch Governors of
NEW AMSTERDAM; Being the Only Authentic History of the
Times That Ever Has Been Published

By DIEDRICH KNICKERBOCKER

De Waarheid die in Duister lag,
Die komt met Klaarheid aan den Dag
*[The truth that in the darkness lay
With clarity becomes the day]*

In this *History* St. Nicholas flies over Gotham City in a magic wagon, an early sighting of Santa Claus. The account of New York, with its invented narrator and mix of history, legend, and implausibility, stands alongside Irving's romantic history as a substantial contribution to a new fiction. Scott, thanking a friend for sending him the book well before he met Irving, read it aloud to his wife and two friends and declared, "I have never read anything so closely resembling the style of Dean Swift . . . our sides have been absolutely sore with laughing. I think, too, there are passages which indicate that the author possesses powers of a different kind, and has some touches which remind me much of Sterne." Readers may be put in mind, also, of the Carlyle of *Sartor Resartus*.

Old Mrs. Archer in Edith Wharton's *The Age of Innocence* valued the polite, humorous, and social Irving. She "was always at pains to tell her children how much more agreeable and cultivated society had been when it included such figures as Washington Irving, Fitz-Greene Halleck and the poet of 'The Culprit Fay.'" What she, and we, most relish in his work is not his evocation of the frontier, the native American, and buffalo and bison—not Paul Bunyan and Babe the blue ox or Leatherstocking—but a tentative world of close detail and response, in which the American dream is haunted by older dreams, European and primeval, but the dreamer wakes into a literal world.

He knows things change, including language itself. Thus, in one sketch, falling into conversation with a book in the Abbey library at Westminster, he writes, "Language gradually varies, and with it fade away the writings of authors who have flourished their allotted time." The only writers who survive such "mutability" are those, like Shakespeare, who "rooted themselves in the unchanging principles of human nature."

Irving began his published career at the age of nineteen as Jonathan Oldstyle, writing for the *Morning Chronicle* nine "Observational Letters" full of the kinds of social reflection that presented Mrs. Archer and her circle with an image of their own values and prejudices, and indeed of themselves. He satirized styles of dress, of ritual, of theater (he was addicted to the theater as a young man), and caused mirthful controversy by raising matters of taste and manners in a city (it was he who first, in 1807, dubbed it Gotham) that was becoming self-aware. His pieces had antecedents, in the essays of Addison and in Benjamin Franklin's "Silence Dogood" letters. They were distinctive in tone and effect.

As far as the novel is concerned, Irving's most original exploits were in satirical history of the Knickerbocker type, and in the historical writing he undertook as a novelist might, researching but also supplying unattested incident, dialogue, and color, romanticizing a narrative that included historical figures. Scott gave him courage. The lineaments of his narratives, rather than their wider context, were historical. An unreliable narrator has seldom been more trusted. His biography of Christopher Columbus sold well on both sides of the Atlantic, running through more than 170 editions before 1900 and persuading the world that, before Columbus, everyone imagined that the world was flat. Irving showed the way for Cooper: *Mercedes of Castile* profited in the wake of his *Columbus*.

Some American writers—Poe and Cooper among them—felt that Irving had become too European; his books about the American West, written after his seventeen years abroad, went some way toward reassuring them. In 1832, almost in a penitential spirit, he went west and had the experiences we associate more with Cooper's big-boned heroes. He hunted buffalo, saw "savages," ate native dishes, including skunk, and was puzzled by the conflict between pioneers and "the red men," his sympathies going "strongly with the latter." This journey did not find its way into his best fiction.

He became an advocate of a new American literature and of a copyright law strong enough to protect it from piracies. In this campaign he made common cause with Dickens, among others, and helped bring about the fundamental reform required. He also reached an agreement with his American publisher, Putnam, for a 12 percent royalty on retail price on the collected edition of his work, the first such deal to be struck with a publisher by a major writer.

He was thus the first American writer talented and astute enough to live primarily by the pen, to set the best loved of his tales in the New World, and to invest the language with American speech. Not a moralist, he wrote for pleasure and to give it. "I have been so accustomed to associate you with my pleasantest and happiest thoughts," Dickens wrote to him, "and with my leisure hours, that I rush at once into full confidence with you, and fall, as it were naturally, and by the very laws of gravity, into your open arms." He spent some years in Spain and was deep in Spanish literature and history: no wonder Don Quixote was his patron saint, and the humor of Knickerbocker is not unlike that of Cervantes. William Dean Howells, looking back, remarked, "I did not perceive then that Irving's charm came largely from Cervantes and the other Spanish humorists yet unknown to me, and that he had formed himself upon them almost as much as upon Goldsmith"—about whom he also wrote a biography. "Afterwards," Howell adds, "I came to see it, and at the same time to see what was Irving's own in Irving; to feel his native, if somewhat attenuated humor, and his original, if somewhat too studied grace." Yet, he said, Irving along with Cervantes and Goldsmith (a natural constellation) had been his "first three loves in literature." Perhaps he touches on the appeal Irving had for Mrs. Archer: "There was the beautiful manner, but the thought seemed thin."

Thought, perhaps: but beyond thought, the compelling force of the visual and aural imagination and the power of a clear style to plant it in the reader's imagination as deep as memory? Robert Louis Stevenson pays Irving the least ambiguous tribute, for his way of telling took root in him. "It is my debt to Washington Irving that exercises my conscience, and justly so, for I believe plagiarism was rarely carried farther. I chanced to pick up the *Tales of a Traveller* some years ago with a view to an anthology of prose narrative, and the book flew up and struck me: Billy Bones, his chest, the company in the parlor, the whole inner spirit, and a good deal of the material detail of my first chapters [of *Treasure Island*]—all were there, all were the property of Washington Irving. But I had no guess of it then as I sat writing by the fireside, in what seemed the spring-tides of a somewhat pedestrian inspiration; nor yet day by day, after lunch, as I read aloud my morning's work to the family. It seemed to me original as sin; it seemed to belong to me like my right eye."

———•———

Until the middle of the twentieth century young readers often came to the novel by way of James Fenimore Cooper (1789–1851). His Leatherstocking Tales, intended for adult readers, became fodder for adventure-loving adolescents. They were assumed to be good books for reading aloud: my father read *The Last of the Mohicans: A Narrative of 1757* to my brother and me, and the magic conjuration of huge forests and perilous waters stays like an actual memory. There were also scenes of brutality that disturbed our sleep and, rereading the book, I came upon one that has haunted me, when Cora witnesses Magua's duplicity and the brutality of a frustrated Huron:

> The savages now fell back, and seemed content to let their enemies advance without further molestation. But, as the female crowd approached them, the gaudy colors of a shawl attracted the eyes of a wild and untutored Huron. He advanced to seize it without the least hesitation. The woman, more in terror than through love of the ornament, wrapped her child in the coveted article, and folded both more closely to her bosom. Cora was in the act of speaking, with intent to advise the woman to abandon the trifle, when the savage relinquished his hold of the shawl, and tore the screaming infant from her arms. Abandoning everything to the greedy grasp of those around her, the mother darted, with distraction in her mien, to reclaim her child. The Indian smiled grimly, and extended one hand, in sign of a willingness to exchange, while, with the other, he flourished the babe over his head, holding it by the feet as if to enhance the value of the ransom.
>
> "Here–here–there–all–any–everything!" exclaimed the breathless woman, tearing the lighter articles of dress from her person with ill-directed and trembling fingers; "take all, but give me my babe!"
>
> The savage spurned the worthless rags, and perceiving that the shawl had already become a prize to another, his bantering but sullen smile changing to a gleam of ferocity, he dashed the head of the infant against a rock, and cast its quivering remains to her very feet. For an instant the mother stood, like a statue of despair, looking wildly down at the unseemly object, which had so lately nestled in her bosom and smiled in her face; and then she raised her eyes and countenance toward heaven, as if calling on God to

curse the perpetrator of the foul deed. She was spared the sin of such a prayer for, maddened at his disappointment, and excited at the sight of blood, the Huron mercifully drove his tomahawk into her own brain. The mother sank under the blow, and fell, grasping at her child, in death, with the same engrossing love that had caused her to cherish it when living.

Such writing, unsentimental in the midst of the lurid and picturesque, literal in delineating motive and action, with the "grasping at," the incompleteness of the attempt even in death, epitomizes the spell Cooper cast. Anthony Trollope cut his teeth on *The Prairie*. Thackeray admired Cooper; Disraeli and Gladstone were of one mind at least in their enthusiasm for him. Late in life Matthew Arnold read *The Pioneers* aloud to his family, finding a real sense of the America he had visited, though acknowledging that the book did rather drag.

His twentieth-century heirs include Chinua Achebe and Cormac McCarthy. Some of the vilest scenes in *Blood Meridian* (1985), for example, seem to originate in Cooper, as does the sense of a confluence of mutually hostile cultures preying upon one another and collecting scalps. Both writers portray the Indians in savage detail, but juxtaposed with the murderous deeds of the white men. Their scenarios are separated by a century (1757, the French and Indian Wars, and the Mexican borderlands in the 1850s). They are set in territories at the edge of the expanding country, where law and order are yet to be established and where America's "Manifest Destiny" is not a theory or an aspiration but a dark reality.

The warriors, the bandits, collect mementoes, scalps or ears, which are tokens of taken lives. Chingachgook's actions are described: "Another groan more faint than the former was succeeded by a heavy and sullen plunge into the water, and all was still again as if the borders of the dreary pool had never been awakened from the silence of creation. While they yet hesitated in uncertainty, the form of the Indian was seen gliding out of the thicket. As the chief rejoined them, with one hand he attached the reeking scalp of the unfortunate young Frenchman to his girdle, and with the other he replaced the knife and tomahawk that had drunk his blood. He then took his wonted station, with the air of a man who believed he had done a deed of merit." Matter of fact, unemotional, it made the Victorian reader squirm: elsewhere in the novel there is elaboration, a system of rhetorical filters. Here plain statement, its plainness underlined by the Indian's sense of the noble normality of the act, shocks the reader but suspends judgment. In *Blood Meridian* the language is more extreme, the withholding of authorial judgment more shocking. "They rode up into the dripping hills and in the first light Brown raised the rifle and shot the boy through the back of the head. The horse lurched forward and the boy toppled backward, the entire fore plate of his skull gone and the brains exposed. Brown halted his mount and got down and retrieved the sack of coins and took the boy's knife and took his rifle and his powderflask and his coat and he cut the ears from the boy's head and strung them onto his scapular and then he mounted up and rode on. The packmule followed and after a while so did the horse the boy had been riding."

Cooper can write thriftily, his adjectives to the point: "reeking," for example, and "young," each touching a nerve, prove that writing is still coming from a recognizably human zone, with an implicit sympathy. We are on side. McCarthy is in another place. His imagination is Homeric but his figures are for the most part ignoble.

It is appropriate that a new literature should be launched with an epic, and the scale, the stateliness, the heroisms and sacrifices, and the remoteness of the Leatherstocking Tales are all indisputably epic, as is the history they recount, bringing together the Trojans and the Greeks, as it were—native Americans in their various tribes and languages and their duplicitous allies, English and French. The chapters all carry classic epigraphs, the majority drawn from Shakespeare. Cooper's new subject matter thus borrows legitimacy and suggests a lineage. And the legitimacy was recognized: Balzac turns to Cooper with admiration, finding in the linked Leatherstocking novels the formal principles of his own vast accordion, *La comédie humaine*. Writing in the *Revue parisienne* in 1840, Balzac declared that Leatherstocking was "a monument, a magnificent moral hermaphrodite, born half-savage, half-civilized. I do not know if the extraordinary work of Walter Scott has given us any creation as magnificent as this hero of the savannahs and the forests." It is possible that Balzac's writings affected Cooper's as well: the traffic may have run in both directions.

Certainly the French took Cooper to heart. His admirers saw in him the father of the *roman d'aventure:* Cooper fueled the imagination of Alexander Dumas, for example. He was sculpted by Pierre Jean David, who sent copies of the bust to his native Angers and to other French towns where he knew Cooper was loved. Schubert and Berlioz were among the composers who could not get enough of him. Berlioz's overture *Le corsaire rouge (The Red Rover)* is a signal tribute. By 1855 four collected editions of Cooper's work had been published in French.

The books, like Scott's, are informative and edifying, packed with particulars and incidents based in history. They evoke places and people not previously made real in fiction, increasing a reader's tolerance and understanding. They also convey the author's contentious vision, republican and individualist, expressed outside fiction too, comprehensively in 1828 in *Notions of the Americans*. He did not avoid controversy and fought several successful libel suits.

As with Scott, so with Cooper, elaborate construction in the margins of recorded history, the effortful movement through vast landscapes of the New World, fascinating to American and European readers of the nineteenth century, have come to seem labored. The comic figures—Duncan, for example—are doggedly, repetitiously unfolded: laughter dries up in the adult throat when, for the umpteenth time, he begins to intone a reedy psalm; fear, love, courage, and other passions find a great deal of language but only limited embodiment, and one sex remains uncreated, beyond a set of pretty templates.

Cooper's style is deliberate compared with Irving's, more constructed, less voiced. Nor is he as generous: there is the not-unhealthy animosity toward England that Irving warned against. In the fourth chapter of *The Prairie* Cooper writes of the old country: "The hive has remained stationary, and they who flutter around the venerable straw are wont to claim the empty distinction of antiquity, regardless alike of their tenement and of the enjoyments of the numerous and vigorous swarms that are culling the fresher sweets of a virgin world." His style retains the "empty distinction of antiquity" he condemns, but in some novels he culls the fresher sweets of theme with a vengeance.

For this he was celebrated by some. Wilkie Collins (scornfully quoted by Mark Twain) calls him "the greatest artist in the domain of romantic fiction yet produced by America," a limited encomium because American literature, as far as the British reader was concerned, was still in its infancy. Cooper's Leatherstocking world is projection rather than observation or re-creation. Trees and paths, rivers and islands, prairies and mountains, are props in a vast set where the author, in the guise of a romantic historian, sets in motion aspects of himself awake, and of his selves culled from his anxieties and dreams. It is the "him," the gendered imagination, that marks the bounds of his inventing.

Herman Melville laments not having met or even seen Cooper in the flesh. He is as wholly alive to his writings as though he had been an old acquaintance. He liked the sea stories, of which only *The Red Rover* has a (small) modern readership, and also the Leatherstocking Tales, whose impact on his own writings about native peoples in the South Seas and the varieties of people in *Moby-Dick,* is marked. Cooper widened the subject matter of fiction and understood and honored differing worldviews. Writing to a friend in 1851, Melville says: "His works are among the earliest I remember, as in my boyhood producing a vivid, and awakening power upon my mind." Again, this sense of *awakening* power: the awakening of landscapes and literatures, dark faces and half-understood voices, but also the awakening from dream. Melville regrets that Cooper has fallen from favor with American critics (his books were still popular). "He was a great, robust-souled man, all whose merits are not even yet fully appreciated. But a grateful posterity will take the best of care of Fenimore Cooper." Tolstoy was in his debt, but more secretly so, using his work in paraphrase in *The Cossacks,* for example.

A longer posterity has not proven grateful. It is hard to agree with Joseph Conrad, who in *Notes on Life and Letters* celebrates the romantic conviction of the work. "For James Fenimore Cooper nature was not the frame-work, it was an essential part of existence. He could hear its voice, he could understand its silence, and he could interpret both for us in his prose with all that felicity and sureness of effect that belong to a poetical conception alone." He never regretted his infatuation with Cooper: "His method may often be faulty, but his art is genuine. The truth is within him."

That spell has failed, the voices of nature are no longer audible in the work. For a while the abundant figurative language, the "poetic" elements, seemed fresh; they now have a projected feel. This is what Mark Twain with malicious delight set out to demonstrate. In 1894, traveling to Europe and short of money, he drafted "Fenimore Cooper's Literary Offences," and by the time he reached London it was complete: one of the bloodiest hatchet jobs one author has ever committed on another. The hatchet is an appropriate metaphor in the context of Cooper. Twain takes the scalp and much of the cranium with it.

He begins by suggesting that writers and professors who praise Cooper ought to read him. "Cooper's art has some defects. In one place in *The Deerslayer,* and in the restricted space of two-thirds of a page, Cooper has scored 114 offences against literary art out of a possible 115. It breaks the record." Twain the humorist is in earnest. He proceeds to enumerate the eighteen violations of the nineteen (or twenty-two: an arguable point) "rules governing literary art in the domain of romantic fiction" in *The Deerslayer.* The most demanding rule is that "the personages in a tale shall be alive, except in the case of corpses, and that always the reader shall be able to tell the corpses from the others." For Twain being alive means speaking and moving in the human sphere, without ceremonious posturing; epic incident is at odds with the living, up-close demands of the novel.

And he despises Cooper's tendency to mix register in his always mannered dialogue: "When a personage talks like an illustrated, gilt-edged, tree-calf, hand-tooled, seven-dollar Friendship's Offering in the beginning of a paragraph, he shall not talk like a negro minstrel in the end of it." Cooper's dialogue can, within a single speech, move from the poetic and flowery to a labored replication of dialect and accent. Twain anatomizes incidents of malpractice. His points are repetitive, but he is building a rhetorical case:

12. Say what he is proposing to say, not merely come near it.
13. Use the right word, not its second cousin.

14. Eschew surplusage.
15. Not omit necessary details.
16. Avoid slovenliness of form.
17. Use good grammar.
18. Employ a simple and straightforward style.

Cooper: guilty on all charges. Twain endured a furious Atlantic crossing, waking each morning with his enforced companion and hating him more in his heart. He hated the way that in the Leatherstocking Tales the same customs of pursuit and capture were deployed time after time, a stock of tropes that the author pulled out of his box whenever required. He did not invent but reused. "If Cooper had any real knowledge of Nature's ways of doing things, he had a most delicate art in concealing the fact. For instance: one of his acute Indian experts, Chingachgook (pronounced Chicago, I think), has lost the trail of a person he is tracking through the forest. Apparently that trail is hopelessly lost. Neither you nor I could ever have guessed out the way to find it. It was very different with Chicago." It was a simple trick, and always a surprise. "Chicago was not stumped for long. He turned a running stream out of its course, and there, in the slush in its old bed, were that person's moccasin-tracks."

Dealing with implausibilities of a particular descriptive passage, Twain is lethal. He summarizes the qualities of *The Deerslayer*. "A work of art? It has no invention; it has no order, system, sequence, or result; it has no lifelikeness, no thrill, no stir, no seeming of reality; its characters are confusedly drawn, and by their acts and words they prove that they are not the sort of people the author claims that they are; its humor is pathetic; its pathos is funny; its conversations are—oh! indescribable; its love-scenes odious; its English a crime against the language. Counting these out, what is left is Art. I think we must all admit that."

Twain is not Cooper's only hostile posterity. For D. H. Lawrence, Cooper is vexing. Though his world is large, his imagination is puny, he brings new material into a morally pinched space, applies the wrong labels, not realizing in himself, in his amoral imagination, what his basic themes actually are, or the radical value of his enterprise. Like Scott, he has problems in creating women. In *The Last of the Mohicans* the sisters dark Cora and pale Hetty are referred to as the "females" and seem iconic, without bodily or spiritual identity, their presence in the books primarily to stimulate the manly virtues and vices of the chief protagonists. They embody vulnerability, purity, innocence of an old-fashioned, well-scrubbed, and starched kind. They are to be revered and served by men, they may even kindle passions in them, but few sparks fly between. A father's love for his daughters is more real than a man's love for a woman, even (or especially) such women as these paragons.

A man's love for a fellow man is another matter: the love Chingachgook and Natty Bumppo the Deerslayer feel for each other, their voiceless communication and calm intimacy, provide the emotional bedrock of the Leatherstocking Tales. This love lies at the root of a whole line of American fiction, from *Moby-Dick* and *Adventures of Huckleberry Finn* to *Fear and Loathing in Las Vegas*. In *Love and Death in the American Novel* Leslie Fiedler draws attention to it: "This is the pure marriage of males—sexless and holy, a kind of counter-matrimony, in which the white refugee from society and the dark-skinned primitive are joined till death do them part." Cooper had a resisted impact on D. H. Lawrence: the relationship of Birkin and Gerald in *Women in Love* is not innocent of Cooper, or as innocent as Cooper.

Though Lawrence tells us to trust the tale and not the teller, he cannot resist lingering over Cooper's privileged social antecedents, using them to discredit him. Cooper's father was a man of substance and character; he founded Cooperstown on Lake Champlain. "And Fenimore was a gentleman of culture. No denying it." The novels, Lawrence insists, follow a wish-fulfillment formula, in plot development and in the patterning of relationships, and these formulas conceal "the real thing." His account of the author is partial: Cooper the child of privilege squandered much of it. He was expelled from Yale, he joined the merchant navy and at eighteen the American Navy. These experiences he used in conceiving the sea stories that enable Melville's exotic, remembered, and imagined early novels. By the time Cooper was twenty-one, he was married and writing. He had found his vocation.

Lawrence divides Cooper's novels into two categories, the white novels (hardly read at all today) and the Leatherstocking Tales. The white novels *(Homeward Bound, Eve Effingham, The Spy, The Pilot)* are peopled by characters not too remote from Henry James's early sketches, though James seems hardly aware of Cooper's existence when he writes of American literature. The old-class Effinghams return from Europe: father, daughter, uncle, an admirable, faithful nurse. Eve Effingham has concluded her education. On the ship she encounters Septimus Dodge, self-made and on the make; he has ingested Europe differently from Eve, encountering its artifacts without responding. A man of Cooper's background would naturally write the white novels. But where did the Leatherstocking Tales come from? What was his imagination doing, seeking consolation in the pathless woods with Natty Bumppo, while his wife was struggling into a new dinner gown in the next room?

The books form a sequence, though the sequence was not composed in chronological order. First came *The Pioneers; or, The Source of the Susquehanna: A Descriptive Tale* (1823), *The Last of the Mohicans: A Narrative* (1826), *The Prairie: A Tale* (1827), a thirteen-year gap, and then *The Pathfinder; or, The Inland Sea* (1840) and *The Deerslayer; or, The First Warpath* (1841). The last of these, formulated upon the earlier ones, provides the earliest back-narrative: Natty and Hurry Harry are young, out hunting in the unspoiled wild. They chance upon two white females. *The Last of the Mohicans* is second in the cycle, with more history and politics of a credible, indeed a historical kind. We spend much of the novel on Lake Champlain, where Cooper's father's settlement was located, and as with Hawthorne we sense that we are in a landscape that, though idealized, has been inhabited by the author. The British and French are at each other's throats and the British are clearly in retreat. The daughters of the British general, dark and smoldering Cora, pale and virginal Hetty, come in search of their papa. When it is time for them to flee, Natty becomes their scout and protector, along with Major Hayward, Chingachgook, and the handsome young Mohican warrior Uncas, the "Last" of the title. There is deceitful, handsome Magua, who longs for Cora and abducts her, and is humiliated and fatally punished for his effrontery. The noble tribes are endangered species: the Delawares and the Mohicans are almost extinct. We follow them into their final agony. There are as many, and as melodramatic, deaths as in a Jacobean tragedy, but Hetty the White Lily reassuringly survives, to bear white children. Third in the saga is *The Pathfinder,* set in the Great Lakes in 1759 when Natty in his thirties falls unsuccessfully in love.

The penultimate book in the sequence is *The Pioneers,* set in a raw frontier village. With the different classes of frontier folk, the village inn, the bone-chilling church, Christmas games, pigeon-shoot, we are in the human and thematic neighborhood of Dickens's Christmas in *The Pickwick Papers.* The move west begins in earnest in *The Prairie:* a huge wagon of Kentucky folk jolts its way into the unopened prairie among Indians. An ancient Natty Bumppo dies magnificently, "seated on a chair on the Rocky Mountains, looking east" to where he came from, having been Leatherstocking and Pathfinder and Deerslayer. Fluid identity is a theme, as in Waverley it is one of Scott's. The pioneers, for their part, get a certain way, their progress stalls, and they settle: endurance is tried when they fall short and find destiny right there.

Lawrence reminds us that Cooper would never have been at home with the native American: the love between Natty and Chingachgook was in the head. "It is wish-fulfilment, an evasion of actuality," Lawrence says. How true is this? Cooper was happy enough on shipboard, with its mixed tribes, and he knew the area of Cooperstown and the diverse people there. Lawrence intellectualizes the author because it suits him to do so; though Cooper was a man of the polite world, he had got his hands dirty.

Cooper does not directly acknowledge nor perhaps quite understand the central theme of his work; he was waking up, says Lawrence, but not entirely awake. "What did Cooper dream beyond democracy? Why, in his immortal friendship of Chingachgook and Natty Bumppo he dreamed the nucleus of a new society. That is, he dreamed a new human relationship. A stark, stripped human relationship of two men, deeper than the deeps of sex. Deeper than property, deeper than fatherhood, deeper than marriage, deeper than love. So deep that it is loveless. The stark, loveless, wordless unison of two men who have come to the bottom of themselves." It is a gradual process, not a sudden change. Lawrence writes this passage in a voice like that of Birkin in *Women in Love,* for this is an intensified and unacknowledged version of a key desire in Lawrence's own novel.

Mrs. Trollope, recovering from a serious illness during her tour of the United States, was brought some American novels to read. She found Mr. Flint's *Francis Berrian* "excellent; a little wild and romantic, but containing scenes of first-rate interest and pathos." *Hope Leslie* and *Redwood* by Miss Sedgewick "have both great merit." In her convalescence she read, too, "the whole of Mr. Cooper's novels." Not wise: "By the time these American studies were completed, I never closed my eyes without seeing myriads of bloody scalps floating round me; long slender figures of Red Indians crept through my dreams with noiseless tread; panthers flared; forests blazed; and which ever way I fled, a light foot, a keen eye, and a long rifle were sure to be on my trail. An additional ounce of calomel hardly sufficed to neutralize the effect of these raw-head and bloody-bones adventures. I was advised to plunge immediately into a course of fashionable novels. It was a great relief to me; but as my head was by no means very clear, I sometimes jumbled strangely together the civilized rogues and assassins of Mr. Bulwer, and the wild men, women, and children slayers of Mr. Cooper." Such was Cooper's residual magic.

Fortunately her ebbing fever did not encounter Edgar Allan Poe (1809–1849). He touches another level of fear. Elizabeth Barrett, writing from Wimpole Street, already an intimate but not yet the bride of Robert Browning, thanked Poe in 1846 for a book he had sent her: "There is a tale of yours ('The Case of M. Valdemar') which I do not find in this volume, but which is going the round of the newspapers, about mesmerism, throwing us all into 'most admired disorder,' and dreadful doubts as to whether 'it can be true,' as the children say of ghost stories. The certain thing in the tale in question is the power of the writer, and the faculty he has of making horrible improbabilities seem near and familiar." This ability to haunt, the spell Poe cast over America and Europe, was expressed primarily in short stories rather than the novel form, yet it is the distillation and Americanization of the Gothic, an extension of the magic Washington Irving had performed in his American tales, but more intense, deranging, seemingly deranged. His one novel, *The Narrative of Arthur Gordon Pym of Nantucket* (1838), about the extreme adventures of a character who starts out as a stowaway on a whaling ship, was well known to Melville. The protagonist vanishes into an unresolvable mystery that haunts several Anglophone and French writers. "The darkness had materially increased, relieved only by the glare of the water thrown back from the white curtain before us. Many gigantic and pallidly white birds flew continuously now from beyond the veil, and their scream was the eternal *Tekeli-li!* as they retreated from our vision. Hereupon Nu-Nu stirred in the bottom of the boat; but upon touching him we found his spirit departed. And now we rushed into the embraces of the cataract, where a chasm threw itself open to receive us. But there arose in our pathway a shrouded human figure, very far larger in its proportions than any dweller among men. And the hue of the skin of the figure was of the perfect whiteness of the snow." The novel was translated into French in 1857 by the poet Charles Baudelaire.

Poe belongs in this account as one who drafted and signed an American declaration of literary independence from Europe. His assessment of his contemporaries, European and American, formed a basis for an independent American criticism as well. He gave credit where it was due, but sometimes withheld it, too, in the interests of his larger goal, the discrimination of American from British literature. The "graphic effect" of Poe's prose that Irving praised is also present in the criticism with its minute attention to style and its panoramic attention to the new tradition.

As a reader Poe closely engaged the text as he went along, pen in hand, conducting a dialogue with it. "In getting my books," he says, "I have been always solicitous of an ample margin; this not so much through any love of the thing in itself, however agreeable, as for the facility it affords me of penciling suggested thoughts, agreements and differences of opinion, or brief critical comments in general." If his comment is too extensive to be accommodated in the margin, he uses the nineteenth-century equivalent to a post-it note: "I commit it to a slip of paper, and deposit it between the leaves; taking care to secure it by an imperceptible portion of gum tragacanth paste." He adds, "In the *marginalia,* too, we talk only to ourselves; we therefore talk freshly—boldly—originally— with *abandonnement*—without conceit—much after the fashion of Jeremy Taylor, and Sir Thomas Browne, and Sir William Temple, and the anatomical Burton, and that most logical analogist, Butler, and some other people of the old day, who were too full of their matter to have any room for their manner, which, being thus left out of question, was a capital manner, indeed,—a model of manners, with a richly marginalic air." His essays and sketches grow from these alert responses: having attended to the surface of a text, he risks going deeper.

Henry James was in no doubt about the value of the "collection of critical sketches," though he covers his nose when he describes it: "It is probably the most complete and exquisite specimen of *provincialism* ever prepared for the edification of men. Poe's judgments are pretentious, spiteful, vulgar; but they contain a great deal of sense and discrimination as well." Poe, in his refinement, his dandyism, is not comfortable with the imitative, anglophile writing of his time, though clearly he responds to the British authors he reads; among American writers he is not quite at home, either, with the homespun, the pseudo-primeval, the effortfully American. What he hungered for was American forms. Those forms did not require American settings or an American idiom, but they did require a fundamental adjustment of the imagination.

D. H. Lawrence noted that the "Gothic-horror tradition to which Poe belongs, and to which he gave a powerful impetus, is replete with good-bad writing . . . The predictability of the rhetoric, its very lack of originality, guarantees the reliability of the narrator and makes his uncanny experience more believable." He sees Poe as having a disintegrative, sloughing imagination, unable to shape and form a new consciousness. He can read style but not form; he can witness to the new but not get a handle on it. He becomes "more a scientist than an artist," because he lacks wholeness of imagination: "In true art there is always the double rhythm of creating and destroying." Poe has only the latter; his "tales" are not "stories": they are "a concatenation of cause and effect." Lawrence is impatient with the predictable logic of their progression. The style is "meretricious," mechanical, aestheticizing the human, turning the figures into predictable, predicted automata. "He never sees anything in terms of life, almost always in terms of matter, jewels, marble, etc.,—or in terms of force, scientific. And his cadences are all managed scientifically." With scorn he adds, "This is what is called 'having a style.'"

The first of the modern southern novelists, Ellen Glasgow, reminds us that Poe is a southerner. "The formalism of his tone, the classical element in his poetry and in many of his stories, the drift toward rhetoric, the aloof and elusive intensity,—all these qualities are Southern. And in his more serious faults of overwriting, sentimental exaggeration, and lapses, every now and then, into pompous or florid style, he belongs to his epoch and even more to his South." Her capital "S" protests too much. For he was also an American in a fuller antebellum sense, and the first American writer to go to the heart of Paris and of French literature. He may never have visited Paris in fact, though legend says that during one of his invisible years (his life is full of unlit passages) he did. He imagined Paris, the Bois de Boulogne, the Faubourg St. Germaine, the lamps, carriages, book-closets, the Rue Morgue. His great friend was the Chevalier

Auguste Dupin, a Sherlock Holmes *avant la lettre*. "Books, indeed, were his sole luxuries, and in Paris these are easily obtained."

Posthumously, it is in Paris that he has found his place most confidently, and it is there that his Gothic found its heirs. He arrived decisively in 1852, in French translations by—among others—Charles Baudelaire, who had become obsessed with him during the previous five years. Poe had the effect of raising Baudelaire's spirits after the coup d'état of December 2, 1851, when the president became the emperor. Disillusioned, the French poet put politics behind him and threw himself into advocacy and translation. He had been familiar with the fringes of Poe's work even while Poe was still alive. He read him first in 1847 and experienced "a strange commotion." Poe wrote works that Baudelaire himself had already half-thought, half-imagined. In 1852 Baudelaire published his first translations of Poe's tales and articles on him. In France, Poe's own essays, Edmund Wilson reminds us, "provided the first scriptures of the Symbolist Movement." The indefinite, the deliberately imprecise, the refusal to provide a *sens trop précis;* the development of synaesthesia. "What made Poe particularly acceptable to the French, however, was what had distinguished him from most of the other Romantics of the English-speaking countries: his interest in aesthetic theory. The French have always reasoned about literature far more than the English have; they always want to know what they are doing and why they are doing it: their literary criticism has acted as a constant interpreter and guide to the rest of their literature."

The Goncourt brothers in their *Journal* entry for July 16, 1856—Poe had been dead a mere seven years—wrote with prescience: "After reading Edgar Allan Poe. Something the critics have not noticed: a new literary world, pointing to the literature of the twentieth century. Scientific miracles, fables on the pattern A + B; a clear-sighted, sickly literature. No more poetry, but analytic fantasy." This is Borges's point in his lecture on the detective story: not only did Poe invent a genre, he invented, by extension, the reader of that genre; and in the aftermath, that reader (multiplied a million times) impacts upon the future writer with demands of a narrative kind, and with techniques of suspicious reading, where every detail is interrogated and weighed. "Something monomaniacal," the Goncourts continue. "Things playing a more important part than people; love giving way to deductions and other sources of ideas, style, subject, and interest; the basis of the novel transferred from the heart to the head, from the passion to the idea, from the drama to the denouement." They had certainly understood his radical, subversive, and irreversible presence. They had not, however, registered how Poe "makes use of what is at hand, the banalities filling the popular reader's mind." They were reading Poe from the distance of another language.

He belongs with Melville, Hawthorne, and Dickinson on the dark side of American writing. But he was kicking against the same irritants as Emerson and Whitman and Longfellow, the dominance of English models in American literature. He said, a little prematurely, "We have snapped asunder the leading-strings of our British Grandmamma."

Poe's lucidity as critic and story writer is contrived. The Goncourts note the deliberation, the construction of his writing. Is this not, in fact, the necessary condition of any writer fighting out from under a "colonial" literary yoke? Nothing can be second nature, all the tools need to be cleaned, appraised, and new ones invented where necessary; everything is acquired, language itself has to be remade. The "tun dish," as Stephen Dedalus reminds us, must be reclaimed. Poe was before his time in the United States, but also in Europe, as Willa Cather reminds us: he "belonged to the modern French school of decorative and discriminating prose before it ever existed in France. He rivalled Gautier, Flaubert and de Maupassant before they were born. He clothed his tales in a barbaric splendor and persuasive unreality never before heard of in English."

France, a French setting, the use of French phrases, the insistence on a difference the reader cannot readily verify, give Poe a rare freedom, and he populates this freedom with voices. There is something of the actor in him. N. Bryllion Fagin long ago placed Poe in the experimental Francophile tradition of American letters: in constructing a story, "Poe, who usually uses the first person for vividness, did not imaginatively *live* the parts but *acted* them—hence the impression of reality while we read and the feeling when we finish the story that it never happened." We are back with the Goncourts' judgment: "Things playing a more important part than people." His is the first fiction of this type in English.

# 16

# The Fiction Industry

Charles Dickens, Harrison Ainsworth, Elizabeth Gaskell, Wilkie Collins

"Make 'em laugh, make 'em cry, make 'em wait," says Wilkie Collins. Dickens adds, make 'em pay. Make 'em pay as often as possible. The trick is to find enough of 'em: each pays a modest weekly or monthly sum and develops an addiction. Business depends on steady supply and quality control. Many products of the age remain popular a century and a half later.

Gustave Flaubert wrote to George Sand in 1872, "I have just read Dickens's *Pickwick*. Do you know it? There are superb passages in it; but what defective composition! All English writers are the same; Walter Scott excepted, all lack a plot. That is unendurable for us Latins." Arthur Hugh Clough, urging Matthew Arnold to forget about Empedocles on Aetna and attend instead to the poetry of the modern city as revealed in, for example, *Bleak House,* counsels against Flaubert. "The novelist does try to build us a real house to live in; and this common builder, with no notion of orders, is more to our purpose than the student of ancient art who proposes to lodge us under an Ionic portico." Artistic form is to be found in life: "The true haunts of the poetic powers are no more upon Pindus or Parnassus but in the blank and desolate streets, and upon the solitary bridges of the midnight city, where Guilt is, and wild Temptation, and the dire compulsion of what has once been done . . . There walks the discrowned Apollo, with unstrung lyre." Still there are the large allegorical figures, but here scabby, threadbare, literal. Dickens is read. William Dean Howells speaks for his generation: "I have had my time of thinking Dickens, talking Dickens, and writing Dickens, as we all had who lived in the days of the mighty magician." He concedes that "it was a very rough magic now and again."

Dickens divides writers. Is his popularity vulgarity, a compromise of artistic rigor? And his forms are—look at the early books—as baggy as Cervantes's. Max Beerbohm imagines George Bernard Shaw's tetchy objections, high-handed and political. "Charles Dickens had lucid intervals in which he was vaguely conscious of the abuses around him; but his spasmodic efforts to expose these brought him into contact with realities so agonizing to his high-strung literary nerves that he invariably sank back into debauches of unsocial optimism." Ford is hard on Dickens's formal sense: "Along with all his contemporaries, as a constructive artist even of the picaresque school, Dickens was contemptible."

Forster is harsh about Dickens's drawing of character. Ancient Egyptian friezes, he says, always show faces in profile; Dickens always shows them boldly from the front. Pickwick seen from the side, Forster adds, would be "no thicker than a gramophone record." He allows that sometimes, infected with the author's vitality, they start "to vibrate a little, so that they borrow his life and seem to lead one of their own." This modest concession undermines Forster's case, that the flatness is deliberate, designed to engage, but not too deeply, the broad readership. Does he, as this suggests, *patronize* his readers? The critic F. R. Leavis grants that Dickens is a great—entertainer. He lacks "a total significance of a profoundly serious kind." In his writing, humor and seriousness are ill-assorted. Teaching by means of social satire is one thing; but a laughter that is social, humanizing, even sentimental in the eighteenth-century sense familiar from Goldsmith, sells the reader short. And yet, how would we recognize "a total significance" if we came across one? And "profoundly serious" makes us ask whether a shallowly serious significance might be found, in which laughter is permissible.

Writing as a different kind of novelist, V. S. Pritchett declares: "While the word *Dickensian* lasts, the English novel will be suffocated. For the convivial and gregarious extravagance and the picaresque disorder which are supposedly Dickensian are not Dickens's especial contribution to the English novel. They are his inheritance from Sterne, Smollett and, on the sentimental side, from Richardson, an inheritance which may be traced back to the comedy of Jonson." Evelyn Waugh, in *A Handful of Dust,* creates for poor Tony Last the dreadful life-sentence of reading Dickens aloud to the crazed Mr. Todd in the South American jungle. Thus he exorcises that towering spirit. But novelists from other cultures take Dickens to heart without precautions. He was crucial to Nikolai Gogol, and Joyce valued particularly his Cockney eye and ear and draws some of Bloom's construction, and the sense of Dublin itself, from Boz and the abundance of his London. In *The Idiot,* Dostoyevsky, creating the character of Prince Mishkin, learned lessons from Mr. Pickwick, detecting beneath the humor of his innocence something of Don Quixote's benign but perilous fantasy. Dostoyevsky is closer to Dickens and Balzac than to Tolstoy and James. Form matters less to him than the lived *agon.*

Dickens's point of departure is often people whose insignificance in the social order is clear. Orwell notes that his social range is various but not wide: "The aristocracy and the big bourgeoisie exist in his books chiefly as a kind of 'noises off,' a haw-hawing chorus somewhere in the wings, like Podsnap's dinner parties." He wonders whether a love of Dickens is not also a nostalgia for childhood, and declares: "No grown-up person can read Dickens without feeling his limitations," adding with grateful exasperation, "and yet there does remain his native generosity of mind, which acts as a kind of anchor and nearly always keeps him where he belongs." *Generously angry,* Dickens knows how things could be, is disappointed, but never loses hope.

Something else gives the lie to Forster's sense of flat characters and reminds us how close Dickens is, in his sense of scene and character, to the world of theater. The widow Betty Higden says of the clever orphan Sloppy in *Our Mutual Friend,* "He do the Police in different voices." If, as Stevenson notes, early Dickens falls easily into iambics that dissolve different voices in a homogenizing rhythm, he develops in time a style based on differentiated speech, his own diverse pitch as narrator, and those habits of delivery peculiar to characters and rendered as accent, dialect, or more subtly in patterns of phrasing, diction, pace, and refrain. Each novel is full of character-narrators making sense of experience as best they can. Their interpretations are an index of their illusions, hopes, and desires, and they stay in precarious harmony thanks to the main narrator's governing voice, which is loud, alert to them and to us, readers conceived as audience. He is an "out loud" writer, and in reading him to ourselves we suddenly speak to hear a voice, or move our hands to see a gesture; so cunning is his puppetry that he moves us physically, too.

In a letter to Wilkie Collins in 1856, Dickens says he was "a writer when I was a mere baby, and always an actor from the same age." The editor of *Revue de Deux Mondes* wanted a biography, and Dickens provided as much as he wanted to be known. He omits facts that inform the fiction. His mother he mentions not at all. His father is described as having been "in the Navy Pay Office," but his problems with debt and prison are passed over. The blacking factory trauma of his childhood is not mentioned. At the age of twelve or thirteen he was "put to a school near London. Where (as at other places) I distinguished myself like a brick." He allows himself a moment of pride recalling his time as a parliamentary reporter: "I left the reputation behind me of being the best and most rapid reporter ever known," and, an afterthought, "(I daresay I am at the present writing the best shorthand writer in the world.)" Another touch of hubris (it was the year before his separation from his wife): he reports that he married the daughter of a close friend of Scott's. Looking back over his undisclosing letter, he says, "I feel like a wild beast in a caravan describing himself in the keeper's absence."

The letters exercise all his voices. He writes to close friends, a mother-in-law, business associates, publishers, critics, a Jewish lady disturbed by his characterization of Fagin; to his own children, with whom he maintains distinct relationships; to other children; to friends on the Continent and in the United States. Each requires an adjustment of address, a diction, a set of common memories. Reflected in so many mirrors, refracted through so many lenses, Dickens discloses more of himself than did any other author of his time.

He was born at 387 Mile End Terrace (now 293 Old Commercial Road), Portsea, near Portsmouth, Hampshire, in 1812, the second child and first son of John Dickens, a naval pay clerk, and Elizabeth, a lively woman who could not resist going to a dance the night before his birth. The Portsmouth house is now a museum. It contains the green velvet upholstered chaise longue on which in the long light of summer he slowly died at the house he loved best in the world, Gad's Hill Place, Higham by Rochester, Kent, in 1870.

His family moved to London when he was four years old, then to Chatham, the first place he clearly remembered; and later to various domiciles in London, particularly in Camden Town. John was committed to the Marshalsea Prison off Borough High Street in Southwark for debt. Dickens never forgot the situation or the place. John Dickens is evoked in the character of Wilkins Micawber in *David Copperfield* as someone always exceeding his means and "waiting for something to turn up." Thus, in the Marshalsea, John, like Wilkins, waited and, sure enough, a small legacy came, an answer to patience and a dogged self-belief rather than to prayer. There are touches of his wife in Mrs. Micawber. Dickens gives Wilkins a happy destiny, a concession that betrays the comic permanence of the character. Personal overrode artistic necessity. Charles provided for his parents' needs in ways they never provided for his.

Mrs. Micawber was not a sufficient exorcism of his mother. Mrs. Kate Nickleby contains more of Dickens's sense of her. "Mrs. Nickleby, sitting bodily before me, once asked whether I really believed there ever was such a woman," Dickens says. The shoe did not seem to fit and she chose not to wear it. The damage she did to her son may have catalyzed the art, based as it is on hurt, resentment, and a longing for trust, constancy, and affection.

Life in Regency London was hard for a boy whose father was in jail and, once out, still in debt. The sins of the father were visited on the son: at the age of twelve Charles was put to work labeling bottles at Warren's Blacking (shoe polish) Manufactory at Hungerford Stairs, near Charing Cross, London, one street and a world away from the thriving, fashionable bustle of the Strand. Warren's opened out at number 30; around the corner, at the warehouse toward the river, the boy worked for six shillings a week. Murdstone and Grinby's wine warehouse in *David Copperfield* is indebted to the memory of that hell.

Four months was a long time in the boy's life. Rats infested his days, arbitrary cruelty terrified and enraged him. Worst of all, his parents condemned him to continue when there was no longer a pressing need for the modest income he brought in. Those who should have protected him abandoned him. He was a middle-class boy among the desolate poor. His father fell out with the employer and the boy was freed. Dickens never forgave his mother for urging that the argument be resolved so he could return to work. In Mrs. Nickleby he settled scores, but nothing could allay the pain that deepened all the shadows in his books, so that Dostoyevsky understood, even in the character of Pickwick, that more than good cheer and laughter were entailed.

When in *Martin Chuzzlewit* Dickens writes how, on entering Mrs. Todger's boardinghouse, one experienced "a sensation of cabbage," it is clear how well he knew his subject: it registered not on all his senses, but on his being. He retained a feeling for the circumstances of the poor even as he understood the hypocritical values of his own class, and how the worlds connected. Abandoned and orphaned children occupy center stage, children delivered from nightmare either by life, like Oliver Twist, or by death, like Jo the *Bleak House* crossing sweeper. A "threshold revolutionary," Dickens tells truths almost neurotic in their lived intensity.

Not all readers warm to his vulnerable creatures. Regarding Jenny Wren, the dolls' dressmaker in *Our Mutual Friend,* Henry James declared: "Like all Mr. Dickens's pathetic characters, she is a little monster; she is deformed, unhealthy, unnatural; she belongs to the troop of hunchbacks, imbeciles, and precocious children who have carried on the sentimental business in all Mr. Dickens's novels; the Little Nells, the Smikes, the Paul Dombeys." John Cowper Powys calls him "a shameless sentimentalist. Why not? It is better to cry than to comb one's hair all day with an ivory comb."

After Warren's, Charles was returned to school. At fifteen he learned shorthand and started in the world, working first in a lawyer's office. Dandyish, good looking, he amazed his fellow clerks by his wide knowledge of geography. Later he became a reporter. His first courtship, of Maria Beadnell, daughter of a banker, ended when the father objected. Meeting her some decades later, now a plump, voluble, unamusingly married woman, he vowed from then on to leave the past in the past. Was young Charles like the clerk Mr. William Guppy in *Bleak House,* scheming, biddable, and not quite couth? He had, more than his wits about him, a gift for narrative. In 1833 his first story, "A Dinner at Poplar Walk," was published by *New Monthly Magazine*. It went down well. He became a regular contributor of *Sketches* under his *nom de plume* Boz. Dickens's first book, *Sketches by Boz, Illustrative of Every-Day Life and Every-Day People,* was published by John Macrone in 1836, on Dickens's twenty-fourth birthday. Six weeks later, at the end of March, Chapman and Hall began serializing in monthly parts *The Posthumous Papers of the Pickwick Club, Containing a Faithful Record of the*

*Perambulations, Perils, Travels, Adventures and Sporting Transactions of the Corresponding Members.*

Dickens's ambition was to be an actor. The crucial audition that might have led to a stage career was ruined by a cold. He had to content himself with amateur dramatics, but conducted over time at a nearly professional level and to acclaim, even before the Queen; and later with his famous public recitals of his own work. He possessed an exceptional ear, inferring a whole character from a voice. It is not surprising that, when he produced plays in earnest, he started with Ben Jonson's *Every Man in His Humor,* in which he played Captain Bobadil (1844). This was a benefit production on behalf of impecunious Leigh Hunt. A double bill of *Merry Wives of Windsor* and *King Lear* followed. His delight in performance was unfeigned and flamboyant, on and off stage. He could never resist what he called "those great piled-up semicircles of bright faces, at which I have lately been looking—all laughing, earnest and intent."

A year after writing that, he witnessed a different audience. "When the sun rose brightly—as it did—it gilded thousands upon thousands of upturned faces, so inexpressibly odious in their brutal mirth and callousness, that a man had cause to feel ashamed of the shape he wore, and to shrink from himself, as fashioned in the image of the Devil." The occasion was the public hanging of Maria and Frederick Manning at the Horsemonger Lane Gaol in Southwark, the first husband and wife execution to have been conducted for a century and a half. It drew an audience of 30,000. Pritchett declares, "We are bound to become fascinated by the thing we punish." Certainly Dickens was, but as a writer with a moral purpose, he harnessed, even as he darkly satisfied, that fascination. He hired an upstairs apartment to get a good view; the experience galvanized his public campaign against capital punishment. He conjured Henry Fielding, one of his masters in fiction but also—as chief magistrate for Westminster—in public morals, as a witness. John Cowper Powys notes, "The world of Dickens' fantastic creations is all the nearer to the truth of our life because it is so arbitrary and 'impossible.' He seems to go backwards and forwards with a torch, throwing knobs, jags, wrinkles, corrugations, protuberancies, cavities, horns, and snouts into terrifying illumination." The things he illuminates were really there, physically or morally.

He tied himself to the theater by friendships, productions, performances, and, starting in 1857, a clandestine love affair. For him the stage was where characters came wholly alive to one another and to an audience. Life grew conscious of itself, three-dimensional. Theater was a place of embodiment. In his public readings—a source of income and eventually of the exhaustion that hastened his death—he found his dramatic métier. Illustration, carefully commissioned and "orchestrated," added dimensions to a reader's experience of his books; so performance lifted them off the page; an audience's experience was different in kind and intensity from a reader's. The performed and printed story were different: he understood the art of adaptation.

A few days after Mr. Pickwick first appeared before the public, Dickens married Catherine Hogarth, daughter of Scott's friend the music and drama critic of the *Morning Chronicle*. Dickens had courted her for some time; he loved her and her family: her sisters were dear to him. When, a year later, Catherine's younger sister Mary died, Dickens was overwhelmed with an inordinate grief that he invested in his fiction. Many of his young heroines spring from that innocence arrested by death. He conducted a long, emotional correspondence with his mother-in-law. "I have never had her ring off my finger by day or night, except for an instant at a time, to wash my hands, since she died. I have never had her sweetness and excellence absent from my mind so long."

Besides grief, he had other pastimes. He forged a lasting friendship with John Forster, a literary critic and journalist who became his literary executor and first biographer. And now that he was getting well known, he was courted by hostesses and became a member of the Gore House set, presided over by Lady Blessington and the Count D'Orsay, makers and arbiters of fashion. He was elected to the Athenaeum. His social success, given where he came from and how limited his formal education had been, was remarkable.

He was restless. Unlike Pip in *Great Expectations*, he did not abandon his roots: he avoided putting down any until he acquired Gad's Hill, the house he had coveted since he was a boy. Even then he needed to feel unconfined, that he could go where he liked without social obstacle. It was a matter of mastering the social registers of English, as an actor might. He had mastered them as a writer. His discipline was as severe as Scott's. Pathologically punctual, for dates, deadlines, assignations, he despised unpunctuality in others, whether authors, children, or friends. He insisted, too, that he would walk as long every day as he wrote: a hard day's writing was followed by a major excursion. His letters delight in motion: taking a steamboat to work between Broadstairs and London, climbing Mount Vesuvius, visiting Niagara Falls, life-changing panoramas. With his close business colleague W. H. Wills he spends a night at Bow Street Police Court gathering impressions, observing what he calls the "internal economy of the station house all night," going to the police cells and soaking up "from twelve tonight to four or five in the morning" the whole scene.

Fame came quite suddenly in 1836. After the sketches and operettas, *The Pickwick Papers,* which started unpromisingly, developed a broad readership. Chapman and Hall offered him an emolument ("too tempting to resist!") of £14 per month, each (monthly) issue with four woodcuts. The installments added up to an expansive, informal, and familiar book, made the more accessible by the pictures. To begin with, Dickens was asked to illustrate with words the cheerful graphic work of Robert Seymour. He negotiated with the publisher to give him more space than his predecessors had enjoyed, so that the pictures might seem to emanate from the text; then he introduced certain characters specifically to engage Seymour's wit and skill—Mr. Winkle, for example. The publisher wanted country and sporting anecdotes; Dickens made it clear that he had only a limited experience of the countryside and did not wish to restrict himself to this area, which was, anyway, already well supplied with sketches.

In *The Posthumous Papers of the Pickwick Club* Mr. Samuel Pickwick, founder and chairman, and the three other members, resolve to make it a corresponding society: they will record their travels and adventures. This provides a commodious, relaxed framework for an entertainment. "All very well but damned low," grumbled John Lockhart in the *Quarterly Review,* the same Lockhart who had contributed to the gloriously low *Noctes Ambrosianae.* Characters in *Pickwick* (and in later Dickens) sometimes appear and disappear in reaction to public response. To the Pickwick Club members' adventures are added supplementary narratives, but the focal adventures include: a visit to Rochester, where we encounter the strolling, lascivious player Alfred Jingle, and where Nathaniel Winkle very nearly has to fight a duel; a visit to Dingley Dell, where the agreeable Mr. Wardle entertains us, Jingle elopes with the gentleman's sister, who is recovered, and we meet Sam Weller; then on to Eatanswill, where democracy is sorely tried in a parliamentary election and Dickens discharges some of the accumulated venom of his journalistic days; to Bury St. Edmunds, where Jingle and his servant Job Trotter again deceive Mr. Pickwick and Sam; in pursuit of the miscreants to Ipswich and the most hilarious of Mr. Pickwick's adventures, where he inadvertently finds himself late at night accidentally in the bedroom of a lady, resulting in a suitor's outrage, a visit to the magistrate, another almost-duel, and an averted abduction; the famous Christmas back at Dingley Dell; a specious "breach of promise" suit with Mrs. Bardell, who takes Mr. Pickwick to the cleaners; a visit to Bath; Mr. Pickwick's imprisonment in the Fleet (informed by John Dickens's time at the Marshalsea) for refusing to accept the court's ruling in favor of Mrs. Bardell; Sam Weller's own separate adventures; and after further divagations Mr. Winkle, who has been in quest of a bride throughout, finally weds his Arabella. This in brief is the fever chart of the narrative, Dickens responding to what he thought the widest public would enjoy. The spike in sales when Sam Weller made his entrance proved it was possible to play an audience, to improvise; readers were interested in the surface of the story, adventure by adventure, in the humor rather than overarching form.

During the writing, the illustrator committed suicide. William Makepeace Thackeray submitted sketches, hoping to succeed him, but Dickens did not like his work. Had Thackeray been appointed, English fiction might have looked different, but Dickens and Thackeray were to have an on-off relationship. Hablot K. Browne (Phiz) took Seymour's place and became a close friend of Dickens: they were to travel together to research the stories and get things right in the drawing and the writing—for example, as regards the schools of Yorkshire for *Nicholas Nickleby*.

Sam Weller, Dickens's first Sancho, rather than Mr. Pickwick, captured the popular heart, however irritating his mannerisms are for modern readers. With his arrival the series focused upon character. Illustrations showed the writer's and artist's view of a character; they also restricted readers' freedom to imagine a scene. Graham Greene says the pictures are a distraction, a distorting lens. Between us and the language Dickens wrote, Phiz's or Cattermole's or Cruikshank's version is interposed. But the letters between Dickens and his illustrators show how completely he tipped the scales in the writer's favor. He supervised the illustrators tactfully, but severely. To George Cattermole, who illustrated *The Old Curiosity Shop*, for example, he suggested changes and corrections. "The child lying dead in the little sleeping-room, which is behind the open screen. It is winter time, so there are no flowers but upon her breast and pillow, and about her head, there may be strips of holly and berries, and such free green things. Window overgrown with ivy. That little boy who had that talk with her about angels may be by the bedside, if you like it so; but I think it will be quieter and more peaceful if she is quite alone. I want to express the most beautiful repose and tranquility, and to have something of a happy look, if death can."

With *Pickwick* Dickens understood the challenge of writing "parts" that would add up to a successful book. He registered "the constant drawback of my monthly work," which interfered with larger planning, the problem of creating a *form,* to which Ford referred. A series of cliff-hangers (each installment had to end in suspense of one kind or another) might not settle naturally into novel form. And how tie up the loose ends? "It is very difficult, indeed, to wind up so many people in 'parts,' and make each part tell by itself," and yet he hoped to "get out with flying colors notwithstanding."

Serial publication, in monthly or weekly measures, accounts for some of the qualities and defects. Writers *had* to entertain. If they preached a social or political lesson, they had to reach clear conclusions. The density and richness of style, installment by installment, worked against publication as a single separate volume. Wilkie Collins celebrated and resented the artistic formula of the serialized novel. There is the challenge of word count: some weeks the material was too abundant for 3,000 or 5,000 words, some too thin, but the extent of the installments, once agreed upon, was nonnegotiable.

The period before *Pickwick* was not a rich one for the novel. Scott's ghost loomed. Between *Crotchet Castle* and Dickens's early masterpiece there was activity that pointed in Dickens's direction but fell quite short. Historians remember (readers do not) the journalist-novelists Pierce Egan (*Life in London*, 1821–1828) and Theodore Hook (*Sayings and Doings*, beginning in 1824, and *Gilbert Gurney*, 1836). They had an impact on Dickens, a journalist turning to novels. Less forgotten are George Payne Rainsford James (1799–1860) with his historical novels and romances, whom Thackeray parodied; and the still-read Manchester-born writer Harrison Ainsworth (1805–1882), the shape of whose career foreshadowed, and then shadowed, Dickens's. His first novel, *Rookwood* (1834), was a success on a hybrid Scott-Radcliffe model, with embedded balladry. He edited magazines, *Bentley's Miscellany* (1840–1842; where he succeeded Dickens) and the longer-lived *Ainsworth's Magazine* (1842–1853), going on to acquire the *New Monthly Magazine*. In London he was a gracious host, advancing his career by cultivating friendships and including Dickens, John Forster, and Bulwer-Lytton among his guests. He left thirty-nine published novels, some illustrated by Phiz and Crickshank, most of them indebted to Scott; among the unforgotten, *Crichton* (1837) and *Jack Sheppard* (1839). He was present at Dickens's celebrated Dombey Dinner on April 11, 1846, along with Dickens's closest friends and some competitors (including Thackeray).

Giuseppe de Lampedusa, the great Sicilian novelist, author of *The Leopard*, loved *Pickwick,* the whole, meandering book, reading it as a predictive catalog of the characters and landscapes of Dickens's later novels. "It is a fairy tale without the supernatural which has as its genie a warm-hearted and bespectacled old man." He adds, "There is all the gaiety and appetite of Rabelais without his lasciviousness": Rabelais in abundance, and fairy tale in threatened innocence and eventual "deliverance." Here *in utero* is the whole Dickensian world. We have in *Pickwick,* Lampedusa claims, 300 characters, thirty-five inns, laughter, wholesome love, controlled salaciousness, sentiment, despair, redemption.

From *Pickwick* we pass to the dark world of *Oliver Twist.* A child is the center of merciless attention, and the good do not necessarily receive their expected desserts. This fairy-tale world abuts the actual world of Dickens's childhood, from which magic and enchantment have vanished. Dickens enchanted his public with *Pickwick,* giving them what they wanted. Now it was his turn: he has something to say, or rather, to do: the first of several exorcisms.

He was writing for *Bentley's Miscellany,* which he himself edited for Richard Bentley (1794–1871), the publisher responsible for the 127-volume Standard Novels. His son George followed him, bringing out the novels of Wilkie Collins and of Mrs. Henry Wood, among others. For Bentley, Dickens (as "Boz," with Cruickshank as illustrator) edited and introduced the two-volume *Memoirs* of the popular pantomimist and ur-clown Joseph Grimaldi (1779–1837). Dickens had to organize the material to greater effect and enhance it, an early act of editorial intervention to improve a work for market. Grimaldi's world was dear to him: Drury Lane, the struggle to rise, the footlights, the pathos of his later years when disability overtook him; the whole drama set in an immediate past, a place more congenial to his imagination than the present or, Scott's and Ainsworth's preserve, remoter history. Grimaldi was "extravagantly natural." His life and art were not wasted on young Dickens.

*Oliver Twist* changes key, not form. "The one defect in that wonderful book," writes Wilkie Collins, "is the helplessly bad construction of the story." Like *Pickwick*, it is picaresque, "gradualist," cohering as it goes along, gathering pace not through symmetries and internal rhymes so much as by an intensification of the protagonist's vulnerability. As he becomes materially more valuable, his peril increases. Oliver's innocence is not challenged, and Dickens's reluctance to test his protagonist at a moral level, while those about him are subject to trial, might seem a weakness in conception. It is in the nature of the successful picaresque that the central figure is consistent. Memory is short, imagination improvises.

Graham Greene is astonished by the transition from *Pickwick* to *Oliver,* the change in style from *Pickwick*'s glittering close-ups "into the delicate and exact poetic cadences, the music of memory, that so influenced Proust" in *Oliver.* Indeed, as a boy of twelve and thirteen, at Illiers, Marcel Proust lay "in the hazel-copse by the asparagus bed" reading Dickens and George Eliot. Greene stresses the sense of material reality, the tenable archetypes that are Fagin and Monk, and by contrast the flimsiness of the "good" characters; each time Oliver is rescued, we know, as any child going to bed knows, dreadful things are in store, shadow friends are waiting and wanting, even as the good friends, those of daylight and lamplight, put us to bed and tuck us up. His characters are solitaries "caught living in a world of their own," says Pritchett. "They do not talk to one another; they talk to themselves . . . The whole of Dickens's emotional radicalism, his hatred of the utilitarians and philanthropists and all his attacks on institutions, are based on his strongest and fiercest sense: isolation."

Dickens wrote to the actor-manager William Charles Macready that his "whole heart for twenty months" was invested in *Nicholas Nickleby* (1838–1839), which he dedicated to Macready. Nicholas is, in a sense, the protector Oliver should have had, a high-spirited lad fallen on hard times due to his impecunious father's death, setting out in the world to make his way. He scores his vivid triumphs and exorcisms as he goes, most memorably turning the physical tables on the wicked headmaster Wackford Squeers, one of those whom Dickens convicts, in the preface, as "traders in the avarice, indifference, or imbecil-ity of parents, and the helplessness of children; ignorant, sordid, brutal men, to whom few considerate persons would have entrusted the board and lodging of a horse or a dog." In several places Dickens characterizes and punishes such men, freeing their slaves, in this case the downtrodden Smike, who be-comes Nicholas's grateful Sancho. Their adventures, on stage and elsewhere, and their battle with Nicholas's usurious uncle end happily. Nicholas saves his sister from a dreadful fate, the good end up married or settled, the bad commit suicide or are transported to the colonies or otherwise disposed of.

Dickens remembered first hearing of the dreadful Yorkshire schools when he was "a not very robust child, sitting in bye-places near Rochester Castle, with a head full of Partridge, Strap, Tom Pipes and Sancho Panza." In short, he was of the tribe of Oliver, and already a reader of the down-to-earth characters in Fielding, Smollett, and Cervantes. To a child enjoying *Nicholas Nickleby* in its serialized form, the author wrote, "I have given Squeers one cut on the neck and two on the head, at which he appeared much surprised and began to cry, which, being a cowardly thing, is just what I should have expected from him—wouldn't you?"

His great productive period had begun with almost pathological intensity. Sometimes major projects overlapped, and given the complexity of plot one might expect more errors in "continuity" than occur. *The Old Curiosity Shop* (1840–1841) was originally conceived as of a piece with *Barnaby Rudge* (also 1840–1841), both books to be narrated by Master Humphrey (*Master Humphrey's Clock),* but this speaking storyteller device he abandoned after the opening chapters. *The Old Curiosity Shop* was published in weekly parts at thruppence, to entice poorer readers, then gathered into shilling monthly installments. Shorter sections dictated a further heightening in dramatic tension to keep readers hooked. Dickens always aimed for the largest readership for commercial rea-sons and because, as a liberal-minded writer, he wanted his causes and charac-ters to gain currency in the other sense.

Declining a friend's invitation he declared, "All next week I shall be laid up with a broken heart, for I must occupy myself with finishing the *Curiosity Shop,* and it is such a painful task to me that I must concentrate myself upon it tooth and nail, and go out nowhere until it is done"; and to his illustrator, "I am, for the time being, nearly dead with work and grief for the loss of my child." Later he referred to it as "Nellicide," the death of Little Nell Trent, one of his innocents, a devoted grandchild caring for her grandfather at his eponymous shop. Here are profligate family members who expose innocence to ruin, and the misshapen money-lender Daniel Quilp. Nell owes something to Mary Hogarth, but she is more a projection of Dickens himself. Grandfather and child flee from the long arm of

Quilp and find peace but, exhausted, find death also in a cliff-hanger that held Britain and the United States in suspense. It is cloying stuff. By the time of Oscar Wilde, cheeks were dry: "One must have a heart of stone to read the death of Little Nell without laughing."

*Barnaby Rudge* was a departure: a historical novel set, like *A Tale of Two Cities*, in a remoter past, in this case the period of the anti-Catholic Gordon Riots of 1780. The book, with more fairy-tale and Gothic properties (birthmarks, supposed ghosts, and such) than ever before, is memorable for its description of the riots themselves and their material and cultural destruction, images particularly vivid to Victorian readers and intended to warn against religious zeal and those of a violent disposition who hitch a ride on public hatreds and bigotries. The idiot Barnaby's raven, Grip, is based on two ravens Dickens kept as pets. His children had urged him to write them into a book. Edgar Allan Poe reviewed the novel in 1841; his poem "The Raven" was published four years later. James Russell Lowell, noting the connection, wrote in *A Fable for Critics:* "There comes Poe, with his raven, like Barnaby Rudge, / Three fifths of him genius and two fifths sheer fudge."

Poe admired Dickens, but he noted "the disadvantages, both to the author and to the public, of the present absurd fashion of periodical novel-writing, that our author had not sufficiently considered or determined upon *any* particular plot when he began the story now under review." Poe detects "traces of indecision" that are artistically damaging to the book, and that might have been avoided had the book been thoroughly conceived and planned in advance. As characters develop, their earlier speeches and actions become out of character. Other problems exist: things are set up for effect but there is "no result," notably Barnaby's horror of blood, insisted on at the beginning, and his relishing of the riots, insisted on later. The method of publication ensures that the serialized book, which sets out on its journey before the destination has been fixed, retains disfiguring traces of the creative process. Poe admires Dickens's skill: when he senses plot is failing, he shifts attention to the riots, as if to shroud the error in the turmoil of history. "The riots," says Poe, "form a series of pictures never surpassed." Here was evidence, more conclusive in *A Tale of Two Cities*, of the friendship and influence of the Carlyle of *The French Revolution* (1837).

In January 1842 Dickens and his wife traveled to the United States, where he lectured in public, advocated the case for reciprocal copyright, and made friendships that survived the publication of his collection *American Notes* (1842) and the novel that drew on his experience of the New World, *Martin Chuzzlewit* (1843–1844), the last of his picaresque books. It includes romance, satire (especially in the figure of Mr. Pecksniff, hypocrite and surveyor), and adventure, the protagonist, Martin, accompanied by his faithful Sancho, Mark Tapley. For once the main character is transformed and improved by experience; indeed, changes occur in a number of characters who seem to have been fully imagined. They share the book with less-developed figures, caricatures of deception and evil. Mrs. Sarah Gamp, the bibulous old nurse and midwife, stands tall among them. Chesterton was sorry that Dickens abandoned the picaresque for "more conventional forms," but what could be more conventional than the picaresque? And the best was yet to come.

While he was writing *Martin Chuzzlewit,* Dickens was also composing what was to become his most popular shorter fiction, *A Christmas Carol* (1843), the first of his Christmas stories, followed by a string of little best-sellers including *The Chimes, The Cricket on the Hearth, The Battle of Life,* and *The Haunted Man.* He became engrossed in composing *A Christmas Carol,* walking fifteen or twenty miles through London late into the night: he laughed and cried, he was deep in the writing. Other stories initially outsold *A Christmas Carol,* but this one stuck. Built like a fairy tale around Ebenezer Scrooge and his moral transformation, it begins with a visit from a ghost. Scrooge has three visions (the fairy-tale number). Established as a killjoy in the opening pages, he is put through nightmare paces, waking on Christmas morning an altered man. Because the book did less well than his publishers anticipated, Dickens broke for a period with Chapman and Hall over the repayment of advances. He was coming to realize how a writer might do well to retain control of the means of production when serializing or publishing work in a journal. He had perfected, too, his method of symbolic character development.

*Dombey and Son,* published in 1848 after a gap of four years, marked a formal change in his writing. The mature Dickens is darker, not because he is older (he was still quite young), but because despite success the wounds of his childhood festered, his bitterness intensified. He became a harsher critic. He develops symbols in a more deliberate way, so foregrounded that at times they displace other elements, including the humor. Perhaps he had taken Poe's criticism to heart: there is forethought in plotting, more patterning, a consistent drama. He no longer responds so congenially to his immediate readership.

He began writing the book in 1846 in Lausanne. He and his family were spending long periods abroad, getting to know the Continent, and Dickens was mastering its languages. He loved Paris, where he continued work on *Dombey and Son.* So intense were his labors and concentration that he suffered depression. He felt more strongly than before his writing's didactic mission, to illuminate "one or two things among the rest that society will not be the worse, I hope, for thinking about a little." In a lesser writer this could have been self-important; in Dickens it is humility, acknowledging his responsibility beyond that of mere entertainer.

The spread of the railways established the circulatory system of industry and commerce, feeding into the corrupt heart of empire. *Dombey and Son* makes the point of transformation real to the modern reader. Mary McCarthy reads the novel as "a parable of Empire, the Dombey fortune extending tentacles of investment overseas while sickening at the centre in the person of poor little Paul and holding somewhere in its clutches Major Joey Bagshot and his servant, called the Native." The British insularity that Dickens touches upon was, McCarthy notes, "a side-benefit of empire."

The reinvention of his art in *Dombey and Son* is not quite complete. The plot is overly deliberate, we see climaxes approaching from a distance, but the skills that will bring us *David Copperfield, Bleak House,* and *Great Expectations* are developing, with a structure of symbols parallel to the action, the effect analogous to counterpoint: a plot structure and a symbol structure harmonize.

Money is a recurring symbol in *Dombey and Son:* what it is in different hands and minds—power, position, influence, survival, neglect. Dombey is the declining form of one kind of moneyman, the merchant; he is being supplanted by the manufacturer and industrialist, with greater power to harm people and the environment, and more potential to do good, hence with a greater moral burden. A telling dialogue on money occurs between Mr. Dombey and his sickly son one evening in chapter 8.

> Mr. Dombey entertaining complicated worldly schemes and plans; the little image entertaining Heaven knows what wild fancies, half-formed thoughts, and wandering speculations. Mr. Dombey stiff with starch and arrogance; the little image by inheritance, and in unconscious imitation. The two so very much alike, and yet so monstrously contrasted.
>
> On one of these occasions, when they had both been perfectly quiet for a long time, and Mr. Dombey only knew that the child was awake by occasionally glancing at his eye, where the bright fire was sparkling like a jewel, little Paul broke silence thus:
>
> "Papa! what's money?"
>
> The abrupt question had such immediate reference to the subject of Mr. Dombey's thoughts, that Mr. Dombey was quite disconcerted.
>
> "What is money, Paul?" he answered. "Money?"
>
> "Yes," said the child, laying his hands upon the elbows of his little chair, and turning the old face up towards Mr. Dombey's; "what is money?"
>
> Mr. Dombey was in a difficulty. He would have liked to give him some explanation involving the terms circulating-medium, cur-

rency, depreciation of currency, paper, bullion, rates of exchange, value of precious metals in the market, and so forth; but looking down at the little chair, and seeing what a long way down it was, he answered: "Gold, and silver, and copper. Guineas, shillings, half-pence. You know what they are?"

"Oh yes, I know what they are," said Paul. "I don't mean that, Papa. I mean what's money after all?"

Heaven and Earth, how old his face was as he turned it up again towards his father's!

"What is money after all!" said Mr. Dombey, backing his chair a little, that he might the better gaze in sheer amazement at the presumptuous atom that propounded such an inquiry.

"I mean, Papa, what can it do?" returned Paul, folding his arms (they were hardly long enough to fold), and looking at the fire, and up at him, and at the fire, and up at him again.

Mr. Dombey drew his chair back to its former place, and patted him on the head. "You'll know better by-and-by, my man," he said. "Money, Paul, can do anything." He took hold of the little hand, and beat it softly against one of his own, as he said so.

But Paul got his hand free as soon as he could; and rubbing it gently to and fro on the elbow of his chair, as if his wit were in the palm, and he were sharpening it—and looking at the fire again, as though the fire had been his adviser and prompter—repeated, after a short pause:

"Anything, Papa?"

"Yes. Anything—almost," said Mr. Dombey.

"Anything means everything, don't it, Papa?" asked his son: not observing, or possibly not understanding, the qualification.

"It includes it: yes," said Mr. Dombey.

"Why didn't money save me my Mama?" returned the child. "It isn't cruel, is it?"

"Cruel!" said Mr. Dombey, settling his neckcloth, and seeming to resent the idea. "No. A good thing can't be cruel."

"If it's a good thing, and can do anything," said the little fellow, thoughtfully, as he looked back at the fire, "I wonder why it didn't save me my Mama."

He didn't ask the question of his father this time. Perhaps he had seen, with a child's quickness, that it had already made his father uncomfortable. But he repeated the thought aloud, as if it were quite an old one to him, and had troubled him very much; and sat with his

chin resting on his hand, still cogitating and looking for an explanation in the fire.

The juxtaposition of father and son, the paradox of their similarity and difference,
is staged: the fire—and the sea, that other symbol that absorbs little Dombey in a
death of the kind that repelled Henry James but reduces less severe readers to
actual tears.

With *David Copperfield* (1849–1850) Dickens was into his mature stride,
having abandoned improvisation for an art in which everything is "subordinated to plot." Mrs. Gaskell's writings, which he admired and published, affected him. Later, Wilkie Collins had an impact. His art had to change. The
growth of the railways and the quality and speed of connections they made in
fact and imagination, the acceleration, meant that the ambulatory picaresque
had expired.

Dickens was heartened by the "bright unanimity" of his new novel's reception, a reward for the again intense concentration required in composition:
"Coming out of *Copperfield* into a condition of temporary and partial consciousness," he wrote to a friend: his absorption was so complete that it effaced the
social world; yet it replicates it convincingly on the page. McCarthy suggests
that he attempted here to write a new kind of novel, but the transformation is
not quite complete. Had he achieved his aim, the focus would have fallen on
the transformation, or revelation, of Steerforth's true nature, which would
have illuminated David's development; but Steerforth's change is a surprise to
David, to us, even perhaps to Dickens.

Yet there is a transformation, one to which Orwell draws attention in his account of the novelist whose politics disappointed him. At the outset all the
characters are seen as huge; gradually they diminish, as the boy, and the reader,
grow in understanding and maturity. Also the book alters in tone when we reread it, our sense of it helps to define where we are when we do so. "Dickens
has been able to stand both inside and outside the child's mind, in such a way
that the same scene can be wild burlesque or sinister reality, according to the
age at which one reads it."

He prepared scrupulously for writing, departing on an "exploring expedition" to make sure the topography was correct. He found a direction-post with
"Blunderstone" on it and planted the very object in his novel. "In some of the
descriptions of Chesney Wold, I have taken many bits, chiefly about trees and
shadows, from observations made at Rockingham," he wrote. And he warned a
correspondent: "Get a clean pocket-handkerchief ready for the close of *Copperfield* No. 3." To another he wrote in 1852, "To let you into a secret, I am not quite
sure that I ever did like, or ever shall like, anything quite so well as *Copperfield*."

Proust's favorite Dickens novel is *Bleak House* (1852–1853), a book whose immediate success with the public outran even *Copperfield*'s by 50 percent. It is a collection of mystery stories and introduces one of the first detectives, in the form of Inspector Bucket; it is also chilling satire on the delays and abuses of the old Court of Chancery, at the heart of the London fog. Around the focal case of Jarndyce v. Jarndyce, an endless suit over the distribution of a once-substantial estate, gather the smaller cases that draw plaintiffs into obsession and death. Miss Flite is a small-time litigant with a symbolic collection of caged birds to be released when justice is done.

The narrative point of view "bounces" us (Forster says) between an omniscient storyteller in the first chapter and Esther Summerson's individual perspective and voice in chapter 2; now diary, now dramatic writing, back and forth; and Esther's tone can be cloyingly naive. The book is "all to pieces logically"—by design. "The novelist who betrays too much interest in his own method can never be more than interesting," Forster tells us. Or less, we must add, especially of novels from this period. Henry James believed that Dickens forced himself to write against the grain from the mid 1850s, starting with *Bleak House*. It was not an easy period for him. He was working on the less than successful *A Child's History of England* at the same time, dictating to an amanuensis. In December 1853 he began his public reading career with *A Christmas Carol* for the benefit of the Birmingham and Midland Institute, drawing an audience of 2,000 people. This in itself marked a major change in his creative life.

Readings became lucrative and obsessive. At the same time he continued his work as an editor, running his popular journal now from London, now from Paris or Gad's Hill. Yet the artistic concentration of *Bleak House,* despite the unsettled narrative technique, and the development of genuine suspense and real characters give it a claim to being his greatest mystery story. He feeds us clues and evidence with a sparing hand, builds the suspense in several story lines at the same time, and leaves us in doubt about identities, and the murder, to the last possible moment. The symbols, again, are telling—for example, Bleak House itself, with the Dedlock portraits on the stairs, the dead-end family represented by a haughty, arrogant Sir Leicester whose comeuppance is tragic, and whose wife is depicted on a truly tragic scale.

Dickens drew some of his contemporaries into the story. Harold Skimpole is lightly based on Leigh Hunt, his self-centeredness emphasized; boisterous Boythorn embodies his friend the poet Walter Savage Landor. Lesser characters include the charitable Mrs. Jellyby neglecting her own family in the abstract interest of others, Mr. Turveydrop personifying hollow deportment, Krook the flammable rag-and-bone impresario, the crafty misfit moneylender Smallweed, and many more. Some critics write off the army of minor figures as so many caricatures. George Santayana insists that many of these "caricatures" are in fact "living grimaces"; he finds a distinction between mimicry and caricature, the one being dynamic and glancing, the other static and reductive. In Dickens we find both, and it is as well not to confuse them or we discard elements of value. Joyce admired the way Dickens presents a character "fundamentally natural and probable with just one strange, wilful, wayward moral or physical deformity which upsets the equipoise and bears off the character from the world of tiresome reality and as far as the borderland of the fantastic." Dickens fails, as George Eliot does, when he inserts characters for "diplomatic value," "correctness," and idealizes or sentimentalizes them, his women in particular. But some peripheral characters are essentialized. When we hear "Lovely woomen, what a sex You are!," we are directly in the corseted, periwigged presence of Mr. Turveydrop.

Money in this book has a rather different value from money in *Dombey and Son*. Here the main money is inherited, certain rules and customs attend inheritance, certain status attends inheritors. The flow of money is dammed up by death and litigation, made stagnant, poisoning the old and the young, nourishing parasites. The embodiments of its spirit are Krook (illiterate, parasitical); Tulkinghorn with his enormous scheming brain, his devoted malignity; and poor Miss Flight with her wretched birds.

In *Hard Times* (1854) the shadowy ancestral culture of *Bleak House* gives way to a different society and story. Dickens struggled to shape the book for periodical publication: "The compression and close condensation necessary for that disjointed form of publication gave me perpetual trouble." Its dynamic is that of an essay. The tension is in argument and proof, the satire of what Carlyle called "the dismal science" of economics, more than in incident or character. McCarthy reads it as an Ideas novel: utilitarianism taken to task. We must see Messrs. Gradgrind and Bounderby as "dangerously insane." But then, "Ideas are utilitarian. They have a purpose. They are formed in consciousness with a regulatory aim, which is to gain control of the swarming minutiae of experience, give them order and direction." Dickens might have concurred: "My satire is against those who see figures and averages, and nothing else—the representatives of the wickedest and most enormous vice of this time—the men who, through long years to come, will do more to damage the real useful truths of political economy than I could do (if I tried) in my whole life."

As he grew older, the challenge of writing a novel became more intense, just as the novels became more complex in texture and structure, more directed in terms of theme. Having aimed to please the reader, he now must also challenge and please himself. *Little Dorrit* (1855–1857), begun in Paris and composed over a long period, elicited one of his most forthright letters (to Mrs. Winter) about the commitment of composition. "I hold my inventive capacity in the stern condition that it must master my whole life, often have complete possession of me, make its own demands upon me, and sometimes, for months together, put everything else away from me." He adds, "Whoever is devoted to an art must be content to deliver himself wholly up to it, and to find his recompense in it. I am grieved if you suspect me of not wanting to see you, but I can't help it; I must go my way whether or no." This is what made Louise Colet so furious with Flaubert; he had no choice (and no desire) but to put his art first.

Dickens now put his own life and passion first. In 1857 he produced *The Frozen Deep,* a play written in collaboration with Wilkie Collins, with his group of amateur actors at the Free Trade Hall, Manchester. For the first time he engaged professional actresses for several parts. These were the Ternans: a mother and two daughters, Maria and Ellen. Ellen Ternan, aged eighteen, lively and intelligent but not enormously talented, became Dickens's mistress. He was forty-five. Mrs. Dickens discovered the romance and left her husband in 1858. There was a narrowly contained scandal that had repercussions on some of his friendships and on his publishing. His wife's sister stayed with him (gossip attached to that friendship as well) and the children, apart from the eldest, Charles Junior, who went with his mother. Even after the separation Dickens kept his affair secret for his and Ellen's reputations, but it was a relatively open secret. They spent much of their time abroad, and *A Tale of Two Cities* (1859) was composed on various tables, desks, and knees in France and England.

In 1859 he had founded a new publication, *All the Year Round,* the successor to *Household Words,* which he acquired and incorporated into the new venture. The first issue included the first installment of *A Tale of Two Cities.* It was successful. Dickens had established a serviceable business model for the Victorian author: the writer-publisher who takes both shares of the profit. His Christmas number for 1863 sold more than 220,000 copies.

The money Dickens successfully accumulated was different from the currency in his novels. *Great Expectations* money is a betrayer of hope, distorting lives when it is promised, withheld, and at last released, an instrument of manipulation and revenge for the dreadfully wounded Miss Havisham, and of furtive love for Magwitch. Pip is humanly perverted by expectation of money, hurting himself and others. When Lucien Daudet remarked to his friend Proust that the relationship of Magwitch and Pip in *Great Expectations* (1860–1861) resembled that of the louche, aging Baron de Charlus and the parvenu son of his valet Morel in *A la recherche du temps perdu,* Proust was pleased. This "queering" of Magwitch and Pip may seem a little far-fetched and contemporary. The elements of power and fear are certainly present, but it is hard to infer an erotic charge in Magwitch's expectations; paternal, not amorous feeling. More on the button is Peter Carey, who in his novel *Jack Maggs* (1997) pulls a bright thread or vein out of Dickens's book, reinflecting Dickens's characters and themes.

The first installment of *Great Expectations* appeared in *All the Year Round* in December 1860, the last at the end of August the following year. He wrote to Macready: "I have just finished my book of *Great Expectations,* and am the worse for wear. Neuralgic pains in the face have troubled me a good deal, and the work has been pretty close." Close in more senses than one: the climate in his imagination seemed to have changed, in response partly to advancing years, partly to the pain of his broken family, but also due to the small losses that accumulate in middle years. When a woman he had admired died, he wrote to a friend: "I think of her as of a beautiful part of my own youth, and this dream that we are all dreaming seems to darken."

He had trouble bringing the book to a satisfactory conclusion and depended on the advice of Bulwer-Lytton, one of his devoted readers and critics, to revise it. It had been a long writing journey before he could address some of the themes developed here, to recognize someone not unlike himself at the beginning of his journey. In his second preface for the book he confessed it was the dearest child of his imagination. As a father he could never resist playing favorites; as a novelist, too.

The moral structure of the early novels is clear, categorical, naive; the morality of the later novels is bold and simple and almost always resolved. The pathos is predictable, contrived for effect. In Europe his contemporaries (some of whom read his work with profit) included Dostoyevsky and Tolstoy, Flaubert and Turgenev. For them the medium was expansive, not resolved. *War and Peace* (1862–1869) and *Crime and Punishment* (1866) were fruits of the same period that produced *Great Expectations* and *Our Mutual Friend*. Dickens was having difficulty finding his way back into the discipline required for extended fiction.

The final novel was published in two volumes and never did please his critics. For Henry James it was "the poorest of Mr. Dickens's works. And it is poor with the poverty not of momentary embarrassment, but of permanent exhaustion . . . Seldom, we reflected, had we read a book so intensely *written,* so little seen, known, or felt." It belongs to a troubled time. Dickens was a public figure with an almost open secret, his relations with Ellen Ternan. In June 1865, when they were returning from Paris, their train plunged into a ravine. Dickens was able to save Ellen and help other passengers, but the experience of the Staplehurst railway accident lodged as a lived nightmare in his memory. In an effort to recover, to escape the gossip, and to make more money (he was certainly well-to-do by now), he undertook a second tour of the United States, this time with no female companion, giving public readings up and down the map. He saw old friends, was cosseted, dined with the president. Though he brought in over $200,000, his health was impaired.

But he loved public performance, the sensation of a rapt audience: the ultimate contact with readers, face to face, and money earned substantially and quickly. He returned to the reading circuit in Britain. In 1869 at his final reading he performed one of his most exhausting feats, the murder of Nancy by Bill Sikes from *Oliver Twist,* a return to his darkest roots. The violence suggests a temperament born of resentment and resistance, issuing in astonishing climaxes that give the reader a rush of adrenalin. In such scenes the author assuages something in himself and us, producing an effect between exorcism and catharsis. That "something" is in part a sense of isolation. The larger scene is displaced by a symbol—the fog, for example. One element, sometimes purely metaphorical, fills the page. "By this dissociation Dickens brings to us something of the fright of childhood," says Pritchett. And Edmund Wilson: "Dickens was more attracted than repelled by horror and violence," for aesthetic and psychological reasons.

In *Oliver Twist* and in his last, unfinished novel, *Edwin Drood* (1870), the movements of the murderer's mind are portrayed in terms of hysteria and nightmare, removed from the daylight zones of comic vision. As he struggled with his last book, he confided, "There is a curious interest steadily working up to [installment] No. 5, which requires a great deal of art and self-denial." He died before the book was complete and, though sequels have been written and filmed, it is not clear what he intended. This is the point, Pritchett says, at which Victorian and modern literary approaches to murder diverge. Here, as in Wilkie Collins's *The Moonstone,* we start to get "murder for murder's sake, murder which illustrates nothing and is there only to stimulate our skill in detection and to distract us with mystery." We enter into the narrowing realm of genre fiction.

Dickens executed his will in May 1870, treating wife and mistress less than lavishly and leaving as principal beneficiaries his eldest son and his devoted sister-in-law Georgina, his confidant and the recipient of some of his warmest and most vulnerable letters. On June 9 he died at Gad's Hill with Georgina and Ellen at hand.

Dickens's impact as an editor and a publisher was decisive for English fiction. He established, in 1844, cheap book clubs so that poorer families could invest three halfpennies a week and share on a rotating basis the sections of the novels as they appeared. He would insist that certain of his readings be open to workingmen. Always the intentions of his art were inclusive. He advised his contributors never to write down to audiences but to assume intelligence; and he expected of writers a moral seriousness.

The eighteenth-century debts of Dickens's later work—to Fielding and Smollett, for example—diminish; the work develops formal complexity, especially in his most nimble construction, *Great Expectations*. Some readers, satisfied with plain entertainment, love a gallery of characters and dislike the distraction of deeper themes and structures; others find the larger *formal* context that Flaubert and Ford overlooked in their impatience with the early work.

Trollope in *The Warden* contrasts the scrupulous, logical reformers of the past, devoted to large statements and great works, to those of his day who move "with a lighter step, and quicker: ridicule is found to be more convincing than argument, imaginary agonies touch more than true sorrows, and monthly novels convince, when learned quartos fail to do so. If the world is to be set right, the work will be done by shilling numbers." Of such men, Dickens, as Mr. Sentiment, "is the most powerful." "It is incredible the number of evil practices he has put down: it is to be feared he will soon lack subjects, and that when he has made the working classes comfortable, and got bitter beer put into proper-sized pint bottles, there will be nothing further for him left to do." What most disgusts Trollope is what he takes as Dickens's necessary vulgarity—necessary, that is, if he intends to address "the millions," for he "must use glaring colors."

Trollope's account, spoken by John Bold with a kind of incensed resignation, is sour but not entirely unfair. Scott created a style for architecture, heraldry, and fictional heroism, a "living past." Dickens created an image of England so convincing that it seemed to overwrite not only what had come before but what actually *was,* with a sufficient, compelling, and consoling vision, richly peopled with characters, caricatures, and figures and in a manner just and forgiving. Lampedusa celebrated it: "Dickens's kingdom is *magic realism,*" he says, long before that term was applied to Gabriel García Márquez and other modern writers. "It is a kingdom infinitely attractive but most difficult to rule." It is a vision charged with sentiment, historically and morally archaic and partial: the novel and its paying audiences do well to resist its enchantment. "I am the limpet on the rock," Dickens writes to a friend in 1844. "My father's name is Turner, and my boots are green."

When Wilkie Collins (1824–1889) was finishing his novel *No Name* (1861–1862), he was unwell and anxious because of the serialization deadline. Dickens, his editor at *All the Year Round,* wrote, "simply to say what follows, which I hope may save you some mental uneasiness. For I was stricken ill when I was doing *Bleak House,* and I shall not easily forget what I suffered under the fear of not being able to come up to time." He offered to return to London and ghost while Collins recovered. He knew the story and style and could (like Johnson with Goldsmith, or Ford with Conrad) do the voice. Collins declined and finished his own work. It earned him an astonishing £4,600.

Like the author, the novelist Nick Hornby found it hard to finish reading *No Name,* describing his encounter with it as a boxing match: "I had to return to my corner to wipe the blood and sweat off my reading glasses." He considered the issue of length: "It could be, of course, that the book seems bloated because Collins simply wasn't as good at handling magazine serialization as Dickens, and that huge chunks of the novel, which originally came in forty-four parts, were written only to keep the end well away from the beginning." Indeed, it could; or it could be that reading styles have changed and attention spans have grown shorter than they were. Two of Collins's novels remain nearly popular, on the page and in dramatic adaptation. *The Woman in White* (1860) was serialized by Dickens in *Household Words,* starting in the same issue as the last part of *A Tale of Two Cities;* and *Great Expectations* was serialized alongside Collins's *The Moonstone* (1868).

Marian Halcombe is a winning protagonist in *The Woman in White,* the equal of the fat villain Count Fosco. Dickens called the book a giant step forward, "and most especially in respect of tenderness." He had criticized Collins for not trusting his readers and for overemphasizing facts, interpretations, and effects. "Perhaps I express my meaning best," says Dickens, "when I say that the three people who write the narrative in these proofs have a *dissective* property in common, which is essentially not theirs but yours." The forensic manner displaced their distinct voices, weakening characterization. "*I* know that this is an admirable book, and that it grips the difficulties of the weekly portion and throws them in a masterly style."

Collins availed himself early of Dickens's advice, whose candor was tactful but unsparing. "I think the probabilities here and there require a little more respect than you are disposed to show them." He praised the consistency and intensity of Collins's engagement with his task. The young man learned from the elder's example and editing, the elder picked up formal clues from the younger. Their collaboration is manifest not only in works they wrote together but in the seeds they planted in one another's minds.

Collins was the son of the painter William Collins, an affectionate man of strict morals who hoped his son would go into business. When his father died, Wilkie wrote his biography, then discarded reverence and went his own way to become a writer of fiction and plays. He met Dickens during a production of Bulwer-Lytton's *Not So Bad as We Seem* in 1851, just after he had been called to the bar. He never practiced law.

In Bulwer-Lytton's play Collins played a small part, Dickens a large one. Despite the gap in ages they became close. Dickens employed Collins on his magazines. Collins dedicated to Dickens *Hide and Seek* (1854), the first of his novels to be recognized; and Dickens in a rash moment of gratitude praised it as superior even to Mrs. Gaskell's writing, of which he had a high opinion. The two men were intimate until their families were united by marriage. Collins's frail brother Charles wedded Dickens's daughter Kate. Then Collins, who liked success, signed a contract worth £5,000 for a novel with the publishers of *Cornhill Magazine*, a competitor to Dickens's magazine, edited by Thackeray. A coolness grew between them, and Collins, who prospered for a time as the inventor of the Sensation Novel, retained in later years an alloyed respect for his mentor. His work after *The Moonstone* (for which Dickens lured him back to his magazine) became increasingly sensational and his reputation went into eclipse.

Dickens destroyed the letters he received from Collins, perhaps because of what they disclosed: the men had visited the darker corners of London and Paris and spent weeks traveling together. Collins's private life was more scandalous than Dickens's. He despised matrimony and ended up with two families—one long-term relationship with Caroline Graves, the original for *The Woman in White,* the other with Martha Rudd. Between them he divided his time, love, and estate. Despite the irregularities in his own life, Dickens would have criticized such conduct in the younger man. Collins also became addicted to opium, at first a relief for physical pains. The plot of *The Moonstone* depends on the effects of laudanum. At the age of nine he overheard Coleridge confessing his addiction to Mrs. Collins; by the age of thirty he was himself taking the drops regularly. It is reported that by the end of his life he was taking a sufficient dose each day to kill a dozen men.

Collins named his three favorite novelists as James Fenimore Cooper, Scott, and Honoré de Balzac, a curious though formally coherent galaxy of godfathers. At its most inventive his work can suggest the intensities of Zola, as when he evokes the troubled Rosanna taking solace at the Shivering Sands in *The Moonstone*. Mr. Betteredge, the benign narrator, has come to call her in to supper and she takes him into her confidence. Their informal intimacy, their characterization through speech, and the haunting description are rare in English fiction. As it was delivered to his office for editing before serialization, Dickens wrote to a colleague, "I have read the first three numbers of Wilkie's story this morning, and have gone minutely through the plot of the rest to the last line. It gives a series of 'narratives,' but it is a very curious story, wild, and yet domestic, with excellent character in it, and great mystery." It was the high-water mark of Collins's unwholesome, suggestive art. No one thought at the time that a novel based around a crime, in this case a theft involving different cultures and classes, was inferior to other forms of fiction. The genre was in its infancy, coming out of stale gothic shadows: it had yet to be brought down to the tight focus and formal conventionality of later crime novels. Like the stories of Poe and Sheridan le Fanu, Collins's were frowned on only when they went too far, violating credibility and credulity.

After Collins, Elizabeth Gaskell (1810–1865) has a wholesome, reassuring aspect. She too was taken up by Dickens and, with greater resistance than Collins, endured his editing; she too fell out with him. By 1854, after sharp exchanges, Dickens exclaimed, not wholly playfully: "Oh, Mrs. Gaskell—fearful—fearful! If I were Mr. G. O Heaven how I would beat her!" She had contributed to the first issue of *Household Words* in March 1850 and became one of his regulars.

Dickens outlined the peculiar nature of his magazine: "No writer's name will be used, neither my own nor any other; every paper will be published without any signature, and will seem to express the general mind and purpose of the journal, which is the raising up of those that are down, and the general improvement of our social condition." He knew Mrs. Gaskell would warm to the objectives. What he did not tell her was that though authors' names would not appear in the magazine, his own name as editor would grace every page.

Dickens admired her direct, ungilded style, but as editor he valued most her ability to produce work to deadlines and in volume (she tended to overrun and he had to cut). Perhaps too he responded to the very quality George Moore found most disgusting in her. For Moore she was "the most commonplace of all English writers," and he came within a hair of calling her "a kettle singing on a hob." Dickens addressed her in very different terms, first with not entirely empty flattery: "There is no living English writer whose aid I would desire to enlist in preference to the authoress of *Mary Barton* (a book that most profoundly affected and impressed me)." She was taken in, but soon grew wise to his manipulative flirtation. Though they fell out, Dickens published almost two-thirds of her essays and stories.

She started late, at the age of forty-three, writing fiction to recover from grief at the loss of her son Willie. Elizabeth Cleghorn Gaskell (born Stevenson) produced, as well as four surviving children, six substantial novels and much other writing. Her father, like the husband she married in 1832, was a Unitarian minister. After her mother died, she was raised by her Aunt Lumb, Hannah Holland, "my more than mother," in the market town of Knutsford, Cheshire. The place bears her mark as vividly as, if more tastefully than, Haworth bears the mark of the Brontës. Knutsford is the setting and source for *Cranford,* and—in *Wives and Daughters*—Hollingford.

She suffered early losses. Her brother John, a sailor intending to settle in India, who encouraged and stimulated her reading, vanished in 1828. The next year her father died, and she was left, still a minor, under the authority of her unloved but not wicked stepmother. Aunt Lumb was among the strong-minded independent women whom Elizabeth admired and whose lives she chronicled in *Cranford* and celebrated in other novels, a theme that culminates not in fiction but in her enormous *The Life of Charlotte Brontë,* the story of the growth of an isolated genius unlike her own. It was the fruit of an uneasy friendship, a tense complementarity. Muriel Spark could not abide her, describing her as "a provincial, materialistic, self-satisfied humbug" who "wrote badly most of the time. In spite of her social zeal it is impossible to take her altogether seriously." Spark calls as witness Jane Carlyle, who spoke of Gaskell's "air of moral dullness."

She had access to a conventional, well-stocked library. The *Edinburgh Review* and *Quarterly Review* were read and sometimes discussed. She enjoyed reading aloud and being read to, especially Shakespeare but much else, dramatic and otherwise. She knew the great novels of the eighteenth century, but apart from Richardson they made only a small impression on the author-to-be. Like Jane Austen and at least two generations of young women after her, she read Goldsmith's *History of England* and *The Vicar of Wakefield.* Furtively she read Byron, and without concealment she devoured each new novel by Scott. He was edifying and safe. Burney, Radcliffe (a slight weakness for the Gothic), Austen, and Bulwer-Lytton she enjoyed, especially the all too sublime *Pelham* (1828) and *Paul Clifford* (1830), and she was astonished by Susan Ferrier's *Destiny* (1831), which she read over and over when it appeared.

What nourished her instinct for storytelling was the culture of gossip, a nosy small-town world where secrets were for disclosing and each small problem was everyone's business, discussed with the concentrated seriousness of state affairs; and then the boarding school, with different intensities. She suffered an unquenchable "thirst for detail," her biographer Jenny Uglow (from whom this account derives) declares, "which she judged so feminine." In her early years she dreaded London, staying in Chelsea with her father and stepmother. Later the city was a haven she hated to leave. There she was somebody other than the minister's wife and mother of four daughters. In London she was invited to parties with the Carlyles, Thackeray, Dickens, and others, because of who she was. Just as Dickens had made a bonfire of his correspondence, Mrs. Gaskell's daughters burned her papers after her death. Whole years and friendships were reduced to ash.

Though she portrays a largely Anglican world, she was, like her husband, Unitarian. Their faith was lived and felt, and much of that feeling was intellectual—caught up in the debate between the conservative, rationalist Unitarianism of Joseph Priestley and the Unitarianism of James Martineau, who talked of knowing through feeling. Martineau took that word not in its enervated Victorian sense but as an expression of the deep source of self-transcendence that Wordsworth, too, evokes and that is at the heart of early Romanticism, transcending mere self through feeling. In Martineau's argument, that feeling is a feeling *for others*. This romanticized Unitarianism deviates from the potentially Gradgrindian approach of earlier Unitarians. Though the Gaskells did not greatly enjoy Martineau's company, or that of his sister Harriet Martineau (1802–1876), friend of Charlotte Brontë and the didactic story writer and novelist whom Elizabeth regarded with skepticism and a touch of envy, they certainly understood the attraction of his less intellectual faith. Martineau's understanding of guilt and how it fetters mind and will is deep, and deeply healing. Gaskell is a great cause-and-effect writer, her art consisting in making credible chains of action, with credible consequences that seem to issue from characters' decisions.

Her husband, William, contributed much to Manchester over several decades. He was minister at the Unitarian Chapel in Cross Street, now encased in a substantial office building. (Unitarians excel at husbanding the talents God entrusts to them.) He was a tall, lean, and, in photographs, *leaning* man, humorous, reserved, insistently positive. It is he who urged his wife to write her way out of grief and then suffered her success and its consequences for the family and congregation. When she became a writer, Elizabeth changed: not only was she seen differently, she behaved differently.

In 1848 Elizabeth published *Mary Barton,* based on the industrial problems of 1842–1843, much closer in time to historical events than Dickens cared to come. The book gave heart to radicals but offended local industrialists, who regarded their paternalism as benign and enlightened and felt misrepresented. Several local grandees were in the Cross Street congregation or among the Gaskells' friends: there was more than momentary embarrassment when the author's anonymity was breached. Initially she had used the complex pseudonym Cotton Mather Mills, honoring the great American Puritan and the contemporary English economic and social philosopher. She noted other women's pseudonyms, especially Charlotte Brontë's and Marianne Evans's, and was glad to find them out.

It was not easy to find a publisher for *Mary Barton.* Finally Dickens's friend John Forster persuaded Chapman and Hall. He had also brought them Kingsley, Thackeray, Carlyle, Browning, Clough, Ainsworth, Trollope: an impressive commissioning record. Elizabeth wanted to call the book *John Barton:* he was her main focus. But could a book properly be named after a murderer? The change to *Mary,* with the impact it has on the reader's focus, was "a London thought," contrary to the author's intentions.

There was nothing to suggest she would write this book in particular. Her letters hardly touched on the dreadful social situation that followed the 1838 crash in Manchester, the unemployment, the housing conditions, prostitution, alcoholism, and crime. When General Napier took charge of the troops in the city, he described it as "the chimney of the world . . . What a place! The entrance to hell realized!" About this city and these people Engels wrote *The Condition of the Working Class in England*. Like *Oliver Twist, Mary Barton* bears witness to the consequences of the Poor Law of 1834 for "actual" people, the emergence of the workhouses and all they stood for. "I bethought me," she recorded, "how deep might be the romance of those who elbowed me daily in the busy streets of the town where I resided." Her interest was not idle curiosity: there was an instinctive identification with their plights and losses, especially those of their children. This manifests the "feeling" Martineau described. She wants to understand the subject and effaces herself. She does not display wit or cleverness: she records. There is humor but no wit: "One is dismayed by the lack of cleverness," says Virginia Woolf. Yet Woolf notes Mrs. Gaskell's authorial reticence in the life and in the art. "It is delightful to see how cleverly she vanishes." She hid away her manuscript work lest visitors think her odd; what was a little odd was that she kept a cow in the back garden, a memento of the rural scene.

Characters in *Mary Barton* are credible in themselves and at the same time stand for their class, interests, and struggle. Symmetries are obvious: two families, the Bartons and the Carsons; two sets of parents and children; the rich and poor bound together through labor and need, a dialectical structure. Mary's sensibility is familiar: Gaskell provides her with values that might seem to belong to a different class. She loves in terms of middle-class fiction; that readers believe all that she says and does shows how cleverly the cuckoo has been installed in the nest. We credit too the various forms of transgression Gaskell portrays: the highly articulate aunt who walks freely in the streets, Mary who loves above her station, her father who fights back with words and actions. Gaskell's melodrama, like her complex working-class characters, has much in common with Dickens's.

On a small scale, *Mary Barton* produced a radical storm, in the way that *Uncle Tom's Cabin* (1852) was to do on a large scale. It took issues and, by hearth-light and with intent, peopled them, making palpable what readers suspected but rather wished not to know. Readers, that is, who had leisure and the luxury of conscience. Carlyle accepted the gift of the book "as a real contribution (about the first real one) towards developing a huge subject, which has lain dumb too long." Charles Kingsley responded to it as if it had been a didactic tract, like one of Miss Martineau's.

For Dickens Gaskell undertook her next big project, the sketches and stories that became *Cranford* (1851–1853). Its opening paragraph contains the kernel of the whole entertainment: "In the first place, Cranford is in possession of the

Amazons; all the holders of houses above a certain rent are women. If a married couple come to settle in the town, somehow the gentleman disappears; he is either fairly frightened to death by being the only man in the Cranford evening parties, or he is accounted for by being with his regiment, his ship, or closely engaged in business all the week in the great neighboring commercial town of Drumble, distant only twenty miles on a railroad." This world of women is drawn from a deliberately female perspective, with no pretense at anonymity. Dickens spoiled the fun Mrs. Gaskell had with Pickwick: the amiable Captain Brown is struck down by a train, so engrossed is he in an installment of *The Pickwick Papers*. The editor changed the mesmeric text to Hood's poems.

Here she has become a little trying: busy, "charming," girlish, spoilt. In *Cranford* the narrator's eyes twinkle, she buttonholes and invites complicity. Like Dickens she flatters the reader. There is a problem: the narrator is not evenly fictionalized. Once again serialization takes an artistic toll. The narrator of *Cranford* does not develop, she is developed. She is, and is not, the social Mrs. Gaskell. The narrative is the fruit of actual memory, but *Cranford* is gendered writing from the outset when the issue is specifically raised. There is no pretend male narrator here. *Cranford* is her most original work, if not her most satisfactory, and her favorite among her books. She loved its world and the self she made of herself in it. Woolf notes, "Too great a refinement gives *Cranford* that prettiness which is the weakest thing about it, making it, superficially at least, the favorite copy for gentle writers who have hired rooms over the village post-office."

*Ruth,* also published in 1853, appeared at the same time as Hawthorne's *The Scarlet Letter,* which eclipsed it. The story is of a seamstress keen to escape her situation, making for herself exposed and vulnerable spaces. The theme was controversial: adolescent love, illegitimacy, and the like. *North and South* two years later is a more reckonable volume. It opens like a story by Katherine Mansfield: "'Edith!' said Margaret, gently, 'Edith!' But, as Margaret half suspected, Edith had fallen asleep. She lay curled up on the sofa in the back drawing-room in Harley Street, looking very lovely in her white muslin and blue ribbons."

*North and South* was a *weekly,* not a monthly serial. It is on the face of it her most conventional work, exploring the cultural gap between the north and south of England, the interests and values of each defined by contrast, the catalysts being love and money. The book was to be titled *Margaret Hale,* but a "London thought" again intervened. The challenge of serial publication proved almost too much for her, and adjustments between the serial and the book were considerable.

*The Life of Charlotte Brontë* (1857) was an important change of gear for Mrs. Gaskell. Some regard it as "her best novel," a mischievous judgment, but her subject was indeed a mystery to her. The plot of the *Life* was ready-made, the subject close to her interests. Early in their acquaintance, Charlotte Brontë invited Mrs. Gaskell to Haworth: "Leaving behind your husband, children, and civilisation, you must come out to barbarism, loneliness, and liberty." Charlotte regarded Elizabeth as a friend; for Gaskell, Brontë was more, and rather less. She was a *type* of woman that fascinated the author, tied as she was herself into domestic and family duties and the continual distractions of a social world. Writing a life of Charlotte Brontë gave her license to explore aspects of womanhood beyond the range of the conventional characters of her fiction, and an imagination quite unlike her own. Woolf draws the contrast in these terms: "The tuft of heather that Charlotte Brontë saw was her tuft; Mrs. Gaskell's world was a large place, but it was everybody's world."

She returned to fiction, and in imagination to Whitby in Yorkshire, in 1864 with *Sylvia's Lovers,* a triumph of romantic melodrama. Feeling of a literary sort, different in kind from the self-transcending feeling Martineau described, has taken over. Gaskell is writing to please readers who enjoyed the verse narratives of Crabbe, with their ill-fated characters, and the elegiac, wet-cheeked world of Tennyson's *In Memoriam.* But *Wives and Daughters* (1866), her last and unfinished novel, has the inventive vigor of the first, and a narrative assurance from the opening paragraph: "To begin with the old rigmarole of childhood. In a country there was a shire, and in that shire there was a town, and in that town there was a house, and in that house there was a room, and in that room there was a bed, and in that bed there lay a little girl; wide awake and longing to get up, but not daring to do so for fear of the unseen power in the next room—a certain Betty, whose slumbers must not be disturbed until six o'clock struck, when she wakened of herself 'as sure as clockwork,' and left the household very little peace afterwards. It was a June morning, and early as it was, the room was full of sunny warmth and light." Written for Thackeray's *Cornhill Magazine,* it is understated and wry. Again the story concerns two families, this time socially closer than in *Mary Barton,* their hopes and disappointments, marriage, money, and the true feeling that underlies misleading appearances.

What the reader remembers from her novels is their world, not individual characters: she has a panoramic skill, more instinctive than George Eliot's but similarly coherent. There is substance and completeness: the industrial and rural worlds uneasily coexist and are acknowledged. James was entranced by this realness, the authority of her art. And Dickens—not in a spirit of flattery, because he knew she would not be taken in—wrote to her in 1855: "It seems to me that you have felt the ground thoroughly firm under your feet, and have strided on with a force and purpose that *must* now give you pleasure." She was, to be-gin with, at least, his "dear Scheherezade," with this difference: she eschewed false magic for the superior magic of the real. She had learned to resist her friend and editor, and to frustrate him. Her resistance made her more like him, certain of the reality she was creating and the lives that unfolded in it. Her art entertained and, at a certain level, served.

# 17

# Gothic Romance

Charlotte Brontë, Emily Brontë, Anne Brontë

"I wished critics would judge me as an *author* not as a woman," Charlotte Brontë said. Asked why she concealed her identity behind a pseudonym: "What author would be without the advantage of being able to walk invisible?" When one first saw her, she could seem invisible. Mrs. Gaskell imagined her wrongly, anticipating a solid, forceful woman. She waited in the Gaskells' cheerful lounge, "a little lady in black silk gown, whom I could not see at first for the dazzle in the room." When Thackeray organized a party for her at his house in London, his daughter remembers, he stooped to offer his arm to go through to dinner, "for, genius though she may be, Miss Brontë can barely reach his elbow."

By then she had learned how to dress for formal occasions. Some years before, rushing to London in a panic with her sister Anne to persuade her publisher, George Smith, that she and her siblings were different writers, not one figure with three pseudonyms, they were taken to the opera by Mr. Smith, clad "in their plain, high-necked dresses," formal and quaint among the exuberance of the London *beau monde*. On that evening at Thackeray's, Charlotte appeared "a tiny, delicate, serious little lady, with fair straight hair, and steady eyes. She may be a little over thirty; and she is dressed in a little *barège* dress with a pattern of faint green moss." (This may be the dress on display at Haworth, with greenish and bluish flowers. It was not admired by the ladies of Thackeray's circle.) The party was a failure. Thackeray had invited his friends, including the Carlyles, but Miss Brontë had no small talk and spent her least unpleasant moments in conversation with the Thackeray governess. Thackeray sneaked away to his club soon after dinner. The atmosphere of his own party oppressed him. He had expected "an austere little Joan of Arc marching in upon us and rebuking our easy lives, our easy morals." But when they met, the cat got her tongue.

Up until their meeting, Charlotte idolized him. The politic, social man was not what she had imagined. "You see by Jane Eyre's letter, don't you," Thackeray wrote to a friend, "why we can't be great friends?" They had corresponded, "and met, very eagerly on her part. But there's a fire raging in that little woman, a rage scorching her heart which doesn't suit me." That fire and rage were gendered: there is a resisting spirit in Charlotte Brontë's writing that put "the High Priest of Truth," as she once referred to him, on his mettle. In 1855 "the delightful

Mrs. Oliphant" (Henry James's epithet), herself a prolific novelist, remarked on the revolution in the writing of female characters that Charlotte Brontë effected, bringing on "the most alarming revolution of modern times." No longer need heroines be "humble and devoted." George Moore imagines her in London where she was introduced to the editors, "a dozen pompous men standing before the fire, their coat-tails lifted, their eyes fixed on the timid girl who had discovered bigamy and written it out all by herself."

Her editor asked Miss Brontë for advice on possible careers for his daughters. Despite her own experience she commended governessing: "A governess's experience is frequently indeed bitter, but its results are precious; the mind, feeling, temper are there subjected to a discipline equally painful and priceless." It was a form of bondage, but within it there might be dignity and independence of spirit, unlike matrimony, which she resisted (she had offers) until, in 1854, she succumbed to her father's large, genial curate Arthur Bell Nicholls (his middle name having already provided the sisters' sur-pseudonym), more for her father's and his sake than her own. In the governess three ingredients central to Charlotte's identity combine: mind, feeling, and temper, the trinity of sentiment. And in governesses Charlotte and her sister Anne found suitable heroines for two novels: *Jane Eyre,* and *Agnes Grey* (which George Moore described as "the most perfect prose narrative in English literature . . . simple and beautiful as a muslin dress"). There are no successful conventional marriages to be found in the Brontës' books, and their women elude novelistic, if not romantic, stereotypes.

Muriel Spark spares a thought for the employers and subjects of the Brontës' teaching exploits, in the light of which Charlotte's benign retrospect looks unconvincing. Charlotte wrote in her diary: "Am I to spend all the best part of my life in this wretched bondage, forcibly suppressing my rage at the idleness, the apathy, the hyperbolical and most asinine stupidity of these fat-headed oafs, and of compulsion assuming an air of kindness, patience and assiduity?" As governesses, Charlotte and Anne suffer, Spark says, from "the usual terrible children," and when Anne introduced their brother, Branwell, into the Robinson's house where she taught, and he contrived an uneasy and perhaps, perhaps not, requited romance with the mistress of the place, she had another anxiety, viewing his conduct. These observations fed into the writing of *The Tenant of Wildfell Hall* (1848). Emily disliked governessing and came home quickly from her first excursion. Though her book does not focus on governesses, like her sisters' it is "unique, unconformable."

Charlotte's first novel, *The Professor,* was published after her death, but the manuscript prompted an encouraging letter from her eventual publisher. George Smith recalls how the parcel containing *The Professor* reached his office "bearing also the scored-out addresses of three or four other publishing houses." It had gone the rounds, and her failure to repackage it "was not calculated to pre-possess us in favor of the MS." Still, the firm's reader, Mr. W. Smith Williams, recognized its promise. By the time she received his constructive rejection, she was just completing *Jane Eyre.*

Charlotte Brontë in Manchester or in London, already a writer "whose small hand," Thackeray's daughter declared, "nevertheless grasped a mighty lever which set all the literary world of that day vibrating," was different from the young woman at Haworth Parsonage in Yorkshire, where she and her siblings grew up. Their circumstances are much romanticized. Matthew Arnold evoked them in verse. Virginia Woolf visited in 1904, composing one of her early articles. The place was "not exactly gloomy, but, what is worse for artistic purposes . . . dingy and commonplace." She was affected especially by the sight of Charlotte's "thin muslin dress" and shoes, material survivals of an unsettling intimacy. "One other object gives a thrill," Woolf notes; "the little oak stool which Emily carried with her on her solitary moorland tramps, and on which she sat, if not to write, as they say, to think what was probably better than her writing." A writer's com-ment: Woolf knew that a finished work seldom lives up to its conception, and may have had in mind a sentence of Charlotte's: "Life is so constructed that the event does not, cannot, match the expectation." Woolf draws attention in Emily's writing to the "suggestion of power underlying the apparitions of human nature and lifting them up into the presence of greatness."

Walking out with Keeper, her bulldog, Emily got close to the landscapes and weathers of the moors. "Hers, then, is the rarest of all powers," Woolf noted. "She could free life from its dependence on facts, with a few touches indicate the spirit of a face so that it needs no body; by speaking of the moor make the wind blow and the thunder roar." A flagstone bridge spanning Sladen Beck was one of the sisters' favorite haunts. Keeper may have been the prototype for Charlotte's Tartar in *Shirley,* though it was about this novel that Charlotte in-sisted a little disingenuously to her friend Ellen Nussey in 1849 that the characters were not drawn from the life. "It would not suit the rules of art, nor of my own feelings, to write in that style. We only suffer reality to *suggest,* never to *dictate.*" That word "suffer"—meaning both permit *and* endure—carries the full heft of Charlotte's reflective sensibility.

The Brontë sisters who survived, Charlotte (1816–1855, writing as Currer Bell and after her marriage known as Charlotte Nicholls), Emily (1818–1848, writing as Ellis Bell), and Anne (1820–1849, writing as Acton Bell), were born in Thornton but removed to Haworth shortly after Anne's birth. At an early age they began drawing maps and pictures and composing verse and prose, a shared activity that brightened with imagined travels and passions their overcast childhood and adolescence. They linked arms and marched around the dining room table composing, or they paired off, brother Branwell with Charlotte, and Anne with Emily. It extended and intensified their lives, as fiction was to do, and they recited to one another what they had written, filling the time with other places and voices.

Initially they shared poetic projects. Emily and Anne composed the Gondal sagas, Charlotte and Branwell the Angria sagas, and this continued into their early adult life. Narrative invention was a pretext for exploring passion rather than creating realistic tableaux. Poems attached to adventures; their larger-than-life figures felt and gestured and never quite died. Of Emily, Virginia Woolf reflected, "Her poems will perhaps outlast [*Wuthering Heights*]." Heathcliff and, to a lesser degree, Mr. Rochester are flawed heroes, Byronic in spirit, of a piece with the saga protagonists whose brimming hearts and earthquake heartbreaks are irrepressibly verbal, like the protagonists of operas.

In their poetry as in their novels they are gothic Romantics. The favored time for crisis is night, the favored season, winter—the long dark winters of the moors. Their somber perspectives were not merely literary. At Haworth they endured a litany of bereavements: early on, two elder sisters; their mother, Maria Branwell, in 1820, at the birth of Anne; in later years their brother; "Aunt Branwell," who had come to take care of them after their mother's death; and then Charlotte lost her remaining sisters and wrote her last two novels without them.

At Haworth, too, they were educated. Their mother and father were both well read, and their father, Patrick Brontë, wrote: he produced verse, volumes of sermons, and a novel. There were books in the house and literary journals, in particular *Blackwood's Magazine*. Charlotte and Branwell brooded upon this other world of writing, criticism, publishing, on the fringes of which they lived. They produced little magazines and tried to imitate the severity, satire, and critical breadth of *Blackwood's*. From their parents they inherited didactic bias and an earnestness that made it hard for them to be detached and ironical in the manner of, say, Jane Austen, or to be satirical with the fantastic wit of the *Noctes Ambrosianae*. Their characters were too *real* to them, the societies in which they placed them too tenuously grasped. There is no urban or county norm. Weathers and settings are made real by states of mind and feeling. The poems adopt somber, popular forms: ballad and hymn stanzas; the novels resort to fable and romance, the diction restricted, if not restrained, feelings running deep but strait.

Charlotte wrote more than half her poetry between her thirteenth and twentieth years; "but I am now twenty-four approaching twenty-five—and the intermediate years are those which begin to rob life of its superfluous coloring."

What carries over from her verse into her prose is a focus on isolated voices: "Again I find myself alone." "What does she dream of, lingering all alone?" Striving is in will and dream; when striving finds plot and action and the dream gives way to a sense of the literal world, she becomes a novelist. Charlotte affected one of the great poets of the nineteenth century in far-off Amherst, Massachusetts. Emily Dickinson wrote:

> All overgrown by cunning moss,
> All interspersed with weed,
> The little cage of "Currer Bell"
> In quiet "Haworth" laid.
>
> Gathered from many wanderings—
> Gethsemane can tell
> Thro' what transporting anguish
> She reached the Asphodel!

The "transporting anguish" of so much loss touched Dickinson, as did the force of Jane Eyre. Again, self-effacement was required if the author intended to speak truthfully: "Currer Bell will avow to Mrs. Gaskell that her chief reason for maintaining an incognito is the fear that if she relinquished it, strength and courage would leave her, and she should ever after shrink from writing the plain truth," Charlotte declared.

Emily Brontë's poems have an emotional vigor of another order from her sister Charlotte's. Arnold celebrates her as one "whose soul / Knew no fellow for might, / Passion, vehemence, grief, / Daring," not since Byron—that dark Romantic name again. Byron's rejection of all he took to be hypocrisy drew her to him, but as a woman with a different sense from his of disabling hypocrisies. She too broke molds and models. Her verse strains conventional form; in fiction, she strained form too. Form is a means, not an end; if the end violates the means, let convention bend. What matters is not fiction but the truth that fiction tells.

The life tells truths as well. Her brother, Branwell, had been a clerk for the Manchester and Leeds Railway but was dismissed for culpable negligence. As a tutor, he fell for a married woman and succumbed to drink and drugs. Emily waited up for him and finally nursed him as he died. Drained of energy, she caught a chill at his funeral and never left the parsonage again, though for her last two months she rose each morning, dressed, and kept house. Even on the day of her death she got up and dressed, then realized that the time had come. The coffin maker reported her coffin was five foot six long by sixteen inches wide. Her last poem begins:

No coward soul is mine
No trembler in the world's storm-troubled sphere
I see Heaven's glories shine
And Faith shines equal arming me from Fear

Emily ("stronger than a man, simpler than a child," Charlotte said) was followed to the grave in 1849 by Anne, who succumbed to tuberculosis in Scarborough and is buried there. Charlotte survived for six more years, dying during her first pregnancy.

Even Charlotte, worldliest of the sisters, was unworldly. Mrs. Gaskell fascinated and a little repelled her. Unused to socializing, Charlotte did not identify those moments of insincerity, irony, or calculation that underlay some of her friend's sisterly effusions. She allowed herself to be manipulated, even asking her publishers to delay releasing *Villette* (1853) so as to give Mrs. Gaskell's *Ruth* uncontested literary space.

She came closer to romance than her sisters did. Aunt Branwell, shortly before she died, gave Charlotte and Emily enough funds to establish a school. They needed more education and polish, so they set out for Brussels to attend (and Charlotte later to teach at) the Pensionnat Héger, an establishment run by a Roman Catholic couple, Zoe Héger and her charismatic (Charlotte thought) husband, Constantin. She fell in love; he did not encourage her. When at last she returned to Yorkshire, she courted him by post, without effect. Her drama is encoded in those details: Protestant girls in a Catholic establishment; inexperienced girls from the provinces exposed to the moral perils of the city and the little Pensionnat community; and finally, fatally, the married couple in positions of authority. This was to be Charlotte Brontë's one story, told in four different novels, the first written after she and Emily had tried to set up their school and failed. Monsieur Héger's impassivity made him a vulnerable protagonist, for Charlotte could make of him, and of Zoe, whom she regarded grimly but without malice as the chief obstacle to her desire, whatever she wished.

In her first novel, *The Professor* (posthumously published in 1857), she started probing the wound while it was raw. She deploys a male narrator, sets the novel in Brussels (aka Villette), and reverses the sexual roles, as if trying to understand from another point of view. The experiment was not a success. Her last novel, on the other hand, recycling material from the first, was closer to the truth she lived; indeed, one has the sense that here truth did not suggest but dictated, and this is one reason the novel never quite takes hold of the common reader and why it is not the main characters but the ancillary ones in which the book comes alive.

The uncommon reader finds in *Villette* rare qualities, indeed rare integrity. Lorna Sage loves it because it is so "miserable": "not a nice novel at all, indeed a bitterly, sardonically old-maidish one, but the braver and more brilliant for that." Lucy Snowe is unbeautiful, unmoneyed, friendless. She goes to Belgium to teach in a girls' school. Madame Beck, the head, comes to respect her. She tries to resist but seems to fall in love with John Bretton, the school's English doctor, who happens to be (a truth withheld with serious artistic consequences) her godmother's son. He in turn is responsive to Ginevra Fanshawe, a flirty, shallow girl who happens to be handsome, and the dependent and diminutive Paulina Home, a "child-woman" stereotype, Sage says. Bretton's response to her is almost like a perversion, so odd, so infantile is she. The heroine finds herself responding to M. Paul Emanuel, ferocious and strict but generous at heart. He moves from despotism to affection. She remains in Brussels, in charge of her own school, when he is called away to the West Indies. We are not told if he returns, we are pretty sure he does not, the author being scornful of those who require happy endings. She does not drown him, but she does not throw him a rope. The use of nature toward the end reflects the state of mind of the protagonist. It is corroborative, even collaborative. It is a grey story, with some sharply drawn characters. Lucy "aches on purpose," says Sage. Woolf declares *Villette* Charlotte Brontë's "finest" novel.

Here and elsewhere Charlotte Brontë, David Cecil suggests, "stretched the long arm of coincidence to the point of dislocation." Arnold questioned the religious and sexual morality of the book, and E. M. Forster objected to how Lucy Snowe, whom we learn to regard as a figure of probity and directness, conceals from us what she already knows, that Dr. John is in fact her childhood playmate grown up. This underlines a problem of conflict between narrative device and plot: for effect, we need to be surprised; yet to have the information withheld by this particular character betrays the character. In *Villette* romance is not completed but deferred, and if M. Paul Emanuel cannot (yet) belong to her, he will certainly belong to no one else.

The years 1847 and 1848 marked the apotheosis of the Yorkshire Bells. In January 1848 the "perverse and morbid" (Orwell's phrase) *Wuthering Heights* began to be reviewed (as did *Agnes Grey* by Anne Brontë). But most significantly, in *Jane Eyre* (1847) Charlotte Brontë altered the direction of fiction, creating a new kind of protagonist—plain, passionate, patient, and rewarded. It is as though Pamela has been reinvented, a girl with greater powers and more self-possession but with far higher emotional, moral, and spiritual mountains to climb. An orphan overcomes early obstacles and becomes a teacher and then a governess at Thornfield Hall to Mr. Rochester's natural daughter. She narrowly escapes a bigamous relationship with her master, more narrowly still eludes a righteous marriage to a vicar bent on missionary work in India, and more narrowly still, thanks to a moment of telepathic communication, marries the now widowed and blind Mr. Rochester. A happy ending: she moves into the ruins of a great house with her sightless and maimed husband. In making him happy, she is herself fulfilled.

Harshly remembered details from her own early life inform the book, not least the evocation of Lowood, based on the boarding school for children of the penurious clergy to which Patrick Brontë sent his girls for a time, there to experience the awful conditions that weakened their constitutions and damaged them for life.

Charlotte started writing *Jane Eyre* in Manchester. Of the Brontë novels it is the most conscious of earlier books, the most literary. In the opening pages we meet with Thomas Bewick's *History of British Birds,* James Thomson's "Autumn" from *The Seasons,* and—most appropriately—Samuel Richardson's *Pamela.* The book is aware of what it is, finding its own shelf in the library. Charlotte's narrator is a continuous presence. First-person, confiding, sometimes buttonholing, not least when she declares, "Reader, I married him": we focus on rather than through her, and the narrative perspective contributes to the drama (we find things out as she does). Woolf remarks that she "never leaves us for a moment or allows us to forget her," rather like Pamela writing her letters at all hours, though here the author has the advantage of retrospect. Emily conducts *Wuthering Heights* by means of a series of interlinked narrative perspectives, a harder formal challenge. "The drawbacks of being Jane Eyre are not far to seek," says Woolf, speaking not only of the character but also of the narrator. "Always to be a governess and always to be in love is a serious limitation in a world which is full, after all, of people who are neither one nor the other." She compares her to Thomas Hardy in terms of her narrow focus and force of personality. But with *Jude,* she reminds us, we reflect ruefully as we go, whereas with *Jane Eyre* we rush to the finish. It is hard to distance us from the narrator to achieve a more objective purchase on her world. In style, too, Woolf says, Charlotte Brontë and Hardy have something in common. They are "self-centred and self-limited writers" and due to this limitation possessed of "a power denied the more catholic and broad-minded." They are narrow, they cannot assimilate but merely adopt; their styles seem to be built out of "a stiff and decorous journalism." Yet they "have forged themselves a prose which takes the mould of their minds entire; which has, into the bargain, a beauty, a power, a swiftness of its own."

Charlotte's *Shirley,* published in 1849, is another matter. It is set in Yorkshire toward the end of the Napoleonic Wars, after the little Corsican had "passed like a wild dream through Europe" (George Moore), at the time of the Luddite riots when the wool industry was unable to export and hardship was intense. This could be the frame for a Gaskell novel; its real interest is, again, romantic. Robert Gérard Moore is half English and half Belgian, another surrogate

Constantin Héger. A mill owner, he continues modernizing in the teeth of circumstance, including extreme labor unrest. Under financial pressure he goes against his heart, which is committed to Caroline Helstone, a conventional Brontë heroine, who reciprocates from her shy perch in her uncle's hostile rectory. He proposes to the wealthy Shirley Keeldar. She repels his advances, history relents, war and labor troubles end, his property is restored, and he marries Caroline, who forgives him. Robert's brother Louis, who has been a tutor in Shirley's house, wins her hand. Charlotte has it both ways, a climbing man and a climbing woman. We have moved out of the Byronic sphere; these characters are more credible, the world they inhabit neither fabulous nor heroic.

Going southeast from Haworth about ten miles, we reach Heckmondwike, the neighborhood of *Shirley*. The book corresponds to the landscape where Charlotte and her sisters were educated and to which she returned as a teacher. The novel's setting has a literal feel, whereas the Ferndean Manor of *Jane Eyre,* based on the ruins of Wycoller Hall, about six miles west of Haworth, is darkened and made fabulous by a Gothic spirit that, in Charlotte's writing, seems at ebb in her later novels.

Three miles to the west of Haworth stands Withens, a weather-beaten pile that became Wuthering Heights, though onto it Emily grafted features of other residences that had impressed her. Charlotte insisted that Haworth and the surrounding moors were responsible for Emily's individual vision and vigor; she was "a nursling of the moors" and the book was "moorish, and wild, and knotty as the root of heath," a naturalization of the Gothic. The figure of Heathcliff, with his emblematic name and dark turbulence, has become a romantic archetype. *Wuthering Heights* is his book. In her preface to the 1850 edition, Charlotte wonders whether it is "right or advisable" to invent a character like Heathcliff. Probably not, yet in Emily's novel she perceives her sister's gift, which "wills and works for itself," like possession. She becomes "the nominal artist" whose "share in it has been to work passively under dictates you neither delivered nor could question—that would not be uttered at your prayer, nor suppressed nor changed at your caprice." Emily submitted to this demon and, having done so, respected the product of that submission. She did not change it, did not scruple and moralize and retreat from the thing it was, a thing of a piece with the heroisms of the poetic sagas she had written, but here in hauntingly credible prose. It is, Forster says, "filled with sound—storm and rushing wind." Muriel Spark chides Charlotte's moral misgivings. She is herself besotted with Heathcliff: how can this villain be so attractive, "perfectly sane and utterly bad," not petty like commonplace villains. "Heathcliff is a big bad man, he is never ridiculous, he is terrible, a real Prince of Darkness. He is not only the villain, he is the hero of the book in the grand Homeric sense."

The passivity that Charlotte speaks of was not artless; on the contrary, a deliberate artist prepared it, and to regard it as passivity is to gender and diminish it. A writer may be possessed but, if original, is never passive. Passive writers make their way by means of clichés. Forster again: "Emily Brontë had in some ways a literal and careful mind. She constructed her novel on a time-chart even more elaborate than Miss Austen's, and she arranged the Linton and Earnshaw families symmetrically, and she had a clear idea of the various legal steps by which Heathcliff gained possession of their two properties." Up to there she was conventional. "Then why did she deliberately introduce muddle, chaos, tempest? Because in our sense of the word she was a prophetess; because what is implied is more important to her than what is said." Dante Gabriel Rossetti saw the action of *Wuthering Heights* as set in Hell, Miltonic sulfur in the air, in the disproportion between mere men and giants. Local, small details because of the intensity of focus fill the imagination's whole retina, monstrous things. A social world is displaced by this lived, living space that includes us by invading us, by—as Romantic and Gothic works seek to do—drawing our anxieties, feelings, and emotions into its patterns of play. Heathcliff gives the book its "fiendish magnitude," as Spark says. Heathcliff is branded from his foundling arrival, "a little black-haired swarthy thing, as dark as if it came from the devil," and when his old nurse Ellen Dean cannot close the dead Heathcliff's eyes and wipe the sneer from his face, we realize how consistent he has been in life and death.

Not all readers take the book to heart. Henry James despised "the crude and morbid story of *Wuthering Heights*." For him a sense that the surrender to the irrational was not counterbalanced by the fairy-tale would-be happy ending meant the book was incomplete. Yet this incompleteness, this withholding of interpretation from areas the novelist intended should remain unexplained, creates space for readers willing to subject to the darkness. If in Charlotte's novels we are always conscious of a narrator, in Emily's the story is given its head, none of the interlocking narrative perspectives controls the reader. The story draws us on and in, until something in ourselves is compromised.

Constantin Héger spoke of Emily's "strong imperious will," she was dauntless, and he thought she should have been a man. But in her fiction she did something quite as unprecedented as Charlotte had done in hers. She created characters with souls (psychological readings of her book are reductive and limiting) that walk about unprotected by irony, to whom the cruelest justice is done. The book is merciless in the way of Homer and Shakespeare, and only the ending belongs wholly to her century and its habits of resolution.

Had Dickens devised Heathcliff, he would have been a villain. In Emily's imagination he is an irresistible protagonist. Good Mr. Earnshaw picks him up in the streets of Liverpool—the orphan theme being central to the Brontës as it was to Dickens—and rears him as if he were a son. Oliver Twist comes to Yorkshire. But Hindley Earnshaw despises the interloper, does him down, and is punished more harshly even than Hardy's protagonists. The coincidences exceed Hardy's in their contrivance and consequence. Heathcliff falls in love with Catherine Earnshaw, overhears her saying she can never marry him, vanishes, and three years later returns rich, to find her married to the meager Edgar Linton. Heathcliff's revenges follow: on Edgar via his sister Isabella, whom Heathcliff marries; on Hindley and his son Hareton; on Cathy, Catherine's daughter by Edgar. In the end Cathy and Hareton are united. We hardly know them: their happiness is required to resolve a far greater artistic tangle than it can.

The form had become versatile and capacious: Scott filled it with history, the Gothic writers with dream. In Emily Brontë the Gothic achieves a complex structural and textural fulfillment. It is of a piece, integrated, with—despite the coincidences—a bold necessity that emerges from characters. They are, though intense and fantastic, also credible; their shadowy world also is credible, existing on this side of the edge of literal vision. Emily Brontë's novel is finished and achieved in the sense that Jane Austen's best novels are, though different in kind. In Austen order is rational and proportionate, applied, as it seems, from the outside, by an ironist. Not Byronic passion but ladies and gentlemen, and when the Gothic gets in, the very shadows are in tatters. *Villette* has in it Gothic scenes, the masked nun, for example, in the cloister of the school, the unironic courage of its conventions. Austen's mystery inheres in the quotidian, it does not require, it repels, mystification. She does not elaborate diction or extraordinary incident, but weaves a subtler spell.

In Emily Brontë order is integral, with a solidity and consistency contained: seasons, cycles of conflict and resolution, image structure, generational symmetries, the devices of poetry extended throughout the novel but contained within its boards. Plot is inseparable from setting and character. The protagonists would not survive outside the elemental environment of their particular book. There could be no sequel or prequel. You would not meet Heathcliff anywhere other than on those moorlands, with the darkness falling. And the poetic structure, as Woolf might call it, exists without violence to the solid credibility of the world evoked. In its integrity, her art comes closer to Stendhal's than that of previous English writers.

# 18

# Real Worlds

Frances Trollope, William Makepeace Thackeray, Anthony Trollope, Benjamin Disraeli

Charlotte Brontë dedicated the second edition of *Jane Eyre* to William Makepeace Thackeray, her "Titan." The variety of characters and classes he portrayed, the authority of his social tones, his sense of decorous register: he commanded a whole orchestra as against her little chamber ensemble; and he had so many themes, his imagination visited so many unfamiliar neighborhoods. She even liked the sketches with which he illustrated his books. Then she developed misgivings about him. "I have come to the conclusion that whenever he writes, Mephistopheles stands on his right hand and Raphael on his left, the great doubter and sneerer usually guides the pen, the Angel, the noble and gentle, interlines letters of light here and there."

In 1848 Thackeray had sent her an inscribed copy of *Vanity Fair,* before he knew who she was. *Jane Eyre* and his book were published in the same year and were reviewed together, a little acerbically, in the *Quarterly Review.* When they met, she found him more approachable than the seven grand, pompous critics who wined and dined her. "Mr. Thackeray," she wrote to a friend in 1852, "is a man of quiet, simple demeanor; he is however looked upon with awe and even some distrust. His conversation is very peculiar, too perverse to be pleasant."

The normative force of nineteenth-century England is manifest in the writer Thackeray became, as against what he might have been, given his colorful antecedents. His books might have included more of India, the relations of parents and children, more of the travails of marriage. Walter Bagehot spoke of the creative poverty of Thackeray's age: it could at best produce "a young ladies' literature," since that was the principal market for the novel, a morally delicate readership whose education in right thinking and action must always be considered. Thackeray confided to a friend that he was "perfectly *free*" in his religion but did not think it wise to own up in print for fear of upsetting readers. The creator of Becky Sharp did take risks, but usually within bounds. Critical and satirical as he can be, he will not violate certain taboos, bad and good actions must (in the end) have moral consequences, just deserts: "Come, children, let us shut up the box and the puppets, for our play is played out": thus, duly infantilized, after 700 pages, we are ushered out of *Vanity Fair.*

Henry James feels in the writing the fact of Thackeray's birth in Calcutta, as though it gave him a different purchase on England from that of his home-born contemporaries. He did write fantastically about India in *Some Passages in the Life of Major Gahagan,* and elsewhere Indian themes occur, though remotely, with some facts still in place and the freedom of romantic invention. At the end of *Vanity Fair* Dobbin is engrossed in his *History of the Punjaub,* and only little Janey is dearer to him than his work-in-progress; ironically, Amelia resisted him for so long that by the time he got her his positive affections were exhausted: bleakest of the *Fair's* vanities.

Thackeray's father was a well-paid collector, following in his own father's footsteps. His wife bore Anthony, their one child, in 1815, when she was just nineteen. She was widowed before the boy was five. In time—not a very long time—she remarried, a Major Henry Carmichael Smyth, whom Thackeray was able to esteem, and in later years mother and stepfather often stayed at the writer's home. Trollope wrote in *English Men of Letters* (1879), "Mrs. Carmichael Smyth was disposed to the somewhat austere observance of the evangelical section of the Church. Such, certainly, never became the case with her son," who nonetheless had the sense not to argue with the old lady.

He might have had other grounds for grievance. Less than two years after his father died he was sent to England, his mother staying behind in India to lead her own life. Thackeray claimed to remember the departure. "A ghaut, or river-stair, at Calcutta; and a day when, down those steps, to a boat which was in waiting, came two children, whose mothers remained on shore." The journey to England was long, with one particular adventure. The boat landed at the island of St. Helena, where a servant pointed out the famous prisoner. Napoleon, the servant said, was very hungry. He devoured "three sheep every day, and all the little children he can lay hands on." Another version has the boy's nurse taking him up a long hill to a farmhouse with a little walled garden. A man was seated in a chair under a tree, dressed in white with a broad-brimmed hat. "That's him," exclaimed the nurse under her breath, "That's Bony!" Later in Paris young Thackeray followed the procession that bore Napoleon to his second burial at Les Invalides. When *Vanity Fair* came to be written, the comical, cowardly Joseph Sedley, fleeing his disgrace at Waterloo and returning to India, visits St. Helena and takes credit among his fellow passengers (who do not know him) for capturing "the Corsican upstart" himself.

Thackeray attended Charterhouse, which he dubbed "Slaughter House." He started off, a schoolmate recalls, "a pretty, gentle, and rather timid boy. I think his experience there was not generally pleasant." He remembered it, and the preparatory school he attended when he first arrived, as purgatorial. He did not distinguish himself except in the intensity of his unhappiness. He disliked games, he disliked the stern headmaster. He wrote proficient verse parodies.

At eighteen he went up to Trinity College, Cambridge. There he made friends with that great English translator and letter writer Edward Fitzgerald ("my dearest old friend," whom he nominated as literary executor and to whom he committed the publication of his Ballads should he die) and with Tennyson. But he failed to stay the course, leaving in 1830. He did leave a modest editorial trace: in 1829 a little magazine, *The Snob,* was produced. It lived for a few weeks. It was succeeded by *The Gownsman,* which lasted rather longer. He may have edited the first and had a hand in the birth of the second. He contributed to them in a spirit of parody.

When Thackeray left Cambridge, the delightful part of his life began. He divided himself, Trollope says, between Weimar, where he was introduced to Goethe, and Paris, intending to become an artist. Thus, before he was halfway through his twenties he had seen the two greatest spirits of the age, the Emperor and the Intellect. He grew proficient in German and read a great deal of German romantic literature. The "Ducal town of Pumpernickel" chapters of *Vanity Fair* owe much to Weimar.

"He was a competent draughtsman," Trollope says, "though never a brilliant one." We encountered him tendering for the job of Dickens's illustrator for *The Pickwick Papers.* "He did illustrate his own books, and everyone knows how incorrect were his delineations. But as illustrations they were excellent. How often have I wished," Trollope adds, "that characters of my own creating might be sketched as faultily, if with the same appreciation of the intended purpose." Thackeray's approximations told more than finished work.

He toyed with taking up the law, and what he learned in this pursuit too he put to use when the time came to write *Pendennis.* His father left him a considerable estate, worth about £17,000, yielding an income of some £500 a year. Part of the principal he spent acquiring in 1833 the *National Standard,* for which he wrote and drew copiously. The journal was soon exhausted, and his private fortune collapsed due to his profligacy and an Indian bank failure, a disaster that proved useful in writing *The Newcomes.* He may—living with a certain risky excess—have contracted gonorrhea (and this in turn may have had a fatal impact on the course of his marriage).

Financial failure made him serious. He aimed to restore his fortune before he died, and this he amply did. He tried to live as an artist in Paris (Fitzgerald kept him up to date with developments in England, writing of his larger and lesser contemporaries) and in London in 1834 and 1835, then began work as a journalist. Trollope remarks: "If a man can command a table, a chair, pen, paper, and ink, he can commence his trade as literary man." With bitter realism he adds: "All that he wrote was not taken, and all that was taken was not approved."

Thackeray contributed to *Fraser's Magazine* a series known as *The Yellowplush Correspondence.* This was his equivalent to *The Pickwick Papers,* an ambitious and delightful work of apprenticeship. Mr. Charles Jeames Yellowplush is a footman. His affected orthography (an early form of cacography) suggests a deficiency in his formal education. He evokes for us a complex social milieu. *Fashionable Fax and Polite Annygoats* by Jeames Yellowplush introduces his master Bullwig, based on Bulwer-Lytton, who urges his man to steer clear of literature.

> "Yellowplush," says he, seizing my hand, "you ARE right. Quit not your present occupation; black boots, clean knives, wear plush all your life, but don't turn literary man . . . Oh!" said Bullwig, clasping his hands, and throwing his fine i's up to the chandelier, "the curse of Pwometheus descends upon his wace. Wath and punishment pursue them from genewation to genewation! Wo to genius, the heaven-scaler, the fire-stealer! Wo and thrice-bitter desolation! Earth is the wock on which Zeus, wemorseless, stwetches his withing wictim;— men, the vultures that feed and fatten on him. Ai, ai! it is agony eternal,—gwoaning and solitawy despair! And you, Yellowplush, would penetwate these mystewies; you would waise the awful veil, and stand in the twemendous Pwesence. Beware, as you value your peace, beware! Withdwaw, wash Neophyte! For heaven's sake! O for heaven's sake!"—Here he looked round with agony;—"give me a glass of bwandy-and-water, for this clawet is beginning to disagwee with me."

We are not a thousand miles from Peacock, though the humor is of the surface, the plotting nugatory. Thackeray could not survive on Yellowplush alone; he also wrote for the *Morning Chronicle,* and *Punch,* which proved lucrative, and reviewed books for the *Times.*

In Paris he had met Isabella Shawe, and they married there in 1836. He was French correspondent for an English periodical that failed, and the couple returned to London, seemingly happy, with no fixed prospects. Three daughters were born in rapid succession. The eldest, Anna Isabella, became Lady Richie (1837–1919), a successful writer of novels and essays. The middle child died at six months. The youngest, Harriet Marian (1840–1875), became the first Mrs. Leslie Stephen, mother of Virginia Woolf's half sister, Laura Makepeace Stephen.

Thackeray separated from his wife in 1840. She had become restive, then listless, then quite blank. After furious rows with her relations and an attempt at suicide, when she hurled herself into the sea, she became unresponsive to him, to the girls, to everyone. He arranged for her to be looked after in France and then in England, at last finding her a safe place. It appears that after they separated, though he had close friendships with women, he generally avoided romantic entanglements. He had his club to go to, and there were the celebrated smokeries on the Strand where he would retire to write, or meet friends. His character Pendennis also spends time there, in an air that is bohemian and un-buttoned but not unsafe; chess, charming ladies, singing choirboys: dives from which one emerged refreshed. There were also the Cider Cellars of Maiden Lane, though socially inferior; Evans's supper rooms in Covent Garden, "the Cave of Harmony" in *The Newcomes,* were another place to withdraw to.

Of his predecessors he most valued Fielding. In his lecture on Fielding in *English Humorists of the Eighteenth Century* he declares: "I should like, as a young man, to have lived on Fielding's staircase in the Temple, and after helping him up to bed perhaps, and opening his door with his latch-key, to have shaken hands with him in the morning, and heard him talk and crack jokes over his breakfast and his mug of small beer." It is possible to read *Vanity Fair* as a response to *Tom Jones,* about whose protagonist Thackeray remained ambivalent, at once loving him and disapproving.

In 1838–1839 *The Tremendous Adventures of Major Gahagan* was serialized, a fantastical, Baron Munchhausen–like adventure that in its form recalls the extremes of Fielding's transcendental *A Journey from This World to the Next.* Fielding was writing near the end and Thackeray near the beginning of his career, but what is wonderful in each book is the courage of invention, setting aside the trammeling quotidian world in the interests of wild, exploratory entertainment. The protagonist is a great soldier and boaster, heightening the hyperboles of the Indian tale with Irish overstatement. He keeps gunpowder in his apartment, "under my bed, with a candle burning for fear of accidents." "Once in Spain," he says, "I ate the leg of a horse, and was so eager to swallow this morsel, that I bolted the shoe as well as the hoof, and never felt the slightest inconvenience from either." A big mouth in every sense.

In *Catherine,* too, the influence of Fielding may be felt. This novel, serialized in 1839–1840, is told by Isaac (Ikey) Solomons, Junior, using dialect and simulated speech once more, and traveling to a layer of society below those Thackeray previously visited. Ikey tells a story with a harsh ending, speaking against the glamorizing of criminals that readers relished in the Newgate Novels of the day, those that grew directly or indirectly out of Fielding's *Jonathan Wild.* Bulwer-Lytton and Harrison Ainsworth had written in this area, and Dickens had created Nancy in *Oliver Twist,* a good thief over whose death we mourn. In *Catherine* the protagonist is based on an actual husband murderer who was executed more than a century earlier. The book is set in the period of Thackeray's ambitious novel, prepared for with exhaustive "collateral research," *The History of Henry Esmond* (1852).

Ikey's is a coarse voice. It does not exonerate Mrs. Cat. But it is not so coarse as Thackeray intends. He is picking his way toward Becky Sharp. Like Fielding, he could never quite win the moral argument with his tender heart. Yet his cap is set against the conventional "humbug" of the sentimentalizers, one aspect of the false feeling and factitious pathos that the readers of the day lapped up. He has his own, contrary sentimentalism. William Dean Howells notes "a property in Thackeray that somehow flatters the reader into the belief that he is better than other people." He has "his air of looking down on the highest, and confidentially inviting you to be of his company in the seat of the scorner he is irresistible." And there is also his continuous literary engagement: "Then, if the boy has read a good many other books, he is taken with that abundance of literary turn and allusion in Thackeray; there is hardly a sentence but reminds him that he is in the society of a great literary swell, who has read everything, and can mock or burlesque life right and left from the literature always at his command."

Like Swift, Scott (the self-reviewer of *Waverley*), the Brontës, Dickens, and others who had their reasons to appear masked, Thackeray used pseudonyms. Some magazines required pseudonymity, where the name was part of the comedy. Thackeray first put his own name on a book, Trollope says, when *Vanity Fair* was published. Earlier, pseudonyms freed him from his own class and voice: he could visit characters and have experiences from which a frock coat would have debarred him. He escaped the mereness of "I" and as narrator became a character. He can in the first person enter the world of Queen Anne's England, a romanticized military India, or the hell of London low life. Names like Ikey and Yellowplush imply voices and accents, the faded britches of service and the uncertain dictions of an underclass or race. Ikey is an offshoot of Fagin. Thackeray deployed many other names. From France he imported Théophile Wagstaff; there is Michael Angelo Titmarsh, George Savage Fitz-Boodle, Dr. Solomon Pacigico. He was a heavy user, at least 25 pseudonyms. Voltaire used more than 170, his name itself being a pseudonym. Defoe (born Foe) holds the current record with 198.

In Thackeray's day, fate provided a measuring stick greater than Fielding. The age of Dickens is almost coterminous with the Victorian era. Thackeray is a favorite among writers, but Chesterton is too partial when he says that Thackeray's style is "singularly easy and sympathetic . . . carried in slow soft curves when Dickens hacked out his images with a hatchet." There is more life and variety in Dickens, sentence by sentence, than in Thackeray; he is not ingratiating. Only one book of Thackeray's, *Vanity Fair,* rivals Dickens's for readership.

They started their assault on Parnassus at much the same time. Thackeray was one year Dickens's senior, but in Trollope's words he was "unsteadfast, idle, changeable of purpose, aware of his own intellect but not trusting it, no man ever failed more generally than he to put his best foot foremost." In writing, "there is a touch of vagueness which indicates that his pen was not firm while he was using it." And though he admired, Thackeray also resisted, Dickens's art, writing to a friend in 1851, "The Art of Novels *is* to represent Nature: to convey as strongly as possible the sentiment of reality . . . in a drawing room drama a coat is a coat, and a poker a poker; and must be nothing else according to my ethics, not an embroidered tunic, nor a great red-hot instrument like the Pantomime weapon." They were acquaintances, then came a gossipy misunderstanding and falling out that lasted a long time, but was mended shortly before Thackeray died. By then the men were, or seemed to be, level pegging in prosperity if not in celebrity.

His next substantial fiction is one of his most enchanting. *The Luck* (later *The Memoirs) of Barry Lyndon* (1844) reverses the *Catherine* formula, creating an extreme villain we cannot help but like because of the way he tells his story. In gambling he cheats, he bullies to get his way, he lies and betrays. There is no glimmer of goodness in him: all we can say is that he refuses to cut and run. He has pluck, if not courage. He speaks for himself with candor like the narrator of Nashe's *The Unfortunate Traveller.* His crude character is matched by the crude conception. Thackeray knew his readership (not Bagehot's young ladies in this instance) and gave it what it wanted. We feel Lyndon's fall not with relief that justice has been done but with disappointment that the merry adventure is done.

Nothing Thackeray had written prepares us for the leap, in terms of form, narrative skill, and social insight, of *Vanity Fair.* Ford Madox Ford proclaims it as possibly "the greatest work in the English language." For Sarah Orne Jewett it was the great Russian and French novelists "all rolled in one." Edwin Muir says: "In naturalness, in consistence with itself, *Vanity Fair* is . . . superior to any English novel of character which precedes it." Margaret Atwood relishes Becky. She "makes no pretensions to goodness. She is wicked, she enjoys being wicked, and she does it out of vanity and for her own profit, tricking and deluding English society in the process." She "uses men as ambulatory bank accounts."

Having been serialized—in twenty-four numbers as against Dickens's usual twenty—and having sold in the end some 7,000 copies a month and been all the rage in London, it was published in book form in 1848. Thackeray at last was taken seriously and reviewed, "his name became common in the memoirs of the time," Trollope said. "Those who are old enough can well remember the effect which it had, and the welcome which was given to the different numbers as they appeared. Though the story is vague and wandering, clearly commenced without any idea of an ending, yet there is something in the telling which makes every portion of it perfect in itself. There are absurdities in it which would not be admitted to anyone who had not a peculiar gift of making even his absurdities delightful."

Thackeray tried out several titles, among them *Pen and Pencil Sketches of English Society* (an extension of his work as a caricaturist in line and language) and *Novel without a Hero* (eventually the book's subtitle). He was staying in Brighton when the actual title came to him in the night, a eureka moment that struck him out of slumber like a bolt of lightning. Bunyan had found his chief secular debtor. We remember how in *The Pilgrim's Progress,* in the town of Vanity, a year-round fair is held. Christian and Faithful confront there various temptations on their journey to the Celestial City. From Bunyan Thackeray might have drawn a moral architecture, a kind of allegorical mansion. In fact the title came last, and the book relates to Bunyan only glancingly.

The prologue is entitled "Before the Curtain"—immediately we see "the manager of the Performance." He looks out into the bustling fairground where human life in all its forms is pullulating and going about its mischief. "Yes, this is *Vanity Fair;* not a moral place certainly; nor a merry one, though very noisy." He looks at the actors coming away, removing their disguises, settling in to dinner: "poor Tom Fool, yonder behind the wagon, mumbling his bone with the honest family which lives by his tumbling." The characters are introduced as doll puppets he manipulates. They have "given satisfaction to the very best company in this empire." Here are Becky Puppet, Amelia Doll, Dobbin Figure, and Wicked Nobleman who in the end belongs to Old Nick. Margaret Atwood sees Thackeray as inheriting the orchestral skills of Shakespeare's Prospero, himself the begetter of Ben Jonson's *The Alchemist,* and she is right to stress the continuity of the novel with the theatrical tradition, its staged nature, the characters as performers under strict direction.

Though the novel is not a thoroughgoing allegory, the allegorical trappings invite continuous commentary from the narrator. Characters' names are emblematic: Sharp, for example, and Dobbin, Crawley and Hornblower and Quadroon. The nature or inner life of characters, if they have one at all, is turned inside out, as if it were a glove. When we meet Miss Pinkerton, briefly but memorably, she is exalted into the realm of legend and myth, and she stays there. And just as later in the novel we are on the edge of the stage of actual history, at Waterloo, here too we are in a parlor of history. "'Have you completed all the necessary preparations incident to Miss Sedley's departure, Miss Jemima?' asked Miss Pinkerton herself, that majestic lady; the Semiramis of Hammersmith, the friend of Doctor Johnson, the correspondent of Mrs. Chapone herself." Mrs. Chapone existed: she hosted "rational, instructive and social" receptions for bluestockings. Johnson allowed her to contribute to his *Rambler,* but apart from *Letters on the Improvement of the Mind,* famous in their day, she was not an outstanding writer. She spent time in Richardson's company, and some regard her as a model for his virtuous and withstanding women. For her part, Miss Pinkerton remains Semiramis for the whole chapter, and Doctor Johnson haunts the novel's shadows, his *Dictionary* a ponderous leaving gift for each girl. "On the cover was inserted a copy of 'Lines addressed to a young lady on quitting Miss Pinkerton's school, at the Mall; by the late revered Doctor Samuel Johnson.' In fact, the lexicographer's name was always on the lips of this majestic woman, and a visit he had paid to her was the cause of her reputation and her fortune." When Miss Sharp "put her pale face out of the window" of the retreating carriage, on the day of her departure, she "actually flung the book back into the garden." The transgression is momentous, monumental.

There is a chronology of events, but incidents do not relate dramatically to one another. The progression is thematic, and two plots counterpoint one another: Becky on her road to glorious ruin and Amelia making her uncertain way toward Captain Dobbin, each progressing at a different pace in contrary directions. Impatience heads for her inevitable fall, while patient merit (Dobbin) takes its spurs and in the end gains a prize that we may feel is no longer quite worth the struggle.

The tale, though more subtle, is in the line of *Moll Flanders* and *Fanny Hill.* But where Defoe and Cleland reward thrift and good husbandry, Thackeray rewards cloying goodness in Amelia and dogged fidelity in Dobbin. Becky, the Moll or Fanny figure, does not fare so well but entertains us far better. The devil, as elsewhere in English fiction, has the best tunes. Readers wanted redeemable elements in Becky, whom they found it impossible to despise. Yet Thackeray knew, as a weekday preacher, that he could do more to improve the reader's morals by showing the workings of vice rather than advocating virtue. Still, at the core of his work, Howells points out, there is something more than a moral conundrum, a "toxic property." "He is himself forever dominated in imagination by the world, and even while he tells you it is not worth while he makes you feel that it is worth while."

The Crawleys are an example of a clan variously rotten in all its branches. Sir Pitt Crawley, boorish and monstrous, and sentimental, is chief spider in a web infested with malicious, unctuous, smug, and scheming relations, with Rawdon

Crawley the most irredeemably self-serving. Was Thackeray surprised by how grotesque his characters grew under his pen? The spirit of Smollett rather than Fielding guides his hand, and the disproportions are of caricature, though always they breathe a literal, sulfury air. Sir Pitt Crawley's proposal to Becky is tense and hilarious. She is always offered what she has wanted just when she can no longer have it. "You must come back. Do come back. Dear Becky, do come," he pleads. "Come,—as what, sir?" "Come as Lady Crawley, if you like. There, will that satisfy you? Come back and be my wife. You're vit for it. Birth be hanged. You're as good a lady as ever I see. You've got more brains in your little vinger than any baronet's wife in the country. Will you come? Yes or no?" And then "the old man fell down on his knees and leered at her like a satyr."

Thackeray is unsparing in his use of ironic repetition. Becky is getting herself set up. "She had been trying the new piano all the morning. The new gloves fitted her to a nicety. The new shawl became her wonderfully. The new rings glittered on her little hands, and the new watch ticked at her waist." Here is Delilah and he the unsuspecting Samson: "and Delilah patted Samson's cheek." Everything is new except the old, old story. In the verses "Vanitas Vanitatum," its wisdom borrowed from the book of Ecclesiastes, Thackeray wrote, "Methinks the text is never stale, / And life is every day renewing / Fresh comments on the old old tale, / Of Folly, Fortune, Glory, Ruin."

Worse than Sir Pitt is Lord Steyne, the steepest and foulest of the social peaks Becky climbs. She has by this point been wholly seduced by the empty charms of Mammon, and at the climax of her ascent she is brought down to terra firma by her husband, himself so corrupted as to be part of the universal cupidity. The evocation of his anger and then his collusion is a high point of English narrative. Indeed, Thackeray was so engrossed in the writing that he was beside himself. Completing the scene, he announced to the empty room, "Sublime, sir! By heavens, it's sublime!"

By contrast, Amelia's life, with its sentimental tragedies and her slow-starting self-interest, feels like part of a design rather than a compelling parallel narration, devised as a necessary balance for Becky's story. Goodness is not much fun in fiction, its patience and resignation leave the reader impatient. We know virtue will get its rewards, material and libidinal. But how will the author punish his wrongdoers? The fate of Amelia's unworthy husband at Waterloo, however, surprises us with an understatement worthy of Evelyn Waugh. "No more firing was heard at Brussels. The pursuit rolled miles away. Darkness came down on the field and the city,—and Amelia was praying for George, who was lying on his face, dead, with a bullet through his heart." The bullet has lodged in the very organ we were persuaded he did not have. When at last Dobbin wears down and gets Amelia, years and quires later, the author calls attention to his artifice. "Here it is,—the summit, the end, the last page of the third volume."

This intrusion of the narrator (or is it the writer himself?) making a point of the novel's fictionality, strikes some contemporary readers as a modern feature, the "mere novelist" archly conceding the limitations of his art. Ford regards it as a cuteness that destroys the spell of the story and draws inordinate attention to the teller. The narrator intrudes frequently and sometimes disastrously. The epilogue is a minor problem, however, set against what Ford calls "the greatest literary crime ever committed," namely, "Thackeray's sudden, apologetic incursion of himself into his matchless account of the maneuvers of Becky Sharp on Waterloo Day in Brussels."

In *Rebecca and Rowena: A Romance upon Romance* (1850) he reverted to pseudonym, this time to protect the achievement of *Vanity Fair* from association with what is in effect a comic exercise on a theme of Walter Scott's. For the purpose of this volume he became Michael Angelo Titmarsh. He set out from Scott's *Ivanhoe* (1819), one of the most popular books of the time, his first novel with a wholly English subject. Trollope says, "No writer ever had a stronger proclivity towards parody than Thackeray; and we may, I think, confess that there is no form of literary drollery more dangerous. The parody will often mar the gem of which it coarsely reproduces the outward semblance." Not so in this case. "Nothing of Ivanhoe is injured, nothing made less valuable than it was before, yet, of all prose parodies in the language, it is perhaps the most perfect. Every character is maintained, every incident has a taste of Scott." Scott himself might have approved.

All the later ambitious and large-scale novels by Thackeray he put out under his own name. In 1850 *The History of Pendennis: His Fortunes and Misfortunes, His Friends and His Greatest Enemy* was published, having been serialized at the same time as *David Copperfield*. Both books are informed by autobiography and touch upon education and first romance. They end with their protagonists beginning careers as writers. Thackeray fell ill and his serialization was halted for three months, a peril for "part writers." He made reference once more to his beloved Fielding in the preface. "Since the author of *Tom Jones* was buried, no writer of fiction among us has been permitted to depict to his utmost power a man. We must drape him, and give him a certain conventional simper. Society will not tolerate the Natural in our Art." His mission was to follow in Fielding's footsteps, to follow Nature in the ways he had said Dickens failed to do.

Yet the larger plot may strike us as bearing some similarity to Richardson's in *The History of Sir Charles Grandison*: early ill-judged marriages that delay happiness, misjudgments, complex antecedents, the shackles of circumstance and heredity. It is as though Thackeray's imagination, which had dwelt so long in the shadow of Fielding, even here calling *Tom Jones* to mind as his archetypal novel, had gone for some Richardsonian freedoms. "Let us have the facts out, and mend what is bad if we can. This novel of Pendennis is one of his loudest protests to this effect." But it is an inert protest. The preface, Trollope says, "is a sort of confidential talk between writer and reader . . . In the course of his volubility the perpetual speaker must of necessity lay bare his own weaknesses, vanities, peculiarities." He does not become a character but makes it hard for the reader to relate to the characters he has created. "The book is robbed of its integrity by a certain good-humored geniality of language, which causes the reader to be almost too much at home with his author." Not for Sarah Orne Jewett, who like many near contemporaries regarded *Pendennis* as Thackeray's masterpiece, "more full of true humanity," she declared, than *Anna Karenina*.

Why is it that novelists often regard their most artful and artificial novels as their best? In 1852 Thackeray published *The History of Henry Esmond*. This book was deliberately not serialized but published in three volumes; a typeface and page layouts were designed to give it the flavor of an eighteenth-century book. He researched it closely. The ending was controversial: the hero married a woman who earlier in the book had seemed a "mother" to him. (His long, pure, but conflictual seven-year relationship with Jane Brookfield, wife of an old friend, was put to work here.) Critics declared the book brilliant. Walter Pater in his essay "On Style" says, "Thackeray's *Esmond*, surely, is greater art than *Vanity Fair*, by the greater dignity of its interests." Trollope agreed: "*Esmond* is a whole from beginning to end, with its tale well told, its purpose developed, its moral brought home,—and its nail hit well on the head and driven in." Trollope told Thackeray that *Esmond* "was not only his best work, but so much the best, that there was none second to it. 'That was what I intended,' he said, 'but I have failed. Nobody reads it. After all, what does it matter?'" What is new about the book is that, though written into the past, it is neither Gothic nor Romantic. It affirms the reality of its recovered world.

How difficult it must have been to write, given the need to turn back the clock of language, forget the encroachments of the modern. The past was not very past, the peril of anachronism extreme. Robert Louis Stevenson compared the challenge of writing *Vanity Fair* with that of writing *Henry Esmond:* "It was easier to begin to write *Esmond* than *Vanity Fair,* since, in the first, the style was dictated by the nature of the plan; and Thackeray, a man probably of some indolence of mind, enjoyed and got good profit of this economy of effort." In short, it was formulaic as to language, and some feel it introduced an artificiality into Thackeray's writing from which he never recovered.

Witnessing Dickens's success as a public speaker and other writers supplementing their incomes in this way, Thackeray undertook a series of lectures on the English humorists, touring them around Britain and to America. He lacked Dickens's charisma and never drew vast audiences, but he was not unsuccessful. He was an anxious speaker. Charlotte Brontë praised the intimate directness of his manner: "a quiet humor and graphic force enlivened it throughout," she reported to her father; "there was quite a *furore*" for the first half dozen lectures. The audience included Dickens and Carlyle, Macaulay, Longfellow, and others. When he brought his lectures to America, he gathered material for his novels.

He enjoyed his American tours, especially the first. Slavery did not repel him as much as it had Dickens. He wrote to his mother that he did not see blacks as his equals, though perhaps slavery was morally wrong. His hosts had quizzed him about the living conditions of English working families, which he knew to be in some areas far worse than the conditions in which slaves were kept. Whipping appalled him, yet he was willing to believe that families were not generally split up and sold separately at the block. Unlike Dickens, he did not turn the American experience to critical or satirical ends. Instead, in 1857–1859, he published *The Virginians,* a novel set before and during the American Revolution, a sequel to *Henry Esmond* intended as a fond acknowledgment of the United States, though his portrait of George Washington did not go down well. The plot gave him difficulty, and here more than before the author continually intrudes. The War of Independence is delayed, Thackeray moralizes about the tired novel form and its challenges. An ambitious book, it is not widely read even as an adjunct to *Henry Esmond.*

Before *The Virginians* came *The Newcomes* (1853–1855), for which Henry James devised the generic term "loose, baggy monster." Thackeray was back to *Vanity Fair* territory and back too in his own age, but without urgency, focal character, or vibrant wit. Writing on a large scale, he again anatomizes snobbery, double standards, opportunism. Clive Newcome is not Becky Sharp. He has some attributes of the young Thackeray: a not outstanding painter, a man unwilling or unable to challenge himself, not driven by the forces that turn *Vanity Fair* into such a Becky-blown whirlwind. It has its memorable passages, in which momentarily he outstrips Dickens in mercilessness. Thus Pendennis toward the end of *The Newcomes* visits the chapel of the Grey Friars and hears the singing of Psalm 37. The 25th verse sounds, *I have been young, and now am old: yet have I not seen the righteous forsaken, nor his seed begging their bread.* "As we came to this verse, I chanced to look up from my book towards the swarm of black-coated pensioners: and amongst them—amongst them—sate Thomas Newcome." His incredulity is conveyed in that stark repetition. "His dear old head was bent down over his prayer-book—there was no mistaking him. He wore the black gown of the pensioners of the Hospital of Grey Friars. His order of the Bath was on his breast. He stood there amongst the poor brethren, uttering the responses to the psalm. The steps of this good man had been ordered hither by Heaven's decree: to this almshouse! Here it was ordained that a life all love, and kindness, and honor, should end! I heard no more of prayers, and psalms, and sermon, after that. How dared I to be in a place of mark, and he, he yonder among the poor?" This pathos is made the more touching by the Colonel's apparent contentment with his situation: he has found a place of belonging. Yet his death is in the sentimental vein, less manipulative of the reader than Dickens's death scenes but still full of intended tears. The novel's satire, tilting at familiar windmills, is weary. With exceptions, the sentiment he introduces is like tired yeast; the loaf rises just far enough not to be a pancake. To his contemporaries, however, this was another pinnacle of his art. Trollope declared, "I know no character in fiction, unless it be Don Quixote, with whom the reader becomes so intimately acquainted as with Colonel Newcome." The Knight of the Sad Figure has been washed of the dust of Spain and swathed in a soft fabric of sentiment.

In 1860 Thackeray was invited to edit *Cornhill Magazine,* which was to become one of the great magazines of the time for fiction. Trollope's *Framley Parsonage* began serialization in the first issue, and Trollope observes, "At this banquet the saddle of mutton was served before the delicacies." Other contributors included Tennyson, Harriet Beecher Stowe, Elizabeth Barrett Browning, Mrs. Gaskell, John Ruskin, Matthew Arnold, Bulwer-Lytton, and the editor's own daughter. Unlike Dickens, Trollope says, "justice compels me to say that Thackeray was not a good editor. As he would have been an indifferent civil servant, an indifferent member of Parliament, so was he perfunctory as an editor." He did not stay the course. After two years he resigned, having published his last completed novel, *The Adventures of Philip* (1861–1862) in the magazine. The incomplete *Dennis Duval* (1864) appeared there posthumously. He died at home in 1863, his lost fortune amply restored. His concern with its restoration and with the material circumstances of his vocation hovers about the novels themselves, as Howells says: "You may read the greatest part of Dickens, as you may read the greatest part of Hawthorne or Tolstoy, and not once be reminded of literature as a business or a cult, but you can hardly read a paragraph, hardly a sentence, of Thackeray's without being reminded of it either by suggestion or downright allusion." Arnold Bennett *avant la lettre*.

"It is nearly twenty years since I proposed to myself to write a history of English prose fiction," Trollope declared in his *Autobiography*. "I intended to write that book to vindicate my own profession as a novelist, and also to vindicate that public taste in literature which has created and nourished the profession which I follow." English readers were prejudiced against novels: entertainments, hardly serious. He wanted to celebrate "their grace, their honesty, and good teaching." He summarizes his arguments and we realize that in not having written the book he left us no poorer.

He did not respect Thackeray's sense of moral propriety, however. He submitted a piece to *Cornhill Magazine*. "The story was sent back to me by Thackeray—rejected. *Virginibus puerisque!* [For girls and boys!] That was the gist of his objection. There was a project in a gentleman's mind,—as told in my story,—to run away with a married woman! Thackeray's letter was very kind, very regretful,—full of apology for such treatment to such a contributor. But—*Virginibus puerisque!* I was quite sure that Thackeray had not taken the trouble to read the story himself. Some moral deputy had read it, and disapproving, no doubt properly, of the little project to which I have alluded, had incited the editor to use his authority." The creator of Becky Sharp had assumed the public role of (albeit mild) censor. And Trollope, morally didactic a moment later, is incensed when the red pen is applied to his own work.

He worked with an energy he had acquired from his formidable mother, Frances Trollope (1779–1863), author of two yards of books, a few of which are still opened. She clocked up, her son estimated, 114 titles. He admired her, though he had reason to resent her in his early years. When she was thirty she married her much older husband, whose affairs were in a state of steady decline until he fled his creditors and escaped to Belgium in 1834. Some years after her death Anthony came into possession of a clutch of her love letters. "In no novel of Richardson's or Miss Burney's have I seen a correspondence at the same time so sweet, so graceful, and so well expressed." Need had not yet made her a public writer. Trollope *père*'s cumulative failure was for Frances a deprivation. She was alert, fun-loving, and adventurous. He, a kind of Casaubon without the benefit of income, was busy compiling an interminable ecclesiastical encyclopedia.

Frances was no Dorothea. She *felt* her way through life and language: reason, says Anthony, was a tool she never mastered. She loved Dante, Spenser, and (with all the women of the time) Byron, and from an early age she "seized with avidity on the novels, as they came out, of the then unknown Scott, and . . . could still talk of the triumphs of Miss Edgeworth." She developed an appetite for adventure, made her own luck, and adventure came. In 1827 she took two sons and a daughter to America in pursuit of a political cause; "a certain Miss Wright," an American lecturer, instilled in her "communistic ideas," and "with her politics were always an affair of the heart." More practically she intended to get her son Henry off to a good start and to escape, without formal separation, a waning marriage. In Cincinnati, Ohio, she established what Anthony called a bazaar, selling "little goods, such as pin-cushions, pepper-boxes, and pocket-knives" to the "still unfurnished States." The experiment was not a success, though Anthony visited the site of the "emporium," a sorry place, when later in life he traveled to that city.

Her response to America, from American perspectives, was harsh, more even than Dickens's in *Martin Chuzzlewit*. She concludes, "A single word indicative of doubt, that any thing, or every thing, in that country is not the very best in the world, produces an effect which must be seen and felt to be understood. If the citizens of the United States were indeed the devoted patriots they call themselves, they would surely not thus encrust themselves in the hard, dry, stubborn persuasion, that they are the first and best of the human race, that nothing is to be learnt, but what they are able to teach, and that nothing is worth having, which they do not possess." Anthony came to know the country; he was fair-minded and he remembered it was a market for his books. "The Americans were to her rough, uncouth, and vulgar,—and she told them so. Those communistic and social ideas, which had been so pretty in a drawing room, were scattered to the winds. Her volumes were very bitter; but they were very clever, and they saved the family from ruin." Her industry was prodigious then and later, and this he admired: "She was at her table at four in the morning, and had finished her work before the world had begun to be aroused. But the joviality was all for others."

The Trollopes' time in Bruges was a doleful exile, his father worrying at his encyclopedia, his brother dying of consumption, and his mother holding things together, writing and nursing, mother and breadwinner by turns. "The doctor's vials and the ink-bottle held equal places in my mother's rooms. I have written many novels under many circumstances; but I doubt much whether I could write one when my whole heart was by the bedside of a dying son. Her power of dividing herself into two parts, and keeping her intellect by itself clear from the troubles of the world, and fit for the duty it had to do, I never saw equalled." His brother died, his father died. Frances was free to find her own way, which she did.

She was a sentimental radical all her life, despite disillusion with America, and her books touched the conscience of the age. *The Life and Adventures of Jonathan Jefferson Whitlaw; or, Scenes on the Mississippi* (1836) was read by Harriet Beecher Stowe: *Uncle Tom's Cabin* was published sixteen years later. She dealt with the issues of child labor in *Michael Armstrong, the Factory Boy* (1840), with the stigma of illegitimacy, and with corruption in the English church. Indeed, in *The Vicar of Wrexhill* (1837) the themes of Anthony Trollope's *Barchester* novels are differently broached. The chief character is an evangelical clergyman, licentious, cold, suave, and cruel, an English prototype for Elmer Gantry. The clarity with which his vices are anatomized, in counterpoint to his proclaimed religion, is harsh because Mrs. Trollope is not a satirist: she is in earnest, believes in her character and makes him real. At the core of her social imagination there is no redeeming comedy.

Her successful novels were less topical: in *The Widow Barnaby* (1838) and *The Widow Married* (1839) the buxom widow of a rural apothecary poses as a woman of fortune to bring off a rich marriage. Vulgar, selfish, cruel, she remains a source of pleasure. Readers have stomached coarser things in Smollett. Her imprisonment is fair enough, her marriage to the hard-drinking and gaming clergyman appropriate rather than cruel. Her niece Agnes, whom she maltreats, marries well, and a conventional, *Vanity Fair* and *Eustace Diamonds* kind of justice is seen to be done. Mrs. Trollope has directness and moral purpose, writing as though Jane Austen had not happened.

Anthony admired her energy, not her style. He was a natural writer, conservative in craft, drab when read *in extenso,* yet his devoted readers turn to him not for escape so much as consolation. Nathaniel Hawthorne—an unlikely advocate—asked a friend, "Have you ever read the novels of Anthony Trollope? They precisely suit my taste,—solid and substantial, written on the strength of beef and through the inspiration of ale, and just as real as if some giant had hewn a great lump out of the earth and put it under a glass case, with all its inhabitants going about their daily business, and not suspecting that they were being made a show of. And these books are just as English as a beefsteak. Have they ever been tried in America? It needs an English residence to make them thoroughly comprehensible; but still I should think that human nature would give them success anywhere."

In the abundant evenness of his work, an evenness in which excellent novels and dull novels are delivered in the same idiom, at the same steady pace, one is put in mind of Fielding's "painful and voluminous historian," who feels himself compelled "to fill up as much paper with the detail of months and years in which nothing remarkable happened, as he employs on those noble eras when the greatest scenes have been transacted." Such histories are like newspapers, with the same count of words whether or not there is news; their writers are like stagecoaches that run back and forth on the same route whether or not they carry passengers.

He was overly proud of his abundance, concluding his *Autobiography* with a list of his books, their publication dates, and an account of the income he derived from them (he watches his pennies as closely as Moll Flanders did, and as Arnold Bennett would do). He declares his "literary performance" to be "more in amount than the works of any other living English author . . . I have published much more than twice as much as Carlyle. I have also published considerably more than Voltaire, even including his letters." But does he hold the absolute record? "We are told that Varro, at the age of eighty, had written 480 volumes, and that he went on writing for eight years longer . . . I comfort myself by reflecting that the amount of manuscript described as a book in Varro's time was not much." Henry James gets his measure, writing in 1883: "He published too much; the writing of novels had ended by becoming, with him, a perceptibly mechanical process." His writing came to have "the virtues of the photograph. The photograph lacks the supreme virtue of possessing a character. It is the detail alone that distinguishes one photograph from another." He was "a good observer, but he is literally nothing else." Cynthia Ozick, reporting James's exasperation, is rather fairer: "Trollope's great theme is people making use of other people, especially in the accumulation of money, and who can doubt the contemporaneity of a novel about money?" His contemporaries reviewed his earlier books with delight but were worn down by an output that, in some years, amounted to four substantial books. He outproduced even Mrs. Oliphant.

Each day Trollope wrote roughly the same number of pages, a quasi-sacramental commitment, James calls it. "I have allotted myself so many pages a week. The average number has been about 40. It has been placed as low as 20, and has risen to 112. And as a page is an ambiguous term, my page has been made to contain 250 words; and as words, if not watched, will have a tendency to straggle, I have had every word counted as I went." He set his watch beside him and decanted 250 words every fifteen minutes, for three hours, consisting of half an hour rereading the previous day's production with the ear, weighing phrases, correcting, and then writing the day's words. James once crossed the Atlantic in the same ship as Trollope and witnessed how he worked. The trip was stormy, but Trollope "drove his pen as steadily on the tumbling ocean as in Montague Square."

V. S. Pritchett sees Trollope as an outsider (like himself), fascinated by the normal, the regulated. He is "sincere, sturdy, shrewd and unhopeful." His novels do not rise to tragedy, but do not descend to satire. They keep an even ground, whether his subject is the rural gentry, the colonial world, or the aristocratic and democratic parties of government. His plots remind Pritchett of Henry James's, though James possesses far greater formal imagination and human tact: Trollope is full of sense, rather than Jamesian sensibility. "The *Spoils* [*of Poynton*] were treasure, the [*Eustace*] *Diamonds* are property." Pritchett adds, "With all his mastery, Trollope only knows what people are like, not what they are for." His characters are real, but not energetically portrayed. Lizzie Eustace could never become Becky Sharp.

There is, however, progression through his work, from daydream to the troubled dreams of his mature writing (beginning with *He Knew He Was Right* in 1869), a world where the consequences are larger than at first they seem, and the underlying forces darker. In the middle period the novels are light and generally comic; they seem to have come easily, and Jane Austen's shadow has passed over them, without lingering. "His good nature was truthful if it grew less and less hopeful," Pritchett remarks. "Trollope is a master of that dramatic art which the English novel seems to have inherited from its early roots in the theatre; the art of putting the right in the wrong and the wrong in the right." There is good and bad, no evil. He is the novelist of "average life."

And his aesthetic, asserted rather than argued in his *Autobiography,* celebrates the consumer. "The writer of stories must please, or he will be nothing. And he must teach whether he wish to teach or no." The novelist is the clergyman's cousin. He instances Dickens, Thackeray, and George Eliot and challenges the reader to "find a scene, a passage, or a word that would teach a girl to be immodest, or a man to be dishonest." His realism is not like the "stippled" naturalism of Flaubert and Zola (what James calls "the sedentary school"); his wide geographical canvas, which includes the British Isles, the colonies, and the United States, distinguishes him, more than his love of the golden mean. Yet he writes, not like Stevenson for surprise, but for recognition. He makes the familiar—familiar.

Stevenson acknowledges the poverty of Trollope's aesthetic but he likes the style. "The web, then, or the pattern: a web at once sensuous and logical, an elegant and pregnant texture: that is style, that is the foundation of the art of literature." We come back to books whose style pleases us even if their sense is thin. He thinks of Cicero; then he thinks of Trollope: "It is a poor diet for the mind, a very colorless and toothless 'criticism of life'; but we enjoy the pleasure of a most intricate and dexterous pattern, every stitch a model at once of elegance and of good sense."

Henry James too was partial to the pattern, yet embarrassed by its partiality, as though Trollope were too easy a novelist, too companionable, a passable wine but not an exceptional vintage. He writes about *Miss Mackenzie* with feeling: the spinster with a fortune, in middle life, doing the right thing and reaping rewards. The sole adventures of significance are pecuniary: she inherits, the inheritance is improper, she signs it over, she marries a cousin. The circumstances and the physical world in which the actions take place (the *web*) are more real than the characters themselves. There is stolidity and even stupidity in the responses of Miss Mackenzie and her friends, a lack of reflection. He did not detect such faults in Jane Austen. "But when a novelist's imagination is weak, his judgement should be strong. Such was the case with Thackeray." Not, alas, with Trollope, who remains so mired in particulars that he lets go the larger scene. "Mr. Trollope's devotion to little things, inveterate, self-sufficient as it is, begets upon the reader the very disagreeable impression that not only no imagination was required for the work before him, but that a man of imagination could not possibly have written it."

In 1865, when Trollope still had much work to come, James insists that "his manner is literally freckled with virtues," but "all virtues of detail." He is exasperated with the Trollopian formula, the similarity with earlier books in theme, characterization if not character, elements of plot. There is abundant plot but no real story. Blandness (despite extreme incidents) James construes as an aspect of his realism, but regrets it nonetheless: "For Mr. Trollope anything is preferable to a sensation; an incident is ever preferable to an event." Exasperation turns to annoyance. *The Belton Estate* infantilizes the reader: it is "a *stupid book* . . . It indicates the manner in which a novel should *not,* on any account, be written." Later, surveying the work as a whole, he recognized Trollope's place in the family of Dickens, Thackeray, and George Eliot, though he was of short stature.

Though Trollope was not a formalist, James is wrong to say that "he had no 'views' whatever on the subject of novel-writing." The *Autobiography* promulgates, if not a theory of the novel, at least many elements that add up to a dogma about integrity of purpose, a Richardsonian prejudice. James speaks of the "almost startling simplicity" of Trollope's dictums: "His robust and patient mind had no particular bias, his imagination no light of its own. He saw things neither pictorially and grotesquely like Dickens; nor with that combined disposition to satire and to literary form which gives such 'body,' as they say of wine, to the manner of Thackeray; nor with anything of the philosophic, the transcendental cast—the desire to follow them to their remote relations—which we associate with the name of George Eliot." The French see as characteristic of the English imagination the quality they describe as *honnête*. "He represents in an eminent degree this natural decorum of the English spirit," says James.

The first Trollope novel to make a real mark was *The Warden* (1855), followed two years later by *Barchester Towers*. In the course of his Post Office work, Trollope traveled to Salisbury, and there, wandering about the cathedral and close on a long bright midsummer evening, he conceived *The Warden* and stood for an hour "on the little bridge," working out just where Hiram's hospital would be situated. The oddness is, he started without knowledge of cathedrals or close life; he invented, he found out. The archdeacon was "the simple result of an effort of my moral consciousness." His "intellectual" motives were an objection to the way the Church had, historically, taken charitable legacies and applied the proceeds to the establishment or embellishment of sinecures; and how emphatically the press attacked individuals in receipt of such emoluments, as though they were culpable. On July 29, 1852, after two years' literary silence, he sat down to *The Warden,* commencing the task at Tenbury, Herefordshire, a year after his visit to Salisbury. The book had a relatively long gestation.

The author was forty, had published three unsuccessful books, and was a responsible employee of the Post Office (how often vividly written letters, delivered on time, play a part in his novels, as if he had been sponsored by the Penny Post he helped to invent). *The Warden* is, in James's words, "simply the history of an old man's conscience," like *The Vicar of Wakefield,* and Mr. Harding, precentor of Barchester Cathedral, Trollope's most successful clerical creation. The theme is not original, but the choice of protagonist and the execution are. He is drawn to protagonists whom, on the face of it, we would not find engaging: not young, attractive, marriage-bound, heroic, nor outstanding in their field. Their ordinariness fascinates him, how as common men and women they deal with a world turned hostile. Thus, Mr. Harding and Archdeacon Grantley are placed in tension, the key conflict of the book. Grantley is real and almost sympathetic, but his "spiritual grossness" (as James calls it) is also exposed. Following Thackeray, Balzac, and others, Trollope carries characters from one novel to the next. The serial thus extended into something like an *ur*–soap opera.

How remote his wit is from Peacock's: in Dr. Anticant he parodies Carlyle and in Mr. Sentiment we see Dickens, yet they have not the voices of their quarries. In Grantley's sons Trollope was sending up three bishops of the day: the fun is lost on modern readers, as it was on many of the author's contemporaries. But the chief miscalculation, which recurs in several books, is the way in which the narrator reminds readers that they are involved in a work of fiction. James finds this the least forgivable fault, quoting derisively a late sentence in *Barchester Towers* where the narrator cheerily declares, "The end of a novel, like the end of a children's dinner party, must be made up of sweetmeats and sugarplums." This sells the book short, the maker of a commodity responding cheerfully to customer requirements, as a maker of meat pies might feel constrained to add more jelly. James finds some of Trollope's preposterous names, as if mined out of Peacock, further evidence of a low sense of his art. Mr. Nersay, Messrs. Stickatit, Rarechild, Fillgrave may amuse; but the illusion of reality is easily shattered.

In a letter of 1868 Trollope wrote against the use of the first-person narrator: "The reader is unconsciously taught to feel that the writer is glorifying himself, and rebels against the self-praise. Or otherwise the 'I' is pretentiously humble, and offends from exactly the other point of view. In telling a tale it is, I think, always well to sink the personal pronoun." Everything conspires to advance the story, which for him is the first principle. If, as he says, "the dialogue is generally the most agreeable part of a novel," it works only "as it tends in some way to the telling of the main story. It need not seem confined to that, but it should always have a tendency in that direction. The unconscious critical acumen of a reader is both just and severe."

In *The Eustace Diamonds* Trollope rises to the stature of Wilkie Collins and approaches the lower slopes of Thackeray. This novel he thought over in bed at night, and in the morning, when he was out walking or sitting by his hearth, to "make the things fit": "That requires elbow-grease of the mind. The arrangement of the words is as though you were walking simply along a road. The arrangement of your story is as though you were carrying a sack of flour while you walked. Fielding had carried his sack of flour before he wrote *Tom Jones,* and Scott his before he produced *Ivanhoe.*" Among the most powerful evocations in the book is Lizzie joining the hunt. In fiction, her riding to hounds is uniquely exhilarating. Trollope made no bones about it: he loved hunting. He tried to ride out at least twice a week.

Thomas Hardy attended a public meeting on "the Eastern Question" addressed by Gladstone, Lord Shaftesbury, the Duke of Westminster, and Anthony Trollope. Trollope outran his time but would not be curbed; he kept on speaking, a kind of filibusterer spoiling his cause. This mature gentleman, "liberal-conservative," risked running for the very Parliament he had created in fiction, and failed as some of his characters fail. Stolid and eminently solid, one would have thought him thoroughly establishment. Yet his understanding of the outsider, of the man or woman trying to secure a place in the social world, is acute, perhaps the most striking recurrent element in his fiction. His childhood and youth had made the theme real to him. He told the story in *Autobiography,* written in 1876, published posthumously in 1882.

The downward bias of his father's life made his boyhood wretched. Starting as a Chancery barrister in London, occupying dingy chambers at Lincoln's Inn, he was unsuccessful, then poor, then destitute. Yet he remained gentry and his sons were to be educated accordingly. His father left London and sunk his money in a house and farm. "That farm," Trollope writes, "was the grave of all my father's hopes, ambition, and prosperity, the cause of my mother's sufferings, and of those of her children, and perhaps the director of her destiny and of ours." His father had attended Winchester School and been a fellow of New College, Oxford. Harrow School was nearer to hand and became the young man's hell; he went dressed in rags and was surrounded by taunting boys whose parents were prompt with fees and rewards. His vulnerability like a scent drew the bully. Even his brother Thomas Adolphus, later a comrade, "as a part of his daily exercise . . . thrashed me with a big stick." His father bullied, but with the boy's interests at heart. "From my very babyhood, before those first days at Harrow, I had to take my place alongside of him as he shaved at six o'clock in the morning, and say my early rules from the Latin Grammar, or repeat the Greek alphabet;

and was obliged at these early lessons to hold my head inclined towards him, so that in the event of guilty fault, he might be able to pull my hair without stopping his razor or dropping his shaving-brush." He contemplated suicide.

Though his father was a writer and his mother would be one, there were few books in the house. He read to rags the first two volumes of James Fenimore Cooper's *The Prairie*. Thus, he experienced America through fiction when his mother and siblings actually went to the New World, and he learned a little about form from two-thirds of a novel. On the whole his education was deficient; he stresses how what learning he got, he got in spite of the dead languages he imperfectly acquired. He nearly became a teacher but by good fortune found employment at the Post Office. It took time to settle: he fell into gambling, then became a victim of moneylenders. Gradually he found his independent feet.

He always entertained himself in solitude by composing long narratives in his head—a structured daydreaming that went on from day to day. The novelist was stirring in him, but it was years before he took pen and paper and set his stories down. Finally, sent on a mission to Ireland in 1841, he took the bit between his teeth. "I fabricated the plot of *The Macdermots of Ballycloran*. As to the plot itself, I do not know that I ever made one so good,—or, at any rate, one so susceptible of pathos." *The Macdermots,* published, though unsuccessfully, in 1847 thanks to his mother's good offices, "is a good novel, and worth reading by any one who wishes to understand what Irish life was before the potato disease, the famine, and the Encumbered Estates Bill."

Travel made it possible for him to write, and he developed his pattern of composition, rejecting Carlyle's injunction that "a man when travelling should not read, but 'sit still and label his thoughts.'" He wrote on a tablet, in pencil, and his wife made fair copies when he returned home. One of his happiest acts of composition was *Barchester Towers*. "The bishop and Mrs. Proudie were very real to me, as were also the troubles of the archdeacon and the loves of Mr. Slope." He recounts how it happened that later on he slew Mrs. Proudie, his supreme comic tyrant. He overheard two clergyman discussing her at his club. "'Here,' said one, 'is that archdeacon whom we have had in every novel he has ever written.' 'And here,' said the other, 'is the old duke whom he has talked about till everybody is tired of him. If I could not invent new characters, I would not write novels at all.' Then one of them fell foul of Mrs. Proudie." The author introduced himself and promised them, "As to Mrs. Proudie,' I said, 'I will go home and kill her before the week is over." She died frozen upright with a paralytic stroke, like a dreadful monitory statue, holding on to a bedpost. Trollope committed a crime of literary passion, and ill-judged, too.

He traveled, and he wrote, the novels piling up, notable among them *Doctor Thorne* (1858), *Framley Parsonage* (1861), *Orley Farm* (published in 1862, and one of his favorites because so rooted in his life at the point at which it began to improve), *The Small House at Allington* (this and *Pride and Prejudice* Virginia Woolf regarded as the most perfect novels in English) and *Can You Forgive Her?* (1864), *Phineas Finn* and *He Knew He Was Right* (1869), *The Eustace Diamonds* (1873), and *The Way We Live Now* (1875). His illustrators included John Everett Millais, an artist who would read the book he had to decorate and render very clearly what the author intended.

Trollope is forthright in declaring what he expects of fiction. Earnest, unoriginal, it gives us the essence of him, the most companionable and least extending of authors. "A novel should give a picture of common life enlivened by humor and sweetened by pathos. To make that picture worthy of attention, the canvas should be crowded with real portraits, not of individuals known to the world or to the author, but of created personages impregnated with traits of character which are known. To my thinking, the plot is but the vehicle for all this; and when you have the vehicle without the passengers, a story of mystery in which the agents never spring to life, you have but a wooden show. There must, however, be a story. You must provide a vehicle of some sort." He concedes, not entirely justly, that humor "has not been my forte."

Among his contemporaries, Trollope rather despised Benjamin Disraeli (1804–1881), the first Earl of Beaconsfield, Knight of the Garter, Privy Counsellor to Her Majesty the Queen, and Fellow of the Royal Society, a man who was twice prime minister, the only British prime minister to date of Jewish origin, though he had joined the Church of England in his teens. For Trollope, quite apart from Disraeli's obnoxious politics, his novels were posed, too theatrical, "a smell of hair-oil, an aspect of buhl, a remembrance of tailors, and that pricking of the conscience which must be the general accompaniment of paste diamonds." In the next century Chesterton described Disraeli as "a genius and not a gentleman," his anti-Semitism heightening his admiration and repugnance.

*Vivian Gray* (1826), Disraeli's first novel, appeared when he was twenty-two and tells the story of a brilliant young man entering the political world. The protagonist commits a murder and flees abroad, and the story has a kind of picaresque movement built by the young author's prepolitical imagination. Trollope's example did not appeal to him: he had been seduced by Byron, he needed a large-scale romantic protagonist. Walter Allen calls it "a monstrously witty book," the sentences epigrammatic in their self-conscious, self-satisfied finish, the style curiously eighteenth-century, not essayistic in the manner of Peacock but possessing a rather too clear clarity. Much of his later writing is satirical, but never merely that. And there is his roman à clef about Byron and Shelley, *Venetia*. He never ceased to be a romantic or to feel himself as walking on a stage before an audience.

He is best remembered for the Young England trilogy: *Coningsby; or, The New Generation* (1844), *Sybil; or, The Two Nations* (1845), and *Tancred; or, The New Crusade* (1847). Taken together, these books constitute one of the few genuinely political fictions in British literature, on a scale not seriously rivaled until Gore Vidal's historical and political writings a century later. The *dailiness* of politics interests Disraeli, how the ideal and the quotidian coexist. *Coningsby* and *Sybil* reveal the political scene at the time of the first Reform Bill, and the state of England. *Sybil's* subtitle, *The Two Nations,* with the theme, if not of class struggle, at least of the conflict between rich and poor, is a phrase that entered common political parlance and is still current. It is worth remembering that *Sybil* predated *Mary Barton* (1848) in revealing what industrial workers were up against, though Mrs. Gaskell was closer to her subject and less grandiloquent. Disraeli's books still have truths to tell.

He writes efficient prose, and his handling of big scenes rivals Dickens's, so that riots, state occasions, epic and big-screen moments stay in mind, theatrical, with a sense of the order that makes for acceleration toward climax, though the more intimate writing is brittle, lingering if at all for the echoes of clever dialogue. "Disraeli's gift is for the superb and operatic," says Pritchett. In *Sybil,* "his people are speaking the language of opera; yet, after a hundred years, how exactly Disraeli has defined the English political situation. He is our only political novelist; I mean, the only one *saturated* in politics; the only one whose intellect feasts on polity." Among modern novelists, Gore Vidal and Frederic Raphael have a similarly acute ear for the caustic, the conscious exchange, though in Vidal and Raphael dialogue is ironized both in itself and in the narrator's stance toward his characters, who thus appear at two removes, as if projected on a screen. How well Disraeli might have written for Hollywood. Anachronisms apart, how well he writes for the page. He has the assurance of a historian and a historian's sense of irony.

The critical response to *Lothair* (1870) led Henry James to enter the lists against those critics whose loathing of Disraeli's politics and, or, his antecedents, darkened their judgment, and against those, his allies, who praised him as a matter of reflex. The book is not one of Disraeli's best. "The author has great cleverness, or rather he has a great deal of small cleverness." He is clever enough to get into complications, formal and aesthetic, but not clever enough to get out of them, "so that in the end his talent lies gloriously entombed and enshrined in a vast edifice of accumulated mistakes." This does not detract from the achievement of his successful novels, however: James is keen to do critical justice to the work, regardless of the man who is himself trying to do justice, according to his always slightly peculiar, wavering lights.

# 19

# *"Thought-Divers"*

Nathaniel Hawthorne, Herman Melville, Harriet Beecher Stowe

Sending his collection of stories *Mosses from an Old Manse* to Edgar Allan Poe in 1846, Nathaniel Hawthorne confesses: "I admire you rather as a writer of tales than as a critic upon them, I might often—and often do—dissent from your opinions in the latter capacity, but could never fail to recognize your force and originality in the former." The year after he received this gift, Poe wrote his essay on allegory, part of a larger polemic against forces he saw as hostile to the new literature: the Transcendentalists, Emerson and the Alcotts and writers whose communities, philosophies, politics, and theologies seemed hostile to invention and independence. Poe contrived his stories, but he did so with dramatic, not moral, intensity. They do not propose a key for interpretation, even when they seem decidedly allegorical and we think, "When he said this, he actually meant that." No, he would reply: "When I said this, *this* is actually what I meant" and there is no "hidden meaning" underpinning the figuration.

The reader of allegory, Poe says, is required to consider the unreal as real, as if in a simile the subject and the thing it is "like" were reversed. What purpose is served, beyond moral obliquity? Drama, psychology, and "realism" are displaced. Bunyan's *The Pilgrim's Progress* survives in spite of its allegory, the pleasure "found in the direct ratio of the reader's capacity to smother its true purpose, in the direct ratio of his ability to keep the allegory out of sight, or of his inability to comprehend it." Sometimes it cannot be avoided because an action insists on having figurative implications, but it must be "judiciously subdued, seen only as a shadow or by suggestive glimpses, and making its nearest approach to truth in a not obtrusive and therefore not unpleasant *appositeness*." It is a matter of proportion, and insofar as allegory does not displace the primary sense, it can be—warily—tolerated.

Hawthorne's major and some of his minor works have allegorical elements, and some ask to be read as allegory plain and simple, what is said and what is meant reaching different ends. The drama is argument, the argument drama; descriptions are symbolic, symbols descriptive. "One thing is clear," Poe insists, "that if allegory ever establishes a fact, it is by dint of over-turning a fiction . . . Under the best circumstances, it must always interfere with that unity of effect which, to the artist, is worth all the allegory in the world." Hawthorne is "too fond of allegory, and can never hope for popularity so long as he persists in it." Poe offered his advice to a living writer: Hawthorne read his comments. So did Henry James, who a generation later wrote a book about Hawthorne for British readers, his one sustained account of an American forebear. He roots his reflections in Poe's evaluation.

Allegory "is at war with the whole tone of [Hawthorne's] nature, which disports itself never so well as when escaping from the mysticism of his Goodman Browns and White Old Maids into the hearty, genial, but still Indian-summer sunshine of his Wakefields and Little Annie's Rambles." Those Transcendentalists nearly drowned him: "*His* spirit of 'metaphor run mad' is clearly imbibed from the phalanx and phalanstery atmosphere in which he has been so long struggling for breath." He has the skills and genius that would fit him to be a mystic; but they equally fit him to be "honest, upright, sensible, prehensible and comprehensible"; and he does not have the metaphysical instinct to be a mystic. With Shakespearean tones Poe exhorts: "Let him mend his pen, get a bottle of visible ink, come out from the Old Manse, cut Mr. Alcott, hang (if possible) the editor of *The Dial,* and throw out of the window to the pigs all his odd numbers of *The North American Review.*"

Certainly Hawthorne's "walk is limited," his work "mannered," "treating all subjects in a similar tone of dreamy *innuendo*," yet he is nonetheless the great original, and Poe is struck by how, in 1846, his name is seldom mentioned in accounts of American literature while lesser and less-demanding figures are celebrated. James Russell Lowell notes as much in headlong critical couplets that prefigure Dr. Seuss: "There is Hawthorne, with genius so shrinking and rare / That you hardly at first see the strength that is there." Lowell senses in him the androgynous spirit of the first order of genius, the genius of Shakespeare and Mozart. Certainly among American writers it is Hawthorne who first creates credible characters of both sexes, who can write children and old people, and who has a developed sense of good and evil. That sense of evil set him apart from the Transcendentalists, whose senses are so insistently fixed elsewhere that they cannot smell the sulfur in the rose or spot the serpent winding through the garden. It was the pungency, the moral realism, that struck D. H. Lawrence. He saw that the allegorical mode was necessary for the kinds of truth Hawthorne had to tell. *The Scarlet Letter* "is to me one of the greatest allegories in all literature . . . Its marvellous under-meaning! And its perfect duplicity." He reflects, "Sin is a queer thing. It isn't the breaking of divine commandments. It is the breaking of one's own integrity." This is the spectacle with which *The Scarlet Letter* entertains us. Edith Wharton refers to it as one of the rare "novels of pure situation," with *Tess of the d'Urbervilles,* which occurs within a different moral frame.

James knew Hawthorne to be at the start of something inescapably American in which he too, despite his expatriation, could not help but participate. He distantly remembers the original publication in 1850 of *The Scarlet Letter* (he was seven at the time): "the sensation the book produced, and the little shudder with which people alluded to it, as if a peculiar horror were mixed in with its attractions."

Nathaniel Hawthorne (1804–1864) was born in Salem, Massachusetts, site of the seventeenth-century witch trials. Before 1688, four so-called witches had been hanged near Boston. But in 1692 a curious shaking disease spread through Danvers, a part of Salem. Doctors could do nothing to stop it, and ministers recognized the devil; great preachers like Cotton Mather began to stir up local fear. By the end of the summer, nineteen people had been hanged; a man called Giles Corey was pressed to death; fifty-five confessed under pressure; 150 were confined to prison and another 200 fell under suspicion. A sizable portion of the population was implicated. As relatives of prominent citizens began to be accused, propriety was affronted and the nightmare gradually ebbed. The trials haunt the New England conscience. When Arthur Miller drew his play *The Crucible* from the history of the period, using it to comment on the excesses of the McCarthy period in 1953, it struck the American conscience: "Are you now, or have you ever been, a witch?"

If we return from the dramas of 1692 and 1953 to 1804, we find a baby, Nathaniel Hathorne. The Hathornes added a "w" to put distance between themselves and their rigid ancestor William Hathorne, whose son John was one of the three presiding judges at the Salem witch trials. Nathaniel evoked William in the "Introductory to *The Scarlet Letter*": "I seem to have a stronger claim to a residence here on account of this grave, bearded, sable-cloaked, and steeple-crowned progenitor—who came so early, with his Bible and his sword, and trode the unworn street with such a stately port, and made so large a figure, as a man of war and peace—a stronger claim than for myself, whose name is seldom heard and my face hardly known."

Behind *The House of the Seven Gables* lies a drama that involved William. "Hawthorne apparently found the idea of the history of the Pyncheons in his own family annals," James says. *The Scarlet Letter* includes elements of his early family history, too. Wiltshire ancestors had emigrated to America to find a new life and the freedom—a paradoxical word in context—to practice their religion, in the company of John Winthrop, with his long nose and beard-lengthened face, author of the sermon "The City on the Hill" and of substantial chronicles of the New World, "the brightest and most amiable figure in the early Puritan annals," who makes an appearance, or disappearance, in chapter 12 of *The Scarlet Letter,* "The Minister's Vigil," where Mr. Dimmesdale encounters the Reverend Wilson, fresh from the old governor's deathbed: "Governor Winthrop . . . had passed from earth to heaven within that very hour. And now surrounded, like the saint-like personage of olden times, with a radiant halo, that glorified him amid this gloomy night of sin—as if the departed Governor had left him an inheritance of his glory, or as if he had caught upon himself the distant shine of the celestial city, while looking thitherward to see the triumphant pilgrim pass within its gates—now, in short, good Father Wilson was moving homeward, aiding his footsteps with a lighted lantern!" The allusion to Winthrop's great sermon is quiet but unmistakable.

Hawthorne's father, a sea captain, died in Dutch Guiana when the boy was four. His mother grieved long and hard, her mourning the environment in which the boy grew up, secluded, in a house of concentrated whispers and privacies. "If ever I should have a biographer, he ought to make great mention of this chamber . . . because so much of my lonely youth was wasted here, and here my mind and character were formed; and here I have been glad and hopeful, and here I have been despondent. And here I sat a long, long time, waiting patiently for the world to know me." Hawthorne was reticent and arrogant, expecting the world to come to him, as adolescent writers do.

A serious reader of poetry and romances from an early age, he relished Edmund Spenser's *The Faerie Queene* and Bunyan's *The Pilgrim's Progress*. They gave an allegorical bias to his imagination. He detected symbolic structures and meanings in observations and events. He was curious about and then unsettled by his Puritan heritage, growing up in shadows cast by a culture still nourished by Europe. Young Nathaniel spent happy time away from home, in Maine. In the woods he recorded small details of an almost primeval world. But much of his youth was spent in Salem, musing and writing in his attic, walking out in the gloaming, keeping company with his retiring mother and his more forceful sister, who, some speculate, was almost a wife to him.

Considering Hawthorne's formative years, Henry James evokes "a little unadorned parlor, with the snow-drifts of a Massachusetts winter piled up about its windows, and a group of sensitive and serious people, modest votaries of opportunity, fixing their eyes upon a book full of Flaxman's attenuated outlines." These were outlines of figures that belonged in narratives, some of them classical compositions and images of the statuary that later abounded as plaster casts in municipal galleries and was removed to basements early in the twentieth century, when even the best copies became unfashionable and a worship of originals took hold. Some of Flaxman's engravings have a gothic aspect, in particular the Dante prints, which viewed by candlelight in a close parlor contributed to the boy's darker thoughts.

He was concerned, almost to the point of obsession, with issues of *conscience*. Like his friend Herman Melville's, his sense of evil is rooted in man and nature: it follows upon estrangements from the divine. One need not be European to feel a modern impatience with Emerson's overly illuminated paradoxing. James says, "Emerson, as a sort of spiritual sun-worshipper, could have attached but a moderate value to Hawthorne's cat-like faculty of seeing in the dark." And of seeing the dark itself.

Even in the early work, a sense of sin shadows what he writes, a residue of Puritan antecedents. He has, James says, the ability "to transmute this heavy moral burden into the very substance of the imagination." This may be why he insists on calling his key novels "romances": they belong in a tradition different from conventional social novels, being founded on legend and possessing a strong metaphysical dimension, and—most importantly—being susceptible to figurative interpretation. He is more directly out of Bunyan than out of Defoe or Fielding. This is the curiosity of his great novels, as of the mature Melville's: their symbolism is not limited to a particular passage or chapter but coheres throughout, and by means of this coherence the stories signify.

In his preface to *The House of the Seven Gables* he says, "The point of view in which this tale comes under the Romantic definition lies in the attempt to connect a bygone time with the very present that is flitting away from us." "The very present" is D. H. Lawrence's "urgent insurgent now" of the radical writing of the twentieth century.

In Scott the past echoes in the present; in Hawthorne it finds its consequences there. The same preface stresses the need not to overemphasize moral elements: "The author has considered it hardly worth his while . . . relentlessly to impale the story with its moral as with an iron rod,—or, rather, as by sticking a pin through a butterfly,—thus at once depriving it of life, and causing it to stiffen in an ungainly and unnatural attitude." The moral need not be stated if the narrative has done its work. The reader should be trusted. From an early age Hawthorne had outstanding readers. He studied at Bowdoin College in Brunswick, Maine. His contemporaries included the poet Henry Wadsworth Longfellow, Horatio Bridge, who wrote memorably about him in later years, and Franklin Pierce, who became the fourteenth president of the United States. Hawthorne graduated in 1825.

At his own expense he published his first novel, *Fanshawe*, in Boston in 1828. His formal skills fell short of the earnest themes and spiritual self-pity of the plot. The book is theme- rather than character-driven, exploring self-denial and the impartiality of true love in determining what is best for the beloved rather than the self. Sacrifice, with a doleful burden of pathos: the book went unnoticed, and the author, with solid grounds now for self-pity, found a way out of the cul-de-sac his novel represented by means of editorial and journalistic du-ties (including writing for children) and short stories, which were successfully collected in *Twice-Told Tales* (1837, enlarged edition 1842), the first great collec-tion of short stories in American literary history. With Poe and Irving he proved a master of a genre that was to become distinctively American.

During Hawthorne's early adult years, no New England writer, says James (omitting the example of Irving), was looking to explore the issues entailed in the enjoyment of life for its own sake. It would have been an incomplete theme. Life was a trial, and how the writer responded to the charges it leveled at characters, how he questioned and cross-questioned them, was what mat-tered. The writer was a step away from the minister. In the United States an excessively moral respect was paid to writers and writing, respect so exagger-ated that it made demands. Books were published and read for moral propri-ety. Good writing for its own sake was not encouraged (hence Irving was not properly valued on the literary bourse and had to content himself with the mute approbation of contented readers). A serious culture of literary reception was just beginning, represented in a few journals and notably in the critical writings of Poe and the advocacies of Irving. Critical culture, according to H. L. Mencken, starts with Samuel Lorenzo Knapp, LLD, "the first native critic of beautiful letters—the primordial tadpole of all the later." His *Lectures on American Literature with Remarks on Some Passages of American History* was pub-lished in 1829. It is alert to every clergyman, historian, and poet who left a writ-ten record, and makes slow reading.

In 1839–1841 Hawthorne filled a post at the Boston Custom House. He spent several months at Brook Farm in West Roxbury, Massachusetts, the experimen-tal community established in 1841 by George Ripley and his followers, inspired by the ideals of Transcendentalism. Emerson did not join them, out of a "convic-tion the Community is not good for me." Margaret Fuller was also reluctant. Henry David Thoreau confided to his journal, "As for these communities, I think I had rather keep a bachelor's room in Hell than go to board in Heaven." At Brook Farm for three years the residents explored collective living and rural disciplines (physical and intellectual work being seen as complementary) in a spirit of tense comradeship, though with poor husbandry. After a fire devastated the common farmhouse in 1847, the original community was effectively over.

Hawthorne risked joining the community, but he was no more suited to com-munal life than Emerson. A solitary, reflective individual, he thought he would have time there to read and write. Things turned out otherwise and the value of the experiment to his writing came later, when he had reflected on it. He wrote the novel that opens a fictional window on the experiment, *The Blithedale Romance* (1852). He had one important success there: he married the artist and illustrator Sophie Peabody, a native of Salem associated with the founders of Brook Farm, and this relationship, though it brought him no closer to Transcendentalism, transformed his life: he had a companion so close that at times she seemed almost a collaborator. They settled at the Old Manse in Concord, and there he began to write in earnest, developing a new dimension in the American Gothic in the wake of Irving's and Poe's successes.

Appointed surveyor of the Port of Salem, he wrote little but observed, and when "ejected" from his post, he was ready to undertake the big works. In the following years he rapidly produced his masterpieces *The Scarlet Letter* (1850), *The House of the Seven Gables* (1851), and *The Blithedale Romance*. His publisher, James Fields of Ticknor and Fields, editor of the *Atlantic Monthly,* encouraged him to complete *The Scarlet Letter.* In February 1850 Hawthorne wrote to Horatio Bridge: "I finished my book only yesterday; one end being in the press at Boston, while the other is in my head here at Salem, so that, as you see, my story is at least fourteen miles long."

For a time he lived in the Berkshires and there became a friend of Herman Melville. In 1852 he wrote the biography of his college friend Franklin Pierce, who, once elected president of the United States, paid his propagandist with the lucrative American consulship at Liverpool. In 1853 Hawthorne traveled to England, where he spent four years, proceeding to the Continent, and finally returning to Concord in 1860. *The Marble Faun,* his most significant later work, set in Italy, was published in that year. There are four substantial posthumous fragments, of which *Septimus Felton; or, The Elixir of Life* is the most interesting.

On his death in 1864 he had earned the respect Poe wished upon him two and a half decades before. To have young Henry James commissioned as biographer-advocate to the British in 1879, fifteen years after his death, was a mark of his acceptance. James is a meticulous critic, even though Hawthorne is, on the face of it, remote from him in kind. James insists on the darkness of *The Scarlet Letter,* its categorical morality, the one spot of color being the lurid A. It is a novel of consequences ending not in marriage but in something more savagely instructive than a carillon. Hester Prynne and little Pearl with her puckish crown of flowers continue to act in the mind, they follow us out of the book. This first great *original* work of American fiction "belonged to the soil, to the air; it came out of the very heart of New England."

The fact of Hester Prynne and Arthur Dimmesdale's love, drawn convincingly, was of less consequence to Hawthorne than the fascination of its moral consequences. *The Scarlet Letter* is a novel of revenge: Roger Chillingworth exacts a relentless penance from Dimmesdale, "conjoining himself with his wronger, living with him, living on him, and while he pretends to minister to his hidden ailment and to sympathize with his pain," James says, "revels in his unsuspected knowledge of these things and stimulates them by malignant arts." This triangle may have been in James's mind when he planned *The Golden Bowl,* with its relentless delicacy of design. Lawrence is close behind James in his fascination with the characters' fates: "Yet [Hester's] only marriage, and her last oath, is with the old Roger. He and she are accomplices in pulling down the spiritual saint." In this book Lawrence defines the constraints of the American imagination: "They give tight mental allegiance to a morality which all their passion goes to destroy. Hence the duplicity which is the fatal flaw in them, most fatal in the most perfect American work of art, *The Scarlet Letter.* Tight mental allegiance given to a morality which the passional self repudiates."

Hawthorne takes setting for granted: local color is dim, he writes more in the spirit of Hardy than of Scott or Dickens. James finds an unreality in the fiction, with its preference for symbolism over detail, "an abuse of the fanciful element." Hawthorne declared that his tale existed "somewhere between the real world and fairy-land, where the Actual and Imaginary may meet, and each imbue itself with the nature of the other." This "meeting" can be forced. Hawthorne overstresses the *heat* of the scarlet letter, for example, making it into a kind of branding on the flesh, hellfire. Lawrence for his part celebrates the symbolism as crucial to the tale. The confession and death of Dimmesdale are merciless; yet the impulse that led to his and Hester's love was natural, and the code that made it sin exposed them to guilt's enslavement.

*The House of the Seven Gables* has never enjoyed the popularity of *The Scarlet Letter.* It has a shorter dramatic time span but grows out of a longer history, whose pertinence to the plot provided Hawthorne with a narrative challenge. His cast of characters is large, yet their lives are predetermined. At first they seem static, enacting or enduring consequences of actions not their own. Particular family histories shadow them. The composition is effortful. The house itself is elaborate and insistently symbolic; characters and scenes balance one another: a Gothic tale classically told.

James visited the house on which the novel was based and was disappointed; the book had disappointed him already. It seemed a prologue to a great novel rather than a great novel itself. The *donnée,* the pretext, was insufficient to sustain 100,000 words of charged, slow-moving narrative: there was a frustrated sense of larger purposings. The book sets out to give a New England vision; it works on a big canvas, but the *dramatis personae* are "figures rather than characters." The central incidents are aftermath, not action. Hepzibah Pyncheon "dragging out a disappointed life in her paternal dwelling," opening a little shop to make ends meet, being destitute due to a bankruptcy not of her making. Her brother is released from prison, where he has been punished for a crime he did not commit, and a lovely young country cousin arrives in the old mansion. Time for redemption, but the Fall occurred offstage, in another time and theater. The story is elegiac and unfolds with "a kind of humorous tenderness" at odds with the themes. Judge Pyncheon is more an ancestral portrait than a character, "a superb, full-blown hypocrite, a large-based, full-nurtured Pharisee, bland, urbane, impressive."

Chapter 11 contains some of Hawthorne's most precise symbolic writing. Old time-ravaged Clifford, freed from prison and slowly regathering his faculties, sits with his by now beloved country cousin Phoebe, out of range of his parched, devoted sister. From the window over the main door he watches the street. His listless vigil is interrupted when an Italian boy with a barrel organ stops under the emblematic elm, having spotted the watchers in the house, and

> opening his instrument, began to scatter its melodies abroad. He had a monkey on his shoulder, dressed in a Highland plaid; and, to complete the sum of splendid attractions wherewith he presented himself to the public, there was a company of little figures, whose sphere and habitation was in the mahogany case of his organ, and whose principle of life was the music which the Italian made it his business to grind out. In all their variety of occupation,—the cobbler, the blacksmith, the soldier, the lady with her fan, the toper with his bottle, the milk-maid sitting by her cow—this fortunate little society might truly be said to enjoy a harmonious existence, and to make life literally a dance. The Italian turned a crank; and, behold! every one of these small individuals started into the most curious vivacity. The cobbler wrought upon a shoe; the blacksmith hammered his iron, the soldier waved his glittering blade; the lady raised a tiny breeze with her fan; the jolly toper swigged lustily at his bottle; a scholar opened his book with eager thirst for knowledge, and turned his head to and fro along the page; the milkmaid energetically drained her cow; and a miser counted gold into his strong-box,—all at the same turning of a crank. Yes; and, moved by the self-same impulse, a lover saluted his mistress on her lips!

The sense could hardly be clearer, but Hawthorne must make sure we understand precisely what this description is doing.

> Possibly some cynic, at once merry and bitter, had desired to signify, in this pantomimic scene, that we mortals, whatever our business or amusement,—however serious, however trifling,—all dance to one identical tune, and, in spite of our ridiculous activity, bring

nothing finally to pass. For the most remarkable aspect of the affair was, that, at the cessation of the music, everybody was petrified at once, from the most extravagant life into a dead torpor . . .

The monkey, meanwhile, with a thick tail curling out into preposterous prolixity from beneath his tartans, took his station at the Italian's feet. He turned a wrinkled and abominable little visage to every passer-by, and to the circle of children that soon gathered round, and to Hepzibah's shop-door, and upward to the arched window, whence Phoebe and Clifford were looking down. Every moment, also, he took off his Highland bonnet, and performed a bow and scrape. Sometimes, moreover, he made personal application to individuals, holding out his small black palm, and otherwise plainly signifying his excessive desire for whatever filthy lucre might happen to be in anybody's pocket. The mean and low, yet strangely manlike expression of his wilted countenance; the prying and crafty glance, that showed him ready to gripe at every miserable advantage; his enormous tail (too enormous to be decently concealed under his gabardine), and the deviltry of nature which it betokened,—take this monkey just as he was, in short, and you could desire no better image of the Mammon of copper coin, symbolizing the grossest form of the love of money. Neither was there any possibility of satisfying the covetous little devil. Phoebe threw down a whole handful of cents, which he picked up with joyless eagerness, handed them over to the Italian for safekeeping, and immediately recommenced a series of pantomimic petitions for more.

The monkey's tail is in the end too distressing to Clifford, its ugliness making the worshipper of beauty withdraw. The scene has a lively reality, though Hawthorne strives to reduce it to meaning.

*The Blithedale Romance* is in a lighter vein than the other great novels. It comes "nearest to actuality" and yet is ill judged in portraying the community. Lawrence undermines the book with a synopsis. "There," he says, "the famous idealists and transcendentalists of America met to till the soil and hew the timber in the sweat of their own brows, thinking high thoughts the while, and breathing an atmosphere of communal love, and tingling in tune with the Oversoul, like so many strings of a super-celestial harp. An old twang of the Crevecoeur instrument." It was a doomed experiment. "Of course they fell out like cats and dogs. Couldn't stand one another. And all the music they made was the music of their quarrelling." The problem is, "You *can't* idealize hard work. Which is why America invents so many machines and contrivances of all sort:

so that they need do no physical work." In no time "the idealists left off brook-farming, and took to bookfarming." You cannot idealize real men, Lawrence says. He overstates the case: *The Blithedale Romance* is lyrical, comic, and in part believably peopled. The narrator, Miles Coverdale, is specific, unlike the "disembodied spirit" of the earlier books.

He shares much with Hawthorne himself, "half a poet, half a critic, and all a spectator." When he decides to leave Blithedale, the first person comes close up, so close that the reader feels author and narrator are almost one. Coverdale has had a decisive disagreement with the arrogantly patriarchal Hollingsworth and resolves to leave the community, at least for a time. He goes to say farewell to the pigs he has minded. "There they lay, buried as deeply among the straw as they could burrow, four huge black grunters, the very symbols of slothful ease and sensual comfort. They were asleep, drawing short and heavy breaths, which heaved their big sides up and down. Unclosing their eyes, however, at my approach, they looked dimly forth at the outer world, and simultaneously uttered a gentle grunt; not putting themselves to the trouble of an additional breath for that particular purpose, but grunting with their ordinary inhalation." Each word is subtly chosen, none so effectively as "Unclosing," which is not the same thing as "Opening": the participle suspends the pigs between the world of their comfort and the world that surrounds them. "They were involved, and almost stifled and buried alive, in their own corporeal substance. The very unreadiness and oppression wherewith these greasy citizens gained breath enough to keep their life-machinery in sluggish movement appeared to make them only the more sensible of the ponderous and fat satisfaction of their existence. Peeping at me an instant out of their small, red, hardly perceptible eyes, they dropt asleep again; yet not so far asleep but that their unctuous bliss was still present to them, betwixt dream and reality." It is a place where to some extent all the characters in this book dwell, the dream gradually loosening its hold. "'You must come back in season to eat part of a spare-rib,' said Silas Foster, giving my hand a mighty squeeze. 'I shall have these fat fellows hanging up by the heels, heads downward, pretty soon, I tell you!'" To this Coverdale's response contains the larger moral of his story. "'O cruel Silas, what a horrible idea!' cried I. 'All the rest of us, men, women, and livestock, save only these four porkers, are bedevilled with one grief or another; they alone are happy,—and you mean to cut their throats and eat them! It would be more for the general comfort to let them eat us; and bitter and sour morsels we should be!'"

Coverdale contrasts with unsubtle, forceful, ideological, indifferent Hollingsworth. The historic Margaret Fuller is the source of Zenobia, "the nearest approach that Hawthorne has made to the complete creation of a *person*," James says. When he came to Brook Farm, Hawthorne found Fuller, self-assertive and one of the best-educated women of her time (and she knew it), irritating and he was glad to avoid her. Oscar Wilde recalls how, visiting the United States, someone told him that when Margaret Fuller had an essay to be published, "the printers had always to send out to borrow some additional capital 'I's.'" She was the first woman to be given access to Harvard College Library. In time she began to fascinate Hawthorne, as she had others before him. He recalls a day when he'd left a book at Emerson's: "I returned through the woods, and, entering Sleepy Hollow," a place haunted by Irving's legend, "I perceived a lady reclining near the path which bends along its verge. It was Margaret herself. She had been there the whole afternoon, meditating or reading." They start a philosophical discussion. That is how we remember her, not "her vivacity of desire and poverty of knowledge" but rather "the glare of her understanding." Coverdale sees himself as through Zenobia's eyes, and again it is as though Hawthorne was writing of himself as a writer, his position and perspective in relation to the observed world: "She should have been able to appreciate that quality of the intellect and the heart which impelled me (often against my own will, and to the detriment of my own comfort) to live in other lives, and to endeavour—by generous sympathies, by delicate intuitions, by taking note of things too slight for record, and by bringing my human spirit into manifold accordance with the companions whom God assigned me—to learn the secret which was hidden even from themselves." Here too is a foreshadowing of Henry James.

Zenobia is a handsome woman; Margaret Fuller was not, by any stretch of the imagination, that. But Hawthorne did not complete the translation of his experiences into fiction. Some onetime inhabitants of Brook Farm, after *Blithedale,* felt that the taciturn, reclusive Hawthorne, whom they had elected to positions of responsibility within the community, had fed off their ardor, a kind of spy. (Fuller herself went on to become a distinguished journalist, the first full-time female employee of the *New York Tribune* and then the first full-time American foreign correspondent. By then she had shaken the dust of Brook Farm out of her petticoats.)

Hawthorne's years of exile began after Brook Farm. When he set out on his travels, James says, he had trouble "unlearning" his nationality; his Americanness was ingrained, so that in Europe, "the strife between his sense of beauty," intense but unengaged, "and his sense of banishment" from any natural inclusion in that beauty, left him in a state of anxious imaginative inertia. Irving abroad discovered America and felt almost at home in England. For Hawthorne, and then for James, it was a different story. In a passage with personal resonance, James declares: "He is outside of everything, and an alien everywhere. He is an aesthetic solitary. His beautiful, light imagination is the wing that on the autumn evening just brushes the dusky window." His writing thrives on familiarity, not entitlement.

It took him years abroad to free himself from dependence on the familiar. Yet he never addressed the subject of what it meant to be an American, a New Englander, as he might have been expected to do in Europe; he is the first thoroughly rooted major American novelist, constrained in that nationality with its cultural resources and its strict determinants. What are those determinants? James is fascinated to see, by contrast with Hawthorne, what he has himself managed to transcend in and through Europe. Yet he is drawn to the peculiar integrity of Hawthorne, who always wanted to write a kind of novel different from the ones he did write, but could not find a way.

To British readers James defined Hawthorne's Americanness in ways that alienated American readers. Poor Hawthorne, he says, having to write "a romance about a country where there is no shadow, no antiquity, no mystery, no picturesque and gloomy wrong, nor anything but a commonplace prosperity, in broad and simple daylight, as is happily the case in my dear native land." James speaks of the *blankness* of the canvas that the American novelist is required to fill with figures. He must invent because nothing is given, nothing is second nature. Clearly Hawthorne read plenty of good books: he describes them in the *Notebooks*. He developed his "charming, expressive, slightly self-conscious, cultivated, but not too cultivated, style." He is correct always, out of a thorough politeness. In his diaries he refers even to close friends as Mr. X or Y, preserving their privacy almost from himself.

The blankness of the canvas, the need to invent, were borne in on James when he visited the building that inspired *The House of the Seven Gables*. He drew from the experience something of use to his own art: a writer forgets the actual in order to remember it as fiction. Thus, James insists, Hawthorne is not a proto-realist. Flaubert and Zola wrought their revolution after Hawthorne's main work was done; and Hawthorne did not dwell on a wider social or material world: "His touch on such points is always light and vague, he has none of the apparatus of a historian, and his shadowy style of portraiture never suggests a rigid standard of accuracy." His symbols, too, are "images which shall place themselves in picturesque correspondence with the spiritual facts with which he is concerned." He "turned up the underside of common aspects—the laws secretly broken, the impulses secretly felt, the hidden passions, the double lives, the dark corners, the closed rooms, the skeletons in the cupboard and at the feast." This is the way of Thomas Hardy, undermining commonplaces to show the dark side.

The American imagination is naturally "oppressed by the burden of antiquity in Europe" yet craves a burden of its own. Art cannot travel light. From the "little unadorned parlor" to the cultural abundance of England and Italy was a huge step. Hawthorne looks at an English high street, "an emblem of England itself. What seems new in it is chiefly a skillful and fortunate adaptation of what such a people as ourselves would destroy. The new things are based and supported on sturdy old things, and derive a massive strength from their deep and immemorial foundations, though with such limitations and impediments as only an Englishman could endure. But he likes to feel the weight of all the past upon his back; and moreover the antiquity that overburdens him has taken root in his being, and has grown to be rather a hump than a pack, so that there is no getting rid of it without tearing his whole structure to pieces." James is one of those "such a people as ourselves"; he fights the destructive impulse with consequences for himself and his art. Virginia Woolf quotes a very different passage about the Englishman, from *Our Old Home* (1863): "It has required nothing less than the boorishness, the stolidity, the self-sufficiency, the contemptuous jealousy, the half-sagacity, invariably blind of one eye and often distorted of the other, that characterize this strange people, to compel us to be a great nation in our own right, instead of continuing virtually, if not in name, a province of their small island."

When Hawthorne went abroad he gained, but he also lost something central to himself, a sense of the adequacy of the world he came from, innocence. "Bored by the importunity of Italian art," he loathed nudes in sculpture; he disliked Rome and its layered culture; he was happiest in a rural villa near Florence where he conceived *Transformation,* which in America became *The Marble Faun,* a faulty novel with fine passages. "Strange that Europe should have made a most experienced author write such nonsense" as the *French and Italian Notebooks,* says the Franco-American novelist Julian Green. "At the very bottom of Hawthorne lurked a provincial, brought to light by this journey."

He returned to a no longer united United States in 1860. The Civil War was to destroy forever the world that had formed him, a world he, like many other Northerners, had found tolerable; like Pierce, and like Emerson and Fuller and Thoreau, he would have preferred secession or "amputation" to the civil strife that ensued. He said of his frustration in continuing to write: "There seem to be things that I can almost get hold of, and think about; but when I am just on the point of seizing them, they start away, like slippery things." He repeats the word "things": he is defeated by the difficulty of his themes. He intended to write *The Dolliver Romance,* about the elixir of life, for serialization in the *Atlantic Monthly.* He longed for a restorative journey to England, he was weary, the fire in his eyes was dim. His publisher sent him to consult Dr. Oliver Wendell Holmes: they walked together in Boston (Hawthorne did not like to be physically examined). Holmes reassured him but told his publisher that "the shark's tooth is upon him." His old friend Pierce, now an ex-president of the United

States and a vigorous opponent of Lincoln, took him away for a change of air in New Hampshire. On their journey Hawthorne died in his sleep. He was buried at Concord, his funeral attended by Longfellow, Emerson, James Russell Lowell, Oliver Wendell Holmes, and Bronson Alcott. American fiction, in part thanks to him, existed, with its own themes, and formal properties, its own classics.

Much is made by critics and biographers of the intense but brief friendship between Hawthorne and Herman Melville. They met in 1850, remained close friends during the period in which Melville was writing *Moby-Dick,* a copy of which he presented to Hawthorne on an afternoon in November 1851 when the two men dined together (a happy launch party of two) at the Curtis Hotel in Lenox, Massachusetts. Melville had dedicated the book to Hawthorne:

IN TOKEN
OF MY ADMIRATION FOR HIS GENIUS,
THIS BOOK IS INSCRIBED
TO
NATHANIEL HAWTHORNE

He wrote, "I have written a wicked book, and feel spotless as the lamb." Then their friendship cooled and by the end of 1852 there was little commerce between them, apart from a visit Melville paid to Hawthorne in 1856 in Liverpool, where Hawthorne was American Consul and Melville was halting on his pilgrimage to the Holy Land.

Melville, in the surviving letters to Hawthorne (Hawthorne's letters to him do not survive), poured out his heart, and a confused heart it was: the letters vulnerable, ingratiating. Taken with Melville's published writings, they have given rise to speculation about the author's psychology and sexuality. Beyond question is Melville's not-uncritical engagement with Hawthorne's work, which he continued to read and annotate after the friendship was over, and after Hawthorne's death. He wrote in 1851 to his friend Evert Duyckinck (also a correspondent of Hawthorne's), having just read *Twice-Told Tales,* "Their deeper meanings are worthy of a Brahmin. Still there is something lacking—a good deal lacking—to the plump sphericity of the man. What is that?—He doesn't patronize the butcher—he needs roast-beef, done rare." Despite this desire for something *more,* Melville insists, "I regard Hawthorne (in his books) as evincing a quality of genius, immensely loftier, & more profound, too, than any other American has shown hitherto in the printed form. Irving is a grasshopper to him—putting the *souls* of the two men together, I mean."

It was Melville's always pessimistic insistence on the "soul" that eventually tried Hawthorne's patience. After their last meeting in Liverpool and on "the monotonous sand hills" of Southport, Hawthorne wrote with distaste of a changed man, an unsuccessful and no longer sympathetic man. At first he looked "much as he used to do (a little paler, and perhaps a little sadder), in a rough outside coat, and with his characteristic gravity and reserve of manner." They fell into something like their earlier intimacy. But Melville was unwell, having "suffered from too constant literary occupation, pursued without much success, latterly; and his writings, for a long while past, have indicated a morbid state of mind. [He] began to reason of Providence and futurity, and of everything that lies beyond human ken, and informed me that he had 'pretty much made up his mind to be annihilated'; but still he does not seem to rest in that anticipation; and, I think, will never rest until he gets hold of a definite belief." Melville went on his way to Italy and the Holy Land more troubled than before.

Herman Melvill was born in New York in 1819 of Dutch and English stock. Both his grandfathers had been generals in the War of Independence, and Grandfather Melvill attended the Boston Tea Party. A merchant working on commission, Herman's father was often absent; business did not prosper, the War of 1812 being a final straw. He moved to Albany. When his fur business failed, he declared bankruptcy, his mental balance went, and he died, leaving destitute a young family. (Four years after his death Melville's mother added an "e" to the family name, a modest social makeover reminiscent of the Hawthornes'.)

The boy was twelve when his father died. His schooling continued under straitened circumstances. He had an independent spirit and set out as soon as he could to earn his own keep. He became a cabin boy on a ship to Liverpool and back, an experience that would feed into his fourth novel, *Redburn: His First Voyage* (1849, with "no metaphysics, no conic-sections, nothing but cakes & ale," he wrote in a letter). In January 1841 he set to sea again, this time on a whaler, the *Acushnet,* bound for the Pacific. On that January day, he said in later years, his life began in earnest. Here, too, started a gestation. Just over a decade later, it would issue in *Moby-Dick.*

Melville jumped ship in the Marquesas Islands after eighteen months at sea. He spent a brief time on Typee among courteous natives whose neighbors described them as cannibals. *Typee: A Romance of the South Seas* (1846), his first book, was an imaginative expansion of this experience, "calculated for popular reading, or for none at all." His South Pacific books were published as novels, in part because readers found them too far-fetched to be credible, and Melville could call no witnesses. The liaison with the lovely naked Fayaway, based in experience, added to the appeal of *Typee,* his most popular book. It does not conform to our expectations of a novel. It is now factual, now polemical. Like Irving and Cooper among fellow Americans, Melville in Typee, and later in Hawaii, is at home. Missionaries and colonials (especially the French) inflict spiritual poverty and material greed upon these prelapsarian citizens. When his adventures in Typee were over, he "escaped" and joined another whaler, continuing his travels in the Pacific, then found an American naval frigate to take him home with material for three novels.

*Typee* did not find an American publisher. It was brought out in England and sold well. *Omoo,* his next book, was published in 1847 the United States. The author-adventurer became a contentious celebrity. He maintained that the works were based in truth. Between 1857 and 1860 he supplemented his earnings by giving public lectures, largely on the theme of his travels. It may have been the public doubt that induced him to provide exhaustive authorities and the celebrated "Extracts" to prove the bona fides of the incredible, largely factual *Moby-Dick.* Whatever they represent, there is solidity to the symbols.

In 1847 Melville married Elizabeth Shaw, whose father was chief justice of the Supreme Court of Massachusetts. They had four children, two sons who died in youth, one at his own hand, and two daughters. Elizabeth in time became manager and provider. His writing life foundered, a post as customs inspector was secured, and for nineteen years he was paid a salary and exercised his honesty in a highly corrupt organization. Here Bartleby the Scrivener, sad protagonist of the story of that title, was conceived. Melville, like his faded protagonist, would have "preferred not to."

His wife stayed with him through periods of alcoholism, violence, and breakdown. In 1872 she wrote to a friend, "Herman from his studious habits and tastes being unfitted for practical matters, all the *financial* management falls upon me." She and her brother regarded his writing as a failure; they humored him, and in later years he was permitted to print his own poems, which kept him busy, though when he was writing, especially *Clarel,* he seemed at times to be mad with concentration and near despair. He described the poem to a friend as "a metrical affair, a pilgrimage or what not, of several thousand lines, eminently adapted for unpopularity." Inspired by his trip to the Holy Land, it was twice as long as *Paradise Lost.* An uncle's bequest paid for publication in 1876. It hardly sold, and the unsold copies were eventually burned.

Melville's poems are worked up. They contribute to the rumor of an "unspeakable" theme that has to do with a radiant sexual irresolution, manifest in the relations of Ishmael and Queequeg, in the last novel *Billy Budd,* and in some of the more peculiar goings-on in *The Confidence-Man.* More insistently even than Conrad, Melville after *Typee* depicts a male world: intimacy is between men and types of men: at sea, in the army, and elsewhere. He celebrates, laments, touches—and occasionally foresees, not with the big vision of Walt Whitman, but with narrowed eyes. He sees, beyond a bad age, to the other side of evil.

The facts of Melville's life suggest without telling a story. This is a reason Hart Crane called him a "fabulous shadow." It is a modern presumption to assign specific weight to the known—because of the unknown—facts: his affection for Hawthorne, his strained marriage, the suicide of one of his sons, and the loss of another. What we have solidly before us is the prose and verse: what it says and does not say. His seriousness deepens with candor, some elements gain definition, elements that contribute to his eclipse as critics and readers turn from what they do not quite comprehend or feel comfortable with. This writer, a Unionist hostile to slavery, with a definite sense of evil and good (in that order), and a feeling for his country and the people involved at all levels in a murderous turbulence, foresaw some of the bad consequences of just action. "But the Founders' dream shall flee," he says: what will take its place? In his poem "The March into Virginia" he shows the initial confidence—carriages accompanying the solders to battle to watch the spectacle—in all its unsuspecting innocence; and the consequences of battle itself. The wind blows one way, he says, but with unpredictable back-currents. "It spins against the way it drives." This is history's way. The great novels—*Moby-Dick; or, The Whale* (1851) and *The Confidence-Man: His Masquerade* (1857) before the war, and *Billy Budd, Sailor* (begun in 1886, unfinished at his death in 1891, published in 1924) after it—deal with these themes.

*Moby-Dick* proved exhausting to write. Melville knew it was original and understood that it was good. Published in 1851, it was not a success; until the first quarter of the twentieth century it was neglected. *Pierre; or, The Ambiguities* was published in 1852 and it also disappointed the critics and the author. D. H. Lawrence summarizes it: "He wrote *Pierre* to show that the more you try to be good the more you make a mess of things: that following righteousness is just disastrous."

This becomes a key theme in *The Confidence-Man*, though there it went down no better than in *Pierre*. The failure of *The Confidence-Man* was incomprehensible to him, as it is now to us. The critics turned and turned away editors and readers: nothing he could write would have stemmed the tide. His fiction writing was more or less done. In 1863 he moved with his family from the farm at Pittsfield, Massachusetts, where his greatest work was produced, to 104 East 26th Street in New York City. Here he spent the long remainder of his life writing (when he did write) principally poetry. He frequented the secondhand bookshops on Canal Street. In neglect he died in 1891. To a friend he had written, "All ambitious authors should have ghosts capable of revisiting the world, to snuff up the steam of adulation, which begins to rise straightway as the Sexton throws his last shovelful on him." In his case the steam rose long after the body had been digested by the earth of Woodlawn Cemetery in the Bronx.

Edmund Wilson admired and resisted *Moby-Dick*: "like going down the funnel of Dante's Inferno, with no Purgatory or Paradise to follow." It is in this spirit that schoolchildren are ushered on board the *Pequod,* their eyes alert to symbolism and in a hushed and solemn mode, and how many of us resisted it. Yet in the light of *Typee* and *Omoo,* and especially *The Confidence-Man,* how can students and teachers fail to respond to the humor of the narrative? Ishmael is aware of the absurdities of the wide world and the narrow, epitomizing world of the *Pequod,* and as tension increases (pace hardly does), the elements of humor change. Dark they can be, but humor, now frankly comic, now eerily incongruous, survives even in the dark. Lawrence rails against Melville's sententiousness: he did not hear the tonal leavening, when after disaster Ishmael survives to tell the tale. The bigness of the climax, the smallness of the aftermath. The sinking ship sucks Ishmael into its vortex, but: "When I reached it, it had subsided to a creamy pool. Round and round, then, and ever contracting towards the button-like black bubble at the axis of that slowly wheeling circle like another Ilion I did revolve." Then the "cunning spring" releases the vehicle of Ishmael's deliverance: "Owing to its great buoyancy, rising with great force, the coffin life-buoy shot lengthwise from the sea, fell over, and floated by my side." The sharks, so fierce before, are now unharming, "with padlocks on their mouths"; the sea hawks "sailed with sheathed beaks." And the novel ends with a play upon the name of the familiar ship that rescues him, the *Rachel,* who in him finds not her missing children, just another orphan.

The language of *Moby-Dick* is different in kind from the language of Melville's earlier novels. It is richly Jacobean, with the kinds of unsentimental concerns with mortality and the physicality of the body that we experience in the drama and religious writing of an age in which the King James Bible and the Book of Common Prayer were entering the bloodstream of English, when Rabelais and Cervantes were being translated. The language was making itself, and here in *Moby-Dick* language is making itself. The archaic feel is in part due to an anachronistic impulse of comprehension.

In a letter to a friend written in 1849 Melville reports, "I have been passing my time very pleasurably here, but chiefly in lounging on a sofa (à la the poet Grey) & reading Shakespeare. It is an edition in glorious great type, every letter whereof is a soldier, & the top of every 't' like a musket barrel." Before, Shakespeare was a closed book to him because the editions available were so hard on the eye. "I am mad to think how minute a cause has prevented me hitherto from reading Shakespeare. But until now, every copy that was come-atable to me, happened to be in a vile small print unendurable to my eyes which are tender as young sparrows." The writer, on the very gangway of the *Pequod,* was overjoyed, "chancing to fall in with this glorious edition, I now exult in it, page after page."

Shakespeare's rhythms affect Melville's prose. Many paragraphs are virtually in blank verse; he risked subtler and more complex sentences, his building of the language became at once more natural and more deliberate, varying pitch, placing climaxes, making voices. In the description of the giant squid and elsewhere, Melville creates a sense of utter stillness into which some unexpectedness, a monster or a thought, irrupts: placidity, unpredictability. He grants, as Shakespeare does, an appropriate tone to each scene, and to each character an appropriate diction. They speak in accordance with their age, culture, and class. He kept Shakespeare by him, writing almost two years later to the same friend how he was writing his book:

> I rise at eight—thereabouts—& go to my barn—say good-morning to the horse, & give him his breakfast . . . Then, pay a visit to my cow—cut up a pumpkin or two for her, & stand by to see her eat it—for it's a pleasant sight to see a cow move her jaws—she does it so mildly and with such a sanctity.—My own breakfast over, I go to my work-room & light my fire—then spread my M.S.S. on the table—take one business squint at it, & fall to with a will. At 2 1/2 P.M. I hear a preconcert knock at my door, which (by request) continues till I rise & go to the door, which serves to wean me effectively from my writing, however interested I may be. My friends the horse & cow now demand their dinner—& I go & give it to them. My own dinner over, I rig my sleigh & with my mother or sisters start off for the village . . . —My evenings I spend in a sort of mesmeric state in my room—not being able to read—only now & then skimming over some large-printed book.

The large-print book is that glorious edition of Shakespeare, attending him on his long voyage.

Ishmael knows it is time to put to sea "whenever it is a damp, drizzly November in my soul." He sets a scene: the modern city of Manhattan, and the histories that inhere in it: Indian, Dutch, English, American. His interest is in the history not of privilege but of the common man; and when he goes to sea, with his manifest intelligence and experience, he insists on shipping as "a simple sailor, right before the mast, plumb down into the fore-castle, aloft there to the royal mast-head. True, they rather order me about some, and make me jump from spar to spar, like a grasshopper in a May meadow. And at first, this sort of thing is unpleasant enough."

He is fueled by curiosity to see remote places and unusual things, in particular (a phrase that recurs) "one grand hooded phantom, like a snow hill in the air." Repetition creates leitmotifs that stitch memory together. Queequeg is "headpeddling," for example; other figures have their epithets as in epic, which the novel in a sense is: a close-up epic, told not by a singer of tales but by an insignificant participant. A democratic epic.

Melville starts building the story with a series of set-piece evocations: the Spouter-Inn, the first night with Queequeg, the sermon, Nantucket: the book proceeds by quite discrete chapters. One can take them as singly strung upon a narrative string, but they also build toward a rapt wholeness. Chapter 14 celebrates Nantucket and the Nantucket whaler, ending, "He lives on the sea, as prairie cocks in the prairie; he hides among the waves, he climbs them as chamois hunters climb the Alps. For years he knows not the land; so that when he comes to it at last, it smells like another world, more strangely than the moon would to an Earthsman. With the landless gull, that at sunset folds her wings and is rocked to sleep between billows; so at nightfall, the Nantucketer, out of sight of land, furls his sails, and lays him to his rest, while under his very pillow rush herds of walruses and whales." Many chapters are part of the narrative and at the same time essay summaries of the symbols and concerns of the whole book. The ship, the disposition of its mates and harpooners, all are dealt with in turn, participating in the symbol pattern and the narrative.

Melville's story is one of reversals (the theme of *The Confidence-Man* was already in his mind as he composed *Moby-Dick*). One expects certain things of a headhunter and a cannibal. Expectation is to be disappointed. The first adjustment comes when Ishmael recognizes the man in Queequeg. "For all his tattooings he was on the whole a clean, comely looking cannibal. What's all this fuss I have been making about, thought I to myself—the man's a human being just as I am: he has just as much reason to fear me, as I have to be afraid of him. Better sleep with a sober cannibal than a drunken Christian." This is the first step in recognizing the humanity of the ship's variegated crew. The agent of transformation is humor: Ishmael teases himself out of fear and prejudice, and in doing so raises interesting questions about Christianity, sexuality, marriage ("You had almost thought I had been his wife"), friendship, and trust. Remembering Queequeg's strong, reassuring embrace, he says: "My sensations were strange. Let me try to explain them."

One brilliant description follows another: of the street, of the entrance to the chapel, and the chapel itself. Then comes the organ blast of the sermon. E. M. Forster says that it "has nothing to do with Christianity. It asks for endurance or loyalty without hope of reward." Such a sermon has much in common with the traditions of Old English; it has almost a pagan tenor, establishing a dark order of being. No wonder when the preacher kneels and prays, it is as though his murmurings bubbled up out of the very depths of the sea. The irony is not lost on Ishmael, nor on us later in chapter 64, "Stubb's Supper," when Stubb orders the ship's cook to preach to the sharks that noisily pick at the hulk of the first whale slain. The parody is humorous and sinister, contrasting two versions of English, of God, of the Devil, two races, two ages, and two elements.

> Sullenly taking the offered lantern, old Fleece limped across the deck to the bulwarks; and then, with one hand drooping his light low over the sea, so as to get a good view of his congregation, with the other hand he solemnly flourished his tongs, and leaning far over the side in a mumbling voice began addressing the sharks, while Stubb, softly crawling behind, overheard all that was said . . .
>
> "Your woraciousness, fellow-critters. I don't blame ye so much for; dat is natur, and can't be helped; but to gobern dat wicked natur, dat is de pint. You is sharks, sartin; but if you gobern de shark in you, why den you be angel; for all angel is not'ing more dan de shark well goberned. Now, look here, bred'ren, just try wonst to be cibil, a helping yourselbs from dat whale. Don't be tearin' de blubber out your neighbour's mout, I say. Is not one shark dood right as toder to dat whale? And, by Gor, none on you has de right to dat whale; dat whale belong to some one else. I know some o' you has berry brig mout, brigger dan oders; but den de brig mouts sometimes has de small bellies; so dat de brigness of de mout is not to swallar wid, but to bit off de blubber for de small fry ob sharks, dat can't get into de scrouge to help demselves."
>
> "Well done, old Fleece!" cried Stubb, "that's Christianity; go on."

Earlier, in chapter 44, when Captain Ahab has drawn the crew into complicity with him, playing upon their greed, bringing them to his level, he descends to his quarters and there unrolls charts and begins to study them. We gaze in through Ishmael's eyes at the damaged old captain at work. Melville is careful to provide illumination for a scene, sometimes literal, sometimes mysterious. "While thus employed, the heavy pewter lamp suspended in chains over his head, continually rocked with the motion of the ship, and for ever threw shifting gleams and shadows of lines upon his wrinkled brow, till it almost seemed that while he himself was marking out lines and courses on the wrinkled charts, some invisible pencil was also tracing lines and courses upon the deeply

marked chart of his forehead." The transformation here, in which Ahab becomes continuous with the topography the maps describe, is integrated in this
moment into the very pattern of the world through which he travels, so that its
nature and his nature come into conjunction. Against Ahab's head we might set
chapters 74 and 75, in which whales' heads are considered, a meditation on vision
itself, the two huge craniums balancing one another on each side of the ship and
suggesting different philosophies and values. We must hurry our observations,
for soon one head will be cut free and sink to the ocean bottom. This close-up
observation and close-up symbolism are many steps beyond the allegory Poe
argued against. Here evil is embedded in nature itself, with a sense of wonder
that points back to diminished man.

Lawrence celebrates the symmetries of *Moby-Dick*. Indeed, this book appeals
to him so strongly that it blunts his polemic. He looks at the captain, possessed
of a purpose so strong that, like the humors of a Shakespearean tragic hero, it
will not release him. Ahab asks, "But do I look very old, so very, very old, Starbuck? I feel deadly faint, and bowed, and humped, as though I were Adam stag-
gering beneath the piled centuries since Paradise—." All of human failure and
alienation are piled into and upon him, a beast of human, not like Christ transcendent, burden. In chapter 134 Melville says Ahab has "food for thought, had
Ahab time to think, but Ahab never thinks; he feels, feels, feels, *that's* tingling
enough for mortal man." This fascinates Lawrence about Ahab, it makes him
terrifying, his inability to step outside obsession.

His three mates are human aspects of this figure whose fate renders him inhuman. Starbuck the Nantucketer comes first, a Quaker always responsible,
respected—afraid. He contrasts with Stubb, "fearless as fire, and as mechanical." Then Flask, a man without imagination, "stubborn, obstinate." In his eyes
"the wondrous whale was but a species of magnified mouse or water-rat." They
manage a crew of "renegades, castaways, cannibals." There are people of various ages, too: what's missing except in memory is women.

Then, crucially, come the harpooners, whose skills and presence draw into
play three continents, worlds of unfamiliar culture. Queequeg is a native of the
South Sea Islands, "all tattooed, big and powerful"; then Tashtego, the mighty
red Indian; and finally Dagoo, the enormous African. "Many races, many peoples, many nations, under the Stars and Stripes. Beaten with many stripes," Lawrence says. No wonder the Trinidadian historian C. L. R. James used Melville,
and especially *Moby-Dick,* as a lens through which to read the history of the
century preceding his in *Mariners, Renegades and Castaways* (1953). "The miracle
of Herman Melville is this: that a hundred years ago in two novels, *Moby-Dick*
and *Pierre,* and two or three stories, he painted a picture of the world in which
we live, which is to this day unsurpassed."

Meanings in *Moby-Dick,* some stated, some emerging from paradoxical juxtapositions, from echoes and cross-references, are inexhaustible. But does the book itself mean anything? It means what it does, the impact of individual dramas and how they play into the climactic events, the struggle with the white whale himself. After all that we have learned, to the culture we acquire in the progress of the book, the layered fellowship into which we have been initiated, destruction comes. This huge, uncomprehended presence of evil has an unacknowledged psychology about it, a lived sense of the fall.

Melville's last, posthumously published short novel, *Billy Budd,* takes place aboard a ship as well. Here the symbolism is more transparent than in *Moby-Dick.* A conflict is staged between good and evil. The very justice that ought to protect and preserve the good is the force that destroys it. Billy is impressed (kidnapped for conscription) from an American ship, *The Rights of Man,* into service on a British ship, the *Bellipotent.* He is innocent and beautiful. He is loved by Captain Vere and the crew, except for Claggart, the master at arms, who engineers his downfall. Captain Vere could not be more remote from Captain Ahab, and yet his rigidity in implementing the law proves as destructive as Ahab's zeal in pursuing his obsession and can be read as a parallel madness. The novel ends with an official account that turns Billy into a mutineer and Claggart into a hero.

"He isn't quite a land animal," Lawrence says of Melville, watching him "going home to the sea" as though he were a Viking. Melville was weary, and Lawrence hears him, as he embarks on *Moby-Dick,* declare, "Basta! It is enough. It is enough of life. Let us have the vast elements. Let us get out of this loathsome complication of living humanly with humans. Let the sea wash us clean of the leprosy of our humanity and humanness." Ironically, of course, the sea intensified rather than washed away the complications. Yet with some reason Lawrence says, "Never man instinctively hated human life, our human life, as we have it, more than Melville did." Furthermore, "the ugliest beast on earth is the white man, says Melville."

His last full-length novel, *The Confidence-Man,* deals with that ugliest beast. It is the first of April (the book was published on April Fool's Day 1857, the day of the action itself), and we are on a boat, the *Fidèle* ("the Faithful" or "the Fiddle"), this time a steamboat on the river that drains the American heart of darkness, the Mississippi. In forty-five chapters we meet the confidence man in various guises and disguises, and with him a number of travelers en route to New Orleans in pursuit of tawdry desires. The chapters carry suggestive and comic titles: "A Gentleman with Gold Sleeve-Buttons," "Worth the Consideration of Those to Whom It May Prove Worth Considering," "Containing the Metaphysics of Indian-Hating, according to the Views of One Evidently as Pre-possessed as Rousseau in Favor of Savages," "Ending with a Rupture of the Hypothesis," for example.

It is as though we were in imaginative regions mapped by Rabelais and Cervantes, Fielding and Sterne, worlds where grotesques with heightened human features meet, or collide, and define one another. But this is set in the New World, the grotesques are peculiar to it, and we recognize the beginning of an American version of the genre. Mark Twain develops it, with greater specificity than Melville in terms of the butts of his satire, as in *A Connecticut Yankee in King Arthur's Court;* and later writers—Nathanael West in *The Day of the Locust,* Ralph Ellison in *The Invisible Man* with its "unrealistic effects" that make the conflicts resonant beyond the immediate narrative, Katherine Anne Porter in *Ship of Fools* (drawn from a dozen sources), John Barth in *The Sot-Weed Factor* where the type and intensity of the alienating humor change from section to section. They share the American karma of a book that in its day bombed. It also may have affected the manner and matter of writers from beyond the American shore, such as Flann O'Brien in *The Third Policeman.* Only in the twentieth century, and not at its beginning, was the originality of *The Confidence-Man,* with its interrelated grotesque and comic narratives, recognized.

Certain writers recognize another legacy. It sails against the tide of American empiricism. Here when the narrator sees or says something, we can be sure that by the end of the paragraph or chapter the form will have changed, the initial sense will have been contradicted by what follows and another nature revealed. This instability is what puzzles readers keen for the narrative certainties of *Typee* or the moral consistency of *Billy Budd.* Everything is appearance: the closer we look, nothing in fact *is.* The herb doctor and the Missourian, a rustic but (unexpectedly) a true philosopher, encounter one another in chapter 21 and engage around the theme of slavery (a recurrent subject). The Missourian demands to know whether the herb doctor is an abolitionist, and the casuistry begins: "'As to that, I cannot so readily answer. If by abolitionist you mean a zealot, I am none; but if you mean a man, who, being a man, feels for all men, slaves included, and by any lawful act, opposed to nobody's interest, and therefore, rousing nobody's enmity, would willingly abolish suffering (supposing it, in its degree, to exist) from among mankind, irrespective of color, then am I what you say." This is a starting position: the argument goes in tightening circles until the hypocrisy is nailed. The confidence man of the title changes nature and shape. The word *confidence* is used in all its senses, from instinctive and unreflecting trust to the plays the confidence man makes upon it. In the end, on the paradoxically named *Fidèle* the only thing we can be sure of is that, on the first of April of this fiction, we can be sure of nothing. The confidence man himself may be a deliverer or a devil, the Deliverer or the Devil.

If Melville miscalculated his readership with *Moby-Dick,* with *The Confidence-Man* he went one better. It marked the end of his road as a novelist, even though, from where we read, the book is a vigorous and compelling beginning. Americans were not ready for this road. The Civil War was about to start, the Mississippi steamboat would not, for some time, carry so culturally and socially diverse a cargo of monsters.

In a short time the Melville who charmed British and then American readers with the seascapes and landscapes of the South Pacific, the soft-focus savages, the lived adventures, had gone into the deeps with *Moby-Dick* and into the absurd with *The Confidence-Man.* He was impatient always, artistically and spiritually. He wanted to play the game of art by rules of his own devising. His America finds an earnest, apocalyptic focus in the *Pequod* on the high seas of the world and a metaphysically comic one in the *Fidèle* plying the inner waterways of the continent itself. We are all tempted to invest in the Blue Sky Mines, we share in ideological confusions, most of us are moderate folk, with the limitations Melville discloses. There are things we should not like and should not do, but we like and do them unreflectingly. The anger that fueled the book was prescient. The war that brought the themes of *The Confidence-Man* to the surface was about to begin.

*The Confidence-Man* should be read in the same month as *Huckleberry Finn.* They share themes. For Twain the river is the way out, a place to escape to; in Melville's imagination it is where con men congregate en route to the rich human fishing grounds of New Orleans. Melville knew what he was doing in creating the claustrophobic, caustic world of this book. Early on he had been asked whether he went along with Emerson, a mind whose cast could hardly be farther from his own. "Nay, I do not oscillate in Emerson's rainbow, but prefer rather to hang myself in mine own halter than swing in any other man's swing." The image is of suicide, and also of freedom. Yet he loves Emerson who takes intellectual and imaginative risks. "I love all men who *dive.* Any fish can swim near the surface, but it takes a great whale to go down stairs five miles or more; & if he don't attain the bottom, why, all the lead in Galena can't fashion the plummet that will." Not Emerson: it is "thought-divers," himself among them, "that have been diving & coming up again with bloodshot eyes since the world began."

———·———

In the early 1850s American fiction came of age. *The Blithedale Romance* and *Uncle Tom's Cabin; or, Life among the Lowly* were published in 1852, a year after *Moby-Dick.* The first was a gradual *succès d'estime,* the second an unprecedented *succès fou,* the third (commercially) a turkey. Mrs. Harriet Beecher-Stowe wrote the book by which American fiction was defined in the popular mind in the United States and in Europe. Her success among contemporary readers, set alongside Melville's failure in his more ambitious writings, reveals the character of a reading public hungry for a contemporary literature directly relevant to the issues of the day, and an appetite for melodrama, which it has never lost. Stowe may not seem to dive so deep as Hawthorne and Melville, but her almost accidental book, set alongside their meditated and crafted work, provides a cautionary tale to writers.

Stowe's book might not have taken book form had it not been for the editor of the *National Era,* who serialized it week after week. It grew like a narrative blog and was immensely popular. He insisted on book publication. William Dean Howells remembered reading it in serial form, how it had begun "to move the whole world more than any other book has moved it." And this was before it was a book. "I broke my heart over *Uncle Tom's Cabin,* as every one else did . . . I felt its greatness when I read it first, and as often as I have read it since, I have seen more and more clearly that it was a very great novel." He concedes "certain obvious lapses in its art," its simplicity and even primitiveness, but these factors do not diminish it. It is "still perhaps our chief fiction," and it filled him with national pride.

It met with resistance from other writers, but that resistance her advocates regarded as highbrow, persnickety. After all, what do writers know about writing? Flaubert lamented her moralizing: Had she presented the narrative without finger-wagging, it would have been more eloquent. Had she trusted the tale, and the reader, rather than manipulated them. Chekhov said in a letter: "Madame Beecher-Stowe has wrung tears from your eyes? I read her once, and six months ago read her again with the object of studying her—and after reading I had an unpleasant sensation which mortals feel after eating too many raisins or currants." But his correspondent had wept, as many readers did. Reviewing *We and Our Neighbors* by Mrs. Stowe, Henry James exclaimed, not without admiration, at how she succeeded without aspiring to literary value at all; the writing seemed to flow from its themes, serve its cause, and accidentally to compel as a novel. Its themes are urgent, not only the root theme of slavery but also the exploration of Christian duty and freedom and of the moral role of women. John Updike notes, "Christianity in Dickens or Trollope is just a lick and a promise compared with Christianity for Stowe." She was surrounded by theologians: her father, her brother, her husband. She too did service as a teacher. The novel's divine burden was as much part of its popularity as its abolitionist one.

She was born in Connecticut into a large family five years before Emily Brontë's birth. Her brother became a significant preacher and then was involved in a scandalous adultery suit in which he was the correspondent. She married, had a family. They traveled, staying for a time in Cincinnati, Ohio, a staging post on the Underground Railroad by means of which slaves, with great peril and hardship, escaped bondage. There was much hearsay, much legend around the traffic out of slavery; she read the newspapers and met and spoke with escaped and freed slaves. This exposure inspired her, and she took the experience east with her when her family moved back to New England and her husband took a chair in religion at Bowdoin College in Maine. She was complaining of how literature was "removed from the parlor," where together women and men participated in it, and children might fruitfully overhear, to gentlemen's clubs and universities from which women were excluded. Her books were for parlor reading.

Published in March 1852, *Uncle Tom's Cabin* sold 300,000 copies in a year. Marveling at these sales, Updike reminds us that America was smaller at that time—less than a tenth of its present population, and lacking much of its land mass. "Everyone" read it. In 1862 Lincoln is said to have remarked, in welcoming the author to the White House, "So you're the little woman who wrote the book that started this great war?" *Uncle Tom's Cabin* sold equally well in Britain: first published in May 1852, it promptly sold 200,000 copies; a few years later more than a million and a half, though the author benefited less than she might have, because over half were in pirated editions.

*Uncle Tom's Cabin* drew fire from anti-abolitionists. They attacked it as inaccurate and opportunistic. The author, to defend herself, wrote *A Key to Uncle Tom's Cabin* (1853). She described the books she had read and the resources she had used. Subsequent scholarship has shown that some of the texts she refers to she did not read until after the book was serialized. A chief source was the autobiography of the escaped slave Josiah Henson, who, once identified, republished his book as *The Memoirs of Uncle Tom* and lectured publically on being Uncle Tom. He had made his way to Canada in 1830 and helped free others.

A crucial influence on her writing was Dickens, whose books she read aloud to her children. Her dialogue can be brilliant, especially that of her black characters and the language used by white bigots. From Dickens she learned about comedy and the force of melodrama as well as the irresistible impact of sentimentality on common readers. She also mastered the art of creating types: Uncle Tom himself, Eliza, Eva, villainous Simon Legree the slave owner, and many of the minor and comic characters. After the Civil War the prototypes she had established became stereotypes. An anti-Uncle-Tom literature evolved, provided first by writers keen to paint a rosier picture of slavery and discredit Stowe, and in the second half of the twentieth century by critics for whom her characters were reductive, harmful to an emerging apprehension of *real* black characters and black experience in fiction. If we set the book in the scales with Mark Twain's *Huckleberry Finn,* its essential lightness as a novel, whatever its force as a tract for the times, is revealed.

In "Everybody's Protest Novel," the first full essay in his first book of essays, *Notes of a Native Son* (1955), James Baldwin described it as a "very bad novel, having, in its self-righteous, virtuous sentimentality, much in common with [Louisa May Alcott's] *Little Women.*" It is on artistic grounds that Baldwin finds it wanting, though it is also, he makes clear, racially obtuse, culturally reductive. Wet-eyed sentimentalists are averse to actual experience. The demands of the theme, which he praises her for attempting, were beyond her. He says, "The failure of the protest novel lies in its rejection of life, the human being, the denial of his beauty, dread, power, in its insistence that it is his categorization alone which is real and which cannot be transcended." Almost worse than its racial categorization is its harsh, repressive Christianity.

Like Mary Shelley's *Frankenstein,* and for some of the same reasons, *Uncle Tom's Cabin* after a period of neglect has been restored to readership, to that canon of books we read because of what they say and when they said it. We read them with ideological attention. For George Orwell it is the best example of a "'good bad' book": "ludicrous . . . full of preposterous melodramatic incidents," yet it moves the reader and is "essentially true."

There is a tendency to imagine Mrs. Stowe as a sententious, remote moralist. Mark Twain admired her as someone with a popular touch and liked her as a person. He left a corrective in his autobiography: When he lived near her, she would come into the Twain house "at her own free will, and as she was always softly slippered and generally full of animal spirits, she was able to deal in surprises, and she liked to do it." When least expected, "she would slip up behind a person who was deep in dreams and musings and fetch a war-whoop that would jump that person out of his clothes."

# 20

# The Human Comedy

Victor Hugo, Stendhal, Honoré de Balzac, Gustave Flaubert, Émile Zola

"We were at Victor Hugo's house last Sunday week," Dickens writes to a friend in 1847, "a most extraordinary place, looking like an old curiosity shop, or the property-room of some gloomy, vast, old theatre." The place turns to fiction before our eyes. "I was much struck by Hugo himself, who looks like a genius as he is, every inch of him, and is very interesting and satisfactory from head to foot." Victor Hugo (1802–1885) was already famous as the author of important plays and poems and (among others) the novels *Le dernier jour d'un condamné* (1829, translated as *The Last Day of a Condemned Man*) and *Notre-Dame de Paris* (1831, known in English as *The Hunchback of Notre-Dame*). *Les misérables* (1862), culminating in the melodramatic redemption of Jean Valjean, a novel savaged by the critics but loved by the reading public, was fifteen years away. Dickens admired Hugo's work for its dramatic aspirations, and his personality for its dramatic shape: he was what a writer should be in scale, fame, and influence. (Dickens was also drawn to Hugo's handsome wife and daughter, who seemed out of keeping with the prevalent Gothic mood. "Sitting among old armor and old tapestry, and old coffers, and grim old chairs and tables, and old canopies of state from old palaces, and old golden lions going to play at skittles with ponderous old golden balls, they made a most romantic show, and looked like a chapter out of one of his own books.")

Upton Sinclair was the most vocal American advocate of *Les misérables*, reading the almost 2,000 pages of the unabridged French edition as a great sermon and echoing Hugo's own assessment of the work, not so much a novel as an orchestration of a human ascent from hell to heaven, an ascent secular in rhetoric but with a Dantesque ambition and even a glow of transcendence. Here is the imagination of Sir Walter Scott Gallicized, politicized. The history recounted is still a little in the past, but a past that is close enough to overlap with many readers' personal memories.

A life of the novel in English would be incomplete without some account of the key works and writers in other languages that give it shape and sustenance. Cervantes and Rabelais are constant companions to writers of English fiction, just as every French writer of the eighteenth century traveled with Richardson and some with Defoe and Swift, and of the nineteenth with Scott. The commerce between French and Anglophone literature was quite direct, and when American writers were intent on kicking the British grandmamma downstairs they turned to French literature as an informing resource equal with the English, a writing whose social concerns and tonal ironies were of a different kind from the English, yet possessed the same formal variety. Restless innovative American writers went to Paris and found their feet there. If some of them settled at last in England, it was with a strong residual investment in France, where the cultural imagination, especially in the nineteenth century, was itself in a mighty transition and was, as a result, less trammeled than the English in a skein or snare of insistent social, linguistic, and formal continuities, more apt to take risks and to experiment with subject matter and form.

Hugo's famous preface to the play *Cromwell,* written while he was little more than a boy (1819), hinges on the view that the traditional genres of tragedy and comedy belong to a (hierarchical) past. Modern drama, modern fiction, entail a Shakespearian mixing of styles and genre, abandoning the classical obsession with generic decorum and "beauty"—but for what?—for the Gothic, for a poetry of the "grotesque." This is not so remote in impulse from the realism of Balzac, whom Edmund Gosse described as "a realist haunted or attacked by phantasms and nightmares of romance," and whose realism itself tilts against stable genres; but observation is the key for Balzac, imagination and invention for Hugo: the accountable versus the emancipated artist.

The life of the novel in English is a complex and ragged story. It develops in contrary directions, it becomes almost impossible to hold the limbs together, each with its own impulses and intentions, struggling with the rest. Taxonomists and novelists themselves are always hunting for a tidier account, one that is not afraid to say *this is not a novel, this development is not true to the story.* Such versions exist and, however partial they are, they are worth attention if a major writer proposes them. Edith Wharton, writing in 1934 at the end of her creative life and troubled by the inexorable changes in the world of fiction, changes that she feared might obscure the achievement of her generation and the writers that meant most to it, came forward with her history. The French line, though not that of Hugo, is crucial to her. Her view was shared, at least in part, by other Americans, including Henry James. A wave of British writers keen to carry the novel as little altered as possible into the twentieth century might have made common cause with her.

Modern fiction, she declares, began when "the 'action' of the novel was transferred from the street to the soul," namely with Madame de La Fayette's *La princesse de Clèves* (1678) in the seventeenth century, the Abbé Prévost's *Manon Lescaut* (1731) in the eighteenth, and decisively with Diderot's *Le neveu de Rameau.* What separates the fiction of the early period, right up through "Defoe, Fielding,

Smollett, Richardson, and Scott," is "the great dividing geniuses of Balzac and Stendhal." She says, "Balzac was the first not only to see his people, physically and morally, in their habit as they lived, with all their personal hobbies and infirmities, and make the reader see them, but to draw his dramatic action as much from the relation of his characters to their houses, streets, towns, professions, inherited habits and opinions, as from their fortuitous contacts with each other." In fiction the material world assumes importance and weight equal with that of the moral world; fiction becomes a language of decisive embodiment.

Where do the French novelists belong in the plot of this story? After Scott? It was Scott, Balzac insists, who enfranchised him. And Honoré de Balzac stands rough and fleshy in Rodin's great casts of him like the still-damp and clayey maquette out of which Flaubert, Maupassant, and then Zola—and eventually even Proust—help themselves for their novels. Balzac affects English writers early, during his own lifetime. Thackeray, for example, watched the spectacle of *La comédie humaine,* with its more than 2,000 characters and ninety-five finished books (drafts, fragments, and disembodied titles have followed), rise out of the French language.

Yet it is a strain of emerging *American* fiction, rather than the British *Vanity Fair* and *The Eustace Diamonds,* that the radical nineteenth-century French writers recognized. They translated Poe. Irving and Hawthorne more or less comfortably took the French air, James and Wharton found there some of the energies they required, both technical and thematic. In due course Meredith and Stevenson, Conrad and Ford, Joyce and Woolf, Stein and Fitzgerald, Richard Wright and James Baldwin, found there elements crucial to their sense of self and their art. France was a space apart from their provincial, increasingly monoglot cultures, and apart from the constraining demands of the British legacy.

Twain laughs at French language and literature, the yellowing pages of a new French novel that delivers filth to unsuspecting readers. French: a language with which to entertain cats. France was in fact proof against such self-satisfied provincialism. After Richardson and Sterne, English fiction tended, says Wharton, "in the direction of an ample and powerful novel of manners." And so, "the great, the distinguishing gift of the English novelist was a homely simplicity combined with an observation at once keen and indulgent; good humor was the atmosphere and irony the flavor of this great school of observers, from Fielding to George Eliot." Part of the good humor and irony had to do with the moral ending, a sense that justice must be done and rewards doled out at the novel's end. Contrariwise, in France we find Balzac with his passion for extension, to get everything in; Stendhal with his for concentration, focusing in; and Flaubert after precision, to get it unambiguously right. That rightness is in thrall to no moral imperatives and is resolutely anti-sentimental. The energy of these writers and their monomania are intimidating and exemplary. Beside Scott and Dickens, the *formal* ambitions of Balzac, to bring an interconnected world to birth, were hubristic, but no less laudable for that. John Cowper Powys, a great laborer in language himself, was fascinated by *"the idea of his undertaking. Just the torrent of his energy, just its tide and every detail of that coffee-drinking."* Balzac drank coffee by the tureen.

So too Flaubert's exhaustive drafting, his inching toward the right, the precise phrase, his instinct for details that fix a real world in imagination; and there is the rolling organ blast of Victor Hugo as poet, novelist, and dramatist, and the flute-tones of Maupassant. And the Goncourt brothers and Sainte-Beuve, a critical literature and a literary culture whose priorities are aesthetic even in a highly politicized age, and for which morality, as expressed in literature, could be contrary to orthodox teaching, the imperative being another kind of truth and the happily-ever-after endings over.

What most troubles Edith Wharton in English fiction of the nineteenth century is the writers' reluctance to confront the reality of sexual relations. Jane Austen's "delicate genius flourished on the very edge of a tidal wave of prudery," she says, and the first great conformist to that prudery is Sir Walter Scott himself. Thackeray was not alone in complaining of the loss of freedom since Fielding's time. Wharton calls such self-censorship a "reaction against truth." Had it not been for this reaction, "this sudden fear of touching on any of the real issues of the human comedy and tragedy, Thackeray's natural endowment would have placed him with the very greatest." Trollope might have achieved work of greater maturity and moment, "and George Eliot, perhaps born with the greatest gifts of any English novelist since Thackeray, might have poured out her treasures of wit and irony and tenderness without continually pausing to denounce and exhort."

Denunciation, exhortation, the preaching of conventional morality (even by George Eliot, who was hardly conventional in her own life) tended to sell short a fiction that had been capable of whole vision, and to infantilize the reader. Wharton's favorite Continental novelists, among them Stendhal (Marie-Henri Beyle, 1783–1842), Tolstoy, and Balzac, perceived their duties differently: "to see life whole" was what they set out to do; "they took the English novel of manners in its amplitude, its merriment and pathos, and in their hands 'the thing became a trumpet.'" The psychological novel, Wharton insists, is born in France, the novel of manners in England, and "out of their union in the glorious brain of Balzac sprang that strange and chameleon-creature, the modern novel, which changes its shape and color with every subject on which it rests."

Stevenson agrees with Balzac, Scott empowered nineteenth-century French fiction. Voltaire's "starveling stories" were abstract, tending to parable; after

Scott the French story swells with fact and detail. "The introduction of these details developed a particular ability of hand; and that ability, childishly indulged, has led to the works that now amaze us on a railway journey." What was added by Balzac was one kind of detail; but Émile Zola (1840–1902), in order to "afford a popular flavor and attract the mob . . . adds a steady current of what I may be allowed to call the rancid."

In chapter 19 of *Le rouge et le noir,* anticipating Stevenson's and Twain's objections, Stendhal develops a theme he introduced six chapters earlier as an epigraph: "A novel is a mirror carried along a high road. At one moment it reflects to your vision the azure skies, at another the mire of the puddles at your feet. And the man who carries this mirror in his pack will be accused by you of being immoral!" The novelist's mirror "shows the mire, and you blame the mirror! Rather blame that high road upon which the puddle lies, still more the inspector of roads who allows the water to gather and the puddle to form."

Certainly young Julien Sorel, protagonist of *Le rouge et le noir* (*The Red and the Black,* 1830), stood in need of a little literature of indecency to advance his courtship of Madame de Renal. In chapter 7, with young Julian being tied in knots with indecision, shyness, lust, and ambition, the narrator—a devotee of *Don Quixote*—reflects: "In Paris, Julien's position with regard to Madame de Renal would very soon have been simplified; but in Paris love is the child of the novels. The young tutor and his timid mistress would have found in three or four novels, and even in the lyrics of the Gymnase, a clear statement of their situation. The novels would have outlined for them the part to be played, shown them the model to copy; and this model, sooner or later, albeit without the slightest pleasure, and perhaps with reluctance, vanity would have compelled Julien to follow." "Some people," La Rochefoucauld says, "would never have fallen in love if they had not heard love discussed." Most people, one is tempted to say. Poetry and fiction tell the reader how to feel, how to simulate feeling, and how to perform it. Julien has read holy works, histories, and some of the classics. There are parts he is fit to play. But he stumbles into the life of feeling without a guide. Stendhal's book depends on the innocence of entirely natural protagonists, for Madame is as green as Julien. Here in a pure form Rousseau is ironized. As Gore Vidal says, "The genius of suspicion has made his entrance on the stage." And Mary McCarthy, who writes so well on Stendhal's protagonists, insists that his main theme is, as with Lawrence—though how different their styles—the gulf between what one expects to feel and the feeling one actually experiences. This disproportion obsesses Flaubert, who did not like Stendhal's novels at all, and Proust, who did.

"Stendhal marks the boundaries of the more traditional nineteenth-century novel," says the American novelist and critic Francine Prose, "and then proceeds to explode them. Just as Fabrice [the protagonist of *La Chartreuse de Parme* (*The Charterhouse of Parma,* 1839)] keeps discovering that his life is taking a different direction from what he'd imagined, so the reader keeps thinking that Stendhal has written one kind of book, then finding that it is something else entirely." His omniscient narrator is epistemologically challenged: "He can't see why everything—politics, history, intrigue, the battle of Waterloo, a love story, several love stories—can't be compressed into a single novel. The result is a huge canvas on which every detail is painted with astonishing realism and psychological verisimilitude."

The poet Paul Valéry is right: "One is never done with Stendhal." Wise and wry, Stendhal is unable to be sentimental. The electricity that flows between Julien and Madame de Renal when at last Julien summons up the courage to touch her in the dark garden seems to proceed from a lightning bolt. Perhaps it was his avoidance of easy tears and easy satisfactions that delayed Stendhal's popularity in France and abroad until the end of the nineteenth century. Chesterton speaks admiringly of "the thread of irony which runs through all the solemn impossibilities of the narrative." This response to tone and manner by an English reader indicates his appeal for English and Anglophile writers. Without him, Lampedusa would not have composed *Il gattopardo* in the form, or with the unsparing tone, that he did. Stendhal was read by writers and those who knew about literature—those, for example, who went beyond the more famous volumes of Balzac and entered into the larger *Comédie*. Francine Prose, a great modern reader, says, "I love the way Stendhal uses 'Italian' to mean passionate, and how he falls in love with his characters, for all the right reasons. One can only imagine how Tolstoy would have punished [Fabrice's aunt] Gina, who is not only among the most memorable women in literature, but who is also scheming, casually adulterous, and madly in love with her own nephew. Each time I finish the book, I feel as if the world has been washed clean and polished while I was reading, and as if everything around me is shining a little more brightly." The cleanliness of the washed world is not moralizing: we see it as it is.

Not only is Stendhal's writing frank and uncompromised; it possesses a steady, engaged eroticism. Indeed, it draws on the author's erotic experiences not so much in detail as in occasion. On August 3, 1838, he writes, in English, that his beloved of eleven years "gives wings." They part in September, and back in Grenoble, over a period of fifty-two days, he dictated *La Chartreuse de Parme,* surprising himself with the plot as it unfolded, never sure what turn it would take. Italo Calvino calls it "the best novel ever written"; he ought perhaps to have called it "the best novel ever extemporised." Other novelists, James and Stevenson among them, have experimented with dictating their texts, but usually with forward planning and notes. Stendhal's improvisation, twenty-five pages a day, is astonishing: the book is so well organized that some critics doubt his account. The effort, like the story itself, is Byronic. (He met Byron in Milan in 1816, though the novelist-to-be was too in awe of the poet to do more than jibber.)

The noble protagonist of *La Chartreuse,* Fabrice del Dongo, is born in 1798 and is thus fifteen years younger than the author. His life is spent entirely within the span of the author's own, though he is Italian, and his Parma, a fictional version of the city, is remote from Stendhal's native Grenoble. Still, to Fabrice the author assigns a number of experiences from his own life, not least his service in the armies of Napoleon. Fabrice is able to experience firsthand many of the intrigues and events that for the young writer had been hearsay. The novel brings alive his time and, with a nuanced obliquity, aspects of his own life. Gina, the Duchess of Sanseverina, and Count Mosca are like characters out of opera, only credible, prosaic: as patrons they scheme in their adultery to advance Fabrice in the church, for which he has no vocation—certainly celibacy is not on his agenda. A failed affair leads to his killing a man and his detention in the Farnese Tower high above the city of Parma. The plots for Fabrice's release are elaborate, while he enjoys a charming, if complicated, love affair with Clélia Conti, daughter of the prison commander. He is sprung from prison, loses his love. Fabrice becomes a man of the cloth and a successful preacher, hoping to draw Clélia into his congregation. Clélia bears him a son and they try to devise a way of claiming him, faking his death. But the child does die, and Fabrice, alone, withdraws to the eponymous Charterhouse, where he dies. Gina follows soon after.

"I admire him, not as a model, but as a better self, one that I shall never really be, not for a moment," said Elias Canetti. Inspired by the Russian writer Nikolai Gogol, he used to turn to Stendhal, reading a few pages of *Le rouge et le noir* each day to keep his language fit and the detail precise and sufficient. For his part, Stendhal did not go to fiction, but getting himself in voice to dictate *La Chartreuse* he told Balzac in 1840 that he read two or three pages of the *Code Napoléon* to establish the objective tone *(pour prendre le ton),* to be always natural, and never to use factitious means to intrigue the reader. No wonder Ford described him as "a cold Nietzschean."

Stendhal frees himself of dogmas of all kinds and as a result is very hard to classify. In his *Notes on Life and Letters* Joseph Conrad, impatient with the way critics try to enlist writers in specific movements, celebrates the protean as the only free imagination. "It is a weakness of inferior minds when it is not the cunning device of those who, uncertain of their talent, would seek to add lustre to it by the authority of a school. Such, for instance, are the high priests who have proclaimed Stendhal for a prophet of Naturalism. But Stendhal himself would have accepted no limitation of his freedom. Stendhal's mind was of the first order.

[He] was pre-eminently courageous." One aspect of his freedom was his use of pseudonyms. Marie-Henri Beyle (his real name) became—among other pseudonyms—Stendhal. A pseudonym is a renunciation: the author as fiction, in most cases defensive but in Stendhal an aspect of detachment.

All that liberty and, as Proust points out, so many images of cells and prisons in which, paradoxically, the protagonist feels free of the contingent, of social compulsion. Some things are out of place in the novel, and Stendhal knows this, writing in *La Chartreuse,* "Politics, amidst the interests of the imagination, are a pistol shot in the middle of a concert. This noise is ear-rending, without being forceful. It clashes with every instrument." His own artistic error in this novel, from Balzac's point of view, was to include his personal experience of Waterloo, passages that had their impact on Tolstoy in his composition of the Battle of Borodino in *War and Peace* but that are extraneous to the novel. "M. Beyle," declares Balzac, "has chosen a subject which is real in nature but not in art." It was these passages that Hemingway enjoyed, "an accidental piece in a book that had much dullness."

It would have been hard not to write about that traumatic experience. Orwell reflects, "Among the flames of Moscow [Stendhal] read an English translation of *Paul et Virginie*"—for he survived Napoleon's disastrous retreat from Russia in 1812—"and during the revolution of 1830 he sat listening to the gunfire in the streets without, apparently, feeling any impulse to join in." Orwell finds in this detachment a charm. "There is something about him, a kind of mental climate, that makes it possible for him to get away with all the vices that ruin the ordinary sensitive novel." He is a beguiling narcissist, beautiful, we cannot resist watching him, he commands our *libidinal* attention. Paradoxically, the theme of *La Chartreuse* is magnanimity. The careful proportioning of the plot makes the improbabilities work. The protagonists are, according to Orwell, "spiritually decent." Apart from Waterloo, the book is timeless. The Duchess of Sanseverina may have bad deeds to her credit, but she has done nothing *meanly,* Orwell insists, nor has Mosca or Fabrice, each condemned despite his qualities.

The *charm,* as Orwell says, has much to do with the way Stendhal secures our complicity. From a superior and encompassing perspective he does not, as Tolstoy might, hector or lecture us; he draws us into his company, as a narrator he has a presence we share. It is this flattery, this collusion we enjoy: he makes us feel on his scale as well as in his company. "I implore the reader, if ever I get one," he says in the autobiographical *Life of Henry Brulard,* "to remember that I make no claim to veracity except in so far as *my feelings* are concerned." He speaks about the shadows of real facts, where his memory lives. Yet the *Life* is full of little maps, sketches, and diagrams where he tries to reconstruct the precise spaces in which the real facts somehow persist and trouble memory. It is clear how large a presence he was for those Anglophone writers impatient with the moral imperatives of the reading public as legislated by the lending libraries and the moralizing critics of their day.

Yet only Balzac celebrated his work while he was alive and maintained an interest in it after Stendhal died, from syphilis and other ailments. Balzac's essay on *La Chartreuse* became an introduction to later editions. Different as the two writers are, there is complementarity between them, one refined and perfected, a narrative reticence, the other copious, sprawling, universal, always at our elbow.

It was to Victor Hugo, equally copious, that Honoré de Balzac (1799–1850) dedicated *Illusions perdues* (1843), the third and last of his *Scènes de la vie de province* (*Scenes of Provincial Life*, which also includes *Ursule Mirouët* and *Eugénie Grandet* and is one of the thirteen subsets of *La comédie humaine*). He admired Hugo for standing up against oppression and asked his blessing on a book that is "an act of courage as well as a truthful history." Hugo visited Balzac as he lay dying seven years later. The story of this visit fascinated Samuel Beckett. Balzac had been abandoned even by his Russian wife, "a bitch of a woman," Beckett said. Hugo felt under the bedclothes for his friend's hand, squeezed it—no response. The body was already decomposing, though he was still shudderingly alive. "That's why there is no death mask of him," Beckett added. "When they went the next morning to take his death mask, applying the plaster to his face, his nose fell off. It was impossible. He was too far gone." With Balzac a death mask is a contradiction in terms.

In *Illusions perdues* he explores provincialism, a theme central to European and then American fiction. It has to do as much with attitude as with location. We have experienced its effects in Stendhal, where Julien Sorel slowly rises out of it, and is then destroyed by it. Balzac does not trust the reader as Stendhal does: he underlines what he means with essayistic strokes. "Far away from the centres of light shed by great minds, where the air is quick with thought, knowledge stands still, taste is corrupted like stagnant water, and passion dwindles, frittered away upon the infinitely small objects which it strives to exalt. Herein lies the secret of the avarice and tittle-tattle that poison provincial life. The contagion of narrow-mindedness and meanness affects the noblest natures; and in such ways as these, men born to be great, and women who would have been charming if they had fallen under the forming influence of greater minds, are balked of their lives." A powerful indictment—and if we are to believe the force of Balzac's human comedy, a true one, proven by example. Madame de Bargeton is taken to be a crackpot, given her enthusiasms and eccentricities, "but in these extravagances of hers a keener observer surely would have seen the broken fragments of a magnificent edifice that had crumbled into ruin before it was completed, the stones of a heavenly Jerusalem—love, in short, without a lover." The crescendo to the final paradox is irresistible: the rhythm of the prose persuades. Then Monsieur du Châtelet: "There was nothing that he did not know—nothing that he really knew." In such a world, when Lucien and Madame de Bargeton are drawn to one another, they have a common uncommon experience. "The obstacles at the outset of a passion of this kind are alarming to inexperience, and those in the way of the two lovers were very like the bonds by which the population of Lilliput throttled Gulliver, a multiplicity of nothings, which made all movement impossible." This did not make them any the less real. Thus later, in Paris where he has failed, Lucien "the poet" is seen writing drinking songs to pay for the funeral of his mistress; she lies dying in the next room. And his own death, in a later novel, is for one of Oscar Wilde's voices (in *The Decay of Lying*) among his greatest sorrows

To get Dickens, Trollope, Thackeray, and their British and American contemporaries into qualitative perspective, we must understand some aspects of Balzac, his formal ambitions, range, accomplishment, and failure. Trollope's novels relate one to another, characters and themes carry forward, but then the author moved on to a different setting and cast. Concerning *La comédie humaine*, Balzac declared, "J'aurai porté une société toute entière dans ma tête" (I have carried a whole world in my head). Excepting Proust whose world is, thanks to Balzac, more complex, other novelists go to him as to a credible, habitable world. The better we get to know his books, the more we understand how scrupulously differentiated his characters are. Some are observed, some imagined, yet unlike in Dickens, there is a lived as well as a sketched reality even in the smallest specks of his humanity. His characters cast shadows. The suffering of the virtuous characters in *La cousine Bette,* for example, or in *Le père Goriot,* goes unrewarded on earth and, one suspects, in the afterlife. Theodore Dreiser's Sister Carrie, on the brink of the love she never quite finds, begins to grow wise on *Old Goriot:* "She caught nearly the full sympathetic significance of it," even as her second, estranged partner is starving to death in the snowy streets outside. Hunger is more real, in experience, than love, except for the incorrigible old roué Baron Hulot—yet his last (is it his last?) marriage is to the aggressive and worse-than-plain provincial cook's maid.

Balzac's novels were serialized, and serialization took ambitious risks. The action of *La cousine Bette* begins eight years before the novel began serialization, in 1846. It ends in February 1846. Balzac risked the near past and almost the present. Readers were invited to measure the fiction against the reality they lived, the weather, the politics, the scandals of the day, to walk in imagination down the very streets of their cities and towns with new buildings and old leaning together. When the serialized episodes were gathered into books, even then they had the mud of yesterday's streets and the scents of yesterday's flowers about them.

In his preface to *Roderick Hudson,* Henry James, remembering his early failure to create credible places, recalls how he "nestled, technically, in those days, and with yearning, in the great shadow of Balzac; his august example, little as the secret might ever be guessed, towered for me over the scene." That example has in part to do with fidelity to things as they are. It made him useful to the philosopher Friedrich Engels, who wrote of a materialism that understood the connections between spirit and physical worlds.

Balzac took real places and made them more real, trying to replicate rather than represent them. A heroic attempt, doomed at best to partial success. "The idea of *La comédie humaine* was at first as a dream to me, one of those impossible projects which we caress and then let fly," he says in his "General Introduction." He was insufficiently an ironist to realize the impossibility of his project. There is something of the scientific investigator in his presentation of his program. "For does not society modify Man, according to the conditions in which he lives and acts, into men as manifold as the species in Zoology?" Not even two misers, or two cuckolds, are quite the same. "The differences between a soldier, an artisan, a man of business, a lawyer, an idler, a student, a statesman, a merchant, a sailor, a poet, a beggar, a priest, are as great, though not so easy to define, as those between the wolf, the lion, the ass, the crow, the shark, the seal, the sheep, etc."

He sets himself up not as a creator but on the one hand as a scribe, on the other as a taxonomist. Individuals can be classified, understood, in themselves and in relation. He knows the aristocratic curve of Lucien's instep, and contrasts it with the flatter foot of David in *Illusions perdues.* This is incontrovertible evidence of their difference in temperament and their complementarity. He dresses his characters for the sake of decency, but he knows them in their nakedness, even the dusty, frayed-genteel people, scented, powdered, and pomaded against age and pockmarks, who turn up at Louisa's party wearing as well their prejudices, carrying their title deeds. Two things compel the reader in these itemizations: their reality, and the concreteness of expression, a style content to name rather than decorate. Balzac was not writing "literature."

Zola, writing in 1880 in *Le roman expérimental* regarding the nature of fiction, describes *La cousine Bette* as "the report of an experiment that the novelist conducts before the eyes of the public." The nature of the experiment is like those he sets out to conduct. Zola sells Balzac short: "The whole operation," he says, "consists in taking facts from nature, then in studying the mechanism of these facts, acting upon them, by the modification of circumstance and surroundings, without deviating from the laws of nature." Zola's conclusion is that of a mad scientist, intoxicated by his power: "Finally, you possess knowledge of the man, scientific knowledge of him, in both his individual and social relations."

Balzac declared: "French society would be the real author; I should only be the secretary. By drawing up an inventory of vices and virtues, by collecting the chief facts of the passions, by depicting characters, by choosing the principal incidents of social life, by composing types out of a combination of homogeneous characteristics, I might perhaps succeed in writing the history which so many historians have neglected: that of Manners." In his view, no one had ever written a proper *history* of manners, how they emerge, how they change, how they connect in the material and social worlds.

George Moore sees the *Comédie* as a vast city: "As a traveller in the unknown East, standing on the last ridge of the last hill, sees a city, and in awe contemplates the walls fabulous with terraces and gates, the domes and the towers clothed in all the light of the heavens," so to the "imaginative reader" appears *La comédie humaine*. Fanciful, but accurate too: there is a four-squareness and material presence about the world of Balzac's books, and in his more mysterious and speculative fiction, such as *La peau de chagrin* (*The Wild Ass's Skin,* 1831), it is this solidity that makes believable his excursions into the transcendent. Moore pushes his image of the city further, speaking of endless suburbs and at last the center of this comprehensive world, where we find *Eugénie Grandet.* Unlike most novelists, Balzac revised to include *more* world—not to speak with greater complexity, not to poeticize, but to make it more real. His author proofs were a nightmare for editors and typesetters. Fat text balloons bulged out of the type areas into the wide proof margins: he added words, sentences, paragraphs, changed the order to lead more immediately into a scene, complete a movement. In one case the draft first sent to the printer was as little as a quarter of the eventual text published. The typesetter (it was a laborious and time-consuming task, and worse to correct) went mad; the printer was required to absorb at least some of the unbudgeted, though no doubt anticipated, costs. Balzac was not unaware of this, for more than any earlier author except Cervantes and Richardson, he understood the industry, as *Illusions perdues* with its detailed evocation of print works makes clear. He had *been* a printer: he ought to have known better.

Being lazy (this most industrious writer of all time), Balzac found revising the printer's proofs easier than making fair handwritten copies and correcting them. He could work fast, at times faster even than Sir Walter Scott. But when George Moore affirms that *La cousine Bette* was written in six weeks, the writer working eighteen-hour shifts, we might ask how long he took over proofs, and how many sets were required. The second part of *Sur Catherine de Medicis: La confidence des Ruggieri,* was "composed in one night." Do we believe this? It runs to about 30,000 words. Again, he must have spent longer correcting than composing it.

His father initially intended him for the legal profession, and he studied, probably in the same spirit as Eugène de Rastignac in *Le père Goriot,* not to follow the calling but to understand the institution. He was interested in the laws of property, and on bankruptcy he focused the closest attention. It is the force of money he understands. He is the first novelist with the artistic skill to foreground it, to use it to sharpen rather than diminish the human drama. Thus in *Illusions perdues* Lucien's minute spendings are enumerated, every centime significant. George Moore concludes, "Civilisation in the nineteenth century is money, and Balzac, with his unerring wisdom which saw into the heart of things, knew, or rather felt, that money would be the stake for which Christianity would fight its last great battle." And lose, from the evidence of his and later fiction. If, as Conrad says, "the fair truth of human delicacy can be found in Mr. Henry James's novels," then "the comical, appalling truth of human rapacity let loose amongst the spoils of existence lives in the monstrous world created by Balzac."

It is monstrous in part because it is merciless. Mary McCarthy contrasts Victor Hugo's engaged compassion with Balzac's detachment, the clinical observation of character that in Zola would acquire a sadistic edge. We read the dark passages of Balzac with the fascinated complicity we bring to viewing photographs of accidents: had the cameraman dropped his camera and intervened at some risk to himself, he might have averted a disaster. The thought crosses our minds, but we cannot take our eyes off the image.

In Venice, one midcentury summer, the *beau monde* dressed up as Balzac characters, speaking and acting their favorite roles. His impact on the imagination and fiction of Britain, the United States, Russia, Poland, and Hungary is great. As with Scott, it went beyond writing to couture, furnishing, and style. All this Sainte-Beuve concedes in his obituary, while attacking the man for lack of real knowledge, his "physiological *intuition,*" a good phrase to describe the way in which the novelist enters into the very bodies of his characters, as, for example, in the Baroness Hulot in *La cousine Bette* he feels her tremors, fears, and fevers. He "lived in" his work, as if it were a capacious but portable dwelling, like a snail shell to a snail. Proust knows that Balzac is in his art. "There was no dividing-line between real life (the one which is not so, in my opinion) and the life of the novels (which is alone real for a writer)." Listing artists or doctors, he mixes real-life names with those of characters from his novels, real too—like painters who include portraits in a crowd, or their own face on, say, the figure of Goliath. He praises Balzac's discriminated dialogue, leaving his characters' language to speak for itself, an artistic reticence that at first strikes us as out of keeping with his explanatory manner. He leaves characters remarkably free. "So in Balzac we shall continue to feel and almost to satisfy those passions from which the best literature ought to cure us." It is as well that his object is not literature, then.

Gustave Flaubert (1821–1880) read Balzac while he was still a schoolboy: *La comédie humaine* began publication in the 1830s. "What a man Balzac would have been, had he known how to write! But that was the only thing he lacked. An artist, after all, would not have done so much, would not have had that amplitude." It was the moralizing, the buttonholing, that Flaubert objected to: "He is a legitimist, Catholic, aristocrat. An author in his book must be like God in his creation, present everywhere and visible nowhere." Still, his world was congenial to Flaubert, to such an extent that Flaubert was shocked to find in him, notably in *Louis Lambert* (1832) and *Le médecin du campagne* (1833), passages close to his own, though when he wrote his passages he had not yet read the Balzac. Balzac's death affected him: he had hoped to get to know him. He had hoped Balzac would approve him.

Henry James met "poor Flaubert." "I shall always be so glad to have known him; a powerful, serious, melancholy, manly, deeply corrupted, yet not corrupting, nature. There was something I greatly liked in him, and he was very kind to me." James's adjectives are deliberately paradoxical. He engages the artist and the man primarily at a moral and psychological level: "He stopped too short. He hovered forever at the public door, in the outer court, the splendor of which very properly beguiled him, and in which he seems still to stand as upright as a sentinel and as shapely as a statue. But that immobility and even that erectness were paid too dear. The shining arms were meant to carry further, the outer doors were meant to open. He should at least have listened at the chamber of the soul. This would have floated him on a deeper tide; above all it would have calmed his nerves." It is as though James, of all novelists, wanted a looser, more obstreperous writer, one who elbowed his way into the drawing room and even the better-class boudoir. "He felt of his vocation almost nothing but the difficulty." It is hard to think of a writer who got closer to the heart of the matter, with such seeming objectivity. Lemot caricatured Flaubert as a surgeon, dissecting Madame Bovary: he holds on the end of a fork an organ that looks like her dripping heart. For his mercilessness James calls him "a writer's writer." Without Stendhal and especially Flaubert, Henry James might have been a very different kind of writer and English literature might have had quite another aspect.

Flaubert grew up in Rouen, where his father was a respected surgeon. As a child he was devoted to history and was writing precociously by the age of fourteen. His juvenilia and adolescent work connects thematically and in terms of narrative with the work of his maturity: he was hewn from a single tree.

Expelled from the lycée in 1839, he passed his exams with the help of private tutors and became a law student in Paris. Law did not engage him, but Paris did. In 1842 he composed a covertly confessional work, *Novembre*, switching experimentally from first to third person and including an encounter with a *fille de joie* who teaches him the facts of life and is rewarded by a life story not unlike his own to that point. He wrote the first *L'éducation sentimentale* (which shares little but its title with his great novel) and experienced has first major epileptic fit in 1844. In his three-volume biographical analysis *L'idiot de la famille: G. Flaubert de 1821 à 1857* Jean-Paul Sartre portrays it as "hysterical," a psychosomatic way of escaping the legal profession and adult responsibilities. Flaubert was treated gently after his illness. Sartre suggests that it licensed him to be irresponsible as a writer.

Giving up legal studies, Flaubert retired to Croisset, a house his father acquired for him outside Rouen, described by the Goncourt brothers as "a pretty homestead situated half way up a hill on the banks of the Seine," where he read to them for hours on end from his exotic novel *Salammbô* (1862). In their *Journals* they penetrate the sanctum: "Here we are at last in the study, which has been the silent witness of so much hard work, and which turned out *Madame Bovary* and *Salammbô* . . . In a corner is the camp bed, covered with a piece of Turkish embroidery, and heaped up with cushions." This is where he slept sometimes, between bouts of composition. "In the middle of the room is the work table, a large round table covered with a green cloth; the ink-stand is in the form of a toad." Here he wrote and lived. His father and sister died in 1846; his mother and niece Caroline remained his devoted family. The Goncourts admired them both, the one a little archaic, the other serious and hospitable. They visited again years later and gave an account of a household able to accommodate a whole literature under its roof.

In 1846 Flaubert met the writer and poet Louise Colet, with whom he had a sporadic affair and (on and off) an intense eight-year correspondence that elicited some of his essential statements about fiction and some acid lines about women—Louise in particular, a clinging mistress because he pushed her away so often—and love. "I write a love letter," he said, "to write, and not because I love." He enjoyed a more relaxed relationship with Maxime du Camp: they went on a walking tour and wrote a book of "notes" in which they alternated chapters; then they went on an eighteen-month expedition to Egypt and the Middle East, a period during which Flaubert developed his sense of artistic purpose, saw the world, and experimented in a variety of debaucheries. Upon his return to Croisset he set to work on *Madame Bovary*. Five years' work, it turned out. The early part of this slow, massive effort is documented in his letters to Louise Colet.

*Madame Bovary,* originally subtitled *Moeurs de campagne (Country Habits),* was serialized in 1856 in the *Revue de Paris* (though by the time it began publication, the book was complete, unlike the novels of Dickens, Collins, or Dostoyevsky, which were written during serialization with the risks that that entailed). He conceived a book "at the limits of possibility," the subject on the verge, or over the verge, of propriety; a subject of total insignificance, a *"livre sur rien"* (a book about nothing), held together by *"la force interne de son style"* (the inner strength of its style). "The best works," he declared, "are those with least matter; the nearer the expression approaches thought, the more the word is silenced by it and disappears, then the more beautiful the work becomes . . . Form as it grows skilful becomes attenuated; it abandons all liturgy, rule, metric; it abandons the epic for the novel, verse for prose; it no longer recognises orthodoxy and is as free as the imagination that produces it."

D. H. Lawrence criticized this very aspect of *Madame Bovary,* what he saw as a disproportion at the book's heart: "Emma Bovary and her husband Charles simply are too insignificant to carry the full weight of Gustave Flaubert's sense of tragedy." James agrees with Lawrence: Madame Bovary is made to bear too much on her restless, provincial shoulders. When Flaubert declares, *"Madame Bovary c'est moi,"* he means it, more or less, because through her he is excising from himself the romanticism he came to reject, what had made him love and later revile Victor Hugo. She is Don Quixote's god-daughter, led astray by reading.

As Proust says, *Madame Bovary* might have been called *L'éducation sentimental.* The challenge Flaubert faced was narratorial: his stance was to be virtually invisible. Stylistic and formal concerns were paramount, *"les affres du style,"* style's intense sensations. The absence of moral comment in so morally charged a book, about a provincial woman who marries, commits adultery and then suicide, and about her husband and his disappointments, required the absence of a directive authorial voice.

Flaubert developed the *style indirect libre;* as in Joyce, the thoughts of a character are set down without preamble, without "he reflected" or "she felt," so that inner elements carry the same weight as "objective" detail. The narration moves, without the reader being consciously aware, between "omniscient" or "objective" and the subjectivities of characters. Their sincerity or candor coexists with the narrative's irony. Jane Austen did something of the sort, but Flaubert developed it into the central principle of his art and reflected on its practice. Gore Vidal finds here "no such thing as a subject, style in itself being an absolute manner of seeing things." John Cowper Powys compared his prose to a "great cracked bassoon," which has something of Flaubert's tone about it. Here is Flaubert's own instrument: "Human language is like a cracked kettle on which we beat out tunes for bears to dance to, when all the time we are longing to move the stars to pity."

Proust takes us to the heart of Flaubert's manner. He resists the strong metaphors that lend "a kind of immortality to style" and seldom rises above the level of the speech of his most common characters. He does not entertain the possibility that this is the point of them, that they are—in *Madame Bovary* at least—in character, and their colloquial weakness does not draw us away from a character whose perspective we have assumed. Proust concentrates on elements in the prose that are hard to translate, the nature of the language that creates "the great moving pavement that are the pages of Flaubert." There is, he says, "a grammatical beauty (as there is a moral or a dramatic beauty) which has nothing to do with correctness." A sentence can begin in one place and end in quite another, and the forward movement of the style is not a progression of completed sentences but an interlocking pattern; a prepositional phrase or subordinate clause rises above its station and governs what follows. Proust speaks of the "hermetic continuity of style" achieved, hence the moving pavement.

He lingers over Flaubert's use of tenses, in particular the imperfect or past continuous, with things in the perfect past sometimes written as participles, withdrawn from the continuous past (the night advancing) and arrested. Often the subject is not human, the objects discussed have an apparent will of their own: "the hills were rising on the right," "the ocean was pounding on the left." Such things—phenomena or objects—are endowed with an agency equal to that of human characters. The imperfect tense helps to neutralize the narrator, things overheard or said can be reported without quotation marks. Proust speaks of the elegiac effect of such writing (we experience it with special power in *L'éducation sentimental*). And then there is the dissolve, achieved by verb changes: from the past continuous Flaubert suddenly emerges into the simple past or the present. The abundant conjunctions, adverbs, and prepositions function as a kind of rhythmic notation, defining the prosody, over and above their contribution to the literal sense. The syntax, Proust says, is "distortive." The distortion often imitates the process of perception. We spy out the young Charles Bovary in chapter 1, concealed behind a little screen of phrases and subclauses, hidden, shy. *"Resté dans l'angle, derrière la porte, si bien qu'on l'apercevait à peine, le nouveau"*— there he *is,* a very simple verb—*était*—and then the gathering of reductive ironies, so that by the end of the sentence we have not only seen but framed and judged the protagonist.

One must also take into account the nature of the *mot juste* as practiced by Flaubert. It is not only denotative precision and correctness that he is after. The *mot juste* entails appositeness of sound and tone: it must be mimetic and also correct in terms of register, the perspective from which it is being perceived and delivered; the loss of the French sound is the loss of part of the justness, part of the sense. The appropriateness of the sound (voice, depictive phrasing, larger cadence) binds it in. In the French sentence above, the perspective is that of a boy who belongs to the group, observing a new boy who is a bit absurd and who does not belong, and who may well become a fit target for teasing and bullying.

*Madame Bovary* "gave moral offense" and Flaubert was tried in 1856 for writing an obscene and blasphemous book. The censor's case was fundamentally against the alleged nihilism of the book that a "present narrator" might have mitigated. When Flaubert was acquitted in 1857, the novel was promptly a success, thanks in part to the trial. Flaubert's lawyer argued for a higher morality: Madame Bovary's fate was a moral caution rather than an incitement. Robert Louis Stevenson called it "a masterpiece of appalling morality," an unredeemed vision of a marriage and of adultery that presents the irresistible demands of the imagination and the flesh and the intractable social and spiritual consequences of those demands.

In the red and blue corners, respectively, are Emma, a selfish, silly, inadequate, sensual, and (to some) irresistible farmer's daughter, and Charles, dull, inarticulate, a prey to desire and low-grade ambition, capable of an inexpressible love. Rodolphe and Léon are selfish, mediocre, and, as lovers of married women often are, insincere. Monsieur Lheureux, the coarse moneylender, exploits Emma's depression and drives on the suicide. Bournisien the priest and Homais the chemist in Balzac's sense epitomize the provincial at its most impoverishing. In the end the priest sprinkles holy water, the chemist disinfectant, on Emma's body. Charles's unbridled grief occurs offstage and the reader is harrowed as much by the ironies as by the anatomization of the corpse. We experience it so intensely because the narrator and the husband have withdrawn: the narrator provides detail and sequence without tonal inflection. We are left with the appalling neutrality of it. Kafka was fascinated by Flaubert's "restriction of the field": How absent can the narrator be? The less he provides, the more the narrative demands of the reader's construction and engagement. In *L'éducation sentimentale,* Proust says, the spaces between the words rather than the words themselves, the rhythms and not the specific adjectives, create what he calls the "poetry." Flaubert provides templates, the reader invests them, a further perfection of the style developed in *Madame Bovary.*

His vocation was all-engrossing, he was a writer twenty-four hours a day, with or without a pen in hand. Some close friends accompanied him in his rituals and vigils. He continually reminded himself of what the tradition entailed. "I read Rabelais and Don Quixote every Sunday with Bouilhet and never tire of them . . . The more one contemplates them the bigger they grow, like pyramids, and in the end they almost frighten you." In such company he was bound to grow tall or wither. His horror of marriage was part of his discipline: "Elle pourrait entrer dans mon cabinet!" (She might invade my study!) His vocation was demanding, like a mystic's or stylite's. What kept him going were the "rages" of composition in a day-to-day life he flattened out with discipline. To his mother, Flaubert wrote, "If one gets mixed up with life, one cannot see it clearly; one suffers too much, or enjoys it too much. The artist, in my opinion, is a monstrosity, something outside nature." He respects the characters he makes. He told George Sand, "We must, by an effort of the mind, go over to our characters, as it were, not make them come over to us." Madame Bovary's integrity is independent of him. "It is one of my principles that one must not write oneself into one's work."

Madame Bovary took five years, L'éducation sentimentale seven. Other works crept in between times. To George Sand, whom he addressed as "Dear Master" and for whom he composed Un coeur simple, though she died before he finished it, he declared: "The only way not to be unhappy is to shut yourself up in art, and count everything else as nothing." This was, then, where he shut himself away, and Henry James found it intolerable. While Madame Bovary was a brilliantly successful application of Flaubert's theory (he saw it in such cold terms, from the point of view of a fellow practitioner, as Zola was to do), he pronounced L'éducation sentimentale "elaborately and massively dreary." He dismissed Salammbô, Flaubert's least-read and from posterity's point of view least-successful major work, as an accomplished fruit of detached erudition. This it is: years were spent in getting up its archaeological and historic details. There he invested the best of his experiences of the East. At the time it appealed to critics and readers and it sold. It is, Julian Barnes says, "what it is—a jeweled contraption that draws you in, and which you have to accept on its own terms. There is no point as a reader trying to compromise."

Madame Bovary and L'éducation sentimentale are also works of erudition, and Bouvard et Pécuchet (Cyril Connolly called it "that Baedeker of futility"), his most delightful novel, appropriately incomplete, is a work that takes erudition to and then beyond the edge of reason: 1,000 volumes were read for the notes of the first volume, and Flaubert is said to have killed himself by the labor of his unfinished investigations. "But my everlasting novel bores me sometimes in an incredible manner! These tiny details are stupid to bother with! Why annoy oneself about such a miserable subject?" Yet he did. George Sand encouraged him with the warmth of a mother and the coquettishness of an old mistress. It was Joyce's favorite among his novels. With Madame Bovary, "in terms of artistic control—the control of narrative voice and the use of style indirecte libre—Flaubert shows a new line and says, Now we are starting again," says Julian

Barnes. "And if *Madame Bovary* is the start of the modern novel, then . . . *Bouvard et Pécuchet* . . . is the start of the modernist novel."

The more he studies, the more he finds himself in history and imagination, with the reality of memory: "It seems to me . . . that I have always lived! And I possess memories that go back to the Pharaohs. I see myself very clearly at different ages of history, practicing different professions and in many sorts of fortune." Imagination is not a matter of acquisition but of recovery. "My present personality is the result of my lost personalities." He liked the quote from Goethe, "Go forward beyond the tombs." There are startling images of the kind that irritated Proust: he writes of his dead, "I am gorged with coffins like an old cemetery." And then, "Each one of us carries within himself his necropolis." A necropolis that clings to a stone: "I live absolutely like an oyster. My novel is the rock to which I attach myself, and I don't know anything that goes on in the world." And in bactrian mode: "I am like the camels, which can't be stopped when they are in motion, nor started when they are resting." He reverted to the long-suffering camels he encountered in North Africa on several occasions. "I do not expect anything further in life than a succession of sheets of paper to besmear with black. It seems to me that I am crossing an endless solitude to go I don't know where. And it is I who am at the same time the desert, the traveler, and the camel." The late *Trois contes* is an index of Flaubert's range, especially *Un coeur simple* where Flaubert's parrot is beatified.

*Madame Bovary* was less dramatic than descriptive: an edition restoring 200 passages that Flaubert had discarded reveals how the book might have inched forward, like those novels of René Béhaine (1880–1966) that so appealed to Ford Madox Ford and in which the fiction seems to occur in real time. *L'éducation sentimentale* is far more dramatic, the cast of characters vast, with larger geographies and important historical events lived through. In *Madame Bovary,* as he said to Louise Colet, "it is no small thing to be simple." Yet it was hard to be complex in the way of *L'éducation sentimentale,* where plot is secondary to the large social and psychological transactions, the outside and the inside, that contain it. Plot is also secondary to the aesthetic intent of the novel, which Flaubert describes synesthetically. The Goncourt brothers recall a meeting with the novelist in which he spoke with such lucidity that one wishes they had been his Boswells on a more regular basis. "The story or the plot of a novel is quite indifferent to me. When writing a novel my aim is to represent a color or a shade. For instance, the tone of my Carthaginian novel [*Salammbô*] is purple. In *Madame Bovary* I was anxious to produce a musty shade, suggestive of the life of vermin. The moral of the whole thing affected me so little that a few days before beginning to write the book I had a conception of Madame Bovary, which was quite different from the one eventually given to the world. Though the tone of the picture and the surroundings would have been the same, I had thought of her as a pious, chaste old maid . . . I realised, however, that that would make an impossible heroine." In *Madame Bovary* he had tried to stand apart but had become entangled with his protagonist, who outgrew his intentions. He could not be clinical: her protracted death filled him with physical pain and nausea. In *Bouvard et Pécuchet* (1881) he comments, "The author erases his work by shining too much light on himself."

But *L'éducation sentimentale*—Ford calls it "the greatest novel ever written"—is also a "nearly perfect group novel." The author escapes the fascination of the singular to a detached engagement with the group, and it is possible for him to be more evenhanded because he despises his subject matter, even though it implicates him. In a letter of 1866 he said, "Depicting the modern French bourgeois is a stench in my nostrils! And then won't it be time perhaps to enjoy oneself a bit in life, and to choose subjects pleasant to the author?" That choice had to wait for *Bouvard et Pécuchet,* whose experience of late middle age and retirement reflected the progress of his own imagination, from its naive and optimistic beginnings to the disabused clarity of old age. He had learned what was insufficient and what was untrue without ever quite finding what was sufficient or true. And the fault lay in part in the culture of his class. In 1867 he wrote: "Axiom: Hatred of the bourgeois is the beginning of virtue. But I include in the word bourgeois, the bourgeois in blouses as well the bourgeois in coats." It was bourgeois society as a whole, in its relations upward and down, and its carefully differentiated and nuanced subclasses within the class, that he anatomizes. After apostrophizing the illusions of the society his books portray and are read by, he sees them as "a consequence of romanticism, predominance of passion over form, and of inspiration over rule." A succinct definition of romanticism: "the predominance of passion over form"? Or if not passion, then seeming passion, the show of feeling, the Byronic excess that attracted and repelled Stendhal. "They extolled an actress not as an actress, but as a good mother of a family! They asked art to be moral, philosophy to be clear, vice to be decent, and science to be within the range of the people."

Ironically, *L'éducation sentimentale* more than any of his other mature works draws upon his own experiences of Paris. The young Frédéric Moreau, tenderly and mercilessly portrayed, is Flaubert's own youth, the relationships based on his. The education of the title is his, the reluctant law student, the romantic whom the world answers with its literality. The insistence of the body's needs, the might of money, history's fickle ways, are anatomized. Madame Arnoux's complexities far exceed those of Emma Bovary in part because the narrator does not presume to know her, or any of the characters he is portraying, in such depth as he did the characters in *Madame Bovary.* There is, as a result, much more imaginative space for the reader, more leisure, intensities of quite a different kind.

The social *range* is fascinating: the ways classes and ideologies readjust in relation to shifting patterns of wealth and power are a lesson in skepticism.

The book wearied Henry James, who returned with relief to *Madame Bovary*. And readers divide between the two books, or stroll on to *Bouvard et Pécuchet* and enjoy the eccentricities of two men of contrasting temperament who meet by accident (they both write their names on their hatbands, a sufficient coincidence to form a bond on a hot day by the Canal) and become inseparable. Chance, again, privileges them: they are able to escape their Paris lives and retire to an estate in the country, there to pursue a series of entertaining dead-end enthusiasms of the most instructive kinds in every field from farming to art, from architecture to literature. Flaubert has advanced to a gentler satire, comic but no less moving, that cuts into the human organism and finds there the almost indestructible organs of hope and optimism. Subject to time and to the vagaries of culture, the organism, aware of the world, lacks self-awareness. That is its redeeming grace. Flaubert dies, their story remains open, and the diagnosis: Are they "dangerously insane" or are they "two harmless imbeciles"? If insane, they partake of a higher sanity; if dangerous, only to themselves.

Flaubert enjoyed researching and writing *Bouvard et Pécuchet*. The encyclopedic challenge was of a different order from that of his dramatic narratives: this is in fact a series of dialogue essays with experiments embedded, moving from a known world of social intercourse to a space that, while literal, touches on the legacies of Rabelais that realism had pushed well out of practice. He seems to have set out to entertain himself and, incidentally, the reader. And he has returned to the company of Cervantes and the Knight of the Sad Countenance. Flaubert escaped the realism he perfected in his two great novels: "I curse what they agree to call realism, although they make me one of its high priests." And to Ivan Turgenev he wrote, "It isn't enough merely to observe; we must order and shape what we have seen. Reality . . . ought to be no more than a spring-board . . . This materialism makes my blood boil." This was to be Vladimir Nabokov's view, precisely.

It was partly through Émile Zola (1840–1902) that Balzac's and Flaubert's impact on English fiction was distorted and transmitted. In Zola we move from realism to naturalism, categories whose definition has exhausted critics and told us little more about the art of fiction than that "-isms" are treacherous unless they stay close to actual works. Zola's *Le roman expérimental* (1880) is a key. He regarded the technique he developed as continuous with scientific techniques of investigation. Henry James, writing about Stevenson, says, "The doctrine of M. Zola himself, so jejune if literally taken, is fruitful, inasmuch as in practice he romantically departs from it." His "naturalism," curdled romanticism, is anti-idealist and more uncompromising than Hardy's, though Hardy owes Zola a sour debt. He admired Zola's novels but condemned him for being untrue to his unworkable theories, for the disparity between what he argues and what he does: "to subscribe to rules and to work by instinct."

Reading Zola's great novel "about" alcoholism, *L'assommoir* (1877), Flaubert too was annoyed. Zola "has principles which are shrivelling his brain," he says, with a touch of jealousy: in his *Monday* articles Zola suggests he had discovered "Naturalism." He never mentions poetry or style. Guy de Maupassant is also impatient with Zola. There is no way a novelist can be wholly objective or express everything: "Selection is therefore necessary,—and that is the first blow to the theory of 'the whole truth.'" Neither Balzac nor Zola (and certainly not Hardy) manages to be as dispassionate as the theories of fiction require. Dostoyevsky and Tolstoy recoiled from this numbering of the lines in the tulip, this suggestion that with the right information and discipline, everything can be known and shown; Zola knew there was a limit to how much detail actually made sense, and how much began to unmake it.

This fascination with detail Zola brought to Britain in 1898–1899. Wearing a bowler hat and pince-nez, he spent his time observing nursemaids in Upper Norwood, preparing them for translation into the kind of fiction of which he was the great exponent. The book in which they would appear, in a translation by Ernest Alfred Vizetelly, son of the publisher Henry Richard Vizetelly, who was twice fined and went to prison for three months at the age of seventy for publishing the unbowdlerized English Zola, was *Fécondité* (*Fruitfulness,* 1899). Zola had absented himself from France in the wake of his celebrated letter to *L'Aurore* now known as "J'accuse," publically supporting Dreyfus. Zola, tried for libeling the General Staff and sentenced to a year's imprisonment, on balance preferred England. Vizetelly *fils* found him accommodation, and he enjoyed cycling in Weybridge and environs, wearing his bowler hat and changing his name once a week. He ended up at the Queen's Hotel, Church Road, Crystal Palace, "a popular haven for distinguished foreign guests travelling incognito," David Arkell tells us. Vizetelly recounted Zola's visit in the *Evening News.* They discussed the English birthrate and child-rearing customs. "Zola was all for breast-feeding: he was sad to note that in this respect Englishwomen had started on the same downward path as their French sisters. Indeed the ladies of Upper Norwood seemed hardly to see their children at all," so well-served were they by their nursemaids. He observed these gangs of girls and their charges "during his afternoon strolls to Beulah Spa. He told me how they neglected their charges and stood about, endlessly flirting and gossiping." This is why "the old master of *naturalisme* . . . amused himself by counting the number of hairpins left lying about the pavement." It was in London that he completed *Fécondité,* returning to France in June of 1899.

# 21

# Imperfection

George Moore, George Eliot, Louisa May Alcott,

George Meredith, George Gissing, Samuel Butler, Edmund Gosse

Zola's principal disciple in Britain was the Irish novelist George Moore (1852–1933). Contentious, opinionated, his knowledge of France, of London, of the arts and music, made him a churlish dandy. In *Conversations in Ebury Street* he remembers a chat with Zola: he was ingratiating himself with the author, being "almost a boy," and making Zola grumpy when he agreed that Zola's essay on Balzac was inadequate. Zola was fishing for a compliment, not the truth. Edith Wharton remembers Moore in full malicious flight at a luncheon party: "John Hugh-Smith with seeming artlessness drew Moore out on his great contemporaries, and James, Conrad, Hardy, and all others of any worth, were swept away on a torrent of venom."

In style, and diction in particular, Moore defends English against French incursions. He remembers a grouse-shooting expedition in northern England where he was inattentive to the sport because enchanted by "the beautiful English your gamekeeper speaks." He made his host admit that he too liked this earthy native idiom better than the acceptable social idiom of the day. Like many writers moving in higher social circles, his experience of the rustic was in privileged contexts where it was possible to be sentimental and sententious in the same breath. His father died when he was seventeen, and on reaching his majority he enjoyed a substantial annual income of between £500 and £4,000 per annum. "My object," Moore declares, "is to separate myself as far as possible from the language spoken in good society." Disingenuous: he is a perfectionist, but always in a bohemian spirit, always deviating from the norms of fashion. "Let the critic not inveigh against excess; let him remember rather that everything carried to excess is genius." And as a general escape clause, "Who should know better than you that we do not live by knowledge but by illusion." Gertrude Stein mentions him in *The Autobiography of Alice B. Toklas:* "Gertrude Stein and George Moore, who looked like a very prosperous Mellon's Food baby, had not been interested in each other." One can believe much of the gossip about his dandyism and ruthlessness. He was an intimate of Arthur Symons when he was writing *The Symbolist Movement in Literature* (1899), and he spent time with William Butler Yeats. They probed one another's Irishness. Moore returned to

Ireland for a decade early in the twentieth century to assist in the Renaissance. In 1911 he published *Ave,* the first of this three-volume memoir *Hail and Farewell* (1911–1914) marking his departure from Ireland and his decisive return to 121 Ebury Street.

Rebecca West moved to Ebury Street in her twenties, and there George Moore, her neighbor, became a kind of friend, dropping in some evenings for a chat. "They were not so much conversations as monologues; George Moore enjoyed talking about himself; but, luckily for me, his monologues in my house usually"—not always—"took the form of literary rather than amorous experiences." These entailed his unfolding the plots of planned and forthcoming books, including *Héloïse and Abélard* and *A Story-Teller's Holiday.* Then at last he asked her about her writing, which was near its beginning and less interesting to him than his own. Ebury Street he twice calls "a long, lean and lack-luster street." He made his nest there. He preferred conversation and a good bottle to the labor of composition.

Ford Madox Ford admired him (but in parentheses) as "probably the greatest and most dispassionate technician that English Literature has ever seen." He laments his neglect, due perhaps, he suggests, "to the fact that he belonged to no school in England; perhaps to his want of personal geniality, perhaps to something more subtle." He was hated by Hardy, who wrote his last angry poem in response to him, by Meredith and others for his criticism of them in his *Confessions of a Young Man* (1888)—a fictionalized autobiography that had a formative impact on Joyce—and elsewhere. His Continental affiliations, the fear that he might be Meredith's natural heir, his Roman Catholic origins, his exquisite taste in painting, his refusal to suffer fools (though he was not always a good judge of who the fools were and could sometimes be mistaken for one himself) put him beyond the pale.

Orwell does not share Ford's admiration for Moore. Of *Esther Waters* (1894), which he saw as Moore's best novel, he says, "It was written by a man whose fingers were all thumbs and who had not learned some of the most elementary tricks of the novelist, for instance, how to introduce a new character, but the book's fundamental sincerity makes its surface faults almost negligible." His sense of pity, not overdeveloped, avoided sentimentality, and as a result he has a just evenness of manner, ruthless when necessary. How can a great technician be all thumbs in his greatest novel? Ford respected Moore's attempt at an English realism, modeled on Zola or any other source; to Orwell it seemed crudely conceived and executed.

From the beginning Moore was a realist in something like a French manner, publishing *A Modern Lover* (1883) and *A Mummer's Wife* (1884) and drawing the disapprobation of the lending libraries for his detailed investigation of seduction and its aftermaths. He attacked the censoring spirit of those libraries and its effect on readership and writing. Esther Waters is a girl from Plymouth sent into service. She becomes pregnant, delivers the child, survives, and becomes much sought after as a bride. Like Mrs. Gaskell's *Ruth,* the novel is about a woman who passes from innocence to ostracism, and then returns to a kind of grace. It became popular and was one of the few of his works that he reread without disgust. It is one of the rare pure English realist novels in an age in which English realism was getting a bad press. He did not make common cause with fellow realists. Hardy, Gissing, and others who might have seemed natural artistic allies were unwelcome. When Hardy and Walter de la Mare dined at Ebury Street, they did not taste the food or wine, so intellectualized were they, so self-engaged: "an excellent Barsac was, speaking figuratively, turned to water by *Tess of the D'Urbervilles* and *Jude the Obscure."* Moore loathed the opening scenes of *The Return of the Native,* finding the description of Egdon Heath wholly without content and written for effect, a factitiousness that beset Hardy's ill-made melodramas, feebly written, the grammar bad: "Ours is after all," he tuts, "the literature that includes Shakespeare." Arnold Bennett, on the other hand, reading Moore's *Mike Fletcher* in 1897, declared it "vicious, meretricious, and—delicious." At this distance in time that last adjective recommends him for revival. Worth dusting down too, whatever he thought of them or they of him, are his contemporaries George Meredith, George Gissing, Samuel Butler, and Edmund Gosse, whose lights lie hidden under the wonderfully abundant bushel of George Eliot.

"It is a possible contention that after those two perfect novels, *Pride and Prejudice* and *The Small House at Allington,* English fiction had to escape from the domination of that perfection, as English poetry had to escape from the perfection of Tennyson," Virginia Woolf suggests in 1928. "George Eliot, Meredith, and Hardy were all imperfect novelists largely because they insisted upon introducing qualities, of thought and of poetry, that are perhaps incompatible with fiction at its most perfect." Fiction had to move beyond perfection to grow and survive. It took a variety of directions through the jungles of realism and naturalism.

Trollope regarded George Eliot (Mary Ann, later Marian, Evans, 1819–1880) as the second-best novelist of his time, after Thackeray. Her partner, George Henry Lewes (in honor of whom she chose the first of her pseudonyms), was his friend and "the acutest critic I know,—and the severest . . . He is essentially a doubter, and has encouraged himself to doubt till the faculty of trusting has almost left him." And Eliot was of a similar cast of mind. Her "permanent fame" would be based upon her novels, but this was a paradox, because "the nature of her intellect is very far removed indeed from that which is common to the tellers of stories. Her imagination is no doubt strong, but it acts in analyzing rather than in creating." She dissects things to see, then show, what is inside. V. S. Pritchett refers to her as "the great schoolmistress." If we attend her class, we feel in the presence more of a philosopher than of a novelist, something one might say of those later writers who have learned from her, Iris Murdoch, for example, and A. S. Byatt, for whom exploring ideas is at least as important as developing narrative. How difficult for young readers her novels must be, Trollope reflects; hard to extract pleasure from *Felix Holt, Middlemarch,* or *Daniel Deronda:* "I know that they are very difficult to many that are not young," too, among whom he numbered himself. It is worth persevering, and Trollope takes particular pleasure in George Eliot's most rebarbative work, her historical novel *Romola.* She could hardly be less like Trollope. Stevenson is a reluctant admirer: "A high, but, may we not add?—a rather dry lady. Did you—I forget—did you have a kick at the stern works of that melancholy puppy and humbug Daniel Deronda himself?" He goes on to anatomize this awkward Eliot character, her final major creation, "the Prince of prigs; the literary abomination of desolation in the way of manhood; a type which is enough to make a man forswear the love of women, if that is how it must be gained." He adds: "Hats off all the same, you understand: a woman of genius."

Arnold Bennett strikes an offensively contrary note: Eliot is *a woman.* The style of *Adam Bede* is "feminine in its lack of restraint, its wordiness, and the utter absence of feeling for form which characterizes it"; even though, unlike other women writers, Eliot does not season the text with italics, she creates the same effect as if she had. He brings the Brontë sisters into the sweep of his generalization. Elsewhere he says Eliot "was too preoccupied by moral questions to be a first-class creative artist. And she was a woman. A woman, at that epoch, dared not write an entirely honest novel! Nor a man either! Between Fielding and Meredith no entirely honest novel was written by anybody in England. The fear of the public, the lust of popularity, feminine prudery, sentimentalism, Victorian niceness—one or other of these things prevented honesty."

Her chief defect, Trollope declares, is that "she struggles too hard to do work that shall be excellent," not a struggle Trollope ever conducted as he dropped one novel after another behind him, seldom looking back. "She lacks ease. Latterly the signs of this have been conspicuous in her style, which has always been and is singularly correct, but which has become occasionally obscure from her too great desire to be pungent." He wrote about her while *Daniel Deronda* was still being serialized; he was struggling with its considered opacities sentence by sentence.

If she was as Trollope paints her, then she failed on her own terms. She expressed herself against "purposive" literature, in the 1870s scorning "that dead anatomy of culture which turns the universe into a mere ceaseless answer to questions." Yet with Goethe's her own writing does share a kind of purposiveness: no description is ever there for its own sake; it has a metaphorical or symbolic function. This sense of intent and design, the sparseness of innocent detail, puts certain effects and certain kinds of character beyond her. The gratuitous is absent. Everything is itself, plus.

In *Adam Bede* Proust was struck by "the attentive, meticulous, respectful, poetic and sympathetic portrayal of the humblest, most hard-working life." Homely qualities, the importance of domestic hygiene and a respect for life's dailiness, the duty and dignity of it, stayed with him. Here Proust found a sense of the larger order that makes sense of the seeming inconsequentialities, injustices, and tragedies of daily life. And he makes a natural connection with Emerson's "Compensation": in *Silas Marner,* Silas loses the gold and this opens for him the love of the child. Her feeling for nature "animates rather than depicts it"; hers is "a quite new and affectionate view of things." Eliot demonstrates the gradual development of sympathy and affection. The harm we do is wrong; the harm done to us can lead to our improvement, part of "a greater good that God wanted to do us." In writing of her, Proust himself turns moralist from the sweet contagion of her manner. George Moore, reading *Silas Marner,* grew impatient: "Ah, if she had been less purposeful!" How could she be otherwise? Mary McCarthy reminds us, "The popular novelist (and there was no other kind, the art novel not having been discovered) was looked up to as an authority on all sorts of matters," and with Eliot, as with Dickens and earlier with Fielding, this entailed a didactic strain. What may irritate Moore, and the modern reader, is the rigor of the moral inflection.

Born in Nuneaton, Warwickshire, the landscape of much of her fiction, she was brought up in a strict Anglican low-church environment. Her father was a successful estate manager and she traveled about with him, attentive to the cottages, the people and fields, the plants and seasons, the creatures: an education supplemented by reading. Her father secured her access to the library of his employers at Arbury Hall. She read in a not disorganized, wide-ranging way. She and her elder brother Isaac (they are not unlike Maggie and Tom in *The Mill on the Floss*) were sent to local boarding schools. In her early, pious phase, like Dorothea Brooke in *Middlemarch* ("that priggish lioness is my favorite female character in any fiction," says Nadine Gordimer), whom she creates with such tenderness, both in her naivety and in her slow-garnered maturity, she studied what she believed would enhance her Christian knowledge and understanding. Romances and novels were unthinkable. Unlike Dorothea, Mary Ann Evans was certainly unconventional to look at, even "plain."

The family moved to Coventry, at that time a handsome old town. She walked along wider streets inhaling "the air of old-fashioned provincialism." Writing late in life, she imagines the pasts of people clad in anonymizing costumes, their particular histories not unlike her own, "among the midland villages and markets, along by the tree-studded hedgerows, and where the heavy barges seem in the distance to float mysteriously among the rushes and the feathered grass." Such writing refutes those who say her style is pleasureless. These fellow provincials and she have seen much since childhood, but "joy in our native landscape" remains "one deep root of our national life and language." Her Midlands ("Loamville": not a memorable name) are comparable to Bennett's Five Towns and Hardy's Wessex: she has, unfussily, her landscapes; imagination faltered when she moved outside them.

She encountered the dissenters of her day active in the Midlands. Her faith weakened. She continued to attend church with her father. She kept up appearances for his sake. Five days after he died, she traveled to Switzerland with friends to pursue her studies.

Moore read Eliot's style as born of "a conflict between theory and conduct," a struggle that began in her late teens and continued unresolved into her last writings: it might have been settled had she opted for a frank paganism, or set out in pursuit of pleasure, something to move her decisively away from the Christian imperatives. Her crisis is not peculiar to her sex, her country, or her age. Albert Camus wrote in French a century later, "What interests me is knowing how we should behave, and more precisely, knowing how to behave when one does not believe in God or reason." Had Eliot been able to make public her irregular domestic arrangement with Lewes, that too might have had an impact on the freedom with which she thought and wrote. But though she had the courage to follow her inclinations in life, she could not write candidly from them. Lord Leighton provided the illustrations for *Romola*. Ideal, says Moore, since Leighton and Eliot were both "workers in wax."

She is still at the heart of our sense of the novel but is more honored than read for pleasure. Virginia Woolf speaks of her with respect, but—apart from *Middlemarch*—without affection. She resists her dialogue except in dialect; she finds her too often humorless and unsubtle, not *driven* the way the Brontës are. There is something foursquare about her. Edmund Gosse sees her as heavy-featured, crowned by a hat "always in the height of Paris fashion, which in those days commonly included an immense ostrich feather." Woolf says, "To read George Eliot attentively, is to become aware how little one knows about her."

*Silas Marner* and *Middlemarch* are studied and discussed; the other novels appeal more narrowly, and her verse, critical writings, and translations are specialist territory. Her "rich and well-balanced" prose and solid construction "were not enough to save her from the whirling, bubbling flood of Time; her books have gone down like the mill." Moore overstates the case, but her books have grown stiff with intention—artistic, yes, but more pressingly philosophical and moral. She was naturally inclined to philosophy, and Lewes suggested "prose narrative as an outlet for her genius": a philosopher novelist is what she became. Reading her is a task of comprehension. The functionality of the prose, in which she surpasses Trollope, and her sweet, sometimes ironic earnestness—story and moral, not language and construction, being the object—set her in a didactic frame. Serious response to her work entails interpretative engagement. The novels are never ends, always means.

The publisher John Chapman, with whom Marian Evans lodged when she returned to London from Switzerland in 1850, was at the center of a radical milieu congenial to her. As a young man of twenty-three, Thomas Carlyle had singled Chapman out to be the British publisher of Emerson. Chapman was not an intellectual, though he wished to be. He was slippery and sincere, scheming yet committed. He tried his authors' patience, picked their pockets, and strove to shine and to be seen to shine among them. He was a philanderer: when Mary Ann Evans came to lodge, he lived with his wife, two children, and their nanny, who moonlighted as his mistress. Wife and nanny were uncomfortable with Mary Ann's presence, not without reason. She was for a time more than Chapman's assistant. He was excluded from Eliot's first biography, written by her short-lived husband and long-lived American widower, the banker John Cross, twenty years her junior and a devoted memorialist. He worked with her and Lewes as bookkeeper and adviser, and it seemed a natural step to take her on once Lewes died. He was unsettled in mind and on the honeymoon journey to Italy, where they were translating Dante together, he threw himself off their hotel balcony into the Grand Canal in a suicide attempt. He was rescued by their quick-witted gondolier.

Chapman's house on the Strand—publishing house, lodging house, bookshop—was a place of soirées. Emerson, Horace Greeley, G. H. Lewes, T. H. Huxley (who devised the term *agnostic*), J. A. Froude (troubled younger brother of Richard Hurrell Froude, Newman's intimate), F. W. Newman (troubled younger brother of John Henry Newman), Mrs. Gaskell, the poet Arthur Hugh Clough, and radical exiles including Mazzini, Pierre Leroux, and a Mr. Merks all passed through. Chapman met Mr. Merks at a friend's house for dinner. He was to be recognized in time as Karl Marx, and Chapman nearly published his work.

He did publish David Friedrich Strauss's *The Life of Jesus* in Miss Evans's translation, a book that contributed to theological ferment (he paid her £20 for two years' work on it). Mary McCarthy says this exercise left a deep mark of discipline on Mary Ann Evans: "I think that this kind of training really makes one more interested in the subject than in the style. Her work certainly does not suffer from any kind of stylistic frippery. There's certainly no voluminous drapery around." And it is excessive attention to "drapery" that for McCarthy announces intrusively the gender of a writer. An interest in décor, on the other hand, indicates a feminine sensibility: "You notice the change in Elizabeth Bowen. Her early work is much more masculine. Her later work has much more drapery in it. Who else?" Then she begins blotting her copybook: "Jane Austen was never a 'woman writer,' I don't think."

Chapman also published Auguste Comte and other innovative thinkers from the Continent. One of the few novels he brought out was J. A. Froude's *The Nemesis of Fate,* a story of brotherly sadism, at once insufficiently fictional and insufficiently autobiographical to work. The theme is close to Mary Ann Evans's concerns: What happens to a young man who discovers he cannot in conscience preach or administer the sacraments of the Church of England? An Oxford don burned a copy of the book before the students of Exeter College. Marianne Evans read it with minute attention. "If any one under the sun has a magical, magnetic, glamour-like influence, that man has. He's 'aut Mephistopheles aut nihil' [either Mephistopheles or nothing], that's what he is." A friend described Froude's "strange elfin beauty," and how he never looked at you directly but saw everything nonetheless.

She was close to Froude, to Herbert Spencer (to whom she wrote plaintively, "I can be satisfied with very little, if I am delivered from the dread of losing it"), and at last to Lewes, a married man with whom she chose to spend her life despite the social stigma. Her love for Lewes ended her relations with Chapman. She knew what she was doing and did not casually decide. "Light and easily broken ties are what I neither desire theoretically nor could live for practically. Women who are satisfied with such ties do not act as I have done— they obtain what they desire and are still invited to dinner." She stopped being invited and after a time ceased to care.

Always independent, she was not drawn to a sisterhood of writers. In "Silly Novels by Lady Novelists," Gaskell and Charlotte Brontë excepted, George Eliot discriminates four kinds of fiction writer she was required to read: "the frothy, the prosy, the pious, or the pedantic." Her least favorite variety is "the mind-and-millinery" novel. This essay precedes her first serious efforts in fiction but seems by negatives to map out a personal creative and moral space. "Every art which has its absolute *technique* is, to a certain extent, guarded from the intrusions of mere left-handed imbecility. But in novel-writing there are no barriers for incapacity to stumble against, no external criteria to prevent a writer from mistaking foolish facility for mastery. And so we have again and again the old story of La Fontaine's ass, who puts his nose to the flute, and, finding that he elicits some sound, exclaims, 'Moi, aussi, je joue de la flute'—a fable which we commend, at parting, to the consideration of any feminine reader who is in danger of adding to the number of 'silly novels by lady novelists.'" She knew what to avoid, writing toward the end of her life, "bad literature of the sort called amusing is spiritual gin." Her most eloquent female seconder in the twentieth century was Dorothy Parker, who in an interview, briefly absenting herself from her sex, said of women writers, "They gush. Norris said she never wrote a story unless it was fun to do. I understand Ferber whistles at her typewriter. And there was that poor sucker Flaubert rolling around on his floor for three days looking for the right word."

In September 1855 George Eliot began writing fiction. "I always thought I was deficient in dramatic power, both of construction and of dialogue"—and in a way she was right. Still, she took a chapter she had drafted early on, when she went to Germany with Lewes to firm up their relationship and do research for his Goethe biography, and one day she read it to him. He encouraged her. Later, at Tenby, he pressed her to start a story. She resisted. "But one morning as I was thinking what should be the subject of my first story, my thoughts merged themselves into a dreamy doze, and I imagined myself writing a story, of which the title was 'The Sad Fortunes of the Reverend Amos Barton.'" She told her dream to Lewes. He approved. She was thirty-seven. This most rational creature started her first novel from a dream.

In her fervently religious youth she was filled with guilt when she read a novel, as when she read Byron, the spiritual equivalent to masturbation, contaminating the mind and spirit. Dorothea in *Middlemarch* is like this. When at last she marries she is free to read whatever she likes. Before that, preparing for the married state, her reading, like a diet, was for moral development and fortification.

Once Mary Ann Evans outlived adolescent scruple, she read Scott's novels and poems, sharing them aloud with her father each evening. From Scott she learned that descriptions should have more than literal significance. When she went to London she read novels by George Sand and Balzac, some with pleasure and instruction, others with distress. *Scenes from Clerical Life,* a projected series of stories, begins with *Amos Barton. Scenes* was published anonymously. Dickens, reading with his usual clarity, sensed from the language that it was the work of a woman.

When she sent the first *Scenes* to John Blackwood, she began one of the most congenial relations an author has ever enjoyed with a publisher. It profited both parties. Beyond material ambitions, a sense of responsibility settled on her. James notes how she came to accept "the great obligations which to her mind belonged to a person who had the ear of the public, and her whole effort thenceforth was highly to respond to them—to respond to them by teaching, by vivid moral illustration and even by inner exhortation." This moral purpose is part of her legacy: she wants her books to be good and do good, with the earnestness of one of her more energetic fictional clergymen. The year before *Scenes* appeared, *Madame Bovary* survived its trial and became a best seller in France. The distance between the two literatures could hardly be more accurately measured than by the distance between these two works, their sense of form, moral intent, and readership.

*Adam Bede* (1859), her first full-length novel, is a significant development in scale and purpose: a moral tale in which the good carpenter Adam's steadfastness and virtue are tried through his love of a woman who slowly and painfully becomes worthy of him. The opening passage proclaims the world of imagination, then a wholly recognizable scene unfolds, as though the real surrenders its full sense to this enchantment: "With a single drop of ink for a mirror, the Egyptian sorcerer undertakes to reveal to any chance comer far-reaching visions of the past. This is what I undertake to do for you, reader. With this drop of ink at the end of my pen, I will show you the roomy workshop of Mr. Jonathan Burge, carpenter and builder, in the village of Hayslope, as it appeared on the eighteenth of June, in the year of our Lord 1799." All the reader's senses are alerted. "The afternoon sun was warm"—yes, but it was warm "on the five workmen"—its warmth not only declared but registered on a group of people who are at work on "doors and window-frames and wainscoting"—building houses. The smell of the worked wood, and wafting in from outside the senses register "the scent of the elder-bushes" in bloom, "spreading their summer snow." It is a luminous confusion of senses, "seem" and "is" in tension.

The reader is deep in the scene in no time, that drop of ink dilating into vision, like a pupil coming awake. It is through the eyes of "a rough, grey shepherd dog" drowsing, "his nose between his forepaws," that we first see "the tallest of the five workmen, who was carving a shield in the centre of a wooden mantelpiece." He is singing in a "strong barytone," singing a hymn ("Awake, my soul, and with the sun . . ." by Thomas Ken) to the accompaniment of the noise his tools make. He stops, focuses, measures, starts again, the voice louder, and we follow it into the man himself: "Such a voice could only come from a broad chest, and the broad chest belonged to a large-boned, muscular man nearly six feet high, with a back so flat and a head so well poised that when he drew himself up to take a more distant survey of his work, he had the air of a soldier standing at ease." We see his strong arm, his "long supple hand." And then he is named: "In his tall stalwartness Adam Bede was a Saxon, and justified his name." Lest we think he has been idealized, the narrator, clearly in thrall to the magic herself, brings the tone back a little: "The face was large and roughly hewn, and when in repose had no other beauty than such as belongs to an expression of good-humored honest intelligence." This at first remarkable man is, in the end, not so remarkable: he is a type as well. A man and an every-man. A. S. Byatt regards the narrator in Eliot not as omniscient but possessing, rather, the kind of knowledge the chorus has in Greek tragedy, speaking in the "common human voice," thus drawing attention to Eliot's subtlety relative to Thackeray, Trollope, and other contemporaries.

Adam's beloved Hetty, evoked with equal tact, is seduced by Arthur Donni-thorne, son of the local squire. Adam sees him off but not before Hetty has got pregnant. When she realizes, she goes in search of Arthur, fails to find him, bears the child, and is arraigned and condemned for its murder. She is reprieved, Adam's virtue and her penitence are rewarded, and the novel ends by restoring a somber normality more reflective than the vigorous hope with which it be-gins. The plot, had Hardy handled it, would have ended darkly, but there is a redeeming warmth in Eliot's moral. Almost any man or woman can be redeemed if sin is acknowledged and repented. *Adam Bede* is a simple tale, satisfying in structure and the economy of the telling. "As time goes by," Pritchett says, "*Adam Bede* looks like our supreme novel of pastoral life." In it Eliot owes a debt to Scott's *The Heart of Midlothian,* but her book is more credible in acknowledging, mutedly, the instincts and needs of her characters, and at the level of characters in relationship it has, Pritchett shows, a more adult appeal than Scott's. He brings history alive, but Eliot, limning a smaller canvas and using a truer palette, tells the reader about several kinds of love and their consequences in a moral world.

The task of the novelist is close to that of the reconstructing historian, work-ing with facts; her "veracious imagination" sets out to detect sequence, connec-tion, and significance. How complete are her sequences and how tight the con-nections? What does she omit? She gets the scale of her characters right. Hetty Sorrel is modestly conceived and credibly developed. She is among James's favorite heroines. The fact that Adam does not suffer sexual jealousy, though, mars his characterization, James says. "He is meant, I conceive, to be every inch a man; but, to my mind, there are several inches wanting. He lacks spon-taneity and sensibility, he is too stiff-backed." He stands beyond temptation, out of evil's reach: he can *only* be good and faithful, like Gabriel Oak in Hardy's *Far from the Madding Crowd.* Jealousy should be a key to action, or if not, the absence of jealousy should be interrogated, and it is not. Pritchett says, "The failure to record jealousy and the attempt to transmute it so that it becomes the ambigu-ous if lofty repugnance to sin, springs from the deeper failure to face the nature of sexual passion."

We have come a long way, but there is still a distance to go. "The unremit-ting ethic of self-improvement," Pritchett reminds us, "has been the sepulcher of all mid-Victorian fiction except *Wuthering Heights.*" The impact of Eliot's book was less decisive than it might have been. Henry James leafs through it with limited pleasure: Eliot has not yet found her strength. "It is as a picture, or rather as a series of pictures, that I find *Adam Bede* most valuable. The author succeeds better in drawing attitudes of feeling than in drawing movements of feeling." More than her larger intentions, James admires "the touches." William Dean Howells, who was young when the book first appeared, remembers "the day when *Adam Bede* was a new book, and in this I had my first knowledge of that great intellect for which I had no passion, indeed, but always the deepest respect, the highest honor; and which has from time to time profoundly influenced me by its ethics." The aesthetic and ethical have found a pale congruence.

"I wish the book to be judged quite apart from its authorship," George Eliot said, hence her choice of the male pseudonym, which has become her permanent moniker: plaques marking places of her residence in Switzerland and in Britain accept the fiction of herself. The pen name fended off inappropriate curiosity, gossip, and journalism. It meant (until she was rumbled) that she could say what she meant without being judged as a lady of her day. It concealed her improper lifestyle. Early readers of *Scenes from Clerical Life* assumed her to be a clergyman and read the book as a book. Modern readers "hear the voice of a woman, a free-thinker, a religious skeptic." Which of these readers hears Eliot's book more clearly?

*Adam Bede* was followed in close succession by *The Mill on the Floss* (1860) and *Silas Marner* (1861). *The Mill on the Floss* she intended to call *Sister Maggie*. Reflecting on the book, and on her dislike for Balzac's *Père Goriot,* James realized that at this time she was interested in painting a picture of life, not in producing a real-seeming "moralized fable" to "teach by example." "We feel in her, always, that she proceeds from the abstract to the concrete; that her figures and situations are evolved . . . from her moral consciousness, and are only indirectly the products of observation." It is the absence of the gratuitous touch that makes a scene real beyond moral intention and design, that ties the book in more narrowly to its moral intention even than Bunyan is in *The Pilgrim's Progress.* There the allegory has a typological resonance, here it is formulaic and two-dimensional. The *Bookseller* review in 1860 says that, had the book not been advertised as "by the author of *Adam Bede,*" it would have been passed over. It was a disappointment. The relationship between Maggie and Tom, sister and elder brother, is complex; so too is Maggie's relationship with her father and other characters who, in one way or another, are charmed by the independent and forceful person. Her choices, first spiritual and later romantic, lead her into isolation and alienation, resolved by a river flood in which she makes peace with her brother; they attempt to save Lucy Deane and her family and are drowned. "Conclusions are the weak points of most authors, but some of the fault lies in the very nature of a conclusion, which is at best a negation."

The literal culmination of Maggie's desires, needs, courage, and failure in swirling death makes her a type for all of Eliot's heroines, though the later ones are less melodramatically thwarted. "Save for the supreme courage of their endeavor," writes Virginia Woolf, "the struggle ends, for her heroines, in tragedy, or in a compromise that is even more melancholy. But their story is the incomplete story of George Eliot herself." James notes a lack of passion in Eliot's women, who are "marked by a singular spiritual tenacity," apart from Maggie Tulliver.

*Silas Marner*, James and Pritchett argue, is "more nearly a masterpiece" than any of her works before *Middlemarch* (1872). It makes real a material world of the kind Proust admired her for, her low to middle life, and most of her novels encompass both levels. The narrative method she adapted from Wordsworth's poem "Michael," with its plain, understated pace and classical sense of inevitability. Her peasant dialogue is not realistic, the exuberance of rural life is absent; but much else is to be found, and she avoids caricature and condescension. Fred's conversation about dialect with his sister Rosamond is a vindication of dialect and slang, and a wise account of what "correct" English really is.

> "Are you beginning to dislike slang, then?" said Rosamond, with mild gravity.
> "Only the wrong sort. All choice of words is slang. It marks a class."
> "There is correct English: that is not slang."
> "I beg your pardon: correct English is the slang of prigs who write history and essays. And the strongest slang of all is the slang of poets."
> "You will say anything, Fred, to gain your point."
> "Well, tell me whether it is slang or poetry to call an ox a leg-plaiter."
> "Of course you can call it poetry if you like."
> "Aha, Miss Rosy, you don't know Homer from slang. I shall invent a new game; I shall write bits of slang and poetry on slips, and give them to you to separate."
> "Dear me, how amusing it is to hear young people talk!" said Mrs. Vincy, with cheerful admiration.

Though he does not speak dialect, Silas Marner is credibly a linen weaver, Adam Bede a carpenter, Maggie Tulliver a miller's daughter, Felix Holt a watchmaker, Dinah Morris a factory worker, Hetty Sorrel a dairy maid. George Eliot knows the common folk of "Loamshire": "she promises no heaven and threatens no hell," Pritchett says; "the best and the worst we shall get is Warwick-shire. Her world is the world of will, the smithy of character, a place of knowl-edge and judgments."

Her characters, unlike those in eighteenth-century novels whose fortunes are governed by chance, work in a more measurable *bourse,* indeed *in a bourse.* Economic and moral worlds, like circles in a Venn diagram, overlap. It might almost be said that the economic model provides the moral template. The au-thor's moral confidence and clarity, Pritchett says, ironically enlarge the charac-ters because none of them quite conforms: rules do not govern but measure conduct, and the ways in which characters act deepen our sense of types.

Her judgments are narrow not because she is inflexible but because she ap-praises the individual him- or herself, not only the individual in society and in relation. Even in *Middlemarch,* where there is such extensive interaction, it is the private trials of each character that interest her: the social scene frames and catalyzes, but the drama takes place in the isolation of the human heart and conscience, which are often at odds with one another. Characters reflect in complex ways, challenge themselves, come to self-knowledge. Conscience, the favorite resort of the protestant and dissenting imagination, is where she operates to greatest effect. Her larger moral purpose can be in conflict with her aesthetic purpose. She is reluctant to dismiss or damn. Even to Bultrode she gives the benefit of a dozen doubts before he is finally condemned. "Her intellect is sculptural": Pritchett has in mind the sculptor working in stone, not clay. "The clumsiness of style does not denote muddle, but an attempt to carve decisively." We see, toward the ends of her story lines, not only what is but what might have been; the mature characters see as well, aware of their fallings-short.

*Romola* (1863) is her aberrant novel. It strays from Warwickshire, from En-gland and her century, it travels to Italy, drawn by a fascination with the kinds of evil that flourish openly in warmer climes, upon which Catholic shadows fall, where ambition, lust, and superstition thrive. And it was popular. *Cornhill Mag-azine,* under Thackeray's editorship, serialized it in 1862–1863 and Eliot re-ceived £7,000, a huge fee, before it was published in book form. Howells re-members how he read it "again and again with the sense of moral enlargement which the first fiction to conceive of the true nature of evil gave all of us who were young in that day." This, from the countryman of Hawthorne and Mel-ville! There is much in the book that is remote, false, and cloying, but at the heart of it is Tito Malema: "Not only a lesson, he was a revelation, and I trem-bled before him as in the presence of a warning and a message from the only veritable perdition. His life, in which so much that was good was mixed with so much that was bad, lighted up the whole domain of egotism with its glare."

Eliot can speak of his "loathsome beauty," but she does not go into its consequences except indirectly. "The characters stop at the waist," says Julian Green.
For Howells the memory of the book is moral, "how near the best and the worst
were to each other, and how they sometimes touched without absolute division
in texture and color."

Eliot has a politics, most transparently explored in *Felix Holt: The Radical*
(1866), a welcome return to the wide canvas of "midland country life," interested
in its reality as well as the dramas it affords. In 1866, the year of its publication,
James wrote his most penetrating review of Eliot, illustrating her creative gifts
and vices. Characterization by gesture irritates him. It epitomizes an aspect of
a larger failure. "Her plots have always been artificial—clumsily artificial—the
conduct of her story slow, and her style diffuse." He finds the conclusions to her
books peremptory, contradicting the current of "facts" she has set in motion;
and "a certain sagacious tendency to compromise," he says, "pervades the author's spirit" and contributes to "the meager effect of the whole and the vigorous
character of the different parts which stamp them as the works of a secondary
thinker and an incomplete artist."

Even so, he is in thrall to the book and its author for solid reasons. He admires the firmness of her character drawing, its completeness. He is affected
by "that extensive human sympathy," how her "humanity colors all her other
gifts—her humor, her morality, and her exquisite rhetoric." For him the style
is not neutral but a contributing merit. He commends its range and control, for
the author "writes from a full mind, with a wealth of fancy, of suggestion, of
illustration, at the command of no other English writer, bearing you along on
the broad and placid rises of her speech, with a kind of retarding persuasiveness which allows her conjured images to sink slowly into your very brain."
There is her humor, which is quiet and irresistible. And finally he admires her
"constant, genial and discreet" morality. He places her in the tradition of the
novel of manners, of Edgeworth and Austen. She "is stronger in degree" but "not
different in kind" from them. Her superiority is a "masculine comprehensive-
ness," though she retains feminine—delightfully feminine, he adds gallantly—
qualities. She "has exquisitely good taste on a small scale, the absence of taste on
a large."

Fortunately in this final assessment James was wrong. She had begun work
on *Middlemarch*, expansive, profligate, yet in remarkable taste, the formal challenge she had set herself unprecedented, and unreplicated by later novelists.
James could and could not stomach it, so he repeats his paradox: it "is at once
one of the strongest and one of the weakest of English novels . . . a treasure-house
of detail, but it is an indifferent whole." There is no evidence that he spent much

time appraising the whole: he knew his mind about her shortcomings, rooted, it may seem to us, in a gender prejudice. In her *Impressions of Theophrastus Such* she may directly address James's *idée fixe* about her originality, for as a critic he represented the "dear public" of her ironic address: "The dear public would do well to reflect that they are often bored from the want of flexibility in their own minds. They are like the topers of 'one liquor.'"

Some advocates preface praise for *Middlemarch* with an apology, as when Woolf calls it "the magnificent book which with all its imperfections is one of the few English novels written for grown-up people." Is it necessary to concede "all its imperfections"? In the case of *Middlemarch* no such allowance is required. It is among the most complete and replete novels of the nineteenth century, and though it is slow, that very pace is part of its enchantment. Seasons turn, the years pass, the detail is coherent and holds; nature and the social world proceed in their inevitable, hardly perceived reciprocities. The whirligig of time brings round its revenges, to be sure, but also its rewards; and men and women grow older and come to understand where they have been and where they have not. The "grown-up people" Woolf invokes are unworthy of her and of the novel form, which has, by now, a remarkable and mature backstory.

In *Middlemarch* Eliot tells two stories in particular, that of the education, sentimental and otherwise, of Dorothea Brooke, and that of the innovative physician Lydgate, the first led astray by an inordinate regard for learning, the other—original and visionary—by sexual desire and a corrupting ambition. Several subplots qualify the principal stories, among them the moral romance of Fred and Mary Garth, the fall of Mr. Bulstrode into the abyss of his past, Mr. Farebrother and his unfulfillable desires, the amusingly contrasted Cadwalladers.

In romantic novels hero and heroine meet, are kept apart, and finally at the end unite. Art abets nature in a happy ending. Eliot takes two attractive young characters who are conventionally ideal for one another. They live in the same society, are of a similar class, have congruent instincts and desires, their consciences and ideals are attuned. Yet—they do not get together. What are the consequences, for each of them? Out of this failure the novel flows, with all it sees, does, and forgives in its protracted course. Here there is more diversity and vitality than in all the Barchester novels combined; more than in Wessex, too, and the Five Towns. Because the two main narratives, the halves that might have made a romantic whole, do not fit, do not consciously meet until it is too late, because the circle is not closed, the novel gathers in more and more. There are closing chapters in which scores are settled, rewards given, but the tension between the main stories remains unresolved. Plots matter less than the world that informs them, its languages, how it comes into being. William

Gass remarks, "I think I forgot the basic plot of Middlemarch hours after I read it, and it was of course a terrific book. But the impression, the quality of its style, that I think I shall remember forever."

Gass is interested in the movement of the prose. David Lodge explores the rhythm of the narrative, which seems "to approximate to the rhythm of life itself, since so much of it consists of extended scenes in which the characters speak and interact as they would have done in real time." For such writing, serialization was ideal: "For the original readers of that novel, buying it in bimonthly installments over a whole year, the correspondence in tempo between life and art would have seemed even closer," says Lodge. James is not giving it sufficient oxygen when he complains of its lack of "concentration" and declares that its "diffuseness . . . makes it too copious a dose of pure fiction. If we write novels so, how shall we write History?" Yet compression and concentration were inimical to her way of seeing.

In *Middlemarch* the gap between fiction and history closes. Eliot strove for this in the faked Italy of *Romola* and finally in *Daniel Deronda*. But in *Middlemarch* the variety of interrelated stories presents a fictional world answerable to an actual world. Eliot recognized the tension between the literal "sequence of associations" and the "sense of proportion," between story and plot. Here the "reconstructing historian" is after her quarry: knowledge and understanding. She recommends "indirect ways" of arriving at them. Like Saint Teresa of Avila, her tutelary spirit, she knows that in daily actions the real *becomes* real. A "fine imagination," she says, "is always based on a keen vision, a keen consciousness of what is, and carries the store of definite knowledge as material for the construction of its inward visions. Witness Dante, who is at once the most precise and homely in his reproduction of actual objects, and the most soaringly at large in his imaginative combinations."

When she was composing, Eliot said, she became possessed of a "not herself." She was *acted through*. The scene between Dorothea and Rosamond in *Middlemarch,* inevitable, long in the buildup, was possible only when she knew the characters and could entrust the chapter to them. She wrote the scene without a single erasure: it emerged red-hot, even white-hot, from the kiln. Rosamond was the hardest character for her to draw, because she is so remote from the author. Dorothea was easier, being (like others of her heroines) not unlike Eliot herself.

In creating Lydgate, Eliot conducted the right research: she defined his social place in terms of family and community, precisely, and what followed from those givens, especially in his fateful relations with Rosamond Vincy, has an air of tragic inevitability. James has great regard for the reality and intelligence of Lydgate's creation. Taking the characters generally, "their impressiveness and (as regards Lydgate) their pathos, is deepened by the constantly low key in which they are pitched. It is a tragedy based on unpaid butchers' bills, and the urgent need for small economies." The word "tragedy" becomes appropriate even in this bourgeois setting because the characters have been so meticulously placed. Ladislaw, on the other hand, James regards as an "eminent failure": the author did not know him; he remains as evanescent as the impressions he leaves, great-uncle of Peter Pan. Pritchett, too, acknowledges the occasional Achilles' heel, but *Middlemarch* is a centipede and can absorb into its movement a few weak heels without developing a serious limp. "Bulstrode's moral ruin, and his inability to confess to his dull wife, is portrayed in a picture of dumb human despondency which recalls a painting by Sickert. One hears the clock tick in the silence that attends the wearing down of two lives that can cling together but dare not speak."

The solidest, most taciturn and stale character in *Middlemarch,* whose attraction the author best understood, is the reverend Edward Casaubon. We are reluctant to give him up, until it becomes impossible not to do so. We do not imagine that he can be redeemed, but we hope that he might be. "I can think of no other English novel before or since which has so truthfully, so sympathetically and so intimately described the befogged and grandiose humiliations of the scholar, as he turns at bay before the vengeance of life," says Pritchett, with a vulnerability all historians must feel in the midst of their more impossible projects. He is not an easy or a complete villain, and there is more to him, he is bigger even, than Eliot expected him to be. He sees himself, "Poor Mr. Casaubon," plainly: he "had imagined that his long studious bachelorhood had stored up for him a compound interest of enjoyment, and that large drafts on his affections would not fail to be honored; for we all of us, grave or light, get our thoughts entangled in metaphors, and act fatally on the strength of them." The image of the treachery of metaphor has its English sources in Bacon's essays; it is a caution that Eliot repeats to herself because she never quite takes it to heart. She is a master of metaphors, and when there are entanglements she is generally in control of the raveling and unraveling.

"And there is the pathos," she writes, "the heroism often accompanying the decay and final struggle of old systems, which has not had its share of tragic commemoration." *Middlemarch,* one of the unambiguously accomplished English novels of the nineteenth century, keeping company with Balzac and even Flaubert, is an elegy that does not appeal to every readers. Howells recommended it to his friend Mark Twain. "I bored through *Middlemarch* during the past week," he retorted, "with its labored and tedious analyses of feelings and motives, its paltry and tiresome people, its unexciting and uninteresting story, and its frequent blinding flashes of single-sentence poetry, philosophy, wit, and what not, and nearly died from the overwork." It was not entertaining in an up-front way. "I wouldn't read another of those books for a farm. I did try to read one other—*Daniel Deronda*. I dragged through three chapters, losing flesh all the time, and then was honest enough to quit, and confess to myself that I haven't any romance literature appetite, as far as I can see"—then remembering who he was writing to—"except for your books."

*Middlemarch* is as wonderful as Eliot gets. Her final major novel is *Daniel Deronda,* and it is possible to agree with Twain on this one. James puts his criticism in the voice of Pulcheria, a girl who, conversing with her friends, releases several telling darts, though in their anti-Semitism some tell against James, not Eliot. Fido the dog is sitting on *Daniel Deronda.* Much that Pulcheria says about the late writing is true. Clearly Eliot, moving from Warwickshire into unexplored political areas, has not adjusted her technique to the material: "A picture is not a person," Pulcheria says of Daniel. "And why is he always grabbing his shirt-collar, as if he wished to hang himself up? The author had an uncomfortable feeling that she must make him do something real, something visible and sensible, and she hit upon that clumsy figure." Characterization by gesture riles Pulcheria: "Deronda clutches his coat-collar, Mirah crosses her feet, Mordecai talks like the Bible; but that doesn't make real figures of them. They have no existence outside the author's study." Eliot, she says, "is very fond of death by drowning. Maggie Tulliver and her brother are drowned, Tito Melema is drowned, Mr. Grandcourt is drowned." *Daniel Deronda* "has nothing that one can call a subject. A silly young girl and a solemn, sapient young man who doesn't fall in love with her! That is the donnée of eight monthly volumes." The "silly young girl" may point at George Eliot's essay on the Silly Novelists, but Pulcheria knew better than to abandon George Eliot in their company.

It was an age of silly young girls and boys in fiction, and of sentimental and sententious parents. In 1875, reviewing Louisa May Alcott's *Eight Cousins; or, The Aunt Hill,* James writes, "Miss Alcott is the novelist of children—the Thackeray, the Trollope, of the nursery and school-room." She is also a gentle satirist. He dislikes the book because of its attitude to children, its inviting them into a complicity that is in his view perverse: "this unhappy amalgam of the novel and the story-book," he calls it. Considering her novel *Moods* ten years earlier he said, "The two most striking facts with regard to *Moods* are the author's ignorance of human nature, and her self-confidence in spite of this ignorance." *Little Men* and *Little Women* remain stuck in the craw of many readers who, as I did, experienced them in a pre-television childhood, read to us by parents to whom they had been read. Our parents emerged rather embarrassed from the experience: the texts had been so compelling to them when they were small; they had assumed that writing retains its effects. In this case it did not. Mr. Bhaer remembers how, when he lied, his grandmother used to snip the end of his tongue with her sewing scissors until it bled. Little Nat, who cannot help lying, offers his tongue. But Mr. Bhaer contrives a much worse punishment. Nat shall be required to punish Mr. Bhaer. Not only will he have lied, he must then cause physical pain to the caring adult. The book abounds in punishment. Jo remembers her mother whipping her. In rage, she tells her mother she "ought to be whipped as much as me," and instead of a second helping her mother is all contrition. "You are right, Jo, I am angry; and why should I punish you for being in a passion when I set you such a bad example? Forgive me, dear, and let us try to help one another in a better way." What a lesson Jo learned that day! "I never forgot it, and it did me more good than a dozen rods." James dislikes Alcott's precocious children, and if one brings them into company with the haunted brother and sister in *The Turn of the Screw* or with Maisie in *What Maisie Knew* or Maggie in *The Mill on the Floss,* the distance between sentimental and credible is clear, even when Peter Quint's face appears at the adult window in a sulfurous cloud.

And George Meredith? "His boys and girls," says Virginia Woolf of *Richard Feverel* (1859), his first major work, "may spend their time picking daisies in the meadows, but they breathe, however unconsciously, an air bristling with intellectual question and comment." And then *Harry Richmond* (1871): "The story bowls smoothly along the road which Dickens has already trodden of autobiographical narrative. It is a boy speaking, a boy thinking, a boy adventuring." The progress is faultless, "without a kink in it. Stevenson, one feels, must have learnt much from this supple narrative, with its precise adroit phrases, its exact quick glance at visible things." But in the end his boys are not real like David Copperfield. They are, she says, "sample boys," types of boy, off the peg. "Meredith's characters," Edmund Wilson says, "while yet remaining individual and unmistakable, often rise to represent something universal." In *The Egoist,* according to Edith Wharton, "his Willoughby Patterne is typical before he is individual." Pritchett sees this as Meredith's legacy to D. H. Lawrence: "people are not individual characters, but psychic types, flames lit by the imagination." For that very reason, perhaps, they are easy to follow into fantasy. Woolf speaks of his "intermittent brilliancy," and Oscar Wilde, setting Meredith beside Balzac, speaks of his style as "chaos illumined by flashes of lightning."

In other respects, Wilde is on the side of George Moore regarding Meredith: "As a writer he has mastered everything, except language; as a novelist he can do everything, except tell a story; as an artist he is everything, except articulate. Too strange to be popular, too individual to have imitators, the author of *Richard Feverel* stands absolutely alone." Aphorism stalks aphorism, each true up to a point. But Wilde was inclined to love him; he says with some bitterness:

"It is easy to disarm criticism, but he has disarmed the disciple. He gives us his philosophy through the medium of wit, and is never so pathetic as when he is humorous. To turn truth into a paradox is not difficult, but George Meredith makes all his paradoxes truths, and no Theseus can thread his labyrinth, no Oedipus solve his secret." George Moore takes this contrary view further, without mitigation, speaking of Meredith's "crackjaw sentences, empty and unpleasant in the mouth as sterile nuts." Modern readers must be satisfied with intermittency or set his books aside. In *Women in Love* Lawrence evokes the master ironically: "And then round the bushes came the tall form of Alexander Roddice, striding romantically like a Meredith hero who remembers Disraeli."

The characters are like that, they do not grow; and there are few moments of repose, the writing is effortful, early and late. The comic Meredith, however, is excepted. In *The Egoist,* Woolf says, Meredith "pays us a supreme compliment to which as novel-readers we are little accustomed." Namely, "he imagines us capable of disinterested curiosity in the behavior of our kind." Yet Moore's optimism was out of date in 1928 and perhaps will also be out of date in 2028. Thomas Hardy's was a powerful antidote to his fanciful vision. The questing, unstable novels of Meredith with periphrases and heightened phrasing, their poeticism, are experimental, seeking ways out of the deadened symmetries and balances of "the well-made" novel that had become a buffer, a dead end. Mary McCarthy sees Meredith's aphoristic style as an aspect of experimentalism. "He went counter to the 'stuffy' realist tradition" and played against conventions, broke rather than refined the rules. He hinted at interior monologue. Such procedures can also be "meretricious," Woolf says, and the excesses of Meredith are more obvious and unsatisfying than the flatness of a moribund Trollopian tradition. He would be discussed from time to time, Woolf declared, but his decisive hour would never come.

Woolf as Virginia Stephen knew Meredith well: he was a close friend of her father's. Vernon Whitford in *The Egoist* is based on Leslie Stephen (just as Meredith's ex-father-in-law Peacock suggested Dr. Middleton). He spent summers with the Stephen family in Cornwall; Virginia was his favorite of the girls, and it is tempting to associate him with Mr. Carmichael in *To the Lighthouse,* ceremonious, undemonstratively affectionate. When he died she wished to do him the kind of justice he had done her father. With Henry James and Samuel Butler, she says, Meredith "despised the public" yet like them desired its "beefy" recognition. Sadly, "each failed to attain a public; and each wreaked his failure upon the public by a succession, gradually increasing in intensity, of angularities, obscurities, and affectations which no writer whose patron was his equal and friend would have thought it necessary to inflict." Each devised his own stylistic aberrations. "Their crocuses, in consequence, are tortured plants, beautiful and bright, but with something wry-necked about them, malformed, shriveled on the one side, overblown on the other. A touch of the sun would have done them a world of good."

The letters support Woolf's argument. At the start of Meredith's fiction-writing career, the neglect of *The Shaving of Shagpat* (1856) had an impact on the direction his fiction took. In his case as in that of some of his contemporaries the public played a role in his self-perception of failure. Thirty-three years later he wrote to Edmund Gosse: "The English have hardened me outside, and there has been a consequent process within. I do my work to the best of my ability, expecting the small result for the same, which I get." In the more than three decades of his writing life, he says, "I have seen no varying in our public." By now he has forgotten *Shagpat* and sees *The Ordeal of Richard Feverel* as his first *real* novel. He can commiserate with Gosse, because in his view *Richard Feverel* and Gosse's own controversial *Father and Son* explore the same generational theme and suffered the same denunciations and neglect. The subscription libraries refused to stock such books, a form of censorship, making the books unprofitable and limiting readership. Meredith had "good hope of the Americans"; certainly he had a following in the United States—and on the Continent. He had an eye for Europe: he was sent to a Moravian boarding school in Neuwied on the Rhine at the age of fourteen (his mother died when he was five). His first surviving letter, miserable and correct, is written in German. In 1894, the year before he stopped writing fiction, he invited Paul Valéry to dinner: "Cuisine anglaise, malheureusement: mais pour le vin, il est bien français." Like his contemporaries he read contemporary literature from the Continent and keenly followed Anatole France's progress.

Meredith studied law but preferred to follow a literary vocation, as poet first of all, then as journalist and novelist. He met his first wife many pages back: Mary Ellen Nicolls, the widowed daughter of Peacock, whom Meredith revered for his wit and ease. Seven years Meredith's senior, Mary Ellen was and remained his difficult Muse. They married in 1849. In 1856 the Pre-Raphaelite painter Henry Wallis, popularly known for his lurid depiction of Chatterton's suicide (the young Meredith modeled for the "marvelous boy," portrayed as a marbled corpse), made a bold pencil sketch of her. Her frank gaze engages his with a seriousness that led, two years later, to her leaving Meredith. She lived with Wallis for three years and then died. Meredith's *Modern Love* (1862, a poem sequence for which he invented the sixteen-line "Meredithian" sonnet) and the novel *The Ordeal of Richard Feverel* relate to his double loss.

He married again in 1864 and settled in Surrey. The family home, Flint Cottage at Box Hill, was substantial and congenial, with big windows, big trees round about, and a friendly, wisteria-clad aspect. There he wrote his *Essay on*

*Comedy* (1877) and his two most durable novels, *The Egoist* (1879) and *Diana of the Crossways* (1885). Its countryside lives in his work. Edward Thomas reminds us of a brilliant passage in *Diana of the Crossways*: "Through an old gravel-cutting a gateway led to the turf of the down, springy turf bordered on a long line, clear as a racecourse, by golden gorse covers, and leftward over the gorse the dark-ridge of the fir and heath country ran companionably to the south-west, the valley between, with undulations of wood and meadow sunned and shaded, clumps, mounds, promontories, away to broad spaces of tillage banked by wooded hills, and dimmer beyond, and farther, the faintest shadowiness of heights, as a veil to the illimitable. Yews, junipers, radiant beeches, and gleams of the service-tree or the white-beam, spotted the semicircle of swelling green Down black and silver." Such writing made him a determining presence for his contemporaries, and not only the novelists among them.

Robert Louis Stevenson wrote, "I have just re-read for the third and fourth time *The Egoist*. When I shall have read it the sixth or seventh, I begin to see I shall know about it." What attracted him? "I had no idea of the matter—human, red matter he has contrived to plug and pack into that strange and admirable book. Willoughby is, of course, a pure discovery; a complete set of nerves, not heretofore examined, and yet running all over the human body—a suit of nerves." That image, true to Meredith's spirit, is Gothic in the manner of Jekyll and Hyde. He loves the other characters. "The manner and the faults of the book greatly justify themselves on further study . . . Vernon's conduct makes a wonderful odd contrast with Daniel Deronda's." Like Woolf, he notes a continuity between Eliot and Meredith. He came back to *The Egoist* in 1905: "From all the novels I have read (and I have read thousands) [it] stands in a place by itself. Here is a Nathan for the modern David; here is a book to send the blood into men's faces." It goes beyond its genre. "Satire, the angry picture of human faults, is not great art; we can all be angry with our neighbor; what we want is to be shown, not his defects, of which we are too conscious, but his merits, to which we are too blind." It may be satire, but "it is yourself that is hunted down; these are your own faults that are dragged into the day and numbered, with lingering relish, with cruel cunning and precision." He records, "A young friend of Mr. Meredith's (as I have the story) came to him in an agony. 'This is too bad of you,' he cried. 'Willoughby is me!' 'No, my dear fellow,' said the author; 'he is all of us.'"

And he was aware of sharing with his contemporaries certain key themes. Pritchett says, "Meredith is above all a novelist of youth and growth; for he accepts with pleasure the conceit, the severity, the aggressiveness and self-encumberedness of young men and women, the uncritical impulses and solemn ambitions." This acceptance is an index of his strength as a writer of character (he does not judge) and his weakness as a writer of social relationship; the subject and the subjective in his characters have more hold on him than the world through which they move; it serves as backdrop and provides stimuli. He is impatient with Dickens's characters, who are so much more integrated into the entertainment of relationship and plot: he sees them as caricatured; Dickens's popularity is incomprehensible to him.

Gore Vidal resolves Meredith into one paradoxical dominant theme: "education and ordeal." There is something theatrical in the writing of this repetitive *agon,* the characters facing the audience rather than one another to deliver their arias and soliloquies. And Meredith always upstages his characters, breaks across the limelight to direct the action. Yet Vidal also insists on a kind of politics in his writing, an awareness of the self-destructive egoism of the dominant class and its types, the formalized nature of social roles and the distortion these impose on the living self of his characters.

Given the isolation of his characters, Edith Wharton says, he had the greatest difficulty when trying to figure out "how to pass from the mind of one character to another without too violent a jolt to the reader." That art acquired with such difficulty by Flaubert was never quite mastered by Meredith. So Rhoda Fleming in the eponymous novel (1865) and her stuttering suitor at last plight their troth, but find it hard to speak, so the author puts in brackets what they are thinking and in standard quotations their unsatisfactory spoken phrases: we get inner *and* "objective" dialogue, we can infer a tone. In *The Egoist* at last "the fantastic novelist, whose antics too often make one forget his insight, discarding most of his fatiguing follies, gives a rich and deliberate study of a real human being."

The fiction of the first part of the nineteenth century was mostly set in the past, a past often still in reach of memory, but far enough away to be closed. There is something collusive about most of it, the novel on the side of the establishment and its readers, accepting political and social structures even as it satirizes and corrects. With Eliot, but more so with Meredith, Gissing, Hardy, and others, resistance begins. Fiction risks the present or near present, the values of some primary characters and their fates are at odds with what the age demanded. Novelists had sided with Creon; Antigone's hour had come. Respectability and its formal accoutrements are recognized as tyranny. In the eighteenth century, tyranny was one man lording it over others, corrupt man thriving in corruption and—it was fiction, after all—being brought to justice. The nineteenth century experiences an increasingly callous and alienating political and economic system, individual tyranny displaced onto institutions. The moral burden becomes more personal, less categorical: how to survive, improve, if possible, change.

Meredith's heart was light at the start. *The Shaving of Shagpat,* earliest of his fictions, in its exuberance and lively unrealism owes debts to Peacock. He remembers how it came about: "Some one gave me *The Arabian Nights,* and I lived and lived in them until I said to myself, 'Why, I can write a story in that vein,' and I wrote a book called *The Shaving of Shagpat.*" It opens with beguiling assurance. "It was ordained that Shibli Bagarag, nephew to the renowned Baba Mustapha, chief barber to the Court of Persia, should shave Shagpat, the son of Shimpoor, the son of Shoolpi, the son of Shullum; and they had been clothiers for generations, even to the time of Shagpat, the illustrious." Magic and the circumstantial meet in a confident and charming style, at once exotic and familiar. "Now, the story of Shibli Bagarag, and of the ball he followed, and of the subterranean kingdom he came to, and of the enchanted palace he entered, and of the sleeping king he shaved, and of the two princesses he released, and of the Afrite held in subjection by the arts of one and bottled by her, is it not known as 'twere written on the finger-nails of men and traced in their corner-robes?" Earnest readers tried to make it into allegory. Meredith dissuaded them. "I suppose [*Shagpat*] does wear a sort of allegory. But it is not as a dress-suit; rather as a dressing gown, very loosely." Again, as in *The Egoist,* he refused to confine himself within generic boundaries. Reflecting on his novels a dozen years after he had stopped practicing the art, he recognized faults, but he had not striven for perfection: that "would have cramped my hand."

Vidal recalls James's words: "He did the best things best." And James wrote to Stevenson, Meredithian through and through, of his "charming *accueil* [welcome], his impenetrable shining scales"—a reptile's? a musician's?—"and the (to me) general mystery of his perversity." This perversity is obvious to modern readers: a stark disparity between the literal world he is presenting and a kind of symbol world that shadows it and breaks through, selectively, at points of climax.

Meredith worked as a reader for Chapman and Hall. Thomas Hardy's first novel was sent to him. He recognized the writer's talents but urged against publishing "so pronounced a thing" as *The Poor Man and the Lady,* which would cause a furor and make Hardy's future hard. Hardy asked to meet the reader, and he and Meredith became friends. Meredith told him that the style of that early book had "the affected simplicity of Defoe's" (as did Stevenson's, years later). Naive realism in fiction gives it, for the general reader, a kind of factual authority. To write of troubling themes in that unadorned manner was to court mischief. When *Desperate Remedies,* Hardy's first published novel, came out, it was less ambitious than *The Poor Man* and, as Meredith had advised, more contrived in terms of plot.

The "chief way" to "the art of expression," he told a young writer, is "by merely writing until you are full of your subject. Then the right words come of nature." Responding to this spirit, Stevenson composed *Prince Otto*, "an experiment in style, conceived one summer's day when the author had given the reins to his high appreciation of Mr. George Meredith." It is James's most *literary* work, a "coquetry," "a kind of artful inconsequence." James emphasizes his own debts to Meredith in the area of description, and this is what Wharton regards as Meredith's "distinguishing merit": "He always made his art as a landscape-painter contribute to the interpretation of his tale"—for example, "the sunrise from the top of Monte Muttering" in *Vittoria,* chapter 1, "and the delicious wall-flower-colored picture of the farm-house in *Harry Richmond*," necessary to the novels, portrayed "as the people *to whom they happened* would have seen them." Objective, but subjectively portrayed, a synthesis of outer and inner worlds. Stevenson and James learned also from Meredith's dialogue, which Vidal calls "beautifully concentrated" and "elliptical": "It continues to sound in the work of Ivy Compton-Burnett and her imitators." When Max Beerbohm parodies Meredith in *A Christmas Garland,* this is what he finds irresistible.

> He waved hand to the door. "Lady, your father has started."
> "He knows the adage. Copy-books instill it."
> "Inexorable truth in it."
> "We may dodge the scythe."
> "To be choked with the sands?"
> She flashed a smile. "I would not," he said, "that my Euphoria were late for the Absolution."
> She cast eyes to the carpet. He caught them at the rebound.
> "It snows," she murmured, swimming to the window.
> "A flake, no more. The season claims it."

Sherlock Holmes was infected with this bacillus when it came to dialogue, cryptic and inferential. Sir Arthur Conan Doyle admired Meredith, and when Holmes says to Dr. Watson, "And now let us talk about George Meredith, if you please, and we shall leave all minor matters until to-morrow," we know what he means. After *Shagpat,* there were few minor matters to hold over.

So large was Meredith's reputation among writers that John Cowper Powys found it necessary to dislike him, his "jeering" style: "I don't like his kind of mind." And E. M. Forster has it in for him with such vehemence in *Aspects of the Novel* that the modern reader recognizes the eminence he held at the turn of the twentieth century: "He will never be the spiritual power he was about the year 1900." His philosophy is dated (Chesterton called it "barren"); his anti-sentimentality looks heavy-handed. His vision of nature, unlike Hardy's, is Surrey-rich, "fluffy and lush." Everything is newly decanted, there is no real vintage in it. "When he gets serious and noble-minded there is a strident over-tone, a bullying that becomes distressing." "What with the faking, what with the preaching, which was never agreeable and is now said to be hollow, and what with the home counties posing as the universe, it is no wonder Meredith now lies in the trough." Yet Forster must concede that "he is in one way a great novelist. He is the finest contriver that English fiction has ever produced, and any lecture on plot must do homage to him." He did not command a large readership in his own day, but he was the *novelists' novelist,* one of the original authors of "liter-ary fiction."

And what of George Gissing (1857–1903)? His early life is more appalling than a Zola plot. *Workers in the Dawn* (1880), his first novel, Meredith recom-mended to Chapman and Hall, and he revered his elder as much as Thomas Hardy did. Gissing wrote twenty-three novels, one of which is remembered and read more often and eagerly than anything by Meredith, including *The Ego-ist;* this is *New Grub Street* (1891). The book, says David Lodge, "as a study in the pathology of the literary life . . . is unequalled, and still surprisingly relevant." Its more than equal modern descendant is Martin Amis's irresistible, appalling *The Information* (1995).

In Gissing the actual business of writing and writers becomes a subject: the process, its temptations and pitfalls, are explored. Gissing told Thomas Hardy, "In literature my interests begin and end"; here he epitomized what had become of the commercial world of literature in which integrity cannot long survive, given the nature of the public and of those who pander to it. Margaret Atwood celebrates it as an early example of a book "in which writers write about writers writing." She is taken with his understanding of writer's block as experienced by Edwin Reardon, pushed by his wife, then abandoned by her, his death as much from a broken talent as from a broken heart. Most of the characters write or are connected with writing. But Gissing focuses on two contrasted individu-als, Edwin Reardon, who has some talent as a writer but is not commercially minded, and Jasper Milvain, who is reticent and intellectual and acts from an unattenuated understanding of the ways of the world. Milvain's scheming cyni-cism triumphs; Reardon hopes, fails, and dies, having drawn himself and those he loves into poverty. His estranged widow, now an heiress, ends up marrying Milvain, a love-skeptic enjoying unmerited prosperity. That's how the world wags: moral and material rewards are out of sync. Happy endings are not justly distributed.

Milvain's philosophy of the literary marketplace is simple: "I maintain that we people of brains are justified in supplying the mob with the food it likes. We are not geniuses, and if we sit down in a spirit of long-eared gravity we shall produce only commonplace stuff." Poor Reardon is of the long-eared tribe. Milvain urges, "Let us use our wits to earn money, and make the best we can of our lives. If only I had the skill, I would produce novels out-trashing the trashiest that ever sold fifty thousand copies. But it needs skill, mind you: and to deny it is a gross error of the literary pedants." Reardon meets a successful writer who plunges him even deeper into self-doubt, "Well, the novelist was a rotund and jovial man; his dwelling and his person smelt of money; he was so happy himself that he could afford to be kind to others."

Planning to make a fortune, Milvain has a great idea whose time came a century later. He has been writing *An author's Guide.* It will sell, even though his fiction has not done so. And beyond that he is inventing the Creative Writing course in which he will teach technique, subject matter, and tone. He is even aware of gender issues. "I'm going to advertise: 'Novel-writing taught in ten lessons!' What do you think of that? No swindle; not a bit of it. I am quite capable of giving the ordinary man or woman ten very useful lessons . . . The first lesson deals with the question of subjects, local color—that kind of thing. I gravely advise people, if they possibly can, to write of the wealthy middle class; that's the popular subject, you know. Lords and ladies are all very well, but the real thing to take is a story about people who have no titles, but live in good Philistine style. I urge study of horsey matters especially; that's very important. You must be well up, too, in military grades, know about Sandhurst, and so on. Boating is an important topic . . . I shall teach my wife carefully, and then let her advertise lessons to girls; they'll prefer coming to a woman, you know." Eighteenth-century Grub Street, where writers toiled without profit and starved, no longer existed, but its spirit survived, intensified in an age with such enormous demand for product, variety, and competition. Bad writers and the talented unsellable writers lived in adjacent garrets and starved together.

Virginia Woolf reflected on Gissing's unusual readership: not only general readers but people who read little fiction: governesses, mechanics, working men, dons, professional men, "the daughters of farmers in the north." These rather private, rather depressive people found the world of his novels real: disappointment and unfulfillment are the rule, not the exception, and in Gissing's even style he tells it as they know it to be. "His books are very sad; that is the first thing that strikes the reader." Gissing had "one great theme. It is the life of a man of fine character and intelligence who is absolutely penniless and is therefore the sport of all that is most sordid and brutal in modern life." Here we learn the "terrible importance of money, and, if you slip, how you fall and fall and fall." Only Dickens and Mrs. Gaskell before him got poverty so right, and he is not sentimental like Dickens or profligate like Gaskell. Bitterness and disappointment are in proportion to original possibility, hope, and expectation.

Gissing's later years were successful. He was ranked with Meredith and Hardy; Henry James and H. G. Wells were his friends. Conrad and Stephen Crane responded to his work. His last book, *The Private Papers of Henry Ryecroft,* autobiographical and autumnal, was successful in its day and remains readable. Though his books did not reach happy endings, his life did. Wells nursed him toward the end and writes with the cool attention of a scientist in his *Experiment in Autobiography* of his dying friend: "It is one of the many oddities of my sheltered life that until the death of Gissing I had never watched a brain passing through disorganization into a final stillness." He takes us through the process.

The formative years of Samuel Butler (1835–1902) were more conventionally unhappy than Gissing's. "We are a nation of father haters," Pritchett declares. "The eighteenth-century father is a pagan bursting a blood vessel in the ripeness of time; the nineteenth-century father is a Jehovah dictating an inexhaustible Deuteronomy. Money, as Butler saw it, makes the difference." We pass from the illusion of fate, luck, and fortune in the eighteenth century, with its speculations, profits, and losses, the good receiving sentimental and material rewards, to the wary husbandry of the nineteenth, when money gains an ordering autonomy and men have at last refined an abstract master to serve, a master whose demands outweigh all others. Endings are no longer tidy: after Balzac the conventional happy ending is suspect and classical closure to which readers had become accustomed could no longer be depended upon.

Butler's grandfather was a bishop and his father a reluctant minister of the Church, keen to force his own son into God's service as he had been forced (his real ambition had been to go to sea). Butler grew by painful contraries into a liberalizing spirit, curious, eagerly unorthodox. A gifted amateur, he engaged in science, advocated Darwinian theories, and claimed to be a Homeric scholar. When he sides with Eratosthenes, his verdict is just: "Homeric commentators have been blind so long that nothing will do for them but Homer must be blind too. They have transferred their own blindness to the poet." But Butler's theory of the female author of the *Odyssey,* Homer in a frock, is itself not wholly without a white stick. Still, he translated the *Iliad* and the *Odyssey* into highly serviceable prose. Borges reminds us that he knew the *Iliad* by heart.

He also wrote fiction and satire. Two of these works are read today, and Pritchett introduces the first in these terms: "*The Way of All Flesh* is one of the time-bombs of literature. One thinks of it lying on Butler's desk at Clifford's Inn for thirty years, waiting to blow up the Victorian family and with it the whole great pillared and balustraded edifice of the Victorian novel." Graham Greene, a writer haunted by his father, relishes it: "Read *The Way of All Flesh* for the sa-vour of hatred," he declares. We must also read *Brewton* "for the brilliant re-porting of the opening chapters." *Erewhon; or, Over the Range,* was published anonymously in 1872 and sold well in part because readers imagined it to be by Bulwer-Lytton. It is a dystopian odyssey that begins in Butler's experience of New Zealand (where he was a sheep farmer on the South Island for four years) and ends in a country whose name is (almost) "nowhere" spelled backward. (Some of the down-under Erewhonian names can be reversed, so that Yram who helps Higgs and Senoj Nosnibor his host are readable in a mirror, while the at-tractive Arowhena might have been more judiciously named, and the goddess Ydgrun is an anagrammatic Grundy.)

The most compelling satire of its kind since Gulliver traveled, it does not ri-val Swift because Butler is not sufficiently an artist, Greene says, to make it credible. Swift measured and mapped and diagrammed, proportions hold, and the worlds Gulliver visits are consistent; Butler is content with impressionism, his conceits do not build toward coherent satirical vision. But there is satire and amusing contrivance in the book, which itself assimilates Butler's speculative essays on the evolution of machines (passages that much appeal to the theorist Giles Deleuze).

In a way the book answers *Robinson Crusoe*. Here we follow the fate, not of a man punished for youthful hubris; indeed, young Higgs the protagonist's depar-ture from Britain was a proper colonial excursion, to farm sheep and make his fortune. Though he strives and climbs and suffers in the mountains, the story is about the narrator only insofar as he becomes an everyman. The flat-toned manner is Swift's, though we do not believe in Erewhon as we do in Swift's otherworlds. Had the book been true to its opening, the prose as transparent as that of W. H. Hudson, Butler might have proven a lyric novelist or memoirist of the first order. A Wordsworthian recrudescence of memory, the beginning that takes us to his beginning, is there: "I am there now, as I write; I fancy that I can see the downs, the huts, the plain, and the river bed—that torrent pathway of desolation, with its distant roar of waters. Oh, wonderful! wonderful! so lonely and so solemn, with the sad grey clouds above, and no sound save the lost lamb bleating upon the mountain-side, as though its little heart were breaking." An old ewe thinks the lamb is hers, they run to one another; both are mistaken, and they part to their solitudes once more. Anyone familiar with New Zealand high country, how range opens on range, will find the climb toward dystopia convincing and the descent into Erewhon itself a wrenching of genre.

Butler makes no bones about his intentions in *The Way of All Flesh*. His man-ner is forensic and essayistic. He directs us to the opening of the nineteenth century when, though the "violent type of father, as described by Fielding,

Richardson, Smollett and Sheridan" is no longer common in literature, subtler forms persist. "The parents in Miss Austen's novels are less like savage wild beasts than those of her predecessors, but she evidently looks upon them with suspicion, and an uneasy feeling that *le père de famille est capable de tout* makes itself sufficiently apparent throughout the greater part of her writings." The roots are in the Old Testament fathers, revived by the Puritans. "Moreover, Puritanism restricted natural pleasures; it substituted the Jeremiad for the Paean." This provides a psychological dimension for those who argue that the novel thrives at a time when the values of Protestant individualism and bourgeois capitalism are growing and changing.

Even so, Butler held off publishing *The Way of All Flesh*. It appeared posthumously, and when it did the editor had had to reconstruct the book because Butler left no authoritative final draft. He withheld it because "it dealt soberly but sincerely with the chief springs of human conduct," and such dealing seemed unspeakable, even as the great edifices of the Church were crumbling. The most subversive element in Butler may be his tone: "The amusement we get," says Pritchett, "comes from his stand for Common Sense, Equanimity, Worldliness and the Plain, and from comparing its downrightness with its underlying timidity." The quietness, the sidelong half-smile of the writing, puts us in mind not of the vehemence of Carlyle or the bitterness of Dickens but the evenhanded autobiographies and biographies of the eighteenth century. Greene objects to the ways in which Butler's argument dwarfs and "burns dry" his characters: it is certainly a roman à thèse, and its technique of embodied argument, over four generations of the Pontifex clan, though not peculiar to Butler, was much used by lesser writers of the time. The fate of Ernest Pontifex is harsh, his partial triumph in overcoming with a whole, if maimed, spirit the tyrannies of family and society is told with care and quiet interpretative rigor by his friend and godfather, Mr. Overton. We stand on the very edge of the human precipice and look over. It is no surprise that Ernest becomes an author of radical books.

Contrasting Butler's book with *Father and Son* (1907), the memoir by Edmund Gosse (1849–1928), the difference between the needs of fiction and of "fact" becomes clear. Gosse's book is the product of affection, an attempt to mend rather than explore a rift, with a severe, loving parent: "not a clash of wills so much as a division of principles; and, since the breach was tragic, its agony was without resentment." Butler lived and died loathing his father, and vice versa, but the Gosses, Pritchett says, "gazed helplessly, emotionally across the gulf of history between them." The opening words are stable with understanding: they intend to examine what has happened. "This book is the record of the struggle between two temperaments, two consciences and almost two epochs. It ended, as was inevitable, in disruption. Of the two human beings here described, one was born to fly backward, the other could not help being carried forward." Is it a memoir? Much of the material does not square with known facts. Truth to the impression, perhaps: a halfway house between autobiography and fiction, a mixed genre that comes into its own in the twentieth century with Proust, Gide, and Genet, with Woolf, Lawrence, and Powell, with Bellow, Updike, and Roth. *Father and Son* directly inspires novelists in the twentieth century, in particular Peter Carey, whose *Oscar and Lucinda* draws on it.

# | 22 |

## *Braveries*

Robert Louis Stevenson, W. H. Hudson, Bruce Chatwin, Richard Jefferies,

William Morris, Charles Kingsley, Henry Rider Haggard, Rudyard Kipling

Edmund Gosse and Robert Louis Stevenson (1850–1894) first met in their teens, and after 1879, when he moved to London, Stevenson would on occasion stay with Gosse and his family. Both men were attentive readers and critics, generous, open, and restless; formal experimentation is to be found in their best work, mechanical fluency marks their journeyman's work, though Stevenson is seldom flat or a *mere* writer. Stevenson is neglected, Edith Wharton says, because of his versatility and omnicompetence. She admired him and did not misvalue him just because his best books belonged to what were regarded as secondary genres: children's literature, adventure, and horror.

He died relatively young, but he lived young, too, taking risks, going west (until he reached the East) in his life and writing. Henry James suggests that all his writings answer for boyhood, "the age of heterogeneous pockets." He notes "the singular maturity of the expression that he has given to young sentiments": his "constant theme is the unsophisticated," evoked with sophistication of means and manner. His are not fireside children: they are out of doors, after adventure. Muriel Spark quotes his lines "it is but a child of air / That lingers in the garden there" and remembers how she and her friend Frances Niven as little girls in Edinburgh used to sneak into the garden of the Stevenson birthplace house next door to Frances's because they liked him so. Andrew Lang noted Stevenson's "buoyancy, the survival of the child in him. He has told the world often, in prose and verse, how vivid are his memories of his own infancy." The fantasies of the boy "ripened into imagination: he has also kept up the habit of dramatizing everything, of playing, half consciously, many parts, of making the world 'an unsubstantial fairy place.'" Hence, Lang suggests, the freakishness of the work, the Mr. Hydes and Long John Silvers, the evil uncles: "He plays at being an Arabian tale-teller, and his 'New Arabian Nights' are a new kind of romanticism—Oriental, freakish, like the work of a changeling." Stevenson: most erratic of the Victorians, most urgently at work because he knew, if not the actual number of his days, that they were surely numbered, due to his tuberculosis. All this talk of fairy places should not mask the fact that his essays and fiction lead deep into experience.

We find Stevenson the actual boy in his native Edinburgh furtively reading Whitman in a coffeehouse away from the supervision of his strict parents, haunting the dark steep streets of the Old Town; in England in the company of Gosse, James, even Meredith ("the only man of genius of my acquaintance"); in the Cevennes with his bad lungs and the famous donkey; in California gazing like Balboa at the Pacific; in Dorset with his new wife, dropping in on Hardy and his not so new one; then back in California, setting out for Samoa, where he was to construct his tropical equivalent to Abbotsford at Vailima and write himself to death to fulfill responsibilities, real and assumed, much as Scott had done. Scott sailed with Stevenson's grandfather in 1814 to view lighthouses, notably the Bell Rock (1811), one of fifteen he built. His son, Stevenson's uncle Alan, built thirteen. Scott haunted Stevenson and his work.

Mark Twain, not in general well disposed to British writers, made an exception of Stevenson. "He was most scantily furnished with flesh, his clothes seemed to fall into hollows as if there might be nothing inside but the frame for a sculptor's statue." To this wonderful metaphor, with its appropriate hollowness, given the subject's tuberculosis, he adds a "long face and lank hair and dark complexion and musing and melancholy expression." The whole impression "seemed especially planned to gather the rays of your observation and focalize them upon Stevenson's special distinction and commanding feature, his splendid eyes. They burned with a smoldering rich fire under the penthouse of his brows, and they made him beautiful." A fire burns there with minimal fuel, an image of the man and of the working of his imagination.

The fuel Stevenson burned he described in his essay about his literary antecedents. Set beside Coleridge's *Biographia Literaria,* Trollope's *Autobiography,* or Hardy's *Life,* his brief ledger of indebtedness is a literary confession that provides a reading list and lucid pointers for modern readers keen to penetrate not only Stevenson's imagination but his age.

Stevenson's wife, Fanny, ten years his senior, an American with three children, was a woman who had suffered much and expected much. Biographers deal as harshly with her as life did. She was in later years overweight, her hair turned grey (it happens), she was loud, coarse, and unladylike (Stevenson had without too much fuss frequented the prostitutes of Edinburgh and felt at home with unpolished people, even to the extent that he crossed America in an immigrant train, roughing it); she was volatile and at times unstable. Yet he loved her, whatever his friends thought, and he loved her children. She mothered him and they fulfilled one another's needs. We cannot know much more than that they stayed together through difficult years and put more than a brave face on it.

We do know without doubt what he read and how, what words he responded to and saw the world through. Few writers give so clear an account of their formation as Stevenson does. Because he is one of the "exquisites of style," his *catalogue raisonné* is also an account, a balance sheet. Apart from fiction, the first book that marked him was Montaigne's *Essais* (read, we must assume, in French: he mentions no translation). Young readers "will find in these smiling pages a magazine"—he uses the word in its French sense of storehouse—"of heroism and wisdom, all of an antique strain"; they will have their "linen decencies and excited orthodoxies fluttered." After Montaigne, not before, despite his strict upbringing, he names the New Testament, with special emphasis on Matthew's gospel, which he urges us to read "freshly like a book, not droningly and dully like a portion of the Bible." Immediately after the gospel comes Whitman's *Leaves of Grass,* which we know he regarded as a formally and morally liberating text; it "tumbled the world upside down for me, blew into space a thousand cobwebs of genteel and ethical illusion, and, having thus shaken my tabernacle of lies, set me back again upon a strong foundation of all the original and manly virtues." It is for those "who have the gift of reading." Why mince words? "The average man lives, and must live, so wholly in convention, that gunpowder charges of the truth are more apt to discompose than to invigorate his creed." The average man will either reject the work for indecency and blasphemy or embrace it as a new gospel and lose his way. "New truth is only useful to supplement the old; rough truth is only wanted to expand, not to destroy, our civil and often elegant conventions."

After Whitman, he must mention the philosopher Herbert Spencer. He cannot vouch for the durability of his teachings but he can for the unadorned authority of his style: "There dwells in his pages a spirit of highly abstract joy, plucked naked like an algebraic symbol but still joyful." And then George Henry Lewes's *Life* of Goethe, a writer who repelled him for a dozen reasons, but the life reminded him "of the truly mingled tissue of man's nature, and how huge faults and shining virtues cohabit and persevere in the same character." The poems of the Roman poet Martial delighted him, and the stoical *Meditations* of Marcus Aurelius, whose "dispassionate gravity," self-effacement, and "tenderness of others" move the reader to the core.

Wordsworth puzzles him. A peculiar "innocence, a rugged austerity of joy, a sight of the stars, 'the silence that is in the lonely hills,' something of the cold thrill of dawn, cling to his work and give it a particular address to what is best in us." He does not teach a lesson but casts a spell, and this is what Stevenson does, he aims "to set a 'dream' going in the reader's mind," as John Gardner puts it. Readers are not passive. They hope, they judge. Their engagement should be deeper, in ratio to how much space the author leaves in the novel for them to occupy imaginatively. "Such," says Stevenson, "are the best teachers; a dogma learned is only a new error—the old one was perhaps as good; but a spirit communicated is a perpetual possession." He adds Meredith, his first novelist, and he adds Thoreau; the Hazlitt of "On the Spirit of Obligations," which changed his life; William Penn's aphorisms; and Algernon Mitford's *Tales of Old Japan.*

Samuel Butler grumbles that writers like Stevenson "seem to have taken pains to acquire what they called a style as a preliminary measure—as something that they had to form before their writings could be of any value." He is not that kind of writer himself! "I should like to put it on record that I never took the smallest pains with my style, have never thought about it, and do not know or want to know whether it is a style at all or whether it is not, as I believe and hope, just common, simple straightforwardness."

The question of style and its limitations arises in discussions of Stevenson and his contemporaries, Meredith in particular. Stevenson in his formative years "played the sedulous ape" to other writers, to Hazlitt, Sir Thomas Browne, and Montaigne, for example. This was his poet's instinct: poets learn by imitation, and writers of fiction can do so as well. What does the writer attentive to the work of other writers concentrate on? In parody and *homage,* it is *style* they strive to replicate. This is a quality Borges admires in Stevenson, how he understood that "in a well-written page all the words should look the same way." The wrong, the archaic or crudely chosen word breaks the spell. "All our arts and occupations lie wholly on the surface," Stevenson declares; "it is on the surface that we perceive their beauty, fitness, and significance." If one gets the surface right, it will imply the depths; to try to penetrate the depths is to endanger the whole craft of the novel. Equally dangerous—though he risks it—is critically anatomizing and analyzing the text.

John Galsworthy took Stevenson's creative reticence as an aesthetic excuse for a psychological reticence: "He felt life, I believe, too keenly to want to probe into it; he spun his gossamer to lure himself and all away from life. That was his driving mood; but the craftsman in him, longing to be clear and poignant, made him more natural, more actual than most realists." Stevenson would have resisted this characterization. He is a theorist of style, metaphors enact his meaning. When he says, "The true business of the literary artist is to plait or weave his meaning, involving it around itself; so that each sentence, by successive phrases, shall first come into a kind of knot, and then, after a moment of suspended meaning, solve and clear itself," he is not being fanciful. We can read him, or Shakespeare, or Carlyle, sentence by sentence, and see this process occurring, the delivery of clear meaning or clear sense, no matter how mimetic the style. "In every properly constructed sentence there should be observed this knot or hitch; so that (however delicately) we are led to foresee, to expect, and then to welcome the successive phrases."

The design should not be too contrived: the writer must be "ever changing, as it were, the stitch" while giving "the effect of an ingenious neatness." He insists that "style is synthetic; and the artist, seeking, so to speak, a peg to plait about, takes up at once two or more elements or two or more views of the subject in hand; combines, implicates, and contrasts them"—the image of weaving again—"and while, in one sense, he was merely seeking an occasion for the necessary knot, he will be found, in the other, to have greatly enriched the meaning, or to have transacted the work of two sentences in the space of one." The "synthetic writer" can be the more penetrating artist, with "a far keener sense of the generation and affinity of events." We are persuaded: "That style is therefore the most perfect, not, as fools say, which is the most natural, for the most natural is the disjointed babble of the chronicler; but which attains the highest degree of elegant and pregnant implication unobtrusively."

Stevenson, James says, "regards the literary form not simply as a code of signals but as the keyboard of a piano, and as so much plastic material." We are required to consider first his *manner,* and then his *matter.* Foregrounding *manner,* medium used in a particular way, sets him apart from writers who seek to disappear in their writing. He *appears.* James calls it a "bravery of gesture." And beneath his "dancing-tune," James insists, there is a depth. "Much as he cares for his phrase, he cares more for life, and for a certain transcendently lovable part of it." He is an extraordinary critic, but in his creative work "his feelings are always his reasons." This should put us in mind of Lawrence: the two writers, critically, creatively, and in their lives and deaths, have much in common. Reflecting on his letters, Greene, whose early novels are in Stevenson's debt, and who grew impatient with the adolescent concerns of his books, their "spurious maturity," despairs of the exaggerations in his language, but detects a maturing as the writer enters the darker years, in parentheses including cruelly: "(for suffering like literature has its juvenilia—men mature and graduate in suffering)."

A major challenge for Stevenson was to graduate out of Scott. James complains that the language of *Catriona* (1893), the sequel to *Kidnapped* (1886), which traces David Balfour's subsequent adventures, lacks "visibility": "It subjects my visual sense, my *seeing* imagination, to an almost painful underfeeding." With his accustomed tact, Stevenson conceded the point, then told James in a letter *why* he was writing in this way. "I *hear* people talking, and I *feel* them acting, and that seems to me to be fiction. My two aims may be described as, 1st. War to the adjective; 2nd. Death to the optic nerve." He concedes that his is "an age of the optic nerve in literature," yet literature got on without so much description in the past: it can do so again. Scott is the main initiator of excessive description. Making it visible is not necessarily making it real, and Stevenson resists work of many realists of his time. Even Zola: his use of description is a dissipation of style, a way of drowning fiction in a thick "rancid" tide of "visibility." This was at the heart of Stevenson's reaction against Scott, whose works stand at an odd angle behind all his own, a fact he acknowledges even in resisting it. "After Scott," he says, "we beheld the starveling story—once, in the hands of Voltaire, as abstract as a parable—begin to be pampered upon facts."

The legacy of Scott half a century later was a prose that confused thickness with depth; and part of Stevenson's originality is in perceiving and defying the tendency. Yet *Kidnapped* stands in a clear relationship to *Waverley,* and *The Black Arrow* to *Ivanhoe.* There was no way a Scottish writer could come out from under Scott's abundant shadow altogether. Stevenson provides sufficient detail, readers are allowed space in which to visualize for themselves. In *Strange Case of Dr. Jekyll and Mr. Hyde* we become one with Mr. Utterson, puzzling the narrative together. The reader collaborates, the story a joint venture with what turn out to be three narrators: when Mr. Hyde is described as having an "unexpressed deformity," we provide it, each in our own way. Stevenson speaks conventionally of "my paymaster, the Great Public," but he puts that public to work, and his cordial contract paid: after *Treasure Island, Kidnapped,* and *Dr. Jekyll* were in print, Stevenson was clearing £5,000 a year, about £60,000 or $85,000 in today's values.

Henry James read all of Stevenson's fiction as if it addressed a mature audience—which in a sense it did. The faults in the writing he took to be less aspects of the adventure story genre, more consequences of Stevenson's resistance to Scott's legacy. In characterization Stevenson says that James "treats, for the most part, the statics of character, studying it at rest or only gently moved; and, with his usual delicate and just artistic instinct, he avoids those stronger passions which would deform the attitudes he loves to study." His own case is different: there are few statics, and thus through action the adventure stories keep their proportion: he does not "change his sitters from the humorists of ordinary life to the brute forces and bare types of more emotional moments." They are stable in action or in repose. He certainly uses strong emotions and passions, but he will not display them. They are in the background, under the surface of characters. The fiction discloses their effect on the surface, which is all we can monitor. We know the deep adjustments and disruptions by their consequences in tone and action. He was indeed the disciple of Marcus Aurelius.

Much of his writing is collaborative in its creation. His first successful book, *Treasure Island* (1883), he began in a holiday cottage. There was a lad staying (who would become his stepson and formal collaborator): he was not a bookish boy but he liked to paint. Stevenson joined him from time to time with watercolors at the easel. "On one of these occasions, I made the map of an island; it was elaborately and (I thought) beautifully colored; the shape of it took my fancy beyond expression; it contained harbors that pleased me like sonnets; and with the unconsciousness of the predestined, I ticketed my performance 'Treasure Island.'" The story came to him. The boy became excited about it, and so did Stevenson's father, the engineer, who contributed materially to it—for example, the precise contents of Billy Bones's chest. He is never precious about the sources of his ideas; the collaboration with the reader is also a collaboration with other writers. "No doubt the parrot once belonged to Robinson Crusoe. No doubt the skeleton is conveyed from Poe . . . The stockade, I am told, is from *Masterman Ready* [by Captain Marryat]. It may be, I care not a jot." His main debt was to the painted map, whose specific geography, as that of an actual island might have done, determined the narrative: "It was because I had made two harbors that the *Hispaniola* was sent on her wanderings with Israel Hands."

Of the fiction that followed, the series *The Black Arrow* (which he began in 1883), an adventure story set during the Wars of the Roses, and *Prince Otto* (1885), an action romance set in Grünewald, a state he invented (James called it a "coquetry"), are effortlessly researched and constructed. With *Strange Case of Dr. Jekyll and Mr. Hyde* (1886) Stevenson emerges as an original artist. The story is simple and terrifying, the telling a gradual piecing together of clues. In its theme of psychological division, it visits the territory Hogg did in *True Confession*, though Stevenson is structurally tidy, without the confusions of theology, though underpinning its psychology is the troubled spirituality of an earlier period when beneath the smoothed surface of the Enlightenment flowed turbulent, unacknowledged psychospiritual currents. *Kidnapped* (1886), his most complete achievement, has drama and economy of style but explores a wider map: David Balfour pursues his just inheritance, works alongside the memorable, swashbuckling Jacobite Alan Stewart (Breck), and engages in Scottish history with the Jacobite theme. Stevenson, imagining his country, creates it whole, Highlands and all, on a human scale. Readers who dislike dialect writing find Stevenson's invention of various simplified Scottish demotics persuasive and necessary to the differentiated drama. Even James is dazzled by the way he has created a sound for the Scottish eighteenth century. He does not cry out for a glossary. Though the book was serialized in a "boys' paper" in England, it satisfies, James insists, the demands of "higher criticism." The miserly uncle is a caricature drawn less from life than from Scott; James does not like the way the action is left suspended at the end, but the book can "stand by *Henry Esmond* as a fictive autobiography."

There is none of the sense of set pieces we get in Scott: the adventure ties closely in to character, history, and landscape. His most ambitious novel, *The Master of Ballantrae* (1889), works on the largest canvas he attempted, creating a tale of revenge on three continents. The later novels, collaborations with his stepson Lloyd Osbourne, attempts at sequels, the suggestive unfinished torso of *Weir of Hermiston* (1896), and *St. Ives* (1897), which he dictated to his stepdaughter Isobel Strong, often performing the parts as he developed them, and which Arthur Quiller-Couch completed, are of interest. But nothing lives up to *Kidnapped.*

Each of his books is a new start, only *Catriona* building on the characters of an earlier book. Yet how often he succeeded with his readers, the marketplace, and posterity. Greene admires the writing of the last six "Samoan years," during which "his fine dandified talent began to shed its disgusting graces, the granite to show through." This is a very English and moralistic judgment: between graces and granite, is granite always to be preferred? He preferred (and he said so) Dumas to Balzac, adventure and action to the grinding reality of urban life. The ambivalence of Stevenson's narratives appeals to less-censorious readers than Greene, as it had appealed to Greene when he was setting out. Like Poe, Stevenson has been popular abroad, perhaps more popular there than at home, taking home to mean Scotland first and Great Britain second. In Latin America, Borges is only his most translated advocate. From Russia, or from Russian, comes Nabokov's vivid lecture on *Dr. Jekyll and Mr. Hyde.*

Many of his works were composed when he was an invalid, writing in bed, in places traveled to for his health. He seldom alludes to these circumstances in his books. His early life was full of incident and adventure, his later marked by vicariousness, yet he knew how to live fully in the imagination, and in style. James recalls the first time he read Stevenson's work: "I seemed to see the author, unknown as yet to fame, jump before my eyes into a style." In *Dr. Jekyll* it will not let the reader's interest flag, tenacious like the ancient mariner in the eponymous poem, until it releases us at the end wrung out and as weary and tried as Mr. Utterson the solicitor.

During his years in Samoa, where he took the Samoan name Tusitala, "teller of tales," Stevenson produced *Catriona,* hoping to make money; and he worked on *Weir of Hermiston,* which pleased him greatly. In December 1894, opening a bottle of wine, he seems to have suffered a cerebral hemorrhage. He died within a few hours.

Taking issue with Walter Besant and Henry James in his great essay "A Humble Remonstrance" (1884), Stevenson blurs the line between fiction and factual narrative, not only on the grounds of the instability of facts. The art of narrative, he declares, is continuous: *Tom Jones* and Boswell's *Life of Johnson.* In an aside he calls Boswell's *Life* "a work of cunning and inimitable art," and it succeeds because of its coherent characterization, its selection and ordering of incident, and "the invention (yes, invention) and preservation of a certain key in dialogue." So, he asks with Pilate, *What is truth,* when the means of its delivery is language? In taking issue with James's opposition between *art* and *life,* Stevens is paving a way for some of his most original and, today, least valued successors, for in the oblique debate James was the victor, not because his argument is stronger but because Stevenson, his peer as a critical theorist and a writer less given to subtilizing, was carried off by life to Samoa and then to the shades.

First among the writers whose work Stevenson seems to prepare a way for is William Henry Hudson (1841–1922). Ford looks to him with gratitude: his temperament "is the most beautiful thing that God ever made." In his memoirs, nature writing, and fiction he is "totally undramatic in his methods": the word is subordinate to the sentence, the sentence to the paragraph, the paragraph to the page. His is a forbearing style, subjecting itself to what it has to say. In *Hampshire Days* he declares, "My flesh and the soil are one, and the heat in my blood and in the sunshine are one, and the winds and the tempests and my passions are one." Conrad says "his writing was like the grass that the good God made to grow and when it was there you could not tell how it came." His editor Edward Garnett noted that "Hudson's nature writings appeal to the mind, to the heart, and the senses together." One feels *individually* addressed, singled out as by a letter writer.

Even in fiction Hudson tells the truth, what his eyes see and his ears hear. His memory is alert and present because he is alive in the present and sees by analogy. How he misses the great birds of South America; every high-flying English bird—he helped to found the Royal Society for the Protection of Birds—brings back to mind whole species observed with minute attention on the other side of the world.

Hudson was born not far from Quilmes in the province of Buenos Aires (or Ayres as he spelled it in the Anglo-Saxon manner), Argentina. His parents were English and Anglo-American. He spent his early, idyllically Spartan years on his father's *estancia* or ranch, Los Veinticinco Ombúes, on the pampas. Indeed, twenty-five of these large, evergreen Ombú trees marked a kind of avenue, visible from a distance. As he grew older he explored farther out, beyond the avenue, coming in time to know a wide area, its topography, plant and animal life, and especially its birds. Typhus and rheumatic fever weakened him as a boy; he was solitary, mild, and self-sufficient. His father failed at many things, decisively as a sheep farmer, and life was poor and unrestricted.

His brother encouraged him to read Darwin as a naturalist, without much care for the theological issues raised. He started collecting specimens, riding into Argentinean Patagonia, Brazil, and Uruguay. He writes of his early years in my favorite of his books, the autobiographical *Far Away and Long Ago* (1918). The author was seventy-four when he wrote it, and the book is not an elegy but a labor of recovery composed with intense concentration during the First World War, as if this happy elsewhere could be recovered and made available to the contemporary reader.

A single sentence must stand for the clarity and connectedness of his seeing language: "There was a field of alfalfa about half an acre in size, which flowered three times a year, and during the flowering time it drew the butterflies from all the surrounding plain with its luscious bean-like fragrance, until the field was full of them, red, black, yellow, and white butterflies, fluttering in flocks around every blue spike." This is an image but also the template of a recurrent experience gratefully witnessed. He insists on the accuracy of the objects observed and of their environments: nothing is isolated. He disliked photographs: they degraded what they portrayed, especially natural things, arresting them in time, removing them from being. The artist had to see and communicate, not just point a lens.

He can seldom resist the pressure of anecdote, even when it is not quite germane to his argument or scene: he refuses to edit out memory and digression. There is a natural transparency about the progression of his writing. The protracted, happy, threadbare idyll of childhood passes. We arrive at a grim chapter in *Far Away and Long Ago* entitled "Boyhood's End." The boy arrives not at puberty but at the city, its notorious slaughterhouses, the destination to which the gaucho's long rearing and herding of livestock, all the human legend and lore of the Pampas, are directed. It is hard for a young reader—any reader—to forget the description of the Saladero in Buenos Ayres, the great area where the meat was carved and salted. The killing ground spread over three or four square miles, where the flocks of sheep, cattle, and horses were driven. He sees it in the same transparent, unironic language with which he has presented the paradisal world. Now the huge herds are driven together, cruelly slain, skinned, and butchered, the pariah dogs and ubiquitous vultures and gulls gorging themselves. "The blood so abundantly shed from day to day, mixing with the dust, had formed a crust half a foot thick all over the open space: let the reader try to imagine the smell of this crust and of tons of offal and flesh and bones lying everywhere in heaps." High walls of skulls and bones surrounded the *quintas* in these areas, as a farmer would build a wall of the stones cleared from his fields. This was, after his unrestrained childhood, a city of most dreadful night, the scenes and smells, the heartless cruelty familiar from the war.

In 1869, his parents dead, Hudson traveled to England. He was twenty-seven and poor, and London was a misery for him. He married a woman who owned a lodging house. Sixteen years passed before he published his first book, *The Purple Land That England Lost* (1885); like Kipling he was suspended between two cultures, two natures, two politics. It was not an easy situation, and it contributed to his dependence on memory, his celebration of years when he was free to wander and explore, invisibly dependent on his father. That freedom, when his imagination and his skills in observation took shape, remained a paradise from which the fall into maturity, into England, material hardship, and advancing years, had to be endured. It was *The Purple Land* that led astray Robert Cohn in Hemingway's *The Sun Also Rises*. "*The Purple Land* is a very sinister book if read too late in life," the protagonist Jake Barnes says. "It recounts splendid imaginary amorous adventures of a perfect English gentleman in an intensely romantic land, the scenery of which is very well described." Some books are treacherous when read too young, some when read too old.

Hudson had to acquire the language in which he wrote. He learned to speak English as a boy, but while in Argentina spoke principally Spanish and perhaps Guaraní. How did he spend the sixteen years between his arrival and his first book? Was it the prose of Darwin and Huxley that shaped his own lucid sentences? Was it his rapt attention to the English countryside? His first pieces for the scientific papers were written in a mannered idiom. Yet the language of his later nature writing and fiction is not effortful. He became a naturalized British subject in 1900. A year later he received a Civil List pension. By then he had written his early fiction. The stories of *El Ombú* (1902) and *Green Mansions: A Romance of the Tropical Forest* (1904) followed.

"I'm not one of your damned writers," he said irritably to Ford. "I'm a naturalist from La Plata." And he teased, "It's perfectly simple to write down what one has seen." It is to this simplicity that the damned writers and critics come back repeatedly, wondering how he does it. Nothing is harder than to be unaffected. In 1932 John Galsworthy, anything but unaffected, praised *The Purple Land* as "the best Picaresque novel in English of the last hundred and more years." Picaresque is not wrong: his Spanish tradition included that. Galsworthy admired *El Ombú* and *Green Mansions* as "tragic recital" and "rarest fantasy." He is sui generis, free of the restraints of school or group, "nomadic records." In an "age of specialisms" he insisted on remaining a generalist, free to walk and look as he liked. His is the prose of a naturalist, even a scientist. The pressure of content refines it, a palpable intelligence governs it, so that the sense is spread out evenly through it, the writing not for effect but for accuracy. The only writer of his time who shares his virtues is Stevenson.

The only modern writer who belongs in Hudson's company is (Charles) Bruce Chatwin (1940–1989). The affinity is less of subject matter, though both wrote about remote places and about nature, than of style. Hudson died old, however, Chatwin before he was fifty, of AIDS. Greene wrote of Stevenson, "He left behind him what mainly amounts to a mass of juvenilia. Gay, bright, and perennially attractive though much of the work may be." A "spurious maturity" is evident in Chatwin, too, when the writing is too artful, but his maturity and stylistic clarity advance from book to book.

Chatwin grew up largely in Birmingham. He was restless, first of all for Wales, where he later set his one conventional novel, *On the Black Hill* (1982), and then for places farther afield. Travel provided a basis for form: a beginning, middle, and end; the middle is full of lesser beginnings, middles, and ends. It is the picaresque made literal. It is Mandeville and Don Quixote and Scott and journalism.

He attended private schools he did not much like and did not immediately go up to university. Instead he was found work at Sotheby's, first as a porter and then, proving he had an acute eye, as an assessor and valuer. It was the ideal situation for one fascinated by objects, their sale and collection, and also by collectors. He became an expert on impressionist art and eventually a director of the company. He suffered eyestrain and was given a six-month sabbatical, during which he traveled to Africa. Later he spent two years reading archaeology at Edinburgh University, but it was not for him.

As a child he remembered a cabinet of curios in which was preserved a hank of red hair that once belonged, he was told, to a brontosaurus. It had been sent to the family by a relation in Patagonia. Later he discovered it was in fact the fur of a sloth. Later still the precious hank was lost, and he set off to Patagonia to find a replacement for it, the occasion for his first book, *In Patagonia* (1977), which changed the course of travel writing. In the same cabinet was some porcelain, and from that small collection germinated the legendary collection at the heart of his novel *Utz* (1988). It may also have contained trinkets from Dahomey, hence *The Viceroy of Ouidah* (1980) centered around the slave trade, and from the Australian outback pointers to *The Songlines* (1987). What makes Chatwin such a close cousin of Hudson is the materiality of his imagination. Each object tells a story, story leads to story, and a community can be inferred, fact and fiction. Naturalist and anthropologist coexisted with the novelist. In 1972 the *Sunday Times Magazine* hired him as an adviser on architecture and art and his travel assignments began. He discovered an aptitude for travel writing. In 1974 he broke loose and spent six months in Patagonia. His book appeared three years later.

*In Patagonia* he intended to make a series of "snapshots," people and places observed, a focused album. Inevitably the fact and trajectory of the journey linked them, and as they accumulated they connected to one another. The album became moving pictures, the narrator zigzagging and spiraling down the foot of South America, discovering the European, in particular the Welsh, residue at the end of the Earth. In Britain the book was a success, but when it reached Patagonia there was resentment: he had invented things, and his precise account was undermined by invention. Describing *On the Black Hill* he said, "Very little I've invented but on the other hand there are new combinations," including, incidentally, Lewis and Benjamin, the twin brothers who, though Welsh in ancestry, he'd encountered in Patagonia. This is what Picasso called "the lie that tells the truth," and Hudson practiced it, too, but in the absence of witnesses: Ford's truth to the impression. *The Songlines* is frank about its weaving of fiction and fact, though despite its candor it still provoked controversy in Australia. His ethnographical disciplines helped him alienate himself from received views of the Aborigines and their culture.

His last novel, *Utz,* is a kind of displaced autobiography. He was suffering from AIDs, though his condition was not made public, and *Utz* is a kind of intense, brief elegy. Set in Prague, it is narrated by a young man from England come to meet a collector of Meissen porcelain. Like *The Viceroy,* this book is so short it might almost count as a novella. In these different brief novels the effect of Flaubert's *Trois contes,* one of Chatwin's favorite books, is felt. The economy, intensity, and apersonality of the narrative means that the stories exist with great freedom and the reader must participate in the process of connection and interpretation.

Edmund White recalls his first meeting with Chatwin in New York. The introduction was arranged by the photographer Robert Mapplethorpe, to whose book *Lady Lisa Lyon* Chatwin had contributed an essay. As soon as they met, they "fooled around" sexually, and that cemented their tense friendship. White was jealous of Chatwin's looks, accent, social success. In Paris Chatwin would talk about his books, giving "oral drafts" of them, and in retrospect White noted how much less gay the print version was from the one he told over dinner. After *The Viceroy* failed, Chatwin retreated to his conventional Welsh novel; the twins were initially lovers (Updike took this as given), though in the printed version they were presented as chaste.

His death was marked by a Greek Orthodox church service on St. Valentine's Day 1989, the day the Ayatollah Khomeini of Iran declared the fatwa against Salman Rushdie, one of Chatwin's close friends. Rushdie attended the service, his last public engagement before he went into hiding. Martin Amis describes the service as "a torment in its own right, with much incomprehensible yodelling and entreating . . . The robed clerics waved their fuming caskets in the air, like Greek waiters removing incendiary ashtrays." This was, he concluded, Chatwin's "last joke" on those who loved him, "his heterodox theism had finally homed in on a religion that no one he knew could understand or respond to." The Rushdie affair doubly buried him.

There are five books, and each starts (as Stevenson's do) from scratch, a new invention, a new combination of elements and a different narrative strategy. *The Songlines* is sprawling, inventive, "anthropological," sentimental; *Utz* was a corrective, tight, crafted, Mozartian. It was written in bed in the south of France as he was dying. For the protagonist Utz, his collection of porcelain was more real than the current events raging (and passing) around him in Prague. Collection is no more futile than engaging with the ephemeralities of history or the treacheries of life. Asked by an interviewer, "Where in your work is the division between fiction and non-fiction?" he replied, "I don't think there is one." The narrative "I" of *Utz*, a journalist, is vague, half erased. He vanishes altogether in the radiance of the fairy-tale final scene. Listing things the proposed blurb for the book omitted, he noted, "One of the principal themes of the book is that the Old Europe 'survives.'" This was also a theme of *In Patagonia*. "The novel is a catalogue of the recondite, the arcane, the forgotten." It is also an act of remembering, validated by a rapt irony.

———

Edward Thomas describes the structure of Richard Jefferies's essays in terms of instinct, second nature: "Even if it were all nightmare, the very truthfulness of the agitated voice, rising and falling in honest contemplation of common sorrows, would preserve it, since it is rarely given to the best of men to speak the truth." We are a long way from the disciple of Marcus Aurelius: Jefferies is at once a romantic and a modern. The essay's shape "is the shape of an emotional mood, and it ends because the emotion ends. It is music, and above, or independent of, logic." Yet like Stevenson Jefferies wrote for young readers; he chafed at the conventions of fiction, either because he could not master them or because he would not be mastered by them.

(John) Richard Jefferies (1848–1887) is often mentioned as a nature writer in the same breath with Hudson, though he was a generation older and his manner and matter are different. He is a naturalist with a gun, suspected of being a poacher by some (*The Amateur Poacher* was published in 1879), while Hudson was a naturalist without, and at his worst a harmless trespasser. Jefferies was a native of rural Wiltshire, his father being a farmer near Swindon, and he draws on his boyhood in *Wood Magic: A Fable* (1881) with talking animals and fable-based fantasy, and in the altogether more grounded *Bevis* (1882), one of the favorite children's books of the time, and for some time to come. John Fowles read and reread it until he was in his mid teens. An 1897 edition was trimmed down from the original three-volume format by the children's novelist G. A. Henty. Bevis and Mark (based on Jefferies himself and his younger brother) are a doughty pair; it is worth noting, given the raft and the "Mississippi" scenes, that the book appeared three years before *Huckleberry Finn*. The protagonists do not linger over the natural world; they impose on it the force of their imaginations, drawing on Homer, the Wars of the Roses, Cooper, Cervantes, geography lessons, and much else.

*The Story of My Heart* (1883) is a book of studied intensity, quite the opposite of *Long Ago and Far Away*. It probes less the world than Jefferies's responses to it. "In the glow of youth there were times every now and then when I felt the necessity of a strong inspiration of soulthought. My heart was dusty, parched for want of the rain of deep feeling; my mind arid and dry, for there is a dust which settles on the heart as well as that which falls on a ledge." This landscaping of the self would be intolerable were it the effort of a lesser writer. "Sometimes I came from the Reading-room, where under the dome I often looked up from the desk and realized the crushing hopelessness of books, useless," compared with the smallest "soulthought"-inspiring scenes of nature. He was always in search of new ideas, and "the simile of a new book of the soul is the nearest to convey the meaning—a book drawn from the present and future, not the past." Hence his stabs at a kind of fiction unusual in Britain, post-apocalypse, early sci-fi, in *After London; or, Wild England* (1885). Yet it is a fantasy that fulfills a deep wish: that nature should reassert itself over human depredations; after barbarism, the natural world returns and heals the wounds man has made. "Instead of a set of ideas based on tradition, let me give the mind a new thought drawn straight from the wondrous present, direct this very hour." So in *After London*, having experienced the ruined city, the phosphorescent yellow light like a thick illumined fog, Felix the protagonist (the irony of his name not wasted) moves on: "Ghastly beings haunted the site of so many crimes, shapeless monsters, hovering by night, and weaving a fearful dance. Frequently they caught fire, as it seemed, and burned as they flew or floated in the air. Remembering these stories, which in part, at least, now seemed to be true, Felix glanced aside, where the cloud still kept pace with him, and involuntarily put his hands to his ears lest the darkness of the air should whisper some horror of old times." It is a conventional image of terror, but heightened. "The earth on which he walked, the black earth, leaving phosphoric footmarks behind him, was composed of the mouldered bodies of millions of men who had passed away in the centuries during which the city existed. He shuddered as he moved; he hastened, yet could not go fast, his numbed limbs would not permit him."

What could be more reactionary than an ecological utopia in which man has at best a residual role to play? Not agrarianism but primevalism. Nature's final refutation of man and all his deeds. Jefferies's imagination was snared in custom and tradition, and these very abstractions, against which he kicked, drove him inward and away from the object-reality of things he loved.

Jefferies began earning his living as a reporter on local newspapers. One of his editors encouraged him to read widely and, though he had left school in his mid teens, he became an unconventionally learned man. He wrote local history and was confident enough in 1873 (he was twenty-five) to publish *Reporting, Editing, and Authorship: Practical Hints for Beginners in Literature* (1873)—a textbook for a New Grub Street writers' group. His own novels found a publisher a year later when *The Scarlet Shawl* appeared. It did not make his fortune. His early success as a writer was based on essays and nature writing. Several collections of his pieces appeared and sold considerably. The first of his adult novels to be noticed, *Greene Ferne Farm* (1880), also drew on autobiography, the lives of his parents and others he knew; thus in *Amaryllis at the Fair* (1887), regarded as his best novel, imagination is an agent more of translation than invention, the writing rooted in memory. The scenes are short, the family inches toward disaster in a series of little climaxes. He could not sustain a composition on a large scale. He was poor, lived with tuberculosis, but unlike Stevenson never quite prospered. In hardship he resisted a Civil List pension, being against the dependence patronage imposes. Necessity drove him to surrender even that principle.

William Morris (1834–1896) was "strangely moved" by Jefferies's *After London* and it may have contributed to his 1890 *News from Nowhere; or, An Epoch of Rest,* though his plotting and politics are more coherent than Jefferies's, in part because he was responding to the American writer Edward Bellamy's phenomenally successful novel of 1888, *Looking Backward: 2000–1887,* an American best seller of its time, a forebear of Ayn Rand.

Morris's protagonist William Guest falls asleep and wakes up in a future state. The science fiction is burdened not with futuristic gimmicks but with ideas, and the socialist utopia has been wished rather than won. "I must now shock you by telling you that we have no longer anything which you, a native of another planet, would call a government." He witnesses in the first person: a state in which structures are socialistic, private property a thing of the past, and what holds society together is a "love one another" ethic and the given world's delights. Morris, it is worth remembering, was the British representative at the Second Socialist International in Paris in 1889. His socialism was public and engaged: the author of *The Earthly Paradise* may have described himself as a "dreamer of dreams, born out of my due time," but he also preached Marx in the open air to the unemployed. His first substantial novel attempted a popular vindication of his beliefs, projected into the future, a world of happy consequences. Morris addresses in narrative terms many popular objections to socialism. There is low-key romantic interest, but what really engages Morris is ideas. His is a Swiftean experiment in symbolic narrative, but without anger or satire. It was serialized in *Commonweal* and then issued in book form. The book is still read, but not for its narrative. In its cliff-hangers, the cliffs are not high nor the waves below turbulent.

There is more to Morris's fiction than one classroom fantasy, and that more is a developed fantasy world, in three dimensions, various and variegated, and on a larger scale than *News from Nowhere*. His novels include *The Wood beyond the World* (1894), *The Well at the World's End* (1896), and published posthumously, *The Sundering Flood* (1897). These engaging romances, with their entirely imaginary geographies, were the too-sweet and poetical fruit of Morris's final decade. They set a taste for fantasy and inevitably had an impact on the fantasy and romance writers who succeeded him. He is a crucial begetter of C. S. Lewis's Narnia novels, and J. R. R. Tolkien expressed a debt to him in the conception and execution of *The Lord of the Rings*. Indeed, some of Tolkien's characters take their names from Morris's creations. James Joyce, too, drank of the waters of *The Well at the World's End* (1894), though to him it tasted differently.

In 1886 Morris declared a love for books that were in one way or another "Bibles": the Old Testament itself, the poems of Homer, Hesiod, the northern poems including *Beowulf*, the *Edda*, the *Kalevala*, and the traditional poems of Wales and Ireland. He aspired to add to that tradition with his fanciful wisdom books. They were not to be judged primarily on *literary* grounds: "To me they are far more important than any literature. They are in no sense the work of individuals but have grown up from the very hearts of the *people*."

---

Charles Kingsley (1819–1875) suffered a more comfortable failure than Jefferies's, the falling short of his artistic vocation. For Andrew Lang he is "Canon Kingsley," "the greatest of all boys," his humor acceptable to the ten- or twelve-year-old but embarrassing to the grown man revisiting the enthusiasms of his youth. James in his obituary suggests that he made and then unmade his reputation as a writer. Three of his books are still read: *Hypatia* (1853), *Westward Ho!* (1855), and *The Water Babies: A Fairy Tale for a Land Baby* (1863). The last of these, with its strongly monosyllabic, Old English diction and its lively rhythms, is excellent for reading aloud to children. The protagonist, a chimney sweep, escapes and has adventures among water creatures. Social reform was Kingsley's motive in writing, and the charm of the tale is undermined by heavy moralizing: the book does not hold up against the weird, amoral-satirical worlds of Lewis Carroll or the verse fantasies of Edward Lear. Kingsley is not exactly *earnest,* but he plays always with serious intent. *The Water Babies* is just one book he addressed to young people. He also popularized classical stories, in *The Heroes,* for instance, honoring by example one of his favorite writers, Thomas Carlyle, whose philosophy he simplified and Christianized in a muscular spirit. Young Edmund Gosse recalled how "Kingsley, a daring spirit, used sometimes to drag us out trawling with him in Torbay, and although his hawk's beak and rattling voice frightened me a little, his was always a jolly presence that brought some refreshment to our seriousness."

The adult novels are also insistently moralized. *Hereward: The Last of the English* is, James suggested, wrecked by didacticism. Mrs. Gaskell's *Mary Barton* he read as a work of radical history, not fiction. His own *Alton Locke,* with less penetration, visits her themes: the starved poet-tailor, a pathetic hero. Kingsley's heart was big, and a fox's bark could wring it. He prophesied that the days of fox hunting were numbered. They still are.

The moral obligation he feels does not entail truth to character, to subject matter or form, but to a dogmatic sense of duty courageously embraced that hobbles his plots and limits the range of his protagonists. He is not a philosopher, and when he thinks he is philosophizing, he is usually delivering clichés. James dislikes much of Kingsley's manner and matter, but he respects the skills his moralizing misdirects: "He wrote with an air of high animal spirits, and often in an admirably picturesque style; but to our sense, which was perhaps fastidious, the note of simple sincerity was rather wanting." In the end, "a capital novelist was spoiled to make a very indifferent historian."

He entered the church. His attack on John Henry Newman for hypocrisy elicited from the cardinal-to-be his famous *Apologia pro vita sua:* he served thus as a theological catalyst, and his foursquareness elicited one of the century's most subtle and coherent spiritual self-disclosures. He was Regius Professor of History at Cambridge, resigned his post to become a canon of Chester Cathedral (abandoning the West Country that had shaped his imagination), and devoted his intellectual effort to furthering the dialogue between religion, art, and science.

There is something gung-ho and unfinished about him. Thackeray called him a "fine, honest, go-a-head fellow, who charges a subject heartily, impetuously, with the greatest courage and simplicity; but with narrow eyes (his are extraordinarily brave, blue and honest), and with little knowledge of the world, I think." A genial evocation. Lang is too generous also. Boys when they read Kingsley "hurry on with the adventures, and do not stop to ask what the moralizing means. They forgive the humor of Kingsley because it is well meant.

They get, in short, the real good of this really great and noble and manly and blundering genius."

———•———

The novelist Ngũgĩ wa Thiong'o went to an independent Gikuyu missionary school in Kenya. There he read the work of Dickens and Stevenson, initially in abridged form, and Henry Rider Haggard, whom he describes as one of the blundering "geniuses of racism," in full. The formative impact of these authors (even those that were abridged and simplified) on him and other African writers who, in the middle decades of the twentieth century, read so "unfashionably" and, in ideological terms, archaically, was to impart a sense of big themes, open narrative, a historical imagination, and a sense of place. They also instilled a respect for the reader. There was nothing precious about becoming a novelist: it was an adventure in the world. Though "language and literature were taking us further and further from ourselves," they were taking them "to other selves, from our world to other worlds." So long as, on many by-ways, in the end they found the first self, the first world and language, often in furious reaction against the literature absorbed and its degrading effect on their own sense of self, the resources gained in the long excursion did not impoverish.

Sir Henry Rider Haggard (1856–1925) was the highest-earning British author between 1887 and 1894, bringing in more than £10,000 per annum, roughly equivalent to £170,000 ($250,000) in today's values. He was read avidly by boys of all ages. Writing to a schoolboy at Eton College in the late 1880s, Lang—who shared Rider Haggard's interest in the paranormal and collaborated with him on three novels—declares, "I am glad you like *She,* Mr. Rider Haggard's book which I sent you. It is 'something like,' as you say, and I quite agree with you, both in being in love with the heroine, and in thinking that she preaches rather too much." It's the problem we met with in Kingsley, but here Ayesha, "She Who Must Be Obeyed," is a commanding figure who in different ways both Sigmund Freud and Carl Jung admire, and who elbows her way into modern psychology. "But, then, as she was over two thousand years old, and had lived for most of that time among cannibals, who did not understand her, one may excuse her for 'jawing,' as you say, a good deal, when she met white men. You want to know if *She* is a true story. Of course it is!"

There is no doubting the warmth of Lang's response (backed up by H. P. Lovecraft, who described the novel as "actually remarkably good") or the justice of Ngũgĩ's verdict. Yet *She* has sold in the region of 90 million copies since it first appeared in 1887. Margaret Atwood, another postcolonial writer who discovered *She* as a child among her father's books, contributes an introduction to a recent new edition. She was haunted by the powerful female figure (whose literary legacy is considerable, certainly and ironically, on John Mortimer's *Rumpole*). Atwood was excited and engaged, "then I graduated from high school and discovered good taste, and forgot for a while about *She*." When she redis-covered bad taste, she thought about it some more: where did She come from, "old-young, powerful-powerless, beautiful-hideous, dweller among tombs, ob-sessed with an undying love?" Here was a key to a broad cultural sensibility: the book's popularity was due to the fact that the nerves it touched were common nerves. Ayesha is an archetype peculiar to our most complex hang-ups.

Haggard set many novels in Africa, where his father sent him when it was evident that the boy—who failed to make it into the army or the Foreign Office—was without talent: he might be able to make his way in the colonial service. This he did. He returned to England with a young family in 1881, studied law, and was called to the bar in 1884. But his energies had begun to be channeled into fiction. In 1885 he published his phenomenally successful *King Solomon's Mines,* introducing a lost-culture adventure genre. Its later manifestations include Edgar Rice Burroughs's *Tarzan* and the 1933 film *King Kong*. It celebrated actual explorers he had encountered in Africa. The Allan Quatermain novels (modeled at several removes on Cooper's Leatherstocking and Scott's Waverley novels in creating a series in which one book sold another) followed, along with other nov-els of real commercial moment, some of which retain a dedicated readership, though not in modern Africa. Indiana Jones is, apart from the name, effec-tively Haggard's creation. Rudyard Kipling enjoyed his plots and adventures and was his friend. He wrote for effect and was successful at eliciting the re-sponses he intended. It is not always clear which of his novels are meant as adven-tures for boys and which for men. In this he is like some of his near contempo-raries who wrote a fiction that appealed at several levels.

In 1889, when Kipling arrived back in England, he and Rider Haggard became close, sharing as they did, in different parts of the empire, colonial experiences. Haggard's civic contribution to the colonies, especially in agriculture, took him to many outposts, and he was awarded a knighthood. His heroes are heroes of empire; his stereotypes the caricatures of the 1930s and empire's unraveling: the good African served the cause of progress, which meant the colonial enterprise; the bad African stuck by his own culture, presented, if at all, in simplified terms. At home in the colonies and dominions, Haggard was not at home with the cul-tures colonized and dominated, until, as with the Zulu culture in *King Solomon's Mines,* Ignosi proves his goodness as restored king of Kukuanaland when he lis-tens to counsel and makes some fundamental Westernizing adjustments to his subjects' culture.

Modern readers are reluctant to pick up his books. They are hard to put down. The writing is engaging. In the market at Bungay, Suffolk, Thomas Wingfield learns of the defeat of Spain and in no time he is off in New Spain engaged in saving the Aztec king Cuauhtémoc (Gautama), experiencing the wild exoticism of the Aztec capital, being in one scene prepared for sacrifice, in another deified, and proving himself superior and English in his wiles, fortune, and survival. This occurs in *Montezuma's Daughter*, which he wrote with Lang. His first forays were into historical writing, but by 1884, the year he was called to the bar, his fiction career began with *Dawn*. He wrote more books than Scott, and for five years after he died in 1925, a new book or two appeared each year, so well-stocked was his larder. He was the most commercially and ideologically successful of Stevenson's generation of writers. Was he also one of the "juggling priests" that Stevenson warned against, an "esurient book-maker" who in the interests both of financial gain and imperial commitment resolved, consciously or not, to "continue and debase a brave tradition, and lower, in their own eyes, a famous race"? The words *esurient* and *race* are prophetic: Stevenson, as a Scot, stood at an angle to English concerns, though he liked and admired many of his English contemporaries. Notable among the others was Sir Anthony Hope Hopkins, better known as Anthony Hope, whose *Prisoner of Zenda* (1894) and the less successful sequel *Rupert of Hentzau* (1898) were widely popular as well. And there was, above all, Rudyard Kipling, upon whom an excessive blame was to be visited.

When Stevenson was on his way to Samoa, stopping in Adelaide, a number of letters caught up with him, and he discovered that the space he had left in English writing was rapidly being filled by Rudyard Kipling (1865–1936). Sidney Colvin, who had been a champion of his work, was backing this new horse; James too informed his friend and protégé about him. William Ernest Henley, his editor, publisher, and collaborator, described by Kipling's biographer Harry Ricketts as "a rumbustious, domineering character, a literary bullock looking for a china shop," was now working with "The Kipperling." How did Stevenson feel, traveling to his afterlife, at this evidence of succession, of life's inexorability, the water, as it were, closing over him? Kipling admired Stevenson and paid him every compliment, including imitation. Kipling intended to visit Stevenson in Samoa but never arrived. They met only in books.

As far as Greene is concerned, most of the bad things about Kipling can be laid at the door of his evil Aunt Rosa: "revenge rather than justice seems to be the motive" of his books. Greene is hard on Kipling's prose, seeing it as undermined by "the tricks of the reporter," loss of context, concentration on single details and effects. "There is almost an inability to experience truly: observation is ruined time and again by the pretence of personal emotion." Does this harsh judgment extend to the *Jungle Books*? to the short stories and the poems? to *Kim*? Greene intends that it should. "Surely Tinker Bell danced when Kipling was born. Of greatly gifted writers perhaps the two who have written with most falsity of human relations are [J. M.] Barrie and Kipling." This take on Kipling, summary and ideological, excluded him from polite readership even as Haggard's novels were being taught in missionary schools to boys in Kenya, Nigeria, and South Africa. Robert Buchanan, a Gladstonian Liberal, characterized Kipling as "the voice of the hooligan." But "Just is the Wheel!" as Kim's beloved Lama, follower of the Middle Way, proclaims; it turns, and readers can again admit to reading Kipling (with certain provisos) for pleasure. His story engages much of the world and the history of his time, that indefinite interface between the British and the American centuries. Stevenson, a Scot, married an American from the West: an adventure; Kipling, apologist for empire, married a member of the settled New England oligarchy: a slow, inexorable misadventure. Philip Burne-Jones is most famous for his "Vampire"; his portrait of Carrie (Caroline Balestier, Mrs. Kipling) is forceful, like Milton's Dalila, who "Comes this way sailing / Like a stately Ship." And Kipling, in this scenario, occupies the role of Samson. Burne-Jones's portrait of him is conventional, slightly less than human in scale.

The first English-language recipient of the Nobel Prize in Literature (1907), Joseph Rudyard Kipling (1865–1936) was born in Bombay in 1865. His parents had courted in Staffordshire, walking beside the reservoir Lake Rudyard, and named their firstborn for that body of romantic water. His father, a professor of architectural sculpture (and later principal) at the Bombay school of art, became principal of the School of Arts and curator of the Lahore Museum, Kim's "Treasure House." His mother was sister of Lady Burne-Jones and of Stanley Baldwin's mother. He did not come from the prosperous branch of the family but had culture and influence at his disposal.

India in his early years was sufficient and wholly real to him. It provided the foundation of his imagination and memory. He was under the care of Indian servants and spoke Hindustani better than English. This was more than a "below stairs" experience of the Raj. Kim is the boy he would like to have been, the boy he imagined being. When he was packed off to England as a little sahib, India became his lost world. He could revisit but never quite reenter it. Much of his best writing is devoted to the effort of reclaiming it.

He stood in an awkward relation to the colonial world; the country he came to lacked the warmth, color, and easy intimacy of the one he left. He was "only six," but by that age the deepest layers of imagination were in place. He went from the active affection of his family home to live with an elderly evangelical relation in Southsea. The miserable time he spent there was relieved by occasional visits to the Burne-Jones's near Brighton. "The circumstances of his early childhood in fact were uniquely valuable in his growth as a writer," Kingsley

Amis declares; "without them, he would have been not only different but diminished." Would he have been happy?

From the misery of this life he passed at the age of fourteen to the United
Services College at Westward Ho! (the one town in Britain with an exclamation
mark in its name, the name itself a tribute to Charles Kingsley's novel), in Dev-
onshire, a minor public school. There he began writing verses. *Schoolboy Lyrics*
was printed privately when he was sixteen. The following year he returned to
India to serve on the staff of the Lahore *Civil and Military Gazette,* contributing
articles and verse.

A colleague describes him at this time as "a short, square, dark youth," bespectacled, and with "an unlucky eye for color . . . He had a weakness apparently
for brown cloth with just that suggestion of ruddiness or purple in it which
makes some browns so curiously conspicuous." No matter: "The charm of his
manner . . . made you forget what he looked like in half a minute." He had a habit
of rubbing his spectacles because "he was always laughing; and when you laugh
till you nearly cry your spectacles get misty. Kipling, shaking all over with laughter, and wiping his spectacles at the same time with his handkerchief." He liked
to invent pseudonyms, among them Esau Mull and Jacob Cavendish, and to indulge in parodies of his elders: "Come under the Punkah, Maud."

Kipling spent time with soldiers to find out how they thought. That colleague
again: "He watched them at work and at play and at prayer from the points of
view of all his confidants—the combatant officer, the doctor, the chaplain, the
drill sergeant, and the private himself." His approach was to learn firsthand, as
a journalist does; journalism was his chief vocation, practiced in India, in the
South Africa of the Boer War, in the Far East, America, and England. In relation
to his Indian stories and to *Kim,* he saw deep into "the strangely mixed manners
of life and thought of the natives of India. He knew them all through their horizontal divisions of rank and their vertical sections of caste; their ramifications
of race and blood; their antagonisms and blendings of creed; their hereditary
strains of calling or handicraft." He quickly inspired confidence, so that even
religious figures opened up to him. "In two minutes the man—perhaps a wild
hawk from the Afghan hills—would be pouring out into the ear of this sahib,
with heaven-sent knowledge and sympathy, the weird tale of the blood feud
and litigation, the border fray, and the usurer's iniquity, which had driven him
so far afield." It is difficult for the nonspecialist to have an opinion about the accuracy of his portrayals, but there can be no doubt of their fictional coherence.
Kim is his surrogate.

In 1887 he became foreign correspondent for the Allahabad *Pioneer* and began his travels. The sense that Kipling is a writer with inside information is due
to this journalistic training. So too his sense of detail and a generally public

tone that carries into his fiction. By the time he arrived in London in 1889, after a terminal row with the *Pioneer,* he had a reputation for verse and prose. *The Story of the Gadsbys, Plain Tales from the Hills,* and *The Phantom Rickshaw and Other Eerie Tales* had all appeared the year before, and *Departmental Ditties* (1886) had found its way to England as well. He had extensive introductions on arrival, met with and was fêted by writers, artists, and political figures. Early popularity did not earn him the distrust of fellow writers. It was not then considered *de trop* for him to fix his eye on readership. He developed his demotic Cockney dialect, experimental forms, and mastered traditional verse. James writes, with reserved approbation: "No element assuredly in the artistic temperament of Mr. Rudyard Kipling but operates with the ease and exactitude of an alarum clock set to the hour."

By 1895 his reputation as a poet was so high, he may have been offered the laureateship in the wake of Tennyson, one of several honors he rejected. In later years he turned down the Order of Merit, and when his remains finally came to rest in Westminster Abbey in 1936, he was plain Rudyard Kipling. The completeness of his experiences—of the Raj, of the empire for which he was apologist and elegist, of England, of the United States—gave him an apartness, even when he seems to speak familiarly. This contributes to the impersonality of his writing, a reluctance to dwell on subjective experience, a preference for completeness, and a tone of truth-telling.

His politics, if they did not change, intensified. The American failure contributed to a hostility to America that mars some productions; a strain of misogyny follows his unsteady marriage (like Stevenson, Kipling found female characters hard to write); a constant sense of the mission of the empire, and of Britain's falling short, rouses him. He was not a conventional reactionary, a successful man growing old and wanting the world to stabilize and time to slow. For him there was urgency in arguing the case for the empire even in its decline. He had seen it, understood its cultures and potential, and foresaw the consequences of its failure. His reports—for instance, during the Boer War—are brilliant, because he was a fine correspondent, presenting surface events while understanding underlying causes. His *Letters of Travel* (1920) are full of fact and form.

But when in 1902 he retired, still a young man, to Bateman's in Burwash, Sussex, and called it home for his remaining thirty-four years, his sense of himself in the world, and of England, was arrested. Amis regards the move to Bateman's as fatal: all of the best work, he says, was composed before that lowbrowed house cast its enervating shadow over him and Carrie. In this manorial retirement, beyond the fray, he was increasingly alone with his disappointments. Duty, sacrifice, and devotion, his recurrent themes, were elicited particularly by the First World War, in which his only son was killed at the Battle of Loos. Hatred was one of the negative emotions that fed into his stories (less into the novels), and he was frank about it. Somerset Maugham was his not-ungrateful beneficiary, speaking of "Old Kipling, whom everyone despises so much these days," and wrote a valuable introduction to a selection of Kipling's fiction.

Kipling wrote *Kim,* a book that more than any other argument for the defense exonerates him, or at least significantly lessens the magnitude, of the political charges generally leveled against him. "*Kim* I must have read many times as child and man," writes the poet Peter Scupham: "a book whose embracing sympathies become richer with each successive reading as Kim himself changes from my childhood image of an alter-ego adventurer to my adult sense of him as a lodestone for many kinds of love." This is a boy's book that becomes, like other novels of the period, a book for adults as well. Scupham notes the "manylayered tolerance and understanding in *Kim*—not always associated with Kipling." Critics construct his politics selectively to find a crude consistency that some works flatly contradict. As novelist he is neither philosopher nor ideologue. He is not Rider Haggard and claims the freedom to start a new book, find a new path, or reopen an old one.

*Kim* was published in 1901. Kimball O'Hara lives his picaresque life begging and running dubious missions in a Lahore based closely upon the city Kipling knew. Kim is an orphan, his late father a dissolute Irish soldier, his mother also dead. Various natives, ignorant of his identity, patronize him, notable among them Mahbub Ali, a Pashtun or Afghan involved in the Great Game between two empires vying for influence in the subcontinent, the British and the Russian, and trading horses across borders. The book begins with a meeting between Kim and the man who becomes his master and his responsibility, an unworldly Tibetan Lama seeking the mysterious River of the Arrow to wash himself clean and transcend the Wheel of Things. They take one another under their wings, Kim becomes his *chela* or disciple without forfeiting his cunning. Protecting and leading his master, the boy experiences all the peoples and places of India and comes to understand how the British systems of control and repression work. He is drawn into the secret service, tested and proven, his coming of age a various and exciting process. Though it becomes known that he is English, he is never reduced but, like Mowgli in the *Jungle Book,* preserves his uniqueness and lives between the many worlds that are India and the other world of Britain and its empire. The characters he encounters are defined by speech, costume, caste, and their place in a not quite stable hierarchy. Kim is at home in their languages and cultures. The events that take place in Simla, where he encounters Lurgan Sahib and learns about gemstones, are especially vivid. It was at Simla that Kipling spent his vacations from the heat of summer: "Pure joy—every golden hour counted. It began in heat and discomfort, by rail and road. It ended in the cool evening, with a wood fire in one's bedroom, and next morn—thirty more of them ahead!—the early cup of tea, the Mother who brought it in, and the long talks of us all together again."

In the Simla scenes in *Kim* the protagonist discovers his true karma. As Lurgan Sahib performs incomprehensible magic with the gemstones, Kim—to retain his courage—makes a decisive shift and we know he is changing form: "So far Kim had been thinking in Hindi, but a tremor came on him, and with an effort like that of a swimmer before sharks, who hurls himself half out of the water, his mind leaped up from a darkness that was swallowing it and took refuge in—the multiplication-table in English!" That exclamation mark expresses the narrator's own surprise at his protagonist's instinctive defenses. When his education is complete, Kim's Lama wants to let him go, but Kim wishes to stay with this man who is his spirit's beloved and his father. "I am not a Sahib. I am thy chela," he insists. The boy who was the Friend of All the World is inexorably becoming a young Englishman.

When in 1889 Kipling left India for a second time, having lost his job, he traveled east, to Burma, China, Japan, and then San Francisco. He wrote sketches and articles for the *Pioneer*. Unlike most British travelers to the United States, Kipling arrived on the West Coast, then traveled north to Canada, exploring the continental American West and the frontier, befriending Mark Twain when he finally reached Elmira, New York. In the autumn he arrived in England once more, traveled down to London, and found himself known as a writer. A plaque in Villiers Street, above a sherry wine importer and wine bar, marks where he lived and conceived some of his books. Here he completed his first novel, *The Light That Failed* (1890), about a painter who loses his sight and meets a particularly melodramatic death—in battle. "His luck had held to the last, even to the crowning mercy of a kindly bullet through his head." There is a paragraph break in which we wipe our eyes. "Torpenhow knelt under the lee of the camel, with Dick's body in his arms." *Finis* in both senses.

This intense, uneven novel was followed by a nervous breakdown, and then a close friendship with the American book agent Wolcott Balestier, who collaborated with Kipling on another novel. In the interests of his mental health, he resumed his travels. In India, on learning of Balestier's early death, he hurried back to England, having proposed marriage to Balestier's sister Carrie by telegram. She accepted by the same medium, a succinct exchange. They married in early 1892 and their life together started rosily enough, they traveled widely and then, after financial reversals, settled in Brattleboro, Vermont, near Carrie's family, renting Bliss Cottage and setting it to rights. Their first child was born there, and Kipling wrote some of his best work, including the *Jungle*

*Books,* indebted for its inspiration in part to Haggard's *Nada the Lily.* The Kiplings built their own house, and he wrote there a favorite book of many boys of my generation, *Captains Courageous* (1897), in which Harvey Cheyne Jr., a spoiled rich kid, falls overboard from his father's yacht and is picked up by a fishing boat and subjected to manly discipline, finding his true nature once the veneer of snobbery, affectation, and indulgence has been harshly rubbed off. This story too ends in melodrama, and we realize that the superiority of *Kim* is in its understatement and open-endedness. In the sea writing of *Captains Courageous* there are touches worthy of Marryat and Melville. Life in Vermont ended, due to many factors but especially a quarrel with his wife's family. In 1896 he and Carrie left the United States for good.

It is conventional to present Kipling's later years as grim, fluctuating between anger and resignation, his politics a mess of prejudice. After his son's death, his anger with the Establishment, of which he was such a formidable representative, burst out in ways that alarmed his friends. But his later years were not uniformly sour. Success is a tonic, even for a lonely heart. Hugh Walpole remembers the sixty-one-year-old Kipling at the Athenaeum, seated among the reviews of his most recent book, "beaming like a baby." He still wrote, and could write well, even if he did not think as much as he had done and no longer read the runes with the clarity he had in his days of travel. Was H. G. Wells satirizing Kipling in that chapter of *The Island of Dr. Moreau* in which "the Beast-Men are seen mumbling their pathetic Laws," since the actual rhetoric of the *Jungle Book* had become rooted in the popular mind along with many of the poems, "If—" in particular?

Pritchett puts Wells and Kipling together. They are "obviously divergent branches of the same tree. Wells the Utopian, Kipling the patriot—they represent the day-dreams of the lower middle class which will either turn to socialism or fascism." This is the same dialectical irresolution that marks the British imagination in the 1930s and again in the 1970s. "Opposed in tendency, Wells and Kipling both have the vision of artists; they foresee the conditions of our time. They both foretold the violence with a certain appetite."

Kipling lost some popularity when he began to stigmatize his core readership by insisting on the hard truths underlying his—and their—ideology. At the victory ceremony after the Boer War ended, outside the Transvaal Parliament 10,000 soldiers gave voice to the poem "Recessional." The apparently wholesome "what oft was thought but ne'er so well expressed" gave way, in some works, to "what was never flushed out into the open before." Kipling's poem "The Islanders" was a poisoned chalice for his political admirers: Angus Wilson describes how it "takes each sacred cow of the clubs and senior common rooms and slaughters it messily before its worshippers' eyes." J. M. Barrie acidly declared, "Mr. Kipling has yet to learn that a man may know more of life staying at home by his mother's knee than swaggering in bad company over three continents." Barrie was a "mother's knee" chap who kept charming company.

Kipling is still read, even during the decades when it was not pukka to read him. The Definitive Edition of his works had gone through sixty impressions by 1982. Unit sales of the most popular of his books remain substantial. This little, often lonely man is caricatured by Max Beerbohm in his Savile Club cartoon as a dwarf, his thinning hair combed flat on his outsized skull, aggressively attentive to a debate: an unlikely redeemer of British masculinity (the Nobel Prize citation praised his "virility of ideas"), and physically an implausible champion of the imperial ideal. In the same cartoon a pointy-faced Thomas Hardy looks on, unamused, and there is Gosse, too, and other players in that parallel Great Game, the *fin de siècle* literary comedy.

# 23

# Smoke and Mirrors

Charles Dodgson (Lewis Carroll), Rudolf Raspe, Bram Stoker,

Ouida, Marie Corelli, Walter Pater, Oscar Wilde, Denton Welch,

Arthur Conan Doyle, J. M. Barrie, Max Beerbohm, Kenneth Grahame

Queen Victoria read *Alice in Wonderland* with pleasure. Two anecdotes, one or both apocryphal, followed from her response. The first is that, in the manner of the Red Queen, she commanded that other works by Lewis Carroll be brought to her forthwith. Her servant brought her one of his mathematical books, possibly *An Elementary Treatise on Determinants, with Their Application to Simultaneous Linear Equations and Algebraic Equations,* by the Rev. C. L. (Charles Lutwidge) Dodgson (1832–1898), for indeed the mathematician and the author of *Alice* were manifestations of the same person, on the face of it as different as Jekyll and Hyde. The other story tells of how the Queen suggested he dedicate his next volume to her, and he did so: it was entitled *Condensation of Determinants* (1866). This should not strike us as a deliberate irony. The artist Trevor Winkfield reminds us that Carroll "should be remembered (but is not) for his books on Euclid and symbolic logic. *Alice* is a continuation of science into different realms." His intelligence and imagination are consistent; readers force a division upon him.

His great-grandfather, grandfather, and father were clergymen. His father, a conservative high-church Anglican who admired Newman and was affected by the Oxford Movement, had a contrary influence on his son, who, though a practicing Anglican, was of a less hectic temperament. The son read *The Pilgrim's Progress* when he was seven, and its structured allegory left a mark. He produced handmade magazines for his brothers and sisters, notably *The Rectory Umbrella.* (When he got to Oxford he revived the creative-editorial habit with the scrapbook *Mischmasch.*) His mission was to entertain and to satirize domestic authority, the *don'ts* that dog any child's life. He kept various kinds of unusual pets, including snails, toads, and earthworms, and observed them closely. (A poem contributed to a college magazine is full of animals with human resonance: "She has the bear's ethereal grace / The bland hyena's laugh, / The footsteps of the elephant, / The neck of the giraffe.") He was sent as a boarder to Rugby School, where he suffered "annoyance at night" but was outstanding in mathematics. He went up to Oxford, and though he did not, or could not, work hard, he excelled and remained associated with Christ Church for the rest of his life. There he was required by college rules after a fixed time to take full religious orders; this he was unwilling to do, yet he remained. His imagination recovered, darkened, from his time at Rugby.

In 1862 he began telling the story of Alice to Dean Liddell's three daughters Lorina (Ina), Alice, and Edith. By then Mrs. Liddell had become uneasy about his continually photographing the girls and wary of his attention. The second daughter, Alice, once she was safely Mrs. Reginald Hargreaves, remembered, without sinister inflection, "one summer afternoon when the sun was so burning that we had landed in the meadows down the river, deserting the boat to take refuge in the only bit of shade to be found, and which was under a new-made hay-rick." The three girls required a story, and Mr. Dodgson (they were accompanied by a second clergyman) obliged. After a while he broke off and promised more "next time." "Oh! but it is next time," the girls exclaimed, and the story recommenced. Sometimes he pretended to fall asleep while he told the story and the girls worried him until he resumed. In 1865 the book was published, enhanced with John Tenniel's initially reluctant services as illustrator.

It is now difficult to mention Lewis Carroll without alluding to pedophilia. There are those photographs, and some biographers suggest he proposed marriage to an eleven-year-old child (others that her married mother was his quarry). Because diaries are missing and some pages were deliberately removed, biographers feel licensed to speculate despite the tone and manner of Mrs. Hargreaves's testimony—she would have known had Dodgson been a Victorian Humbert Humbert, as she would have been his Dolores Haze. Like much biographical supposition, speculation leads away from the work to a zone in which we have no bearings or (in the absence of fact) business. In 1906 Mark Twain set up a club for young girls that were his imaginary granddaughters and called it the Angel Fish and Aquarium Club, with members from the ages of ten to sixteen. The old writer sent them letters, took them to concerts and plays, and organized games. It was, he said, the chief delight of his life. Admittedly, there was no boating on the Mississippi and not the same interest in photographs, but the burly American and the lean, shy Englishman shared a passion that modern critics read in terms of their own sexually overattentive, suspicious, and prurient age.

The adventures in *Alice's Adventures in Wonderland* have much to do with the logic and forms of card games, while *Through the Looking-Glass and What Alice Found There* (1871) is formally indebted to chess in its characters and rules, to the extent that the list of Dramatis Personae is presented in terms of chess pieces and the moves are specified in a preliminary table. Alice ranges the board as a not quite free but highly experimental agent, confronting some pieces, conversing with others, and briefly entering the identity of the sheep and finally the Queen. The pairings provide much of the humor. As the White Knight approaches, the

White King explains, "'He's an Anglo-Saxon Messenger—and those are Anglo-Saxon attitudes. He only does them when he's happy. His name is Haigha.' (He pronounced it so as to rhyme with 'mayor.')" Alice riffs on the letter "H," and the King further explains, "'The other Messenger's called Hatta. I must have TWO, you know—to come and go. One to come, and one to go.'" Wordplay and word-spinning, punning, the expressiveness of typographical variation (italics, small caps), and other elements expressing tone, irony, or parody, and the seeming nonsense that shadows sense but will not be pinned down: no wonder Carroll was taken up by the surrealists and other language experimenters.

The moralizing Duchess in *Alice's Adventures in Wonderland* is an ancestor of the French poet Apollinaire. Jabberwocky is the most memorable of Carroll's fantasy creations. In 1941 Harold Levin suggested Humpty Dumpty as "the official guide" to the language of Joyce's *Finnegans Wake*. Carroll invented the portmanteau word ("You see it's like a portmanteau—there are two meanings packed up into one word") and the arbitrary movement of language in the mind. Humpty could "explain all the poems that ever were invented—and a good many that haven't been invented just yet." But Joyce claimed that he had not read Carroll until 1927 when his last book was well on its way. Once he did read him, and the biography, there was no escape for the Oxford don and Alice Liddell: they must be swallowed by Joyce's assimilative imagination. There they are, "loose carollaries," "Lewd's carol" appearing as "old Dadgerson's dodges," "wonderland's wanderlad," and Alice, "liddel oud oddity." There are subtler variations, allusions, echoes, distorted quotations. "Though Wonderlawn's lost us for ever. Alis, alas, she broke the glass! Liddell lokker ["looker" in the revised edition] through the leafery, ours is mistery of pain." It is a context Charles Dodgson provided late, though he might have been uncomfortable to appear there at all. There is a logic, true or false, to Carroll's procedures; Joyce by contrast is not after clarities but, to the best of his abilities, creating the messy, blurred consistency of consciousness through language.

Carroll's later work lacks the interest or permanence of the *Alice* experiments. He was not keen to be known as their author. When people came looking for him, he went to ground or hurried off like the March Hare. Or his smile faded into the lush foliage of a tree. Best to find him in his books, a man of paradox, logic, and reverse logic, contrariness and wit. He was a serious mathematician and a defender of Euclid against all comers, and his more popular mathematical writings are laced with humor of a disarming kind. No wonder Mervyn Peake, creator of the Gormenghast trilogy (1946–1959), illustrated *Alice,* learning tones and gestures from his Victorian forebear.

The Welsh essayist Idris Parry discusses Lewis Carroll in company with the fantastic tales of Baron Munchausen, begun by Rudolf Raspe (1736–1794), though later lavishly enhanced by other hands. Raspe was a German librarian and archivist turned scientist, working in the Cornish tin industry (having fled disgrace at home). He writes well in English (Horace Walpole commented on the quality of his style) for a man who was in his forties when he came to England. He got little return for his labors, because the first publication, an octavo booklet of about fifty pages, sold cheaply. It came out in the 1780s under the grand title: *Baron Munchausen's Narrative of His Marvellous Travels and Campaigns in Russia, Humbly Dedicated and Recommended to Country Gentlemen; and, If They Please, to Be Repeated as Their Own, after a Hunt, at Horse Races, in Watering-Places, and Other Such Polite Assemblies; round the Bottle and Fire-Side.* This German-seeming book, written in England, in English, was based on stories published in a German comic magazine a few years earlier, so among his many felonies the roguish Raspe is guilty also of plagiarism, unless those earlier anonymous stories were also his work. It is hard to believe this man, who fled Germany for pilfering from his patron, was expelled from the Royal Society for loose morals, fled to Scotland from Cornwall after a mining fraud, and perpetrated another fraud there.

He did not contribute to the expanded collection of stories: Munchausen grew wings and flew away from his author or kidnapper. He attracted illustrators and has been much embellished in the years since. The title of an early edition was changed to *Gulliver Reviv'd: The Singular Travels, Campaigns, Voyages and Sporting Adventures of Baron Munnikhouson Commonly Pronounced Munchausen; as He Relates Them over a Bottle when Surrounded by His Friends—A New Edition Considerably Enlarged with Views from the Baron's Drawings.* Munchausen is the master of epic lies told with a straight face. He is a cousin of Thackeray's Major Gahagan, at two removes or so from Kafka, whose *The Metamorphosis* makes the extreme metaphor into a literal-seeming truth. Dickens at Tavistock House had, among his imitation book backs, "*Munchausen's Modern Miracles.* 4 vols." shelved with "*Paxton's Bloomers.* 5 vols., *Drowsy's Recollections of Nothing.* 3 vols., *Growler's Gruffiology,* with Appendix. 4 vols. and *Lady Godiva on the Horse.*"

Dickens is never tonally neutral in the way of the Munchausen storyteller or of Lewis Carroll, whose logic is so rigorous as to elude the trammels of probability without ever losing the reader, who is happy to agree for the duration. The real becomes surreal in their hands. What makes Carroll prodigious is the coherence of the world he creates, as "answerable" and truthful because as consistent as Swift is in *Gulliver.* The rabbit hole and looking-glass worlds, which Anthony Burgess relates to Kafka's more literalizing vision, with puzzles and mazes and metamorphoses, with strange creatures that are monstrous but never monsters, reflect vividly (if not always advertently) on Victorian conduct.

The popularity of the Alice novels and, on a diminishing scale, of *Munchausen,* depends as much on the page as animation and film.

———•———

An unlikely number of the novels of the later nineteenth century found their way into the films of the twentieth. Some are great books translated into the clichés of Hollywood; some helped to define those clichés, because Hollywood is in some respects the dazzling natural child of the fiction industry, a child that became guardian of an aging, sometimes ailing parent. Film revives a flagging book and gives credibility to a bad one.

The Colombian novelist Gabriel García Márquez describes *Dracula* as "a great book," one he came to not as a boy but as a grown-up reader: earlier, he says, he might have regarded it as "a waste of time." Earlier, he might have been the better judge. It is a compelling set of images, and the narrative at the right time on a windy moonless night with a thorough suspension of disbelief is unsettling—one of those "good bad books" that litter English-language fiction and subsidize the publication of less popular work. (Abraham) "Bram" Stoker (1847–1912) was a journalist and a man of the theater, the great Henry Irving's manager and a director at the London Lyceum. He started writing novels early in the 1890s. *Dracula,* the book for which he is remembered, appeared in 1897. His other horror novels are less gripping and less durable.

*Dracula* is a book for which Stoker prepared: he studied vampire lore and visited some of the locations. He took the subject seriously in a calculating spirit, the spirit of the *Grand Guignol,* recognizing in the success of earlier horror and gothic works of fiction and theater (for his was a *theatrical* imagination, every element audience-directed) a substantial market. *Alice* is full of invention, *Munchausen* of surprise and humor; *Dracula* shares the dark of Walpole's gothic, but with designs on a reading audience. As commercial horror, film serves it better than the modern page.

For the page, to add a sense of veracity, Stoker tried something different, an unattenuated narrative in which the protagonists are given an immediate presence, without authorial intervention. Thus, we begin with four chapters of Jonathan Harker's journal. Harker writes like a novelist, however, and the illusion of the journal is hardly maintained, though the writing has an element of novelettish immediacy.

> He said to the driver, "You are early tonight, my friend."
> The man stammered in reply, "The English Herr was in a hurry."
> To which the stranger replied, "That is why, I suppose, you wished him to go on to Bukovina. You cannot deceive me, my friend. I know too much, and my horses are swift."

> As he spoke he smiled, and the lamplight fell on a hard-looking mouth, with very red lips and sharp-looking teeth, as white as ivory. One of my companions whispered to another the line from Burger's *Lenore.*
>
> "Denn die Todten reiten Schnell." *("For the dead travel fast.")*
>
> The strange driver evidently heard the words, for he looked up with a gleaming smile. The passenger turned his face away, at the same time putting out his two fingers and crossing himself. "Give me the Herr's luggage," said the driver, and with exceeding alacrity my bags were handed out and put in the caleche. Then I descended from the side of the coach, as the caleche was close alongside, the driver helping me with a hand which caught my arm in a grip of steel. His strength must have been prodigious.

The clichés—the German accent, for example, the red lips, sharp teeth white as ivory, the steel grip—are part of Harker's journal voice, but all the (written) voices we hear, from Mina Murray's and Lucy Westenra's ("Well, my dear, number One came just before lunch. I told you of him, Dr. John Seward, the lunatic asylum man, with the strong jaw and the good forehead"), to the protracted extracts from the *Dailygraph* newspaper, the alarming log of the ship *Demeter* bound for Whitby cargoed with mystery and fear ("If we are wrecked, mayhap this bottle may be found, and those who find it may understand. If not . . ."), and Dr. Seward's diary, are studded with clichés of language and vampiric tropes— clichés that did not start here but gained currency thanks to the book's success.

*Dracula* attempts indirection, to let the reader construe the story from the documents provided. But those documents are not realized as fictions in themselves. The author pulls the strings to achieve his effects, the reader's freedom as illusory as that of the victims, who move the tale forward with their vulnerable throats and napes. The epistolary novel of yesteryear— Richardson's, for example—allows the reader actual freedom to engage in the moral and dramatic movement of the narrative; in *Dracula* what matters is a succession of spinal shivers implicit in the tale. Stoker's journalistic instincts were acute, his formal skills unequal. In Whitby today visitors can have the Dracula experience: it takes less time than reading and, like the screen versions (except that we are physically entailed), is quite as frightening, or not, as the novel itself.

---

Film has not taken possession of *Marius the Epicurean* by Walter Pater (1839–1894), the ill-favored Oxford don, the "Caliban of letters," who is seen literally dropping to his knee to present his pupil, Oscar Wilde, with a lily. He was among the tutors of a disquieted Gerard Manley Hopkins, and it is necessary to recognize his disproportionate impact on the Oxford of his day and on later generations (Edward Thomas's, Ford Madox Ford's, Somerset Maugham's) if the scented peculiarities of the *fin de siècle* are to be understood in relation to the vigor they engendered in the following century. In 1890 the freshman Max Beerbohm, not yet the insouciant ironist of the Edwardian age, amused his Oxford tutor when he said he wanted to attend Pater's lectures. A few days later, at the print shop, he saw, "peering into a portfolio, a small, thick, rock-faced man, whose top-hat and gloves of bright dog-skin struck one of the many discords in that little city of learning or laughter. The serried bristles of his moustachio made for him a false-military air." Clearly the city was ready for Zuleika's arrival. "I think I nearly went down [dropped out of university] when they told me that this was Pater."

Pater was an illuminating reader of Flaubert. Yet his own world and his way of addressing it are remote from Flaubert's in all respects except one: the pleasures of style. In "The School of Giorgione" he speaks of art, and the life from which it emanates, as "a kind of listening." In his own essays and fiction, style becomes a means of expelling voice from written language, rendering it timeless. Every bit as much as that precious Elizabethan writer John Lyly, Pater constructs sentences. The indulgent, intellectual languor of *Marius the Epicurean* (1885) is never a voice, Pater's sentences unfold in the direction of Latin. Marius is appalled to see, in ancient Rome, the gladiators. Not the smell and dust and blood: something more refined troubles him, their impact on his sensibility, an affront that takes a moral direction. "But the gladiators were still there. Their bloody contests had, under the form of a popular amusement, the efficacy of a human sacrifice; as, indeed, the whole system of the public shows was understood to possess a religious import. Just at this point, certainly, the judgment of Lucretius on pagan religion is without reproach—*Tantum religio potuit suadere malorum* [Religion was so strong in persuading them to evil]."

Due to such affronts and disillusionments, to such subordinate clauses, qualifiers, and contrived epiphanies, Marius evolves and matures. That more beguiling protagonist Stephen Dedalus in *A Portrait of the Artist as a Young Man*, a breathing character remote from Oxford in all but erudition, would have been very different without Pater's precedent. Back to the gladiators at the end of the second part of *Marius:* Pater is ungrounded and abstract when he speaks of concreteness, but—as we are—he is ready to move on. "Yes! what was needed was the heart that would make it impossible to witness all this; and the future would be with the forces that could beget a heart like that. His chosen philosophy had said,—Trust the eye: Strive to be right always in regard to the concrete experience: Beware of falsifying your impressions." Marius passes through the stages of belief, each time tempted, persuaded, mastered, and then mastering and moving on.

Pater's architectural prose yields a stilted, too-refined sense. This would be the apotheosis of the Classics, proof that they provide a realm in which an individual can mask human and spiritual inadequacies, decked out in eloquence as substantial as the king's new clothes, except that the clothes are old. They smell only of lavender. With Ronald Firbank it is all shrill delight and lightness, the world embraced with delicacy and affection. That sense of delight in the writing, and of discovery, we miss in Pater's fiction, though the manner serves him in his essays, which are approached still with raptness by young readers disposed to enjoy sensually alert intellection. "Long after the very latest roses were faded, when 'the town' had departed to country villas, or the baths, or the war," how cleverly he arranges the series: husbandry, self-indulgence, duty, "he remained behind in Rome; anxious to try the lastingness of his own Epicurean rose-garden; setting to work over again, and deliberately passing from point to point of his old argument with himself, down to its practical conclusions." So Marius begins his own life in aestheticism directed toward beauty, achieved through self-effacement of the ascetic kind he praised in Flaubert as "martyrdom." Transposing religious into aesthetic terms, Pater participates in the late-Victorian translation of the spiritual into the aesthetic.

—•—

"One should not be too severe on English novels," Oscar (Fingal O'Flahertie Wills) Wilde (1854–1900) declared; "they are the only relaxation of the intellectually unemployed." John Cowper Powys calls Wilde "the Uranian baby" who never grew up; he is always speaking, speaking out, his voice prepared, self-conscious, self-satisfied. The framing of epigrams is his forte in theater and on the page, making distinctions, being distinguished and distinct. Again, we are in a world far from natural speech and from "nature" as we understand it from writers of the period who are not wits, who have an inclusive, less aloof vision of the world and of their responsibilities within it.

Wilde expanded from thirteen to twenty chapters the original 1890 periodical version of *The Picture of Dorian Gray,* some of the changes in response to suggestions made by Pater, who was, after his own experiences at the hands of critics, anxious about the response to the book. Wilde added a "Preface," a series of aestheticizing aphorisms in the form of a free verse text, set out with elaborate, if not quite functional, indentations.

> The nineteenth century dislike of Realism is the rage of
> Caliban seeing his own face in a glass.
> The nineteenth century dislike of Romanticism is the rage of
> Caliban not seeing his own face in a glass.

On publication in 1891 of Wilde's one completed novel, the *Bookseller* reviewer was puzzled, as he might have been with *Marius,* though *Dorian Gray* was a good deal more coherent in form: "Is it a novel, or a philosophy, or a criticism?" Booksellers need to categorize a book, to put it on the appropriate shelf: cross-generic titles are a problem. "The whole story from beginning to end," the review adds, "breathes an unwholesome hothouse atmosphere, though its cleverness and artistic qualities are not to be denied." Some would very nearly deny, however: John Addington Symonds wrote to Edmund Gosse of the book's "morbid and perfumed manner of treating such psychological subjects." He calls it "an odd and very audacious production, unwholesome in tone, but artistically and psychologically interesting. If the British public will stand this, they can stand anything. However, I resent the unhealthy, scented, mystic, congested touch which a man of this sort has on moral problems." The objections were to its eroticized aestheticism, a step beyond Marius's exquisite restraint, and the full flowering of what Wilde had almost said elsewhere. The expanded book version is tamer than the magazine version in terms of explicit homosexual elements; in revision Wilde underlined the aesthetic themes. It was still provocative and rarefied.

John Galsworthy confided to his diary that he could "never stomach Wilde's personality nor his writing." In his *Essays* he is more ambivalent: "Return to the consideration of the nature and purposes of Art! And recognize that much of what you have thought will seem on the face of it heresy to the school whose doctrine was incarnated by Oscar Wilde in that admirable apotheosis of half-truths: 'The Decay of the Art of Lying.'" "The seeing of things as they really are—the seeing of a proportion veiled from other eyes (together with the power of expression), is what makes a man an artist." Galsworthy begs a philosophically untenable question when he says, "Things as they really are." "What makes [Wilde] a great artist is a high fervor of spirit, which produces a superlative, instead of a comparative, clarity of vision." Comparative, superlative: undependable counters. What we have in *Dorian Gray* is an unusual, a superlative, gothic clarity of—yes—vision, even if, as Joyce says, the book (which he calls *Dorian Grey*) "is rather crowded with lies and epigrams." The charges of Galsworthy and Joyce would not have touched Wilde. In a letter to W. E. Henley, an angry editor and a jealous and resentful *littérateur,* Wilde wrote, "Work never seems to me a reality, but as a way of getting rid of reality." This is an extreme version of what Nabokov insists is the condition of real fiction.

What reality was Wilde getting rid of? In part it was his particular Irish antecedents. Gore Vidal evokes Wilde's mother, Jane, in Wildean terms: "Self-dubbed Speranza Francesca, [she] was, if not larger than life, a good deal larger than average." With so many writers, Vidal says, it is a matter of: *Cherchez la mère*. Colm Tóibín remarks that Lady Wilde could have been a grand dame but dressed dreadfully: always out of fashion, too much fabric, too many accessories; "her paint and tinsel and tawdry tragedy-queen get-up" made her "a walking burlesque of motherhood" and, more importantly, of fashion. And his father? He "resembled a monkey, a miserable-looking little creature . . . apparently unshorn and unkempt." Opposite the Wildes' mansion in Dublin were the Turkish baths. The Wildes did not frequent them.

There was all that to get away from. A fiction of self to grow into. With the assistance and inspiration of Pater and John Ruskin, different teachers whose styles led in the direction of elaboration, he made rapid progress, moving into more *particular* circles. Soon he was in London and getting famous. The character of Bunthorne in Gilbert and Sullivan's *Patience* sends up Wilde, who at the age of twenty-seven was a celebrity big enough to poke fun at. In 1881 he set sail for America, "famous for being famous," and was a success. He met many notables, including Walt Whitman, with whom he claims to have exchanged a manly kiss, and his popularity grew, preparing the international high-diving board for his fall. He met his nemesis, Alfred Douglas (Bosie), in 1891, after writing and revising *Dorian Gray*, and their relationship became intense in 1893. Bosie is irrelevant to the conception and execution of the novel and plays; it is unnecessary to recount the intense pursuit of the petulant youth, the broken promises, broken heart, trials, and broken will of one of the brittlest talents of its time. Borges notes "Wilde's *technical* insignificance" yet cannot resist his "invulnerable innocence."

Like Don Quixote, Dorian is led astray by fiction, a "poisonous French novel" that may have been by Joris-Karl Huysmans (1848–1907), *À rebours* (1884), translated into English as *Against Nature* or *Against the Grain*, a book that left a perfumed stain on André Gide and other writers who found respite in the decadents. The protagonist Jean Des Esseintes, an aesthete impatient with the bourgeois environment, in a novel with even more inaction than *Marius*, imagines his world, in which he explores and unfolds his tastes and prejudices. Naturalism is discarded in favor of an artificial stage where the protagonist is in control because he is imagining it. Wilde blurs the connections between his and Huysmans's books, but *À rebours* is a more likely source of primary infection than *Marius*.

Dorian's portrait has been painted by Basil Hallward, an artist transcendently inspired by Dorian's beauty. The hedonistic Lord Henry Wotton, the artist's friend, attracts Dorian, who wishes to arrest his own physical beauty, and his wish is fulfilled. His aging and the physical consequences of his sins, in a Gothic masterstroke, are transferred to the painting. Hidden behind a screen, it gathers his decay while he enjoys an unblemished good time in the world. Like Dr. Faustus's, his contract has an expiry date. Dorian's fate has been translated to film, television, and theater. Wilde saw aspects of himself in the three principal characters; their dialogue (much of the book is dialogue) is a communing among his selves. The coldness of the ending, with Dorian, a knife in his shriveled heart, discovered dead beneath his portrait restored to its original luster and youth, is worthy of Walpole.

Gosse wrote to André Gide regarding his *Oscar Wilde: In Memoriam* published in March 1910: "Of course he was not a 'great writer.' A languid romancier, a bad poet, a good (but not superlatively good) dramatist,—his works, taken without his life, present to a sane criticism, a mediocre figure." There is more to him than that. In *A Critic in Pall Mall* Wilde admires Turgenev's and Tolstoy's panoramas, but when he starts to write about Dostoyevsky he cannot conceal his feelings. His aphorisms cease and he is drawn into the story, astonished: "Where there is no exaggeration there is no love, and where there is no love there is no understanding."

———

Wilde overshadows the fine, small achievement of Denton Welch (1915–1948). Welch's prose is full of paradoxes, his stories of themes that are more telling for being undeclared. His world is fallen, yet there are moments of release, if not epiphany. Occasionally he perceives the "horrible, beautiful immortality that we've been looking for. The never-ending of our race on earth." Born in Shanghai, he fictionalizes his childhood spent in China in *Maiden Voyage* (1943). A year later *In Youth Is Pleasure,* his most accomplished novel, an evocation of adolescence, appeared. His stories are his most distinctive work, but there is an integrity of purpose and vision in all that he wrote in a difficult, short life. *A Voice through a Cloud,* another autobiographical novel, appeared posthumously in 1950. William Burroughs dedicated to him *The Place of Dead Roads* (1983; the second of the trilogy that includes *Cities of the Red Night* and *The Western Lands*) and declared that Welch was in fact Kim Carson, his protagonist: "a unique literary abduction." He had read Welch back in 1946 without realizing the lasting impact of his work until he reread it and found himself in its pages; he had "memorized whole passages" without intending to. Those who compare Welch to Ronald Firbank, says Burroughs, sell Welch short. He is "so much better." "I can't remember a sentence from *Prancing Nigger;* all that remains is a faint nauseating whiff of whimsy." He is unfair to Firbank, but Burroughs's advocacy of Welch remains prophetic: his hour will come. Firbank's decisively has. Burroughs sets Welch alongside Jane Bowles in terms of original phrasing and distinctive vision. "And they never deviate into whimsy."

———•———

That most narrative of modern poets Tony Harrison writes, in "Thomas Campey and the Copernican System," of an old house-clearance man who "drags away" the unvalued once-read classics and faded accoutrements of the dead: "Marie Corelli, Ouida and Hall Caine / And texts from Patience Strong in tortoise frames. / And every pound of this dead weight is pain / To Thomas Campey (Books)." The most popular novelists of their age have become books by the pound, dead weight. In their writing there is, not whimsy, but a continuous calculation of tone, an adjustment to readership, whose sentimental disposition can be played upon like an instrument. Such mass readerships can develop in cultures where literacy is widespread, and the creators and purveyors of literature as commodity learn to condition demand and provide the suitable emollients. The implicit contract between reader and writer invigorates Scott's, Dickens's, and George Eliot's work, for example, sharpening their sense of responsibility and guaranteeing the complexity and intended three-dimensionality of their triple deckers. But as literacy becomes less hard-won, more a cultural given, and as entrepreneurs understand its potential, dangers arise. The "literary novel" emerges in reaction to the appropriation and exploitation of common readers by writers who play to and then with them: those whom Scott and Dickens with their writing consolidated and educated, later popular novelists target.

In Stratford-on-Avon at the start of the twentieth century, Mason Croft, today the Shakespeare Institute, was the grand house of Marie Corelli (1855–1924; born Mary Mackay) and in Corelli's time rivaled Shakespeare's shrines in popularity. Corelli was keen to preserve the old buildings of Stratford and did much to make the town what it is for the modern visitor. At the time, people stopped to gawk at her house and, if they were lucky, at her and her long-term companion and the beneficiary of her will, Bertha Vyver.

Not only English visitors were fascinated: Corelli was widely translated and universally admired by readers, even while her "glad books," as Mencken called them, were derided by critics. Indeed, when Meredith was reader for Chapman and Hall, he made sure that her submission was rejected, to his editorial credit but their commercial loss. Once she was successful beyond most writers' imaginings, she would be seen sometimes in a gondola on the Avon, poled along by a gondolier specially imported from Venice. Her vanity and bad taste were unrivaled. She knew she was a genius and her public agreed. She had an enormous entry in *Who's Who*—longer than anyone else's. In commercial terms she was major, one of the most major in our literature. Her sales exceeded the combined sales of the popular male writers of the day. The term *best seller* started life in the 1890s in the United States. Charles Garvice's romances sold a million copies a year in English and translation; Nat Gould's 130 horse-racing novels by 1927 had sold 24 million copies. Before him, however, Corelli's *The Sorrows of Satan* was "the best-selling novel of the English-speaking world."

She started as a musician and retained her performance name as a *nom de plume*. From *A Romance of Two Worlds* in 1886 through *The Soul of Lilith* (1892), *The Sorrows of Satan* (1895), and *God's Good Man* (1904), right up to *Innocent: Her Fancy and His Fact* (1914), she was unstoppable; but the First World War marked a decline in her fortunes. What most repelled her critics and, after the war, her erstwhile readers was the strained melodrama of her books, and their continual moral tussle, given their Christian bias, with pseudoscience and parapsychology. She is an early high priestess of New Age concerns: New Age with tinsel and heady scents. Conscience, Soul, and Thought put on capital letters: we are in deep. She was a phenomenon, a priestess, a forerunner of Ayn Rand, in crinolines.

Among Ouida's more conventionally spiritualist contemporaries was Arthur Conan Doyle (1859–1930), a real "trained doctor." Novelist-physicians abound, in the last century, notably, Bulgakov, Celine, Alfred Döblin, Somerset Maugham, and A. J. Cronin, and in earlier centuries Rabelais, Goldsmith, and Smollett. All share a forensic bias, a cool eye. Conan Doyle had something of Jekyll about him. Stevenson was a friend, a fellow Scot. It is hard not to hear Prufrock prefigured in the descriptions: "See how the yellow fog swirls down the street and drifts across the dun-colored houses." Holmes is addressing Doctor Watson. Perhaps T. S. Eliot's gothic "you and I" refers to the drug-taking detective and his physician. Or not.

Sherlock Holmes uses copious clichés—we may want to call them commonplaces—so that anyone with the remotest sense of London (whether the place is known to them or not) can fill his empty phrases with Dickens's or other ready-made impressions: London has already been imagined, and Conan Doyle does not need to reimagine it. Indeed, his London, like Dr. Jekyll's, has much in common with Edinburgh and as such is a generic place. Holmes inhabits a city of the mind and does not see anything but the connections that our fuller vision obscures.

Conan Doyle told the *New York Times* that the purpose of fiction is "to amuse mankind, to help the sick and the dull and the weary." H. L. Mencken lists the popular British writers of the day, including Barrie, Caine, Mrs. Ward, Quiller-

Couch, "one and all, high and low, they are tempted by the public demand for sophistry, the ready market for pills." They sell *literature* short. Stevenson, as if to agree with Mencken, wrote to Conan Doyle in 1893 from Vailima about the Holmes stories: "That is the class of literature that I like when I have the tooth-ache. As a matter of fact, it was a pleurisy I was enjoying when I took the vol-ume up; and it will interest you as a medical man to know that the cure was for the moment effectual."

Even at his most spiritualist, Conan Doyle is a material man. He earned, he was happy to report, three or four times as much from serial as he did from book rights, evidence of the power of unresolved suspense over the weekly read-ing public. He did not trouble much about editorial process and hardly resisted correction and emendation; and he cared little how the text looked on the page. For him fiction entertained in the composition and proved a not too effortful source of income. Once the story was told, it had no further hold on him. Holmes and Watson were like friends: they visited, they departed. At last he wrote to his publisher in 1896 with what seems like feeling: "Poor Holmes is dead and damned. I couldn't revive him if I would (at least not for years), for I have had such an overdose of him that I feel towards him as I do towards pâté de foie gras, of which I once ate too much, so that the name of it gives me a sickly feel-ing to this day." His readers had to wait until the new century for his stomach to settle, in 1901, with *The Hound of the Baskervilles*.

There is more to Conan Doyle than Sherlock Holmes, though Sherlock Holmes is his durable legacy. His 1912 novel *The Lost World* contributes to a long tradition of fantasies in which history and prehistory come into implausi-ble conflict. It may all have begun with Jules Verne's *A Journey to the Center of the Earth* (*Voyage au centre de la Terre,* 1864) and been continued in various forms by Rider Haggard, but *The Lost World* (1912) gives plausible new currency, not to ancient cultures, but to ancient natures, to dinosaurs and their contemporaries. Edgar Rice Burroughs's *The Land That Time Forgot* (1916) takes its cue from Conan Doyle, and there are elements of his story (including the title) in Michael Crichton's 1995 sequel to *Jurassic Park* (itself indebted to *The Lost World*).

Doyle's recorded voice survives, to tell us how as a young doctor in Edin-burgh he was under Dr. Bell, an acute physician who could, by merely observing a patient, discover not only their illness but their social position and even their work. Until then (he makes an exception of Edgar Allan Poe) detective stories were resolved mainly by luck: he wanted to write stories in which science took the place of chance. So real was Holmes to readers all over the world that he received copious letters, one offering marriage. While visitors to Marie Corel-li's house at Stratford now go there for quite other reasons, the procession of tourists in search of 221B Baker Street has never abated, yet none has ever found the house.

———•———

The immensely productive Maria Louise Ramé (or de la Ramée) (1839–1908), better known as Ouida, is a decade and a half Marie Corelli's senior and, as a writer, her superior, less pretentious, more engaging, and she takes herself rather less seriously. She is not a priestess and, instead of spiritual vanity, has a conscience and an erratic heart. A spendthrift, she died in relative poverty in Italy, having got through a great deal of earned money.

She collected stray dogs, her fluctuating pack numbering as many as thirty. In 1870 she published *Puck,* in which the following affectionate exchange occurs between the protagonist and her dog. Short paragraphs give a sentimental staccato to the prose, a designed tremor:

> She kissed the dog on the forehead; then pointed to the kreel of shells and seaweed on the red, smooth piece of rock.
>
> "Take care of them, dear Bronze," she murmured; "and wait till I come back. Wait here."
>
> She did not mean to command; she only meant to console him by the appointment of some service.
>
> Bronze looked in her face with eyes of woe and longing; but he made no moan or sound, but only stretched himself beside the kreel on guard. I am always glad to think that as she went she turned, and kissed him once again.

Bronze is not unlike Kipling's canine in *Thy Servant: A Dog,* though Kipling's is less sentimentally rendered.

Ouida in early work could be quite (comparatively) risqué in idiom and theme; she stood apart from the more overtly didactic of her contemporaries. But she had other designs on her readers, less to instruct than to excite and entertain. Hers was a fiction of sensation and sentiment. She moved in the direction of Scott and the historical romance, with more unlikely invention than her predecessors.

It was impossible to ignore her, and she continued to surprise. Chesterton, comparing her writing with that of Mrs. Oliphant, gives her the edge in terms of oddity: "Ouida, with infinite fury and infinite confusion of thought, did fill her books with Byron and the remains of the French Revolution." In 1875 Henry James was taken by surprise when asked to review *Signa: A Story:* "Let no man hereafter despair of anything; even Ouida improves! She began several years ago with writing unmitigated nonsense, and now she writes nonsense very sensibly mitigated." A dyed-in-the-wool charlatan, she improved thanks to intelligent reading of Victor Hugo and some of Swinburne's lucid and rhythmical prose. The essence of her art is to seem to mean without meaning anything in particular: each sentence exists in a kind of tense hope that it may follow the one before and perhaps precede the one following. The plots are wild and sometimes dotty. But Chekhov was reading the books in Russian translation with pleasure in 1891, wishing he knew English so he could do them justice. At around the same time Oscar Wilde was paying her a reluctant tribute in the teeth of critical good sense: "*Guilderoy,* with all its faults, which are great, and its absurdities, which are greater, is a book to be read."

Norman Douglas had for her a tenderness writers sometimes feel, rueful, paying a debt too late. In *Alone* he reflects on her death: "Smollett lies yonder, at Livorno; and Ouida hard by, at Bagni di Lucca. She died in one of these same featureless streets of Viareggio, alone, half blind, and in poverty." He calls to mind the Suffolk of her youth: in Bury St. Edmunds, life was so boring that people, she said, rang their own doorbells to keep them from rusting. Douglas writes, "I know Suffolk, that ripe old county of hers, with its pink villages nestling among drowsy elms and cornfields; I know their 'Spread Eagles' and 'Angels' and 'White Horses' and other taverns suggestive—sure sign of antiquity—of zoological gardens; I know their goodly ale and old brown sherries." In Bury he is tempted to knock at the house where she was born, but he passes by and seeks the memorial fountain, a drinking place for dogs and horses, "among the drooping trees. The good animals for whose comfort it was built would have had some difficulty in slaking their thirst just then, its basin being chocked up with decayed leaves." Tenderly—Norman Douglas can sometimes be tender—he says, "If her novels are somewhat faded, the same cannot be said of her letters and articles and critiques. To our rising generation of authors—the youngsters, I mean; those who have not yet sold themselves to the devil—I should say: read these things of Ouida's." How against the grain of fashion he writes! "Read them attentively, not for their matter, which is always of interest, nor yet for their vibrant and lucid style, which often rivals that of Huxley. Read them for their tone, their temper; for that pervasive good breeding, that shining honesty, that capacity of scorn." In these pages he finds "qualities which our present age lacks, and needs." And he sees her as clear-headed and unfashionable. "How right about the Japanese, about Feminism and Conscription and German brutalitarianism! How she puts her finger on the spot when discussing Marion Crawford and D'Annunzio! Those local politicians—how she hits them off! Hers was a sure touch."

———

The apotheosis of Edwardian sentimentality is J. M. (James Matthew) Barrie (1860–1937), so successful that he was knighted and given the Order of Merit.

Conan Doyle wrote to his publisher, "No one has said enough, as it seems to me, about Barrie or Kipling. I think they are fit—young as they are—to rank with the highest, and that some of Barrie's work, *Margaret Ogilvy* and *A Window in Thrums,* will endear him as Robert Burns is endeared to the hearts of the future Scottish race." This valuation was generally shared. Barrie was a phenomenon. Mrs. Humphry Ward trumpeted *The Window in Thrums* as "a masterpiece to set beside the French masterpiece, drawn likewise from peasant life, of almost the same date, *Pêcheur d'Islande.*" He is not on a very large scale, admittedly: "Barrie's gift . . . has been a gift making for the joy of his generation; he too has carried the flag of the True Romance—slight, twinkling, fantastic thing, compared to that of Kipling, but consecrate to the same great service."

Born in a four-room weaver's cottage (his father was a weaver and cloth dealer) in Kirriemuir, near Glamis Castle, he became, he reminded himself and his readers, a guest of kings. It mattered to him, but not to his imagination. "Nothing that happens after we are twelve matters very much," he said: puberty and all the complications it brings efface the creature we *really* are and, beneath the confusions and paradoxes of adulthood, remain. He left Kirriemuir at the age of eight for Glasgow, where his elder brother was teaching. Then Forfar at ten and at thirteen (life being over) to Dumfries. The reason things end for him after twelve may be connected with the death of his brother in a skating accident. James was six. Getting over that loss was impossible: the irretrievable and *actual* "lost boy."

His mother's experience of Kirriemuir was more real to him than his own years there, and her grief at his brother's death expanded his own. He felt when she was talking to him that she was sometimes trying to talk to his brother. He regarded himself to be "as Scotch as peat" but became a Londoner. Scots saw him as an escapee: his compass needle lost its northern bias. His books, in particular *Auld Licht Idylls* (1888), *A Window in Thrums* (1890), and *The Little Minister* (1891), drawing on his mother's experience and religion, troubled Kirriemuir folk for the picture they presented of their world. These books trouble their few modern readers for their inordinate indulgence of the child's "little lonely voice." "Little," the sentimentalist's trademark. Gosse sees "the influence of Sterne everywhere. The pathos of Sir James Barrie is intimately related to that of the creator of Uncle Toby and Maria of Moulines." This note is lost on modern readers.

An attentive friend of Hardy, of Conan Doyle and Jerome K. Jerome, he wrote in a way that invited interest of a kind that has dogged Lewis Carroll also, and as with Carroll the verifiable facts can be read in various ways. Are we dealing with a pervert? The answer is, as with Carroll, probably not. He loves his characters intensely; the control he exerts, how he grooms them and puts them through their paces, his puppetry, create in modern readers a continuous unease. In his "Scrutiny" of Barrie, the poet Edgell Rickword moves out of dazzlement with the style into a sense of the connection between the writer and his subjects: "The skill with which Barrie handles the half-human material he selects for use on the stage, to some extent dazzles the spectator into accepting a sleight of hand." But we come close, "a cotton thread becomes visible, running from the puppets' breeches to the showman's waistcoat; for it is Barrie's heart that pumps into them what vitality they possess. He loves them, and wants them to be loved so very much." They and their author "swim in the sweet oily liquor of universal pathos which is his philosophy of life."

Rickword's concern is largely with Barrie's theater work. *Peter Pan: Or the Boy Who Wouldn't Grow Up,* first staged after Christmas in 1904, became a novel only in 1911 as *Peter and Wendy.* George Bernard Shaw, puzzled but not displeased by the play, saw it as rather more than a children's entertainment. So did Rickword, but in a darker spirit. For him, "The apotheosis of Barrie was a social phenomenon, hardly a matter for literary criticism at all, and as a society's criticism of itself hardly to be bettered. When such glamor is at work, the spectator is impervious to any demonstration of the falsity of the creation." The spell holds for the duration, but the shadow rejoins the body that casts it, the lost boys wake up in their own beds.

In 1911, a good year for popular middle-brow Edwardian literature, Sir Henry Maximilian Beerbohm (1972–1956), "the incomparable Max," artist, one of the great social caricaturists in the English tradition, published *Zuleika Dobson.* "You all know Miss Dobson—not personally," says Forster, "or you would not be here now. She is that damsel for love of whom all the undergraduates of Oxford except one drowned themselves during Eights Week, and he threw himself out of a window." In that summary the frame and substance, if not the content, are clear. This is a book that arises from a narrowly based, rich and brittle class culture.

Zuleika—Beerbohm insisted the name be pronounced "Zu-*leek*-a"—arrives at Oxford by train in paragraph three. Amid the steam, she is a flash of light: "Into the station it came blustering, with cloud and clangor. Ere it had yet stopped, the door of one carriage flew open, and from it, in a white travelling dress, in a toque a-twinkle with fine diamonds, a lithe and radiant creature slipped nimbly down to the platform." The world is instantly spangled. Fun is promised and delivered. He takes a "real" world that is familiar to many readers and portrays it in an archaized idiom. He enchants, he mythologizes it, standing apart. He writes a passage and reflects, "Has not a passage like this a beauty unattainable by serious literature?" Updike comments on Beerbohm's 1919 collection of stories *Seven Men* (which includes "Enoch Soames," about a poet who wants to know what his reputation will be a century thence and makes a Faustian pact with the devil to find out) and his parodies in *A Christmas Garland* (1912): "Minor artistry became in him a determination, a boast; like Ronald Firbank and Nathanael West, he remains readable while many mightier oeuvres gather dust. The filigree is fine, but of the purest gold."

Comparing himself with Stevenson, Beerbohm reflects, "I, in my own very inferior boyhood, found it hard to revel in so much as a single page of any writer earlier than Thackeray. This disability I did not shake off, alas, after I left school." He never engaged a past remoter than the mid-nineteenth century. "There seemed to be so many live authors worth reading. I gave precedence to them, and, not being much of a reader, never had time to grapple with the old masters." He learned by parody, hence the *Garland,* the best place to get to know him, so long as we are familiar with the thinly veiled writers garlanded, among them:

> THE MOTE IN THE MIDDLE DISTANCE, H*NRY J*M*S
> P.C., X, 36, R*D**RD K*PL*NG
> A SEQUELULA TO 'THE DYNASTS,' TH*M*S H*RDY
> SCRUTS, ARN*LD B*NN*TT
> THE FEAST, J*S*PH C*NR*D
> EUPHEMIA CLASHTHOUGHT, G**RGE M*R*D*TH

Conrad was delighted to be guyed in such company; a parody of the quality of Beerbohm's was a compliment. Beerbohm's skills were those of an essayist, and Woolf puts him in the company of Montaigne and Lamb, writers who gave themselves to the reader. Hence the familiar nickname, the easy intimacy we feel in his company. "Serious literature" is not on the agenda. Woolf reflects, "Thus, some time in the nineties, it must have surprised readers accustomed to exhortation, information, and denunciation to find themselves familiarly addressed by a voice which seemed to belong to a man no larger than themselves."

Beerbohm understands what style might be and do, remembering in his essay on Walter Pater how even in the days when he honored him he did not admire his style. "Even then I was angry that he should treat English as a dead language, bored by that sedulous ritual wherewith he laid out every sentence as in a shroud—hanging, like a widower, long over its marmoreal beauty or ever he could lay it at length in his book, its sepulchre." It took him time to get over his regard for "the couth solemnity of his mind . . . his philosophy, his rare erudition."

—•—

At this time, adult literature and writing for children could be close. Adult taste was sentimentalized, children and their assumed innocence were idealized and made vulnerable. After the Alice books the great children's novel of its age is *The Wind in the Willows* (1908) by Kenneth Grahame (1859–1932), another self-exiled Scot. He was born in Edinburgh in the same year as Doyle, in a house opposite to one that Scott occupied for several years in Castle Street. He was a descendant of Robert Bruce, and his father was an advocate.

He arrived in England after his mother's death and his father's turn to alcoholism, to live with grandparents by the Thames at Cookham. He went into banking, retired in 1908, and then wrote his fifth and finest book. His own child, Alastair, may have been the occasion for composition—the troubled, bossy, and sickly child of a difficult marriage who killed himself just before he was twenty, while an undergraduate in the wide world that was Oxford. The boy inspired the intractable and willful character of Mr. Toad, while Mole, Ratty, and Badger step out of nature and society to companion him. There are no female animals, and the women who help and hinder Mr. Toad are portrayed with asperity. It is a bachelor world. (Mrs. Mole was erased in revision.)

Parents who read to their children learn that a good book is one you can read aloud with pleasure dozens of times. The Beatrix Potter books survive endless reiteration, and their phrases enter the family lexicon—Mr. Jackson's reassuring words to Mrs. Tittlemouse, "No teeth, no teeth, no teeth"; Jemima Puddleduck's "foxy gentleman"; the Flopsy Bunnies' "Lettuce is soporific"; and Mrs. Rabbit's classic injunction, "Now, my dears . . . you may go into the fields or down the lane, but don't go into Mr. McGregor's garden: your Father had an accident there; he was put in a pie by Mrs. McGregor." And from *The Wind in the Willows,* Mole's "Oh my, oh my, oh my," and phrases like, "messing about in boats," "the artful toad," the car claxon's "poop poop"; and the cautionary, "Beyond the Wild Wood is the Wide World . . . And that's something that doesn't matter, either to you or me." Some say the scenes are set on the bank of the Thames, some on the banks of the River Fowey in Cornwall. In fact, the river can only be reached by crossing the Wild Wood in the other direction.

There is a more tenable, almost palpable transcendence and mysticism in *The Wind in the Willows* than in Marie Corelli or spiritualist Conan Doyle, embodied in the Piper at the Gates of the Dawn, who, at rather greater length than most children can endure, meditates on nature. The prose is heightened, one is tempted to call it purple, but that would seem to ironize the continuous pleasure to be had from it, a repeatable pleasure different in kind and in degree from what we experience from the wily precisions of Lewis Carroll. The world of *The Wind in the Willows* seems real rather than enchanted, in a minor key. It has the elegiac feel of a place that, though we were so much there, we cannot return to.

# 24

# Pessimists

Thomas Hardy, Joseph Conrad, Stephen Crane

Robert Louis Stevenson with his wife, Fanny, visited Thomas and Emma Hardy at their new house Max Gate in Dorset in 1885. Fanny wrote to her mother-in-law about the "pale, gentle, frightened little man, that one felt an instant tenderness for, with a wife—ugly is no word for it, who said, 'Whatever shall we do?' I had never heard a living being say it before." The Stevensons took away a vivid impression of Emma, but only sympathy for her husband, whom James referred to as "the good little Thomas Hardy." He was already a celebrated novelist. *The Mayor of Casterbridge* (published the following year in book form) was being serialized. Stevenson wanted to dramatize it. Hardy was flattered, the suggestion made him feel "several inches taller" (Stevenson towered over him; this metaphorical growth redressed proportion). Stevenson had admired *Far from the Madding Crowd* (1874), Hardy's first major novel. Hardy's books included *Desperate Remedies* (1871) and *Under the Greenwood Tree* (1872), published anonymously; *A Pair of Blue Eyes* (1873) under his own name, in which Elfride Swancourt leaves the devoted writer Henry Knight literally hanging from a cliff at the end of chapter 21, the first "cliffhanger" in serial fiction; *The Hand of Ethelberta* (1876), *The Return of the Native* (1878), *The Trumpet-Major* (1880), *A Laodicean* (1881), and *Two on a Tower* (1882). It was a substantial bibliography for a writer in his mid-forties, and Stevenson, ten years his junior, admired the Wessex world Hardy was creating. Later, Hardy was to refer to James as the Polonius and Stevenson as the Osric of novelists. This left the role of Hamlet suggestively open.

The greatest European actresses of their day, Eleonora Duse and Sarah Bernhardt, each wanted to play the role of Tess in dramatizations of *Tess of the D'Urbervilles* (1891), though the furor surrounding *Jude the Obscure* (1895) darkened public enthusiasm for the writer. Stevenson is among those who found *Tess* rebarbative, the rape having been, in his view, ill conceived and its evocation unconvincing. Hardy the Dorset pessimist was now an immoralist as well, a charge redoubled with *Jude,* a harrowing book but not one of his best: it steps away from Wessex, the antagonists are unworthy of the protagonist. Woolf notes, "Jude carries on his miserable contest against the deans of colleges and the conventions of sophisticated society. Henchard"—in *The Mayor of Casterbridge*—"is pitted, not against another man, but against something outside himself which is opposed to men of his ambition and power."

After the moral buffeting he took in 1895, Hardy renounced fiction (he had referred to his fiction, half seriously, as "ephemeral" in any case) and gave himself over entirely to his first love, poetry. In the eighteenth century a novelist might double as a pamphleteer, but few aspired to excel as poets in the manner of, say, Scott, the Brontë sisters in their formative years, George Eliot, Melville, Meredith, Stevenson himself, Kipling, and Stephen Crane.

Stevenson and Hardy in 1886 may have discussed the vagaries of novel serialization. Stevenson was to have his own traumas with the serial editors of the *Illustrated London News* later on. Hardy reckoned that of all his novels the one most damaged by the exigencies of serialization was *The Mayor of Casterbridge:* the need for *incident* week after week made for too much plot; also, the absence of gentry led to some difficulty in placing the completed novel with a publisher. (We remember the counsel of the New Grub Street writing course: "I gravely advise people . . . to write of the wealthy middle class; that's the popular subject, you know.")

In a notebook Hardy wrote, "I am convinced that it is better for a writer to know a little bit of the world remarkably well than to know a great part of the world remarkably little." Most of his fiction is set in "a little bit of the world," his native Dorset fictionalized as Wessex. He was born in the center of that world, at Higher Bockhampton, in 1840, the third year of Queen Victoria's reign. He was set aside as stillborn but the midwife heard a movement and rescued him. His father was a musician and builder. His first clear memory dates from 1844: his father gave him a toy accordion. Hardy partly acquired both his father's skills, making music—a source of imagery in his novels—and being articled as an ecclesiastical architect from 1856–1861, specializing in the Gothic revival and becoming a competent draftsman.

His family was originally from Jersey, "le Hardy's." Hardy considered restoring the "le," like Daniel Foe with his "De." There was something dynastic going on in the family: Thomas was the third. The boy's sense of formal language began in church with the liturgy, the Bible, and in particular the hymns. When he started schooling at home, his mother gave him *Rasselas* and, as a corrective, Jacques-Henri Bernardin de Saint-Pierre's melodramatic *Paul et Virginie* in English. He loved the romances of the elder Dumas; and he enjoyed Shakespeare. His maternal grandmother was steeped in Bunyan, Fielding, and Richardson and the eighteenth-century essayists.

His mother regarded herself as a cut above her husband (the attitude of his own wife to him). She had ambitions for her son: he received the best education that could be afforded, in Dorchester and later at King's College, London. For five years he worked in London at an architect's office and became a prizeman of the Royal Institute of British Architects. During this period he wrote the earliest of the poems he was to collect decades later in *Wessex Poems* (1898). He was reading fiction and making the capital his own. He was conscious of walking the streets of Dickens's and Thackeray's novels. In 1863, aged twenty-three, he wrote to a friend: "You must read something of [Thackeray's]. He is considered to be the greatest novelist of the day—looking at novel writing of the highest kind as a perfect and truthful representation of actual life." But the novels of Thackeray do not invariably have "an elevating tendency": he is unable to make "perfect" characters, a fault in a moral teacher but a virtue in a portraitist.

In 1866 Hardy was reading Trollope and was in a state of indecision about what to write. Blank verse plays? In 1867, living back in the West Country, he embarked on a novel. *The Poor Man and the Lady,* by "the Poor Man," was completed. He copied it out and received a clear and helpful rejection. Fragments of the book survive. When *Desperate Remedies,* his first accepted book, an attempt at the "sensation novel" Wilkie Collins had made popular, was to be published, Hardy was required to provide a £20 guarantee against loss. It began well and was then stopped in its tracks by a *Spectator* review. The disaster was material and psychological: he had to find a further £75 for the publisher. In 1870, crossing Hyde Park one June morning, he learned Dickens had died.

In 1873 Meredith's friend Leslie Stephens of *Cornhill Magazine* asked the young novelist for a serial. He got *Far from the Madding Crowd.* Hardy's friend Horace Moule urged him to publish *Desperate Remedies.* Virginia Woolf, writing over half a century later, understood the promise of this imperfect project. "He already proves himself a minute and skilled observer of Nature; the rain, he knows, falls differently as it falls upon roots or arable; he knows that the wind sounds differently as it passes through the branches of different trees." In this he is like George Eliot, whose seasons are correct, her nature instantly real.

He was writing in earnest and at speed. Because he had not published his poetry, he was able from time to time to mine it for his fiction. His poetic concerns are evident in his shaping of scenes, the oblique economy of satirical and tragic payoffs, and most of all in the rhythm at points of lyrical or dramatic heightening. Michael Henchard's sparse, merciless "Will" in *The Mayor of Casterbridge* is a case in point:

> That Elizabeth-Jane Farfrae be not told of my death, or made to grieve on account of me.
>> & that I be not bury'd in consecrated ground.
>> & that no sexton be asked to toll the bell.
>> & that nobody is wished to see my dead body.

& that no murners walk behind me at my funeral.
& that no flours be planted on my grave,
& that no man remember me.
To this I put my name.
'Michael Henchard'

As an adolescent, Hardy attempted to translate Ecclesiastes into Spenserian stanzas. Biblical images, subject matter, and echoes of the rhythms of the Authorized Version sound throughout his prose. Accused of pessimism, he called himself an "evolutionary meliorist," quoting a line from his "In Tenebris ii": "If way to the better there be, it exacts a full look at the worst." Yet there is in his sense of time and memory something that no evolution could ameliorate. The world might become more tolerant and tolerable, but the human condition hardly improves. His novels spend so much time looking at "the worst" that "the better" fades. Joseph Conrad, no optimist, understands the perils of a pessimism so settled as to be either willful or pathological. Perhaps with Hardy in mind he wrote, in *Notes on Life and Letters:* "It must not be supposed that I claim for the artist in fiction the freedom of moral Nihilism. I would require from him many acts of faith of which the first would be the cherishing of an undying hope; and hope, it will not be contested, implies all the piety of effort and renunciation. It is the God-sent form of trust in the magic force and inspiration belonging to the life of this earth. We are inclined to forget that the way of excellence is in the intellectual, as distinguished from emotional, humility. What one feels so hopelessly barren in declared pessimism is just its arrogance." He objects to the hubris of pessimism, like the extreme Protestant who insists he is the greatest sinner, demanding a larger portion of God's ire and Christ's mercy than anyone else. D. H. Lawrence admired Hardy's obdurate consistency, seeing him more as an idealist than a godless Protestant: his pessimism "is an absolutely true finding. It is the absolutely true statement of the idealist's last realisation, as he wrestles with the bitter soil of beloved mother-earth." Truth, then, not willful distortion. "He loves her, loves her, loves her. And she just entangles and crushes him like a slow Laocoön snake. The idealist must perish, says mother-earth. Then let him perish."

The openings of Hardy's books have an air of evenhanded neutrality, but a dark stain soon shows. There can be little doubt what direction we are headed in when a book begins, "One evening of late summer, before the nineteenth century had reached one-third of its span, a young man and woman, the latter carrying a child, were approaching the large village of Weydon-Priors, in Upper Wessex, on foot." We know what season and roughly what year we are in; three characters have been seen, if not introduced; we assume their humble station from the way they travel; the (imagined) provincial setting is specifically estab-lished. Hardy begins to fill in the rough outline. "They were plainly but not ill clad," modest but not penurious; and they have come a long way, "the thick hoar of dust which had accumulated on their shoes and garments from an obvi-ously long journey lent a disadvantageous shabbiness to their appearance just now"—a nice semantic clash between the hoar we associate with frost and the season and fact of dust. The "disadvantageous shabbiness" indicates that they are in some kind of peril. Hardy begins to color in the image, the man first, his physical aspect, his clothing, each detail adding physical but also social informa-tion and moral hue. "At his back he carried by a looped strap a rush basket, from which protruded at one end the crutch of a hay-knife, a wimble for hay-bonds being also visible in the aperture." The vocabulary belongs to a rural vocation and a locality. Characters emerge from landscape, its customs and communi-ties. As they are differentiated and defined, their lives are trammeled in the downward bias of Hardy's plot.

In *Far from the Madding Crowd* it takes five short paragraphs for us to meet, like, and trust Gabriel Oak. Then in the sixth paragraph, with and through his eyes, from his very place in the landscape, we experience a first vision of Bath-sheba, the scene created as if a statue were being erected to celebrate a Roman triumph; the unfolding drama of the description leaves the observer (Gabriel and the reader) transfixed as by the arrow of Cupid himself when his eye reaches "the apex": "The field he was in this morning sloped to a ridge called Morecombe Hill. Through a spur of this hill ran the highway between Emmin-ster and Chalk-Newton. Casually glancing over the hedge, Oak saw coming down the incline before him an ornamental spring wagon, painted yellow and gaily marked, drawn by two horses, a Waggoner walking alongside bearing a whip perpendicularly. The wagon was laden with household goods and win-dow plants, and on the apex of the whole sat a woman, young and attractive. Gabriel had not beheld the sight for more than half a minute, when the vehicle was brought to a standstill just beneath his eyes." Half a minute is enough to seal his fate. As in the previous opening, a protagonist has been measured for his fate.

It is here that Woolf sees Hardy achieving his fullest maturity. "The subject was right; the method was right; the poet and the countryman, the sensual man, the sombre reflective man, the man of learning, all enlisted to produce a book which, however fashions may chop and change, must hold its place among the great English novels." She draws attention to his unprecedented sense of the physical world, and how the landscape can frame and magnify the little lives of people. "The dark downland, marked by the barrows of the dead and the huts of shepherds, rises against the sky, smooth as a wave of the sea, but

solid and eternal." The protagonists are Hardy's fullest and most solid characters: they "stand up like lightning conductors to attract the force of the elements." Inevitability is built into the images and symbols. "When Bathsheba
sits in the wagon among her plants, smiling at her own loveliness in the little
looking-glass, we may know, and it is proof of Hardy's power that we do know,
how severely she will suffer and cause others to suffer before the end." Arnold
Bennett praises *The Woodlanders* (1887), its plot "one of the most exquisite examples of subtle symbolic illustration of an idea that a writer of fiction ever
achieved; it makes the symbolism of Ibsen seem crude."

In notes and marginalia Hardy says what he is up to, and up against, as a
writer. "Art is a disproportioning . . . of realities, to show more clearly the features that matter in those realities, which, if merely copied or reported invento-
rially, might possibly be observed, but would more probably be overlooked."
The word "disproportioning" has a Gothic energy. "Hence 'realism' is not Art."
No wonder Lawrence responds while Conrad demurs. Some of Hardy's critical
opinions are provident and—given the mid- and late-Victorian milieu—radical.
In 1887 he wrote, "I begin to feel that mere intellectual subtlety will not hold its
own in time to come against the straightforward expression of good feeling"—
this at a time when his own fiction was growing in intellectual range and formal
ambition. He is never technically straightforward: he sets himself challenges,
continually exploring form, not playfully, for its own sake, but morally. The
avoidance of affectation and mere decoration is axiomatic: "The whole secret of
living style and the difference between it and dead style, lies in it not having too
much style—being, in fact, a little careless, or rather seeming to be, here and
there." Answering Matthew Arnold on the subject of rootedness, he wrote: "A
certain provincialism of feeling is invaluable. It is the essence of individuality,
and is largely made up of that crude enthusiasm without which no great
thoughts are thought, no great deeds done." He said in 1888, "The besetting sin
of modern literature is its insincerity. Half its utterances are qualified, even
contradicted, by an aside, and this particularly in morals and religion." He
highlights "the principles that make for permanence," namely "the value of organic form and symmetry, the force of reserve, and the emphasis on understatement, even in his lighter works." A more concise description of the Hardyesque, conventionally English temperament would be hard to find. It results
from his reading of a French writer, Anatole France, whose novels and critical
concerns affected Meredith, Galsworthy, Gosse, and others.

Emma Lavinia, née Gifford, was the sister-in-law of a parson whose church
in Cornwall Hardy helped to "improve" in the Victorian manner, architectur-
ally vandalizing it with the best intentions. Remembering her first view of
Hardy, she said, "I was immediately arrested by his familiar appearance, as if I

had seen him in a dream—his slightly different accent, his soft voice." For two years their marriage was apparently happy. The problem was less that they drifted apart than that they were bound together too tightly. Hardy may not have behaved badly to her, but he did not behave well. Endurance replaced love, and more than thirty-five years of unhappiness elapsed before Emma died. Hardy had renounced fiction seventeen years before. After Emma's death, in 1914 he married a younger woman, Florence Dugdale, his amanuensis, and she in turn recorded his *Life*. "The world does not despise us; it only neglects us," he says. If this is true (there was no indifference in the way the world responded to Hardy and his books), tragedy is impossible. There are no just gods to offend or serve. There is no sin against a given rule, there is only sin, repeated day after day, against self: failure to choose rightly and act in pursuit of a happiness. This is not far from George Eliot's stance, though Hardy is less rueful than she, more committed to the predicament.

When *Far from the Madding Crowd* was serialized anonymously in *Cornhill Magazine* in 1873, some readers and critics attributed it to George Eliot. She was "not a born storyteller by any means," Hardy said. Her country folk seemed "more like small townsfolk than rustics." Still, the confusion of new readers can be understood: Hardy is more somber, but the main difference is that an external fate weighs on Hardy's characters. It is always in waiting. Eliot's vision is balanced. "The English peasant lived and still lives in a milder, flatter world than Hardy's," says Pritchett, "a world where conscience and self-interest keep down the passions, like a pair of game-keepers." Hardy's world is the more dramatic, Eliot's the more just. Some of her characters make good, some are good. Hardy's dominant theme is individual unfulfillment in time. His vision is of a past unrealized, full of potential: "Everything glowed with a gleam," but "we were looking away." The past with its choices is placed beside a present those choices impoverished. Life is ever "a thwarted purposing."

The stress Hardy lays on thematic issues is crucial, because his aesthetic is inseparable from the themes, indeed is continuous with them. Edith Wharton holds Hardy up as an example of the importance of specifics and of the *diction* of those specifics: "The impression produced by a landscape, a street or a house should always, to the novelist, be an event in the history of a soul," which is fair enough, "and the use of a 'descriptive passage,' and its style, should be determined by the fact that it must depict only what the intelligence concerned would have noticed, and always in terms *within the register of that intelligence* [my italics]." Thus she endorses as entirely appropriate the description in *The Return of the Native* of Egdon Heath as Eustacia Vye gazes out at it from Rainbarrow. This she contrasts with what she sees as a miscalculation in *Tess of the D'Urbervilles* of the description, geological and agricultural, "of the Wessex vale through which . . . unseeing, wretched, and incapable at any time of noting such particulars [the protagonist] flies blindly to her doom." Wharton fails to see that Hardy's intention was precisely that, to underline the fact that the landscape and the victim are disconnected, existing as it were in disdain of one another. This is what, when the crisis arrives, happens to Hardy's heroes and heroines: individual and environment are expressed in deliberately alienated registers. Lodge shows how Hardy with his strong sense of new science, geology in particular, juxtaposes the fragilities of a fleeting present with fossils, things long dead. "His work is notable for such breathtaking shifts of perspective, which display the fragile human figure dwarfed by a Universe whose vast dimensions of space and time were just beginning to be truly apprehended." Only in an art governed by rules rather than responding to experience would such a disjunction be seen as an artistic fault.

When writing *Far from the Madding Crowd,* not realizing at the time to what extent it would become the principal world of his fiction, Hardy created Wessex. It gave unity to the provincial, or what he calls the "local," novels that followed. It amused him how soon Wessex caught on and became not imagined but a "real" place. It was credible. W. H. Auden admired Hardy's "hawk's vision, his way of looking at life from a very great height. To see the individual life related not only to the local social life of its time, but to the whole of human history gives one both humility and self-confidence." This "hawk's vision" is also the cartographer's. He "conceives of his novels from an enormous height," says Pritchett. "They are to be tragedies and tragi-comedies, they are to give out the sound of hammer-strokes as they proceed; in other words Hardy arranges events with emphasis on causality, the ground-plan is a plot, and the characters are ordered to acquiesce in its requirements." This is a limitation, the characters too tied to contingency and circumstance ever to *live* in the way Eliot's characters do, teetering on the edge of wrong decisions, then choosing rightly. If things can go wrong, they will: "He has emphasized causality more strongly than his medium permits." We might resist this notion of the medium having implicit regulations that a novelist transgresses at peril. The theme that obsesses Hardy (no weaker expression will do) is life's ironies, how intention and execution never quite coincide.

Ford notes how in his stories Hardy comes up very close; he rivets us, his eye fixed on ours and, strangely, through us, on the story he is telling: he and we too are vehicles of the telling. That directness means we read novel after novel not with satisfaction but continuing hunger. For what? For—perhaps—the relief of positive closure that is deferred. "Novel-writing as an art cannot go backward. Having reached the analytic stage it must transcend it by going still further in the same direction," he tells himself in his *Personal Notebooks.* Reviews of his last two novels, and of *Jude* in particular, were harsh. Wrote "the delightful Mrs. Oliphant" in *Blackwood's Magazine*: "There may be books more disgusting, more impious as regards human nature, more foul in detail, in those dark corners where the amateurs of filth find garbage to their taste; but not, we repeat, from any Master's hand." Stephen King a century later shared her view: "When I read *Jude the Obscure,* that was the end of my Hardy phase. I thought, This is fucking ridiculous. Nobody's life is this bad. Give me a break, you know?"

Hardy's impact on English fiction is felt rather later than Mrs. Oliphant's strictures. Graham Greene reads him to discover points of aesthetic and moral clarity, when they coincide and produce affecting simplicity. "In all writers there occurs a moment of crystallisation when the dominant theme is plainly expressed, when the private universe becomes visible even to the least sensitive reader." In Hardy he instances such moments as: "The President of the Immortals . . . had ended his sport with Tess" and (from the preface of *Jude*) "the fret and fever, derision and disaster, that may press in the wake of the strongest passion known to humanity." He comments too on Hardy's thematic similarity with a novelist who at first seems remote in every way from him. "There is much in common between the pessimism of Hardy and of James; both had a stronger belief in the supernatural evil than in supernatural good, and if James had, like Hardy, tried to systematize his ideas, his novels too would have lurched with the same one-sided gait." James does not emerge unscathed from the comparison. His novels "retain their beautiful symmetry at a price, the price which Turgenev and Dostoyevsky refused to pay, the price of refraining from adding to the novelist's distinction that of a philosopher or a religious teacher of the second rank."

James criticized Hardy for various faults, most tellingly his overuse of dialogue in *Far from the Madding Crowd,* where he loses sight of the fact that "dialogue in story is after all *but episode*" (my italics). He makes the crucial distinction between dialogue used crudely to advance narrative and dialogue integrated into the movement of the novel. James finds Hardy "inordinately diffuse." He prefers metaphorical and symbolic description, where characters merge with the scene. Ivy Compton-Burnett, whose novels are the apotheosis of dialogue and who disliked descriptive passages, made an exception of Hardy, for "surely his presentation of natural features almost as characters puts him on a plane of his own, and almost carries the thing into the human world." Austen, on the other hand: she hurries through or skips descriptions in order to get back to the people.

James's case against *Far from the Madding Crowd* illustrates a widening gap in English fiction between provincial and modern sensibilities. James contrasts the small plot with the huge extent of the novel, the result in part of too many conversations, "descriptive padding and the use of an ingeniously verbose and redundant style. It is inordinately diffuse, and, as a piece of narrative, singularly inartistic." Into the excesses of Hardy he reads a need to return to Aristotelian principles of unity and to continue the struggle against the tyranny of the "triple decker," the novel published in three volumes. He concludes with a seeming compliment: "Mr. Hardy has gone astray very cleverly, and his superficial novel is a really curious imitation of something better."

Hardy had readers abroad. In 1893 he was in London for a lecture on Tolstoy by Sergei Stepniak and learned that the Russian translation of *Tess* had earned the approval of the master himself. He speculated that he might have influenced Proust, whom he read in French. *A Pair of Blue Eyes* (1873), "more lyrical and psychological" than his other novels, drawing on his courtship, was among Proust's favorite books, partly because it was invigorated by autobiography. William Dean Howells "came rather late, but I came with all the ardor of what seems my perennial literary youth, to the love of Thomas Hardy." He began with *A Pair of Blue Eyes* and hurried on to the rest of the oeuvre. "I love even the faults of Hardy; I will let him play me any trick he chooses . . . if only he will go on making his peasants talk, and his rather uncertain ladies get in and out of love, and serve themselves of every chance that fortune offers them of having their own way." Hardy touches a primitive note, appeals to a hardly acknowledged but no less real susceptibility in the Anglophone reader. "We shrink from the unmorality of the Latin races, but Hardy has divined in the heart of our own race a lingering heathenism, which, if not Greek, has certainly been no more baptized than the neo-Hellenism of the Parisians." How remote he is from George Moore—and is this one of Moore's dark resistances to Hardy? This English heathenism? "His heroines especially exemplify it, and I should be safe in saying that his Ethelbertas, his Eustacias, his Elfridas, his Bathshebas, his Fancies, are wholly pagan." Less fancifully, he declares, "His people live very close to the heart of nature, and no one, unless it is Turgenev, gives you a richer and sweeter sense of her unity with human nature." He responds to the humor in Hardy, and it is as well to remember, after the solemnity of many critics, that like Eliot, though less subtly and less continuously, his tone is complicit with the reader.

Woolf understands that Hardy's achievement is unique; she lists his shortcomings, all of them by-products of his larger vision. We pass through the "open air and adventure" of Defoe, into the drawing rooms of Austen, conversations, things said and left unsaid, and "the many mirrors of their talk revealing their characters." Then "we turn to Hardy," and "we are once more spun round. The moors are round us and the stars are above our heads." This is not all, for in Hardy, "the other side of the mind is now exposed—the dark side that comes uppermost in solitude, not the light side that shows in company. Our relations are not towards people, but towards Nature and destiny. Yet different as these worlds are, each is consistent with itself."

———•———

Graham Greene described Edward Garnett as "the greatest of all publishers' readers." In 1898 Garnett visited Ford Madox Ford at Grace's Cottage, bringing him a new novelist. "Conrad came round the corner of the house. I was doing something at the open fireplace in the house-end. He was in advance of Mr. Garnett, who had gone inside, I suppose, to find me. Conrad stood looking at the view. His hands were in the pockets of his reefer-coat, the thumbs sticking out. His black torpedo beard pointed at the horizon. He placed a monocle in his eye. Then he caught sight of me."

Joseph Conrad (Józef Teodor Konrad Korzeniowski, 1857–1924) is the most Slavonic of English novelists, in language roots and in themes. Pritchett takes him, in his mature work, to be a "prophetic novelist," for whom the individual being is timeless, and is thus more a soul than a person, "and good and evil and fate fight for the possession of their future." England is impatient, he says, with prophetic writers, Conrad and Lawrence in particular, between whom he detects an affinity. Conrad's characters "live on the edge of a great anxiety, an unbearable exasperation, a threatened loss." He is as out of place among the British novelists of his day as Ford himself was, and Thomas Hardy. He stands apart from what Mencken calls "the hysterical splutterings and battle-cries of the Kiplings and Chestertons, the booming pedagogics of the Wellses and Shaws, and the smirking at key-holes of the Bennetts and de Morgans"—apart, "and almost alone, observing the sardonic comedy of man with an eye that sees every point and significance of it, but vouchsafing none of that sophomoric indignation, that Hyde Park wisdom, that flabby moralizing which freight and swamp the modern English novel." Arthur Symons allegorizes his manner: "At the centre of his web sits an elemental sarcasm discussing human affairs with a calm and cynical ferocity . . . He shows the bare side of every virtue, the hidden heroism of every vice and crime." Conrad does not judge: his is "an implacable comprehension, as of one outside nature, to whom joy and sorrow, right and wrong, savagery and civilization, are equal and indifferent." There can be a high tone and swelling cadence in the criticism of Conrad by writers moved and dwarfed by him.

Much has been written to explore his Polish nature, not to reclaim him but to deliver him from too English a reading. His family background was impoverished aristocratic. His father wrote plays and translated French romantic literature, and Shakespeare and Dickens, two writers at the heart of Conrad's imagination. The boy grew up in a literary household, urged to read in his own language and to master French. The family was close, driven still closer by exile: the father's politics led to his arrest by the tsarist police and he, followed by the family, took a long involuntary trip to Vologda, far to the north of Moscow. After four years they were allowed to return nearer home. Conrad's mother died and four years later his father followed. The boy was eleven. No wonder he was skeptical of Russian political culture, its imperial pretensions, its ideological exports. *Under Western Eyes* (1911) evokes a faux-radical world of exiles and intrigues, political and spiritual terrorism, a world familiar from Dostoyevsky and from the story of Nabokov's years of exile in the wake of the 1917 Revolution. Conrad's world of exiles lost in miasmic idealism has a palpable, timeless reality about it, as in another sense does *The Secret Agent* (1907), dealing with displacement and alienation at another social level and in a city whose fogs Dickens had prepared for the violent, mindless intrigues of the anarchists. Conrad's take on imperial politics is colored by his understanding of the Great Game between Russia and Britain, which Kipling explored in *Kim*. When Kipling seemed to suggest that the Boer War "was undertaken for the cause of democracy," Conrad commented in what is always described as his "second language," French: "C'est à crever de rire [It's enough to make you die of laughter]."

His first language was Polish; his second, spoken language, Russian, he did not write in. His third writing language, after French, was English. He began to learn it when he was twenty-one. He arrived aboard a ship in Lowestoft in 1878. He had read some English classics in Polish and French; he had heard English spoken on shipboard, but now it was the lingua franca of the people he moved among, and he had no choice but to learn. English was never second nature to him. Ford was instrumental as editor and collaborator, notably in *The Inheritors* (1900), *Romance* (1903), and *The Nature of a Crime* (1923). He helped Conrad master his medium. He recounts how in composing his more elaborated sentences Conrad translated in his head from the French. He spoke the sentences aloud to make sure of the sound and sense, trusting his friend as quality controller. At times Conrad felt contempt for English. Even during the writing of *Nostromo* he told Ford how he regretted that it was too late for him to become a French writer. (Ford himself believed that English was superior for poetry, French for fiction.) Conrad, Ford tells us, "used to declare that to make a direct statement in English is like trying to kill a mosquito with a forty-foot stock whip when you have never before handled a stock whip." Conrad distrusted the blurring edges of English, how every word carries moral and semantic baggage, ambiguities that cannot be focused except by precise contextualizing, and sometimes not even then. H. G. Wells urged Ford not to spoil Conrad's "Oriental style," his anxious way with the language.

Conrad became a British subject in 1886 (in the same year, he received his Master Mariner's ticket). Ten years later, having abandoned the mariner's life in favor of authorship, he married Jessie George, an Englishwoman with whom he had two sons and who, like many writers' wives, was unpopular with his friends and critics. By the time he published his first novel, *Almayer's Folly* (1895—he had begun writing it in 1889), he was known as "Joseph Conrad." He had considered alternatives, including the single name Kamudi, which is Malaysian for "rudder." He ends his "Note" on this first book with the words: "the curse of facts and the blessing of illusions, the bitterness of our wisdom and the deceptive consolation of our folly," an epigraph for his entire oeuvre. Garnett kept Conrad going after *Almayer's Folly* failed, "and one suspects it was Garnett," says Greene, "who organized critical opinion so that Conrad had the support of his peers during the years of popular neglect."

*Almayer's Folly* is dedicated to the memory of "TD" (Tadeusz Bobrowski), the uncle who looked after Conrad when his parents died and who left him a legacy substantial enough to pay off his debts. Conrad's act of pious memory insists on the connection between the discrete chapters of his life, divided by time, vocation, and language. It was this uncle who agreed that Conrad should leave Poland when he failed to get an Austro-Hungarian passport and was liable to call-up in the Russian army. The young man made his way to Marseilles and began the life of adventure that preceded the long sedentary years of invention and memory. Gunrunning, romance, storms, solitudes, the enervating tropics, colonial worlds: he moved through them in fact and then in fiction. His best novels have, like Melville's, Kipling's, and Hudson's, lived authority. When he was buried in 1924 in Canterbury City Cemetery, his tombstone bore his Polish name. The epitaph is Edmund Spenser's "Sleep after toyle."

*Heart of Darkness,* described as a novella or a story in some editions, but with the scope and force of a novel, develops directly from his experience, for in 1889 he made the journey he describes, fulfilling a long ambition to penetrate into the unmapped heart of Africa. He gave shape to his adventure by means of formal devices. The story in the first person is told by an everyman lolling with others on the deck of a cruising yawl on the Thames. Between them there is "the bond of the sea," making them tolerant of one another and their "yarns." Several people are defined by profession, Lawyer, Accountant, Director; and then there is Marlow, "cross-legged right aft, leaning against the mizzen-mast. He had sunken cheeks, a yellow complexion, a straight back, an ascetic aspect, and, with his arms dropped, the palms of hands outwards, resembled an idol." A malarial individual among "types," it is he who, as they await the turn of the tide, begins the story.

And he continues it for its full length, with occasional interjections from the first narrator, who becomes, like us, a listener. Already we have a story and a story within it, two frames, two chronologies: the great historical chronology in which the River Congo and the Thames, in different eras, penetrate to analogous darknesses, and the chronology of Marlow's story, which begins in 1890, shortly after the Belgian king Leopold with his "great genius for evil" has established the Congo Free State, a free-for-all state for Europeans. The situation caused concern, and *Heart of Darkness* functions as an essay as well as a travel narrative and novel.

Why the storytelling devices? To underline the authenticity of the witnesses: both the hearer and the adventurer who lived to tell the tale. Because the anonymous first narrator neither doubts nor cross-questions Marlow, we do not doubt him. How can we doubt a voice that recounts the experiences in the order in which they became real to him, in a voice that registers the very surprise he felt? He hears things and gradually registers what they are, then what they must mean: it is a continual coming into consciousness of extreme experience, disbelief displaced by the undeniable evidence of cruelty, slavery, and death. Marlow represents the spirit of efficiency, of doing a job responsibly, against the odds; but he is vulnerable, subjected to Kurtz's narration, and the extremity of what he hears and sees cuts deep into him, and us. Much of the power of the story is the result of a symbolism that makes the Congo a kind of recurrent archetype, including among its antecedents those nations now "civilized" that carry in their hearts the residue of analogous aberrations; indeed, we are tempted to ask through the ironies whether such aberrations are not the inevitable law of colonial development.

It is largely to the symbolism Marlow uses that the Nigerian novelist Chinua Achebe objects in his challenging 1975 lecture "An Image of Africa: Racism in Conrad's *Heart of Darkness*" and in later writings on the subject. No one previously questioned Conrad's ideological bona fides. Writing as an African, Achebe found the degraded image of the native people of the Belgian Congo degrading. Reflecting on his essay later on, he said, "Some people imagine that what I mean is, Don't read Conrad. Good heavens, no! I teach Conrad. I teach *Heart of Darkness*. I have a course on *Heart of Darkness* in which what I'm saying is, Look at the way this man handles Africans. Do you recognize humanity there?" In portraying how Belgian administrators and adventurers dehumanized the native people, Conrad becomes complicit with them in his language and symbolism. "People will tell you he was opposed to imperialism. But it's not enough to say, I'm opposed to imperialism. Or, I'm opposed to these people—these poor people—being treated like this." Achebe responds to the *incomplete* radicalism of Conrad's representations: "Especially since he goes on straight away to call them 'dogs standing on their hind legs.' That kind of thing. Animal imagery throughout. He didn't see anything wrong with it." He failed to register the connection between his terms and the oppressors' means. "So we must live in different worlds. Until these two worlds come together we will have a lot of trouble." To come together, the language of representation needs to work at a different level. Metaphor is treacherous. How much more natural, instinctively humane, is the language Aphra Behn deploys in *Oroonoko,* a much earlier account of colonial atrocity. Achebe has been much criticized for defining Conrad's racism. Let Philip Roth obliquely defend him. He says tetchily, "Jews who register strong objections to what they see as damaging fictional portrayals of Jews are not necessarily philistine or paranoid."

The realities Conrad portrayed were various. His first novel, he says in *A Personal Record* (1912), was developed on an overly long land-leave while he was still a second officer. He took rooms on a square in Pimlico and there, without his landlady's knowing, he was visited, he tells us, not only by Almayer and his wife and daughter: "It was my practice directly after my breakfast to hold animated receptions of Malays, Arabs and half-castes. They did not clamor aloud for my attention. They came with silent and irresistible appeal—and the appeal, I affirm here, was not to my self-love or my vanity." They were hauntingly corporeal to him, bringing with them a pungent scent of their landscapes, "their obscure sun-bathed existence." In *Written Lives* the Spanish novelist Javier Marias recounts the extraordinary concentration with which Conrad focused. He sat too close to the candle and his book caught fire as he was reading; indeed, he was a continual fire hazard. He was intensely irritable (for instance, when he dropped his pen), then obsequiously deferential. When one of his sons was born he urged the maid to get the child to shut up, it might disturb his wife, not realizing that the cry belonged to the newborn. Flaubert and Maupassant were his touchstones. Dostoyevsky he despised.

But *things* were real: the spray from the sea, the infant, the stories words made on the page, whether he was reader or writer. In a preface to *The Nigger of the "Narcissus"* (1897), a brilliant *ars poetica* and an abiding challenge to every novelist, he says: "My task which I am trying to achieve is, by the power of the written word to make you hear, to make you feel—it is, before all, to make you *see.* That—and no more, and it is everything." No writer before him, and none after until Vladimir Nabokov, who disliked his work, so insists on the materiality of effect he wishes to achieve. "If I succeed, you shall find there according to your deserts: encouragement, consolation, fear, charm—all you demand—and, perhaps, also that glimpse of truth for which you have forgotten to ask." Conrad begins with words that haunt his century, and are alluded to by Saul Bellow in his Nobel Prize acceptance speech. "A work that aspires, however humbly, to the condition of art should carry its justification in every line. And art itself may be defined as a single-minded attempt to render the highest kind of justice to the visible universe, by bringing to light the truth, manifold and one, underlying its every aspect." The artist knows the world but must descend into the self to find what is true, and he appeals "to our less obvious capacities."

Greene cites approvingly Conrad's axiom about art rendering justice to the visible universe. What *kind* of justice is the highest? The forensic? Trial motifs recur, the visible universe stands before a judge. Conrad demands completeness. Apart from Kurtz and Nostromo, most of his major characters have long and detailed backstories so that we can understand their psychological and moral trials. *Lord Jim* (1900), for example, is a full portrait, one that deeply engages the reader and empowers our judgment.

Conrad's financial and critical success came after he had already done his best writing. His breakthrough book was *Chance* (1913). Edward Garnett regarded it as his most insular novel and his least accomplished, yet it gained a popular readership, after which his career was on an even keel. Of the later books, *The Shadow Line* (1917), a powerful story of coming of age at sea, feels like a younger man's book, with something of the purity of Stephen Crane's narratives. The melodramatic *The Arrow of Gold* (1919) engages the reader and is, like many of his stories, suitable for filming. His protagonists are Peter O'Toole and Anthony Quinn types, strong, with an Achilles' tendon in their souls. *Victory* (1915) was his first novel to be adapted for the (silent) screen, in 1919. The best-known treatment of Conrad's fiction is Francis Ford Coppola's *Apocalypse Now* (1979), based on *Heart of Darkness,* transposed to Vietnam.

Of his longer novels "the most anxiously meditated" was *Nostromo* (1904). It is ambitious in form and goes furthest in exploring his themes. He regarded it as a turning point, "a subtle change in the nature of the inspiration." It was composed between 1903 and 1905, after the more or less linear novels that focus on solitary protagonists confronting fate in an extreme natural environment.

*Nostromo* might have taken a similar form, focusing on the single flawed protagonist. Conrad heard a story when he was eighteen or nineteen, sailing in the Gulf of Mexico, about "some man who was supposed to have stolen single-handed a whole lighter-full of silver, somewhere on the Tierra Firme seaboard during the troubles of a revolution." He forgot the story until, a quarter of a century later, "I came upon the very thing in a shabby volume picked up outside a second-hand bookshop. It was the life story of an American seaman written by himself with the assistance of a journalist." The seaman's tale is not unlike Nostromo's. The man in the original story is a rogue. But what if the man had not been a total rogue, what if he had been either good, or believed to be good? The story of that single crime and its consequences was not sufficient, however: this was the sand grain, not the pearl.

In Costaguana with its little capital of Sulaco Conrad creates a complex, populous social environment, a plausible Latin American republic in which Europeans and Americans have come to make their lives or fortunes or both (the native population plays little dramatic part). Removed from their natural environments into this perilous, unstable world, its nature not quite tamed, its lineaments not quite knowable, his characters reveal what they are in the unfolding political and spiritual dramas. Conrad's Latin America is remote from Rider Haggard's fantastic and Hudson's natural worlds. Romance here is treacherous. The absence of binding traditions and the presence of many conflicting ideals seal men and women (for here Conrad has drawn women, among them Mrs. Gould, his most complex female character) in their discrete selves, like characters in Hardy except that, because most of them are in a kind of exile, they do not have even the consolation of a natural belonging, of a surrounding Wessex.

The Scottish writer, politician, and traveler Robert Cunninghame Graham (1852–1936) provided some of the information needed in the creation of Costaguana. He had contacted Conrad after reading his story "An Outpost of Progress" and remained his friend, first introducing him to Garnett. Graham was ten Conrad protagonists rolled into one: "When I think of Cunninghame Graham," Conrad declared, "I feel as though I have lived all my life in a dark hole without seeing or knowing anything." Graham, a friend also of Ford and Hudson, of George Bernard Shaw and Chesterton and Galsworthy, was a man of action. An aristocrat and the first socialist member of the British Parliament, he helped to found the Scottish Labor Party at the end of the nineteenth century and the National Party of Scotland in 1934. His maternal grandmother was Spanish and his first language was hers, though he was reared in Scotland and educated at Harrow. He emigrated to Argentina to become a rancher and make his fortune. While Hudson stayed close to the ground, to the grasses and birds and the unpeopled places, Graham moved among men and cattle and developed a reputation. His adventures were numerous, in North Africa, in Europe. He returned to Britain upon his father's death and began his political career. He died of pneumonia in Buenos Aires after an excursion to Hudson's birthplace.

Ford contributed materially to *Nostromo*. It was originally serialized in *T.P.'s Weekly* from January through October 1904. The April 8 installment fell due, and Conrad's gout and "nervous depression" made it impossible for him to continue. He wrote later, "The creation of a world is not a small undertaking except perhaps to the divinely gifted. In truth every novelist must begin by creating for himself a world, great or little, in which he can honestly believe." Ford came to the rescue and contributed several pages on Conrad's behalf. He knew his style and shared this imagined world sufficiently to ventriloquize him. Ford's genius as an editor was this ability to get inside a writer's project, to see what was needed and to encourage or—at times of crisis—to provide it.

Costaguana began in Conrad's mind as "a twilight country which was to become the province of Sulaco, with its high shadowy Sierra and its misty Campo for mute witnesses of events flowing from the passions of men short-sighted in good and evil." As he wrote, the anxiety of concentration he always suffered made him fear that he might lose himself in the vast reality of the world created. He portrays himself concluding his book as Gulliver returning from his travels. He was writing from imagination and research—though he had traveled in the Gulf, landfalls were few and he had not known the people or places well. He brought to bear on his narrative elements of the history of Paraguay and other Latin American countries, the life of Garibaldi that helped in the formation of Viola and Hirsch, and technical works to make the landscape, the climate, and the mining credible.

All of the protagonists are tested, and all but a few are found, or find themselves, wanting. The moments that determine their fates are intense but fleeting; once passed, characters are changed in their own eyes, and that self-knowledge is irreversible. Señor Charles Gould, the "Idealist-creator of Material Interests," becomes enslaved by those interests and is unable to escape the Mine "in this world." Introduced in earnest forty-odd pages into the novel, Nostromo is portrayed riding past an equestrian statue of Charles IV: the Capataz de Cargadores ("Gian Battista," who becomes Captain Fidanza, or Trustworthy, just when he is least to be trusted) "made incorruptible by his enormous vanity." Conrad emphasizes his racial and social difference from Gould and all the others. It is fascinating how, in a macaronic spirit, Conrad with phrases of Spanish, Italian, French, sometimes fused in a Costaguanan Esperanto, creates an authentic sense of foreignness. Old Giorgio Viola, child of Garibaldi's betrayed revolution, has learned that power is within people, not above them. Then there is Decoud, with whom it is hard not to identify, and whose corruption is unbearable and inevitable; and Hirsch, who is in equal degrees pathetic and heroic; and Monygham, most damaged of all the characters yet also most redeemable.

The constants in Conrad's experiment are Señora Emilia Gould, introduced performing an act of kindness, giving Giorgio glasses, and continuing kind and forbearing throughout; and Captain Joseph Mitchell of the OSN (Oceanic Steam Navigation Co.), who is solidity itself, a man with a job to do, undistracted by imagination and with whom, as with Marlow, Conrad identifies. Such men survive and serve. Also, though they are not major characters, Don

José Avellanos, author of the *History of Fifty Years of Misrule,* a survivor of torture, speaks from the corrupt continuing history of the land, and his daughter Antonia Avellanos ("Antonia the Aristocrat and Nostromo the Man of the People are the artisans of the New Era") engage the reader. After the changing characters and the constants there are the shadow characters: Mrs. Teresa Viola, Giorgio's wife, always wringing her hands; his daughters Linda ("indignant and angry") and "the fair Giselle"; there is the charming, sensual Morenita to whom Nostromo gives his silver buttons, and the common folk who compose the crowd scenes. There are too the emblematic figures, types with a function rather than an identity within the novel: Ribiera the dictator, the rebellious Montero brothers, and Mr. Holroyd the American, the capitalist endower of churches.

The time structure of the novel is unusual: Conrad starts the narrative, reaches a climax and suspends rather than resolves it, goes to another part of Costaguana, to the mine, to the city of Sulaco, to the three Isabels, the islands that play such crucial, mute parts in the drama, and the lighthouse, to pick up a different thread in the complex narrative of a country. "In his big elaborated books he is always avoiding his climaxes," Pritchett notes. Here the avoidance is dramatic, a principle of structure: weaving rather than spinning, orchestration rather than plain melody. There are three movements, echoing the structure of the old triple-decker novel: "The Silver of the Mine," which establishes the geography and the main themes of the novels; "The Isabels," in which the crucial drama of the theft of the lighter of silver and its immediate consequences are recounted; and "The Lighthouse," a denouement, a settling of accounts.

One character cannot bear isolation: liberal, delicate, the engaging flâneur Decoud, hungry for Europe, somewhat in love, and as fate would have it, it is he who suffers literal and fatal isolation as a kind of castaway with the stolen silver. Nostromo, on the other hand, can happily exist alone; his transformation from a monster of seeming virtue to a monster of actual vice is the most compelling metamorphosis Conrad achieves, especially because he uses metaphor to clarify but not displace the story. At the end of chapter 7 a weary Nostromo rests, then, as evening falls, wakes in a full recognition of his new being, like a lion after slumber. "At last the conflagration of sea and sky, lying embraced and still in a flaming contact upon the edge of the world, went out. The red sparks in the water vanished together with the stains of blood in the black mantle draping the sombre head of the Placid Gulf; a sudden breeze sprang up and died out after rustling heavily the growth of bushes on the ruined earthwork of the fort. Nostromo woke up from a fourteen hours' sleep, and arose full length from his lair in the long grass. He stood knee deep amongst the whispering undulations of the green blades with the lost air of a man just born into the world." Up until now, he has been of the landscape. Now he is seen, himself apart: "Handsome, robust, and supple, he threw back his head, flung his arms open, and stretched himself with a slow twist of the waist and a leisurely growling yawn of white teeth, as natural and free from evil in the moment of waking as a magnificent and unconscious wild beast. Then, in the suddenly steadied glance fixed upon nothing from under a thoughtful frown, appeared the man." Evil dawning upon him defines the man.

Edith Wharton admires Conrad's variation of point of view in *Nostromo,* the movement from Captain Mitchell's stolid, efficient vision to the more refined and nuanced perspectives of other characters. In Henry James's writing there is what she calls a "hall of mirrors" or "a series of reflecting consciousnesses, all belonging to people who are outside of the story but accidentally drawn into its current," like the Assinghams in *The Golden Bowl,* as eavesdroppers in one way and another. Their objectivity is guaranteed, even if their accuracy cannot be depended upon because they are becoming conscious of things and are not omniscient from the outset. In *Nostromo* the first-person-singular narrator, who is omniscient, breaks in only at times of acute solitude, as when Decoud is going mad on the island or Nostromo is waking up a changed man. The source of Conrad's technique, she says, is in Balzac.

Like Balzac's, some of Conrad's fiction is overly metaphorical. Metaphor develops an impetus of its own, producing a grandiloquent note when the writer's attention turns from subject to effect; return to sense can be forced and unconvincing. Thus Conrad writes, "The creative art of a writer of fiction may be compared to rescue work carried out in darkness against cross gusts of wind swaying the action of a great multitude." The writer is on a roll and nothing can stop him now. "It is rescue work, this snatching of vanishing phases of turbulence, disguised in fair words, out of the native obscurity into a light where"—and he must come back to his subject somehow—"the struggling forms may be seen, seized upon, endowed with the only possible form of permanence in this world of relative values—the permanence of memory." Yet that same approach can create an engagingly wry tone, as when he writes, "I have now on my shelves a book apparently of the most valuable kind which, before I have read half-a-dozen lines, begins to make a noise like a buzz-saw. I am inconsolable; I shall never, I fear, discover what it is all about, for the buzzing covers the words, and at every try I am absolutely forced to give it up ere the end of the page is reached." Conrad is conscious of the sounds books make, their harmonious disposition, always reading aloud in Ford's company, their own words and those of the writers they admired. Some books are too musical and the nature of the prose overwhelms the sense. Ugly noise, like overly pretty noise, makes a book unreadable.

Orwell declares, "One of the surest signs of [Conrad's] genius is that women dislike his books." This is untrue, though the books are, beyond Mrs. Gould, poor in realized female characters and cool to those themes that are supposed to engage women readers. Orwell's judgment is false in terms of its own day and ours. But much of the outstanding writing of the end of the nineteenth and early twentieth centuries, with its insistence on adventure and crisis, does have a gendered appeal. Forster speaks of Conrad's "dread of intimacy," a character-istic of Victorian, especially late Victorian, writing. Conrad "has a rigid concep-tion as to where the rights of the public stop." That sense too establishes barri-ers in the fiction.

In the later preface to *The Nigger of the "Narcissus,"* where he celebrates the scope and efficacy of art, Conrad writes, "The artist appeals to that part of our being which is not dependent on wisdom; to that in us which is a gift and not an acquisition—and, therefore, more permanently enduring." This notion is at once romantic and at the same time classical, impersonal because shared: "He speaks to our capacity for delight and wonder, to the sense of mystery sur-rounding our lives; to our sense of pity, and beauty, and pain; to the latent feel-ing of fellowship with all creation—and to the subtle but invincible conviction of solidarity that knits together the loneliness of innumerable hearts"—to which one may respond, would that it were so, or would that it could be so today; and he concludes: "to the solidarity in dreams, in joy, in sorrow, in aspirations, in illusions, in hope, in fear, which binds men to each other, which binds together all humanity—the dead to the living, and the living to the unborn."

---

"It was, I think, in the spring of '94," writes Willa Cather, "that a slender, narrow-chested fellow in a shabby grey suit, with a soft felt hat pulled low over his eyes, sauntered into the office of the managing editor of the *Nebraska State Journal* and introduced himself as Stephen Crane." Six years later Conrad said his farewell to Stephen Crane (1871–1900), the American poet and fiction writer. "I saw him for the last time on his last day in England. It was in Dover, in a big hotel, in a bedroom with a large window looking on to the sea. He had been very ill and Mrs. Crane was taking him to some place in Germany, but one glance at that wasted face was enough to tell me that it was the most forlorn of all hopes. The last words he breathed out to me were: 'I am tired. Give my love to your wife and child.' When I stopped at the door for another look I saw that he had turned his head on the pillow and was staring wistfully out of the win-dow at the sails of a cutter yacht that glided slowly across the frame, like a dim shadow against the grey sky." That tactful, understated story is Conrad at his truest, the visual and the symbolic fuse.

"He knew little of literature," Conrad remarks, "either of his own country or of any other, but he was himself a wonderful artist in words whenever he took a pen into his hand." Admired by Ford and James as well as Conrad, Crane has retained a readership on account of his manner and matter. Pritchett is precise in his praise: "Writers are always faced by two sets of words before they write; those which will draw a literary curtain over reality, and those which will raise the veil in our minds and lead us to see for the first time. Crane's gift for raising the veil is clear." There is the impersonality here that we get in a different degree in Conrad. Crane is unwilling to dramatize, to falsify: "He goes . . . for the anonymous voice in the heart," Pritchett says. An unalloyed truth in his manner, he is more modern than Hardy—indeed, in some respects more modern than Conrad. "God is cold," says a refrain to a late poem, discovered after Crane's death. His directness, the absence of "literary" definition, impresses. He has many stories and six novels to his credit, the best-known being *The Red Badge of Courage* (1895). He also wrote two volumes of verse before he died of tuberculosis in a German sanatorium. Ralph Ellison is haunted by Crane's own Civil War–hauntedness in *The Red Badge* and elsewhere, and the originality of his style, a legacy that outlives the myth of his intense short life and the mystery of his having written, at the age of twenty-one, a novel regarded as "one of the world's foremost war novels when he had neither observed nor participated in combat." John Dos Passos admired his courage and the sounds the language made, close to the speech of the characters.

Crane's father, a Methodist minister in New Jersey, died when Stephen was eight. Stephen studied at Lafayette (military) College, and then at Syracuse University, rejecting his father's values. He was drawn to journalism as a career, and—a quiet, gentle man—he was fascinated by poverty, violence, and war. His first novel, *Maggie: A Girl of the Streets* (1893) was infatuated with sordid realism, more Hardyesque than Hardy in its deterministic pessimism: "It tries to show," he says in a dedicatory note, "that environment is a tremendous thing in the world and frequently shapes lives regardless." This thematic element appealed to Conrad. "If one proves that theory," Crane adds, "one makes room in Heaven for all sorts of souls (notably an occasional street girl) who are not confidently expected to be there by many excellent people." In Jacksonville, Florida, he married such a girl, Cora Taylor, a brothel madam, whom he brought to England in 1897. They settled at Brede Place, Sussex. Like gunrunning and being a war correspondent, it was an adventure. He committed himself in earnest.

His fictions depend on Hardyesque irony, the irony of life, not of style. In prose the longer form is a problem for him: his talents are in creating what Cather calls "episodic, fragmentary life"; he is a modernist *avant la lettre*, and building a sustained longer narrative is not a gift he acquired. The discipline of responsible journalism had its downside; but it sharpened his language and eye for hard truths. His prose is free of class and national bias.

In *The Red Badge of Courage,* Pritchett says, "Crane starts a bugle call and sustains it without a falter to the end of the book. The scene is a single battlefield in the American Civil War, and the purpose of the novel is to show the phases by which a green young recruit loses his romantic illusions and his innocence in battle, and acquires a new identity, a hardened virtue." Crane wrote the book in nine days, but it was a long time gestating: he claimed it had started in his imagination when he was a boy, and was natural to him because his forbears were soldiers and one of his brothers an expert in the Civil War. Cather remembers him saying, "The detail of a thing has to filter through my blood, and then it comes out like a native product, but it takes forever." His story of his protagonist, Henry Fleming, is that of "a lonely individual's struggle for self-definition, written for lonely individualists," Ralph Ellison says. It puts us in mind of the protagonist of another short, lonely novel, Holden Caulfield, Henry's distant cousin in American fiction.

The version we read today was much improved by Crane's editors, among them Cather, who recalls her experience of the book when it was serialized. "*The Red Badge of Courage* had been published in the *State Journal* that winter . . . and the grammatical construction of the story was so faulty that the managing editor had several times called on me to edit the copy. In this way I had read it very carefully, and through the careless sentence-structure I saw the wonder of that remarkable performance. But the grammar certainly was bad." One day, after lying in wait for him and trying to trip him into a serious conversation, she succeeded. She asked if stories could be written to formula. "You can't do it by rule any more than you can dance by rule. You have to have the itch of the thing in your fingers, and if you haven't,—well, you're damned lucky," he said, "and you'll live long and prosper, that's all." Whereupon he yawned and made his exit. Cather was smitten—she was a junior in college and he was the first real man of letters, despite his bad grammar, that she had met. "His eyes I remember as the finest I have ever seen, large and dark and full of lustre and changing lights, but with a profound melancholy always lurking deep in them. They were eyes that seemed to be burning themselves out." On his last night in town he talked to her at length and with great bitterness. All this she remembered and wrote down six years later upon his death. He was only twenty-eight when he died, an age at which Conrad had not even begun writing fiction, and when Hardy had yet to publish a novel. Had any American writer done so much so early? He was twenty-one when *Maggie* appeared, twenty-four when *The Red Badge of Courage* was published.

Ernest Hemingway regarded *The Red Badge of Courage* as part of his essential genealogy, seeing it as whole and integrated in the same way a major poem might be. Crane's Henry Fleming is a natural forebear of Hemingway's Frederic Henry in *A Farewell to Arms*. Courage Hemingway described as "grace under pressure," a notion close to Crane's belief in duty and the individual's duty stoically to accept its disciplines. Crane's writing itself, the order of the words, sentences, paragraphs, and incidents, taught Hemingway things, in particular Crane's story "The Blue Hotel," the style of which he discussed at length with John Dos Passos when they were together in Paris.

# 25

# Living through Ideas

Nikolai Gogol, Ivan Turgenev, Fyodor Dostoyevsky, Leo Tolstoy

Ivan Turgenev explained to Henry James how his imagination worked. Like Dante passing through Hell, he would "see" a person or persons who "solicited" him, putting themselves body and soul at his disposal. To bring them to being, he had to find the right places and relations for them. This became their story. Many readers, he acknowledged, found his pretexts too frail, his novels lacking in architecture. "But I would rather, I think, have too little architecture than too much—when there's a danger of it interfering with my measure of the truth." The persons, the soliciting figures, were his first interest, the setting secondary: to be interested first in the setting would have been to put the sled before the horse, the demands of form before the "measure of the truth."

In the teens of the twentieth century, Virginia Woolf, dissatisfied with the narrow, material measure of such British public prophets as Arnold Bennett, H. G. Wells, and George Bernard Shaw, found in the Russians the serious intent and wholeness of vision that had marked the novels of Hardy and Conrad. Their work was coming into vogue. The awakening of Anglo-Saxon readers to Russian literature between 1885 and 1920, according to the poet and critic Donald Davie writing in the 1950s, "should rank as a turning-point no less momentous than the discovery of Italian literature by the generations of the English Renaissance." There had been for centuries a fairly steady exchange between English and French, Italian, German, and Spanish fiction. Many Anglophone writers spoke some at least of the languages of the Continent and kept abreast of literary developments. This was not the case with Russian, though for their part the Russians read Europe attentively into their culture and language, remote as they were. European forms and thoughts turned unfamiliar there. The novel came back into French and English transformed.

Curiosity about Russia and its culture grew as it became clear what the vast Eurasian autocracy might represent and become; when the First World War was complicated by the October Revolution and a new political order seemed to be emerging, the witness of those humanly engaged writers of the previous century was full of information and radical foreshadowing. The sudden efflorescence of translations gave access to a world that reflected and distorted European forms. Skepticism and deep belief coexisted in the nineteenth-century

Russian writers. Their distrust of abstractions, their faith in particulars and in the irreducible force of contingencies, was paradoxically underwritten by an instinct for civic and spiritual transcendence. There might be ironies of tone and larger ironies of formal construction, but they were neither reductive nor ingratiating. Comedy too—and there is much comedy in the great Russian novelists—is generally affirming and humanizing.

For Doris Lessing, "the highest point of literature was the novel of the nineteenth century," and she focused among "the great realists" upon Tolstoy, Stendhal, Dostoyevsky, Balzac, Turgenev, Chekhov, as though they formed a kind of continuum. "I hold the view that the realist novel, the realist story, is the highest form of prose writing; higher than and out of the reach of any comparison with expressionism, impressionism, symbolism, naturalism, or any other -ism." She added, "The great men of the nineteenth century had neither religion nor politics nor aesthetic principles in common. But what they did have in common was a climate of ethical judgment; they shared certain values; they were humanists."

In the speech he wrote accepting the 1970 Nobel Prize in Literature, the exiled Russian writer Alexander Solzhenitsyn redefined what realism, and especially socialist realism before it was suborned by the Soviet authorities, meant to the Hungarian critic György Lukács, who was called upon to defend his views by the Communist authorities. Realism was something quite distinct from the propaganda disguised as fiction that was neither realistic nor socialist: "Literature is the memory of peoples; it transmits from one generation to the next the irrefutable experiences of men. It preserves and enlivens the flame of a history immune to all deformation, far from every lie." What is durable, what goes to the shaping of Solzhenitsyn's own art, is the realism of Tolstoy, of Dostoyevsky, at once deeply Slavic and dyed through and through with a complex, lived Christianity. Their novels are at once works of fiction and of history.

The earliest translations into English were for the most part indifferent, often conducted at two removes, from Russian to French (the texts cut and edited for the French market), to English (with further adjustments). Turgenev's landscapes, tones, and attitudes were conveniently Anglicized. Dostoyevsky's peculiarly dilated style was made more conventionally varied, less distended, with grave tonal consequences.

Some of the later translations proved major works in their own right, particularly those by Constance Garnett (1861–1946), the wife of Edward Garnett, himself the great editor and advocate of Hardy, Conrad, and others. She translated dozens of books by Tolstoy, Turgenev, Dostoyevsky, Chekhov, and Gogol. Her work accelerated the change in English fiction that Woolf records with such emphasis. Many of her translations remain available. Those novels and stories, in artistic and ethical scale, decisively raised the bar for English fiction. Constance Garnett's only contemporary rival, and this only in the area of Tolstoy's writing, was Louise Maude, who with her husband, Aylmer, Tolstoy's first English biographer, worked on a projected collected writings of Tolstoy in English. Louise Aylmer's *Anna Karenina* appeared in 1918, her *War and Peace* in 1922–1923; Constance Garnett's appeared a good deal earlier, in 1901 and 1904, respectively.

The Russian novelists brought something "other" into English—formal and thematic challenges, social vision, spiritual seriousness. They insisted on scale, historical, philosophical, and moral. The most congenial and familiar-seeming arrival in English was Ivan Sergeyevich Turgenev (1818–1883), an aristocrat who made his way first into French. He collaborated with his French translator, residing in Paris for years and becoming a member of the Goncourts' and Flaubert's circles.

Henry James read and conversed with Turgenev in French and was drawn to the man, to his precision and succinctness; Tolstoy was "a reflector as vast as a natural lake" while Turgenev in scale and definition was more European, an ironist. "In his little green salon nothing was out of place." Yet his sense of the "superfluous man," unaccounted, unaccountable, full of self and self-delusion, resembles Chekhov's provincial characters, as much in the stories as in the plays, and Tolstoy's characteristic metropolitan official Ilya Yefimovich Golovin, "Privy Councillor, superfluous member of various superfluous institutions" in the novella *The Death of Ivan Ilyich* (1886). Such men leave hardly an impression on a vast, indifferent world. Turgenev "felt and understood the opposite sides of life; he was imaginative, speculative, anything but literal," said James. There was something momentous in the "anything but literal" way he drew out the lives of those "superfluous men." His 1850 book of stories is entitled *The Diary of a Superfluous Man,* translated by Garnett in 1899. In the village of Sheep's Spring on March 20, 18–, Tchulkaturin writes: "The doctor has just left me. At last I have got at something definite! For all his cunning, he had to speak out at last. Yes, I am soon, very soon, to die. The frozen rivers will break up, and with the last snow I shall, most likely, swim away . . . whither? God knows!" The dramatic occasion gives way to reflection, and the narrative of inconsequence, which is highly consequential in its detail and insight, begins. "Well, well, since one must die, one may as well die in the spring. But isn't it absurd to begin a diary a fortnight, perhaps, before death? What does it matter? And by how much are fourteen days less than fourteen years, fourteen centuries? Beside eternity, they say, all is nothingness—yes, but in that case eternity, too, is nothing. I see I am letting myself drop into metaphysics; that's a bad sign—am I not rather faint-hearted, perchance? I had better begin a description of some sort. It's damp and windy out of doors." As he writes on, the very act of writing absorbs him, he becomes his own reader and critic. "I have read over what I wrote yesterday, and was all but tearing up the whole manuscript. I think my story's too spun out and too sentimental," he writes on March 25 of his long March 24 entry. And on April 1: death "flits about me, like the light breath which made the prophet's hair stand up on end."

The "superfluous men" in *Fathers and Sons* (1862, translated by Garnett as *Fathers and Children* in 1895), which Vladimir Nabokov described as "one of the most brilliant novels of the nineteenth century," are of a different order. The moral heroism of a seeming nihilist like Yevgeny Bazarov exceeds that of any mere epic hero, especially when he is presented in the affectionate, ineffectual company of his university friend Arkady Kirsanov. They disappear into the provinces, where we encounter two very different kinds of families and values, one ineffectually conservative, the other ineffectually progressive, and Bazarov's slow death, like Madame Bovary's written eight years earlier by Turgenev's friend Flaubert, is one of the harshest in fiction.

James, who met him in the 1850s, became Turgenev's admirer, disciple, friend, and English champion. James's several essays, filtered through the American editor William Dean Howells, prepared readers for the author also of *A House of Gentlefolk* (1859, translated by Garnett in 1894) and *On the Eve* (1860, translated by Garnett in 1895), his celebrated stories and, among his plays, *A Month in the Country*. "Our Anglo-Saxon, Protestant, moralistic, conventional standards were far away from him," James said, "and he judged things with a freedom and spontaneity in which I found a perpetual refreshment." Howells for his part regarded Tolstoy as "the noblest of all [my] enthusiasms."

Conrad read the Russians in Russian. For Turgenev he felt an unalloyed affection. He read him as an unsentimental elegist for an order that "social and political events in Russia" were bringing to a messy end. Turgenev recorded "the deep origins" of those events, "the moral and intellectual unrest of the souls," throughout his three decades' work with what Conrad calls "the unerring lucidity of a great national writer. The first stirrings, the first gleams of the great forces can be seen almost in every page." His art is characterized by "mastery" and "gentleness": "He brings all his problems and characters to the test of love," and there are so many kinds of love to draw and to betray them. Turgenev confessed to the Goncourt circle that his first introduction to sensual love was with a serf girl on one of the family estates, and later a serf woman gave birth to a child he had fathered. He never married but spent his adult years in platonic sensual thrall to the opera singer Pauline Viardot, whom he heard in *The Barber of Seville* in Russia in 1843 and whom he followed to France two years later, settling into her household, beloved of her children, and tolerated by her partner.

Conrad admired particularly Turgenev's women characters, who seemed to grow out of patient respect and spirtualized sensuality: "Women are, one may say, the foundation of his art," said Conrad. "They are Russian of course. Never was a writer so profoundly, so whole-souledly national. But for non-Russian readers, Turgenev's Russia is but a canvas on which the incomparable artist of humanity lays his colors and his forms in the great light and the free air of the world."

Conrad distinguishes Turgenev from that other Russian writer, to whom men appear as "strange beasts in a menagerie or damned souls knocking themselves to pieces in the stuffy darkness of mystical contradictions." Turgenev is not Dostoyevsky. Perhaps for this reason, Conrad suggests, while protesting his ignorance of things Russian, Turgenev was "beaten with sticks during the greater part of his existence . . . When he died the characteristically chicken-hearted Autocracy hastened to stuff his mortal envelope into the tomb it refused to honor, while the sensitive Revolutionists went on for a time flinging after his shade those jeers and curses from which that impartial lover of *all* his countrymen had suffered so much in his lifetime." The irony of it! "In truth it is not the convulsed terror-haunted Dostoyevsky but the serene Turgenev who is under a curse." Because Turgenev lived in France and developed a large reputation there, he was the first and for some years the only Russian writer widely known in Europe. Exile suited him. When fellow Russian writers turned up, there was a sense of rivalry, and serious disagreements with Dostoyevsky, Tolstoy, and others occurred. In Russia itself he had many devoted readers but few critical advocates. Because his writing was widely read in translation, he was condemned for his literal portrayal of Russia: his fiction was treacherously unaffirmative and unhopeful about Mother Russia.

On January 10, 1861, Turgenev lectured on "Hamlet and Don Quixote" in Saint Petersburg, an event to raise money for the Society for the Aid of Indigent Writers and Scientists. In the wake of Tsar Nicholas I, there were plenty of indigent writers and scientists to aid. Fyodor Mikhaylovich Dostoyevsky (1821–1881), recently returned from four years' imposed exile at a prison camp in Omsk, Siberia, was in the audience. Turgenev quoted Goethe, "To comprehend a poet, one must enter that poet's environment." The lecture began with an error of fact: that the first quarto of Shakespeare's *Hamlet* (1603) and the first part of Cervantes's *Don Quixote* (1605) were published in the same year. To him, the (near) concurrence "seems momentous. The proximity of time in this instance induces a consideration of a whole series of events." Not unnaturally Turgenev, himself a reader of Spanish who once considered translating *Don Quixote* into Russian, and whose temperament is more at home with the Knight of the Sad Figure than with the soliloquizing Prince, wonders whether Shakespeare in retirement might have read *Don Quixote,* in Spanish or in translation. How archaic, and how modern, the Spaniard would have seemed to him.

The indulgent instincts that irritated Tolstoy and Dostoyevsky in Turgenev are evident here: "The poetic masterpieces created by the genius of superior minds, and endowed with an eternal vitality, have this peculiarity . . . one's conceptions of them, as of life in general, may differ greatly from another's, may even be diametrically opposed, yet at the same time be valid." To the responsive reader, though the meanings of these two works cannot be confined, paraphrased, or reconciled, their valid contrary directions are undeniable. Turgenev regrets that the Don is often read merely as a figure of jest, the embodiment of "idealistic nonsense": "In reality one ought to see the Quixotic as a template of self-sacrifice, even though Don Quixote himself has been drawn as ludicrous." Here is the source of Bazarov, who expresses Turgenev's own gentle, insistent radicalism, unabetted by the illusion of some metaphysical redemption.

Hamlet and Don Quixote, Turgenev concludes, embody "two contrasting basic tendencies, the two poles of the human axis about which they revolve. All men, to my mind, conform to one type or the other; one to that of Hamlet, another to that of Don Quixote, though it is true, no doubt, that in our era the Hamlets are far more common."

Turgenev is civilizing, a creature of his century who brings it alive in ours. He is consistently translatable. The challenge of Dostoyevsky is of a different order. He speaks like a near contemporary of our own even when the world he evokes, with its ghastly deprivations, is imaginable to us, not in the literal terms in which it was experienced and written but, as it were, figuratively, allegorically. We read him as an aftermath of Dickens (whose work he was occasionally allowed to read in military hospital in Omsk) and a prelude to Franz Kafka. In translation it is possible to forget that he can be humorous, even comic, in dark ways. And unlike Turgenev, he does not write in an easily transferable style. Some critics suggest he did not write well, the prose deliberately repetitious, flat, low-key, a language often appropriate to and mimetic of the world on which it drew. His novels can seem programmatic, theme-driven. George Moore, who wrote a preface to *Poor Folk* in 1894, later dismissed Dostoyevsky as "little more than Gaboriau"—the inventor of crime fiction—"with psychological sauce, and that of an inferior kind." The panoramic overview was not his métier. Hemingway notes, "In Dostoyevsky there were things believable and not to be believed, but some so true they changed you as you read them; frailty and madness, wickedness and saintliness, and the insanity of gambling were there to know as you knew the landscape and roads in Turgenev." He asks a friend, "How can a man write so badly, so unbelievably badly, and make you feel so deeply?" V. S. Pritchett understood this conundrum: a better writer would have overdefined or crowded out his characters. "Dostoevsky's style: it is a talking style in which his own voice and the voices of all his characters are heard creating themselves, as if all were narrators without knowing it." The connection with Virginia Woolf is not far to seek.

Dostoyevsky is the most prosaic of novelists. There is nothing pretty, no picturesque, little of that natural description, the sense of widening distances, that at once dilates and racks up the tension in Turgenev. His first novel, *Poor Folk* (1846, translated by Garnett in 1914), is conducted in letters between two almost penniless relations, an older man called Makar Devushkin and his second cousin Varvara Dobroselova. Both have literary pretensions, and their experiments in style while vivid and entertaining are also parodic. Makar makes himself responsible for Varvara, expecting nothing from her but love and fidelity. Their relationship, which despite its language of love seems to be without libidinal urgency, is their only wealth, and they are profligate with it. Their letters explore numerous themes, political, literary, romantic, religious. It is not what the letters say or the writers know, but what the letters say *about* the protagonists, that matters. They exchange books. Varvara sends Makar a volume of stories that we infer is by Nikolai Gogol (1809–1852) because the story that repels poor Makar is "The Overcoat" (1842). There Akakiy Akakievitch, a scrivener like Makar, threadbare and obsessive, perishes and takes a metaphysical revenge. Makar quite fails to recognize himself despite his own problems with an overcoat. "We all emerged from Gogol's *Overcoat*," a statement tradition assigns to Dostoyevsky, may be apocryphal, but there can be no doubt of the impact of Gogol on his writing. In *Crime and Punishment* Gogol is a regular point of reference. *Poor Folk* is an extended tribute to Gogol's example, with his kind of remorseless, dark humor, and merciless understanding of urban poverty.

It is the "measure of truth" that makes a kind of poetry of the squalid rooms and wet and windy streets of Dostoyevsky's Saint Petersburg and Moscow. He was the first writer systematically to map and then inhabit the nightmare possibilities of the visionary city, a nightmare from which the novel will not be shaken awake. This is what makes his characters so much more than just tormented slaves of their passions and situations. Acts of violence grow out of the conjunction between extreme intelligence and savage deprivation. Isolation becomes so intense and complete, despair so acute, that the only deliverance available is by means of Christ, himself a suffering servant, divine and at our bidding when need is most intense.

Woolf was drawn to Dostoyevsky's moral intensity and the scale of his writing. After experiencing Russian reality the English protagonist, male or female, could no longer come home to comfortable slippers and a posset. She could not imitate the Russians, but she could strive for a comparable originality. Jack

Kerouac, more ambitious and hubristic, compares his own mature style to Dostoyevsky's in *Notes from the Underground* (1864), "confessional madness," and sells the Russian short. J. M. Coetzee in *The Master of Petersburg,* by contrast, honors the spirit of his master without vaunting his own achievement.

Dostoyevsky, the insubordinate son of a temperamental minor aristocrat, began by creating closely focused, deliberately narrow worlds whose borders were drawn by the characters themselves. The more complex his characters, the greater their self-knowledge, the larger the canvases he worked on. His exile, his obsession with gambling, his epilepsy ("the epileptic monster . . . more dangerous than cocaine," Edmund Gosse told André Gide), his hunger for transcendent belief and for social change, all feed into his fiction, including *The House of the Dead* (1862, Garnett translation 1915), *Crime and Punishment* (1866, Garnett translation 1914), *The Idiot* (1869, Garnett translation 1913), and his supreme masterpiece *The Brothers Karamazov* (1880, Garnett translation 1912). Many of his stories and novels, the last in particular, were suggested by a newspaper report of some sordid event. Others grow directly from his own experience. Some years ago at a casino outside Frankfurt, during an afternoon of roulette, I was startled to see an admonitory bronze tondo commemorating the fact that Dostoyevsky had spent time and most of his money in the room where I had just parted with much of mine. The fateful year for Dostoyevsky was 1865. He lost 3,000 gold rubles in a very short time, then dictated *The Gambler* at speed, in twenty-six days, to earn an advance he had already squandered.

Because the world of hardship was familiar to him, he could see before him a detailed narrative of streets and tenements, of thoughts and obsessions. Thus, Dmitri Karamazov's one relief from his stifling, impecunious provincial existence is the inn at Mockroye where he visits the voluptuous Grushenka and the gypsies. The place may be a dead end, a pit into which he pours his resources, but for him it is where sunless Dionysian intensities occur. Released by alcohol from all inhibition, he is transfigured, even in so tawdry a place. On his last visit, his money spent or lost, quite drunk, Dmitri falls asleep and starts to dream. He dreams of children, of an innocence he himself has lost. On waking, he finds his accusers there to charge him with his father's murder. "Mitya's entire soul was as if shaken by sobs and tears. He approached the table and declared that he would sign whatever we required. 'I had a good dream, gentlemen,' he declared somehow strangely, with a face somehow new, as though illumined by joy." A reader who sees Dmitri merely as a reckless half-pay officer, a victim of his own vices, will not understand the independence and urbanity of "I had a good dream, gentlemen." Dmitri does not panic. He possesses Dantesque gravity and self-knowledge, as if the flame of his true self had flared up from the wreck his vices had made of him.

Dostoyevsky's publisher and friend A. S. Suvorin records a visit to his author in 1880: "He lived in a shabby little apartment. I found him sitting by a small round table in the drawing-room, he was rolling cigarettes; his face was like that of someone who had just emerged from a Russian bath, from a shelf on which he had been steaming himself." Dostoyevsky said to Suvorin, "I have just had an attack. I am glad, very glad, to see you." He was composing *The Brothers Karamazov* and reflecting on whether, had he known that an assault had been planned on the Winter Palace, he would have informed. "Weighty, solid reasons" argued for informing, "absolutely trivial," social reasons would have inhibited his telling. Yet the trivial reasons, which entailed social interaction and uncertainty, prevailed.

He spoke, or preached, in Moscow earlier that year, at the unveiling of the Pushkin memorial. Toward the end of his highly charged oration, he declared, "Let our country be poor, but this poor land 'Christ traversed with blessing, in the garb of a serf.' Why then should we not contain His final word?" Turgenev, who had spoken on Pushkin with less effect the night before, was deeply moved. He overcame their tetchy rivalry and embraced him. The next year Dostoyevsky died. At his funeral there was a vast attendance.

Dostoyevsky was first translated into English in 1881. Almost two decades earlier, in the high Victorian period, the first, poor translation of Lev Niko-layevich Tolstoy (1828–1910) appeared. His time had not come, his radicalism was unwelcome. Religious and cultural certainties became less certain with the years. *War and Peace* in an anonymous and faulty translation from the French was published. Then, in 1887–1890, eight further fictional works by Tolstoy appeared, in among his essays and prophetic utterances. Count Tolstoy became a living presence in English letters, his aristocratic title lending weight to social and religious teachings that became more emphatic and eccentric as he tried to live out his Christian anarchism in his later years.

Tolstoy, says Virginia Woolf, is "the greatest of all novelists," her touchstone. "It is not the samovar but the teapot that rules in England," she says; "time is limited; space crowded; the influence of other points of view, of other books, even of other ages, makes itself felt. Society is sorted out into lower, middle, and upper classes, each with its own traditions, its own manners, and, to some extent, its own language." For English novelists there were social structures that made shorthand possible: a single detail might reveal the class, income, and taste of a whole family: "There is a constant pressure upon an English novelist to recognize those barriers, and, in consequence, order is imposed on him and some kind of form; he is inclined to satire rather than to compassion, to scrutiny of society rather than understanding of individuals themselves." Her rhetoric falls into a habit of binary oppositions; Tolstoy's does not. He is exempted by a culture that had not experienced the Reformation and Enlightenment except at second hand, that borrowed European forms and carried them like lamps into a vast reluctant dark that was his element.

Edmund Wilson calls Tolstoy "one of the greatest impersonators in literature." Impersonation is central in "stream of consciousness" to an even greater degree than in the dramatic monologue or free indirect narration. He could put on the voice, the mouth and head and neck and hands of his characters. They were not Dostoyevskian projections of self, even when informed by memory; nor are they Turgenev's soliciting figures. They entail rigorous self-effacement and intense intellectual effort. Tolstoy's image of the self-wasting pain of composition could almost be Woolf's: that one should write only at moments when one leaves "a bit of one's flesh in the inkpot" with each dip.

A bad student at school, a soldier and a would-be writer, Tolstoy was deeply affected by his meetings in Paris (1860–1861) with Victor Hugo, who had recently completed *Les misérables*. Here was a work on a scale, and with a clarity, that Tolstoy found inspiriting. Without *Les misérables, War and Peace* (1869) might not have been written. It was his fifth novel, and in scope and achievement a great step forward from *The Cossacks* (1863).

E. M. Forster reflects on how *War and Peace* ought to be depressing: it is concerned with the passage of time, the inexorable physical, and in most cases the spiritual, decay of its protagonists. Yet it is not depressing, because of its proportions, its scale in space and time; it induces something like fear and wonder at the vast sweep of the world it depicts. And its characters live continuously: Pierre Bezuhov and his foil Prince Bolkonsky, Natasha, Kuragin and his seductive sister, stay with us after the novel is put back on its shelf. *War and Peace* has an effect like music because of the large cast of characters, the time span, and Tolstoy's sense of world. Woolf saw much of his power as being the result of a philosophical pessimism at odds with the vitality of his language. He incorporates different registers, so that as in a piece of music where the key feels inappropriate to the descriptive context, a deliberate, sustained irony is created. Tolstoy himself did not regard *War and Peace* as a novel. Its combination of fictional and expository, essayistic material was formally hybrid. Dostoyevsky admired it as "landlord's literature," the last of its kind. Turgenev, who at first resisted the book, became its advocate in France and was instrumental in getting Tolstoy's work translated. As a result Flaubert read and admired it. The writing about war in straightforward, unsentimental terms gave Hemingway important lessons.

In *What Is Art?* Tolstoy says that what gets in the way of realism is, ironically, the very detail intended to convey the real. "Imitation cannot serve as a standard of the value of art, because, if the chief property of art is the infection of others with the sensation described by the artist, the infection with the sensation not only does not coincide with the description of the details of what is being conveyed, but for the most part is impaired by the superabundance of details." Strict imitation is not art, as Tolstoy knew, and Dostoyevsky rather differently, and as Nabokov teaches time after time in lectures and essays and by fictional example. When the romantic novelist Ouida remarks, as a caution, that Tolstoy's "morality and monogamy are against nature and common sense," and adds that he is dangerous, an "educated Christ," she is remarking on the treachery of a morality that proceeds from or issues in aesthetics, a phenomenon with which the twentieth century—from the modernists to Alexander Solzhenitsyn—became too familiar.

*War and Peace* is a book of essays and a book of lives in time—and not just in fictional but in historical time, lives touched, shaped, and maimed by events: Tolstoy is right to distance it from more conventional novel forms. Its impact on American fiction, in particular on Norman Mailer's, is acknowledged by Mailer himself. Christopher Isherwood confesses, "I love Tolstoy's furious essays." By contrast, *Anna Karenina* (1877)—Nabokov dubbed it "the supreme masterpiece of nineteenth-century literature," while Rebecca West called it "a ridiculous book"—is more dramatically whole than *War and Peace,* coming down to the single, dreadful focus that it shares with *Madame Bovary,* the fate of the adulterous heroine whom we have come to love as it were against the grain. Tolstoy makes no secret of the plot we have ahead of us when, in the very first sentence, he declares, "Happy families are all alike; every unhappy family is unhappy in its own way." We do not immediately go to the Karenin household. We start in a more conventional place, with the Oblonskys, where Mrs. Oblonsky has discovered her husband's infidelity with (inevitably), "a French girl, who had been a governess in their family, and she had announced to her husband that she could not go on living in the same house with him." The well-ordered Karenin establishment is then gradually reduced by Anna's passion to an epic unhappiness. Edna O'Brien remarks, "Anna Karenina is the most believable heroine. The last scene where she goes to the station and looks down at the rails and thinks of Vronsky's rejection is terrible in its depiction of despair." Terrible, and credible.

Whatever the place of his overcoat in the history of Russian fiction, in some ways Gogol remains, though first among the great writers of his time, also the most modern and challenging. His unevenness is not in dispute. For Nabokov he is treacherous indeed. "I was careful *not* to learn anything from him. As a teacher, he is dubious and dangerous. At his worst, as in his Ukrainian stuff, he is a worthless writer; at his best, he is incomparable and inimitable." The shapelessness and fantasy of his novels became less rebarbative to readers toward the end of the nineteenth century and in the twentieth. His story of a nose that detaches itself and develops a life independent of the face where it grew, spiting it, as it were, is entirely logical except in its first premise, like Kafka's *The Metamorphosis,* David Garnett's *Lady into Fox,* or Philip Roth's *The Breast.*

In 1852, before his major novels had been composed, Turgenev contributed an obituary for Gogol to a Saint Petersburg magazine. The censor forbade publication in Saint Petersburg, but it was published in Moscow. Turgenev got into trouble with the authorities as a result of the piece and spent a month in prison and two years in exile—comfortable exile on one of the Turgenev estates. Gogol gave him the time, his estate and its peasants the occasions to write.

Gogol took a perverse pleasure in revealing not the injustice but the absurdity of everyday experience. Sometimes the absurdity takes the form of fantasy, as in "The Nose," sometimes the literal world is left more or less intact. Chichikov, the round, comfortable antihero of *Dead Souls* (1842, Garnett translation 1922) embodies the provinces at their materialist worst. He intends to make his place and fortune. The dead souls of the title are the deceased serfs who remain on the books of the landowner and can be used as collateral for mortgages; they can be bartered with or hoarded up. If he can get title to enough of them, he will be able to borrow substantially and acquire the estate and status he craves. He fails, flees, and the novel continues in a different province but in a similar vein. Just as he is receiving his comeuppance the novel halts, like Laurence Sterne's *A Sentimental Journey,* in mid-sentence. *Dead Souls* is original, dramatic, comic, enduring; his first novel, *Taras Bulba* (1835), is more like apprentice work, the exaggerations more controlled, the Ukrainian politics to which Nabokov took exception bluntly present.

In the better stories and in *Dead Souls* there are none of the resolving coincidences that make Dickens's fiction so pleasant in its resolutions, so bracingly sentimental. There are no particularly happy endings, but there is laughter and, occasionally, a kind of metaphysical revenge. Gogol's fiction is economical, a quality he bequeathed to Turgenev. It is hard for the contemporary reader to regard Gogol as a realist. True, sometimes his descriptions are foregrounded, but they are not always as integrated and thematically functional as they are in Turgenev's work. He is, we now see, "a fantasist, a satirist, a master of the grotesque," as the translator and critic Peter France describes him, "maybe a surrealist before the event, an inspired 'folk' entertainer (like Dickens but more so)." That "more so" points to American fiction and to the exuberance of Mark Twain. But first, the legacy of Turgenev.

# 26

# The Fate of Form

William Dean Howells, Henry James, Cynthia Ozick, Mrs. Humphry Ward,

Edith Wharton, Sinclair Lewis, Marcel Proust, Dorothy Richardson,

Anthony Powell, Henry Williamson, C. P. Snow

William Dean Howells (1837–1920) was born into a big family in Ohio where his father was a newspaper publisher and printer, and he became, at an early age, an editor in his own right; he was also a writer, his first book being a collection of poems written with a friend. He was a patriot keen to promote American writing. He was an advocate of new writers (Stephen Crane, for example, though his judgment was not invariably so sound) and revalued older ones. His "Editor's Study" essays, followed by the "Editor's Easy Chair," were popular literary journalism. There was a substantial readership for polite essays and for fiction. *Century Magazine* in the 1880s when it published Henry James's *The Bostonians* (1886) and Howells's best novel, *The Rise of Silas Lapham* (1885), about the emergence of an American man of business, had a circulation of 100,000. Formidable influence, then, the note always moral. Confronted with his portrait, young and old, Oliver Hardy comes to mind: the aspect of a large comedian overlaid by an earnest straight man. The mustache changes from portrait to portrait but is always like Twain's, well combed and out of proportion to the face. His essays buttonhole and patronize the reader at the same time. Mencken speaks sardonically of "the wraith of the later Howells, the virtuous, kittenish Howells, floating about in the air," poisoning it with ill-directed enthusiasm, affirmative piety. Kittenish as a bear.

When Sinclair Lewis was awarded the Nobel Prize in Literature in 1930, he rendered the *coup de grace* to Howells in his address, "The American Fear of Literature." He began in a friendly, patronizing voice, almost like Howells's. "Mr. Howells was one of the gentlest, sweetest, and most honest of men," and then, to the jugular, "but he had the code of a pious old maid whose greatest delight was to have tea at the vicarage. He abhorred not only profanity and obscenity but all of what H. G. Wells has called *the jolly coarsenesses of life*." Only the Great War put an end to his stifling influence on American letters. His greatest achievement was "to tame Mark Twain, perhaps the greatest of our writers, and to put that fiery old savage into an intellectual frock coat and top hat." His type survived. Lewis's medicine, magisterially administered, tried to purge the republic of American letters of one of its most persistent types.

Howells enjoyed collaborative writing (editor-writers often do, drawing energy from working in tandem). With a friend he prepared a campaign biography of Abraham Lincoln. His reward was a consulship in Venice. Howells was in Venice during the Civil War and experienced the upheaval remotely. Fascinated by Europe, he was never at home there, unlike James who became French and then, though some English writers could not bring themselves to welcome him, English. Howells returned to an unfamiliar United States quite transformed by its trauma. His mission as editor, critic, and then novelist, became emollient, curative rather than diagnostic or analytical.

He only started to write novels, his friend Henry James declared, when he had lived abroad, then edited, and "lived considerably." And when he began, "he continued to practice the cabinet-picture manner" of his sketches, though adding broader strokes in later works. He contributed to *Harper's* and to the *Atlantic Monthly,* of which he became editor in 1871, a post he retained for a decade, exercising influence and ensuring that his own writing was read with craven respect. He began with *Suburban Sketches* (1871). He was an assiduous *describer,* rendering the picturesque and essentializing incidents or scenes. "I know of no English novelist of our hour whose work is so exclusively a matter of painting what he sees," James remarks, "and who is so sure of what he sees."

"Out of the tension between the adventurousness of Flaubert and the edgy reticence of Hawthorne came the novels of William Dean Howells," Gore Vidal fancifully says. How can his realism remind Vidal first of Turgenev's, then of Zola's? Does he forget Bazarov, Thérèse Raquin? Howells favors resolved endings, as in *A Modern Instance,* about the consequences of divorce, a relatively unexplored subject at the time. This book is a finger post: down that road we come to the far more solid achievement of Theodore Dreiser and later realists. The *real* American realists have made the mode American and need not be read as footnotes to a European movement. Vidal quotes Howells describing how a character "discovered in himself that dual life, of which everyone who sins or sorrows is sooner or later aware: that strange separation of the intellectual activity from the suffering of the soul, by which the mind toils on in a sort of ironical indifference to the pangs that wring the heart; the realization that in some ways his brain can get on perfectly well without his conscience." It is schematic, more theological than psychological.

Howells, keen as editor and author to strengthen American literature, borrowed formal energies from Europe. In *The Lady of the Aroostook* (1879) American and English circle one another fascinated, a theme easily pursued and easily exhausted. His novels remain readable but not, on the whole, memorable. He lacks James's purchase on American characters. He likes them too well and gives them the benefit of too many doubts, a fiction of good fellows of both sexes, since even his villains are redeemable.

In his sixties Howells "strung out" in the *Ladies' Home Journal* a series of short essays entitled *My Literary Passions*. Willa Cather had no time for them: "'Passions,' literary or otherwise, were never Mr. Howells' forte," she remarked. He used the occasions to please himself as much as his readers, who were, Cather says, accustomed to reading "those thrilling articles about how Henry Ward Beecher tied his necktie and what kind of coffee Mrs. Hall Cain likes." Ladies were confronted with the name of "the great Zola, or call him the immense Zola," presented as "the prime mover in the attack upon the masters of the Romanticistic school." Furrowed brows.

"The Realists," says Howells, "who were undoubtedly the masters of fiction in their passing generation, and who prevailed not only in France, but in Russia, in Scandinavia, in Spain, in Portugal, were overborne in all Anglo-Saxon countries by the innumerable hosts of Romanticism," who control the field "to this day." Howells, patron of the severe un-Romantic Crane, was himself tinged with Romanticism. "He adores the real, the natural, the colloquial, the moderate, the optimistic, the domestic, and the democratic," says James. This is realism of a limited kind; and he does dislike tidy resolutions, elaborate plot, coincidence, elements that in order to engage readers distort plausibility. But he has a vice: more than just living, his characters always seem to be performing, even if only half aware of the footlights that at any moment might highlight them. They stay doggedly in character. Development is at a premium.

*Their Wedding Journey* (1871) was a charming step into fiction. It follows a couple across New York State, their eyes opened by their change of condition and the adventures they encounter at stations, in streets, on steamboats, and in hotels. It is not Pickwick, it certainly is not Zola, but the world they move in is plausible. American life is framed and represented, and is wholesome. *A Chance Acquaintance* (1873) was more ambitious, but travel, this time along the Saint Lawrence and Saguenay Rivers, is still the narrative core, and Howells has not yet learned to hold his characters still. There is Quebec! And look, the Falls of Montmorenci! The guide distracts us from the story. But story does not interest him. By the time he came to *A Modern Instance* (1882) and *Indian Summer* (1886) he was writing novels of manners. Class friction, incompatibility of custom: there is something Forsterian about these novels, their anguished misunderstandings, yet what they lack is irony to heighten the comedy and impart proportion. *A Modern Instance,* Howells's convincing novel, creates tenable characters, their fates determined by how they react to one another. This realism is in the spirit of Eliot, not Zola. Howells's early writing—the Venice sketches, for example, with fresh delight in minutiae—is far from the engaged writing: it is as though, James says, in returning to America he has lost his lighthearted Muse.

Given the hail-fellow-well-metness of Mark Twain, it is curious that he and Howells remained lifelong friends. How could a writer as keen on *earning* as Twain sit down at table with the man who declared, "I do not think any man ought to live by an art. A man's art should be his privilege, when he has proven his fitness to exercise it, and has otherwise earned his daily bread; and its results should be free to all." They could hardly be more remote in kind or class. Yet when Howells gave a good review to Twain's *The Innocents Abroad,* Twain appallingly said, "When I read that review of yours I felt like the woman who said that she was so glad that her baby had come white." He saw himself in Howell's charming charlatan Bartley Hubbard, who tells the tale and tells it true. But even Twain's support was not enough to keep Howells's star in the sky.

In the twentieth century Mencken is only the most virulent of Howells's detractors, impatient with the effeteness and the European fixation in some American fiction. He linked him with James as an influence, and identified a female and doubtfully male progeny of writers made second rate by their example. "As for Howells and James, both quickly showed that timorousness and reticence which are the distinguishing marks of the Puritan, even in his most intellectual incarnations," he says, and his linking of their fastidiousness with the residue of the Puritan spirit is suggestive. They fail in creating characters, producing puppets. "They shrunk, characteristically, from those larger, harsher clashes of will and purpose which one finds in all truly first-rate literature. In particular, they shrunk from any interpretation of life which grounded itself upon an acknowledgment of its inexorable and inexplicable tragedy." We do not recognize James in this.

In American literary journalism Howells and Henry James (1843–1916) were lumped together, as though they shared a project. How different they are in kind Jorge Luis Borges makes clear in his little 1945 essay on James's *The Abasement of the Northmores.* "I have visited some literatures of the East and West; I have compiled an encyclopedic anthology of fantastic literature; I have translated Kafka, Melville, and [Léon] Bloy; I know of no stranger work than that of Henry James." At first he seems conventional and flat compared with the unrealists Borges evokes; gradually we see that we are in the presence of "a resigned and ironic inhabitant of Hell." Glad Howells gets no nearer Hell than reading Zola. James might say, with Mephistopheles, "I myself am hell, nor am I out of it." In his novels and stories "we are dealing with the voluntary omission of a part of the novel, which allows us to interpret it in one way or another; both premeditated by the author, both defined." In *The Turn of the Screw* and *The Lesson of the*

*Master,* we do not know, or we know for certain two contradictory things. The acutest pain a character can suffer in James is *not to know* or *not to know for sure:* for the reader this is his fiction's intensest pleasure.

James distanced himself from Howells's notion that American freedom from custom, class, and ingrained tradition was liberating for the novelist. In the first place, did such freedom, could such freedom, really exist in society? "It is on manners, usages, habits, forms, upon all these things matured and established, that a novelist lives—they are the very stuff his work is made of; and in saying that in the absence of those 'dreary and worn-out paraphernalia' which I enumerate as being wanted in American society, 'we have simply the whole of human life left,' you beg (to my sense) the question. I should say we had just so much less of it as these same 'paraphernalia' represent, and I think they represent an enormous quantity of it." The only refutation he would accept is the emergence of actual books "on a par with those of Balzac or Thackeray." He says in his essay on Emerson, "We know a man imperfectly until we know his society." Saul Bellow in a *New Yorker* interview in 1988 made a parallel claim, with at least one foot in his mouth, trying to respond to multiculturalist polemic with its tendency to relativize values, or "values": "Who is the Tolstoy of the Zulus? The Proust of the Papuans? I'd be glad to read him." One is reminded of the grumpy brigadier writing to the *Times:* "How can we trust those Russians? Why, in Russian there isn't even a word for *détente."* Yet James has a point and a point of actual reference, Hawthorne, who spoke of the difficulty of "writing a romance about a country where there is no shadow."

Hawthorne is the American writer crucial to James. James's story "The Passionate Pilgrim" is based on an incident narrated by Hawthorne in "Consular Experiences," about an American coming to England expecting to find a tangible heritage, something that belonged to him and to which he belonged. It was not to be found in the form anticipated. In a letter James conceded that he had perhaps exaggerated the merits of Europe: "It's the same world there after all and Italy isn't the absolute any more than Massachusetts. It's a complex fate, being an American, and one of the responsibilities it entails is fighting against a superstitious valuation of Europe." Hawthorne was an American antidote. Writing about him James is nostalgic, he wishes *to have been American* in the antebellum way that Hawthorne was, to have grazed more fully in innocent pastures and understood the landscape and the variety of its people better. An inversion occurs: a man endowed with "metropolitan" values desires the assumed liberties of the "provincial." Town mouse and country mouse. James insisted, "It takes a great deal of history to produce a little literature . . . it needs a complex machinery to set a writer in motion." *Roderick Hudson* was rooted in Hawthorne's last novel, *The Marble Faun;* more telling, in James's late work, is the elaborated symbolism indebted to Hawthorne, a touchstone of Americanness.

A reader approaching James for the first time will find him startlingly different from his contemporaries and nineteenth-century antecedents. He did not attend a private school or, except briefly and uncommittedly, Harvard. He received an education via tutors in New York and Albany, and in London, Paris, Geneva, Bonn, and Bologna. He did not serve in the armed forces, and the only male societies to which he belonged, in his English years, were the gentlemen's clubs. He liked theaters and galleries and cycling in the country rather than music halls, hunting, and fishing. Above all is his absolute devotion to his writing. Like Flaubert, he existed in and for writing and was nothing without it. Unlike Flaubert, though he had a number of long and intimate correspondences, he did not keep, or even keep at bay, mistresses, or visit prostitutes. His fiction is chaste: there is intense intimacy but the temperature is controlled.

Edmund Wilson at nineteen wrote his first essay on Henry James. He comments on his prosperous boyhood. His father, who lost a leg when he was still a child, became a theologian who rebelled against his Presbyterian forebears and turned into a radically democratic Swedenborgian, fascinated by the Brook Farm experiment and by Fourier. Henry's older brother was the philosopher William James, to whom he remained close. There was his sister, Alice, a diarist, mentally unstable and dead at forty-three from breast cancer. She died in England in 1892, and Henry, who had helped support her and until that time had paid his way by writing, benefited from her will; thereafter his royalties were augmented by rental income from properties in New York State. Susan Sontag wrote her only play, *Alice in Bed,* about this troubled victim of the age.

Then there were Garth Wilkinson (Wilky) and Robertson (Bob), Henry's two written-out brothers, damaged—one physically, the other emotionally—by the Civil War, each a failure in the eyes of their demanding father and their brothers. Central to the American world James abandoned was his first cousin Mary (Minny) Temple, the young, lively, tubercular relation, whose clarity and cheerful, observant, self-effacing mortality touched the writer; she may have inspired some of his female characters, notably Daisy Miller and Millie Theale in *The Wings of the Dove.* Three letters from her survive—"My darling Harry"— and make clear the easy rapport between them; Henry wrote to her about serious encounters—with George Eliot, for instance—and as she grew more ill she longed to see Europe, and to see him in Europe: " 'Words is wanting' to tell you all the affection & sympathy I feel for you," she said in her last letter, in 1869.

She was used to his absences. In 1859 he was enrolled in a school in Boulogne. Among his classmates was a boy who became the great French comedian (Benoît Constant) Coquelin. His culture remained profoundly French when he settled in England. In *The Ambassadors* (1903) Lambert Strether, a widower in his mid-fifties, a figure close to James himself, is dispatched to France on a mission: his patroness and friend Mrs. Newsome wants him to recover her wayward son Chad, seduced in every sort of way by that treacherous country. Time for him to return and start a real life in the family business. But even, or especially, in his fifties Strether, with imagination and heart, is himself seduced. France has made Chad into a different quality of man; and Strether is likewise altered.

*The Awkward Age* (1899), Wharton says, is James's "convinced attempt . . . to write 'a little something in the manner of Gyp,'" that is, conducted largely in dialogue. He certainly is very nearly a French writer here. No wonder Flaubert received him, and Ivan Turgenev, another Francophile friend who helped insulate him from becoming too English. Flaubert entertained him in his dressing gown, an informality for which James never quite forgave him. Wharton reports that James "was particularly popular among his French friends, not only on account of his quickness and adaptability, but because his youthful frequentations in the French world of letters, following on the school-years in Geneva, had so steeped him in continental culture that the cautious and inhospitable French intelligence felt at once at ease with him." They were astonished at his "mastery of the language. French people have told me," Wharton added, "that they had never met an Anglo-Saxon who spoke French like James; not only correctly and fluently, but—well, just as they did themselves; avoiding alike platitudes and pomposity, and using the language as spontaneously as if it were his own."

James Thurber remarked, "I have a reputation for having read all of Henry James. Which would argue a misspent youth *and* middle age." James's output was certainly copious. Twenty completed novels and two unfinished when he died, 112 stories or "tales," some so substantial that we regard them as novels in their own right (among them *Daisy Miller,* 1878; *The Aspern Papers,* 1888; *The Lesson of the Master,* 1892; *The Turn of the Screw,* 1898; and *The Jolly Corner,* 1908), fifteen plays, and hundreds of reviews, essays, and miscellaneous writings constitute his oeuvre. In 1906–1910 he had the luxury few authors afford themselves of revising his work for a definitive American edition. Revision is often substantial: many of the novels were formally or stylistically marred by the demands of serialization, in terms of both what serialization required and the speed at which he had had to write. In a letter to Wharton in 1912 he spoke of his fear of deadlines and schedules. To have the opportunity (and energy) to revisit and reshape his work was for him momentous: he got the full run of his work in view, four decades' writing, and he was able to provide prefaces that seem to disclose everything we need to know, and yet withhold (as Conrad's do) the very things we are most curious to know. He set parameters within which he wanted to be read, evading questions modern readers raise. He was largely responsible for creating modern readers.

Edwin Muir regards James as the father of many of the "question-begging terms" used in discussing fiction: "He was an incurable impressionist; and he has infected criticism with his vocabulary of hints and nods." He used words like "pattern" and "rhythm" without defining them, assuming that we would go along, which we did for almost a century. "The danger of a practicing theorist on the novel like James is that he ends by doing exactly what he wants to do. He excludes three-quarters of life where another would make some effort to subdue it. His plots will no doubt be very neat; but they will not have the organic movement, the ebb and flow, of a plot in the main tradition." This was written by the first English translator of Kafka. Had he read further, Muir would have found James sharing his very terms. "The Art of Fiction," one of the great theoretical statements about the novel, was provoked by Walter Besant, who in an article laid down restrictive shoulds and shouldn'ts, dos and don'ts, for the writing of fiction. James enunciates, using the same metaphor as Muir, an open intention. "A novel is a living thing, all one and continuous, like every other organism, and in proportion as it lives will it be found, I think, that in each of the parts there is something of each of the other parts." It is as though Coleridge had transmogrified into a writer of fiction, bringing that large romantic metaphor in his rucksack. But James did apply rules to his own fiction. He was wary of first-person narrative because of its "terrible fluidity of self-revelation." He had Thackeray in mind, perhaps. He developed the "indirect oblique style," largely in response to the inadequate alternatives available and under the spell of Flaubert in particular and Balzac generally. Mary McCarthy remarked on the eccentricity and containment that James's work epitomized. "He did not broaden a way for his successors but closed nearly every exit as with hermetic sealing tape." Considered in the light of his antecedents, too, she lists what is missing, starting with "battles, riots, tempests, sunrises, the sewers of Paris . . ." and the little gratuitous details that, as Barthes would say, make the fiction "real."

In the preface to *The Portrait of a Lady* James speaks of "the house of fiction," which has not one window but numberless windows, it being capacious and perhaps expanding. The windows at the front have been "pierced" or are still "pierceable" "by the need of the individual vision and by the pressure of the individual will." And "at each of them stands a figure with a pair of eyes, or at least with a field-glass"—his famous "point of view"—"which forms, again and again for observation, a unique instrument, insuring to the person making use of it an impression distinct from every other." This is one of the points at which we are being created as readers: "He and his neighbours are watching the same show, but one seeing more where the other sees less, one seeing black where the other sees white, one seeing big where the other sees small, one seeing coarse where the other sees fine." There is no question-begging here but an observation of such *creative* simplicity and use that it dazzles. Edith Wharton acknowledges how important this is to James's, as to her own art. Other novelists have "intermittently" been aware of it; but James formulates it by asking, "Who saw this thing I am going to tell about? By whom do I mean that it shall be reported? It seems as though such a question must precede any study of the subject chosen, since the subject is conditioned by the answer." The consequences for James were plain: he "sought the effect of verisimilitude by rigorously confining every detail of his picture to the range, and also to the capacity, of the eye fixed on it." Wharton admires the subtlety with which he contrives point of view, so that "the reader's visual range was continually enlarged by the substitution of a second consciousness whenever the boundaries of the first were exceeded." In *The Golden Bowl* Colonel and Mrs. Assingham ("this insufferable and incredible couple") are like spies piecing together the narrative from separate perspectives. "I don't quite see, my dear," says the Colonel to his wife; and we elide from his into her point of view.

Vidal is less impressed than Wharton: "Famously, James made a law of the single viewpoint; and then constantly broke it." If he broke it, he never abandoned it. "The choice of the point(s) of view from which the story is told is arguably the most important single decision that the novelist has to make," David Lodge insists, "for it fundamentally affects the way readers will respond, emotionally and morally, to the fictional characters and their actions." James's development of point of view is subtler than many of his followers'. Lodge contrasts Maisie's style in *What Maisie Knew* (1897) with Holden Caulfield's in J. D. Salinger's *Catcher in the Rye,* of which it is a subtle ancestor. Maisie is unable to express in "skaz," a personal language, dialect, or "voice" rendered mimetically, what she perceives and understands. James writes for her a language that exceeds her articulateness but accurately reflects the complex nature of her understanding and response.

We can show where information resides and even how it resides there, but we cannot paraphrase it. It belongs to a subjectivity and resists entering the "objective" world of discourse. T. S. Eliot called it "thinking with his feelings." James's speakers are not usually discriminated by dialect or diction, yet they are, even without "he said" and "she said," clearly differentiated, because dialogue is "organic and dramatic" in the sense that "it expresses the disturbing impact the characters have on each other once they emerge from their private self-communings and seek some form of mutual comprehension." This too is a product of point of view. Lodge demonstrates how, in *The Ambassadors,* through consistent point of view, James makes extreme coincidence credible. "If it doesn't *seem* contrived, in the reading, that is partly because it is virtually the only twist in the entire plot (so that James has large reserves of credulity to draw on), and partly because the masterly narration of the event from Strether's point of view makes us experience it, rather than merely receive a report of it." Lodge takes us through the three stages of his "slow motion" perception of it, and shows how by careful economy, by making everything *else* credible, we believe what is least plausible. This is a lesson learned, very differently, by Kafka; both writers root their understanding in the example of Flaubert.

It is now commonplace, and certainly convenient, to see James's writings as dividing, like Caesar's Gaul, into three parts. The first, in which he concentrated upon serial novels, runs to *The Portrait of a Lady* (1881), regarded by many as his greatest novel. The second period includes much of his best shorter fiction. He had tired of the rigors of serial deadlines and succumbed to an enthusiasm for theater, producing several plays. James I and James II. The return of the Old Pretender came with the later novels, James III, the discipline of serialization reimposed, the late, characteristic James style, elaborated, extended: the period primarily of *The Wings of the Dove* (1902), *The Ambassadors* (1903), and *The Golden Bowl* (1904).

Vidal is most at home with James I, the American, evoking his countrymen in Europe. The first of the novels, *Watch and Ward* (serialized in the *Atlantic Monthly* in 1871, published as a book in 1878), James came to despise: a kind of proleptic *Lolita,* about a man who raises up his ward and marries her. His first celebrated novel was *Roderick Hudson* (1875), which he saw as his début. He was changing, exposing himself socially at every opportunity and like the young Proust keeping ears and eyes wide open. In late 1878, the year of *Daisy Miller,* and early 1879 he accepted 140 dinner invitations in a single season. He was a large presence, entertaining with a kind of Pickwickian *thereness*. One noticed Henry James, and despite his formality he could be spontaneous; one remembered him. "While James's critics were complaining that he was no longer American and could never be English," Vidal says, "James was writing *The Portrait of a Lady,* as nearly perfect a work as a novel can be." The hardest task for the novelist, James realized, "consists in giving the sense of duration, of the lapse and accumulation of time. This is altogether to my view the stiffest problem that the artist in fiction has to tackle, and nothing is more striking at present than the blankness, for the most part, of his indifference to it." This he wrote in connection with Gissing. He had learned by the end of the first phase to follow Balzac, the master of time passing. He kept faith with the world-making Frenchman. The first period also included *The American* (1877), *The Europeans* (1878), and

*Washington Square* (1880). He had moved well beyond the baggy Victorian novel of his time, even though like other novelists he was writing for serialization.

Mrs. Henry Adams wanted James back in America, away from the seductions of the "injudicious old ladies" of London, Vidal says. She wanted him to defend himself against his detractors. Bret Harte found him poisoned by Englishness through and through. After *Daisy Miller,* the protagonist of which he called "an inscrutable combination of audacity and innocence," James began to lose confidence in his ability to create contemporary American characters. This loss of grip on crucial elements in his imaginative world contributed to his move away from detailed realism, and the formal perfection of *The Portrait of a Lady* marks his decisive transformation. He becomes less interested in the contingent world and more narrowly focused in, more intensely aware of what does fill the (more selective) frame, as if seeking figurative significance not through but in select elements of the material world. We never come to "understand" the world of *The Turn of the Screw;* we never discover precisely what the spoils of Poynton are. Things are left unsaid and undefined between characters; they also remain unsaid to the reader. What is omitted we assume to be insignificant, or its significance is, paradoxically, its absence: what Maisie *did not* know even as she knew so much. In *The Ambassadors,* the Newsome fortune is based on manufacture of a little useful item for the home; we never learn what it is, though the action of the novel is financed from it. James does not say because it is irrelevant except to our curiosity: "Life being all inclusion and confusion, and art being all discrimination and selection," as he reminds us in the preface to *The Spoils of Poynton* (1897).

We are to accept what our narrator tells us, not to ask for more. The ownership of some furniture is being contested, but we are not told much about it. Another novelist might have given us a catalog, but James is interested in the theme of possession, not in the things possessed. If we take what is given in the terms in which it is offered, we find a rich sufficiency. If we ask for what is not germane, we lose the novel. E. M. Forster's objections are very English and rather selfish. He comments on the limited range of characters we encounter, and they are "constructed on very stingy lines," he says. They do not have the sort of fun we have, they do not run, they are not shown about to embrace sexually or die for a cause. They keep their clothes on. (This is a point Updike also underlines: "Sex existed for James mostly as a rumor, a hidden center of ado, and some impatience attends his treatment of it.") Forster concludes, "Maimed creatures can alone breathe in Henry James's pages—maimed yet specialized." Other writers' characters might exist in another novelist's novel; James's characters are nontransferable.

James II wrote another clutch of novels, but his attention was on the stage and shorter fictional forms. *The Tragic Muse* (1890) failed; he renounced novel writing (though his vow was only briefly kept). Greene is fascinated by this failed, self-deluded pursuit of theater, James's attempt to address a more immediate audience and earn a bigger fee for less effort. Given the success on stage, screen, and in the opera house of adaptations of James's work, why was he unable to effect the transformation himself? The failure of *Guy Domville* marked him for life. It was an eighteenth-century costume drama ridiculed by audiences, though it was not disliked by Shaw or the then-unknown H. G. Wells or by Arnold Bennett.

He should have applied his own rule about fiction to stage writing: he warned novelists off historical fiction, against abandoning (in a phrase that foreshadows Lawrence) "the palpable present-*intimate* that throbs responsive"; and reading *The Tory Love* by Sarah Orne Jewett, he writes to her, "You have to think with your modern apparatus a man, a woman—or rather fifty—whose own thinking was intensely otherwise conditioned, you have to simplify back by an amazing tour de force—and even then it'll all be humbug." "You may multiply the little facts that can be got from pictures & documents, relics & prints, as much as you like— *the* real thing is almost impossible to do, & in its absence the whole effect is as nought," he insists. "I mean the invention, the representation of old CONSCIOUS-NESS, the soul, the sense, the horizon, the vision of individuals in whose minds half the things that make ours, that make the modern world were non-existent." He urges her to return to the near, lived world of her earlier fiction.

Greene overstates the case: *Guy Domville* is not "unmistakably trash." It was less a disaster than some would-be playwrights experience. It ran for five weeks, and when it was taken off it was to make room for another untried piece that looked more promising, *The Importance of Being Earnest* by Oscar Wilde. James's problem was that he was too busy *being* the dramatist, moving his players like chess pieces in a slow contest for material and social prizes. The mechanics of dramatization got in the way and there was no space for his instincts. James's last novel was a novelization of the play *The Outcry* (1911), whose performance was canceled due to the death of King Edward VII. Said Updike, "The cumbersome though finely painted charabanc of the late James style is pulled swaying along by a frisky pony of plot, farcical and romantic, designed for stage-lit action." His collaboration in the early translation into English of Ibsen's plays was more valuable than his original stage work.

Colm Tóibín's novel about Henry James, *The Master* (2004), takes the failure of *Guy Domville* as its point of departure: the protagonist goes on stage the first night to acknowledge applause and is booed. *The Master* follows the four years from theatrical and human humiliation, through isolation, to his transformation into the later novelist, dictating his work to amanuenses. The notebooks that he produced between 1890 and 1895 have the germs of most of his major later work in them. The theater years were seeding time for his last phase. Whatever the quality of his stage writing, Gore Vidal insists, it helped purge his prose of its commonplace excesses; there was a new economy, even an ecology, in his language. This moved him into an "oral tradition of narrative," Vidal proposes, wryly portraying James as a kind of bourgeois bard. More than the language, his writing for stage affects the structure of his work, its scene-by-scene development that owes much to the example of French classic drama. The spoken and internal monologues, the symmetries, become crucial, and the drama rises out of the structure rather than being subjected to it. "As he became more and more preoccupied with the architecture of the novel," Wharton writes, "he unconsciously subordinated all else to his ever-fresh complexities of design, so that his last books are magnificent projects for future masterpieces rather than living creations." One would like to correct that last phrase of Wharton's to read "*as well as* living creations," though with a kind of life different from that of his earlier fiction, from that of most fiction, with the exception of Richardson's and that of his French followers.

Willa Cather knows how to value the late novels. She concedes that they can be "sometimes a little hard, always calculating and dispassionate, but they are perfect." Unfortunately they do not address modern issues, "'degeneracy' and the new woman and all the rest of it." (She forgot that he contributed to *The Yellow Book*.) But he can "turn on so many side-lights" (another relic of theater). "And then his sentences! If his character novels were all wrong one could read him forever for the mere beauty of his sentences." She admires the evenness, one might say the realism, the refusal to rise to climaxes or to dramatize. His phrases, "never dull and never too brilliant," remain in solution, as it were: "He subjects them to the general tone of his sentence and has his whole paragraph partake of the same predominating color. You are never startled, never surprised, never thrilled or never enraptured; always delighted by that masterly prose that is as correct, as classical, as calm and as subtle as the music of Mozart." The Mozart of *Cosi fan tutti* and *La nozze di Figaro*, perhaps. Conrad commends "the absence of shouted watchwords, clash of arms and sound of trumpets" in James, "an imaginative effort finding its inspiration from the reality of forms and sensations." At the heart of such fiction there is an "energetic act of renunciation. Energetic, not violent: the distinction is wide, enormous, like that between substance and shadow."

Here Greene locates the originality of James's work. "In all writers there occurs a moment of crystallization when the dominant theme is plainly expressed, when the private universe becomes visible even to the least sensitive reader." But it is hard to find such crystallizations in James, those points of lift-off and resolution: he was intent on dramatizing and "was more than usually careful to exclude the personal statement." From *The Ivory Tower* Greene instances the phrase "the black and merciless things that are behind great possessions." This is a value statement peculiar to the writer rather than to the narrator. James shows through in glimmers of darkness.

James's self-effacement is crucial to the art. "To most of us, living willingly in a sort of intellectual moonlight, in the faintly reflected light of truth," says Conrad, "the shadows so firmly renounced by Mr. Henry James's men and women, stand out endowed with extraordinary value, with a value so extraordinary that their rejection offends, by its uncalled-for scrupulousness, those business-like instincts which a careful Providence has implanted in our breasts." Artists who sacrifice their gods to their passions may produce passionate, unrepeatable work—*Wuthering Heights,* say, or *Moby-Dick,* or *Kim;* if they sacrifice their passions to their gods they may produce dozens of competent works with their "business-like instincts," as Trollope did. The ideal, if there were abstractable ideals in art, is to make the passions and the gods collude, yet "make" runs in the teeth of the reality of most fictional composition.

James developed acute writer's cramp in his hand and shoulder and took to dictating his work to a typist. Raymond Chandler remarks, "My revered HJ rather went to pieces a bit when he began to dictate." He was a natural stutterer, so he had to dictate slowly, precisely. This third creative phase centers on Rye, East Sussex, where he settled at Lamb House. He had three principal amanuenses at Rye. All of them worked straight onto the typewriter. Miss Weld took down four novels, numerous articles, stories, a biography, and some letters in her three-and-a-half-year stint with him. *The Wings of the Dove* was 194 days' dictating. *The Golden Bowl* took thirteen months of mornings. He smoked and paced, and his amanuenses could pass the time as they wished—knitting, reading, crocheting, themselves smoking—between the slow storms of words. The daughter of Miss Weld reports that Mr. James had a lovely voice and that typing for him was like being a piano accompanist to a singer. James referred to his later, dictating style as "Remingtonese," after the make of typewriter. We see the portly James pacing up and down, his accompanist clattering on her alphabetical piano, the little bell signaling another line end, the steel arm tapped, the bale, whizzing back, like the shuttle mechanism on a weaving machine, back and back, making the carpet and the figure in it.

He dictated in his favorite space at Lamb House, the Garden Room. It was like going out to work, crossing the modest lawn to his comfortable literary space, pretty and bow-windowed, with a view of the street where he could keep an eye on the peaceful village. In World War II a German bomb fell directly on the room, destroying it, James's pictures, and the large collection of his books, and doing severe damage to the house itself. The Garden Room was never rebuilt.

One might have expected that writing for the stage or dictation might have shortened James's sentences. If we remember blind Milton unfolding the huge periods of *Paradise Lost* to his daughters, we will know that the writer aloud need not become laconic, though Milton had the mnemonic of meter and for James the units of energy are not the foot and line but the phrase, sentence, and paragraph, and some of the sentences run on for half a page or more. James Thurber regarded this as the chief problem with the late style: he got bored. "James is like—well, I had a bulldog once who used to drag rails around, enormous ones . . . He loved to get them in the middle and you'd hear him growling out there, trying to bring the thing home." The problem was the garden gate: "*Crash,* he'd come up against the gateposts." James sometimes tries to get the rail through a gate not wide enough. Hardy agrees: James "has a ponderously warm manner of saying nothing in infinite sentences." In his journals Arnold Bennett, having read a story by James, noted, "His mere ingenuity, not only in construction, but in expression, is becoming tedious, though one cannot but admire. Also his colossal cautiousness in statement is very trying, If he would only now and then contrive to write a sentence without a qualifying clause!"

In the twentieth century James divided readers, in part at least because he marks in his work a crucial transition from traditional to modern, and from a literature dominated by British to one dominated by American writers. In *Ideas and the Novel* Mary McCarthy addresses the issue of originality, without broaching the political theme. James, "almost single-handed, invented a peculiar new kind of fiction, more refined, more stately, than anything known before, purged, to the limit of possibility, of the gross traditional elements of suspense, physical action, inventory, description of places and persons, apostrophe, moral teaching." He "etherealized" and—she cannot resist the elision—"etherized" the novel. In a sense James gives us templates. He withdraws as much as possible from his later work the material specifics of his characters' worlds, even the sense of location. We participate in supplying the visualization. If his characters enter a gallery, we must provide the occasions for their aesthetic rapture. McCarthy compares James to Psyche, averting his attention from certain self-forbidden zones. In his preface to *Wings* he dwells on indirection, his circuitous approach. He regards Millie with passion and respect but always "through the successive windows of other people's interest in her." This is the essential late James, looking through their eyes to see only what that person is seeing. The narrator sees into each character's process of seeing. And, McCarthy remarks, we must accept the protagonists of the later novels "on faith" because of the indirectness of their presentation, accept them "as ectoplasms emanating from an entranced author at his desk, in short as ghostly abstractions, pale ideas, which explains, when you come to think of it, the fever of discussion they excite in the other characters." They exist as "ideas" "expelled by a majestic butler at the front door." The majestic butler: such an apposite image of a public aspect of James, caricaturable yet even thus reduced still formidable.

James ended his writing life with an attempt to return to the first years. Where did his journey start, of what was he made? His three late autobiographies, like Hudson's *Far Away and Long Ago*, were written to fend off gathering loss. *A Small Boy and Others* in 1913 and *Notes of a Son and Brother* in 1914 look into formative relationships. He became a British subject in 1915 to mark his solidarity with his adoptive country when World War I began, and to protest against America's neutrality. The third volume, *The Middle Years*, appeared after his death, in 1917.

His artistic and wider cultural revolution was, like all the great modernist "moments," not wholly conscious of its radical character. He knew "a tradition is kept alive only by something being added to it," and not everyone—as Joyce and Pound and Picasso were to find—responds to addition with gratitude or understanding. Addition was not James's explicit aim but the inevitable result of his way of reading and writing. To the English reader he seemed alien even as he became more Anglophile. Woolf claims that the reader (presumably the rooted English reader) can tell from the way he writes about Britain that James did not grow up in his adoptive land; his criticism too has a transatlantic (she might have said, cross-Channel) feel, a sense of distance and different values, perspectives. Woolf's is a naive comment in its assumption of a unitary English sensibility. What distinguishes James from this supposed Englishness? "A special acuteness and detachment, a sharp angle of vision the foreigner will often achieve; but not that absence of self-consciousness, that ease and fellowship and sense of common values which make for intimacy, and sanity, and the quick give and take of familiar intercourse." We might extrapolate from this a view of James as a writer lacking in intimacy, sanity, speed, ease. Yet from Woolf's perspective Kipling, Stevenson, Hudson, Lawrence, and most of her distinguished contemporaries would not be admitted to her aboriginal club. Her exclusion is aggressive—and defensive.

Woolf sensed a trend. Of the great modernists only she is English in the terms she proposes. Lawrence, and later Auden, gravitated to America. Immigrants and the descendants of colonials, Irish and American, were no longer deferentially coming forward. When Henry James chose Lamb House and settled in Rye, the war was lost: Yeats and Wilde, Shaw and Synge were all at work; Joyce and Katherine Mansfield were laboring in the very field she considered hers;

T. S. Eliot was her friend, and there was awkward Ezra Pound, and soon the poets H.D. (Hilda Doolittle), William Carlos Williams, Robert Frost, and Wallace Stevens, and the novelists Faulkner, Hemingway, Fitzgerald. Already from Poland had come Conrad. The Great War put an end to many things, not least to the English purchase on high culture: England's high culture lay dreadfully wounded. The Woolfs were great editors and publishers, but the most brilliant editor of all went into the war with the name Ford Madox Heuffer. His German background and his irregular lifestyle did not stop him from creating the elegiac figure of Christopher Tietjens, "the last English Tory."

The poet and critic William Empson, too, recognized the change that was afoot and resisted it. His hostility to James is fueled by his hostility to what Americans were achieving on the very ground of England and in its language: "Americans are a good deal out of line with Western as well as Eastern Europe," he wrote, adding, to quarantine them further, "and as well as the rest of mankind, in assuming (verbally at least) that socialism is inherently bad, but naked individualism and competition good." He acknowledges an irony: "Actually, you find splendid public works being done in the States, and the world's most spectacular operations of organized charity; but all this has to be treated as a kind of brothel which the President winks at." A child of that brothel settled down in (James's own description) "the little old cobble-stoned, grass-grown, red-roofed town, on the summit of its mildly pyramidal hill and close to its noble church," Lamb House, Rye, East Sussex.

European novelists remain fascinated by James—the man, the writer, the American—even when not especially interested in his writing. David Lodge learned, as he was writing his novel about James, *Author, Author* (2004), that other novelists were pursuing the same quarry. Colm Tóibín scooped the prizes, overshadowing Lodge's compelling book. Tóibín puts a good deal of body back into the American author, recharging his libido and writing in the light of it. There was also Emma Tennant's *Felony* to contend with, and Alan Hollinghurst's *The Line of Beauty*, its hero obsessed with James. Lodge confessed that no book had given him more pleasure to write than *Author, Author*, or less pleasure to publish. Joyce Carol Oates, in a more fragile and heightened spirit, is fascinated by the Master. At Rye he walked out with his fat little dog Tosca, into the countryside, talking to her and getting tangled in her leash.

There is a novel waiting in those conversations: What did he confide, what did Tosca know? She may prove as eloquent as Elizabeth Barrett's *Flush*, speaking through Woolf in *A Biography* (1933). But who would have the affectionate stomach for such a task? Enter the dedicated Cynthia (Shoshana) Ozick (b. 1928), James's sensitive interpreter and devotee.

Ozick thrives in the shadow of James. Her first novel, *Trust* (1966), was "heavily influenced by compulsive reading and rereading" of *The Ambassadors*. She is by turns passionate and exasperated by the Master. The plot of her sixth novel, *Foreign Bodies* (2010), she describes as a reversal of *The Ambassadors*. Her relationship with James is deep, mischievous, critical, but faithful. She loves and berates him for many things, including his sexual indeterminacy, and understands the late novels as few other readers do. She is also a devoted Jewish-American god-daughter of Edith Wharton.

In her own fiction she resists editing, especially editorial cuts, and this resistance has not been good for her six novels, in which architectural can displace dramatic balance. It is more for her poems, working traditional forms briskly, efficiently, like Rubik's cubes, and her essays that she is valuable to contemporary readers, though her love of phrase-making, which sometimes stifles in satisfaction the flow of her fiction, is in evidence as she revisits her favorite books, her touchstones. As with Lionel Trilling, who was once her teacher, the foundations of her literary imagination are narrow and deep. Certain books recur in her critical writing. She would rather excel in the novel, yet there are fewer accomplished critics than there are novelists. In this, and this only, she resembles Jonathan Lethem, unresting, busy, a critic and theorist first, and of the first rank, his fiction a by-product. He "began writing," he says, "in order to arrive into the company of those whose company meant more to me than any other," which he does, in a crucial but ancillary genre. "I read in order to write," Ozick said, and as a reader she arrives in their company: "If the novel were to wither—if, say, it metamorphosed altogether into a species of journalism or movies, as many popular novels already have—then the last trustworthy vessel of the inner life (aside from our heads) would crumble away." A tremendous statement, it enjoins belief rather than agreement.

---

When Mrs. (Mary Augusta) Humphry Ward (1851–1920) tells of other writers, among them James, Meredith, and Barrie, in *A Writer's Recollections* (1918), it is generally to report what they thought of her, not to deliver her view of them: gratitude, not judgment. Similarly, her dislike of Wells and others hostile to her is personal. She opposed women's suffrage and, with that other industrious antisuffrage novelist Mrs. Oliphant, kept her otherwise lethargic, predominantly male family in style by her literary earnings, advertising in her writing name her marital status and subordination. She was not popular among other writers of her day, but she enjoyed a formidable presence in the marketplace. According to Arnold Bennett, Gladstone, "a thoroughly bad judge of literature, made her reputation, and not on a post card, either! Gladstone had no sense of humor—at any rate when he ventured into literature. Nor has Mrs. Humphry Ward. If she had she would not concoct those excruciating heroines of hers. She probably does not know that her heroines are capable of rousing temperaments such as my own to ecstasies of homicidal fury." His temperament is to be read in his afterthought, "Moreover, in literature all girls named Diana are insupportable."

Mrs. Ward's memoirs celebrate, more warmly than the facts justify, her friendship with "Beloved Henry James!" Her daughter as a child fell trustingly asleep in his arms. After she sent him each of her numerous books he wrote her a friendly letter and sometimes rose to a review. He noted how the huge and rapid success of *Robert Elsmere* (1888), the book by which she is best remembered, led to a significant alteration in how women writers were perceived and what was expected of them. The book's publication was "a momentous public event" and changed things in the marketplace for good. She earned £4,000 in royalties, a fortune in modern terms. For a later novel, *The History of David Grieve* (1892), she was paid £7,000 for American rights. The book, after the success of *Robert Elsmere*, bombed. In any case, in the decade following her first great success she earned a dozen times the first £4,000; had international copyright been in better working order, she would have been still richer from her American editions, but piracy picked her pocket along with many others.

Her success and that of other women writers, James says, is that "they have at last made the English novel speak their language." It is telling that James puts it this way round: he knows that women have effected a change in the idiom and form of the novel, and have not merely adapted to it. He emphasizes too how the new women novelists, like George Eliot before them, are characterized by *intellectual* rather than sentimental energy. *Robert Elsmere* is a tightly and neatly laden ship, full of "intellectual and moral experience."

She remembers learning of James's death. It was the thick of the First World War and she was in France. Theodore Roosevelt had suggested that a number of prominent English writers should travel to the Front to report their impressions, and her reports were later collected as *England's Effort*, a volume of informative propaganda. "We came down ready to start for the front, in a military motor, when our kind officer escort handed us some English telegrams which had just come in. One of them announced the death of Henry James," she writes, "and all through that wonderful day, when we watched a German counter-attack in the Ypres salient from one of the hills southeast of Poperinghe, the ruined tower of Ypres rising from the mists of the horizon, the news was intermittently with me as a dull pain, breaking in upon the excitement and novelty of the great spectacle around us."

She is the first Australian-born novelist to appear in this volume: Hobart, Tasmania, but she went to England when she was five and the antipodes left no mark on her. Family ties with England were strong: her grandfather was Thomas Arnold, the eminent Victorian headmaster of Rugby. Uncle Matt (Matthew Arnold) helped the family on its return. Her father Tom, Matt's elder brother, was a weak-spirited professor of literature, a weathervane of the Oxford Movement, converting to Roman Catholicism, losing his post in Australia, finding a post in England with difficulty, reconverting to Anglicanism, then re-reconverting to Catholicism. His wife only just tolerated his changes of faith, after the first one lobbing a brick through the window of a Catholic church in Hobart.

Mary was consigned to boarding school while her siblings remained at home. Her strong character (as she became famous, her reputation as a harridan was established in literary circles) may have led her parents to send her away lest she unsettle the quieter children. She returned in her late teens to Oxford, where her family had settled, and married before she was twenty-one. Humphry Ward, whose Mrs. she became, was not much of a catch. He had been neglected as a child, as Mary was. He managed to get to Oxford, where he was intimate (perhaps for a time very intimate) with Walter Pater, and after his marriage to Mary and his unsuccessful career as a journalist and art speculator, he and later their son depended on Mary's earnings.

She began with a children's book and wrote articles for *Macmillan's Magazine*. Her first novel, *Miss Bretherton* (1884), about an actress, was neither ambitious nor successful. But in a short time she became a best seller on both sides of the Atlantic. *Robert Elsmere* (1888), which tells of the intimate battle between the eponymous pastor and his wife over issues of faith and religious form (her parents' conflict providing the themes), she thought she could write in five months. It took three years to complete the 800-page novel, reduced from a draft of 1,358 pages. The concerns are spiritual in the way of the late nineteenth century: spiritual by argument and attempted proof. Heterodoxy made the book controversial. It was a period in which religious content sold books.

Beyond her novels she was interested in education. She played a role in establishing Somerville College, Oxford, and worked hard as an advocate of education for disabled children, a passion that provided her last great public triumph, lobbying Parliament to include physically disabled children in the 1918 Education Bill. But she became more Victorian as that age passed, and her antisuffrage stance was one of several causes she actively promoted. For Lytton Strachey she was a soft target, and he was happy to take potshots at her; Max Beerbohm dubbed her "Ma Hump."

Intellectual seriousness rather than novelistic qualities recommended her books. As the public issues were resolved, the interest of the novels receded, though what she achieved for women writers, even as she opposed voting rights of women at large, is indisputable. In her later years punitive tax laws and the demands of her husband and son ate into the fortune she had earned. She was compelled to rent out her London residence, where she had entertained James, and her country house as well. And her tenant? A novelist of quite a different stamp, expatriate Edith Wharton (1862–1937), the American writer who valued James most as writer and friend.

Like James, Wharton late in life wrote autobiography, in her case not self-exploratory but full of zest, anecdote, the adventure of having lived, especially in the years before the Great War, and the chanciness of her unplanned vocation. As in her long-chaptered essay *The Writing of Fiction* (1924), she is making a case, then for her kind of writing, later for her kind of living. *A Backward Glance* (1934) tells less than we would like, or indeed feel entitled, to know about the inner workings of the people whom she lived among and wrote about. In her friendship with James there is laughter, charming social awkwardness, but she approaches the writer in him only anecdotally. "The real marriage of true minds is for any two people to possess a sense of humor or irony pitched in exactly the same key, so that their joint glances at any subject cross like interarching searchlights." She has James in mind as "perhaps the most intimate friend I ever had, though in many ways we were so different." The texture of their lives, the accidents that threw them together, their fortune to have lived when they did, are lightly traced. Updike says she wrote lying in bed, shedding her pages (as old Verdi did his Requiem) on the floor, where her secretary harvested them and carried them off for transcription.

She was more comfortable in an intellectually and artistically too-bright society than James ever was. The social circles she moved in, in London and Paris, included American, British, French, and other European voices, a natural, easy, always polite cosmopolitanism and multilingualism; the names of Bourget, Daudet, Rodin, and Monet move as it were through the same rooms as James, Percy Lubbock, Mary Hunter, Theodore Roosevelt, and Madame de Fitz-James. Wharton was, simply, *at home.*

The memoir bears three epigraphs. The first, Whitman's "A backward glance o'er travell'd roads," is there both to source the title and to underline from the start her American origins. The second, from Chateaubriand's *Memoires d'outre tombe,* "Je veux remonter le penchant de mes belles années," states precisely her longing, more urgent than nostalgia, in an *entre deux guerres* ugly and mean with aftermath and premonition, once more to ascend the stairs of her best years. The third epigraph, from Goethe's *Wilhelm Meister,* establishes her intellectual bona fides and her Bergsonian sense of the durability of experiences: "Kein Genuss ist vorübergehend"—no pleasure is ephemeral, a seductive axiom, meaningful primarily for an imagination with the means to translate lived experience into art. We note the absence of a British epigraph: these markers establish a territory sufficient to the American expatriate.

When she was a shy, socially awkward girl and a reluctant debutante in New York, the family library contained her grandfather's books, the English and other classics, the bindings for the most part undisturbed. Writers did not frequent the prosperous Wharton home, apart from "Washington Irving, that charming hybrid on whom my parents' thoughts could dwell at ease, because, in spite of the disturbing fact that he 'wrote,' he was a gentleman, and a friend of the family." But other writers, my goodness, no. "Mrs. Beecher Stowe, who was so 'common' yet so successful," said Mrs. Wharton, without irony. "Success" itself was a kind of ostentation. The girl picked up these inflections and prejudices. When she began to write, she anatomized them. She developed a real interest in the essays of Sainte-Beuve.

The New York in which she grew up was in every feature remote from the city it was to become. She portrayed it as a "cramped horizontal gridiron of a town without towers, porticoes, fountains or perspectives, hide-bound in its deadly uniformity of mean ugliness." And so remote is it from the city she knew as an adult that it was like an imaginary world, coherent, consistent, and entirely lost, except to imagination. Things that had seemed repellent at the time are viewed with leniency, understood if not condoned. Had *The Age of Innocence* (1920) risked saga length, like Thomas Mann's *Buddenbrooks,* giving us the father, the son, the grandson, we might have witnessed the moral and cultural as well as the physical transformation in her American world.

Americans, Ozick reflects in an essay on Wharton, often seek and think they find in their lives the narrative coherence of a novel, shape in the trajectory between birth and where they are on their path to the other place. In Wharton, "despite certain disciplines, [life] was predicated on drift, and fell out, rather than fell into place." It was not defined by crises, it was "a setting all horizon," "a perpetual noncircumstance clear of external necessity." So much culture and amenity went into Wharton's life that one is put in mind of the beginning of *The Education of Henry Adams* when, on the ten pounds of the baby's flesh, all the forces of American history and privilege converge. Adams, and Wharton, would not have had it otherwise. This satisfaction with circumstances is neither smug nor complacent, but it may be one reason for the neglect of Wharton's work, Ozick notes, among feminist critics. Yet the way Wharton removed herself from the culture that shaped her, moved out of its gravitational field, was exemplary. "The publishing of *The Greater Inclination* broke the chains which had held me so long in a kind of torpor. For nearly twelve years I had tried to adjust myself to the life I had led since my marriage; but now I was overmastered by the longing to meet people who shared my interests." Placing the word *overmastered* after, and in such close proximity to, the word *marriage* suggests the intensity of nonconforming desire: art is a kind of infidelity to class, to marriage: fiction as a first, intense adultery. This is the reader's experience of it—Madame de Renal, Madame Bovary. It took Wharton that way.

After the years of formation, the emergence of the writer of fiction, came a period of creativity, then after-years when it became easy, she prospered, and the work settled into convention. Wharton was formed and, the memoir makes clear, remained at heart pre–World War I. Her efforts for the war-wounded in France, inspired by Whitman's activity in the American Civil War, were noble, but they did not find a place in her major fiction. Though James predeceased her by two decades, he goes deeper into the twentieth century than she could and remains contemporary in ways she cannot.

Both writers in their maturity responded to Proust. As soon as Wharton read the first volume of *À la recherche du temps perdu*, she sent a copy to James, "and his letter to me shows how deeply it impressed him." His judgment "had long been hampered by his increasing preoccupation with the structure of the novel, and his unwillingness to concede that the vital centre (when there was any) could lie elsewhere." He had always been an abstemious reader of contemporary English fiction—exceptions including H. G. Wells, with whom he had a vexed friendship, and Conrad—and he could hardly hide his impatience with them: "As time passed, and intricate problems of form and structure engrossed him more deeply, it became almost impossible to persuade him that there might be merit in the work of writers apparently insensible to these sterner demands of the art." But, she declares, "he seized upon *Du côté de chez Swann* (1913) and devoured it in a passion of curiosity and admiration. Here, in the first volume of a long chronicle-novel—the very type of the unrolling tapestry which was so contrary to his own conception of form," and this very contrariety is what detained him, "he instantly recognized a new mastery, a new vision, and a structural design as yet unintelligible to him, but as surely there as hard bone under soft flesh in a living organism." It was a triumph to have insinuated such a radical presence into Lamb House. "I look back with peculiar pleasure at having made Proust known to James, for the encounter gave him his last, and one of his strongest, artistic emotions."

In *The Writing of Fiction* Wharton knew that the tide had turned not only against her but against all that she most loved in literature. She had to distinguish among the moderns between those who belonged in the central tradition, *her* tradition, and those who did not. She devotes the whole concluding portion of *The Writing of Fiction* to Marcel Proust (1871–1922). The book was published two years after Proust's death when *À la recherche* was not yet published in full. Proust was nine years her junior and had been used by younger writers as a stick with which to beat nineteenth-century relics like herself. Her essay, written when she was seventy, is counterattack, reclamation, and vindication. Proust is in the central French tradition of Stendhal and Balzac. He is not different in kind; on the contrary, his social world, his concerns and themes, and his very structural principles are a development of, rather than a break with, what came before. She asserts this even before the work was published in full. The long years between the beginning of publication, with *Du côté de chez Swann,* and the later books reminded her more of Balzac's steady world-making than of the work of the moderns, fragmentary, achieving accelerated effects. Even from where she stood she could insist that Proust was not an innovator but "that far more substantial thing in the world of art, a renovator." He develops "without disowning the past"—this is her chief concern, to show Proust as part of a living and still-viable continuum. In her sense he was; in another he was not.

Nabokov sees Proust's work as playful—seriously so, but teasing: "The whole"—and he had the benefit of the whole—"is a treasure hunt where the treasure is time and the hiding place the past." Proust's passion and love of material abundance contrast sharply with his indirectness; he speaks rationally and expansively and at the same time conceals; he takes a strong moral tone and yet there is what Wharton must have recognized as a not so very modern depravity about the project. When she first read him, Wharton had, in fact, resisted Proust. Now her strategy was to splice him onto the family tree that included Balzac and Thackeray along with their ancestry and issue. She admired the narrowed, closely focused range of "his social admirations" and saw in him the ironic dazzlement at "contact with the very society" he anatomized and satirized. She never tried to meet him: she did not like what she had heard of the man. But she could not forgive herself for not having addressed a letter to him. "Proust is in truth the aware and eager inheritor of two great formulas: that of Racine in his psychology, that of Saint-Simon in its anecdotic and discursive illustration. In both respects he is deliberately traditional."

Proust's characters are wholly alive. Wharton directs us to the scene in volume 5 when Swann tells the Duchesse that he may not be able to accompany her and the Duke on holiday next year because he is dying; she is on her way to a party and has no way of responding to this news; she is surprised at his bad manners in choosing such a time to tell her his unwelcome information. Wharton also dwells on *petit Marcel*'s grandmother, her rushing out to walk alone in the rain at the start, and later her slow and detailed death, watched over by Françoise; also Saint-Loup and Rachel, and the Baron; the Wagnerian effect, they all live to such a degree that "each time they reappear (sometimes after disconcertingly long eclipses), they take up their individual rhythm as unerringly as the performers in some great orchestra!" Proust establishes trust in the narrator's voice: first the child, and then, in part because of the credible child, the adult. He possesses the "power to reveal, by a single allusion, a word, an image, those depths of soul beyond the soul's own guessing."

There are in Proust "defects in the moral sensibility, that tuning-fork of the novelist's art." She was speaking not of his sexuality but of something more crucial. The evidence for this defect is in how occasionally characters step out of character to eavesdrop, to do something untoward in the service of the narrative. Characters lose their *"probableness"* and move like actors trying to make sense of a faulty play. This was magnified in the work of hostile younger writers. "It is as much the lack of general culture as of original vision which makes so many of the younger novelists, in Europe as in America, attach undue importance to trifling innovations."

What troubled her in younger writers was that they were ready to abandon form as she and the French novelists before her conceived it. Form is "the order, in time and importance, in which the incidents of the narrative are grouped; and style is the way in which they are presented, not only in the narrower sense of language, but also, and rather, as they are grasped and colored by their medium, the narrator's mind, and given back in words." She disliked "the present quest for short-cuts in art," such as stream of consciousness, that facile experiment that "contains its own condemnation, since every attempt to employ it of necessity involves selection, and selection in the long run must eventually lead to the transposition, the 'stylization,' of the subject." In *À l'ombre des jeunes filles en fleurs* (1919) Proust evokes the (fictional) novelist Bergotte who "analyses the art of fiction." He is after gauged effect: *"C'est doux."* For Wharton this means harmonious, sweet as a dunked tea biscuit and, we might add, proportionate. A serious novelist, she says, "will never do his best till he ceases altogether to think of his readers (and his editor and his publisher) and begins to write, not for himself but for that *other self* with whom the creative artist is always in mysterious correspondence, and who, happily, has an objective existence somewhere, and will some day receive the message sent to him, though the sender may never know it." That *other self* in this definition must be posterity.

The world of fiction is insistently concrete; writers have not (until Ivy Compton-Burnett, and not really even there) returned to the abstractions of the eighteenth century, its unity, its concern with the substance and not the accidents of experience. Thus, "the great, the distinguishing gift of the English novelist was a homely simplicity combined with an observation at once keen and indulgent; good humor was the atmosphere and irony the flavor of this great school of observers, from Fielding to George Eliot." In such fiction the writer refrains from saying some things, for fear of offending the reader, and therefore allows reception to determine (censor) the thematic and verbal limits of a book. Such self-censorship was no less than a "reaction against truth." "But for this reaction against truth, this sudden fear of touching on any of the real issues of the human comedy and tragedy," Thackeray might have been great, Trollope might have vied with Austen, and George Eliot more a novelist and less a teacher.

There was also the insistence on the centrality of *plot,* and this irritated Wharton. Her novels have often inevitable progression and incident, but they are not constrained, as Dickens's and Trollope's are, by a mechanical narrative patterning. Stendhal and Tolstoy and Balzac set out "to see life whole"; they "took the English novel of manners in its amplitude, its merriment and pathos, and in their hands 'the thing became a trumpet.'"

Wharton wants literary history to be orderly. Her book is schematic, and though she chides the taxonomists who classify literature, she provides various phyla, classes, and orders of her own. In particular she regards the subjective writer, whose works are autobiographical however they package themselves, as lacking the "objective" faculty crucial to the novelist. The link between the real novel and the autobiography done up as a novel is Goethe's *Werther,* a book she valued from the no-man's-land between fiction and life writing. But she was a child of the French nineteenth century. Edmund Wilson answers critics who object to the material solidity of her world by saying she is more New York than Balzac is Paris or Thackeray London. Her worlds are real so that *The Age of Innocence* (1920, for which she won the Pulitzer Prize for the Novel, the first woman to do so) is the "severest of American novels," exposing the corrosive power of respectability by grounding it firmly in "the real." Newland Archer and May Welland announce their engagement and pay a visit to the Welland family matriarch, Mrs. Manson Mingott, whom we meet in a cruelly familiar description, not without an affectionate recognition of her "once upon a time":

> The immense accretion of flesh which had descended on her in middle life like a flood of lava on a doomed city had changed her from a plump active little woman with a neatly-turned foot and ankle into something as vast and august as a natural phenomenon. She had accepted this submergence as philosophically as all her other trials, and now, in extreme old age, was rewarded by presenting to her mirror an almost unwrinkled expanse of firm pink and white flesh, in the centre of which the traces of a small face survived as if awaiting excavation. A flight of smooth double chins led down to the dizzy depths of a still-snowy bosom veiled in snowy muslins that were held in place by a miniature portrait of the late Mr. Mingott; and around and below, wave after wave of black silk surged

away over the edges of a capacious armchair, with two tiny white
hands poised like gulls on the surface of the billows.

The flight of double chins would have been brilliant; the addition of the adjective "smooth" gives them a texture at once marmoreal and fleshly, the metaphorical and the literal elements existing in an illuminating, incongruous tension. This is followed by a paragraph in which we, as readers, are addressed as
"you" and brought as close to the actors as if we were, not in the front row of
the theater, but on the stage. Her use of dramatic irony often takes this form.
"The burden of Mrs. Manson Mingott's flesh had long since made it impossible
for her to go up and down stairs, and with characteristic independence she had
made her reception rooms upstairs and established herself (in flagrant violation
of all the New York proprieties) on the ground floor of her house; so that, as you
sat in her sitting-room window with her, you caught (through a door that was
always open, and a looped-back yellow damask portière) the unexpected vista of
a bedroom with a huge low bed upholstered like a sofa, and a toilet-table with
frivolous lace flounces and a gilt-framed mirror."

When later May's cousin Madame Olenska moves to her little, almost unre-
spectable house beyond the neighborhoods of propriety, we have another vision
from within, as it were, again in Welland's company, and see through the material surroundings all the moral perils among which that remarkable protagonist
has allowed herself to wander, drawing admirers in her wake. Wharton's early
"technical" writings had been gathered in *The Decoration of Houses* (1897), a book
she wrote with a collaborator, and the illustrated *Italian Villas and Their Gardens*
(1904). This knowledge fed into her use of metaphor and her sense of spatial relations, internal décor, and settings.

The world of women, too, she creates with tact in the first paragraphs of
the novel: the son privileged by his widowed mother and sister, who squeeze
in, in order to give him space. "In an unclouded harmony of tastes and interests they cultivated ferns in Wardian cases, made macramé lace and wool
embroidery on linen, collected American revolutionary glazed ware, subscribed to *Good Words*, and read Ouida's novels for the sake of the Italian atmosphere." Polite, right down to Ouida. In parentheses, Wharton adds, to
clarify their literary taste and their social views, "(They preferred those [nov-
els] about peasant life, because of the descriptions of scenery and the pleas-
anter sentiments, though in general they liked novels about people in society,
whose motives and habits were more comprehensible, spoke severely of
Dickens, who 'had never drawn a gentleman,' and considered Thackeray less
at home in the great world than Bulwer–who, however, was beginning to be
thought old-fashioned.)"

Fifteen years earlier she had written *The House of Mirth* (1905), a merciless account of the suffocating tyranny of the old Knickerbocker culture in which she grew up, its values, and those of the new unprincipled millionaires buying a spurious legitimacy. New money looks brashest when it is trying to establish itself in a ceremonious and stately context. Beauty—the irresistible, unconventional beauty of Lily Bart—is time-sensitive and gossip-sensitive; the goods are gawped at, handled, and each time devalued, yet Lily in her tragic end is a lady in the old sense, having found high principle in an excess of the material poverty she and her class most fear. And the protagonist Selden, who might have rescued her? Wharton knows him to be of a sexually indeterminate nature without needing to say "he is not the marrying kind." Some readers find him inadequate as a balance to Lily and treacherous in his seeming desertion of her in her need, but there is a deep realism in Wharton as in James, an instinct about the (unstated) sexual compatibility of characters. Wharton in her formative years as a writer had suffered intense friendships with men of this cast, one in particular. She knew the things these friendships could provide, and where they stopped.

Virginia Woolf reviewed the book early in her critical career, recognizing familiar elements in the community of the novel, bound together by its wealth but also by something Woolf found in her own culture, quoting Wharton: "a force of negation which eliminated everything beyond their own range of perception." These "affinities" connect and isolate characters; here are "the elect" as much as among the Puritans, only now defined by lineage and possession, "a curiously cold and vicious society." That coldness and viciousness had helped to destroy the mind of Wharton's husband, a "real gentleman" from an established Boston family, whom she married in 1885. Edward Robbins Wharton was devoted and openhanded to his "Pussy," carrying always a $1,000 bill in case she wanted anything. He grew subject to depressions, which confined them, and later him, to their now-famous house The Mount, which they built in 1902 between Stockbridge and Lennox, Massachusetts, with its white façade and "a little gray cupola with a weather-vane," alluding to rather than imitating the features of a French chateau, in one of which she would end her days. Now restored, The Mount is a record of her taste and subtlety as a designer. It remained her primary residence until 1912. There she wrote *The House of Mirth,* much of *Madame de Treymes* (1907), and other fiction. There too she entertained, when her husband no longer traveled: people came to her. By 1908 Edward Wharton was beyond help, and they divorced in 1913. By then Edith had an intimate companion, a journalist with whom she had much in common intellectually.

Her connections in France meant that when the war began she could travel to the front and see what was going on. She wrote articles collected in *Fighting*

*France: From Dunkerque to Belfort*. For her relief work she was made a Chevalier of the Légion d'honneur. After the war she left Paris for Provence, and there she rediscovered her roots in *The Age of Innocence*. In 1923 she returned to the United States to receive an honorary degree at Yale. That was her last visit home. She finished her life fourteen years later in Hyères, in the far south of Provence. The journalist Ned Winsted, Welland Archer's friend in *The Age of Innocence* and a man based in part on Wharton's companion, voices a quandary that was real for her, for James and Howells, and perhaps for Irving, Hawthorne, and Melville before them. Speaking as an American he exclaims: "Culture! Yes—if we had it! But there are just a few little local patches, dying out here and there for lack of—well, hoeing and cross-fertilising: the last remnants of the old European tradition that your forebears brought with them." What to do? "But you're in a pitiful little minority: you've got no centre, no competition, no audience. You're like the pictures on the walls of a deserted house: *The Portrait of a Gentleman*. You'll never amount to anything, any of you," not until "you roll up your sleeves and get right down into the muck. That, or emigrate . . . God! If I could emigrate."

The one novel in which she gets "right down in the muck" is *Ethan Frome* (1911), her most outright American book, much loved at one time by the American educational establishment—we certainly read it at school in the early 1960s. Mencken calls it "brave and tragic," "so rare as to be almost singular." In subject it is her most radical novel, working against her grain. "In the arts, as in the concerns of everyday, the American seeks escape from the insoluble by pretending that it is solved. A comfortable phrase is what he craves beyond all things," and *Ethan Frome* is a bleak and uncomfortable book. However dramatic its ironies, it lacks humor. She came to resent its success because it seemed to devalue her characteristic work, just as Henry James was vexed by the success of *Daisy Miller*.

There is less affinity between Wharton's and James's novels than one might expect. Despite their regard for one another, they admire those of each other's works that most resembled their own. As James became more nuanced, less descriptive, more insistent on the present and real time, Wharton's concerns with detail became more defined, her sense of past period and place fuller, more documentary. She resisted abstraction; her characters are not types but defined with particularity. It is to them we look, not to ourselves in them. Stylistically, too, her writing makes lighter demands and the pace of her mature work is brisker than James's. In technique and manner, there is more in common between her and George Eliot than James.

Yet Wharton speaks not only for herself. "The truth is that [James] belonged irrevocably to the old America out of which I also came, and of which—

almost—it might paradoxically be said that to follow up its last traces one had to come to Europe." Why did neither of them go home, or rather, why did home become Europe? The writing that was on the American wall before World War I caused James to change nationality and Wharton to become a French patriot. She reflects in a late essay, "One is sometimes tempted to think that the generation which has invented the 'fiction course' is getting the fiction it deserves. At any rate it is fostering in its young writers the conviction that art is neither long nor arduous, and perhaps blinding them to the fact that notoriety and mediocrity are often interchangeable terms." In such a culture there was no place for what she did or who she was.

———·———

Edith Wharton's pleasure upon receiving the Pulitzer Prize in 1921 for *The Age of Innocence* was checked when she learned that the judges had voted to give the award to *Main Street* by the young Sinclair Lewis (1885–1951; though it was his eighth work, he was only thirty-six). Columbia University's advisory board had overridden the judges' choice (Lewis's book was not "wholesome" enough) and given her the prize because *The Age of Innocence* revealed the "wholesome atmosphere of American life and the highest standard of American manners and manhood." Lewis, an admirer of Wharton, wrote to congratulate her. "When I discovered that I was being rewarded—by one of our leading Universities—for uplifting American morals, I confess I did despair," she replied: had they actually understood the book at all? Lewis's letter reassured her, "the first sign I have ever had—literally—that 'les Jeunes' at home had ever read a word of me . . . Some sort of standard *is* emerging from the welter of cant & sentimentality, & if two or three of us are gathered together, I believe we can still save Fiction in America." To this pious sentiment she added an invitation to Lewis to visit her in France with his wife. After that visit Lewis asked if he could dedicate his novel *Babbitt* to her. "No one has ever wanted to dedicate a book to me before—& I'm so particularly glad that now it's happened, the suggestion comes from the author of *Main Street*." In 1923 the Pulitzer judges chose *Babbitt* but again the trustees refused, and Willa Cather's "wholesome" war novel *One of Ours* prevailed. At last, in 1925, when the judges chose *Arrowsmith* and the trustees reluctantly concurred, Lewis turned the prize down on the grounds that it rewarded boosterish books, propaganda for America and the American way of life, and his book was not in that category.

Wharton and Lewis drifted apart, but for a time the expatriate and the determined native, who saw the American dream with such nightmare clarity, made common cause. Despite his thematic novelty, Lewis belonged to the mainstream as she saw it, though he belonged also to something new and transformative. When he was awarded the Nobel Prize in Literature five years after *Arrowsmith,* the first American to be thus honored, he was forty-five and he knew that his best work was behind him. Already with *Dodsworth* (1929) he sensed that he was losing control. Still, he had a case to make and scores to settle. In his Nobel lecture, "The American Fear of Literature," he characterizes the kinds of readers he was up against, though he does not enumerate the death threats he received after the publication of *Main Street* nor does he quantify its enormous success, 2 million copies sold in two editions, a quarter of a million words written in fourteen weeks, 30,000 discarded at the beginning. The novelist John Hersey, who was for a time his amanuensis, was shocked at how much Lewis was willing to excise from a book, not least because Lewis was a two-finger typist and on the old manual typewriters the percussive pressure hurt his fingers. He taped up his fingers and kept on doggedly typing.

Lewis's nickname, "Red," was less for his politics than for his ginger hair and rosy complexion. His chief political contribution is in capturing the diction and the emphatic, bullying philistinism of a culture that wore down and defeated certain kinds of innocence. He was a skilled mimic but sometimes went too far and on too long. Frederick Raphael notes, "Babbittry entered the American language as the style of salesmanship and humbug to which John Updike surely paid rhyming tribute in his creation 'Rabbit' Angstrom, a salesman in the Lewis tradition."

Lewis spared his Nobel audience in Stockholm the whole story of his struggle: "Now and then I have, for my books or myself, been somewhat warmly denounced." But he does concede, "There was one good pastor in California who upon reading my *Elmer Gantry* desired to lead a mob and lynch me, while another holy man in the state of Maine wondered if there was no respectable and righteous way of putting me in jail." He comes from a country in which "most of us—not readers alone but even writers—are still afraid of any literature which is not a glorification of everything American, a glorification of our faults as well as our virtues." That phrase "even writers" is gentle to the older generation; "in our contemporary American literature, indeed in all American arts save architecture and the film, we . . . have no standards, no healing communication, no heroes to be followed nor villains to be condemned, no certain ways to be pursued, and no dangerous paths to be avoided." In *Travels with Charley* John Steinbeck, who revered Lewis, reflects on how he was hounded out of Sauk Centre, Minnesota. There Lewis was born and bred. It was the prototype for Gopher Prairie and Elk Mills, and it might aspire in the emptiness of time to become like Zenith where Babbitt lived. Midwestern towns pass through different stages in their inexorable, leveling evolution. A decade after his death Sauk Centre boasted on a road sign that Lewis was born there, but in town, Steinbeck discovered, the young people had no idea who he was.

"One may safely class him with writers termed 'advanced,'" E. M. Forster wrote, "with people who prefer truth to comfort, passion to stability, prevention to cure." He compares him with Wells, describing them as photographers, snapshot takers. "They have just the same gift of hitting off a person or place in a few quick words; moreover, they share the same indifference to poetry, and pass much the same judgments on conduct." Their talents took them in different directions. With Lewis we follow his eye, not his voice, and we come away less with a sense of his social criticism than of the society he criticizes. His sentences are, in an old-fashioned, Whartonian way, often—beautiful. In *Main Street* the drabness comes alive as Carol Endicott walks along it; Erik Valborg seduces us as he seduces her. Edmund Wilson places the book next door to *Madame Bovary.*

He wanted to "lodge a piece of the continent in the world's imagination," Forster said of *Main Street,* to portray a nation in its human complexity, including the concerns of women, black people, the neglected. He was a committed researcher into people and places: he lived among them, taking notes, assembling evidence with forensic care. Imagination came into play after the facts were understood. Rebecca West noted that he gave himself no leisure; he was so busy looking and noting that he read little to set a standard; after 1929 he skittered and was no longer able to "give his genius a chance." Yet there are the major novels before decline set in with *Dodsworth* in 1929, when the scene moves to Europe and Lewis enters a territory that James and Wharton inhabited naturally but he could not. His self-doubts and loneliness drove him deep into alcoholism. None of the eleven novels he wrote between 1929 and his death was of a standard with his great books—*Main Street* (1920) in which he found his feet decisively, *Babbitt* (1922), and *Elmer Gantry* (1927).

Though his fiction is not self-reflexive, Lewis does have scores to settle, and he settles them. As a boy he was badly bullied, and he ran away from home at thirteen to go serve as a drummer in the Spanish-American War. He did not get beyond the train station. He began keeping a diary. He did well enough at school to go to Yale and begin publishing his writings. At Yale he was bullied, an ugly boy from Minnesota with chips on his shoulder. The bullying his protagonists suffer, both from malevolent individuals and as a result of a leveling pressure in society, he understood. Elmer Gantry and George Babbitt are two of the great bullies in literature, and they thrive: natural selection obeys no moral imperative, the good and the fittest are seldom the same. He has what Wharton describes as "the objective faculty" in extreme form.

Lewis's fiction can be rearranged and read in an unfolding chronology like the Leatherstocking novels, providing a vivid picture of the rapidly evolving and eroding world he portrays. From the struggle of settlers to the drab comforts of Main Street ("the climax of civilization") little more than half a century passes, a kind of sequel to the accelerations Mark Twain witnessed with astonished unease. And like Twain, Lewis, earnest in theme, is a great entertainer because he writes uncompromisingly about this world of dead-end promise, the American dream from which Carol Kennicott or George F. Babbitt and Martin Arrowsmith struggle to wake, and which Elmer Gantry understands and plausibly manipulates.

Lewis represents the culmination of a current in the tradition Wharton celebrates. Proust is another, stronger current that flowed and still flows directly into English fiction and the literatures of Europe and the Americas. His presence, given his snobbery, his methods, his languor, seems to empower many of the formal revolutions of the twentieth century. Because Proust's narrating voice is so defined and self-involved, it is not the teller that engages writers but the ways of telling. By 1937 Cyril Connolly could declare, "The greatest Mandarin was Proust who has become so familiar as almost to rank as an English writer." Thanks to the C. K. Scott Moncrieff translations (published between 1922 and 1930), since revised and but never quite displaced by others, Proust was as good as Anglophone. Had he not learned some of his profound lessons from John Ruskin? Connolly adds, "He was modern enough to attack the values of this world but he had nothing to put in their place, for their values were his own, those of the narrator of the book who spends his life in going to parties and watching snobs behave but is never a snob himself." But he is, always, in choice of parties, of clothes, in his insistence on old and new class and money. Patrick Bateman in *American Psycho* is merely a perversion of little Marcel, a stickler for brand names and propriety, but with the addition of the sharpened coat hanger, nail gun, mace can, and chainsaw.

Proust cannot see beyond, but he can see what is actually there. Unlike André Gide (1869–1951) and other near contemporaries in France, his artistic intentions were not didactic or ideological, though his sensibility is rooted in a profound conservatism of a kind in which few readers willingly collude. The snobbish incongruity of his social values means that we take them as a given, as we do the social order in an Austen novel, not an element we must argue with. Here we focus on the narrow, luminously real social world that fuels the narrator's politics; individual memory comes alive in its own terms. If we question those terms, the spirits the author conjures will vanish. "But when from a long-distant past nothing subsists, after the people are dead, after the things are broken and scattered, still, alone, more fragile, but with more vitality, more unsubstantial, more persistent, more faithful, the smell and taste of things remain poised a long time, like souls," the very souls he has shown us ensnared in a tree, an object, waiting to be freed like Ariel or Sycorax, to come back and travel with us; "ready to remind us, waiting and hoping for their moment, amid the ruins of all the rest; and bear unfaltering, in the tiny and almost impalpable drop of their essence, the vast structure of recollection." And more than recollection.

The reflective precision of the writing includes each tone and inflection of feeling. There is the prurient coming-of-age comedy of little Marcel waiting to see "whether the unlikely insect"—a bee he wanted to observe—"would come, by a providential hazard, to visit the offered and neglected pistil," witnessing as well a paunchy, aging Baron de Charlus, distracted on his way from visiting the ailing Mme. de Villeparisis by Jupien, the ex-tailor, conduct a similar, strange ritual, an elaborate, flirtatious dos-y-dos, before vanishing for some furtive pleasure. "At the same instant as M. de Charlus disappeared through the gate humming like a great bumble-bee, another, a real one this time, flew into the courtyard." Charlus returns, and little Marcel loses both the bee and his human quarry at the same time. There is the fragile world of little Marcel and his grandmother; the tense, brilliant world of Swann and his harrowing by Odette, the maturing of aristocratic Robert de Saint-Loup, to whom the young Marcel becomes intensely attached, and whose relations with Gilberte contrast with those of Swann and Odette and—to come—Marcel and Albertine. There are the brilliant essayistic pages in which painting, writing, and music are considered through the figures of Elstir, Bergotte, and Vinteuil, and throughout the theme of love in all its variations, and memory with its treacheries, its lacunae and falsifications. (One of the last notes that Proust dictated, "There is a Chinese patience in Vermeer's craft," recalls Marcel's favorite painting, *A View of Delft,* which like his novel configures itself around any point on which one chooses to focus.)

Harold Pinter's *The Proust Screenplay* (1978), a précis of the novel, is a kind of magic flower that, beginning as a little rectangle of paper, draws shape and color out of the element of memory and by capillary action expands into "all the flowers in our garden and in M. Swann's park, and the water-lilies on the Vivonne and the good folk of the village and their little dwellings and the parish church and the whole of Combray and its surroundings," and the world of Swann and much (everything) else besides. Just as in *A Portrait of the Artist as a Young Man* Joyce shows the growth of an imagination through the evolution of an individual's language, so in *À la recherche* Proust shows a man coming into full possession of himself through recovering the fullness of his experience, which entails so many congruent and incongruous experiences and lives.

Some English novelists try to play variations on Proust's form. Dorothy Richardson (1873–1957) in *Pilgrimage,* her magnum opus, had reached 2,000 pages when Graham Greene wrote about it in 1935, "I should imagine Miss Richardson in her ponderous unwitty way has had an immense influence on such writers as Mrs. Woolf and Miss Stein, and through them on her disciples." The second paragraph of her first volume opens, "Her new Saratoga trunk stood solid and gleaming in the firelight. To-morrow it would be taken away and she would be gone. The room would be altogether Harriett's. It would never have its old look again." Four "would" constructions so early in a fiction might seem exhaustively proleptic. Her style as she wrote on became less awkward, less abundant, more austere, over twelve volumes: had she gone back and revised, the book might have been shorter and more readable, but it would have lost its process, the learning curve that is also its theme. It is Proustian in scale, but circumstantial, with Miriam, Richardson's little Marcel, doing this, doing that, events forming a long chain of—inconsequence. The project was radical in conception but the passage of time rendered it laborious. The stream of consciousness, Greene suggests, had passed its sell-by date, and though the escape from the tyranny of plot into the sea of subjectivity was at first refreshing, it drowned any author too long immersed in it. And so, Green says, "we are turning back with relief to the old dictatorship, to the detached and objective treatment."

Another English writer often called Proustian is Anthony Powell (1905–2000). His twelve-volume *A Dance to the Music of Time,* the title borrowed from one of Nicolas Poussin's most beautiful and suggestive canvases, was published between 1951 and 1975. The repetitive theme is the interplay between privileged people and the bohemian set that exploits and seasons them. Powell, an old Etonian who came from landed gentry and married into the aristocracy, was more at home in the world he portrayed than Proust had been in his; a sense of entitlement and his connections took him far, and after the relative failure of his early freestanding novels the relative and prolonged success (*d'estime,* if never *fou*) was welcome. He was praised by his friends, including Evelyn Waugh and Kingsley Amis, revered by some younger writers, including A. N. Wilson, and reviled by others, Auberon Waugh among them, as "tedious and overpraised," a litmus test of affectation. Before he was well established, Edmund Wilson wrote of him: "A watered-down British Proust, the Proustian observations on human life are largely unsuccessful." He was "far from profound or poetic," and—something that struck those of us who read first one or another of his four volumes of autobiography (I came in with *Messengers of Day* in 1978)—"these books are full of bad writing and even bad grammar." Edmund Wilson mildly enjoyed the "lightweight comedy" of earlier volumes, but unlike Powell's friend Evelyn Waugh, and unlike Angus Wilson, "he has no literary importance whatever." The judgment is harsh and does not quite dispose of Powell. He was always irritated to be compared with Proust because it denied him credit for originality. In an interview he conceded, "I'm a great admirer of Proust and know his works very well. But the essential difference," style and form and genius apart, we want to interject, "is that Proust is an enormously subjective writer who has a peculiar genius for describing how he or his narrator feels. Well, I really tell people a minimum of what my narrator feels—just enough to keep the narrative going—because I have no talent for that particular sort of self-revelation." This, on the face of it, seems to be Christopher Isherwood territory, the "I" as camera, but Isherwood is less conservative and formally more astute and adventurous. Also in his early writing he has a wider scene, more to reveal and to encode.

Like James's, Proust's effect is, at its most potent, less on structure and style than on ways of seeing, of refiguring the past and through it the present. He teaches, to borrow the Irish poet Eavan Boland's phrase, "object lessons," and this has been of special importance to women, gay, and postcolonial writers, trying to read away from conventional valuations, to see in ways that penetrate a thing or theme without pre-seeing, pre-reading, pre-speaking. Nadine Gordimer is one such debtor: "Proust has been an influence on me, all my life—an influence so deep it frightens me . . . not only in my writing, but in my attitudes to life." More specific is Edna O'Brien: "Proust's influence on me, along with his genius, was his preoccupation with memory and his obsession with the past. His concentration on even the simplest detail—like one petal of a flower, or the design on a dinner plate—has unique, manic intensity." She puts him in company with Joyce: "Joyce and Proust, although very different, broke the old mould by recognizing the importance of the rambling, disjointed nature of what goes on in the head, the interior monologue. I wonder how they would fare now. These are more careless times."

Proust and Powell are novel sequence or series writers, and in the first half of the twentieth century there was something of a vogue for writing in this extending form that made it possible to consider the great transformations wrought by one or two world wars, the end of innocence, the birth of new kinds of modernity. Readers were expected to buy into the series as into a serial, though the novels also aspired to be freestanding. Some of the best writing of the period, and some of the worst, is lost and found in these expansive works.

Henry (William) Williamson (1895–1977) is best remembered for *Tarka the Otter* (1927), best forgotten for his politics. After the First World War, where he rose to lieutenant in the Machine Gun Corps and experienced the Christmas truce of 1914 when German and British troops sang "Silent Night, Holy Night," renewing battle the next day, an irony that told so bitterly on the conflict that he regarded it as a mission to work after the war to heal the breach between England (his England was rural, epitomized by Devon and a West Country unstained by industry and the depredations of capitalism) and Germany. In 1935 he attended the National Socialist Congress in Nuremberg (one of the "key dates" omitted from the Henry Williamson Society on its website). He revered Hitler, admired the Hitler Youth with the nostalgia of a born-again Boy Scout, and joined Sir Oswald Mosley's British Union of Fascists. He never quite lost his admiration for the Führer or his belief that history, or History, took a wrong turning when Germany signed the Instruments of Surrender in 1945.

He became a writer after the First World War, moved by Richard Jeffries's *The Story of My Heart,* which turned his mind to memoir and to fiction. In his rural tetralogy *The Flax of Dreams* (1921–1928), his account of the protagonist Willie Maddison draws on his own life. Already the sense of identification with the land, the literal soil of the West Country, is established, the atavism that precedes and underpins the politics that were to follow. The fifteen-volume *A Chronicle of Ancient Sunlight* (1951–1969), a fictional autobiography, is his little-read magnum opus, the story of Phillip Maddison. It redeploys material from the tetralogy, seeing it from a later perspective. *The Gale of the World* (1969), melodramatic and epically self-indulgent, concludes with the protagonist on the brink of starting his fifteen-volume *Chronicle.* He "has been untouched by the spirit of modernity," Anthony Burgess remarks: given the scale and scope of his major work and its deliberate circularity, this is not quite true. Those who advocate Williamson feel they must somehow exonerate him of his political views. Better to acknowledge them: they were not naively held, and his apologists do him a disservice by patronizing him. They are complex views, they have a historical and a Spenglerian philosophical context, and they underpin his vision of the world quite as much as Roman Catholicism underpins Waugh's, Greene's, and Burgess's, Marxism Edward Upward's, or a particular view of the South Faulkner's. Take them away and you have just another nature writer. His politics are a problem, but the real problem is an overbearing egotism. No matter how clearly he sees or shows, he always interposes his presence, he never stands back and lets the beloved landscape have its own say.

He took great pains with *Tarka,* redrafting it (by his own count) seventeen times. His novel sequences give the impression of lyric potency: his hands are rough from the soil, his eyes reflect the ancient sunlight. Ted Hughes delivered the address at his funeral: clearly Williamson spoke directly to the nature writer and eco-critic. He is fervent, and that outweighs, for readers who stay with him, much that repels. There but for the grace of God goes D. H. Lawrence, a sexual and sensual man whose landscape was sufficiently marred by industry to frustrate idealization and atavism.

The least sentimental and atavistic British novelist of the period was C. P. (Charles Percy) Snow (1905–1980), Baron Snow of the City of Leicester (he liked to be introduced by his title), who also wrote a substantial novel sequence, the eleven volumes of *Strangers and Brothers* (1940–1970), an appropriate work for a

biographer of Trollope, which he was (1975). The novelist J. G. Ballard remembers the deadening impact of Powell and Snow in that "heyday of the naturalistic novel" on emerging writers: "I felt that maybe the novel had shot its bolt, that
it was stagnating right across the board. The bourgeois novels, the so-called
'Hampstead novels' seemed to dominate everything." In 1978 Snow published a
series of essays entitled *The Realists,* a term he applied variously to Stendhal, Balzac, Dickens, Dostoyevsky, Tolstoy, Benito Pérez Galdos, James, and Proust. The
purpose was to situate himself in a succession of major writers.

There is no dance or music to speak of in *Strangers and Brothers.* Inexorable
time is historical; each book sets out to tell a truth about the age. The conceit
is that we are reading the autobiography of Lewis (later Sir Lewis) Eliot, a scion
of the working-class Midlands (Snow himself was born in Leicester, second of
four brothers, in relatively modest circumstances, and went on to the University
of Leicester and then to Cambridge, where in 1930 he became a Fellow of Christ's
College). The world of provincial brothers is contrasted with the world of strangers into which Lewis goes to make his life. He becomes a barrister; he is widowed and bereft of his closest friend by the war. Lecturing at Cambridge he experiences academic politics *(The Masters).* He loves again, marries again, gets
involved in developing nuclear "defensive" weapons, and suffers crises of conscience. He paces the *Corridors of Power* (1964); the Moors Murders inspire *The
Sleep of Reason* (1968), about which Pamela Hansford Johnson (Lady Snow, 1912–
1981) wrote a reflective study, *On Iniquity* (1967).

Snow knew whereof he wrote. He served in the British government in various roles that exploited his technical knowledge. The world he knew had little
myth or poetry in it, and his fiction is quite without them. The contingent world
exists, and it is out of those contingencies that fiction is built. His art is closer to
Trollope's than Disraeli's, written in a language of unemphatic prose. What is
remarkable is the way in which he portrays class and class difference, a reef on
which many greater novelists have foundered through idealization or condescension. He is the novelist of social mobility, and there is a kind of life in his
novels that we miss in Powell's. Marghanita Laski (1915–1988), herself a readable
novelist and a caustic critic, admires Snow's attempt to write political novels but
judges his efforts "unsuccessful for pervasive egotism and poor pacing." After
all, Sir Lewis is as close to Lord Snow as Phillip Maddison is to Henry Williamson. It may be that the novel sequence, rooted in Proust, is the ultimate egotisti-
cal form. There is the evidence of Ford, Priestley, Hartley, Isherwood, Waugh.
But there is contrary evidence as well. Martin Amis, unlike Laski, is inclined to
forgive Snow his egotism, his "howlers," tonal, idiomatic, and otherwise, admiring the way his fiction is rooted in actualities, real corridors, and engages the
issues of the day.

# 27

# Prodigality and Philistinism

Artemus Ward, Mark Twain, George Washington Cable,
Theodore Dreiser, Frank Norris, Jack London, Upton Sinclair

A recurrent theme in this history is the adoption of literary pseudonyms for reasons of class, sex, privacy, or other calculation. A pseudonym also offers writers
a Jekyll and Hyde freedom, the ability to release certain impulses without owning up to them. In his Pulitzer Prize–winning 1991 biography *Mr. Clemens and
Mark Twain,* Justin Kaplan explores this division, which is also a splitting off of the
antebellum adventuring southerner and the man who rediscovers what Kaplan
calls "the usable past" and makes of it his best books. Especially among the humorists the pseudonym was of use, and if it fit, it concealed the original as decisively as a mid-nineteenth-century mustache concealed an author's mouth with
its plume. The name of Charles Farrar Browne (1834–1867) has vanished under
the much better writing name Artemus Ward. It was Ward who in 1865 encouraged Samuel Clemens, then thirty-one and a jobbing journalist and writer of
"pieces," to send off his frog story to New York. Clemens used his pseudonym,
Mark Twain.

Like others of his generation (more grandly Howells, more modestly Clemens, among them) Artemus Ward began his professional life in printing, as a
type compositor. The concentration involved in assembling words and sentences
from the slugs of type brought him close to text. He began writing and at
twenty-four published the first of his comic pieces in Cleveland, Ohio. Two years
later he was in New York editing the weekly humor magazine *Vanity Fair,* unsuccessfully. His English imitated a generalized dialect or accented speech, as Edgeworth, Hogg, and, in *The Yellowplush Correspondence,* Thackeray had done.

It is as an entertainer that Artemus Ward is remembered, if at all, and for the
impact he had on Samuel Clemens, who heard him speak in Nevada and
thought *he* might do that sort of thing. He got to know Ward: their mustaches
are compatible, though Clemens's was to become, in Garrison Keillor's phrase,
"the most beloved mustache in America."

Ward went before Clemens in the United States and Europe, a lecturer,
jokester in the papers, entertainer on the circuit, the circuit that Dickens and
Thackeray helped to develop. Abraham Lincoln, himself an accomplished mimic,
relished Ward's manner and voice, and he read to his cabinet the latest Artemus

Ward before presenting them with the text of the Emancipation Proclamation. Ward survived the war and the president but died young of tuberculosis in England, where he had grown popular as a speaker and as a writer for *Punch*.

Other writers enjoyed a similar American success, though they did not export as Ward had done. There was Josh Billings, born Henry W. Shaw; and Petroleum V. Nasby, in the flesh David R. Locke (Philip Roth reports that Lincoln admired Nasby's "letters" so much he said he'd have "given up the Presidency to have written them"). Billings and Nasby each used phonetic spelling (cacography) as a way of drawing out the accents of characters. The author puts on a consistent voice, and that voice becomes the narrator and a character in his own right. In the twentieth century the language thus invented came to be known by the Russian term "skaz." Orpheus C. Kerr (Robert H. Newell) and Mark Twain (Samuel Langhorne Clemens) put extreme cacography aside, using it (as Dickens had done more sparingly) principally in dialogue. They created broad, informal, distinctively American idioms. By its judicious use, Twain became something more than the great comic writer and novelist of his time.

He had to outgrow some of his early habits before he could undertake extended fiction in earnest. What he considered the "fun" of writing in, for example, *Innocents Abroad; or, The New Pilgrim's Progress* (1869) was the "irreverent application of modern, common sense, utilitarian, democratic standards to the memorable places and historic associations of Europe." The name of the Everyman here is not Christian but American. It is a kind of humor that today rebounds upon the teller. Great art is ridiculed, the exaggerations of the *cicerone* and the guidebooks are so parodied that the things they describe are degraded at the same time. Twain does not polish the lenses of perception, restoring clear vision. He and his kind of comic writers, unlike Dickens, Irving, and Thackeray, distort. They do not make the familiar new but build upon the unfamiliar in a rhetoric of paradoxes.

Mencken admires and is exasperated by Twain: "There was in him something of that prodigality of imagination, that aloof engrossment in the human comedy, that penetrating cynicism, which one associates with the great artists of the Renaissance," but "his nationality hung around his neck like a millstone; he could never throw off his native Philistinism." Mencken finds the source of this limitation, and his reiterated Francophobia, in his birthright, as it were, born in a "Puritan village of the American hinterland": "Try as he might, being what he was, he could not get rid of the Puritan smugness and cocksureness, the Puritan distrust of new ideas, the Puritan incapacity for seeing beauty as a thing in itself, and the full peer of the true and the good." "A Southern Puritan? Well, why not."

Willa Cather admired the best novels: "I would rather sail on the raft down the Missouri again with 'Huck' Finn and Jim than go down the Nile in December or see Venice from a gondola in May." But *Innocents Abroad* and his later critical strategies she did not enjoy. In 1895 she wrote defending Max O'Rell (Léon Paul Blouet), whose *Outre mer,* "a book which deals more fairly and generously with this country than any book yet written in a foreign tongue," Twain had attacked in characteristic form. "Mr. Clemens did not like the book, and like all men of his class, and limited mentality, he cannot criticize without becoming personal and insulting. He cannot be scathing without being a blackguard."

Thomas Alva Edison visited Twain in Redding, Connecticut, the year before he died and filmed him smoking and taking tea. Part of the footage was used in *The Prince and the Pauper* (1909), a two-reel short movie. He thus provided the story for one of the incunables of cinema and played a bit part in it as well. He was among the earliest writers, perhaps the very first, to submit a book to his publisher in typescript. He had *Life on the Mississippi* (1883) transcribed from his manuscript by a typist working on an early Remington, a massive, handsome Victorian structure. (The original Sholes & Glidden Type Writer, a decade earlier, came on a special table with a foot treadle for carriage return and resembled an old Singer pedal sewing machine.) Later on he dictated his memoirs "to a type writer" (the noun, not yet compounded, still contained the operative), an act more second nature to him than it was to the architect of prose, Henry James, with his pacing, pausing, harrumphing approach to dictation.

A fascination with the mechanical reproduction of text led Twain, an injudicious entrepreneur like his father, once his writing and publishing were successful, to invest heavily in a typesetting machine, a masterpiece of design. Into this undependable contraption he sank a fortune over a period of fourteen years before the development of linotype superseded it. He lost his and much of his wife's money. His publishing venture, which began successfully, also failed in 1894 after some unwise editorial decisions. Like Sir Walter Scott after the failure of Ballantynes, Twain felt a duty to repay all his creditors in full and spent several years writing, lecturing, and giving public readings to do so. He began an ambitious round-the-world lecture tour in 1894, going from East to West, to Cleveland, Vancouver, and thence to Australia, New Zealand, Sri Lanka, India, South Africa, and Britain, and lived for a time in Europe. He returned to the United States in 1900, his debts under control.

In 1904 Henry James spoke at Bryn Mawr College about the changes in English accent and expression; from his increasingly "apart" perspective he lamented the syllabic elisions, strong voicing of the "r" and other elements in American speech. Susy Clemens, Mark Twain's favorite daughter, who wrote an intimate life of him and died at twenty-four of cerebral meningitis while her parents were on their world tour, might have taken James's part. Her father in 1891 had addressed a different group of young Bryn Mawr women and insisted on telling them a story in a dialect that Howells might have described as "the realest kind of black talk." She begged him not to perform "The Golden Arm," one of his favorite recital pieces.

Something peculiarly American happens in that language gap between Henry James and Mark Twain, even in the "literary" Twain who stalks the jobbing humorist. Twain brings back into literary usage, in "this age of mass literacy," Updike says, some of the properties of speech. "In utterance there's a minimum of slowness. In trying to treat words as chisel strokes, you run the risk of losing the quality of utterance, the rhythm of utterance, the happiness." His example is from Twain: "He describes a raft hitting a bridge and says that it 'went all to smash and scatteration like a box of matches struck by lightning.' The beauty of 'scatteration' could only have occurred to a talkative man, a man who had been brought up among people who were talking and who loved to talk himself." The diction and cadence of written speech are of course *not* speech but artful contrivance, yet the art tends toward placing the speaker back in the text *as* speaker: not James's celebrated "point of view," but something basic to older traditions of storytelling. The *telling* is foregrounded and slowness at all costs avoided. Cervantes and Defoe, not Richardson and Cooper, are back in favor. *Don Quixote* was one of Twain's "beau ideals" of writing, he declared in 1860, and he never recanted.

Samuel Langhorne Clemens (1835–1910) was born in Florida, Missouri, a village then of twenty-odd provisional houses on Salt River. As an infant of three, Samuel is said to have chewed uncured tobacco with his milk teeth and learned to spit like a man. Judge Clemens, as Samuel's father was generally known, an optimist and speculator, believed in Florida's future: Salt River would be made navigable, the little town would become a metropolis; and there was always the railway. The future was farther off than he calculated, and in 1839 he took his family to Hannibal, Mississippi, a modest river port familiar as St. Petersburg, the lightly fictionalized setting of *The Adventures of Tom Sawyer*. Samuel's formal education ended when he was eleven, with the death of his father. He was apprenticed at twelve to a printer called Ament for board and clothing, "more board than clothing," thus following his brother Orion into the trade. Nothing from his boyhood, no scrap of early writing, has come to light except a penciled SAM CLEMENS, laboriously lettered on the inside of a little purse that probably saw less coin than the effort of inscription.

Of the seven Clemens children only three survived to adulthood. Orion lived to a ripe age but Henry, who began as a printer, died just short of his twentieth birthday. Orion acquired the *Hannibal Journal,* a paper combining entertainment and information, and published it from the Clemens home. He invited Samuel to help and in his mid-teens the writer-to-be was composing type and occasional sketches. At eighteen he pretended to go to St. Louis but in fact went farther, to New York, Philadelphia, Washington, then west to Cincinnati. He decided to travel to South America and took a little steamboat on the Mississippi to New Orleans in order to catch a ship south. He decided instead to become a river pilot. He set out over two years to learn the 1,200 navigable miles of the treacherous, shifting waters between St. Louis and New Orleans. Pilots needed to land at the ports, of which there were hundreds, and the large and little lumberyards where cargo and passengers were taken on and deposited. Here he got his pseudonym and his memorial: in taking depth, "mark twain" or "two fathom" was a common cry; his tomb is marked by a twelve-foot (two-fathom) monument. He received his pilot's license in 1859, the year after his young brother Henry, who followed him into the river service, died in a steamboat explosion. Twain blamed himself, and his fascination with parapsychology was enhanced by a desire to make amends or connections.

His piloting career ended with the Civil War. He had been reared in a slave state and enlisted with the Confederacy but soon resigned and rejoined Orion, who had conveniently moved north to Iowa. Twain then went west to establish a journalistic career in Nevada (where in 1863 he first used his *nom de plume*) and California. He had numerous adventures and acquired further skills, including those of a miner. He befriended Bret Harte writing for the *Californian* in San Francisco (they later fell out). In 1867 his first book, *The Celebrated Jumping Frog of Calaveras County,* named after his most popular story and including other sketches, appeared. As is often the case with first books, the excitement was laced with disappointment over detail. He wrote to Harte, "The book is out, and is handsome." Then, "It is full of damnable errors of grammar and deadly inconsistencies of spelling in the Frog sketch because I was away and did not read the proofs; but be a friend and say nothing about these things. When my hurry is over, I will send you an autograph copy." It was a success, despite misprints, and sold, he said, 100,000 copies in three years, forming the basis of a fortune he made, and lost, proving himself a son of his more unsuccessful father.

He went to Europe first in a spirit of exploration, writing regular entertaining travel reports for the newspapers. "1 about Pazzuoli, where St. Paul landed," he says in his list, "the Baths of Nero, and the ruins of Baia, Virgil's tomb, the Elysian Fields, the Sunken Cities and the spot where Ulysses landed." His traveler's reports were laced with textbook history and flashes of wit and skepticism about the value Europeans placed upon their cities, landscapes, and histories. These reports were gathered in *Innocents Abroad.* In conversation with Kipling, Twain remarked, "Get your facts first," the voice goes low, "then you can distort 'em as much as you please."

A fellow passenger on his trip to Europe, Charles Langdon, showed him a photograph of his sister Olivia. Twain fell in love with the picture, and in 1868 returned to Elmira, New York, to court and win her hand. In 1870 they married, and four children followed. The first, Langdon, died while a baby. Of his daughters, Susy died young.

Olivia was of a well-to-do liberal family, and through her he got to know the sorts of people he had missed in his earlier years, some passionate about abolition, social justice, women's rights. Some declared themselves atheists and egalitarians. He encountered Frederick Douglass, the escaped slave whose mission was to bear witness to what slavery meant for the slave. And he made a lifelong friendship with William Dean Howells, who described him as "the Lincoln of our literature."

After a spell in Buffalo, New York, Twain and his family moved to Hartford, Connecticut, where he built a home next door to Harriet Beecher Stowe's. He was already an established celebrity, and there he wrote his best-loved books, starting with *The Adventures of Tom Sawyer* (published in 1876). Of the novels, this was followed by *The Prince and the Pauper* (1881); *Adventures of Huckleberry Finn* (1884), regarded by some as *the*, if not the *great*, American novel; and *A Connecticut Yankee in King Arthur's Court* (1889), in which the writing began to seem effortful, his natural energy to abate.

In 1874 he was hard at work on the first of these projects. It absorbed him with a continuous creative labor different from any he had experienced before. This was not a collection of sketches or a collaboration but a novel entirely his own, spun out of memory and shaped by a plotting instinct. It took him away from the immediacy of journalism into an area of careful, continuous shaping, the creation of characters and voices given a large space in which to become themselves. "I have been writing fifty pages of manuscript a day, on an average, for some time now, on a book (a story)," he told a friend, "and consequently have been so wrapped up in it and so dead to anything else, that I have fallen mighty short in letter-writing." The reality of the imagined and remembered world of Hannibal was such that he fell out of the quotidian world of journalism and family life as well and was happily lost. He remembered his writing room as an enchanted space, "a snug little octagonal den, with a coal-grate, 6 big windows, one little one, and a wide doorway (the latter opening upon the distant town)." The welcome *distance* of the town enables him to compose. "On hot days I spread the study wide open, anchor my papers down with brickbats and write in the midst of the hurricanes, clothed in the same thin linen we make shirts of. The study is nearly on the peak of the hill."

Twain had known a Tom Sawyer in San Francisco, hence the name; he built the protagonist of his book out of three childhood acquaintances and imbued him with some of his own qualities. Though the first *Adventures* ends with Tom still a boy, his popularity secured his return to later novels, most importantly to *Huckleberry Finn,* but also, for commercial reasons, because his name combined with Twain's would sell books at a time when the author was in need, to *Tom Sawyer Abroad* (1894), and *Tom Sawyer, Detective* (1896), and to three unfinished works, notable among them *Tom Sawyer's Conspiracy.* Several of Twain's young protagonists are almost indistinguishable from Tom except in their different contexts.

He had a strong sense of dramatic and characteristic incident. Aunt Polly's hard thimble and quick temper go together: symbolic object and action. The scene in which Tom dupes other boys to paint the fence for him has a moral clarity comparable to Don Quixote's encounter with the windmills. The hidden boys watching the townsmen sound the river for their bodies forget themselves, fascinated and frightened at the possibility of ghosts. They witness the unexpected grief to which their own funerals give occasion, fulfilling a universal fantasy, that of being present at one's own funeral. Then they are revealed to the congregation:

> There was a rustle in the gallery, which nobody noticed; a moment later the church door creaked; the minister raised his streaming eyes above his handkerchief, and stood transfixed! First one and then another pair of eyes followed the minister's, and then almost with one impulse the congregation rose and stared while the three dead boys came marching up the aisle, Tom in the lead, Joe next, and Huck, a ruin of drooping rags, sneaking sheepishly in the rear! They had been hid in the unused gallery listening to their own funeral sermon!
>
> Aunt Polly, Mary, and the Harpers threw themselves upon their restored ones, smothered them with kisses and poured out thanksgivings, while poor Huck stood abashed and uncomfortable, not knowing exactly what to do or where to hide from so many unwelcoming eyes. He wavered, and started to slink away, but Tom seized him and said:
>
> "Aunt Polly, it ain't fair. Somebody's got to be glad to see Huck."
>
> "And so they shall. I'm glad to see him, poor motherless thing!"
>
> And the loving attentions Aunt Polly lavished upon him were the one thing capable of making him more uncomfortable than he was before.
>
> Suddenly the minister shouted at the top of his voice: "Praise God from whom all blessings flow—SING!—and put your hearts in it!"

Sentimental, cloying: broad, American-gothic horror and humor slip into soft focus. As at the end of a comedy, music is cued and a dance of relief. It is too easy. Readers are left to provide the irony: what awaits these resurrected children is a drab adulthood, a *Main Street* for which even these pages prepare. This may not have been the author's intention when he has the minister start off the singing.

Jorge Luis Borges disliked *Tom Sawyer.* It is not fully *imagined,* it manipulates the reader at the end and sells the main story short. He loved *Huckleberry Finn:* "I think that Mark Twain was one of the really great writers, but I think he was rather unaware of the fact. But perhaps in order to write a really great book, you *must* be rather unaware of the fact." *Tom Sawyer* is like *Treasure Island,* a memorable but not entirely satisfying narrative. Both appeal as children's books, while *Huckleberry Finn* and *Kidnapped* appeal as much, and differently, to adults. "In our national imagination, two freckle-faced boys, arm in arm, fishing poles over their shoulders, walk toward the river or one alone floats peacefully on its waters, a runaway Negro by his side," Leslie Fiedler writes. "They are on the lam, we know, from Aunt Polly and Aunt Sally and the widow Douglas and Miss Watson, from golden-haired Becky Thatcher, too—from all the reduplicated symbols of 'sivilisation.'"

*Tom Sawyer* was the practice run, *Huckleberry Finn,* designed as a sequel, the major expedition into a world reimagined, with its inherent themes. When Fiedler declares, "It is maturity above all things that the American writer fears, and marriage seems to him its essential sign," we demur: what Twain fears in *Huckleberry Finn* is what he was willing to accept at the end of *Tom Sawyer:* abandoning his characters to the kind of "maturity" represented in the ideologies, the fixed and fixing institutions of American life "on shore," especially as they existed in the apparently stable antebellum south. In *Huckleberry Finn* his writing, because of the solidity of his memory and imagination, learns to resist at a formal level. The characters he introduces, not only the outsiders Huck and Jim and Pap and the confidence men, but ill-fated Buck whose death is one of Huck's defining losses, the feuding families, the gullible and vindictive townsfolk, redefine a center of interest: the social novel and the novel of manners are displaced by a fiction in which society is the thing that the protagonists must escape, its enervating or corrupting models of maturity and conformity rejected, characters inventing their own manners and affections and speaking in their own voices. Huck's instinct for right and wrong is, more importantly, an instinct for good and evil: when he trusts it things go right; when he tries to follow prescriptive rules, they go awry. He can elude cultural imprisonment, ineradicable racial prejudice, when he is on the river with Jim; the challenge is bringing that natural instinct ashore.

*Huckleberry Finn* has more in common with *Moby-Dick* and *The Confidence-Man* than with *Tom Sawyer,* despite the characters and style, and even though Melville's evil is transcendent and his characters unredeemed. Ishmael for his part explores the whole map to perdition; when Huck decides to "light out for the territories," he must go—not west, because the river is disobliging and flows south, the singular route of Melville's *The Confidence-Man.* And the Mississippi is not just any river: it is a vast American waterway, a crucial artery and at the same time a frontier that at flood stage redefines itself, a natural force that links and divides. It rolls like time in one direction, despite eddies and whirlpools. Pilgrims who embark on it will, if they survive, all attain a similar journey's end. There is the chanciness of weather and season but the certainty of direction. Such choices as exist are of limited consequence, though in terms of survival, as Twain the navigator knew, they are crucial.

For Hemingway modern American fiction descends from *Huckleberry Finn.* Faulkner is less categorical, more personal. In New Orleans, where he made a living by odd jobs, he recalled, "I met Sherwood Anderson. We would walk about the city in the afternoon and talk to people." Evenings they met again, drank together, and Faulkner listened. He liked the writer's life as he saw it in Anderson and began to follow it himself. Anderson "was the father of my generation of American writers and the tradition of American writing that our successors will carry on. He has never received his proper evaluation. Dreiser is his older brother and Mark Twain the father of them both." That is, the Mark Twain of *Huckleberry Finn.*

The book is, Stevenson says, a "whole story of a healthy boy's dealings with his conscience." Its wholeness detains him, not for only a picaresque sequence of incidents but for a completed narrative. It has engagement in its humor that sets it apart from the successful sentimental and moralistic writing of its time and of Twain's other books. From the first page, Huck, who tells the story in his own voice, identifies his author, a man who tells the truth, for the most part. He introduces this Twain only to dismiss him, establishing his own style. Lawrence describes this as "Obeying from within."

The narrative incorporates dialects appropriate to characters, "to wit: the Missouri negro dialect; the extremest form of the backwoods Southwestern dialect; the ordinary 'Pike County' dialect; and four modified varieties of this last." The author insists on the precision with which these different aural colorings have been applied to the language, Huck's and those of the characters whose dialogue he reports. *Huckleberry Finn,* which comes into existence in part by the grace of *Uncle Tom's Cabin* and the liberties Stowe took with subject matter and voice, is the first thoroughgoing novel of its kind in English, part of the liberation from British novelistic conventions in which a dominant, privileged dialect reports and thus subordinates variations. J. D. Salinger acknowledges that Holden Caulfield has a forebear in Huck. So, in a more complex way, do Scout Finch, Augie March, and even Humbert Humbert.

John Updike contrasts Twain's tone and manner with Stowe's. "Religion, in Huck's mouth, melts to a joke, and nature, heedless and carefree, takes over the canvas. America has never looked as broad, fresh, and majestic as the Mississippi does from Huck and Jim's raft." The book goes disastrously, though not fatally, wrong when we get to the Grangerford-Shepherdson feud; the treacherous, lazy undercurrent of Twain's imagination takes hold, says Updike. As Tom appears and breeds his usual mayhem, plotting when plotting is unnecessary and making a game of liberty, Huck recedes; it is Huck who has given the book its integrity.

The masterpiece is marred by a defective ending. Hemingway is uncompromising: "If you read it, you must stop where the Nigger Jim is stolen from the boys. That is the real end. The rest is just cheating." A happy ending is implausible, the world does not work like that. Yet the ending might be seen as forced on him by the genre in which Twain thought he was writing, the audience he thought he was addressing, readers who had enjoyed *Tom Sawyer,* many of them children. They had to be let off the hook. Others too note the treachery of genre, the cheating it imposed. "I've often wished that someone would rewrite the end of *Huckleberry Finn,*" Paul Bowles declares, "delivering it from the farcical closing scenes which Twain, probably embarrassed by the lyrical sweep of the nearly completed book, decided were necessary if the work were to be appreciated by American readers." Bowles, skeptical of the American common reader, also understands the calculation that a writer of Twain's commercial nature would make, trying to predetermine its *effect* on the reader. "It's the great American novel," he continues, "damaged beyond repair by its author's senseless sabotage." Twain sabotages the endings of several books, standing beside his common readers and second-guessing their expectation. Ralph Ellison has quite a different take on it: the moral quandary Jim's situation puts Huck in, and his decision to deal with it anarchically, is a key transformation of conscience and consciousness in nineteenth-century American literature.

In *Huckleberry Finn,* though the plot is dramatic, it is never—even with the corpse on Jackson's island, the Duke and Dauphin duping townsfolk, the coincidence of Tom's return to the scene, and the unsatisfactory concluding pages—unbelievable. The theme of slavery could hardly be more real, Jim's fear of being sold south by Miss Watson precipitating a series of events each of which probes deeper into the mind of the enslaved and the slave-dependent. The extreme situations remain credible in the context of the action and in the voice of the narrator; irreverence inheres in characters, and their alienation tells us more than the novelist's explicit moralizing could do. The oppressive theme is material greed, greed as a religion. The novel demands more than a novelist setting out to entertain bargained for. Themes darken. No longer satirical, the book touches on things profound, timeless, and irredeemable. Twain gives himself up to the novel, and it draws on other books, not only his own earlier writings. He despised Cooper, but this book would not have taken the form it did without Cooper's example, and Irving's, both willing to engage cultural and tribal difference; and Meredith is said to have had an effect on the formation of the conmen Duke and Dauphin.

Yet the crucial inspiration, the informing spirit, if we are to believe Twain, was literal. Asked about the "original," Twain replied, "'Huckleberry Finn' was Frank F. . . . Frank's father was at one time Town Drunkard [at Hannibal], an exceedingly well-defined and unofficial office of those days." He insisted, "In *Huckleberry Finn* I have drawn Frank exactly as he was. He was ignorant, unwashed, insufficiently fed; but he had as good a heart as ever any boy had. His liberties were totally unrestricted." Then he acquires an emblematic quality in retrospect: "He was the only really independent person—boy or man—in the community, and by consequence he was tranquilly and continuously happy, and was envied by all the rest of us. We liked him; we enjoyed his society." Here is Huck himself. "And as his society was forbidden us by our parents, the prohibition trebled and quadrupled its value, and therefore we sought and got more of his society than of any other boy's." There had to be a happy ending even in the reconstruction of "real life": "I heard, four years ago, that he was Justice of the Peace in a remote village in the State of——, and was a good citizen and was greatly respected." The distance between Huck's voice and Twain's is mainly a matter of dialect. Both buttonhole the reader. We reject or accept complicity and belief: "There was things which he stretched," Huck says of the author, "but mainly he told the truth. That is nothing. I never seen anybody but lied one time or another, without it was Aunt Polly, or the widow, or maybe Mary."

<hr />

Faulkner in New Orleans celebrated Anderson but made less of the work of New Orleans–born George Washington Cable (1844–1925), though Cable was, Edmund Wilson insists, "unique in dealing realistically, before Faulkner, with the problem of the mulatto in the South." He served the Confederacy. After 1865 he became a journalist for the *New Orleans Picayune*. Sympathetic to the freed slaves, he criticized the conditions they endured, making himself unpopular with *Picayune* readers. Like Kate Chopin, he showed the city that was to develop a bohemian and liberal reputation as repressive and, in matters of race, a closed and ruthless environment. At forty he removed to Massachusetts. He befriended and toured with Twain, who especially praised his novel *The Grandis-simes* (1880), set in New Orleans soon after the Louisiana Purchase. A historical-romance-cum-saga, it traces the stories of a creolized French-American family. The racial mix includes Native American, African, and European elements. In Cable, Twain declared, "the South has found a masterly delineator of its interior life and its history. In truth, I find by experience, that the untrained eye and vacant mind can inspect it and learn of it and judge of it more clearly and profitably in his books than by personal contact with it." Literature thus so clarifies that it can displace actual experience. Mr. Cable will do our seeing for us.

Did Mark Twain really spawn what Sinclair Lewis called "that grizzly bear Theodore Dreiser" (1871–1945), a writer so earnest, so keen to trace the truth at its wartiest, so unengaging and yet compelling to read? In 1916 H. L. Mencken, commenting on the difficulty Dreiser had with publishers, editors, and critics, remarks how all the attacks "have scarcely budged him an inch. He still plods along in the laborious, cheerless way he first marked out for himself . . . his later novels are, if anything, more unyieldingly dreiserian than his earliest." There is something rudimentary about his imagination: "He is still in the transition stage between Christian Endeavor and civilization, between Warsaw, Indiana and the Socratic grove, between being a good American and being a free man," a situation he experienced acutely when his first novel was so badly mauled, "and so he sometimes vacillates perilously between a moral sentimentalism and a somewhat extravagant revolt."

Fourteen years later Sinclair Lewis declared in Stockholm that Dreiser's *Sister Carrie* (1900) marked a radical shift in American fiction. "Dreiser more than any other man, marching alone, usually unappreciated, often hated, has cleared the trail from Victorian and Howellsian timidity and gentility in American fiction to honesty and boldness and passion of life. Without his pioneering, I doubt if any of us could, unless we liked to be sent to jail, seek to express life and beauty and terror." There was the issue of daring to choose the subjects Dreiser chose, as there had been for Flaubert in *Madame Bovary*. Flaubert may have inspired Dreiser to eke out *Sister Carrie,* written under pressure from a friend who believed in the project and the author more than the author did himself. "My great colleague Sherwood Anderson has proclaimed this leadership of Dreiser," says Lewis. "Dreiser's great first novel, *Sister Carrie,* which he dared to publish thirty long years ago and which I read twenty-five years ago, came to housebound and airless America like a great free Western wind, and to our stuffy domesticity gave us the first fresh air since Mark Twain and Whitman."

Twain: but he is usually such a *cheerful* presence in his books, buttonholing. When something dreadful happens, he reassures the reader, he creates places of refuge for us to retire to—a subplot, for example, where we can distract ourselves. He spoils the end of *Huckleberry Finn* to leave us, he hopes, satisfied, in the cocksure company of Tom, with Huck put back in place. Dreiser would have stuck by Huck and Jim to the bitter end, and the end would have been bitter. Borges describes him as a Prometheus so long chained to the crag that it has entered into him and is there, "a fundamental component of rock that is pained by life." Little fiction is as bleak as Carrie's and other characters' quest for gainful employment. Martin Amis says the novels "sometimes feel like a long succession of job interviews," most of them unsuccessful and those that are successful ill-fated.

But in his choice of humble and rough subject matter and his sense of place, writing always on the brink of cliché without (for the most part) falling into it, and using a language that stays close to common speech, Dreiser has no American antecedent so close as Twain. It is in Europe that analogies with his practice are to be found. John Cowper Powys sees him as out-Balzacking Balzac "in his contempt for the rules; but just as none of the literary goldsmiths of France convey to us the flavor of Paris as Balzac does, so none of the clever writers of America convey to us the flavor of America as Mr. Dreiser does." Powys discerns in "this formidable American" something like Balzac's "obstinate tenacity of purpose, the same occult perception of subterranean forces, the same upheaving, plough-like 'drive' through the materials of life and character."

Dreiser, son of German immigrants, understood the popular taste for writing that did not preen as "art," which is not to say that it was artless. In an essay-memoir collected in *Twelve Men* (1919) he writes of his elder brother, Paul Dresser, a celebrated songwriter ("On the Banks of the Wabash" and "My Gal Sal" are his best-known compositions), the only member of his family "who truly understood me, or, better yet, sympathized with my intellectual and artistic point of view," a thoroughgoing nonintellectual, portrayed as rather below middle brow. He did not understand what Dreiser was up to, being at home with "popular song, the middle-class actor or comedian, the middle-class comedy," and with the entertaining writers, "Bill Nye, Petroleum V. Nasby, the authors of the Spoopendyke Papers, and 'Samantha at Saratoga.' As far as I could make out . . . he was entirely full of simple, middle-class romance, middle-class humor, middle-class tenderness and middle-class grossness," tastes and proclivities that charmed and delighted the literary brother. Why? "I should hesitate to try to acknowledge or explain all that he did for or meant to me." In the person of his brother he met, he understood and loved, a representative of his main subject matter, the average person.

What he did not love was the world of American publishing, that metonym for the larger ordering of society according to rules of a hierarchy defined by greed, competition, and moral hypocrisy. To this he had had to submit his work, for it he had been required to revise, expurgate, and distort his work, and in it he was to become, for a few hard years, an employee. When he was an editor, a young writer caught his attention, he hoped to help him, to save him from the experience he himself had had with *Sister Carrie,* "the fierce opposition or chilling indifference which, as I saw, overtook all those who attempted anything even partially serious in America." Unembellished, unironic truth telling was an offense. Twain told the truth sometimes, but distracted the reader with laughter, adventure, historical information, pasteboard scenery. But undecorated truth? "One dared not 'talk out loud,' one dared not report life as it was, as one lived it." And, one might add, in the language that belonged to that hard life. Dreiser had been warned by his boss, "a most eager and ambitious and distressing example of that American pseudo-morality which combines a pirate-like acquisitiveness with an inward and absolute conviction of righteousness," that he wanted novelty, not the "mush" of other magazines. But nothing should be accepted that did not strongly appeal to the common reader, and everything had to be *"clean,"* "a solid little pair of millstones which would unquestionably end in macerating everything vital out of any good story."

Dreiser was reluctant to obey. He was different. He was the first major American novelist with an un-American name (which he kept) and non-Anglophone antecedents. E. L. Doctorow calls him "a naïf who stared and wondered at everything, managed to connect it all in as unitary a vision as has been produced by American literature." Gertrude Stein, three years his junior, took her voice-bearings from him, especially in *Three Lives.* He mastered English, but never strove to nuance his usage, to develop those musical and semantic instincts that make a text a continuous pleasure in itself. We go to him for his breathing, always uncommon common characters, for the reality of his cities, Chicago and New York in particular, and for the wholeness of a vision that includes squalor, violence, sex, a world degraded by a system of dominance and subservience, of having and not having. And not giving.

Saul Bellow is his debtor. In the school of realism that formed his own aesthetic, Bellow says, "Dreiser, a realist of course, had elements of genius. He was clumsy, cumbersome, and in some respects a poor thinker." One is expected to clear one's throat before speaking warmly of Dreiser, as though the air around him is slightly fetid. "But he was rich in a kind of feeling that has been ruled off the grounds by many contemporary writers—the kind of feeling that every human being intuitively recognizes as primary." And for such feeling a primary, unartful language is appropriate. "Dreiser has more open access to primary feelings than any American writer of the twentieth century . . . He blunders, but generally in the direction of truth. The result is we are moved in an unmediated way by his characters, as by life." He touches depths, Bellow adds, previously accessible only to Shakespeare, Balzac, few others. He, like they, saw a great deal and lived in the present world.

He was among the earliest American writers to be born and raised in deep poverty. Doctorow speaks of the "ethnic and lower-depth writers out of Chicago," and makes him a kind of godfather to Richard Wright, Nelson Algren, and Bellow. He saw the big world in relation to the little man, remaining innocent of East Coast orthodoxies. George Santayana's "genteel tradition" was not for him. He haunted newspaper offices until he was allowed to become a reporter. He learned to write in the school of efficient expression and sensational subject matter, a language of selective precision and calculated understatement. One of the strengths of his fiction is that he sees how things are without offering systematic remedies. There is almost none of that relenting we get after crisis in Hardy or Conrad. He strikes a Homeric note, leaving to the reader the business of feeling and response.

In his formative years he was a disorganized and omnivorous reader. Irving and Hawthorne were favorites. "I used to lie under a tree and read *Twice Told Tales* by the hour. I thought 'The Alhambra' was a perfect creation, and I still have a lingering affection for it." He also read Bret Harte and, in a more serious mood, T. H. Huxley, from whom he learned how a dispassionate, clear style works, the style of a trained biologist. Dreiser did not acquire that style but he learned clarity. In 1896 he made the "enchanted discovery" of Thomas Hardy, whom he piled onto Balzac: a novel could work on a large scale, and it could be answerable at the tribunal of history. Mencken notes similarities of theme and tone between *Tess of the D'Urbervilles* and Dreiser's *Jennie Gerhardt* (in a letter Dreiser conceded that Jennie was partly based on Tess) and between *Jude the Obscure* and *Sister Carrie.* "All four stories deal penetratingly and poignantly with the essential tragedy of women; all disdain the petty, specious explanations of popular fiction." Dreiser's female characters are realized.

Like his protagonist L—— in *Twelve Men,* he seemed "literally obsessed . . . with Continental and more especially the French conception of art in writing." He liked reading the lives of writers, but he liked the work as well, of "de Maupassant, Flaubert, Baudelaire, Balzac, de Musset, Sand, Daudet, Dumas junior, and Zola, as well as a number of the more recent writers." But Dreiser insists that when he wrote *Sister Carrie,* he had not yet read Zola. And there is nothing French about his style. Critics apply Teutonic stereotypes to him as well: "He shows all of the racial patience and pertinacity and all of the racial lack of humor," Mencken declares. "Here is the very negation of Gallic lightness and intuition, and of all forms of impressionism as well. Here is no series of illuminating flashes, but a gradual bathing of the whole scene with white light, so that every detail stands out." Mencken finds no "charms of style." For Dreiser language was a medium; he was enough of a journalist to find that an off-the-peg phrase would often do. To linger, to refine and prettify, would have worked against pace and theme.

His *Trilogy of Desire* comprises *The Financier* (1912), *The Titan* (1914), and the incomplete posthumous novel *The Stoic* (1947). He portrays the world of finance and its emblematic tyrant Frank Cowperwood, based on Charles Tyson Yerkes. The life Yerkes lived in his youth, in its libidinal and criminal turns, resembled that of George Hurstwood, the man unraveled by affection in *Sister Carrie*. Yerkes, however, recovered and did much to develop mass transport systems in Chicago and London. Dreiser's banking world is as authoritative as Thackeray's world of politics. He writes in a style that is direct, undecorated, appropriate. Dreiser was patient, did his research; and he can be dull. Like one of Shakespeare's colder heroes, Coriolanus, for example, Cowperwood enjoys power and exercises it without mercy. He triumphs against the odds, though he does not linger over victory. Dreiser understands Cowperwood's other desire, the sexual one, expressed without obfuscation. Already in *Sister Carrie* and *Jennie Gerhardt* (1911) he had studied, from the female perspective, the nuances of sexual affection. But the scale of *Trilogy of Desire* is epic, the theme American in ideology and in its implicit critique. A number of women fall prey to Cowperwood: Dreiser neither condones nor condemns, it is a function of biology with social consequences. And by the time he wrote these books he had read Zola closely.

Dreiser's moral kin are Melville and Hardy, but his sense of evil differs from theirs. For Hardy it is life's little ironies, an inherence in the way things are, and for Melville evil is transcendent, finding embodiment and symbol in the world. For Dreiser there is the possibility of rectifying things, because man has made the very structures and systems, the streets and tenements, around the eager accumulating of money. Inherent in all his fiction is the possibility of change if values change, though the demands of the sensual citizen are less susceptible to mitigation. Still, they too can be adjusted, just as his female characters emerge from dependence and develop a will of their own. Carrie achieves a large-scale solitary success as an artist and, unfulfilled, is mistress of her fate; Jenny rises higher in terms of her moral struggle, and finds a dramatic (though it can seem a specious) fulfillment in the death of the man she loved but could not stay with. Even Roberta Alden in *An American Tragedy* (1925) rises up and reclaims the moral high ground as she perishes. Doctorow speaks of Dreiser's "Balzacian population unified by the rules of commerce and the ideals of property and social position." As in Balzac, the libido remains a volatile part of the equation. The worlds of Zola, and of Ibsen, who often comes to mind when we read Dreiser's long, slow novels, are not so subtle as his. "I do not know what truth is, what beauty is, what love is, what hope is," Dreiser wrote to Mencken. "I do not believe anyone absolutely and I do not doubt anyone absolutely. I think people are both evil and well-intentioned."

Truth is never conclusive: Dreiser does not identify with the characters he depicts. Weak and inadequately villainous characters, Hurstwood for example, or Clyde Griffiths in *An American Tragedy,* continually seem about to change, to rise out of their moral inertia. When they do—as, for example, during the tram strike, that traumatic chapter in *Sister Carrie*—they are overwhelmed by circumstances they did not, could not, anticipate. Hurstwood's suicide and Carrie's success are given equal weight by this evenhanded "critical distance" that is not stiffened with irony. Dreiser never made a narrative persona for himself, or foregrounded a version of himself as Hemingway and Faulkner do within their narratives. It is no wonder that after *Sister Carrie* and its difficult progress to publication he had a nervous breakdown. The absence of a separable narrator makes Dreiser's world complete and vertiginous because it *includes* him. New raw-edged cities, teeming crowds, open spaces themselves create less a sense of potential and opportunity than of abandonment. *Sister Carrie* is unalleviated: no subplots distract us from two protagonists going along together and then, brought down as low as they can go without arriving at destitution, separating and following different fates. And how much more so is the story of *An American Tragedy* the ultimate thwarting of the American dream. Again Dreiser borrowed his plot from an actual news story. The overturned boat, the dead pregnant girl, the trial and execution, were matters of record. After a substantial false start in 1920, Dreiser set out to provide the backstory, meticulously constructed and so slow and riveting it feels almost like real time as the reader follows the adventures of Clyde Griffiths, the beguiling, resourceful protagonist, from a hard-up revivalist childhood to execution, from abjection through promise to a martyrdom that implicates the educational, commercial, and social institutions that first tempt and then patiently, deliberately destroy him. It is not only his story but that of the women of various types and classes who attract him, and whom he corrupts, each a breathing presence. Dreiser visited the places in which in 1906 the crisis events of the actual drama occurred. The manuscript was extensively revised and re-revised by the editors and then by the author, who finally made a trip to Sing Sing prison, lived in imagination his protagonist's final days, and completed the book, or abandoned it to his publisher, in the autumn 1925. They got it out just in time for Christmas.

His publishers at Boni and Liveright were much less cautious than Harper Brothers had been a quarter of a century earlier when they turned down *Sister Carrie* on grounds of its morality, Carrie's "successful" adultery. Doubleday, Page had agreed to publish *Sister Carrie* after severe editing, in as neutral a livery as possible, and then tried to withdraw it. No review copies were distributed and the salesmen made little effort to move the stock. Just over a thousand copies were printed, but less than half of them sold. Frank Norris, an editor at Harper Brothers, got hold of some copies and sent them to a few reviewers. Those who responded saw Dreiser as a naturalist and, in Doctorow's phrase, a barbarian, a reputation he never quite outgrew and in a sense merits. The book did not sink entirely without trace, and its time did come. But Dreiser was damaged. Doctorow included Dreiser as one of the historical characters in his novel *Ragtime.* He recounts how he rented a furnished room in Brooklyn and, like Hurstwood, went quietly mad. "He put a chair in the middle of this room and sat in it. The chair didn't seem to be in the right position so he turned it a few degrees, and he sat in it again. Still it was not right. He kept turning the chair around and around, trying to align it to what—trying to correct his own relation to the universe? He never could do it, so he kept going around in circles and circles." Eventually he went to a sanatorium in White Plains. Doctorow contents himself with the novelist adjusting and readjusting his chair.

—·—

Frank (Benjamin Franklin) Norris (1870–1902), Dreiser's first public advocate, was himself a novelist. His novel *McTeague: A Story of San Francisco* (1899) has thematic affinities with *Sister Carrie.* Norris, born in Chicago, educated partly in Europe, at Berkeley, and at Harvard, a man attuned to the culture of the day and especially to French literature, is less trusting than Dreiser as a writer: he always makes sure that readers catch the sense of a symbol, a gesture. There is nothing ambiguous about the grainy end of *McTeague,* where the protagonist is fatally attached to the corpse of his nemesis. "Looking down, he saw that Marcus in that last struggle had found strength to handcuff their wrists together. Marcus was dead now; McTeague was locked to the body. All about him, vast, interminable, stretched the measureless leagues of Death Valley." *Vast, interminable, measureless:* that's not quite enough: "McTeague remained stupidly looking around him, now at the distant horizon, now at the ground, now at the half-dead canary chittering feebly in its little gilt prison." The docent is anxiously solicitous in his tautological manner and tone. Dreiser is not inclined to such considerations. He was "a bigger man than Norris from the start," says Mencken; "it is to the latter's unending honor that he recognized the fact instanter, and yet did all he could to help his rival."

Willa Cather welcomed *McTeague* as soon as it appeared: "A new and a great book has been written." Once you have read the book you appreciate "the stiff, uncompromising commonplaceness of that title." Subject matter is not important. The eponymous central figure is a dentist. This is how we meet him. "It was Sunday, and, according to his custom on that day, McTeague took his dinner at two in the afternoon at the car conductors' coffee-joint on Polk Street. He had a thick gray soup; heavy, underdone meat, very hot, on a cold plate; two kinds of vegetables; and a sort of suet pudding, full of strong butter and sugar. On his way back to his office, one block above, he stopped at Joe Frenna's saloon and bought a pitcher of steam beer. It was his habit to leave the pitcher there on his way to dinner."

McTeague had grown up in a mining camp in the mountains, trundling heavy cars of ore for his father, who worked hard and then drank and hit hard. His mother apprentices him to a dental quack, and when she dies he has just enough to set up his "Dental Parlors" on Polk Street, where over time he collects "a clientele of butcher boys, shop girls, drug clerks and car conductors." He was a giant, blonde figure, he could pull teeth with his thumb and finger. "His hands were enormous, red, and covered with a fell of stiff yellow hair; they were as hard as wooden mallets, strong as vises, the hands of the old-time car boy."

Norris evokes Polk Street in all weathers, at all times of day, a place the clock and calendar make into every modest place in the world, a microcosm. Cather admires how "in four pages he reproduces the life in a by-street of a great city, the little tragedy of the small shopkeeper." His description "is a positive and active force, stimulating the reader's imagination, giving him an actual command, a realizing sense of this world into which he is suddenly transplanted. It gives to the book perspective, atmosphere, effects of time and distance, creates the illusion of life." These economies and precisions Norris and Dreiser share, an unusual objectivity. Most young writers, she says, "observe the world through a temperament, and are more occupied with their medium than the objects they see. And temperament is a glass which distorts most astonishingly." McTeague wants a shortcut to prosperity, and what appears to be his good fortune, when his wife wins a lottery prize, begins the dreadful chain of events that leads to her death and his fate. It is impossible not to feel here, more acutely than in Dreiser, the active presence of Zola. "The story becomes a careful and painful study of the disintegration of this union, a penetrating and searching analysis of the degeneration of these two souls, the woman's corroded by greed, the man's poisoned by disappointment and hate." A subplot underlines and intensifies the themes. Norris "seems to have no ambition to be clever. His horizon is wide, his invention vigorous and bold, his touch heavy and warm and human. This man is not limited by literary prejudices: he sees the people as they are, he is close to them and not afraid of their unloveliness." This genius, Cather declared, here and in her reviews of his later work, need not hurry: he was developing just fine. But he *did* need to hurry: he died of peritonitis at thirty-two, after his appendix ruptured.

Forty years later Edmund Wilson took a dimmer view of Norris. He represented the emerging sensibility of the American West Coast: "Buoyancy, mysticism, lack of solidity, feeling of not going anywhere, of the California writers: *McTeague* . . . and Saroyan, the relentlessly hopeless and ridiculously hopeful, equally purposeless." *The Octopus: A Story of California* (1901) is powerful but less coherent than *McTeague,* developing an unequivocally global scenario and tentatively using some of the techniques Dos Passos would embrace a couple of decades later. The final shoot-out takes place at the ranch Los Muertos (The Dead) in California, but the Octopus (capitalism at its most rapacious) manifests itself all over the world: "The great harvest of Los Muertos rolled like a flood from the Sierras to the Himalayas to feed thousands of starving scarecrows on the barren plains of India." A Panglossian conclusion, that this will all be to the best in a longer perspective, provides a touch of Marxist irony.

In 1904 Jack London (1876–1916) was elected a member of the Bohemian Club in San Francisco. Rudyard Kipling was kidnapped and taken there (to his relief) in 1891. Frank Norris had been a member, as was the satirist Ambrose Bierce. Norris had been plagiarized by London and was now dead. London too was to die relatively young, of uremia aggravated by chronic alcoholism, or by an accidental or deliberate morphine overdose. Just as his cause of death cannot be ascertained, so too his parentage is mysterious. He was born John Griffith Chaney, but the father whose name may have appeared on the birth certificate (lost in the aftermath of the 1906 San Francisco earthquake) denied paternity when the boy tracked him down in his late teens. Meanwhile John, now Jack to distinguish himself from his stepfather, had taken that stepfather's surname, London.

He lived pell-mell: an oyster poacher, he turned into a piscine gamekeeper for the state Fish Patrol; a college dropout (from Berkeley), he became an omnivorous reader and assembled a library of 15,000 titles. He was by turns a canner, a jute mill worker, a hobo. He contracted scurvy in the Klondike gold fields. As a journalist for the Hearst newspapers in his twenties he covered the war between Russia and Japan in Korea; in his early thirties he sailed with his wife to Tahiti and the Marquesas, following Melville's footsteps into "the valley of the Typee," though he brought his romantic interest with him. He lived in Alaska and Canada and Hawaii; the Far East attracted him. Like Mark Twain he invested in unworkable inventions and was a poor businessman, though he turned failures to account in his writing. His family leeched from him. Doctorow, a firm and forgiving advocate of the man and his work, wonders whether he might have been a model for F. Scott Fitzgerald, for one of those characters "who brought to exquisite perfection the writer's sacrifice of his talent to his expansive style of living." He died at forty having produced fifty books, ten times as many articles and essays, 200 stories, nineteen novels.

"Jack London," Doctorow says, "was never an original thinker. He was a great gobbler-up of the world, physically and intellectually, the kind of writer who went to a place and wrote his dreams into it, the kind of writer who found an Idea and spun his psyche around it." He could not help himself: genius and hack, original writer and plagiarist. Egerton R. Young claimed that *The Call of the Wild* was taken from his book *My Dogs in the Northland*. London acknowledged using it as a source and claimed to have written a letter to Young thanking him. He drew directly on Kipling, even on works like *Thy Servant a Dog*. It is undeniable that, like many of his contemporaries writing for the popular press, he borrowed, recycled, and took shortcuts. A journalist, he was attuned to the reader. Artistic and other forms of integrity could look after themselves. As epigraph to his memoir *The Road* he quotes Kipling's demotic "Sestina of the Tramp-Royal":

> Speakin' in general, I 'ave tried 'em all,
> The 'appy roads that take you o'er the world.
> Speakin' in general, I 'ave found them good
> For such as cannot use one bed too long,
> But must get 'ence, the same as I 'ave done,
> An' go observin' matters till they die.

Experience turned London into a radical. In 1896 he joined the Socialist Labor Party, then moved on to the Socialist Party of America. Translated into Russian, his stories were among Lenin's favorites: tales of unlikely survival, hardness and shrewdness combined; and the weather in *The Call of the Wild* and the other northern novels and stories had a Siberian inflection. The story "Love of Life" was read to the Soviet leader in his final illness. The next day he demanded more, and the day after that he died.

In his essay "How I Became a Socialist" London explains that he lived among what H. G. Wells had called *the people of the abyss,* the phrase used as the title for London's 1903 account of living rough in Whitechapel and the East End. To gather material he went as native as an American could do in that harsh neighborhood for several months. He understood the urgent need for change. In *The People of the Abyss* he juxtaposed an account of the Coronation to the abjection of the inhabitants of the East End. He wrote the book, in the line of Defoe's *Journal of the Plague Year,* in seven weeks. Orwell acknowledged a debt to it and to *The Road* in his less rigorous life experiments and in writing *Down and Out in London and Paris* and *The Road to Wigan Pier.*

London's style is engagingly direct. In *The Road* he writes simply, "I rode into Niagara Falls in a 'side-door Pullman,' or, in common parlance, a box-car." He crosses the whole of America. And he sees the inside of a prison, where he suffers a traumatic assault. This is not far from the world of Saul Bellow's Augie March.

> "Never again a hobo. I'm going to get a job. You'd better do the same. Nights like this make rheumatism."
>
> He wrung my hand.
>
> "Good-by, Bo," said he.
>
> "Good-by, Bo," said I.
>
> The next we were swallowed up from each other by the mist. It was our final passing. But here's to you, Mr. Swede, wherever you are. I hope you got that job.

A visceral socialist, London was equally visceral in other opinions. Prosperity and alcoholism took a toll of his ideals. There is no ideological stability in his work; elements of racism are as undeniable as the liberal and radical passages. Doctorow acknowledges these contradictions: "So he was by his mid-twenties, a carrier of the fashionable and mutually exclusive ideas of his time—democratic socialism and pseudoscientific racism—in the body of his own burning vitality." He writes *in response* and does not seek the distance from his subjects required for consistent analysis. Subjects remain real and resist abstraction. He is, after all, a storyteller and novelist; a witness, not theorist. His novels have a picaresque quality: vivid separate incidents are strung together, in the manner of short stories linked by recurrent characters and themes. He remains readable, especially in *The Call of the Wild* (1903), *The Sea-Wolf* (1904), and *White Fang* (1906), and then—a change of gear marked by his wonderful autobiographical *The Road* (1907)—*The Iron Heel* (1908), which was revived in the late 1930s because it seemed to foresee the rise of fascism. His later autobiographical narrative *John Barleycorn* (1913) explores his alcoholism. This book burned into Hemingway's imagination.

London was eight years old, he says, when he discovered his vocation. He borrowed Ouida's novel *Signa* (1875) from the library, and its excesses took him by the throat. "As passion yet unknown thrills in the adolescent, as maternity yet undreamed of stirs in the maiden; so the love of art," Ouida declared, "comes to the artist before he can give a voice to his thought or any name to his desire." Passion, poetry, implausible kitsch, he could not resist: "Signa heard 'beautiful things' as he sat in the rising moonlight, with the bells of the little bindweed white about his feet." This, London said, set him on the way of writing. He is an heir, but an inadvertent one, of Cooper, who was thick and dense compared to him. He studied what he liked best and saw how it worked, copying it out by hand, and then tried to do similar things himself. In 1900 his first book of stories was published.

It was a good time to be a writer: weekly demand for "product" from the cultural and entertainment papers was high, and a competent writer could expect to make a good income. He sold *The Call of the Wild* for $750 to the *Saturday Evening Post,* then the book rights to Macmillan for $2,000. It was his first success, a cornerstone of his considerable, soon-exhausted annual income.

*The Call of the Wild* Doctorow calls "Jack London's fervently American variant of the novel of sentimental education." Whatever its plagiarisms, he ranks it (far too high) alongside *Huckleberry Finn.* "The voice of the book is the voice of insistent wisdom," Doctorow says. It is certainly insistent, with the unselfconscious confidence, the assertive self-importance that marks much of London's work. As a writer he does not create a space for readers to linger. He marches them, encouraging them to see only what they are told to see, toward a destination. Lawrence might have devoted a chapter to him in his *Studies in Classic American Literature.* There is something Lawrencian in London's search for the "great Man-Comrade," that call of a deeply American wild. He expresses it to his women and wives: they have as much difficulty understanding it as Ursula Brangwen does Rupert Birkin's needs in *Women in Love.*

London and Hemingway share a direct style, but London pulls the whole melting mess of the iceberg up on shore for us to see, while Hemingway keeps the larger mass submerged in the sea for the reader, viewing only the tip, to infer. Hemingway expected imaginative engagement from readers. London, accustomed to writing for consumers of journalism, had different expectations. London is profligate of detail. Hemingway gives away no more than is absolutely necessary.

Shortly before he died, London invited Upton Sinclair (1878–1968) to stay at his ranch. Theirs was an undemonstrative, watchful friendship, but some disagreement between them had to be resolved. He promised Sinclair as much privacy as he wanted, and also straight talking. It was not to be: London was already unwell, and his sickness accelerated.

Norris and Dreiser left a clearer mark than London on the writing of Upton Sinclair, at his best and worst the most politically dogmatic writer of his day, and for more than a decade the best-known American writer in the world. Edmund Wilson noted that reading one of his novels is "like eating a half-ripe melon: the social thesis spoiled the story and the simple-minded stories spoiled them as pamphlets." Yet on a young reader, living in a politically troubled world, his effect was galvanizing. The South African novelist Nadine Gordimer took her bearings from him. "It was Sinclair's *The Jungle* that really started me thinking about politics: I thought, Good God, these people who are exploited in a meatpacking factory—they're just like blacks here. And the whole idea that people came to America, not knowing the language, having to struggle in sweat-shops . . . I didn't relate this to my own father, because my father was bourgeois by then . . . but I related it to the blacks. Again, what a paradox that South Africa was the blacks' own country, but they were recruited just as if they had been migrant workers for the mines. So I saw the analogy. And that was the beginning of my thinking about my position vis-à-vis blacks." His work, unsurprisingly, was blacklisted, and that opposition (like the "banned in Boston" that set so many careers in motion) toughened his arguments. Those who like his work say that resistance to it improved his art: he gave up being lyrical, appealing, and resolved to call it as he saw it. He saw it through specific spectacles and was usually didactic, whether he was trying to change his reader's politics or their take on the paranormal.

Sinclair was a writing factory with almost a hundred books to his credit, and a Pulitzer Prize for one of his less successful, *Dragon's Teeth* (1942), third of the Lanny Budd books, which are packed with history, event, and analysis and were international best sellers. They are about how the system can be subverted from within by a powerful and well-to-do communist who entertains and promotes his ideology by harnessing the very energies of the hostile system he seeks to overthrow.

His first great and, some argue, durable success, *The Jungle* (1906), his twenty-fourth novel, appeared three and a half decades before *Dragon's Teeth*. He intended, by focusing on the meatpacking industry of Chicago, to indict the system of which it was an extreme expression. The success of his portrayal subverted his larger aim: the novel became a catalyst for reform, not revolution. *The Jungle* had immediate impact on legislation to regulate the production and inspection of food. He had aimed for the nation's heart, he later said, but hit its stomach.

Sinclair's novels before *The Jungle* were based on historical and military incidents; a jobbing novelist, he put adventure before politics. *The Jungle* marked a change of gear. When W. H. Hudson saw the stockyards of Buenos Aires in *Far Away and Long Ago,* he was appalled; Sinclair is angry, with the cold anger of the righteous. Hudson saw and retreated whereas Sinclair waded in and got his hands bloody. He went under cover and worked for almost two months in 1904, collecting material—voices, smells, and images—in the hands-on way Orwell used later. He is in the preacher tradition, cajoling and hectoring, continuing to cajole and hector after the argument is won. The number of his books is proof that he would not shut up. His ground changed, each book persuading us of something rather different from the one before. In this he resembles the even more prolific Aldous Huxley, who came from England to share his adopted

California landscape and an interest in psychic phenomena, though in Huxley's case the interest led, as with Christopher Isherwood, into areas of Eastern spiritual discipline. Sinclair's *Mental Radio* (1930) recounts psychic experiments conducted with his second wife, Mary Craig Kimbrough. Albert Einstein wrote a preface confirming the Sinclairs' bona fides while hedging his bets. Mary provided the subject matter for *Sylvia* (1913) and *Sylvia's Marriage* (1914): early on he learned, as a jobbing writer, the importance of series, how once a popular character was established, readers would follow from book to book. Though *his* name appeared on the books, they were joint efforts: such collaborations were ideologically sound, though it might have been thought more fair had both names appeared on the dust jacket.

It was around this time (1930–1932) that Sinclair, who was engaged in the film industry, produced Eisenstein's *Que Viva Mexico!,* one of the less happy collaborations between creative cultures. All through the 1930s he was politically engaged. He backed Prohibition, he supported the Croppies. Irrepressible American optimism balanced his rage against the system. He ran as a Socialist candidate for Congress and in 1934 tried for the governorship of California, polling 900,000 votes. Carl Van Doren sets Sinclair among "the ragged philosophers." He is not a misanthrope and certainly not an ironist. His bold naivety is an aspect of his accessibility. When he takes up the cause of those Americans, many of them recent arrivals unable to speak English and all the more vulnerable for that, caught in the trammels of the Chicago stockyards, he chooses a scenario in which the moral categories could hardly be more clearly defined. The struggle is not staged, as in his earlier novels, but lived. Here witness, not satire, is his technique. The documentary comes into its own. We are dealing with types and prototypes: "Ona was blue-eyed and fair, while Jurgis had great black eyes with beetling brows, and thick black hair that curled in waves about his ears—in short, they were one of those incongruous and impossible married couples with which Mother Nature so often wills to confound all prophets, before and after. Jurgis could take up a two-hundred-and-fifty-pound quarter of beef and carry it into a car without a stagger, or even a thought; and now he stood in a far corner, frightened as a hunted animal, and obliged to moisten his lips with his tongue each time before he could answer the congratulations of his friends." Their drama is no less intense for that. Yet it is odd, as Jurgis gets angrier and his love for Ona curdles, to have Sinclair quoting Wilde's "The Ballad of Reading Gaol." Wilde is evoked, not named, as "a poet, to whom the world had dealt its justice." The borrowed words fit neither the circumstances nor the characters. The novel ends with the exhortations of the orator, a moment of political optimism from which it is not to be reclaimed. We are far now from the great rivers and generous mustaches of the age of Twain. Modern industrial

America demanded a fiction of engagement. It has more to do with the realities of politics than with the transformations of the art of fiction, yet the setting chosen provided, as it had half a century earlier for Mrs. Gaskell in *Mary Barton* and other novels, a functional basis for form.

Among Sinclair's later works his retro *Another Pamela* (1952), an epistolary novel, is a wry tribute published 210 years after Richardson's *Pamela*. This restrained and eventually married heroine is reincarnated in midcentury southern California. Sinclair has happened upon her letters, which he presents to us faithfully, altering only her spelling and occasionally her punctuation (after all, she never went to high school). Pamela's voice and her moral qualities are not much altered. It is fun to find her in an "auto camp in Arizona"—a motel—and to hear her responding to the sunny, temptation-laden Hollywood world like a time-traveler arrived not only from another age but from a different genre. God gets the glory here as in Richardson's novel, though less plausibly now. The setting and the descriptive strategies of the book remind us of the impact of film on fiction, especially popular fiction that aspires to the condition of film and ties in with it rather than, as in *Another Pamela,* with earlier fiction. Film does much that a novel cannot do; it is to the novel what photography is to painting, and as Gore Vidal says, as a result "the novelist must go deeper, must turn into the maze of consciousness where the camera cannot follow." Sinclair had no map for that maze. Like many modern novelists he came to see the reader as part of an audience, to be exhorted or instructively entertained by plot and image. The writer comes to see himself as cameraman: efficient language does as little as possible to distract from the direction and directness of narrative. Even in *Another Pamela,* rooted in an earlier text, the language is distinguished by a stiff old-fashionedness, a nod in the direction of Richardson, but it does not rise to pastiche or parody.

The truths Upton Sinclair tells are given; unlike Twain's, they preexist his books, are political, grounded in a theory of history whose patterns ideology can transcribe. His characters live within and for those larger verities, and their lives are a disclosure of consequences. We are close to the world of allegory, in which figures exist as instructive and sometimes affecting illustrations of what dogma knows to be true.

# 28

# Blurring Form

Willa Cather, Sarah Orne Jewett, Marilynne Robinson, Janet Lewis,

Kate Chopin, Sherwood Anderson, Gertrude Stein, Laura Riding, Mary Butts

Willa Cather (1873–1947) disliked the 1936 side-on portrait Carl Van Vechten took of her wearing a fluffy dark fur ensemble and looking Russian and effort-fully feminine. She asked her publishers to tell him to burn the prints. She liked Edward Steichen's immediate 1926 portrait. She smiles attentively at the viewer, arms crossed, her shirt (not a blouse) open at the neck, with a large loose-knotted cravat. Her hair is approximately parted in the middle, with wisps of grey; she seems to listen, emanating her own informal light.

"In the beginning," she wrote in 1920, "the artist, like his public, is wedded to old forms, old ideals, and his vision is blurred by the memory of old delights he would like to recapture." Something of a tomboy from the start, dressing in boys' clothes, she was fascinated by all sorts of creatures, then by surgery, ampu-tation, embalming. Given the legacy of the Civil War, in which amputation was practiced even when a bandage might have been sufficient, she saw limbless veterans everywhere. After the family moved from Virginia to Nebraska, she played in her uncle's Confederate uniform. From an early age she learned the force of gossip in the small communities where her family lived.

She attended the University of Nebraska. An avid reader, she particularly en-joyed Stevenson and Flaubert. In 1930, after she had become an established American novelist, at the Grand Hôtel d'Aix in Aix-les-Bains she got to chatting with an old lady, who turned out to be the octogenarian Caroline Commanville, the niece Flaubert loved. Cather said how she liked the closing sentence of the last of the *Trois contes,* "Hérodias." The old lady recited it with Flaubert's own emphases: "Comme elle était très lourde, ils la portaient al-ter-na-tive-ment." The final adverb, Cather remarks, "is so suggestive of the hurrying footsteps of John's disciples, carrying away with them their prophet's severed head." English cannot quite get this: "since it was very heavy, they took turns in carrying it."

Back in Nebraska, Cather became an editor and a reviewer. She never doubted she would be a writer. Like Twain, she started in a contemporary American vein, then moved into the past and other cultures. Her lifestyle was unconventional. In 1901 she befriended a well-to-do young woman, Isabelle McClung, and lived with her in the family mansion in Pittsburgh. This removed financial pressure and she was able to plan projects for the longer term while continuing journalism. When Isabelle married, Cather contrived another "Boston marriage" and set up house with Edith Lewis at 5 Bank Street in Greenwich Village, New York.

She was sent on a journalistic assignment that proved important in her development as a novelist. With Georgine Milmine she researched and wrote a series of articles (1907–1908) published in 1909 in book form, *The Life of Mary Baker G. Eddy and the History of Christian Science*. The articles so incensed Christian Scientists that they tried to buy up every copy of the issue of *McClure's Magazine* in which they appeared; then book publication prolonged the controversy. Mrs. Eddy lived just outside Boston, and Cather made Boston her base for research.

Once in Boston she took the opportunity to meet Sarah Orne Jewett (1849–1909), the best-known woman writer of the day and a favorite of Cather. Jewett, a correspondent of Henry James and a protégé of William Dean Howells who much admired her ear for dialogue, invited Cather to the house she shared with Annie Fields, widow of the publisher and editor of the *Atlantic Monthly*, where Jewett had published her first story when she was just nineteen. James described the house at 148 Charles Street as "the votive temple of memory." It was worth a visit: Jewett showed Cather the books inscribed by Dickens, the lock of Keats's hair. Thackeray stayed there on his visit to Boston and sketched a self-portrait. This Cather was invited to admire. Poe, had he visited, might have noted the European provenance of the relics: the temple faced east.

Jewett read Cather with approval, but also gave advice. She urged her to be clearer about her landscapes, to see and write them more from the outside, making them contain her characters instead of leaving them internalized in her characters. Her own best writing focused on the world in which she grew up, South Berwick, Maine, where she would accompany her father, a physician, on his rounds.

A defined setting releases the energies of Cather's *Death Comes for the Archbishop*: history inheres in landscape, characters from different times connect with one another through it. Its clarity can provide unity and resonance quite independent of plot. James was impatient with the "humbug" of Jewett's historical plots, but Cather was less categorical. She dedicated her first major novel, *O Pioneers!*, to Jewett's memory, forging a link with a foremother now neglected. One of Jewett's Flaubertian mottos stayed with Cather: "Écrire la vie ordinaire comme on écrit l'histoire" (To write about ordinary life as one would write history). How do women and men live, Jewett asked, not only up to but on into marriage, with its provincial vicissitudes. South Berwick is the "Deephaven" and "Dunnet Landing" of her stories. She published nineteen books and made a decent living as a writer.

*The Country of the Pointed Firs* (1896), serialized and praised, created a believable New England. Kipling called it "the realest New England book ever given us." Its twenty-one relatively brief chapters are still of value. Because they are separate, the book straddles genres: a collection of sketches and a novel at once, shorter and more concentrated than Mrs. Gaskell's *Cranford,* more modest, more artful, less humorous. Between unspoiled natural worlds of land and sea, beautiful, harsh, are set the dedicated, threadbare lives of country people who live on the margin and come to terms with their isolation, their losses, their foreshortened future. In the last chapter, Dunnett Landing dwindles, the sights and characters fade out one by one. The writing is clear and sad. James described the book as a "beautiful little quantum of achievement." The lyricism of its prose is of the kind Edith Wharton found sentimental but Cather knew to be tempered and sincere. A structural looseness about this, her first and best work of fiction, is notable. Jewett was writing about a fishing community and a threatened way of life. She refused to bend and knit the material into a prescribed form. Cather liked Jewett's sense that truth to theme and setting were sufficient guarantors of formal wholeness. This quality she had admired in Stephen Crane: it was the measure of his originality. Jewett's example licensed Cather, those odd elements in the novels that feel right but cannot be critically wrestled into place.

Jewett died in 1909, having suffered a severe accident eight years earlier that put an end to her decent and committed, if attenuated, creative life. In part attenuation was part of her subject matter, a community nearing extinction—organic, vulnerable to change, and apart from the clattering world of industry and its depredations.

"Life began for me," said Cather, "when I ceased to admire and began to remember"; she did not go for conventional or closed forms. She sought appropriate "shapes" for her subject, as in *O Pioneers!* (1913; the title from Whitman). *The Song of the Lark* (1915) is distorted by the absence of conventional form: an excessive interest in subject matter (opera) in the second half diminishes her interest in her protagonist, the opera singer Thea Kronborg.

*My Ántonia* (1918) deliberately avoids conventional form. The title tells us where to focus, but we begin with the narrator's return to his own roots, and only then do we meet the Shimerdas, Ántonia's family; and how slowly she emerges! There is a passage in which Ántonia tells an Old World story about a boisterous winter wedding party returning late at night in several sledges to the groom's village. The wolves, famished, almost invisible shadows, overrun all but the first sledge; and that first sledge, which the wolves are approaching, is lightened by Peter and Pavel, who cast the two newlyweds into the wolves' path, human jetsam. It is a clear and brutal story of survival at all costs (though Peter and Pavel are themselves destroyed by their deed). Ántonia's narrative does not relate to the main story. Cather insists in a later preface to *Alexander's Bridge* that the material of memory is already shaped, one ought not meddle or make it conform to a closed structure. "In working with this material [the writer] finds that he need have little to do with literary devices; he comes to depend more and more on something else—the thing by which our feet find the road home on a dark night, accounting of themselves for roots and stones which we had never noticed by day." The nocturnal nature of the aroused imagination, and the ways in which, as in dream, unexpected associations occur, the involuntary and therefore justified irregularity, make Cather's best passages surprise. In theory, fiction should be natural, not effortful; unnecessary detail should be jettisoned, and the writer develop an instinct to follow imagination. But she could not kill her darlings—the ravening wolves, for example—and so the narrative flows around some embedded elements, what she referred to as "insets," beautiful but not logically germane.

In 1922 she published what was her most commercially successful novel, though certainly not her best. Patriotic, naive, mawkish, time-serving, *One of Ours* (1922) won the Pulitzer Prize for the Novel. Here she steps out of memory into research that feeds a sentimental inventiveness. Claude Wheeler dies on the battlefields of France. The First World War gave Cather an opportunity to write about a war. The War Between the States had fascinated her; here she could orchestrate events in a European theater where she need not take sides, because the sides were already fixed in history.

In her later years her views became conservative and in some areas reactionary; yet the artist survives within the older woman. *The Professor's House* (1925) Louis Auchincloss describes as "a mine for symbol seekers," effortful and not very engaging. Then comes the momentous *My Mortal Enemy* (1926), thematically a miniaturized *The House of Mirth;* with the final estrangement of the lovers and their reversal of roles there is a seeming echo of *Sister Carrie*.

Her most popular book, *Death Comes for the Archbishop,* was published in 1927. Memory and research prepared its way. Her plot is historically informed, the landscape drawn by memory, familiar even in the dark. Landscape here is never mere background or context: it exerts a force, whether it be the Sabine hills, Clermont in France where the archbishop started his life's journey, or the powerful character of New Mexico where, even as death is coming, "he always awoke a young man."

"Father Joseph had come to love the tamarisk above all trees. It had been the companion of his wanderings. All along his way through the deserts of New Mexico and Arizona, wherever he had come upon a Mexican homestead, out of the sunbaked earth, against the sunbaked adobe walls, the tamarisk waved its feathery plumes of bluish green. The family burro was tied to its trunk, the chickens scratched under it, the dogs slept in its shade, the washing was hung in its branches." Cather writes seemingly without effort, invisibly: scenes rise before us vast and complete. The effect she was after, she said, was that of the narrative paintings in which a series of panels—in a church, a refectory, or public building— might represent the key events of a life. She loved the rural themes and characters of the paintings of Jean-François Millet, and in *Death Comes for the Archbishop* she evolved her theories from the more iconic work of Puvis de Chavannes, whose sequence based on the life of Saint Geneviève led her to seek a prose equivalent, "something without accent, with none of the artificial elements of composition."

———

By reading ten pages a day first thing in the morning, Bret Easton Ellis got through one of Jonathan Lethem's books (it had put him off at first) and realized how good it was. He was trying to get into Marilynne Robinson's *Gilead*. "I have been carrying it around now for four or five months. And every time I think, *This is so boring, I'm not going to read any more of it.* But I have to pick it up again because it's so beautifully written, the prose gives me the chills when I read it." He tries, but the book lacks "that kind of propulsive energy . . . that I require from a novel. And it's very meditative and very—a very different experience from most contemporary novels." That it certainly is, strenuous in salutary ways.

Robinson (b. 1943) has three novels to her credit, *Housekeeping* (1980), *Gilead* (2004), and *Home* (2008). The twenty-four-year gap between the first and second seems to indicate how meditative and careful she is as a writer, deliberate and unspontaneous. Yet she claims to be a rapid writer in her fiction, and a natural one. She summons her muse: "What to say about Melville? He transferred the great poem at the end of Job into the world of experience, and set against it a man who can only maintain the pride of his humanity until this world overwhelms him. His God, rejoicing in his catalog of the splendidly fierce and untamable, might ask, 'Hast thou seen my servant Ahab?'" This is the moral and spiritual tradition she, too, writes from and for. It is not the casuistical, dogmatic faith of Flannery O'Connor but something more earnest, muscular, devolved to the believer. Protestant. Her engagement with the uses of metaphor in Dickinson, Thoreau, and Melville and her sense of how the Bible informs their writing makes her read Faulkner with a spiritual commitment his books support. "The Easter service that is the climax of *The Sound and the Fury*," she says, "is a study in the workings of fiction and Scripture as reciprocal interpretation." Christ says, "I was hungry and you fed me, I was thirsty and you gave me drink," and he adds, "Insofar as you did it unto the least of these, you did it also unto me."

Robinson declares, "In the moment Christ's grandeur is revealed, his identity is conflated with those most profoundly in need. So Faulkner's Benjy and every Benjy in the world is in fact Christ, *not metaphorically but metaphysically* [my italics]." The believing grandeur of her statement, delivered without the least reserve of irony, is an index of her originality. Narrative is, for such a writer, embodiment: it is not an easy art, and as Bret East Ellis says, it is "meditative" and decidedly not "propulsive." It chills only those readers who are sensitive enough to register the fundamental challenge it entails. "Dilsey, in assuming her endless burden of care for [Benjy], has fed and clothed Christ himself, and she has been Christ in her care of him. She must have known this all along—the text is not obscure—but a good sermon changes even known truth into profound realization." The critic (Elaine Showalter) who describes her fiction as "a stunningly original exploration of the classic forms and formulas of American writing" has not felt the chill. Robinson is impatient with modern critical and political "condescension toward biblical texts and narratives, toward the culture that produced them, toward God." It is another denial of enabling continuities and of community, the values that champion the vulnerable and protect both Benjy and Dilsey.

Melville is her sometimes tutelary spirit. In *Housekeeping,* she said, "I thought that if I could write a book that had only female characters that men understood and liked, then I had every right to like *Moby-Dick.*" The values of sisterhood are not congruent with her values. *Housekeeping* is set in a West we are conditioned to expect to be full of cowboys, bandits, and Indians. In this laconic world of large skies, "isolated towns and single houses," refocused through the lives and perceptions of women, language itself changes, and mother Earth again becomes motherly, which is not to say she is without severity. "The great assumption of literary realism," Robinson says, "is that ordinary lives are invested with a kind of significance that justifies, or requires, its endless iterations of the commonplace, including, of course, crimes and passions and defeats, however minor these might seem in the world's eyes." The lives of fictional characters provide true and false patterns for living and for action.

As a child growing up in Sandpoint, Idaho (prototype for Fingerbone, Idaho, where her first novel is set), she felt that in some way she broke in on nature's enchanting integrity. She longed for inclusion. She was pious, too, and there is much of her youth in the characters of her novels. Being alone was a good place to be. "I looked to Galilee for meaning," she says, "and to Spokane for orthodonture." (Her family was worldly enough to be concerned about her looks.) She was raised Presbyterian and became a Congregationalist, engaged by the writings and example of John Calvin, the demanding figure behind

John Ames in *Gilead,* whose ancestors were abolitionists in "Bleeding Kansas" before the Civil War.

Ruth (the biblical figure is not far away) tells the story of her and her younger sister's upbringing (her older sister is a missionary in China) in Fingerbone, after their mother's suicide. Aunt Sylvie, a wanderer, comes to look after them, and when she leaves, Ruth follows her, as her namesake followed Naomi, back to her natural home, which is not Bethlehem but wandering. Themes of house and home, husbandry, self and family, are explored. The book features a novel, Morton Thompson's best seller *Not as a Stranger* (1954). "That isn't the sort of thing you should be reading," Sylvie declares; "I don't know how it got into the house!" She adds it to the pyre of reading material that goes up in flame before she and Ruth abscond in chapter 10. *Housekeeping* has some of the blur and disorder of early Cather, and some of the formal freedom.

*Gilead*—the title is the name of the town in Iowa where the protagonist lives—is more conventional and certainly more singly focused than *Housekeeping,* the fictional autobiography, charting the spiritual battles of John Ames, a midwestern congregationalist pastor now growing old. He is writing the book for his little son, sharing the memories of his grandfather and father and trying to extend through narrative the vocational continuities they had fostered. The book asks, What is right action? The grandfather was a militant abolitionist, the father a staunch pacifist, and each had the spiritual task of justifying his actions in relation to man and God. The symbolism is straightforward, the book a kind of appalling and enthralling discipline for the reader, evoking the emergence of America and an alternative tradition of American values. John Ames has suffered great pain and loss and been sorely tested, too. The relationship with his best friend's son, his namesake John Ames Broughton, seen at first as a challenge to his late marriage and family, is crucial: in the change that has occurred in this seeming black sheep, his faith in man's ability to choose and choose rightly is partly restored. He too learns to forgive, not only the young man but his own father and grandfather. The book is true to Ames's language, rich in biblical allusion and cadence. Robinson's PhD was in Shakespeare. This, with her intimate knowledge of Melville, particularly the mature Melville of *Moby-Dick,* is evident in the writing, which is anachronistic in its elaboration and contemporary in its urgency.

In *Home,* set in 1957, the civil rights movement gaining momentum, the once prodigal John Ames Broughton has come back to Gilead. His partner is black, they have a child. Their story extends *Gilead* and its social and spiritual concerns. The narrator, Glory, Broughton's sister, is also returning to Gilead. *Gilead* and *Home* overlap in time and incident. Moral and spiritual rigor are enacted in Robinson's novels. Her essays provide a gloss that does not distract from the fiction but deepens our understanding of the spiritual dimension of her novels.

———•———

Had Janet Lewis (1899–1998) survived another year or so, she would have been, briefly, a citizen of three centuries. She had, however, a very specific location in time and culture. Her fiction shares some of the concerns and strategies of Cather's. Born in Chicago, she set out as a writer from the same town (Oak Park) and school, and at the same time, as Ernest Hemingway. The two writers published early work in the same high school magazine. In later years their paths hardly crossed: he was destined to go wide, she deep. There is a residue of the pioneer in her and the independence of a writer who insists on concentrating only on experience crucial to her. A novel engages experience when it matters in some moral way. The plight of the Indians, for example, and of Japanese interns in the Second World War, mattered to her and to her severe and brilliant husband, the poet Yvor Winters.

Though she was a poet, she wrote five novels, four of them historical. *The Invasion* (1932) is about the relations between the Ojibway Indians and the Americans, British, and French in the later eighteenth and the nineteenth century, set on an island near the confluence of Lake Superior and Lake Michigan. Problems of legitimate authority and justice are explored through this and her later historical narratives, *The Wife of Martin Guerre* (1941), her most celebrated book, based on actual documented events, set in sixteenth-century France and dealing with love, absence, and identity; *The Trial of Sören Qvist* (1947); and *The Ghost of Monsieur Scarron* (1959). Her second novel was made into an opera, and she was an active librettist. The novel *Against a Darkening Sky* (1943) concerned itself with her world, the period of the Great Depression in California. She needed the longer perspective and never perfected an art for dealing with matters close at hand.

In the year of Lewis's birth, Willa Cather reviewed *The Awakening* by Kate Chopin (1850–1904); the book disappointed her at the time. Chopin could have been a far more useful foremother for Cather than Jewett was, but Cather was not ready. She was still writing undistinguished poetry and her first novel was thirteen years away. In Chopin she detected a French influence. It produced a different timbre from the East Coast novels that maintained regular commerce with a British tradition. Cather calls *The Awakening* a "Creole *Bovary*," and she sounds for a moment like one of Flaubert's early critics: "I shall not attempt to say why Miss Chopin has devoted so exquisite and sensitive, well-governed a style to so trite and sordid a theme." The style has "no great elegance or solidity; but [is] light, flexible, subtle and capable of producing telling effects directly and simply."

The story of Edna Pontellier from Kentucky is tired (she is a girl whom literature has led to false dreams of romance), and Leonce Pontellier is hackneyed as the insensitive, caring husband. Edna gets used to her husband, even gets rather to like him, and the children, though she can really take them or leave them, and indeed she does. At their summer holiday retreat, with other prosperous Creole families, enter the young, handsome Robert Lebrun. Complications follow. Edna becomes impatient with her husband and gradually works toward what seems to her a point of independence. Her lover is only half-hearted and abandons her, the world proves increasingly inhospitable to her desires and imagination. She returns to the place where Robert taught her to swim and swims away. Cather suggests that she is, on a smaller scale, following in the footsteps of Anna Karenina. She advances a feminist argument against this kind of protagonist. Such romantic illusion afflicts "only women of brains, at least of rudimentary brains, but whose development is one-sided; women of strong and fine intuitions, but without the faculty of observation, comparison, reasoning about things." She goes further, angry not at Chopin, who was herself angry, but at the situation: "These are the people who pay with their blood for the fine ideals of the poets, as Marie Duplessis paid for Dumas' great creation, Marguerite Gauthier [in *La dame aux camellias*]. These people really expect the passion of love to fill and gratify every need of life, whereas nature only intended that it should meet one of many demands." But Edna's fate also relates to Don Quixote's, and to Dorothea Casaubon's. "And next time," Cather admonishes, "I hope that Miss Chopin will devote that flexible, iridescent style of hers to a better cause."

The succinct thirty-nine-chapter novel ends predictably, the melodramatic symbols assert themselves. Edna steps into the dark shallows. "The foamy wavelets curled up to her white feet, and coiled like serpents about her ankles. She walked out. The water was chill, but she walked on. The water was deep, but she lifted her white body and reached out with a long, sweeping stroke." There can be little doubt of where she is going, with only six short paragraphs left.

About Chopin Marilynne Robinson reaches quite a conclusion quite different from Cather's. "In discovering herself Edna is discovering her fate. In exploring Edna's regression, as she puts aside adult life, retracing her experience to its beginnings, for her its essence, Chopin describes as well a journey inward, evoking all the prodigal richness of longing, fantasy, and memory. The novel is not a simulated case study, but an exploration of the solitary soul still enchanted by the primal, charged, and intimate encounter of naked sensation with the astonishing world." The ending cannot spoil a novel vivid with moments of freedom and social violation. Edna has courage, spirit, spirituality, and an artist's desires and skills. At her most imaginative and assertive she speaks beyond her individual condition. Her land- and seascapes are lived, the spaces in which Edna moves as wife and mother, and then as an independent woman, are genuinely habitable; there are compelling characters, notably the sour, ambivalent Mademoiselle Reisz, a talented pianist thwarted in her humanity, whom Edna recognizes and to whom she is drawn. She represents a departure from the destructive norms of society, though a departure that leads not to fulfillment but to isolation.

Kate Chopin is the first of the notable southern women writers. Her *fin de siècle* Louisiana with its foliage and fireflies, its erotic charge, the presence of French (her passion for Maupassant is evident in her stories and novels), of the Creole and an almost tropical sea, is a territory as specific and realized, on a small scale, as Hardy's Wessex. And in Edna she has begun to draw a new kind of character in American fiction, the fully sexual, intelligent woman keen to establish independence yet unable quite to achieve it, even in New Orleans with its cultural and racial mix. Edna learns at once the loneliness of the rebel and the gruesome consequences (a witnessed childbirth) of social conformity. She finds that bohemian New Orleans, if it exists at all, is for men and another sort of woman. Women like Edna had had few roles to play in an American fiction now well established. *The Awakening* (1899) caused scandal. It was banned from libraries and severely dismissed (Cather's was one of its milder reviews). The furor stopped Chopin from writing: the attacks on her book and on herself were a measure of how far her themes and her sex had yet to travel.

It was in a different New Orleans, down-at-heel, hard-edged, that William Faulkner began writing, supporting himself with odd jobs. Modernism had arrived in the French Quarter, which with its mix of races and cultures itself seemed a natural incidence of what modernism was made of and for. The magazine *Double Dealer,* established in 1921, provided a forum for the movement and published work by Faulkner and Sherwood Anderson. Without Anderson, Faulkner would have started in a different direction. Anderson asked a lot of the young man, and when Faulkner sensed his approval he knew he was on to something. Henry Miller too speaks of his love for Anderson, his favorite American writer, with whom he was continually at loggerheads (but he was at loggerheads with most of his contemporaries), especially on the subject of America: Anderson loved America, the very idea of it, its places, its people.

Sherwood Anderson (1876–1941) as a visitor in England cut an odd figure. He lunched with Arnold Bennett in 1926, and Bennett describes in his journal his "outrageously untidy and long grey hair, all over his eyes, etc., blue shirt and darker blue silk necktie in the arty style of the 90's, with a pink-stoned ring to hold the tie." He disliked "evil arty association," but Anderson "had sound sense on lots of things, and I liked him." The word "arty" in connection with the 1890s was a kind of shorthand for decadence; it is inappropriate in the context of Anderson, whose one "arty" weakness was his unconditional enthusiasm for Gertrude Stein. They were fiercely protective of one another. Hemingway recalls, "Anderson's stories were too good to make happy conversation." *Winesburg, Ohio* (1919) is one of the great story collections of the century, and in its sense of place and economy of means it made different formative marks on Hemingway, Faulkner, Steinbeck, and others. "I was prepared to tell Miss Stein," Hemingway says, "how strangely poor his novels were, but this would have been bad . . . because it was criticizing one of her most loyal supporters." He parodied *Dark Laughter* (1925)—"so terribly bad, silly and affected," and Anderson's only best seller—in his second novel, *The Torrents of Spring* (1926), a book whose judgment of writers gave early evidence of his caustic manner. It was subtitled *A Romantic Novel in Honor of the Passing of a Great Race*.

In Anderson's early novels, *Windy McPherson's Son* (1916), *Marching Men* (1917), and *Poor White* (1920), rebelling against naturalism, he established a narrative pattern that proved useful to his successors. A generation and a half later Saul Bellow in *Augie March* (1953) brings the pattern to a paradoxical apotheosis. Anderson's novels focus on a character, a young man who is intelligent, not very articulate, and ambitious, leaving his hometown in a picaresque spirit to seek the city, not for the bright lights so much as in quest of wealth, because this he has been told is what really matters in the world. Once there he finds a range of unfulfillments: he gains what he wants, and still he wants. Want is stilled in service to others, nurturing, organizing, attempting to make the world a better place for all, not just for the first person singular, who, on his own, is a nought.

In 1923 Anderson wrote the largely plotless *Many Marriages* and then, having read Joyce's *Ulysses,* he embarked, with some of Joyce's disorientations affecting his style, on *Dark Laughter* (1925). In part it reimagines *Huckleberry Finn* (Faulkner is aware of the debt). John Stockton, a reporter from Chicago, asks what Twain would have chosen to write about in the transforming America of the 1920s, his river and the villages he had known turning into cities, the petty greeds and tyrannies growing and intensifying within the economic and political structures. Stockton records a land "of song killed, of laughter killed, of men herded into a new age of speed, of factories, of swift, fast-running trains." He finds solace among the common people and ends up running off with the boss's wife. In 1920s America this counts as a happy ending.

His advocacy of Gertrude Stein (1874–1946) remains important. Here was a writer weary of naturalism, fascinated by the voices and lives of common people. His politics kept getting in the way because he was angry at those forces that impoverish and enslave commonfolk. "And what I think is that these books of Gertrude Stein's do in a very real sense recreate life in words." His introduction to her work credits her with what he would himself like to have done. He makes a case for her in a speaking voice. "Since Miss Stein's work was first brought to my attention I have been thinking of it as the most important pioneer work done in the field of letters in my time . . . every artist working with words as his medium, must at times be profoundly irritated by what seems the limitations of his medium. What things does he not wish to create with words! There is the mind of the reader before him and he would like to create in that reader's mind a whole new world of sensations, or rather one might better say he would like to call back into life all of the dead and sleeping senses." In Stein's *Three Lives* (1909), for example, the reinvention of fiction is complete. Anderson speaks of "the extension of the province of his art," which serious writers set out to achieve. "One works with words and one would like words that have a taste on the lips, that have a perfume to the nostrils, rattling words one can throw into a box and shake, making a sharp, jingling sound." He does not stress how few words are needed in the box, and how they work by graded, spoken repetition, incrementally, like notation in music, like dabs of paint in different configurations on a canvas. When words speak from the page, they "have a distinct arresting effect upon the eye, words that when they jump out from under the pen one may feel with the fingers as one might caress the cheeks of his beloved." He writes so close to the writing that he seems to be touching the face of the writer. Such advocacy goes beyond its subject. The best of Stein is astonishing; the worst (rather greater in volume) is astonishing. The paradox is that they sound so similar when read aloud.

From *Three Lives* on, Cyril Connolly says, Stein's method became "a simplification, an attack on order and meaning in favor of sound but of sound which in itself generated a new precision." He speaks of her impact on Anderson and on Hemingway. She is anti-mandarin, and despite the seeming opacity of her modernism, a voice made out of the variegated particulars of common speech. From common speech she refined something unprecedented. Mina Loy, her contemporary in Paris, likens her to a Marie Curie, extracting "a radium of the word." This is not quite right. Stein refines only down to the phrase. The word is significant only in combination, and the combination gains in significance with reiteration, subtle variation, and in combination with other not entirely stable phrases that carry a narrative and emotional burden, the writing seeming to take form in the ear rather than the heart. When the language signifies, it seldom does so conventionally: it remains aware of the fact that it is language and that the sense inheres in how it is delivered and in the causes behind that actual form of delivery. To try to paraphrase is to pour it away. Stein's combining of phrases without indicating subordination or precedence is parataxis taken to extremes. In her longest and least controlled work, *The Making of Americans* (1925), which inspired Thornton Wilder's Pulitzer Prize–winning play of 1938, *Our Town,* the technique is taken beyond the sense of sense and makes a text that is *in extenso* unreadable. She showed Hemingway the dozens of her manuscripts; no publisher could keep up with her output. She wrote, her partner Alice B. Toklas typed, and the piles grew. Publishing became intermittent, difficult; she grew restive.

Hemingway persuaded Ford to serialize sections of *The Making of Americans* in the *Transatlantic Review* (pretending it was part of a long short story or novella), and he himself, with the assistance of Miss Toklas, prepared the first installment. It fell to Hemingway also to proofread the text, a task he found tedious, though Stein claimed he benefited from it. Ford learned something, too: not to trust Hemingway, a lesson he never really put into practice. The link between Ford and Stein was less intense and more durable than that between Hemingway and either of them.

It is one of the miracles of the modernist period that Stein found publishers at all. The photographer Alfred Stieglitz published early Stein, giving "Matisse" and "Picasso" their first airing in America. Stieglitz liked them because they charmed him and he could not make sense of them. We read them today as a series of rapt refrains, with small variations, focused, unfocusing, refocused. She described the technique as not repetitious but insistent, and this was right. The diction is simple, and what emerges is not a verbal repetition so much as an emphasis. She speaks of Whitman's avoidance of names: he "wanted really wanted to express the thing and not call it by its name." This refusing to tie a thing to its name, even though the name was correct, this preference for rendering the thing in and as language, accommodating it within the medium rather than subordinating the medium to it, was one of the radical and resonant modernist gestures, insisting that the medium be acknowledged in every phrase.

Diderot wrote his books, he said, for a world of friends: "C'est pour moi et pour mes amis que je lis, que je réfléchis, que j'écris" (It is for my friends that I read, reflect, write). Stein said she wrote for herself and for strangers. She did not crave the remote intimacy of a devoted readership, she said: such a transaction would have been confining for both parties. Then she declared that she wrote only for herself. William Gass wishes she had taken one final step and declared that she did not write for *anybody.* He is Stein's closest reader and most complex contemporary disciple. He says of directed language, "People who send you bills do that. People who want to sell you things so they can send you bills do that. People who want to tell you things so they can sell you things so they can send you bills do that."

She developed a private language with her brother, Leo. When they fell out in 1914 and he departed for Italy with the Renoirs while she stayed in Paris with the Picassos, she developed another kind of language with Alice B. Toklas. This is the language of some works, such as *Tender Buttons,* which is informed by an immediate, erotic privacy that remains at once private and suggestive: the sense is clear though meaning may not be.

Paris was relatively inexpensive. There she and her brother, with the modest fortune inherited from their Jewish-German-American parents' labor as clothing merchants, could live well and contribute to the world of art. 27, rue de Fleurus, which she and Leo originally shared and where she stayed on with her companion, Alice B. Toklas, became a domestic museum of contemporary French art, the walls covered in works by Picasso (one of her close friends), Matisse, and Cézanne. In later years there was usually a poodle called Basket in attendance: Basket I, Basket II: the name survived the dog (Paul Bowles remembers a Basket III, and was photographed with it). Hemingway and his wife went to call on Miss Stein and Miss Toklas. Miss Toklas entertained Mrs. Hemingway while Miss Stein made herself responsible for the young man. The apartment, Hemingway wrote, "was like one of the best rooms in the finest museum except there was a big fireplace and it was warm and comfortable and they gave you good things to eat and tea and natural distilled liqueurs made from purple plums, yellow plums and wild raspberries." Everything was ceremonious: the carafes, the lovely little glasses, more a sacrament than a tea party.

Picasso and Stein argued; she sat endlessly for him so he could paint his remarkable hollow-eyed portrait of her. She chided him for stepping outside his medium and writing poems. They celebrated one another in their best work. Edmund Wilson was not persuaded that Picasso, or Paris, were good for Stein. "She is a first-rate literary talent to whom something very strange and probably unfortunate has happened—perhaps it is the basic emptiness of the life of the artistic foreigner in Paris." She resembles late Henry James in that, had her stories not taken the form and manner that they did, had they "not been told in this queer way," they would not have been written at all. This is a useful connection: some late James and most of Stein's writings exist as instances of themselves, in Stein's case instances of inherencies in a language that does not only attenuate but ceases to connect with conventional rules and is permitted what Hélène Cixous calls a "libidinal" dynamic; ceases to connect simply with the things it names. Of James, Stein writes, "I am I not any longer when I see."

She made different impressions on her visitors. Hemingway wrote, "She had beautiful eyes and a strong German-Jewish face that also could have been Friulano and she reminded me of a northern Italian peasant woman with her clothes, her mobile face and her lovely, thick, alive immigrant hair which she wore put up in the same way she had probably worn it in college." She was voluble while he was shy and listened. Later, as his patience wore thin, he became less shy than sullen. He took John Dos Passos to meet her. "I wasn't quite at home there. A Buddha sitting up there, surveying me," he said, evoking prophetically the statue of her in the park behind the New York Public Library, where she looks like a Native American Gautama.

Julian Green, like Hemingway, fixed on her eyes. They were "large and beautiful, there is something brave and *open* in her expression." She told him about an early, enormous, and influential book she had written, which had affected a large swath of writers. "'It's a rather formidable book,' she tells me, 'it moves rather formidably. It is an epic.'" She was praising *The Making of Americans*. She told Green she admired Cocteau but would not say which works; in fact, "she does not declare herself outright about anything in a precise way." Only on rare occasions did she feel confident enough to offer criticism. She visited Hemingway's rooms and looked over a story. It was all very well, she declared, but *inaccrochable*. This seemed to mean that it did not hook or fix in the way it should, it did not, like a tare, stick in the reader's mind.

In "Une Génération Perdue," a chapter of his memoir *A Moveable Feast*, Hemingway recounts that there was no arguing with her fixed ideas of who and how his generation was. He began to see through her: "She wanted to know the gay part of how the world was going; never the real, never the bad." And later, "She quarrelled with nearly all of us that were fond of her except Juan Gris and she couldn't quarrel with him because he was dead." The impact of her work depended on her personality, her insinuating, passive aggression, hard for a man to counter. She was, he came to see, profoundly lazy.

Among her novels *Three Lives: Stories of the Good Anna, Melanctha and the Gentle Lena* is the most consistent, original, and approachable. Each story is told not in the voice but in the language of the protagonist. This has the effect of depersonalizing the telling from the narrator's and the subject's point of view: both are submitted, or subjected, to an appropriate language, and the reader comes to terms with it, its diction, rhythm, repetitive syntax, with a sense of total presence. The diction is reduced to an extremely narrow range of simple repeated words, some of them consistently used according to the rules of a constructed dialect. Stepping into this language space, she was surprised in composing the second story, of Melanctha (who is not given an adjective in the title, and whose narrative is subtitled *Each One as She May*) that the narrative voice worked in a "prolonged present," without past or future, the life unfolding in language as it is lived in time, without the calming distances before and after. This is why the story is immediate, its end so troubling.

She wrote it at a time when she was posing for Picasso's famous portrait at his studio; she meditated on it and walked back to rue de Fleurus composing sentences, and her biographical cat's-paw Alice B. Toklas reports that "the poignant incidents she wove into the life of Melanctha were often those she noticed in walking down the hill from Ravignan," her poor black American imbued with the universal experiences of poor people. Toklas is Stein's cat's-paw because she never could get round to writing the projected *Life,* so at last (at the end of the book) the character of Stein abruptly declares: "I am going to write it for you. I am going to write it as simply as Defoe did the autobiography of Robinson Crusoe." We return with a sharp elision to the voice of Alice B. "And she has and this is it."

E. M. Forster speaks of Stein as the one novelist who "has tried to abolish time." She "has hoped to emancipate fiction from the tyranny of time and to express in it the life of values only. She fails, because as soon as fiction is completely delivered from time it cannot express anything at all, and in her later writing we can see the slope down which she is slipping." If you forfeit time sequence, inevitably you forfeit the elaborate syntax whose articulations exist in time. But there is this other syntax, and there are the patternings of parataxis whose repetitions (which she called insistences), those brushstrokes, do create a stable pattern in the perpetual present that each of us actually inhabits. Donald Barthelme locates in repetition, insistence, the uniquely painterly element, or analogy, in Stein's writing, "a pointillist technique, where what you get is not adjacent dots of yellow and blue, which optically merge to give you green, but merged meanings, whether from words placed side by side in a seemingly arbitrary way or phrases similarly arrayed, bushels of them."

Virginia Woolf is less categorical than Forster, less generous than Barthelme. She sets the image of the clock ticking at the heart of fiction: Emily Brontë tried to conceal it, Sterne turned it upside down, Proust kept changing the hands to make things happen at the same time. Stein destroys it altogether, and when the clock is broken, syntax and all the other pacing elements perish with it.

Looking at *Melanctha* and beyond, William Gass reflects, "She made me understand how little I knew about what could be done with the basic units of all writing. And she raised philosophical questions about what the basic unit really was, or whether there was one, and about the functions of grammar." Here Flaubert's challenge, to see how *little* the novelist can work with to create full effects, is most cheerfully met: "One of the wonderful things about Gertrude is that her repetitions rearrange the aesthetic grammar of the sentence and impose this new or special grammar upon the ordinary syntax of English." He naturally uses the analogy of painting. "I realized that I had to begin to get a feel, the way a painter would, of what happens when you try a sentence this way or try it that."

In her collaboration with the composer Virgil Thomson on *Four Saints in Three Acts,* originally with an all-black cast, she subjected him to the same radical considerations. Grace Paley records, "Gertrude Stein's *Three Stories* impressed me. The use of the 'other voice.'" Richard Wright insisted that Stein's language helped him find his own voice. She helped in other ways, too: their epistolary friendship, culminating in their meeting in 1946, shortly before her death, was one of her last projects. Making common cause, she helped him get a visa to go to Paris. "I've got to help him . . . You see, we are both members of a minority group." Those minorities within the literary community were based on race, sex, and lifestyle, so that Europe could be home though the imagination remained elsewhere, in a country from which it could never escape, even had it wished to.

When *The Autobiography of Alice B. Toklas* appeared in 1933, it sold well and provided an occasion for both women to travel back to the United States for a protracted speaking tour. The photographer and writer Carl Van Vechten, a close friend who wrote the introduction to Stein's 1946 *Selected Works,* accompanied them on part of the journey and reported on the effect they had on audiences, converting the skeptics and disbelievers by giving voices to those texts, and on how Stein enjoyed airplane travel, gazing down at the United States as at an enormous map, the elements reduced to patterns, shapes, and forms, emptied of their vernacular dailiness and purpose.

When the Second World War began, Stein and Toklas, both Jews, stayed in France but removed to Bilignin, in the Rhône-Alpes. No one seemed to bother much about them. They knew a man with connections under whose protection they were safe. Stein's politics were always conservative: she despised Franklin D. Roosevelt, spoke up for General Franco at the time of the Spanish Civil War (complicating her relations with Picasso), and went so far as to translate some of the French Vichy leader Marshall Pétain's speeches into English: she likened him to George Washington. In 1938 she expressed hostility to the "fathering" Fascist, Communist, and National Socialist leaders of Europe, gendering and dismissing the authoritarian. Her opinions have not been held against her to the same degree as those of other modernists, contemporaries, though they appear to have been no less virulent, and her position, not least as a Jew, equally vexed.

Of all her books, *Paris France,* meditating on expatriation, is her most American. Her techniques and theories would not have occurred to her in the United States. John Ashbery, less programmatic than she is, whose exile in France, and in French, lasted a decade, knows that the rigor of her program, of her voices, is essentially French, the subtle phrasal metamorphoses, the way she moves through sounds to a resolving sound as in "Lifting Belly," how she encodes a sexuality, creating a language that maintains a sense of distance from what it touches and holds. Her notion of a "cubist literature" was to abandon "meaning" for a multidimensional, new art: simplified syntax, series not sequence, reversals, inconsequentialities, hesitancies, surprises, numerous, cumulative. The draining away of content, the word thing in and as itself.

It was Stein who pointed Robert Graves and Laura Riding, both poet-novelists, to Majorca, where they created—far from Paris and competition—another place of exile for English-language writing, though here primarily a British enclave. When they founded the Seizin Press there in 1927, one of the earliest books they brought out was Stein's *An Acquaintance with Description*. Laura Riding (1901–1991) at first found Stein astonishing. The charm wore off. "Some of my experience of Gertrude Stein and Alice Toklas was in the Haute Savoie area of France," she recalls, "Mont Blanc in view, and Gertrude Stein uprearing herself as another mountain, Alice Toklas a foot-hill without whom there would have been no Gertrude Stein mountain." From irony she proceeds to invective: she could not abide what she saw as naive pretension. "Gertrude Stein wanted to be seen as a mountain of sophistication in the form of a new simple-mindedness—a wisdom for the new time dispensing with all the stale complexities of the past. She was, in actual personal force of mind, a wise-cracker." Riding's attacks, given how generous Stein had been, are disproportionate: the old queen bee is vulnerable to the attack of the new. "She had the fluent *bonhomie* of a fraud who wanted only lots of love without requirements of proof of meritedness. It could all seem so sensibly, even beautifully, *natural*." *Seeming* most offended Riding, and she never bit her tongue or minced her words. "In time, I came to know the inner poverty of it all, and took the stand that effusions about her dog 'Basket' did not do, with me, as stuff of devoted communication."

Riding had written fiction, the stories in *Lives of Wives* and *A Progress of Stories,* the novel *A Trojan Ending* (1937), and later co-authored with her third husband, Schuyler B. Jackson, the massive epistemological tome *Rational Meaning*. A poet who publically renounced poetry as a language of untruth and expanded that renunciation over and over until the rationale much exceeded in word-count the whole wonderful rejected poetic oeuvre, was repelled by Stein's slack, unfocusing ideas of language and its usefulness to the exploratory imagination. "She showed, and as if it were a triumph to do this, that the rational impulsion in the use of words was resistible. Her planned incoherencies can make a strong initial impression of liberation from banal syntactical logicalities." "Planned incoherencies," almost a contradiction in terms, describes precisely what Stein is after. Riding is not praising her onetime friend: "Actually, her sentences are formed of cliché fragments. And it is a significant peculiarity of her personal talk, and of her conversational writing, that both abounded in statements of banal generalizedness of sentiment or opinion." Stein could not be tied down and therefore could not be directly engaged in conversation or argument. Language was a medium to swim in, without footing on any terra firma.

Other, more just and useful readings are possible. The poet Ron Silliman arrived—by way of Stein—at a prose sentence that functions like a verse line, at once connected to and disconnected from the adjoining sentences in the same suggestive way as the strophes of a highly enjambed text are. Writing ceases to be representational. As Stein says in "Composition as Explanation," with the logic of "Rose is a rose is a rose" (that is, the girl is a rose, and "the girl is a rose" is itself "a rose"), "The composition is the composition of the composition."

Stein is not a dead end, but she does go to the very edge of the map. Those who have learned most from her in later years have been poets and composers. She is one of the strangest yet most direct heirs of Flaubert; he remarked in a letter of 1852 to Louise Colet: "The best works are those with least matter; the nearer the expression approaches thought, the more the word is silenced by it and disappears, then the more beautiful the work becomes."

The American expatriate writer and publisher Robert McAlmon (1895–1956) published work by Ford, Djuna Barnes, Hemingway's first book of stories, Stein's *The Making of Americans,* and the first novel by Mary Butts (1890–1937), *Ashe of Rings* (1925), about the First World War. A "war fairy tale," it draws on her own life, her prosperous, privileged Dorset childhood (recalled in detail in her memoir *The Crystal Cabinet: My Childhood at Salterns*), on a London where she suffered severe privations, and then back to the mansion in Dorset where the settled world was changed by her own changes. The book explores elements of the occult (she had a messy relationship with the "magician" Aleister Crowley). Her style works in short cadences and phrases, as if it has been assembled out of lines of free verse, and the characters and voices are expressed, and express themselves, in a mannered idiom. This and her other books survive as engaging footnotes to modernism. Butts writes good stories and memoirs, but she does not sustain longer forms. Each of her works is a curate's egg. Emotionally and materially she was needy, but the materialism of her contemporaries repelled her, that of H. G. Wells in particular, with his "hells of Materialism," "pitiless technocrats," and enervated utopias. The past was too much with her, the world of legend, of objects made sacred by history and survival. Socialism repelled her because it denied "all spiritual and all *individual* values." Her emphases became stronger and the world closed in on her. She seemed to promise much in the 1920s, when Gertrude Stein was making Paris over, and practicing, in a more settled and systematic way, experiments not unlike Butts's, but always with her strange paratactic style digesting them into language, without self-pity. As in the portrait of her by Picasso, the eyes see without looking.

# 29

# Social Concerns

H. G. Wells, Rebecca West, Arnold Bennett, John Galsworthy, Somerset Maugham,
Hugh Walpole, Frederic Raphael, Aldous Huxley, Arthur Koestler, George Orwell

Writing fiction, Henry James told a wayward protégé in terms that Stein and Cather would both have found agreeable, "is art that *makes* life, makes interest, makes importance . . . I know of no substitute whatever for the force and beauty of its process." His protégé was Herbert George Wells (1866–1946), now breaking rank with the older writer. James came to seem a bit absurd, ponderous: "Leviathan retrieving pebbles" Wells called him, adding with rancor, because he no longer liked to be patronized, "a magnificent but painful hippopotamus resolved at any cost, even at the cost of its dignity, upon picking up a pea."

In the old country, revolutions more spectacular than Gertrude Stein's were gathering force. But readjustments in the mainstream of fiction had to do with subject matter and social emphasis, and only consequently with form. Arnold Bennett reflects on H. G. Wells's celebrity abroad, but at home? There is the little lady in Bayswater who declares, "Wells? No! I draw the line at Wells. He stirs up the dregs. I don't mind the froth, but dregs I—will—not have!" The homogenizing power of the lending libraries had diminished, but the market for fiction that it created and conditioned knew by reflex what it wanted. Wells was among those redirecting fiction, turning it away too from the implausibly high art of Flaubert as transmitted by James. James said of Wells, "Everything he writes is so alive and kicking." He was in line for some of its kicks.

Aesthetic priorities were put in the balance with social and political concerns. "In claiming to speak for the unspeaking," says the novelist Frederic Raphael, "and affecting to denounce the unspeakable, too many writers have excused themselves from developing their art on the old Wellsian grounds that they had better things to do than excellent work." It is no wonder that Wells's writings appealed, as the best British fiction often did, to younger readers. In 1941 Orwell generalized the impact Wells had had on him: "Back in the nineteen-hundreds it was a wonderful experience for a boy to discover H. G. Wells." Orwell's was not unlike the boyhoods of Wells's own characters setting out on their picaresque adventures: "There you were, in a world of pedants, clergymen and golfers, with your future employers exhorting you to 'get on or get out,' your parents systematically warping your sexual life, and your dull-witted schoolmasters sniggering over their Latin tags." You opened Wells's books, "and here was this wonderful man who could tell you about the inhabitants of the planets and the bottom of the sea, and who *knew* that the future was not going to be what respectable people imagined." Anthony Burgess was reared on Wells's *The Outline of History* and responded to Mr. Polly's view that "human history becomes more and more a race between education and catastrophe." Education need not entail privilege: for Burgess, Wells is "patron saint of all who scribble fast for a living, of all guttersnipes and counterjumpers who make the literary grade," who did not attend Oxford, the apotheosis of the omnivorous and omnicompetent Edwardian.

Edwin Muir contrasts the traditional picaresque "traveling hero" with Wells's "climbing hero," the novel mapped not onto a landscape but onto a society, the hero's progress exploring and anatomizing the vicissitudes of that more or less stable and certainly repressive social world. Adventure is no longer in survival but in success or failure, Mr. Polly's taking action to escape from the imperatives of the social world, or success and failure on an imperial scale as in *Tono-Bungay*. The social world is at once context and theme of Wells's picaresque. At the end of *Tono-Bungay,* as the cruiser *X2* makes its way down the Thames, the narrator (incidentally providing the composer Ralph Vaughan Williams with a kind of descriptive libretto for his *London Symphony*) declares, "Again and again in this book I have written of England as a feudal scheme overtaken by fatty degeneration and stupendous accidents of hypertrophy." Moving down the river, he reads England. "To run down the Thames so is to run one's hand over the pages in the book of England from end to end." He unfolds the panorama of church, gentlemen's clubs, sport, and gradually the newer neighborhoods, "squalid stretches of mean homes right and left and then the dingy industrialism of the south side, and on the north bank the polite long front of nice houses, artistic, literary, administrative people's residences, that stretches from Cheyne Walk nearly to Westminster and hides a wilderness of slums." At last the fiction that is history asserts itself. "For a stretch you have the essential London; you have Charing Cross railway station, heart of the world, and the Embankment on the north side with its new hotels overshadowing its Georgian and Victorian architecture, and mud and great warehouses and factories, chimneys, shot towers, advertisements on the south. The northward skyline grows more intricate and pleasing, and more and more does one thank God for Wren. Somerset House is as picturesque as the civil war, one is reminded again of the original England, one feels in the fretted sky the quality of Restoration Lace." Celebration, elegy, satire: the passage is full of knowledge, love, fatigue, and as it enters the area of the slums, anger.

The new writers saw the English novel, as George Eliot (more nicely) had done, as instrumental, didactic: defining, then taking sides. That current of

English fiction that flows strongly through Fielding, Austen, Dickens, Eliot, and Hardy remained a dominant current, streaming on despite French, American, and Irish countercurrents. Wells brings in not new forms but a new genre, what V. S. Pritchett's calls "scientific romance," predictive rather than prophetic, a fiction that works itself free of the laws of contingency only to create contingencies of its own. Ruefully Pritchett says, "There was a time, one realizes, when science was fun." We must go back to the Swift of *Gulliver's Travels* to find science (of a rather different sort, untainted with the gothic or the romantic) inspiring fiction and providing a basis for satire. "The influence of science, in the 150 years that lie between those two writers, is philosophical, not factual." *Frankenstein* came from a different source. Here we are on the threshold of science fiction, but the exigencies of conventional fiction hold. Wells's route-map to the future took him down a political road, but it ran parallel to the road that Don Quixote, Christian, Robinson Crusoe, and Waverley had traveled.

The new writers lived differently from James, or Proust, or Mrs. Wharton and Mrs. Ward, who stood apart, getting into the large world of their fiction by creating stable perspectives. Their distance was not irony; on the contrary, they were witnesses of life's ironies, their fiction explored them but did not commit its style to irony. It resisted complicity. When Wells and other contemporaries put their art at the service of social concerns, when they chose a fiction governed by political or philosophical logic rather than the intractable human experience that in different ways Flaubert and Zola charted, they took a decisive step in the reader's direction. Wells put first what he took to be the reader's civic health. What the French call "la littérature engagée" (which paradoxically describes a literature that is disengaged from the texture of the "real" and propelled by ideological energies) was anathema to James, whose effort was in seeing. Wells's writing is "about," James's at its best "is": James creates experience. His art is primary; in these terms, Wells's is secondary, as secondary as criticism can be.

Wells met James in 1898. Three years earlier, in the company of George Bernard Shaw, Wells had walked away from the first night of James's play *Guy Domville*. Wells was English, born in Bromley, Kent, and the fact that he was lower middle class weighed on him: his mother had undeniably been a housemaid, his father (thanks to an inheritance like Mr. Polly's) an unsuccessful shopkeeper, risen from domestic gardener, and an avid cricketer with the county team, earning extra income from playing. With a freethinking father and a devout Protestant mother, Wells in his early years experienced recurrent domestic turbulence. His parents finally separated, his mother going back into service, and the four children, of whom Bertie was the youngest, went their ways. Young Wells was apprenticed to a draper from 1880 to 1883, and his experiences fed into his Jerome-K.-Jeromish comic cycling novel *The Wheels of Chance* (1896) and a decade later *Kipps: The Story of a Simple Soul*. ("I tell you we're in a blessed drain-pipe, and we've got to crawl along it till we die," says the apprentice Minton.)

He did not succeed as a draper. He had already botched his chances as a chemist's assistant, though he had learned lessons that would prove valuable in writing *The Invisible Man*. After each failure he returned home and stoked the fires of disillusion with more reading: fiction, philosophy, history. He made two stabs at becoming a schoolmaster, the second time succeeding, going to London, and studying with the Darwinian biologist Thomas Henry Huxley, one of the clearest minds and prose stylists of his time. He started earning an almost reasonable income but remained in every sense hungry. Eventually, in 1890 he attained a BSc in zoology. He found another teaching post and numbered among his favorite pupils the young A. A. Milne (the school was run by Milne's father), who would create *Winnie the Pooh* for his son Christopher.

He married a cousin, divorced her, and married one of his pupils, on whom he fathered two sons, and though they remained married until his wife's death, he proceeded through a series of affairs, most famously with Rebecca West (1892–1983), with whom he had a writer son, Anthony West. The dynamics of sex intrigued him as a writer and a zoologist. There is something cinematic in his occasional portrayals of intimacy. Pritchett writes, "The love scenes between the giants in *The Food of the Gods* are the most embarrassing in English fiction, and one wonders that the picture of the awful Princess, goggling in enormous close-up and fanning herself with half a chestnut tree, did not destroy the feminist movement." Swift would have written such a scene with comic intent, but Wells's intentions are dramatic.

He admired D. H. Lawrence as a writer and a life, seeing in him a man with social disadvantages similar to his own. Wells's early social and material insecurity informed his imaginative world: the movement of his fiction is toward release or escape from trammeling circumstances. His social fiction and his science fiction follow a similar trajectory. The first twenty years he regarded as crucial to the growth of his imagination: they also left him chronically uneasy in well-heeled drawing rooms and set him, in his own estimation, at a disadvantage in the London literary world of the time. Mrs. Humphry Ward looks all the way down her handsome nose with condescension: "Mr. Wells seems to me a journalist of very great powers, of unequal education, and much crudity of mind, who has inadvertently strayed into the literature of imagination." She almost endorses *Kipps* ("almost a masterpiece"), *Tono-Bungay* ("a piece of admirable fooling, enriched with some real character-creation, a thing extremely rare in Mr. Wells's books"), and *Mr. Britling Sees It Through* ("perhaps more likely to live than any other of his novels, because the subject with which it deals comes home so closely to so vast an audience"). Yet as a character Mr. Britling "has neither life nor joints," and she throws in gratuitously, "like the many other heroes from other Wells novels, whose names one can never recollect": the book survives because of its subject, the living experience of the war. He lacks *charm,* and without charm, Mrs. Ward says, his journalistic fiction has no hope of lasting. Mr. Bennett, on the other hand . . .

Wells belonged to a rising generation that included Bennett, Galsworthy, and other writers Woolf described as "materialists." Wells's mind "is too generous in its sympathies to allow him to spend much time in making things shipshape and substantial. He is a materialist from sheer goodness of heart, taking upon his shoulders the work that ought to have been discharged by Government officials, and in the plethora of his ideas and facts scarcely having leisure to realize, or forgetting to think important, the crudity and coarseness of his human beings." His sense of economy was more than a legacy of Balzac: it overrode the metaphysical instinct with a sense of the sufficiency of the given world: it was everything that was the case. Transcendence was a province for theologians and hypocrites. If a projected future is his subject, the "actual" world prefigures and determines it, an extended materiality. Wells, Bennett, and Galsworthy "are concerned not with the spirit but with the body," and "the sooner English fiction turns its back upon them, as politely as may be, and marches, if only into the desert, the better for its soul."

Essentially, "they write of unimportant things" or, as C. P. Snow does in a later materialist generation, make important things inconsequential; "they spend immense skill and immense industry making the trivial and the transitory appear the true and enduring." There is a problem here with Woolf rather than Wells and his contemporaries: for her "the unimportant" seems categorical rather than aesthetic. She has read the Russians and wants English writers to stand up in their company, with comparable spiritual and existential seriousness. For Hudson, Hardy, and Conrad, "we reserve our unconditional gratitude." They know what matters and do not ignore the darkness.

Ford notes Wells's contrary nature, his recurrent outrages, as part of his interest in things; he lacks a sense of proportion, hence his enlarging of little lives, foregrounding of what is generally obscured. He contrasts in Wells the *imaginer* and the bitter *remembrancer:* "the difference precisely between a pure genius and a damned journalist" (damned in the sense of cursed). Pritchett reads him in the same way: "I think the best Wells is the destructive, ruthless, black-eye-dealing and house-burning Wells who foresaw the violence and not the order of our time." In *The Island of Dr. Moreau,* a generic forebear of Conan Doyle's *The Lost World* and Edgar Rice Burroughs's *The Land That Time Forgot* (1924), the eponymous doctor is, Pritchett declares, "of course, a sadist." Borges called the book "an atrocious miracle" and imagined it finding its way into the center of English literature. So far it has not, though Margaret Atwood has written an essay suggesting ten divergent readings, approaching a fictional territory marked out by Calvino and, differently, by Julian Barnes.

Only occasionally does Wells put one in mind of Stevenson—for example, in *The Invisible Man* when the mystery of the protagonist is handled in a Mr. Hyde spirit, though Wells's science is more convincing than Stevenson's and the explanation of the ways in which he achieves invisibility feels plausible. More than Stevenson, Wells recalls Kipling. Though "opposed in tendency, Wells and Kipling both have the vision of artists; they foresee the conditions of our time. They both foretold the violence with a certain appetite," Pritchett says.

Wells's profligacy, his rapid inventiveness and reluctance to refine, came to irritate James, who became avuncular. His assumption of authority and seniority in turn riled Wells, whose books, after all, outsold James's. Class, even suppressed, still makes political choices and politics color a writer's work. James said of Wells, not without reason (and with disappointment), "so much life" but "so little living." Living has to do with consistency, fidelity, and concentration; it has moral dimensions.

Wells's ten-year relationship with Rebecca West coincided with her writing and publishing her admiring biography of Henry James (it appeared in 1916); James would have been a recurrent topic of discussion. The affair began in 1913, a year before relations with James began to cool. West had given a harsh review to Wells's *Marriage*. She was irritated by his mannerisms. Wells invited her to lunch and they fell tetchily, precipitately into a love of a kind that did not destroy his marriage and accelerated his already formidable literary productivity. He published over fifty novels in his lifetime, and dozens of books on other subjects, from history and science to zoology, political polemic, and attempts at autobiography. The years he shared with West were among his most creative. (She was to take a different view of them.)

One strand of his writing leads into classic science fiction and includes *The Time Machine* (1895), *The Island of Doctor Moreau* (1896), *The Invisible Man* (1897), *The War of the Worlds* (1898), and *The First Men on the Moon* (1901). Another strand, in which James heard Wells's true voice, explored the insistent *present*, which reminded James of his own sense of the present. The more conventional novels were well plotted, topical, and written with directness. They include *Kipps* (1905), *Tono-Bungay* (1909), *The History of Mr. Polly* (1910), *The New Machiavelli* (1911), *Marriage* (1912), and several more. His later life he gave over to nonfiction, popular history, political science, and prophecy. "I flung myself into futurity," he announced in his bright new voice at the start of the bright new century; by the

end, with the Second World War, whose ideologies and machines he had prophesied half a century earlier, he was giving up on mankind: *Mind at the End of Its
Tether* (1945) is ashen, disenchanted. He is in some ways quite as logical as Zola,
but while Zola unfolds lives in their bleak declension, Wells unfolds ideas, moving less from people than from premises. *The Outline of History* (1919) sold over
3 million copies, better than all his other books together.

In September 1914 the government invited well-known writers to make public declarations of the case for war. Wells (with Barrie, Bennett, Galsworthy,
Hardy, and Masefield) complied. He was at home with arguments, his imagination tending to generalize but never quite to coalesce. Alongside radical new
ideas, old prejudices persist. Like Maugham, Greene, and others, until the rise of
Hitler he participated, as it were by reflex, in the anti-Semitism of the age, a
bleak aspect of cultural laziness that survives in British intellectual life.

Wells invented a number of utopias, from the little epiphany of Mr. Polly's
happy deliverance from the urban world, to elaborate, implausible worlds he
made, from *Men Like Gods* (1923) to *The Shape of Things to Come* (1933). Contented,
ordered, reasonable lives are devoid of the negative emotions, the deadly sins;
things are temperate and bland. Social change, Wells thought, would gradually
alter human expectation and human nature itself. But he could not fail to learn
from history, and by 1941 the hopes of Fabian Socialism were over: social me-
liorism had proven illusory. Orwell returned, in a memorable 1941 essay, to this
writer who had been his mentor. He quotes with deadly effect. Wells called
Hitler "that screaming little defective in Berlin" (the word "defective" reminding us of his interest in eugenics before the war), and said the German army
was inefficient, its air power largely spent, when the facts were otherwise.
Wells was simply too sane to understand the world, Orwell said, a generous
reading that detects, too, the limits of his fictional imagination. "Creatures out
of the Dark Ages have come marching into the present," said Orwell of the Nazis, "and if they are ghosts they are at any rate ghosts which need a strong
magic to lay them." Wells lacked that magic and he did not like Orwell's essay.
He called his critic a Trotskyist with flat feet. (In fact, inside his size-twelve
shoes or boots, Orwell did have flat feet.) It would be wrong to judge Wells on
his last years. Conrad, against Forster's verdict that Wells was quite without
poetry, insists, "Mr. Wells, the writer of prose whose amazing inventiveness we
all know, remains a poet even in his most perverse moments of scorn for things
as they are. His poetic imagination is sometimes even greater than his inventiveness, I am not afraid to say." And Bennett revered him, writing in 1917 of
*The New Machiavelli:* "To me the welcome accorded to his best books has always
seemed to lack spontaneity, to be characterized by a mean reluctance. And yet

if there is a novelist writing today who by generosity has deserved generosity, that novelist is H. G. Wells."

Wells could be generous as an advocate. He praised another ex-draper writer, the Welsh novelist Caradoc Evans (1878–1945), for his "brutal thoroughness" as a realist, a rare example of someone writing directly from experience of the squalid shops, the tyranny of the employers, the spiritual brutality of the chapel, the long hours, the meagerness and injustice of the life. His stories *My People* (1915) and the novel *Nothing to Pay* (1930) are his key works. "I remember things: badly-paid farm labourers; stunted pale-faced children, whose bodies are starved and whose intellect is stifled at the hands of the village schoolmaster; sexless women whose blood has been robbed by the soil; little villages hidden in valleys and reeking with malice."

---

Rebecca West was born Cicely Isabel Fairfield in 1892 in London. Her novel *The Fountain Overflows* evokes her background, though the characters of the parents are altered in the interests of fiction. The family's relative poverty contrasted with the material solidity of her surroundings: "We had furniture and we had masses of books, and we had a very good piano my mother played on." The furniture was from her father's Anglo-Irish side of the family. It is out of that impecunious solidity that her material ambition came. Her father, well educated and widely talented, died when she was twelve. Her piano-playing mother returned to her native Scotland, learned typewriting, and provided for her family with an alternative keyboard skill. She worked for an American evangelist team as secretary and then hymn accompanist when they toured Britain. Later she ran a typing business, and her clients included Edinburgh academics. There was a sense of emancipation in a household abandoned by its menfolk: the women managed to make do, and more. Cicely left school at sixteen with tuberculosis, and her formal education was over. She missed out on advanced Latin and on Greek, but her early fascination with historical and poetic romance, and with drama, presaged much. She had performed for her parents, their friends, and the servants. Her play on the death of Chatterton she printed and performed alone in the attic, moving herself to tears.

The lack of formal structure in her learning shaped and limited her originality. She went as far as curiosity took her, then veered off another way. Her instincts were those of a journalist and her fiction celebrates the sufficiency of facts. In *Beginnings* she speaks of the "foolscap ledgers" where from an early age she wrote her books. She preserved them: "They stand in a row at the bottom of my bookshelves, getting dusty and more dusty as time goes on." She revisits them and is astonished at their energy and their scrupulous tidiness, an aspect of the "priggishness" of the young writer: "I realized that I had worked out my first plays and my first poems much as I drew maps of the river system of France for the classes I attended in London." Her historical novels were written then, some running to 300 sheets of foolscap. At twenty-five she attempted a modern novel: "Prose was still a contemptible stopgap for the days on which I could not write poetry."

Her relations with Wells, and later affairs with, some say, Charlie Chaplin and, without doubt, the press baron Lord Beaverbrook, gave her no qualms. She became the most prolific of critics, writing for British and American newspapers and magazines. American work kept her in the money. So did marriage in 1930 to a banker, a relationship that survived until his death in 1968. She amassed a fortune through writing. In 1948 President Truman, dubbing her "the world's best reporter," gave her the Women's Press Club Award for Journalism. She was fascinated by trials, in particular the Nuremberg trials (which she reported on for the *New Yorker*). Some regard as her best book, combining history, travelogue, political commentary, and autobiography, *Black Lamb and Grey Falcon* (1941), more than 1,100 pages about the Balkans. For the *Sunday Times* she wrote on South African apartheid. Her last novel, *The Birds Fall Down* (1966), is a spy story set in Russia before the Revolution. It is based on the life of the turn-of-the-century Belarussian Jewish agent provocateur and double agent Yevno Azef, a figure Conrad more sinisterly evokes in *Under Western Eyes*.

Virtually alone among intellectuals she believed Senator McCarthy was not wrong to conduct the anticommunist investigations in the brutal way that he did, and she never adjusted this opinion. Her politics remained left–right: floating, though she normally voted with the left. While her anticommunism alienated her from the liberal-left establishment in Britain, she retained a more secure presence in the United States. She could be harsh about American culture, but she recalled, "I longed, when I was young, to write as well as Mark Twain. It's beautiful stuff and I always liked him."

Her first novel, *The Return of the Soldier* (1918), was the first Great War novel by a woman, written while the war was still being fought. Her protagonist has lost part of his memory and longs to return to his first love, a humble woman, rather than to his wife, who belongs to his own class. In the ensuing four decades she published another four "problem" novels and some novellas about class, money, what the Collects call "inordinate desires," and the impact of social pressures on the individual. Her 1956 novel *The Fountain Overflows* remains most readable, depicted from the life: her own. A pianist mother struggles to make ends meet, a brilliant father unsettles things, the exceptional children come alive. The best and least dependable elements of a culture are metonymized in the Aubrey family story. The posthumously published novels (*This Real Night* in 1984 and *Cousin Rosamund* in 1985) add to the account.

———•———

Late in life West suddenly, sourly remembered Arnold Bennett (1867–1931): "He was a horrible, mean-spirited, hateful man. I hated Arnold Bennett." T. S. Eliot was equally repelled by Bennett. One evening, "sitting on a mat . . . discussing psychical research with William Butler Yeats (the only thing he ever talks about, except Dublin gossip)," Eliot was affronted: "A red-faced, sprucely-dressed man with an air of impatient prosperity and the aspect of a successful grocer came up and interrupted us with a most disagreeable Cockney accent," and he adds parenthetically, "( . . . the lower middle class cockney beats them all)." How did a man from the Potteries, who spent much of his life in Paris, develop a cockney accent? "I was so irritated," Eliot says, "that I left for another part of the room almost at once—later I found out it was Arnold Bennett."

The image of the successful grocer fits Bennett like a silk hat on a Five Towns millionaire. Inventory is his vocation. On January 2, 1905, he does his annual stock take: "Last year I wrote 282,100 words, exclusive of rewriting. This comprises . . ." and he enumerates the plays, novels, stories. It is the precision of the final 100 words that is tellingly specific. He loves catalogs: in his *Journal* he lists the reviews he receives, his completed stories in different series, his expenses. Often minutely, day by day, we see a work growing statistically before our eyes, and then the harvest in terms of money advanced and earned. "Tonight," he wrote on Tuesday, September 29, 1896, "I am to begin my new novel, *Sir Marigold,* a study of paternal authority." He knows, as if it is in the past, the hour of commencement, the title, the theme of the book. It is there already, waiting for him to come and inflate it. But he is anxious about influence: he's unwisely been reading George Meredith and Mrs. Humphry Ward and they have infected him, Meredith with a style that is "splendidly fantastic," Mrs. Ward with her realism "by dint of laborious and carefully ordered detail," both out of key with "my natural instincts towards a *synthetic impressionism*" derived from the Goncourts.

One feels the impressionist in his perspectives, when, for example, the narrator walks behind a group of people and infers their expressions. This creates a sense of space: in following, one is measuring distance before, and if the distance behind has already been created, space opens out. The narrator is subject to the larger context of the novel. "Bennett's gift as a writer," Pritchett says, "is to abolish the rôle of spectator." We see and know with the character. Without the omniscient perspective, we are muddled and resolved with and in the characters. Point of view is dilated.

The French naturalists, too, made their mark on Bennett. But the excess of "laborious and carefully ordered detail" works against the "truth to the impression" he seeks: the rooms are too full of enumerated furniture, and many of the landscapes starved of moving air. "Usually the documentary eye served him only too well": Greene is disappointed at the vivid scene painting, where characters are less realized, or not realized at all. A material world that is too real, too solid, makes it hard for characters to emerge, their individual response is disabled. "What we make out Mr. Bennett as doing," says James, "is simply recording his possession or, to put it more completely, his saturation." This material saturation is important to recognize because his contemporaries, too, "whether by his direct action on their collective impulse or not, [are] embroiled, as we venture to call it, in the same predicament." This is what Pritchett means when he speaks of the solidity of Bennett's world, its circumstantial foursquareness: "He is the connoisseur of normality, of the ordinary, the awkward," and Pritchett stresses his "fidelity" to the seen, if not the visualized, world and his insistent "sincerity." The reader is entitled to ask, does sincerity have a place in this kind of art?

Wells and Bennett are complementary manifestations of the period. Bennett's origins were less modest than Wells's, but were joyless. He was born in the Potteries in a town subsumed into modern Stoke-on-Trent. His father became a solicitor when Arnold was nine, and they took a stiff step up in the world. He showed early promise, composing a sonnet while still a small child. He was educated locally and started working for his father, an abstemious, even a miserly man. Bennett remained in his father's employ until he was twenty-one, sometimes acting as his rent collector. Elements from his autobiography color *Anna of the Five Towns* (1902), making the character of the protagonist Anna Tellwright and of her father unsentimentally real. His father haunts even his later fiction. He provides a distant model for Henry Earlforward, the hard old spirit of *Riceyman Steps* (1923). Perennial conflict between parents and children is here, and in others of Bennett's books, given a new vitality. As often as not, the conflict originates in the child.

Bennett escaped to London in his twenty-first year to become a solicitor's clerk, then a journalist, and at last a writer. He could not shake the Potteries out of his imagination. His first novel was *A Man from the North* (1898). Its protagonist admires Maupassant in the way that Bennett did. In 1900 he was supporting himself full-time as a writer, and in 1903 he moved to Paris, where he did some of his best writing. He chronicled "the Five Towns" rather in the spirit in which Hardy chronicled Wessex, homing time after time in fiction, never so vividly as in *The Old Wives' Tale* (1908), an international success that gained him an American readership. The seven decades' trajectory of the narrative is a provincial history and includes, too, a metropolitan counterpoint in the history of France.

He prospered and was generous to other writers. He retained a nineteenth-century sense of the civic and moral duties that accompany the writer's vocation. For him, to a greater extent than for Wells, the conflict with Henry James had to do with the place accorded the reader in the writer's creative enterprise. "I can divide all the imaginative writers I have ever met into two classes," says Bennett magisterially, "—those who admitted and sometimes proclaimed loudly that they desired popularity; and those who expressed a noble scorn or a gentle contempt for popularity. The latter, however, always failed to conceal their envy of popular authors," the "noble scorn" revealing itself as ironic, "and this envy was a phenomenon whose truculent bitterness could not be surpassed even in political or religious life." This aloof tone is one reason Wyndham Lewis described him as "a kind of book-dictator," repelled by his narrow certainty, his hostility to experiment, and his obsession with money.

He is obsessed. It has been suggested that he may have been the prototype for the extreme cultural materialist Mr. Nixon in Ezra Pound's poem *Hugh Selwyn Mauberley*. In 1898 Bennett surveyed the earning power of his contemporaries: Wells was outstripping Hardy at "12 guineas per thousand," like some seriously down-market entertainers, and Stanley Weyman, with an American following, got 16 to 18 guineas per thousand words. "Kipling stands solitary and terrible at £50 per thousand, £200 being his minimum for his shortest short story." Money is the measure. "Some, indeed many, of the greatest creative artists," he says, including himself, "have managed to be very good merchants also, and have not been ashamed of the double *rôle*." He was one of the earliest novelists to employ an agent, the great J. B. Pinker. By 1913 Bennett was earning £17,000 per annum. He acquired a Queen Anne House—in Essex, admittedly—and a yacht, traveled widely, and outstripped most of his contemporaries in material terms. The aesthete who does not engage with the commercial aspects of his vocation knows "no more about reality than a Pekinese dog on a cushion . . . Let him mingle with the public, for God's sake! No phenomenon on this wretched planet, which after all is ours, is meet for the artist's shrinking scorn." The words *must* and *should* fall lightly from his pen, instructing the writer what to do, the reader what to demand. D. H. Lawrence's criticism can be equally cajoling, but always in the interests of breaking rather than reinforcing norms; his average man is anything but average in Bennett's terms. Lawrence loves the potentiality of the independent, ignitable intelligence.

Unsettling in Bennett's expository writing are his assumptions about writers and about "us" readers, with whom he aligns himself. This is what John Carey, trying to restore Bennett in 1992 in his antimodernist *The Intellectuals and the*

*Masses* (1992), warmed to in the writer, a forgotten hero in the battle against "high culture." Rebecca West was unconvinced by the ideology and the books: "Mr. Bennett can never work happily on a character which is not socially and personally mediocre." For Woolf, despite his insistence on the material world and characteristic characters, he fails to get inside them: he tries to "hypnotize us" to believe that, once he has constructed the house, "there must be a person living there."

At the start Bennett admired Flaubert, but he developed a dislike for him. His "unreality" was intolerable, Bouvard and Pécuchet do not live down the street, any street: in literal terms their story is impossible. He writes, without irony, this most English of judgments: "If Flaubert had been a greater artist he might have been more of an amateur." Yet he is willing to accept, with regret, other kinds of unrealism, such as the view that in matters of sexual representation the public's prejudices need to be considered.

Bennett is modern, servicing the public and urging other writers into the same collusion. He was, Bellow says, one of the "exceedingly proficient and dependable servants of the reading public." Lacking "is the impulse to expand." He wrote a piece entitled: "Literary Taste: How to Form It, with Detailed Instructions for Collecting a Complete Library of English Literature." Read on: the completeness is, as such completenesses necessarily are, partial in both senses. Yet he knew what the new reader wanted: authority, instruction, a way of feeling safe in the world of books, of not being wrong-footed by a natural liking or an exposed ignorance. With the lending libraries in decline and criticism increasingly highbrow, the *How To* age had arrived. He also produced the successful *How to Live on 24 Hours a Day* where the novel too has its moment: "A good novel rushes you forward like a skiff down a stream, and you arrive at the end, perhaps breathless, but unexhausted. The best novels involve the least strain." And from the preface: "The proper, wise balancing of one's whole life may depend upon the feasibility of a cup of tea at an unusual hour."

There is another side to him. Novelist Margaret Drabble's biography shows him responding to modern movements in art and literature (usually abroad). In 1908 he praised Chekhov, the Russian Ballet, Romain Rolland, André Gide, Paul Valéry, and Paul Claudel. He may have encouraged Constance Garnett to translate Dostoyevsky. He cannot resist the natural realism of the Russians, Turgenev in particular. Visiting the United States, where Dreiser's *Sister Carrie* had sold a tiny number of copies, Bennett (welcomed as the greatest British novelist to tour since Dickens) hailed the book and raised it from the dead. He spoke up for T. S. Eliot and Robert Graves and gave D. H. Lawrence money, something that Lawrence had not accepted from Wells.

When Sinclair Lewis saw Bennett's manuscript of *The Old Wives' Tale,* "written in the most delicate script, legible as typing, with almost no changes in it, and decorated with coloured initials by him, so that it's like a monkish scroll," he was puzzled that anyone could draft at speed with such meticulousness. Bennett, in turn, marveled at the blue-and-red revised tangle of Lewis's scripts. Bennett's manuscript physically manifested what Virginia Woolf claimed of his art: "He can make a book so well constructed and solid in its craftsmanship that it is difficult for the most exacting of critics to see through what chink or crevice decay can creep in. There is not so much as a draught between the frames of the windows, or a crack in the boards." Such structure! "And yet—if life should refuse to live there? That is a risk which the creator of *The Old Wives' Tale,* George Cannon, Edwin Clayhanger, and hosts of other figures, may well claim"—we expect the worst, but she turns niftily—"to have surmounted. His characters live abundantly, sometimes unexpectedly, but it remains to ask how do they live, and what do they live for?"

In his introduction to *The Old Wives' Tale* Bennett recalls reading *Une vie* by Maupassant, how the author told the whole life history of a woman. The technical achievement fascinated him and he proposed to go one better and tell, in a single novel, the whole life story of two women, sisters, working out their very different salvations. Two young girls become two stout and stiff old ladies. "Constance was the original; Sophia," who elopes with a traveling salesman, heir of a modest fortune, "was created out of bravado, just to indicate that I declined to consider Guy de Maupassant as the last forerunner of the deluge." Bennett could compose with an almost Trollopian celerity, and the first part of this book took him six weeks to draft. It grew naturally out of his own experience: "In the first decade of my life, I had lived in the actual draper's shop of the Baines's, and knew it as only a child could know it." When he knew his subject so well, he wrote with authority; later in the book when Sophia, in France where she had fled with her cowardly, pretentious husband, Gerald, is made to witness the execution of the murderer Rivain at Auxerre, his imagination lets him down. He is uncomfortable with invention. The execution that does not convince us does finally unman Gerald, and from this moment on he is beyond sympathy. Sophia gains independence, remains in Paris, and refurbishes a faded guest house, making a personal fortune out of her unfulfillment.

When, at the end of the novel, Sophia having died and Constance having survived to witness the attempt to federate the Five Towns, the demands of progress come up against the settled conservatism of the communities. She fears that federation cannot be resisted; her last efforts as a sentient citizen are to vote against it, risking her life to go out, and as a consequence falling into her final

illness, though the outcome brings a quiet joy to her last hours. "Only the pro-
foundest philosophers had not been surprised," says the narrator, "to see that
the mere blind, deaf, inert forces of reaction, with faulty organization, and
quite deprived of the aid of logic, had proved far stronger than all the alert enthusiasm arrayed against them. It was a notable lesson to reformers."

This novel possesses an ending that is English to an almost parodic degree.
It ends, literally, in a dog's dinner. Tottery old Fossette, the only residue of Sophia's years in Paris, muses, as dogs do in Kipling and Woolf, on her neglect
now that her mistress is dead, and on dog life generally. This last connection
with Sophia's life abroad provides an unintentionally comic echo. At first the
dog rejects what is put out for her, sulks, but then, because nobody seems to
care, she addresses her bowl of food. It is not the sisters or the dog who are the
protagonist of the book, E. M. Forster says. "Time is the real hero of *The Old
Wives' Tale.*" He stresses the novelist's devotion to sequence, the lived tyranny
of sequence that Scott also understood. What the novel compels us to acknowledge is that time passes: we start off full of hope but in the end we die. Pritchett
writes of how he conveys the sense of time passing, "a passing which blurs our
distinctiveness and quietly establishes our anonymity."

Bennett specialized in female characters. He understood some of the difficulties women from different backgrounds experienced and also how general
circumstances were changing in empowering ways. Of the twenty-odd novels,
seven identify their heroines in the title: *Anna of the Five Towns* (1902), *Leonora*
(1903), *Teresa of Watling Street* (1904), *The Book of Carlotta* (a 1911 revision of *Sacred and Profane Love* from 1905), *Hilda Lessways* (1911, second in the celebrated
Clayhanger trilogy), *The Pretty Lady* (1918), and finally an ironic goddess, *Venus
Rising from the Sea* (1931). "There are writers whose last novels are very like the
first," Saul Bellow says. "Having learned their trade, mastered it once and for all,
they practice it with little variation to the very end. They can be very good novelists." But will they continue to be read? Only if this great figure of fun, sent up by
the modernists as a pompous critic and conventional writer, can be reconceived,
a sense of his originality restored to the novels. Ford sees him as a *Homo duplex,*
the opinionating journalist with a moral mission and, on the other hand, "a real
genius, which is a much quieter affair." The novels had the intended effects on
readers. In his diaries John Cowper Powys describes Phyllis Playter, his partner, reading the opening of *Clayhanger* at breakfast and reducing them both to
tears. "She read about the little Darius being saved from the Workhouse by Mr.
Shushions. She cried & I cried. It was a triumph for 'A.B.'!"

Pritchett speaks for "us" much as Bennett does, but more wisely: "Our final
impression of him is as a kind of estate agent's valuer walking with perfunctory
step through the rooms of our lives, ticking his inventory and treating us as if

we were long deceased." This lesson a generation of English writers mislearned from French naturalism: to begin when the character is safely dead, to retrace the life. Fiction as a coroner's art.

Unlike Wells and Bennett, the Nobel Prize–winning novelist John Galsworthy (1867–1933), O.M., rejecter of a knighthood, first president of PEN International, and most clubbable of men, was born into a wealthy county family and grew up on a handsome estate in Surrey. He studied at Harrow School and then trained for the law at New College, Oxford, where his memorial stone in the cloisters was carved by the great sculptor Eric Gill. In 1890 he was called to the bar, but he preferred travel and work in the family shipping business. In Australia he met the novelist-to-be Conrad, still a sailor, and they became friends. Conrad never lost an opportunity to promote Galsworthy's work. Galsworthy's love life was complex and intense and fed into his fiction.

He started as a storywriter, using a pseudonym for seven years. In 1904 he owned up to a book and in 1906 to a successful play. In that year a notable novel, *The Man of Property*, first of the three Forsyte novels, was published. He was better known as a playwright, alert to social problems, than as a novelist. The plays and the novels inhabit a social zone where a gradually unraveling lower aristocracy and the high bourgeoisie with social aspirations circle around each other, scheming. He is engaged by his characters; modern readers are often repelled by their sophistical and predatory materialism, their exquisitely insincere good manners, and their furtive flouting of conventions. Many of his women are snared in unsatisfactory marriages (as his wife-to-be had been, conducting an affair with him for a decade before they were able to marry). Irene Forsyte is one of the women their long affair inspired. Not all readers warmed to her. Lawrence declared her "a sneaking, creeping, spiteful sort of bitch."

Lawrence contrasts human being and social being and suggests that novelists conceive character in one way or the other, but seldom combine both. Galsworthy's characters are social beings, alive only in one another's company, while Dickens's, Austen's and even, he suggests, Meredith's share a world with us, and we with them. The social being as opposed to the human being follows the rules and patterns of the slave of old. Obedience. Servitude to one master. Money: it filters into every fiber of character. Money contributes, deeply, to human characterization, "but in the last naked him it does not enter." Yet in Galsworthy, as in Bennett (though not in Wells), it does. Most readers might agree that only characters with the defined will and self-awareness of Irene somehow, just, manage to transcend it. The others are subject to "the money-sway" and "the social moral," both of which are in Lawrence's book "inhuman." He had been reading Nietzsche when he ambushed Galsworthy, a writer whose work he had read with pleasure before he was commissioned to reread it with displeasure.

When he says that "the later novels are purely commercial," he underlines how much Galsworthy's imagination has sold out. What begins as satire, Lawrence says, fizzles out because the author "gave in to the Forsytes." Orwell puts it differently: "The bitterness of his earlier vision of life gave his books an undeniable power" but in the later books he becomes complacent and benign.

Even in his early work he was not "dangerously subversive," more "morbidly pessimistic." The characters were, after all, not unlike the Galsworthys themselves. "Satire exists for the very purpose of killing the social being, showing him what an inferior he is"; and Galsworthy could not go through with that. In the end he was "dishonest to life." His male protagonists are "afflicted with chronic narcissism." Sex in the novels is "doggy," its trajectory from desire to consummation without nuance. Despite pomade and aftershave, the Galsworthys are sniffers and leg-cockers. At the level of sex, had his satire run deep, he might have triumphed, but at that level he sentimentalizes. Because he is so rooted in a single class and landscape, his novels do not connect with England at large.

Writing about him during the First World War, in which—having been passed over for active service—he went to France to tend the wounded, Mrs. Ward expressed a hope that he might still have "the harvest of his literary life before him." He had what made for greatness: "passion and style, and varied equipment, whether of training or observation; above all, an individuality it is abundantly worth while to know." He was socially acceptable and she could be generous to him in ways she could not be to Wells and Bennett. Orwell wanted him to be more savage, less polite: "The picture he was trying to build up was a picture of a money-ruled world of unspeakable cruelty—a world in which an obtuse beef-eating race of squires, lawyers, bishops, judges and stockbrokers squatted *in saecula saeculorum* [age upon age] on the backs of a hypersensitive race of slum-dwellers, servants, foreigners, fallen women and artists." He projects the writer he would have preferred, and when his quarrel with society came to an end, his imaginative power dwindled; "or perhaps it was merely that the oppressed classes began to seem less oppressed."

He wrote essays in which he tried to show the countryside, to evoke England, but the self-satisfaction of this prose, the little epiphanies that the author deems worth sharing, Edwardian, poised, benign, are also false. "For though to you, for instance, it may seem impossible to worship Mystery with one lobe of the brain, and with the other to explain it, the thought that this may not seem impossible to others should not discourage you; it is but another little piece of that Mystery which makes life so wonderful and sweet." Sweet. Golden. Such words do overtime in description and interpretation. The infrequent industrial scenes are clichéd also. And he addresses us as "you," not patronizingly in the manner of Bennett, but politely, as if we are in his company admiring him. His essay "A Novelist's Allegory" is like one of Wilde's children's stories, but without charm, the style and manner here inappropriate to the subject. For him the novelist-essayist must make sense in "fictional" terms, hence the generic diversions, reminiscent narratives, and other effects. "Sensibly, or insensibly, we tune our songs to earn the nuts of our twilight forest." Bambi is just over there, in the thicket. "We are, I think, too deeply civilized, so deeply civilized that we have come to look on Nature as indecent." In his essays he covers his Nature with gesture and mannerliness to avoid indecency. There are moments of clarity that might have spoken to Eliot and other modernists for whom Galsworthy was a dinosaur: art, he says, stimulates "impersonal emotion," an unexpected idea. Indeed, an *idea*.

Bennett understands Galsworthy's originality. It bores him rather, yet he cannot deny it. Generally, he says, the best novelists are repelled by and do not actually write about the middle class, the class that buys their books, a class that, though he aspired and "rose" to it, he also despises. "As for John Galsworthy, the quality in him which may possibly vitiate his right to be considered a major artist is precisely his fierce animosity to this class." Nowadays that animosity looks like an accepting near-complacency. "Major artists are seldom so cruelly hostile to anything whatever as John Galsworthy is to this class. He does in fiction what John Sargent does in paint; and their inimical observation of their subjects will gravely prejudice both of them in the eyes of posterity." It is ungrateful of posterity (which includes us), Bennett says, because the class is the paymaster of most successful novelists. He revisits *The Man of Property* in 1917. "Well, it stands the test," he declares. "It is certainly the most perfect of Mr. Galsworthy's novels up to now. Except for the confused impression caused by the too rapid presentation of all the numerous members of the Forsyte family at the opening, it has practically no faults." He finds "no places where the author has stopped to take his breath and wipe his brow. The tension is never relaxed. This is one of the two qualities without which a novel cannot be first class and great. The other is the quality of sound, harmonious design." It is all those things, and yet the modern reader is more likely to go with Lawrence's vehemence than with Bennett's polite, politic commendation.

One of the highest-earning English writers of the 1930s, (William) Somerset Maugham (1874–1965), came closer than most to the spirit of French writing handed down from Flaubert to Maupassant. Not that his *style* partakes of particular refinement, but as a narrative artist he practices an economy and achieves a focus we look for in vain in Bennett and Galsworthy. "There was something unsaid in all his work which gave it a kind of snarl and charm," says Frederic Raphael, a judicious advocate. "His stories are fatter than Guy de Maupassant's, and always suggest that there is more that could be said, which leaves the reader an emotional participant even when he is not an aesthetic admirer." Given Maugham's style, no reader can be an unconditional admirer, yet it is hard not to read to the end, impatient with the narrator yet absorbed by the narrative. Orwell said Maugham was the contemporary who most influenced his writing. Burgess used elements of Maugham's life to make the buttonholing octogenarian protagonist and undependable narrator Kenneth Toomey in *Earthly Powers* (1980).

What keeps one reading Maugham, says Greene, is "not characters, not the 'atmosphere,' not style but the force of the *anecdote*," less the how than the what of the telling. Lawrence Durrell was surprised that Maugham copied out "a page of Swift every day when he was trying to learn the job, in order to give himself a stylistic purchase, as it were." The choice of the acid and caustic Swift is telling, like Stendhal's choice of the *Code Napoléon* for similar purposes. But it did not work for Maugham. His grasp of English was idiomatic; it lacked semantic depth. "His prose is sometimes dismaying," Raphael says. And Rebecca West: "He couldn't write for toffee, bless his heart," but she liked him as a man and misread his manners as evidence of a good heart. They were manners: "To write good prose is an affair of good manners," he insisted. "It is, unlike verse, a civil art." Still, for West he was "not a bit clever or cold or cynical. I know of many affectionate things he did. He had a great capacity for falling in love with the wrong people. His taste seemed to give way under him so extraordinarily sometimes." Not to mention his judgment, sentence by sentence. She adds, "Occasionally his conversation was beautifully funny and quite unmalicious." He was not "quite unmalicious" in fact, as West realized when in a late memoir he vilified his late ex-wife. At that point he became for her "an obscene little toad."

There was calculation in his "good manners," a form of concealment, of manipulation, ceremonious, at once self-despising and despising the object of ceremony. The cruelty of his marriage, his parenting, and his treatment of many people close to him entailed treachery, a velvet glove on a bony fist. His beginnings had promised a trajectory with social concerns of another kind, somewhere between those of Wells and Bennett. The themes of his short stories, Greene says, are "adultery in China, murder in Malaya, suicide in the South Seas, the colored violent stories which have so appreciably raised the level of the popular magazine." Many of Maugham's stories, Greene adds, "sprawl into the proper region of the novel." The stories sold. A 1923 contract with Hearst magazines (American money was crucial) guaranteed him $2,500 per story. From what is still one of his most famous stories, "Rain," he earned more than $1,000,000 in copyright fees in his lifetime. The stories were adaptable for film, and Maugham was, among novelists, one of the great beneficiaries of and contributors to Hollywood.

Maugham was aware of his shortcomings. A good writer is his own best critic, Greene insists, and after noting that "there is at the heart of his work a humility and a self-distrust rather deadening in their effects," he quotes Maugham's preface to the stories: "I knew that I had no lyrical quality. I had a small vocabulary and no efforts that I could make to enlarge it much availed me. I had little gift of metaphor; the original and striking simile seldom occurred to me." This sense of limitation becomes a point of departure; had Bennett possessed it he might have been more succinct.

He did apprentice himself to French masters; in fact French was his first language. He was born in Paris, where his father worked in the British embassy and his mother was a sociable and popular woman. His mother died when he was eight, his father when he was eleven, leaving him a solid private income. He went to England and was reared by his uncle (a vicar in Whitstable, Kent) and aunt, whose world he did not find sympathetic and evokes many times in his fiction, in particular in *Cakes and Ale,* where a sense of its unmalicious severity and of his not-quite-belonging are conveyed, and in *Of Human Bondage* (1915), a kind of English *A Portrait of the Artist.* With its relentless libidinal tensions, it is arguably his masterpiece, though it is hard not to find it long, repetitive, a curate's egg of prose. The story told runs parallel to the life he led; in it his sexual concerns had to be heterosexualized, his patterns of desire at times projected onto female characters.

He persuaded his guardian to let him study abroad, in Germany, where he developed a passion for music and enjoyed his first homosexual encounters. At eighteen he began as a medical student at St. Thomas's Hospital in London. He was at home in London: away from his uncle's influence he could do as he wished, meet a more varied portion of humanity than in Whitstable or indeed in Heidelberg, and observe and write as well as study. His writing benefited from what he saw as a doctor. He contracted tuberculosis and spent many months in a Scottish sanatorium.

At twenty-three his first novel, *Liza of Lambeth* (1897), was published. It owes debts to Maupassant, but here a relatively short idea is stretched on the rack of the novel form. He wrote as a doctor in Lambeth and tries in the dialogue, awkwardly, to reproduce the dialect he heard. The book traces the brief life of his humble but lively protagonist, Liza Kemp, a factory worker, the last of thirteen children left to provide for her drink-fuddled, doddery old mother. Liza, half in love with Tom, is seduced by a married man called Jim. A married friend is beaten by her husband, and Liza herself sustains blows from her lover and her lover's wife. Liza has got pregnant, miscarries, and, Maugham being in thrall to Zola as well as Maupassant, dies. It was on the strength of this novel that Theodore Dreiser called Maugham "an earnest thunderer in the cause of naturalism and himself a Zolaesque writer of constipated power." (It was also Dreiser who, after bad reviews had almost sunk it, praised *Of Human Bondage* and made sure of its place in the modern canon.) Maugham had also been affected by Arthur Morrison's *Tales of Mean Streets* (1894), common stories plainly told, using elements of dialect, the reader allowed no sentimental escape. This was literature as confrontation. Having become accustomed to watching the unraveling lives of the poor without getting directly implicated, he became a vivid analyst. Lack of imagination, he said, made him a literalist, a transcriber. Later he was to give a self-deprecating and implausible sexual inflection to his uninventiveness: "The homosexual," he declared, has "small power of invention, but a wonderful gift for delightful embroidery." There is little embroidery in *Liza,* though it proved popular and convinced the young doctor to become a writer.

Famous for his books but too old to enlist as a combatant when the Great War began, Maugham joined other writers (including, among the Americans, John Dos Passos, Hemingway, Dashiell Hammett, and E. E. Cummings) in the ambulance corps. Malcolm Cowley notes that "one might almost say that the ambulance corps of the French military transport were college extension courses for a generation of [American] writers." Here he also met Frederick Gerald Haxton, a young American who remained his companion until 1944 when he died. It was due to Haxton's arrest on charges of indecency that Maugham left England and, seriously well-to-do at the end of the war, purchased the now-famous Villa Mauresque and its dozen acres of park and garden at Cap Ferrat on the French Riviera. Here he held soirées and gatherings to entertain writers, artists, royalty, politicians, his nephew Robin, and the occasional lovely young man who raised the erotic temperature for Maugham and some of his guests. Rebecca West declared the house "very pleasant and quiet and agreeable." The view was spectacular, so much so that he had to seal the windows of his writing room to avoid that distraction.

He was not an exquisite like Noel Coward, though he would like to have been; he was more in the role of one of Coward's hosts, recessive, predatory. And he was at the Villa one of Coward's many hosts. Raphael insists on his independence of "any coterie or ideology" and portrays him as standing "at a slight angle to the Anglo-Saxon world." This is not quite right: he had and has a coterie, and however inadvertently a gendered ideology. "The book of his that seems to me most homosexual is *The Narrow Corner* (1932). I think it's my favorite," said Christopher Isherwood. It was the third and final "exotic" novel in a run that began with *The Moon and Sixpence* (1919) and included *The Painted Veil* (1925), and it was the last because this type of novel moved too close to the heart of Maugham's matter. "A very romantic book," Isherwood continues. "It's set on a ship. There's this beautiful boy who's wanted by everybody, including the police. There's a wonderful doctor with a Chinese assistant who smokes opium. Very glamorous. I adore that book."

West was fascinated by Maugham's appearance, "he was so neatly made, like a swordstick that fits just so." Because he wrote so close to life, the swordstick was sometimes drawn in the fiction, wounds were dealt. *The Magician* (1907) very nearly elicited a libel suit from Aleister Crowley. Thomas Hardy's widow Florence was appalled when she read *Cakes and Ale: Or the Skeleton in the Cupboard* (1930) and recognized so much truth, and falsehood, in the book.

It was the elements of truth that made the fiction feel like history, so much so that its plausibilities seem to displace history. A man of secrets, Maugham had little compunction in exposing the hypocrisies and duplicities of others, whether their roots were in class, in organized religion, or in some other institution of social nurture. He took little care to protect the living. In *Cakes and Ale* he based Alroy Kear, the would-be biographer of Edward Driffield (the Hardy character) on his bemused friend the novelist (Sir) Hugh (Seymour) Walpole (1884–1941). "What I mind," Walpole meekly said, "are a few little things—little things that Willie and I had together—only he and I knew—those he has put into print." Walpole hardly survived the attack; his books are little read today.

He merits a digression. Henry James, borrowing an image used first by Bennett and then by Wells, compares Walpole's technique to squeezing an orange, the juice of which is "quite remarkably sweet." He squeezed, then squeezed again. "*The Duchess of Wrexe* reeks with youth and the love of youth and the confidence of youth." James itemizes what this confidence moves among, a wonderful male world of places, institutions, possibilities. But the book leaves James dissatisfied: "The tract . . . affects us as more or less virgin snow, and we look with interest and suspense for the imprint of a process." There could hardly be a clearer aesthetic desideratum than "the imprint of a process." It is something James looked for, and missed, in many of the new novels he was asked to read. Missing from Walpole too is the reek of the human one gets in Lawrence and, in a more mannerly form, in Bennett. Walpole's novels, James says, "smell of the romantic."

But James liked Walpole, an ambitious and personable young man, also solicitous. He wrote to him generously, affectionately, in May 1912 advising him, "Don't let anyone persuade you—there are plenty of ignorant and fatuous duffers to try to—that strenuous selection and comparison are not the very essence of art, and that Form *is* [not] substance to that degree that there is absolutely no substance without it." He was counseling him against the critics who spun his wind vane about with contrary counsel. "Form alone *takes,* and holds and preserves, substance—saves it from the welter of helpless verbiage that we swim in as in a sea of tasteless tepid pudding, and that makes one ashamed of an art capable of such degradations." Like Woolf, James too had been reading the Russians. "Tolstoi and Dostoievsky are fluid puddings, though not tasteless, because the amount of their own minds and souls in solution in the broth gives it savour and flavour, thanks to the strong, rank quality of their genius and their experience." Their imitators are bland, their vice their "lack of composition, their defiance of economy and architecture." Walpole, despite James's hope for and belief in him, lacked also.

His enormous literary output in a not very long creative life included thirty-six novels. He pushed himself hard and proved successful in his own day on both sides of the Atlantic. Born in Auckland, New Zealand, the son of a clergyman who later rose to be bishop of Edinburgh, he was educated in England and contrary to his father's wishes decided not to enter the Church, taking up writing instead. His invented town of Polchester in Glebeshire is the setting for several books, a composite of places he had lived, and of their religious characters. It is hard not to remember Trollope (of whom he wrote a biography) when looking at a shelf of Walpole, noting the recurrent ecclesiastical themes. He lived well and a little ostentatiously, and kept his homosexuality generally to himself. Maugham's fictional assault on him must have been doubly painful, given that they were on to one another's secret. He is best remembered for Rupert Hart-Davis's discreet biography published in 1952. He remains a remarkable literary phenomenon, a substantial-seeming planet that turns out to have been a meteor.

In *Cakes and Ale* Edward Driffield's widowed second wife tends the late writer's flame and wants a hagiographical biography to be written. Kear, the Walpolian "literary operator of the day," undertakes the commission, treating it like another bland novel, seeking only such information as will contribute to an edifying, sentimental, and commercial success. Kear understands literary hierarchy and sees an eventual place for himself at the top of the tree, so long as he plays his cards wisely. In Maugham's fictional world, things are seldom what they seem. "Bad" characters are good: they are themselves, live as fully as they can, and know that others are *as they are,* not as we would have them. Their moral clarity is misread by society and they are stigmatized. The narrator begins with conventional perspective and gradually learns to read the truth.

Strickland, the protagonist of *The Moon and Sixpence,* is like a character out of D. H. Lawrence strayed into the wrong imagination. The narrator, an ironic and rather sour Englishman, pieces together, initially at the abandoned wife's behest, the life of the complex character. Strickland has dropped out of the English establishment. He has thrown away respectability, wealth, wife, and family in pursuit of a vocation for which at first he has no aptitude. The story, transposed, grows out of the life of the French painter Paul Gauguin. The narrator in Paris experiences Strickland's appalling monomania, the way he uses people and discards them, his unsentimental and unconditional devotion to his art. At last in Paris he is permitted to visit the artist's threadbare studio and see his works. This is his response. "Even I, in my colossal ignorance, could not but feel that here, trying to express itself, was real power . . . I fancy that Strickland saw vaguely some spiritual meaning in material things that was so strange that he could only suggest it with halting symbols. It was as though he found in the chaos of the universe a new pattern, and were attempting clumsily, with anguish of soul, to set it down. I saw a tormented spirit striving for the release of expression." After a burst of dialogue, he draws a momentous conclusion that may be not his only, but the author's:

> Each one of us is alone in the world. He is shut in a tower of brass, and can communicate with his fellows only by signs, and the signs have no common value, so that their sense is vague and uncertain. We seek pitifully to convey to others the treasures of our heart, but they have not the power to accept them, and so we go lonely, side by side but not together, unable to know our fellows and unknown by them. We are like people living in a country whose language they know so little that, with all manner of beautiful and profound things to say, they are condemned to the banalities of the conversation manual. Their brain is seething with ideas, and they can only tell you that the umbrella of the gardener's aunt is in the house.

Stevenson is not far away. He wrote, "No man lives in the external truth, among salts and acids, but in the warm, phantasmagorical chamber of his brain, with the painted windows and the storied walls."

Maugham was not Strickland, and he did not write entirely convincingly about him. Despite his social arrogance, more than once he placed himself only on the foothills of Parnassus. "I know just where I stand," he said, "in the very front row of the second-rate." It is possible to take issue with him. Strickland is not in the end Gauguin, Driffield is not Hardy, but what stays with us from his novels is fiction, not distorted fact. "It has never been Maugham's characters that we have remembered." Greene says, "so much as the narrator, with his contempt for human life, his unhappy honesty." We remember and come back to the compelling narrators, voices Greene finds at once disagreeable and irresistible.

———•———

Born in Chicago the year of Bennett's death and of the publication of his *Venus Rising from the Sea,* the British writer Frederic (Michael) Raphael (b. 1931), Maugham's biographer and advocate, shares with Bennett an abundant and diverse body of work, including a vast, expanding memoir, and unabating energy. Active as an essayist-reviewer, a polemicist, a translator, and, above all, a novelist, he is generally identified as "the Oscar-winning screenwriter." That's the work that pays the bills.

He has written over twenty novels, the most famous, because made into a highly successful television series, being his fourteenth, *The Glittering Prizes* (1976). It follows a group of Cambridge undergraduates, not long after the war, making their ways into the world. Adam Morris is the character closest to Raphael himself, who took Waugh's advice: "Never kill people off in your books, because you never know when you might need them again." The book and its sequels *Fame and Fortune* (2007) and *Final Demands* (2010), which continue their story to 1979 and then to the 1990s, though published more than three decades apart, attest to the continuity of Raphael's approach, the later books, darker, life-soiled, and soured, being clearly of a piece with the high-spirited ironies of youth, conducted in his characteristic clever, hard-edged dialogue, characters competing and at odds with one another in the immediate and the long term. Their medium is language, and they are brilliant. They are full of themselves, their irony is a form of hubris. This fiction makes the demands, not of modernism, but of the acute essayist who requires continuous attention and engagement. A classicist by training, Raphael uses language with what is today an unnatural fastidiousness. And he treats us as his equals. "If my fiction has unity," he says, and he expects his work to add up to an oeuvre, "it is in the use of irony and my reluctance to play the emotional card without a tincture of contrariness. I am a sentimental man, but a tearless writer."

The protagonist of *A Double Life* (1993), a novel of understatement and elegy, is a French diplomat reflecting on a life rich in historical and personal incident yet now emotionally spent. The distance between the cold account and the life it accounts for is one of those formal paradoxes that Raphael practices. Prostitution, the simulation of desire and courtship, become metaphors for diplomacy and other human rituals carried out with formal conviction, but without belief. The modern condition of intelligent men or women is to stand outside themselves, the mind—like Paul Valéry's Monsieur Teste—emancipated from the body's pains, pleasures, and decays. The meditation is conducted in dialogue and reflection that are witty, for here as in Maugham we are in the realm of knowing social comedy, with tragedy's mask hanging on the wall, in wait as it were. Even in making love, the mind still works, so that the act of love happens without the lover engaging except mechanically. He notes the effect it has had on the woman: her color has changed. Repression has seldom been so convincingly exposed.

Among his own works, *Like Men Betrayed* (1970), described by Paul Theroux as "Proust with machine-guns," and *Lindmann* (1963), "which is 'about' the Shoah [but] does not contain the word Jew," are among the best. "I favour indirection, when possible, but I like to be going somewhere." In his essays he throws indirection to the wind, but in fiction, prose is in counterpoint with dialogue, in dialogue with it, as it were, the director's presence. His advice to writers is generally sound. Description, he says, must "enrol the reader's imagination. Makeweight description (for instance, P. D. James's obese inventories of her characters' furniture) is patronising and narcotic."

The developments of Continental modernism were unpalatable to Maugham, as to Greene and others among the heirs of Maupassant and Zola. On January 23, 1920, Aldous Huxley (1894–1963) attended in Arnold Bennett's own Paris the *Première vendredi de littérature,* the famous Dada "manifestation" at which Tristan Tzara recited "phonic poems to the accompaniment of an eight-inch electric bell which had completely drowned his voice." Huxley knew that Italian futurism as represented by Marinetti and now Dada were the fault of his contemporaries, their stolid shockability, their pragmatic Anglo-Saxon imagination. He knew the differences between the nihilism of the dadaists (he enjoyed their satire, though not their apocalyptic utterances: no need, he thought, to destroy literature itself) and the potentialities that futurism recognized, even after the First World War.

In "Water Music," an article in the *Athenaeum,* Huxley, great-nephew of Matthew Arnold, grandson of T. H. Huxley, nephew of Mrs. Humphry Ward, was among the earliest English writers to consider aleatory principles in art, and the dadaists provided the occasion. A tap dripping made to his wakeful ears music of a kind, without form, "asymptotic to sense." Always there is the chance that it will make sense, that we will make sense of it. For him at the time "making sense" was still something akin to paraphrase, finding the "hidden key," because sense is made in prose. Yet he was already advancing toward America, emigrating to California in 1937, and *The Doors of Perception* in 1954. He was restless, optimistic, disoriented, impatient with predetermined forms and genres. In his second year in California he published *After Many a Summer,* a fable-novel in which a man rich beyond most, in his California Mandalay, acquires an eighteenth-century aristocrat's diary in which he learns the secret of long life. The raw minced innards of ancient carp, consumed regularly, are the key. But the price to be paid for longevity is regression to a simian state. Still, apes enjoy themselves sexually, leaving behind the human world for a sensual life in which time ceases to matter. Scientist and pessimist conspire together in this story, there is an excess of essayistic reflection, the novel's humor and pace are not sprightly. This happens to be the novel that George, the protagonist of Christopher Isherwood's 1964 novel *A Single Man,* is teaching to his students at a college in California during the single day the novel takes. Bereaved, solitary, George has ironic time for Huxley, his once fellow countryman.

Back in 1920, young Huxley was in a Paris rather different from that of the American contingent. Stein remarked to Hemingway, "Huxley is a dead man . . . Why do you want to read a dead man? Can't you see he is dead?" He was not experimenting with form, he was intellectually rather than imaginatively engaged. Ideas were bad for art, he seemed to say. He was, in Stefan Collini's description, a man physically lethargic but unstoppable, with remarks and opinions about everything. His encyclopedism would seem Johnsonian, but he lacked Doctor Johnson's morose, aphorizing stability of being. His first completed novel, *Crome Yellow* (1921), he wrote out of the experience of working at Garsington Manor, Lady Ottoline Morrell's home and the focus for many of the Bloomsbury writers. There he met D. H. Lawrence, whose letters he was to edit in 1933, Bertrand Russell, Lytton Strachey, and the rest. His book is an effortful social comedy in the manner of Peacock, but without Peacock's focus; it has too many quarries, too much cod-psychology, and it allows itself protracted riffs: the long sermon in chapter 5, the historical divagations, the teasing out of aesthetic arguments, the ponderous, unbearable Mr. Bodium, the insistent reflections on sex and love. He is in a kind of rapt dialogue with issues of the day that, not being issues of our day, entertain but do not engage. Lady Ottoline recognized herself and her friends and never forgave him.

His second novel, *Antic Hay* (1923), written rapidly after he moved to Italy, is set in postwar London where, deploying an ennervated cast not unsimilar to that of *Crome,* he explores related themes. The protagonist Theodore Gumbril is an inventive, remote cousin of Edward Ponderevo, purveyor of Tono-Bungay in Wells's novel. Gumbril's "Patent Small-Clothes" with pneumatic seat-cushions, and his confidence-instilling beard, are less plausible than Tono-Bungay: from Wells's scientific romance and comedy we have descended to farce. Ideas are caricatured rather than fictionalized. The sexual content is foregrounded (he was, after all, seeing a good deal of his friend Lawrence). His sense of *love* does not quite connect with sex; sex is a problem rather than the culmination of a process. In the end, Cyril Connolly says, "Huxley the intellectual pulls the lower self along like a man pulling a dog by a leash; there are glimpses of other dogs, lamp-posts, green grass, trousers and tree-trunks; then comes a jerk, 'eyes look your last' and a scientific platitude."

Lawrence catalyzed the changes in Huxley's thought and nature. Huxley wrote his most famous novel, *Brave New World,* shortly after Lawrence's death, while he was editing the *Letters.* It was published in 1932 and set at a time six centuries in the future. Wells's *Men Like Gods* provoked the book: Wells's scientific optimism is qualified and reversed in Huxley's dystopian book. Transparent behind their paired names (Benito Hoover, Bernard Marx), characters and issues of the then-present day appear and enact the merged consequences of their ideas. His satire is less against the totalitarian ideologies of Europe than the reductive material imperatives of American capitalism and the culture to which, in the 1930s, it was giving rise.

The science is so thoroughly developed that it convinces: the standardization and industrialization of the reproductive cycle stand for the greater freedom achieved, in which it is unnecessary for the human being to reflect at all: enjoyment is the end. *Brave New World* is the ultimate consumption novel. Huxley remarked, "All's well that ends Wells." His last novel, *Island* (1962), provides another imagined world in which harmony is achieved by implementing a generous, forward-looking morality as tenable and untenable as his other intellectualized futures. Burgess notes, "The people themselves are a sort of ideal Eurasian race, equipped with fine bodies and Huxleyan brains, and they have read all the books that Huxley has read." Huxley, says Burgess, "more than anyone helped to equip the contemporary novel with a brain." The philosopher C. E. M. Joad sees it differently. "The trouble with Huxley is and always has been intellectual whole-hoggery. Ideas will go to his head."

For a year Huxley was an ineffectual French master at Eton, unable to keep order in class but possessing a peculiar turn of phrase that impressed one of his pupils, Eric Arthur Blair (1903–1950), who became George Orwell. Huxley and Blair were not friends, but Huxley wrote a letter of congratulations after *Nineteen Eighty-Four* was published. Orwell in a relatively short life—he died at forty-seven—wrote copiously. His political and cultural essays survive their long-past occasions. The adjective "Orwellian" describes a disabused approach, that of the civic agnostic who has passed through ideological conviction and witnessed the duplicity of those who seek to *apply* rules and force history to obey predictive patterns. He was an editor, a travel writer, and, for our purposes, a novelist. The last two of his six novels, *Animal Farm: A Fairy Story* (1945) and *Nineteen Eighty-Four* (1949), envisaged the directions the world was taking. They are perennial best sellers.

Blair was born in India, where his father worked in the Civil Service. His mother, half-French, was raised in Burma, and part of her family remained there. As an infant Eric went with his mother and two sisters to England, settling in Henley-on-Thames. His formal education began at a convent school when he was five. In a haphazard way he progressed to Eton, where he did not distinguish himself and thus avoided university. Cyril Connolly was a boyhood friend, and though they did not see much of one another at Eton, Connolly later published him in *Horizon* and talked up his work.

The "old boy network" worked for Orwell: he was not above soliciting reviews and doing favors in return. Henry Miller benefited from this comradely perfidiousness, and more transparently still Connolly, to whom he wrote, as in more formal language Fanny Burney had done two centuries before, "You scratchy my back, I'll scratch yours." To his friend Jack Common he confesses to feeling like "a sort of Gerald Gould [owner of the rich silver mine in *Nostromo*] selling my intellectual virtue at constantly-decreasing prices." In an essay Orwell quotes a passage of Miller and generalizes: "There is a fine rhythm to that. The American language is less flexible and refined than the English, but it has more life in it, perhaps." That closing "perhaps," hedging his bets, is proof of his argument as it relates to English English. Miller's response is first warm, "a wonderful chap in his way," but the temperature drops: "In the end I thought him stupid. He was like so many English people, an idealist, and, it seemed to me, a foolish idealist. A man of principle, as we say. Men of principle bore me." And Orwell could be as scathing and ungenerous, referring to Edward Carpenter as a "pious sodomite" and (in 1936, of all years) to Hemingway's "disgusting rubbish."

Casting about for a career, Orwell chose to go to Burma and work with the Indian Imperial Police. He had family there, the posting was not entirely lonely. Orwell needed his family; after each experiment in living and every professional and medical setback he returned home, while he had a home to go to. Burma gave him responsibility, authority, and subject matter for essays and for his first novel, *Burmese Days* (1934), composed well after his return, when he was thirty, though conceived long before. His classic essays "Shooting an Elephant" and "A Hanging" share the matter of *Burmese Days* but have drama and directness that it lacks.

In 1927 he contracted the excruciating dengue or break-bone fever and returned to England. Having been an outsider in Burma, he assumed an outsider stance in relation to England, moving out of his own class, his own neighborhoods, choosing the slums of Paris and London and the north of England. From the outside Friedrich Engels, Henry Mayhew, and the Victorian collectors of underclass history had entered these zones, and more instructively Jack London, who went native in his own country and then in England, dressing down and living with the poor, sharing their lice and diet in *People of the Abyss* (1908). *Down and Out in London and Paris* (1933), and the more artful *The Road to Wigan Pier* (1937), with its social vision and then the account of the author who is, as Raymond Williams observes, both outside and inside the world he writes of, were the products of this strategy of going native, though Orwell's immersion was not total. He came up for air, good meals, and the occasional visit to London and home and never quite lost, or found, his bearings among the poor. Williams calls Orwell's "a successful impersonation of a plain man." Having resigned from the Burmese police, he wanted to expiate his years "as an agent of imperial oppression" in novels and essays; a similarly eloquent process was enacted at home.

His family and a few friends contrived his mental and physical survival. The sense of independence that marks his writing was illusory. He was still dependent in 1934 when, after a serious bout of pneumonia, he gave up school teaching, which in any event he had not enjoyed. After another stay at home, an aunt found him a job in a London bookshop. Before the war there was always a way forward and out for him.

He wrote novels eagerly, in rapid succession and with modest success: *A Clergyman's Daughter* (1935), *Keep the Aspidistra Flying* (1936), and—published after his return from the Spanish Civil War, where he saw active service, was seriously wounded, and shed many of his political expectations and ideals—*Coming Up for Air* (1939). He admired Maugham's straightforwardness, insisting on the story over the telling. He wrote to Julian Symons, "I am not a real novelist anyway . . . one difficulty I have never solved is that one has masses of experience which one passionately wants to write about . . . and no way of using them up except by disguising them as a novel." The kinds of experience he had in mind, such as fishing, belonged more naturally in his essays. But pressure of politics had made his essays less capacious, more serious. Now the pressure of history put his fiction on hold.

When fiction became possible again after the war, the experience of Spain, of the war, and the rise of the Soviet Union had transformed his imagination and purpose. He was deeply marked by *Darkness at Noon* (1940) by Arthur Koestler (1905–1983), based on the late 1930s Moscow show trials but informed by Koestler's experience as a prisoner in Franco's Spain. Orwell took *Darkness at Noon* as informed, journalistic fiction, not as the allegory it was intended to be, in which characters stand for familiar ideological types, the old revolutionary who sees through it all, the tin-pot commissioner, the idealist betrayed. Orwell reviewed it. *Nineteen Eighty-Four* is well aware of it. Koestler's No. 1, a thinly disguised

Stalin stand-in, lurks behind Big Brother. Koestler's and Orwell's protagonists both die with the ruler's image in their mind's eye.

*Animal Farm: A Fairy Story* and *Nineteen Eighty-Four* were as topical as Evelyn Waugh said all Orwell's work was, and political, but the politics was more than thematic: it had entered into the forms themselves, creating modern allegory of two kinds, the animal fable and the dystopian narrative with trappings of science fiction but with designs on his own world. He was in the zone of Butler's *Erewhon* ("One sees what a tremendous advantage is gained simply by not trying to be clever," Orwell said of him) and the fiction of H. G. Wells. Julian Symons describes his trajectory to these surprising destinations: "His career has a particular fascination because it shows a clumsy writer becoming a delicate one, a man unsure of his aims and attitudes becoming a great moral force, and the finest English social critic of his generation."

*Animal Farm* was completed in 1944 and widely rejected. Publishers on the left were worried that the book would alienate their main readerships. Frederic Warburg, who became Kafka's and Mann's publisher, was a man of the anti-Soviet left. He had become a supporter of Orwell's and published the book in 1945. Four years later *Nineteen Eighty-Four* appeared. "Every line of serious work that I have written since 1936," Orwell declared in 1946, "has been written, directly or indirectly, *against* totalitarianism and *for* democratic socialism, as I understand it." E. L. Doctorow, who distrusts the motives of Orwell's writing, says, "The story Orwell tells is not of good nations against bad nations but of governments against individuals." There is a "totalitarianism implicit in the structure of the entire postwar industrial world," and part of this ideology entails "the political manipulation of reality through the control of history and language." The neologisms and popular expressions that come from *Nineteen Eighty-Four* include *newspeak, doublethink (blackwhite,* the embodied oxymoron), *thought-crime, prole, unperson, Big Brother, The Ministry of Truth.* It is a world familiar and unfocused by the opening sentence: "It was a bright cold day in April, and the clocks were striking thirteen."

Orwell insists, "Every writer, especially every novelist, *has* a 'message,' whether he admits it or not, and the minutest details of his work are influenced by it. All art is propaganda. Neither Dickens himself nor the majority of Victorian novelists would have thought of denying this." Most of them would not have thought of affirming it, either. Their mission was as much to entertain as to instruct. Politics is present in every page, but so too is the continual surprise of invention, a refreshing plainness of language, especially in *Animal Farm,* that is restorative, as though English is being delivered back to a kind of innocence in which the ways in which it is perverted by ideology as by art become lucidly clear. Julian Symons notes the permanent urgency of Orwell's last two books.

"Prophecy, I believe, was something not at all in Orwell's mind when he was writing. He was concerned with what was for him the present, not the future." This was not science fiction. It was 1948 (the year he completed the book) with an inversion of digits, still close in time, in detail, in memory and possibility. In his obituary notice Pritchett dubbed him "the wintry conscience of a generation" who, to tell the truth, "had 'gone native' in his own country."

# 30

# Portraits and Caricatures of the Artist

James Joyce, Wyndham Lewis, Samuel Beckett, G. K. Chesterton,
Anthony Burgess, Russell Hoban, Flann O'Brien, Donald Barthelme

It is not possible to postpone the high tides of modernism any longer. Gertrude Stein has appeared, a disputed harbinger. The pressure of convention resisted her, the kind of pressure that in different forms recurs each decade, determined to recover a *status quo ante* by erasing or discrediting the new. It was possible to marginalize and caricature Stein. But when Joyce, Woolf, Ford, and Lawrence made revolutions as various and decisive as Richardson's, Scott's, or Flaubert's, convention retreats for a time.

The modernists were not all friends; their personal and artistic animosities remain instructive. At 27, rue de Fleurus, Hemingway said, "If you brought up Joyce twice, you would not be invited back. It was like mentioning one general favorably to another general." Gertrude Stein had a problem with Mr. James Joyce. "Joyce is good. He is a good writer," she says. But she goes on, she cannot let it rest. "People like him because he is incomprehensible and anybody can understand him." He flatters with seeming difficulty, like a crossword puzzler. But the real issue is this: "Who came first, Gertrude Stein or James Joyce? Do not forget that my first great book, *Three Lives,* was published in 1908. That was long before *Ulysses.*" She makes one last stab at fairness, but it is a stab pure and simple. "Joyce has done something. His influence, however, is local. Like Synge, another Irish writer, he has had his day."

Celebrating her own originality, she defines an element in modernism that her work refuses to share and from which it thus stands apart. "You see it is the people who generally smell of the museums who are accepted, and it is the new who are not accepted, you have got to accept a complete difference," she noted in an interview. "It is hard to accept that, it is much easier to have one hand in the past. That is why James Joyce was accepted and I was not. He leaned towards the past, in my work the newness and difference is [sic] fundamental." In *Stephen Hero,* the precursor of *Ulysses* published posthumously in 1944, Joyce says of the present age that "the spirit wherever it is able to assert itself in this medley of machines is romantic and preterist," suggesting in the neologism "preterist" a manner and tone leaning toward a familiar, irrecoverable past. When Hemingway, who knew and for a time believed in Miss Stein, wrote that

Joyce was the writer who "made it possible for us to break away from the restrictions," he was contrasting Joyce's additions with Stein's subtractions from the resources of fiction. She took Flaubertian economy to one extreme, he to another. She was a miser of diction while, as Borges says, he is "a millionaire of words and styles" and "less a man of letters than a literature . . . within the compass of a single volume." Yet he binds himself with different formal chains.

In the 1920s and 1930s James Joyce and D. H. Lawrence were often mentioned in the same breath, as were Joyce and Stein. In 1926 Wyndham Lewis advanced the mischief. Joyce was as impatient of that "intellectual woman" as she of him. She claimed precedence, and Lewis granted it to her in "Mr. Jingle and Mr. Bloom" in *The Art of Being Ruled*. "Miss Gertrude Stein," he declares breezily, "is the best-known exponent of a literary system that consists in a sort of gargantuan mental stutter." He likens her process to the speech of the mad. "Her art is composed, first, of repetition, which lyricises her utterances on the same principle as that of hebrew [sic] poetry. But the repetition is also in the nature of a photograph of the unorganized word-dreaming of the mind when not concentrated for some logical functional purpose." This describes at once her method and what it works away from.

Joyce, says Lewis, successfully employed a similar technique, "(not so radically and rather differently)," in *Ulysses*. "The thought-stream or word-stream of his hero was supposed to be photographed." Joyce too displayed symptoms of madness, Lewis concedes; and in his Nobel Prize address another Lewis, Sinclair, speaks of writers "a little insane in the tradition of James Joyce" (by then Stein had been shrugged out of the equation). Anthony Burgess, denying Joyce's direct influence, concedes his long-term effect: "Joyce can't be imitated, and there's no imitation Joyce in my work. All you can learn from Joyce is the exact use of language." The deliberate out-of-focus of his inventions in *Finnegans Wake* is part of this exactness, not delimiting but assimilative. Even proper names can release in epiphanies whole essays of sense. Sterne and Swift should have exchanged names, he who loved them both remarked.

Joyce aims at naturalism without the "semi-lyrical" freedoms taken by Stein. What is odd about Leopold Bloom is his wordiness: "He *thought in words*, not images, for our benefit, in a fashion as unreal, from the point of view of the strictest naturalist dogma, as a Hamlet soliloquy." Pretended naturalism forces Joyce into "something less satisfying" than Steinian arbitrariness, something at once comic and penetrating. Back into fiction flow the energies of Rabelais and Cervantes, those that had been ironed, bleached, and beaten out of the novel in over a century of moralism and propriety. "I do not know if you are a fountain or a cistern," William Butler Yeats is reported as saying to the novelist.

The older generation was, to begin with, puzzled and dazzled by Joyce. H. G. Wells, reviewing *A Portrait of the Artist as a Young Man* in 1917 in the *New Republic,* noted a coarseness of language and theme, but he was astonished, too: "The interest of the book depends entirely upon its quintessential and unfailing reality. One believes in Stephen Dedalus as one believes in few characters in fiction." Eleven years later, in November 1928, his patience was exhausted. He sent Joyce an angry, disappointed letter. In *Ulysses* (1922) and the fragments from *A Work in Progress* that began appearing in 1924 and in 1939 would be published together as *Finnegans Wake,* Joyce had "turned [his] back on the common man"—the "common man" in his various uncommon forms being Wells's prime quarry. The books provide time- and intelligence-poor readers with "vast riddles" and were clearly much more "amusing and exciting to write than they will ever be to read." Setting himself up as the "typical common reader," he gets no pleasure: "Who the hell is this Joyce who demands so many waking hours of the few thousand I have still to live for a proper appreciation of his quirks and fancies and flashes of rendering?" He went as far as *A Portrait* but could progress no further.

In his *Journal* Arnold Bennett mentions Joyce twice, first as "a very important figure in the evolution of the novel" and then to place him with Lawrence (he was reading *Lady Chatterley's Lover* at the time) as one of the most original novelists of his time. He speaks without enthusiasm, salutes, and passes on. Rebecca West uses him as a pretext. Comparing Proust and Joyce, she speaks of *Ulysses* "representing the spirit by the unstained boy Stephen Dedalus and matter by the squatting buffoon Leopold Bloom." She finds in this a "myth that perfectly expresses the totality of facts and emotional effects of the Augustinian complex. It is the ring-fence in which the modern mind is prisoner." She is captivated by "Marion" Bloom. Reading a description by Joyce, she sets off on one of her own, a riff so conventional as to epitomize the distance between them in formal and semantic intelligence. For effect she makes "Marion" out to be a "Dublin slut" and comments on the dinginess of the Dublin room in which she lies.

For her Joyce (and Lawrence) are "prepolitical" writers despite the "tundish," the Jewishness of the "squatting buffoon," the merging of languages and much else. In the light of her conclusion, it is hard to believe she read Lawrence at all. Hemingway said Joyce "would only explain what he was doing to jerks. Other writers that he respected were supposed to be able to know what he was doing by reading it." There were "jerks" among the older generation, but all the significant writers of the time made the effort with Joyce.

Virginia Woolf's early response to *Ulysses,* when T. S. Eliot urged it upon her, was exasperation. After the first three engaging, puzzling chapters, she lost patience in a rage fueled by all her snobberies. It was, she declared in 1922, "an illiterate, underbred book . . . the book of a self-taught working man, and we all know how distressing they are, how egotistic, insistent, raw, striking, and ultimately nauseating." She changed her views, but this first response is telling: the text was too hard to be pleasurable, and the readiest way of dismissing it was by dismissing the author. Lawrence, too, angrily disliked *Ulysses* and described the Molly Bloom soliloquy as "muck." He wanted to do it without "muck." Over acres of prose, Joyce's characters "strip their smallest emotions to the finest threads, till you feel you are sewed inside a wool mattress that is being strongly shaken up, and you are turning to wool along with the rest of the wooliness."

Orwell suffers less moral than aesthetic qualms: "Joyce is a kind of poet and also an elephantine pedant" who nonetheless dared "to expose the imbecilities of the inner mind" and managed by this exposure "to break down, at any rate momentarily, the solitude in which the human being lives." It is refreshing to leave the moralists behind. John Cowper Powys, his imagination always sexually alert, cannot resist "the mingling of that almost ecstatic sense of word-play—word-implications, word-conjuring, word-coining, word-marrying, word-murdering, word-melting, word-hypostasizing—which takes up the basic facts of sex and perpetually ravels them and unravels them, with passages of almost Shakespearean imagination." And Katherine Anne Porter, as if for her whole generation, upon learning of Joyce's death writes in a notebook, "What would we have done without him?" She watched him at a reading T. S. Eliot gave at Sylvia Beach's bookshop in Paris: "He sat as still as if he were asleep, except for his attentive expression. His head was fine and handsome, the beard and hair were becoming to the bony thrust of his skull and face, the face, the face of a 'too pained white wit,' as he said it, in the bodily affliction of prolonged cureless suffering of the mind." "Laden with the loot of learning."

James (Augustine Aloysius) Joyce (1882–1941) was born in Dublin. Most of the early life that matters is contained in *A Portrait of the Artist as a Young Man* (1916). A schoolboy essay entitled "Trust Not Appearances" (he was fourteen when he wrote it) opens with the prophetic sentence, "There is nothing so deceptive and for all that so alluring as a good surface." What follows is exquisite, delicious, the commonplaces of decadence. At the top of the page he has written *AMDG,* the motto of the Jesuit order: *ad majorem Dei gloriam* (to God's greater glory). Augustine as his second name, but the severely chaste Jesuit Saint Aloysius contributed his third. He had little control over the young man who goes astray as early as the end of chapter 2, but reclaims him with hellfire a chapter later. When the poet George Barker in 1942 declared that "the clue, the whole clue, and nothing but the clue to James Joyce is not Dublin but Rome," he was on to something. And Flann O'Brien writes that later, "with laughs he palliates the sense of doom that is the heritage of the Irish Catholic."

He attended what is now University College, Dublin, and studied philosophy and languages. Like Flaubert, he was convinced of the importance of his work even before he started writing. At eighteen he contributed his first article, "Ibsen's New Drama," on *When We Dead Awaken,* to the London-based *Fortnightly Review.* He was paid twelve guineas, with which he took his father to London, where he met the editor. Ibsen himself read the review, sent his thanks via his English translator, and eventually Joyce wrote him a letter in Norwegian, having mastered the language in order to do so. Arnold Rubek from Ibsen's play contributes to the character of Stephen Dedalus in *A Portrait of the Artist,* raptly observing the young woman who takes him in imagination "near to the wild heart of things" and whom he observes as an artist, stealing her spirit, aestheticizing her, but never touching her even in imagination. What chastity he has learned! Rubek is dead and wakens, interesting "not because of himself, but because of his dramatic significance." After the excitement of Ibsen, the Dublin stage gave itself over more and more to Irish writing. Joyce regretted the narrowing. Ibsen's sense of characters in specific situations and places informs the delimited, stifling worlds of Joyce's socially and spiritually maimed *Dubliners* (1914).

He left Dublin for Paris in 1902, like Stephen Dedalus "to encounter for the millionth time the reality of experience and to forge in the smithy of my soul the uncreated conscience of my race." It was a foretaste of his long exile, in which he first refigured his own past and then was able to begin his real immersion in Dublin, the place his imagination continued inventing. He returned to Ireland in 1903 for his mother's death, took a teaching job in Dalkey, had a date with Nora Barnacle on June 16, 1904—the day chosen for the action of *Ulysses*—which led to their eventual marriage, then returned abroad, first to Zurich, later to Trieste, teaching English as a foreign language. At twenty-five, in the Berlitz language school in Trieste, with nothing particularly substantial published under his name, he taught a Jewish businessman called Ettore Schmitz, better known by his *nom de plume* Italo Svevo (1861–1928). He was a self-published novelist writing in Italian. He was also a considerable linguist, speaking French and German as well as Italian, and with enough English to read the printed and unpublished stories, given to him by Joyce, that would compose *Dubliners.* Joyce read a book Svevo had issued in 1898 and liked it, encouraged the writer, and became an advocate of his best-loved novel, about the metaphysical difficulty of stopping smoking, *La coscienza di Zeno (Confessions of Zeno,* 1923). He made sure it was translated into French and reviewed. The French reviews led to Italian reviews; gradually Svevo's wry laughter spread. He was a model for Leopold Bloom, and his wife Livia contributed her middle name to Anna Livia Plurabelle in *Finnegans Wake.* The narrow Triestine focus of Svevo's fiction and the deliberate imperfection of his language affected Joyce; the short round author and his tall, lean English teacher might have been seen walking out together, as though Don Quixote and Sancho Panza had exchanged ages and shapes.

*A Portrait of the Artist,* written in part during the years in Trieste, drew on the epiphanic exercises of *Stephen Hero.* This book of rehearsed epiphanies was published only after Joyce's death and described by Edmund Wilson as a "schoolboy's production," interesting primarily in the way its tone foreshadows *Finnegans Wake* and in its early account of Joycean "epiphany." *A Portrait* is end-dated 1904, though not published until 1916. In 1912 he returned to Dublin and tried to find a publisher for *Dubliners.* The book did not appear until 1914 because printers were afraid that some elements in the stories might prove actionable and printers were held responsible for the material printed. The same hesitancy beset the publication of *Ulysses* (1922). *Finnegans Wake* (1939) was seventeen years in the making and appeared as the Second World War began. Joyce died two years later.

The life he chose for himself and his family was hard. His failing eyesight remained a problem, and at last he contracted the Miltonic or Homeric disability. The Joyces lived a Spartan existence, their daughter Lucia suffered mental illness, and at no stage were they financially secure, though the love and respect accorded to Joyce, a difficult man, by other difficult contemporaries, among them Ezra Pound, Wyndham Lewis, Ford Madox Ford, and T. S. Eliot, gave a sense of distant, necessary collegiality. It was a resisting group of writers and artists, disenchanted with cultural and political establishments and bent on changing them. Each writer chose, for much of his life, exile, and each laboriously made his own luck.

As an Irish writer he became aware, as *A Portrait* makes clear, that the language of his imagination was in some sense imposed; his English was differently inflected from that of the dominant English culture. Its norms needed resisting. The Roman Catholic Church presented another kind of colonialism. It informed and constrained Irish culture. He needed to work both legacies into his own terms. The first Christian martyr, Stephen, provides his first name; the patronymic draws on the great maze-maker, Dedalus, father of Icarus. Joyce codifies a fusion, suggesting persecution, flight, escape, another kind of martyrdom in Icarus's wild abandon and fall. He loosens the bonds further with Leopold Bloom, a Jew set down in an alien geography that Joyce knows as well as a place can be known, by heart, the literal city and the city of the mind: a stable, responsive geography. As Bloom and Stephen make their ways through defined space, Joyce is with them every inch of the way, clearing their sight. After the age of twenty Joyce spent little time in Dublin, and it may seem that he avoided it for fear that erasures of buildings, streets, trees, the changed curtains in the windows, would somehow mar the stability he required for his imagination to work, and not only in *Ulysses* but in *Finnegans Wake,* in which the geography, often specific in *Ulysses,* is taken for granted, becoming a literal and a dream space at the same time. John Updike notes that just before *Ulysses* went to press, Joyce was still writing to people in Dublin for more detail. His questions were specific: his book wanted to be materially, factually "true." Approximation would undermine that purpose: what was imagined was not the world but mind and imagination *in* the given world.

*Dubliners* he wrote mostly in Trieste in 1905, out of notes made earlier. The stories follow a progression of experiences, from childhood to maturity. They end not in a lift-off but in the settling snow of "The Dead," the most resonant long short story of the twentieth century. The stories refuse to dramatize: they bind themselves to a literal world and the dailiness of experience. The artistry is to honor the literal so that what it releases, the "epiphanies," are not contrived but realized. There is openness in the structure of the stories, which themselves explore eventlessness, entrapment. Joyce's own favorite among them was "Ivy Day in the Committee Room."

*A Portrait of the Artist* appeared first in New York in 1916. It had been serialized in the *Egoist* (with its 185 subscribers) and the Egoist Press bought sheets and issued it in Britain the following year. At last in 1924 it was published by Cape and began to enjoy wider circulation. For many writers, this book—about working through languages toward an individual, possessed language—is a handbook in figuring and refiguring the early years as the mind interprets them, learning to resist the dominant language of each period. Beginning in the language of family and childhood narrative, Stephen passes through the language of school with its arbitrary disciplines, of the church, the academy, of politics and literatures. His progression is particular to himself and of general interest to every conscious reader and writer. Specific detail becomes for the reader typical, inclusive.

Joyce focuses narrowly in on the protagonist in what is a third-person narrative until the closing pages. Readers experience his world, apprehend it with his apprehension. The effect is of first-person narrative. This discipline he acquired in writing *Dubliners. A Portrait*—especially the fourth chapter—grew out of notebooks and journals Joyce kept at college. The book embodies what Eliot calls the "intolerable wrestle with words and meanings." The precision and slipperiness of language were clear to him, its protean treacheries, from his Jesuit education.

*A Portrait* begins with hearing, sorting out words and how they sound, how they connect with one another, and finally how they relate to the world, a world increasingly complex as the first chapter progresses from simple narrative into adult conflict. Every element is under strain, from the punctuation to the diction, syntax, paragraphing. In the second chapter language connects to and communicates images, the visible and sensual world begins to exist in it. Then language starts to convey deeper, nonsensual meanings, a language of categories, thoughts, and another kind of feeling, of moral discrimination, responsibility, guilt, and the emergence of a limited, a prescribed self-perception, culminating in a surrender to the language of the liturgy and faith, the "grammar of assent" in which the individual is effaced and merged in the historical communion of saints and believers. Such language makes Stephen *passive,* the self subsumed. Here at its most potent is the temptation of religious *vocation,* overcome when he understands his true vocation and dedicates himself to something language is and does in a noninstrumental way. He has a vision of what is in the world and where he corresponds with it. The final chapter enacts the preparation of his language for art. Here occur the debates on nationhood, family, and language itself and the affirmation of the wholeness, harmony, and radiance *(integritas, consonantia, claritas)* necessary to contain and make apprehensible that beauty.

The destiny of such an artistic vocation is aloneness, and the final transition to it is marked by the dramatic move into first-person narrative. Alberto Manguel quotes in *A Reading Diary* that passage from *A Portrait* where the artist's personality reveals itself: "at first a cry or a cadence or a mood and then a fluid and lambent narrative, finally [it] refines itself out of existence, impersonalizes itself, so to speak." A comic spirit underlies the earnestness of the venture: it contains its own parody. "The artist, like the God of creation," says the lapsed Roman Catholic Joyce, using an image Flaubert would have admired, "remains within or behind or beyond or above his handiwork, invisible, refined out of existence, indifferent, paring his fingernails." Joyce, in "locating" the artist "within or behind or beyond or above" embodies his omnipresence and his disappearance, repositioning becoming in effect an erasure. But he still has fingers, and nails that need paring.

*A Portrait* demands much of its readers, readjusting their expectations and taking them to the threshold of a new fiction. That fiction is *Ulysses.* Faulkner advises us, "You should approach Joyce's *Ulysses* as the illiterate Baptist preacher approaches the Old Testament: with faith." Borges is less amenable. "Plenitude and indigence coexist in Joyce." He is incapable of construction (by which he means narrative construction) and so resorts to labyrinths and symmetries. Martin Amis, reminding us that the novel began as a story to be added to *Dubliners,* makes an observation not out of key with Borges's: *Ulysses* is "a short story of a third of a million words."

Like the stories, *Ulysses* is a day, and we remember how Stephen Dedalus re-marks, "Every life is many days, day after day. We walk through ourselves, meeting robbers, ghosts, giants, old men, young men, wives, widows, brothers-in-love, but always meeting ourselves." So we do. Some of those meetings are prosaic, others miasmic, as when Bloom wanders through the kind of neighbor-hood where, in *A Portrait*, young Stephen first encounters a prostitute and avails himself of her tenderness. Eroticism here is of another order, intense, hilarious, rousing. The language enacts, the words flutter on their wicked pinions.

> *Bloom plodges forward again through the sump. Kisses chirp amid the rifts of fog a piano sounds. He stands before a lighted house, listening. The kisses, winging from their bowers fly about him, twittering, warbling, cooing.)*
> THE KISSES: *(Warbling)* Leo! *(Twittering)* Icky licky micky sticky for Leo! *(Cooing)* Coo coocoo! Yummyyum, Womwom! *(Warbling)* Big comebig! Pirouette! Leopopold! *(Twittering)* Leeolee! *(Warbling)* O Leo!
> *(They rustle, flutter upon his garments, alight, bright giddy flecks, silvery sequins.)*
> BLOOM: A man's touch. Sad music. Church music. Perhaps here.
> *(Zoe Higgins, a young whore in a sapphire slip, closed with three bronze buckles, a slim black velvet fillet round her throat, nods, trips down the steps and accosts him.)*

When E. M. Forster delivered the Clarke Lectures (later *Aspects of the Novel*) in Cambridge in 1927, *Ulysses* was unavailable in full in England. It had been banned for obscenity (it arrived legally in 1936). Portions of it had been pub-lished in the American *Little Review* between 1918 and 1920, and in February 1922 Sylvia Beach published it in Paris. Forster, a decade before the book could be bought over the counter, characterizes it as "that remarkable affair—perhaps the most interesting literary experiment of our day," though he found it hard to enjoy. He repeated a formal mantra that has continued to distract readers from the book. *Ulysses* "could not have been achieved unless Joyce had had, as guide and butt, the world of the *Odyssey*." Clearly the *Odyssey* was in Joyce's mind, but to establish and maintain the novel's continuous connections with the Homeric poem is to miss the book itself. After composition had begun, Joyce's thoughts of Homer were intermittent. Occasionally, as Anthony Burgess suggests, a formal challenge presented itself, and such moments of connection, or response, were informing. Others were mechanical, or gratuitous, or exist only in the critics' eager imaginations.

A formal effect, Burgess says, begins "from the Cyclops episode on," when the author starts "to lengthen his chapters to make the reading time correspond with the imagined time of enactment." This formal change of gear and pace means that "the book is technically not so much a unity as people like to think. Compare the Aeolus episode with the Oxen of the Sun and you'll see what I mean." In other words, the technical aim is not unitary, different impulses are pursued, and throughout elements of parody and homage affect tone and pace and disrupt a conventional sense of "unities." The book has more in common with Rabelais, say, than with Thackeray. Forster responds ambivalently to its uneven purpose: it is "a dogged attempt to cover the universe with mud, an inverted Victorianism, an attempt to make grossness and dirt succeed where sweetness and light failed, a simplification of the human character in the interests of Hell." Henry Miller is less ambivalent than Forster. "I see [Joyce] as a broken vomit, a precious sewer, a medieval stew."

Virginia Woolf got the measure of Joyce's radicalism: the intention was not shocking effect but a previously unattempted *realism*. She singles out the cemetery scene, "with its brilliancy, its sordidity, its incoherence, its sudden lightning flashes of significance," how it comes "so close to the quick of the mind that, on a first reading at any rate, it is difficult not to acclaim a masterpiece . . . If we want life itself, here we surely have it." Her excitement was local, attaching to scenes and not to the whole book. Later she called it "a memorable catastrophe—immense in daring, terrific in disaster." Given her own technical experiments and competitiveness, she cannot but have been troubled by the depth and range of Joyce's imagination as compared with her narrower experience and tidier architecture, a tidiness that works against authentic stream of consciousness. "Joyce was not the first writer to use interior monologue," David Lodge reminds us, "(he credited the invention to an obscure French novelist of the late nineteenth century, Edouard Dujardin), nor the last, but he brought it to a pitch of perfection that makes other exponents, apart from Faulkner and Beckett, look rather feeble in comparison." Against the stagey, exquisite procedures of Woolf, *Ulysses* reeks of the human in every chapter. It is a book of smells and stenches, one reason it so affects the readerly imagination. "*Ulysses* is a psychological rather than a heroic epic," Lodge says. "We become acquainted with the principal characters not by being told about them, but by sharing their most intimate thoughts, represented as silent, spontaneous, unceasing streams of consciousness." We also breathe through their noses. Orwell's verdict: "Now and again there appears a novel which opens up a new world not by revealing what is strange, but by revealing what is familiar." In a letter, he wrote, "Art implies selection and there is as much selection in *Ulysses* as in *Pride and Prejudice*. Only Joyce is attempting to select and represent events and thoughts as they occur in life and not as they occur in fiction." But, as Woolf did, he sensed a failure of continuity—"the book does seem to me to split up into a lot of unrelated or thinly related incidents." The language works at different intensities, and sometimes it is on the brink of breaking into verse.

One thing Orwell surprisingly did not mention, though Saul Bellow does, not without a certain disbelief. How is it that *Ulysses,* written during World War I, proceeds with so little acknowledgment of the war's realities? How could a person living through that cataclysm not register it in his writing? "Could the fury of such a war be ignored?" Evidently, yes: the date of the action and the reality is 1904. But the elegy the book represents, or becomes, is released in part by the changes war effected in sensibility and memory. What Bellow calls "the force of tradition" in Joyce does indeed carry "realism into parody, satire, mock epic— Leopold Bloom." Yet parody opens up a bold realism of a different order in which disproportion and caricature deliver the world back to its natural unpredictable disproportions. As in Rabelais, art is made to take a dose of reality, and again to contain, rather than reflect, the world. Real life intrudes in dozens of gratuitous details.

A reader who sets out to read *Finnegans Wake* as a story, or for its story, will be thwarted. There are many elements of narrative, but they matter less than the things the novel is doing at the same time. It is founded on popular and ballad culture: the writer is not included as a voice; his is a magician's presence, an orchestrator's: no "I" directs or catechizes us. It is like a cauldron in which bubble the languages and literatures of Europe and beyond, as in a seafood soup when you recognize now a clam, a bit of cod or haddock, an antenna, an oily eye: a broth full of familiar things apprehended beyond the reach of description.

For *Madame Bovary* Flaubert chose the lowest and least sympathetic subject he could find on which to build a world. Here Joyce chooses Timothy Finnegan, a tipsy workman who falls from a ladder to his death, then builds him up and out, of ballad, legend, myth, of real places and the stories that inhabit them, and of the many languages that pass through the port and the ear. Finnegan wakes at the word *whisky,* subsides again, and the wake becomes a funeral wake, only it never settles down to being just that. The setting is the same city that *Ulysses* explores, but miasmic, refracted through languages and traditions suggested by analogy, synergy, and irony. A builder dies. Literal, symbolic. He falls, literally, but with all the implications that building and falling have in religious, civic, and cultural traditions. His funeral is a funferal. (In a letter he calls himself Jeems Jokes.)

A delightful and instructive way into the book is the passage in which we are shown by a drunk guide around the Wellington Monument Museum, called The Willingdone Museyroom. Many of the themes and much of the geography are evoked with precision of detail; only the language is in strange, ecstatic focus, each word brings into play a variety of meanings. It is useful to read aloud and, slowly, in a various group to which every member contributes a different hearing and the particulars of a distinct culture. It is also valuable to use Burgess's 1969 *A Shorter "Finnegans Wake"* and *Here Comes Everybody: An Introduction to James Joyce for the Ordinary Reader* (1965), also published as *Re Joyce*. In 1973 he wrote *Joysprick: An Introduction to the Language of James Joyce*. These books help us keep company with H. C. Earwicker (HCE) and Anna Livia Plurabelle (ALP), to understand the recurrences and evolutions of image, phrase, and theme, the circularity of construction.

Joyce uses etymology and punning to subvert the stability and autonomy of his language and deliver it back to a place before Babel, in which it is again expressive across borders of register and denotation, a place where grammars of sound and rhythm compete. It is as though Joyce were trying to write a book that did not need to be translated, that would create and exist in a common language. It is not in English as we understand the term: each word is rediscovered with its contingent riches, which the context acknowledges and welcomes. We understand the whole project, or we fail to understand altogether. If language can be transfigured, then what it expresses is similarly susceptible. Joyce is not reacting against the limitations of conventional English but celebrating its potential, how much more it is and can do. Echoing the philosopher Vico, he developed further the metaphor of language as a river; there is no doubting the centrality of the image of rivers and their confluences in his book.

Samuel Beckett transcribed parts of *Finnegans Wake* for Joyce and helped to make the first French version of the Anna Livia Plurabelle passage under his supervision. About Joyce he declared that the writing "is not about something; *it is that something itself.*" This notion, beyond mimetic enactment, of creative embodiment defines the hubris of the great modernists. Each passage, in the *Wake* particularly, aspires to be an instance of itself and not "about" itself. Joyce's later works aspire to the condition of primary creation. In this too he is heir to Flaubert.

———•—

Wyndham Lewis (1882–1957), dubbed by Auden "that lonely old volcano of the Right," intended subversions as well: "to be busily balking / The tongue-tied Briton—that is my outlandish plot!" he declared in *One-Way Song,* his one significant poem. His 1937 novel *The Revenge for Love,* clearheaded about the Communist mission in Spain, is hostile to those English intellectuals (Auden among them) who sympathized. Each of his books is wedded to issues of the day, not in the way that Joyce's *Ulysses* is tied to 1904 Dublin but in the way that Pope's satires are specific to their age. This *topicality* requires that the modern reader be familiar with context in order to get a purchase both on the narrative reality and the satirical intent. Orwell in 1945 recognized the problem: "Enough talent to set up dozens of ordinary writers has been poured into Wyndham Lewis's so-called novels, such as *Tarr* and *Snooty Baronet.* Yet it would be a very heavy labor to read one of these books right through." They lack "some indefinable quality, a sort of literary vitamin." Even his last significant "so-called" novel, the autobiographical *Self-Condemned* (1954), lacks that whatever it is.

Hardy once remarked that a book "is not at bottom criticized . . . as a particular man's artistic interpretation of life, but with a secret eye on its theological and political propriety." This goes some way toward explaining the neglect into which Lewis's writing has fallen. T. S. Eliot called him "the greatest prose master of style of my generation." C. H. Sisson praised his "appreciation of the role of the human mind" in the twentieth century. There is something distinctive about his approach, hectoring and white hot, witty and unresting, and about his direct language. This bigmouth is more than an heir to the hooligan streak in Kipling and to the ranting streak in Ezra Pound.

Meeting him in Paris, Hemingway was (in retrospect) repelled. Here was a character out of *La Bohème,* but without the jollity. "He had a face that reminded me of a frog, not a bullfrog but just any frog, and Paris was too big a puddle for him." They spent grudging time together and Lewis "watched superciliously" while Pound and Hemingway boxed. "I do not think I had ever seen a nastier-looking man," Hemingway declared. "Lewis did not show evil; he just looked nasty." He was smaller than his swagger and big ideas. Peter Ackroyd is less merciless, but says, "There is something too heated and assertive about his writing, and it often suffers from an excess of point. He knows what he is saying, but not who he is saying it to." Or when to stop. The eyes, Hemingway reported, were "of an unsuccessful rapist." Long before this attack, Lewis had described Hemingway—as a writer—in just but degrading terms.

Saul Bellow, who values Lewis highly, recalls the distinction he made in "his intellectual biography" *Rude Assignment: A Narrative of My Career Up-to-Date* (1950), between small-public art and great-public art. The latter represented by Dickens, Balzac, Tolstoy, perhaps Bellow himself, the former by Flaubert, Baudelaire. There is a national public and a series of smaller publics, selected or self-selecting. Division grew and small-public artists began to feel superior, set not only apart but above, even stimulated by the indifference of the large public. Like Joyce (and like Hemingway) Lewis seems to address the large public but reaches, and that fitfully, a small one.

Lewis, the self-styled Enemy of the subjective, irrational, and affected, took a fatal step in 1931. He published *Hitler,* a book that described the National

Socialist program approvingly. It was not a prophetic book: it misread the facts. In the 1930s context, his misreading was literary suicide. No one refuted him. His anti-Semitism, for which he later atoned, was not commented upon. Instead he was ignored, and his later books suffered the same fate. When in 1937 he wrote *The Hitler Cult,* about the reality of Hitler's program, it was too late. Lewis was not a fascist, not even in the shorthand sense the word has acquired, but he shared an interest in political structures with most of the modernists. He acknowledged his error, but the damage was permanent.

Percy Wyndham Lewis was born aboard his father's yacht off Nova Scotia. His American father—Lewis called him a "professional idler"—had a private income. He and Lewis's mother separated when the boy was eleven. Percy went with his mother to England, had a governess, and was sent to public schools, finally to Rugby. He did not distinguish himself. He went on to the Slade School of Art (1898–1901). Then he escaped from England, living in Paris and elsewhere in Europe. Paris, he said, was his university. He attended the lectures of Henri Bergson and, as a corrective, read Nietzsche. In 1909, back in London because his father had cut off his allowance, he began to try to make a living as a painter.

His first story was written while he was painting and took him less time than the canvas. He included it in *The Wild Body: A Soldier of Humor and Other Stories* (1927). "It was the sun, a Breton instead of a British, that brought forth my first short story—'The Anjou' I believe it was: the Death-god of Plouilliou." The story "was the crystallization *of what I had to keep out of my consciousness while painting.* Otherwise the painting would have been a bad painting." In other words, the ideas in the story were not plastic ideas and would have distorted the plastic expression.

Ford published Lewis's stories in the *English Review;* Lewis knew Pound, the poet-philosopher T. E. Hulme, the sculptor and artist Henri Gaudier Brzeska, and other writers and artists. With Pound, Lewis established "Vorticism," a movement in painting and literature that took up where Imagism left off and had elements in common with Italian Futurism. He published *Blast,* a periodical that ran for two fat, rumbustious issues. Lewis was among the first English artists to accept the challenge of cubism and, in a spirit quite different from Stein's, to transpose it into prose. In *Blast,* his and Pound's aim was to shake what they considered the somnolent British into recognition that the arts needed renewal; sentimental conventionality was unequal to the age of the machine and the difference it made to the human spirit. "We stand for the Reality of the Present—not the sentimental Future or the sacripant Past," the manifesto proclaimed. *Blast* was the destructive phase of his work—attempting to wipe a smug public-school grin off the Academy's face, to purge English art of introverted irony and renew it with extrovert wit. His first novel, *Tarr* (written between 1909 and

1911, expanded and serialized in the *Egoist* from 1916, published as a book in 1918, revised 1928) grew with him, the English (Tarr) and the German (Kreisler) protagonists in tension in a heightened Paris. Their loves and other activities serve to reveal their characters and national characteristics, and the German proves a sinister figure. Lewis kept adjusting, the figure of Tarr not unlike his haughty early self, the Nietzschean artist.

When *Tarr* was completed the second time, Lewis enlisted and saw service in France. And he *saw* service, becoming an official War Artist for the Canadian War Records Office, and his sketches, exhibited in 1919, were among the most original: true to the aspect of men turned into fine-tuned, disposable instruments of war. By the time he revised *Tarr* a third time, it was in the interests of form, the urgent themes and occasions that gave rise to it having relaxed. Rebecca West called the 1918 version a "beautiful and serious work of art." It reminded her of Dostoyevsky. The figure of Kreisler "is worthy to stand beside Starveling." "We watch him turning life into blood-stained *charivari* exactly as we watched Germany during the war."

After the war, through sporadic magazines (*The Tyro* and *The Enemy*) and in a number of books, Lewis became the satirist of his day and an erratic philosophical and political thinker. *The Art of Being Ruled,* his most important cultural and political work, appeared in 1926; *Time and Western Man,* a philosophical investigation of his obsessive theme, where he breaks with Bergson, in 1927. *The Childermass,* the first major piece in his trilogy that came to be known as *The Human Age,* was published in 1928 and completed many years later, more a fantasy apocalypse than a novel, and his devastating novel-satire on the Sitwells and the literary coteries of the day, *The Apes of God,* came out in 1930. Here he embodies the distinction between what Goethe calls "puppets" and "natures," something more profound than Forster's "flat" and "rounded" characters. The first are men (and fictional characters) who follow clockwork patterns, cogs in the giant machine; and the others are unpredictable, creatively alive. The Apes belong to the former category.

Thus systematically he made his position on politics, philosophy, and aesthetics clear. He collected many enemies, including Roger Fry and the whole of *bien pensant* Bloomsbury, the Royal Academy, the aesthetes, the Sitwells, and others. He rejects the historical man-centered art that flows from romanticism. As a portrait painter, he made figures true to vision, portraits drained of subjectivity: they are contained energies apparently impatient to return to motion. Aware of the allure of the subjective, he sees it as finally solipsistic. Lawrence was naturally among the *bêtes noires,* and in *Paleface* (1929), written in an informal style reminiscent of Lawrence, he includes his decisive attack on writers who privilege the emotions, the abdomen and groin, over the head as the "vital centre."

Poverty began for him in the mid- to late 1920s. It was a frayed and fraying rather than a desperate poverty, and it dogged him for the rest of his life, later compounded by blindness. "What has befallen me, or rather, my books," he wrote in *The Writer and the Absolute,* "proves what is my contention: namely, that the mid-twentieth-century writer is only nominally free, and should not fail to acquire a thorough knowledge of the invisible frontiers surrounding his narrow patch of liberty, to transgress which might be fatal." He had his *Hitler* in mind.

He does not imitate the "wholeness of nature" but breaks it up, shuffles objects or ideas, juxtaposes them so they question or ironize one another. The organic metaphor is for him a convenient falsification, resorted to only in a spirit of irony. In his fiction he often focuses a single aspect of a character, fragmenting the whole; the selective data he provides serves as a clause in a larger idea or pattern. The emerging pattern is finally stable but never static. It is an art, as I. A. Richards said, always in sharp focus, but perspective changes continually, bewilderingly. The reorienting effects Joyce achieves by compounding language Lewis brings about by refocusing. This art rewards close engagement, and one approaches in the work of Lewis specific understanding in ways that Joyce evades. Lewis's technique is alienating. We do not identify with character, or enter into conventional human drama. Our attention is deflected to the drama of ideas. A "hyper-daylight" (Pound's phrase) is trained upon them. They are volatile and dangerous and must be handled professionally. In *Men without Art* Lewis declared that his contemporaries could "write *satire* for *art*—not the moralist satire directed at a given society, but a metaphysical satire occupied with mankind."

Like Lewis, Samuel (Barclay) Beckett (1906–1989) had two métiers, in his case drama and fiction; unlike Joyce, he wrote in two languages, English and French. His French composition began in earnest with his translation with Alfred Péron of the Anna Livia Plurabelle passage in 1930, a version Joyce did not immediately approve, and of his own novel *Murphy* some years later. These exercises alerted him to how the other language leaves behind much of the dead semantic burden that adheres to the words and structures of one's native language, the residues in habitual usage. Joyce made constant use of these heavy residues, the blur they create around words, everything from etymology to idiomatic and dialect usage. The "language of the night" Joyce called it, working by association, libidinally. Translation, sloughing one semantic history and imposing another, had to find the blur not in stimulated aural memory and instinct but by design. Giambattista Vico (1668–1744), whose anti-Cartesian belief that the truth is approached through creation, not through observation, and whom Beckett adduces in his first published writing on Joyce, insisted that "anyone who wishes to excel as a poet must unlearn his native language, and return to the pristine beggary of words." In writing in French, Beckett declared, "without all the old associations English has for me, I was able to get at it more clearly, the outlines were clearer." When Oscar Wilde wrote *Salomé* in French, he had a comparable experience of liberation into clarity; and Ford practiced this same "pristine beggary" when he translated *The Good Soldier* into French without consulting his own original text.

After the exercise of translation, collaborative translation in particular, working with a native speaker of the host language, Beckett saw the possibilities of composing in the first place in the host language, then bringing the work back into English. Some of his earliest works in French, translated into English in collaboration with the American writer and publisher Richard Seaver, are included in *First Love and Other Novellas*. Beckett revised the translations later, but not the originals. This suggests that French was in more than one sense a medium.

In translating *Molloy* (1951), Beckett worked with another Anglophone writer (he did not want a translator as such). In 1994, Patrick Bowles recollected the conversations they had, he a young man of twenty-six. It was four decades after the event but Bowles had kept notes. Composing his trilogy—*Molloy, Malone Dies* (1951), and *The Unnamable* (1953)—Beckett said, was like "writing on top of a lot of dust." He "loathed" English as a medium, its "stilted idiom," and claimed to have lost the facility to write in it (though much of his later work, especially for the stage, was composed in English). The 240 pages took fifteen months to translate, which suggests how exigent Beckett was. Beckett, Bowles reports, called his books "a positive statement of a negative thing." His was "pre-logical writing. I don't ask people to understand it logically, only to accept it." He felt the need for isolation from his native language, so that in time the choices a writer made were actual choices rather than reflexes: "Anything that makes writing more difficult is helpful."

What made writing most difficult for Beckett was James Joyce, his greatest blessing and curse. By November 1, 1928, they had met. At the first meeting Joyce was out of sorts. He was holding court, there were other young writers present, and sardonically he demanded of the young Beckett whether he was composing an *Iliad* or a *Divine Comedy*. He had no idea he was addressing a man already in possession of Joycean attributes and then some. Beckett was also a promising athlete (chosen for the Trinity College, Dublin, Cricket First XI), a Senior Exhibitioner who received a First Class Moderatorship in Modern Languages, a gold medal, and travel grants. When he declared himself an avatar of failure, he had a considerable fall to get there.

Beckett survived his early encounter. His first letters to Joyce are those of a modest research assistant, respectful, distant. In time he got as close as anyone could to Joyce; adopting French as his language of composition a decade later was in part to break out of Joyce's orbit. Beckett's first, abandoned novel, *Dream of Fair to Middling Women* (1932, not published until 1993, and reworked into the stories of *More Pricks than Kicks* of 1934), reflects (mutedly) the kinds of humor and the sense of place that he learned from Joyce. Belacqua Shuah, a Trinity student, wanders through the city. Stephen Dedalus has gone before, but the closer Joycean proximity of these stories is to *Dubliners,* with more dialect. Beckett also adapts here some of the extrovert elements of style he has acquired from *Ulysses* and *Finnegans Wake.* He includes letters, invitations, dates that might seem to ground the text, but then he uses archaic words and neologisms, music, foreign languages. He has not decided which way to turn, toward the semantic lavishness and formal openness of *Finnegans Wake,* or toward the lavishness of Proust, whose great novel he has not only read but written about extensively (his little book *Proust* was published in 1931), or in a direction as yet undefined. It was another decade before he accepted that Joyce was a wonderful dead end, his abundance, his continual embellishment of his work ("He was always adding to it; you only have to look at his proofs to see that"), his control, were inimitable.

Beckett recognized that *his* challenge was "impoverishment," deliberate "lack of knowledge," and "taking away." In his Proust book he remarked, "Only he who forgets remembers." He distinguishes between "endings" and "conclusions." The latter are what a tidying memory can make of the former, falsifying because of the instinct for form, the hunger for completion. The inconclusion of his trilogy, consciousness extending into the aftermath of material existence, the mind still working not in a spiritual realm but in the murmurous exile of undeath, rejects conclusion. In *Play*—the play of the three urns with faces *"so lost to age and aspect as to seem almost part of urns. But no masks"* protruding—the voices reach a dreadful, parallel, untranscendent conclusion:

> M: Perhaps they meet, and sit, over a cup of that green tea they both
>     so loved, without milk or sugar not even a squeeze of lemon–
> [Spot from M to W2.]
> W2: Are you listening to me? Is anyone bothering about me at all?
> [Spot from W2 to M.]
> M: Not even a squeeze of–
> [Spot from M to W1.]
> W1: Is it something I should do with my face, other than utter?
>     Weep?
> [Spot from W1 to W2.]
> W2: Am I taboo, I wonder. Not necessarily, now that all danger is
>     averted. That poor creature–I can hear her–that poor creature–

[Spot from W2 to W1.]

W1: Bite off my tongue and swallow it? Spit it out? Would that pla-
cate you? How the mind works still to be sure!

This is an extension of the themes of the *Unnamable,* not a reductio ad absurdum so much as a paralyzing apotheosis.

From Joyce he retains the traits of "silence, exile and cunning." And like
Joyce's, his own work is a dead end. Hugh Kenner compares the Beckett cul-de-
sac not so much to James Joyce's as to Henry James's, and as soon as James's name
is mentioned the appropriateness is overwhelming. It is fastidious, utter refinement that marks the mature work of both men, our two "virtuosi of the dead
end, playing there each man hand after hand of his own intent necessary soli-
taire, intricate in its quasi-colloquial abstractions, minimal in its referentiality,
inauthentic for anyone else to attempt." It is as dead an end as Ivy Compton-
Burnett's, or Jean Rhys's, only more deliberate, more theorizable. It is also rooted
in certain experiences of which he could not "make" sense, so that they haunted
him and he revisited them, approaching from different angles, listening. He recalls one experience in particular: "For five months I watched my brother dying
in pain. All that time he was uttering a kind of low cry. He certainly wasn't uttering it for anyone else. Only for himself. And not even for himself. Not *for* anything at all. He merely uttered it. He couldn't *not* have uttered it, he couldn't stop
uttering it, he didn't *want* to utter it, he uttered it, in spite of himself, and yet not,
since he didn't *want* not to utter it either. The cry escaped him, all the time, from
where he was, in his room."

Molloy retains movement. Is Beckett's brother a prototype of Malone, on his
long deathbed? In *The Unnamable* the cycle of paralysis is completed. The French
critic, theorist, and writer of narrative Maurice Blanchot (1907–2003) writes that
in *Molloy,* "what is expressed still to some extent conforms to what we think of
as a story"; in *Malone Dies,* "the space explored has none of the resources available in the first novel, being reduced to just one room"; and in *The Unnamable* at
last, "the stories do not even try to stand on their own, but 'circle mechanically
around the vacant centre occupied by the nameless "I." ' " The question of point
of view is now terminally vexed. There is no protagonist, there is no separable
narrator. An exasperated Martin Amis declares, "Beckett was the headmaster of
the Writing as Agony school. On a good day, he would stare at the wall for eighteen hours or so, feeling entirely terrible, and, if he was lucky, a few words like
NEVER or END or NOTHING or NO WAY might brand themselves on his
bleeding eyes."

To get the measure of Beckett, who in 1969 suffered "the catastrophe" of being awarded the Nobel Prize in Literature, it is worth revisiting his early enthu-

siasm. It is hard for inventive poets to find their way to the surface. As much effort can go into emerging as a writer as goes into the writing itself. Sometimes the process becomes literature. In the 1920s the Toulouse poet Jean du Chas established the Concentriste school of writers. They were a late outgrowth of symbolism and shared some of the qualities of the Anglo-American Imagists and of the Vorticists. Beckett lectured on Jean du Chas in Dublin in 1930. The lecture was collected in the volume of his writings entitled *Disjecta*.

Du Chas resembles Max Beerbohm's Enoch Soames in one respect. He also resembles Anne Knish and Emanuel Morgan of the Spectra group. When Ethel Malley sent the papers of her modernist brother Ern to Australian editors, she too was active in Jean du Chas territory. In short, du Chas was Beckett's invention. Beckett delivered his lecture without expression, its exemplary pedantry a parody of the academic life he was to leave. This was his declaration of intent. It defined a self-serving poetic economy in which a movement, a writer, and the works that go with them are contrived, their reception orchestrated. Like God in the overarching world, so in the microcosm the creator-critic has unusual power. He invents what facts are needed for explication; readers can appeal to the highest authority, and none can gainsay him.

"It is useless for the aesthete (or any other anarchist) to urge the isolated individuality of the artist, apart from his attitude to his age," says G. K. Chesterton. "His attitude to his age is his individuality: men are never individual when alone." In this sense, then, we can regard Beckett's isolated figures as universals. Greene was not the first to mention Gilbert Keith Chesterton (1874–1936) in connection with James Augustine Aloysius Joyce: "A generation that appreciates Joyce finds for some reason Chesterton's equally fanatical play on words exhausting. Perhaps it is that he is still suspected of levity, and the generation now reaching middle age has been a peculiarly serious one." Kafka was entertained by Chesterton's allegorical fiction. Borges relished the Father Brown stories, and like Borges, Chesterton began in a hopeful liberalism of which the remainder of his writing life seems like an eloquent denial. Because of such modernist connections, the idea that Chesterton, who would have felt comfortable in the newspaper offices of the second chapter of *Ulysses,* somehow belongs in Joyce's creative company grows louder. Thomas Hardy, whom Chesterton described as a "village atheist," spent a few happy minutes on his deathbed constructing an epitaph for his rival: "Here lies nipped in this narrow cyst / The literary contortionist."

Hugh Kenner, the great expositor of Pound, Joyce, and Eliot, published his first book in 1947. *Paradox in Chesterton* included an introduction by Herbert Marshall McLuhan, also in the morning of his career. Kenner wipes the smile off Chesterton's face and McLuhan in his introduction reads into him a man of much more serious dispositions than most readers, a "metaphysical moralist." Inside his substantial (six foot four, 130 kilo), genial frame, he suggests, "all the time there was a very thin man indeed struggling to get out." There is a "toby-jug" aspect of Chesterton, but something more too. Two penetrating Canadians could read his meanings but were less sure of his tones. Chesterton is a true Edwardian, witty, lively, wasted on a period neither serious nor profane enough for him. His gestures were anachronistic. He became a "metaphysical jester," and as Naipaul and Bellow both remind us, the most effective jesters are often those who are closest to the fatal edge, laughter and gestures expressing a displaced hysteria.

Joyce is indisputably *there* on the permanent map of fiction. But those who would make Chesterton count imagine that if Joyce could be reduced down to *Dubliners* and *A Portrait,* it would be as though he were relatively *not* there. The molds would have been stretched and rattled but not quite broken. It has proven harder to diminish him than it was to diminish Stein. But what if there were an *alternative* modernism, or an alternative *to* modernism, and an English one . . .

One problem for Chesterton fans is their writer's abundance—he wrote more than eighty books and hundreds of reviews, articles, and poems—and he failed in his profligacy to challenge conventional forms. In her "Scrutiny" of his work Dorothy Edwards chides the writer "who believes that truth is something completely objective, a kind of treasure that one may light upon by some outrageous accident," and she notes that he does not change from book to book. His ideas develop but his writing does not. Peter Ackroyd acknowledges him as a "journalist of genius. But he was so prodigal of his genius that he scattered it in all directions—a master, someone said, who never wrote a masterpiece."

Chesterton's advocacy of Victorian fiction, with its ill-judged, condescending chivalry toward female novelists, anachronizes him. Of George Eliot he wrote that she sees her characters clearly but "not through an atmosphere": they exist in imagination but not in the world. Atmosphere excited him, and he can create atmosphere more convincingly than character. His conservative satisfaction with the allegorical mode sits uncomfortably with his painterly love of specific detail. He did, after all, go to the Slade to become an artist rather than to Oxford to become a writer. It is as though his writing was a Manichean exercise, an uneasy tension between a love of particulars and a devotion to Thomist ideas. His distributist ideals, "three acres and a cow," were hardly rooted in philosophical or political realism.

There is the matter of his religious belief, as he moved toward and then embraced his wife's Roman Catholicism. This attracted Greene but repelled Arnold Bennett: "Not all Mr. Chesterton's immense cleverness and charm will ever erase from the minds of his best readers this impression—caused by his mistimed religious dogmatism—that there is something seriously deficient in the very basis of his mind." This deficiency is manifest in his books' construction. Father Brown, unlike Sherlock Holmes, is an assembler of puzzles, not an analyst of clues. He has or stumbles upon evidence that points him in certain directions; he does not seek it out and unpack it. The knowledge he possesses, beyond revelation, is always a fact that no one else has access to. It is an art of withholding rather than discovering information. The books are full of symbols, many of them conventional, their meaning arbitrarily assigned.

His popularity is rooted in conventionality. *The Napoleon of Notting Hill* (1904), dedicated to his close friend and co-religionist Hilaire Belloc, went through 118 editions in English and translation between publication and 2010. Its bizarre protagonist, Auberon Quinn, is a common clerk, but the story is set conveniently in a future in which the impoverishments of spirit and imagination entailed in capitalism are well advanced. Auberon is randomly chosen to occupy the throne and sets out to bring the past alive in a reinvigorated present. Chesterton was always drawn to what he calls "the festive antiquarianism of Sir Walter Scott," but to create it in the past would have been counterproductive. Because it had happened before, it might recur, for as he wrote elsewhere, "Roman Britain and Medieval England are still not only alive but lively; for real development is not leaving things behind, as on a road, but drawing life from them, as from a root." The social and spiritual impulse behind this cheerful-seeming book is elegiac, dark; it may have had an impact on George Orwell when he came to write *Nineteen Eighty-Four*.

Chesterton's second and best-known novel, *The Man Who Was Thursday: A Nightmare* (1908), portrays a road gone starless indeed. Again the mode is fantasy, though the book is set in the period of writing. Gabriel Same, the protagonist, is called upon by Scotland Yard to help deal with the anarchist threat. Published a year after Conrad's *The Secret Agent*, the book has a weak grasp on its themes, a tenuous sense of the world in which radical ideologies sneak toward actions with human consequences. The police themselves are stereotyped. The plot is complex and works satisfactorily, Chesterton creating, within his schematic and symbolic structures, some plausible characters and surprises. Syme and Lucian Gregory, the anarchic poet, conduct dialogues and Chesterton develops essayistic ideas in their exchanges. Gregory appears in the end to be a genuine anarchist, but not in the way Conrad's characters are. The book's challenge is less political than theological. It serves Chesterton's higher—religious—purpose in ways that diminish it as fiction. *Manalive* (1912) brings in the holy man who is also a symbol of vulnerable simplicity, his integrity demonstrated rather than tried. It is again a book whose ideas first shape and then stifle. The action occurs and is then explained, a happy ending arrives with logical, not dramatic, necessity. In *The Flying Inn* (1914), Chesterton goes back to a future in which Islam has come to power in England, and against its prohibition on alcohol the protagonists make it their mission to rumble about the country in a mobile "inn," or cart, dispensing rum.

In 1969 Anthony Burgess wrote a theologically troubled introduction to Chesterton's *The Autobiography,* puzzled, as a Catholic himself, at the spirited innocence of the man. Chesterton was alert to the treachery of simplification and sentimentality but never recognized it in his own writing: a disillusioned Liberal, a sentimentalist of the common man at a time when some common men read and thought, a foe of capitalism and of the gathering energies of totalitarianism, a little Englander who at the same time rejected Anglicanism and took the Roman road. He was popular but was not taken very seriously. His politics, suffused with theology, were a dead end, his anti-Semitism no less repugnant for being culturally conditioned. It was into a province of a world like the one Chesterton addressed, a world he spoke for and reflected, that Leopold Bloom made his awkward entry on June 16, 1904.

The problem with *Ulysses,* Anthony Burgess (1917–1993) says, is that "Joyce spent too long on the book." Where it starts out from and where it arrives, even though the day is the same, seem to belong to different journeys. Still, there is about Joyce a monumental containment: four major books, each complete, and the material published after his death illuminating rather than dissipating what is there. Burgess is notable for the dissipation of his vast oeuvre. Like a customs officer fascinated by the four suitcases that the almost-blind Joyce is pushing through Nothing to Declare, he stops him, unpacks each bag in turn in full view, and tries on all the apparel. His Joyce books have been mentioned. In 1965 he went to Dublin to make a documentary about the author. In 1986 he produced his *Ulysses* musical, *Blooms of Dublin.*

As a color-blind child, Burgess found "an auditory compensation" listening on his wireless at the age of twelve to the gamut of Debussy's orchestral timbres. Even the word *alphabet* (French pronunciation) "is a yellowish color and sticks to the teeth in a delicate, thick paste that smells of butter biscuits." He could not pronounce the word "without chewing a little of language itself in a concentrated form." This is his account, in any case, and he is no less believable than Ford in his backward projection of the self.

"I wrote much because I was paid little," Burgess said. In fact he wrote much because he loved to read, and everything he read was pretext to his writing: after he prospered he continued writing and wrote more than ever. In 1966 Philip Larkin said exasperatedly to a friend, "The whole of English Lit. at the moment is being written by Anthony Burgess. He reviews all the new books except those by himself." Larkin was wrong. When Burgess was a reviewer for the *Yorkshire Post,* his editor gave him a book to review by Joseph Kell entitled *Inside Mr. Enderby.* Kell was a pseudonym masking the fact that Burgess was producing too many books. He enjoyed the freedom of identities. And he reviewed the book. Did not Sir Walter Scott review his own *Waverley* at length? Burgess used several pseudonyms, male and female. His writing name itself was a construction. Born John Anthony Burgess Wilson, he saw an abundance of Wilsons in the marketplace. His editor at Heinemann, Roland Gant, removed the conventional husk and revealed: Anthony Burgess.

For a time Gore Vidal regarded Burgess as the most interesting English writer of the previous half century. "Like Meredith," he says, "Burgess does the best things best." He has a soft spot for his worst things, too, and there are a lot of them. The bulk of his writing is out of literature. Kenneth Toomey, the old homosexual narrator in *Earthly Powers* (1980), Burgess's vast and best novel, which might have won the Man Booker Prize the year that Golding's "bloody awful" *Rites of Passage* did, is a projection of Somerset Maugham. Burgess too was a natural expatriate, Martin Amis says, culturally and otherwise, "developing freely under the lax and spacious influences of Europe"—those influences decidedly literary. Amis adduces American influences, too, of Herman Wouk's *War and Remembrance,* of Saul Bellow. The book "meshes the real and the personalized history of the twentieth century (more earnestly and intimately than E. L. Doctorow's *Ragtime* or Tom Stoppard's *Travesties*)." Toomey, a second-rate writer himself, bumps into the great: Joyce in particular, but also Hermann Hesse, Forster, et al. He is seduced by AE (George Russell) on the very day when Russell makes his appearance in Joyce's *Ulysses.* Toomey's name-dropping rivals Ford's.

*Nothing Like the Sun: The Story of Shakespeare's Love Life* (1964) was a roman à thèse in which the bard's developing imagination and amours are colored with New World syphilis. *A Dead Man in Deptford* (1993) more straightforwardly resurrects Marlowe. The pretexts for *Napoleon Symphony* (1974) were Beethoven's *Eroica* and the little Corsican's life, full of comedy that downplays historical incident. *1985* is a *riposte* to Orwell's *1984,* though Burgess gets it as wrong as Orwell did; and *Man of Nazareth* (1979) is the book of the film of the book. His twenty-second novel, *Abba Abba* (1977), brings together Keats and the Roman dialect sonneteer Giuseppe Belli. The title is a self-referential indulgence (the author's initials forward and reversed, twice; the rhyme scheme of the Petrarchan sonnet, *Eli Eli,* and so on). Throughout his work there is more revisioning than vision, language projects (verb and noun) in many forms. And there is F. X. Enderby of the Enderby novels, a personal creation, a poet whose poems have merit but, produced by a fictional character, have yet to receive their due.

Indeed, Burgess was an accomplished poet, a painter, and most of all a musician. He was at home before and after modernism, though critics who call him modernist give him too much credit.

He was not, by his own account, a reviser of whole works: he revised in advance: "I like to run a scene through in my mind before writing it down, seeing everything happen, hearing some of the dialogue." Then he wrote page by page, and when a page reached final form and was added to the pile, it was done, there was no reworking. He had a *whole* sense of his books, project by project, though his memory of where his language had been was imperfect and he repeats gestures and phrases. Martin Amis is scathing about his stylistic conflations, asyndetons, the "paraded muscularity," "needless vividness," "horribly Hopkinsian neologisms and 'kennings,'" elements Burgess probably regarded as brilliantly poetic.

His journalism and his critical books, about Shakespeare, Lawrence, Hemingway, and others, share the virtues and faults of the fiction. A voracious reader, he took shortcuts (given the encyclopedic scale of his projects, how could it have been otherwise?). He surveyed literature for different readerships, domestic and foreign, and wrote summary histories of the novel. He explored the theme of pornography, one of the literary arts to which he did not significantly contribute, being rather squeamish, despite his Shakespeare and the violence of *A Clockwork Orange*.

In 1944 his pregnant first wife was assaulted and robbed by four American deserters in blackout London. This was the occasion for *A Clockwork Orange* (1962), a book he claimed to have written in three weeks for the money and the film. The book is less gratuitous than his account makes it seem. It explores responsibility and free will. The protagonist is finally "cured" of thuggery, and of his ability to hear the powerful undercurrents in music. The relationship between art and violence, imagination and anarchy, Thomas Mann explored at length in *Doctor Faustus,* a lucid novelistic expositions of the rise of Nazism. Burgess was a close reader of Mann, a subtle novelist-essayist each of whose fictions worked as a philosophical argument even as the story emerged. Each of Mann's novels inhabits a specified historical moment. Too much of Burgess's fame rests on *A Clockwork Orange,* memorably filmed and then suppressed by Stanley Kubrick. The American and British editions of the novel are different: Burgess was talked into dropping the final chapter for the American edition: the symbolism of twenty-one chapters, coming of age, was sacrificed, and the conclusion of the philosophical argument was sacrificed to melodramatic necessity.

Martin Amis has fun with Burgess's distinction between the A novelist, who is conventional, mainstream, emphasizes narrative, senses the reader's presence, and reaches moral conclusions, and the B novelist who approaches from a less calculated angle. "Serious" novelists often want to move from A to B or between A and B. Burgess is of this sort, from the early Malayan trilogy of novels and Enderby by way of the *Orange* to *Abba*. In *A Clockwork Orange,* for example, neither the American nor the British versions ends in a morally comfortable place. David Lodge quotes Burgess: "I saw that the novel would have to have a metaphysical or theological base . . . the artificial extirpation of free will through scientific conditioning; the question whether this might not . . . be a greater evil than the free choice of evil." At one level the unalloyed brutal manner recalls *A Handful of Dust* or *Brighton Rock,* even *Lord of the Flies.* The relationship between art and evil can be close; art need not lead toward "the good," and the aesthetic has no necessary moral component.

The reader is conditioned to accept the Russianized language Burgess developed. "A bonus," says Lodge, "is that the stylized language keeps the appalling acts that are described . . . at a certain aesthetic distance, and protects us from being too revolted by them—or too excited." In short, it distances and thus aestheticizes them, which makes it possible for the reader to understand the novel as an essay or a fiction at one remove. The dystopia of *A Clockwork Orange* is taken a step further in the cacatopia of *1985,* a novel that comments on Orwell's book and politics, written at a time when Burgess feared the foe was on the Left, before Mrs. Thatcher's reforms had pointed the trembling needle in a different direction. His Bev Smith, unlike Orwell's fully drawn Winston Smith, is innocent and therefore not a protagonist but a victim.

Anthony Burgess admired *Riddley Walker* (1980), a book after his own heart. Russell Conwell Hoban (1925–2011) devised a language, the dialect for "an as yet unborn England," postindustrial, postnuclear, post *next* millennium. When critics compare Riddle's riddling, stripped-down, disrupted language to Joyce's overstuffed pillow in *Finnegans Wake,* they miss a crucial point. Connections with Burgess and Joyce are chimeras: a truer analogy would be with Tolkien, though Hoban lacks the rich semantic mulch of Hobbitry. A still closer analogy might be with the thick idiom Dylan Thomas uses in his radio drama *Under Milk Wood* (1954). But in fact the main feature of Riddley's speech is a relatively simple phonetic and typographical disruption of Standard English. How would it be if we translated it back into standard language? How much of the book's magic is entailed? "I dont have nothing only words to put down on paper. Its so hard. Some times theres mor in the emty paper nor there is when you get the writing down on it. You try to word the big things and they tern ther backs on you. Yet youwl see stanning stoans and ther backs wil talk to you."

Hoban's dystopian vision is less focused than Burgess's in *A Clockwork Orange,* more comprehensive. He created his, or our, new culture by deductive invention. The rituals, events, and relationships play with a kind of preemptive nostalgia on our world and customs, which for the sake of the narrative have been destroyed. England is now "Inland," and the inhabitants in a kind of new Iron Age are, Riddley the narrator reveals, trying to recreate the big weapons that saw off the earlier world. This and others of Hoban's books made him a cult writer. He began to dress the part, to live the part, and when he died at the age of eighty-six his face was as familiar as, for example, Terry Pratchett's is today. His books for children, including the series about Frances the badger (1960–1970), and *The Mouse and His Child* (1968), and for adults (sometimes for both: Riddley is twelve years old and despite his circumstances has not altogether put off childish things) occupy a world of pure imagination. When they engage the day-to-day world, they do so tangentially. His best writing, Burgess declared, is "what literature is meant to be."

Hoban was born near Philadelphia into a family of Ukrainian-Jewish extraction and served as a radio operator in the Philippines and then on the Italian Front in the Second World War. He became a prominent illustrator, providing covers for leading magazines, including *Newsweek* and *Time*. In November 1962 his image of Joan Baez appeared on *Time*. In 1961 he produced an image of Holden Caulfield, cap reversed, to accompany an article. He also provided Jackie Gleason, and a double portrait of Mickey Mantle and Roger Maris that was not used. He was a professional illustrator, excellent with sports subjects. He worked in advertising and became an artistic director at J. Walter Thompson. He wrote books for children in collaboration with his first wife. In 1969 he and his family arrived in London for a short stay. His family returned home, he took up permanent residence in the United Kingdom. His sixteen adult novels were produced in Europe. Harold Pinter adapted Hoban's third and most naturalistic novel, *Turtle Diary* (1975), as a film. *Riddley Walker,* the fourth, was a long time in the making, requiring careful invention and coordination. *Pilgermann* (1983) goes into the medieval past and presents us with a Jewish pilgrim, freshly castrated by a Christian mob for sleeping with the consenting wife of a merchant, on his way to the Holy Land. He has had a vision of Christ. The fantasy is extreme and the Christians, in particular the Crusaders, are a brutal nemesis for Jew and Muslim alike. Taken with *Riddley Walker,* Hoban's vision is consistent, the past and future virtually intolerable. Science fiction and historical fiction arrive at similar ends.

Joyce did not generally speak up for his contemporaries. He made an exception of Anita Loos (1888–1981), author of *Gentlemen Prefer Blonds: The Intimate Diary of a Professional Lady* (1928), of which he allowed himself—almost blind—to read short portions while drafting *Finnegans Wake.* He also excepted Brian O'Nolan or Brian Ó Nualláin or, as the *Irish Times* satirical columnist, Myles na gCopaleen, but best known today as Flann O'Brien (1911–1966), whose *At Swim-*

*Two-Birds* (1939) he struggled through with a magnifying glass, finding in it "a true comic spirit." As William Gass says, "There aren't many funnier books." Anthony Burgess declared that a taste for O'Brien's fiction is *de rigueur* for anyone who claims to understand and appreciate the modern.

O'Brien's publishing history is sad. *At Swim-Two-Birds* was accepted for publication by Longman's on the recommendation of their reader, Graham Greene, who suggested some adjustments, some bowdlerizing, so that "all balls" became "all my bum." It was 1939, the year of the publication of *Finnegans Wake,* and the beginning of the Second World War. O'Brien claimed Hitler hated the book so much he contrived the war as a way of stopping it in its tracks. His second novel, submitted in 1940 following on the commercial unsuccess of the first, which sold 244 copies in the first six months, Longman declined. They had wanted something less fantastic, and he had become even more fantastic in *The Third Policeman* (1967). Frustrated, he sent the manuscript through William Saroyan to an American publisher who lost it. Rejection stopped him in his novelistic tracks. He wrote in Irish, but during his remaining years as a civil servant (that is how he earned his living and one of the reasons for his adopting a pseudonym: civil servants were not allowed to write in public under their own name), he more or less gave up on the wider Anglophone world. *The Third Policeman* was not to be published until 1967. He had been dead for over a year. When William Gass describes him as seeming "too satisfied to be Irish to be sane," he does not take into account the rejections that drove him mad. He compares O'Brien with Joyce and Beckett: like them he was a great linguist, a comic writer, an accomplished pasticheur.

The third and fourth novels were less complex and inventive than their predecessors. *The Hard Life* (1962), drawn in part from life, was dedicated to Greene, who responded with delight and frustration at so long a gap between books. *The Dalkey Archive* (1964) cannibalized *The Third Policeman* for material. Readers who encounter *The Third Policeman* first suffer a series of déjà vus when they come to it. The order of publication suggests a dilution of O'Brien's wildly inventive mode, as though Joyce had written *Ulysses* first, left *Finnegans Wake* in the bottom drawer for later, and followed on with *A Portrait*. In *The Dalkey Archive* James Joyce appears in a public house not entirely unlike the one in *At Swim-Two-Birds,* and the protagonist and he converse about the weird misanthropic philosopher-inventor De Selby, about bicycles and money and pneuma. Joyce is old, out of touch. He is smoking a cigar, quietly drinks, dimly chuckles. He is on the brink of joining the Jesuit Order (a "late vocation") and taking his *Ulysses* royalties with him as a dowry. Did he, or did he not, publish those hard books? "The only thing you must never reveal is my address—particularly not to any of those lascivious pornographic blackguards."

In his two principal novels, deadpan presentation of improbable and impossible things has never been deader—in a good way. In *The Third Policeman* the tone derives from the "objective" stance of classic journalism, only reported speech conveying the subjectivities affected by facts. But when the facts do not cohere, we want a guiding voice, an omniscience or an ironist to point the way. Our need is so urgent that in the end as readers we assume a narratorial role.

Borges describes *At Swim-Two-Birds* (the title referring to the pub through which the novel focuses) as the most complex verbal labyrinth he has encountered. "A student in Dublin writes a novel about the proprietor of a Dublin public house, who writes a novel about the habitués of his pub (among them, the student), who in their turn write novels in which proprietor and student figure along with other writers of novels about other novelists." Out it spreads, we all end up booked in alarming ways that remove our agency. Because there are several narratives, the book has several beginnings and open ends. Agency is additionally removed because many of the figures are drawn from legend and literature and have a preexistence to the bodies in the pub they now occupy. The student annotates the manuscripts. Different styles are explored, parodied; the book is a stylistic compendium of Irish literature. The influence of Joyce, says Borges, is "undeniable but not disproportionate in this manifold book." John Banville notes, "Irish prose has a certain tone, a tone of high rhetoric and high comedy which, when successful, is a wonderful heady blend." William Gass asks, "Where will you find—these days—as joyous a throat, so that saying the song to yourself, if not daring its full singing, will make you happier than a sniff would?"

In his essay "Two Diction Novels," which grows out of his enthusiasm for Philip K. Dick's writing, Jonathan Lethem describes reading *The Third Policeman* for the first time. "The book's main character is, without his knowledge, murdered in the first chapter. He proceeds to enter a bizarre and shadowy mirror-world, and experiences there a bewildering array of 'impossible' events. He spends most of the novel in pursuit of an elusive policeman, who is supposed to possess the ability to enlighten the protagonist in his confusion. Mysterious signs of this policeman are everywhere. In the end, the protagonist learns he is dead, only to have this awareness immediately stripped from him. The novel ends with our character back where we first found him: newly murdered, on the verge of the events of the novel we've just finished reading." It is a fine pancake, as the policeman says when each new conundrum emerges in the narrative. The word *pancake* signals comfortably to the reader that one line of fantasy and absurdity has come to an end and another will begin.

O'Brien has had few direct heirs. B. S. Johnson's *Travelling People* alludes to and borrows from him in a spirit of affectionate tribute, and there are verbal echoes. Jonathan Lethem owes him a debt of love, which is not the same thing as a direct creative debt. O'Brien's true heir, possibly inadvertent, is Donald Barthelme (1931–1989), the great modern cataloger, out-cataloging Whitman, the hero of parataxis, the funniest writer in American literature.

Finnegan in *Finnegans Wake* is dead. He dreams, is dreamed about, resurrects and dies again, little deaths, big deaths. The protagonist of *The Third Policeman* dies and then is dead, a continuous, active, and perplexed death of the kind Samuel Beckett dreaded. The book's epigraph is taken from the intolerantly brilliant De Selby: "Human existence being an hallucination containing in itself the secondary hallucinations of day and night . . . it ill becomes any man of sense to be concerned at the illusory approach of the supreme hallucination known as death." The novel is a chronicle of that "supreme hallucination." In *The Dead Father* Barthelme takes up the theme, but the dead father in this case stumbles about carrying his death with him, accompanying and weighing down his inventive, resourceful, but continually frustrated children. He is Finnegan, he is Cronos, God the Father, he is Lear, Hamlet the elder reeking of sulfur, Rabelais's Grangousier, Dostoyevsky's Fyodor Pavlovich Karamazov, he is the burden of Faulkner's *As I Lay Dying,* surrounded by the voices of her pallbearers, and he is the cruel cause of unstanchable hilarity. Most of all he is Donald Senior. Gabriel García Márquez's *Autumn of the Patriarch* was published in the same year as *The Dead Father*: "It was his genius to stress the sorrows of the dictator," Barthelme said, "the angst of the monster." It was Barthelme's genius to make his dead father figure elicit, despite his monstrosity, pity, regret.

In his essay "After Joyce," he wrote, "Play is one of the great possibilities of art; it is also . . . the Eros-principle whose repression means total calamity." The first and most effective repressor is the father. "The humorless practitioners of *le noveau roman* produce such calamities regularly, as do our native worshippers of the sovereign Fact. It is the result of a lack of seriousness." In lumping the equation of the French avant-garde of the day together with the American "realists," he is defining with great clarity a distinctively Joycean and Nabokovian zone for fiction. In 1963 he locked horns with Saul Bellow, who argued that modern fiction is "predominantly realistic" because "realism is based upon our common life." Barthelme objected to the reductiveness of that word *common* and to the nominalist fallacy that underlies realist fiction conceived in Bellow's spirit. In 1981 Barthelme ran through the mutations of realism in an interview, concluding, "In fact, everybody's a realist offering true accounts of the activity of mind. There are only realists."

He noted how a "mysterious shift" occurs when we declare that "art is not about something but is something," the finished text "becomes an object in the world rather than a commentary upon the world." It is the argument of the

New York School poets, who influenced and were influenced by Barthelme's writing. John Ashbery, speaking of Frank O'Hara's poetry, noted how each poem frustrated paraphrase and was "an instance of itself." His own long poem *Girls on the Run* (1999), based on the strange cartoon rolls of Henry Darger, is a first cousin of Barthelme's *Snow White*. The connections between Barthelme's verbal imagination and the visual (and other) arts is subtle and central. He worked as a gallery director in Houston for a time. His own fiction might be described as "cubist" in the ways in which—especially in the four novels, *Snow White* (1967), *The Dead Father* (1975), *Paradise* (1986), and *The King* (1990)—the many narratives that collide and coalesce into the cacophony of voices that constitute the novel exist on a single plane, without perspective, without coherent time structure, in a kind of ecstatic parataxis. The enormous catalogs (no novelist since Rabelais gives us raucous, infuriating, and delightful digressive lists, which themselves lead off into further digressions) provide a surface that insists that all time is present. The longer fiction is marked by the discipline of the short story, but the short story dilated among other stories. The novel is an anthology that disrupts and redistributes the fragments of its constituent narratives over a large verbal area, spattering and weaving. Barthelme was irritated when Joyce Carol Oates quoted the narrator of his story "See the Moon?," "Fragments are the only forms I trust," attributing this confession to the author himself. Fragmentation occurs, to be sure, but the fragments are used not in the way T. S. Eliot does in *The Waste Land* ("These fragments I have shored against my ruin") but as strands that disappear and reappear, not always in chronological order, not always in a logically answerable fashion, yet making the thing that is the novel.

After his contretemps with Bellow, one senses his suggestive contrariness to "the main stream" in every luminous utterance. "Writing is a process of dealing with not-knowing, a forcing of what and how . . . The not-knowing is crucial to art, is what permits art to be made." This is not a knowing agnosticism but a discipline harder than any, a road of aesthetic denial without metaphysical reward: "The not-knowing is not simple, because it's hedged about with prohibitions, roads that may not be taken. The more serious the artist, the more problems he takes into account and the more considerations limit his possible initiatives." There is no place for cliché or off-the-peg language, for "content" as conventionally conceived. "I think the paraphrasable content in art is rather slight—'tiny,' as de Kooning puts it." His authority is as a painter, and an abstract painter at that. "The change of emphasis from the what to the how seems to me to be the major impulse in art since Flaubert, and it's not merely formalism, it's not at all superficial, it's an attempt to reach truth, and a very rigorous one."

Jonathan Lethem lists Barthelme with the "self-declared postmodernist school of U.S. fiction writers." It also includes Robert Coover, John Barth, Stanley Elkins, William Gass, and John Hawkes, among others, most of them male, friends or acquaintances, and teachers. It is a connected and (because inventive and intellectually rigorous) a generally benign infestation of the body-literary. But because privileged by the academy, especially in writing programs, it is potentially pernicious. Lethem adds Thomas Pynchon as a tutelary spirit, but a nonteacher.

There are novelists who find the movement malign in the extreme. John Gardner in *On Moral Fiction* sets his cap against it. About Barthelme in particular, whom he grudgingly finds amusing, he writes, "The world would be a duller place without him, as it would be without F.A.O. Schwartz," the famous Fifth Avenue toy store. "His world is not one of important values but only of values mislaid, emotions comically or sadly unrealized, a burden of mysteries no one has the energy to solve. It is a world he seems to have little wish to escape." Gardner adds, "His writing has emotional control, clarity of style, and at least an impression of life's tragic waste; but even at his best, as in *The Dead Father,* Barthelme goes not for the profound but for the clever." For Gardner profound and clever are antithetical (he is certainly not clever). Like other profound pragmatists, moralists, and conservatives, he purports to speak for a silent majority of readers. Against Gardner and those like him Barthelme affirmed, "I believe that my every sentence trembles with morality in that each attempts to engage the problematic rather than to present a proposition to which all reasonable men must agree." His art leads not to the Ten Commandments: we know them already. It may, however, lead to new ways of reading them.

Uncharacteristically joyless is Gore Vidal's assault on Lethem's "self-declared postmodernist school of U.S. fiction writers," the essay "American Plastic: The Matter of Fiction" (1974). He seems to have been assigned the task of doggedly reading through all the stories and novels, and dogged the reading is until he reaches, in *The Dead Father,* which he takes to be a response to Roland Barthes's *The Pleasure of the Text* and not to Barthelme's own loving, volcanic father and his paradoxical legacy, the section entitled "A Manual for Sons": "There is no doubt that beneath the mannerisms, the infantile chic, the ill-digested culture of an alien world, Barthelme does have a talent for, of all things in this era, writing." Embedded in American Plastic, Barthelme is dismissed, but first separated off and read for, of all things in this era, pleasure, a quality in which few modern writers equal him.

Born in Philadelphia, Barthelme as an infant was removed to Houston, Texas, where his father, Donald Barthelme Sr., an architect, became a professor at the University of Houston. The family house he built was ostentatiously modernist outside and in, people traveled to gawk at it, and the boy and his younger siblings (two of his three brothers are also writers, his sister is successful in business) grew up there. They were, he says, "enveloped in modernism." The house "was modern and the furniture was modern and the pictures were modern and the books were modern." His father gave him while he was an adolescent a copy of Marcel Raymond's *From Baudelaire to Surrealism*. Barthelme's father was a man of strong opinions, his mother an inspiriting and well-read woman and writer. The house was a modern space full of modern thought, only the music was classical. The vehemence of the architect's views and his resistance to the developing views of his son (he disapproved of his postmodernisms) would develop into the monstrous psychological thematics of *The Dead Father* and *The King*.

The son studied journalism at the University of Houston and took other courses but never graduated. In Houston he wrote for the local newspaper. He was drafted and went to Korea, arriving on July 27, the day the Korean armistice was signed. On his return he worked for the university and edited the university-published magazine *Forum* (1956–1960), a wide-ranging cultural magazine of philosophy, literary criticism, economics, anthropology, psychology, biology, mathematics, architecture, film, music, and theater. Contributors included Leslie Fiedler, J. K. Galbraith, William Gass, Hugh Kenner, Marshall McLuhan, Walker Percy, and Harold Rosenberg, a friend and close associate. In 1961 he became director of the Contemporary Art Museum in Houston. He was, he said, "always a little drunk" and spent his evenings in Houston's black jazz clubs, hearing some of the great southern musical innovators. "From Barthelme to Pynchon," Gore Vidal reports, "there is a sense of booziness, nausea, hangover." But, we must add, in Barthelme's case there has been a gregarious and carnivalesque "night before."

In 1961 the *New Yorker* published the first of many of his stories. (He proved crucial to the reinvention of the *New Yorker*. The editor William Shawn was eliding the distinctions between poetry and fiction and declared that Barthelme's stories should be read as poetry. In 1967 the full text of *Snow White* was included, "a huge chunk of real estate," Pynchon called it, "almost insurrectionary in its impudence," which "helped liberate the whiz brains in the office and scramble the genetic code of the magazine's humor and fiction irregulars.") Barthelme moved to New York and lived there (also traveling widely) for eighteen years, running through three wives and several creatively fruitful affairs (including one with Grace Paley and another with his literary agent) before returning to Houston in 1980. He had begun teaching early in the 1970s and enjoyed the work, being naturally a lucid talker and a brilliant reader. He was popular and gregarious as a mentor. He became a professor at the University of

Houston, developing the creative writing program. He died of throat cancer in 1989. (His father survived him by seven years.)

Samuel Beckett, he declared, was foremost among his literary predecessors, a kind of father figure: "I'm just overwhelmed by Beckett," he said in an interview, "as Beckett was, I speculate, by Joyce." A literary genealogy, full of anxieties and ecstasies, is proposed. It goes back all the way to Rabelais, and the family tree includes, variously, Kafka and Stein, O'Brien, Gass, Barth, Pynchon, the poets Kenneth Koch, Frank O'Hara, and John Ashbery. From Beckett, specifically, he learned a sense of timing. Beckett, dramatist and novel-writer, has an acute ear especially for the pause. Barthelme's prose is speakable, its obscurities generally resolved by the voice.

There is a melancholy about Barthelme's Snow White waiting for her prince with her Rapunzel tresses dangling to the ground, and the Dead Father kept from watching the porno film suffers a similar *noncoitus tristis*. Thomas Pynchon writes, "As any Elizabethan could tell you if they all weren't dead, melancholy is a far richer and more complex ailment than simple depression." Also funnier: Jacques, Orsino, Don Quixote. But "Barthelme's was a specifically urban melancholy, related to that look of immunity to joy or even surprise seen in the faces of cab drivers, bartenders, street dealers, city editors, a wearily taken vow to persist beneath the burdens of the day and the terrors of the night." He is "an alchemist of the banal baroque," the redeemed cliché. The fiction writer and essayist George Saunders (1958–) is one of Barthelme's brightest expositors. He speaks of his "vaudevillian manner" and notes that Barthelme gives readers "a series of pleasure-bursts." This happy phrase is not quite adequate, unless those bursts are in a minor key or are laced with melancholy, part of the unconventional catharsis of Barthelme's best fiction.

# 31

# Tone and Register

Virginia Woolf, E. M. Forster, Paul Scott, J. G. Farrell, Norman Douglas,
Ronald Firbank, Pelham Grenville Wodehouse, Kazuo Ishiguro,
Elizabeth Bowen, Edna O'Brien, Jeanette Winterson

Virginia Woolf starts her 1921 "Unwritten Novel" with a pane of glass: "Plate-glass windows. Carnations; chrysanthemums. Ivy in dark gardens." Are we looking through it or seeing reflections? "Milk carts at the door. Wherever I go, mysterious figures, I see you, turning the corner, mothers and sons; you, you, you. I hasten, I follow. This, I fancy, must be the sea. Grey is the landscape; dim as ashes; the water murmurs and moves. If I fall on my knees, if I go through the ritual, the ancient antics, it's you, unknown figures, you I adore; if I open my arms, it's you I embrace, you I draw to me—adorable world!" Things seen, the "I" that sees, that celebrates and feels. The world exists in the end to substantiate the I.

Eudora Welty described Woolf as "the one who opened the door. When I read *To the Lighthouse* . . . I was so excited by the experience I couldn't sleep or eat." The novelist Edna O'Brien was "overwhelmed first by the generosity of her mind and its perspicacity. Later I read *To the Lighthouse* and my favorite, *Mrs. Dalloway,* which is very spry and sprightly . . . I began to read everything she had written—diaries, letters, etcetera . . . I realized that she gave of herself so utterly, so shamelessly." She leaves nothing out, the daily detail or the earth-shattering observation. "So I came to know her and to love her." Woolf's younger contemporaries read the novels as they appeared and believed they were witnessing evolution in the novel form. But the next generation was repelled by her knowing tone as a critic, her self-conscious, often preening style, her return to what they perceived as a discredited tradition of belles lettres.

(Adeline) Virginia Woolf (1882–1941) continues to polarize writers, female and male. Progressive, or retrograde? Progressive and retrograde. Contemporary academic critics and theorists make a dinner of her even more than of Joyce and Lawrence. The connections between her writing and her exhaustively chronicled life (in her letters and diaries she provided a copious daily record) raise issues of gender, incest, mental illness, intentionality, racism. Her anti-Semitism is all the more grotesque because though she married a Jew, she stereotyped Jewish characters and reiterated her revulsion in a reflex she never overcame.

In her essays and reviews Woolf reflects on the act of reading, her particular act, its place, its season; she remains a pragmatic *reader,* seldom adopting the tetchy, tutting distance of the critic. She puts the book aside and then reflects upon it. She does not specialize, even when in *A Room of One's Own* she explores the tradition of women writers. She is interested in engagement, the extension provided by a book, and in its merits, the two not necessarily connected. Edna O'Brien, like many modern readers, approached her first by way of her collection of essays *The Common Reader.* Here she discovered "a woman who loved literature, unlike many critics who just use it."

Jeanette Winterson suggests that the best way in is through *Orlando* (1928), dedicated to Vita Sackville-West, for whom she had contrived a passion and who remained a friend after their affair. *Orlando* grows out of her informal scholarship. The protagonist in his/her transitions over three centuries, locked into a libidinally charged youth less fantastic, because on the face of it less serious, than Dorian Gray's, celebrates the object of her obsessive passion. Bernard Malamud says that "in essence she was avoiding a subject," but such obliquity, hardly uncommon among writers exploring sexuality, made it durable in fiction. "They sublimate and so become sublime," a novelist of thoroughly heterosexual persuasion commented, with a trace of resentment.

The readers she addresses are not well-educated scholars and critics. Those she has in her sights read for pleasure, not to instruct or to "correct the opinions of others." "Above all, he"—she uses the male pronoun in a gender-neutral spirit—"is guided by an instinct to create for himself, out of whatever odds and ends he can come by, some kind of whole—a portrait of a man, a sketch of an age, a theory of the art of writing." The common reader's enthusiasm can get the better of his discrimination. No matter, "second-rate works of a great writer are worth reading because they offer the best criticism of his masterpieces." Due to her Victorian legacy, not least her father's sense of the non-negotiable responsibilities the writer has to readers, her "address" remained more "directed" than that of Joyce, say, or Stein. Her readers learn from the quality of her critical attention, and find little of "the vagueness which afflicts all criticism of novels." Peter Ackroyd, who should know from his own youthful experience, has her in mind when he remarks, "One of the nervous ailments which precedes success is the need to review as much and as often as possible." She could not turn down a commission.

She was interested in form more than plot and came to trust her insights, those sudden connections that revealed larger continuities of imagination in time and space. The exercise is public, actual or simulated dialogue. She experimented with what she described as "Otway conversation." Taking an imaginary common reader called Penelope Otway, she set her talking with a male friend.

The "I" of the critic, like the "I" in the fiction, devolves authority to two individuals of different sex, in the interests of creating a depersonalized, more nuanced view. Her approach, according to her editor the poet Andrew MacNeillie, is to begin in sympathy and "become the writer's accomplice. One may say it is to possess expert instincts; it is certainly not to espouse theories," since the integrity of the work being read would be distorted by *a priori* expectation: "She writes too from the point of view of an educational outsider, a woman set to school in her father's library, denied the privileges of her male siblings. Her reading is uncanonical," and this has much to do with its independence and freshness.

Her lack of formal schooling can be overplayed (she overplayed it herself). She was among the best-read writers of the twentieth century and her deprivations were in many respects more enabling than rote learning, the regimented and forced growth of her brothers and their contemporaries whose originality, if they had any, was not encouraged by schoolmasters. In *A Room of One's Own* she says, "I thought how unpleasant it is to be locked out; and I thought how it is worse perhaps to be locked in." From an early age she had the freedom to come and go.

Virginia Stephen was the daughter of Sir Leslie Stephen (1840–1904), who is remembered as an Alpine mountaineer and the first editor of the *Dictionary of National Biography*. A significant critical presence, he was trained for the priesthood but renounced his vocation at twenty-five, becoming a writer on science, philosophy, mountaineering, and literature (biographer of Thomas Hobbes, Johnson, Alexander Pope, Swift, and George Eliot), and editor of *Cornhill Magazine,* where he numbered Hardy, Stevenson, and James among his contributors. His first wife, Thackeray's daughter, died in 1875, leaving him one daughter, Stella, who, having gone the same way as her grandmother, was institutionalized in 1891. He married the handsome widow of Herbert Duckworth, who had three sons, and the new family grew to include Julian (who went by his middle name, Thoby, and died at twenty-six of typhoid fever), Vanessa (later surnamed Bell), Virginia, and Adrian.

In his three volumes of *Hours in a Library* Stephen included chapters on authors whose work Woolf herself was to quarry, among them the novelists and narrative poets Defoe, Richardson, Fielding, Walpole, Crabbe, Cowper, Scott, Hawthorne, Balzac, and Disraeli. In the drawing rooms of her childhood she encountered living writers. Henry James, James Russell Lowell (her secular godfather), and George Henry Lewes visited; the spirit of George Eliot was never far away. When in 1904, the year of her father's death, a decade after her mother's, she began writing for the *Guardian,* and a year later reviewing for the *Times Literary Supplement,* she was confident, independent, and more than a match for her conventionally educated contemporaries.

The deaths of her mother and her half-sister, Stella, in Virginia's mid- and late teens led to her first mental disturbances; her father's death, after ten years' dependence on Virginia and Vanessa, had even worse consequences. It was bereavement and deliverance, but so complete a change left her briefly institutionalized and she remained subject to recurring mental problems for the rest of her life. Soon after her father's death the siblings, free to make their own way, removed from Kensington to Gordon Square in Bloomsbury. Here they came into regular contact with Thoby's contemporaries from Trinity College, Cambridge—Lytton Strachey and Clive Bell, and with Duncan Grant and Roger Fry, the critical, literary, and artistic core of that most English cultural phenomenon, the Bloomsbury group, based on intimacy, social class, political disposition, and cultural aloofness. Vita Sackville-West, wife of the diplomat and writer Harold Nicolson, was also of their number, and E. M. Forster was one of several associate members or camp followers. Thoby's friend Leonard Woolf, the "penniless Jew" Virginia was to marry in 1912, was present in 1904 but went abroad in October to civil service work in Ceylon and India, not returning until 1911.

Roger Fry coined the term "Post-Impressionist" and in 1910 curated an exhibition at the Grafton Galleries in London entitled "Manet and the Post-Impressionists." He featured work by Cézanne, Gauguin, Matisse, and Van Gogh. Woolf, who wrote a life of Fry, was profoundly affected: "On or about December 1910 human character changed," she said, recognizing in the new art a challenge for fiction as well. A second exhibition followed in 1912, and Fry founded the famous Omega Workshop in Fitzroy Square the year after. His insistence on continuities between the arts and his willingness to look abroad inspired Woolf. She trusted Fry's judgment and vision.

The Post-Impressionists, rooted in Impressionism, were keen to restore to art elements that had been purged from it and to answer Impressionism with something at once more personally weighted and more economical. Fry addressed it in the 1910 catalog. "You have explored nature in every direction, and all honor to you; but your methods and principles have hindered artists from exploring and expressing that emotional significance which lies in things, and is the most important subject matter in art." In freeing themselves from the requirements of representation, they "had found a new immediacy by suppressing all explanatory transitions, bridge passages, inert segments of the canvas that are mere picture-building." These terms were not lost on Woolf.

In 1917 she and Leonard acquired a manual printing machine and established the Hogarth Press. It grew into one of the significant literary publishing houses of the day. One of her younger authors, Christopher Isherwood, whose books *The Memorial, Mr. Norris,* and *Lions and Shadows* the Hogarth Press published, found

Virginia fascinating. "She was one of the most beautiful women I've met in my life, really absolutely stunning, in a very strange way. Of course she was middle-aged when I knew her. She had the quality that manic-depressive people have of being up to the sky one minute, down into despair and darkness the next." He celebrates "her tremendous animation and fun, on a gossipy level. She loved tea-table talk." So enchanted was he that one evening, pressed to stay to dinner, he did so, forgetting that he was "supposed to be going on a very romantic trip to Paris with somebody who was in fact waiting at the airport at that moment . . . She had that effect on people."

Virginia's first novel, *The Voyage Out,* appeared in 1915. It existed in draft in 1912 as *Melymbrosia.* She worked and reworked it. It is tempting to compare it with Aphra Behn's *Oroonoko,* with its colonial themes, but the journey of discovery Virginia's initially closeted protagonist Rachel Vinrace undertakes is modern, and it is a roman à clef insofar as we meet Clarissa Dalloway on board the ship, and a fictionalized Lytton Strachey (St.-John Hirst) and Vanessa (Helen Ambrose). Woolf was already "drawing from life" and beginning to shape her mature characters. The ship-of-fools convention serves well for revealing Edwardian foibles. Forster saw it as "strange, tragic, inspired," and found in it a value well in excess of its promise. Like many first novels, it has too many plans, too much thought has gone into its themes and structures; it is stiff with intention. It is important primarily in relation to what was to follow. Its immediate successor was *Night and Day* (1919), described by Forster as "the simplest novel she has written, and to my mind the least successful."

In 1919 the Woolfs acquired Monk's House in Rodmell, East Sussex, not far from the River Ouse, for £700. The view remains as it did, and Jeanette Winterson writes, "If you concentrate, then gradually the present will fade and the day trippers will fade, and you, with the peas and beans on your right and the pear tree beside you, will be able to narrow your eyes across the flats and catch the distant wind of the river and its sentry of trees." Winterson stands there as a writer herself, reflecting how Woolf saw and did not see this "stretch with no man-made interruption to qualify her gaze," her imagination still at work in another place. Monk's House was as inconvenient and without amenity as those houses endured by Orwell and others for whom creature comforts were of little interest. Fitting out the house and establishing work routines were fulfilling activities. The Woolfs divided their time between London and the country until, with the Blitz and the destruction of Virginia's London home, they moved to Monk's House more or less permanently. It was here, under an elm tree, that Leonard deposited her ashes in 1941, her drowned body having been recovered from the water three weeks after her suicide and cremated. Angus Wilson, infatuated with the Bloomsbury group, honored the pieties that held the group together, protecting frail reputations for years. Of the suicide he declared, absurdly, "This was Hitler's triumph . . . the blackest moment of the war."

*Jacob's Room* (1922), her most experimental early novel, creates space around the protagonist by presenting him from others' points of view with very little of the protagonist himself: how he is seen, how he is reacted to, a projection. Forster speaks of the deliberate constraints: "The objection (or apparent objection) to this sort of writing is that it cannot say much or be sure of saying anything. It is an inspired breathlessness, a beautiful droning or gasping which trusts to luck, and can never express human relationships or the structure of society." But this book defies precedent with its economy of means. "So at least one would suppose, and that is why the novel *Jacob's Room* comes as a tremendous surprise. The impossible has occurred," he said, still astonished. "A new type of fiction has swum into view."

With *A Room of One's Own* (1929), a new type of essay emerged as well. It was composed for delivery as lectures in 1928 at the Arts Society at Newnham and the History Society at Girton, Cambridge's two women's colleges, on the topic "Women and Fiction." The title gave Woolf maximum freedom. For the purposes of her essay she was not the Virginia Woolf whose name people were beginning to recognize: she remained almost anonymous; the reader can call her "Mary Beton, Mary Seton, Mary Carmichael or any other name you please"— everywoman, so long as that personification is English, cultured, relatively independent, and with the benefit of social privilege.

*A Room of One's Own,* a room occupied by the articulate narrator, is experimental in the novelistic form in which she frames the argument. She builds it in accordance with rules of fiction, dramatized in a plot with subplots, characters, and Aunt Sallies. The narrator buttonholes the reader and remarks, "Fiction here is likely to contain more truth than fact." Her refrain is: "A woman must have money and a room of her own if she is to write fiction." She addresses the Cambridge ladies as one who regrets her lack of their privilege, yet is also aware how limited their conceded freedoms are in comparison to men's. Even so, "It was absurd to blame any class or any sex, as a whole. Great bodies of people are never responsible for what they do . . . they too, the patriarchs, the professors, had endless difficulties, terrible drawbacks to contend with."

Part of the essay's Englishness is its awareness that it is class-specific, part its insouciance. Woolf is more interested in sexuality than class, and so she argues that male and female writing are at their best "when sex is unconscious of itself"; she asks women to write "all kinds of books, hesitating at no subject however trivial or however vast." In a whisper she asks, "Are there no men present? Do you promise me that behind that red curtain over there the figure of Sir Chartres Biron is not concealed? We are all women you assure me? Then I may tell you that the very next words I read were these—'Chloe liked Olivia . . .' Do not start. Do not blush. Let us admit in the privacy of our own society that these things sometimes happen. Sometimes women do like women." The rabbit is out of the hat: this speaker was herself the lover of Vita Sackville-West, who had accompanied her to Cambridge for the lectures. She was the author of *Orlando*. Here, with modest libidinal exposure, almost theoretically, she shares with women more institutionally privileged than herself the themes she had embodied in her wittiest and most rhapsodic fiction. Inventing Shakespeare's sister Judith, an equal genius but marked for disappointment by sex and society, she is developing a personal space that she had come to understand through her developing fiction.

Four years earlier, in 1925, Mrs. Dalloway was back from *The Voyage Out* to make her way through her eponymous novel, the "supreme mystery": "Here is one room: there another." Forster writes of Clarissa Dalloway (her given name a debt to Richardson, creator of the first "real" female character in English fiction) and Septimus Warren Smith: "The societified lady and the obscure maniac are in a sense the same person." Forster says, "His foot has slipped through the gay surface on which she still stands—that is all the difference between them." In a single day, from morning to night, Mrs. Dalloway's conscience flows, with discrete revelations of a life only partly lived, toward the party she is hosting. Meanwhile Septimus advances to suicide. Many of Woolf's recurrent themes, rooted at once in her daily life and in her experience of mental turbulence, develop. Forster starts to summarize the "plot" of *Mrs. Dalloway* and then retracts: summary suggests stability, a fixity out of keeping with Woolf's intention and manner. It emphasizes structure, and "emphasis is fatal to the understanding of this author's work."

In *To the Lighthouse* (1927), her most transparently autobiographical novel, the Ramsays are on holiday in a very Cornish Scotland, reminiscent of the St. Ives, Cornwall, where Woolf's family spent every summer until 1895, the year of her mother's death. Efforts to fictionalize are rigorous, but so is the effort to remember and re-create. This tension contributes to the close-up feel, an engrossing effect. The very syntax of the passage in which, briefly, for Mrs. Ramsay the whole world comes into focus, is mimetic in its pacing, in its phrased parceling out of sense, which is also time, and in its withholding of the object until it cannot be withheld any longer and the moment—ends.

> But the voice had stopped. She looked round. She made herself get
> up. Augustus Carmichael had risen and, holding his table napkin so
> that it looked like a long white robe he stood chanting:

> To see the Kings go riding by
> Over lawn and daisy lea
> With their palm leaves and cedar
> Luriana, Lurilee,

and as she passed him, he turned slightly towards her repeating the last words:

> Luriana, Lurilee

and bowed to her as if he did her homage. Without knowing why, she felt that he liked her better than he ever had done before; and with a feeling of relief and gratitude she returned his bow and passed through the door which he held open for her.

It was necessary now to carry everything a step further. With her foot on the threshold she waited a moment longer in a scene which was vanishing even as she looked, and then, as she moved and took Minta's arm and left the room, it changed, it shaped itself differently; it had become, she knew, giving one last look at it over her shoulder, already the past.

The secular liturgy of Mr. Carmichael's chanting, his ceremoniousness, moves her, and us through her, into an epiphany as vivid as any in Joyce, and the release of Woolf's most sympathetic and whole character back into the quotidian world, with its darning, gardening, and maternal and conjugal anxiety, is breathtaking. Writing of a passage in Jane Austen, Woolf could be describing her own: "It fills itself; it shines; it glows; it hangs before us, deep, trembling, serene for a second; next, the housemaid passes, and this drop, in which all the happiness of life has collected, gently subsides again to become part of the ebb and flow of ordinary existence."

The book is peopled with Woolf's familiars, ghosts whom she revives and then releases once more. In the brothers and sisters, James the ruthless, Cam the wicked, Jasper, Prue the fair, Rose, Andrew the just, she has redistributed characteristics of her siblings. The other protagonists—Lily Briscoe, whose painterly endeavor is not unlike Woolf's own challenge in language, problematic Charles Tansley, and Mr. Bankes—emerge in their own voices and among the voices surrounding them on this vacation from daily life. The conventional setting for a social novel, the country house, Woolf transforms into a world of exposed subjectivities.

The three-section structure is almost schematic: "The Window" creates a vivid sense of presence; the brief, harrowing interlude entitled "Time Passes," with the lighthouse light pulsing steadily through the empty house, acknowledges loss, the chance deaths of key protagonists, the change in the lives of the survivors. Then "The Lighthouse," the concluding section, acknowledges absence and the beginning of recovery. The novel perfects Woolf's version of stream of consciousness and her use of a symbolism that, while almost too clear in intention, is also persuasively light, lyrical. "It is easy for a novelist to describe what a character thinks of; look at Mrs. Humphry Ward. But to convey the actual process of thinking is a creative feat," says Forster, "and I know of no one except Virginia Woolf who has accomplished it." The Peruvian novelist Gabriel García Márquez began his experiments in fiction under the spell of Joyce, but as he grew he turned for more digestible sustenance to Woolf.

Cyril Connolly did not much like *To the Lighthouse.* "Virginia Woolf seemed to have the worst defect of the Mandarin style, the ability to spin cocoons of language out of nothing," he said. "The history of her literary style has been that of a form at first simple, growing more and more elaborate, the content lagging far behind, then catching up, till, after the falseness of *Orlando,* she produced a masterpiece in *The Waves.*" What raised this book to classic status? She was growing away from the Forsterian "artlessness and simple poetical, colloquial style, into patterns of her own. The reveries of a central character come more and more to dominate her books. In *The Waves* (1931), originally to be called *The Moths,* she abandoned the convention of the central figure and described a group of friends, as children, as young people and finally in late middle age." He adds that *The Waves* "is one of the books which comes nearest to stating the mystery of life and so, in a sense, nearest to solving it."

Its form is the interweaving monologues of Bernard, Susan, Rhoda, Neville, Jinny, and Louis, the absence of the catalyst Percival, with nine interludes in which the sea with neutral continuity through successive times of day, like the lighthouse light (we are no longer on the shore but in the indifferent tide), underscores the growth and decay of the protagonists. The movement of time and the neutrality of the natural world create in the characters intense longing, anxiety, raw-nerved desire. They long to hold their various worlds in place. Woolf's characters live, says Forster, "but not continuously" in the way that, say, Tolstoy's characters live continuously. Discontinuity is a result of two concerns: the defining moment, preceded by striving and succeeded by indefinition; and the anguished sense of separation between people and other people, between people and their memories.

In 1933 Woolf wrote *Flush: A Biography,* a life of Elizabeth Barrett (Browning)'s cocker spaniel, taken from its birth in the country through its confinement with Miss Barrett in Wimpole Street to a happy old age in Italy. Flush shares much in common with Pinker, a dog Vita gave to Woolf at the height of their intimacy in 1926. Some readers might, not without reason, regard this as a reductio ad absurdum of the stream of consciousness. It is followed in 1937 by *The Years* and in 1941 by *Between the Acts*. The unraveling of the last few years of her life, the less than ecstatic reviews of her new work, the arrival of the Second World War, the Woolfs' permanent removal to Monk's House (over which the German air force flew regular sorties en route to London), the destruction of her London home in the Blitz, the prospect of a German invasion, her husband's Jewishness, all weighed with her until she decided, after the disruption of her earlier breakdowns, not to repeat them. Had Leonard complied with her suicide note instructions, "Will you destroy all my papers," our sense of the twentieth century would have been very different.

In a bad sentence all his own, Truman Capote declared, "From the point of view of ear, Virginia Woolf never wrote a bad sentence." With Stein, Joyce, Woolf, Lawrence, and their beneficiaries, the ear of the writer, and thus of the reader, does work of a kind it has done before in the fiction of Sterne, Flaubert, and few others. The writer is less interested in the distance between reader and narrative, writer and narrative: the challenge is to enact, establishing aesthetic *presence*. The lips move as the novel is composed, and the ear (dramatically and musically attuned) must be satisfied before the sentence is complete. This constituted what T. S. Eliot, in conversation with Arnold Bennett, called "the 'Virginia' school of fiction." The rules of irony, the habit of keeping a knowing distance, that set Bennett and Wells and Galsworthy on our side of the story, directing our attention, clearing our path so that we enjoy the fullest view and retain moral purchase, an essentially social, sociable perspective, is not for her.

---

Edward Morgan Forster (1879–1970), in whom the formal spirit of Jane Austen, regendered, came back to life, delivered the Clark Lectures at Cambridge in 1927. The lectures were attended both by the poet A. E. Housman, as oblique and thematically challenged a writer as Forster, and F. R. Leavis, who was finding his new bearings at the time. In the book of the lectures, *Aspects of the Novel,* Forster proved a coherent theorist of the new fiction. By 1927 his own novels (apart from the posthumous *Maurice,* written in 1913–1914, revised in 1919, 1934, and 1960–1961, and published in 1971) had all appeared. In 1956 Dorothy Parker remarked, "As for living novelists, I suppose E. M. Forster is the best, not knowing what that is, but at least he's a semi-finalist, wouldn't you think?" He had been dead as a novelist for over three decades.

Forster imagines the company of novelists outside time, sitting together and writing in the British Museum Reading Room, that great round space now full of memory, the mausoleum of the book surrounded by Lord Foster's luminous atrium. For him, the "demon of chronology" is "our enemy"—his "us" is the novelist and the engaged reader. He likes to juxtapose, for example, Richardson and James, Wells and Dickens, their books conducting a dialogue outside the sequence of history. "History develops," he says, "Art stands still." This paradox he expresses in the image of the mirror that is not itself changed by what passes before it. "We must refuse to have anything to do with chronology," he declares, though the challenge is ultimately beyond him. Still, he makes some useful comparisons. Taking Richardson and James, "each falls short of the tragic, though a close approach is made." Neither Dickens nor Wells "has much taste: the world of beauty was largely closed to Dickens, and is entirely closed to Wells." Forster compares the way that Dickens in *Bleak House* "bounces" us in point of view from omniscience in the first chapter to Esther's partial perspective in the second, and back again, to André Gide's approach in *Les faux-monnayeurs* (1925): both novels are "all to pieces logically." He warns: "The novelist who betrays too much interest in his own method can never be more than interesting." Such a judgment implicates Stein, Joyce, and his friend and publisher Virginia Woolf herself.

His lectures are not free of dogma. He insists that the novel, "this low atavistic form," always "tells a story," an immutable rule, a common denominator. But for Woolf, Stein, and others, telling a story in Forster's sense is what a modern novel does not do, and what writers since Sterne have been sending up. Even when Forster discriminates between "story" and "plot," he does not quite do justice to the potentialities of the form.

When listening to a compelling story, we attend with our mouths ajar, we are passive, and as soon as we question the teller the spell is broken. But we *read* plots, we assemble the pieces and participate in the act of creation, indeed we are required to negotiate lacunae, to make connections, to leap here and step back there, to recognize, adjust, and correct. The better the plotting, the more space it leaves the reader to engage, the more it requires of us. A story recounts events in time sequence, a plot disposes the facts of the story in such a way as to make sense. That sense can be dramatic, moral, enactive. The story tells us, "The King dies and then the Queen dies." The plot adds cause: "The King dies and then the Queen dies of grief." Thus, "what the story does is to narrate the life in time. And what the entire novel does—if it is a good novel—is to include the life by values as well." Plot elicits intelligence and memory. Plot denies the reader the freedom of passivity. It is "the novel in its logical intellectual aspect; it requires mystery, but the mysteries are solved later on; the reader may be moving about in worlds unrealized, but the novelist has no misgivings. He is competent, poised above his work."

This *control* unsettled Forster. He laments that the novelist is required to tie up loose ends. Why can he not just walk away? In the notebooks he used in preparing the Clark Lectures he poses himself the question, "Can nothing liberate English fiction from conscientiousness?" Fantasy is crucial to many novel writers, it characterizes the work of Sterne and Melville, remote as they are from one another; "fantasy asks us to pay something extra" and we are rewarded. Without fantasy the novel is diminished. Fantasy is not prophetic; it can entail the supernatural, says Forster, "but it need not express it." In *A Passage to India* we remember the little wasp that Mrs. Moore finds on a peg and releases into the night, and how two hundred pages later, without making a connection, Professor Godbole, not present at the first incident, alludes to it. This second sense, this inadvertent knowledge, is given to his reflective characters. They know beyond the story, they read the plot from the inside.

V. S. Pritchett says that Forster refuses "to speak in a public voice. This has given the personal a startling strength." His "personal" is peculiarly sociable. Isaiah Berlin remarked too, "He lacked the gift of intimacy." We are in his company but not in his confidence. The personal in Forster is specific, instinctive; it resists compulsion and yet is not quite free to rebel. "All that is pre-arranged is false," he declares. Yet fiction must come to terms with that falsehood and even capitulate to it, however reluctantly. Stuart Hampshire shows how the early novels "have the delicacy of being composed from within the assumptions that they implicitly question." Into the brittle artificialities of the novel of manners irrupts the reality of a felt emotion, or an experience for which the characters can find no words, or only words that are true but in polite terms inappropriate. Virginia Woolf was not satisfied with *A Room with a View,* not because of its settings or the working of plot, but because of "some belittlement, which seems to cramp the souls of the actors," to do with the mildly satirical *de haut en bas* tone, a superiority, a quality of class. "Lucy's conversion becomes a thing of trifling moment, and the views of George and his father no longer spring from the original fountain." Nadine Gordimer notes Forster's "peculiar understanding of the hollowness of the Haves and the strength-without-power of the Have-nots."

A decade after *Aspects of the Novel* he wrote in "Notes on the English Character" that "the character of the English is essentially middle-class," marked by "solidity, caution, integrity, efficiency. Lack of imagination, hypocrisy." It had traveled a long way in that direction, from Bunyan, Defoe, and Fielding. "And even Saint George—if Gibbon is correct—wore a top hat once; he was an army contractor and supplied indifferent bacon. It all amounts to the same in the end." What of the compelling corrective of D. H. Lawrence? Is he only the exception that tests the rule? "For it is not that the Englishman can't feel," says Forster, "it is that he is afraid to feel." His no longer creative sensibility displaces a more vigorous reality. He failed to take his own counsel: "Provincialism in a critic is a serious fault. A critic has no right to the narrowness which is the frequent prerogative of the creative artist." He had become what the critic Oliver Staly-brass describes as a "slightly uncommon reader"; he was no longer a novelist, except that he kept tinkering with *Maurice,* the thematically contentious novel published during the year after his death.

Born in London, Forster lost his father when he was still a baby. At the age of seven he inherited a small fortune from an aunt. It freed him later on from the necessity of earning a living: he could write. He went from Tonbridge School to King's College, Cambridge, where he read history and classics and became an "Apostle," one of a group that celebrated the individual conscience and became notorious a few decades later for the idealistic Soviet spies who were sourced from it. Forster's Cambridge world is evoked in the opening pages of *The Longest Journey,* his second and slowest novel. Norman Mailer learned a great deal from this book: you turn a page and suddenly find Gerald has been killed, a focal character wiped out as it were by nature itself: "It taught me that personality was more fluid, more dramatic and startling, more inexact than I had thought." It changed his sense of the stability and, one might say, the sculptural presence of characters. Though Forster never wrote a first-person novel, he knocked Mailer out of third and into first.

Forster traveled in Europe. In the First World War he was a conscientious objector, volunteered for the International Red Cross, and went to Egypt. But well before the war began, at the age of thirty-one, he had completed four of his five principal novels, starting with the first sensual encounter between Italy and the Forsterian English in *Where Angels Fear to Tread* (1905), and then *The Longest Journey* (1907), *A Room with a View* (1908), and his most ambitious novel, *Howards End* (1910), about the problems of inheriting a house with its history and ghosts, an emblem of a vulnerable and changing England. Early in the 1920s he went to India as private secretary to the maharajah of Dewas and *A Passage to India* followed in 1924.

From Proust, and in different ways from the Alexandrian poet Constantin Cavafy, and the French novelist André Gide, who came to terms at such elaborate length with his own sexuality, Forster took important lessons in tone and strategy. From Gide's *Les faux-monnayeurs* he quotes the character Edouard's description of his novel. "'A slice of life,' the naturalistic school used to say. The mistake that school made was always to cut its slice in the same direction, always lengthwise, in the direction of time. Why not cut it up and down? Or across? As for me, I don't want to cut it at all." The attempt to achieve presence at once in time and space, the ambition of inclusiveness as in Proust, fascinated Forster. He realized he lacked the energy and concentration for invention at that level of sustained intensity. "You see what I mean," Edouard continues, "I want to put everything into my novel and not snip off my material either here or there."

The modern novelist had fallen from the grace of tradition and precedent. The writer who continued accepting the conventions of the novel as Bennett and Galsworthy had was working with echoes. After Joyce and Woolf, after Proust, the alert novelist knew that to create entailed not imitation but a greater risk. Forster defined it, for himself and for his British contemporaries, as the modern imperative of irony, the distance a writer creates between the saying and the thing said. That distance entails a conscious manipulation of readers' understanding of form. It acknowledges the artificiality of the work it makes. This has consequences for a reader engaged in experiencing the narrative while remaining continuously conscious of that engagement. The writer's irony, and consequently the reader's, Forster describes as a negative mysticism. He is the most conservative-seeming of the modernists, and at times his modernism failed him altogether. The structure of *Maurice* is closed, it is a novel with a lesson to teach, and characters become representative types. Mr. Ducie embodies the poverties of education, Dr. Barry of medicine, Mr. Borenius the vicar of Penge of the Church, in relation to the theme of sexual unorthodoxy. Art might take us outside the claustrophobic hamlet of nurture, but it can only indicate, and only briefly, the connections that might be made. Such arcadias as exist—Cambridge with its seasons, terms, and terminus, ancient Greece with imagined freedoms, and the womanless Greenwood into which the protagonist and his handsome deliverer escape—are temporary or imaginary. *Maurice* is stifled by its themes, so much more compellingly, because obliquely, explored in other novels, especially in the relationship of Fielding with Dr. Aziz in *A Passage to India*.

Woolf spoke of the most essential gift of the novelist, "the power of combination—the single vision." She adds, "The success of the masterpieces seems to lie not so much in their freedom from faults—indeed we tolerate the grossest errors in them all—but in the immense persuasiveness of a mind which has completely mastered its perspective." In *Maurice* Forster knew he had failed, and each time he revisited it he failed again. In other novels he makes a virtue of necessity. Woolf admires how, in *A Room with a View,* he induces us to endorse and wish success to the coarse and hairy Emersons: "To be able to make one thus a partisan is so much of an achievement." The more so at a time when the Emersons' point(s) of view among the Hogarth Press's readers would not have been immediately sympathetic, however they seem today. When Lucy Honeychurch emerges from "the muddle" of her emotions and society's expectations and chooses the vigorous, sub-Lawrencian George Emerson over shrill Mr. Vyse, she responds to the kind of sudden illumination that Austen gives to Emma, but Lucy is stepping out of her class's expectations while Emma is stepping back in.

There are unexpected incidents in *A Room with a View,* notably the murder, the kiss and crushed *pince nez,* and, supremely, the swim in the woods, moments in which what is expected loses its power and, when it is reestablished, irreversible changes have occurred below the surface. Irony inheres as much in the rebellious plot as in the style, and each irony suggests not cynicism but the emergence of possible alternative choices, actions and values.

When it was published, *A Passage to India* read very differently from the way it does today. Apologists for the Raj were offended by Forster's depiction of the British community. Rose Macaulay, among the first enthusiastic reviewers of the book, declared Mr. Forster "the most attractive and the most exquisite of contemporary novelists." Readers might have feared that "his peculiar gifts" would be wasted on so unpromising a subject as India, but they can be reassured. "He can make even these brown men live; they are as alive as his Cambridge undergraduates, his London ladies, his young Italians, his seaside aunts; they are drawn with an equal and a more amazing insight and vision." If she had momentarily forgotten Kipling, she had in full measure the smug, condescending, and unironic liberal tolerance of the time.

Today what in the novel was satire can seem like stylized description because of changes in prejudice and ideology, and the irony is all the more potent. The opening chapter begins in guidebook language, dismissing Chandrapore (based on Banikpore) as a particularly worthless place; there is a change of perspective and style, and the place becomes magical. This juxtaposition of perspectives establishes a luminous paradox: the experiences of the book exist between two incommensurable points of view. In the second chapter we meet Aziz and Mrs. Moore, the paradox of their different points of view in a different key from the introductory passage.

The novel takes its title from Whitman, and its dedication *"to Syed Ross Masood,"* whom Forster had tutored and for whom he felt intense affection, suggest a theme encoded if not directly stated. It is only in the final paragraphs, when Fielding returns to India and is out riding with Aziz, that the theme almost surfaces, concealed in the playfully angry debate about colonialism. It gives to this displaced love story a libidinal current far in excess of the explicitness of *Maurice,* entailing as it does not only two men but two cultures in a passionate, destructive embrace.

In his notes for the novel Forster described the three-part structure he favored in this as in earlier novels.

| MOSQUE | Cold Weather |
|--------|--------------|
| CAVES  | Hot Weather  |
| TEMPLE | Rains        |

The loose ends, the "intermediate and unrecognized connections," interest him most in *A Passage to India,* Lawrencian concerns, the closed form that refuses to close. Its openness is enforced by the diversity of cultures it accommodates— British, Muslim, Hindu. Certainly Forster knew the diverse cultures of the Muslims well, from his time not only in India but also in Egypt; yet the magic of Professor Godbole's singing, and the mystery and unassimilated otherness of the Hindu scenes, have a potent, unsettling force. Forster does not interpret: he presents the ceremony, his lucidity unclouded by disbelief. Only the most theorized reader would take it for irony or condescension.

The literary agent and novelist Paul Mark Scott (1920–1978) found his theme after several competent, unsuccessful novels. *The Jewel in the Crown* (1966) is a kind of reimagining, two decades later, of *A Passage to India.* Here Chandrapore is replaced by Mayapore, Adela Quested by characterful, unprepossessing Daphne Manners, and humble, excitable Aziz by the articulate, Anglicized Indian Hari Kumar. The controlling character is police superintendent Ronald Merrick, who bears no similarity at all to Fielding. Merrick is ambitious, a social climber who at first pays court to Daphne. His hatred for Hari Kumar is based on race and sexual jealousy and may also have in poisoned form some of the repressed nuance of Fielding's fondness for Aziz. The reader participates in assembling the story from documents—interviews, reported conversations, and narratorial fact-finding—surrounding the romance of Hari and Daphne, followed by her gang rape and its aftermaths. What for Adela was a hysterical, unexplained experience in the Marabar Caves is for Daphne a hideous, witnessed assault in a public park. There is, as in Forster's novel, a complicated trial, but one in which the politics are more subtle and Daphne a formidable figure of resolution. The aftermath is bittersweet: as in *A Passage to India,* no lasting reconciliation between the cultures and races is yet possible after so long and unequal a history. Love occurs, but circumstances thwart it.

Many of the numerous characters, fictional and historical, introduced in *The Jewel* reappear in the subsequent volumes of Scott's Raj Quartet, *The Day of the Scorpion* (1968), *The Towers of Silence* (1971), and *A Division of the Spoils* (1974). The main action takes place between 1942 and 1948, a period that included British withdrawal and Partition. India finds itself and in so doing the English too are changed, some collapsing into their prejudices, others understanding, if not embracing, change. Scott's last novel, *Staying On* (1977), which received the Man Booker Prize, examines what happens to the English who chose to remain in an independent India, and the changing Indians themselves. An unhappily married couple stays behind to spend their retirement in India. Their life in a changing townscape and the isolating tension of their relationship make this book an unsentimental elegy to long relationships, intimate and political. The conclusion is more bitter than sweet. The end of too-long exile is the beginning of another kind of exile.

Introducing a whiff, no more, of cordite: Mary McCarthy felt that J. G. (James Gordon) Farrell (1935–1979) could have stood up for himself more staunchly when critics disparaged his Booker Prize–winning *The Siege of Krishnapur* (1973). "Farrell's motto might have been stated thus: If because of ideas and other unfashionable components your novel is going to seem dated, don't be alarmed—date it." Ideas mattered to him, however vivid his characters. His first book was a staged encounter between two aspects of existentialism, his unfinished last a fragment and notes that would have been entitled *The Hill Station* and made his colonial trilogy, *Troubles* (1970), *The Siege of Krishnapur*, and *The Singapore Grip* (1978), into a quartet broader in scope (starting with Ireland and including Malaysia in its span) than Paul Scott's, but narrower in novelistic achievement. Of the novels in this undertaking, only *The Siege of Krishnapur* is original and durable. Farrell was intellectually consistent: he used the occasion of his Booker Prize acceptance speech to attack the sponsors for their activities in the Third World.

Of Scott's books Rebecca West enjoyed "the Indian one" (the title slipped her mind); but although "very funny because it's all about people making a fuss about nothing," that "isn't really enough." She is bemused that readers consume Proust and Forster "at the same time." The one is food for all seasons, the other a bagatelle. The book of the period she valued was *They Went* (1920) by Norman Douglas (1868–1952). "It's about the king of a legendary country. I've read it several times and I've always found it beautiful." She makes it sound like Nabokov's *Pale Fire*. Her own voice in interview, self-parodying, self-communing, sounds like that of a Nabokov narrator inventing himself.

Douglas, with Forster, is among the last British writers to experience the special relationship between the British sensibility, with its burden of caveats and inhibitions, and the Mediterranean. From Alexandria late in 1917 Forster wrote to Douglas about his earlier book, *South Wind*. Alexandria, he told Douglas, "rather resembles Nepenthe," a heightened version of Douglas's beloved Capri, where the action—and inaction—of the novel takes place. There, "ideals and principles gently relax," the emollient effect of the Mediterranean and the sirocco on the tight-laced British spirit can be celebrated. Forster shares with Douglas an Alexandrian anecdote quite as bizarre as the incidents and conversations that occur in Nepenthe, except that Forster's tall tale was presented as true. Forster was writing to a man with whom he shared unacknowledged proclivities, and whose exile was not by choice but by necessity. Four times Douglas fled from British jurisdiction as a result of peccadilloes, two of them committed with boys.

The book begins like a short story, establishing a tone. "The bishop was feeling rather sea-sick. Confoundedly sea-sick, in fact." The adverb *rather,* used for deliberate understatement in a certain class of English discourse, is immediately corrected by another adverb, also rooted in class usage, which exaggerates. Between the two the reader can deduce an unhappy medium: the Bishop of Bampopo has had a rough crossing to Nepenthe. In the more effortful opening of Anthony Burgess's *Earthly Powers* (1980), as throughout that book, there is a coarsened residue of Douglas, whose seductive delicacy many have tried to replicate but the filigree is generally lost. "It was the afternoon of my eighty-first birthday," says Burgess's first-person narrator, Kenneth Toomey, "and I was in bed with my catamite when Ali announced that the archbishop had come to see me." That sentence establishes much more than a tone of voice; it is ostentatiously constructed, not spoken. Too much information, however arresting it may be. Douglas's voice is at ease with itself, amused; he is an assured, contentedly decadent aphorist, a polysexual sensualist without a conventional conscience. We encountered him before, defending the prose of Ouida against her detractors, especially Henry James, "this feline and gelatinous New Englander." It is as well to keep on the right side of such a writer.

Among his effortful heirs was Lawrence Durrell, an admirer of his "writing personality," whose *Panic Spring* owes much to *South Wind.* He describes Douglas as "unsnobbish, and yet he was the extreme stylist of the silver age." We associate snobbishness with the class to which Douglas belonged, and to the voice. This is our prejudice, that a writer cannot be "a good stylist" in Douglas's sense "without being snobbish. The delicacy and tact and the stylish gentlemanly thing was so well matched in Douglas that it carried no affectations; he was not trying to be pompous or anything." Again, the word *gentlemanly* has become polluted for modern readers. Durrell insists, "He is the happy example of the style perfectly married to the man. I never met him, but I'm sure his speaking tone was exactly like his writing tone. That easy informal Roman Silver-Age style is something everyone should be able to enjoy and appreciate." He compares it with chamber music, as against the orchestral ambitions of Tolstoy and Dostoyevsky.

Woolf, reviewing *South Wind* when it first appeared, compares Douglas with Peacock, and also with Wilde. He agreed with Ouida that Wilde was a *cabotin,* a ham actor, while at the same time reviling the laws that landed him in prison, the same laws that put him to flight. Woolf gives Douglas a pedigree of antecedents and then insists, "His book has a distinguished ancestry, but it was born only the day before yesterday." The day before, because he was clearly not born yesterday: he is too canny, he has the air of nurture about him. Ford, who considers Douglas alongside Wyndham Lewis and D. H. Lawrence (who sends Douglas up in *Aaron's Rod* and with whom Douglas was to have a notorious spat), talks about his freedom from the influence of Conrad, Gissing, James, and Flaubert. He begins to compare him to Anatole France, whose *analytical* imagination produced the ideological and political hilarity of his parallel history of France, *Penguin Island* (1908), but then they work on different scales, France is always a civic writer while Douglas never is. Douglas's characters generally exist on the edge of caricature; they are credible for the duration of their scenes in the sunlight of the narrative. When Ford speaks of "the author's savage, mordant dislike for humanity," he exaggerates: it is more impatience than dislike, but it is true that he cannot spend too much time in a character's company. He prefers the souls of *places,* unlike the "human-centred novelist of today." Like Wyndham Lewis, who in this respect he resembles, Douglas began, Ford reminds us, as an essayist.

"Viewed from the clammy deck on this bright morning, the island of Nepenthe resembled a cloud." We approach the setting of *South Wind* wonderingly. "It was a silvery speck upon that limitless expanse of blue sea and sky. A south wind breathed over the Mediterranean waters, drawing up their moisture which lay couched in thick mists about its flanks and uplands." Transported here, his characters display their eccentricities. They are drawn from the areas of his experience, a German childhood, a period in his ancestral Scotland, the diplomatic service which he abandoned precipitately in St. Petersburg to avoid his first major, and heterosexual, scandal, the English world, and the expatriate community with its foibles and vices. In its abundant eccentricities the book reveals, as Woolf says, "what a narrow convention the novelist is wont to impose on us."

*South Wind* with its humor, verging on the camp, its bright colors, its wry formal intelligence, came into the age of Bennett and Wells, Conrad and Galsworthy, as something different in kind, in scale, intent, and seriousness, something closer to James and Stevenson in terms of art than to the mainstream of the day, something liberating—indicative, if not of a new, then of another, manner, voice, approach, a coming into natural shape and size. Huxley's *Crome Yellow* lives in the same neighborhood but lacks the assurance and, with its digressions, the proportion of *South Wind*. It had its impact. Graham Greene says, "My generation was brought up on *South Wind*." Douglas's life was "consistently open, tolerant, unashamed." Given the things he got up to, he might have been ashamed:

certainly he enjoyed life. His last book was an anthology of aphrodisiac recipes. His collection of obscene limericks with spoof-scholarly annotations is an underappreciated classic.

His travel books possess the qualities of style that Durrell notes. *Siren Land* (1911), *Fountains in the Sand* (1912), and *Old Calabria* (1915) are of a piece with the lightness of *South Wind*. In *Alone* (1921) he wrote a credo that challenges the modern writer as it did the writers of his own time.

> I know full well that this is not the way to write an orthodox English novel. For if you hide your plot, how shall the critic be expected to see it? You must serve it on a tray; you must (to vary the simile) hit the nail on the head and ask him to be so good as to superintend the operation. That is the way to rejoice the cockles of his heart. He can then compare you to someone else who has also hit the nail on the head and with whose writings he happens to be familiar. You have a flavor of Dostoyevsky minus the Dickens taint; you remind him of Flaubert or Walter Scott or somebody equally obscure; in short, you are in a condition to be labeled—a word, and a thing, which comes perilously near to libeling. If, to this description, he adds a short summary of your effort, he has done his duty. What more can he do? He must not praise overmuch, for that might displease some of his own literary friends. He must not blame overmuch, else how shall his paper survive? It lives on the advertisements of publishers and—say those persons, perhaps wisely—"if you ill-treat our authors, there's an end to our custom." Commercialism.

In his eighties Douglas died in Capri. He had been sick for a time and chose to go. Nancy Cunard, to whom he was kind and supportive, attended his burial. She puzzled over Horace's words cut into the blue-green stone below his name: *Omnes eodem cogimur.* Douglas would have translated it for her: "We all reach the same destination." His own last words were also in character: "Get these fucking nuns away from me."

Arthur Annesley Ronald Firbank (1886–1926) resisted the Roman Catholic Church (to which he converted in 1907) with greater delicacy than Douglas and for different reasons. He loved the pomp, the choirs and processions and icons, gowns and incense, all the accoutrements. In Rome he even thought he might have a religious vocation. But however much he wanted the church, it did not want *him*. His revenge is most luminous in the character of Cardinal Archbishop Don Alvaro Narciso Hernando Pirelli. The exquisite little novel *Concerning the Eccentricities of Cardinal Pirelli* (1926, Firbank's last) opens with His Holiness christening a police puppy called Crack in the presence of all the grandest people of Clemenza, and ends with him dying, dressed only in his grand miter, having failed in pursuit of Chicklet, the enchanting and *almost* biddable choirboy. His doting housekeeper preserves his modesty by coiling over it "her brier-wood chaplet," reflecting on the uses of beads but lamenting how they do not go far "with a gentleman." In an ecstatic stroke we leave him gazing his last on the untrammeled heavens, "a blue like the blue of lupins." How many taboos are violated, and with what ingenuous innocence.

Firbank died young, in his fortieth year, having written stories, plays, and nine (or ten) short books that his admirers call novels. They nearly constitute a genre of their own, rich in voices and inconsequential incident, yet shorter than novels are expected to be. Narrative is of little consequence: what matters is atmosphere, reflection, the magic qualities of language in terms of evocation and tone, unraveling late Victorian values and reconfiguring them, a process that reaches, in languid ways and attitudes, well beyond the reach of Wilde's satire. They are not satire but celebration of what it might be to be human in a body unburdened of a Christian soul, untrammeled by the Ten Commandments and their litany of "nots." What a long way the Firbanks had gone in a mere three generations. Firbank's great grandfather was an illiterate Durham miner, his grandfather pulled himself up by his bootstraps, built "beautiful railways," and became an enormously rich baronet, dying the year Ronald was born. His father was a Conservative member of Parliament who died unlamented by his son, except that he had steeply diminished the family fortune and the independence Ronald received was less than he had anticipated. His mother, who died two years before her son, was the cultivated daughter of an Irish Protestant. She was able to spend some of her father-in-law's fortune on collecting prints and porcelains, communicating her taste and enthusiasm to her son. She was protective of little Ronald wherever he went, anticipating him, sending a servant to sweep the way and make his bed in new places. His health and comfort were assiduously catered for.

In the household where he grew up, industrialists and artists visited, *The Yellow Book* and prospectuses for railways and factories were displayed. The boy Ronald was brittle and sickly, cosseted by his mother and despised by his father. As he grew older he briefly attended Uppingham School, as Norman Douglas was to do. Two terms were enough to persuade his mother that he needed a private tutor. He was sent to France to learn the language for a possible career in the Diplomatic Service. France refined his dress sense and dandified his manners. He devised a mask of mannerism and gesture to protect himself and blur, as Woolf did at roughly the same period, the distinction between legend and reality. It was easier to perform than to be Ronald Firbank. There was more than a little of his revered Oscar Wilde about him, and Lord Orkish in his one-act play *The Princess Zoubaroff* (1920) is Firbank's version of a Wilde delivered from punishment, inhabiting a polysexual utopia.

When the First World War came, he went to ground, composing several novels in a short space of time. He lived in Oxford. Current events do not enter the fiction at all. The writing emerges with a *fin de siècle* detachment, in disregard of the contingent world. "Firbank worked in fragments all the way through," Alan Hollinghurst says, "amassing phrases in notebooks, and supposedly compiling his early novels on narrow horizontal strips of paper, which could be shuffled and rearranged in a way that sounds prophetic of much later experiments with the cut-up." (We might think also of Vladimir Nabokov with his filing cards, and some of their technical resemblances.)

In *Vainglory* (1915), Forster's favorite among the early works, Mrs. Shamefoot strives for immortality through art, a stained glass window devoted to her life at St. Dorothy's Cathedral. "It is frivolous stuff," says Forster, "and how rare, how precious is frivolity! How few writers can prostitute all their powers!" David Lodge shows how the book, published on Henry James's seventy-second birthday, breaks all Jamesian rules: "no centre of consciousness, no unity of effect, no 'action,'" but it would have been hard for him "to call it loose and baggy when it was so agile, so indirect, so evidently if mysteriously 'designed.'"

*Inclinations* (1916) evokes Miss Geraldine O'Brookomore, author of curious fictions including *Six Strange Sisters* and *Those Gonzagas:* her plans for a happy lesbian romance with adolescent Miss Mabel Collins are dashed when Mabel marries Count Pastorelli instead. *Caprice* (1917) pursues another female protagonist, Miss Sarah Sinquier, an aspiring actress who debuts triumphantly as a husky Juliet and dies in a quite fortuitous accident with a trap door. It is with *Valmouth* (1919), his first utopian world, that his major work, if so filigreed a genius can do "major," begins. The setting is a resort on an imaginary south coast of an imaginary England, a place for affairs and pleasures, all out of the ordinary in terms of sexual combination. Under the aegis of the black masseuse Mrs. Yajnavalkya (known as Mrs. Yaj), the exquisite conversations and landscapes pass before us. It ends in a bridal pursuit of a butterfly.

The novel that had success in Firbank's lifetime was *Sorrow in Sunlight* (1924). Carl Van Vechten, a devoted advocate, found an American publisher, who retitled it *Prancing Nigger.* The ambitions and affectations of a provincial, prosperous English matron are vested in Mrs. Almadou Mouth, who takes the whole Mouth family from their innocent tropical paradise (the novel opens with young Miami Mouth in a hammock, meditating on her slow world—we gradually realize that she is naked) to the metropolitan capital of the island (in some respects like colonial Haiti) so that her children can enter society. The inconsequential hilarity of the novel violates every sexual and social norm. The book sold in the United States. It provided the only real income from writing that Firbank received. His other books in tiny, uncommercial editions were, if not self-published, certainly underwritten by the author.

Firbank died in Rome in 1926, enfeebled, alcoholic. His friend Lord Berners did not know he was Roman Catholic. He was buried in the Protestant Cemetery, where Keats and Shelley lay, but quite soon transplanted to the cemetery of San Lorenzo.

His writing exemplifies "camp" in its most natural form, the seemingly unaffected affectation of it, inversions of word order, continual ellipses ("I think nothing of filing fifty pages down to make a brief, crisp paragraph, or even a row of dots"—Flaubertian profligacy!), an excess of punctuation (including exclamation marks) that insists on inflection over sense, fragmentation of narrative, a deliberately inorganic structure with parallelisms and paradoxes, the pretense of speech ironized through diction, unexpected combinations of words and ideas, incursions of foreign words, parody. And always a sexual undercurrent, but never a conventional one. Forster notes that the writing is marked less by its intelligence than by its continuous, unresolving imagination: "He was incapable of totting up life." What moves us is his tact, his ability to build a fantasy phrase by phrase in a dream language where every term is unexpected and apposite. Firbank moves, and moves deeply, those readers he does affect (not all readers, certainly) by his language: diction, phrasal balance, governing cadences, unexpected runs and tickles, beauty. Truman Capote remarks, "To some degree all writers have style—Ronald Firbank, bless his heart, had little else, and thank God he realized it." Firbank himself remarked, "I am all design—once I get going." He moves back and forth between "the colored glint and the naughty tweak," Forster says, the voice of the butterfly and the voice of the beetle. Fantastic literature in every genre shares one quality, what Forster calls "the absence of a soul."

Forster calls Firbank a glow worm. He is more a firefly, but it is never actual fire: he comes on tantalizingly, now here, now there; the eye follows and joins up the dots he makes. They exist in time, the shapes we finally trace between them are in space, the embroidery of his writing. Alan Hollinghurst says, "The technique is compositional rather than narrative." Evelyn Waugh says the compositions are "built up, intricately and with a balanced alternation of the wildest extravagance and the most austere economy, with conversational nuances." "Nuance" needs to be stressed. W. H. Auden, who shuns the company of readers who do not respond to Firbank, points out that the voices are not characters but attitudes. Certain symbols or images define a character, but their voices are interchangeable: they could easily exist in another novel, apart from the occasional color bar. Auden speaks of the earthly paradise Firbank uniquely created, a place in which "without having to change our desires and behavior in any way, we suffer neither frustration or guilt." In *Orlando* Woolf may owe him a debt, not least in her chronological liberties.

David Lodge compares Firbank's effect on later writers with that of Hemingway. It is a matter of economy, different though the textures they achieve are. Waugh, he recalls, compared Firbank's narratives to "cinema films in which the relation of caption and photograph is directly reversed; occasionally a brief vivid image flashes out to illuminate and explain the flickering succession of spoken words." This reversal of the roles of description and dialogue is telling. "His art is purely selective. From the fashionable chatter of his period, vapid and interminable, he has plucked, like tiny brilliant feathers from the breast of a bird, the particles of his design." Does not the image, though delicate, apply to Hemingway's selective technique as well? And perhaps to that of Nathanael West, and of Burroughs at his most oblique.

Firbank despised the commentary and criticism that did not "get" what he was up to. In the wake of Oscar Wilde, who apart from those who understood the encoded "double talk" could have understood? He kept his counsel, he did not review books, he did not issue statements. There is the work, there are the letters; there is no mediating public prose. This restraint is an engaging aspect of his complex integrity.

Discursive restraint, for different reasons, marks the work of P. G. (Sir Pelham Grenville) Wodehouse (1881–1975). In 1920 Lukács identified a cuckoo in the literary nest: "The novel has a caricatural twin 'the entertainment novel' which has the outward features of the novel but which in essence is bound to nothing and based on nothing, i.e. is entirely meaningless." The caricatural twin sometimes proves itself stronger than the more conventional product. Increasingly persuasive efforts are made to elevate Wodehouse's fiction to the category of "literature." If Wodehouse is to be elevated, what genre does he practice? Is his a parodic reversal of the Quixote-Sancho dynamic? Is it a new picaresque? It seems more natural to place him alongside Richard Crompton's *Just William* (Ginger as a scruffy Jeeves, William as accident-prone Bertie Wooster, and an abundance of aunts) and other examples of well-made children's fiction that depends on the predictability of caricature: a public school, a schematized class system, a place of knocks and tumbles without durable pain or suffering. Wodehouse's world is brittler than Trollope's cathedral close, too narrow to keep company with *Cranford*. Martin Amis speaks of his "comic pastoral," a category that Kazuo Ishiguro's butler Stevens in *The Remains of the Day* parodies, having no Bertie Wooster to serve and being devoid of banter.

Waugh says Wodehouse had a direct effect on his style of writing. Certainly the early novels owe him something, not least in caricature and dialogue. Lawrence

Durrell admired Wodehouse's merry potboiling, comparing it to his own "Antrobus nonsense." The writer needs to remain "absolutely sincere and honest towards the form." Even if it is at one level trivial, a committed execution can dignify it. Wodehouse urges the would-be comic writer, "Get to the dialogue as soon as possible." He hears his characters and takes a kind of dictation from them, as though they were speaking in a play. It is another version of the "point of view of ear." Again there is dramatic three-dimensionality in the composition that makes narratives adaptable to stage, radio, and television. And he potboiled for a long time. He lived almost to the middle of his ninety-fourth year and sold his first story in 1902, at the age of twenty, when he became a full-time writer. "I don't remember what I did before that. Just loafed, I suppose."

He admired a writer who also potboiled for the Empire, George MacDonald Fraser (1925–2008), author of the dozen Flashman novels that were believed to be authentic history by some reviewers and readers in Britain and America, deceived by the author's inventive consistency and the apparatus he provided, the notes, Afghan glossaries, and the conceit that the author was editing and amending a preexisting script. "If there was a time when I felt that watcher-of-the-skies-when-a-new-planet stuff," Wodehouse said, "it was when I read the first Flashman." Though different in theme and form, there is a connection between Flashman's and Bertie Wooster's cultures. Bertie lived in an indeterminate *entre deux guerres*—a fatuous, perpetually Edwardian England unthreatened by the Great Depression and Hunger Marches, where the Blackshirts are figures of mockery and the Second World War never happens. It's impossible to imagine Bertie in a military uniform except at a costume ball.

One reason Wodehouse's vision remained unclouded and complete is that, due to a political misjudgment during World War II, he felt compelled to leave Britain for the United States, where he became naturalized. His error had been that during the year he was a prisoner of war in a German internment camp, at the request of the Germans he broadcast about conditions in the camp. He had hoped to reassure those who had relations or friends in detention, but his broadcasts were seen as treacherously supporting the German cause. He did not repent of having told the truth. Even in 1975 he kept his nerve. "Everybody seems to think a German internment camp must be a sort of torture chamber. It was really perfectly normal and ordinary. The camp had an extraordinarily nice commander, and we did all sorts of things, you know. We played cricket, that sort of thing." The only thing he ever wrote about the experience was the notorious broadcasts.

Stevens in the Booker Prize–winning novel *The Remains of the Day* (1989) is Jeeves crossed with the lugubrious donkey Eeyore from *Winnie the Pooh*. Or Jeeves fallen out of Bertie Wooster's employ and into the grinding wheels of history.

Jeeves who still imagines himself indispensable yet fails slowly, totally, on every front. He perseveres, even as the book ends, striving for dignity like Malvolio cross-gartered, ingratiating, riding for a fall. "Jeeves was a big influence," says Kazuo Ishiguro (b. 1954). "Not just Jeeves, but all butler figures that walked on in the backgrounds of films. They were amusing in a subtle way. It wasn't slapstick humor. There was some pathos in the way they would come out with a dry line for something that would normally require a more frantic expression."

This was Ishiguro's third novel, and he was keen to address "an international audience." How better to do so than to choose a familiar, specifically British but universally familiar trope and redevelop it, building out from the parochial: "There was a conscious feeling among my peers that we had to address not just a British [audience]." Ishiguro belongs to a generation made not only self-aware but self-conscious in part by Malcolm Bradbury and the University of East Anglia creative writing program, a center at once of excellence and of promotion. Ishiguro attended in the wake of Ian McEwan, a writer he admired, and he recalls how Angela Carter secured him an agent and pushed his work in the direction of the magazine *Granta,* where he was listed in 1983 and again in 1993 as one of the twenty most promising new British writers of the decade. Lady Bracknell might have had a view on this jumping, or being jumped, up and down on the same spot twice.

Ishiguro was born in Nagasaki, where his mother, conventional and cultivated, with prewar memories, was brought up and survived the bombing. His father grew up in Shanghai and became a distinguished physical oceanographer. When Kazuo was five his family emigrated to Guildford, Surrey, and his father did secret work in the National Institute of Oceanography. Japan is to Ishiguro a few fragments of memory. The Japanese setting of his first two novels is imagined. He did not return to Japan for almost three decades and his knowledge of the language is at best rusty. Japanese literature has had little impact upon him; Japanese cinema, on the other hand, he acknowledges as a formative source.

*A Pale View of Hills* (1982), his first full-length novel, is set largely in Nagasaki. It was an immediate *succès d'estime.* It is about a mother with a problem child: she is torn between mother love and a desire to get her own life back. Its was originally set in Cornwall, but setting mattered less than character. He had met such people in his work with the homeless and understood their quandaries, which could amount to tragedies. He transposed the story to an imagined Japan. Japanese women, his mother had told him, "traditionally used a slightly different formal language from men," though nowadays the differentiation is lost. Ishiguro was intrigued by this notion of a gender-specific inflection, the obliquity and self-effacement it entailed. The narrator is a woman of his mother's generation.

Her adult daughter has killed herself. How can the mother tell such a tale? She tells it as though it belonged to someone else, entering only at the end, in an experimental fusion of scenes in the present that does not quite work, creating confusion instead of the clarification intended. But the third person lets the novel take in more world than it could have done as confession.

His second novel, *An Artist of the Floating World* (1986), is also about coming to terms. The title ties the artist Masuji Ono into the Japanese wood-block print tradition of the *ukiyo-e,* "pictures of the floating world," of pleasure and cheerful vice centered on the geishas, sumo wrestlers, kabuki actors, and the high and low life that frequented them. The Japanese *ukiyo-e* sounds very much like "sorrowful world," the cycle of death and rebirth from which the enlightened seek release. Ishiguro's protagonist belonged to and served the traditions represented by the *ukiyo-e.* Worse, he departed from the path of purity and became a propagandist and activist in the projects of extremist factions that led Japan into the war. Events come back to him, a dimming failure, and he must come to terms with them. It is a short step from Mesuji Ono to Stevens in *The Remains of the Day.*

The main difference is that Stevens chose to serve, rather than choosing the cause he served. He followed a master, which is what a servant does, and is implicated in his master's actions without bearing responsibility for them. He comes to terms at second hand but is no less implicated for that. The novel has little action. As Stevens goes on his tour in his late master Lord Darlington's car, dressed in his late master's clothes, his memory moves into the past and reconstructs the events that undid his Lordship's reputation, his secret championing of appeasement and therefore of the German cause. We dabble at the edge of history and historical imagination; the book celebrates a disappearing habitat in the voice of a disappearing species. It is essay as well as novel, marked by an Austenish economy at crucial moments in which the enormity of Lord Darlington's actions becomes clear, and the pathos of Stevens's human failure. Ishiguro's economy is built on the expectation that readers have stored up sufficient historical knowledge, and doubt, to understand change in the moments in which it is occurring. Stevens and Miss Kenton almost touch, and that touch would have broken the fatal meniscus containing Stevens and the values that seal him in his vocational bondage. His desolation, when he last sees Miss Kenton, is appallingly poignant.

Ishiguro's protagonist is again the narrator. He interposes himself, his values and prejudices, which become the subject of the novel, a knot of unreflecting, committed, and inadvertently despairing Englishness. All the characters, including the narrator, are secondary. This is the world of Rosencrantz and

Guildenstern. The plot is inferred rather than revealed, and we trust the undependable narrator because we recognize from the opening words, with their elaborate politeness, that he is undependable and we must look through and around him. He misreads events in revelatory detail. The slow release of facts and the gradual emergence of themes show Ishiguro's almost excessive mastery. One reviewer spoke of the book as too controlled, too perfect.

The consequences of this verdict were unfortunate. The next novel he published, *The Unconsoled* (1995), is ambitious in the way that "literary novels" are, its readers specialist and academic. Anita Brookner resisted, then declared it (hedging her bets) "almost certainly a masterpiece." A. S. Byatt notes, "Ishiguro is a perfectionist. One of the things I loved about *The Unconsoled* was that it was the nightmare of an artist who is stopped from exercising his or her art." It is this perfectionism that Ishiguro was writing against in this book where he pursued "the logic of dreams" for more than five hundred pages, a protracted, muddied stream of consciousness. The idea of the two plots might have worked: Ryder is the son trying to save his unhappy parents' marriage by fulfilling their hopes for him as a pianist—in short, a man about to fail; and Brodsky, an old man trying to repair damage already done by conducting with tender brilliance. "Those two stories take place," Ishiguro explains, "in a society that believes all its ills are the result of having chosen the wrong musical values."

Teenage writers learn through mimicry. As a boy, Ishiguro admired Arthur Conan Doyle. In his gap year traveling across North America he kept a Kerouac-style diary. His song writing imitated Leonard Cohen's. Not being Kerouac or Cohen, he had to get them out of his system. But Conan Doyle is another matter, his legacy comes through in *When We Were Orphans* (2000), at one level a detective story that visits Ishiguro's father's formative cityscapes of Shanghai in the 1930s. Christopher Banks's parents have vanished in Shanghai and he sets out to find out what he can. In *Never Let Me Go* (2005) he strays into the world of cloning, science fiction set in the recent past, not the future, less in the spirit of H. G. Wells, who explains unusual phenomena, more in the zone of Dolly the sheep. His protagonists have three decades, not threescore year and ten, to live; their concern for one another displaces the self-interested scheming of standard man and woman planning for survival, even at the expense of others. Sci-fi is a useful, if implausible, shortcut.

Ishiguro began in thrall to Bloomsbury, his novels crafted, his themes weighed; he writes as one might play chess, never getting in the way. Impatience with perfection can be treacherous. Even Forster succumbed to it from time to time. Yet for writers to move forward, they must reject what appears familiar and accept risk. In the case of Ishiguro, he deliberates and seeks out risks and shapes the kinds of risk he intends. He is like his British contemporaries wary of unexpected risk, unplanned detours.

———•———

Elizabeth (Dorothea Cole) Bowen (1899–1973) was born in Dublin. When her father became mentally ill in 1907, she and her mother moved to England. Her mother died, she was looked after by aunts, attended art school in London, and quite early on chose a life of writing. She existed in the neighborhood of Blooms-bury, and her imagination, rooted in the particulars of her own life, goes to Woolf for formal resources. At first she concentrated on short stories, but novels began to come. She was not a fluent writer of longer fiction and there is a sense of effort in all her books.

She and her husband enjoyed an extremely open relationship. One of her extramarital affairs lasted thirty years. She built her characters out of herself and the people she got to know with the ready intimacy of her group. Her favorite among her novels was the second, *The Last September* (1929), dealing with Anglo-Irish affairs and ending with the burning of the big house at Danielstown, based on her own family home of Bowen's Court, which she inherited and which did not burn but nearly bankrupted her; after she sold it, it was pulled down. The time structure of *The House in Paris* (1935), with its concentration on in-between periods, when key incidents have occurred or are about to occur, focuses time present and past in ways that relate to *Mrs. Dalloway* and *To the Lighthouse*. Woolf remains an earnest foremother. *The Death of the Heart* (1938) is an effortful romance with another too-young heroine. *The Heat of the Day* (1948), about spying and romance, seems in its title (like the earlier novels) to revel in the definite article and has a categorical feel. All of the books, with their sense of uneasy belonging and Anglo-Irish inflection, are at home in a given world and accept, without Woolf's uneasy play with language, that words attach to things in a simple way, an aspect of her natural conservatism.

Raymond Chandler regarded *The Heat of the Day* as "a screaming parody of Henry James" and watched how the critics were "tying themselves in knots" to be polite, realizing she was potentially good but here "the poor girl is giving an exhibition of what happens when an over-earnest writer completely loses her sense of humor." One imagines that James's Maisie and others of his younger heroines spoke directly to Bowen's sense of abandoned self. Anthony Burgess, unlike Chandler, was impressed: "No novel has better caught the atmosphere of London during the Second World War," he said, "that drab suffering world." He was intrigued by a type that Chandler found unrealized, the character of a man reduced to being a traitor.

*Eva Trout, or Changing Scenes* (1968), her last novel, is based directly on her own experience as a girl and young woman coming to terms with a life where everything is paid for with money but, in the formative years, a sense of love has been wanting. Eva causes everyone, including herself, trouble. The book lends itself to various thematic and symbolic readings, with its immature heroine who seems charming to some readers, affected to others. In 1968 it had an archaic feel. Shortlisted for the Booker Prize, it was critically her most successful book. She is described as a bridge between Woolf and Iris Murdoch, an obvious, earnest span. When she died, Bloomsbury was over.

Yet among the works Edna O'Brien (b. 1930) found enabling as a writer were "the early books of Elizabeth Bowen—especially the one she wrote about her home in Ireland, Bowen's Court." She added, "Unhappy houses are a very good incubation for stories." Her own severe childhood in Tuamgraney, County Clare, Ireland, found itself recast as subject matter for her fiction, once she had read Joyce's *A Portrait of the Artist* and realized that the story it told was true. By then she was in London, married to a Czech writer and beginning to raise a family. She started to look into herself and found many of the awkward, questing women she would write about. She took work as a publisher's reader. Her sharp, well-written reports got her a novel contract. *The Country Girls* (1960) was the first book in a trilogy. Baba and Kate, close friends but contrasting figures, grow up together. They leave the security of convent school and go into the world, seeking different kinds of freedom. Baba wants to be independent, Kate is a romantic.

O'Brien, having taken her Stephen Dedalus wings and left Ireland, arrived in a wholly alien London, in November, and feeling lost wrote the book of definition and valediction "in those first few weeks after my arrival." The pages sped under her pen, the energy of memory no longer restrained. "All the time I was writing it I couldn't stop crying, although it is a fairly buoyant, funny book. But it was the separation from Ireland which brought me to the point where I had to write." On publication, the book was banned by the Irish censor on account of its sexual content. *The Lonely Girl,* retitled *Girl with Green Eyes* (1962) and *Girls in Their Married Bliss* (1964) completed the trilogy. They were also disobedient and liberating for younger, emerging Irish writers.

Part of the charm of London was the opportunities it gave O'Brien to read and develop her style. She had trained as a pharmacist, and her early writing was thickly lyrical. She attended a lecture on Fitzgerald and Hemingway—her road to Damascus, she said—and the impact was immediate. She understood the power of economy in prose and set about making herself a serious writer. *A Pagan Place* (1970), written in the second person, was her own *A Portrait of the Artist*. To this book she points new readers as a way in. Tuamgraney is credible, as are her no-saying parents, her no-saying church, yet her protagonist becomes—a nun. It was hard to write against, but this she did in fiction and dramatic work. Biographies were a source of strength: she wrote a play about Virginia Woolf and a biography of Joyce. In 2009, marking the bicentenary of Byron's devastating satirical review *English Bards and Scotch Reviewers,* she published *Byron in Love. House of Splendid Isolation* (1994) was based in part on the terrorist Dominic McGlinchey: here she broadened her concerns to include current events and political concerns of a different kind. She began to produce urgently themed novels, including *Down by the River* (1996), about rape and abortion. The connections between repression and violence became clear to her in actual events, and she challenged her fiction to make sense of it. The space she has helped to clear for modern Irish fiction is now populous. Yet she is rueful: "Nowadays there are too many writers, and I think one of the reasons for the deterioration of language and literature in the last forty years has been the spawning of inferior novels." Literature, no longer sacred, is a business: "The dwelling on emotions, the perfection of style, the intensity of a Flaubert is wasted on modern sensibility . . . There is hardly any distinction between a writer and a journalist—indeed, most writers are journalists."

Jeanette Winterson (b. 1959) was invited by Vintage to commission new introductions for Woolf's major works. Why Winterson? Because her star is in the ascendant, she is a woman writer, a selling name, she is strong in her opinions, anti-academic in bias though the author of widely studied texts. She is not frightened of originality, old or new. She tells us that Woolf "was an experimenter who managed to combine the pleasure of narrative with those forceful interruptions that the mind needs to wake itself. Familiar things lull us. We do not notice what we already know." This is certainly Woolf, but the subtext is Winterson: "In art, newness and boldness is [*sic*] vital, not as a rebuke to the past but as a way of keeping the past alive. Virginia Woolf was keenly aware of what she had inherited but she knew that her inheritance must be put to work." The terms used, the projection onto Woolf of points of view and values that are not hers, are aspects of Winterson's polemic. "Every generation needs its own living art, connected to what has gone before it, but not a copy of what has gone before it." Her editorial strategy was imaginative: she invited two contributors to comment on each book, an academic or scholar (emphatically not a *theorist*: they are anathema to her) and a creative writer. Four of the writers chosen were poets. For herself she kept *The Waves.*

Winterson inscribed a copy of *The Passion* (1987), her third novel, set in the time of Napoleon, to my daughter: "What you ask reveals what you value," above the bold squiggle of her autograph. It was more than a "thought for the day": it pointed to the book, to the author, and to the reader. Generous, to add not only a signature but an idea to the title page. The next but one book, *Written on the Body* (1992), the title itself a declaration, fictionalizes an affair Winterson had, after a long-term relationship had ended, with her married literary agent. Her onetime friend and fellow novelist Adam Mars-Jones characterizes her as either "the outsider who gatecrashed the canon, or alternatively the self-sabotaging golden girl and egomaniac who could never match that first success."

"That first success" was *Oranges Are Not the Only Fruit* (1985), based on her formative experiences, and it came as a thematic surprise, its candid, engaging narrator savvy about literary techniques before she has any reason to be (a thinly veiled stand-in for the author, many of whose life experiences she shares, but not the education). The subject matter and the point of view were new. Her story starts sad but proves a fortunate one, a series of conflicts and happy endings. Born near Manchester, she was adopted by a couple belonging to the Elim Pentecostalist Church, biblical fundamentalists. The stepfather worked in a factory. The stepmother ("She was a very unhappy woman. And I was a happy child") looms large in the writing, a woman who raised the child in a bookless, cultureless home, without manifest affection, to be a missionary, encouraged all that was austerely godly, and threw her out when the church did, publically, after it was discovered that at sixteen she was sleeping with another woman. She made her own way, took A-levels at a technical college, found temporary work, and got into St. Catherine's College, Oxford, on a scholarship to study English.

In 2012, with the memoir about her mother, *Why Be Happy When You Could Be Normal?*, she was back in the same territory, with a grinding mix of styles: slapstick, journalistic, didactic, preacherly. It is written to be read aloud, and it works especially well in her persuasive performance. Revisited, *Oranges* is not as good as it first seemed: one longs to edit it, make it less moralistic, less flowery, less rhetorical (the introduction of Pol Pot's Cambodia is so disproportionate, for example, that it overwhelms what it is meant to accentuate). She hectors; it is sometimes best to regard her as a narrative persona. Proud of her first novel, she claims in the introduction to a 1991 reissue, "In structure and in style and in content *Oranges* was unlike any other novel," which is true of any novel. It is not as unprecedented as she believes. For her it must be "an experimental novel: its interests are anti-linear. It offers a complicated narrative structure disguised as a simple one, it employs a very large vocabulary and a beguilingly straightforward syntax . . . *Oranges* is a threatening novel." The teller and the tale are not in sync.

*Gut Symmetries* (1997) and *The PowerBook* (2000), ambitious projects, fail, though she remains committed to them. What can be said for them is that they take risks, some of which are worth taking even though the books do not work. The experiment that works best is her third novel, *Sexing the Cherry* (1989), which is comic, surprising, poetic but not to excess, and novella-length so that it does not outstay its welcome. Since then it is her journalism and controversialism that have fed her considerable reputation, more than the fiction. A prophet without divine mission, she survives: she flies continually through clouds of flak, she is wounded by friendly as often as by hostile fire and stays airborne with smiling, self-justifying righteousness.

She is frank too about the pleasure principle that underlies her aesthetic, a kind of relenting morality. "I try not to tell lies to people I love, and I try not to tell lies where it matters, but I will sacrifice a fair bit of fact if I can tell a good story." And this is where, in the twenty-first century, the author still has a point that needs to be made over and over until it is unnecessary to make it any more. "When Paul Auster and Milan Kundera put themselves in their work it's called metafiction, when I do it it's autobiography." She is *expected* to be confessional, in Mr. and Mrs. Muck *(The PowerBook)* quite as much as in Mr. and Mrs. Winterson. Her achievement so far is sensational. It is not yet fully registered as literary, though on the strength of her first and third novels it ought to be.

# 32

# Teller and Tale

D. H. Lawrence, John Cowper Powys, T. F. Powys, Sylvia Townsend Warner, Henry Miller,

Anaïs Nin, Lawrence Durrell, Richard Aldington, William S. Burroughs, Jack Kerouac

On March 29, 1928, Arnold Bennett records in his journal, "I promised to sub-scribe to the private edition of D. H. Lawrence's new indecent novel, to be printed 'in Florence.'" Bennett found Lawrence's style compelling but the larger design of the novels disappointing; he lost his temper when Lawrence attacked Wells but recovered it when he read some new piece by Lawrence that delighted him. *Lady Chatterley's Lover* he declared a curate's egg. "Generally speaking, the lechery scenes are the best." Today they do not read as "lechery"; Henry Miller, pub-lishing at the same time, provided more focused genital stimulation. Lawrence addresses women and men, Miller largely a male readership. The intimate scenes in *Lady Chatterley's Lover,* if they embarrass or repel us, tell us as much about ourselves as about the author. V. S. Pritchett unfairly holds Lawrence responsi-ble for the modern novelist's inability to write about sexual love.

In the centrality he gives to women characters Lawrence resembles Forster, a point T. E. Lawrence underlined. Though some of his harshest critics have been women, some who have learned most from him in a positive spirit are women. Doris Lessing read him as a girl in Rhodesia, starting with *Aaron's Rod* (1922). She retains the reality of the novel even while she has forgotten its themes: "He spellbinds, he knocks you over the head with the power of his identifica-tion with what he sees." She stresses his seeing, the thing in itself, the thing in relation to what surrounds it and to what it ignites in memory or imagination, how it talks in itself and how it talks to the singular individual. She does not forgive him his excesses, but she can explain them. "I have read theses and tracts, and analyses about Lawrence, which never mention the consumption that was eating him up." The illness that took him young sharpened his responses and provoked his impatience: he hated criticism because he was an egotist, but also because it delayed him, it wasted his precious time and he had so little. He has, Lessing says, what critics call "the defects of his qualities," and she exclaims, "Yes, but what qualities." Pritchett is generous to his faults too: "His angry paganism of demi-gods released a repressed religious imagination in English literature. He re-introduced the direct apprehension of experience. He wrote from within—from inside the man, the woman, the tree, the fox, the mine."

Many of the writers he affected speak of him in a religious tone. John Fowles remembers Lawrence's impact in the shaping of *The Magus*. He was on the island of Spetsai, and he found *himself*: "My own experience on the island was dense, pregnant with existingness." The whole paragraph is rapt, that unpronounceable "existingness" repeated several times with unironic naivety. Because Fowles is not Lawrence and does not share his world, his earnestness is inadvertently comical. It is hard to become Lawrencian, as hard as it was for Benjamin Franklin to become truly American. Lawrence describes Franklin's existential struggle: "He wanted to be American. But you can't change your nature and mode of consciousness like changing your shoes. It is a gradual shedding. Years must go by, and centuries must elapse before you have finished. Like a son escaping from the domination of his parents, the escape is not just one rupture. It is a long and half-secret process."

Another writer who failed to become Lawrencian, though because of his intelligence came much closer, is Anthony Burgess. *Flame into Being,* his Lawrence book written opportunistically like his quick-fire volumes on Orwell, Hemingway, and others to cash in on a centenary, identifies his own antecedents and mission with Lawrence's. He does not convince either. The profound debts of some of the black writers of the 1940s and 1950s are another matter. They were as much outsiders as Lawrence, making their way, exploring their themes. Claude McKay, Jean Toomer, Langston Hughes, Richard Wright, James Baldwin, and Ralph Ellison were helped by Lawrence, who showed them what could be done within the novel form by imaginations shaped beyond the usual pales. Bernard Malamud's 1979 novel *Dubin's Lives* is about a Jewish biographer—differently beyond the pale—engaged in writing a life of Lawrence, a book in which the biographer is overcome by his subject and in middle age experiments with sex, intense jealousy, infidelity, concealment. Dubin is alive, but not on his own terms. The life of the imagination betrays him; this is also a parable of the lies and betrayals of American society in the Nixon period.

"It is hard to hear a new voice, as hard as it is to listen to an unknown language." Lawrence reflects on how readers misread because they do not listen. The only way we can hear is through unconditioned ears, alert to making. He brings to the novel less a new subject matter than a new way of regarding subject matter and, especially, a new way of including the reader. Says Pritchett, "He put the reader more or less in the position of writing the novel for himself, by giving him instantaneous observation and by slackening the strings that move the puppets." Pritchett then makes a crucial association: "Like the Russians, he made the days of his characters' lives more important than the plot." Certainly, like those writers who took key bearings from him, his novels are a quest for the truth of perceptions and relationships, between people, between objects. Plot is incidental. A novel's truth may be inferred even when it is not seen. Lawrence declares in *Studies in Classic American Literature* (1923), "The artist usually sets out—or used to—to point a moral and adorn a tale. The tale, however, points the other way as a rule. Two blankly opposing morals, the artist's and the tale's. Never trust the artist. Trust the tale. The proper function of a critic is to save the tale from the artist who created it." Later: "An artist usually intellectualizes on top, and his dark under-consciousness goes on contradicting him beneath."

The novels are marred by preacherly intrusions and hectoring inconsistency: he has no stable doctrine. Mary McCarthy observes that "reasoning occupies a large part of the narrative, exerting a leverage that seems to compel the reader's agreement." Incidents "press home like gripping illustrations of the point being proved. There is something of parable in most of Lawrence's plots." His characters are individuals and types at once, not constructed but imagined. He described them as allotropic, borrowing the chemical term for the existence of two or more different physical forms of a chemical element. A character's nature is to be detected at a "deeper" level than we normally expect in a fiction. Pritchett sees this as part of Lawrence's debt to Meredith: "People are not individual characters, but psychic types, flames lit by the imagination." But they *are* individual characters, too: Lawrence has and eats his cake. This is his freedom as a critic, too. "There are other men in me, besides this patient ass who sits here in a tweed jacket. What am I doing, playing the patient ass in a tweed jacket? Who am I talking to? Who are you, at the other end of this patience?"

McCarthy at first puzzled at his hatred of the intellect, "the 'upper story' (there is maybe a class prejudice here)," how strange it is "in a man who himself lived almost wholly for ideas." But they were his ideas, he discovered and tested them, or thought he had. And they do not settle into detachable "truths." Each novel has a mouthpiece character who is opposed and interrogated in dialogue and action (Birkin in *Women in Love* and Richard Somers in *Kangaroo* are examples) and is vindicated; the ideas remain dynamic. They are not "proven" at the novel's end. Many novelists give the appearance of having found their form; Lawrence is always searching, provisional, and grows formally more provisional as he progresses toward his apocalyptic themes. It is wrong to suggest he does not work toward closure: he does, but his sense of closure changes. He has more in common with American than British writing, particularly in his repudiation of stylistic irony. The infection of Walt Whitman goes deep. By this we can measure his distance from Forster on the one hand and Lewis on the other. To echo Mary McCarthy, "there may be a class prejudice against those voices made slippery by an education in evasion and obliquity."

As a girl Carson McCullers could not resist Lawrence's writing, and when Pritchett welcomed her early work in Britain he drew the immediate comparison;

in the *New Yorker* in 1941 she was accused of plagiarizing Lawrence's short story "The Prussian Officer" in *Reflections in a Golden Eye*. The charm he cast had to do with the particularity of his seeing and the sense of presence his novels have, either repelling or drawing less-formed talents into his orbit. Iris Murdoch distinguishes between writers with style and no presence (she mentions Shakespeare), and writers with presence like Lawrence, of whom we are always aware as we read. She describes him as "bossy": his presence damaging because it privileges one or another character as the author's spokesman. "Bad writing is almost always full of the fumes of personality," she says.

Those fumes have driven out several writers whose work is similarly toxic. "I tried to read his novels. He's impossible. He's pathetic and preposterous. He writes like a sick man." Gertrude Stein's impatience was implacable. Virginia Woolf was less obdurate, but he tried her patience. "Mr. Lawrence, of course, has moments of greatness, but hours of something very different." Muriel Spark referred to him as "dreary old creeping Jesus." At eighteen Martin Amis has already learned to call *The Rainbow* "The Rainbore," a judgment he may have shared with his father. When I chaired a roundtable discussion at the Hay-on-Wye Book Festival some years ago, the panel was asked to name the most over-rated "great" writer. Iris Murdoch and John Bayley, without hesitation, nomi-nated Lawrence. The most underrated? John Cowper Powys. The narrator of Martin Amis's *The Information* uses the phrase "a monument of neglect, like a Powys" and asks, "How many Powyses *were* there? Two? Three? Nine?" The answer is, probably, eleven.

David Herbert Lawrence (1885–1930) was born in Eastwood, Nottingham, close by ten working pits. He was the fourth child of a coal miner and a former schoolteacher who was ambitious for her children and short-tempered with her not always sober or couth husband. Lawrence found security with his mother, though the relationship complicated his relations with women. His boyhood was marked by contradictions: the misalliance between his father's attitudes and values and his mother's; between the rural and industrial landscapes that co-existed around him; and between sexual and moral obligations that seemed—in those early years—at odds. He remembered that time "as if there was a sort of inner darkness," or was it outer, "like the gloss of coal in which we moved and had our being." The gloss made darkness visible: "The spirit of place is a great reality," he declared, and of all the places he writes of it is this first smudged, damaged landscape that is most real to him.

From a coeducational local council school where he was unhealthy, un-happy, and bullied, he won a scholarship to Nottingham High School for Boys. He spent three undistinguished years there. In 1901 he was withdrawn, but not to go down the pits as his father intended. Shortly after his promising elder brother William suddenly died in London, Bert contracted pneumonia, weakening him for the tuberculosis that would prove fatal. He became a clerk in a surgical appliances factory at thirteen shillings a week. Soon he followed in his mother's footsteps, becoming a pupil teacher and finally a fledged schoolmaster. Until 1912 he taught, all the while working on stories, poems, and his first novel. He had befriended the Chambers family, Alan becoming his best friend and Jessie the confidant with whom he discussed everything and under whose name some of his early writing was published. He was reticent about his writing, fearing exposure, the anomaly of the son of a collier writing at all having impressed itself upon him.

Teaching took him south, to Croydon, Surrey, into landscapes and among accents foreign to him. "How can I answer the challenge of so many eyes?" he asks in a poem. The challenge of eyes later on, when he was invited to read his poems at Harold Monroe's Poetry Bookshop in London, made him turn his back to the audience, a form of modesty that focused attention even more narrowly upon him.

How is it that he was reading at a bookshop in London? In 1909 Jessie sent a story and poems to Ford Madox Hueffer, editor of the *English Review*. Later Hueffer remembered reading Jessie's letter: "I can still see the handwriting—as if drawn with sepia rather than written in ink—on grey-blue notepaper." He glanced from the letter to the submission and read the first paragraph of "Odor of Chrysanthemums." "I was reading in the twilight in the long eighteenth-century room that was at once the office of the *English Review* and my drawing room. My eyes were tired." He dropped the story into "the basket for accepted manuscripts." His secretary asked, "You've got another genius?" He brought in a great harvest of geniuses that year: Norman Douglas, Wyndham Lewis, and Ezra Pound among them. "It's a big one this time," he replied and went upstairs to dress for dinner. At dinner he recommended his new discovery to Wells, Chesterton, and others. At least that's how he recalled the day he discovered Lawrence, his memory being always heightened. "Before the evening was finished I had had two publishers asking me for first refusal of D. H. Lawrence's first novel."

What Ford responded to was the particularity of the fiction, the fact that the writer seemed actually to see what he evoked, with precise and sufficient detail. It was *real,* the prose enactive. And the subject matter, dealing with realities not usually touched upon in fiction (the death of a collier, the widow's painful recognition) had a lived feel. Ford went on to meet Lawrence, an awkward social moment, the chinless, threadbare patrician and the ferret-faced miner's son. Lawrence suddenly appears before Ford as "a fox," preparing "to make a raid on the hen house before him." A moment of deep embarrassment for both of them, followed by an interview: Lawrence thought he had arrived, not knowing how much more is entailed in literary arrival than mere acceptance. He saw "a fairish, fat, about forty" man. That "ish" provides the blur that accompanies Ford, a man not *out* of focus but always about to come into it.

Lawrence's background set him apart from the Anglophone writers of his time. Even Wells was a cut above him. Without cultural or material advantages, emerging from the turbulent household of Mr. and Mrs. Lawrence, he possessed an earnestness he never lost. Not for him the ironies of Oxbridge or insouciant Bloomsbury, its mild experimental luxuries, always busy with itself. Absent from his prose is a deliberated elegance: it confronts reader and subject, bracing and eventually wearying. He is direct and *in* his writing, he makes no bones about it. When he writes humorously, he does not play with the medium, belittle his subject matter, or diminish his characters for effect. One has the sense, in his formal writing and in his erratic, brilliant letters, of a man for whom writing is less an art than an act with moral consequences.

As ill health took firm hold on him, he began to seek climates friendlier than the British. His writing grew urgent. Readers must bring to his work more of themselves than writers usually require, and it is possible to balk—for some readers it is impossible *not* to—at the ethical demands that can obscure the artistic risks he takes. The largest risk was to take his art seriously, and to ask us to do so, to read him as we would a philosophical or religious text. This, as much as the vigor and consistency of his work, drew so perceptive and sour a critic as F. R. Leavis to admit Lawrence to the upper reaches of a Parnassus that he guarded against less definite mortals.

But Leavis's encomia came later. In the early years, teaching children reluctant to learn irritated Lawrence. He began to suffer the emotional and physical strain of an employment for which he had no vocation. The death of his mother in 1910 had left him worn out and near despair. These experiences provided plot, imagery, and themes for the books that many regard as his best—*Sons and Lovers* (1913), his most personal novel, and *Women in Love* (1920).

His first novel, *The White Peacock,* Ford handed to Messrs. Heinemann. It duly appeared in 1911. Set in the landscape of his boyhood, the provincial reality it creates is as tangible and credible as one of Hardy's or Bennett's. It identifies and explores themes that were to be central to his work, including dysfunctional relationships and the havoc they wreak. It is narrated in the first person by Cyril Beardsall. The unsociable character of Annable prefigures the gamekeeper Mellors in Lawrence's last novel, *Lady Chatterley's Lover* (1928). With a literary mind and opinions unconnected with the main action but prophetic of later themes, Annable dies before the novel is over. We may experience his death as a relief, but without his direction and indirection, the novel loses its way. A flawed debut, it is not where a new reader of Lawrence should start.

In 1911 Lawrence had a recurrence of pneumonia. In 1912 he wiped the chalk from his fingers, abandoned the classroom and his fiancé of two years, and traveled abroad for the first time. His self-discovery involved him in running away (after a six-week affair) with Frieda von Richthofen, the aristocratic German wife of a Nottingham professor. As a misalliance all his own, this relationship (one hesitates to call so reposeless a yoking of wills and fates a romance) became the central imaginative reality, the volatile *stability,* of Lawrence's imagination. His contemporaries looked to France; he turned his attention to German culture when it was perilous to do so. His second novel, *The Trespasser* (1912), a collaboration between Lawrence and the diary of a friend, Helen Corke, recounting her adultery with a married man, was originally entitled *The Saga of Siegmund,* and the shadow of Thomas Mann fell on it as surely as the shadow of Ibsen fell on early Joyce. Yet he also resisted Mann, that late disciple of Flaubert, who as an artist fed off the living man like a parasite.

It was to be Wagner *contra* Flaubert (Lawrence had very little time for Flaubert, who "stood away from life as from a leprosy"), or Nietzsche *versus* Bergson. He eloped to Germany with Frieda and wrote *Sons and Lovers* with the freedom he gained with her. He had grown up, says Pritchett, "in a community and indeed in a country where the biography of an imagination embarrasses and is despised." Here he was writing a book that would find a place alongside those unusual attempts by Butler, Gosse, and—supremely—the Joyce of *A Portrait,* a most un-English undertaking. Frieda helped in conversation, in person, to define the female figure in the novel, the protagonist's mother, Mrs. Morel. The themes of family and loss come alive through Frieda's own estrangements (she was forbidden access to her own children when she ran off with Lawrence). Malcolm Bradbury uses the expressionist term "I-drama" to describe this "tale of coming to being." Frieda had been through psychoanalysis, and though Lawrence had not read Freud, he came to know about him. Frieda is responsible for his radical sense of female characters, liberated from Bennett and Galsworthy.

In 1914 Frieda and Lawrence became husband and wife. He completed *The Rainbow,* which originally bore the Wagnerian title *The Wedding Ring* and included material that later went into *Women in Love.* The books were thus from the outset parts of a saga. In *The Rainbow* a forthright symbolic narrative runs parallel with the historical narrative. The debt to the prophetic language of the Authorized Version of the Bible, in cadence and imagery, is clear, but the language changes through the book, Bradbury remarks, "Genesis turning to Revelation." Forster saw Lawrence as among the prophetic novelists: "The novel through which bardic influence has passed often has a wrecked air, like a drawing-room after an earthquake or a children's party." To appreciate prophecy we must be humble readers (deactivating ironic reflexes), and we must be in earnest.

He wrote his study of Thomas Hardy, one of the writers who shaped his descriptive style and vision and whom he adopted as a kind of familiar, Lawrencing the old man who stopped writing novels after the scandal of *Jude the Obscure* two decades before but still wrote poems and watched the world; and he turns on Bennett, despising *Anna of the Five Towns:* it ought to kick out, it ought to be a tragedy and not a social comedy told from a privileged perspective, another bitter fruit off Flaubert's tree.

In 1915 he met Bloomsbury: Forster, Bertrand Russell, Lady Ottoline Morrell, and Lady Cynthia Asquith in particular. Some of them became lifelong correspondents, others played into the characters of his fiction. Hermione Roddice in *Women in Love* grew out of Lady Ottoline, and her unbuttoned romance with a stonemason called Tiger, employed to make bases for the statuary in her garden, provided the basis for the story of Lady Constance Chatterley. There were closer friends, too, John Middleton Murry and Katherine Mansfield, who were drawn upon in the same novel. Ursula is often identified with Frieda, Gudrun with Mansfield, and his friendship with Murry is vividly realized in the relations between Gerald and Birkin. Richard Aldington, writing as a Marxist, says that *Women in Love* shows Lawrence's satirical skills for the first time, but satire is more consistent and less cruel than his treatment of Hermione.

Lawrence lived in Hampstead and began to enjoy the writer's life. Then *The Rainbow* was prosecuted under the Obscene Publications Act, his publisher buckled, and the book was withdrawn. 1,011 copies were destroyed, 766 of them still in unbound form. The bonfire was built and kindled by critics who saw their aesthetic as inseparable from their moral duties. The *Sporting Times* was at the front with the flaming torch.

Why Lawrence in particular? He said what he meant, he explored common passions, and his accessibility made him dangerous. "The magic he performs is transmuting something that is utterly his own into something that is utterly our own," V. S. Pritchett says; his characters are the size we are, they are not looked down on or up to. He was the opposite of Wilde, a greater danger to the *res publica* because he was in earnest. It would have been surprising if, at that period, sensitive to his insubordination, he had not been censored. After the suppression of the book, disappointed by the response of his new friends, penniless, he withdraw to Cornwall and continued work on *Women in Love*. It is the great novel of "as if": that grammatical construction occurs dozens of times, refocusing sometimes to clarify, sometimes to blur the sense. He considered calling the book *Dies Irae* or *The Last Days*. World War I had put an end to respect for experiment in the arts. Between *The Rainbow* and *Women in Love* falls the shadow of the war itself. One novel belongs to the old world, one to aftermath. "In the winter of 1915–16," he wrote in *Kangaroo* seven years later, "the spirit of old London collapsed. The city, in some way, perished from being the heart of the world and became a vortex of broken passions, lusts, hopes, fears, and horrors." Cyril Connolly sees the war as a refining fire. "Lawrence, as the early lyricism of his pre-war books evaporated, became a master of the colloquial style." Saul Bellow with reverence quotes Lawrence: "The sympathetic heart is broken. We stink in each other's nostrils."

He drafted *Women in Love* in Cornwall at great speed in the spring and summer of 1916. It was his fifth novel; he rose like his fabled Phoenix from the ashes of the prosecution of *The Rainbow* and the anger, disillusion, and poverty that followed. Aldington calls the persecution Lawrence suffered the "official patronage of the greatest and most original English writer of the age." Fortunately *The Lost Girl* (1920), the book he had been working on, was left behind in Germany, and the manuscript could not be recovered. Into its absence flowed his greatest novel. He revised it in the autumn, and it weighed in at about 200,000 words. Then came the problem of finding a publisher for this "end-of-the-world" fiction. Better that it be published later, he said, than halfheartedly. He knew it was a book that would "laugh last," after acceptable voices had died away. His public hostility to war at a time of swaggering nationalism, and the echoes of *The Rainbow* affair, told against him. The book was published in November 1920 in an American limited edition, in 1921 in Britain. There was legal opposition, but Martin Secker, unlike his previous publisher, refused to bend and the book was never withdrawn.

In *Lady Chatterley's Lover* he registers the change the war wrought on England and on his imagination most vividly. The book opens with one of his most remarkable paragraphs. "Ours is essentially a tragic age, so we refuse to take it tragically. The cataclysm has happened, we are among the ruins, we start to build up new little habitats, to have new little hopes. It is rather hard work: there is now no smooth road into the future: but we go round, or scramble over the obstacles. We've got to live, no matter how many skies have fallen." And this is where Lady Constance Chatterley finds herself, uttering a truism that time has made true once more: "The war had brought the roof down over her head. And she had realized that one must live and learn." The triviality of what survived, and of the literature of that survival, repelled Lawrence. Clifford Chatterley is a writer, and his physical impotence colors his second-rate imagination. A doting Mrs. Bolton looks after Clifford and talks to him endlessly. Her gossip "was Mrs. Gaskell and George Eliot and Miss Mitford all rolled in one, with a great deal more, that these women left out." She knew so much, she had "such a peculiar, flamey zest in all their affairs," but it was "just a *trifle* humiliating to listen to her." Clifford was not only being entertained but "listening for 'material.'" And Connie finds that "his so-called genius" is no more than "a perspicuous talent for personal gossip, clever and apparently detached." And here emerges Lawrence's higher morality, invested in the reflections of his protagonist.

> After all, one may hear the most private affairs of other people, but only in a spirit of respect for the struggling, battered thing which any human soul is, and in a spirit of fine, discriminative sympathy. For even satire is a form of sympathy. It is the way our sympathy flows and recoils that really determines our lives. And here lies the vast importance of the novel, properly handled. It can inform and lead into new places the flow of our sympathetic consciousness, and it can lead our sympathy away in recoil from things gone dead. Therefore, the novel, properly handled, can reveal the most secret places of life: for it is in the *passional* secret places of life, above all, that the tide of sensitive awareness needs to ebb and flow, cleansing and freshening.
>
> But the novel, like gossip, can also excite spurious sympathies and recoils, mechanical and deadening to the psyche. The novel can glorify the most corrupt feelings, so long as they are *conventionally* "pure." Then the novel, like gossip, becomes at last vicious, and, like gossip, all the more vicious because it is always ostensibly on the side of the angels . . .
>
> For this reason, the gossip was humiliating. And for the same reason, most novels, especially popular ones, are humiliating too. The public responds now only to an appeal to its vices.

Lawrence is not nostalgic. He and his protagonists live in the present and invite, and would have us invite, the future.

In Cornwall in 1916 the Lawrences were suspected of being German spies. They left England. He felt persecuted because he *was* persecuted. Together Frieda and Bert, the ill-assorted couple, a scrawny, gingery, consumptive collier's son and a substantial, emphatic German lady, traveled, sustaining one another in retreat from critical and moral opprobrium at home, from poverty, and in flight from death. Had their complex love not been deep-rooted, Lawrence would not have survived. After the war they continued traveling. England was never home for them again. Lawrence wrote travel books, essays, introductions, novels, and poems; he painted. Wyndham Lewis called him "an incompetent Gauguin," a just verdict, but his bold incompetence has a strong erotic charge: the bodies in his paintings are as human as his fictional characters; they emerge from their narratives with an attempt at fullness. He does not caricature. (We are put in mind of Maugham's Charles Strickland.) Exhibited in London, they were duly banned by the police, the pictures confiscated, providing Lawrence with his final direct experience of English morality in action.

Much of his prose occurs in essays written at white heat; the ideas retain a sense of occasion and the provisionality one experiences in reading Nietzsche. One idea releases in the reader a cascade of subsidiary ideas. These detonations of sense are the product of sharp, partial insights that dazzle one area of a work at the expense of others. His *Studies in Classic American Literature* retains its freshness, its alarm. It increases in potency with the years. It looked less unconventional in an age when Wyndham Lewis was a co-conspirator and sparring partner. Lewis and Lawrence were less unlike than they seem, the one more visceral, the other more intellectual. But Lewis had no patience with Lawrence the sentimentalist of, for example, *Mornings in Mexico* (1927). John Fowles, on the other hand, is drawn to the later Lawrence, the one who as a philosopher risks the big aesthetic gestures and errors.

He completed his least successful book, *The Plumed Serpent,* in Oaxaca, Mexico, in February 1925. Its original title was to be *Quetzalcoatl* and the intention was to bring the philosophy and fiction back together, to prevent the "split" he knew imperiled his art. After writing it he nearly died of malaria and dysentery; his tuberculosis was confirmed, and in order to reenter the United States he had to rouge his cheeks so immigration would not suspect his condition. It was only with *Lady Chatterley's Lover,* his late great novel, that he very nearly succeeded in repairing the "split."

Yet his essays have encouraged profound adjustments in later writers, heightening their sense of presence and presentness, of how the language of imagination needs to be *enactive,* expressing its subject in the complex mimesis of syntax, rhythm, and diction. When he traveled to France, Germany, Italy, Australia, New Zealand, the South Seas, California, Mexico, and New Mexico, he came not as a tourist with a verbal camera but as himself, an active intelligence, tubercular, keen to apprehend a culture. His reaction to landscape and custom, in Australia, in Mexico, is extreme and illuminating. Living in new places enlivened him; he would never be at home again. This was the exile of a major wholly English modernist, working-class, largely self-educated, frank, sexual and spiritual without irony, serious, playful but never playing. He spent his final years in Europe, trying to retard what he refused to acknowledge as tuberculosis. In 1930 he died in a sanatorium in Vence, in the south of France, and was buried. In 1935 the body was exhumed and transported to Taos, New Mexico.

———•———

John Cowper Powys (1872–1963) dedicated his first novel, *Wood and Stone* (1915), to Thomas Hardy. "Where Mr. Hardy is so incomparably greater than Meredith and all his modern followers," said Powys, "is that in these Wessex novels there is none of that intolerable 'ethical discussion' which obscures 'the old essential candors' of the human situation." He is himself addicted to "ethical discussion," and unlike Hardy he has not the habit of irony. Hence his poems, which preceded his novel writing, were already excessively in Hardy's debt, and the huge books for which he is remembered he grouped together as Wessex novels: *Wolf Solent* (1929), published when he was fifty-seven, *A Glastonbury Romance* (1932), *Weymouth Sands* (1934), and *Maiden Castle* (1936). He moved to Wales and lived on, reaching the great age of ninety-one. He wrote two substantial Welsh novels, having, at the behest of his admirer the largely neglected novelist James Hanley (1897–1985), moved to and fallen in love with the country that provided his surname and his imagination's sentimental subsoil.

P. J. Kavanagh compares *A Glastonbury Romance* to *South Riding* (1936) by Winifred Holtby (1898–1935), Vera Brittain's early companion and author of one of the first studies of Virginia Woolf. The large provincial canvas and the multiple points of focus on a community half in hock to the past, half groping toward a future, is a subgenre indebted to Bennett, to the Russian novelists, and to the vexed aesthetics of socialism. Kavanagh also likens Powys's book to *The Good Companions* (1929) by J. B. Priestley (1894–1984), a Yorkshire novel that attempts orthographically to differentiate varieties of local speech. Priestley admired Powys, and Angus Wilson set him beside James and Lawrence (an awkward pairing).

His most vehement advocate was Henry Miller, whose attentions may have done as much harm as good. "John Cowper Powys, of course, had the most tremendous influence on me; but then I never knew him, never cultivated him. I didn't dare! I was a midget and he was a giant, you see. He was my god, my mentor, my idol." Miller was in his twenties when in 1916 he paid a dime to hear Powys lecture on the Russian novelists at the Cooper Union in New York City. It changed his life. When he went to meet Powys thirty years later, the old writer said he knew and admired his work. C. H. Sisson called Powys a "pornographer" when his popularity swelled in the 1970s. Miller was a more opencast pornographer; his master is skilled at innuendo and elaborate foreplay but shy of climax. *Three Fantasies* (1985) entails some callisthenic sex among angelic creatures that puts us in mind of Milton's interpenetrating angels and, equally, of the antics of William Burroughs's oversexed *Wild Boys*. Powys's brother Theodore told a friend that in *Wolf Solent* "he thought John kept teasing his characters, not like 'an honest Sadist,' but lecherously." There is something atavistic, heady, and fetid in the Wessex air, something we associate neither with Hardy nor with Lawrence, neither with Joseph of Arimathea nor with Arthur in Avalon.

John Cowper Powys was born in Shirley, Derbyshire, the eldest of the ten surviving children of a well-to-do clergyman. It was a writerly family and his siblings include three other significant writers, Theodore Francis (1875–1953), to whom he remained closest, Llewellyn (1884–1939), and (Catharine Edith) Philippa (1886–1963). When John was eight the family removed to a village near Glastonbury, Somerset, and this was to inform the world of his fiction. He attended Sherborne School and Corpus Christi College, Cambridge, graduating in 1894. He made an unsuccessful marriage and supported his wife and child largely from a distance, lecturing on cultural and philosophical subjects up and down the United States for three decades. He settled at last with Phyllis Playter, who became the companion of his long declining years, and who was with him when he stopped lecturing to write *A Glastonbury Romance* in Hillside, near Philmont, in the remote corner of New York State where Theodore Dreiser sought him out.

Theodore Powys in 1927 published *Mr. Weston's Good Wine*. Its critical and commercial success may have galvanized John to pause his hectic lecture schedule and concentrate on writing. Theodore took his title from a line in *Emma*: "She believed he had been drinking too much of Mr. Weston's good wine, and felt sure that he would want to be talking nonsense." (Sylvia Townsend Warner, to whom credit must be given for teasing Theodore out of reclusion, remarked that he talked like Mr. Woodhouse in Jane Austen's novel.) Mr. Weston and his helper, Michael, arrive in the village of Folly Down to sell their wines, white (of love) and dark red (of death). The village is allegory, the inhabitants good souls, bad souls, and those somewhere between who need redeeming. The book is full of argument, digression, fancy, the style whimsical, the action contrived and cruel in the ways that allegory and fairy tale can be. Mr. Weston provides choices, and what people choose determines their fates. There is disparity between a style that is brittle and trivializing and themes that are schematic but universal: Good and Evil.

When a friend suggested to Lawrence that this book was better than Hardy, Lawrence described Theodore's novel as "a wooden Noah's-Ark world, all Noah's Ark." One thing that contributes to its woodenness is the attempt at dialect. When Mr. Gunter digs up Ada's grave in a cloddy, literalized Gothic, he addresses the corpse. "'Ada,' he said, stepping to the coffin again, ''tain't I that have moulded 'ee, 'tain't I that have rotted thee's merry ways wi' wormy clay. I bain't to be talked of no more.'" Elsewhere, speaking for himself and his siblings, Theodore declared, "We have a love for the individual, but a dislike of humanity." In his *Soliloquies of a Hermit* (1918), a puzzling combination of literary and theological argument, Theodore is his clergyman father's son in terms of rhetoric and theme, but the modern reader is drawn to his paradoxes and subversions. "Though not of the Church, I am of the Church. Though not of the faith, I am of the faith. Though not of the fold, I am of the fold; a priest in the cloud of God, beside the Altar of Stone." He concludes: "I am without a belief;—a belief is too easy a road to God." Dogma does not lead to God, or even point in a divine direction. Yet the individual like a compass needle wavers and points and wants to know why.

When John compared Flaubert's prose to a "great cracked bassoon," he was, like Lawrence, hostile to the *self*-effacement entailed in Flaubert's technique. He loves Balzac but expresses this love more in response to the headlong life than to the novels: "*The idea of his undertaking*. Just the torrent of his energy, just its tide and every detail of that coffee drinking." The teller, not the tale, engages him. In his diary in 1934 he writes: "I read *One of Our Conquerors* and was struck by how the jeering mental fanciful word-mongering style of Meredith has a certain resemblance to Joyce. But the writing was not obscure to me." (Joyce's could be.) He disliked Meredith's soul, his nature: "I don't like his kind of mind." Judgment of the artist entails the art.

Powys wrote *A Glastonbury Romance* with a map beside him so he could localize the characters, the flora, and fauna in an "objective" topography. He had Joyce's approach in mind, but unlike Joyce's Dublin, where an imaginative necessity compelled the accuracy to space and time, a day and the minutes of that day being the evolving occasion of the book, the constraints Powys imposes have not that imaginative necessity. In *Suspended Judgments* (1916), written for American readers who liked his baggy lectures, he used the word *genius* more than 200 times, applying it to a score of writers to mean very different things, until it has less meaning than a gesture.

In reading Rabelais with the great abstracting eye of his essays he suddenly declares, "From the noble pleasures of meat and drink and sex, thus generously treated; we must turn to another aspect of Rabelais' work—his predilection for excrement." He begins to use the big voice of the sermonizer. "This also, though few would admit it, is a symbolic secret. This also is a path of initiation. In this peculiarity Rabelais is completely alone among the writers of the earth. Others have, for various reasons, dabbled in this sort of thing—but none have ever piled it up—manure-heap upon manure-heap, until the animal refuse of the whole earth seems to reek to the stars! There is not the slightest reason to regret this thing or to expurgate it. Rabelais is not Rabelais, just as life is not life, without it." G. Wilson Knight in his essay "Lawrence, Joyce and Powys" (1951) suggested a link between anal eroticism and mystical ecstasy. Fecal matter becomes a transcendent issue. Another explanation is possible. When selecting from his diaries, the editor must decide whether to retain the daily record of bowel movements, often worryingly irregular, of interest to him in mapping the progress and regress of his ulcers. Does the editor spare the reader at least some of the anxiety of effluence, which he shares with the Earl of Rochester and, differently, with Joyce?

Powys loved Joyce's writing. He defended his work in the United States when controversy broke around *Ulysses*. The chapter order of *Ulysses,* its answerability to Homer, he found too schematic, but *Finnegans Wake* was a continual resource, and he regarded it as he did *Don Quixote* and *Gargantua and Pantagruel* less as a book, more as an element to immerse himself in intellectually and imaginatively. The thoughts of the corpse in its coffin at the beginning of *A Glastonbury Romance* owe much to *Finnegans Wake*. Despite his love of Joyce, the "rules of art" he promulgated in *The Complex Vision* are romantic, willful, and retrograde except in their inclusion of the needs of the physical body in the experience of art.

> A thing to be beautiful must form an organic totality, even though in some other sense it is only a portion of a larger totality.
>
> It must carry with it the impression, illusive or otherwise, that it is the outward form or shape of a living personal soul.
>
> It must satisfy, at least by symbolic association, the physical desires of the body.
>
> It must obey certain hidden laws of rhythm, proportion, balance, and harmony, both with regard to color and form, and with regard to magical suggestiveness.
>
> It must answer, in some degree, the craving of the human mind for some symbolic expression of the fatality of human experience.

And so on. In *Wolf Solent* we are from near the outset in a world no longer literal but layered with history, legend, myth. "This 'sinking into his soul'—this sensation which he called 'mythology'—consisted of a certain summoning up, to the surface of the mind, of a subconscious magnetic power which from those very early Weymouth days, as he watched the glitter of sun and moon upon the waters from that bow-window, had seemed prepared to answer such a summons."

Capitalism, collectivism of various kinds, and atavism all lay claim to Powys's settings, their legendary, historical, and natural resources. They are microcosms of ideological, spiritual, and psychosexual struggles. Rather too much character and incident, not to mention politics conceived on an abstract basis, are packed into the tight fictional chronology. One reader, owner of the Wookey Hole caverns, thought he recognized himself in the character of Philip Crow and sued for libel. Damages were awarded against author and publisher, and the financial and psychological effects on Powys were serious. He was forced to make changes to *Weymouth Sands,* to remove the literal world. In Britain it was to be entitled *Jobber Skald;* when it appeared, all references to Weymouth were removed.

Beside this physiological mysticism, the skeptical, ironic, and politically radical imagination of Sylvia Townsend Warner (1893–1978) works on a more manageable scale, though her world too is largely rural and parochial and much of it is untouched by the twentieth century, despite her engagement in its politics. She was a musicologist, one of the editors of the ten-volume *Tudor Church Music* (1923–1929), work on which took her down the railway line from Harrow, where her father was a master at Harrow School, the few miles to London, where she came to know the writers and artists of the day and experienced the fringes of Bloomsbury. T. F. Powys introduced her to Dorset, where she met her life companion, Valentine Ackland. She began as a poet but turned her attention to stories (she was a regular contributor to the *New Yorker*) and novels.

Charles Prentice, her editor at Chatto and Windus, in 1926 accepted the novel *Lolly Willowes,* which, like *Mr. Weston's Good Wine* of the following year, became promptly a lasting success in Britain and America. *Mr. Fortune's Maggot* (1927) and *The True Heart* (1929) followed. Warner's sense of "time" and "timing" in and between books was not limited to her musical studies or her verse, and her interest in narrative form makes her, if not experimental, at least innovative, in the way that her friend David Garnett could be, in generic impurity (allegory, parable, and symbolism having sporadic work to do) and variety of register. As with T. F. Powys there is the peril of preciosity. A passage from *The Corner That Held Them* (1948), describing a medieval scene in which the bishop lies on his deathbed, illustrates a rather too charming inventiveness: "The crowd wept and swayed, telling each other how even now, at death's door, he would not lie in a bed but lay on the ground with nothing but straw beneath him. None was more fervent than the harlots whom he had cast out of the city, and who now came in a procession, combed and clean and wearing their best clothes, to pray for the man who had taken them seriously. Walking among these crowds Henry Yellowlees felt himself someone apart, a ghost perhaps, or more truly a figure in geometry, a stalking displeased triangle among these swelling curves of emotion." In an introduction to a book of her stories T. F. Powys said, "Her witty writings are formed of good things, being in their natures like a piece of patchwork, sewn together in 1746, a tall pair of candlesticks, a fire of driftwood, a bottle of old wine, a needle and thread—And a red slipper."

A more obvious, outspoken heir of Lawrence was Henry Miller (1891–1980). He and the beautiful, arrogant Anaïs Nin (née Angela Anaïs Juana Antolina Rosa

Edelmira Nin y Culmell, 1903–1977) established in Paris an undisciplined, irregular nexus that included French, American, and British writers, with several of whom—Antonin Artaud, Edmund Wilson, James Agee, and Gore Vidal among them—Nin had dalliances. "We must flow deeply from the core of our inner being," Vidal has the character Marietta, loosely based on Nin, declare in *Two Sisters*. She recognized herself, though she claimed not to have read the book. This is how it was with the group: they provided one another's subject matter. Nin's famous *Diaries,* Miller's novels, key elements in Lawrence Durrell's, Wilson's, and Vidal's fiction complement the lives they led and the people they knew in ways less transmuted, less *fictionalized,* than in the work of earlier fiction writers. It is hard to read them, as it is Dos Passos and Hemingway, whose success Miller resented, without bringing to the reading a literal curiosity. It is a clef à roman rather than the other way around, as also and more "cleverly" is the fiction of Christopher Isherwood and his kind.

Nin was coyly arresting, unrestrained, prosperously and tolerantly married. She patronized writers and artists while becoming a writer herself, conducting a life of passion and culture, and keeping the journals that, more than her fiction, make her famous. She and her husband bankrolled Miller for almost a decade, paying his rent at the famous address 18, villa Seurat, and arranging to underwrite the first edition of *Tropic of Cancer.* And Miller painted, too, watercolors that are bold in a childish way and ugly, without the sudden focus of Lawrence's oils. But he was proud of them, and many more of his than Lawrence's survive.

Nin was influenced by each of her lovers but especially by Miller. D. H. Lawrence was a subject they shared: "How I have racked my brain over him!" Miller wrote to a friend in 1933; he had plumbed him more deeply than anyone before, "and why should I not, since there is so much in common between us, even to the obscurity." His brain-racking was shared with Nin, whose first published book, *D. H. Lawrence: An Unprofessional Study* (1932), swam against the current of fashion in two respects. Lawrence's reputation was in posthumous decline, and on the whole women writers gave him a wide berth. His courage drew her equally to his work and his person.

Miller missed no opportunity to pay his respects to that other crucial polestar "Cowper Pow Wow," as he calls John Cowper Powys. First the voice of the lectures and essays, with their Emersonian afflatus, struck him, and later the novels. Orwell said Miller "had put the spoken language back into literature and gotten rid of the language of protocol." "True enough, up to a point," Saul Bellow remarked in a letter to John Cheever, "but Henry poured his peculiar cafeteria fruit salad—his 'philosophy' and his 'poetry'—over everything." This we owe to the public Powys.

To Durrell, Miller said, "I am writing exactly what I want to write and the way I want to do it. Perhaps it's twaddle, perhaps not." He was attempting "to reproduce in words a block of my life," a block that appeared significant to him. Vidal sees in this declaration the impact of Miller on Orwell, Nin, Durrell, and others. He also notes Miller's, and by extension the others', extreme political naivety in the 1930s. "Five minutes with Hitler and I could have solved the whole damned problem," Miller proclaims with a species of Wilhelm Reichian hubris: "They don't know how to deal with the guy. He's temperamental—and terribly earnest. Somebody has to make him laugh, or we're all lost." From his early years he was a devotee of the neo-romantic fiction of Norwegian Nobel Prize winner and Germanophile Knut Hamsun (1859–1952), described by Isaac Bashevis Singer in an introduction to Hamsun's great novel *Hunger* as "the father of the modern school of literature in his every aspect—his subjectiveness, his fragmentariness, his use of flashbacks, his lyricism." Hamsun too wanted to talk to Hitler, and sent his Nobel Prize medal as a gift to Joseph Goebbels, the Nazi propaganda minister. Miller read Spengler's *Decline of the West* hungrily.

Miller's sentimentalizing optimism, the belief in himself as tonic and healer, are less out of Whitman (as he would have us believe), more a toxic residue of the intellectual solipsisms that made the 1930s such a "low dishonest decade," as Auden called it. Being a writer was as much a public performance as a private discipline. "I got myself married overnight, to demonstrate to all and sundry that I didn't give a fuck one way or another." What can seem playful about Miller, the entertainment of his big speaking voice, takes on quite another aspect when restored to its historical moment. In her diaries Nin is high-handed with her lover, but not unjust: "He is an intellectual." How harsh the word sounds when a woman speaks it of her lover! "He seeks simplicity and then begins to distort it, to invent monsters, pain, etc. It is all false, false, false." Miller's repellent machismo undermines a modern reader's trust in him.

In 1922 he wrote his first novel, a modernist mess that was rejected and left Miller depressed, but he rose from his ashes declaring, "I knew at least what it was to fail." The books that retain their interest are his accounts of the difficult early years, *Black Spring* (1936) and *The Rosy Crucifixion* (consisting of *Sexus, Plexus,* and *Nexus,* 1949–1960), and *The Colossus of Maroussi* (1941), whose critical and commercial success in Britain diminished his Anglophobia. The accounts of the Paris years upon which his notoriety is still based, *Tropic of Cancer* (1934) in particular, described by Ezra Pound as "a dirty book worth reading," still is both those things.

Miller's father was a genial alcoholic tailor, his mother bitter and repressed, his sister feebleminded. He grew up streetwise in Brooklyn and later thought he might become a "Brooklyn Proust." He was not seriously poor, but he was rebellious and this entailed both self-denial and indulgence. It was when he decided to become a writer—giving up his safe, tedious job at Western Union, having left his second wife, who had supported him devotedly during his late apprenticeship, to live permanently in Paris—that he sometimes, by his own account, was reduced to begging in the street. Orwell admired this willed penury and what it taught Miller about the other half—rather more than half at the time. For Orwell such writing, out of experience rather than ideology or literature, possessed the value of witness.

In Paris in the 1930s Miller was one of the most audible and visible Americans. In 1932 he said of himself, "Written three books, none of which accepted thus far. Also about a hundred short stories, some of which appeared in various American magazines." With *Tropic of Cancer* he emerged from neglect to notoriety, no longer unpublished but banned. There followed some of the defining fiction of his time, evoking its mind and habits. His books, literal and realistic, cut to the libidinal and dramatic chase. The "I" is strong and indistinguishable from the author's self-image. "I am a patriot—of the 14th Ward, Brooklyn, where I was raised," *Black Spring* opens. "I was born in the street and raised in the street." Hence he was "free."

"What is not in the open street is false, derived, that is to say *literature*." Yet his work is deliberately literary, performative, its subtleties not in the nuances of style or relationship. This is the literal *picaro,* his narratives taking their place in the descriptive, satirical, comic tradition of *Lazarillo* if not of the great, civilizing *Don Quixote.* He is as didactic as Lawrence, but unlike Lawrence's characters who find themselves in relationship, Miller's sense of the whole man, the fulfilled man, issues in solipsism. His anarchic politics cannot accommodate the kinds of order that secure a functioning civil society. He is contemptuous of the very forces that underwrite his irresponsible freedom. Fellow travelers with him include William Saroyan, though he outgrew Miller's loud gesturing. Jack Kerouac loved the younger Saroyan and is, at a remove, a relation of Miller's. Saroyan, he says, got him "out of the nineteenth-century rut I was trying to study." Saroyan—and Hemingway. And Thomas Wolfe.

Orwell compares Miller to Nero "fiddling with his face towards the flames" of Rome, "completely negative, unconstructive, amoral," the Jonah inside Orwell's whale; "a passive accepter of evil," his is "the human voice among the bomb-explosions, a friendly American voice, 'innocent of public-spiritedness.'" In this it is possible to discern a root energy of the Beats and of the New Journalism and other groups and movements that dramatize and exaggerate the claims of the first person. William Gass says of "our time's greatest aggrandizer of Lust," that he "talks too much, compulsively, his memory is made of suspiciously precise lies, the overlarge anecdotal detail—yowl, stance, and quim size, garlic and onion, vestibule or stairway—like one of those guides at the Vatican."

Beside this bold, insistently American, seeming literalist, chance placed as *confrère,* as in those American war films where a Brit is introduced for wit and intrepid *sang froid,* Lawrence (George) Durrell (1912–1990). Except that Durrell was not quite British. He was born in India and lived in Britain only for his schooling; he was a "non-patrial" and considered himself, if anything, a citizen of the Mediterranean. From Corfu he published his first novel in 1934. It was then that he wrote a fan letter about *Tropic of Cancer* to Miller and their friendship began. He remained Miller's creature, and yet on the face of it he is artificial, baroque, exotic, and experimental. Of Durrell Nin was able to say, from the altitude of her wealth and her relationship with Miller, "He is unsure of himself, but we are sure of him," the generous condescension of a patroness. To believe and be believed in, for many in the *entre deux guerres,* was more necessary even than to be well reviewed or to sell. It was part of the discipline of the avant-garde that one's work was recognized and esteemed by the few individuals whose recognition one respected. Such recognition was a charm against the bad opinions of others. To be believed in by Stein, or Riding, or Nin (if their belief was solicited) was sustaining, sufficient.

In the late 1930s, when Miller was exhausted and needed a change, Durrell introduced him to Alexandria, to the Greek poet George Seferis and other writers and characters. They traveled, and from this experience Miller wrote the *Colossus* with its lush sense of living transitions. Durrell stayed on when war began, experiencing the "limbo" that Egypt became. He was employed as a press attaché by the British Embassy, starting in Cairo, then in Alexandria, where he met Eve (Yvette) Cohen, an Alexandrian Jewess, the prototype for the eponymous Justine and the second of his four wives.

In *The Alexandria Quartet,* consisting of *Justine* (1957), *Balthazar* (1958), *Mountolive* (1958), and *Clea* (1960), the reader experiences the same incidents from different perspectives, as in Robert Browning's long, mechanically executed verse novel *The Ring and the Book.* Durrell described the metaphysical and physical background of his tetralogy in the *Paris Review.* Freud, Einstein, and Eastern and Western philosophies were accomplices. It is a grand statement of intent. Readers are expected to involve themselves in construction and collation, like historians seeking less a single line of narrative than a completed texture. Time passes but can be revisited and reevaluated, and we can (as in the magic lakes of C. S. Lewis's Narnia) dive between disparate points of view, if not between worlds. The effortfully tragic affair of the rather needy narrator of the first book with Justine, a handsome, passionate, married Jewish woman, becomes, in the relative calm of *Clea,* where aesthetic and psychological conclusions are drawn in an aftermath, a *point de repère,* a key to the fulfillment and failure of their lives. Narrators change, and there is thematic variety, not least in Durrell's hostile take on the British administration and secret service. As the *Quartet* progresses, the linear narrative is "interleaved" with memory, reflection, and slabs of descriptive prose of the enriched kind for which Durrell's travel writing prepares us. He suggests that the first three novels are "space" and the fourth "time." Certainly the needle has jumped out of the groove and the music has progressed to a different key in *Clea.* The *Quartet* is a slow, cumulative experience in which, we are told, the protagonist is in fact Alexandria, that great emollient city in which every race and vice is at home. It is the kind of intellectual project Clifford Chatterley might have imagined. Burgess's verdict is generous: "It is the exoticism of the setting and the bizarreness of the events which impress the reader more than the somewhat pretentious theorizing about the structure."

*The Black Book* (1938), Durrell's third novel, earned Nin's and Miller's particular approval. Durrell wrote, not facetiously, that he had set out to produce "the NEW BIBLE." He sent his only manuscript copy to Miller with instructions to throw it out if he did not like it. Miller advised him in future to use carbon paper and not risk losing his work in the post. He and Nin typed it out again and arranged for its publication by Jack Kahane's Obelisk Press in Paris, publishers of *Tropic of Cancer,* of Richard Aldington's *Death of a Hero,* and of books by Nin, Connolly, Joyce, Frank Harris, James Hanley, and Norman Douglas (the immortal *Limericks*).

Richard Aldington (1892–1962) was another of Durrell's older intimates. In 1950 he published the controversial, "corrective" biography of Lawrence entitled *Portrait of a Genius but . . . ,* which like his biographies of Wellington, Sainte-Beuve, and T. E. Lawrence cut to the bone. Aldington was pathologically disappointed by what he perceived as his failure as a writer compared with those who had been his close contemporaries, among them T. S. Eliot, whom he helped edit the *Egoist* and whose cat he minded; Pound, with whom he fought the Imagist battles, and of whose poem "Hugh Selwyn Mauberley" he wrote to Durrell much later, "I spit on that particular effusion of a draft-dodging Yank"; and Lawrence, with whom he and his first wife, H.D. (Hilda Doolittle, the Imagist poet and novelist, author of arch, classicizing novels, continuations of her "Imagist" and associative poems by other means) had a close relationship. He had to endure Durrell's accruing success with the *Quartet* and other books. Of Aldington's numerous books, one makes singular claims on our attention. His first novel, *Death of a Hero* (1929), may not be "the best war novel of the epoch" (Durrell's claim that cemented their friendship), but it should not fall from view.

For reasons akin to Durrell's, Aldington did not want to live in England. He served in the First World War and suffered severely. Like many of the Great War books, *Death of a Hero* appeared a decade after the events that occasioned it. Its urgency has to do with a need for closure. Aldington started work on the book soon after the war but could not get a purchase on the story. Living in Provence, he returned to the early draft and began to reexperience in earnest. The tone is harsh, critical, cynical; his resignation is not that of defeat or despair; the final gesture, when the protagonist George Winterbourne is mown down by the German machine guns, is shocking but inevitable. From the moment he enlists, just as the war begins, his will surrenders.

The novel is divided into three "books." George is born into a family marked by disappointment, its failures those of a class snared in Victorian materialism and morality. He innocently accepts the rhetoric and values that veneer the actualities of social life. He reels sufficiently to reject his father's lifestyle and go to London in pursuit of an artistic career. In the second book, like Birkin in *Women in Love,* George is exposed to a variety of ideas and lifestyles, marries, and as his relationship unravels war is declared and he enlists, a convenient escape. He goes through training and is posted to France, fights, and finds on leave that he is entirely alienated from the London milieu. Back at the front, due to officer casualties, he is rapidly promoted. The title of the novel grows in irony with each paragraph, and the author, who can be as preachy as Lawrence, does not let us forget the fact. The novel ends with a poem—Aldington was a poet first and last—on the sameness of wars from Troy to 1918.

Durrell was a generous writer. Just as he encouraged and helped Miller, so with Aldington he tried to revive the literary artist in him. He endured peevishness and grumpiness. What mainly survive of Aldington are letters and the sense of him as one of the adjuncts of poetry and fiction, a comrade, a catalyst, a day laborer, but not the manager of his own estate. Durrell knew better. He watched with dismay as Aldington veered toward the Mosleyites, who seemed to admire him. Like Durrell himself he needed affirmation, and if he had to settle for zany ideologues, so be it. But he was in the end intelligent enough to keep, if not a safe distance, at least some distance from them. Ironically, his books, especially *Death of a Hero* with its indictment of a society and a war, appealed in the Soviet Union. Maxim Gorky was a big advocate, and Aldington was officially fêted in Moscow in 1962 on his seventieth birthday. His solidarity with common soldiers was proof of his bona fides, whatever games he played with the Blackshirts.

---

The giddy slide from Lawrence through the Powys brothers and Miller ends in William (Seward) Burroughs Jr. (1914–1997). His celebrated, notorious *Naked*

*Lunch* (1959) was originally published in Paris by the Olympia Press, which also brought out work by Miller, Beckett, and Durrell, and Nabokov's *Lolita,* and a range of pornographic literature in English and translation that was prosecuted when imported into Britain or the United States. It is one of the last books to have been subjected to an obscenity trial in the United States. This hero of 1960s counterculture is now legal and licensed. Even in his lifetime, once he was under control, he dressed in suit and tie and might have been confused with a bank clerk or an adding machine operative.

In her review of *Naked Lunch* Mary McCarthy stressed Burroughs's vaudeville humor. She also noted that his fear of female genitalia aligned him with Jonathan Swift, a gratuitous-seeming but on reflection illuminating juxtaposition. Mailer called the author a genius, better than the run-of-the-mill literary "homosexual villain." Bellow's contrary verdict is expressed in a letter: the novel "is shocking for a few pages and then becomes laughable because it's so mechanical. Grand Guignol. It doesn't have much human content." Deliberately, in a spirit of desecration, it responds to the "goody" qualities of America: "On one side the scrubbers and detergent-buyers, and on the other the dirty boys, equally anal." Martin Amis calls it "the world of spectral rhetoric, drug withdrawal, urban breakdown, rampant vandalism, and no women." In *The Wild Boys* (1971), "a whole generation arose that had never seen a woman's face nor heard a woman's voice."

J. G. Ballard found Burroughs life-changing. When he encountered *Naked Lunch,* "I read about four or five paragraphs and I quite involuntarily leapt from my chair and cheered out loud because I knew a great writer had appeared amidst us." He read all the Burroughs he could lay hands on. "I knew that this man was the most important writer in the English language to have appeared since the Second World War, and that's an opinion I haven't changed since." Ballard remained an advocate and became a friend. Beckett, on the other hand, accused him of turning writing into plumbing.

Burroughs is not a systematic experimental writer: he set out to disrupt the relationship between language and the world we are conditioned to see through it. In "The Future of the Novel" he described himself as a "cosmonaut of inner space," his mapping of psychic zones entailing a redrafting of the novel form itself, using techniques from painting and cinema. That redrafting was already well advanced; he has an exaggerated sense of his revolution. *Queer,* written around 1952 but not published until 1985, is a kind of proleptic key to the later novels, the mulch in which his later works germinate. It is not a good novel; portions of it were intended to be included in *Junkie* but were left out of the original edition. Jack Kerouac calculated that it should be published because it would appeal to homosexual East Coast critics. At this point in his writing life his style was not remote from the voice in which he wrote letters to close friends, the style that made Ginsberg encourage him to write fiction.

The unconsidered quality of his "spectral rhetoric" is audible in his later *obiter dicta* when he has adopted the role of prophet. "If anybody ought to go to the extermination chambers definitely scientists, yes I'm definitely antiscientist because I feel that science represents a conspiracy to impose as, the real and only universe, the Universe of scientists themselves." (*"If anybody ought to go to the extermination chambers?"*) He continues, "They're reality-addicts, they've got to have things so real so they can get their hands on it." Burroughs is not a reality addict. He wants to change perception.

In conversation with fellow-Beat writers Gregory Corso and Allen Ginsberg in 1961 he explained his "vision." "I feel that the change, the mutation in consciousness will occur spontaneously once certain pressures now in operation are removed." Those pressures are categorical and vague at the same time. "We" all know what he means; we are expected to nod in assent. "I feel that the principal instrument of monopoly and control that prevents expansion of consciousness is the word lines controlling thought feeling and apparent sensory impressions of the human host." He wanted to resist the tyranny of language itself, a steep challenge for a writer. "The forward step must be made in silence. We detach ourselves from word forms—this can be accomplished by substituting for words, letters, concepts, verbal concepts, other modes of expression; for example, color." There is film, noise, sound, fragmentation, cut-ups: "man must get away from verbal forms to attain the consciousness, that which is there to be perceived at hand." "Forward steps," he says, retaining a sense of progression that underpins and undermines his argument, "are made by giving up old armor because words are built into you—in the soft typewriter of the womb you do not realize the word-armor you carry; for example, when you read this page your eyes move irresistibly from left to right following the words that you have been accustomed to." So he disrupts, arbitrarily, and meaning comes from different combinations, language released from sequence and syntax. The discussion proceeds in continuous, dialogue form. If, he argues, the species is reluctant to change, well, it can be forced to do so.

Ballard understood this aspect of Burroughs, his awareness of how "language could be manipulated to mean absolutely the opposite of what it seems to mean." He aligns him momentarily with Orwell, but Burroughs's distrust of language went deeper than Orwell's. "He was always trying to go through the screen of language to find some sort of truth that lay on the other side. I think his whole cut-up approach was an attempt to cut through the apparent manifest content of language to what he hoped might be some sort of more truthful world." The paradox was that, to transcend language his medium remained, however fragmented, language. In *Naked Lunch,* for instance in the "Benway" chapter, he echoes other writers who turned language against itself, Kafka and Lewis Carroll for example.

What keeps Burroughs in print and talked about is the company he kept, the force of his rhetoric, and the accidental nightmarish life he led. The work and the life are inseparable because the one so directly feeds the other, its addictions, rages, and disconnections. If one takes away the life story or interrogates the rhetoric, the work deflates. His most famous book was assembled by his friends and then wrestled with and abandoned by its author. In 1992 with the industrial metal band Ministry he recorded "Quick Fix," an apocalyptic series of short cuts of human violence, from the Holocaust to nuclear weaponry, with ritual and social violence intercut, and scenes of blue, beautiful Earth rolling in space beside the Moon, its sterile sidekick. His voice is old, slow, angry, monitory, resigned, accompanied by a heavy, metallic rhythm. He was a provider of titles to pop culture, if not a purveyor of stronger substances. Among his offspring are The Heavy Metal Kids, The Insect Trust, The Soft Machine.

William Burroughs was born in St. Louis, Missouri, into the Burroughs adding-machine fortune. He was sent to Harvard, then lived on a monthly allowance from his parents in Chicago and New York. His circle began to form in 1943 when he met Allen Ginsberg, who was inspirited by his learning, energy, and acid reticence and the gap between where he came from and who he was. Burroughs was the group's elder and teacher, and not initially its writer, taking under his wing Jack Kerouac and others.

In the teeth of his privileged background he resolved on a life of transgression, defining himself by contrary actions, rather as the French novelist and playwright Jean Genet did, but without Genet's insistence on public theater and with the ability, when circumstances threatened to overwhelm him, to move on, because he had the means. His early, more or less conventional writings and collaborations did not find publishers. He stepped out of the frames of convention. There was something of the celluloid cowboy about him, or the Prohibition gangster in a would-be "community of outlaws." But it was hard to shock the bourgeoisie. His addictions, to morphine and other substances, were vices of the well-to-do. He and his partner, Joan Vollmer, also an addict, in pursuit of cheap drugs and an unpoliced existence, went south, had a child in Texas (the autobiographical novelist William S. Burroughs III, with a "real" life more dreadful and confused than any of his father's fictions, and dead at thirty-three), then gravitated to Mexico. He wrote to Kerouac, "Mexico is sinister and gloomy and chaotic with the special chaos of a dream." There, under pressure from his friends and of circumstance, he composed *Junkie: Confessions of an Unredeemed Drug Addict,* about his fourteen-year addiction, his first published book. It appeared in 1953 under the pseudonym William Lee. "The original edition had a number of disclaimers, a number of expurgations," Burroughs explained; "they expurgated all the four letter words, and so on. So we decided to bring out an unexpurgated edition—as it originally was written." The restored edition, which included passages about homosexuality, was published by Penguin Books in 1977. In less than a quarter of a century the radical underground had been assimilated and Burroughs was that awful thing, "literature," and a subject of academic study.

Ginsberg originally edited and agented the book and got *Junkie* published by Ace Books, a pulp publisher, after Burroughs killed his partner in a William Tell–style accident with an apple and a Star .380 automatic pistol in Mexico in 1951. "I would never have become a writer but for Joan's death, and to the realization of the extent to which this event has motivated and formulated my writing. I live with the constant threat of possession, and a constant need to escape from possession, from control." In a kind of miasmic new-speak her death becomes "this event" whose real subject is "I": it "manoeuvred me into a lifelong struggle in which I have had no choice except to write my way out." He jumped bail in Mexico and continued his odyssey in pursuit of drugs. After Latin America his destination was Tangiers, Morocco, where he settled in 1952 and got to know Paul Bowles a couple of years later. There drugs were plentiful and he was undisturbed by the authorities. And he wrote. "We must find out what words are and how they function. They become images when written down, but images of words repeated in the mind and not of the image of the thing itself." Language vanishes into itself. Ultimately we have the talking asshole, boys without character buggered without passion, toothed vaginas, all those different languages from the body's several mouths.

He wrote by hand. In 1957 Kerouac went to stay near him and typed out the chaos of manuscripts that became *Naked Lunch*. Burroughs saw the writing as an act of evacuation, "shitting out my educated Middlewest background once and for all," though it was not once and for all, just the first or second movement. Cathartic relief, like drug addiction, required increasingly extreme expression to produce the desired effect. Once Kerouac had typed and ordered the pages, Burroughs revised and re-revised until 1959 when it was published. He regarded it as a picaresque story told by William Lee, the pseudonymous author of *Junkie*. The writer-outlaw wrote from the drugged miasmas of the "outlaw" life he lived, his outlaw experience being intensely subjective. Viewed from the outside he feeds upon himself. All his books, he insisted, are in fact part of one book.

Some readers insist *Naked Lunch* is a deliberate artifact, fragments following, in planned discontinuity, the consciousness of an addict living from fix to fix. They contend that the theme is all sorts of addiction, here expressed in terms of drugs. Thus read it is political, satirical. Clearly it is political, but whether the artistry is intentional and intentionally his is another matter. In the face of so jagged a text and so friable a plot and time sequence, many approaches are plausible, none authoritative. The authority is the author, who becomes a celebrity, much sought out in Lawrence, Kansas, where he hunkered down, interviewed, photographed, and always mentioned with Kerouac and Ginsberg, a charmed triangle of institutionalized resistance.

As he grew older, Burroughs was unable to fight off his literary enthusiasms. *Place of Dead Roads* (1983), the second volume in his homosexual western trilogy that opens with *Cities of the Red Night* (1981) and ends with *The Western Lands* (1987), features Kim Carson, who shares an identity with Denton Welch, one of Burroughs's favorite writers. "I sort of kidnapped him to be my hero. And so much of it is written in the style of Denton Welch. It's table-tapping, my dear. He's writing beyond the grave and I should certainly dedicate the book to him." The book shores up fragments, not in the spirit of T. S. Eliot in *The Waste Land* but in a more tramplike, elegiac spirit, lines and phrases from poets including Rimbaud and Wordsworth and fellow novelists, including Conrad. Lord Jim was a hero, Gatsby another. Burroughs thought he understood their social and spiritual worlds. "Sometimes some lines of verse would light up a scene from his past, like a magic lantern," he says; we are briefly reminded of Proust.

It is almost an irrelevance to say that *Junkie* or *Naked Lunch* is not a *good* novel. For Burroughs and his admirers qualitative aesthetic judgments are reductive, though he feels their bearing on him later on. His formal and stylistic legacy is limited, whatever thematic impact he had. Hubert Selby Jr. (1928–2004) published *Last Exit to Brooklyn* (1964) five years after *Naked Lunch*. It was enabled by Burroughs, who cleared a space for its exploration of homosexual and drug themes, but Selby's book remains "real": in it a variety of characters new to fiction and a world never before so bluntly witnessed come alive and stay alive today. The book led to a celebrated obscenity trial in Britain in the 1960s. The frankness of its lived language and its serious purpose offended. The world of the novel comes alive to the degree that the author effaces himself. Set beside *Naked Lunch,* with which it shares a city and a period, the contrast in terms of narrative and moral seriousness could not be clearer. Burroughs's other beneficiaries include Bret Easton Ellis, Hunter S. Thompson, and Cormac McCarthy, though all three work on a scale and with a rigor beyond his.

In 1945 (Jean-Louis) Jack Kerouac (1922–1969) collaborated with Burroughs on the novel *And the Hippos Were Boiled in Their Tanks,* the title drawn from a news report of a fire at a zoo in which the hippos *were* boiled in their tanks. It sounds like a surreal moment from one of Burroughs's late novels, though it grew out of a murder in 1945 about which the writers-to-be knew but failed to report to the police and sent them both for spells in prison. *Hippos* was a kind of apprenticeship for them; Kerouac came to understand Burroughs's style and method so well that he could draw together the scattered, scrawled pages on the floor of Burroughs's lodgings in Tangiers and shape them into *Naked Lunch.* Kerouac chose the title: the book was even more of a collaboration, though accidentally, than their earlier deliberate attempt. It was the best thing Burroughs did, Kerouac said; "[he] hasn't given us anything that would interest our breaking hearts since he wrote like he did in *Naked Lunch.* Now all he does is that 'breakup' stuff; it's called . . . where you write a page of prose, you write another page of prose . . . then you fold it over and you cut it up and you put it together . . . and shit like that." By 1968 when Kerouac was interviewed by the poet Ted Berrigan for the *Paris Review,* the Beat thing was over.

Kerouac, in a religious spirit, used the word *Beat* to mean "beatific," though earlier it had meant less-transcendent things: exhausted, poor, beaten. Religious readings of *On the Road* (1957), *The Dharma Bums* (1958), and *Desolation Angels* (1965) exist, alleging that a spiritual inner world and an unbuttoned, self-indulgent outer world are poles of an intense dynamic. Kerouac drew his fellow Beats into Zen Buddhism. Then he fell out with the counterculture, reconverted in his later years to an actively devotional Roman Catholicism, and became in his brief middle age the kind of man his youth would have despised. He supported the Vietnam War and died of cirrhosis of the liver at the age of forty-seven. "I contradict myself?" asked Whitman, "Very well then, I contradict myself." Kerouac is a knot of contradictions. Like Burroughs he is read still as a writer because of the legend; his later years are forgiven or ignored, just as Burroughs's enthusiastic libertarianism is played down, his sympathy toward Scientology, his public opposition to gun control, his detailed knowledge of firearms, and much else.

Kerouac blamed Ginsberg for pushing the Beat thing too far. "Ginsberg got interested in left wing politics . . . Like Joyce, I say, as Joyce said to Ezra Pound in the 1920s, 'Don't bother me with politics, the only thing that interests me is style.'" But it was Kerouac who changed, grew impatient of "intellectuals," and found his way back to religion, alcohol, and America. Weary of being questioned about the past, he declared, "Oh the Beat generation was just a phrase I used in the 1951 written manuscript of *On the Road* to describe guys like [Dean] Moriarty [based on Neal Cassady] who run around the country in cars looking for odd jobs, girlfriends, kicks." The phrase found its way into the language of "West Coast Leftist groups and turned into a meaning like 'Beat mutiny' and 'Beat insurrection' and all that nonsense." He insists he was not part of that. "I was a football player, a scholarship college student, a merchant seaman, a railroad brakeman on road freights, a script synopsizer, a secretary." All of which was part of the truth. The puzzling whole is more interesting. The image of Kerouac watching Senator McCarthy's committee deliberations on television, smoking cannabis and cheering the prosecutor, is as unsettling as his committed, ideologically rooted support for the Vietnam War.

Kerouac was born in Lowell, Massachusetts, into a French-Canadian family. His elder brother Gerard died of rheumatic fever when he was nine and thereafter became an angel companion to his younger brother. Kerouac remembered his boyhood in *Visions of Gerard* (1963), a short, too-sweet novel. He claims not to have learned English until he was six and was hesitant in speech until his early maturity. He wrote poetry and fiction in his Quebec dialect (two unpublished novellas exist), and he began *On the Road* in French. He was a good athlete and earned himself sports scholarships, then dropped out of Columbia University after an injury and problems with his coach. He did indeed do the jobs he listed in his late interview, in which he erased the Beat phase. It began shortly after he dropped out: he became friends with the nascent poet Allen Ginsberg, the "cowboy" Neal Cassady (1926–1968, Dean Moriarty and Cody in Kerouac's novels), John Clellon Holmes (1926–1988, author of the first "Beat" novel, *Go* [1952]), the hustler and storyteller Herbert Huncke (1915–1996, Elmer Hassel in *On the Road* and a key figure in *Junkie,* and probably the first person to use the word *Beat* in the sense it was to acquire), and Burroughs. He wrote his first novel in 1942, but it was not published until 2010, and then in Slovak translation. He regarded it as "a crock" filled with standard fare, but he did not destroy the manuscript. He wrote two further early novels, which appeared posthumously, and then as John Kerouac he published *The Town and the City* (1950) and as Jack *On the Road*. *The Town and the City* had overdosed on Thomas Wolfe and is a thick read; *On the Road* picks up speed and clarity: a new picaresque has arrived. Joyce, he said, showed him the way: if so, it was a way of contraries, given the formal, stylistic, and semantic approaches of the two writers.

Lawrence Durrell made no bones about it: he disliked the Beats: "They are turning the novel into a skating rink; I am trying to make it a spiral staircase," he said. He lumped together Kerouac and J. D. Salinger as scions of a worthless generation of "self-pitying crybabies." Joyce Carol Oates resists the Burroughsian quality of Kerouac's "memoirist novels." He did not *compose* but instead would "plunge head-on into them, typing compulsively through the night fuelled by alcohol, Benzedrine, and mania to create what he called 'spontaneous prose.'" *On the Road* he composed on an enormously long roll of Chinese art paper, sheets taped together to the length of 120 feet, so that it would pass through his typewriter without the need to reload page by page, a material fact that affected the precipitate flow and sequence of the writing. "Went fast because the road is fast," he wrote to Cassady. It was a well-prepared spontaneity and allowed him to write without chapter or paragraph breaks. His second wife kept him awake with pea soup and coffee during the days and nights of straight composition. ("That's not writing, it's typing," Truman Capote said.) He adopted the same approach when writing *The Dharma Bums*.

*On the Road* was completed in 1951, but six years passed before a publisher brought it out. Its experimental intent, its uncritical approach to the world of drugs and to homosexuality, made it a dangerous proposition. The "anaesthetized fifties" said no.

Most of what he wrote was based on lived and remembered experience. Unlike Burroughs's fiction, his keeps its feet more often than not on the ground, whatever the mind is up to, whatever pills he has taken. Kerouac followed Burroughs into other media, film especially. The 1959 "slice of life" short film *Pull My Daisy* includes Kerouac and Ginsberg as themselves, and Kerouac's voice-overinterprets the characters' movements and speech. The film has an unrehearsed feel. Warhol, whose experiments in the medium began in the early 1960s, took this short work as a point of departure. It was Kerouac who famously said, "First thought, best thought."

Ginsberg encouraged Burroughs to write on the strength of his letters; for his part Kerouac was inspired by the letters of Neal Cassady, "all first person, fast, mad, confessional, completely serious, all detailed, with real names in his case, however (being letters). I remembered also Goethe's admonition, well Goethe's prophecy that the future literature of the West would be confessional in nature." Kerouac refers to a 40,000-word letter, "better'n anybody in America, or at least enough to make Melville, Twain, Dreiser, Wolfe, I dunno who, spin in their graves." That amazing letter was lost. "We also did so much fast talking between the two of us, on tape recorders, way back in 1952, and listened to them so much, we both got the secret of LINGO in telling a tale and figured that was the only way to express the speed and tension and ecstatic tomfoolery of the age." Malcolm Cowley was his first editor and "corrected" his punctuation, syntax, and grammar in *On the Road* and *The Dharma Bums*. After that Kerouac did not allow editing and his books appeared with his fingerprints all over them.

Kerouac's main legacy is empowerment. His rapid style includes in its flow original and clichéd material and runs the gamut from the colloquial through to the excesses of Thomas Wolfe, a kind of elder brother with whose spirit he remained committedly in touch. His dissenting Americanness kept its appeal. To him and to Burroughs, whose work he did so much to shape, New Journalism and other movements and individuals owe their sense of space and language and new transgressive thematic freedoms.

*On the Road* is taught in schools, a consequence of which is that when people are asked to choose their favorite novels, it inevitably features, recently at number

55, just behind *Catcher in the Rye*. The attraction of the book is part nostalgic, part biographical and political; and part must be the quality of the fluent writing, redolent of Whitman and Wolfe, the sense it gives of being "true" in ways that novels generally are not: true to its particular occasions, to an uncensored world of literal contingencies, to a present tense that stays in the present. The book appears to grow out of the very substance of the time in which it was lived and written. Younger readers respond to the romance of its composition and to its durable dissent. It is a book that does not bear rereading, in part because it is not written to be reread. Nor is it quite so spontaneous as it seems: Kerouac edited and reedited even before Malcolm Cowley got hold of it and spattered it with commas. Kerouac's editing was strategic, to lessen the chance of libel; aesthetic, to remove elements that were distortingly personal and painful; and moral, especially as related to the homosexual subject matter, which he toned down.

It is possible, as the impact of the first reading, usually in adolescence, wears off, to wonder whether the book is not a good deal more literary than it wants to seem. Haunting Kerouac's highly, if erratically, cultured mind, ghosting Dean Moriarty and Sal Paradiso (as with their monstrous cousins Raoul Duke and Dr. Gonzo in *Fear and Loathing in Las Vegas*), do the examples of those first subjects of the road novel Don Quixote and Sancho Panza not hover? What is the road novel if not a four-wheel, internally combusted picaresque? There is, too, an additional ingredient: substance abuse, with its parallel acceleration. "Man, I've had a good time!" Kerouac exclaimed. "God, man, I rode around this country free as a bee."

*On the Road* ends by the water, like *The Great Gatsby* with its distant light and all of American history banked against the disappointment. Kerouac may have had Fitzgerald's ending in mind when he wrote, "So in America when the sun goes down and I sit on the old broken-down river pier watching the long, long skies over New Jersey and sense all that raw land that rolls in one unbelievable huge bulge over to the West Coast, and all that road going, all the people dreaming in the immensity of it." It is a different America, one that expresses the broken-down aftermath of Gatsby's world of excess and disparity. Now space, not history, is what we inherit; Moriarty's father has not been and will never be traced. There is disconnection, longing, depth turned on its side.

# 33

# Truth to the Impression

Ford Madox Ford, Ernest Hemingway, Jean Rhys, Djuna Barnes,
John Updike, Don DeLillo, Joyce Carol Oates, Anne Tyler, Julian Barnes

In 1914 Richard Aldington was Ford Hermann Hueffer's fellow hack, preparing a government-commissioned propaganda book, and taking Ford's dictation of *The Good Soldier,* originally to be entitled *The Saddest Story* (1915). Aldington's wife at the time, the American Imagist poet and novelist H.D. (Hilda Doolittle), had given up the task, finding the novel harrowing.

For Hueffer the act of writing involved other people. If he helped Conrad with his art and his English, it contributed to his own development—his sense that composition depends on speaking words aloud, getting their aural impact as pace, rhythm, the creation of suspense and resolution. Analogies with music are clear. An art that takes shape aloud shares characteristics with products of the oral and dramatic traditions. Dictated language must be immediately clear. In the transcriber's response (Conrad or Aldington would have responded) collaboration starts.

Katherine Anne Porter "never knew him when he was not writing a book." He was also editing literary magazines. Graham Greene notes that he also "found time to be the best literary editor England has ever had: what Masefield, Hudson, Conrad, even Hardy owed to the *English Review.*" John Gross called the *English Review* "as brilliant a literary magazine as there has ever been in this country." Ford's unspoken motto was, "Suggestions not dictates." The mission of the *English Review* was "to make the Englishman think," the title "a contradiction in terms."

Ford negotiated a transition from the *fin de siècle* taste of his boyhood environment to the disciplines of early modernism and then, as Greene puts it, after World War I "in the *Transatlantic Review* he bridged the great gap, publishing the early Hemingway, Cocteau, Stein, Pound, the music of Antheil, and the drawings of Braque," smoking those bent Gauloises that tasted and smelled of "dust and dung." It is less that he moved with the times than that he understood change and its consequences in art. Having lived the war, he knew the world was changed. Change is his hallmark. H. G. Wells says that he became "a great system of assumed personas and dramatized selves." First there are the literal selves: English and German resolving in English (had the war not intervened, he might have taken German nationality), outsider becoming insider, "who I am" trying to efface itself so truth might emerge rather than be told.

Ford Hermann Hueffer became Ford Madox Ford (1873–1939). As a young man he replaced "Hermann" with "Madox" to honor his grandfather the painter Ford Madox Brown. After the war, "Hueffer" sounded too Teutonic. The age had changed; he changed his surname to "Ford."

His German-born father, music critic for the *Times* and a correspondent for German and French papers, wrote about the Troubadours, was a close friend of the poet and scholar Frédéric Mistral, who championed the Occitanian language, and was a joint recipient of the Nobel Prize in Literature in 1904. Hueffer's house and that of Ford's maternal grandfather were frequented by artistic and intellectual luminaries, British and European, and Ford's memoirs are full of recollections of encounters with them. At the age of three he offers a chair to Turgenev; a little later his chair is taken from him by the Abbé Liszt. The boy was precocious, with a strain of self-ironizing snobbishness.

When his father died, Ford's mother removed to Ford Madox Brown's establishment in London. The boy was nephew by marriage of Christina and Dante Gabriel Rossetti, and the Pre-Raphaelite brotherhood, by then beyond their prime, had a formative impact on him, as Brown had had on them. At nineteen he published three books, the first a kind of fairy tale in the manner of Wilde. *The Queen Who Flew* (1894) included a sepia frontispiece by Edward Burne-Jones. He published a further book at twenty, and one at twenty-one. He was working on the—is it?—eightieth title (Gore Vidal refers to his "awful copiousness") of his life's work in 1939, when he died; to these eighty have been added letters and other *disiecta membra*. Ford's prose "lay so natural on the page that one didn't notice it," said Ezra Pound in an obituary. This quality he shared with some of the great writers he admired, notably Hudson. The sentence is more important than the word, the paragraph than the sentence, the page than the paragraph, and so on. His is essentially a forbearing style, subject to what it has to say, and marked by a *progression d'effet*: acceleration, every word carrying things forward. "You must therefore write as simply as you can—with the extreme of simplicity that is granted to you, and you must write of subjects that spring at your throat." He said of judging sentences with Conrad, "We thought just simply of the reader. Would this passage grip him? If not it must go."

In *Joseph Conrad: A Personal Remembrance* (1924), of which Mrs. Conrad made such a fuss, he remembers the publication of their 1903 collaboration *Romance* and "its *succès d'estime*"—or rather, "not much of that even, for the critics of our favored land do not believe in collaboration." Ford was by instinct a collaborative artist, sometimes across generations and cultures (Conrad was forty-one, he was twenty-four, when they met), sometimes across media. In collaborations one can never assign authorship of any part, even when manuscripts survive. Between collaborators there can be firmly shared views and values. He and Conrad, for example, "agreed that the novel was absolutely the only vehicle for the thought of our day. With the novel you can do anything: you can inquire into every department of life, you can explore every department of the world of thought." But there is one absolute interdiction: "The one thing that you cannot do is propagandize, as author, for any cause. You must not, as author, utter any views; above all, you must not fake any events. You must not, however humanitarian you may be, over-elaborate the fear felt by the coursed rabbit." Also: "It is obviously best if you can contrive to be without any views at all: your business with the world is rendering, not alteration."

While working with Conrad, Ford was developing his impressionistic manner in writing three book-length essays exploring one of the dominant themes of his fiction: Englishness. He has all the enthusiasm of a convert in *The Soul of London* (1905), *The Heart of the Country* (1906), and *The Spirit of the People* (1907), brought together in one volume as *England and the English* (2003). In the "Author's Advertisement" to the last volume he was able to define his manner: "It is all one whether the artist be right or wrong as to his facts; his business is to render rightly the appearance of things. It is all one whether he convince his reader or cause to arise a violent opposition." He affirmed, even when he misrepeated himself, changed facts, embroidered an anecdote, that he was exercising fidelity to impressions, achieved (paradoxically) by effacing the very self whose impressions they were. Readers cannot judge the truth of a statement: its authenticity is located in a suppressed subjectivity. Ford's argument is clever and sincere, and not untrue.

Had he not written his great novels, the early fiction might burn brighter than it does in their proximity. In *A Call* (1910), for example, the telling is richly inventive. The epistolary epilogue explains to us, and also to himself, the technique and theme he was developing. "There is in life nothing final. So that even 'affairs' never really have an end as far as the lives of the actors are concerned." His historical novels, in particular the Fifth Queen series (based on the life of Henry VIII's fifth queen, Catherine Howard), appeal to readers of historical fiction. C. H. Sisson is no more keen on the genre than Henry James was, but he admires Ford, here for "a tone and language which certainly owe something to a Pre-Raphaelite reading of Malory." Here also Ford is looking for Englishness and coming to understand the kinds of character he wanted to write about. Other substantial early fiction included *Ladies Whose Bright Eyes: A Romance* (1911) and *The Young Lovell* (1913); an early book about Henry James further clarified his thinking. He was writing his implausible memoirs, too, the first volume in 1911.

This was part of the long preparation for *The Good Soldier* (1915), where, Graham Greene notes, Ford found his true subject, the English "gentleman," the "black and merciless things" that "lie behind that facade." The nature and construction of that facade, and its raison d'être, fascinate him: "the ravages wrought by a passionate man who had all the virtues but continence." For nine years John Dowell and his wife have spent the summer season at a German spa town in the respectable company of the Ashburnhams. Behind the decorous manners, passions turn poisonous. When Dowell's world breaks apart, he recounts his story intimately, as to a silent, attentive interlocutor. He is the Marlow of a domestic Congo; or the speaker of *The Turn of the Screw*. "Who in this world knows anything of any other heart—or of his own?" The story is about, not lies, but the fact that nothing is what it seems. Vidal marks the debt to Flaubert and to James in this book that, Vidal says, Ford had called "his great Auk's egg; into this he put everything that he knew about the novel, whose art is entirely dependent on what is left out." That last phrase describes the economies of Kafka and Hemingway.

By the time *The Good Soldier* appeared, the world it described was over. The war had begun and Ford enlisted, becoming an officer in the Welch Regiment from 1915 to 1919. He was into his forties, one of the few mature writers to fight on the Western Front. His perspective was different from that of the poets and painters. He saw limited combat, but he was in the Battle of the Somme. Under continuous bombardment, it is not surprising that he suffered shell shock. Greene declares, "The first war had ruined him. He had volunteered, though he was over military age and was fighting a country he loved; his health was broken, and he came back to a new literary world which had carefully eliminated him." The war ruined him, and it made him, too: it gave him a subject through which all of his passionate concerns were focused and savagely rearranged.

*No Enemy* (1929) was largely written in 1919, between *The Good Soldier* and the first volume of his greatest composite work, *Parade's End*. He regarded it as "in effect my reminiscences of active service under a thinly disguised veil of fiction." It began in "English Country," a series of articles on his recurrent theme, as England emerged altered from the *agon* of the war. He added fictional elements: the narrator tries to set down the story of Gringoire, a poet who served at the front. The impact of war on the alert imagination is recorded, first the ways in which in moments of calm landscape reasserts itself in its altered essence. There follows an account of moments of closeness with common people, in which their humanity and heroism are celebrated. Those people are not only fellow combatants but the civilians whose homes are razed, whose lives are ploughed over. This is a book of transformation, in which the author of *The Good Soldier* starts to change into the author of *Parade's End*. It is hybrid, neither quite fiction nor quite essay.

*Parade's End* consists of four books: *Some Do Not . . .* (1924), *No More Parades* (1925), *A Man Could Stand Up* (1926), and *Last Post* (1928). He was provoked into starting what he called "my prolonged effort" after Proust's death in 1922. He had not read *À la recherche du temps perdu* as the volumes appeared in French, for fear of being derailed by a work he knew so much about from hearsay. The deferred project is Ford's most ambitious: it took him five years to complete, writing a decade after the five years of the war, almost as if replicating, in process, the real time of the books' occasions. Sisson says, "The grand plot of the sequence of novels is, from one point of view, to show what is stirring below and how, as 1914 moves to 1919, the whole of this superficies is carried away or rather, left along the shore as scattered sea-wrack." Beyond this transformation, or re-formation, not only of England but of Europe, "there is a personal plot too, related to certain changes in Ford's personal fortunes—reflected in the war scenes and in the long-drawn-out replacement of Tietjens's wife Sylvia"—Greene calls her "the most possessed evil character in the modern novel"—"by the trim, athletic and altogether un-Pre-Raphaelite Valentine." This is his *summa*. One of its chief themes is the power of the lie, how it changes those who tell the lie and those who are lied to, in love or in war.

He wrote significant novels after this (*The Rash Act,* 1933, in particular) but nothing to equal it in range or formal accomplishment. It is a culmination of the aesthetic he outlined in the Conrad book. Sisson says, "Inadequate dogmatisms— and most dogmatisms are inadequate—melt before him. There is this solvent property in the texture of his prose, and its strength is that it does not arise from any passion to destroy, or to win a cheap victory, but from an effort, admittedly fallible, to render what is. The result is always something provisional." His writing compels us to be *readers,* negotiating with the provisional, agreeing, disagreeing, never passive.

Graham Greene persisted in calling *Parade's End* a trilogy, on the grounds that Ford wrote the fourth volume as an afterthought, and under financial pressure (though he wrote all his later work under financial pressure). Greene's high-handedness was one bone Anthony Burgess had to pick with him. Burgess called it "the worst example I know of unjustified translation." Greene "doesn't think *The Last Post* works" and "he feels perhaps Ford would have agreed with him; and therefore he has taken the liberty of getting rid of the final book. I think Greene is wrong; I think that whatever Ford said, the work is a tetralogy, and the thing is severely maimed with the loss of his final book. An author is not to be trusted in his judgment of this sort of thing." And neither is an editor.

The novels, in Greene's words, tell "the terrifying story of a good man tortured, pursued, driven into revolt, and ruined as far as the world is concerned by the clever devices of a jealous and lying wife." That was for him the focal drama, and not the larger, historical transformations that underlay it. Ford wanted to see the book printed in one volume, comparable in scale to *War and Peace.* Christopher Tietjens is the last of his breed, the Johnsonian Tory gentleman. The war, a sincere and harrowing marriage, and other circumstances undo him; war provides no escape from his circumstances. McMaster stands opposite to Tietjens, a Scot, from a different class and culture, a friend and an increasingly absurd antithesis, a Sancho Panza who is knighted and inherits his tinsel kingdom.

*Some Do Not . . .* introduces Tietjens, his wife Sylvia and the young suffragette Valentine Wannop, a figure of the future drawn into the living past represented by Tietjens. Tietjens and Valentine are unexpectedly and perilously brought together. By the end of the novel—a slow, compelling course—the two are on the verge of becoming lovers and Tietjens is returning to the Front. It is 1917: the dangers for him are extreme, thus heightening the lovers' attachment. *No More Parades* takes up the story with Tietjens back at the Front. The contrast with the first book could not be bleaker; the proximity of death, the confusion, organizational failures, "muddles" and "follies" displace the tensions and the promise of love. Tietjens weakens and falls: Sylvia is betrayed. *A Man Could Stand Up* mirrors the old three-decker novel in its parts. In London Valentine hears the Armistice Day fireworks; in part two there is the violence of bombardment, Tietjens, an unlikely hero, bearing a wounded man through the mud and stench of no-man's-land; and then we come back to Armistice Day and its riotous excess, a kind of dance of death. *Last Post* is the story of one summer's day in which the characters advance out of the war into an altered present, detached from its past by five turbulent years whose memory haunts and distorts. His theme is England, this time a country that no longer knows itself, unraveling as Tietjens is.

"Mr. Ford is unable to write narrative," Greene declares; "he is conscious of his inability to write, as it were, along the line of time. How slipshod and perfunctory the joins between his dramatic scenes would seem if they were not put into the minds of the characters and their perfunctory nature 'naturalized.'" But Ford makes a virtue of necessity, especially in this novel where events rapidly move into the past. "The memory *is* perfunctory," says Greene; "you do not lose verisimilitude by such a bare record as this if you are looking back to events which have become history. The trouble with a novel which follows the chronological sequence is that your events are never history. You are condemned to write of a perpetual present and to convey the shrillness of its emotions." Ford

declared that "on the whole, the indirect, interrupted method of handling interviews is invaluable for giving a sense of the complexity, the tantalization, the
shimmering, the haze, that life is." This is that "impressionism" of which he
was accused and which he resisted.

David Garnett found the physical Ford, chinless, florid, lips "too mobile,"
quite repellent. Hemingway, his protégé in the years of the *Transatlantic Review,* makes him a preposterous monster in *A Moveable Feast:* "He was breathing
heavily through a heavy, stained moustache and holding himself as upright as
an ambulatory, well clothed, up-ended hogshead." He returns to the attack: "I
had always avoided looking at Ford when I could and I always held my breath
when I was near him in a closed room." It was more than the stale Gauloises
that trouble him. It was his saggy, lumbering self-importance, the tall tales he
expected one to believe, or to pretend to believe. It was at once his huge achievement as a writer and editor, and his sense of failure. Ezra Pound reassured
Hemingway that Ford "only lied when he was very tired, that he was really a
good writer and that he had been through very bad domestic troubles." This
did not help with the "heavy, wheezing, ignoble presence of Ford himself."

But Ernest (Miller) Hemingway (1899–1961) in retrospect projected onto
Ford his own sense of disappointment. For his part, Ford admired Hemingway
the man and writer. He watched the stories come to light. As raconteur, Ford
says, remembering 1920s Paris, "Hemingway spoke slowly, choosing his words
with care," then uttering them "gently but with great decision." This frugality
of speech is also a quality of his prose; there is space between the predominant
monosyllables, each word is given its proper weight. Truman Capote calls him
"a first rate paragrapher," the paragraphs generally short, self-contained, but
creating suspense that heralds the next paragraph, and the next. In *A Farewell to
Arms* (1929) he wrote of a hospital, "There were not enough stretchers. Some of
the wounded were noisy but most were quiet. The wind blew the leaves in the
bower over the door of the dressing station and the night was getting cold.
Stretcher-bearers came in all the time, put their stretchers down, unloaded them,
and went away." He explained how, in the circumstances and in relation to the
theme, "abstract words such as glory, honor, courage, or hallow were obscene
beside the concrete names of villages, the numbers of roads, the names of rivers,
the numbers of regiments and the dates."

His second wife had a terrible childbed, the occasion for *A Farewell to Arms.*
He revised the ending several times, writing the subjective out of it. The book
was more developed and formally ambitious than *The Sun Also Rises* (1926). Gore
Vidal grudgingly concedes that in *A Farewell* he "did a few good descriptions,
but his book too"—like Mailer's *The Naked and the Dead*—"is a work of ambition,
in which can be seen the beginning of the careful, artful, immaculate idiocy of

tone that since has marked both his prose and his legend." In another context he inquires, "What other culture could have produced Hemingway and not seen the joke?"

Edmund Wilson, a critical friend of Hemingway, noted how acute his "geographical and strategical vision" was, "what may be called his sense of terrain." The evocation of specific place and specific earth is crucial: from each emerges a different smell, a different spirit. And he knows what time it is, page by page. If a train is running late, he says so. The miracle of *A Farewell to Arms* is that it is sustained, after the short stories, for as Wilson argued, Hemingway's imagination is that of a lyrical writer; he founders when story and structure demand too much. According to Gertrude Stein, Hemingway said, "I turn my flame which is a small one down and down and then suddenly there is a big explosion. If there were nothing but explosions my work would be so exciting nobody could bear it."

A book he returned to as a touchstone was Frederic Manning's *Her Privates We,* about the First World War. He claimed to reread it every year "to remember how things really were so that I will never lie to myself nor to anyone else about them." The book was bowdlerized when first published; later editions restored the force (not contemporary in its virulence) of the vulgar tongue Manning makes the soldiers use: their own language not made polite for the consumer but real for the reader.

Some readers resist Hemingway's sparseness, the limited diction, the repetitions, the refusal of nuance and ambiguity, the avoidance of "literature." Wyndham Lewis dismissed it as "babytalk": no wonder Hemingway rounded on him maliciously in his memoirs. His own understanding of what he was doing is clear: "He thought that 'fine writing' falsified experience," David Lodge notes, "and strove to 'put down what really happened in action, what the actual things were which produced the emotion that you experienced' by using simple, denotative language purged of stylistic decoration." Ford knew how graceful this style, so remote from his own, could be, how it was proof against incursions of the merely subjective. Bellow satirized it: "Do you have emotions? Strangle them." It was not about strangulation, however; more a matter of keeping oneself out of it, giving the story its space and readers theirs. "Hemingway's words strike you, each one, as if they were pebbles fetched fresh from a brook. They live and shine, each in its place." Ford sensed how *contemporary* the style was. "It is indeed the supreme quality of the written art of the moment." The unemphatic endings did not issue in closure but let the stories continue in the head. There was no proscenium arch. Malcolm Cowley places Hemingway in the context of Poe, Hawthorne, and Melville, "the haunted and nocturnal writers."

The crucial tact came in revision. Hemingway recalls an early story he called "Out of Season": "I had omitted the real end of it which was that the old man hanged himself. This was omitted on my new theory that you could omit any-thing if you knew that you omitted and the omitted part would strengthen the story and make people feel something more than they understood." In a later story, "Hills Like White Elephants," he submerged not the ending but the occa-sion itself, to great effect. "Anything you can omit that you know you still have in the writing and its quality will show. When a writer omits things he does not know, they show like holes in his writing." This abstemious fullness character-izes the early fiction, which is, in William Golding's phrase, "excessive in every-thing but vocabulary." *The Old Man and the Sea* (1951), his last great book, might have been enormously long—he knew so much about the subject. He drafted quickly because, later in his writing career, he practiced economy at the point of creation itself, though he revised and revised it. "The luck was that I had a good man and a good boy and lately"—the interview took place in 1958—"writ-ers have forgotten there still are such things."

By then he had received the Nobel Prize in Literature (1954) and was too ill to travel to Stockholm. He had been absent too in 1930 when Sinclair Lewis conjured him up in his Nobel acceptance speech. At that time Hemingway had published stories, *The Sun Also Rises,* and *A Farewell to Arms.* He was in his early thirties, and Lewis listed the objections to including him in his roll call of American writers worth their weight in Europe. He was "not only too young but, far worse, uses language which should be unknown to gentlemen . . . he acknowledges drunkenness as one of man's eternal ways to happiness, and as-serts that a soldier may find love more significant than the hearty slaughter of men in battle." Lewis portrays him as a harbinger, "a bitter youth, educated by the most intense experience, disciplined by his own high standards, an authen-tic artist whose home is in the whole of life." In *The Green Hills of Africa* (1935) Hemingway repays this favor with gall. "Sinclair Lewis is nothing," he writes, and Hemingway's last wife was merciless about Lewis's ugliness. Meeting him in Venice, she fitted him with a violent metaphor: "His face was a piece of old liver, shot squarely with a #7 shot at twenty yards."

In Hemingway's own Nobel acceptance speech, spoken in Stockholm by the American ambassador and recorded by Hemingway in Cuba on a hissing ma-chine that provides a sense of remoteness and applause, he declares, "For a true writer each book should be a new beginning where he tries again for something that is beyond attainment. He should always try for something that has never been done or that others have tried and failed. Then sometimes, with great luck, he will succeed." He was aware his words would be spoken by a diplomat, and he did not want any cadences that could be ridden in the wrong direction. The speech is brief and unambiguous. "How simple the writing of literature would be if it were only necessary to write in another way what has been well written.

It is because we have had such great writers in the past that a writer is driven far out past where he can go, out to where no one can help him." It is hard not to think of the fisherman in his novel-parable about risk and endurance, *The Old Man and the Sea,* adventure in the manner of Crane and allegory in the manner of Bunyan. Harry Morgan puts it succinctly in *To Have and Have Not* (1937), Hemingway's most Conradesque novel: "A man alone ain't got no bloody fucking chance."

His people will speak *their* words, not his. "No matter how good a phrase or a simile he may have, if [a writer] puts it in where it is not absolutely necessary and irreplaceable, he is spoiling his work for egotism. Prose is architecture, not interior decoration, and the Baroque is over." A great writer should know everything. "If a writer of prose knows enough about what he is writing about he may omit things he knows and the reader, if the writer is writing truly enough, will have a feeling of those things as strongly as though the writer had stated them. The dignity of movement of an iceberg is due to only one-eighth of it being above water."

Hemingway remembers his beginnings, where the continuity between the world he wrote in and the settings he created was complete. "I was writing about up in Michigan and since it was a wild, cold, blowing day it was that sort of day in the story." At first "the story was writing itself and I was having a hard time keeping up with it." After a break, he went back and "entered far into the story and was lost in it. I was writing it now and it was not writing itself and I did not look up nor know anything about the time nor think where I was nor order any more rum St. James." That was the creative time he lived for, fully engaged in making. "Work could cure almost anything, I believed then, and I believe it now." After he concluded a session of composition, the first thing he did was to read something *else,* to turn off the tap of his own work in progress, so he could take it up again the next day. There was always a danger that one would write on in one's head and lose the next day's words. "I had learned already never to empty the well of my writing; but always to stop when there was still something there in the deep part of the well, and let it refill at night from the springs that fed it." The springs did fail, but not until he had written seven novels (four of them major), six books of stories, and nonfiction, as well as the journalism with which it all began. After his death his papers were mined and other books appeared, novels and memoirs, only two of them adding significantly to his achievement. *A Moveable Feast* is indispensable; *The Garden of Eden* was heavily edited, but it is worth attending to for the way in which it pushes the boundaries with its themes of gender roles, androgyny, sexual transference, and much else.

He was born and raised in Oak Park, Illinois, a Chicago suburb. He liked sports and, as a teenage writer, based his style on that of the sports columnists he admired: direct, emphatic, fast-paced. In the mature prose, John Updike says, "he gave those of us who would write in this century lessons in dialogue, in blunt and elliptical verity, in gallows humor, in risk as a kind of corporeal poetry, in the pencil-wielder's daily patience." Gabriel García Márquez liked the analogy Hemingway drew between boxing and writing, the artful aggression in relation less to the reader than to the resistant subject matter. Sports journalists taught Hemingway to seek out "unnoticed things that made emotions," the gratuitous detail that brings the experience alive. This is one thing Márquez got from him. Hemingway's first job was as a reporter for the *Kansas City Star,* and when he enlisted as a Red Cross ambulance driver in 1918, his trained eye saw grisly service toward the end of the First World War in Italy. He was wounded and returned home with material that a decade later informed *A Farewell to Arms.*

In 1922 he married Hadley Richardson, the first of his four wives. They moved to Paris, where he earned his living as a foreign correspondent. He made the most of the city, its international writers and artists. Stein referred to him and his contemporaries—who had suffered the war and had doubtful manners and conditional respect for their elders—as "the lost generation." "I thought of Miss Stein and Sherwood Anderson and egotism and mental laziness versus discipline and I thought 'who is calling who a lost generation?'" He loved the new and not-so-new art, finding, like Stein, in modern painters technical ideas for his own writing. He went to the Jeu de Paume gallery most days. "I was learning something from the painting of Cézanne that made writing simple true sentences far from enough to make the stories have the dimensions that I was trying to put in them."

It is agreeable to remember Hemingway in this first extended halcyon stay in Paris, young, handsome, not unhappily married, with his son, his puzzling friendships with Ford and Stein, heavy drinking with Pound, Joyce, and Fitzgerald, and all those walk-on parts including Picasso, Gris, Wyndham Lewis. There was the Shakespeare and Company Bookshop and Sylvia Beach, books loaned and discussed, everything full of hope. A decade later, in the same bookshop, he read "The Dumb Ox," an essay on his work by Lewis, and punched a vase of tulips into shards.

He befriended F. Scott Fitzgerald. The success of *The Great Gatsby,* a copy of which Fitzgerald lent him, meant he had to write a novel, too. "The story was about coming back from the war but there was no mention of the war in it." Hemingway went to the village of Schruns in the Vorarlberg in Austria to revise it. "I did the most difficult job of rewriting I have ever done there in the winter of 1925 and 1926, when I had to take the first draft of *The Sun Also Rises* which I had written in one sprint of six weeks, and make it into a novel." He loved

Schruns: "I remember the smell of the pines and the sleeping on the mattresses of beech leaves in the woodcutters' huts and the skiing through the forest following the tracks of hares and of foxes." The book appeared in 1926. Fitzgerald said he liked it, but Zelda, his wife, shrewd and sometimes shrewish, declared it "phony as a rubber check," characterizing *The Sun Also Rises* as "bullfighting, bullslinging and bullshit." Hemingway believed that Fitzgerald, with whom he drank and caroused rather too often, sometimes wanted to keep him from writing in the same way that Zelda, out of jealousy, tried to destroy her husband's creativity by encouraging him to drink, flirting with other men, and undermining his sexual confidence.

Zelda misvalued Hemingway. If the importance of writers is measured by their influence, few Anglophone writers of the twentieth century are as important as Hemingway. His aesthetic of Flaubertian economy is unmarred by the aestheticism and decadentism that took it up in the late nineteenth century and continued to embroider it in the twentieth. Hemingway's work engages themes that are anathema in a culture of policed correctnesses. In this he is like Lawrence, but without the mystical pretensions or the political arrogance. The sexual charge of male friendships, the difficulty of relations between the sexes, of relations between races and cultures, are part of a lived reality his fiction seeks to remake in language. His commissions and omissions are numerous, and many modern readers experience an undeniable toxicity in his concentration on characters and their realities, his wariness of solving general ideologies. And yet the first half of the twentieth century in American and Latin American fiction, and farther afield, is Hemingway's age. It is not his hard-boiled style that makes him durable so much as his sense of economy: a refined diction and a supple syntax make him such a resource to American writers of all backgrounds. His life story is by now a cautionary tale, a self-created legend. The more he is read apart from the hectoring, hubristic he-manliness of the life, with its appalling gaps and contradictions, the better his writing will be understood and the more vitally the legacy of his writing will continue to be radical and enabling.

It must have been galling to Zelda that he drafted *The Sun Also Rises* so quickly and confidently. He wrote it out of actual experience: his years in Paris, his friends and acquaintances, their excursions to Pamplona for the annual Festival of San Fermín (his original title was *Fiesta,* under which it appeared when first published in Britain), and the evocation of the Pyrenees and the river fishing. What he had originally conceived as a book on bullfighting, a work of evocative journalism, became a novel because the 1925 return to Pamplona was so intense and troubling an experience for the author. He had to make sense of it.

At the heart of the book is the relationship of Jake Barnes, an American journalist living in Europe, who suffers from an emasculating war wound, and the divorced and sexually adventurous Lady Brett Ashley, who appears to be in love with him. Her amorous relations with her Scottish fiancé, with the American Jew Robert Cohn, and with a young Spanish bullfighter lead to Barnes's crisis. Hemingway's models in life are not far to seek: they were his companions on the brief third visit to the Fiesta in 1925. Hemingway's process of imaginative transformation entailed the kinds of distortion and refinement that bring into focus the underlying tensions in relations that are finally displaced by the alternative, durable reality of the fiction. The three-act structure is brilliantly understated. When the fog of complex desire and alcohol burns off, the protagonists are left starkly, singly defined, or diminished, into their separate selves. In its second draft the book was to be called *The Lost Generation*, borrowing Stein's phrase. Among the things that Hemingway wisely loses from his novel are the ballasting adjectives that sink the work of some of his contemporaries, and the authoritative central narrative perspective. *The Sun Also Rises* is inexhaustible in its formal invention, some of it inadvertent and instinctive, some the result of judicious editing.

When he divorced Hadley in 1927, Hemingway gave her the proceeds of *The Sun Also Rises* as part of the settlement. He married again, for a decade, but divorced on returning from the civil war in Spain, after which he wrote *For Whom the Bell Tolls* (1940), published the year he married his third wife. The book sold 360,000 copies in the United States in the year of publication. It was the best novel to come directly out of the Spanish Civil War, a romance in a postromantic age, aware of its anachronism. Maria and Pilar are Hemingway's most convincing female characters, and he catches a sense of Spanish speech.

The feisty journalist Martha Gelhorn was the third Mrs. Hemingway. He met her in Key West in 1936. They were in Spain together, under fire. She did not humor him but held her own ground for a decade and more. He followed her on assignments, to China for instance, a country for which he felt no affinity. Florida and Wyoming had been the poles of his earlier world, Florida for fishing (he sailed out with John Dos Passos and was close to him until they fell out over Spain) and Wyoming for hunting. The map was redrawn with Cuba and Idaho as poles. In 1939 they established their home at Finca Vigía outside Havana, Cuba, a country Hemingway loved. When Martha Gelhorn finally tired of him, she told him he was a bully; besides, his eye had wandered again and Mary Welsh, another journalist, became his last wife.

Fidel Castro took power in Cuba. Hemingway befriended him: he was a fisherman, after all, and the fall of the superannuated dictator Fulgencio Batista was mourned by foreigners and the rich. When the expropriations of American property began in earnest in 1960, however, Hemingway departed to Ketchum,

Idaho. His depressions had become intense ("raging through his life against his mother," says Joyce Carol Oates): a series of physical accidents over the years, and accelerating psychological crises associated with them and with drink, preceded his suicide in 1961, ten years after his last masterpiece, a small novel printed in full in *Life* magazine, *The Old Man and the Sea,* about "courage maintained in the face of failure," Burgess says. His father had committed suicide in 1928, and his first wife's father had done so too. "I'll probably go the same way," he predicted.

But the story runs ahead of itself. *For Whom the Bell Tolls,* started in March 1939, was completed in July 1940. Some critics declared Hemingway back on form. Edmund Wilson saw it as a new departure, a real novel of characters with a convincing story, a powerful *new* sense of "social and political phenomena." It provided "not so much a social analysis as a criticism of moral qualities." But the book was too long and unevenly paced, he said, bulging and emaciated by turns. Hemingway's was seen as a short-story talent: he found it hard to get through the longueurs between incidents with an even pressure on the prose accelerator. Vidal dissented, calling it "a thoroughly superficial book with all the profundity of *Rebecca.*" In Vidal, Daphne du Maurier more than once moonlights as Aunt Sally.

In 1948 Hemingway and his fourth wife traveled to Venice, and there he fell in love with a nineteen-year-old girl. The issue was a novel, *Across the River and into the Trees,* published in 1950 to bad reviews. The tight-lipped sparseness of style had the air of affectation, without the nuance required for such a subject. The title draws on the last words of "Stonewall" Jackson (1863). The delirious general imagines he is in the recent battle where he was accidentally shot by his own men; suddenly he smiles and says calmly, "Let us cross over the river, and rest under the shade of the trees." Titles gave Hemingway problems, but this provenance, the man of action passing into a state of grace (or illusion), and these words fitted the tired author who had survived many serious accidents, some of them self-inflicted.

The worst were yet to come. *The Old Man and the Sea* he drafted in eight weeks and regarded as the best he could do, the best he had done. Faulkner made no bones about it, reviewing it briefly in *Shenandoah:* "Time may show it to be the best single piece of any of us. I mean of his and my generation." Hemingway was awarded the Pulitzer Prize in 1952 and in a surge of hope revisited Africa, where he had safaried before. He suffered two successive plane crashes, and when he at last reached Entebbe with bad injuries and burns he found a little crowd of reporters covering the story of his death. He reread his obituaries while he recovered. Another resurrection of sorts occurred. In Paris he recovered a trunk he had stored there in 1928. It was almost as good as if he had recovered the bag of manuscripts his first wife lost a quarter of a century before. The lumbering, alcoholic, and prematurely old author found the young man's writing. He took the material back to Cuba and began to compose *A Moveable Feast,* the posthumously published book that had, in a manner of speaking, his imprimatur. He submitted it to his publisher, then withdrew it: it was too harsh, the truths it told made cruel by retrospect. It became his *mémoires d'outre-tombe.* Raymond Chandler wrote a sentence true of Hemingway and himself: "I suppose the weakness, even the tragedy of writers like Hemingway is that their sort of stuff demands an immense vitality; and a man outgrows his vitality without unfortunately outgrowing his furious concern with it."

When George Plimpton for the *Paris Review* went to interview him outside Havana in 1958, he found Hemingway standing "in a pair of his oversized loafers on the worn skin of a lesser kudu," a parody of himself. He wrote at a tall desk, by hand; as he grew older his handwriting got larger, and his punctuation more sparse but effective. He always needed a supply of sharpened pencils. Plimpton elicits from him, just three years from his suicide and all his best work behind him, some savage truths about writing and about himself. But there were places even the nimble and brilliant Plimpton could not penetrate. Hemingway told him, "There is one part of writing that is solid and you do it no harm by talking about it, the other is fragile, and if you talk about it, the structure cracks and you have nothing." Also, as if to answer Zelda Fitzgerald, he said, "The most essential gift for a good writer is a built-in, shockproof, shit detector. This is the writer's radar and all great writers have had it." Also editors—Plimpton had it; and readers.

Those who edited the posthumous books did not quite have it. Hemingway abandoned work for a reason. The books extracted from the posthumous papers did the author harm. William Boyd questions the motives of those digging out unfinished and defective drafts. These publications are acts of treachery. A flabby Hemingway displaces the fit pugilist. "Hemingway was subsisting on 'Hemingway' . . . the writer had become more important than the work itself." For Ralph Ellison, writing in 1946, Hemingway was Twain's heir and "has done most to extend Twain's technical influence upon our fiction." The great source of modern American writing was *Huckleberry Finn.*

"When he describes something in print, believe him; believe him even when he describes the process of art in terms of baseball or boxing; he's been there." His style "affected whole generations of us," Mailer said, "the way a roomful of men are affected when a beautiful woman walks through—their night is turned for better or for worse. His style had the ability to hit young writers in the gut, and they weren't the same after that." Joan Didion described how he "changed the rhythms of the way both his own and the next few generations would write and speak," and language is "a certain way of looking at the world."

———•———

Jean Rhys liked Hemingway the man, remembering how with "wolfish so-licitude" he helped her into her coat after one of Ford's *Transatlantic Review* "dances." She was less persuaded by his writing, though she enjoyed *A Moveable Feast,* reading it as fiction. Jean Rhys (born Ella Gwendolen Rees Williams, 1890–1979), one of whose novels has achieved classic status, and whose life as a writer is read as a monitory parable, suffers too from the way the biography, or the myth of the writer, colors the reader's approach to the actual writing. Her fiction is about a vulnerable, helpless, mad, abused—and largely blameless—female protagonist. On first reading the five novels—*Quartet* (1928), *After Leaving Mr. Mackenzie* (1930), *Voyage in the Dark* (1934), *Good Morning, Midnight* (1939), and after more than a quarter century's gap *Wide Sargasso Sea* (1966)—are compelling; read again, they are stifling; not that what they tell is untrue but that the truth told is repeated, partial, contrived, as though there was a purpose in the writing beyond fiction: oblique autobiography, revenge. The protagonists change names but their backstories are similar, their fates variations on a theme.

Ford Madox Ford, who plays a major role, first positive and then negative, in her life, wrote in the preface to her 1927 collection, *The Left Bank and Other Stories,* of "her profound knowledge . . . of many of the Left Banks of the world," and how she had come "from the Antilles, with a terrifying insight and a terrific—an almost lurid!—passion for stating the case of the underdog." She had an unusual sympathy for "law-breakers." Against Ford's advice she tended to edit out contingent details, words that evoke a particular atmosphere, a specific topography, and concentrated instead on "passion, hardship, emotions: the locality in which these things are endured is immaterial." She made an exception in her last novel, *Wide Sargasso Sea,* her prequel to Charlotte Brontë's *Jane Eyre,* for the Antilles, where Rhys was born and raised in Dominica (the novel begins in Jamaica and moves to Dominica, then for its tragic denouement to England), assuming her readers were not familiar with them. They could have been in no doubt about the connection between *Jane Eyre* and three hard sentences in the last part of Rhys's novel: "Now at last I know why I was brought here and what I have to do. There must have been a draught for the flame flickered and I thought it was out. But I shielded it with my hand and it burned up again to light me along the dark passage."

On the strength of *Wide Sargasso Sea* V. S. Naipaul, the most exigent novelist of the Caribbean, praised her work in 1972. The writer who had vanished the year World War II began was back, and she has remained on the edge of vision ever since. The story of her life caught up with her fiction and even now threatens to displace it. First there are the islands, evoked in *Wide Sargasso Sea* in terms of a corrupted Eden: "Our garden was large and beautiful as that garden in the Bible—the tree of life grew there. But it had gone wild. The paths were overgrown and a smell of dead flowers mixed with the fresh living smell." She was sent to England at the age of sixteen full of anticipation. Of course it disappointed her, but she would not return. She was ridiculed at her ridiculous public school in Cambridge, where her "nicest" memory was being run down by an undergraduate on a bicycle: "I wasn't hurt, but he picked me up so carefully and apologized so profusely that I thought about him for a long time"; every silver lining retained a dark cloud.

She was laughed out of RADA, the acting school, for her accent; she struggled hard to make ends meet. For a time she worked as a chorus girl, then as a prostitute, generally maintaining a threadbare illusion of gentility. Her first husband was thrown in prison in Paris, where Ford met her, encouraged her writing, and invited her to stay with him and his partner, Stella Bowen. Ford could not resist the vulnerable and grateful Rhys, and they had an affair that finished her marriage and his relationship, the experience providing Rhys with material for *Quartet*. The end of the affair and the difficulties that ensued gave her material for *After Leaving Mr. Mackenzie*. Her own favorite among her novels was *Voyage in the Dark,* in which the protagonist tours the way she did as a chorus girl and has a relationship with a young man who does not marry her. The unsettled years of her second marriage, marked by her sense of inadequacy, rage, guilt, and excessive drinking, contributed to *Good Morning, Midnight*. After that she lived alone, her third husband getting on the wrong side of the law and spending much of their married life in prison.

Her resurrection in the 1960s was on the basis of a novel rooted less in her immediate life and its disappointments, more in her exotic past and in her reading. Antoinette Mason, the protagonist of *Wide Sargasso Sea,* is eventually buried by her husband in the name Bertha. Initially their relationship is sensual and passionate, but the journey to England, caught in a by-then exhausted marriage, her husband's embarrassment at her exotic otherness, her traces of Negro blood, his decision to lock her away like a bad secret, make for familiar tragedy. The pages at Thornfield leading to the fire are brief and nightmarish.

Of the American writers in Paris at the time, Ford notes: "Their egotism takes the form of making them insist on writing in their own way." Among those he published in the *Transatlantic Review* and he had in mind when he wrote this was Djuna (Chappell) Barnes (1892–1982), like Rhys known principally for one of her several books, like Rhys presumed dead, rediscovered in a reclusive life, and read in terms of her life as well as her writing. In 1924 Hemingway noted sarcastically that Djuna Barnes, "that legendary personality that has dominated the intellectual night-life of Europe for a century is in town." Town was Paris. "I have never met her, nor read her books, but she looks very nice." He did meet her, and she was. Faulkner called her "a fine one."

She was born in Cornwall-on-Hudson and raised in a rich, eccentric, and treacherously unbuttoned household. She was educated at home by her suffragist grandmother and pestered by her own father. She moved to New York in 1911. She studied at the Pratt Institute of Art for a short time (she illustrated some of her books in a distinctive style) and began to make a living as a writer of articles, stories, and—her avocation—poetry and short plays. In the 1920s she gravitated to Paris and the expatriate world there, writing the works that are still read today, *Ryder* (1928, her ambitious mock-Elizabethan novel, briefly a best seller), *Ladies Almanack* (1928), and *Nightwood* (1936, though begun as early as 1927). *Ladies Almanack* was light and playful beside *Ryder*, which touched on the themes of her troubled childhood. *Ladies Almanack* was a book *"which all ladies should carry about with them, as the Priest his Breviary, as the Cook his Recipes, as the Doctor his Physic, as the Bride her Fears, and as the Lion his Roar!"* She described it in a foreword as a "slight satiric wigging" for the entertainment of her (mainly women) friends. Evangeline Musset takes her whip in hand to "set out upon the Road of Destiny." The plump, medievalizing, wryly erotic illustrations are part of the parody, and the humor heightens rather than counteracts the sensuality, a celebration of love between strong-limbed, intelligent, and original women. Marianne Moore remarked that "reading Djuna Barnes is like reading a foreign language, which you understand."

Returned to the United States, she began erasing her work, rejecting offers to republish it. She called herself "the most famous unknown writer" of her time, an identity she had to work for. In June 1958 Edmund Wilson ran into her "looking like the Red Queen" at "what used to be the Minsky Theatre" in New York. They dined in Greenwich Village, and he found her "broader and gentler," not soured as he had expected. She was lame from a fall and used a cane and had suddenly become considerate and attentive: "She was trying to be a kind old lady." This was not the high-spirited or the despairing Djuna he had known before. When the poet Stanley Moss last saw her in New York, she bade him farewell, waving her cane in the air and calling after him, "Follow the heart, Stanley, follow the heart!" Upon her death in 1982 it became possible to resurrect her work.

She had been one of the loves of the long-lived avant-gardist Charles Henri Ford, America's first thoroughgoing surrealist. They met in New York, then he lived with her in Europe and Morocco and typed up the first version of *Night-wood,* correcting her bad spelling (there were three versions before the text was edited, one of them written at the Café de la Mairie in Paris, a place rich in Anglophone literary associations). She was never her own best critic. Henri Ford was not much of a critic either, being in love. She told him, "I consider myself more important than you. You're nobody and I'm somebody." He records a number of deadpan truths she spoke. "With a hangover it's inevitable that one chooses the most reckless cab driver in Paris."

The 140-page novel *Nightwood* survives, itself all that remains of a 190,000-word draft. The opening sentence is also the opening paragraph, a huge unfolding structure with the architectonic features of Firbank, and a lightness of tone Barnes had achieved to a lesser degree in *Ryder,* characteristic of the subgenre of parodic autobiography to which Woolf's *Orlando* also belongs. It promises a different kind and scale of novel from the one delivered; it is an irony that what follows is so tightly written and on such a reduced scale. T. S. Eliot published it at Faber and Faber, pressed to do so and puzzled by it. He was also aware that it contained material that might be libelous. He and Barnes's friend Emily Coleman, who had done so much to purge the original version of "sentimental shit of the worst kind" and revise toward brevity and precision and had "practically forced the book down my throat" (as Eliot put it), cut passages and reordered the material. Writing about it over half a century later, Jeanette Winterson sees no sutures. "It is its own created world, exotic and strange, and reading it is like drinking wine with a pearl dissolving in the glass. You have taken in more than you know, and it will go on doing its work." Clearly the removal of the merely contingent and confessional heightened the account of "my life with Thelma," as Barnes called it, based on her relations with the St. Louis silverpoint artist Thelma Wood (the Robin Vote of the novel: Barnes is Nora Flood). Did the St. Louis connection resonate with Eliot, a native of that city? Did he really like the dense language, the "poetic" character of the prose, the homosexual themes, the false Jew, the drama of Jenny Petherbridge stealing away the frail happiness of two women, one constant, the other flighty but at the same time profoundly needy of a steadying love? We turn from this to Barnes's poem "Twilight of the Illicit" whose second stanza reads:

> Your knees set far apart like
> Heavy spheres;
> With discs upon your eyes like
> Husks of tear;
> And great ghastly loops of gold
> Snared in your ears.

The symmetries of rhythm, the triple rhyme, the metaphorical thrift: had Eliot published Barnes's poetry he might have done her and us a lasting service.

———•———

John (Hoyer) Updike (1932–2009) wrote poetry, too. He resembled Kingsley Amis in wanting his poems to be better loved, because he loved them. They are clear and plain, and speak humorously, needily. His first book and one of his posthumous books were verse. He had aptitude but little genius. Did he have genius for novels? He had genius for sentences, none more than he. Martin Amis speaks of the "the fizzy pungency of his prose." He knew how to join sentences together into brilliant paragraphs that one copied into one's commonplace book; no writer more naturally, artlessly, creates scenes in three dimensions and in time: a decaying building that tells the whole history of a neighborhood, familiar woods in which a family's past, its games, picnics, moon-dappled romances, and brittle dejections live on. Few writers have so evenhandedly included explicit (and copious) sex in their books, understanding the distance between the expectant passions of the heart and the physiological systems of delivery. When he won the Bad Sex award from the *Literary Review,* the joke was more on them than on him.

In a late *New Yorker* review of *Ten Days in the Hills* (2007) he did register unease when Jane Smiley, four decades on, took sex beyond where he left it in his celebrated-notorious fourth novel, *Couples* (1968), in which he gave the organs of increase their vernacular names and lingered over, on, and in them. In a New England suburb the no longer young drink, "frug," reconfigure, and couple in and out of wedlock because they are bored, as people were in the late 1960s. Smiley's book is twenty-first century, *all* coition and dialogue, and this, he hinted, was not quite enough. In four decades fiction and language had become so much looser of limb, so much looser altogether.

His own fiction writing and his reviews believe in his subjects and his readers in old-fashioned, uncomplicated ways. Taking them for granted, he is free to concentrate on his subjects without needing to tip a postmodern wink. As critic, he has most to say about people most like himself, Dreiser and Anderson, for example. He can rise to a grand style. But has he a proportionate sense of formal scale? Is the brilliant easel painter up to the challenge of a large mural? Gore Vidal cannot abide his ingratiating obedience to the reader. His conservative politics and his comfy aesthetics express "blandness and acceptance of authority in any form." He "describes to no purpose," aspiring to be "our good child." His final verdict: "Updike's work is more and more representative of that polarizing within a state where Authority grows ever more brutal and malign while its hired hands in the media grow ever more excited as the holy war of the few against the many heats up."

The childhood reading of "our good child" was, the child reports, "cowardly." He stayed a coward because language made things real. He later learned from Nabokov, whose "amorous style" he loved, and from Proust. Even so, and though he admired Henry Green and loved Borges, he remains a nominalist through and through. He has a more innocent sense of the continuity between words and the world than any of his contemporaries. As a boy he hated to encounter things he did not want to know or feel. First came the terrors of illustrations. *Alice in Wonderland* he experienced in images that chilled his blood. (As a grown-up he wanted to become a cartoonist, and he was a competent graphic artist.) He was traumatized by an account of Shelley's boyhood, and by *Peer Gent.* Like all bookish children he enjoyed being sick in bed, but books like these spoiled the fun. He went off Mark Twain when Injun Joe chased Tom and Becky and never liked Twain after that, except when he had to, as a student or reviewer. When he got his library card he went for unreal and exciting mysteries, the humorists (he mentions fifty volumes of Wodehouse: Rabbit Angstrom as Bertie Wooster?). It was then that he created his first serial character, Manuel Cirraro, famous detective. He avoided the Gothic (though he did conjure witches in due course). He came to like science fiction. He pretended to read *The Waste Land* because it made him look cool, but when at the age of fifteen he came across *Ulysses* at a relation's house he was filled with anxiety. He remained addicted to how, what, and why books: the consolation of facts.

Reading and writing were family things. His mother was a would-be writer ambitious on his behalf; his tolerant, humorous schoolteacher father looked on, listened to them and to the radio with equal attention. It was a small town, lower-middle-class family, conservative, patriotic. Its values remained his values, down to supporting the Vietnam War in the 1960s and acknowledging his paradoxically upbeat American Lutheran Christianity. Reflecting on his childhood and the short fiction, one is put in mind of Norman Rockwell's all-American illustrations, those covers of the *Saturday Evening Post* that children of my generation would gaze at until they could step into scenes that were safe, bright, and wholesome, always suggesting narrative. His was a supportive environment in which he thumbed through magazines as if waiting for the invitation from the *New Yorker,* which came. Most things went his way eventually. He became a famous novelist, more famous than some of his favorite writers, and a brilliant, evenhanded critic whose reviews were an initiation for many younger writers and writers in translation.

Margaret Atwood enjoys *The Witches of Eastwick* (1984), which, like *The Centaur* (1963), moves away from realism and reminds her of *The Wizard of Oz.* It "redefines magical realism," she says; and she is right, it stylizes and contains it. *The Centaur* is Updike's *Ulysses.* The protagonists are a father and son, the father a depressive schoolteacher obsessed with the better times of his youth as a foot-ball star and a First World War soldier, the son a would-be artist, acutely self-conscious and suffering from psoriasis. Both men are keen to get away.

Updike's boyhood keeps breaking through the elaborate marquetry of his fiction. Joyce Carol Oates admires his memoir *Self-Consciousness* (1989), a key to many of his recurrent themes and anxieties; it describes his stutter, how his writing was a way of outwitting it. In her own essay "Inspiration," she says that for Updike "story" comes as a "packet of material to be delivered." In 1957, after his grandfather had died, he revisited the ruins of an old poorhouse: "Out of the hole where it had been there came to me the desire to write a futuristic novel." His first novel, *The Poorhouse Fair* (1959), was not autobiographical, though its occasion was. Mary McCarthy admired it, though it suffered from a "point-of-view" problem, striving too hard for formal effect, "the whole virtuosity of do-ing it through the eyes of this old man sitting on the veranda of the poorhouse, through his eyes with their refraction, very old eyes, and so on. I think, in a way, this trick prevents him saying a good deal in the book." That was of course the intention, to limit the saying.

He makes no bones about it: "A fiction writer's life is his treasure, his ore, his savings account, his jungle gym," and when fellow novelists, Styron or Oates, for example, agree to cooperate with a biographer, it is like helping a thief rifle your own closet. He wrote *Self-Consciousness* when he heard someone was writ-ing his life and he was not about to let it go unchallenged. He laid claim to what was his, fortified against the trespasser. His narrative is richer in reflection than in the kinds of circumstantial detail that make his fiction solid.

He wrote runs of books in which the same characters live their lives in places that become familiar. *Bech: A Book* (1970), *Bech Is Back* (1982), and *Bech at Bay* (1998) constitute the Bech series, linked short stories about a hirsute Jewish writer who spends a great deal of energy examining himself, his marriage, and all the surrounding problems, and who wins the Nobel Prize. He is not prolific, so the model cannot be Bellow or Roth. As a character he is remote from Up-dike himself, an escape from autobiography. There is the witchy pair of East-wick books and the Scarlet Letter adultery trilogy.

His most celebrated series he called the "Angstrom novels," better known as the Rabbit novels, named after their protagonist, Harry "Rabbit" Angstrom, and include *Rabbit, Run* (1960), *Rabbit Redux* (1971), *Rabbit Is Rich* (1981), and *Rab-bit at Rest* (1990). The last two won Pulitzer Prizes. In 2001 a novella, *Rabbit Re-membered*, an after-tremor, appeared in the collection *Licks of Love*. Updike set out over four decades to create the details of a life that on the face of it is not worth the effort of fiction (Flaubert wrote his novel about the nothing that is Madame Bovary), and to show how rich and instructive that negligible life is. It is like his own father's, and his fictional mission is in some sense to bring that invisible existence to the kind of life it actually was and to show that its being mattered. Here is Ford's Tietjens without the ballast of British history, Bellow's Augie March without eagles and prohibition, Roth's Nathan Zuckerman without typewriter, and Heller's Bob Slocum times three. Harry Angstrom is inconsequential, yes. But also, no. After being a high-school basketball star in a dwindling Pennsylvania town not unlike the Shillington where Updike grew up, he was not class valedictorian and he did not go to Harvard like his author: Rabbit spent the rest of *his* life in the normal suburban declining trajectory, never getting what he wants. There's the Toyota dealership he runs, his not-numerous love affairs, his sallow marriage that manages to endure, his unsatisfactory son. Out of this Updike spins novels with effortless abundance. He was deeply touched by Proust.

Ian McEwan's tender obituary declared, "The tetralogy is Updike's masterpiece and will surely be his monument. In all its detail, homely or hard-edged, and all its arenas—work, politics, retirement, and above all sex—the metaphysical is always there," a point the too-literal reader tends to play down, "sometimes a mere gleam buried in the fold of a sentence, at other times overtly, comically." He compares Updike to Bellow as "a master of effortless motion—between third and first person, from the metaphorical density of literary prose to the demotic, from specific detail to wide generalization, from the actual to the numinous, from the scary to the comic." No doubt in his mind about the novelist's genius.

In terms of subject matter, Don DeLillo (b. 1936) is a child of his age. Not many modern developments slip through the net of his fiction, which lives as much as it can in a present, recent past, or future time frame. It's not just mobile phones and ATMs but the whole digital thing. It's terrorism, linguistics, baseball, nuclear holocaust, 9/11. The universe is his oyster, a Blue Point from Great South Bay, Long Island. His first novel (he described it as "overdone and shaggy") is entitled *Americana* (1971), and even when he is writing in Greece his inflections remain American. He does not like being called postmodern: the one adjective he welcomes is "American." He does not like Updike's consolatory *New Yorker* style; he cannot have liked Updike's take on him when he reviewed *Cosmopolis* (2003) in the same magazine: "Though always a concept-driven writer, whose characters spout smart, swift essays at one another, [DeLillo] has shown himself—in large parts of *Underworld* [1997], in almost all of *White Noise* [1985]—capable of realism's patient surfaces and saturation in personally verified detail." Updike intended the condescension that flows from the phrase—tactfully interrupted by a subordinate clause—"shown himself capable of."

DeLillo is from the Bronx, an Italian, Roman Catholic background still close enough to the old country for his grandmother, half a century in the United

States, never to have learned English. He came relatively late to reading, and through reading to writing. His early work was marked by Hemingway sentence by sentence, if not in form. Also J. T. Farrell's Studs Lonigan trilogy "showed me that my own life, or something like it, could be the subject of a writer's scrutiny." He was drawn to Faulkner, to Flannery O'Connor, and fatefully to Joyce, as *Cosmopolis* was to prove. He started his writing life, however, in Madison Avenue as an advertising man, quitting his job at the age of thirty because he decided it was bad for him. Here he realized that there is "something nearly mystical about certain words and phrases that float through our lives. It's computer mysticism." It invades the ear and stays there, infuriating, consoling, uncontrollable. He did not quit advertising to become a writer, but he became a writer. Once he started publishing novels, his output in the first decade was prodigious: seven books. Then he slowed. He began taking pains. He remains prolific by most writers' standards, and he plays his part in a literature on which he has a distinctive perspective.

"The novel's not dead," he declares, "it's not even seriously injured, but I do think we're working in the margins, working in the shadows of the novel's greatness and influence." Despite an abundance of promise and talent, "when we talk about the novel we have to consider the culture in which it operates. Everything in the culture argues against the novel, particularly the novel that tries to be equal to the complexities and excesses of the culture." He chooses four books that succeed against the odds: William Gaddis's *JR*, Norman Mailer's *Harlot's Ghost*, Thomas Pynchon's *Gravity's Rainbow*, and Robert Coover's *The Public Burning*. "They offer many pleasures without making concessions to the middle-range reader, and they absorb and incorporate the culture instead of catering to it." The middle-range reader is, then, in the latter half of the twentieth century, the enemy of the best, even as in American fiction up to the middle of the twentieth century it is precisely that reader who follows and applauds the great American writers. Something has happened: the middle-range has become more conservative, fiction more experimental; prestige is measured less by popular success than high-brow critical recognition. To his list of reckonable writers he adds Robert Stone, Joan Didion, and Cormac McCarthy, who "show us that the novel is still spacious enough and brave enough to encompass enormous areas of experience. We have a rich literature. But sometimes it's a literature too ready to be neutralized, to be incorporated into the ambient noise." He cries out for resistance in writers, who create resistance in readers, "the novelist who writes against power, who writes against the corporation or the state or the whole apparatus of assimilation. We're all one beat away from becoming elevator music."

His favorite among his early books was not the one about the TV producer in search of a big subject, or the dark comedy about football and nuclear annihilation, or about yuppies and terrorism, or the thriller about hunting for the film reel of Hitler's sex life, but *Ratner's Star* (1976), which the critics likened to the work of Thomas Pynchon. It was the first of his books that was taken seriously. It took him two hard years' work. Like Cormac McCarthy he loves science and "was drawn to the beauty of scientific language, the mystery of numbers, the idea of pure mathematics as a secret history and secret language— and to the notion of a fourteen-year-old mathematical genius at the center of all this." It lacks the fluidity of his early books; it is carefully designed and constructed. "The walls, the armature, the foundation—I wandered inside this thing I was building and sometimes felt taken over by it, not so much lost inside it as helpless to prevent the thing from building new connections, new underground links." One is put in mind of a prototype computer game, and indeed, reading the book today there is an archaic quality to cope with. Technology has more than kept pace with art.

To DeLillo's 1977 novel *Players* we owe the birth of Jonathan Franzen. By Franzen's own account, this strange book about ennui and its remedies (affairs, terrorism, suicide) gave him "one of the purest aesthetic responses I've ever had." He was on a Christmas visit to the in-laws. "I'd finally found somebody who was putting on the page the apocalyptic, postindustrial urban aesthetic that I'd been looking for in film and photographs and had found expressed in music, particularly by Talking Heads. And here was somebody who was getting it on the page and writing like a dream." Or nightmare. "His prose was like a call to duty: You must write better. Here, see, it can be done. I find it remarkable that people don't talk more about *Players*. In certain ways, DeLillo never wrote better." Colm Tóibín praises "the deadpan radiant perfection in the sentences of Don DeLillo." In these books of the 1970s he mastered his style.

For *Amazons* (1980), DeLillo's first novel of that decade, which he has now disowned, he adopted the pseudonym Cleo Birdwell for the mock memoir of a female hockey star. He could have made it as a ghostwriter. His Middle East thriller *The Names* (1982) was followed by *White Noise* (1985), his breakthrough campus novel that received a National Book Award and placed him ineradicably on the map. It helped to define a new generation of writers, from David Foster Wallace (for whom DeLillo and Cynthia Ozick were two of the greatest living writers in English) to Paul Auster (who dedicated *In the Country of Last Things* and *Leviathan* to DeLillo) and Zadie Smith. Updike praises it to strengthen his case against *Cosmopolis*: "The surreal supermarkets are the real thing, hilariously familiar, and Jack Gladney's paeans to family life, from within his nest of impudently precocious children and spooky ex-wives, are not ironic."

Jack Gladney, a Hitler scholar (who cannot read or speak German), lives with his fourth wife, Babette. He has three ex-wives, numerous precocious stepchildren, and a clutch of his own kids. He and Babette are terrified of dying. Jack's colleague and friend Murray Jay Siskind runs a seminar on "car crashes," no doubt attended or suggested by J. G. Ballard, whose novel *Crash,* published in 1973, must have been a set text. Jack and Murray have unconsoling but funny conversations: "There are full professors in this place who read nothing but cereal boxes," says Murray. "It's the only avant-garde we've got," says Jack.

In the first section of the book there is academic satire, dialogue, musing. He describes it as "an aimless shuffle toward a high-intensity event—this time a toxic spill that forces people to evacuate their homes. Then, in each section, there's a kind of decline, a purposeful loss of energy." The novel is ingenious and in parts difficult, the science and politics building against one another as he enters a world of corruption, consumption, the even dissemination of meaningless, busy "sound." The idea of "white sound" is carried into the styles, avoiding consolidation around a single voice but at the same time catching the humor of contemporary American language.

After the success of *White Noise,* DeLillo, not the most public of writers, has had nowhere to hide. Each subsequent book is subjected to immediate and extensive reviews. *Libra* (1988), in which he digested the vast Warren Report on the assassination of John F. Kennedy to bring us a fictionalized portrait of Lee Harvey Oswald, was subject to political disapproval and DeLillo's American bona fides called in question. *Mao II* (1991), dedicated to his editor Gordon Lish, takes its title from Andy Warhol's silkscreen series of primary-color portraits of Chairman Mao. Two acts of terrorism sparked it off: one, the press photographers' ambush of J. D. Salinger, an invasion of the privacy of that very private man; two, the fatwa declared against Salman Rushdie after the publication of *The Satanic Verses* (1988). "The future belongs to crowds," DeLillo says in the wake of the Unification Church mass wedding at the stadium. "In *Mao II* I thought about the secluded writer, the arch individualist, living outside the glut of the image world. And then the crowd, many kinds of crowds, people in soccer stadiums, people gathered around enormous photographs of holy men or heads of state."

His most successful novel is one that he least expected to succeed, though it caused him considerable labor. He handed in the hefty typescript without expectations. *Underworld* (1997) is 827 pages in extent, informed by historical fact and character, epic in range but lacking, perhaps, the palpable *reality* of Doctorow's *Ragtime* (1975) and its reinvented innocence. As in *Ragtime* there is a baseball game, DeLillo using the Giants versus the (then Brooklyn) Dodgers pennant struggle in 1951 as a kind of overture to his portrait of half a century of discord. The baseball game is the high point of his writing, effortless, humorous, the engagement of factual characters in fictional situations. The body of the book is written at another level, the epilogue again achieving, in its prophetic intent, a powerful effect. By contrast, *The Body Artist* (2001) was small-scale, intimate, but memorable.

In *Cosmopolis* (2003) the impact of Joyce is most damagingly recorded. It is billed as a "rewrite" of *Ulysses,* set in New York at the dawn of the new millennium, before 9/11 (the subject of *Falling Man,* 2007) but at the time when digital industries were suffering on the stock exchange. It is dedicated to Kurt Vonnegut and Paul Auster, representing older and younger generations. It went down badly with readers. What was said unfairly about *Underworld* could be said fairly about *Cosmopolis,* the first major traffic-jam novel. A twenty-eight-year-old dot .com billionaire, a next-generation American Psycho, is crossing town to the barbershop in his limo. It's slow because the president is in New York and security is tight. The limo has all the modern conveniences: science fiction and metafiction are passengers along with the impatient protagonist, Eric Packer. DeLillo borrows his epigraph from the Polish poet Zbigniew Herbert: "a rat became the unit of currency." How coarse that borrowing from war-ravaged Poland seems in the chrome context that Updike describes as "this farce of extravagant wealth and electronic mysticism."

Lacking here is the solidity of conception and the character that grounds the earlier novels: "The trouble with a tale where anything can happen is that somehow nothing happens," Updike remarks. This book is not one of his "chunky, garish, anxious-to-please" efforts, but cyberpunkish. Only a quarter the length of *Underworlds,* it is thematically straightforward: the world is in the clutch of computers—they predict it, they shape and reshape it. As the limo inches through the traffic, the yen falls, there are demonstrations, Packer manages to get out and have breakfast, get out and have sex, and much more, pass through an anticapitalist demonstration, take advice, give orders. A series of short interpretative paragraphs, mini-essays, impart meaning to the incidents. Updike notes that DeLillo cannot commit wholly to the fantastic plane, as Vonnegut might have done. The attraction of "the quotidian mundane" is irresistible. He ends up in a barbershop as real as those DeLillo went to with his father as a boy in the Bronx.

———————

Reprinting an interview entitled "Blonde Ambition" in her book *The Faith of a Writer* (2003), Joyce Carol Oates (b. 1938) retains the headnote, which declares, "Her novel *them,* winner of the 1970 National Book Award, culminated in the depiction of the Detroit race riots of 1967; *Because It Is Bitter, and Because It Is My Heart* (1990) dramatized an interracial teenage romance; and the Pulitzer Prize–nominated *Black Water* (1992) offered a fictional rendition of the Chappaquiddick incident, from the viewpoint of the drowning young woman. Oates's short, grisly

1995 novel, *Zombie,* suggested by the Jeffrey Dahmer case, explored the psyche of a serial killer in all-too-convincing detail." She has time for newspapers, for popular, dramatic human concerns. She is a distinguished teacher, too, and for many years she was involved with her late husband, Raymond Smith, in editing the *Ontario Review,* which they had founded. When Robert Phillips interviewed her for the *Paris Review,* "Ms. Oates answered all questions openly while curled with her Persian cats upon a sofa."

She is anxiously aware of herself in the world. She said that when she started publishing books in 1963, "I dreaded to present myself as feminine." She published her first stories and essays genderlessly as "J. C. Oates." After all, "the woman who writes is a writer by her own definition, but a woman writer by others' definitions." She has put this thought more or less behind her, though she does brood sometimes, as in her *Journal (1973–1982)* (2007): "Is my work in its scope and ambition and depth and experimentation really less impressive than that of, say, Bellow or Mailer or Updike?" It worries her; but she remains an apparently self-effacing author, foregrounding the work and refusing to do what Mailer does, making "a conscious effort to direct critical assumptions." Human beings constitute, she says, a "species that clamors to be lied to." And she insists, "Art by its nature is a transgressive act." Writers as thieves: in this scenario she is seven nights a week a cat burglar. One of her poems begins, "What is most American is most in motion!"

She is impatient with critics who go on about her productivity. "What is ultimately important is a writer's strongest books. It may be the case that we all must write many books in order to achieve a few lasting ones . . . Each book as it is written, however, is a completely absorbing experience, and feels always as if it were the work I was born to write." Her more than fifty novels are not, for the most part, novellas. *Blonde* (2000, the third of her novels to be nominated for a Pulitzer Prize) was intended to be a novella in poetic prose based on the life of Norma Jeane Baker and running to no more than 150 pages. In the end it exceeded 700 pages, written and revised in under a year. It is one of Oates's novels that works, the story told by a posthumous first person, as is Roth's twenty-ninth novel, *Indignation* (2008). Norma Jeane never becomes Marilyn Monroe, that projection she performed and then sloughed off in the act of suicide.

Her 1971 novel *Wonderland* (the American and English editions have different endings because she got it wrong in the first printing) takes her back to her own reading origins. Her grandmother, the one who provided her with her first typewriter when she was fourteen, gave her *Alice in Wonderland* and *Through the Looking-Glass,* which she remembers as her first books. Norma Jeane has a touch of Alice in *Blonde;* indeed, many of Oates's female protagonists do. "Carroll's wonderful blend of illogic and humor and horror and justice has always appealed to me, and I had a marvelous time teaching the books last year in my undergraduate course." Teaching is at the heart of her experience of writing, in Texas, Detroit, Windsor Ontario, Princeton. "Anyone who teaches knows that you don't really experience a text until you've taught it, in loving detail, with an intelligent and responsive class." Her own students at Princeton include several writers, notably in recent times Jonathan Safran Foer.

During a year in London, she acquainted herself with the country and its writers, completing *Do with Me What You Will* (1973). She conceived a great respect for the novelists she met, Drabble, Lessing, Murdoch, and Colin Wilson among them, characterizing the English novelist as "almost without exception an observer of society . . . Apart from writers like Lawrence (who doesn't seem altogether English, in fact) there hasn't been an intense interest in subjectivity, in the psychology of living, breathing human beings." The American novel "is radically different. We are willing to risk being called 'formless' by people whose ideas of form are rigidly limited, and we are wilder, more exploratory, more ambitious, perhaps less easily shamed, less easily discouraged." She adds something that goes against one's experience of Bellow, Roth, Doctorow, McCarthy, and many others, including herself: "The intellectual life, as such, we tend to keep out of our novels, fearing the sort of highly readable but ultimately disappointing cerebral quality of Huxley's work . . . or, on a somewhat lower level, C. P. Snow's."

All of the things one is urged to avoid discussing at dinner parties—illness and medicine, politics, religion, law—Oates broaches in her fiction, from specifically American perspectives. These themes do not grow together, as they would have done under Balzac's pen; they are discrete and cumulative. Vanguard Press published her first novel, *With Shuddering Fall* (1964), when she was twenty-six. Her first major success came five years later with *them* (1969). Set in Detroit, which she knew well in the troubled 1960s when she taught there, she evokes three decades of the city's underlife in black ghetto districts, and addresses directly the conflicts around race, drugs, and crime. The novel has a compelling solidity, based as it is in actual places and people the author knew.

Updike made a habit of reviewing the novels of Anne Tyler (b. 1941) in the *New Yorker*. He compared her art to John Cheever's: She "has sought brightness in the ordinary, and her art has needed only the darkening that would give her beautifully sketched shapes solidity." Her fascination with the movements of light and dark are like Cheever's, and her seeming lightness, the compelling undertone to the evenness of her imagination. The books are memorable as an ensemble, a tone of narrative that hovers between major and minor key, steadily unsettling. We come to know the threadbare genteel world of Baltimore, where she and her fiction now live, much as we know the scattered landscapes of

Hardy's Wessex or Bennett's Five Counties. We do not come to know the author: she is reclusive and resists interviewers.

We learn from John Barth that she always drafts her books by hand, what she refers to in one place as "the muscular cursive," in another as "quite small and distinct handwriting—it is almost like knitting a novel." She is, says Franzen, a writer whose artistic creed requires reticence. She remains turned toward her work, not her public. If she were a priest, she would conduct the communion in the old way, with her back to the congregation and her face to the altar.

Raised in Quaker communities where books were at a premium, she says she read *Little Women* twenty-two times, a number so precise it must have been invented. Her novels proceed from character to plot, her characters contribute to and to some extent control their circumstances. She is less inclined than Oates to reflect on her standing vis-à-vis male contemporaries. It is Tyler's admirers, including Eudora Welty ("my crowning influence"), Roddy Doyle, Sebastian Faulks, and Nick Hornby, who insist on her centrality. For British male followers she may be a charm against postmodern experimentalism.

Her concern with the shaping realities of individual lives contrasts with her contemporaries' work on larger canvases and themes, as though they lack the close detail she provides, and her close domestic observations were without reference outward. There is a clear difference in intent and in formal imagination, but Tyler and Roth, Tyler and Updike have almost as much in common as Wharton and, say, Henry James. Her sense of melancholy, of homesickness for the vanished world of the first home, and for all the subsequent sloughed pasts, and her writing in and of an unspecified, ahistorical present, about people of a certain class and kind that are recognizable but not easy to grasp or love, are compelling. A familiar and not unforgiving America is her setting; she takes it for granted, grateful but not sentimental. Jane Austen's ghost rather than Louisa May Alcott's hovers near her and is at once richly entertained and safe: there are no erotic affronts in Tyler's books, they work by understatement, there is no gratuitous offense. But Austen's is a busy ghost nowadays. Tyler is not "original": Anita Brookner, Carol Shields, Alice Munro, and other writers work in the same human neighborhoods, though in different city- and landscapes, and addressing slightly different markets. The scale of Tyler's oeuvre, however, its cumulative power, which begins with *If Morning Ever Comes* (1964), published when she was twenty-three, followed by eighteen more novels, sets her apart. *The Accidental Tourist* (1985) is her best-known novel, thanks to Hollywood.

In 1989 she won the Pulitzer Prize for *Breathing Lessons*, a novel that takes place over a single summer's day as Maggie, almost fifty, as the author was when she wrote it, and her husband, Ira (they have two children, as Tyler and her husband did), set off from Baltimore to attend the funeral of the husband of

Maggie's childhood friend off in Deer Lick, Pennsylvania. The delays, detours, and rising tensions of the day might put one in mind of DeLillo's *Cosmopolis,* but the traffic moves more freely, in every sense, and life and love are renewed around the occasion of the funeral. Her favorite among her novels was Eudora Welty's, too, *Dinner at the Homesick Restaurant* (1982). Welty wished she had written the closing sentence: "And high above, he seemed to recall, there had been a little brown airplane, almost motionless, droning through the sunshine like a bumblebee."

—— ◆ ——

Gabriel Josipovici says that reading many of the established names of current British fiction gives him a "sense of prep-school boys showing off." He writes that, reading Julian Barnes, "like reading so many other English writers of his generation, Martin Amis, Ian McEwen, Blake Morrison, or a critic from an older generation who belongs with them, John Carey, leaves me feeling that I and the world have been made smaller and meaner." It is less the critical assault on modernism that worries him than the chronic modern English disease of "irony." "The irony which at first made one smile, the precision of language, which was at first so satisfying, the cynicism, which at first was used only to puncture pretension, in the end come to seem like a terrible constriction, a fear of opening oneself up to the world." In an interview he declared that the success of Barnes and his contemporaries has to do with "an ill-educated public being fed by the media—'This is what great art is'—and they lap it up."

Julian (Patrick) Barnes (b. 1946), and some of his characters, might be inclined to agree with Josipovici, up to a point. "I *hate* the way the English have of not being serious about being serious, I *really hate* it," says Adrian in Barnes's 2011 Booker Prize–winning novel (or is it a novella?), *The Sense of an Ending.* Tony, his protagonist, might have had as a motto a correction of Forster's "Only connect," an imperative "Disconnect." Barnes is impatient with Forster's indulgent self-forgiveness. In *The Sense of an Ending,* as often in Barnes, the protagonist is recalled to a past in which everything glowed with a gleam but the character was looking away. The novel confronts this act of omission whose diminishing consequences are the rest of the protagonist's life. The reflections can be narrowly self-referential, the solipsism tight but engaging, as though it manages, by means of tone, of which Barnes is a master, to attach to and activate the reader's own solipsism. Though many of his books are short, the effect can be comparable to that of a passage of Proust, readers finding themselves refiguring elements in their own past in response to Barnes's characters'.

Barnes, born in Leicester, grew up in suburban London. Northwood, Middlesex, is the *Metroland* (1980) of his first novel. After reading modern languages at Magdalen College, Oxford, and working as a lexicographer for the *Oxford English Dictionary* ("I spent three professional years with the language post-1880, in letters *c* to *g*"), he wrote a guide (unpublished) about writers who went to or through Oxford. He read for the bar while writing and reviewing. He ended up back in London, though in football he still supports Leicester. His first novel appeared when he was thirty-four.

In the long library of his house in North London in 2000, among the Boxer caricatures and the photographs (including one of George Sand by Nadar) on the walls, was a manuscript letter from Flaubert, a present to the author from his publisher when his third, his breakthrough novel *Flaubert's Parrot* (1984), had sold a million paperback copies. This novel is the story of a man doing his best to distract himself from his wife's infidelity and death. Because the novel is in the first person, the narrator, the widowed physician Geoffrey Braithwaite, does his best to distract us as well. The plot evades the story, and that evasion and oblique disclosure is what the novel is *about*. Braithwaite is obsessed not only with Flaubert, his ostensible subject, but with the nature of fact, what we can actually *know* about another person, ourselves, and the world. He takes as his subject the most rigorous novelist of all time and tries to establish the truth of his life. In the end it is impossible even to identify the actual (stuffed) parrot at the heart of his long short story *A Simple Heart*. *Flaubert's Parrot* asks about the nature of a writer's life, about any life; about the stability of fact and what a fact contains, what it can truthfully tell. Language stabilized in a work of fiction is the one (temporarily) dependable medium in what it chooses to contain, what it discloses and omits.

Behind the book at an uncertain, monumental distance stands Flaubert. There is the civic Flaubert in the market square, cupreously stained and disregarded, with his history of sculptors and foundries; there is the Flaubert of the letters, a reluctant lover, dispenser of wit and aphorism; there is the Flaubert of the books and the aesthetics that surround them. A greater, unacknowledged presence is that of John Dowell, narrator of Ford Madox Ford's *The Good Soldier*, a novel Barnes reveres. Dowell, though a better class of man and a greater naïf than Braithwaite, suffers the same epistemological reluctance to come clean with the reader, and with himself.

*Flaubert's Parrot* combines literary criticism, biography, and the narrator's "tragedy." Eccentric Flaubertian dictionaries play back to the author's lexicographical years; there is an exam paper, there are three formal chronologies of Flaubert's life, each accurate, each telling a different story. Fact and fiction exist in a symbiotic relationship that the narrator in part controls. For him, a fictional character whose story is the novel's "factual" basis, the interest of Flaubert is less his fiction than his life and how it relates to his art. Braithwaite turns a bitterly ironic face to the world; yet the world responds with a larger irony: the unknown and unknowable that underlies our most vivid perceptions of others, the evanescence of objective fact. The point in the novel at which Braithwaite divulges most about his wife, her infidelity and his part in her death, Barnes entitles "Pure Story." The language of this assured speaker breaks into syntactically centrifugal phrases as he tells: "The patient. Ellen. So you could say, in answer to that earlier question, that I killed her. You could just. I switched her off. I stopped her living. Yes." He is a physician as well as a husband, and the euthanasia he performs has an aspect of suicide as well. The language after this passage "pretends to recover." We read the maxims for life, a maxim upon maxims. Little tags from Larkin's poems are scattered through *Flaubert's Parrot* (as through Martin Amis's fiction, part of the furniture of the mind of their generation). A further dimension of reality is added by the incursion of real people, actual scholars—Dame Enid Starkie (Flaubert's biographer) and David Hockney, for example.

The parrot is important because it belonged to Felicité, the servant woman in *Un coeur simple* with whom Braithwaite identifies Flaubert. Her parrot is his parrot, her projection onto it of the Holy Ghost itself is his projection. He lines up Flaubert's four encounters with parrots, not to mention his relations, imaginative and otherwise, with other animals, as the book progresses: bear, camel, sheep, "The Monkey, the Donkey, the Ostrich, the Second Donkey, and Maxine du Camp" (his friend who becomes a beast), dogs. He eats animals, and to his crab lice he becomes dinner. The numerology and the symmetries of the book, the balancing of chapters, as a piece of baroque planning, give pedantry a good name.

His second novel, *Before She Met Me* (1982), is a thematic rough draft for *Flaubert's Parrot*. The historian husband chugs down wine and weeps, obsessively imagining the lovers his wife had before he came on the scene. The distance between fact and fiction is slight, sometimes imperceptible. Once imagination is let loose, things acquire a compelling reality. In a later book the narrator says, *"I began to form a mental picture of his lodgings."* From such a mental picture no objective fact will rescue you. Remember Othello. Remember Swann. And there is no such thing as unfictionalized fact: as soon as a fact finds a context, it behaves in accordance with it.

In *Talking It Over* (1991) and, a decade later, its sequel, *Love, Etc.* (2000), Barnes conducts an experiment. Stuart is a tubby young banker, unimaginative, dependable. Oliver, best man when he marries Gillian, is an offbeat charmer. Gillian throws Stuart over for Oliver. In the love triangle the young buck succeeds; in time, however, the beta male prospers, and prosperity raises his mark, while failure knocks the alpha out of his rival. This is a variation on the theme of *Flaubert's Parrot* and of *Arthur and George* (2005), the mystery relating to Arthur

Conan Doyle. It is also the theme of Martin Amis's much more ambitious *The Information* (1995).

By the time Barnes reaches *The Sense of an Ending* he puts obliquity of plot aside, lets irony go, and probes into the heart of missed occasions. Tony Webster is divorced. He is careful, slow-paced, he wanted to go through life without being troubled or taking trouble, and thinks he has succeeded until he receives a small legacy that sucks him into his past, there to address questions he left dangerously open. Piece by piece, like Braithwaite thirty years before, Tony rebuilds the past, Veronica is there, Adrian, restored from fragmentary recollection, conversations, until he begins to understand the place of loss he now occupies. The title of this, his Booker Prize–winning novel, he borrowed from Frank Kermode's 1967 critical book about fiction in time, subtitled *Studies in the Theory of Fiction*. Tony is a tight-lipped Englishman, his voice not like Braithwaite's, out of Ford, where a fullness, a history, a tradition of manners, a custom of reserve make him laconic; here is emptiness, thinness. A sense of superiority is displaced by a fear of being mocked.

Beyond the continuities in his writing, there are a few interesting detours. *A History of the World in 10 1/2 Chapters* (1989) is a collection of stories in different styles that explore a single theme (Flaubert's theme in *Trois contes*): how forms of expression determine and redetermine how we receive content and shape meaning. *The Porcupine* (1992), set in an almost modern country, which may be Bulgaria, is about the trial of a formidable communist leader who subtly plays his captors and defends himself. *England, England* (1998) is a satirical biography of Martha Cochrane and of England as it is going. "England as an idea has become somewhat degraded and I was interested in what would happen if you pushed that, fictionally, to an extreme," he said. "You take some of the tendencies that are implicit in contemporary Britain, like the complete dominance of the free market, the tendency of the country to sell itself and parody itself for the consumption of others, the increasing dependence on tourist dollars; then you add in one of my favorite historical notions, the invention of tradition." You mix these ingredients and then push the resulting dough "as far as it can go and set it in the future. It's a garish, farcical, extremist version of what the country seems to be getting like now. But that's one advantage of fiction, you can speed up time." It was shortlisted for the Booker Prize.

Barnes's default position seems to be the complex romance that travels up and down its own (generally short) length in time, where characters are given a second chance to see where things went wrong, if not to put them right. He seems to be European because of Flaubert. But it is not Flaubert. It is Flaubert's *parrot,* and that elusive parrot, taken with Barnes's well-bred suburban Francophilia, makes him the most English of writers. He, and the Nobel Prize committee, may grow impatient with the cultural and psychological introspection and self-forgiveness of American fiction, but the introspection of Barnes's protagonists is no less solipsistic, the difference being one of tone. He has more in common with Updike than with Sartre or Gide. A love of the French nineteenth century and of French antiquities, an enthusiasm for the novels of Michel Tournier, even a huge French audience and a book about an apocryphal Bulgaria, do not constitute a European sensibility, though they make the English sensibility more beguiling. However reluctant, he is a Forsterian: "The novel is essentially a realist form, even when interpreted in the most phantasmagoric manner," he insists. "A novel can't be abstract, like music. Perhaps if the novel becomes obsessed with theory (see the *nouveau roman*) or linguistic play (see *Finnegans Wake*) it may cease to be realistic; but then it also ceases to be interesting."

# | 34 |

## *Elegy*

Thornton Wilder, William Faulkner, Ellen Glasgow, Eudora Welty,
Carson McCullers, Flannery O'Connor, Harper Lee, Ralph Ellison,
Toni Morrison, Thomas Wolfe, Malcolm Lowry, Joyce Cary

At the memorial service for British victims of 9/11, the British prime minister read the concluding paragraphs of Thornton Wilder's *The Bridge of San Luis Rey*. It meditates on the collapse of an old suspension bridge and the deaths of five people. "A witness to the deaths, wanting to make sense of them and explain the ways of God to his fellow human beings, examined the lives of the people who died, and these words were said by someone who knew the victims, and who had been through the many emotions, and the many stages, of bereavement and loss." He ends, "There is a land of the living and a land of the dead, and the bridge is love. The only survival, the only meaning."

The novel, written by a young academic and would-be dramatist in the same year that Willa Cather published *Death Comes for the Archbishop,* was awarded the 1928 Pulitzer Prize. The imaginary Peru in which the book is set shares qualities with Cather's western landscapes through which move characters of a different cast from the standard protagonists of American fiction. Here was another America, not unfolding a blueprint of the future but provided with slower, more expansive skies, mountains, and spaces for reflection on the large actions and events of human life. In the context of 9/11, Wilder's words gained an archaic resonance. Sinclair Lewis, in his Nobel Prize acceptance speech, spoke of Wilder as one "who in an age of realism dreams the old and lovely dreams of the eternal romantics." This does him scant justice: he dreams away from the romantics toward an earlier time and a longer, common eternity.

When asked to comment on his own life story, Wilder compared the challenge to that of composing fiction: How was one "to employ the past tense in such a way that it does not rob . . . events of their character of having occurred in freedom. A great deal of writing and talking about the past is unacceptable. It freezes the historical in a determinism." Wilder's philosophical concerns illuminate his fictional procedures. "Today's writer smugly passes his last judgment and confers on existing attitudes the lifeless aspect of plaster-cast statues in a museum. He recounts the past as though the characters knew what was going to happen next." This is one reason for his love of dramatic writing: it insisted on the present tense and the seeming freedom, word by word, of the characters.

Thornton Niven Wilder (1897–1975) in his major plays (especially *Our Town*, 1938) and his best novels, *The Bridge of San Luis Rey* (1927), *Heaven's My Destination* (1935), *The Ides of March* (1948), and *The Eighth Day* (1967, National Book Award), writes with apparent directness and human warmth. True, he was a scholar and an intellectual. As a boy his schoolmates ridiculed him for retreating to the library, where he found company among books. His mature pursuits included researching and elegizing *Finnegans Wake* (he was in fact accused of borrowing from it in his 1942 play *The Skin of Our Teeth,* for which he won his third Pulitzer Prize, or Joyce his first); another sport was trying to date the plays of the Spanish Golden Age playwright Lope de Vega. Wilder was a lover of Cervantes, and the picaresque became his chosen model when he was trying to escape the overstaged character of his early fictions. But his learning was joyful, playful. In 1949 at the Goethe Festival held in Aspen, Colorado, Wilder lectured in his own person and also translated Albert Schweitzer's and José Ortega y Gasset's lectures, from German and Spanish respectively. He spent no more time in Europe than Hemingway or Fitzgerald did, but there was about his sense of the world and his learning the kind of European tone that one finds in a philosopher like George Santayana or, in a previous generation, a novelist like Henry James. He did not place himself at the center of his narrative or show off: fiction deepened his concern with human situations, it led away from an "I" with which he was not wholly at ease.

He was born in Madison, Wisconsin. A twin brother died at birth. His elder brother became a Wimbledon tennis player and a well-known poet and professor of theology at Harvard Divinity School, taking after their father, a Calvinistic presence, who was alarmed when Thornton was asked to play the role of Lady Bracknell in a school play and hostile to travesties of any kind. John Updike, introducing *The Eighth Day,* evokes the Wilder household as benign, cultured and not illiberal. Young Wilder grew away from dogma but retained the values that faith had inculcated. He could never affirm, but he could never bring himself to deny. "I am an awful wobbler," he declared. No one "serious" took him seriously in this respect. Updike speaks of his last major novel: "Untidy, self-delightingly, it brims with wonder and wisdom, and aspires to prophecy. We marvel at a novel of such spiritual ambition and benign flamboyance." Wilder told his sister it was "as though *Little Women* were being mulled over by Dostoyevsky."

The conceit of the title is that the seven days of creation are increased by one in which man starts to undo the works of God. "Man is not an end but a beginning. We are at the beginning of the second week," says the town doctor as the twentieth century dawns. "We are the children of the eighth day." Here the didactic elements are less integrated than in *The Bridge of San Luis Rey,* though there is a single crisis, the murder of Breckenridge Lansing, superintendent of the almost exhausted mines of Coaltown. That catalyzes the remaining action. The story moves back in time to examine the psychological and spiritual nature of John Ashley, accused of the murder and sprung from detention, traveling right down the spine of the Americas to the copper mines of Chile. It also touches on the nature of his victims and their wives. The novel's six sections, some of them very long (this was his wordiest novel), are more exemplary essay than conventional novel. Ideas have got the better of him at last. He was able at the end to avoid what might have been his most troubling subject had he been less intellectually agile and optimistic. His father's example and then his memory were powerful closet keepers for Thornton as his unconventional sexuality evolved. We read, "From the first, Lansing admired John Ashley and imitated him, stumblingly. He went so far as to pretend that he, too, was a happily married man. Society would have got nowhere without those imitations of order and decorum that pass under the names of snobbery and hypocrisy." The candor does not quite reach its subject matter.

Wilder père became a diplomat, and the world fanned open before young Thornton, from Wisconsin to Hong Kong, from Berkeley, California, where he spent much of his boyhood, to Shanghai, where his father was consul general. In Updike's words, "he played upon the world's map as on the keyboard of a clavier." He studied for a short time in a private school for the children of the administrative classes 450 miles north of Shanghai and found it lonely, strange, the native people debilitated, with the Sun Yat-sen revolution in progress. Back in California he completed his schooling and went to university, served in the Coast Guard in World War I, and finally took a BA at Yale and an MA in French at Princeton. Then he found himself at the American Academy in Rome, reading Latin and getting into hands-on archaeology, actually participating in digs. He remembered later the intense excitement of exposing an ancient bend in a road along which, millennia before, human traffic bustled in a then modern world. His first novel, *The Cabala* (1926), was taking shape.

He went on to teach, at a famous private school, at the universities of Chicago and Hawaii, Harvard, and elsewhere. He regarded himself as first a teacher and then a writer and was the most successful academic among the writers of his generation, though he did not become an academic novelist. Still, he had to squeeze writing in among other duties and called it "writing on the run," a sort of modern Trollope unstoppably writing, whether in a hotel room, a stateroom, or a term-time office.

He was generically restless, too. He translated from the French play scripts of André Obey and Jean-Paul Sartre, he worked on a libretto with Paul Hindemith, and Louise Talma made one of his plays into an opera. Alfred Hitchcock invited him to write the screenplay for *Shadow of a Doubt.* He was always up for a challenge. In Paris with Gertrude Stein he attended a poetry reading by Picasso, and he met through Stein the novelist, academic, tattooist, and gay pornographer Samuel Steward (pen name Phil Andros), with whom he had an intimacy.

*The Bridge of San Luis Rey* is as much an essay as *On the Eighth Day,* but the young fiction writer rather than the old philosopher is in charge. In 1714 a friar, Brother Juniper (named after Father Junipero Serra, founder of many of the California missions with which Wilder was familiar as a boy), about to cross the ancient rope bridge in Lima, Peru, witnesses its collapse. He wonders about the victims and starts inquiring into their identities and lives. As a Christian he hopes to find a connection in their coincidental deaths. His vast book of interviews is burned by the Inquisition, and he with it. Wilder's book is brief and focused, a remarkable invention.

In 1956 Wilder reflected on the danger in which the American writer increasingly found himself, "almost exclusively thrown in with persons more or less in the arts. He lives among them, eats among them, quarrels with them, marries them." There is an unreality about his "man in the street," shown "as he remembers him from childhood, or as he copies him out of other books." Wilder invented the common man and made him credible partly at least due to his theological and philosophical concerns, and in this his father's legacy is clearest. He may have trouble with the present tense and the contemporary world, and he is best when working at an oblique angle to his subject. He speaks of *Heaven's My Destination* as his main attempt to grapple with "the pious didacticism that would now be called narrow Protestantism." He does not call it that because from his point of view the writer needs a fixed point from which to push off, a point of orientation that is not a point of arrival. "The comic spirit is given to us in order that we may analyze, weigh, and clarify things in us that nettle us, or that we are outgrowing, or trying to reshape. That is a very autobiographical book," he remarks. The comic spirit for him must have a moral dimension, with no space for the merely gratuitous.

When the curtain fell on Faulkner's novel-play *Requiem for a Nun* at the Royal Court, London, the English theater critic Kenneth Tynan imagined an epilogue by the corncob-pipe-smoking Stage Manager from Wilder's play *Our Town.*

> Well, folks, reckon that's about it. End of another day in the city of Jefferson, Yoknapatawpha County, Mississippi. Nothin' much happened. Couple of people got raped, couple more got their teeth kicked

in, but way up there those far-away old stars are still doing their old cosmic crisscross, and there ain't a thing we can do about it. It's pretty quiet now. Folk hereabouts get to bed early, those that can still walk. Down behind the morgue a few of the young people are roastin' a nigger over an open fire, but I guess every town has its night-owls, and afore long they'll be tucked up asleep like anybody else. Nothin' stirring down at the big old plantation house—you can't even hear the hummin' of that electrified barbed-wire fence, 'cause last night some drunk ran slap into it and fused the whole works. That's where Mr. Faulkner lives.

Wilder wrote novels among other things, but William Faulkner (1897–1962), born Falkner, was a fiction writer through and through. For him the challenge of each story and novel is formal: he sets up narrative hurdles, he challenges himself at the level of diction, dialect, and syntax and especially life and language in time. The way language works to deliver character, narrative sequence, and the processes (there are seldom definitive conclusions) of sense fascinates him. Wilder explores the lives of several characters in *The Bridge of San Luis Rey*, a series of discrete narratives sparked by an incident and a set of themes. Faulkner works through voices, sometimes teased out into discrete sections, sometimes interwoven. He plays on different strings and instruments and avoids repetition. He thrives on the struggle, on overcoming (or not) the obstructions of character and the tyranny of time. Eudora Welty describes him as a "divining" writer. His work "increases us," she says, illuminating the past and the present in the process of moving into the past. She is talking about his core sense of the passage of time, how the intermittencies of language arrest, imitate, and are thwarted by its flow.

Faulkner regarded writers as a large family. Melville was Sherwood Anderson's grandfather and Twain his father, Dreiser an elder brother and he himself a younger brother, or a son or nephew; the sense of these connections, some easy and some difficult and destructive, is at the root of his sense of vocation. A family (as we know from his novels) is seldom functional. There are estrangements and incests, kissing cousins can kiss too passionately, fathers reject their children. In *The Sound and the Fury* (1929) the sole character we can more or less depend upon is the black servant Dilsey. In the 1933 introduction he writes that she was "to be the future, to stand above the fallen ruins of the family like a ruined chimney, gaunt, patient and indomitable." She is based on Mammie Caroline Barr, the servant who helped nurse him, bring him up, who endured his adult excesses and errors and died in 1940, and for whom he preached a short "Funeral Sermon" that is exquisite, sincere and compassionate, concluding, "She was born and lived and served, and died and now is mourned; if there is a heaven, she has gone there." He restrains himself, keeps himself out of it as Ford Madox Ford says a writer must, and is able thus to tell a truth not about his feelings but about her being.

How does a writer "keep himself out of it," especially a writer with the burden Faulkner carries? In a sense it is easier for him than for ideologically or aesthetically driven, self-effacing writers, Christopher Isherwood, say, or Henry Green. There is no pretense of objectivity but an acknowledgment and a celebration of the intractable subjectivity of character. Rendering them entails not construction but surrender to what they see, feel, to their history and to the cadences of their language, because they make sense with language and we see them in their language, length of period, diction, complexity of syntax, completion or incompletion. This is his political incorrectness and his imaginative wholeness, a belief that he has a right of access to the most protected areas of the spirit. Ralph Ellison in "Twentieth-Century Fiction and the Black Mask of History" celebrates the ways in which Faulkner "fights out the moral problem" that, after the nineteenth century, literature had generally resolved in platitude or ideology. Faulkner wrote beyond the South and "was actually seeking out the nature of man. Thus we must turn to him for that continuity of moral purpose which made for the greatness of our classics." He would start with the stereotype of the Negro, "accept it as true, and then seek out the human truth which it hides." Faulkner might be a starting point for black writers, "for in his work technique has been put once more to the task of creating value."

Faulkner's characters, unlike those of the young writers he apostrophizes in a 1958 address at the University of Virginia (making an exception of J. D. Salinger, whose *Catcher in the Rye* he admired), "function, live, breathe, struggle, in that moil and seethe of simple humanity," and he lists the novelist's natural ancestors as they occur to him, regardless of chronology: "Dickens, Fielding, Thackeray, Conrad, Twain, Smollett, Hawthorne, Melville, James." James in "that moil and seethe"? Well, yes. But if James, then why not Joyce, whose work he read with fascination in his formative years, and Woolf, whose stream of consciousness he came to prefer to Joyce's because it seemed purer and less contrived, and Thomas Mann whose capacious narrative, metaphorical and thematic architecture even in the stories and novellas challenged him. He approached *Ulysses* without reservation or irony, he said, "as the illiterate Baptist preacher approaches the Old Testament: with faith." This is how we approach Faulkner's books, not because they are obscure but because they have the luminous, close-up clarity of a mind engaged, with all the music of consciousness, its elisions and syncopations; and it should be read aloud.

Faulkner is compellingly impure, mud in the stream, the way consciousness really works before manners constrain and make it mannerly. The authors he loved in his maturity were those he had loved early on, including Cervantes, Flaubert, Balzac, Dostoyevsky, and Tolstoy. He knew his Scott, as southerners generally did. In *Absalom, Absalom!* (1936) riders set off to the Civil War, one mounted upon a black stallion "named out of Scott." We do not learn the name: what matters is the antebellum sensibility in which Scott, his sense of value, figured large. The Authorized Version of the Bible Faulkner had recourse to, drunk and sober; it is responsible for the sometimes overbearing sonority of his prose. His essays, letters, and speeches can be sermonic, hortatory, with big abstractions and devoid of irony, earnest and in earnest. "He has the most talent of anybody and he just needs a sort of conscience that isn't there," Hemingway said: sound and fury in abundance, but . . . He is unable to *end* his books: "I wish the christ I owned him like you'd own a horse and train him like a horse and race him like a horse—only in writing. How beautifully he can write and as simple and as complicated as autumn or as spring," Hemingway wrote to a friend in 1945. During a later misunderstanding between the men, Hemingway defined Faulkner's "great and incurable defect": "You can't re-read him." On a second reading you always see "how he fooled you the first time." In great writing you cannot "dissect-out" the mystery; with Faulkner he thought you could.

Despite differences in volume and scale, Faulkner and Hemingway have in common an originality of the kind that redirects the art they practice. Both are *fighters*. Each wants to be best and wants his generation to outdo the generations before. The better the field, the larger their triumph. Like Hemingway, Faulkner uses metaphors of boxing and other forms of fighting, competition expressed in terms not of relative sales but of relative strength and range. They have another thing in common, an artistic instinct: both are always, always aware of the time of day, the weather of the world in which they and their characters move, the landscape. For Faulkner the reality of the case of Emmett Till, the fourteen-year-old boy from Chicago who was lynched in Mississippi for flirting with a white woman, is palpable.

Hemingway's was a wider, not a deeper, world to travel. Faulkner had the American South, specifically Mississippi, and a portion of Mississippi centered on Lafayette County, which he, in the spirit in which Hardy called his fictional Dorset Wessex, called Yoknapatawpha County (Hemingway dubbed it Ano-matopeoio County). He establishes Yoknapatawpha in *Sartoris,* his third novel, in 1929, combining *Yocona* (the obsolete name of a river) and *petopha* from the Chicksaw Indian language signifying divided or split land. It meant, "water flowing slow through the flatland." Out of Yoknapatawpha, where all but three of his later novels and many of his stories are set, he teases a variety of character and a wealth of history. A divided land it is, and the divisions are unexpected and revealing. Wilson apostrophizes Faulkner as "the inventor of Yoknapatawpha County," "the greatest American novelist and perhaps the best novelist living," who created "a complete imaginary community." He notes the gulf between the stories he wrote doggedly and sometimes brilliantly for magazines to make a living, and the novels he wrote when he had bought enough time.

Virginian Ellen Glasgow (1873–1945) was among the earliest novelists to insist upon the distinctive southernness of southern writing. She stands behind Margaret Mitchell's best seller, *Gone with the Wind* (1936), and identifies a tradition. Later she reviles it, largely due to Faulkner, for its thematic candor and naturalistic language. "One may admit that the Southern States have more than an equal share of degeneracy and deterioration," she says, "but the multitude of half-wits, and whole idiots, and nymphomaniacs, and paranoiacs, and rakehells in general, that populate the modern literary South could flourish nowhere but in the weird pages of melodrama." She remains a first strut of the bridge that leads from popular sentimental writers to Faulkner, Katherine Anne Porter, Eudora Welty, and Tennessee Williams. *Barren Ground* (1925) and the very different *The Romantic Comedians* (1926) still reward the reader who can endure her overemphasis on the suffering of the protagonist in the first and the stereotypes of the second. She had her own melodrama. And after she achieved this artistic maturity in her early fifties, she began to rail against youth: her spirit and her work curdled. The South, as expressed by Faulkner particularly, had become a setting for what was "too vile and too degenerate to exist anywhere else." Sinclair Lewis in his Nobel Prize speech calls Faulkner the man who "freed the South from hoopskirts."

On Faulkner's behalf and her own, Eudora Welty (1909–2001) resisted the way that southerners and, for different reasons, readers from outside the South characterized them as "Southern" and "regional" writers. These terms she found condescending and "careless," an outsider's perspective wary of endorsing writing from so aberrant a history, its themes both inflected and infected deeply by defeat and an ongoing struggle. Welty says she and Faulkner were "simply writing about life" as they experienced it. One southern characteristic she did concede. It had to do with storytelling. "Our people"—she meant the people of the Mississippi Delta and of the South more generally, with their mix of cultures— "our people talk that way. They learn and teach and think and enjoy that way. Southerners do have—they've inherited—a narrative sense of human destiny."

Faulkner the "diviner" sees into things and understands what they are and what they figure. He "throws light on the past and on today as it becomes the past . . . This being so, it informs the future." The past is a heavy burden for Welty also, but she is a detector more than a diviner, a writer whose métier is the short story and novella and whose role in this story is small despite her four adult novels, of which the most engaging is *Delta Wedding* (1946), which plays to her short narrative strengths. There is hardness in her delicacy: she will not sentimentalize. She is the kind of writer who excises, and the thrift of her stories is accentuated by the large canvases of Faulkner, with his stylistic blemishes that we tolerate as expressive roughnesses of voice.

Edmund Wilson draws attention to Faulkner's "inveterate misuse of words ending in '-ate,' such as 'postulate' and 'aberrate'"; he uses "mitigate" for "militate." But he had an editor, someone must surely have drawn his attention to the problem, so why did he insist? Elaborate clauses are suspended without syntactical connection, and danglers of a nonparticipial kind occur. He bases neologisms on archaic usage; for example, "surviven." The syntax is stretched rather than shaped: not James or Joyce but a verbal Procrustes at work. Wilson says, "The big picture is everything" for Faulkner. Characters can be carried away in dialogue, the author's grandiloquence breaking the bounds of their dialect. For Steinbeck the overreaching style made him a species of hypocrite. In 1933 he declared, "The festered characters of Faulkner are not very interesting to me unless their festers are heroic."

Welty loves his style. Celebrating *Sanctuary* when it was published in 1931, she declared, "It's likely that Faulkner's prose can't be satisfactorily analyzed and accounted for, until it can be predicted." She finds it "intolerantly and intolerably unanalyzable and quite pure, something more than a possum in a tree—with its motes bright-pure and dark-pure falling on us, critics and non-critics alike." The image is wonderful, seeming to prophesy the mesmerizing opening of *Absalom, Absalom!*: "From a little after two o'clock until almost sundown of the long still hot weary dead September afternoon they sat in what Miss Coldfield still called the office because her father had called it that—a dim hot airless room with the blinds all closed and fastened for forty-three summers because when she was a girl someone had believed that light and moving air carried heat and that dark was always cooler, and which (as the sun shone fuller and fuller on that side of the house) became latticed with yellow slashes full of dust motes which Quentin thought of as being flecks of the dead old dried paint itself blown inward from the scaling blinds as wind might have blown them." Such a seemingly profligate sentence, sparsely punctuated, heavily adjectived, full of important information, history, introductions, atmospheres, 122 words to get the novel moving, is the essence of *economy*. Welty is aware of this paradox when she talks of the originality of Faulkner's style.

The sentence also prefigures, in its back-and-forth in time and space, the form the novel will take as the huge drama that precedes it grows scene by scene into a history of old-fashioned energies and values with epic features, and their decline, in the aftermath of the Civil War, into the enervation of the present. In a letter Faulkner says, "I am trying to say it all in one sentence, between one Cap and one period." In his novels a narrative mystery and an appropriate formal experiment develop together.

Faulkner wrote at urgent speed, Welty wrote abundantly but slowly. She was shy of exposure; seeing proofs of her work, she said, made her feel she was getting sunburn. One of her wisest remarks is about speech in fiction as "another form of action." Even in a comic novel, dialogue either advances or arrests the narrative. Each word must reveal something about the speaker, the addressee, the action, and sometimes the author's relations to all these. Dialogue is not where the writer rests on her oars, it is never *mere* banter. She was a reviser. "The hardest thing for me is getting people in and out of rooms—the mechanics of a story. A simple act of putting on clothes is almost impossible for me to describe without many false starts." She tries to work from the inside out; she never knows what a character looks like, how she walks, how he dresses, until she knows "exactly what's in their hearts and minds." Updike likens her to Wright Morris as a photographer-writer. She is a portrait reader who reads her subjects in specific places, sews them into their context. William Maxwell told Updike that when Welty submitted stories to the *New Yorker,* she *pinned* the sheets together. Updike saw her as a metaphorical dressmaker, pins pinched between her lips. Richard Ford was her friend and leaves a cheerful picture of the writer. "She does voices, she mimics, she has a sensitivity to the absurdities of language. She also has a vivid memory for song lyrics. She's a performer who simply didn't choose to perform upon a conventional stage." The humor is of a rare and subtle kind. "Her work often doesn't seem funny, but then is funny under the surface—sometimes even quite grave stories."

Nothing came easily to Faulkner, and when the things he had longed for at the start did in fact arrive, it was always too late. He had a temperament predisposed to disappointment. Nothing he did was as good as he felt it ought to be, and he registered few moments when he felt the release of composition. "Ninety-nine percent talent . . . ninety-nine percent discipline . . . ninety-nine percent work," he said, generalizing about serious writers from his experience: "He must never be satisfied with what he does." In New Orleans at the start of his writing career he liked the writer's life as he saw Sherwood Anderson living it, on his own terms, without compromise and with severe frugality.

His first novel, *Soldier's Pay* (1926), did not make him rich or famous, but with it, he says, "I found out writing was fun. But I found out afterward not only that each book had to have a design but the whole output or sum of an artist's work had to have a design." As he wrote on he realized how immensely full of content was "my own little postage stamp of native soil" and how he would not ever exhaust it. *Mosquitoes* (1927) and *Sartoris* made a modest mark. With *The Sound and the Fury* he came creatively of age.

The title carries a Shakespearean irony: life, Macbeth concludes, is in the end "a tale / Told by an idiot, full of sound and fury, / Signifying nothing." The first voice we hear speaking at length is that of Benjy, the idiot child of the Compsons, a once-prosperous and respected family in terminal decline. Faulkner wrote an introduction to the novel in 1933 describing how he tried both to escape the situation of the southern writer, and also to pass judgment, through the development of the characters. This was "the turning point: in this book I did both at one time." He started without a plan, indeed, without knowing he was engaged upon his fourth novel. After the unsuccess of the first three, he felt the bleak freedom of a writer who resolves to please himself. And he did: the experience of writing the Benjy section was never repeated, "that ecstasy, that eager and joyous faith and anticipation of surprise."

The novel has four separate narrators, and the reader builds a world from their telling. They touch upon the same events, each bringing different information, different psychological and moral inflections, to bear. The last narrative is straightforward, but it works on the vivid palimpsest of the first three. Benjy is followed by Quentin, the son upon whom hopes were pinned, who went to Harvard and took his own life as a result of the weeds of prejudice, tradition, morality, and pride planted in his nature. His obsession with time and its arrest provides compelling symbolism. He breaks his watch and takes it to the mender. The language in which he feels makes his world vivid.

> There was a clock, high up in the sun, and I thought about how, when you don't want to do a thing, your body will try to trick you into doing it, sort of unawares. I could feel the muscles in the back of my neck, and then I could hear my watch ticking away in my pocket and after a while I had all the other sounds shut away, leaving only the watch in my pocket. I turned back up the street, to the window. He was working at the table behind the window. He was going bald. There was a glass in his eye—a metal tube screwed into his face. I went in.
>
> The place was full of ticking, like crickets in September grass, and I could hear a big clock on the wall above his head. He looked up, his eye big and blurred and rushing beyond the glass. I took mine out and handed it to him.

Caddy, the sister, catalyst of the moral and psychological action, seems to escape, but in an alarming and destructive way, and her daughter, called Quentin also, comes under the avaricious, abusive guardianship of Jason. His is the third voice, callous in the extreme: without the idiocy of Benjy, he is no less addicted to self-gratification, and the demands he makes, because he has understanding, are the immoral core of the novel, Faulkner's indictment. Benjy is not a moral agent and his castration is a practical way of dealing with his uncontrollable instincts; Jason is a moral agent, and in a state of continual indignation moralizes greedily, misogynistically. He embodies, and he partly causes, the impoverishment of the other characters. Faulkner begins with the least capable character, whose language can articulate only a world of sense impressions in which he moves, the central figure. Intense, brief anxieties mark his utter dependence.

Each successive character is alive in a language and thrall to its limitations. Faulkner ends with an "omniscient" narrator, the point of view moving close to that of the faithful servant Dilsey. She is the most stable, the least vexed, presence in the book, holding together the frayed threads of the family. John Gardner finds Dilsey sentimental; she epitomizes a sentimentality he finds more widely in Faulkner, which leads to his missing the human target. Gardner likes and believes in Dilsey, but he asks whether Faulkner "understands her or really cares." She stands more as a symbol than a person; Faulkner leaves too much unsaid. "Mythologizing her—or accepting the standard mythology of the age— he slightly skews the inevitability of his story. He does the same thing *every time he turns on his mannered rhetoric*—distorts the inherent emotion of the story and thus gets diverted from the real and inevitable progress of events." Again, the issue is one of language and proportion.

Is it mannered rhetoric? Read aloud as Faulkner conceived it, taking a kind of dictation first from Benjy and then risking the other voices, it is something quite different. It does not possess the properties of a script in the way that *As I Lay Dying* or, more obviously, even in format, *Requiem for a Nun* (1951) do, but the handling of voices, of time and timing, and withholding a corrective narratorial point of view to the end, hand crucial responsibilities to the reader. We meet Caddy first through the dependent voice of Benjy, who sees what is there but never why, who cannot infer the emotional content of situations and whose own emotions run the gamut from need to fear, not knowing what he needs or what he fears. Caddy is scents to him, and textures; she attends to him, she is there for him, and then she is gone. When Quentin and then Jason evoke her, she is the same person differently experienced. Though Quentin loves her, her disgrace and absence exacerbate his self-destructive state of mind. What for Benjy is a simple impression for Quentin becomes heavily symbolic. The stained drawers are as virulent to him, in memory, as a scarlet letter. And Jason, who was cruel to Caddy from the outset, drives her away. She is not a symbol of the end of his family's distinction but the cause. There are no contradictions between narratives, just different ways of reading the facts. Each way defines a character. One narrative could not have done justice to so complex a theme. Time for Faulkner cannot be linear.

*As I Lay Dying* (1930) has become Faulkner's most popular novel. It is relatively short and once the technique is understood its form appears straightforward. The narrative is parceled out between fifteen voices, each distinguished by diction and pace, each with a different temperament and a defined relationship with the burden, the dead body of Addie (who retains her voice, too), carried to her final resting place. Again it is a play of voices that define themselves in the act of speaking, creating identities on the ear.

If we are to believe the author, the book was composed in six weeks. He worked at an electric power plant. Occasionally he had to shovel coal into a furnace; otherwise his time was his own in a quiet, separate place. He claimed to have written it "without changing a word." Because *The Sound and the Fury* had not sold well, he set out now "deliberately to write a *tour de force.*" He began knowing exactly where the book was going and how it would end: the whole was there before he started writing. Brevity was in part a charm against his getting bored during writing; also against his marring the writing by authorial presence. Of all his books, this most resembles one of Hemingway's: there is an iceberg under the weathered tip. Its popularity may have something to do with its deliberated wholeness. It is a book that can be *talked about.* It is also dramatic and contains a compelling conflagration (Faulkner has an almost Gothic compulsion in burning down barns and houses). From Donald Barthelme it elicited the jocular complementary *The Dead Father.*

But *As I Lay Dying* did not immediately prosper. *Sanctuary* (1931) "was deliberately conceived to make money," and with its vulnerable female characters, its warped eroticism, and the theme of rape, it certainly did that. When he got galley proofs he was appalled, rewrote it, and had to foot the bill for resetting. That year he noted in a review that defeat is not necessarily an end, a judgment; it can be a moral and psychological instructor, an agent not of destruction but of transformation. The tyrannical Popeye is Faulkner's only unredeemable villain, and after injustice and a lynching, justice is done, though not for the crimes committed, and not in the place where evil occurred.

*Light in August* (1932) begins as a road novel, but a pedestrian one, the pregnant girl in search of the man who she thought loved her and who certainly left her. She has faith and innocence, which carry her through one of Faulkner's harshest novels, about history, race, family, and justice. And how time works. As she walks, the girl hears far off an approaching wagon. She knows the driver will take her part of the way. She inhabits anticipation, then the actuality, and finally the aftermath, in a kind of Daoist meditation. As in the earlier novels the full narrative emerges slowly. We encounter a series of overlying strata, characters diversely related and all defined and redefined as the novel advances. Unlike the four narratives of *The Sound and Fury,* and the intermeshing of *As I Lay Dying,* here the narrator has a limited omniscience and must listen hard to his characters and build them out from their perceived cores.

And he continues at this level of invention, if not of formal clarity, in *Absalom, Absalom!,* the title establishing the theme, the fateful treachery of the beloved son. The revelations are essentially through dialogue, and the core themes are sex and love, carnal and romantic, conventional and transgressive. Jorge Luis Borges wrote in 1937: "There is an infinite decomposition, an infinite and black carnality, in this book. The theatre is the state of Mississippi: the heroes, men disintegrating from envy, alcohol, loneliness, and the erosions of history." Those erosions are accelerated by defeat: the defeated cause or country has no way of shoring up its identities; they wash away, ghosts prattle, men act in a world in which their actions make sense only in relation to the past. Borges compares it to *The Sound and the Fury.* "I know no higher praise." It stays in mind as movements, images, connections: the plump, hungry wagons; the runaway architect, the interracial wrestling, the house fire; and Sutven like Ahab or Judge Pynchon or Judge Holden. It also stays in memory as sound, especially the astonishing iambic rhapsody of Miss Rosa. Faulkner's women, in character and variety, are as unsentimentally achieved as his men. Most fiction, Borges notes in a review of *The Unvanquished* (1938), accepts the pastness of the past, but sometimes (given the past's failures and betrayals) Faulkner seeks "to recreate the pure present, neither simplified by time nor polished by attention." The racial, sexual, and political mix, the Civil War defeat: "There are books that touch us physically, like the closeness of the sea or of the morning." Faulkner has become the Latin American American: Europe can make do with Joyce. Faulkner displaces him. Gabriel García Márquez says, "Only a technique like Faulkner's could have enabled me to write down what I was seeing," returning with his mother to his birthplace, Aracataca, where he spent his early years and found himself "reading" the place. In his view it was a coincidence of techniques.

*The Wild Palms* (1939); the Flem Snopes trilogy *The Hamlet* (1940), *The Town* (1957), and *The Mansion* (1959), in which low triumphs over high, a pyrrhic victory over the Sutpens and Compsons and the other great spent families of the county; the "sequel" to *Sanctuary, Requiem for a Nun,* written as a play with prose introductions to each act; Pulitzer Prize–winning *A Fable* (1954), which Hemingway scornfully dismissed, saying, "I would be a little more moved if he hunted animals that ran both ways"; and *The Reivers* (1962), a posthumous Pulitzer, are variable achievements. But there is no doubt that *Intruder in the Dust* (1948) is a great one. Welty wrote, "The separate scenes leap up on their own, we progress as if by bonfires lighted on the way, and the essence of each scene takes form before the eyes, a shape in the fire." She wrote discreet scenes, but his emerge from a single conflagration, are burnished by the same flames. The story prefigures Harper Lee's more famous, more conventional, *To Kill a Mockingbird*. Welty speaks of Faulkner's "comprehensive sense of the whole deep, deep past" and "far-reaching, bred-in country knowledge." What makes the book excruciatingly anxious to read is its slowness, at the climax almost in "real time," the imminence of the perils faced, the palpable darkness of the night and the patient, settled hatred the common folk feel for the man they have condemned without trial on the basis of his color.

Saul Bellow remembers how he admired people with "ideas" when he was young, everyone bowed down before "ideas." "Sidney Hook . . . once said to me that Faulkner was an excellent writer whose books would be greatly improved by dynamic ideas. 'I'd be glad to give him some,' he said. 'It would make a tremendous difference.'" In Faulkner ideas are lived, part of a historical given. Ideas in Hook's sense, things to be entertained, advanced or refuted, would have been anathema. Faulkner never read Freud, arguing that Shakespeare and Melville got on fine without him.

---

Lula Carson Smith is Carson McCullers (1917–1967), a fiction writer and dramatist, a writer on a very different scale and from quite another South. Gore Vidal places her in the company of those writers of the 1940s who "tend to devote themselves to the drama within the boat, the encompassing cold sea ignored in the passions of the human moment." He links her writing with that of his friend Tennessee Williams, who became her friend in Paris in the 1940s and whose characters and tones come from the same root stock as hers. He admires how, "using the small scale, the relations of human beings at their most ordinary, [she] transcends her milieu and shows, in bright glimpses, the potentiality which exists in even the most banal of human relationships, the 'we' as opposed to the meager 'I.'" Her novels disclose in its complexity the particular southern experience of relation and alienation. He disliked the person herself, her insistent talk always of her own work, her questions always relating to his response. A centripetal artist: Jane Bowles was, he said, similarly self-insistent but with a less singsong, less grating manner.

McCullers was born in Columbus, Georgia, scion of a grand antebellum family on her mother's side and on her father's of French protestant extraction. Her father liked the idea of her becoming a writer, and when she was fifteen he gave her a typewriter. In the same year she contracted rheumatic fever and her life of ill health began. Soon she started having the series of small strokes that gradually incapacitated her. She wrote plays in the manner, she believed, of

Eugene O'Neill. Her first novel has an autobiographical bias and one of the great titles in English fiction, *The Heart Is a Lonely Hunter* (1940), taken from a poem by the Scottish writer William Sharp under his pseudonym Fiona Macleod. The book was an immediate success and was adapted for the stage. Her other notable novels included *Reflections in a Golden Eye* (1941), *The Member of the Wedding* (1946), and the novella *The Ballad of the Sad Café* (1951), all of which were made into films. *Clock without Hands* (1961) works on a larger scale and is her most Faulknerian novel, delving into the theme of ingrained racism. It was not Graham Greene's favorite among her books. He admired her, with Faulkner, as one of the few writers with "an original poetic sensibility." He preferred her to Faulkner because of her clarity and to Lawrence "because she has no messages."

She showed musical talent and at seventeen set off from Savannah by ship for the Julliard School of Music in New York. She lost her tuition money and hunkered down, did odd jobs, and studied writing at night classes at Columbia University and elsewhere in the city. She was drawn to Djuna Barnes and followed her about like a stalker.

She was only nineteen when she went back South to marry the onetime soldier and would-be writer Reeves McCullers, as much a bisexual as she was. They moved to Charlotte, North Carolina. They lived also for two years at Fort Bragg, where she wrote *The Heart Is a Lonely Hunter* and developed the ideas that matured into the charged, bleak eroticism of *Reflections in a Golden Eye*. She was twenty-two. The first marriage was short-lived. When she separated, she returned to New York and lived with the *Harper's Bazaar* editor George Davis, sharing lodgings with the poet W. H. Auden and the composer Benjamin Britten, with Jane and Paul Bowles and the entertainer and striptease artist Gypsy Rose Lee. There she completed *Reflections in a Golden Eye*. In the *New Yorker* that year she was accused of plagiarizing D. H. Lawrence's short story "The Prussian Officer" in her new novel. There were thematic affinities, but the works were on different scales and in different keys. Louis Auchincloss remarks on how her characters "are reflected in the golden eye of Private Williams who looks in the window, an eye that does not judge, but that simply gives them back as they are. That eye is not only nature; it is death." In not judging, it is not Lawrencian, Greene's point. McCullers remembered her Lawrencian phase: at sixteen she wrote a novel entitled *Brown River,* strongly influenced by *Sons and Lovers.*

Fatefully in 1945 she remarried Reeves McCullers, entering once more the tense, unsatisfactory world of his needs and disappointments. In 1946 at the writers' retreat Yaddo she met the young Truman Capote and they got on, two southerners, one established, the other on his way (he was writing *Other Voices, Other Rooms*). When she and her husband were setting out for France later that year, Capote made himself useful, staying over for several days with the McCullerses in Nyack, New York. Reeves enjoyed the company of the young Capote, as later of Tennessee Williams. Carson McCullers promoted Capote's work and felt ill-thanked when, later, she reckoned he had plagiarized from her. She broke with him, though he was steadfast in his affection and attended Reeves's funeral in France and, years later, her own in Nyack, New York. McCullers ran away from her husband's plan for a double suicide. He had followed through with it alone.

By 1948 she was suffering from partial paralysis as a result of her strokes, and her later years were frail. She dictated a memoir, *Illumination and Nightglare,* left unfinished, published more than three decades after her death. "Life could become one long dim scramble just to get the things needed to keep alive," she wrote in *The Ballad of the Sad Café.* "Often after you have sweated and tried and things are not better for you, there comes a feeling deep down in the soul that you are not worth much."

Judging a writer so much of a piece with her sad and strange life as was Carson McCullers is a delicate matter. As her reputation and Capote's have gone through phases of revision, both have diminished. Joyce Carol Oates, reviewing *Illumination and Nightglare,* is in no doubt that Flannery O'Connor's hour is, ironically, coming even as McCullers's unfairly passes. The so-called Southern Gothic they ushered in is now a subject for parody. "McCullers may be perceived in some quarters as a writer of young adult classics whose work has not transcended its era," one of those quarters not being Oates's. For her *The Member of the Wedding* remains "an exquisitely rendered, haunting work that surpasses anything O'Connor has written." She cannot but admire the modern, unsentimentally drawn "lonely, eccentric, sexually ambiguous men and women"—self-portraits, portraits of a marriage, in the manner of Frieda Kahlo's—which "achieve a mythopoeic power largely lacking in the two-dimensional portraits of 'grotesque' Southerners who populate O'Connor's backwoods Georgia fiction." Oates takes an agreeable risk in her concluding, against-the-tide judgment: "McCullers's characters are like us: human, hapless, hopeful, 'real.'"

The characters (Mary) Flannery O'Connor (1925–1964) created are certainly not "like us," Oates says, but "actors in an ideologically charged theological drama (she was a fiercely polemical Roman Catholic), tending toward allegory (or caricature)." In terms of her moral parables they are harrowingly "real." O'Connor's eccentric, entertaining essays with a playful, firm Roman Catholic slant hardly prepare us for the moral and spiritual extremes of her novels. The style is still thrifty and evocative, as in her stories. In her first novel, *Wise Blood* (1952), she cobbled together three short stories with elements of others into a single-seeming fiction. The book opens simply: "Hazel Motes sat at a forward angle on the green plush train seat, looking one minute at the window as if he might want to jump out of it, and the next down the aisle at the other end of the car. The train was racing through treetops that fell away at intervals and showed the sun standing, very red, on the edge of the farthest woods. Nearer, the plowed fields curved and faded and the few hogs nosing in the furrows looked like large spotted stones." The specific detail of the description, the man's name, his posture, the space in- and outside the train, the intermittent landscape visible through trees, the woods receding to the skyline, the sun through them, red intensified by the darkness of the woods; then closer, the hogs: the eye draws its focus back from the transfigured distance to the middle distance, the familiar world that Hazel Motes inhabits. We see not from Hazel's point of view but with an immediate omniscience that proves to be more than that of a standard omniscient narrator. When Hazel becomes "a member and preacher to that church where the blind don't see and the lame don't walk and what's dead stays that way," "the Church Without Christ," his message is simple. "I preach there are all kinds of truth, your truth and somebody else's, but behind all of them, there's only one truth and that is that there is no truth . . . No truth behind all truths is what I and this church preach!"

The purity of the plotting, its simplicity and heartless directness, remind the reader that O'Connor was astonished by Nathanael West's *Miss Lonelyhearts,* a kind of formal pattern-book to which she remained indebted as she felt her way forward in her writing. "My own approach to literary problems is very like the one Dr. Johnson's blind housekeeper used when she poured tea—she put her finger in the cup." Anthony Burgess liked the writing's spareness in which he experienced so directly "the physical world of the fundamentalist south." The elements that drew O'Connor to West, says Joyce Carol Oates, were "his acerbic style, his cruel genius for caricature, and his young male Miss Lonelyhearts as a Christ-fanatic in denial of his faith very like O'Connor's young Christ-fanatic Hazel Motes." His impact on her work persisted in "Westian turn of phrase, sharp, revealing yet funny; a comic tone abruptly turned savage in the story's concluding paragraphs." The fundamental difference between them was that O'Connor was a believer and could, as a result, be even more brutal than West with the world of the body, given the dour endurance of the spirit that the body existed to test and shape. To her correspondence friend Betty Hester, who confessed guilts of a sexual nature to O'Connor, she wrote, "The meaning of our redemption is that we do not have to be our history." The novels lay down the history the characters do not have to be. As a Bible Belt Roman Catholic, O'Connor observes characters of a fundamentalist Protestant persuasion, either practicing or lapsed, who undergo trial and experience transformations.

Oates speaks of "the sadistic punishment of 'disbelievers'" in the books. It is cruel, but to a Christian who has read the Old and New Testaments it will seem scriptural rather than sadistic. O'Connor remarks in an essay, faith "frees the story-teller to observe. It is not a set of rules which fixes what he sees in the world. It affects his writing primarily by guaranteeing his respect for mystery." The writer is thus imbued with "the sharpest eyes for the grotesque, for the perverse, and for the unacceptable."

In 1946 O'Connor enrolled in the University of Iowa on a journalism scholarship. Journalism was not for her. She approached Paul Engle, head of the legendary Writers' Workshop, to ask if she might enter his program. Her Georgia accent was wholly incomprehensible to him: she had to write down her request so he could read it and reply. After looking at her work, his response was affirmative. Her supportive circle of (mainly male) friends included John Crowe Ransom and Andrew Lytle, both editors (Lytle regularly published her in *Sewanee Review*), and the poet and novelist Robert Penn Warren.

When she became established, O'Connor did not sell as well as McCullers. Like McCullers, she suffered ill health. She preferred to stay at the family farm in Georgia writing and tending her peacocks ("It is hard to tell the truth about this bird") rather than struggle in the wider world. She was chronically unwell, increasing in frailty, dwindling like a character in a Gothic novel. She died when she was thirty-nine, having suffered painfully—as her father had before her—from lupus (SLE).

Kurt Vonnegut provided a list of the eight rules for writing short stories. He added that O'Connor broke all the rules except the first, and that great writers (he regarded her as one) can do this. The one rule she kept was, "Use the time of a total stranger in such a way that he or she will not feel the time was wasted." Her essays have the structure of short stories: they are dramatic, persuasive; they have a narrator who is characterized and formed. She says, "In the South there are more amateur authors than there are rivers and streams. It's not an activity that waits upon talent. In almost every hamlet you'll find at least one lady writing epics in Negro dialect and probably two or three old gentlemen who have impossible historical novels on the way." Each sentence takes satire further, deeper into the actual society, its concerns and values.

*Wise Blood* is not a satisfactory novel, its characters sketched with a caricaturist's pen, the incidents of plot thematically, not dramatically, contrived, the lives and deaths unattenuatedly brutal. Yet the book is hypnotically readable, its dynamic being that of dream, where the rightness is felt but not understood. Her second novel, *The Violent Bear It Away* (1960), is remorseless in a different way. Francis Tarwater is fourteen and lives at Powderhead, a homestead farm in a clearing in a remote forest in Georgia. His tyrannical, fundamentalist grandfather Mason, who has forced upon the child a dreadful responsibility, to be a "prophet" of a very specific kind, dies. The book is the story of how the child fulfills an awful duty, which entails locating his uncle and baptizing his own imbecile first cousin Bishop. The battle between faith and reason is waged between grandfather and grandson, uncle and nephew, dead and living, abetted by attendant voices and the pressure of individual histories that cannot be sloughed without judgment and access to grace. Some of the extreme experiences—the drowning of Bishop in a ritual baptism, the rape of young Tarwater when he is picked up while hitchhiking by a predatory motorist (the devil, perhaps)—feel gratuitous. The punishment of the hapless uncle is excessive in other ways. As with *Wise Blood,* however, the writing is hard to resist, its focus and simplicity bringing alive the physical world in such a way as to body forth the dark spiritual elements at play. In an interview, Truman Capote patted her on the head with, "She has some fine moments, that girl." His hand should have been badly charred.

*To Kill a Mockingbird* (1960) is the one book (Nelle) Harper Lee (b. 1926) wrote. It contains ideas of the kind Sidney Hook approves, ideas that would not have occurred to McCullers or O'Connor as matter sufficient for fiction. It was published at as opportune a historical moment as Harriet Beecher Stowe's *Uncle Tom's Cabin* (1852). John F. Kennedy had just been elected president of the United States; the civil rights decade that accelerated the ongoing transformation of the South (and the North) had begun. The book's success (well over 30 million copies sold and a Pulitzer Prize) stopped its author in her tracks. *The Long Goodbye,* of which she had drafted a hundred pages, got no further. The author maintained a dignified distance from the literary world.

Ingrained racism in the American South is witnessed through the eyes of Scout, an articulate girl whose father, Atticus, is the attorney to whom it falls to defend a black man charged with attempted rape. Lee's own father was a onetime newspaper editor who had become a lawyer. Like the narrator of her novel, Lee as a girl was a tomboy who also loved reading. One of her neighbors and playmates was the young Truman Capote, on whom Scout's friend Dill in the novel is based. Lee helped Capote with research for *In Cold Blood* just after she had finished writing *To Kill a Mockingbird.* Capote himself remembers the original for Boo Radley, the ultimately benign monster who lends, with his haunted house, a Gothic dimension to the novel. There is little ambiguity in the book. Straight away we know that Tom Robinson is innocent of rape, that Atticus is benign, wise, and full of high sentence, that Scout is smart and attentive. What governs the book is less the credibly drawn characters than a plot that must have a just outcome and a theme that is morally compelling. It is in the *Uncle Tom's Cabin* tradition: its popularity will decline if and when racism is decisively unlearned and it is possible to pull the book from the school and university syllabus. Even then it will, like *Uncle Tom's Cabin,* continue to find readers. Flannery O'Connor commented, "It's interesting that all the folks that are buying it don't know they are reading a children's book." I was thirteen when it came out and I had no idea it was a children's book when I read it.

At university Lee worked on the newspaper and in her junior year transferred to law. She then realized that she wanted to be a writer, not a lawyer. She went to Oxford on a summer exchange, and on her return dropped out of college and moved to New York, got work, and reconnected with Capote. They wrote, he grew famous, and when her fame arrived, for a few years she retained her ambitions. Interviewed in 1964 Lee said in a voice very like that of Atticus, "I want to do the best I can with the talent God gave me. I hope to goodness that every novel I do gets better and better . . . In other words all I want to be is the Jane Austin [*sic*] of south Alabama." We can blame the "Austin" on her interlocutor.

---

In a memorial statement in 1995, Saul Bellow, a close friend, quotes Ralph [Waldo] Ellison (1914–1994): "We did not develop as a people in isolation. We developed within a context of white people. Yes, we have a special awareness, because our experience has in certain ways been different from that of white people; but it was not absolutely different." Bellow as a Jew understood what he was saying. Ellison added, "Too often they fear to leave the uneasy sanctuary of race to take their chances in the world of art." He took the chance decisively once; for the rest of his life he kept threatening to take it again, but what survived in manuscript was a string of clichés beside the durable originality of *Invisible Man* (1952), which won the 1953 National Book Award and made Ellison the leading black author of his generation. Burgess called *Invisible Man* "without doubt the most important post-war novel on the condition of the black man in an intolerant white society." He responded to the symbolism and to the irreversible circumstances of the plot. As a man of formal patterning himself, Burgess will have noticed the principle of threes on which the book is built, the three main sections, the subsections also progressing in threes, as if following the rules of Roman rhetoric.

Ellison is an uncompromising critic. He debated with theorists of black writing, Stanley Edgar Hyman for example, who argued for the distinguishing qualities of black folklore as a required resource for black writers. Ellison contended that in the interests of participating in the larger world, in literature as a whole, a larger belonging was available: "My point is that the Negro American writer is also an heir of the human experience which is literature, and this might well be more important to him than the living folk tradition." Even so, he came to regard American Negro history as "a most intimate part of American history. Through the very process of slavery came the building of the United States. Negro folklore, evolving within a larger culture which regarded it as inferior, was an especially courageous expression." In song, in speech, "it announced the Negro's willingness to trust his own experience, his own sensibilities as to the definition of reality, rather than allow his masters to define these crucial matters for him." It is possible to condescend to it "as something exotic, folksy, or 'low-down,'" but for his own part he sees it as "intertwined, diffused" in the "very texture" of American experience. This sense of indelible inclusion preceded and survived the defining impact of *The Waste Land* and of Joyce, though he had found nothing of "equal intensity or sensibility by an American Negro writer." He also owed debts to Stein and especially to Hemingway. When, in the mid-1950s, he said, "I wasn't, and am not, *primarily* concerned with injustice, but with art," he was at his most political, holding his art away from the debate on the grounds that it is art and cannot be made instrumental without violation of its integrity. Yet, like much great art, *Invisible Man* is a work of protest. The imagery of darkness and light, the move from South to North as a process of liberation, and other elements of black culture and experience he drew upon, but the process was slow and he took his bearings here from Eliot and Joyce. "When I started writing, I knew that in both *The Waste Land* and *Ulysses,* ancient myth and ritual were used to give form and significance to the material; but it took me a few years to realize that the myths and rites which we find functioning in our everyday lives could be used in the same way." He gives us "a novel about innocence and human error, a struggle through illusion to reality."

Ralph Ellison was born in Oklahoma City and named after Emerson. His parents were quietly cultured, ambitious, and American. He aspired to be a musician. Indeed, he aspired to be a renaissance man, but the Great Depression changed things. He was admitted to the celebrated Tuskegee Institute to study music and availed himself of the library to read widely among the modernists. In 1936 in New York he was brought with Langston Hughes, Richard Wright, and others into the Federal Writers' Project. Wright took him up and encouraged him to read Conrad and James, not to imitate but to enjoy them and measure himself against them. He appears to have gone a long way with Dostoyevsky, *Notes from the Underground* in particular, and Gogol, out of whose famous "Overcoat" he too steps as a writer.

In the "Black Mask of Humanity" Ellison elaborates a theory of creativity that builds on Eliot's notion of the "objective correlative" but psychologizes it. "The irony of the 'lost generation' writers is that while disavowing a social role it was the fate of their works to perform a social function which re-enforced those very social values which they most violently opposed." The work of art "like the stereotype, is personal; psychologically it represents the socialization of some profoundly personal problem involving guilt" (he enumerates, parricide, fratricide, incest, and homosexuality), seeking to transcend them through expressing them. What was it Nietzsche said? "Guilt is a substitute for thought." It can be engaged through art, and once it is it can become subject to thought.

His period as a Communist, working closely with Wright, ended as Wright's did with the Second World War. He began his novel out of disillusion, encouraged by Wright. It took him from 1945, when the idea came to him, to 1951 to complete it. Ellison's characters are, as he and his circle were, educated, engaging culture and prejudice in their complexity and recognizing the different varieties of racial hatred and exclusion in different parts of the United States. The nameless narrator's invisibility is figurative: he is not registered. The book touches on other proscribed themes, including Communism. He knew what kind of gauntlet he was throwing down. "Perhaps the discomfort about protest in books by Negro authors comes because since the nineteenth century, American literature has avoided profound moral searching. It was too painful and besides there were specific problems of language and form to which the writers could address themselves. They did wonderful things, but perhaps they left the real problems untouched. There are exceptions, of course, like Faulkner who has been working the great moral theme all along, taking it up where Mark Twain put it down."

When *Invisible Man* won the National Book Award, Ellison was ineradicably visible and audible. He lectured, toured, and was in demand. Success inhibited him as it would Harper Lee seven years later, and he never completed another novel, though he struggled with *Juneteenth* for years, traveling, becoming a professor of American and Russian literature at Bard, then teaching at Rutgers, Yale, New York University, and the University of Chicago, publishing essays on literature, music, and aspects of the black experience. He claimed to have lost 300 pages of his second novel in a house fire in Plainfield, Massachusetts, in 1967. After he died, Ellison's executor carved out of 2,000 pages of manuscript a book entitled *Juneteenth* (1999). Eventually the manuscripts themselves were published, a vast archival quarry of uneven interest entitled *Three Days before the Shooting* (2010).

"I sensed vaguely and with a flash of panic that the moment I walked out upon the platform and opened my mouth I would be someone else," says the protagonist of *Invisible Man* at his most visible, his most absent. He is free only when, at the end, he burns the documents that stamped upon him a partial identity, that *told* him who he was, worst of all the Brotherhood documents because the Brotherhood understood and exploited his need.

Ohio-born Chloe Ardelia Wofford (b. 1931), who became Toni Morrison, winner of the Nobel Prize in Literature in 1993, the first black American woman to be so honored, has produced ten novels and a good deal of ancillary work.

One of her novels, *Beloved* (1987), outstrips *Invisible Man* in terms of celebrity and shares with it a basic theme. Ellison's controlled, unnamed protagonist, continually possessed, acts out with more or less success roles others give him. "For the next few months our new brother is to undergo a period of intense study and indoctrination under the guidance of Brother Hambro." Morrison's Sethe, by contrast, being a single black woman, is below the radar of the controllers, not written off but simply unacknowledged, and thus paradoxically in a place where she can be free if she can summon the strength and will to find her own identity. "In this here place, we flesh; flesh that weeps, laughs; flesh that dances on bare feet in grass. Love it. Love it hard. Yonder they do not love your flesh. They despise it . . . hear me now, love your heart. For this is the prize." The key words are *flesh* and *love*.

"What is exciting about American literature," Morrison says, "is that business of how writers say things under, beneath, and around their stories. Think of *Pudd'nhead Wilson* and all these inversions of what race is, how sometimes nobody can tell, or the thrill of discovery?" Always, too, there is Faulkner, how in *Absalom, Absalom!* he "spends the entire book tracing race and you can't find it. No one can see it, even the character who *is* black can't see it."

Though she returned a publisher's advance for an autobiography on the grounds that her life was not of sufficient interest to sustain such a book, as a novelist she is content to have her fiction considered as personal narrative alongside memoirs and autobiographies. She is "deadly serious," she insists, about establishing "the milieu out of which I write and from which my ancestors actually lived." She has in mind the slave narratives in which milieu entails "the absence of the interior life, the deliberate excising of it from the records that the slaves themselves told." Those voices, which reach us filtered by the white mediums who transcribed them, she tries to coax alive. "Like the dead-seeming cold rocks," Zora Neale Hurston said, "I have memories within that came out of the material that went to make me." This licenses Morrison's fiction: out of the hitherto mute soil of self it grows, truthful, if not factually true.

Her first novel, *The Bluest Eye* (1970), grew out of a short story she wrote as an undergraduate in a writing group at Howard University in segregated Washington, D.C. The story stayed with her as she completed her MA at Cornell (her thesis being on the theme of suicide in Faulkner and Woolf) and into her teaching career in various institutions. It was published when she was working at Random House in New York. It surprised her colleagues, who had no idea that this editor of, among others, Toni Cade Bambara, Gayl Jones, and Angela Davis was herself an author until her book was reviewed in the *New York Times*. Her editor at Holt took her on, she surmised, because in the late 1960s a lot of black men were being published, and he thought to take a risk. "He was wrong.

What was selling was: Let me tell you how powerful I am and how horrible you are, or some version of that." Her book was quiet by comparison, well made. She was a slow writer and her third book, *Song of Solomon* (1977), established her as a writer. It was the main selection of the Book-of-the-Month Club, the first book by a black woman ever chosen, and the first by a black writer since Richard Wright's *Native Son* in 1940. It tells the life story of Macon Dead III (nicknamed "The Milkman" because he breast-fed into his childhood) from cradle to maturity in Michigan. His best friend and eventually his possibly fatal enemy is Guitar, a Huck Finn sort of boy to Macon's Tom Sawyer, but their boyhoods pass too quickly for this story to build. Here and in her other novels she reveals the end at the beginning, so that the reader is curious not about what but how, attention trained on process.

*Beloved* is Morrison's fifth and most popular novel. Though she is not interested in "real-life people as subjects for fiction," there is a real-life figure, Margaret Garner, behind her protagonist Sethe. "I really don't know anything about her," says Morrison, though a name is something and the fact of her tragedy is something too. These are adequate occasions and do not entail appropriation. She read, in fact, two interviews and said to herself, "Isn't this extraordinary. Here's a woman who escaped into Cincinnati from the horrors of slavery and was not crazy. Though she'd killed her child, she was not foaming at the mouth. She was very calm; she said, I'd do it again. That was more than enough to fire my imagination." Too much knowledge would have stopped the novelist's mouth: "There would have been no place in there for me. It would be like a recipe already cooked."

The author experienced fear in writing, fear slowed her down. She told herself that if the original characters had lived it, she should be able to write it. She tells a ghost story, set in the time of Reconstruction with flashbacks to the days of slavery. Set in the outer suburbs of Cincinnati, the countryside near at hand, its past is the Kentucky plantation ("Sweet Home," as in the song "My Old Kentucky Home," where it's summer and "the darkies are gay"). Several voices, several points of view, deliver the story. Sethe, the main protagonist, is in her thirties. Denver, her daughter, we tend to identify with the author's own (unprivileged) point of view. Baby Suggs is Sethe's mother-in-law. The baby silenced in flight from Kentucky, to avoid recapture, is Beloved, the name on her headstone. Sethe could only afford one word, and paid the stonemason with a sexual favor.

By using several voices Morrison avoids what she calls "a totalizing view. In American literature we have been so totalized—as though there is only one version. We are not one indistinguishable block of people who always behave the same way . . . I try to give some credibility to all sorts of voices, each of which is profoundly different. Because what strikes me about African American culture *is* its variety."

The ghost Beloved is not sinister but angry, creating mayhem the reader accepts at face value. Paul D from the old Kentucky Home rematerializes, and Sethe's life is compelled to join up with its own past. His voice helps her come to terms with her deeds. The writing has sensual and sexual presence, the style economical, impassioned, as though the author is herself surprised by what she sees and hears. Magic is part of the characters' reality and intensifies rather than undermines it, a kind of Gothicized realism. The novel through Sethe's life aspires to tell "the story of the sixty million." Sethe hid the trauma deep in memory, swathed it in "Sweet Home" thoughts. Denver is haunted by the unspoken secret. It puzzles her and drives her out into her secret spot in the garden where she plays and thinks. The stories passed on to Denver by Sethe about her birth, and by Baby Suggs about her father, start to give her a history better than the legacy of the slave trade and the middle passage.

*Beloved* is unsettling not just because of the brutal central event, but because the story is nonsequential, skipping about in time. Memory cuts across the present. The past is not over. Without a single narrator, characters' thoughts interweave. In the closing paragraphs of chapter 2, with no dialogue, the memories and thoughts of Paul D and Sethe slip between past and present, into another voice who addresses "you": "No matter what all your teeth and wet fingers anticipated, there was no accounting for the way that simple joy could shake you." Beloved's own section is unpunctuated, technically incoherent. One is put in mind of Benji in *The Sound and the Fury,* though Beloved's story is unresolved.

Revisiting history to make it one's own, not somebody else's: that is Morrison's mission. America entailed "a deliberate and sustained erasure of the past." It needs to be recovered. If the gaps in memory persist, so will the haunting, the ghosts will not be laid to rest but will continue to rage and disrupt not only those who suspect that they exist but also those who are innocent of suspicion, the daughters, the granddaughters.

*Jazz* (1992) is, stylistically, her most ambitious book. It tries to establish in the language of narrative an analogy for the musical strategies of jazz. Like jazz, the best stories withhold the final note and thus remain unresolved. The avoidance of resolution, no happily-ever-afters, is part of what makes a story truthful. The jazz musician always "has more but he's not gonna give it to you. It's an exercise in restraint, a holding back—not because it's not there, or because one had exhausted it, but because of the riches, and because it can be done again." One stops when instinct instructs one to stop: it is a sense that cannot be theorized. And it is true that as she has progressed, Morrison has become a thriftier writer. In *Jazz* she learned to "blend that which is contrived and artificial with improvisation." The analogy is appropriate: "I thought of myself as like the jazz musician—someone who practices and practices and practices in order to be able to invent and to make his art look effortless and graceful."

*Home* (2012) takes place in the 1950s, when Chloe Wofford was becoming deeply troubled with race relations. She saw a newsreel in which white mothers in the South tried to overturn a bus carrying black children. She tried to think herself into the minds of these women. She could only do it by analogy, and even then not satisfactorily. Is the book a novel or a novella? The publishers claim the latter, the length and singularity of theme the former. It is full of easy symbolism. Frank Money is a young veteran of the Korean War. He's going home. But where, and what, is home? He has bad memories and few hopes, making his way to Lotus, Georgia, only because his sister, the one person he has loved and whom he protected as a boy, is in trouble. "Down deep inside her lived my secret picture of myself—a strong good me." He is certified insane in Seattle, and as he flees south and east the possibility of madness hounds him. He is given leave to argue with the narrator in little italicized inter-chapters. Morrison tells the reader what has happened, after it has happened, in case we missed it. In general, we have not, and could handle a little more trust.

Ellison and Morrison proposed ideas of the kind Sidney Hook looked for in fiction. Thomas Wolfe did not: his work is lavishly dissipated. Dylan Thomas's Llareggub in *Under Milk Wood* is tame in its teeming verbal sonorities when set beside the populous, mimetic excesses of Altamont: *Look Homeward, Angel: A Story of the Buried Life* (1929) is the first and one great novel of Thomas (Clayton) Wolfe (1900–1938). He was an unstanchable writer, emitting as many as 10,000 words per day. No wonder the life was buried. He was an editor's nightmare when it came to cutting—arguing, agreeing, and arriving the following day with even more words to suture the cuts his editor had made. Maxwell Perkins at Scribner's, who edited Wolfe's first two novels (and Hemingway's and Fitzgerald's books as well), remembers the exasperating white nights of revision, the energy of an author without an instinct for literary form. "His whole impulse was to utter what he felt and he had no time to revise and compress." His three subsequent novels, two published posthumously, his plays and stories, mine his life experience. Each protagonist is a version of himself and he comes of age over and over again.

He became famous in his own brief life and he continues to mark American writers. In their formative years they find in him a vibrant self with which to identify. Few reread him in maturity. Faulkner as a near contemporary, Jack Kerouac, Philip Roth, and Cormac McCarthy as heirs, acknowledge him. "I rated Wolfe first, myself second. I put Hemingway last," said Faulkner. "I said we were all failures. All of us had failed to match the dream of perfection and

I rated the authors on the basis of their splendid failure to do the impossible." Wolfe's impossible goal had been "to reduce all human experience to literature." A decade or two later Harold Bloom declared, "One cannot discuss the literary merit of Thomas Wolfe; he has none." Faulkner's claims are too grand, Bloom's dismissal too categorical. There is no doubt about Wolfe's influence, particularly on the American writer's anxious sense of the first person. And some sentences are breathtaking.

Asheville, North Carolina, where he was born, or Altamont, Catawba, was his Yoknapatawpha County. He cannot get back there, yet it possesses his imagination, so that he cannot leave it either. He writes toward it, thinly fictionalizing his growing up, to the age of nineteen. In *Look Homeward, Angel* he is Eugene Gant, whose father carved stone monuments and sold gravestones and made the stone angel who haunts the book and provides, with Milton's elegy "Lycidas," the title. Wolfe's mother kept a boarding house called My Old Kentucky Home, the "Dixieland" of the novel. Of his brothers, Wolfe was closest to Ben, and Ben's death at the age of twenty-six was the occasion for the book.

Thomas was precocious, going up to the University of North Carolina at Chapel Hill when he was fifteen, eager to become a dramatist. He went on to Harvard to study playwriting. He moved to New York, eager to see his work performed there, and began teaching at New York University. He was in Europe in 1924 and 1925, and returned in 1926, beginning work on *Look Homeward, Angel* (*O Lost* was a working title, drawn from the opening rhapsody, which concludes, "O lost, and by the wind grieved, ghost, come back again") and making the transition from theater to fiction.

Ironically, his great Broadway success was Ketti Frings's adaptation of *Look Homeward, Angel,* which opened two decades after his death, ran for a year and a half, and was awarded a Pulitzer Prize for Drama. His death from tuberculosis was sudden and unexpected. Hemingway speculated that in fact the cause was syphilis and that Wolfe's huge abundance as a writer was abetted by those notoriously creative spirochetes.

"Hemingway was fascinating, the pearls of words on a white page giving you an exact picture," said Kerouac, "but Wolfe was a torrent of American heavens and hell that opened my eyes to America as a subject in itself." In his Nobel speech Sinclair Lewis patronizes Wolfe as "a child of, I believe, thirty or younger, whose one and only novel, *Look Homeward, Angel,* is worthy to be compared with the best in our literary production, a Gargantuan creature with great gusto of life." His reputation is still contested: To what extent was his great novel a collaboration between the author and his editor? To what extent did he provide raw material for Maxwell Perkins's editorial pen? He paid Perkins too fulsome a tribute, and critics could latch on to it and discredit him.

Perkins was clear about his role, with the editor's proper humility, but Wolfe came to resent the imputation that without Perkins he would be unable to function and so changed publishers and effectively ceased to function. Attempts to present *Look Homeward, Angel* in its unrevised form, to reveal the Gargantuan proportions of the unedited Wolfe, have not helped his case. But he is a crucial presence in the lives of his contemporaries who saw him as a novelist *maudit* and admired, even envied, him.

The energy of the British writer (Clarence) Malcolm Lowry (1909–1957) at one level resembles Wolfe's. His one substantial novel he described as "a prophecy, a political warning, a cryptogram, a preposterous movie, and a writing on the wall." Yes, but: There is nothing spray-can about *Under the Volcano* (1947) despite its apocalyptic abundance; it was struggled for, sentence by sentence. Lowry's victory is tenuous: He held on to the whole thing too long. He needed a version of Maxwell Perkins to take it off his hands. Instead, he kept returning and returning, revising a chapter here, there, weaving it into a dense, static mass that one inhabits more than reads.

He came from a well-to-do Cheshire background. At an early age he learned to resist authority, an authority first amused and then bemused by his resistance. He demonized those he felt restrained or directed him. All his writing is undependably autobiographical. *Under the Volcano* protagonist Geoffrey Firmin is the ultimate self-justification of the undependable narrator. Under pressure from his family Lowry agreed to go up to St. Catharine's College, Cambridge, on the condition that he could travel first to the Far East. His father arranged the passage. He was a Melville with privileges, resented by other members of the crew. He came back with simple narrative plans, which he wrote, over and over, into a dense, nonlinear work, *Ultramarine* (1933). He went up to Cambridge in 1929. Everyone soon knew he was to be a great prose writer, though the evidence was slim and he took a poor third-class degree. He was under the spell of the American writer Conrad Aiken (1889–1973), who "saw him over" the difficult period from 1927–1929. Aiken's 1927 novel *Blue Voyage* lay behind *Ultramarine*, and Aiken opened American literature and America to the young Englishman. Both were heavy drinkers. Aiken encouraged the ornate and baroque in Lowry. Lowry was also drawn to the work of the once-popular Nordahl Grieg (1902–1943), the Norwegian novelist, playwright, and poet, who was killed on a bombing mission over Berlin. Grieg was a man of action and an intellectual at the same time, and much influenced (as few English writers at the time were) by Kipling. Lowry admired and imitated him in the early 1930s, especially Grieg's 1924 novel *The Ship Sails On,* translated into English in 1927.

Lowry succeeded only once, in a work that took him the better part of a decade to complete and with which he was never happy, and whose success he lived to resent. His other works are peripheral. *Lunar Caustic* (written 1934) is about his detention in Bellevue Hospital, New York, for alcoholism after the crisis of his first marriage. His second visit to Mexico in 1945–1946 with his second wife, when he stayed in the same streets and met some of the same people he had known in what had come to seem the blissful then the blighted months of his first visit, provided him with material for *Dark Is the Grave wherein My Friend Is Laid* (published posthumously in 1968). His main place of residence from 1940 to 1954 was at Dollarton, British Columbia, where he lived a settled squatter's existence in a community to which he felt he belonged. He was virtually an exile from the British literary world. He died in England in 1957.

It "gets off to a slow start," he says. It is hard to break into *Under the Volcano.* He was "obsessed with certain things. All great writers are," says William Gass. "Lowry put down those obsessions on the page, and because they are there, he believes they will have an effect. It is the kind of error the beginning writer makes too—all this stuff that is so important to him never really gets to the page at all." The reader's difficulty shadows the trouble the author had in writing. Like other novels of its kind—*Moby-Dick* and *Nostromo* (Melville and Conrad meant a great deal to the young Lowry), *The Rainbow,* and Thomas Mann's *Doctor Faustus*—it requires repeated attempts. Those who knew the book's "terrain"—landscapes, plazas, buildings—were impressed by the miasmic clarity of the descriptions, though time has altered the settings.

Naivety of conception extends to the rhythmic prose in which Lowry composed the book. He read passages aloud to wife and friends. His is not the natural, if fussy, elaboration of James, whose longest sentences retain contact with a speaking voice, but syntax as architecture, a strained high baroque. He will break into a long iambic run, a Jacobean pace unnatural to fiction; also unnatural are the elaborate time schemes, switchbacks, accreting information. The book begins to make the kind of sense it intends only on a second reading. The problem (and pleasure) is the style itself. What *is* recalcitrant is character—not the *dramatis personae* but the character of the author who concedes that he "is" his protagonist, all of them. The book points back to him again and again, an English Thomas Wolfe, cautious, deliberate in exuberance.

In 1946 Lowry wrote to his publisher defending *Under the Volcano.* Its "irremediable" defect was that "the author's equipment, such as it is, is subjective rather than objective, a better equipment, in short, for a certain kind of poet than a novelist." He compares the novel's allusive manner to that of *The Waste Land.* Lowry's intention was to endow the book with something like a human complexity of consciousness, to make it in effect "creaturely," with a mind of its own as troubled as that of his principal character. The renewable fiesta of alcoholism is enhanced with the soul-eating mescal, which makes even absinthe seem like gripe water. Lowry understands this psychospiritual anthropology. It is endemic in the richly imagined Mexican culture where he plants his characters and it is why Geoffrey Firmin, the British consul, roots there and becomes a Mr. Kurtz: his resources of learning, linguistic genius, and wit he surrenders. A modern tragic hero, he knows what he's doing: there is no moment of recognition. The whole book is denouement.

If *Under the Volcano* feels assembled, this is because it was. In its composition there was none of the flow, the release of pent-up energies that writers such as Wolfe experienced, becoming the medium's passive agent. Lowry imposed on himself a twelve-hour structure (rather loosened by the opening chapter, which looks back from the distance of a year), shorter than the time Joyce allows himself for *Ulysses*. In those twelve hours certain events coincide; at the end of the book, awkwardly, he must narrate events that happen before those narrated in the previous chapter. Each chapter Lowry regarded as freestanding, a structure with verbal and symbolic coherence, belonging to one of his four main characters and with a position in the narrative more geometric than dramatic. The author quarried passages from his poems, from other writings. The book was conceived, he says, in 1936, and he later regarded it as the *Inferno* of a projected Dantesque trilogy, *The Voyage That Never Ends*. The twelve chapters or "blocks" (intended to recall Homer's, Virgil's and Milton's epic structures, as well as some of Lowry's more recherché numerological and mystical concerns) were composed out of chronological order and revised discretely. The drunkenness of Geoffrey Firmin in the twelve hours we share with him is compound. There is beer, tequila, and, crucially, mescal. It is bleak because solipsistic, with the solipsism—we get it in Dylan Thomas and in Sylvia Plath's *The Bell Jar* as well— that allows the situation of the self, its anxieties, alarms, and aberrations, to displace any sense of the "objective." William Gass strives for such an effect: "Like Lowry, I want closure, suffocation, the sense that there is nowhere else to go." Life (he quotes Baudelaire) is "a forest of symbols": but Baudelaire emphasizes the symbols and believes they might yield a consistent sense, whereas Lowry stresses the forest, lost-ness, dark suggestion, rather than emerging pattern.

Canada lays claim to him, not implausibly. But he remains an English writer, and the contemporary he most resembles is Joyce Cary (1888–1957), also a great reviser and rewriter though less caustic than Lowry. Cary wrote brilliantly about Africa, and stimulated Chinua Achebe to acts of admiration and resistance. Henry Reed declares, "His capacity for absorbing himself in his characters and in their *milieu* is unparalleled (save perhaps in Henry Green) in contemporary literature." Reed compares Cary to Defoe. "We do not merely watch a 'character' whose actions and reactions are discontinuous and irresponsible; we become that character." To this skill he gives the name "objectivity," the self-effacement that makes it possible for another self to emerge. There is too a judicious literariness in Cary, he builds, if not on the matter, then at least closely on the manner, of writers he admired. In *Mister Johnson* (1939) he writes a passage that is uncannily close in manner and spirit to the opening of Forster's *Passage to India,* using the same technique of ironic parallelism and much of the same diction. He is seeing things, but through borrowed glasses that retain some of the vision they have seen before. The earlier image of colony and corruption is overlaid by another, with a different geography.

Pritchett remembers visiting Cary in Oxford. "He seemed far too accomplished; he seemed to have everything. He'd been a very distinguished civil servant in Africa. He'd been a great book collector and was a rather able painter— not a genius, but he painted better than most of us." Gulley Jimson, protagonist of *The Horse's Mouth* (1944), was his exuberance fictionalized. "His background was very amusing. He had a rather wild Anglo-Irish background, which was immediately recognizable to anyone who knew Ireland at that time. He was very serious. Oxford made him seem a bit solemn, but he wasn't really solemn. He was very restless." And he recounts how, when they were talking, "suddenly there was a noise at the front door. He clapped his hands and said, That's my cutlet! That's my dinner! Dear old so-and-so's dropped me in my cutlet! Someone had dropped some meat in through the letter drop. He rushed to the door, picked it up, opened the door and said, Oh, she's gone. I heard him shout down the street, Thank you! Thank you! Thank you!"

He composed several novels at the same time, working between them like an artist with several canvases on the go at once. Thus, *Herself Surprised* (1941) tells of Sara Munday, *To Be a Pilgrim* (1942) recounts her affair with Wilcher, and *The Horse's Mouth* her affair with Gulley Jimson. Each novel stands alone, but as a triptych they stand together. Jimson is a fine artist, without the struggle but with the genius of Maugham's Charles Strickland in *The Moon and Sixpence* (1919), also produced at the end of a war. Jimson follows, indeed is obsessed by, William Blake, though Cary is not, so the novel is conventional with a highly unconventional protagonist. Jimson's moral world is described and contained by his art, for which he will commit any crime. Burgess describes *The Horse's Mouth* as "a comic hymn to life, but it has nobility as well." Cary is a great novelist in this celebration of the flesh, says Burgess.

Achebe speaks of Cary as a master of clairvoyance. Lowry possessed neither self-effacement nor clairvoyance. He was unable to stand outside his protagonist or himself. Irony and humor were not his skills. His main character is not created so much as confessed; the created elements are incorporated to plead, to make credible and exonerate. Lowry would like to have been Cary's Gulley Jimson, "rowdy, dishonest, outrageous." "Talk is lies," Jimson says. "The only satisfactory form of communication is a good picture. Neither true nor false. But created." The staccato of his speech, blurted, aphoristic, inviting no reply, is an index of his character. Jimson "is presented as a nuisance, and as a grotesque . . . but he does profoundly represent the visionary, obsessed artist who can never be popular, except among a few of his contemporaries, till after he is dead. In all of these books Cary has succeeded in eliminating himself—the aim of the author of *Finnegans Wake.*"

"Eliminating himself" was certainly not Lowry's objective. His writing was, like his life, continual revision, expression approximate at best, never *quite* what he wanted. His book is wild. It bucks off theorist and critic. *Under the Volcano* is for readers who need to know less than Lowry wanted to tell ("the four main characters being intended, in one of the book's meanings, to be aspects of the same man"; or "the humor is a kind of bridge between the naturalistic and the transcendental and then back to he naturalistic again"); who know that symbols change value in changing contexts, in the advancing light of day; and realize that every object, bottle, leaf and horseman, whore and scorpion, spider and spy, was real in the world where Lowry walked, drank, and was alone, in which he invested Geoffrey Firmin, his angels and demons, fading family and friends.

# 35

# Essaying

Edmund Wilson, Gore Vidal, John Dos Passos, E. E. Cummings, Mary McCarthy,

Katherine Anne Porter, F. Scott Fitzgerald, John Steinbeck, John O'Hara,

Nathanael West, William Gaddis, David Foster Wallace

In Britain economic upheaval did not always register promptly with the creative classes. Fiction was slow to engage the Industrial Revolution. The worlds of Dickens and Gaskell are real enough, but their politics were more sympathetic than radical, an appeal to individual conscience rather than collective action. For writers to embrace radical strategies, to incorporate analysis and propose deep reform, they must be entailed in their subject matter, in the circumstances of the disenfranchised and poor.

American fiction in the nineteenth and twentieth centuries was far more responsive to changing social circumstances. The Great Depression and its aftermaths shook American fiction to its roots. The imperatives of *fact* came to exercise, as they had not done since the time of Defoe, commanding influence. A novel needed to be answerable. Its forms, too, were required in openness and fragmentation to register and sometimes record the realities with which people struggled. Writers whose language and imagination took shape during the Depression, especially if they were old enough to have experienced the Roaring Twenties from the louche side, were marked by a reluctant, inescapable social conscience and a knowledge of the economic volatility of the modern world. In the period between President Herbert Hoover's defeat and Franklin Delano Roosevelt's accession to the presidency, American unemployment reached 25 percent. Social Security did not come in until 1935. The degree of poverty, with people living in city dumps as they do today on the outskirts of Third World cities, is hard to imagine. The American had dreamed that everyone might prosper. The reality of Hoovervilles and dust bowls broke through with imaginative force: a hard, compelling subject, for some the only subject worth addressing.

Among the earliest to report was Edmund Wilson (1895–1972). Politicians and intellectuals had not recognized the extent and depth of the social problems, he said. He had scant respect for belletrists whose reading stopped at style and form. What writers said mattered, even when *how* they said it was part of the what. In 1930 and 1931 he traveled the country and contributed to the *New Republic*. He learned of the epidemic of suicides among working men, saw starvation, nakedness, destitution of opportunity. Marx's predictions were coming true: this was the crisis of late capitalism, the last act. *The American Jitters* (1932) collected his pieces.

Wilson was to become the William Dean Howells and Ford Madox Ford of his generation, the critic, editor, friend, and sparring partner of his major contemporaries, a writer who helps configure a literature even as it is coming into being, his foresight informed by a literary culture that underpins his social alertness. Nadine Gordimer saw how he "sent the blinds shuddering up and flung the door wide on the scholarly preserves of English criticism." He did not simplify to popularize but brought his knowledge of the contemporary world to bear: the writings he considers are brought back into a relationship with the world. He liked to think of himself as a creature of the eighteenth century, but he is more an heir of Sainte-Beuve and the lucid T. H. Huxley of the nineteenth, of Dickens whose particularity and Carlyle whose sense of the writer as hero and man of action appealed to him. At university he mastered English, French, and Italian literature. He piled language on language: German, Russian, Hebrew. At the time of his death he was working up his Hungarian.

This broad *culture* was a guarantee of legitimacy: "No matter how thoroughly and searchingly we may have scrutinized works of literature from the historical and biographical point of view . . . we must be able to tell the good from the bad, the first-rate from the second-rate. We shall not otherwise write literary criticism at all." Wilson championed and criticized the writing of Faulkner and John Dos Passos, of F. Scott Fitzgerald, of Hemingway and Vladimir Nabokov, of Mary McCarthy, his third and most brilliant wife. He kept up with the progress of American literature until 1945, after which he concentrated, as the aging Sainte-Beuve had done, on earlier things, in his case the War Between the States, Pushkin, the Dead Sea scrolls. He identified "the two great enemies of literary talent in our time: Hollywood and Henry Luce" (degraded journalism). His exhausting eight-year marriage to Mary McCarthy was over. His dream of a great American literature, after Fitzgerald's death, seemed just a dream. Late capitalism enlists and consumes the original, the radical and creative. There were exceptions, J. D. Salinger and James Baldwin among them, but he was tired of tracing a decline, after the achievements of the previous decades.

At Princeton Wilson was taught by Christian Gauss, who had known Oscar Wilde and had a dog named Baudelaire, and with whom he maintained a valuable correspondence. He continued his extensive reading, mainly in literature, then enlisted in the army when the United States entered World War I, and served in hospitals as a wound-dresser, purging himself of any sense of privilege he might have had. His politics developed in response to his military experience and his subsequent work as a journalist, first as a reporter for the *New York Sun,* then as managing editor of *Vanity Fair* at the precocious age of twenty-five. Later he was associate editor of the *New Republic* and wrote regularly for the *New Yorker* and the *New York Review of Books*. He made no secret of his ignorance of Cervantes, of the Golden Age of Spanish literature that meant so much to Faulkner, Dos Passos, and other writers he admired. He had no time for *Middlemarch* and was impatient of "viscous prose writing in the early nineteenth century": Scott, Lamb, and even Melville wearied him.

His literary and social writings went hand in hand, and some of his books, mostly assembled from his journalism, remain required reading. *Axel's Castle: A Study of the Imaginative Literature of 1870–1930* (1931), to which he referred as *Asshole's Cactus,* remains an illuminating account of the creative worlds traced by writers from Arthur Rimbaud through Wilson's main quarries, Yeats, Joyce, Eliot, Valéry, Proust, and Stein. In 1940 he published *To the Finland Station* (the title an oblique tribute to Virginia Woolf's *To the Lighthouse* and an indication of his sense of the complex story as possessing a *novelistic* dynamic), an account of the intellectual and social development of socialism from the 1820s to the fateful arrival at the Finland Station in St. Petersburg in 1917 of the sealed train carrying Lenin and the Bolshevik bacillus. Nabokov, when he read the book, characterized Lenin as a "pail of milk of human kindness with a dead rat at the bottom." *Patriotic Gore* (1962) reads the Civil War through its major and minor literature. It attests to the recording power of fiction, not only as witness to events but as provocation and elegy. His criticism seldom limits itself to the literary. Marx and Freud adjusted his ways of seeing. For him, they were complementary thinkers.

The fiction-writing skills he brings to criticism, a sense of the *occasion* of reading, he shares with Doctor Johnson, Ford, and Lawrence. Updike laments the displacement of the fiction writer by the critic in Wilson: would that more such displacements occurred. The animation of Wilson's criticism makes his essays more readable, real, and necessary. His long-range writing (the phrase is from *The Triple Thinkers* of 1938) is seemingly effortless in ways that his contemporaries admired and envied.

Bellow finds his frowning focus slightly comical, referring to "the same gruff Magoo strained way of speaking" and likening his selective myopia to Mr. Magoo's. Wilson if interested in something studied it; if not, it did not register at all. He squinted for particulars of knowledge, what he needed to illuminate an argument or squirrel away for later use. After the dishonesty of the 1930s he distrusted theories. His histories avoid emollient generalization. Chance and free will are always part of the mix. The power of *To the Finland Station* is in the sense it gives of evitability.

Wilson's fiction proved less durable than his critical writing. There is one significant novel, *I Thought of Daisy* (1929). Updike likes this "valentine to the

Greenwich Village of the Twenties." As a character Daisy is "good, if ungainly . . . how charmingly and intelligently she tells of the speakeasy days of a Greenwich Village . . . of lamplit islands where love and ambition and drunkenness bloomed all at once." It was the first and best of his three novels, written while he was balancing his ambitions to be a novelist against a developing career in literary criticism. In a late introduction to *Galahad* and *I Thought of Daisy* Wilson made clear that a roman à clef reading sold his intentions short. The work is based in the real, but what matters are the transformations. Historicizing displaces the experience of the story, making it pretext, gratuitous autobiography.

He had ambitious plans for a three-phase fiction starting with *The Higher Jazz,* but he broke off to write the stories of *Memoirs of Hecate County* (1946), which, Updike says, "possesses a certain saturnine majesty and passages of ground-breaking sexual realism." Mr. Magoo was an erotic virtuoso. A keen recorder of detail, he described in color, as *aides mémoires,* numerous pudenda. The accounts are unsettling in what they suggest of the man. After he and his first wife separated in 1925, he set up with a dancer of Ukrainian origin, the wife of a car thief. She was transformed into the protagonist of a story of straightforward erotic obsession, "The Princess with the Golden Hair," which contributed to the banning of *Memoirs of Hecate County.* The U.S. Supreme Court agonized over Wilson's candor. In 1948 it divided 4–4 instead of reaching a clear verdict on the stories' propriety. Raymond Chandler agreed that the book was indecent, but "in the most inoffensive way—without passion, like a phallus made of dough." The book stayed banned until 1959.

Wilson in Scotland in the 1950s visited the almost-immortal Sir Compton Mackenzie (1883–1972) at the book-crammed flat in which he endured his exile. Like Wilson, he had miscalculated, omitting some of his novel earnings from income tax. Mackenzie was forced to give up his big house and grounds, servants, all the accoutrements that distinguished a laird from the common ruck of men. He received Wilson in bed like a Tulkinghorn or a venerable statesman. He had sold *Whisky Galore* outright to a film company for £500. (J. R. R. Tolkien struck a comparably poor deal for *The Lord of the Rings,* but that fact would not emerge for decades. Wilson's opinion of Tolkien's "juvenile trash" could hardly have been lower: "Dr. Tolkien has little skill at narrative and no instinct for literary form.") In the dim bedroom of the exhausted giant of Scottish writing, both men embattled against tax authorities, Wilson on a straight chair and Mackenzie in a tumultuous bed shared angers and autumnal regrets.

If critical writing is "the world of peripheral letters," those peripheries are crucial in extending or contracting the creative space within which novelists are free to write. (Eugene Luther) Gore Vidal (1925–2012) is a great interpreter of his age. An unanointed successor to Edmund Wilson, whom he described as "the perfect autodidact" who "wanted to know it all," he drew on Wilson's writing for his fiction and oriented himself by it in his essays. Wilson was "proof of the proposition that the more the mind is used and fed the less apt it is to devour itself."

He is more of a journalist than Wilson was, wider in range and as unexpectedly tolerant. As a critic he sparkles at the expense of his subject, but when approaching a masterpiece, such as *The Golden Bowl,* he trains all the light on his subject. He worked with film, occasionally as an actor, mainly on scripts, starting with an adaptation of *Dr. Jekyll and Mr. Hyde* in 1954, and scripting, adapting, or contributing to the scripts of *I Accuse!* (1958), *The Scapegoat* (1959), Tennessee Williams's play *Suddenly, Last Summer* (1959), and his own *The Best Man* (1964). He was a script doctor for *Ben Hur.* He knew that using scripting format in fiction was a risk, yet film affected the way writers visualized, devised transitions, and paced their work. "Every writer of my generation has been influenced by films . . . Find out the movies a man saw between ten and fifteen, which ones he liked, disliked and you would have a pretty good idea of what sort of mind and temperament he has." *Cherchez le film.* Popular fiction relates more closely to the movies than to other (and earlier) fiction. After intertextuality, intercelluloidity. In an age when film does so much that the novel used to do, "the novelist must go deeper, must turn into the maze of consciousness where the camera cannot follow."

Vidal was born in West Point, New York. His father, once an athlete, was then an aeronautics instructor and later worked in the Roosevelt administration and participated in the formation of three commercial airlines. Amelia Earhart had been in love with him. Vidal's mother became a depressive alcoholic; of her he paints a monstrous picture. Vidal had family connections in leading political and artistic circles. After his mother's desertion when he was ten, he was more or less adopted by his maternal grandparents. Grandmother taught him to read. Then, because his grandfather, Senator Thomas Pryor Gore, Democrat, Oklahoma, was blind, Vidal was "required early on to read grown-up books to him, mostly constitutional law and, of course, the *Congressional Record."* Though he admired his athlete father, his grandfather was the focus of his childhood: "He raised me." From him derived the patrician tone and political acidity, the resistance to what he consistently and with increasing vehemence perceived as American imperialism. The Establishment, to which he was born and within whose culture he insisted, as a self-declared homosexual, on remaining, need not be conservative. When John F. Kennedy was elected president, his sense of empowerment soared: twice he ran for office, once—almost successfully—for

Congress (1960), once to be the Democratic gubernatorial candidate in California (1982). *Palimpsest: A Memoir* (1995) and *Point to Point Navigation* (2006) recall friendships with Eleanor Roosevelt, Leonard Bernstein, Princess Margaret, and others, their celebrity being of more concern to him than their actual lives.

He regarded himself as a close friend of his cousin by marriage Jacqueline Kennedy. He was for a time close to Tennessee Williams. Christopher Isherwood, E. M. Forster, and Albert Camus featured in his life. There were also Anaïs Nin (who claimed to have bedded him) and William Faulkner. "Allen Ginsberg kissed my hand as Jean Genet looked on." He was for a very short time a lover of Jack Kerouac, though he claimed later that the Beats bored him.

As a boy Vidal was widely boarded and educated in the United States and Europe. When he graduated from Phillips Exeter Academy, he enlisted in the U.S. Army as a private. His military experience was at sea and informed his first novel, *Williwaw* (1946), written when he was nineteen. The book was dedicated to "J.T.," revealed in his memoirs to have been his intimate school friend Jimmie Trimble, killed in Iwo Jima in 1945, the lost boy who remained immortal in memory, subject of Vidal's first major novel, *The City and the Pillar,* written in 1946 but, because of its themes, not published until 1948. That was the year in which Truman Capote's *Other Voices, Other Rooms* came out, both books presenting clearly homosexual characters. Stonewall was a generation away.

Vidal says the style of *The City and the Pillar* is based upon "the flat, gray, naturalistic style of James T. Farrell," the popular author of the Studs Lonigan trilogy. "Tactically, if not aesthetically, this was for a good reason. Up until then homosexuality in literature was always exotic: Firbank, on the one hand; green carnations, on the other." The emergence of his protagonist's homosexuality was not fun, funny, or consoling. "I wanted to deal with an absolutely ordinary, all-American, lower-middle-class young man and his world. To show the dead-on 'normality' of the homosexual experience." Thus, in a neutral style Vidal's coming-of-age novel tells of good-looking young Jim Willard and his friend Bob Ford, their love which Bob finds unnatural, Jim's enlisting in the Merchant Marine and his efforts, over seven years, to find himself with other like-spirited men and reclaim Bob. Bob, however, is not to be reclaimed. In early drafts of the book Jim murders him; this was commuted to rape in the final revision. Tennessee Williams did not like the ending. "I don't think you realized what a good book you had written." Vidal imagined the ending was "powerful." He provided what he thought editors and readers wanted for "my tale of Sodom, my Romeo and his Mercutio." The title should have been sufficient. "Essentially, I was writing about the romantic temperament. Jim Willard," who stands in for Vidal, "is so overwhelmed by a first love affair that he finds all other lovers wanting. He can only live in the past, as he imagined the past, or in the future as he hopes it will be when he finds Bob again. He has no present." He added, "Nabokov handled this same theme with infinitely greater elegance in *Lolita*. But I was only twenty when I made my attempt, while he was half as old as time." Some review editors boycotted Vidal's later novels. For a time he resorted to pseudonyms, female and male. "Edward Box" wrote three mystery novels that kept Vidal going for a decade.

In 1950 he met his life-mate, Howard Austen. For over half a century they lived together, dividing their later years between Los Angeles and a cliff-face estate on the Amalfi Coast of Italy. Vidal's novels, including the ones rooted in American history, feature gay characters. Those that seem most remote from his experience are obliquely confessional. In *The Judgment of Paris* (1952), "I found my own voice. Up until then I was very much in the American realistic tradition, unadventurous, monochromatic, haphazard in my effects. My subjects were always considerably more interesting than what I was able to do with them."

The novels fall roughly into three generic areas. First are realistic modern stories that illuminate individual lives but that are at the same time emblematic of tensions and concerns in society at large, American and foreign. *The City and the Pillar* (1948) is the most distinctive novel in this category, but there are stockbrokers, adventurers in Latin America (he lived for a time in Guatemala), actors, soldiers, and others in a world not overly endowed with female characters.

In 1964, after ten years spent largely in Hollywood and away from fiction, he published his first thickly researched historical novel, *Julian,* devoted to the short-lived Roman emperor Julianus II, the Apostate, who tried to reverse the tide of Christianity engulfing fourth-century Rome. He wanted to return to Greek and Roman beliefs, too late. Vidal's historical fictions culminate in the "American Chronicles," a national saga of books that runs from the War of Independence through the Second World War. In 1967 he published *Washington, D.C.,* set in the period of the Second World War. He used the third person with great effort, "the constant maneuvering of so many consciousnesses through the various scenes while trying to keep the focus right. It was like directing a film on location with a huge cast in bad weather." He was proud of it. Spoofing Norman Mailer, he declared: "After all, that was the time I got into the ring with Proust, and I knocked the little fag on his ass in the first round. Then I kneed old Leo T. the Great and on a technical KO got the championship. Funny thing, this being the best." In 1973 he published *Burr,* based on Aaron Burr's rise and fall. Out of sequence, Vidal went on to fill the historical gaps in a series of entertaining novels illuminated by the neon variegations of his style. The last in the series was *The Golden Age* (2000), exploring *his* period, 1939 to 1954.

The "highest" sphere is that of his "inventions," and here nest his apocalyptic allegories, his most Golding-like works. His disciples in flight from conventional narrative lack the courage of their conventions. Vidal lacked it from time to time: his work remains restless, uneven but lively even when it pursues chimeras. His metafictions focus his satire. Most notable in this category are *Myra Breckinridge* (1968), *Kalki* (1978), and *Duluth* (1983). He considers the first and last of these among his best work. *Duluth* is fiction responding to the excesses of theory. Italo Calvino relishes the satire and calls Vidal "a master of that new form which is taking shape in world literature and which we may call the hyper-novel or the novel elevated to the square or the cube." From metafiction we step to hyperfiction. Naturally it is about life and death, and death entails moving from one television sitcom to another; relationships enjoy a second chance to fail, clichés take on a new burden of irony. There is science fiction, word processing, and the plot hinges on verb tenses.

More satisfying for general readers is *Myra Breckinridge,* which unexpectedly followed on the heels of *Julian.* Its satire on issues of sexuality are concentrated in the protagonist, a transsexual with ambitions grounded in gender, not in people. Feminism, the claims of and about patriarchy, the culture of machismo, and other issues are, with provocative incorrectness, prodded, most alarmingly with a strap on in a rape scene in which the victim is a macho young man in the process of one of Myra's "corrections." She is herself a subject of transformation. Letitia Van, the hypersexed agent and talent scout, brings sadism to the heart of the story. With its specifically sexual focus, the book is satire at its coldest; also its most hilarious. Vidal knows his "gift for mimicry. The plangent cries of Myra are very unlike the studied periods of Aaron Burr, but the same throat, as it were (deep, deep), sings the song of each." He says that he envies writers like Graham Greene "who, year in and year out, do the same kind of novel to the delight of the same kind of reader." Greene is not so stable as he thinks, and in any case the statement is ironic. Greene committed comparable transgressions, though none so blatant as *Myra.* Posing as Zeus, Vidal says, "then I let *Myra* spring from my brow, armed to the teeth, eager to lose me ladies, book clubs, book-chat writers—everything, in fact, except her unique self, the only great 'woman' in American literature." Compared with Hepzibah Pynchon? The book is "explicit" in ways that guaranteed it would find a general readership in English and translation. It was talked about, and though it has grown tamer, it retains its power to surprise, if not to shock. *Myron* (1974), an opportunistic sequel, is not among Vidal's masterpieces.

As a writer Vidal earned himself a wide generic freedom, moving between history and invention as he explored power, transgression, and the ways in which language transforms not only the record but the very form of experience. His

*Narratives of Empire* (1973–2000)—the American empire—started in Rome. In 1981 he went further back in time, to history's beginning, with *Creation,* a book he returned to and revised, as he has all his fiction over time, some of it radically. Burgess especially admired *Creation,* set in the fifth century BCE. Socrates, Buddha, and Confucius appear. The first-person narrator is Zoroaster's grandson Cyrus Spitama. Vast, detailed, witty, it has none of the historical plausibility, the wayward scholarship that Robert Graves brings to his fiction of the ancient world. It is more about good and evil than about historical realities. Vidal, even in his inventive fiction, is an essayist.

"Except for Thornton Wilder," he says, "I can think of no contemporary American who has any interest in what happened before the long present he lives in, and records." In associating himself with Wilder he makes a point also about style, because Wilder expresses himself in ways that delight at the level of language without ever losing hold of his subject and theme. Vidal feels alone in the value he sets on invention in fiction. His historical novels purport to tell, if not the truth, then a version of it, based on research. To establish veracity Vidal introduces letters into the text undigested, as letters, or transcripts of tape recordings, or diaries. "It makes for immediacy. I know how difficult it is for the average American to read anything. And I'm speaking of the average 'educated' person. It is not easy for him to cope with too dense a text on the page. I think the eye tires easily." In patronizing the reader he sells his own intentions and his art short.

Vidal's artistic instinct and his didactic purpose may owe formal debts to John Dos Passos, dogged recorder "of what happened last summer—or last decade." Dos Passos's claim to accuracy fascinates and amuses Vidal. "Not since the brothers Goncourt has there been such a dedication to getting down exactly what happened, and were it not for his political passions he might indeed have been a true camera to our time. He invents little; he fancies less." Dos Passos is an interpreter and, were it not for his politics, a true one, a moralist for his age. Vidal realizes how out of fashion Dos Passos has become, but other writers feel "unexpectedly protective" of him, out of a natural compassion for the man, and also a self-protective impulse, because of the aesthetically uncaring, incurious, unsympathetic readership he was addressing. The growth of forms and style are simply "a process too slow for the American temperament. As a result our literature is noted for sprinters but significantly short of milers."

Wilson was as close a literary friend as John (Roderigo) Dos Passos (1896–1970) had in his early years. Wilson entertained him, reviewed him, advised him. Their experiences of the war were similar, Dos Passos having joined up as soon as he finished at Harvard and having worked as an ambulance driver, an adventure that accelerated his political development. Wilson did not hugely like him, he was no Fitzgerald or Hemingway, though after the war he stayed in Paris and became part of the "lost generation." But he was an enigmatic reality. Wilson evokes in 1930 "the Dos Passoses' house [in Truro, Cape Cod] in its hollow—the dead trees: 'the sort of place where people would drive old cars into the yard and leave them.'" Like the novels, one is tempted to say, where much comes to rest and is left simply because it was there and its gratuitous presence—in terms of the fiction—underwrites the realism. When the transforming tragedy of 1947 occurred, his wife killed in a car crash that also cost Dos Passos the sight of one eye, Wilson paid him a visit. Dos Passos sat forward in the bed and grasped his friend's hand. "I had never before seen him show anything like emotion."

Wilson's views of Dos Passos's work altered in the light and dark of the politics of the age. "Dos Passos was, so far as I knew, the first American novelist to make the people of our generation talk as they actually did," he said in the 1920s. Two decades later he portrays him as a higher journalist, his "function" being "to take us behind the front pages of the newspapers and provide us with a newsreel of his own, in which we see the drama of history enacted by real men and women instead of in terms of Industry and Labor, Wall Street, the White House, etc." He had, like Steinbeck, a journalist's vocation. For *State of the Nation* (1944) he traveled around the United States for a year, from December 1942 to December 1943, concentrating especially on areas in which there was a distressed proletariat. J. B. Priestley in England had made a similar, if shorter, odyssey to write *English Journey* (1934). Steinbeck too traveled in the same spirit, though he got his hands dirty and focused on individuals to make it real in fiction.

As a reporter and novelist, Dos Passos got a purchase on groups, communities, collectives, operations, rallies, movements. His approach has certain affinities, politically and strategically, with that of Christopher Isherwood, though Dos Passos was less programmatic in his early work and remained attentive to the themes, if not the ideologies, that informed it. There are affinities too with the investigative fiction of Capote, though Dos Passos has none of the ostentatious thoroughness or narratorial infatuation of the author of *In Cold Blood*. Wilson says Dos Passos got the idea to write books about groups, not individuals, from the Russians. His project has a distinctly American face. He looks to the group because his take on the individual and the particular is unstable. The clichés and mechanical descriptions even in his best writing can seem cautious, formulaic: radicalism is in the ideas, and though the fragmentation of elements asks to be compared with contemporary artistic practice, the books are vitiated by an abstracting spirit. He is equally novelist and essayist, one vocation undermines the other. His politics were first questing, then questioning, and finally took on an alarming conservatism that saw in Barry Goldwater a deliverance from the decay of American values.

Dos Passos lived long enough to be several writers, with more than forty novels to his credit, the first published in 1920, the last half a century later. He gained and lost, or outlived, large readerships. At one time he appeared the most formally and politically innovative of American writers. He was for a while, Frederic Raphael says, "the greatest living writer, not least in the opinion of Jean-Paul Sartre, whose narrative technique, especially in the second volume of his uncompleted fictional tetralogy [*Le sursis* (1947, translated as *The Reprieve*), from *The Roads to Freedom*], was indebted to *Manhattan Transfer*." Essayist, painter, musician, and polemicist cohabited uneasily in him. The engaged and active communist transmogrified into a dynamic libertarian.

He started by rejecting privilege. E. E. Cummings describes him taking a bath in a hotel and reflecting on injustice: "Isn't it dweadful of me to lie here in this luxurious warm bath while human welations are being violated all over the countwy—stwikers are being shot down!" Dos Passos was briefly popular in the Soviet Union. In that country, according to Wilson, Jimmy Herf, the newspaper reporter in *Manhattan Transfer* who wants to be a writer and wears many of Dos Passos's chips on his shoulder, was "as well known as any character of Pushkin's." A paid-up member of the Communist League of American Writers, he was written out of the script when he aligned himself with the Trotskyites. Wilson chaired the Trotskyite group set up in the wake of the show trials. Dos Passos's books disappeared from bookshops all over Russia.

Hemingway at first respected him. In Key West he took him fishing and they shared long talks and silences. They went to Spain together in 1937. It was fifteen years since Dos Passos had published *Rosinante to the Road Again* (1922): he knew and loved Spain, its popular and high culture unalienated, compared with pleasureless, cultureless, overly industrious, and emptily prosperous America. That book is marred, as the later novels are, by repetitions that aspire to the effect of musical reprise and refrain, part of the transposition into discursive language of "musical" elements. This mars his first major novel, *Three Soldiers* (1920), where one soldier wants to become a composer. In *Rosinante* the protagonists, contrasted sensibilities more than characters, bump into all sorts on the road, among them a modern Don Quixote and Sancho Panza. The narrator is hardly fictionalized. He is infatuated with El Greco but not familiar with Velázquez. He admires Lope de Vega much more than Calderón de la Barca. He insists that Spanish art is "constantly on the edge of caricature," "a constant slipping over into the grotesque." He lists great works of Spanish art and architecture that "are far indeed from the middle term of reasonable beauty." Most he loves Cervantes. These Iberian enthusiasms irritated Wilson.

*Rosinante* opens with a wandering Telemachus. We half expect an Odyssey to be in the offing, but this son has forgotten the object of his search. He is companioned by Lyceaus, another stray from literature and legend. The book cannot decide what it is up to. Is it an introduction to Spanish history and culture? A picaresque novel? A picaresque essay? A travel book, the picaresque written in? Art criticism, literary criticism, history, amateur anthropology? Is it a critique of alienating American culture and ideology, contrasted with a wholesome and rustic Mediterranean world?

In Spain with Hemingway, Dos Passos felt his infatuation with Communism waning. He broke with Hemingway, he said, because Hemingway lent his name to unexamined propaganda statements and was willing *not* to ask questions about the Soviet agents' part in the murder of José Robles, translator of Dos Passos's work into Spanish and a friend and mentor. His own abstracting political views suffered traumatic adjustment. Hemingway wrote to Fitzgerald that Dos Passos was a second-rate writer with no ear, and a second-rate boxer with no left hand. "Also terrible snob (on acct. of being a bastard)," which indeed he was, his father being a substantial and privately supportive Wall Street lawyer, his mother a long-term mistress of distinguished southern extraction; and Hemingway alleged that he was worried about his black blood when he "could have been our best negro writer."

*Three Soldiers* is about the experiences of American recruits in the First World War. His common man begins in innocence and learns life's treachery, and also that from the army there is no escape, no free will, no space for imagination or repose. The book, mannered and strained, gives a sense of what Americans suffered in the alienating confusion of wartime Europe. The tendency to caricature is something novelists of the Second World War built on, extreme reality having much in common with fantasy and making those who act within it lose some of their verisimilitude. Caricature can heighten; it can also be reductive and repetitious, producing Aunt Sallies whose presence sells the larger project short. Thus Andrews, Dos Passos's most compelling character, who suffers the most reversals in the novel, encounters while convalescing in a hospital from leg wounds a typical monster of the military-spiritual sort: "A little man with chubby cheeks and steel-grey hair very neatly flattened against his skull, stood at the window rubbing his fat little white hands together and making a faint unctuous puffing with each breath. Andrews noticed that a white clerical collar enclosed the little man's pink neck, that starched cuffs peeped from under the well-tailored sleeves of his officer's uniform. Sam Brown belt and puttees, too, were highly polished. On his shoulder was a demure little silver cross. Andrews' glance had reached the pink cheeks again, when he suddenly found a pair of steely eyes looking sharply into his." He protests too adjectivally. "Chubby cheeks" gets it. The "fat little white" hands gilds, but still his anger (from Andrews's point of view, but not quite) builds: "faint unctuous puffing," "little man's pink neck." The "steely eyes" gaze out of this scornful, feminized portrait with understandable indignation.

Then the little man lets rip with language no army padre uses except in comedy: "His voice rose and fell in the suave chant of one accustomed to going through the Episcopal liturgy for the edification of well-dressed and well-fed congregations." Why Episcopal? Is to be well dressed and well fed un-Christian? "'Inasmuch as He has vouchsafed us safety and a mitigation of our afflictions, and let us pray that in His good time He may see fit to return us whole in limb and pure in heart to our families, to the wives, mothers, and to those whom we will some day honor with the name of wife, who eagerly await our return; and that we may spend the remainder of our lives in useful service of the great country for whose safety and glory we have offered up our youth a willing sacrifice . . . Let us pray!'" It will not do. Within the spare, three-dimensional hospital reality, this is poor polemic. Employing an image from shooting that also feels like an image from filming (Dos Passos's screenplays included *The Devil Is a Woman* [1937], starring Marlene Dietrich), Wilson wrote to him of the "short-range" and "close range" of manifestos, editorials, advertisements, and public speeches. The range of fiction should be longer.

The poet Edward Estlin Cummings (1894–1962) wrote one reckonable novel, *The Enormous Room* (1922). In terms of settings it fits into one corner of Dos Passos's expansive *Three Soldiers*. Serving with the Ambulance Corps in 1917, Cummings and a friend, suspected of spying and other misdemeanors, were arrested by the French. Cummings spent over a hundred days in detention in Normandy, his friend a good deal longer. They were kept in the eponymous room. F. Scott Fitzgerald thought this the best literary product by a young American writer involved in the war. It expresses the claustrophobia and irrationality of the situation in ways that proved useful to novelists of the Second World War. Here the picaresque is arrested in one place yet hectically continues to behave as a free agent on the road. No space is covered, but a lot of life is encountered. Gertrude Stein, on the strength of this book, regarded Cummings as "the natural heir of the New England tradition with its aridity and sterility, but also with its individuality."

Dos Passos worked on a different scale. *Manhattan Transfer* (1925, the year of Fitzgerald's *The Great Gatsby*) remains his most readable book. He wrote it at a turbulent time in his own and in American history. The trial of Sacco and

Vanzetti had taken place, and attempts were being made to reprieve them from the electric chair (they were executed in 1927). Dos Passos was arrested for protesting their detention. He had joined the defense committee and wrote in 1927 the 127-page *Facing the Chair: Story of the Americanization of Two Foreign-born Workmen,* reviewing the case that caused protests in the United States and across Europe. He felt a necessary connection between his work as an artist and his activism. The integrity of one entailed the integrity of the other.

*Manhattan Transfer* is theme- rather than character-driven. The elements of formal experimentation drawn from Joyce and from the film techniques of Sergei Eisenstein do not quite make it an experimental novel. They are intended to render the writing more "scientific," answerable less to an imagined than to an observed world revealed in its own language, its very documents (headlines, reports, articles). The multiplication of characters and their symbolic growth and change, some becoming corrupted by the system, some crushed by it, give the book an inexorable and earnest feel. It is blatantly didactic and there is no doubt of its perspectives. The Depression was still a couple of years away, but the New York that emerged exists proleptically in this hectic, alert narration.

In 1938 *U.S.A.,* a novel that combined three earlier books, appeared. Some conservative parents forbade their children to read the book as late as the 1960s because of its political and sexual content and the author's "character." It is Dos Passos's most discussed work, though little read today. He tried to repeat its success fourteen years later with *District of Columbia* (1952), another triptych comprising *Adventures of a Young Man* (1939), *Number One* (1943), and *The Grand Design* (1949). By then he was in retreat from all the beliefs and energies that had shaped his early fiction, and due in part to his disenchantment the book did not catch on.

But *U.S.A.,* its three constituent parts written between the Depression and the Spanish Civil War—*The 42nd Parallel* (1930), *Nineteen Nineteen* (1932), and *The Big Money* (1936)—is thematically coherent. Wilson finds here "almost the thrill of the great Marxists." Remembering his own failed political triptych, he is fascinated to view the huge canvas Dos Passos has worked, risking historical insights that the characters do not share. Missing from the novel are the "pleasures of love, exhilaration of the whoopee period." There is, he says, a "sourness which becomes satire." He is "always holding his characters at arm's length."

Dos Passos described the first volume as social criticism rather than fiction. The 42nd parallel on the map cuts across the middle of America, the nation's midriff. Its theme is the mean, the middle people, what Auden called in 1939 "the average men" endeavoring to advance and improve themselves, to be good and prosper. *Nineteen Nineteen* is also about common people, in the aftermath of the war he characterized in *Three Soldiers.* This volume takes place largely among demobilized, debauched Americans in Paris. Sex of various varieties is evoked with a candor that at the time shocked. *The Big Money* is America off the wagon: more alcohol than water flows through it. The big fish with the big money control and bring others down. The coda is not revolutionary but tends toward anarchy: a striker goes AWOL, hitching a ride down a highway into Huck Finn territory, withdrawing from the fray not in defeat but in abdication; overhead an airplane flies its Big Money men in the other direction toward Los Angeles. The plane traces that middle line, its shadow slicing the continental nation.

Much was once made of Dos Passos's style, his joining up of words, playing with spacing in the spirit of E. E. Cummings. More obviously experimental-seeming, though in retrospect not especially effective, is the way in which he layers narrative. Episodes begin with a "Newsreel," a page or more of actual headlines and lyrics from popular songs to establish a period, a place, and a cultural "reality." Then pages of the Camera Eye follow, a camera that like stream of consciousness without a defining consciousness behind it observes in ways that do not necessarily connect with the narrative proper. It explores the lives of individuals, different in tone and direction in each of the volumes. The "episode" follows, taking the story of a character forward, out of innocence into the bleak uplands of the American experience. This narrative in turn is interrupted to bring us brief biographies of public figures, essays on actual Americans. Each book follows a four-layer formula. No single person dominates and the narrator is not foregrounded. The reader stands in a harsh landscape.

There are eight "public" biographies in *1919,* the ninth devoted to the Unknown Soldier. All were historical, and Wesley Everest ("Paul Bunyan") is the most appalling. It is possible to forget the intensity of anger and concern that writers like Dos Passos and Dreiser, Faulkner and Steinbeck and Lewis felt at a time when such yawning gaps had opened up between the language of value and the values themselves. Everest was a twenty-nine-year-old veteran and activist for the Industrial Workers of the World Union in Centralia, Washington. On Armistice Day 1919 he shot two fellow veterans who were attacking him for his views on the war and on labor. He was released by jail guards to a lynch mob of veterans who tortured him, knocked in his teeth with a rifle butt, castrated him, and hanged him in three different locations, so no one would miss the spectacle. The body was finally riddled with bullets and deposited in an unmarked grave. The death was recorded as suicide.

Wilson regarded *Nineteen Nineteen* as Dos Passos's "most intense piece of writing" about the forces released at the end of the war, a book more radical than *Three Soldiers* or any other book of its time. But he could not help chiding Dos Passos for being so negative; he reminded his friend that he enjoyed banter, good food, and fellowship. Why then was everything in his writing so unrelievedly grim, most of the women bitches, and the ideas simplified so the action could convey them? One cannot entirely display the inside from the outside, as he wished to do. There was simply too much *detail*. Real people in real places get used to where they are. In the 1920s E. E. Cummings was saying that Dos Passos's books "were all made up of externals." Gore Vidal wrote of the "terrible garrulousness in most American writing, a legacy no doubt of the Old Frontier."

As experiment goes, it is of its period. Politically alert readers read the papers. The brisk shorthand of dialogue and conversation Dos Passos renders without fuss, what is politically incorrect being correct in historical register. The introduction of historical figures and public incident was another kind of shorthand. These points of access now provide the obscurity of the texts. *U.S.A.* is of its time, which is why in time it will regain its place at the heart of its decade, an attempt to make sense of the world. If we agree, "our prejudices do the author's work." Of Dos Passos's right-turning *Mid-Century* (1961) Vidal wrote, "There is some truth in everything Dos Passos says. But his spirit strikes me as sour and mean and, finally, uncomprehending."

No American novelist had as great an immediate impact on his contemporaries, at home and abroad, as Dos Passos with the books he wrote before World War II. He was the cause of Lillian Hellman's famous lawsuit against Mary Therese McCarthy (1912–1989). At a party in 1949, McCarthy heard Hellman remark (taking Hemingway's line) that Dos Passos had left the Spanish Republican cause because he did not like the food. McCarthy denounced her. Later she denounced her again on television as a thoroughgoing liar, and Hellman sued. The case ran on until Hellman's death.

McCarthy read *The 42nd Parallel* when she was a student at Vassar, and its impact was immediate and lasting. Like Dos Passos's, her best fiction deals with groups, and though she is more concerned with the inner lives of her characters, more pointed in her satire, she has essayistic instincts in her creative projects. Dos Passos was among the writers she got to know in Greenwich Village, along with Sherwood Anderson, Erskine Caldwell, and Upton Sinclair. The intense engagement of the period educated her in the need for emphasis and clarity. She held her own, and Edmund Wilson when he met her in 1937 was astonished. They married (her second marriage, his third) the same year, Wilson forty-three, McCarthy twenty-six. For the most part it was a marriage made in hell. He put her in a small room, and though he did not lock her in, he told her to get to work. She said, "And I found myself writing fiction to my great surprise," a fiction that risked impoliteness, using vulgarisms, farting. For eight years McCarthy and Wilson battled. By 1945 she was fully fledged and ready for another divorce.

*The Company She Keeps* (1942), her first novel, was about the groups she moved in around Greenwich Village when still with Wilson. The chapters were composed as stories that tended toward their present arrangement. Her fiction was rooted in autobiography, and several of the models for her characters recognized themselves. In 1952 *The Groves of Academe* introduced the campus novel as an American genre, and McCarthy herself, teaching at Sarah Lawrence, is said to have been the protagonist of Randall Jarrell's one novel, *Pictures from an Institution* (1954). In *A Charmed Life* (1955) she chooses a small-town environment, again reading a community and its interactions. Her second major novelistic success, *The Group* (1962), about eight young women graduating from Vassar as she had done in 1933, spent almost two years on the *New York Times* best-sellers list. Louis Auchincloss characterized it as "an encyclopedia of the mannerisms, the fads, the affectations of an era." Both it and *The Company She Keeps* were made into movies. Her fiction is clear, entertaining, astute, containing gossip and tittle-tattle as she thought fiction must, but none of it is innovative. Her contract is with the common reader and with the truths of her subject matter. It does not require the kinds of derangement Dos Passos practiced. "The popular novelist (and there was no other kind, the art novel not having been discovered)," she says, advocating values of an earlier age and of Russian literature, "was looked up to as an authority on all sorts of matters." Much of her later writing concentrates on "real" subjects, in particular the Vietnam War, Watergate, terrorism. Her essays on literature and autobiographical writing complete a remarkable oeuvre.

Her mother and father died in the influenza epidemic of 1918 and she was raised first by her paternal grandparents, Roman Catholics who lodged her and her brothers out with an uncle and aunt. In *Memories of a Catholic Girlhood* she describes the grandparents and relations. A sadistic uncle did not allow her books to read, so she concentrated on him. She became an avid recorder. She and her brothers were duly rescued by her maternal grandfather in Seattle. Auchincloss speaks of her fiction as, like Thomas Wolfe's, "a kind of autobiography." "What I really do," she said, "is take real plums and put them in an imaginary cake." She had, Saul Bellow remarked in a letter, "a taste for low sadism," a desire to *see* punishment done to those who merited it. She realized that progressives and intellectuals were potentially most self-deceiving. Auchincloss concludes, "She saw that the illness of the modern world might be exposed most effectively by showing its ravaging presence in the very minority who believed themselves most immune." Liberalism in teaching and the arts could not counteract the extremism and bigotry she witnessed, if indeed such countering was the "purpose" of art—if art is indeed "purposed" in that sense. In *The Groves of Academe* the monstrous Henry Mulcahy descends on Jocelyn College and destroys its values and culture by his manipulative (hardly ideological) shenanigans. One is put in mind of Nabokov's heartless *Pnin* and of the appallingly plausible Delphine Roux in Philip Roth's *The Human Stain*.

Interviewing her in 1961 in Paris, when she was writing *The Group*, Elisabeth Sifton remarked on the way McCarthy constructed her conversation. Though "remarkably fluent and articulate," she "often interrupted herself in order to reword or qualify a phrase, sometimes even impatiently destroying it and starting again in the effort to express herself as exactly as possible." What was *The Group* to be about? The answer was formal and thematic: "About the idea of progress, really. The idea of progress seen in the female sphere, the feminine sphere." A pause; then, "You know, home economics, architecture, domestic technology, contraception, childbearing; the study of technology in the home, in the playpen, in the bed. It's supposed to be the history of the loss of faith in progress, in the idea of progress, during that twenty-year period." What makes a Woman Writer? The introduction of drapery, description, décor. Not a popular view. Jane Austen was never a Woman Writer, nor was Katherine Anne Porter. But Elizabeth Bowen? She becomes one; and Katherine Mansfield always was one. Some women writers change into Women Writers in midcareer. She loathed those trends in women's writing that harden in figures like Simone de Beauvoir. "I think she's odious. A mind totally bourgeois turned inside out."

She remains skeptical, tentative, even as to genre. "I'm not sure any of my books are novels. Maybe none of them are. Something happens in my writing—I don't mean it to—a sort of distortion, a sort of writing on the bias, seeing things with a sort of swerve and swoop." And there is the problem that her natural mode is satire and comedy; development of character (as opposed to plot) in those modes is challenging. Her main problem is point of view, Flaubert's *style indirect libre,* "the author's voice, by a kind of ventriloquism, disappearing in and completely limited by the voices of his characters." The author absents himself. McCarthy wants the author back, because in the kind of fiction she writes whole areas of feeling and thought are excluded by the narrative choice she feels compelled to make. One reason she loved the Russian writers and advocated Boris Pasternak's *Doctor Zhivago* when other critics were pointing out its narrative impurities was that the problems besetting modern American and Western European fiction were absent from his work: He used his own voice along with those of his characters. He was in the world he was making. She enjoyed writing her travel books, speaking in her own voice about real things.

Katherine Anne Porter (born Callie Russell Porter, 1890–1980) made of her life a fiction that answered better than the facts life dealt her to her sense of who she wanted to be. From self-construction followed her aesthetics. She notes in an essay that Willa Cather preferred the prose of Prosper Mérimée to that of

Balzac on the grounds that, whatever the differences of scale, Mérimée was the greater artist. This was her license, too. She wrote books of stories, the novel *Ship of Fools* (1962), and essays, starting with her focused "The Days Before," a key piece in reclaiming Henry James for American writing, and she engaged and reengaged the work of Stein. A sentence-by-sentence writer, she is epigrammatic and, in her ninety years, less copious than her contemporaries. A summary judge, her verdicts are delivered with artistry. The appraiser is aware of being appraised. Her life is a fiction that produces fictions. She belongs in this book not only for her one novel, a long-anticipated best seller whose force has diminished over time, but for her originality in handling southern subject matter and the themes of race and machismo, her impact as a critic, and her example for emerging southern writers, women in particular. Without her Eudora Welty would have progressed more slowly in the world; Flannery O'Connor, Carson McCullers, and other young writers, too, would have emerged more slowly. But when confronted with the "woman question," she was impatient: "Oh that. I think men and women have their feet nailed to the same deck." The deck of *Ship of Fools* perhaps.

Porter was born poor in Texas and had but one year of formal schooling. She cannot be classed as a Southern Writer as some of her contemporaries and successors can, given the breadth of her subject matter and her rejection of her past. But she does portray herself as "the grandchild of a lost War," a scion of the Confederacy, "and I have blood-knowledge of what life can be in a defeated country on the bare bones of privation." Her actual home was without books and without parental direction. Her mother died when she was small. She invented another childhood, giving herself access to a library, intelligent conversation, graces; she said her family had fallen on hard times. After her mother's death, the family moved in with her paternal grandmother, Cat, a kind of energized Blanche Dubois who fantasized to survive. Porter learned from her to invent herself. Cat died when Porter was eleven, and later she adopted the name Katherine in her honor. The Porter family became nomadic, moving from relation to relation in Texas and Louisiana. She says she was an avid reader of good books: certainly her early style is rooted in serious reading. At sixteen she married unwisely, the first of several bad decisions. At twenty-three she ran away. In Chicago she became Katherine Porter and embarked on a life of travel and crisis, illness, controversy, and brilliant success.

She was convincing: her handsome patrician manner, her old-style ceremoniousness, were aspects of her self-impersonation. This Katherine Anne Porter climbed to the top where she belonged. She knew her contemporaries, big and small. She was asked to the White House, where James Baldwin, rather drunk, said he was in love with her. Many people loved her for a time. Many suffered under the scalpel of her irony. Hers was a practiced duplicity. Truman Capote met her at Yaddo, the writers' colony, when she was in her fifties, he in his early twenties. He conjured her in his unfinished novel *Answered Prayers* as Alice Lee Langman, "an enameled lady" with whom the young, fascinated, and then repelled narrator has an intimacy. This is not his Holly Golightly but a woman who has made her own solid luck. He reflects on her fame: "Like the value of diamonds, her prestige depended upon a controlled and limited output; and, in those terms, she was a royal success, the queen of the writer-in-residence swindle, the prizes racket, the high-honorarium con, the grants-in-aid-to-struggling-artists shit. Everybody, the Ford Foundation, the Guggenheim Foundation, the National Institute of Arts and Letters, the National Council on the Arts, the Library of Congress, et al., was hell-bound to gorge her with tax-free greenery, and Miss Langman, like those circus midgets who lose their living if they grow an inch or two, was ever aware her prestige would collapse if the ordinary public began to read and reward her." Capote is gleeful and bitter in equal measure. In her he sees a version of himself. He too was more Mérimée than Balzac. He might have said with her, "I spend my life thinking about technique, method, style. The only time I do not think about them at all is when I am writing."

She calls *Ship of Fools* "the story of my first voyage to Europe in 1931," from Veracruz, Mexico. She had spent years in Mexico and wrote about it with brio. She is merciless in her handling of characters and types. When she started it in 1941, it might have seemed, with its unappealing Germans (nothing so harsh since Katherine Mansfield's early story "Germans at Meat"), topical. But the time it took to write rendered it timeless. The publisher who commissioned it died well before its completion. The effort, doubt, and redrafting worked to her credit: a best seller in the year of publication, film rights fetched $400,000, and she was in the black for the rest of her life. Not an unhappy ending.

For so long a book it is too rich in memorable sentences and shapely phrases, the novel dissolves in its effects, the sum of which is greater than the whole. The Germans are joined by Mexicans, Americans, and the poor Spanish returning from America. Among the dozens of characters, all classes are represented. Porter was fascinated by their variety and their thwarted interactions, isolated by greed and selfishness. There are several plots but the overarching plot is secondary. The movements between and within scenes, as Isherwood remarked, are keenly cinematic. Porter might be said to have taken form forward in terms of continuity and transition.

Graham Greene regarded her as the best writer to come out of America after early Hemingway. He found in her "the sense of a consciousness open to any wind, a style adaptable to any subject." How different her style is from Hemingway's: Her economy is the product of irony and refinement, of a forensic politeness, a social calculation, rather than a formal, artistic economy.

———•———

Francis Scott Key Fitzgerald (1896–1940) was a remote relation of the author of "The Star Spangled Banner." Vidal takes a dim view of him. "Little of what Fitzgerald wrote has any great value as literature," he says: He is famous more for the life he led than the books he wrote. When he was interested in something, said Vidal, he focused, but he was too wrapped up in himself and "he had no real life in the world." Neither Porter nor Dos Passos was persuaded by his work. Porter said, "I couldn't read him then," when his books were hot off the press, "and I can't read him now . . . Not only didn't I like his writing, but I didn't like the people he wrote about. I thought they weren't worth thinking about, and I still think so." Harsh. Categorical.

Of the writers of the lost generation, Fitzgerald wrote the most elegant, cinematic sentence and paragraph. He should have appealed to Porter, he has the gloss of writers' workshops. But his subject matter disagreed with her. Dos Passos was exasperated by what he saw as Fitzgerald's self-obsession, so that even in the Depression, the Spanish Civil War, and World War Two the suffering subjectivities of his characters, aspects of a troubled self, kept center stage. Fitzgerald, he thought, was not always as drunk as he pretended to be; he pretended to be drunk to license some social outrage. Fitzgerald's was to him the apotheosis of bourgeois sensibility familiar from his own background. Money matters, of course; but history? Fitzgerald recognized this in the second of the three 1936 *Esquire* essays entitled "The Crack-Up": "My political conscience had scarcely existed for ten years save as an element of irony in my stuff."

These self-reflective articles generalize from his experience of celebrity. His problems included alcoholism, the disaster of his relationships, and the malicious genius that now possessed and now rejected him. The essays are without genius, written with a faux candor, a vulnerability that wants to be indulged. The effort to transcend is mired in unshakable self-regard. Wilson collected these and other discursive writings in the posthumous *The Crack-Up*. He regarded Fitzgerald, an intimate at Princeton, as the great writer of his generation. His early death was a life-changing tragedy for Wilson. He also edited Fitzgerald's unfinished novel, *The Love of the Last Tycoon: A Western,* published simply as *The Last Tycoon* (1941). He made claims for it and kept faith with a writer whose work filled him with amazement rather than (as with other contemporaries) professional jealousy. And Fitzgerald valued him: "I had done very little thinking, save within the problems of my craft. For twenty years a certain man had been my intellectual conscience. That was Edmund Wilson." Wilson presents the large fragment of the last book as Fitzgerald's most mature work. His protagonist has a profession, he has gone beyond the college boys and girls growing into the treachery of high society. In *The Last Tycoon,* parties are not central; what matters is a web of changing relationships. This is "the best novel we have had about Hollywood, and it is the only one which takes us inside." It is based on actual people and conflict: Fitzgerald steps into another individual's life.

James Thurber noted "the voluminous, the tiny meticulous notes, the long descriptions of character" that Fitzgerald made for the book, useful to writers who set out to complete the fragment. The story, of a studio boss engaged in a struggle against the trade unions, death, and volatile women (the essential nemesis in Fitzgerald), develops in appropriately cinematic terms, the scene pacing and dissolves, the use of significant image, the lingering shot. He had written for many films and failed to make the big time. He was tied into substantial expenses, educating his daughter and providing for his hospitalized wife. He composed the novel with his whole heart but he had to write short stories to make his daily bread.

All the time he longed to get to bed to write his novel. That's where he went to do the work that mattered to him. "I am deep in the novel," he informed a friend not long before his death, "living in it, and it makes me happy." He did manage to change. Wilson found him in the later 1930s "sober, industrious, completely transformed—just like a well-meaning Middle Western businessman who takes a diffident interest in the better kinds of books." This is hardly the Fitzgerald he had observed at the Plaza Hotel, lying in his bed drunk, watching Wilson "with his expressionless, birdlike eyes." He always had a fear of impotence, a metaphor for the Depression itself, and of his sexual adequacy, including anxiety over his genital dimensions. These anxieties abated in his later years with his last partner, the English-born Hollywood columnist Sheilah Graham, author of *Beloved Infidel,* a bittersweet kiss-and-tell made into a movie with Gregory Peck as Fitzgerald and Deborah Kerr as Graham.

The route to his early death was intense and wasteful. In the essay where he spoke of Wilson as his "intellectual conscience" he mentioned a contemporary who "had been an artistic conscience to me—I had not imitated his infectious style, because my own style, such as it is, was formed before he published anything, but there was an awful pull toward him": Hemingway, whose work he recommended to his editor at Scribner's, acting not as agent but go-between. Hemingway in his memoirs could not deny that in reading *The Great Gatsby* he felt humbled. "When I had finished the book I knew that no matter what Scott did, nor how preposterously he behaved, I must know it was like a sickness and be of any help I could to him and try to be a good friend." Fitzgerald, an attractive and generous man, had many friends. "But I enlisted as one more, whether I could be of any use to him or not. If he could write a book as fine as *The Great Gatsby* I was sure that he could write an even better one." Hemingway said this before he met Zelda and understood Fitzgerald's nemesis. She "was very jealous of Scott's work" and sabotaged it.

Fitzgerald fell in love with Zelda Sayre (1900–1948), an Alabama belle, when during his army service (he was just too late to see action, a fact he regretted) he was posted to Montgomery and met her. He worked hard to get her. She wanted wealth and celebrity and he had neither but set out to acquire both.

Fitzgerald's father had been an unsuccessful man of business, for a time a traveling salesman. His mother had come into an inheritance and the family returned to St. Paul, Minnesota, to live comfortably. Fitzgerald had been given an excellent education (the one thing he wanted his daughter to have, as his finances collapsed). He returned to St. Paul to revise his first novel, *This Side of Paradise,* in 1919. Maxwell Perkins took it for Scribner's, a coming-of-age novel more economical and spectacular, and requiring less revision, than Thomas Woolf's *Look Homeward, Angel.* The book succeeded and the author became a celebrity. Its protagonist, "romantic egotist" Amory Blaine, is a thinly disguised version of the author; Rosalind, who has many of Zelda's characteristics, calls his bluff. He may be all charm, she may love him, but she needs money, too. When Zelda drafted her novel *Save Me the Waltz* (1932), she borrowed the name Amory Blaine for her protagonist. Fitzgerald forbade her to use it. His first novel's success had brought him the fulfillment of his desire and what was to prove fatal, the woman of his dreams. The picture Zelda painted was too intimate for him. She wanted to achieve her own novel, but he revised it, severely. It was published with his reluctant approval. He did for her, it was said, what Maxwell Perkins had done for Thomas Wolfe. Fitzgerald remarked to Perkins, "You're a putter inner and I'm a taker outer." But her novel, frail as it is, was her creation, and like his novels it grows out of their vehement lives. She started a second novel, but stopped this time with decision. She was mentally ill.

Scott and Zelda's early years together were not all unhappiness. Once established, a good writer could live quite comfortably from writing short stories. Fitzgerald was taken up by the agent Harold Ober, a key player for many of the writers of the period. Ober secured him commissions for story writing, especially for the *Saturday Evening Post.* The commercial stories share themes with the more serious work, but they tend to end on an upbeat. He told Hemingway how he wrote good stories "and then changed them for submission" to the better-paying magazines, "knowing exactly how he must make the twists that made them into salable magazine stories." Hemingway called this "whoring." For Fitzgerald it was a way of earning a living and, incidentally, building readership. "The Diamond as Big as the Ritz" and "May Day" are in a different key and can be read alongside the novels.

Once married, Scott and Zelda adopted an extravagant lifestyle they could ill maintain. In New York he completed his second novel, *The Beautiful and Damned* (1922), a book that, by means of Anthony and Gloria Patch, explored and expanded their disorderly life. They were beautiful and the next two decades would reveal them as damned. The book is among his least successful and is portentous, humorless. It hardly prepares us for the decisive achievement that followed soon after.

In Italy and France in 1924 he completed *The Great Gatsby*. He had endured Zelda's emasculating, brief affair, if it was that, with an Italian navy pilot. The narrator of the book, Nick Carraway, is not Princeton but Yale, and did see service in the First World War, unlike the author, but otherwise he and the chastened and sexually challenged Fitzgerald have much in common. Fitzgerald's vision, through Carraway, was androgynous, complete, in the way that Virginia Woolf says an accomplished author must be: active and passive, male and female, credulous and disabused. Also southern, midwestern, and northeastern. Only James Baldwin achieves a similarly comprehensive, 360-degree vision, and that only once, in *Another Country*. Nick Caraway, a dealer in bonds, not in solid things, comes from the indefinition of the Midwest. His neighbor is another midwesterner, the self-inventing James Gatz. Carraway looks in on other lives, misunderstanding his cousin Daisy, her boorish husband, Tom, Mrs. Wilson, and Jordan Baker, the dubious golf star; he is charged with a diffused libidinal energy, and the sensual reality of all those with whom he comes in contact is palpable.

Leaving the party at the love-flat of Tom Buchanan and Mrs. Wilson, after Tom has broken Mrs. Wilson's nose for taunting him with his wife Daisy's name, Nick follows Mr. McKee, an eccentric effeminate photographer with a forceful wife. This, the narrator tells us, is only the second time in his life he has been drunk. The scene comes at the end of a chapter and hangs there, unresolved, for the rest of the novel, a gratuitous, oblique revelation.

> "Come to lunch some day," he suggested, as we groaned down in the elevator.
> "Where?"
> "Anywhere."
> "Keep your hands off the lever," snapped the elevator boy.
> "I beg your pardon," said Mr. McKee with dignity, "I didn't know I was touching it."
> "All right," I agreed, "I'll be glad to."

> . . . I was standing beside his bed and he was sitting up between the sheets, clad in his underwear, with a great portfolio in his hands.
>
> "Beauty and the Beast . . . Loneliness . . . Old Grocery Horse . . . Brook'n Bridge . . ."
>
> Then I was lying half asleep in the cold lower level of Pennsylvania Station, staring at the morning *Tribune,* and waiting for the four o'clock train.

What does this unconnected set of brief vignettes mean? Clearly, unclearly, something has happened. The lever, the sheets, the underwear, the ellipses, the coming-to at Penn Station, suggest a great deal in telling nothing at all. At the end of the following chapter Nick Carraway affirms, "Everyone suspects himself of at least one of the cardinal virtues, and this is mine: I am one of the few honest people that I have ever known." Which is why we cannot trust him.

For one thing, how can he know so much of a neighborhood in which he is only renting a house? When he lists the guests at Gatsby's parties, pages of them like the catalog of ships in the *Iliad* draw in the whole of a social world, all its bright and shadowy inflections. He knows too much. When he never establishes whether Gatsby is in fact a bootlegger, as many of the hangers-on infer, or a bond shark, he knows too little. These epistemological conundrums are part of the fascination of the novel. The more we read it, the more we realize that Gatsby's unfulfillment complements the narrator's emptiness. For a time, at least, Gatsby knows what he wants and sets out to get it. Whatever Gatsby *is,* we are beguiled by his longing, his sacrifice, and the strength of his illusion. He and Citizen Kane have a lot in common: We do not judge (because we do not quite know where it comes from) his wealth.

*Gatsby* was published in 1925 and received good reviews. The first print run of 20,000 copies sold out. The reprint of 3,000 copies lasted for almost fifteen years. Raymond Chandler would have worked on the screenplay had the contract option clause permitted it. Fitzgerald's "charm" was "not a matter of pretty writing or clear style. It's a kind of subdued magic, controlled and exquisite, the sort of thing you get from string quartets."

In the first of his 1936 *Esquire* essays he declared, "The test of a first-rate intelligence is the ability to hold two opposed ideas in the mind at the same time, and still retain the ability to function." In his early adulthood he lived by this rule, seeing "the improbable, the implausible, often the 'impossible,' come true." When Zelda was hospitalized in Baltimore, Fitzgerald rented a house nearby and completed *Tender Is the Night* (1934), formally ambitious but commercially misjudged. Successful Dick Diver is pulled down by his marriage to an unstable woman. His subject is money, its acquisition, its waste. Money is the medium in which everything swims. For many of his protagonists it is new money, leverage and lever, but in the end, for Gatsby, new money is not sufficient to vie with old money, with the settled culture of self-possession. The impregnable established East Coast order, its tolerant hauteur, feeds on and enervates what surrounds it. Maybe Daisy Buchanan's voice *is* "full of money"; though she may be tempted, she cannot be bought, in any case not by Gatsby's ostentation. Or she has already been bought. Zelda belonged to a southern version of that class, as Fitzgerald said to their daughter, "soft when she should have been hard, and hard when she should have been yielding."

Zelda's fate is one form of waking up from the American dream into the living nightmare. Fitzgerald's story, too, has been romanticized to such an extent that, as Cyril Connolly believed, the myth of it eclipsed the novels in the popular mind, the novelist became "an American version of the Dying God." Yet *The Great Gatsby* holds an undiminished readership. It has sold more than 25 million copies worldwide.

---

Fitzgerald took a dim view of the writing of John (Ernst) Steinbeck (1902–1968). He described him to Wilson as "a rather cagey cribber" and sent a marked copy of Frank Norris's *McTeague* to display how Steinbeck had used it in writing *Of Mice and Men* (1937), a book that succeeded unexpectedly and appeared three years before Fitzgerald's death: Steinbeck's star was in a steep ascendant even as Fitzgerald's sank in the Pacific. Fitzgerald lived long enough to witness the early success of *The Grapes of Wrath* (1939). It has now sold over 15 million copies worldwide, though it has a long way to go before it overtakes *Gatsby*.

To begin with, Steinbeck insisted on standing apart. In 1926 he had a caretaker's job at Lake Tahoe that meant he was "snowed up for eight months every year," a genuine privacy in which he wrote his first novel (in the other four months he was a tourist guide). In 1933 he told a friend that writing "is primarily a lonely craft and must be accepted as such. If you eliminate that loneliness of approach, you automatically eliminate some of the power of the effect." Success began to dismantle his privacy and he became nostalgic for the poverty of his early years, when the connection with his parents and his first wife provided a secure creative space. "I hate cameras," he said when asked to provide a publicity portrait. "They are so much more sure than I am about everything." As *Of Mice and Men* began to succeed, he wrote his agent with genuine anxiety: "I simply cannot write books if a consciousness of self is thrust on me. Must have some anonymity." (On the upside he was able to afford a new typewriter, having worked hitherto on a "1912 model.") When he received the Nobel Prize in Literature in 1962, he reflected that only Shaw had written significant work in the wake of this fatal accolade. Faulkner was long spent by the time he got it, Hemingway "went into a kind of hysterical haze," "Red Lewis" became more alcoholic and irascible. He intended to "beat the rap," but he did not.

His trajectory as a writer begins with his historical romance *Cup of Gold: A Life of Sir Henry Morgan, Buccaneer, with Occasional Reference to History* (1929) and ends with the posthumously published, unfinished, and unfinishable *The Acts of King Arthur and His Noble Knights* (1976). These titles remind us that Steinbeck, most American of writers, who never completed his studies at Stanford, fed originally on Milton, and on Thomas Malory. When he first read Malory as a boy, he said, "I must have been already enamored of words, because the old and obsolete words delighted me." There is a sense of continuity between his world and Malory's, his down-at-heel heroes, his moral quandaries, and the Arthurian. In the preface to *Tortilla Flat* he writes, "Danny's house was not unlike the Round Table, and Danny's friends were not unlike the knights of it." The almost simile of "not unlike" stops just short of conceit. Working on the Malory project in 1957, he wrote in a letter, "A novel may be said to be the man who writes it," repeating his 1952 prologue to *Don Quixote,* where he quoted Cervantes on how "the child of my brain" should be exemplary "but I have not been able to contravene the law of nature which would have it that like begets like—"

In the period leading up to *Of Mice and Men* he was observing, then formulating in his fiction a sense of the group and its relations to the individual. He began to develop a serviceable theory of human and social nature. "Until you can put your theme in one sentence, you haven't it in hand well enough to write a novel," he said in 1933. His theme took shape. It informed his politics and kept him skeptical. He spelled it out in a long letter written on June 21, 1933, the culmination of numerous notes and comments-to-self pointing in this direction. "It is quite easy for the group, acting under stimuli of viciousness, to eliminate the kindly natures of its units. When acting as a group, men do not partake of their ordinary natures at all. The group can change its nature." Yet he has discovered that "the group is an individual as boundaried, as diagnosable, as dependent on its units and as independent of its units' individual natures, as the human unit, or man, is dependent on his cells and yet is independent of them." It is an open insight, the adumbration of a law of nature.

Yet he was a figure of the left in the 1930s. He joined the Communist-affiliated League of American Writers in 1935 and met strike organizers and leaders. Other writers associated with the League included Hemingway, Dreiser, and Nathanael West. Vice presidents in the later 1930s included Erskine Caldwell, Langston Hughes, and Upton Sinclair. In 1941 Dreiser was president, but all passion by then was spent. Steinbeck stood by Arthur Miller when he was summoned before the House Un-American Activities Committee and looked back on the period incredulously.

He was born in Salinas, California, in the middle of some of the richest farmland in the world, and he worked during his summers on the farms round about, getting to know the land and those who tilled it, including the migrants. At eighteen he went to Stanford and studied on and off for five years. He left for New York to find a publisher, becoming himself a kind of Grub Street migrant, returning home unsuccessful. He worked at Lake Tahoe, married, and with his first wife took up penurious residence in a house his father supplied for free on the Monterey Peninsula. His parents believed in his vocation and supplied him with stationery for his writing and an allowance.

A character in Elmore Leonard's *Get Shorty* says, "You already learned in school how to write, didn't you? I *hope* so. You have the idea and you put down what you want to say. Then you get somebody to add in the commas and shit where they belong . . . These people do that for you." This might be Steinbeck, who said in 1929 to a writer friend who told him correctness in writing was necessary "good manners," "But I have no interest in the printed word. I would continue to write if there were no writing and no print. I put my words down for a matter of memory. They are more made to be spoken than to be read. I have the instincts of a minstrel rather than those of a scrivener . . . When my sounds are all in place, I can send them to a stenographer who knows *his* trade and he can slip the commas about until they sit comfortably and he can spell the words so that school teachers will not raise their eyebrows when they read them. Why should I bother?" No wonder his writing was susceptible to film treatment: it came to him as images and voices. Those voices, especially in the early writing, belong to people who led harsh lives, close to the earth and to one another.

The first book in which Steinbeck signaled his own direction was the novella *To a God Unknown* (1933). Here he addressed individual readers, not a generalized audience, and the precisions of his narrative, if not his authority as moralist, are established. He never forgot the lesson. Years later he told the *Paris Review* that one must write to someone specific to escape the terror of the amorphous auditorium; and he knew he had to write the whole thing fast and revise afterward, otherwise he might stall. And the writer must speak dialogue aloud, test it on the air. That early unsatisfactory book was a labor to write and the labor shows: it is melodramatic, the themes of belonging, faith, guilt, and sacrifice having an inadvertently parodic, Lawrencian dimension. There are cautious traces of autobiography. It provided him with his education as a writer: in weighing each word, clause, and sentence, and discussing them with his first wife, he shaped a style. The style was not, despite what critics said, Hemingway's. As early as

1929 he declared, "I never read Hemingway with the exception of 'The Killers.'" The next year he talked of reading Xenophon, Herodotus, Plutarch, Marcus Aurelius—and Fielding, working on *To a God Unknown,* "and yet I suppose I shall be imitating Hemingway whom I have never read." He read Hemingway in 1952, *The Old Man and The Sea,* which he admired, noting how lavish "people" had been in pulling Hemingway down, and how lavish they were now in over-praising him. He was suffering a similar fate. Genius, he told the *Paris Review,* is a little boy chasing a butterfly up a mountain. Like Hemingway, he caught his butterfly too early.

His third novel, pieced together out of stories, was tonally more various and effective. Even while he was writing *Tortilla Flat* (1935) he speaks of the plea-sure he took. His father was ill while he wrote, his mother had recently died; he escaped from grief and anxiety into writing. It went "like wildfire," he said in 1933. He had found his manner, and he had found a place away from the human trouble of the time. The book did not make him local friends: indeed, the Chamber of Commerce at Monterey, where the novel is set, instructed hotel employees, when asked for directions, to say Tortilla Flat did not exist. Stein-beck's take on the *paisanos* or natives that inhabit his book is only in part political, as too when in *Cannery Row* (1945) and its sequel *Sweet Thursday* (1954) he draws his postwar California as a place more of consequences than causes. Wilson reflects on how the character Doc in the later book enjoys relations with his neighbors not unlike those Steinbeck has with his characters. But he adds, "It is hard to put one's finger on the coarseness that tends to spoil Mr. Steinbeck as an artist." (Isherwood spoke in his *Diaries* of Steinbeck's skill in killing real charac-ters while writing them.) "When one considers the brilliance of his gifts and the philosophical cast of his mind, one keeps feeling that it should not be so. Yet it is so: when the watcher of life should exalt us to the vision of art, he simply sings 'Mother Machree.'" Yet he had, Wilson conceded in 1940, "a mind which does seem first-rate in its unpanicky scrutiny of life."

If we read the novels as political statements, their inadequacy is clear. But it is unlikely, whatever Steinbeck got up to in his travels, however much his first wife pushed him to the left, that he saw his writing as instrumental, except in revealing injustice. The emphasis on politics in 1930s literature is not helpful. What abide are the themes of individual solitude and the ways in which com-radeship can relieve it. *In Dubious Battle* (1936) was another "learning book," about a strike among the fruit pickers in California in which the Party proves that while it helps foment trouble in the interests of the workers, it seeks to ex-acerbate that trouble in the interests of a wider struggle. The book is hard to enjoy. Even as he completed it he conceded, "I guess it is a brutal book, more brutal because there is no author's moral point of view." He has stepped beyond melodrama. There is too the issue of the "racy speech" of his working men. "I know this speech and I'm sick of working men being gelded of their natural expression until they talk with a fine Oxonian flavor." Mary McCarthy, still cutting her critical teeth, called this book "academic, wooden, inert," also "pompous." He is "no philosopher, sociologist, or strike technician."

The success of *Tortilla Flat* gave the Steinbecks the means to build a home at the ranch in Los Gatos. There he completed *Of Mice and Men* and *The Grapes of Wrath,* and there his marriage to Carol, who had been his amanuensis and collaborator, ended in 1941.

Steinbeck was a dog lover, and a canine accident slowed production of *Of Mice and Men.* His setter puppy cut her teeth on it and "made confetti of about half of my ms book." It enjoyed an unambiguous success in ambiguous forms: a stage adaptation and a film sprung easily from it and gave it enormous circulation. In 1936 he told a friend it was "a tricky little thing designed to teach me to write for the theatre." This is "a play that can be read or a novel that can be played" and was unexpectedly chosen for the Book-of-the-Month Club. Subscribers encountered an uncompromising American scene, characters evoked in plain, unironic style, as though Steinbeck was writing legend rather than literature, with a seemingly artless freshness of the kind we experience when a literature first finds a speaking voice. The Great Depression hit rural communities hard. The migrant workers or "bindlestiff" George and his retarded and dependent companion, Lennie, find work in northern California. "Guys like us, that work on ranches, are the loneliest guys in the world," George declares. Lennie is happy as long as he has George. Their job entails bucking barley for a rancher whose son Curley is an undergrown bully. And there is a woman, Curley's sultry, bored wife. The book, topical in its own day, has become so again in the twenty-first century.

The Steinbecks were at first grateful and then appalled by the flow of earnings from the book, stage version, and film. There was no escaping such success. But the Depression supplied Steinbeck with more unignorable material. In 1937 Horace Bristol, a photographer for *Life* magazine, read *In Dubious Battle* and asked Steinbeck to join him on a photographic excursion to California's Great Central Valley. Steinbeck could write the text for a *Life* feature, basing it on interviews. They traveled during the winter of the year, Steinbeck listening and making notes. Then he backed off. He had other uses for the material he was gathering. Carol, who edited and typed the book and whose mark on it is decisive, found its title in September 1938, *The Grapes of Wrath,* powerful, familiar, resonant. The novel is a kind of battle hymn, democratically American, and as his reputation became more that of a radical, Steinbeck felt it necessary to stress that fact. He had a sense of achievement when he finished it, surprised by the scale of the enterprise. But he did not imagine it would sell or win the Pulitzer Prize, and he warned his agent and publisher to have modest expectations. He had second and third thoughts: "Sometimes, I seem to do a good little piece of work, but when it is done it slides into mediocrity." And then, "I am sure of one thing—it isn't the great book I had hoped it would be. It's just a run-of-the-mill book. And the awful thing is that it is absolutely the best I can do." He completed it in manuscript in five months, at the rate of 2,000 words a day.

Among his acknowledged inspirations were the Dust Bowl photographs of Dorothea Lange, Dos Passos's more literary, less accessible narrative experiments in *U.S.A.*, and the techniques and economies of film writing. In February 1939 Steinbeck wrote to a friend, "I want this book to be itself with no history and no writer." This is an aesthetic and ideological ambition. The form creates an easy dialogue between narrative and exposition, the short chapters and the long, telling chapters counterpointed: dramatic and didactic at the same time, the didacticism Socratic in tone, questioning along the bleak lines of the narrative. There is little doubt where the author stands in relation to the Joads, their ordeal and disappointment. He had worked among these people, reported on them, their hunger, the filth in which they were compelled to live. Lange's documentary photographs include an image of a migrant worker nursing her child. We are reminded of the culminating scene in the novel in which a bereaved mother offers her breast to a starving adult. What was melodrama in *To a God Unknown* is plain history here, and history that uses more or less real voices. Frederic Raphael remembers his first encounter with Steinbeck's Okies. "I found their dialogue, phonetically reproduced on the page, quite incomprehensible. But read it aloud and the voices of the Joad family come out fighting."

Steinbeck did not serve in World War II, but as a war correspondent he literally saw a good deal of action. He was wounded in an explosion in North Africa and returned to the United States. He had become more radical with time, moving curiously to the left, and traveling in 1947 for the first time to the Soviet Union, accompanying the photographer Robert Capa. They collaborated on *A Russian Journal* (1948).

Of his later books, *Cannery Row* and (less successfully) *Sweet Thursday* are bittersweet products of nostalgia for an unrecoverable California. *The Pearl* (1947) was written to be filmed and moves in the direction of parable, like Hemingway's *The Old Man and the Sea*. While in Mexico for the filming, Steinbeck was inspired with the story of the Mexican revolutionary Emiliano Zapata and later wrote his chief film script, *Viva Zapata!* (1952); the film was directed by Elia Kazan and starred Anthony Quinn and Marlon Brando. The politics there are not in doubt. *The Short Reign of Pippin IV: A Fabrication* (1957) is a political satire that Hemingway dismissed as *King Poo Poo,* and *The Winter of Our Discontent*

(1961) is a new departure suggesting a desire for change and yet unable to find the formal means. Only two of the later books add significantly to his oeuvre, *East of Eden* (1952) and *Travels with Charley: In Search of America* (1962), travelogue more than novel.

*East of Eden* is a complex, long, reflective novel that complements its ratiocination with some extreme melodrama. The reader is more artfully played than in *To a God Unknown*, with which it shares themes and settings, a return to first things. Kazan made a film of it, too, in which James Dean played his first major roll. We are back in the neighborhood of Salinas, Steinbeck's echo of Yoknapatawpha County. Here are Good and Evil, Guilt and Forgiveness. The Cain and Abel story is relived in Caleb and Aron; no Eve was ever so evil in nature as Cathy Ames, their scheming mother. Two families fatefully intertwine, and the novelist himself as a young boy makes an appearance. It is a book that resists rereading.

Charley the poodle becomes a character with strong creaturely needs in *Travels with Charley,* in the pickup truck converted into an ur-Winnebago called Rocinante, after Don Quixote's horse. Already ill with several of the complaints that were to kill him, Steinbeck sets out in quest of America, his journey an elegy and celebration. On his return to Monterey he writes, "Tom Wolfe was right. You can't go home again because home has ceased to exist except in the mothballs of memory. I printed it once more on my eyes, south, west, and north, and then we hurried away from the permanent and changeless past."

John (Henry) O'Hara (1905–1970), his past changeless in another sense, is unlikely to reemerge from the shadow he cast upon himself. He not only wanted, he expected, to receive the Nobel Prize, and when Steinbeck was honored his congratulations were frank: "I can think of only one other author I'd like to see get it." Nadine Gordimer and Joyce Carol Oates use his name as a byword for coarse small-mindedness. Gore Vidal paints him as "a great sharer of *idées reçues* with the general population, a man passive to convention, working within the realm of the familiar." John Gardner declares, "There is almost nothing in a John O'Hara novel that couldn't be in the movies just as easily," and O'Hara is remembered best for the movies and musical developed out of his books. Hemingway, on the other hand, valued his first and best novel, *Appointment in Samara* (1934), a book that knows its subject and is well written. And John Updike praised him. Clearly he stood between his best novels (three out of seventeen) and his readers. An increasingly verbose and reactionary journalist, he made a vocation of his failure to go to Yale (after his father's death he could not afford to) and despite contributing dozens of stories to the *New Yorker* and winning awards, never had the success that he believed was his due. His best books are about not belonging, not in the querulous way of his later books but in a way that Hemingway responded to. The plots are schematic and written into, but the writing can be interesting in detail and there is comedy and precision in his social observation. *BUtterfield 8* (1935) and *Pal Joey* (1940) characterize their period. Frederic Raphael admires his power of observation, especially of the Pennsylvania Dutch inhabitants of Gibbs Ville, based on his birthplace, Pottsville, Pennsylvania. He mimed local and class speech, so we overhear voices. Julian English lives fully before he dies in a conflagration of erotic innuendo, the story told with economy. Anthony Burgess admired a later novel, *The Lockwood Concern* (1965), about a family whose wealth is the result of an act of violence. O'Hara is again responsive to the appetites for money and sex, which seem to go hand in hand.

———◦———

Nathanael West (Nathan Wallenstein Weinstein, 1903–1940) wrote four books that despite their shortness are described as novels: *The Dream Life of Balso Snell* (1931), *Miss Lonelyhearts* (1933), *A Cool Million: The Dismantling of Lemuel Pitkin* (1934), and *The Day of the Locust* (1939). None was a success or reprinted in his lifetime. At the age of thirty-seven, returning home after a short trip to Mexico, he died in a car crash with his young wife, Eileen, on the same weekend that his friend F. Scott Fitzgerald, at age forty-four, died of a heart attack while reading the Princeton alumni magazine. Possibly West had learned of Fitzgerald's death and, never a safe driver, was more careless than usual in his hurry to get back. He was under contract with Random House for a fifth novel.

West and Fitzgerald's relationship was one of the many unlikely friendships forged in Hollywood in the years leading up to the Second World War. Fitzgerald's fiction elegizes the world that bankrupted him literally and figuratively, so that he ended his days trying to climb out of debt. In *The Last Tycoon* new notes of satire and resistance sound, but the book was in draft when he died. West, on the other hand, was an opportunist whose luck was on the turn, he was beginning to make it as a Hollywood writer. His novels, however, with their acid take on the American dream, were "caviar to the general." A longer perspective was required to see them. Sixteen years after it was first published, *Miss Lonelyhearts* found its way to Raymond Chandler: "A powerful, strange and unusual book—not pretty, but to my mind definitely in the class of real as opposed to merely calculated writing." West's time was still to come. The American novelist and critic Jonathan Lethem describes him as "the great precursor to Heller, Pynchon, Philip K. Dick, Colson Whitehead and so much else," including, we might add, his estimable self. The great difference between West and Pynchon,

West and his other heirs, is that the "experiment" of West's novels is necessary, not calculated.

West was born in New York City. His father was an immigrant Lithuanian Jew who prospered as a building contractor. Nathan was expelled from Tufts, borrowed the successful transcript of another Nathan Weinstein, and was admitted to Brown in Providence, Rhode Island, where he got through, as he got in, by underhand means, borrowing assignments from other students. When his father died, the funeral was held half in English, half in Hebrew. Nathan was shocked to see the corpse's eyebrows barbered, the face rouged. It wore a fat white tie. "From shortsleeves to shirtsleeves in one generation": a quip worthy of his college friend S. J. Perelman, who married his sister and went on to work with the Marx Brothers and Ogden Nash. Perelman's humor, called "surreal" by those unsure what surrealism meant, left a mark on West.

At Brown, West drew cartoons and wrote sketches more surreal than Perelman's lighthearted *mal* and *double entendres*. Some of the writing he did at the end of his time there in 1924 found its way into *The Dream Life of Balso Snell*. After college he spent two years in Paris, where he completed *Balso Snell*. So short a novel (fifty pages) had an excessive gestation. It is overworked, the humor muffled by economy. It is also an echo chamber, taking its epigraph from Proust's invented writer Bergotte, who himself is quoting somebody quoting somebody, producing the sublime platitude "After all, my dear fellow, life, Anaxagoras has said, is a journey." The novel is set inside the Trojan Horse (access through the fundament). The incidents, told with a heartless objectivity, put the reader in mind less of Homer than of a flatulent Rabelais of the twentieth century, starved by the modern world. Robert McAlmon of Contact Editions, who had published Stein and Hemingway, rejected it: it was "too Anatole France for me." The weirdness does recall *Penguin Island*, the coloring owes much to his reading of French literature and his life in Paris. William Carlos Williams found it a publisher.

When West returned to the United States, he was assistant manager of the Kenmore Hall Hotel from 1927 to 1930 and manager of the Sutton Club Hotel from 1930 to 1933. He attracted and supported writers, giving them free rooms and just-edible food. Guests included Dashiell Hammett, J. T. Farrell, and Erskine Caldwell. Hammett completed *The Thin Man* at the Sutton Hotel. "Dash had the Royal Suite," Lillian Hellman remembered, "three very small rooms. And we had to eat there most of the time because we didn't have enough money to eat anyplace else." The novelist Erskine Caldwell said, "The only writers I ever got along really well with were William Saroyan and a chap by the name of Pep West, Nathanael West . . . they did not talk about their work all the time. They talked about cigars, anything." When Caldwell was enjoying West's hospitality, he was working on his novels *Tobacco Road* (1932) and *God's Little Acre* (1933), books that can be read alongside Steinbeck's accounts of harsh rural realities, this time in the South.

West is a modernist in his sense of fragmentation, of inconclusive narratives. The gulf between Roaring Twenties and Great Depression was deeper than the Marianas Trench. Sudden, grinding misery required a response. Content will out, art becomes exploratory less of its medium than of the human condition. In March 1929, before the Wall Street crash, West was shown some letters sent by the public to "Susan Chester," advice columnist for the *Brooklyn Eagle*. He started *Miss Lonelyhearts* in the turmoil of 1930. In 1932 he published excerpts in two magazines: he needed money. It was finished in 1932 and published. The publisher promptly went into liquidation. The book had begun well but did not recover momentum. West's fiction was thwarted once more.

The nameless male protagonist of *Miss Lonelyhearts,* who gets the post of advice columnist or "agony aunt," is about West's age and carries several of his burdens. "At college, and perhaps for a year afterwards, they"—all the members of his group at Delehanty's speakeasy, educated and disillusioned—"had believed in literature, had believed in Beauty and in personal expression as an absolute end," but there was a change. "When they lost this belief, they lost everything." They began to see and hear differently. When he adds, "Money and fame meant nothing to them," character and author divide. Loss of belief coincided with loss of money. West says, "They were not worldly men," but they were vulnerable to worldly temptations and to a worldly devil in the form of the managing editor Shrike, the taunter who stimulates Miss Lonelyhearts's desolation.

Later, watching Betty at the clothesline wearing only a checked handkerchief tying up her hair, he notes, "Her raised arms pulled her breasts up until they were like pink-tipped thumbs." Nature seems to conspire with Miss Lonelyhearts's lust. "Somewhere in the woods a thrush was singing. Its sound was like that of a flute choked with saliva." When Betty and Miss Lonelyhearts go down, "he smelled a mixture of sweat, soap and crushed grass."

The journalist takes up the mantle of Miss Lonelyhearts in a cynical spirit. He ends in breakdown. Of the many routes of escape, none leads away from the predicament of modern being. The agony aunt, answering readers' vulnerable pleas for help, goes beyond laughter to an unblurred insight into the misery of common lives; he experiences universal heartbreak and becomes a Christ echo—Christ, "the Miss Lonelyhearts of Miss Lonelyhearts"—learning the hollowness of consolation, weeping on his way to Calvary. West is implicated: he continues to write despite what he knows. His protagonist is not surprised when death in its deformity finds him out. The novel, cleanly conceived, is precisely executed. West considered at the outset writing "a novel in the form of a comic strip": it might have been an early and a classic graphic novel.

West was writing quickly now, and his third novel developed a single theme of good intentions and happy circumstances gone wrong. The wheel of fortune turns. *A Cool Million* provides a hero in every sense prosperous who is brought low in a life full of pointless tribulations and defeats. None of the nostrums of conventional fiction holds: Lemuel (a relation of Job and of Gulliver) loses it all, including parts of his body—his teeth, an eye, a thumb, his scalp, and a leg. Eventually he is shot and must forfeit the only thing remaining to him. West is satirizing Horatio Alger's rags-to-riches optimism. In a letter to a friend West described his subject as "a guy who was trying to get one foot on the ladder of success and they were always moving the ladder on him"—but the protagonist remains impregnable: "They couldn't touch the dream." The book comes to West's harshest triumphal conclusion: "Hail, Lemuel Pitkin!" "All hail, the American boy!"

West moved to Hollywood in 1933, to work on a film version of *Miss Lonelyhearts*. He returned for good in 1935, living in a cheap hotel, occupying accommodation on the outskirts of Los Angeles. He started putting down roots. At last he and his wife got a house, a circle of friends, and then died.

West's Hollywood achievement was his final novel, *The Day of the Locust,* another study of the power and treachery of illusion and the fatuity of hope. Tod Hackett, the protagonist, arrives in California to become a scenic artist but in no time finds himself among graying second-raters in the remoter suburbs of the film industry, eking out existences and grimly living for a break. He is drawn to seventeen-year-old Faye Greener, who in turn is living off a doting businessman. "'My name is Homer Simpson,' the man gasped, then shifted uneasily and patted his perfectly dry forehead with a folded handkerchief." Homer is a solid seventy-year-old, in control of neither his lusts nor his body. His hands possess an alarming freedom, he has to trap them between his knees to hold them still.

Satire is present throughout; also desperation. The book was intended to be a kind of *Tortilla Flat,* but West lacks Steinbeck's patience with character. He cannot sidestep his tyrannical themes. He completed the book shortly before his break into well-paid script writing: he had been living hand-to-mouth for a long time. As a Jew with his eyes trained on Europe, he had other anxieties as well. In the real world the American Roman Catholic radio priest Father Coughlin warned Americans against Jews, Jewish influence, and Jewish scheming, promising violence and appearing in public with a flag-waving, armbanded honor guard. In the novel the symbolism is no more obscure, from the cockfighting to the film *The Burning of Los Angeles* on which Tod finds work as a scene painter.

The premiere-night riot with which the novel concludes provides a glaring, generalized apocalypse. It is a comic novel in which laughter is self-reflexive and finally appalled. Tod becomes the screaming siren of the police car that bears him away.

Then there is the news that is still waiting to happen. William (Thomas) Gaddis (Jr.) (1922–1998) is a novelist more honored in the breach than in the observance. At almost 1,000 pages *The Recognitions* (1955), his first novel, written in the late 1940s, has as many readers as Samuel Richardson's *Sir Charles Grandison*. The New Zealand novelist Kirsty Gunn urged on me a copy of the 2003 reprint. It is a great book to have read, not moralistic like Richardson, but disabused, comical in ways less systematic (though more logical) than John Barth, engagingly louche—indeed, critics in 1955 and since have raised the issue of obscenity.

It belongs in an American tradition of apocalyptic writing that includes Hawthorne's *The House of the Seven Gables,* Melville's *The Confidence-Man,* Nathanael West's *Day of the Locust,* and Thomas Pynchon's *Gravity's Rainbow* (on which Gaddis left a mark). Its *dramatis personae* are counterfeiters, fakes, fluid characters, shape shifters. His vision of language, society, the economy, the world itself is terminally entropic. But Wyatt, his forger-protagonist, has a soft, conventional human center, seeking in the art he fakes and the masterpieces he sees the face of his dead mother. In the later novels there is less sentiment. They are the drier for it.

Opening with an untranslated epigraph from Goethe's *Faust* II, *The Recognitions* runs through three sections like a Victorian triple-decker, assuming that we have the informed patience of a Victorian. The challenge is to read it whole. In the hands of Firbank, who might have devised as complex a plot, there would be a leavening camp style and a frisky economy, but Gaddis's style is not light. It can be lumpy in the extended "information" passages; it can be seriously unsubtle. The homosexual art dealer, Recktall Brown, with his black poodle, is one of several false notes Gaddis plays. The book has been dubbed "postmodern," probably because of its allusiveness and fluidity, but it has a conventional solidity of narrative at odds with the term, unless we see it as *thematically* postmodern while stylistically straddling, one foot at least in another camp.

Twenty-five years passed before Gaddis published a second novel, *JR* (1975), and a decade more before *Carpenter's Gothic* (1985), then *A Frolic of His Own* (1994). In the year of his death he completed *Agapē Agape,* a novella in the voice of a caustic expiring man not unlike himself, which appeared four years after his death alongside a volume of his nonfiction writing, *The Rush for Second Place.*

Don DeLillo and especially Thomas Pynchon owe him much; William Gass, David Foster Wallace, and Jonathan Franzen also. *The Recognitions* remains his *pièce de résistance.* Cynthia Ozick remarked on Gaddis's prodigality, "gargan-tuan, exhaustive, subsuming fates and conditions under a hungry logic." He *knows* everything, each statement he makes is rooted in knowledge. Elegiacally he builds into the tradition of Joyce, Woolf, Proust, but also of Mann, also of Henry James. In this hubris consists his originality, a negative originality he shares with Cormac McCarthy, though he has not, sentence by sentence, the irresistible authority of McCarthy's always-realized styles. The last words of *The Recognitions* stand as Gaddis's ironic epitaph: "He was the only person caught in the collapse, and afterward, most of his work was recovered too, and is still spoken of, when it is noted, with high regard, though seldom played."

For the 150th issue of Charles Eliot Norton's *Atlantic Magazine* in November 2007, the editors invited contemporary intellectuals from various quarters to write briefly about "The American Idea." Ten months before he hanged him-self, David Foster Wallace (1962–2008) wrote a characteristic piece that, by rais-ing a series of Socratic questions, detaches readers from the reflexes instilled by the media, realigning their sense of the issues involved. For him the American Idea has to do with forms of liberty. The short piece has footnotes in dialogue with the main thrust of the essay or novel. "Are some things still worth dying for?" he asks, things like "the American idea," which in a footnote he shorthands: "Given the strict . . . space limit here, let's just please all agree that we generally know what this term connotes—an open society, consent of the governed, enu-merated powers, Federalist 10, pluralism, due process, transparency . . . the whole democratic roil." Back to the main questions, the "thought experiment" he wants to put us through: "What if we chose to regard the 2,973 innocents killed in the atrocities of 9/11 not as victims but as democratic martyrs, 'sacrifices on the al-tar of freedom'?" (This phrase, a footnote informs us, is Lincoln's.) "What if we decided that a certain baseline vulnerability to terrorism is part of the price of the American idea? And, thus, that ours is a generation of Americans called to make great sacrifices in order to preserve our democratic way of life—sacrifices not just of our soldiers and money but of our personal safety and comfort?" He continues with his needling questions for another three paragraphs. His think-ing outside the box is an example of what the American Idea is about. "What exactly has changed between Franklin's time and ours? Why now can we not have a serious national conversation about sacrifice, the inevitability of sacrifice—either of (a) some portion of safety or (b) some portion of the rights and protec-tions that make the American idea so incalculably precious?" All questions, no answer is offered: "In the absence of such a conversation, can we trust our elected leaders to value and protect the American idea as they act to secure the homeland? What are the effects on the American idea of Guantánamo, Abu Ghraib, PATRIOT Acts I and II, warrantless surveillance, Executive Order 13233, corporate contractors performing military functions, the Military Commissions Act, NSPD 51, etc., etc.?" The final two questions nudge us with the real: "Have we actually become so selfish and scared that we don't even want to *consider* whether some things trump safety? What kind of future does that augur?"

To speak of Wallace as a novelist is to put his secondary achievement first. He was an essayist whose three novels, *The Broom of the System* (1987, after Pynchon's *The Crying of Lot 49*), *Infinite Jest* (1996), and (posthumous) *The Pale King: An Unfinished Novel* (2011), are uneven, only the second having a secure claim on the general reader. This is not to understate his importance as a writer, only that his value to other novelists is in the essays he wrote and the original ways in which he wrote them. He makes watching paint dry an exquisite protraction. For his last novel he chose what anyone apart from Edmund Wilson or Franz Kafka would describe as the most boring subject available: the Internal Revenue Service, its nuanced and almost impenetrable regulations, its functioning. Wallace's own IRS agents in Peoria, Illinois, are bored. Some readers report themselves bored by the book, though they feel impious to say so. It is as though Kafka had decided to ground *The Trial* and *The Castle* in actual procedures, so that metaphor and fact were in a positive tension, rather than the value being metaphorical. The Pynchon of *Gravity's Rainbow* is near at hand. When the IRS sends out agents with psychic powers, we remember the White Visitation research facility. *The Pale King* has not proved a success, though it was universally reviewed on publication.

Wallace's essays entail the lecture, the sermon, the review, the manifesto, and other genres. He reinvents the form from within, using its own devices, the footnote and the syllogism in particular, and combining genres, bringing confession and review into play with "impartial" journalism whose evident objectivity yields potent satire. He opened his commencement address at Kenyon College in 2005 with a little parable: "There are these two young fish swimming along, and they happen to meet an older fish swimming the other way, who nods at them and says, 'Morning, boys, how's the water?' And the two young fish swim on for a bit, and then eventually one of them looks over at the other and goes, 'What the hell is water?'" His essays recall us to the elements of our social, intellectual, and (he was a churchgoer, wherever he happened to live) spiritual environments. Adam Kirsch characterized Wallace's "self-conscious earnestness," his hostility to reductive ironies ("Irony is the song of a bird who has grown to love its cage") that impoverished an earlier generation. Kirsch's "earnest" is not humorless.

Wallace "came of age" in the wake of the Vietnam War, a period in which discontinuity seemed a rule of life and the writers that most mattered were DeLillo, Pynchon, Robert Coover. He was a postmodernist with premodern values, with Revolutionary values of the 1776 variety, and he was as straight talking as Hunter S. Thompson, but making more sense, trying to engage the concerns of the fiction of earlier times. *Infinite Jest* is over 1,070 pages vast, as the title adjective suggests, commensurate with Gaddis's *The Recognitions*. Jests abound, not least the novel itself, its footnotes, contradictions, idealism, disenchantment. Woven out of three ill-assorted plot lines—Canadian terrorists keen to secure a lethally pleasurable film, a recovering Demerol addict, and (himself?) a tennis prodigy with hang-ups—it is engaging. In eschewing conventional closure, it does not bring a conclusion to the satisfactions it offers.

Closure for Wallace's ashes, or some of them, came by the agency of his friend Jonathan Franzen, entrusted by Wallace's widow to distribute them on an island in the South Pacific where he went to birdwatch, "to recoup his sense of identity after a grueling, boring book tour—and to allow himself to feel, by imposed isolation, the fullness of grief that he had been keeping at bay." The "grueling, boring book tour" would have been, to Wallace, a joke and a subject for research, or both. Franzen's essay measures the distance between his late friend's essayistic skills and his own. Wallace's pathological depressions balance his own manageable grumps and discontents. In the case of Wallace, economic and political upheaval did register. He engaged with the modern with a memory of the American dream and all its promises, which were inexorably reworded, reshaped, until it was impossible to bring them back into true.

# 36

# Enchantment and Disenchantment

Vladimir Nabokov, Ayn Rand, Radclyffe Hall, Ivy Compton-Burnett, Elizabeth Taylor,

Muriel Spark, Gabriel Josipovici, Christine Brooke-Rose, B. S. Johnson, William Gass,

John Barth, Harry Mathews, Walter Abish, Thomas Pynchon, Jonathan Franzen

In 1987 a chess magazine in Moscow published a 2,000-word extract from the memoirs of Vladimir Vladimirovich Nabokov (1899–1977). He had not been acknowledged as a writer in his native Russia before; any presence he had was furtive, his books produced by samizdat or smuggled in from France and Germany. He had been dead for a decade. It is not that he was a purveyor of subversive ideas: his subversions had to do with fiction and its "uses." At last in an out-of-the-way publication he was acknowledged as a grand master of language and metaphor.

When his family arrived in England in 1919, he was writing poems, many of which feature a chess problem of one kind or another. He was the first major writer since Lewis Carroll to invest so much in the game. In 1919–1922 he was an undergraduate at Trinity College, Cambridge, where he started reading zoology, with a private focus on butterflies, and published the first of his learned papers, on the Lepidoptera of the Crimea. He transferred to philology, in particular French and Russian, and got on with his own writing, keeping up his interest in Russian by reading daily in Vladimir Dahl's great *Interpretative Dictionary*.

Nabokov was born into an aristocracy secure enough to see itself as St. Petersburg's "classless intelligentsia." His father was titled, a leader of a liberal faction, and a fluent writer. His mother, an heiress, was cultured and attentive. Their home was a meeting place for cultural and political leaders of the age. The Nabokovs owned large estates and holidayed abroad. They educated their children at home. Vladimir as a child mastered Russian, English, and French. At eleven he went to school with, he tells us, all of Shakespeare under his belt, along with Tolstoy and Flaubert. He was translating freely between his three languages. He was also writing, poetry in the first place. In 1916 he came into his independent fortune and paid to have his verses printed. The Russian Revolution and the Bolshevik coup arrived, and Nabokov père, fearing that his older sons Vladimir, 18, and Sergei, 17, might be drafted into the Red Army, sent them from St. Petersburg to the Crimea. Vladimir had no interest in politics, instead continuing his butterfly expeditions, love affairs, and poetry. By 1918 he had written 334 poems and planned a large volume. In 1918 a small selection was printed; the larger book had to wait until 1923 when the family was in exile.

When the Nabokovs reached England, the boys went to Cambridge and a new life was taking shape. Leaving Vladimir at Cambridge, except during the holidays, the family continued exile in 1920 in the émigré Russian community in Berlin. Life was cheaper there than in London, and the Russian community more concentrated and political. In 1922 Nabokov's father, still politically optimistic and active, was assassinated. Vladimir's imagination lost its lyrical lightness, and though he still shied away from a literature of events and ideas, the world lay heavier upon him, the past was ever less recoverable. In 1925, by now acknowledged to be a promising poet, he married Véra Slonim and began a generally happy life sentence. They spent twelve years in Berlin with him writing, coaching tennis, Russian, boxing and French, and setting chess problems to earn a living for himself, his wife, and his baby son, Dmitri, who would grow into one of his parents' key translation collaborators. Nabokov was a family concern.

At this time he had started writing fiction. The first of his Russian novels to achieve critical success in the expatriate community was *Zashchita Luzhina* (*Luzhin's Defense*, 1930, published in two parts as *The Defense* in the *New Yorker* in 1965). It told, Nabokov said, of "a chess player who was crushed by his genius." Defeated by life but not by chess, the protagonist throws himself out of a building, and as he falls sees the chessboard pattern of the windows of the buildings, and understands the vast and ordered game eternity has laid out for him. Ivan Bunin, the émigré poet and fiction writer, the first Russian Nobel literature laureate, said, "This youngster has taken a gun and mowed down the entire older generation, including me." Nabokov admired Bunin the poet and noted the encomium. He was not friendly to Bunin's fiction.

Of the novels he wrote in Russian, five—in much-changed and never quite satisfactory English translations—are among his best. *King, Queen, Knave* (1928, translation 1968), *Laughter in the Dark* (1933, translation 1936, retranslation 1938), *Despair* (1934, translation 1937, retranslation 1965, where we meet Humbert Humbert's ancestor Hermann Hermann), *Invitation to a Beheading* (1936, translation 1959), and his most complex, celebrated, and obliquely political Russian novel, *The Gift* (1938, translation 1961), recounting satirically in its originally suppressed fourth chapter the life of Nikolai Chernyshevski, father of Russian social realism and Lenin's "favorite author," are central to his oeuvre. The books that hovered between Russian and English gave him the greatest challenge. The languages were like opponents in a game of chess, each with its own plans for the progress of the narrative.

The "truth" told in his memoir *Speak, Memory* (1951), which takes Nabokov from 1903 and his coming to consciousness to 1940 and his emigration to the United States, is a clear indicator of his method of ever-closer approximation to his intent. At the start of 1948 he published fourteen "recollections" in American magazines, the *New Yorker* in particular. These he revised and brought together as *Conclusive Evidence* (1951). Two years later, in the gaps between chasing butterflies and composing *Lolita* (1955) and *Pnin*, two projects undertaken at the same time, he started translating *Conclusive Evidence* into Russian. *Druggy berega (Other Shores)* appeared in 1954 and was welcomed by expatriate readers. He wrote to his *New Yorker* editor that he had promised himself "never go back from my wizened Hyde form to my ample Jekyll one—but there I was, after fifteen years of absence, wallowing again in the bitter luxury of my Russian verbal might." Working in Russian brought the experiences alive from within, they reacquired their own light. So he revisited the English and in 1967 published *Speak, Memory: An Autobiography Revisited,* quite a separate book, richer and differently inflected. His work inhabits the borderland between history and fiction, between Russian and English. And it is ample: Jekyll not Hyde. In Europe before the war James Joyce heard him give a talk, and afterward they chatted. Rachmaninoff lent him money to escape from Germany to America in 1940. Vera's Jewishness was their good fortune: they got onto one of the last Jewish-organized relief ships.

Like Beckett, Nabokov made the transition between languages alive to the different semantic and expressive properties of each. Shortly before sailing to America he completed a novel in English about biography and art entitled *The Real Life of Sebastian Knight* (1941): "Remember that what you are told is really threefold: shaped by the teller, reshaped by the listener, concealed from both by the dead man of the tale." The "atrocious metamorphosis" had occurred, not from pupa to butterfly but from one bright-winged creature to another. In *Speak, Memory* he explained why it was possible for him to become an American and jettison, or ironize, so much of the residue of the European imagination. "I confess I do not believe in time. I like to fold my magic carpet, after use, in such a way as to superimpose one part of the pattern on another . . . And the highest enjoyment of timelessness—in a landscape selected at random—is when I stand among rare butterflies and their food plants." That timeless beauty masks and reveals: "This is ecstasy, and behind the ecstasy is something else, which is hard to explain. It is like a momentary vacuum into which rushes all that I love. A sense of oneness with sun and stone. A thrill of gratitude to whom it may concern—to the contrapuntal genius of human fate or to tender ghost humoring a lucky mortal." Despite the afflatus, he has defined the ways in which space can work in American literature.

Dwindling resources forced Nabokov to leave Europe, but writing in English was for him less a task of reinvention than it was for, say, Conrad. He had learned English early and had studied in a British university. Even so, the creative transition was uneasy. He began writing *The Real Life of Sebastian Knight* on an ad hoc working surface made out of a suitcase propped on a bidet in the studio flat he occupied with his wife and little son in Berlin. It had much in common with *The Gift,* in which he creates the narrator Fyodor, the biography he is writing, his poems, his voice. The invention is a closed system.

Then Nabokov at last landed a summer job, at Stanford. He began preparing lectures on Russian literature. He wrote a story in English, too, which was not published in his lifetime, "The Enchanter," the ur-*Lolita.* The map was drawn for a long creative journey. With these writings and a ballast of sadness the Nabokovs left Europe for California.

The first sentence of his first English novel echoes the intrigue-rich tradition of Gogol, but there is the matter of the date: "Sebastian Knight was born on the thirty-first of December, 1899, in the former capital of my country." Sebastian's half-brother, V., narrates the story of the quest as a biographer to make sense of him. Knight was born the same year as Nabokov and died in 1936. He studied at Cambridge, and V. talks to his friends and contemporaries, describes his books, and tries to redeem him from the attacks of an earlier biographer, the writer's quondam secretary, who depicts him as an ivory tower figure undone by romance. The novel has, as all Nabokov's writing does, a libidinal current (what Updike calls an "amorous style") at once playful and sinister. Sebastian's last novel, *The Doubtful Asphodel,* a book about the unraveling and decline of its protagonist, is evoked. The reader wonders whether V. and Sebastian are not perhaps, *au coeur,* one and the same. The confusions are Shakespearean, and *Twelfth Night* is part of the mulch from which the novel grows. Or is V. perhaps a version of Sergei, the homosexual younger brother Nabokov misvalued, slighted, and in a sense betrayed, here brought back to life as a fascinated witness to his always evasive and treacherous sibling, the novelist's self? The book seems keen to make a kind of ironic amends. Chess is a further pretext, supplying imagery and structure. In ways that *Pale Fire* will take further, this is a mystery story that generates accelerating mysteries as it goes, a narrative that dilates rather than concentrating meaning. As with Knight's concluding work, "the book itself is heaving and dying, and drawing up a ghostly knee." A foreign narrator, from a country in which major upheavals have occurred; much hearsay, much whispering of news and false news as among the exiles, but nothing dependable, nothing as it seems. Immediately the information we need if we are to begin to construe the story is cast in doubt, we are less readers than sleuths setting out to the Zemblan Peninsula of *Pale Fire* and the miasmic college world of *Pnin.*

Something other than the twentieth century is about to start. Spread before us are false accounts, lying books, variant readings, a chessboard, a butterflied upland.

Some critics call this a world of "metafiction," as though something unprecedented and uniquely modern had occurred when the conventions of prose narrative were unsettled in these ways. Yet in how many great novels are the conventions of narrative stable? Writers aspire to be more than storytellers: they play with and against the rules. The "reality" of fiction is unlike the reality of linear narrative and unlike the complex intersecting realities of daily life. Given *Mandeville's Travels, Don Quixote, Gargantua and Pantagruel, Through the Looking-Glass,* "metafiction" begins to look quite long in the tooth. Nabokov's *Ania v strane chudes* (1922) is a translation of *Alice in Wonderland.* That, and Wilde, Pater and Peacock, Wilkie Collins, William Beckford and Horace Walpole, Sterne and Fielding, Bunyan and even Nashe, are his natural English family. His writing resists theoretical reduction even as it defies conventional reading. Art entails artifice, and in form a novel must be true to itself, an instance of itself, its first artistic purpose. Its consistency, its coherence within the conventions it proposes and within which it operates, are paramount. Even parody has to be integrated into the larger purpose. Isaac Babel wrote another kind of fiction altogether: "I have no imagination. I can't invent. I have to know everything down to the last vein, otherwise I can't write a thing. My motto is *authenticity.*" Nabokov's motto might be *consistency,* truth to form.

At Wellesley College (1941–1948) he taught Russian literature, and his translations and advocacies led to publishing projects that altered American perceptions of Russian writing. Among the books he admired and taught year after year at Cornell (1948–1959), starting in 1950, his notes gathered into *Lectures on Literature* (1980) and *Lectures on Russian Literature* (1981), he explores the completeness, coherence, and adequacy of the fictional worlds constructed in terms of their spatial and temporal projections. At Edmund Wilson's behest, among the English books he included in his world literature course was Jane Austen's *Mansfield Park,* the only novel by a woman to find a place in his laconic cannon: Dickens's *Bleak House,* Flaubert's *Madame Bovary,* Stevenson's *The Strange Case of Dr. Jekyll and Mr. Hyde* (which, along with the poems and stories of Poe, exercised a powerful charm on him), Proust's *The Walk by Swann's Place (Swann's Way),* Kafka's *The Metamorphosis,* and Joyce's *Ulysses.* Not being a member of the English Department, he was not permitted to teach American literature. Had he done so he would have had a great deal to say about, among others, Hawthorne and Poe. Still, his "supreme masterpiece" course was popular. Three of the seven books he taught at Cornell were published in his own lifetime: such dust as there was on his reading list was of recent origin. He was furious at the quality of the translations he had to teach from, issuing his classes lists of infelicities and keeping them aware at every moment of the difference between translation and the original. The *integrity* of the book, surviving the places, languages, and landscapes that gave rise to it, affected his sense of the adequacy of fictional creation.

In 1950 he delivered his first Masters lecture. The series caught on despite, or due to, the severity of his delivery and the intellectual demands he made. At times his wife, Véra, was part of the teaching process, distributing handouts, writing on the board, taking office hours, marking papers, and even, on occasion, delivering a lecture from scripts he prepared. She was a decisive woman and after Nabokov's death made editorial and business decisions with the assurance of the master himself. He loved diagrams that proved characters were moving within a coherently imagined space in credible ways. Gregor Samsa's transformation, Stephen Dedalus's Dublin, the disposition of the fatal train in *Anna Karenina* demonstrated the "reality" of the imaginative achievement. The literal has to be right, before the metaphorical, symbolic, or numinous can begin coherently to emerge.

He was reluctant to give up teaching, but in the wake of the success of *Lolita* he accepted that life had dealt him a *forward* hand. At last in the autumn of 1961 he and Véra moved into the Montreux Palace Hotel, where they spent the rest of his life. He was released to pursue his entomological studies, to organize the translation and retranslation of his Russian books, and to write. "My pleasures are the most intense known to man: writing and butterfly hunting," he said. His signature was always butterfly-winged.

New Directions published *Sebastian Knight* and four further books by Nabokov, though in the end he needed more money than they could offer. Henry Holt published the dystopian *Bend Sinister* (1947), the first of his books to be written wholly in the New World. In it politics are foregrounded, too, as hostile to fascism as to communism. The title, taken from heraldry (the line descending from upper right to lower left in a coat of arms) initiates the not-too-subtle wordplay on left and sinister directions. Nabokov's protagonist is Adam Krug, a kind of philosophical Job assaulted not by God but by the tyrant Paduk who is imposing a transparently equalizing, if not egalitarian, ideology called Ekwilism and is trying to get Krug to endorse it. Again a game of chess underlies the action, and again the protagonist and his torturer are opposed and complementary. Nabokov spent four years on the manuscript, and the publishers Doubleday took four months to reject it (*Bend Sinister* was then provisionally titled *Solus Rex*) on the grounds that readers wanted escapist books, not political ones, and it was not the right moment for it.

Eight years passed before his next English novel, *Lolita*, the book that changed his fortune, appeared. The earlier English novels were English in language but were too playful, too philosophical not only in theme but in structure, to satisfy American readers. A road novel, however, would prove more agreeable. A road novel with a controversial theme might entail a useful notoriety. Publishers shied away from it and as a university teacher he was himself wary of putting his name to it. In 1955 the Olympia Press with its list of erotica published it. Nabokov implausibly claimed he was unaware of the reputation of Olympia when he entrusted the book to the publisher, Maurice Girodias. The book was banned in France and listed by Graham Greene as one of the best novels of 1955 in a Christmas roundup. Curiosity became demand. Greene was Nabokov's champion in Britain. The book was commercially published in the United States, and by 1959 Nabokov was at last bought, read, and talked about. Christopher Isherwood regarded *Lolita* as "the best travel book ever written about America." It visits a lot of motels in the internally combusted American variation on the picaresque. It precedes Jack Kerouac's *On the Road* by two years, and Steinbeck's *Travels with Charley: In Search of America* by seven.

*Lolita* must cause any reader moral qualms. The fact that it is engagingly *comic* compounds the thematic offense. How can we enjoy a novel that, exquisitely written, entails murder, pedophilia (or as Martin Amis rightly prefers, nympholepsy), and child rape, and refuses, given the nature of the narrator and editor, familiar figures in Nabokov who always himself stands away from moralizing, to draw *moral* conclusions? The editor tells us that Dolores Haze is dead before we even start reading the confession. Many will consider Nabokov's extenuation—which has to do with the separateness and adequacy of fiction, in which we are free, freed, to disregard moral and other expectations and inhibitions and inhabit the text as *apart*—as unequal to the affront his book provides. The reader is expected to efface not only the habitual self but the whole baggage of predisposition and prescription we carry and that carries us. Suspending disbelief has never been a taller order. This is the liberty Nabokov responds to in Poe's analogous and darkly articulated passions, the liberty he claims for his novels. Edmund Wilson wrote to Nabokov, "Nasty subjects may make fine books; but I don't feel you have got away with this." Here their friendship began to founder.

Throughout his books there is an element of what seems like sadism, a cruelty more extreme than that which Nabokov resists in Cervantes, whose unremitting caricature cruelty to the moonstruck Don appalls him. It seems like sadism because Nabokov does not judge his narrators or editors, the cruelties that happen are presented with an evenhandedness that can seem like approbation. Kafka tells equally cruel things but without a tone of voice or a self-defining narrator; in Nabokov the tone of voice is insistent, a medium and a provocation. In this he is more like Proust, his focus always through a definable lens, and the narrator glancing back over his shoulder to make sure the reader is still there, to gauge effect, to solicit complicity. Humbert Humbert weaves us into the texture of his intrigue. When the narrative spins out of his control, we are disoriented. Nabokov does not allow for squeamishness, which in the 1950s was more acute than it is today. Such provisional heavens as he paints are imperiled by time, his protagonists are damned. He detested Freud, and yet his characters have, for the most part, a Freudian complexion. Humbert is clear about the crime he has committed, but as narrator he comes at us refusing to translate the overwhelming experience into the generality of a prohibited series of actions. It exists in a pre-moral space, like, one is tempted to say, all great art. And it is a space, a mappable space as big as the continental United States. We could plot the route between motels if we wished, as thematically coherent a looping back and forth as Nabokov reveals in his lecture on *Ulysses*.

There is no excess, but rather a revelatory economy sentence by sentence that relates to changing tones as to a character's particular diction. Thus Humbert records the death of his mother in a parenthesis "(picnic, lightning)" and Nabokov leaves it at that. But elsewhere, as Humbert's anguish grows and he knows the limited period of Dolores's flowering is advancing, that she will pass her ripeness and her attraction will go, he tells us how "she would pick out in the book, while I petted her in the parked car in the silence of a dusk-mellowed, mysterious side-road, some highly recommended lake lodge which offered all sorts of things magnified by the flashlight she moved over them, such as congenial company, between-meals snacks, outdoor barbeques—but which in my mind conjured up odious visions of stinking high school boys in sweatshirts and an ember-red cheek pressing up against hers, while poor Dr. Humbert, embracing two masculine knees, would cold-humor his piles on the damp turf." It is hard not to applaud the manipulation of language and reader, the theatrical presentation. Molester and victim in their car, a lovely evening, she looking through the directory with the lambent flashlight, trying to find a place to stay, where he will again abuse her, he fondling her and reflecting on her thoughts, her direction, and his own. The hemorrhoids are an intimate and grotesque touch as the libidinal spell is dissipated by the inexorably advancing single sentence.

We can measure Lolita's loss of innocence by the ways she learns to manipulate language. Her slang, her careless use of words, her dreadfully mispronounced French, at first charm and then increasingly irritate him. Humbert knows how different uses of language are appropriate at different times, but he cannot always tell when Lolita is fighting back using the weapon of his choice. When he is in control he gets the balance right. Charlotte Haze would like to talk like Humbert but cannot. And his archrival Clare Quilty can do it, only better, as if by second nature. He is a writer of plays and controls the action without needing to be a performer himself. No wonder Lolita is at ease with him. We have no idea what demands he makes on her, if any. We do know that in the end he is murdered by Humbert Humbert, though he takes as long to die as Orwell's elephant. Martin Amis did not share his father Kingsley's dislike of Nabokov. Nabokov and Saul Bellow ("Nabokov the classic émigré, Bellow the classic immigrant") are the stars he has learned to steer by. Having enumerated the deaths that are casually recorded in the book, including those of the two protagonists, Amis writes, "In a sense *Lolita* is too great for its own good. It rushes up on the reader like a recreational drug more powerful than any yet discovered or devised. In common with its narrator, it is both irresistible and unforgivable. And yet it all works out."

Four of the seven chapters of *Pnin* (1957) were originally presented as substantial, freestanding short stories in the *New Yorker*. When Nabokov joined them up for book publication, some elements were changed. A few of the oddities in terms of continuity may be due to the somewhat incomplete translation between media. The world that Timofey Pnin occupies is very like the one that Vladimir Nabokov as a Russian lecturer in the United States inhabited. In this novel the American university itself forces the protagonist into caricature: the failure of understanding cuts both ways and distorts his relationships. Comedy intensifies to almost unbearable pathos. So soon after *Lolita, Pnin* is a thematic and tonal relief. Here is the playful, experimental Nabokov back again, humoring the reader at his own expense. *Pnin* was reprinted two weeks after publication and it remains popular. The author seems to take sides with the American reader against his irreducible protagonist. It has weaknesses that Kingsley Amis was not slow to exaggerate, calling it "this limp, tasteless salad of Joyce, Chaplin, Mary MacCarthy [sic]." Amis resented the way Wilson, Randall Jarrell, and Graham Greene cheered him on. What Amis might have responded to are the liberties Nabokov takes with voice and style, the extent of allowable variation. We see Pnin, whose suntan exaggerates his bald dome, whose tortoise-shell glasses conceal his bald eyebrows, whose body mixes mighty (top half) and meager, even feminine (bottom half). He wears flannels and a "tightish tweed coat" along with a "flamboyant goon tie," wide and vulgar, and vivid harlequin socks. "Now he is in America, has he become a clown?" Yet the place is full of contradictions, "the asphalt is infinitely exalted by the wisteria, and the air smells of rubber and paradise."

Many Nabokovians regard *Pale Fire* (1962), which John Cheever describes as a "violet-flavored nightmare," as his masterpiece. Though Cheever was troubled by the unresolved homosexual themes, he thought constructing a novel from footnotes was "a brilliant eccentricity." As with all his later works, Nabokov prepared the book on index cards. Having "a curiously clear preview of the entire novel before me or above me" before he begins, he can compose as he feels inclined, filling in gaps or throwing out a guideline. This book had gestated for thirty years before he began writing. The poem, its pretext, he tried on magazines, which rejected it. Its 999 lines are divided into four cantos.

The poem and novel appeared in the spring and were soon on the *New York Times* best-sellers list. Mary McCarthy threw caution to the winds and proclaimed *Pale Fire* a masterpiece of the century, her review entitled "A Bolt from the Blue." The novel is precariously suspended from a longish poem by John Shade, a make-believe American poet ("by far the greatest of *invented* poets"); the line-by-line commentary prepared by his neighbor Charles Kimbote swathes the opening text in narrative and contention. The poem is full of numerological clues: taken with the extended gloss, this is post-Holocaust Lewis Carroll. Through the ridiculous and charming intrigues, real history and spy-book tropes, puns, and allusions to other books and poems, pulses something urgent and necessary. It is impossible not to be moved in various ways, to laughter, to arousal, to anxiety and concern. Shade's poem appears to be about the suicide of his daughter. Shade is killed before Kinbote undertakes the annotation. Kinbote is mad (or is he?), imagining himself to be the exiled king of an eastern country called Zembla (Russia before the revolution?). He believes Shade was assassinated by mistake, that he himself was the intended target. Here we have a reliable narrative, Shade's, interpreted by the unreliable scholar-narrator Kinbote.

With *Ada or Ardor: A Family Chronicle* (1969) Martin Amis throws up his hands. "At 600 pages, two or three times Nabokov's usual fighting-weight, the novel is what homicide detectives call 'a burster.' It is a waterlogged corpse at the stage of maximal bloat." After her praise for *Pale Fire*, Mary McCarthy's virulently disappointed response to *Ada* is all the harsher. The novel is playful but terrifying, layered so that it is impossible to reach a definitive sense of intention or to resolve the design. The very unsolvability is part of the purpose of the writing, a guarantee of its unbreachable integrity. For Gore Vidal it was unbreachable in a different sense. Asked whether he had read *Ada,* he replied, "No one has read *Ada.*" He admired Nabokov and they conducted an elaborate rivalry. Of the Nobel Prize committee, Vidal said: "It is sad that the dumb Swedes gave their merit badge to Solzhenitsyn instead of Nabokov. Perfect example, by the way, of the unimportance of a writer's books to his career."

Nabokov referred to it as "cosmopolitan" and "poetic," with its several themes and generic registers. It is a family epic of the Russian aristocracy, hence potentially for him a nostalgic exercise; it is a literary history; it meditates on time and how it takes away. The setting tends toward allegory, the language and structure games are played remorselessly, and it is impossible not to agree with Amis that this is a book that has lost sight of its readers. It touches again the sexual themes of *Lolita* but without charm, willfully. He was indulging himself with the language, the form, and a thematics that every time he revisited it (and he did so six times) became more difficult to justify. *Ada* stayed for twenty weeks on the *New York Times* best-sellers list. "In the history of art," Theodor Adorno reminds us, "late works are the catastrophes," no less catastrophic artistically when they succeed in the marketplace.

When he sets out on a journey, the Turkish novelist Orhan Pamuk packs his tattered editions of *Lolita, Pale Fire,* and *Speak Memory:* "Why do I feel as if I am packing a box of my medicines?" They are imbued, each one, with a sinister quality; they are also meticulous in the depiction of detail and in the matching of tone to matter. Cruelty and beauty coalesce. The author's greatness at such points depends upon the reader's answering greatness.

———•———

In January 1964 *Playboy* interviewed Nabokov. In March Ayn Rand was subjected to the same ordeal, and in April the French traitor, novelist, pornographer, and "saint" Jean Genet. Celebrities and, unusually, literary celebrities, though as different as chalk and cheese. Alissa Zinovyevna Rosenbaum (1905–1982), who was to become the American didactic novelist and cod-philosopher Ayn Rand, was six years Nabokov's junior. Her family, like his from St. Petersburg, was rich, but bourgeois and Jewish like Véra's. Both families spent the early Bolshevik period in the Crimea, but when the Nabokovs emigrated to the west, the Rosenbaums returned to St. Petersburg. Alissa studied film but as soon as she could she bolted for the United States. She arrived a dozen years before the Nabokovs made their crossing. She survived real hardship, especially with the language (she had learned Russian, French, and German from her tutors at home, not English). She tried to act in the movies (it was still the age of silent films); she gave up Russian and started writing in English, first plays and after some false starts her first successful novel, *The Fountainhead* (1943), seven years in the writing. Its slow beginnings were transformed when it was turned into a film and became a perennial best seller. *Atlas Shrugged* (1957) was vast and unwieldy, too, but it got read. John Galt, the hero of the novel, is a kind of Tea Party pinup.

For schoolboys of my generation *Atlas Shrugged* was compulsory summer reading. It was on the best-sellers list at roughly the same time as *Lolita*. Rand, who claimed that she valued Mickey Spillane above all modern writers, told *Playboy* that she had read half of *Lolita:* "I couldn't finish. He is a brilliant stylist, he writes beautifully, but his subjects, his sense of life, his view of man, are so evil that no amount of artistic skill can justify them." Nabokov did not record even that much of an opinion of her. Her insistence on square-chinned notions of personal integrity and resistance, on self-fulfillment even at the cost of community, make her politically attractive to those for whom aesthetic considerations are secondary to the moral burden her novels shoulder. Atlas shrugs, which leaves the rest of us shaken.

Two years after Rand arrived in the United States, and the year in which Nabokov published *King, Queen, Knave* in Russian, a scandal in British and then in American publishing occurred. Jonathan Cape in London published Radclyffe Hall's *The Well of Loneliness* (1928), an "openly Lesbian" novel that—if she ever read it—would have attracted as much opprobrium from Rand as *Lolita* did, with even less reason. There is an urgent, melodramatic sincerity about Hall's writing here, a didactic edge as insistent as Rand's. There can be no doubt about the passionate address, nor about the melodrama. She has drunk deep of Emily Brontë and avoided the infection of irony. Earnest and in earnest, she plots. To add something of a red rag of controversial authority to the publishing event, Cape commissioned for the first edition an "appreciation" by Havelock Ellis, well known for his writings on "sexual inversion," and this was included as a preface.

Radclyffe Hall (1886–1943) wrote eight novels. By the time of *The Well* she was established, indeed had won awards for her writing. She thought she was authoritative enough to carry off an unpopular, controversial campaigning novel. Her companion agreed that the risk was worth taking. She warned her editor not to edit her text. *Quod scripsi, scripsi.* And so it was. The only one of her novels still read is not her best. *Adam's Breed* is formally and thematically better achieved. *The Well* is read because of its theme and history.

Even though the action stretches across the *fin de siècle,* the First World War, and the years after, *The Well* has a late Victorian timbre, the language seeded with archaisms, and yet it appeared in the same year as other books exploring lesbian themes—Virginia Woolf's *Orlando* and Elizabeth Bowen's *The Hotel,* for example. Compton Mackenzie's satirical *Extraordinary Women* was also published that year and tried unsuccessfully to shine in some of the limelight Hall's novel generated. We already encountered Djuna Barnes's *Ladies Almanack* (also 1928) in which some of the same characters who feature, more earnestly, in Hall's novel swank about.

The closest Hall gets to a same-sex erotic scene is this: "But Mary turned on her with very bright eyes: 'You can say that—you, who talk about loving! What do I care for all you've told me? What do I care for the world's opinion? What do I care for anything but you, and you just as you are–as you are, I love you! Do you think I'm crying because of what you've told me? I'm crying because of your dear, scarred face . . . the misery on it . . . Can't you understand that all that I am belongs to you, Stephen?' Stephen bent down and kissed Mary's hands very humbly, for now she could find no words any more . . . and that night they were not divided." That's it, "and that night, they were not divided." It was enough to get the book banned. The whole mélange was clearly contrived to deprave and corrupt. The *Sunday Express* was in the denunciatory van, keen to save readers from "the leprosy of these lepers" and to have the book burned. Contrariwise, radical feminist critics today declare that *The Well* established and promoted damaging stereotypes and did much to streamline popular prejudice. Like *Uncle Tom's Cabin* and *Heart of Darkness,* it had a job to do, and those for whom the job was undertaken have come to despise it.

*The Well* stands up less as literature than Conrad's book does, its melodrama is more local and class-bound than Stowe's. There is something nightmarish in the self-sacrifice of the heroine, Stephen, who plots to free her lover into marriage and returns home alone, the saintly vehicle between the "invert" souls and the God she believes in. There they throng, strangers, but, "Surely that was Wanda? And someone with a neat little hole in her side—Jamie clasping Barbara by the hand; Barbara with the white flowers of death on her bosom. Oh, but they were many, these unbidden guests, and they called very softly at first and then louder." She harkens and like the first martyr, for whom she is named, she begins to feel the bruising of the stones. "Rockets of pain, burning rockets of pain—their pain, her pain, all welded together into one great consuming agony. Rockets of pain that shot up and burst, dropping scorching tears of fire on the spirit—her pain, their pain." And they take possession of her, she is their medium: "We have asked for bread; will you give us a stone? Answer us: will you give us a stone? You, God, in Whom we, the outcast, believe," until she herself is addressed: "You, Stephen, who have drained our cup to the dregs—we have asked for bread; will you give us a stone?" Stephen addresses God: "Acknowledge us, oh God, before the whole world. Give us also the right to our existence!"

Leonard Woolf did not like the book, but when the prosecution began he and E. M. Forster drafted a letter and sought signatories to support it, among them T. S. Eliot, Bennett, Dame Ethel Smyth, and Vera Brittain. Hall objected that the letter spoke of censorship but did not affirm the high literary merit of the work, something Woolf, Forster, and Bennett failed to perceive. A more anodyne, brief message was substituted, signed by Forster and Virginia Woolf, about the effects of censorship on creativity. In the United States the publisher played cleverly with censorship, inviting prosecution and selling 100,000 copies in the first year.

Leonard Woolf disliked another woman writer who lived with a female companion and wrote what he regarded as poor books. Dame Ivy Compton-Burnett (1884–1969) was an eccentric heir of Meredith. Her own legacy to Anglophone and other writers is specific: it has to do with economy and embodiment, and the centrality of voices. Updike speaks of her work as "clipped prose, which seemed fit only for cranky, quibbling people pent up indoors in Victorian parlors." But women novelists from Nathalie Sarraute to Francine Prose value her. The Italian novelist Natalia Ginzburg, asked why her own novels always followed one pattern, replied, "I think the best answer I can give is one that an English writer, Ivy Compton-Burnett, one of my favorite English writers, gave to the same question. 'I started that way and I never found it opportune to change.'" The phrase "found it opportune" belongs to a period and a social class. One can hear both arrogance and self-effacement in it. It is not quite true, because Compton-Burnett did change. In 1911 she published *Dolores,* a conventional agonized novel about a young woman trapped in circumstances similar to those she herself had suffered. She came to despise the book for its candor, its lack of imagination. Fourteen years elapsed before her first *real* novel appeared.

In her twenty novels, events—usually entailing family, property, and inheritance—occur offstage like murders in Greek tragedy, but their effects are remorselessly registered in the page-by-page present of the novel. She wrote from the wholeness of the imagined situation, not taking notes and building toward the narrative but spinning the language confidently, a sort of spider. There is remorseless comedy, as in Nabokov, but because her characters are socially rooted, there is more pain in the voices and the laughter. She remarked, "I have not the note-book habit; that is, I do not watch or listen to strangers with a view to using the results. They do not do or say things that are of any good [*sic*]. They are too indefinite and too much alike and are seldom living in anything but the surface of their lives." The assurance of this declaration dazzles. Updike says she wrote sitting on a sofa, slotting the completed pages under a cushion. She always appeared in black, like a Victorian widow. Her imagination lived in a prewar period where her eventless and tragic formative years were spent.

She says, "A plot is like the bones of a person, not interesting like expression or signs of experience, but the support of the whole." Just as casual conversations are of no use to the writer, so too, "as regards plots I find real life no help at all. Real life seems to have no plots. And as I think a plot desirable and almost necessary, I have this extra grudge against life." In a sour spirit, she is of a mind with Nabokov. Real life provides few real characters. Life may provide elements: a face, a portrait, "almost a face in the fire." But nothing more: "People in real life hardly seem definite enough to appear in print. They are not good or bad enough, or clever or stupid enough, or comic or pitiful enough." The writer does not hold a mirror up to nature but generates another nature.

When she submitted work to Leonard Woolf at the Hogarth Press, he could not hear it and said she could not write. Virginia Woolf, threatened by her increasing success, commented, "There is something bleached about Miss

Compton-Burnett: like hair that has never had any color in it." Though chronologically a contemporary of Woolf and Lawrence, she belongs more naturally with the generation in which her first acknowledged novel was published, when she was forty, the generation of Anthony Powell and Evelyn Waugh. And yet her Flaubertian economy of means (spare punctuation, refusing colons, semicolons, exclamation marks, even italics, and limiting her diction) is remote from their profligacy. For her as for her modernist predecessors the reader has responsibilities proportional to the pleasures to be had. *Pastors and Masters* (1925) set the pattern for what was to follow, a whole literature of voices, silences, breathing, of pauses crowded with ambiguity. The scenes are not dramatic, not meditative, not bristling with *bon mots,* but contain characters engaged with one another in a disregard for the protocols of conventional "entertainment." *Brothers and Sisters* (1929) comes closest to her own life in terms of its plots and tonalities. The final book in the series, *The Mighty and Their Fall* (1961), is of a piece with the second: an even integrity of approach, precise, unabating. It is the quintessential transcription of a social class.

Though she claimed to have had "an uneventful life" and refused to talk about it, in fact all her fiction is rooted in its Victorian reality. Her beloved father, a doctor, lost his first wife in childbirth, remarried, and produced in total a dozen children. The second wife sent the children of the first marriage off to school and found her own offspring hard to deal with. Ivy was a child of the second marriage. Her father died suddenly and her widowed mother, like Queen Victoria, vanished in the folds of mourning, taking her own children with her. One of Ivy's favorite brothers died of pneumonia, the other perished on the Somme in 1916. On Christmas day 1917 her two youngest sisters committed suicide together. Of the twelve children, none had children, and none of the eight daughters married. Though the drama of such lives was slow-moving, like that of the Brontë sisters, it was hard to live, not least because Ivy, after her father's death, was put in charge of her younger sisters and when her mother died found in herself the tyrannical strains that had marked her mother, so that her younger sisters fled home as soon as they could.

Much of her mature life she had as companion an expert in the decorative arts, Margaret Jourdain, who died in 1951. She described their relationship as that of "neutrals." When *Pastors and Masters* appeared, Jourdain seemed unaware that Ivy had been working on a book. This furtiveness was less secrecy than a desire not to be seen to fail.

Of her novels, all but two have the word "and" in the title (*A House and Its Head, Manservant and Maidservant, The Present and the Past,* and *A Heritage and Its History,* for example). There is an Austenish sense of balance to do with power and the formal relations that family imposes, and with the ways in which the present is shaped by the past. Her novels are as closely related to one another as R. K. Narayan's Malgudi novels: her work is of a piece. There is little sense of repetition, and out of the spiritually meager material for four decades she teases Victorian and Edwardian voices of a class that has everything except happiness, which can endure only through the exercise of a self-obscuring and obliterating irony. In *A God and His Gifts* (1963) a character remarks, "It is awkward when there is a hush, and you could hear a pin drop, and everyone waits for someone else to speak, and no one does." In a Compton-Burnett novel, someone does. "'What harm is there in hearing a pin drop?' said Joanna. 'And there is little danger of it. When a pin is needed, no one ever has one.'"

Elizabeth Taylor (née Coles, 1912–1975) regarded Dame Ivy as "one of the greatest writers in our history." (She loved books "in which practically nothing ever happens.") Novels by her male contemporaries she ignored. She led a life seemingly eventless. It was more conventionally proper than Compton-Burnett's. She married in 1936 the owner of a company that made confectionary, they prospered, and she wrote twelve novels, starting just at the end of the war with *At Mrs. Lippincote's* (1945). Her subjects are women as middle-class mothers, wives, writers, individuals, finding themselves in new ways after biological and social "obligations" are fulfilled. Her best-known books are *A Game of Hide and Seek* (1951), reissued on the centenary of her birth with an introduction by Hilary Mantel, and *Angel* (1957, reissued as *The Real Life of Angel Deverell*). Angelica, the protagonist of the latter, is a shop girl who develops as a storyteller and finally writes a highly successful, melodramatic novel entitled *The Lady Irania,* honoring the clichés of class and romantic stereotype. She believes she has done something wonderful, but her success is commercial, the publishers cynically manipulate the market that sustained Ouida. She gets money, but the critics and "real" writers regard her with scorn. "The more the critics laughed, the longer were the queues for her novels at the libraries; the power of her romanticism captured simple people." She has become "part of some new and quite delicious joke." She has the golden apples and has won the race. Angelica's sincerity and hubris are indistinguishable. A failure of self-knowledge and irony leave her in possession of the big house and all the trappings of success that greater writers hanker after. Taylor develops the narrative beyond jest into a study of self-deceit and self-belief that at least provided the protagonist with a life not passively accepted but taken in hand, self-made. Active will can unsettle and transform even the most habituated life, and though disruption ensues, so can individual growth and even fulfillment. Her books have too many novelists in them. She writes without sentimentality or nostalgia in a kind of contrary creative spirit, and there is nothing earnest about the precise, witty, and clarifying writing. Her correct, polite characters have human desires and functioning bowels. They even, on occasion, fart.

Updike contrasts Dame Ivy's style with that of Dame Muriel Spark (1918–2006). Both employ an appropriate limited palette. Dame Ivy's palette is somber, with wry highlights. Spark's changes from novel to novel, though there is consistency of technique, the colors and their intensities change, from watercolor through pastel, oils, to acrylics. Dame Ivy has a generalizing, eighteenth-century aspect, like Richardson, whereas Spark is modern in the spirit of Fielding and Smollett, not least when she is ironizing history.

Updike, who likes *Aiding and Abetting* (2000) especially, calls her distinctive writing *"sui generis* novels." There are twenty-two of them. Is it helpful to describe the shorter among them, which run to 128 or 96 pages, generously spaced, as novels? Are they in fact essays, or novellas à thèse? They are not stretched out of shape: she is meticulous about proportions, even when her buildings are of the slightest construction. But some are so poor in incident, so parsimonious of characters—scarcely breathing templates rather than persons—that one wants to find a generic term appropriate to their lightness, intellectual clarity, theological coldness, architecture. Over the almost five decades of her writing life her language changes: "Never ornate, it grows simpler," Updike says, perhaps because life in Italy, far from the dailiness of her medium, has arrested and gradually essentialized it.

And he draws an unexpected comparison. "Has any fiction writer since Hemingway placed more faith in the simple declarative sentence, the plain Anglo-Saxon noun? Hemingway's style sometimes gives the impression of striking a pose, whereas Spark's appears to be merely getting on with it, brushing aside everything she might say but doesn't care to." In this she is more like Nabokov than Hemingway. Her characters fulfill elaborate roles in an argument, balancing within a structure, existing beyond a denoted place in the story that is often unlikely, or secondary to the novel's primary intent. Spark is ironist through and through, merciless, superior, inviting the reader to her plane. William Boyd notes, "The disinterest can also shade into ruthlessness. There has always been a nail-paring objectivity about Muriel Spark's authorial style (this is what drew Evelyn Waugh to praise her first novel [*The Comforters,* 1957])." In some of the later novels, such as *Reality and Dreams* (1996), "the controlling role of Muriel Spark is a little too overt." Spark is more a fantasist than a realist. There is a lot of Gothic in her, first and last. She wrote fiction for almost half a century and found it hard to reread and acknowledge her earlier selves, as though each novel had been committed by a different author and she could not quite take responsibility for it. Readers can recognize a Spark novel at ten paces; but Spark claimed she could not do so herself. Things happen in her novels in ways that call attention to their happening: "Simultaneously, he took off his hat, looked at his watch, and said to Jane, 'What's the news?'" A busy sentence from *The Girls of Slender Means* (1963); also a completely accurate one. A man looks at a woman "with frightened eyeglasses." In her world feelings and responses are registered through objects; how we dress, what we show the world, is as close to an identity as we get, short of theology and what her Roman Catholicism provided.

Spark dusted down the novel form with energy unusual for a British writer. More unusual was that each time she did it, her readership grew; she was not perceived as experimental. Others of her near contemporaries, Christine Brooke-Rose in particular, were up to comparably radical work, only more deliberate, and from within the academy. Did Spark's popularity in fact license work on a much smaller scale than had hitherto been expected of novelists, so that her heirs and successors could be content with cleverness, intellectual contrivance, a poverty of content pretending to answer to poverty as a theme in the modern world? Is she the godmother of that literature of conceit that takes metaphor and develops it ad absurdum? She speaks of her writing as allegory or parable, and given her theological concerns this is plausible. Uprooted from theology, however, her aesthetic as practiced by others is one of diminution.

She had a sacramental sense of her vocation: she surprised herself, then followed that surprise tenaciously. But her legacy is generally to writers without metaphysical intuitions. A natural short-story writer, her novels have those qualities. She understands the world not from a great height but from living in and through it and hearing the language of its crises, tragedies, and so on. She is not out to find a shape, because as a Roman Catholic, for her the shapes are given; she is after form and, at a cost, like Graham Greene, with whom she shared her work, time after time she finds it.

She was born in a genteel quarter of Edinburgh as Muriel Sarah Camberg. Her father was an engineer, half-Jewish, her mother an English music teacher. Her laconic autobiography *Curriculum Vitae* (1992) is not generous in information, but it would seem that the family was frugal, and her education at James Gillespie girls' school was funded by grants. The school was a prototype for Marcia Blaine's, where Miss Jean Brodie (*The Prime of Miss Jean Brodie*, 1961) groomed her "gerrils." The six girls in the novel were in fact a teasing out of the qualities of two, Muriel herself and her best friend. Spark fragments characters and comes close to caricaturing them in the act of fictional refinement. They must fit the form, and no character ever runs away with the story. "Every work of literature should make a world of its own," she declares. "In my view this entails excluding all other worlds." In the theater version of *The Prime*, the adapter cuts the girls off from their families, an isolation from cause that makes them, Spark says, into pure effects.

A hungry reader, she was encouraged to read what was considered the best literature of the past. The past was largely the nineteenth century and featured above all Scott (her first literary award was for a poem composed in honor of his centenary in 1932, when she was fourteen). Browning also featured, and his impact on her development was profound. It was hard to escape Swinburne. Later she composed poems and published a first collection in 1952; from 1950 she wrote on and edited Wordsworth, the Brontës, Mary Shelley, and John Masefield, and after her conversion John Henry Newman demanded her attention. Many of her books were collaborations with Derek Stanford, a man she came to demonize.

When school ended she acquired secretarial skills: going to university was not considered at the time. Bluestockings were not her style. She started work in a large store, then married injudiciously at nineteen "a man who brought me bunches of flowers when I had flu." Sydney Oswald Spark (referred to as "SOS") was much older than she was and was poised to set off to Rhodesia as a schoolteacher. The principal mark he left on her was his surname, preferable to Camberg, and a son, Robin, whom she left behind when she finally got away from Africa. The marriage lasted two years, but she was stuck in Rhodesia for most of the war. With her son an impossible and unmendable relationship developed. She excluded him from her will.

In 1944, back in London, she became one of *The Girls of Slender Means,* living at a club quite like the genteel, threadbare ladies' hostel called the May of Teck in that novel. The war was in its final months, and her first steady job was with the Foreign Office, working for a hush-hush operation whose task was to publish "detailed truth with believable lies" to demoralize the enemy. The stories were disseminated in various ways, notably in broadcast on radio stations that pretended to be German-based. Some of the stories were so good that they appeared as fact in the British press. After the war she did literary hack work, from 1949 onward. Her first novel, *The Comforters,* completed in 1955, was not published until she was almost forty.

*The Comforters* is of its period. It concerns Caroline who comes to imagine that she is a character in the process of being written. She is also a Roman Catholic still in the process of coming over, and to some extent the teleology of Catholicism gave Spark the writer precisely that sensation of mattering in a narrative over which, thanks to the always vexed issue of free will, one had a degree of control, or at least (given the nature of time and the obsolescent human organism), collaboration. Ali Smith speaks of the book as "a dialogue" between Caroline and the Typing Ghost, "a raging, vibrant argument held in a perfectly disciplined matrix, and a near-impossible blend, in the process, of subjectivity and objectivity." This is experimental fiction unlike John Fowles's or Christine

Brooke-Rose's, light, effortless, and no less radical for that. *Robinson* (1958), which follows *The Comforters,* is more slight, about Robinson on an island with only Miguel for company, their existence interrupted by a plane crash and the arrival of three survivors, key among them January Marlow. There is vague love interest, an apparent murder, and a mystery, and some thrifty, telling description that essentializes January's character through her way of seeing: "the mustard field staring at me with a yellow eye, the blue and green lake seeing in me a hard turquoise stone."

There followed *Memento Mori* (1959), which grew out of her relations with her grandmother, whose old age she observed firsthand. Human decline has seldom been told in more mercilessly funny terms. "Remember," says the anonymous telephone message to each mortal victim, "you must die." And die they do, in a world rendered mysterious and intense by blackmail, sex, and extreme brevity. *The Ballad of Peckham Rye* (1960) is also a mystery and an airy study of a dark subject, evil. In the same year appeared *The Bachelors,* which Evelyn Waugh told her was "the cleverest & most elegant of all your clever and elegant books." She had prepared the world for her most popular book, *The Prime of Miss Jean Brodie.*

The circumscribed community, the tight-drawn circle of characters (sometimes as few as two), was her preferred space in which to conduct a plot. In a controlled context the power relations that her novels explore are focused. Miss Brodie's brilliant and brittle tyranny can unfold and collapse under a severe eye. Spark chooses a convent as the setting for her satire based on Watergate, *The Abbess of Crewe* (1974); at its most taut and economical, she chooses the line between a driver's eye and the passenger reflected in the rearview mirror. Power, love, and evil do not need a wide world in which to reveal themselves. This pattern of containment and restraint she shares with Greene and, differently, with Iris Murdoch, whose spaces, though more elaborately drawn, are quite as claustrophobic as Spark's.

Spark left Britain for good in 1963, in the wake of the success of the play and film of *The Prime of Miss Jean Brodie.* The book provided for the rest of her life. The *New Yorker* had ingested *The Prime* in a single issue: she went to New York and became a staff writer for the magazine. In 1967 she moved to Rome, where she lived in style. She and her sculptor partner settled in Tuscany, and she spent the rest of her life there. They acquired an ancient house with religious antecedents, freezing in winter and structurally treacherous. There she developed her writing method, composing books in a steady copperplate hand, in a single draft with minimal correction, on spiral-bound notebooks she had sent to her from the booksellers and stationers James Thin in Edinburgh, thus maintaining a connection with her school days. She tended to write in bed.

In a late interview Spark declared that her writing was driven by an "outside force" that released energies from her memory. She conceded that Proust, a writer she in no formal way resembles, "inspired me more than anything . . . I could see what you could do with memory. I could see what you could do with incidents. It was after reading Proust that I found I rather liked writing prose." Once her debt to her own early years is recognized, her estrangement from her son Robin acquires an aesthetic dimension. As she was converting to Roman Catholicism, he was discovering his Jewish roots and delving into her family past, reading it differently from the way she did. This threatened her very imagination, a space cultivated and kept for herself.

*The Girls of Slender Means,* the last novel she wrote in England, evokes the immediately postwar world she encountered on her return from Rhodesia with its exhaustion, its moribund values and traditions, and its moral lassitude. It helps to explain her departure:

> Long ago in 1945 all the nice people in England were poor, allowing for exceptions. The streets of the cities were lined with buildings in bad repair or no repair at all, bomb-sites piled with stony rubble, houses like giant teeth in which decay had been drilled out, leaving only the cavity. Some bomb-ripped buildings looked like the ruins of ancient castles until, at closer view, the wallpapers of various quite normal rooms would be visible, room above room, exposed, as on a stage, with one wall missing; sometimes a lavatory chain would dangle over nothing from a fourth- or fifth-floor ceiling; most of the staircases survived, like a new art-form, leading up and up to an unspecified destination that made unusual demands on the mind's eye. All the nice people were poor; at least, that was a general axiom, the best of the rich being poor in spirit.

The repetition of the first sentence, ironized and transformed, at the paragraph's end, the direct quote from Eliot's *The Waste Land,* the forensic use of punctuation, especially of commas, so that the tone cannot be mistaken: these are hallmarks of a modernist sensibility at work. Her convert's Roman Catholicism left her, as Burgess, a fellow Roman, puts it, "safe with her theological certainties" so that she can withhold compassion and, when the bomb goes off and Joanna Childe starts to burn up, Spark describes what the victim is wearing.

When she got to New York she lost her bearings. *The Mandelbaum Gate* (1965) won awards, perhaps because for her it was a departure into formal conventionality and an uncharacteristic earnestness about her themes: faith and politics in the Middle East. She wrote each chapter so it could stand as a short story, a good commercial decision because she could sell them one at a time but not as a serial. Her protagonist shares many elements with the author: British, partly Jewish, a Roman Catholic convert, she visits Jerusalem, the spiritual center for her Jewishness and her Catholicism. The focus of confrontation between Jordan and Israel, when the city was still divided before the Six Day War, is the eponymous gate. The war crimes and the trial of Adolf Eichmann provide a pretext. It is long, too long for her style to sustain. Apart from *The Driver's Seat* (1970), a book that seems too taut and short and monomaniacal to be a novel, the late 1960s and the 1970s are productive for her but not as formally inventive as the preceding period, though Graham Greene responded to *Territorial Rights* (1979): "I thought you'd never top *Memento Mori,* but you have."

*Loitering with Intent* (1981) was shortlisted for the Booker Prize, and rightly so. Fleur Talbot makes her way toward becoming an author. This deflected autobiography, part of the project of much of the later fiction, makes sense of and finds form in her experiences. Spark has perfected her clinical irony to examine the severe writer's block that nearly destroyed her in the early 1950s; its resolution produces a joyous release not experienced elsewhere in her fiction. And in Mrs. Hawkins, who narrates *A Far Cry from Kensington* (1988), the rather shrill, always correct and savage voice of her individuality is heard. It is as though one of the several voices of Dame Ivy had escaped and taken over a novel all its own. "I enjoy a puritanical and moralistic nature; it is my happy element to judge between right and wrong, regardless of what I might actually do." Scottish Calvinist but, "At the same time, the wreaking of vengeance and imposing of justice on others and myself are not at all in my line. It is enough for me to discriminate mentally, and leave the rest to God."

For *Aiding and Abetting* (2000), her penultimate novel, Spark chose a real-life mystery. Her villain is a victim, son of a class and culture in terminal decline. His name is Lord Lucan. After the violent death of the family's nanny, he vanished. Here he is found twice over and his fate or fates revealed in a fiction that puts both of him into therapy with a charlatan who is herself magnificently corrupt. We are in the world of false identity that ties in closely with Spark's work at the end of the war, fiction rooted in the partly real, which makes the unreality more credible and more sinister. Here the therapist's falsehood entails false faith as well, the feigned stigmata, the exploitation of naive belief. It is another of her very little novels, but because it ties in to a familiar story, it has a power far in excess of its scale. In her final novel, appropriately entitled *The Finishing School* (2004) and suggesting beginnings and endings, her theme is dissembling. The school is College Sunrise, whose head is writing a novel and whose star pupil is writing a much more successful and vigorous novel. The fashion for writing schools, and questions about the nature of literary talent, its acquisition and transferability, are raised. So too are issues of power, sexuality (variously explored among adults and teenagers), and emotional violence. Here in a tense environment are many of the impulses that run riot in *A High Wind in Jamaica* and *Lord of the Flies*. Spark's experiment remains controlled.

She is an anarchic figure, rejecting labels and "identities" as a woman writer, a Jew, a Scot, though she sees her formation as Scottish, her dialect the decorous propriety of Scottish English: "The Scots have always been among the finest English-speaking writers. Their best language is English. The practice of English by Scots cannot be too seriously promoted." Labels and categories repel and fascinate her, as do characters who are types: Miss Brodie, or in *The Ballad of Peckham Rye* Dougal Douglas (a relation to Humbert Humbert), Lord "Lucky" Lucan, both of him, so to speak.

———•———

"I am a constant admirer of his talent and intellect," Spark wrote of Gabriel Josipovici (b. 1940). Among British writers he possesses a singular pedigree. He was born in Nice, his parents are described as "Russo-Italian, Romano-Levantine," so that his natural languages are several and his geographies, first and second generation, include much of Europe and northern Africa. He lived in Egypt from 1945 to 1956, when he came to Britain. He read English at Oxford and then spent thirty-six years as a teacher at the University of Sussex. He is the author of sixteen novels, three volumes of short stories, eight critical works, and numerous stage and radio plays, and is a regular contributor to the *Times Literary Supplement*. His work has been translated into the major languages of Europe and into Arabic. In 2001 he published *A Life,* a biographical memoir of his mother, the translator and poet Sacha Rabinovitch, with whom he lived for many years until her death. His book *What Ever Happened to Modernism?* questioned the value of the main currents in contemporary British literature. Josipovici's modernism is European, continuous with that of Kafka and Beckett, Picasso, Marcel Duchamp. His first successful fiction was a book of stories entitled *Mobius the Stripper* (1974), and he won the Somerset Maugham Award, only to have it withdrawn when he could not produce a British passport.

Among his significant novels, most of them relatively short and based in the lives of artists, writers, and people of a cosmopolitan, usually a European, disposition, are *The Inventory* (1968), his first, conducted in runs of his characteristic breathless, oblique dialogue and interwoven plot lines; *Contre-Jour: A Triptych after Pierre Bonnard* (1986), based on the life of the painter Bonnard and his hauntingly present nudes; *The Big Glass* (1991), which builds on Duchamp and achieves moments of high comedy (Josipovici is a comic writer in the Continental manner); *In a Hotel Garden* (1993), which treats Holocaust themes; *Moo*

*Pak* (1995) with its sense of the erasures of the English seventeenth and eighteenth centuries and of the Exile burdened with his alien, aching culture; the linked stories of *Goldberg: Variations* (2001); and *Infinity* (2012), the extended interview with the manservant of Tancredo Pavone, a rich Sicilian nobleman and avant-garde composer (one is put in mind of a musical Lampedusa).

By accident (they share a publisher) Josipovici often finds his work lumped together with that of Christine Brooke-Rose (1923–2012), another writer of unconventional fiction, with her taproots like Josipovici's outside the British Isles. Her experimentalism is embedded in the properties of language, however, where Josipovici experiments with limitation of form. At first Brooke-Rose and Spark were taken together, as if growing from a common trunk. In 1965 Spark was awarded the James Tait Black Memorial Prize for *The Mandelbaum Gate*. The following year, for her second experimental novel, *Such*, Brooke-Rose received the same award. In their early careers Spark and Brooke-Rose were friends, but Spark managed her life and her career efficiently, did not bother with husbands after the first one, and after limping along the poor, hard lanes found the main highway. Christine Brooke-Rose became a more obviously experimental and theoretical writer. She was five years Spark's junior. None of her books made a breakthrough; those who praised her—Angela Carter, Frank Kermode, Lorna Sage—came to her with critical and interpretative tools sharper and subtler than general readers are expected to possess.

She was born in Geneva into a household where English, French, and German were spoken. Her father left the family and died when she was eleven. He had been, she later learned, a lapsed Anglican Benedictine monk and a thief with convictions to his credit. Her Swiss-American mother became a Benedictine nun in London. On her later visits to London, even after her mother's death, Brooke-Rose stayed at the nunnery. During the Second World War she enlisted. Because of her language skills she was sent to Bletchley Park with only a school certificate. There she worked alongside leading writers and theorists decrypting coded German messages, an experience more exhilarating and instructive than the highest College high table, the work with immediate consequences for national security in wartime. Somerville College, Oxford, must have seemed tame in the wake of such a differentiating experience. Then she went on to University College, London, where she took her PhD in medieval literature. She lived for several years and through two of her three marriages in London, then moved to Paris, where she taught American and British literature between 1968 (the student troubles) and 1988, when she retired to the south of France and continued writing.

To survive an eventful, difficult life, Brooke-Rose developed a sense of irony and comic endurance, becoming a character within an observed narrative to whom things happened. She is as comic a writer as Spark; but she issues each of her mature fictions with a formal or semantic challenge, a Houdini of the novel choosing obdurate chains.

Her first four novels are conventional in form. *The Language of Love* (1957) coincided with Spark's *The Comforters*. Best of her conventional novels was *The Dear Deceit* (1960, coinciding with Spark's *The Ballad of Peckham Rye*). It told, in reverse chronology, something like her father's story. But she was working on a smaller canvas than Spark's and was frustrated with the scale and conventionality of her work: "Light satires on society, more influenced by Evelyn Waugh and people like that," she said in an interview, and she refused to reissue those books. "From *Out* onwards, I really was trying to expand the possibilities of the novel form." After a short break from fiction, she returned transformed by contact with the French *nouveau roman*. She risked experiments in layout and typography, and on a semantic level. *Out* (1964), *Such* (1966), *Between* (1968), and *Thru* (1975), brought together in a single volume as *The Brooke-Rose Omnibus* (1986), remain a fascinating record of transition, each book distinct yet the experimental project connected as she moved into the mechanics of language, creating a fiction of tenses, of pronouns, of codes and encoding, of withholding (in one novel, for example, the verb "to be" in all its forms is excluded). The experiments are not declared: the reader senses unusual effects and focuses upon the process of writing.

Her memoir-novel *Remake* (1996) reconstructs her life. Though "autobiographical," it uses vulnerable and volatile life material to compose a third-person fiction. Memory is recognized to be distorting and partial, its false certainties held in check by a skeptical language that probes and finds consistent forms underlying the impulses of the subject. It is not a process of chronological remembering. *Remake* dwells less on facts than on what they reveal, the feelings of a wartime child, the textures of her clothing, tastes and smells, her mother, the absent father, a gradual transition into adulthood. Her last novel completes the account. *Life, End of* (2006) was written with acute physical difficulty. She was very old and ill. In it she relives her experiments with narrative, and with the narrative of her life. At the center of the book, in a mock-technical lecture from the Character to the Author, she accepts that her experiments in narrative *are* like life: narrative creates itself even when the subject is the author. Her dark comic imagination explores the meanings and nonmeanings to which, in the end, life and art lead her. Of the intervening novels, those that make a difference to the art of fiction are *Amalgamemnon* (1984), composed entirely in unrealized tenses, and *Textermination* (1991), in which a conference of fictional characters is held to reaffirm the survival of the authors. A being persists only for as long as it is remembered. If memory lets go, texts die. In short, it is the age of the reader and the critic whose attention alone confers life. The confusions are hilarious: Emma Bovary keeps getting into scrapes when she is confused with Emma Woodhouse. There are several closed carriages in which unseen deeds occur. Mr. Casaubon is near extinction. New arrivals include Gibreel Farishta and Saladin Chamcha, bringing trouble with them as they tumble out of the sky. The book was written in the second year of the fatwa against Salman Rushdie and their inclusion was one of Brooke-Rose's rare political gestures.

The name of Bryan Stanley Johnson (1933–1973) is often associated and dismissed with that of Brooke-Rose. His biographer, the novelist Jonathan Coe, tries to free him from this company and from the adjective that has stalked him in life and death, "experimental," as though his books would become more readable if another term could be found. Yet an experimental imagination is his main claim to our attention. That, along with his life and the "almighty aposiopesis" of his suicide. But the books: like Brooke-Rose's and Josipovici's, his (very different) experiments *work*.

Two negative experiences shaped this writer from the working class: evacuation during the war, which left him traumatized and with a sense of having been abandoned by his family; and an unhappy love affair. A contemporary of Alan Sillitoe and John Braine, he left school at sixteen to work as a clerk but studied hard, taught himself Latin, sat the entry exams, and was admitted to King's College, London, from which he emerged with a 2:2 degree and a wounded heart. He was already writing and working collaboratively with Zulfikar Ghose (b. 1935), the Punjabi poet and fiction writer, a significant figure in editorial and collaborative projects in London in the 1960s, who now lives in Austin, where he teaches at the University of Texas.

As a theorist and controversialist, Johnson is always accessible. His radicalism was defined by personal and political, not academic, experience. He wrote seven novels that exploited and undermined the conventional novel form. He cut holes through pages so the reader could see forward. He left unbound chapters to shuffle the text and give it the anachronic quality of memory (though "first" and "last" were named as fixed points). *Christie Malry's Own Double-Entry* (1973) is what its title promises. Johnson by various devices intended not to elude but, as he believed, to enhance realism, to make the printed object a material metaphor for his themes and concerns, to zero *in*. Its cartoonishness and angularity put the reader in mind of Nathanael West's, the sentences concentrated, epigrammatical, and "brutalist." It is not all like that, however: There are comical and tender registers, and as Christie grows up and gets a bank job, he experiences these, before happening upon his "Great Idea," to express his own life by means of the double-entry system familiar to bookkeepers, which maintains a business's balance, only here conducted in terms of human debts and credits, failures and redresses. In the end he is an unsubtle descendant of Raskolnikov, thanks to his adding cyanide to the water supply, killing 20,479 Londoners, and West Londoners (the better class) at that. He intends to blow up Parliament but is diagnosed with cancer and dies. Nothing much is here for tears, however. Old Mum declares, of her daughter who was Christie's girl-friend, "Aaaaer, it was worth it, all those years of sacrifice, just to get my daughter placed in a respectable novel like this." The comedy of the novel is parodic: Johnson did not like the conventional novel, but he also saw the reductive dangers of the experimental, which by 1973 was quite widely practiced. Malry and the author have a lot to tell each other about the modern novel. And about terrorism of the kinds implicit in the capitalist system and those ranged against it.

Unlike his contemporary experimentalists devising strategies to elide the tyrannies of the conventional "I," Johnson's novels move toward that "I," stripping it of convention, refracting the self through diverse lenses. Thus in his first novel, the picaresque *Travelling People* (1963) with its Nabokovian protagonist Henry Henry, the layout lapses into film script format; in the second, *Albert Angelo* (1964), the proleptic holes on the page occur. Exploring time in a different way, *House Mother Normal* (1971), set in a nursing home, takes Woolf's technique from *The Waves* but weaves it tighter, keeping so closely to the tyranny of chronology that the thinking and experiencing of the characters overlap within a paragraph, even within a sentence. The art that precedes the final drafting must entail elaborating conventional parallel narratives that are then braided or skewered on a timeline. His contemporaries acknowledged his novels. David Lodge and Malcolm Bradbury saw them, "got" what they were up to, but none really warmed to what seemed arid exercises. He lacked humor, John Fuller said, and elegance. He talked about seeking truth through fiction and fictional devices, but the nature of that truth wavered and changed, an honorable quarry and a treacherous chimera.

His circle included Wilson Harris, the radical filmmaker, and publisher Stefan Themerson of the Gaberbocchus Press, the novelist Eva Figes, and Orwell's friend Rayner Heppenstall, through whom the French *nouveau roman* made its way into the outskirts of British fiction, along with work by Raymond Roussel, which he translated. Johnson was himself affected by the *nouveau roman* and recognized by the French as an English partisan. Several of his associates contributed to the novel *London Consequences,* a collaboration in which the chapters were assigned to different writers, and which Johnson edited with Margaret Drabble. He made films, wrote plays, and was poetry editor of the *Transatlantic Review.* After his suicide a following slowly grew, and in 2004

Jonathan Coe's biography appeared. The life became the story of a sadly un-availing experiment.

———·———

In recent photographs William H. (Howard) Gass (b. 1924, named after the twenty-seventh president of the United States) looks like a man born to medi-tate, to speak, and not to move very far. He has the aspect of a benign brain with a face on it, to which readers repair for instruction. "LIFE IN A CHAIR" is the title of the opening movement of his magnum opus, *The Tunnel* (1995, 651 pages), a little cousin of William Gaddis's *The Recognitions*. John Gardner speaks of Gass's "emphasis on language—that is, his brilliant use of it in books." What is this "language"? How does it work in criticism, in fiction? He has two novels and several novellas to his credit, as well as stories. His language is of the writ-ten variety, composed and then slowly revised with care. "I write slowly be-cause I write badly," he confessed in an interview. "I have to rewrite everything many, many times just to achieve mediocrity." He is fascinated with shapes and sounds of phrases. As a schoolboy he loved parsing and diagramming sentences. Adam Kirsch notes, in reviewing Gass's essays, "Inevitably, a writer who values style above all will find that the most important element in good writing is not architectonics—the large structure, the deep theme, the buried symbol—but the basic building block of prose, the sentence." If he gets that right, the larger structure will take care of itself. Gass concurs. "*The Tunnel* is about rhetoric too. It's more completely, more single-mindedly about rhetoric, about the move-ment of language and the beauty and terror of great speech."

With a big book it is hard to get the language continuously right, though with an essay or a story one might expect it. Placing Gass in the group to which he is customarily assigned by critics, John Gardner speaks of "the red herring symbols of Pynchon, the structural distractions of Barth, the machine-gun en-ergy of Gaddis. Above all, Gass's verbal glory." It is baroque glory and can be-come congested: the reader's task is divided between appreciation (the virtuoso is always performing to us) and comprehension, and over long periods the two can cease to harmonize. At first Gass relished Nabokov. He saw him plain at Cornell and seemed, in his novellas and stories, if not in his novels (which harbor autobiography), to be of his party. He liked "Transparent Themes" and titled his 1973 *Saturday Review* appreciation "Upright Among Staring Fish." The phrase occurs in a passage where Nabokov discusses ways of seeing. "When we con-centrate on a material object," he says, "whatever its situation, the very act of attention may lead to our involuntarily sinking into the history of that object. Novices must learn to skim over matter if they want matter to stay at the exact level of the moment. Transparent things, through which the past shines!" We must acquire a light tread so as not to sink in the medium. He warns, "Novices fall through the surface, humming happily to themselves, and are soon reveling with childish abandon in the story of this stone, of that heath." The challenge for the stylist, as for the pilgrim in language keen to preserve the "thin veneer of immediate reality . . . spread over natural and artificial matter," is to "remain in the now, with the now, on the now," and not "break its tension film. Otherwise the inexperienced miracle-worker will find himself no longer walking on water but descending upright among staring fish."

Gass's "verbal glory," manifest in essays and meditations, changes in character as he grows older. He distinguished between the languages of Beckett and of Stein, poles between which his own work moves: Stein is garrulous, repetitive. Beckett's economy is less of diction than *volume.* The language of his novels is print, but audible print, prose has its proper volume inherent in pace, style, and pause. Audible within print are the gaps, the white spaces, themselves part of the notation. Gass studied briefly with Wittgenstein at Cornell. In 1917–1918 Wittgenstein wrote, and in 1921 published, the *Tractatus Logico-Philosophicus,* which concludes at the Ultima Thule of language: "Whereof one cannot speak, thereof one must be silent." That silence beyond the meaning language makes is what Gass likes to dwell on; he celebrates writers who, like Stein (he is her prime contemporary expositor) and Beckett, in different ways press at and beyond that limit with their writings.

In an unhappy childhood—his mother a stoical alcoholic, his father an abusive martinet—he read voraciously and indiscriminately. He excelled at school and went to Wesleyan University. For over three years he endured life as a navy ensign, even unhappier than he had been as a boy. Released from service to Kenyon College, he graduated with academic distinction. He was not unharmed by his formative experiences, but he had survived them. At Cornell he took his PhD. He went on to a distinguished academic career and remains active in emeritus retirement.

*Omensetter's Luck* (1966) evokes the life of a little 1890s Ohio town. The book was a critical success, endorsed by Susan Sontag and by Gore Vidal, who calls it a "case of language doing the work of the imagination, but doing it very well." It has not found a general readership because of the demands the writing makes, the slow abundance of its pleasures. David Foster Wallace noted its relative conventionality. Gass began to work against traditional constraints of narrative. In 1968 he published a novella with photographs and experimental typography, *Willie Masters' Lonesome Wife:* he wanted the reader to work free of chronological narrative. *Cartesian Sonata and Other Novellas* (1998) is of a piece with the essays, speculative, troubled.

His largest and most difficult work of fiction, *The Tunnel,* was almost three decades in the making. Accounts differ. It is an oblique autobiography, the protagonist or antihero angry and self-critical, moving at a snail's pace through difficult history. It includes passages of extraordinary writing, but the perfection of the parts does not guarantee the whole. "What I have to tell you is as long as life, but I shall run as swiftly, so before you know it, we shall both be over." When he tells us—something most readers would fail to infer from the text— "*The Tunnel* was built on Schoenberg's 12-tone system—I divided it into 12 chapters, with 12 basic themes," the formal arbitrariness becomes clear. Perhaps this formula was creatively enabling as he inched forward (one remembers how in *Ulysses* Joyce initially ghosted the *Odyssey*), but formal analogies between twelve-tone music and this prose do not hold. Despite Gass's dislike of narrative, this book has one. William Frederick Kohler, whose novel it is, is a professor of history in a Midwest not unlike Gass's native Ohio. Professor Kohler is writing a great book titled *Guilt and Innocence in Hitler's Germany*. *The Tunnel* is his own history, subjective, vulnerable, hubristic. It is a book filled with fear and a paradoxically shared privacy. Views on Gass's achievement in *The Tunnel* remain divided. Its time may come.

Gass belongs to a category of fiction writers whose main readership is in the universities, a category that includes Brooke-Rose, Gaddis, and Pynchon as well. Gore Vidal talks less about the death of the novel than of the novel reader. "Eventually the novel will simply be an academic exercise, written by academics to be used in classrooms in order to test the ingenuity of students. A combination of Rorschach test and anagram." Who does he have in mind? "Hence, the popularity of John Barth, a perfect U-novelist whose books are written to be taught, not to be read." Anthony Burgess describes the 800 pages of *Giles Goat-Boy* (1966, no apostrophe, as in *Finnegans Wake*) as "allegory, parody, didactic treatise, fable, religious codex." It must be taken unseriously to be taken seriously, the postmodern tease. The 768 pages of *The Sot-Weed Factor* (1960) Burgess describes as "an immense spook history of early Maryland." It is also an immense adventure in action and language.

John (Simmons) Barth (b. 1930) is not the dead-end novelist Vidal invents for his polemic. True, he makes demands of his readers and it is an advantage, if one embarks on one of his books, to have the stamina one develops through reading the triple-decker novels of the nineteenth century and through reading and enjoying Joyce, at least as far as the end of *Ulysses*. Barth is aware of the imperiled survival of the novel, though he locates the peril more in the Vidal than in the university camp. In 1967 he published in the *Atlantic Monthly* (hardly a specialist academic journal) his most contentious essay, "The Literature of Exhaustion." He takes his bearings from Jorge Luis Borges, who, were Barth Dante, would be his trusty Virgil. Borges says, "The fact is that every writer creates his own precursors. His work modifies our conception of the past, as it will modify the future." *Tradition and the Individual Talent,* with an Argentinean inflection. Barth looks forward, to the reader, "You who listen give me life in a manner of speaking. I won't hold you responsible." His concerns are three: "intermedia arts," Borges, and the third, which interests us, and entails "what I'm calling 'the literature of exhausted possibility'—or, more chicly, 'the literature of exhaustion.'" His argument is not existential: he concentrates on "the used-upness of certain forms or exhaustion of certain possibilities—by no means necessarily a cause for despair."

He is a rebel along traditional lines: "Art and its forms and techniques live in history and certainly do change. I sympathize with a remark attributed to Saul Bellow, that to be technically up to date is the least important attribute of a writer, though I would have to add that this least important attribute may be nevertheless essential." A modern poet writing in an idiom picked up from Keats or Swinburne would fight for readership despite the familiarity of his means. Yet many contemporary novelists publish what are formally "turn-of-the-century-type novels," last century, that is, though their language, characters, and themes are up to date. To Barth, this formal passivity of artists "makes them considerably less interesting (to me) than excellent writers who are also technically contemporary: Joyce and Kafka, for instance, in their time, and in ours, Samuel Beckett and Jorge Luis Borges." He is dismayed "to see so many of our writers following Dostoyevsky or Tolstoy or Flaubert or Balzac, when the real technical question seems to me to be how to succeed not even Joyce and Kafka, but those who've succeeded Joyce and Kafka and are now in the evenings of their own career."

It is about Beckett and Borges, not Greene and Bellow, and prescriptive only to the extent that it insists on the centrality of *informed* practice. That practice can be self-conscious and remain readable, entertaining, stimulating. Borges speaks of the "contamination of reality by dream," one of his recurrent themes, "and commenting upon such contaminations is one of his favorite fictional devices." Barth is interested through Borges in "how an artist may paradoxically turn the felt ultimacies of our time into material and means for his work—paradoxically because by doing so he transcends what had appeared to be his refutation, in the same way that the mystic who transcends finitude is said to be enabled to live, spiritually and physically, in the finite world." The novel need not be over as a creative genre, but it needs to be refigured. "If you happened to be Vladimir Nabokov you might address that felt ultimacy by writing *Pale Fire:* a fine novel by a learned pedant, in the form of a pedantic commentary on a poem invented for the purpose." He writes himself into the argument: "If you were the author of this paper, you'd have written something like *The Sot-Weed Factor* or *Giles Goat-Boy:* novels which imitate the form of the Novel, by an author who imitates the role of Author." It is the only way open to him, this acute self-consciousness, this acknowledgment that releases the story told from the speculative grip of the theorist, whose questions are incorporated in the form itself.

By the time he was twenty-three Barth was already a professor at Pennsylvania State University, publishing two witty, brief, issue-based realist novels, followed by his two postmodern masterpieces. *The Sot-Weed Factor* is an acquired taste that anyone who loves Fielding and Sterne will find palatable. The opening sentence is the opening paragraph, its elaborated syntax, its *architecture*, powerful preparatory pastiche. "In the last years of the Seventeenth Century there was to be found among the fops and fools of the London coffee-houses one rangy, gangling flitch called Ebenezer Cooke, more ambitious than talented, and yet more talented than prudent, who, like his friends-in-folly, all of whom were supposed to be educating at Oxford or Cambridge, had found the sound of Mother English more fun to game with than her sense to labor over, and so rather than applying himself to be the pains of scholarship, had learned the knack of versifying, and ground out quires of couplets after the fashion of the day, afroth with Joves and Jupiters, aclang with jarring rhymes, and string-taut with similes stretched to the snapping-point." The humor progresses in intensity, as in Alexander Pope's verse satire on education *The Dunciad,* from parody, wordplay, and relative lightness into the thick of cruelty, aberration, and deviancy. The velocity of the book is less a function of narrative than of formal variation and progression. The immense canvas takes us from England to America, through every walk of life, every genre and style.

*Giles Goat-Boy* explores the notion of the university as a species of universe. Its formal contentiousness is underlined by a publisher's message at the start that says (fact or fiction) that two of the associate editorial team resigned over the book's publication. Each editor gives reasons. The protagonist, as is only proper, is called Billy. He is also called George and Giles. Billy is raised by Max as a goat so as to sidestep human misery. The experiment does not work. Billy meets a woman and starts to crave education. He moves into the pass/fail world, proof against the saved/damned world. The structure of the university provides an effective allegorical frame. Barth has even more fun than Dickens did with naming. He has a veritable smorgasbord of sexual incidents of all kinds. Given Billy's goatboy origins, nothing seems too out of the ordinary. He rises by stages from goat to savior.

Barth went on to the State University of New York at Buffalo, a center of literary reinvention for prose and poetry, one of those U-places Vidal deprecates. Here his practice of long fiction was translated into a Borges-inspired practice of short fiction and essay, related forms. He ended his teaching career with over two decades at Johns Hopkins University, retiring in 1995.

It is possible to regard Barth as at heart a parodist. The same might be said of Joyce, or of Nabokov, playing off pretexts and stereotypes, linguistic resurrectionists, composing new bodies out of old body parts like Dr. Frankenstein. Something else is at work: the pressure of memory, a love of language that opens it out in both directions, to the literary past and to a future that it intends should remain rich even when the coinage changes. In 1980 Barth published an essay entitled "The Literature of Replenishment," also in the *Atlantic Monthly*. He reflects that the first essay was written in 1967 during the troubles in the university where he worked and in the country at large. The later essay is calmer, Jimmy Carterish, middle-aged, tenured. He pursues, in a stylish way, the chimera of postmodernism and snares it to his own satisfaction.

The danger in entertaining Vidal's category of U-novelist is that casual readers, empowered with this term, will apply it indiscriminately to any work that is formally unconventional, even by writers as hostile as Vidal is to the tyranny of the U. Harry Mathews (b. 1930) was the first American invited to membership of the French OuLiPo group, which, inspired by Raymond Queneau and Georges Perec, rejected whatever appeared with the face of familiarity in literary form and sought out different approaches to writing that responded to arbitrary and systematic "rules." He is associated with the New York poets, especially John Ashbery and Kenneth Koch. He transforms the novel every time he writes one, from his first, the brilliant, brittle *The Conversions* (1962), which keeps its secrets to and even beyond the very last moment and is delightful despite its opacity; to *Tlooth* (1966), a different sort of mystery, associated among other things with gender, and the title being the sound a boot makes when retracted from deep mud; to his masterpiece *The Sinking of the Odradek Stadium* (1975), an epistolary novel in which the quarry is treasure but the subject is language; and *Cigarettes* (1987) with a taproot, perhaps, in Arthur Schnitzler's *La Ronde*. In all four works, though there is progression and discernible shape, the narrative is richly woven of separate and separable fibers, and in response ideas of form need reformulating.

The Vienna-born American novelist Walter Abish (b. 1931) should also be cleared of Vidal's U charge, even though he has been an academic for much of his life and wears an eye-patch. His first fiction, *Alphabetical Africa* (1974), Updike says, "prankishly took the reader on an intricate trek through the alphabet, with the first and last chapters each confined to words beginning with 'a' and the chapters in between accumulatingly using and then losing words beginning with the remaining twenty-five letters." Vidal might have been justifiably impatient here. Updike sees Queneau and Perec in Abish's tea leaves. Abish ponderously declared, "Feeling a distrust of the understanding that is intrinsic to any communication, I decided to write a book in which my distrust became a determining factor upon which the flow of the narrative was largely predicated."

Abish's family fled Austria in 1940 and traveled as far east as Shanghai. He retains memories of Vienna, and its pastries find their way into his German fiction. They returned to Israel, where he served in the military and began reading and writing. In 1957 he took American citizenship and began teaching in American universities. His early stories are naturally in an absurdist style that has elements in common with Barthelme, though he is not so fluent or funny. His deadpan can be very dead, the humor deliberate; the collaging and plotting of his stories and the form of his first novel are overwrought. For him the New World with its fast-food gratification and ubiquitous materialism feels cheapening, and he is not Humbert Humbert.

What about the old world, though? His best novel, *How German Is It / Wie Deutsch ist es* (1980, no question mark in the title), may be a postmodern classic, though it has slipped from general view. When he wrote it, Abish had never been to Germany. He understood what had happened in Europe, how long-established and prosperous families had fallen from influence and respect. He was steeped in German-language literature of the twentieth century, and he understood that in West Germany the defeat of Nazism had been accompanied by an economic reconstruction based on American models that entailed the importation of American values. The Hargenaus are almost extinct apart from two brothers, a writer and an architect, whose task is to fit their selves and their survival into the alien pattern of postwar German history. The characters are placed in authorial positions, but they are never omniscient and are generally thwarted in their intentions. This is a thriller that, in Updike's words, harnesses "a passionately distrustful concern with modern Germany." Abish presents it as a palimpsest: the new, Americanized Germany is built on the site of a concentration camp. History keeps breaking through the new surface. Postwar democracy is bent out of shape by persistences of class and snobbery, and terrorist explosions mar the idyllic summer of the action. Abish populates the small city of Brumholdstein with people in situations as credible and at once as representative as those we encounter in the realist fiction of the German novelist Heinrich Böll. Sexual relations are numerous and easy, metaphors for power transactions. An unstable world of paradoxes, contradictions, and perils: formal experiment becomes seriously playful, the plot left ragged at the end. There is no question mark in the title because there is no answer to the issues raised, summarized by Updike: "How could the Germans have committed these unspeakable acts? How uniquely German was the Holocaust?"

From Vidal's point of view, bucktoothed, anonymous Thomas (Ruggles) Pynchon (Jr.) (b. 1937) is prime U-novelist. After two years' service in the U.S. Navy, he returned to Cornell (where he had studied science for two years) to read English. He attended classes with Nabokov, who had no recollection of him, though Mrs. Nabokov remembered his handwriting. He is an heir of Nabokov, but of the author of *Ada* rather than of *Pale Fire*. He enjoys, half a century after *V.* (1963), his first book, the reputation of a challenging experimental writer, at least in the U. Writers in the wider world resisted him. He is a shibboleth, marking a breach in modern fiction between writers who, however experimentally, address a general readership, and those who write for readers attuned to theory and the disciplines or reading that some institutions of learning accommodate, in every possible sense.

Anthony Burgess looks on the bright side of experimental writers. He persuaded himself that *V.* and *The Crying of Lot 49* (1966) were "brilliant higher games" and that *Gravity's Rainbow* (1973), despite its rainbow technique of "high color, symbolism, prose tricks," actually had substance. The subject appealed to him, the fictionalized Wartime British Special Operations Executive. In 1944 Tyrone Slothrop, an American lieutenant, is seconded to the Executive to study V-2 dispersal patterns over London: a simple premise, endowed with formal and cross-cultural possibilities. One need only place the book in the context of other almost contemporary and enormously popular American books about the Second World War—*Catch-22* (which Heller started writing in 1953) and *Slaughterhouse-Five,* for example—to see how suddenly fiction could be ingested by and conform to the fashions of the academy.

Peter Ackroyd, a plucky twenty-four-year-old in the year of its publication, took *Gravity's Rainbow* on, noting that it "becomes a specimen of Eng. Lit, as soon as it comes off the presses" and is "an excruciating bore." What kind of book are we dealing with? "It is ostensibly a picaresque version of the last days of the Second World War." But the war itself is not his subject but his subject matter, "the world is Mr. Pynchon's oyster, and his private war radiates through time and space with as much subtlety as a stain." The language is at the root of the problem, "a crammed and choking prose" in which the words relate less to a perceived world and more to gauged effects. "Joyce created a style, and Pynchon merely borrows stylistics."

There are fine lyric moments, but brief and scattered. In the fiction of Barth there is a progression of registers, as the novel advances the dominant key changes. But here modulations are local, the elision between lyrical passages and passages of "pure obscenity" seems unjustified beyond local effect. "This is not, in fact, a terribly 'difficult' book," Ackroyd concludes. "It has its ups and downs but nowhere reaches the level of experimentation of a Joyce or Sarraute.

It remains gloomily and sullenly ensconced within the realistic tradition." Having dabbled in experiment, it "always returns to that bankrupt heritage which it carries as a dwarf would carry a blind giant." Ackroyd in his own fiction would, in due course, play some Pynchonesque games.

Vidal's in his 1976 essay "American Plastic" said, "The energy expended in reading *Gravity's Rainbow* is, for anyone, rather greater than that expended by Pynchon in the actual writing. This is entropy with a vengeance." There is a specific aesthetic issue: "Energy and intelligence are not in balance, and the writer fails in his ambition to be a god of creation. Yet his ambition and his failure are very much in the cranky, solipsistic American vein, and though I doubt if anyone will ever want to read all of this book, it will certainly be taught for a very long (delta) time." The privileging of crankiness and solipsism has licensed a good deal of *mere* experiment and tarred with the same brush the genuinely innovative work of modernism and academically indulged creativity. The backlash, in turn, privileges reaction in contemporary fiction, as though the lessons of the modernisms that flow unbroken from Flaubert through James, Joyce, Lawrence, and Woolf had quite lost their energy.

John Gardner in *On Moral Fiction* contrasts contemporary Continental writers with "writers like Robert Coover in *The Public Burning*, who reduces large and complex forces to humorless comic-strip cartoons"—we are in the zone of earnest art masquerading as comic—"or Thomas Pynchon, who, in *Gravity's Rainbow*, carelessly praises the schlock of the great past (King Kong, etc.) and howls against the schlock of the present, which, he thinks, is numbing and eventually will kill us." Because the tone is uncertain, it is hard to read intention: "We may defend *Gravity's Rainbow* as satire, but whether it is meant to be satire or sober analysis is not clear. It is a fact that, even to the rainbow of bombs said to be circling us, the world is not as Pynchon says it is." Pynchon is aware of some of the problems his work presents, even to him. In an introduction to *Slow Learner* (1984), a collection of apprentice pieces, he seems candid. The early writing is overblown, he says, overly referential. "Make it literary," he would instruct himself, and literary he made it, larding the work with allusions, trying to write in accents and dialects before his ear was attuned, generally writing in excess of the occasion and with an eye always on *effect*. He acquired greater thrift when he came to publish his first two books, and the regression in *Gravity's Rainbow* is to a different strategy, and quality, of overwriting.

*V.* received the William Faulkner Foundation Award as the "best début novel" of 1963. It is a quest, with some of the features of science fiction that abound in his work, and the quest is for the mysterious entity "V" whose material and philosophical nature are elusive. Scientific and technical language is used: the author wrote the book while working in Seattle for Boeing. His background in physics, and the writing he had done for Boeing as a technical journalist, not to mention the manufacturing and big-business environment, contributed thematically and politically to his long-term political coloring. His fascination with the processes of entropy in science and society are defined here. The book is marked by his characteristic game playing, with names first of all.

The theme of the quest, and the epithetic naming of characters, also mark *The Crying of Lot 49.* Pynchon leaned heavily on his undergraduate courses in science and literature when he wrote this relatively short novel, remarkable for its strange incidents and recondite and scattergun erudition. Oedipa Maas is his protagonist, her mission is to be executor for the estate of her onetime lover and late employer Pierce Inverarity. The real names as well as the invented ones draw attention to themselves here; for example, in Mexico the painter Remedios Varo's work is evoked, and her given name takes on a symbolic resonance. Her painting of the eight women, the weavers of reality in their tower, is a potent borrowed symbol. Pynchon continually makes and does not quite make connections with other books that have fed into his imagination, other stories. Oedipa conducts her miasmic mission that leads into unexpected worlds and dimensions. The plot is complicated, sometime with humor and satire. It is a busy narrative highroad, with inevitable switchbacks and collisions. There is substance abuse in the story, and perhaps in the writing some of the digressions, the disproportions, may derive from a Burroughsian excess. When *The Crying of Lot 49* reached 155 pages and seemed finished, he told his agent it was "a short story, but with gland trouble," urging her to "unload it on some poor sucker."

*Gravity's Rainbow* was unanimously selected by the fiction panel for the Pulitzer Prize of 1974, but their decision was vetoed by the board, who described the book as "turgid," "overwritten," and "unreadable" as well as occasionally "obscene." It *is* occasionally obscene, but so are many Pulitzer novels, and being "unreadable" never stopped books from winning prizes. He revisits the themes of his first two novels and the short stories but here at much greater length, and with more complex plotting. Academics have provided ample secondary literature to accompany it, including guidebooks. Though it has little in common with Joyce, his name is evoked by teachers describing the difficulty students will encounter. Technically the most interesting aspect is the handling of time, the way the narrators know only what they know at the time, so that the reader may be continually in a more informed position, seeing how the speaker sees but aware also of what is not, or not yet, visible. Thus the knowledge of major themes, such as the Holocaust, dawns slowly and appallingly over the novel's consciousnesses. This provides an epistemological irony that would be more potent were it not for the cartoonish elements, the overly vivid coloring that diminishes the subject matter.

Some regard Pynchon's 1997 novel *Mason & Dixon,* about Charles Mason and Jeremiah Dixon, the surveyors who plotted the Mason Dixon line, as his best. He spent over twenty years on it, and it is his most straightforward and accessible book. The governing point of view is that of the unorthodox clergyman the reverend Wicks Cherrycoke (no getting away from Pynchon's name games), who wishes to entertain his family on a winter's evening. This Dickensian element contributes to the relative ease with which characters are evoked, their psychological depth and circumstantial coherence, the historical accountability. It seems that Pynchon the philosopher, the game player and orchestrator, has trusted story and character and even effaced himself before their imperatives. Because of the period in which the book is set, on the eve of the Revolutionary War, the world portrayed is simpler, the eighteenth-century coherence of the story is appropriate. It is an age of innocence, unlike the world of 1944 with its permanent distortions that crumple the structures of *Gravity's Rainbow.*

*Against the Day* (2006) is 1,085 pages long. One reviewer said it read "like the sort of imitation of a Thomas Pynchon novel that a dogged but ungainly fan of this author's might have written on Quaaludes." Between the Chicago World Fair of 1893 and the end of the First World War the novel exercises its characters (their names sillier even ever), more than one hundred of them, with worldwide and otherworld geographical span. This is *Ragtime* plus, and minus. Despite its extent, the structure is elliptical, complicated, full of puzzles. If one could reread it, would a grand complexity rise out of the sense of mere complication? It is a book to study, not to read. At the center of its web is Webb, a onetime miner turned radical (bomber, anarchist) killed by agents of a (naturally) evil capitalist. His children set out to avenge his death. It is hard not to think of Webb as a latter-day Finnegan in whose wake so many obscure father-son, parent-child fictions unfold, from Barthelme's hilarious and psychologically acute *The Dead Father* to—this. Here as in *V.* and *Gravity's Rainbow* Pynchon wants to see if and how the past can tell the future (our present) about itself, what might lie latent in events and characters. Webb the terrorist, the justified terrorist we are tempted to believe, read through post-9/11 eyes, is a character different from the one the novel's present proposes. The past rewrites and overwrites itself, yet at some level in the palimpsest, allowing for deep erasures, "original" stories exist. James Wood describes as "hysterical realism" the excess of detail and overkill of contemporary writers, including DeLillo, Rushdie, and Pynchon, each making a full fist of clutched straws: one never knows which detail is to prove finally significant.

Pynchon's legacy is variously read. Some hold him responsible for surrendering the art of experimental fiction and the legacy of modernism to the academy. The modernists and the more adventurous postmodern writers pit art against the commercial imperatives that have driven the fiction industry for years, the habituation of readership, the promotion of fashion. Another reading of the legacy declares Pynchon the father, godfather, or grandfather of cyber-punk, insisting on social breakdown and IT sophistication. The plots have to do with *plotting,* against the establishment or, sinisterly, sweetly, against the electronic media themselves.

"Pynchon was still happening back in the late seventies when I first started thinking of being a writer," said Jonathan (Earl) Franzen (b. 1959), underlining how briefly the new stays new, "though I didn't know about him until a friend quickly pointed out that I was writing like him." Writing like him meant writing badly, elaborately, with his and Robert Coover's "strenuously vivid and all-knowing prose." Pynchon was an influence to be written through. The first full exposure was at university. He had already thought up the plot of his first novel, *The Twenty-Seventh City* (1988), as a college sophomore. He majored in German at Swarthmore, spent his sophomore year in Munich, and went to Berlin on a Fulbright after graduation. That is when he got deeply into Pynchon, after graduation. *Gravity's Rainbow* "utterly consumed me. It was like getting the flu to read that book." So bad was it that his love letters became irritatingly inflamed: "My then-fiancée . . . hated those letters and made her hatred of them known," driving Franzen away from the voice he was imitating. He was also strenuously "copying the sentence rhythms and comic dialogue of Don DeLillo." He adjusted because he was in love. The choice was between brawny comradeship and mature relationship, "in which case that kind of boy writing, however brilliant and masterful, was necessarily subordinate." Later on he registered debts "to various female writers—Alice Munro, Christina Stead, Flannery O'Connor, Jane Smiley, Paula Fox, to name a few," that were more substantial and lasting than those to Pynchon.

His real point of departure was, he later claimed, "Kafka's novel *The Trial,* as taught by the best literature professor I ever had." That book "opened my eyes to the greatness of what literature can do, and made me want to try to create some myself." Kafka's Josef K "is at once a sympathetic and unjustly persecuted Everyman and a self-pitying and guilt-denying criminal" and he became "my portal to the possibilities of fiction as a vehicle of self-investigation: as a method of engagement with the difficulties and paradoxes of my own life." He harnesses Kafka to his own wagon. "Kafka teaches us how to love ourselves even as we're being merciless toward ourselves; how to remain humane in the face of the most awful truths about ourselves." For Primo Levi Kafka was painful to read, for Franzen he is a facilitator.

The first of his four substantial novels, *The Twenty-Seventh City,* draws on the history of St. Louis, in whose suburbs he grew up, the city's century of decline from the 1870s heyday of being fourth in the nation. Franzen describes it as "a sci-fi novel that is all *fi* and no *sci*," and "a concept-driven omnibus fiction in which a group of influential and politically ambitious Indians, led by the former police commissioner of Bombay" (S. Jammu, thirty-five, a strict and effective female officer) "infiltrate the bureaucracy of an unspectacular Midwestern town and terrorize its residents." Martin Probst the successful contractor combines Ibsen's Masterbuilder and Kafka's Joseph K. The book engages Franzen's literary pre-cursors and was critically approved, but nothing more. Set on the East Coast of the United States, *Strong Motion* (1992), about the Holland family and its travails when earthquakes begin to unsettle their world, literally and metaphorically, was also praised but failed to make the big time.

The main personal risk Franzen took in his fiction was to leave satire behind, having neither the earnestness nor the anger required for it. But his fiction has a moral mission, campaigning "against the values I dislike: senti-mentality, weak narrative, overly lyrical prose, solipsism, self-indulgence, mi-sogyny and other parochialisms, sterile game-playing, overt didacticism, moral simplicity, unnecessary difficulty, informational fetishes, and so on." He does not like Joyce. He never liked Lawrence: *Sons and Lovers* because too close to his own experience, its lack of irony makes it "icky" (an adjective he applies also to the effect of McEwan's early novels). He does not read Pynchon anymore.

Before the big success of his midwestern family chronicle *The Corrections* (2001) Franzen was broke, depressed, stuck in an unhappy marriage. The diffi-cult decisions and guilts of divorce passed, and he was released into becoming the "Great American Novelist" cover-boy on *Time* magazine, the first writer to bite the hand of Oprah Winfrey, whose choices of book for her television show he described as sometimes "schmaltzy," though after a decade's feud Oprah chose *Freedom* (2010) and declared herself honored to have him on the show. He declared himself honored to be there and brought the feud to a close. Anne Tyler thinks him "an amazing writer," but sometimes rather "cruel to his characters. I didn't like Patty," the focal character in especially the second half of *Freedom*, "and I wonder if I could have lived with her for however long it took him to write *Freedom*."

Franzen is a champion of third-person narrative: first-person is only permis-sible if the voice is real and compelling, a necessary part of the fiction and not just a means of delivery. He creates strong women characters, and his first wife, herself a writer, and his strong-willed mother remain ghostly presences in his fiction years after his divorce and his mother's death. The success of *The Correc-tions* became a problem in that he felt he had played out its formal inventions—"the hyper-vivid characters, the interlocking-novellas structure, the leitmotifs and extended metaphors"—and yet they constrained him and it took time to break loose. With *The Corrections* he revised his view of the modern reader, whom he had scant respect for in the essays in *How to Be Alone* (2002). Now writing was a kind of collaboration. By the time he broke through to *Freedom,* after false starts and almost false endings, he had learned two things: "that a large novel could be constructed out of multiple short novels, each of them building to a crisis in which the main character can no longer escape reality," and that the reader was his—friend. He himself had once stood in a long queue waiting "to get five seconds with William Gaddis, just so I could tell him how great I thought *The Recognitions* was." That is what being a reader is, the person who invests time and money in a writer, bringing validation. This harmony between producer and consumer has a consolatory, American feel about it: the satisfied client as aesthetic objective.

In his essays and the short memoir *The Discomfort Zone* (2006) Franzen talks like a counselor. This habit he has passed to Jeffrey Eugenides (b. 1960) and other younger writers who practice a detachable moralizing and deliver civic asides. It is good to know Franzen has overcome difficulties in his life, but the fiction does him ampler justice. The staging of his grief after the suicide of his friend David Foster Wallace is disproportionate, or rather, the way he tells it is, in effect how he made time for it, as though the valves of grief could be controlled. Perhaps for some writers they can.

# 37

# Genre

Daphne du Maurier, Barbara Cartland, Catherine Cookson, et al.; Bret Harte,

Zane Grey, et al.; Raymond Chandler, Dashiell Hammett, Elmore Leonard, Agatha Christie,

Dorothy L. Sayers, et al.; H. P. Lovecraft, Stephen King, et al.; Robert A. Heinlein,

Isaac Asimov, Arthur C. Clarke, Ray Bradbury, Philip K. Dick, Ursula Le Guin, et al.

Introducing H. P. Lovecraft, Joyce Carol Oates notes how "readers of genre fiction, unlike readers of what we presume to call 'literary fiction,' assume a tacit contract between themselves and the writer: they understand that they will be manipulated, but the question is how? and when? and with what skill? and to what purpose?" Within the contract, they accept a number of artistic limitations. They expect the story to be "plot-ridden, fantastical, or absurd, populated by whatever pseudo-characters," but the crucial thing is that "genre fiction is always resolved, while 'literary fiction' makes no such promises; there is no contract between reader and writer for, in theory at least, each work of literary fiction is original, and, in essence, 'about' its own language." Something or nothing happens. "Genre fiction is addictive, literary fiction, unfortunately, is not."

The insatiable hungers of Hollywood have done much to stimulate and refine genre fiction. In the eighteenth and nineteenth centuries, within a single novel elements of various genres cohabited more or less comfortably: romance, mystery, adventure, horror, speculation, suspense. A movie makes choices. In relation to audiences, it calculates and makes demands of a writer. In adaptation, certain elements in classic novels are discarded, colors heightened, flavors added. Sometimes it is a matter of correcting attitudes and emphases where politics and prejudices have changed. A film is a collaboration between author, filmmaking industry, and market. The genre novel similarly collaborates with the publisher, who interprets and projects a market's demands onto the author. Most genres of film grew out of, then outgrew, literary conventions. They make their own narrative demands: the big and little screens increasingly determine what happens on the page. "It's the economy, stupid."

A successful genre novel fulfills a series of obligations. Genre novels are not always chastely faithful to a *single* genre. Cross-genre work can fulfill demands of two markets at once. A historical romance, a mystery western, widen a book's market. Genre fiction is where literature and the market unashamedly meet.

Some publishers "subsidize" literary books from the proceeds of genre publishing. Others are happy simply to take the profit.

Romance fiction, rooted in Richardson, Austen, the Brontës, degraded and made lucrative by Ouida, Marie Corelli, and other writers encountered in the nineteenth and early twentieth centuries, has the clearest generic pedigree and is commercially the most significant. In 2004 in the United States, one set of statistics suggests that 55 percent of all paperback books sold were romance novels. In Britain the proportion was said to run at 20 percent. More recent statistics (2012) indicate that 44 percent of romances purchased today are in e-book format, fueling the e-book revolution; of the rest, 46 percent are in paperback, 9 percent hardcover or other binding, and 1 percent audio. The genre is popular throughout the world, but the majority of romance authors is Anglophone. Romance has a generally well-washed and accessorized aspect, and when translated into the world's languages, old-fashioned Hollywood values dominate it. This is one part, and not a small one, of the colonial enterprise, romance winning hearts, if not minds, and conditioning the global libido.

In 2008 in the United States romance fiction is said to have been worth $1.37 billion in actual book sales, quite apart from subsidiary rights income. Over 7,000 novels were published in the genre. The Romance Writers of America association provides the generically flag-waving statistics that 74 million people read at least one romance novel in 2008. Most readers—perhaps as many as 90 percent—are female. Were we to go back in time and scale down our statistics to achieve a kind of like-for-like, the situation a hundred, two and even three hundred years ago would be in line. The great fire in Lilliput, which Gulliver extinguishes with a flood of urine, was caused by a maid falling asleep over a romance novel and overturning her taper. It was by means of such romances that Nastiah, way back in this book's Introduction, managed to endure her hopeless personal life.

And beginning in the eighteenth century, an intelligent and literate woman abandoned or widowed could sometimes make a decent living out of writing novels. The heroine-centered romance remains a largely female tradition of writers catering for a female market, purveying excitement, titillation, and resolution. A close focus is provided in which the microcosm of a relationship decisively displaces the macrocosm of the world (in John Donne's words, "She is all states, and all princes I; / Nothing else is"), and our concern is limited to two (or three) people in the teeth of circumstance and the world at large. The genre is wholesome, heterosexual, nonadulterous. If there is an age differential, it is balanced in favor of the male party. If the writer were to admit homosexuality or adultery or a subversive age difference (an older woman and a younger man, a much older man and a much younger woman), she would trip the novel out of romance and into the realm of literary fiction, where moral formulae and formal constraints make different demands.

Ah, and a happy ending. Or if not happy, then at least emotionally ravishing, where something truly dramatic occurs and the heart is desolated (the heroine's, the reader's), as in *Rebecca* by Daphne du Maurier (1907–1989), a writer who grew on a creative if erratic family tree. Henry James got to know and eventually to like her grandfather, the *Punch* cartoonist George du Maurier (1834–1896), whose writing was in some ways as unexpected and artless as hers. He started late with *Peter Ibbetson* (1891), a novel of separation, reunion, and heartbreak that was made into a successful film in 1917, and again in 1935, and progressed to the more memorable, still curiously innocent, *Trilby* (1894), a Gothic romance in which the eponymous heroine becomes an opera diva thanks to the infernal hypnotic devices of Svengali. Yet Svengali is also tragic, in the manner of Faust: he has to make do with a simulacrum, his assistant Gecko comments, while the real and still implausibly innocent creature belonged to her betrothed: "'He had but to say *"Dors!"* and she suddenly became an unconscious Trilby of marble, who could produce wonderful sounds—just the sounds he wanted and nothing else—and think his thoughts and wish his wishes—and love him at his bidding with a strange, unreal, factitious love . . . just his own love for himself turned inside out— . . . It was not worth having! I was not even jealous!'" The heroine caused a sensation and gave her name to many things, most durably a narrow-brimmed fedora. James makes Trilby sound like a passionate Pre-Raphaelite heroine, alarming and fatal in her coy charm. David Lodge explored James and du Maurier's friendship in *Author, Author.*

Daphne's childhood was surrounded by theater. Her mother was an actress, her father an actor-manager with whom she enjoyed an intense relationship. She herself developed actorly skills to mask and express her personality, or personalities. Details about her romantic life, which included intense relationships with other women, came out after her death, to be set in the balance against her well-mannered married life and motherhood. Often she seemed cold and aloof to journalists and to the public. She was protecting a complicated privacy.

Her first novel, *The Loving Spirit,* was published in 1931. Stories, plays, and more than a dozen novels followed. She is best remembered for the film versions of her books and stories, including *Rebecca, Jamaica Inn,* and *The Birds* (all three directed by Alfred Hitchcock), *Frenchman's Creek, Hungry Hill, My Cousin Rachel, Don't Look Now,* and *The Scapegoat,* starring Alex Guinness. Gore Vidal worked on the screenplay and recalls: "She used to send me helpful memos; and though she could not spell the simplest words or adhere to any agreed-upon grammar, her prose surged with vulgar invention and powerful feeling of the sort that cannot be faked." When he uses the word "vulgar," it is intended as a compliment, sort of; and when P. G. Wodehouse sends her up as Daphne Dolores Morehead, it is without malice. She can evoke the places she most loved, in particular Cornwall and the areas around Fowey and Polruan where she summered for many years and where *Rebecca* is set. She was caught up in the passionate absurdity of her fiction; hers was a Gothic vision rather than a Gothic conceit, and this gives her novels integrity that, if the reader is able to suspend ironic resistance, becomes compelling. If the reader has seen the film, the language matters less.

Her pace as a narrator is instinctive, and she understands how to create suspense. She wrote *Rebecca* in Alexandria, Egypt, where her husband had been posted. It has the intensity of longing in its invention of a landscape. "Last night I dreamt I went to Manderley again," it opens, and we are with her in the dream. Her courtship with Maxim de Winter, their return to the doomed house presided over by Mrs. Danvers with her hostile harping on the late Mrs. de Winter, Rebecca, and the deepening shadows as we shift into a minor key, build as though the story were being told rather than written. There is shipwreck, murder, blackmail, pregnancy, deception, but most of all, true love of a kind that makes the dreadful climax palatable.

Du Maurier's popularity, now waning, was for generations unassailable. Her books were among those most borrowed from libraries. She is not notably original. *Rebecca* owes obvious debts to *Jane Eyre,* and the author was accused of plagiarism by the Brazilian novelist Carolina Nabuco. She would have resisted inclusion in the romance category: after all, she is not mistress of the happily-ever-after ending, and a Gothic element darkens her writing. It was dark enough for Hitchcock. Within the romance category she is both a rule and an exception.

Two romance novelists who stand at opposite ends of the bookshelf, as it were, are du Maurier's older contemporaries Barbara Cartland (1901–2000) and Catherine Cookson (née Catherine Ann McMullen, 1906–1998). Born in Tyne Dock, South Shields, near Jarrow, Cookson experienced life below stairs: she became a Dame of the British Empire and her books have sold—adding those written under pseudonyms—over 120 million copies. She took up writing as therapy after serious physical and nervous troubles, publishing her first novel when she was well into her forties. By the time she died she had written nearly a hundred books. She disliked being called a romance novelist, insisting her books were historical romances in an older, fuller tradition than the commercial romances of the day. They have fed television, and her books followed du Maurier's as most borrowed from the library, dominating until 2002. There is earnest authenticity about her writing, as about her self-effacement, her shunning of publicity, which is more than can be said for Dame (Mary) Barbara Hamilton Cartland, always furred and diamonded, her portraits exquisitely lighted. She insisted that her life was of a piece with her romance fiction, and she knew the value of publicity. She proved a phenomenal best-selling author, starting with the success of *Jigsaw* (1923), which was issued as an e-book in 2011 with the following description: "*JIG-SAW* is the story of a young girl on her first entry into the rich and lavish world of London's society in the 1920s. Her struggle with temptation, and her search for true happiness, makes *JIG-SAW* a must for all Barbara Cartland fans and romantics the world over."

She has fans more than readers, and she may be the biggest-selling author in the world, with more than a billion copies to her credit by the mid-1990s. It is hard to say how many books she wrote, hundreds clearly, and often the same book with variant titles and a different cover, but readers seldom notice or complain. In 1974 her rate of productivity suddenly shot up to fourteen titles per year from a steady flow of between two and six. Something had happened, and it kept happening: in 1977 the flood gates were ajar, twenty-seven books, and so it went, in 1981 twenty-two new titles, in 1982 twenty-seven—years of what had become her rather standard productivity. In 1986 she felt she was flagging but she still managed twenty-six books. She often dictated, which saved her a good deal of labor. Those who remember her clipped staccato know how rapidly she spoke, without pause for breath or thought. One critic said it took longer to read than to write her novels, which may be true, but to dictate them to a proficient secretary? She felt no discomfort at being described as a romance novelist.

Other contemporaries and near contemporaries were also best sellers, with greater claim on attention, such as the punctilious, retiring Georgette Heyer (1902–1974), who created out of laborious research the Regency romance and wrote detective fiction for light relief, one of each every year; and Mary (Florence Elinor) Stewart (b. 1916), who combines romance, history, and suspense in original ways, and who is able to create credible foreign settings, especially on the Greek islands and in the Middle East. Her five Merlin chronicles are highly entertaining Arthuriana. The list of romance novelists runs to several hundred, some highly successful like the very English Barbara Taylor Bradford (b. 1933), who started late in 1979 with *A Woman of Substance* and made her publishers rich, with sales of 32 million worldwide; and equally English Jilly Cooper (b. 1937), who moved into romance and something foreshadowing chick-lit; and others larger than life, like the insistently American Danielle Steel (b. 1947), whose novels wear Prada and seem devised to be filmed, with abundant and colorful locations and well-groomed heroines. These can represent the substantial iceberg.

The permissible erotics of romance fiction are distinctive: the character whose satisfaction engages the reader is generally the heroine: her, rather than his, fulfillment is at issue, and that fulfillment is variously explored. The fruits of a strict but ostentatious chastity are sacramental and orgasmic: it is a matter of calculation, timing, and control. The example of *Pamela* told for something and remains perennial, if not tenable. Romance heroines are generally virgins, whereas the men—generally—are not. All the same, a hero once brought to heel is capable of loyalty and honesty if properly handled, and generally, too, is quite *clean*. According to surveys (and this is an area of writing where it behooves the author to take the findings of surveys to heart in plotting the next book), cleanliness weighs heavier in the balance than a manly physique. A hunk who does not shower does not score.

Feminism is not keen on romance fiction, but sometimes its modern offspring, chick-lit, passes muster. This is a rapidly dating but still contemporary kind of romance in which women achieve a mastery and the web the writer draws is more complex than in the conventional romance, entailing family and other woman friends with whom to share experiences. The term was first used in publishing in 1995 and it has stuck, though claims that chick-lit is postfeminist are exaggerated. The sex in chick-lit books is more frank, sometimes comical, and generally more nuanced than in the traditional romance, where it can be peremptory and is usually out of sight. Helen Fielding (b. 1958) wrote *Bridget Jones's Diary* (1996) and *Bridget Jones: The Edge of Reason* (1999) on the back of her newspaper columns, a kind of ur-blog novel that, thanks to her style and the effects of one entertaining and one dreadful film, sold together over 13 million copies. Like the mis-mem (misery memoir), the chick-lit phenomenon of the 1990s belongs to its period, and both may be on the way out. One or two extraordinary talents could reverse the decline.

The American poet John Ashbery notes how in Britain, "Americans, if they're going to be accepted as writers, have to act 'like Americans.' They have to be loud-mouthed, oratorical." "They loved Bret Harte, whom nobody reads anymore, just because he came to England and walked around in boots and a cowboy hat. *This* is an American, so we can, you know, we can understand this, because the Americans are a bunch of Yahoos." Henry James is equally puzzled by (Francis) Bret Harte (1836–1902), and how he made it as an author by exploiting the Wild West, its characters, the largeness of nature framing the almost unrestrained impulses of man, to the exclusion of other subject matter. Was Harte's production the result of integrity of purpose, or did he calculate on the market? When Dickens died in 1870, Harte wrote a sweet elegy with entire conviction, "Dickens in Camp." It begins in a western setting:

> Above the pines the moon was slowly drifting,
>     The river sang below;

> The dim Sierras, far beyond, uplifting
> > Their minarets of snow.

A conventional western scene is set and then developed. The poet, a Scheherazade figure, entrances the campfire gamblers and loiterers with a familiar story. It is *The Old Curiosity Shop* he shares with them. They are tamed, as is nature itself:

> The fir-trees, gathering closer in the shadows,
> > Listened in every spray,
> While the whole camp, with 'Nell' on English meadows,
> > Wandered and lost their way.

The memory transports the poet back in time, and in space leads him to connect with another country and time.

> Lost is that camp! But let its fragrant story
> > Blend with the breath that thrills
> With hop-vines' incense all the pensive glory
> > That fills the Kentish hills.

> And on that grave where English oak and holly
> > And laurel wreaths intwine,
> Deem it not all a too presumptuous folly,
> > —This spray of Western pine!

It is a well-judged and moving poem, though we no longer respond to Little Nell. Harte's popularity grew, and faded; he took a consular post in Germany, then in Glasgow, finally retiring to London, where he continued to write his westerns with unabated energy and renewed success.

Harte could be a funny writer, as his *Condensed Novels: New Burlesques,* spoofs of Dickens, Wilkie Collins, Cooper, Charlotte Brontë, Conan Doyle, Kipling, Marie Corelli, and Hall Caine, among many others, reveal. His choice of western subject matter and his development of the western genre were not due to a lack of technical skill. Kipling admired his stories; he said of his arrival in San Francisco, "A reporter asked me what I thought of the city, and I made answer suavely that it was hallowed ground to me, because of Bret Harte. That was true. 'Well,' said the reporter, 'Bret Harte claims California, but California don't claim Bret Harte. He's been so long in England that he's quite English.'" Harte's is a wild (far) West of miners and gamblers, which even Oscar Wilde admired, almost without irony. The cowboys come later. They are the real epigones of the western.

Sinclair Lewis's Babbitt likes western movies with their "industrious shooting of revolvers." Frank Norris's McTeague "dreamed of a cowboy's life and saw himself in an entrancing vision involving silver spurs and untamed broncos. He told himself that Trina had cast him off, that his best friend had 'played him for a sucker,' that the 'proper caper' was to withdraw from the world entirely." And his dream, derived from reading the cheap magazines and novelettes of the day, comes true after a fashion, not as he imagined it. Life imitates art but is never quite congruent with it.

Carl Van Doren wrote *Contemporary American Novelists, 1900–1920,* in 1922, relatively near the beginning of the western. He notes that few cowboy stories live up to Harte's tales of gamblers and prospectors: "The cowboy has regularly moved on the plane of the sub-literary—in dime novels and, latterly, in moving pictures." He is type more than character, "largely inarticulate except for his rude songs and ballads; formula and tradition caught him early and in fiction stiffened one of the most picturesque of human beings—a modern Centaur, an American Cossack, a western picaro." A stereotype, he straddles his bronco, waves his six-shooter in the air or twirls his lariat. He is busy, he "rounds up stampeding cattle, makes fierce war on Mexicans, Indians, and rival outfits, and ardently, humbly woos the ranchman's daughter or a timorous school-ma'am." Van Doren portrays him waiting patiently, for as yet he "has no Homer, no Gogol, no Fenimore Cooper even, though he invites a master of some sort to take advantage of a thrilling opportunity." What heroes await their Homer! All the Williams: Buffalo Bill, Billy the Kid, Wild William Hickok, to begin with. Certainly in the foretime of the emerging western genre is Fenimore Cooper, and farther back Sir Walter Scott. The period the western draws on is roughly the last half of the nineteenth century. The first "modern" western was *The Virginian* by Owen Wister, a book that later western writers take as a secure point of departure. It appeared in 1902, the year Bret Harte died.

The enormous list of romance novelists is predominantly female. The western novelists are almost entirely male, with given names like Todhunter, Squire, Courtney, Wade, Bret, Chad, Chuck, Clay, Walt, Dusty, Travis, and Oakley. The readership for westerns is largely male (though there are more women writers of westerns than male writers of conventional romances). One of the earliest successful authors of westerns was Karl May (1842–1912), a German writer who did not visit the United States until his stories were written and never got out West at all, but his books appealed profoundly to German-speakers all over Middle Europe, and to Franz Kafka in Prague, not for their literary qualities but because they traced a wide-open fictional world in which he could almost believe.

The western writer my generation was reared on was (Pearl) Zane Grey (1872–1939). He was a dentist, a baseball player, and at last a novelist with ninety books to his credit. He died, relatively young, a millionaire, but angry and dissatisfied, in part because the critics never gave him what he believed was his literary due. He regarded himself not as a genre novelist but as a novelist plain and simple, and he answered his critics with a vehemence that must have gratified them. The case against him was like the case against Harte, that his West was not *real*. What is real is the fiction of the West that he creates. *Riders of the Purple Sage* (1912) remains his best novel, with descriptions that, though less contemplative, are vivid in the ways that Cather's are. This and others of the earlier westerns read well aloud and appeal to young listeners. Over a hundred films and television adaptations, more and less faithful, have been based on Grey's books.

The western as a literary genre has been in decline for three decades, though the novels of A. B. Guthrie Jr., Jack Schaefer, Louis L'Amour, and others retain their readership and every month a few new westerns are published. The comic book industry, which feeds on the western as it does on romance, continues to thrive, and thanks to film the conventions are kept alive. Writers of the quality of Elmore Leonard, Cormac McCarthy, and Larry McMurtry can assume a shared culture in their readers when they publish books like *Blood Meridian* and *Lonesome Dove* (both 1985).

———·———

Rather than write poetry, Dylan Thomas once said, he would frankly prefer to "lie in a hot bath sucking boiled sweets and reading Agatha Christie." How unstable the romance and the western are as genres: the tradition of the crime and detective novel is more strictly patrolled, and the literary qualities to be found within its constraints are more generally acknowledged. If the romance novel has its roots in Richardson and the western in Scott and Cooper, the crime and detective genre is in a line that includes Dickens and Wilkie Collins, the Poe of the Dupin tales, Stevenson and Conan Doyle and, as it gets grittier, Arthur Morrison. In the nineteenth century there is already an abundance of mysteries requiring detection: What guilty secret is eating away at Jane Fairfax? Why does Mr. Tulkinghorn have Lady Deadlock over a barrel? What does Raffles have on Mr. Bulstrode, and what is the sinister laugh that troubles Thornfield Hall? All that was needed for the genre to develop was less complexity, tighter plotting, narrowed focus, while literary fiction was slowing to the pace of Hardy, Wharton, and James.

It is a genre to which in the last century male and female writers both contribute equally with distinction, the women for the most part being British and colonial, the men American. Among the British males was the Scottish writer A. J. (Archibald Joseph) Cronin (1896–1981), a medical doctor and a slow starter in fiction. Many doctors become novelists: Cronin himself mentions Maugham and Conan Doyle. Cronin fell ill and, given six months off work, started to write, having long wished to do so. "Strictly speaking, then, my first book . . . was the product of a disordered digestion and not, as one lady who wrote to me inferred, a disordered mind."

Play abounds in the area of crime fiction. To begin with, there are official rules. For British writers of the "golden age" (the 1920s and 1930s) these were soberly, ironically set down by the Roman Catholic Monsignor Ronald Knox (1888–1957), himself a dabbler in crime writing. In a Mosaic spirit he incised these Commandments.

> The criminal must be mentioned in the early part of the story, but must not be anyone whose thoughts the reader has been allowed to know.
> All supernatural and preternatural agencies are ruled out as a matter of course.
> Not more than one secret room or passage is allowable.
> No hitherto undiscovered poisons may be used, nor any appliance which will need a long scientific explanation at the end.
> No Chinaman must figure in the story.
> No accident must ever help the detective, nor must he ever have an unaccountable intuition which proves to be right.
> The detective himself must not commit the crime.
> The detective is bound to declare any clues which he may discover.
> The stupid friend of the detective, the Watson, must not conceal from the reader any thoughts which pass through his mind: his intelligence must be slightly, but very slightly, below that of the average reader.
> Twin brothers, and doubles generally, must not appear unless we have been duly prepared for them.

A more detailed list, not of commandments but instructions, was proposed by the American S. S. Van Dine (real name Willard Huntington Wright, creator of the private eye Philo Vance) in "Twenty Rules for Writing Detective Stories," published in 1928 in the *American Magazine,* a journal in which many of the leading crime and literary writers of the day, British and American, published fiction. Van Dine is wordy: two of his rules will suffice.

> 9. There must be but one detective—that is, but one protagonist of deduction—one deus ex machina. To bring the minds of three or

four, or sometimes a gang of detectives to bear on a problem, is not only to disperse the interest and break the direct thread of logic, but to take an unfair advantage of the reader. If there is more than one detective the reader doesn't know who his co-deductor is. It's like making the reader run a race with a relay team.

20. And (to give my Credo an even score of items) I herewith list a few of the devices which no self-respecting detective-story writer will now avail himself of. They have been employed often, and are familiar to all true lovers of literary crime. To use them is a confession of the author's ineptitude and lack of originality. (a) Determining the identity of the culprit by comparing the butt of a cigarette left at the scene of the crime with the brand smoked by the suspect. (b) The bogus spiritualistic séance to frighten the culprit into giving himself away. (c) Forged fingerprints. (d) The dummy-figure alibi. (e) The dog that does not bark and thereby reveals the fact that the intruder is familiar. (f) The final pinning of the crime on a twin, or a relative who looks exactly like the suspected, but innocent, person. (g) The hypodermic syringe and knockout drops. (h) The commission of the murder in a locked room after the police have actually broken in. (i) The word-association test for guilt. (j) The cipher, or code letter, which is eventually unraveled by the sleuth.

---

The most sardonic and instructive writer of crime fiction, one whose literary credit is indisputable, is Raymond Chandler (1888–1959). Always skeptical, he took a dim view of his vocation: "all this desperate building of castles on cobwebs, the long-drawn acrimonious struggle to make something important which we all know will be gone forever in a few years, the miasma of failure which is to me as offensive as the cheap gaudiness of popular success." Yet he insists on its value: just because it is easy to read murder novels does not mean that they are pulp. Properly approached, "They are no easier reading than *Hamlet, Lear* or *Macbeth*. They border on tragic and never quite become tragic. Their form imposes a certain clarity of outline which is only found in the most accomplished 'straight' novels." That "clarity of outline" is analogous to a logical argument or a mathematical formula that makes a good one satisfying; it is why some of the great literary novelists spend so much time in the morgue.

He was born in Chicago. Chandler's father succumbed to drink and fell out of his life quite early. His mother returned to her native Ireland and then went to London, where Chandler was educated at Dulwich College, finishing his studies in France and Germany supported by relations. He passed the Civil Service examination, worked briefly in the Admiralty, then quit to live as a writer. In 1912 he returned to the United States. Nabokov was a tennis coach; Chandler strung tennis rackets. (Unlike Nabokov, he thought chess "the greatest waste of human intelligence outside an advertising agency.") He picked fruit and earned a modest living. In 1917 he joined a Scottish regiment and rose to sergeant. After the war he married a woman twice divorced and much older than he was. Like his father, he became an alcoholic, but not a helpless one. At last in 1939 the long discipline of writing for the pulp magazines came together in *The Big Sleep* (1939), a powerful debut. Philip Marlowe was fully fledged.

Chandler pretends to blame his classical education, acquired at Dulwich, for giving him a sense of restraint and proportion. "I'm an intellectual snob who happens to have a fondness for the American vernacular, largely because I grew up on Latin and Greek. I had to learn American just like a foreign language." In fact the classical discipline, and the deliberate acquisition of Marlowe's hardboiled language, make him a distinctive artist. Nothing is second nature; everything is consciously observed, listened for, and transcribed with a mischievous engraver's precision. Of Marlowe he tells his publisher in 1951, "It begins to look as though I were tied to this fellow for life." (Note that he uses the subjunctive "were" where Hammett might have resorted to the indicative.) In his 1950 polemic "The Simple Art of Murder" he describes the archetypal detective, and it is as though he were giving us a job spec for Marlowe:

> He must be a complete man and a common man and yet an unusual man. He must be, to use a rather weathered phrase, a man of honor, by instinct, by inevitability, without thought of it, and certainly without saying it. He must be the best man in his world and a good enough man for any world. I do not care much about his private life; he is neither a eunuch nor a satyr; I think he might seduce a duchess and I am quite sure he would not spoil a virgin; if he is a man of honor in one thing, he is that in all things. He is a relatively poor man, or he would not be a detective at all. He is a common man or he could not go among common people. He has a sense of character, or he would not know his job. He will take no man's money dishonestly and no man's insolence without a due and dispassionate revenge. He is a lonely man and his pride is that you will treat him as a proud man or be very sorry you ever saw him. He talks as the man of his age talks, that is, with rude wit, a lively sense of the grotesque, a disgust for sham, and a contempt for pettiness.

This is Chandler's own voice, not the one he uses in his fiction. We hear him in his letters, too, unstaged. "Ideas are poison. The more you reason, the less you create." And with a sure instinct: "Expressing yourself is not nearly enough. You must express the story."

A fellow-immigrant to California, Christopher Isherwood, compares him briefly to Faulkner, and then to Walter Mitty—from James Thurber's *The Secret Life of Walter Mitty*—the ineffectual daydreamer Thurber first aired in a short story in the *New Yorker* in 1939 and made into a novel in 1942 with vague-faced Walter, chin on hand, on the cover. Is Marlowe not plausibly a Mitty-ish projection, a fictional fulfillment, hard-drinking, adventurous, surviving, macho, sexually irresistible? If so, Chandler was blessed with a fortunate inadequacy and Isherwood has given us a key.

He wrote his fiction before nightfall. He was easily spooked. After dark he spoke his letters into a Dictaphone for his secretary to type next day. It was a way to have conversations and not be alone. He corresponded for years with Erle Stanley Gardner, that writing machine among detective novelists, who could turn out a book in three days when pressed and who sold in excess of 300 million books over time. Less famous than Chandler and Hammett, he is much more widely read. Chandler praised his skill in making unlikely incidents seem real, as Dumas and Dickens can, and suggested that this quality is "the fundamental of all rapid work."

Rereading his first novel in the "two-bit edition" later on, Chandler remarked to his publisher, "I sure did run the similes into the ground." The magic of his writing remains largely in his similes, which, if they become less numerous, are no less effective. His second novel, *Farewell, My Lovely* (1940), he said was written in "my usual whorehouse style." *The High Window* (1942) was panned by critics for being too fast and furious; when he is slower and reflective, he complains, they pan him for not being fast and furious. You cannot win. He felt he was still "riding around on Hammett and James Cain, like an organ grinder's monkey." *The Lady in the Lake* (1943) and *The Long Goodbye* (1953) complete the run of "major" Chandlers. It is clear from the books that, as he says, he is "fundamentally rather uninterested in plot" and that in his case "the most durable thing in writing is style." Martin Amis describes him as "far too glazed and existential for efficient storytelling," but that is not everything. Amis rather admires how he manages to be "both hot and cool, virile and sterile."

No wonder Chandler loathed the writing of James (Mallahan) Cain (1892–1977), author of several novels that became famous films, some twice over, notably *The Postman Always Rings Twice* (1934), *Mildred Pierce* (1941), and *Double Indemnity* (1943). Perhaps because he disliked Cain's work, he was called to

Hollywood in 1944 to work on the script of *Double Indemnity*. He despised Cain's *faux naïf* approach, which he said was peculiarly American. Yet he brought himself to write a civil letter to Cain, who patronized him. "Personally I think Hollywood is poison to any writer," Chandler remarked, "the graveyard of talent." He worked in Hollywood for four years and became rather famous and quite well off.

The writer he unconditionally admired was (Samuel) Dashiell Hammett (1894–1961). "Hammett is all right. I give him everything. There were a lot of things he could not do, but what he did he did superbly." It was he who, while the English writers were busy dabbing their lips with their serviettes and wondering what the next course might bring, "took murder out of the Venetian vase and dropped it into the alley; it doesn't have to stay there forever, but it was a good idea to begin by getting as far as possible from Emily Post's idea of how a well-bred debutante gnaws a chicken wing." He was restoring the genre to the people to whom it belongs. Compared with the unreal worlds of Agatha Christie, whose *Ten Little Niggers* (1939, the title was changed to *And Then There Were None* when it was released in the United States in 1940) Chandler especially disliked, Hammett was in a different league. He gave characters their own motives, their own language. Chandler admired him also as "an amazingly competent drunk" and, missing the connection, laments the fact that he stopped writing.

Reading Hammett in the wake of Chandler (the wrong direction historically), or out of the context of the genre, the modern reader is not immediately struck. Hammett lacks the linguistic pyrotechnics of Chandler, the abundant metaphor and caustic tone. He seems flat. And there is none of Agatha Christie's charm of setting or the brisk humor of Dorothy L. Sayers. There is economy, we are put in mind of Hemingway, but the sentences do not have his finish. Hammett, Erle Stanley Gardner, and Agatha Christie, like most crime novelists, exist in their genres; Chandler transcends that genre. But Chandler insists on Hammett's virtues, especially in *The Maltese Falcon* (1930): "If you can show me twenty books written approximately 20 years back that have as much guts and life now, I'll eat them between slices of Edmund Wilson's head."

As against Chandler's Philip Marlowe, Hammett gives us Sam Spade and other clearly drawn detectives. All but his last novel were serialized in largish chunks, and this affected the pattern of composition and the structuring of plot. His books reflect his political impatience: he is a radical and though he writes to entertain, he insinuates themes such as greed, exploitation, and injustice, which are not lost even in the films, where a little later there might have been pressure to remove them. Other notable Hammett novels are the first, *Red Harvest* (1929), his own favorite *The Glass Key* (1931), and *The Thin Man* (1934).

More than any of his significant contemporaries, Hammett wrote from experience. At thirteen he left school and after a series of jobs found himself working for the Pinkerton National Detective Agency from 1915–1922, with time off to serve in the Motor Ambulance Corps in the First World War. He contracted Spanish flu and then tuberculosis; he never made it to the battlefield, though in the hospital he met the woman he was to marry. As a Pinkerton man he was troubled that the agency took so prominent a role in strikebreaking as labor in the wake of the war began to flex its muscles.

His marriage broke down after 1926. He turned to drinking, to advertising, and finally to writing. His affair with the writer Nell Martin resulted in his dedicating *The Glass Key* to her, and she to him *Lovers Should Marry*. They did not and he went on to a three-decade affair with Lillian Hellman. She evokes him in her oversweet, de-warted memoir *Pentimento* (1973). Hammett published his last novel in 1934, not long after they got together.

As against the wildly inventive and often implausible Chandler, the energy of whose language persuades us, Hammett is a literalist, basing his characters on people he knew, and although he devises incidents, the characters have a lived solidity. He asks a great deal of them. With Hellman he entered into a life of political activism: he *was* a member of the American Communist Party and had numerous occasions to plead the Fifth Amendment, and to go to prison, where he was assigned to cleaning toilets. The experience accelerated his death. Those later years did not touch the fiction, except to underline its political themes.

Chandler disliked the tone of the English crime writers. Dorothy L. Sayers (1893–1957) declared that the detective story "does not, and by hypothesis never can, attain the loftiest level of literary achievement." It was, she said, always a "literature of escape," not "a literature of expression." Chandler clears his throat: "I do not know what the loftiest level of literary achievement is: neither did Aeschylus or Shakespeare; neither does Miss Sayers. Other things being equal, which they never are, a more powerful theme will provoke a more powerful performance." He suggests that what really troubles her and those like her— Agatha Christie (1890–1976), the New Zealander Ngaio Marsh (1895–1982), Josephine Tey (1896–1952), Margery Allingham (1904–1966), the playful and allusive Scot Michael Innes (real name John Innes Mackintosh Stewart, 1906–1993)— is that their sort of detective story was not novelistic but "an arid formula which could not even satisfy its own implications. It was second-grade literature because it was not about the things that could make first-grade literature." Credible characters, made to conform to a blueprint, became "puppets and cardboard lovers and *papier mâché* villains and detectives of exquisite and impossible gentility."

Among the beneficiaries and heirs of Chandler and Hammett is Elmore (John) Leonard (Jr.) (1925–2013). He has published forty-five novels. A brief visit to the plot of his forty-fourth, *Djibouti* (2010), reveals a key to his success: his very American eyes are on the contemporary world as filtered to him through the American media. The story takes us to the Horn of Africa where a female American filmmaker is doing a documentary on the Somali pirates. Immediately narrative questions arise: How is she to organize and cut the film—that is, how is she to tell the story? Briskly, for Leonard is brisk and often headlong ("If it sounds like writing, I rewrite it"), she meets a mega-rich Texan who has appointed himself to be a one-man antiterrorist marshal in the Wild West of modern Africa. There is the pirate leader and his arms supplier, an Oxford graduate, the newfangled bandidos; and an American-born member of al-Qaeda keen to blow up a tanker the pirates have brought in. The western has moved east and Leonard has written a novel that is already almost a movie. His dialogue, wrote the novelist Philip Hensher, who became a convert when he read Leonard's thirty-seventh novel, *Tishomingo Blues* (2002), "leaps off the page in a magical way." The books have "a perfect, profane articulacy." Margaret Atwood notes how in *Tishomingo Blues* good and bad characters swear differently, and Leonard risks political incorrectness on an epic scale.

If, despite the variety of incident, Leonard has one plot, or one plot shape, nonetheless he "writes re-readable thrillers," says Martin Amis, who identifies a crucial element in Leonard's style, "his use of the present participle." Amis calls it "a kind of marijuana tense," a technique of "slowing down and suspending the English sentence." He will write incomplete sentences, and he refuses, however correct it might seem, to use semicolons and colons in dialogue: they look wrong. For the reader there should be no deflection from the main business of the story.

Jonathan Franzen sets Leonard in the "entertainer" category with P. G. Wodehouse. They are different manifestations of the same literary impulse. We find the same kind of plot, the same kind of tension, and a complicated but usually satisfying resolution. Leonard is sufficiently a realist to blur the line between the enforcers and violators of the law. Good guys are not always law abiding or all good, bad guys are not necessarily below the law if they can use it to advantage, or incapable of human response. The eponymous hero of *Raylan* (2011), Hensher says, "is a drily witty cop who, in another life, might have been a useful and charming armed robber." The nuanced, rough reality of his characters, however repetitively far-fetched the plots, maintained Leonard's popularity over six decades in which he averaged a novel every eighteen months, starting with a western, *The Bounty Hunters,* in 1953 and going on to write crime books and thrillers. More than twenty films have been made of his novels and stories. In 1997 Quentin Tarantino made *Rum Punch* into *Jackie Brown.*

Leonard, born in New Orleans, grew up in Detroit, served in the Navy during the Second World War, then worked in advertising. When he found his way into writing, his approach was energetic and businesslike. He made his calculations and perfected his craft. When characters succeeded in fiction or on the screen, he would bring them back for an encore; there is a reassuring familiarity about each Leonard book, and the promise of surprise, violence, laughter, machismo, and romance. There is room, too, for the inexplicable, the deep mystery of the medium and the healer into which he does not pry, accepting the powers gratefully. *Get Shorty* (1990) is the best book with which to start an addiction to Leonard. Martin Amis calls it "a masterpiece," and within its genre it is; outside its genre, too. Hensher compares it with Calvino and reminds us of the closing lines: "Chili didn't say anything, giving it some more thought. Fuckin endings, man, they weren't as easy as they looked."

Leonard is as famous for his films as his books. Many of those who profess to love the work of Agatha Christie in fact love the television adaptations and her principal detectives, the Belgian Monsieur Hercule Poirot and the irreducibly English Miss Jane Marple. Outside the mystery-book formula she lost her bearings, as her romance novels, published under the pseudonym Mary Westmacott, reveal. Her own crime writing—well over sixty novels in sixty-three years—began three decades after Sir Arthur Conan Doyle's but follows the pattern he established. She plotted her novels carefully, choosing usually a not entirely sympathetic victim, making the means of death not too shocking, and then releasing her shoal of red herrings. The pleasure of detection is considerable: often a reader, returning to a book, has forgotten the sequence and reads with renewed surprise. This may have to do with her low-key style and the spareness of narration. The books have the quality of templates and the reader provides much of the substance. Within the formulaic constraints, we are given considerable imaginative freedom. Her books have sold, it is said, in excess of 2 billion copies.

Women who write crime often create the upper-middle-class world in which a Miss Marple or Poirot are at home. Dorothy Sayers's Lord Peter Wimsey, Ngaio Marsh's Roderick Alleyn, and P. D. James's Adam Dalgliesh are most at home there also. Frederic Raphael speaks of P. D. James (b. 1920) and her "obese inventories of her characters' furniture" as "patronizing and narcotic," adding, "Crime stories, except those of Raymond Chandler, usually reek of what Byron called 'scheme.'" Patricia Highsmith (1921–1995) and Ruth Rendell (b. 1930) explore different areas, with different inflections, though the genteel label and Byron's note may still apply.

Romance and westerns decline, but crime fiction is as common as crime itself, and the subject continues to develop, though the element of nostalgia that draws us back to Poirot and Lord Peter will continue to inform the fiction, just as the hard-boiled America of Hammett and Chandler now has a sepia aspect, and the punks with their pants tight under their arms, the broads with zippered teeth, the unexpected variations on racial and sexual stereotypes, will vie with modern mean streets less susceptible to irony than theirs. Crime has evolved, too: the big-money crime of late capitalism.

———·———

In his evolving essay "Supernatural Horror in Literature," H. P. (Howard Phillips) Lovecraft (1890–1937), working his way down from Ann Radcliffe and Walpole, through Emily Brontë and Poe, to his contemporaries Arthur Machen and M. R. (Montague Rhodes) James, among others, reviled the "smirking optimism" of the literature of uplift with its didactic bent. His stories are not in service of any fixed morality. He celebrates "the weird tale," which can include horror, sci-fi, the Gothic, and which frequently passes into melodrama and self-parody but never lacks the courage of its convictions. "Relatively few," he writes, "are free enough from the spell of the daily routine to respond to tappings from outside," and we are immediately back in Cathy's dark bedroom in *Wuthering Heights,* hearing—is it the branch—tapping at the pane, and all the other spine-chilling Gothic tappings from Walpole and Scott and Austen through Dickens, to the modern Gothic. He speaks of a "literature of cosmic fear" rooted in man, generated by our uncertainties and anxieties. Like Walpole's Gothic, however, Lovecraft's, too, time has partly tamed.

Poe can still frighten a reader, especially late at night. It has to do, as Nabokov understood, with language, with the spaces that vowels carve out of the darkness and the way night loosens the hold of the literal world so that things move and happen in unanticipated ways. Shadows detach from their forms and develop a will. Poe and Lovecraft have much in common. Like Poe's, Lovecraft's favored medium is the tale, not the novel. Poe worked by a faultless instinct, Lovecraft sometimes willfully and by design. He is more interested in places than people, places with inherences; there is a general haunting about his worlds, which start as literal and then degrade. Gothic horror inheres, an aspect of reality, "cosmic" to use his word, rather than of invention. The contemporary French writer Michel Houellebecq touches on this in the very title of his literary biography, *H. P. Lovecraft: Against the World, Against Life.* Borges, borrowing his title from Hamlet's response to Horatio's benign philosophy, dedicates his story "There Are More Things" to the memory of Lovecraft.

Lovecraft had few readers during his lifetime, but his reputation has grown with the world's growing craving for the weird. He is counted among the most influential horror writers of the twentieth century. Joyce Carol Oates makes a large claim: like Poe in the previous century, he has exercised "an incalculable influence on succeeding generations of writers of horror fiction." And Stephen King (b. 1947) calls him the century's "greatest practitioner of the classic horror tale." Lovecraft brought him to horror, King says, and to sales of over 300 million books. Formative influences should receive the percentage that agents claim. In Lovecraft's case it would have come too late.

"I Was a Teenage Grave Robber," King's first published story, appeared in a fanzine when he was eighteen. He had already been writing for more than a decade, and he read, first comic books, then the Nancy Drew and Hardy Boys novels, and watched films and television, which fed his writing, his sense of scene building, dialogue, and dramatic construction. He was enchanted, when the mobile library came to town, to discover the 87th Street Precinct novels of Ed McBain. He was excited by the boldness of the language and the sexuality of the writing. He gave up childish things.

He married, had three children, and worked hard, doing laundry, teaching, and writing. In 1973 he sold *Carrie,* his first novel, and soon it was a best seller. After that he could afford to be a writer: most of his novels and stories have been made into films and television dramas. Since *Carrie* he has published over forty novels and two useful books on the discipline of writing.

Because he was a popular novelist, the only people who took King's writing seriously were readers and booksellers. Critics admired DeLillo's or Styron's or Updike's language. But, hey, King would ask, what about *my* language? I'm in the business. From most critics' point of view, he was not. Like other popular novelists there was, first of all, the issue of the sheer volume of his output. His bibliography is vast, but the novels are generally substantial and serious in intent.

And then there is the issue of genre. Amy Tan urged him to ask and try to answer the questions in public in a book intended for writer-readers and entitled *On Writing: A Memoir of the Craft* (2000). In an age of writers' manuals and writing programs, it is a shrewd and useful book whose authorial informality and hubris tend to get in the way of the substantial truths it has to tell. Central to fiction is a simple paradigm, what King calls in an interview "an intrusion of the extraordinary into ordinary life and how we deal with it." What interests him is not the mechanics of the intrusion—ghouls, rabid dogs, ghosts—but what characters do in response.

Given the amount of mystery and weirdness in his books, it is a surprise to learn that his work room is orderly and bright, his filing system "very complex, very orderly." He tells his *Paris Review* interviewer how with *Duma Key* (2008) he has "codified the notes to make sure I remember the different plot strands. I write down birth dates to figure out how old characters are at certain times. Remember to put a rose tattoo on this one's breast, remember to give Edgar a big workbench by the end of February." It's simply good husbandry, "because if I do something wrong now, it becomes such a pain in the ass to fix later." King pretended to resist his editors, but he was able to say in 2000, not entirely ironically, that to write is human, to edit divine. He has for years solicited his readers' responses to his books, creating what seems like a dialogue, giving readers a place, or the illusion of a place, in the process.

He calls his 1986 horror novel *It* "the most Dickensian" of his books, with a large cast of characters and their "intersecting stories." This effortless complexity eludes him in his later books. Many of his points of reference are to younger contemporaries in the horror and weird-fiction tradition, but he also insists on a wider fellowship, with Dickens, with Faulkner, Dreiser, and Robert Penn Warren, with Carson McCullers. "I love her," he says with simple conviction.

King, so long resisted, has now been honored by the National Book Award committee and published in the *New Yorker*. His novels are taught in schools, displacing the novels by DeLillo, Updike, and Styron. Lovecraft is in print and relatively widely read. The first western to make it onto a Man Booker Prize shortlist was Patrick deWitt's *The Sisters Brothers* in 2011. Romance, especially when tricked out with a little postmodern *chic*, wins big awards. The Betty Trask Award was established in 1984 by a reclusive romance novelist with thirty titles to her name to celebrate "a romantic novel or other novel of a traditional rather than experimental nature," a rubric the judges, often drawn from the hard-core literary classes, have found it hard to honor. The Orange Prize, for women only, celebrates "excellence, originality and accessibility," that last term being the rallying cry that brings genre novelists together to outface the (we must assume) inaccessible literary novels of our time that (until the Booker Prize capitulated) unwholesomely dominated the prize lists. Romance and crime, science fiction, and horror all have their Oscars, but a Betty Trask, a Golden Dagger, an Arthur C. Clarke or Hugo or Nebula, a Spur or Bram Stoker Award, is not the same as a National Book Award, a Whitbread, or a Pulitzer. Critical resistance to genre fiction has been steadily eroding, along with other long-held nostrums to do with what used to be called "literature" and "high culture." Soon genre novels—including science fiction, adventure, cold war, high finance, and spy books—may dominate not only the best-seller lists and book tables but the literary pages and prize lists as well. We hear "the raucous laughter of the strong man," grown proudly proficient with his labeled palette.

———•———

J. G. Ballard declared that only science fiction, as the genre that most distinctively characterized the second half of the twentieth century, would endure, and that the innumerable novels about young people who meet at Oxford and grow up into couples, and recouple, in Hampstead, along with their American, Antipodean, and other equivalents, would vanish.

———•———

Most of the genres described in this chapter are based in a simplification of the rules of realism with its world of stable contingencies. They play with readers' emotions and anxieties and engage their deductive reasoning. Science fiction, like allegory in earlier centuries, addresses the imagination and intelligence at large. The writer earnestly engages the themes, as inventor, as satirist. In the 1920s science fiction increased in popularity, the library of pulp magazines grew with the swelling host of aficionados. It has continued to flourish, now in the wake and now in the van of science. American astronauts and workers in the space industry were brought up on Robert A. Heinlein's "juveniles," potent sci-fi for young people. Their expectation of space travel is shaped by fiction.

Modern as it seems, sci-fi's roots go almost as deep as those of romance: it has been present in this story since Mandeville in his *Travels* strayed off the known map. Wherever the sci-fi writer takes us, we are aware of difference, sometimes generated by a single, simple adjustment of the would-be "real," sometimes by a complete overhaul. The "science" in science fiction does not confine the narrative to the future or to the laboratory; rather, it anticipates that the experiment of the novel will be conducted according to consistent rules. Readers learn to understand and then to anticipate. For the duration of the novel they inhabit an altered or alternative universe. In Philip K. Dick's *The Man in the High Castle* (1962), two characters debate in a futurist staccato whether an imaginary novel called *The Grasshopper Lies Heavy* is sci-fi or not. " 'Oh no,' Betty disagreed, 'No science in it. Nor set in future. Science fiction deals with future, in particular future where science has advanced over now. Book fits neither premise.' 'But,' Paul said, 'it deals with alternate present. Many well-known science fiction novels of that sort.' " What is this book about? The Axis powers have won the Second World War and divided the United States between Japan and Germany, two types of totalitarian tyranny. How does the "free spirit" respond? Different divisions occur in *The Three Stigmata of Palmer Eldritch* (1965), in which two would-be saviors without the courage of their vocations, one with mind-bending substances to draw people into his orbit, the other with defeatist realism, struggle.

Science fiction was one of the promises of Rabelais; *Gulliver's Travels* (Isaac Asimov produced an annotated edition) and the *Alice* books are foundation texts. Defoe, Smollett, Thackeray, Mary Shelley, Poe, Samuel Butler, Huxley, Wells, Orwell, Conan Doyle, Edgar Rice Burroughs, Ford and Conrad in their dystopian collaboration *The Inheritors* (1901), Vonnegut, Lessing, Hoban, and Atwood, among many others, wrote what is sometimes described as "speculative fiction" and can overlap with horror and fantasy. Science fiction begins with "What if?"—a "What if?" that directs narrative away from the familiar world by means of scientific intervention or projection, extraterrestrial visitation, historical reversal, environmental change: something introduced into the experiment of the world to disrupt and redefine it.

Ray Bradbury tells how David Merrick, the film producer, told his scriptwriter Stan Freberg, at work on a musical history of the United States: "Take Abe Lincoln out of the war. He doesn't work." That is the kind of moment in which science fiction might begin. The Nazis win the Second World War, or extinct species are regenerated from preserved DNA, or time travel occurs and history is spatialized, with events as well as places to visit. We attend to ideas, changes; good writing makes us believe and see the world in new ways. Characters function as clauses in arguments or mouthpieces of ideas. As an art of projection, sci-fi requires thinking on the part of the writer and the reader. "Projection": science fiction and film are closely allied.

Six principal writers earned the popular genre its literary credibility, raising it to the level Ballard claims for it. Their most important work tests the thematic and formal resources of the novel form and empowers a vast progeny of contemporary sci-fi writers. Those six are Robert A. Heinlein (1907–1988), Arthur Charles Clarke (1917–2008), Isaac Asimov (1920–1992), Ray Bradbury (1920–2012), Philip Kindred Dick (1928–1982), and Ursula Kroeber Le Guin (b. 1929).

Bradbury calls sci-fi "the art of the possible." He recalls the 1950s and 1960s when students began educating their teachers, bringing Heinlein, Clarke, and Asimov books to class and getting the teachers to read them. Then teachers, like converts, began to teach them and proselytize. The moon landing, front-page scientific and especially space achievements, new weaponry, President Reagan's "Star Wars" defense initiative—all had a bearing on the development of the genre.

To Bradbury, Heinlein exemplifies precise, consistent invention, his novels plausible once the initial premises are accepted. His first stories, like those of his sci-fi contemporaries, appeared in *Astounding Science Fiction*, edited by James Campbell, a legendary figure who broadened the scope of sci-fi and upheld its literary claims. He helped create "golden age" sci-fi, discovering, encouraging, and stimulating young writers. He laid the foundations for some towering reputations. Heinlein he recognized, as did Asimov, Clarke, and others, as a star, *the* star.

Bradbury met Heinlein shortly after graduating from high school. He was dazzled. Heinlein's narratives, whatever their technological trappings, "remained more people-centered than others," he thought, and this affected the development of his own writing. The fate of the individual in a technological age, the importance of individual nonconformity and the threats to it, were key themes, though the male characters he creates are not especially individualized or memorable. When he wrote of political or scientific repression, he was obliquely addressing the theme of religious compulsion, an aspect of his Bible Belt upbringing in Missouri. In life and writing he rebelled. He campaigned for Upton Sinclair, who ran as Democratic candidate for the governorship of California in 1934. Heinlein himself stood unsuccessfully for the state assembly. His early science fiction was branded "social" (that is, "red," "socialist") because of its political and civic concerns.

Heinlein contributed to the *Saturday Evening Post,* and modern sci-fi entered the mainstream. He wrote thirty-two novels (including the testosterone-enriched "juveniles") and dozens of stories. His work was adapted for other media: four films, and radio and television series. He created strong, intelligent female characters based on his third wife, Virginia, his intellectual and travel companion and devoted first reader. They enjoyed liner and freighter travel. His spacecraft resemble ships in their design and the navigation they require. Ginny assisted Heinlein's swing to the libertarian right. Over time, like John Dos Passos, his civic individualism changed emphasis: he campaigned for Barry Goldwater, the conservative Republican presidential candidate in the 1964 election.

At the beginning of his novel-writing career, in 1939, he wrote *For Us, the Living: A Comedy of Customs.* It foreshadows his later themes, but it was not published until 2003. His first published novel was *Rocket Ship Galileo* (1947), which was initially rejected because moon travel was regarded as impossible. There is now a crater on Mars named after Heinlein: his fourth novel, for juveniles and illustrated, was *Red Planet* (1949).

For the first decade of his writing he had no real rivals in terms of the scale of his books and their popularity. He played to the adult and juvenile markets and doubled the odds for success. The juvenile novels entertain the adult in their simple clarity and the memorable Clifford Geary illustrations. The intelligent adolescent is welcome in the adult world and sucked into its dramas. The illustrations remind us how closely the sci-fi genre relates to the comic book tradition. Gore Vidal stressed the impact of film on the fiction-making imagination; but for many writers of the twentieth century, before film came radio, and before radio—and more formative than either because it entailed the act of reading and active imagining—was the comic book. Discrete framed scenes in which a speech-bubble exchange is nuanced by postures, facial expressions, caricature, and backgrounds, where thought-bubbles undermine speech, where loud noises—Biff! Zoom! Bang!—are framed in jagged explosions of color, the volume typographically turned loud, affected how young writers set down their prose, wanting to retain that immediacy and economy.

Heinlein ordered his novels in series. Later sci-fi writers follow suit, constructing large histories, recruiting casts of characters and generations to hook the reader with familiarities and continuities. By the time of *Starship Trooper* (1959) Heinlein had finished with juveniles and was engaged in writing for adults, not avoiding contemporary politics (though refracting it through "future" lenses). He turned against those on the left who were urging President Eisenhower to curb nuclear testing. The later novels have topical occasions that, at their best, they contain and transcend. Most of his books still entertain, and the best of them, *Stranger in a Strange Land* (1961) and *Time Enough for Love* (1973), develop his themes in a novelistic rather than an essayistic spirit, though the morals are detachable and on second reading the didactic ballast rises to the surface. Ayn Rand admired his later work. For his part, Heinlein liked *The Fountainhead*. In both writers intentionality stifled invention, compelling stories gave way to thematic exposition. Heinlein moved beyond the "future history" series into "the world of myth." Sci-fi faded out; ideological fantasy, sci-fi's shadow and nemesis, faded in. Jonathan Lethem suggests that from Heinlein Philip K. Dick derived "a measure of solipsism and paranoia." Dick had his themes, but he was more of a novelist and knew that the story had its necessities and dynamic.

Heinlein left a mark on midcentury sci-fi writers, in particular on Asimov and on Clarke, with whom he conducted a long correspondence until they fell out over American defense policy. Clarke grew close to Asimov, and their friendship lasted. They teased and traded good-natured insults. Neither succumbed to sermonizing, and both retain a wider readership than Heinlein.

Clarke was born in rural Britain, where he learned to stargaze and read American sci-fi. He served in the Second World War, working in radar, and after the war he studied mathematics at King's College, London. He was a significant scientific thinker, visionary, and writer (in an interview in 1974 he described what would become the Internet and many of its commercial ramifications) as well as a popular novelist. He was briefly married in the United States but later emigrated to Sri Lanka, where he lived with a male friend to whom he was devoted. No one made much of a fuss over his orientation, though it was a factor in his exile from Britain.

His sci-fi was first published in *Astounding Science Fiction* in 1946. As his energies gathered for *2001: A Space Odyssey,* he developed a thematic formula: Mankind makes technological advances without developing morally; it comes into conflict with a superior force, and in its struggle to survive it evolves. Jonathan Lethem as a youth loved how in Clarke's books, "Stapledonian socialism thrummed just under the surface of his glossy futures," a reference to Olaf Stapledon (1886–1950), the British philosopher and writer of sci-fi who used popular fiction to explore political ideas. Stapledon's matter and manner affected other writers. Arnold Bennett, Virginia Woolf, Priestley, and Borges admired him. Like other sci-fi writers, he had an actual impact on science: the theoretical physicist Freeman Dyson acknowledged the value of his insights.

Clarke valued two of his books in particular, *Last and First Men* (1930) and *Star Maker* (1937). He shared with Stapledon, and with Heinlein, a conviction that religion had for too long governed morality, directing and distorting the mind and imagination: the time had come to jettison it. In his first critically and commercially successful novel, *Childhood's End* (1953), Clarke introduced the peaceful alien Overlords who come near to Earth and direct the planet toward what seems utopia. That utopia is not the final state: mankind is transformed, absorbed into the Overmind, until finally it and the Earth itself are over. Clarke's fiction and scientific writing developed side by side, but the fiction remains in fascinated thrall to themes his more analytical books could not engage. His fascination with the paranormal and his projection of future worlds have a paradoxically religious (one hesitates to call it a spiritual) dimension not lost on his admirers and exegetes.

His first excursion into film, with Stanley Kubrick, was decisive—*2001: A Space Odyssey* (1968), a major and complex undertaking. Clarke's *Odyssey* borrows legitimacy from Homer's, at the same time suggesting that the characters are bigger than life. They are heroes and creatures of invention, not of nature or nurture. The novel, completed before the film was released, was published after and was read as a novelization. Clarke revised it during the weeks when he and Kubrick were watching the film rushes; inevitably the book exploited cinematic turns in visualization and narrative transitions. Kubrick's spirit merged, not quite comfortably, with Clarke's, and whatever the narrative urgency, the book lacks the formal and stylistic coherence of Clarke's other novels. It spawned sequels, notably *2010: Odyssey Two* (1982), which was also made into a film, though less successfully and not by Kubrick. *2061: Odyssey Three* (1987) and *3001: The Final Odyssey* (1997) exhaust the franchise.

Jonathan Lethem recommends Clarke's 1972 novel *Rendezvous with Rama*, in which a huge alien spacecraft is detected in our solar system. The year is 2130, science is far advanced though human nature has not kept pace. Clarke proves himself a great sci-fi inventor, the world of Rama being one of the most elaborate and consistent in sci-fi literature. Character is secondary. Rama too became a franchise, with a collaborator to do the writing, and three further books followed.

The "Clarke-Asimov treaty" was a joke contract: Clarke undertook always to concede that Asimov was the best science writer in the world (he the second best); Asimov would always concede that Clarke was the best sci-fi writer in the world (he the second best). As modern readers we might wish to reverse this. Few, if any, sci-fi short stories surpass the achievement of Asimov's "Nightfall."

Asimov's is a more fascinating, if a more conventional-seeming, life story. He told it himself in three volumes of autobiography, from which *It's Been a Good Life* (2002), published a decade after his death, was compiled. He was cheerful and optimistic, though he died of organ failure after he contracted AIDS from contaminated blood during a triple-bypass operation. His rate of literary production was prodigious, right into his final illness: a hundred publications in his first sixteen years, a hundred publications in the following nine years, a hundred more in the next five. The velocity increased. In the end he had 500 separate publications to his credit. "When Isaac departs earth and arrives Up There," said Ray Bradbury, "[he will] write twenty-five new books of the Bible. And that only the first week."

Born in Russia, Asimov arrived in the United States at the age of three. His family, millers in the old country, spoke Yiddish. He acquired English and retained little Russian coloring. In the United States his family ran candy shops, and the shy, geeky young Asimov enjoyed "serving": it gave him time to read. By the age of nineteen he was contributing stories to the sci-fi pulp magazines. Modern literary fiction he avoided, though he was a fan of Rex Stout's Nero Wolfe mysteries and of Sherlock Holmes. Crime fiction exercised his deductive faculties within the bounds of convention. Gibbon's *Decline and Fall of the Roman Empire* was formative: he read it "from first page to last at least twice." When he started to write stories early in the 1940s, the world was in ideological ferment and Asimov felt he was in an age not entirely unlike the one Gibbon describes, writing of the present by way of the past; Asimov as a scientist approached the present from an imagined future. The Galactic Empire is unraveling, and the Foundation emerges in the face of anarchy and barbarism to salvage and carry civilization forward. His Foundation trilogy consists, in fact, of discrete stories brought together not in a picaresque sequence but in a ramshackle coherence. When he told Campbell his plans, hatched on a subway ride to see the editor, Campbell foresaw not a story, not a novelette, but "an open-ended series of stories."

Asimov developed a style for his galactic geographies and adventures. "His name was Gaal Dornick and he was just a country boy who had never seen Trantor before." It could be the voice of a time-traveling Chandler with hypervideo, interplanetary travel, and meteor driftage. The world is coherent and imaginatively habitable. Asimov is memorable more for his settings and stories than for his experiments in expression. He uses script format, rhetorical repetitions, and cadences. His vast landscapes open out at times like Cormac McCarthy's: "Arcadia watched the metal rim of the horizon with a stirring of the heart. The village in which the Palvers lived was but a huddle of houses to her—small and primitive. The fields that surrounded it were golden-yellow, wheat-clogged tracts." But his description is seldom excessive. Plot, argument, and forward motion matter. Not that the narrative is linear: Asimov moves around in the story, plotting so that time seems spatialized, with fixed points that can be moved between and returned to like stars. Fifty years ago Asimov was considered modern yet safe to read in school. Thematically controversial, his work had just enough technical complication to talk about, and no sex to speak of. In one of her incautious moments Rebecca West called him a better novelist than Tolstoy.

As a professor of biochemistry at Boston University, Asimov wrote more books about science, astronomy in particular, than novels. These writings were useful to Thomas Pynchon and impressed Kurt Vonnegut, who said Asimov "knew everything." He tried his hand at various kinds of fiction but sci-fi was his métier. He wrote novels in series. The series *Foundation* (1951), *Foundation and Empire* (1952), and *Second Foundation* (1953) traces an empire that spans star systems as they disintegrate and reform; he added further Foundation novels and also the Galactic Empire books (a sort of prequel to the Foundation) and his popular Robot series (a sequel). Large slices of human time are explored. The books enjoy classic status in their genre. From pulp magazines they climb the empyrean: The Everyman edition of the Foundation trilogy gives Asimov the same loving attention as is lavished on Flaubert and Edith Wharton.

Ray Bradbury's first novel, *The Martian Chronicles* (1950), was also a concatenation of stories from the magazines. "The Third Expedition," the sixth chapter of the book, is a revision of the 1948 story "Mars Is Heaven." A third American expedition lands on Mars. The space travelers find a small town, not unlike the Waukegan, Illinois (dubbed Green Town in the fiction), where Bradbury spent his childhood, in which all the crew's childhood hungers and desires can be fulfilled. On the first night, those who succumb to its temptations perish and only the skeptical survive. This moral fable takes its place among others that become a novel because they are marketed as such. There is a trajectory governing their progress. Always a literary man, a lover of Poe and—sentence by sentence—of Wharton, of Steinbeck and Welty and Katherine Anne Porter, Bradbury claimed that the main influence on *The Martian Chronicles* was Sherwood Anderson's *Winesburg, Ohio*.

Born in the same year, Bradbury and Asimov both attended the first World Science Fiction Convention in New York in 1939 (they were nineteen years old). Both contributed to the pulp sci-fi magazines and came under the spell of James Campbell. In the 1960s they moved away from sci-fi, returning to it, altered, in the 1980s. Both hated flying, and because one lived on the East Coast and the other on the West, they seldom met, though they respected one another's work.

Asimov had the candy shop, Bradbury a transforming moment of childhood magic when Mr. Electrico, a carnival magician, touched the twelve-year-old Ray on the head with his electrified sword and commanded him, *Live forever!* The current stood his hair on end and the tingling never stopped. He might have become a magician himself but he turned to writing. As a boy he loved Edgar Rice Burroughs, comic books (Flash Gordon, Buck Rogers), and movies. His second novel, which became a very successful movie in 1966, was the only book of his that he regarded as true sci-fi: *Fahrenheit 451* (1953). It took its title from the temperature at which paper ignites. In this dystopian nightmare, set in an American future but referring to the McCarthy era of suppression and censorship, books have been prohibited. Firemen burn books and the houses with books inside. Books had declined. Abbreviated, simplified, degraded, they became obsolete with television screens everywhere and the irresistible power of shallow entertainment. Books came to seem dangerous. But away from the city and the flickering screens, book lovers have memorized books verbatim, mouthing them until the time comes when books can again be read. The seventeen-year-old Clarisse McClellan is an attractive adolescent protagonist. The book was aimed at young readers. Guy Montag, a fireman and unexpected convert to literature, is a conventional hero and emblem of hope: the obedient evildoer who learns to resist evil.

In 1956 Bradbury wrote the script for John Huston's film adaptation of *Moby-Dick*, an exploration of deeper evil. The experience gave rise to some of his most original reflections on writing fiction and writing for performance, and the different demands each makes. Bradbury enjoyed writing about writing when he was not writing his twenty-seven novels, now available in thirty-six languages, with sales in excess of 8 million copies. "You don't have to burn books to destroy a culture," he said, reflecting on *Fahrenheit 451*. "Just get people to stop reading them."

Philip K. Dick remembered a conversation with Bradbury. They talked about money, the way writers do. Bradbury remembered the meeting differently: "You meet people and you realize they don't like being alive." Dick was such a one. His interesting imagination keeps the reader engaged in the best and the less good of his forty-five novels. The Library of America dedicated three volumes (edited by Jonathan Lethem) to him—he has become a classic too, though in his own day he was by far the least prosperous of the major sci-fi writers. Several of his novels and stories have been turned into blockbuster films: *Blade Runner,* based on his novel *Do Androids Dream of Electric Sheep?* (1968), was released four months after his death, directed by Ridley Scott and starring Harrison Ford. *Screamers, Total Recall* (twice), *Minority Report, A Scanner Darkly, The Adjustment Bureau,* and others followed, all too late for him to enjoy material benefit. He died at the age of fifty-three.

Ursula Le Guin described Dick as "our own homegrown Borges," a curious valuation. As against the exiguous Argentinean, Dick produced a vast body of work. He is not so intellectually refined or formally subtle as Borges, either: His concern with political and material power, with monopoly, and with the possibility of transcendence, reflect a teleological bent. He writes from the perspectives of paranoia, schizophrenia, and those altered states produced by the use (commonly described as abuse) of consciousness-transforming substances. Of his generation of sci-fi writers he was keenest to be read as literature and invested his writing with literary elements that enhance and then obscure his themes. Roberto Bolaño described him as "Thoreau plus the death of the American dream." Dick set out to place real characters, "people I love," in imagined worlds and saw those worlds with uncanny, visionary clarity. Before the Internet came into our studies, Dick surfed the *Encyclopedia Britannica* and Paul Edwards's *Encyclopedia of Philosophy,* finding and forming associations. Of the later novels, *A Scanner Darkly* (1977)—drug-heightened, suburban, nightmarish—ends with an elegiac dedication to those of his friends and acquaintances who had succumbed to substances. Such losses, and his own early death, were part of the price paid for a wildly rich and eccentric oeuvre, a contract made with Mephistopheles. Speculative fiction indeed. R. Crumb and Richard Linklater translated Dick into cartoon form; thus sci-fi returns to the slime from which it originally arose, but a slime enriched, ironized, transformed. At Dick's funeral three of his five former wives and one wife-to-have-been were present. It was a Roman Catholic send-off.

Michael Crichton (1942–2008) had a career that, compared to Dick's, looks almost cynically contrived, fiction as speculation. His father was a journalist, and as a fourteen-year-old Crichton had a travel column in the *New York Times.* Until he was sure he would succeed, he used pseudonyms. After writing conventional, readable novels he came to understand how genre fiction works in the marketplace. In 1969 he published three substantial novels, the second of which, *The Andromeda Strain,* was his first major best seller. Scientists examine a microorganism (dubbed Andromeda) from outer space that can clot human blood. Infected, the patient has two minutes to live. In the same year Crichton attacked *Slaughterhouse-Five* in a review for the *New Republic.* "The ultimate difficulty with Vonnegut is precisely this: that he refuses to say who is wrong . . . He ascribes no blame, sets no penalties." Crichton wants the writer to tell the reader what to think. Or what he thinks. There is no doubt which side he is on. He expects us to be there with him.

His interest is less in people than in biotechnology, corporations, and the ethical issues they raise. He trained as a physician, and his science has the plausibility we associate with Huxley and Wells, though in scale and complexity it surpasses theirs. In the struggle between good and evil, human instinct chooses evil. Crichton's novels became increasingly bleak—the human agent more corruptible, the planet increasingly vulnerable to the combined forces of human greed, immorality, and technological development. Fourteen films, some of which Crichton himself scripted and directed, have been based on his novels. The novel *Jurassic Park* (1993) has sold more than 200 million copies.

In the second half of the twentieth century, science fiction changed from being predominantly a male preserve to being a mixed area. In 1999 more than a third of recorded sci-fi writers were women. Among them, Ursula Le Guin exemplifies some of the thematic and formal possibilities of the genre, readjusted. Le Guin's father was a distinguished anthropologist, and with him she learned to observe the otherness around her. Her mother was a writer too, composing her husband's biography. In Le Guin's *The Left Hand of Darkness* (1969), her first major success, the science fiction element of transformation is based in gender differently conceived and expressed. The book is part of her sci-fi Hainish cycle, set in the Hainish universe. The cycle was begun in 1966 with her first novel, *Roscannon's World*, and eight novels later, in 2000, came *The Telling*. It is sci-fi, but because Le Guin is a woman it is often classed as fantasy. *The Left Hand of Darkness* is set in a future, more than two millennia ahead, in which interplanetary travel and political and civic expansion are pursued. On planet Winter— predictably cold, without the other seasons—the inhabitants are neuter, or androgynous, except once a month when they experience sexual desire and definition. Le Guin explores a world in which the dualities do not naturally exist and freedom is at once enhanced and made terrifying because one cannot *know* what to expect socially—or sexually. Readers are allowed some of the freedoms John Dos Passos offers in his earlier fiction: the book is in part a compendium of information from which we infer, and through which we follow the narrative.

Since the 1960s Le Guin has provided alternative perspectives on politics, nature, gender, and much else, in a spirit not of opposition but of calm redress. She has written for radio and for film. Her concern with gender and gender formation means that she is a novelist of nurture with a belief in the effects on human development of structures, ideas, and words. They make things happen, or they stop things from happening. In one configuration they ensure freedom and creativity, in another they constrain. Understanding is to be deliberately pursued.

Reflecting on the occasional adaptation of her work for cinema, she offers an explanation that is also a point of difference between her work and that of the other sci-fi writers considered here. "In modern fantasy (literary or governmental), killing people is the usual solution to the so-called war between good and evil. My books are not conceived in terms of such a war, and offer no simple answers to simplistic questions."

# | 38 |

## Convention and Invention

David Garnett, J. B. Priestley, L. P. Hartley, Richard Hughes, Storm Jameson, Walter Greenwood,

H. E. Bates, Ethel Mannin, Olivia Manning, Stella Gibbons, V. S. Pritchett, Robert Graves,

Doris Lessing, Angela Carter, Elaine Feinstein, Colm Tóibín, Alan Hollinghurst

In his 1967 *Atlantic* essay "The Literature of Exhaustion," a personal *ars poetica* and a celebration of the brittle, essayistic fiction of Jorge Luis Borges, John Barth declared that realist resources of fiction were exhausted. The "proper novel" has, historically, attempted "to imitate actions more or less directly, and its conventional devices—cause and effect, linear anecdote, characterization, authorial selection, arrangement, and interpretation—can be and have long since been objected to as obsolete notions, or metaphors for obsolete notions."

The case for the "proper novel" is still made, not least by novelists who continue working in what they believe to be an unbroken line that stretches from Defoe and Fielding to—well, to Howard Jacobson, Hilary Mantel, Nicole Krauss. Borges knew that tradition is not synonymous with convention: on the contrary, the dry hand of convention is at the throat of that vital and irreducible thing that is tradition. Taste agrees with convention, judgment is engaged with extending tradition. As Don Quixote shows, the author's tilting-spear against the impotent windmill of convention is irony.

The "proper novel" in this exhausted tradition—which with respect to the twentieth century one can describe as fundamentally humanist—has become a genre, recognizable by the proprieties Barth identified. There is nothing inherently wrong with those properties except that, as John Cage reminds us, habit, convention, and obedience all threaten to stifle the natural desire to discover, indeed our ability to recognize the new when it appears. At the start, writers may resist convention and set out with invention and disobedience, but convention's seductions, social and material, are stronger than the integrity and imagination of most. Also, it can become taxing *always* to be interrogating the "real." On the other hand, accepting the real as a category outside the language that constructs it, a category to which language can confidently refer, begs questions. Impatience with Sterne, Nabokov, and other writers (Christine Brooke-Rose, B. S. Johnson, Mark Z. Danielewski) who reify the medium of writing or the book object itself is hard to justify once the tenets of a philosophical realism are questioned. Writers of conventional "proper novels" to whom Barth refers grow impatient with experiment and are not dissatisfied with a "mainstream," commercially defined, though it flows sluggishly.

This was the case with David Garnett (1892–1981). He belongs to a great literary family. In the 1920s he established the Nonesuch Press, a private press that produced handsome collectible editions of major and minor classics. Books were in his blood. His grandfather was a leading Victorian man of letters; his father, Edward, was the editor who introduced Conrad to Ford, "found" Somerset Maugham, eased both D. H. and T. E. Lawrence into print, championed American writers, and rejected *A Portrait of the Artist as a Young Man*. His mother was the translator Constance Garnett. David busied himself creatively and libidinally with the Bloomsbury Group. His first book, *Turgenev* (1917), marked an apprenticeship to that precise and Maupassantian Russian. His first novel, *Dope-Darling: A Story of Cocaine* (1919), appeared under the pseudonym Leda Burke. Going to meet him at his home in France, Frederic Raphael reflects that he "was born when Queen Victoria still had another nine years to reign. He knew D. H. Lawrence, before the first world war, and rejected—reluctantly—a seductive overture from Frieda. He played at sea captains with Joseph Conrad— a laundry basket for a ship, sheets for a sail—and he was recruited by H. G. Wells for a barnyard variety of badminton invented by 'the Don Juan of the intellectuals.' He test-drove a speedboat designed by T. E. Lawrence."

In 1920 Garnett's most inventive and successful book, *Lady into Fox,* appeared. Recently married, Sylvia and Richard go for a walk in the woods. Sylvia turns into a fox. At first she retains her human nature, continues to dress, converse, play piquet; but gradually she becomes more vixenish, descending onto all fours, until at last Richard out of love releases her into the wild. She gives birth to five cubs, which Richard cherishes, and she is finally killed in a hunt in which Richard himself is injured. Apart from Sylvia's metamorphosis, Garnett's narrative is logical and realistic in conventional ways (he did some research into the nature of foxes to get the details right), so that after the first shock the transformation becomes credible and readers grow anxious for the vixen Sylvia much as they do for the bug Gregor Samsa in Kafka's *Metamorphosis*. This parable novel, about nature and natures, love and relationship, is a pure expression of confident and instinctive and mannerly English modernism. Garnett's style is perfectly clear, his narrator tactfully out of sight.

This style remains the chief virtue of his writing. *A Man in the Zoo* (1924) is about a man who goes on show at the zoo as a specimen of *Homo sapiens*. It possesses some of the charm of *Lady*. The transition into a more realistic mode occurs in *The Sailor's Return* (1925), which in increasingly conventional terms also deals with issues of accommodation. A West Country sailor returns from his travels with a black bride: What does she experience, and how does his community welcome her? George Moore, one of Garnett's masters, urged him to conduct the necessary research and showed him how to write so as to make the action seem inevitable. A reticent narrator is crucial to the effect: the story happens, we are not guided through it.

His later work loses its cool clarity. The tone can be whimsical and ingratiating, and though fantasy recurs in stories and sporadically in the novels themselves, the attempt to integrate modern subject matter into a realist strategy works against his natural grain. *Aspects of Love* (1955) was a vulnerable novel, the pretext, over two decades later, for Andrew Lloyd Weber's musical by that title (1989). The modernist Garnett fades away.

John Boynton Priestley (1894–1984) experimented with time in his plays, but in his novels he hardly toys with modernist notions at all. When he was awarded the Order of Merit in 1977, Dame Rebecca West declared that particular gong devalued. Her distaste for Priestley partook of various kinds of snobbery. Primarily she did not like his insistent address to a general reader who was also a *common* reader; and his popular success with theatrical works that were unabashedly political was a further affront. Priestley had a strong, rudimentary sense of what a writer owes society. His sense of duty dated back to his experience of the First World War, in which he served and was wounded, emerging a vocal critic of the officer class. After studying at Trinity Hall, Cambridge, he set out as a piquant comic novelist.

The third of his twenty-six novels, *The Good Companions* (1929), received prizes, and he was soon widely read. Yorkshire found its voice again, phonetically rendered in Jess Oakroyd, who sets off from a town not unlike Priestley's native Bradford for a series of adventures on the high road to London. The unstable, vibrant world of the music hall is evoked, and Priestley's ear for dialect comes rather too much into its own. The book is engaging, though its sense of class has come to seem patronizing, comforting, if not comfortable. He was ambitious to get into his novel as much of the world as he could: characters, credible setting, and incidents abound. His imagination has the scope, if not the penetration, of Dickens's. *Angel Pavement*, published in 1930, is also conceived on a substantial social scale, the comedy rooted in Depression-era London, the politics taking their bearings from that period.

There was something adversarial in his nature. He felt he was a target of attack and so fought back, even when there was no evident cause. He sued Graham Greene (unsuccessfully) for defamation over what he took to be a portrayal of himself in *Stamboul Train* (1932). He identified with his readers more than with his literary peers. In the autumn of 1933 he set out like his own Jess Oakroyd on a progress around England, publishing the account as *English Journey* and making neglected English places and social conditions public. The project, Orwellian *avant la lettre,* had a radicalizing effect on the political classes, as John Dos Passos's *State of the Nation* did a decade later in the United States.

*Literature and Western Man* (1960) was one of Priestley's most ambitious and forgettable books, a substantial survey of half a millennium of the literatures of the Western world up to Thomas Wolfe. His reflections in *Man and Time* (1964) cast some light and shadow on his work, but his fascination with theories of perception belongs to its period, not ours. His willingness to entertain, and to be entertained by, plausible notions is part of his intellectual innocence. It might have benefited from a touch more irony.

Ian McEwan reports, "L. P. Hartley's *The Go-Between* [1953] made a huge impression on me." The impression, Edwardian, passionate, restrained, was a lasting one. Leslie (named after Leslie Stephen) Poles Hartley (1895–1972) is best remembered for that book, for the Eustace and Hilda trilogy consisting of *The Shrimp and the Anemone* (1944), *The Sixth Heaven* (1946), and *Eustace and Hilda* itself (1947), and for *The Hireling* (1957). The first and last of these were made into what became classic films. Two years after Hartley's death, Angus Wilson recorded an affinity and perhaps a debt when he wrote of "the decaying humanist world of which L. P. Hartley (and, indeed, a great many of us) is trying to make sense under the realistic events of his novels." Sense had to be made in the traditional forms, even though decay might be thought to inhere in the forms themselves.

From 1923 Hartley was a reviewer of fiction, and during his first two creative decades he published stories but no novels. Lovecraft thought him "notable for his incisive and extremely ghastly tale, 'A Visitor from Down Under.'" Like Priestley, though with a narrower politics and a more bounded readership in mind, Hartley had a sense of the novelist's duty to his readers, a duty that as book reviewer he performed with enthusiasm and some severity. In 1967 he published *The Novelist's Responsibility,* a collection of critical essays. The formal and aesthetic limitations of his concerns are revealed in *Facial Justice* (1960), a cacatopian novel set in the wake of a Third World War, a world in which blandness prevails and beauty is deliberately marred. The beautiful protagonist is destined to be reduced to commonplace. A kind of mild reason prevails in this world of neither fire nor ice; the outcome of the cataclysm is not Wellsian tyranny but a further wan portrayal of the decaying humanist world with its lack of conviction.

In *The Go-Between* Leo is a turn-of-the-century boy Mercury and blind Cupid, bearing messages from well-born Marian to low-born Ted, not understanding quite how he is being used but becoming implicated and altered emotionally, learning without a language what love is in its different kinds. Hartley is good at creating vulnerable innocence. Leo is a vigorous relation of frail, inhibited

Eustace Cherrington; we first encounter Eustace in *The Shrimp and the Anemone* as a nine-year-old living in a seaside town at the beginning of the twentieth century, clearly overshadowed by his beloved elder sister, Hilda. In the second volume Eustace goes up to Oxford (Hartley himself went up to Balliol in 1915, befriended Huxley, joined the army in 1916, and for health reasons never marched away) and begins quietly to grow, to stretch his wings, to show literary inclinations; and there is Hilda still between him and his own sunlight. The telling is precise, the psychology persuades, as though we are reading something close to autobiography.

Ali Smith remembers *The Go-Between* as a set text at school, the token modern work in 1979 when she was sixteen. She read the Penguin edition "with Julie Christie under a parasol on the front, a still from Joseph Losey's 1970 film adaptation." Thirty years later she took down the same book. "Can a book ambush you? From the prologue ('Are you vanquished, Colston, are you vanquished?') to the epilogue ('Tell him there's no spell or curse except an unloving heart') it felt, as I reread, uncannily familiar, like something I knew—and had no idea I knew—by heart." It is a book that affixes itself like a burr to adolescence, with Alain-Fournier's *Le Grand Meaulnes* and *A High Wind in Jamaica* (published originally in the United States as *The Innocent Voyage*, 1929) by Richard Hughes (1900–1976). Those books cast spells that continue to work, though the means used are conventional.

*The Human Predicament* is regarded by critics, if not by readers, as Richard Hughes's major achievement, a would-be trilogy of novels (the third roughly sketched and hardly begun at the time of his death). In *The Fox in the Attic* (1961) and *The Wooden Shepherdess* (1973) he interweaves fiction and fact; historical figures are never far away, and twenty-odd years of history, from the 1920s through World War II, are revived. What was original in this heightened history, or heightened fiction, was the way in which the style is consistent between the realms of "fact" and "imagination," giving the books the texture of experience in time, a time whose historical reality is brought up close by the incorporation of fictional elements. It is an insistently political form of writing.

That most ungothic writer Margaret Storm Jameson (1891–1988) was born in Dracula's Whitby, Yorkshire. For her, writing was political exploration, and her chief concerns as a journalist and often as a novelist were with the present and the near future. There is little elegiac clutter in her work, much clarity of thought along defined lines. Ideas are *real* to her in ways that they were for many writers whose social visions developed in response to the economic disasters of the 1920s and the political polarizations of the 1930s.

The two volumes of her autobiography are entitled *Journey from the North* (1969, 1970) and, devotedly English in her radicalism, she was aware of the distinctive perspectives she and other women of her generation were bringing from her province to the civic center of an England often exclusively identified with the Home Counties and subsumed within a Great Britain at the heart of an Empire. Hers was a shipbuilding family, and she centered her trilogy *The Triumph of Time,* which consists of *The Lovely Ship* (1927), *The Voyage Home* (1930), and *A Richer Dust* (1931), on that history, weaving into it elements of her own life, though as it were backdated to the nineteenth century. Yorkshire remained real, though a Yorkshire increasingly of memory, as the center of her life slid south. She created foreign landscapes and cities with authority, but England remained her point of acutest reference.

She studied at Leeds University and was elected secretary of the Women's Representative Council. An active socialist and suffragist, her whole life was given to serving causes. She stands in this context for that northern generation of remarkable radical female fiction and memoir writers that includes Jameson's close friend, Cheshire-born Vera Brittain (1893–1970), best remembered for her *Testament of Youth* (1933) and its two sequels; her close friend Yorkshire-born Winifred Holtby (1898–1935), whose posthumously published novel *South Riding* (1936) is still read; from Derbyshire, Katherine Burdekin (1896–1963), disguised behind a pseudonym and rediscovered for her dystopian, proto-Orwellian *Swastika Night* (1937); and the Edinburgh writer Naomi Mitchison (1897–1999), whose life very nearly touched three centuries.

Jameson began teaching at the Working Women's College in London. She believed "the intellect of the working class" was fresh and energetic enough to give rise to "a new Renaissance" that would come suddenly, decisively. She experienced the First World War at a formative age, the Great Depression and General Strike of 1926 in her early maturity, then the ideological and political divisions and tensions that issued in the Second World War. Her fiction follows her developing concerns and, in *Love in Winter* (1926), it takes a line closely parallel to autobiography, her protagonist Hervey Russell, a writer with a growing reputation ( Jameson's own fiction began appearing in 1919), moving into London literary society, disposing of an inadequate husband (as she did in 1924), and falling in with a cousin whose life needs rebuilding after his devastating experiences of the war. Jameson remarried in 1926.

With other writers she was involved in establishing the *Left Review,* which managed to keep a little distance from the authoritarian British Communist Party. When the Union of British Fascists held a big rally at Olympia, she (along with Brittain, Huxley, and others) was among the five hundred protesters who burst into the hall and heckled the Fascist leader. They were set upon by the black-shirted stewards, some were injured, and all were ejected. The outcry that followed led to the *Daily Mail* ceasing to support the Fascists. Recruitment to the cause diminished. For Jameson the ideological issues of the day could not have been more real. Two years after the rally her novel *In the Second Year* (1936) contributed to the *bien pensant* leftist orthodoxy of the period, projecting five years into the future a Fascist Britain, the "second year" of the title being an allusion to Hitler's momentous second year and its brutal consolidations. Despite the dystopian structure, the novel is peopled by characters rather than stereotypes, and its closeness to the author's present gives it material solidity. Part of the effect is due to this very proximity, the familiarity of a world that politics has shaken like a snow globe. More than a critique of the easily villainized right, the book is severe on the liberal center, whose principles and prevarications become its chief weakness. Though more dated than they, it belongs in the dystopian company of *Brave New World* and *Nineteen Eighty-Four*. Jameson regarded this as her best novel, the one that in the most complex way penetrated and understood the political world she lived in.

Also from the north, from Hanky Park, Salford, Lancashire, came Walter Greenwood (1903–1974), a proper child of the classes for which the liberal and radical middle-class writers sought to speak. His parents were politically committed working-class people. The father died when the boy was nine. Four years later Greenwood left school and began a series of subsistence-level jobs that were wearing and instructional. He spent his spare time, and his unemployed time, in Salford Library and worked hard on behalf of the Labor Party. He wrote stories and, in 1932, his first and best-loved novel, *Love on the Dole*. It was published, after several rejections, the following year by Jonathan Cape, whose main reader was the aging Edward Garnett. It had social consequences (on the Beveridge Report of 1942, for example) in part because articulate witnesses who had experienced extreme poverty were few, and the world it described was made credible in an emphatic, undecorated style, precise with anger yet tempered by fatalism. The novel, set in Hanky Park as it was then, before it became a Salford shopping precinct, was *Road to Wigan Pier* territory: "tiny houses cramped and huddled together, two rooms above and two below, in some cases only one room alow and aloft; public houses by the score where forgetfulness lurks in a mug; pawnshops by the dozen where you can raise the wind to buy forgetfulness." The book is set largely in 1931, the year before it was written. Harry Hardcastle, like the author, in his mid teens works in a pawnshop. He progresses to the local engineering factory, where after a long impecunious apprenticeship he is laid off. It is the Great Depression: no work is to be had. But he has fallen in love with Helen, a local girl, who is pregnant. They marry, though he has been denied the dole. Harry's sister in turn falls in love with Larry Meath, a political activist. At the core of the novel is a march that actually occurred in October 1931. The novel marchers are confronted by the police, and in the fray

Harry receives fatal injuries. After his death Sally accepts the blandishments of Sam Grundy, a scheming bookmaker who has been after her for some chapters, and this liaison makes it possible for her brother and her father, relieved of ideals, to work and survive within an unaltered system. Edgell Rickword, editor of the *Left Review,* saw it as the first genuine expression of the living circumstances of a working-class community, in part at least because, half a century before Irvine Welsh, Greenwood uses in dialogue the Salford language to which these experiences belong, not an emollient standard English.

The north-south divide can be illustrated by comparing Greenwood's work with that of an immediate contemporary, Herbert Ernest Bates (1905–1974), who shared his publisher. In "The Watercress Girl," a story set in something very like H. E. Bates's own childhood, which it romanticizes, a grandfather takes a boy in a pony trap to meet "Sar' Ann" (Greenwood-style, the grandfather speaks in an orthographic Northamptonshire dialect). Bates was born in Rushden. He came of modest antecedents, but nothing in Rushden was so straitened as Hanky Park. The rural could be construed as idyllic in that part of England, and there was a good grammar school. Bates did not proceed to university, but he became a newspaper office clerk (a job he disliked as much as Greenwood did his pawnshop), then worked in a shoe warehouse, and at last became a journalist. When he was twenty he published *The Two Sisters* (1926), the novel having been accepted by Jonathan Cape, again on the advice of Edward Garnett. This was the first of his almost one hundred publications.

In World War II Bates served as an Air Force squadron leader, and his most powerful novels are political in a different spirit from Greenwood's: patriotic, fervent, subscribing to traditional notions of heroism but not forgetful of the truths writers told of the First World War. He went on to write novels about Burma and India, work drawn from his war experiences farther east. The propaganda stories in *How Sleep the Brave* (1943) (published under the pseudonym "Flying Officer X") and his stirring novel *Fair Stood the Wind for France* (1944), his first commercial success, retain their power, but with a black-and-white quality, characters acting rather than living.

In the late 1950s Bates developed a large readership with *The Darling Buds of May,* first of the Larkin family ruddy-faced novels produced between 1958 and 1970. They revert to the landscape and company of his earliest fiction, but with a nostalgia the titles themselves underline (*A Breath of French Air; When the Green Woods Laugh; Oh! To Be in England;* and *A Little of What You Fancy*). In 1971 he published the remarkable short novel *The Triple Echo* (1971), a late return to the home front of war and to Bates's landscapes. The treacle has been drained out of this story of a deserter taken in by a woman whose husband is serving abroad. At her suggestion he assumes a female disguise; they fall in love. He is duly courted by an army sergeant who at a Christmas party discovers the travesty, with tragic consequences. The structure is tight, Lawrencian, and what is potentially melodramatic is in fact sparely, cruelly rendered. The harsh textures of the age are made palpable. The war novels and this late fiction raise Bates out of the category of English nature and short-story writer: his wartime fiction had a political effect, or use, different in kind from Greenwood's.

In the 1930s it was hard not to be drawn into politics, often in ways that felt awkward to the writer. The vast bibliography—some ninety-five books—of Ethel (Edith) Mannin (1900–1984) is a case in point. Born in London of Irish parents, she insisted on her Irish provenance, supported Irish independence, and claimed to be an Irish writer. Ireland is pleased to claim her. At the age of fourteen, asked to write an essay on patriotism, she composed an impassioned attack on king and country and was punished before the whole school. She had reckoned as her reader a favorite radical schoolmistress, not the headmistress.

Her autobiographies, of which several volumes appeared between 1930 and 1977, make her passionate intensity and her privileged perspective clear. Mannin was the daughter of a warmhearted socialist postal worker and belongs, if not in Hanky Park, in a less insalubrious working-class neighborhood, noisy, turn-of-the-twentieth-century Clapham. She was sent to an inexpensive and undistinguished private school where she was bullied and occasionally infatuated with her tormenters. She began to write stories and published one when she was ten in the children's pages of *Lady's Companion*. She achieved a scholarship and at fifteen went to a commercial school. Again she fell in love with a teacher, a socialist who inducted her into the mysteries of Fabianism and the revolutionary Independent Labor Party. She began as a copy typist at an advertising agency and, still in her teens, was promoted to copy writer.

Mannin's memoirs provide considerable detail: in setting herself at center stage she grows larger than life. Sexual liberation being one of her goals, she had more than her fair share of romances, some with people whose names she forgets, some identified with initials, and others rather boldly themselves. She married at nineteen, had a baby, continued writing. She started composing "serialized romantic novelettes," paid as Dickens had been "by weight," a guinea (£1.05) for every 1,000 words. Most of her novels are rooted in romance conventions, though she took the form beyond the popular rulebook and sometimes risked unhappy endings. In 1922 she published her first novel, *Martha,* an overwrought book about excessive love and its consequences, parenting, and the perils an independent girl faces in the world. What begins as a species of ideological misery memoir ends happily ever after. Martha is, of course, a writer, and the novel not unconnected with Mannin's intense, narrow experiences.

Her early books are politically alert but not programmatic. Ten years later, with *Love's Winnowing* (1932), she became a frankly political writer. *Red Rose* (1941), written in 1938, was her fictionalized version of the life of her friend the American radical Emma Goldman. Mannin also wrote more than a dozen travel books, from as far east as Burma and as far west as Morocco. And she wrote books that philosophers regard as social science and social scientists as philosophical. She drifted on from anarchism to Buddhism, the faith in which she died. She had written fifty-one novels.

There is satire in some of her novels, like her use of an index, a convention common to some literature but not to fiction, which she plays with to effect in *Ragged Banners: A Novel with an Index* (1931), but in later life she dismisses it as "a youthful affectation." She toyed with a "new form" in *All Experience* (1932), a portmanteau book designed to include all sorts of writing, generically promiscuous. Again, she did not pursue the challenge far. In *Children of the Earth* (1930) and *Venetian Blinds* (1933) and other novels of the decade her protagonists were working-class women. These were her more original and sustained explorations. Issues of sexuality and gender and the developing role of the independent woman writer remain central in her work. The romantic, melodramatic framework of the novel is unchallenged, whatever play of themes it learns to tolerate.

Mannin came into conflict with the Independent Labor Party. The party leader, James Maxton, tried to dictate her subject matter and approach, finding *Men Are Unwise* (1934) not fit for revolutionary purpose. She began to fear that her early romances were complicit in the exploitation of women. In *Cactus* (1935) and *The Pure Flame* (1936) she strove to meet Maxton's criticism. Then she revisited the Soviet Union in 1935, seeing a future that decidedly did not work. There was no return to the ILP after *South to Samarkand* (1936), a book of dissatisfaction and disillusion. Her pacifism grew, along with a studious and sentimental orientalism. Her final novel, *The Late Miss Guthrie* (1976), concentrates on a working-class woman; the story relates to her mother's life, and her own.

An altogether more substantial Anglo-Irish writer, but shyer, socially less agreeable, is Olivia (Mary) Manning (1908–1980), nicknamed Olivia Moaning by friends because of her continual complaints in later years about her neglect and the greater success of her contemporaries, with some of whom she, or her husband, was intimate. Between 1960 and her death she wrote *The Balkan Trilogy* and *The Levant Trilogy,* which together constitute *The Fortunes of War,* a long and, for tenacious readers, compellingly lived account of the period leading up to the Second World War and of the war itself, with characters drawn from life. Their little histories are magnified by the events they witnessed or in which they engaged. Manning is able to describe in detail the quick, bloody moves of modern warfare and the dislocation of a modern women, suspended between cultures, with no fixed place. Anthony Burgess described *The Fortunes of War* as "the finest fictional record of the war produced by a British writer," a substantial contribution to that popular historical sequence genre to which Ford, Hartley, Waugh, Powell, Durrell, Richard Hughes, Paul Scott, and many others contributed. She regarded her work as close to autobiography.

Harriet and Guy Pringle are based on Manning and her British Council husband, R. G. (Reggie) Smith; their postings take them from Bucharest to Athens to North Africa. Via Harriet we see through Manning's eyes; the author had originally drafted parts of the book in first person, then reverted to third person to achieve greater narrative range. Guy has some of the scale and English pluck that we find in Ford's Ashburnhams and Tietjens, though he is drawn from a lower social class. A defined individual, he also represents the class and culture of which he is a product. Manning began her project before issues of gender and colonialism were foregrounded. Some critics are anachronistically hard on her. What is remarkable is that she produced this comprehensive and readable account of the twilight of Empire and of a war that, from the perspective of one intimately involved in its movements, unfolded in such chaotic ways.

Ethel Mannin and her socially engaged urban and rural "miserabilism," and Olivia Manning and her historical saga, can profitably be set beside the timeless corrective of Stella Gibbons's *Cold Comfort Farm* (1932). It gathers in its satirical sickle-sweep whole swathes of romance fiction from the Brontës to Mannin herself, including grief-laden tales by Hardy and Lawrence. The particular butt of the author Stella (Dorothea) Gibbons (1902–1989) was Mary Webb (1881–1927), whose *The Golden Arrow* (after the success of *Precious Bane*) was revived and serialized in the *Evening Standard*. One of Gibbons's vexing duties in the newspaper office was to summarize the plot for readers who missed a chapter. *Cold Comfort Farm* is the most durable consequence of Webb's work, as *Don Quixote* is a ripe result of the romance tradition and *Northanger Abbey* of the Walpolian Gothic.

It was Gibbons's first novel of the twenty-five she wrote and the only one that is still read. She dedicates it to "Anthony Pookworthy Esq., A.B.S., L.L.R.," a writer whom she professes to respect profusely. She speaks of herself as a tyro interloping on the field of literature after a decade "in the meaningless and vulgar bustle of newspaper offices" (a phrase she uses four times in three pages). "The effect of those locust years on my style (if I may lay claim to that lovely quality in the presence of a writer whose grave and lucid prose has permanently enriched our literature) has been perhaps even more serious." She adds with a fervent humility, "The life of the journalist is poor, nasty, brutish and short. So is his style. You, who are so adept at the lovely polishing of every grave and lucent phrase, will realize the magnitude of the task which confronted me when I found, after spending ten years as a journalist, learning to say exactly what I meant in short sentences, that I must learn, if I was to achieve literature and favorable reviews, to write as though I were not quite sure about what I meant but was jolly well going to say something all the same in sentences as long as possible." She will mark her text with one, two, or three stars, as in a Baedeker guide, to alert readers and more importantly reviewers to points of salient beauty.

She did not resent the success of that first novel but remained a little puzzled by it. Later works cost her more effort and gave her more pleasure, but none of them had the long legs of that lighthearted exercise in literary redress. It is set, she tells us in a headnote, in "the near future," like the best of Storm Jameson. It has more the feeling of being set in a grimy rural past in, say, a wet and pungently manured Dorset. But we are in a version of Sussex where natives speak a version of the dialect of the county (with a number of invented, punning words), as though transcribed by Priestley, Greenwood, or Bates, only the effect here is to heighten comedy rather than render authenticity. Flora Poste is a sophisticated young woman left penniless when her parents die. She wishes herself upon the Starkadder maternal cousins, who live at the eponymous, dysfunctional farm near Howling. The Starkadders feel under obligation and grudgingly receive her. Every Starkadder, and it is an extended family, has some deep-seated problem that needs mending, and Flora with her modern sensibility knows what to do to transform this hotbed of misery into an efficient family farm, and how best to release those whose fulfillment might best be sought elsewhere. The presiding spirit is Aunt Ada Doom, a sort of rural Miss Havisham who at an early stage of her life witnessed "something nasty in the woodshed." The book takes Cold Comfort Farm from dystopia to utopia in roughly 240 pages. The bones of various authors, starting with Emily and Charlotte Brontë, are broken as the world is adjusted and set back on course. By the time Flora is rescued by her cousin Charles, soon to be a clergyman, she has put the world to rights, using *The Higher Common Sense,* and laid waste a whole popular genre.

———•———

Richard Findlater's 1985 anthology *Author! Author!* leaves readers in doubt: Can writing ever be a vocation subject to general laws—even laws of the most practical kind? The Society of Authors' magazine *The Author* devoted its first decade, Findlater says, "to the definition and defense of literary property," by which he means copyright in all its aspects, especially as it benefits the author. "Material interest" was the one thing, Walter Besant declared, that would bring writers together. In 1978 the Society of Authors proclaimed itself a trade union, marking a culmination of effort but not, perhaps, unanimity among members.

Unionization complicated, too, relations between writers, publishers, and agents. Storm Jameson quotes Claudel: "It is indecent to try to live on your soul, by selling it to the mob"; and Coleridge: "Never pursue literature as a trade"— refreshing aphorisms set against the avaricious and garrulous brilliance of Shaw, the pencil-stub calculations of Bennett, and Galsworthy's pompous condescension. Findlater makes a series of *sic aut non* juxtapositions, orchestrating a debate that qualifies and attenuates every point of view. In an article proposing a national publishing house, the critic Herbert Read makes the point: "No patronage can confer greatness on an art whose roots are withering in an impoverished soil." Yet a 1949 editorial, following Read's line without his cavils, declares: "Authorship has fallen on such evil times that a national plan to make it a field of opportunity again may be the only way of bringing life back into our literature." Literature can be legislated for and financed, it would seem, when enough opinion agrees. Sir Osbert Sitwell cautions the writer to be aware of what state patronage involves, "glittering prizes that soon bring his genius level with that of the contemporary politician. It means pandering to the aesthetic sense of the town council, to that of every oaf, who says 'I know what I like.'"

Most prescient was a writer whose views are frequently canvassed in this book, V. S. (Victor Sawdon) Pritchett (1900–1997), writing in 1940. "The real economic struggle is going to begin when popular publishing with a huge public finally destroys the gains in status and income which authors have had under the present system of restricted and expensive publishing." That struggle began in earnest well over forty years ago. Pritchett was president of English PEN and International PEN and president of the Society of Authors. He was knighted in 1975.

As Pritchett progressed, he came to rely on the American market and the income he could earn from teaching in the United States. Stefan Collini asks "whether any English writers have lived by their pen since 1945 without this being true of them." By the 1960s Pritchett earned more than half his income from American sales and engagements. He was aware of this, and that awareness cannot but have affected how he wrote and what he chose, or was commissioned, to write about.

Pritchett's mother, a lively woman full of stories, had expected her fourth child to be a girl and had planned to name her after the queen. The boy became Victor, a name he disliked and resolved into initials. He was born above a toy shop in Ipswich, where his father, an unsuccessful small-scale businessman, was trying to set up another of his shop ventures, in this case a stationers. It was a lower-middle-class environment, the setting of much of his subsequent shorter fiction, and he was the first of his tribe to become a writer. He left school in his mid-teens and went to work in the leather trade. Like some of his own characters and those of his beloved Chekhov, the writer whose short-story art his own most resembles, he was always waiting for life to begin, his wait lasting eighty years. He knew more about the novel in English and the European novel than any of his contemporaries, and while he had a breadth of interest comparable to that of Virginia Woolf, whose essays he began by admiring, went off, then returned to, he reveled in the otherness of the writers he read and did not apply familiar templates to them. The otherness of the Russians, the Spanish and, among the Portuguese, of José Maria Eça de Queirós, engaged him. He also understood the evolution of the forms of fiction and of the industry that first served and then governed them. His time being very nearly our time (he survived to the threshold of this century), there was a great deal to know, and he knew it firsthand. He was an editor as well as a voluminous critic, and his memory did not let him down. The connections among European literatures were in growing disrepair; Britain was reverting to a monoglot culture, fed increasingly on the imaginative works from its former colonies. Pritchett continued to make connections between English and European literatures, to read in German, French, and Spanish, and to struggle with Russian.

Without his critical presence English and perhaps British literature would have a different, diminished aspect. "The duty of the critic is to literature, not to its surrogates," he said. Like Edward Garnett, like Ford Madox Ford, he worked for a good that went well beyond the natural self-interest of the first-person singular. He survives today more as a reader, an interpreter, and an advocate—in his effects, as it were—and as the author of outstanding short stories, than as the novelist he considered himself to be. And yet to be a reader of such diligence and tact is a higher achievement than producing a shelf of B+ novels. When he said that nothing happened to him, he was forgetting how many worlds he had read, how many engagements he kept.

What first marks Pritchett's critical approach is an insistence on limitation and proportion, which taken together constitute form. He values Arthur Hugh Clough (1819–1861), whose verse novel *Amours de Voyage* (1849) remains the most delicate performance in that unlikely genre that we have in English, an epistolary exchange between young, languid, and amorous travelers. He defends Clough against the charge of "shortness of imagination," recognizing instead in the verse novel a calculated determination "not to see beyond his subject," so that the voices remain true to his correspondents whose letters comprise the fiction. He compares Clough's approach to E. M. Forster's and notes the advantage the writer draws from precision, candor, directness, and *limitation*. His tact is to skim off excesses of emotion, those insistences that overshoot the actual runway of subject and theme. "The cat is never quite on the mat, as far as I am concerned," he said.

Pritchett's abundance as a writer tells against him. As Dryden wrote of Cromwell upon his demise, "How shall I then begin, or where conclude / To draw a fame so truly circular?" Pritchett made fun of his own energies. Had they been channeled into creative work, he would have outproduced Trollope. He wrote everything but poetry, a mode for which he had respect and a sharp critical ear but that was not his medium. He avoided writing drama, though he is a master of fictional dialogue: "It comes naturally to me to write dialogue. I'm not a plot writer." But he understood the fundamental difference between dialogue on the page and dialogue for staged performance.

His was the generation of Graham Greene and Henry Green, Waugh and Isherwood, C. S. Lewis and Tolkien. Though he is the most English-seeming of writers in manner and mildness, he is more a broad European than his contemporaries, original like Maupassant and Chekhov for "having something of a foreign mind." He lived in France and Spain when he was in his twenties. He trained himself as a journalist, he became dyspeptic and neurotic, collecting a credible set of writer's complaints. His first marriage unraveled but his second brought respite and cured many of his anxieties. Caustic Gore Vidal gave him an almost unconditional encomium and remains his only equal in critical breadth.

Pritchett's work for the leather company entailed messengering. He was noticed and patronized and allowed to go to Paris with a small allowance; he worked there and began writing for the *Christian Science Monitor,* his father being of that faith, and was well paid. He read *Ulysses* when it was published in Paris in 1922 and found it "frightful." The *Monitor* sent him to Ireland at the time of the troubles (1922–1924) to report less on events than on people, impression pieces. Later he realized what *Ulysses* was doing. He went to Spain, learned Spanish and experienced an alien culture on the pulse, changed by the pace of the country, its sense of community and hospitality, the feeling that earlier centuries coexisted with the present and that history was a matter of accretion, not erasure. He met the philosophers Miguel de Unamuno and José Ortega y Gasset, read their works, and engaged his own beliefs through theirs. On his return he began to write major essays on classical and new writers for the *New Statesman.*

His story lines are generally conventional. Dialogue and its modulations are the core of Pritchett's art, Ben Jonson's "Speak that I may see thee" measuring the reality of his characters. The situations are plausible in the sense that they do not distract from the emergence of character. "Dialogue is my form of poetry." His construction of dialogue is from the inside out, so that it carries the inconsequentialities, the strange transitions and tangents, that speech contains. He was an avid listener, not to replicate what he heard in the shop, street, or office but to understand the way speakers, even as they speak, mingle cliché with original thought, combine idiosyncrasy with commonplace. His love of the short story is fueled by this love of dialogue.

He was "bullied into" writing his first novel, *Clare Drummer* (1929), about his experiences in Ireland. Because he was a great boiler-down of language, he found it hard to be expansive, short fiction being his natural métier. He looked back on *Clare Drummer* without enthusiasm, though in it he invested some of his best recollections of people and places. It dealt with a difficult period, when he married his first wife, who, after a decade's attrition, he went on to replace. He wrote five novels with which he retained a tentative relationship. They were not at the heart of his work. When he talked about them, he immediately went on to talk of their sales. *Nothing Like Leather* (1935) sold 11,000 copies, whereas *Dead Man Leading* (1937), well received, "coincided with Munich and failed commercially." *Mr. Beluncle* (1951), a fictionalized autobiography with his father in it, sold well. It is his best novel. What story there is, is given, and he concentrates on making the world of Mr. Beluncle—from his eccentric church, which he and his family attend, to his furniture company, to his home life—real. His father, never much of a reader, could not get through it.

Not the fiction but the actual autobiographies, *A Cab at the Door* (1968) and *Midnight Oil* (1971), convey the complex, often humorous world in which Pritchett lost and found his way. They take him into the fifth of his ten decades. In his later years he became a servant of writers, a sitter on committees and a sort of hat-rack for laurel wreathes. He was done much reverence and he accepted it with a good grace. His life overlapped with Tolstoy's and Shaw's and Yeats's, and he wrote on Ian McEwan, Salman Rushdie, and Shiva Naipaul. Few writers have so long and so open a span. He claimed that the lack of a university education meant that he had no in-built sense of hierarchy or ranking and approached each writer from the ground up, watching what they do and how they do it. Thus too with his observation of characters, which began no doubt with watching his own ill-assorted and well-meaning parents, his mother desperately, good naturedly trying to keep things together, his father inadvertently blowing them apart with his optimism and scheming. Here are people "floundering amid their own words, and performing strange strokes as they swim about, with no visible shores, in their own lives."

Equally abundant was Robert Graves (1895–1985), though he was more at home in history than in the present or near-present tense. His European vision is rooted in the classics and in his sense of the ways human nature expresses itself in history. Critics have read into his Rome of the Claudius novels prophetic warnings to a continent approaching meltdown. His impatience with the directions the world was taking had to do with his own extreme experience of the trenches in the First World War, followed by the depredations of industrialism and the erosion of the specifics of culture. He became more sentimentally Welsh with time, more a particularist, reading the present through but not into his enormous knowledge of the classical and biblical past, a resource for his fiction. Some regard him as a "green" writer *avant la lettre*.

As a young man Graves admired Thomas Hardy in a different spirit from Powys's, principally for his poetry. His fiction is remote from Hardy's. It grows out of literature and the life of writing. The indefatigable reviser of his poems could also be a reviser of prose, though there were fewer opportunities for republishing novels, translations, and his huge compendia of myth, history, and speculation. In 1934 he published *I, Claudius,* a novel based on the Latin historians he read as a schoolboy at Charterhouse and at Oxford and never tired of rereading. *Claudius the God and His Wife Messalina* (1935) followed. Graves was a rather free translator from classical, Celtic, and oriental texts. He fidgeted, insisting on forming and reforming, revision not vision. He loved to collaborate: with history, with earlier texts, with other writers. His most famous collaboration was with Laura Riding.

The turbulent, fruitful relationship with her and with the poets and artists who came to Majorca to be with them, ended in 1939. By then they had been significant publishers. Their Seizin Press had issued the magazine *Epilogue* and work by Gertrude Stein as well as their own writing. They provided a kind of informal writing school in a comfortable climate; they revised Graves's earlier work, and wrote poems, stories, novels, and criticism. There is an element of impertinence in the speculations of biographers who have tried to reconstruct their lives together. Biography distracts attention from the writing.

Graves was publically courteous about Riding, whatever exasperations he may have experienced. Riding's letters, private and public (there is a public aspect to everything she wrote), could be outspoken. Indeed, she was never less than outspoken on the subject of her years with Graves, a period that, from her point of view, was maliciously misread by journalists and biographers. When as her publisher in 1979 I was preparing an edition of her book *A Trojan Ending* (1937), she remembered the *Time and Tide* review: her book, it proclaimed, was not unlike *I, Claudius.* "In fact," she quoted the reviewer, "it might have been called *I, Riding.*" She adds: "I reproduce this intendedly superior impudence—the writer is Malcolm Muggeridge—for the interest of the *I, Claudius* reference. As working comrade, in the Seizin Press, and an associate editor of *Epilogue,* of which I was editor, and a chosen collaborator in certain writings, Robert Graves, especially among my working comrades, had concentratedly attentive help from me in all his writer's texts, in the period of our working association." She describes the nature and extent of her involvement in editing and shaping the work of those she regarded as comrades, Graves especially; though her use of "sensibility" is anachronistic and the credit she claims immoderate, she did engage passionately in editing the work. So she insists, "Robert Graves, when he came into association with me, set himself to learn all he could from me of the principles of sensibility of the good in language. Robert Graves lacked the instinct of such sensibility, but he was well-supplied with literary ambition. He had got along until he came into association with me with drawing on the varied and deep-reaching material for tricks of the literary trade that the traditional literary stock provided. The story of what, with my assistance, he drew from my sensibility-experience and knowledge-experience, in matters of language is a wide-wandering one. I shall just record as to *I, Claudius* that if I had not worked to extremes of care upon its text for raising it to a level of fair literary civility, it would have been a production of gross and awkward capering, a mess of vulgarities in a sauce of inept stylistics." He suppressed an original preface thanking her, she said, for "the touch of my linguistic and stylistic hand."

Graves wrote fiction for money. The Claudius books were composed, not without conviction, but specifically to pay bills. They succeeded. Early in his career he wrote a savage "Scrutiny" of Kipling (1928): Whatever his reservations as a young man, from Kipling he learned a love of particular detail, of history, and the interaction of subjective man with the political and civic world. He also learned about authorial husbandry. He was hard on Kipling's errors of fact, a score on which Graves himself was not blameless.

He chose his subjects with care. The Claudius novels depict a fascinating, familiar dark epoch in world history, the Roman empire fallen into the hands of incompetent emperors: Tiberius, Caligula, Nero. Graves's hero, scholarly Claudius, weak, with an agonizing speech impediment, pretends to be a fool in order to elude notice. History flushes him out. A first person tells the story, with wry comedy, until, silenced, the remaining testimony is entrusted to others. Claudius understands the forces of history. Propelled into imperial and divine eminence, he witnesses and dies.

Graves's first novel, *My Head! My Head!* (1925) retold the story of Elisha and the Shunammite woman. It amplifies the brief Old Testament pretext and is the first of Graves's personal readings into the early years of the Hebrew and thus the Christian story. Twenty years later, after Riding's departure, he published *King Jesus* (1946), a reimagining of the Gospel stories. "I, Agabus the Decapolitan began this work at Alexandria in the ninth year of the Emperor Domitian and completed it at Rome in the thirteenth year of the same." Jesus has become the charismatic advocate of an ethically and spiritually demanding form of Judaism hostile to the literalism of those who manage the Temple, to Roman authority, and to the draw of older cults. The novel's end is known from the first page. Action serves as argument. Graves's novels can be read as essays by other means.

Given Graves's interest in the issues raised by the treatment of women and his hostility to Milton and the literature and politics he represented, *The Story of Marie Powell: Wife to Mr. Milton* (1943) is one of his durable novels. His Mrs. Milton, the unfortunate first wife, was sixteen when she married. Milton needed her dowry: it did not accompany her and he reacted, emotionally and sensually, against this betrayal. And she was a Roman Catholic. The drama of familiar figures drawn with authorial prejudices as rigid as those he attributes to his poet-villain is exasperating and engaging in equal measure, drawing in the age's political and military turbulence. The execution of Charles I is witnessed in unflinching, if not quite convincing, prose. *Homer's Daughter* (1955) was a further inventive attempt to explore the place of women in literature, building at once on the classics and on Samuel Butler's theory that the *Odyssey* was composed by a Sicilian princess, the original of Nausicaa in the poem. At the same period he was writing his celebrated *The Greek Myths* (1955) and was steeped in the lore invested there, teasing a novel out of the material and using a first person as in *I, Claudius,* an off-center "I" who sees from a new angle what we already think we know. This is Graves's own point of view in fiction, the art of reinvention. In *Homer's Daughter* the narrator tells her story while also working up the epic in the hope that through attribution to Homer the poem might endure.

---

Doris (May) Lessing (née Taylor, 1919–2013) in longevity vied with Pritchett and outstripped Graves. She was born in Persia and raised in Rhodesia. Or she was born in Iran and raised in Zimbabwe. In either case, she came into a world very different from the modern one. "I think it is very good for small children to be batted around the world because they remember it all." She has. She moved to Britain, specifically to England, in 1949. A year later her most celebrated novel, *The Grass Is Singing* (1950), was published.

It was completed in 1949 but rejected, revised down by two-thirds of its extent, and resubmitted. From the outset she was a poor stylist, her hand debauched by the pen, overly fluent (Coetzee gently says she "prunes too lightly"). Like *Look Homeward, Angel* and *Lord of the Flies,* the book required a persuasive and visionary editor. The editor she most generously acknowledges is the one who published her work in the *New Yorker* and then at Knopf, Robert Gottlieb, one of the editorial geniuses of the second half of last century.

Lessing's formative literary debt is to D. H. Lawrence, and not only to early Lawrence but to the one who pushed form into new, apocalyptic shapes. She learned how to isolate and focus in on intense relationships, about the physicality of imagination, its erotic dynamic. Then there was the matter of fluency, of writing the story from beginning to end and discovering inherent flexibilities of form as it responds to different content. Joyce Carol Oates noted how her books became difficult to categorize: "realism," space fiction, parable, autobiography, allegory, fantasy with elements of all these. There is the Children of Violence series (1952–1969), five novels—Burgess calls them her Pentateuch—that explore themes in their time from the changing points of view of ours. The second sentence of *The Golden Notebook* (1962), a friable experimental masterpiece, reads, "As far as I can see everything is cracking up." With *Briefing for a Descent into Hell* (1971) she moves away from realism and starts her space odyssey, or allegory, the deliberate dreaming in which "you can use your mind to tell you things you don't already know." In 2007 she was awarded the Nobel Prize in Literature, the citation characterizing her as an "epicist of the female experience," skeptical, fiery, visionary, who has "subjected a divided civilization to scrutiny." Such language seems remote from the particular and various texture of her work.

Through her father's experience and stories, the First World War was familiar to her. She was born the year after it ended. He had returned wounded and asked his bank to transfer him out of England. He found it constrained and claustrophobic. The family went to Rhodesia, where he believed he would make a fortune. His wife, who had loved rubbing elbows with diplomats in Tehran, found the transition to rural Africa trying. Young Doris Taylor found in her a prototype for the protagonist of her first published novel. The author-to-be might have had a wonderful life there, where "the Africans told stories, but we weren't allowed to mix with them. It was the worst part about being there. I mean I could have had the most marvelously rich experiences as a child. But it would have been inconceivable for a white child." She and her brother, overly supervised by their mother, shared this separation from the living world they inhabited. The main engagement with the land was hunting and shooting its creatures for sport.

By the time she was eighteen she had drafted two novels. When she became a Communist she was a bouncy and cheerful cadre, referred to as "Comrade Tigger," which proves two things, one about her character and another about the penetration of *Winnie the Pooh* in radical circles. Communist recruits, she said, "tended to be people with unhappy childhoods behind them, looking for a substitute family."

A contrary individual, she did much to irritate her family, especially in her choice of husband. Gottfried Lessing was much disliked by them, and then by her. In 1949 she traveled to England. She experienced no adjustment of culture because of the profound Englishness of her parents and the ideological bridge she carried with her, which made sense of England in terms of Rhodesia and vice versa. She was at home even with rationing and bomb damage, and it was a relief to be away from the married life she made and unmade there. Soon enough, Coetzee points out, reading from the second volume of her autobiography, *Walking in the Shade* (1997), she discovered "in the British psyche 'a smallness, a tameness, a deep, instinctive, perennial refusal to admit danger, or even the unfamiliar: a reluctance to understand extreme experience.'" They suffered from "an enduring preference for 'small, circumscribed novels, preferably about the nuances of class or social behavior.'"

Coetzee calls *The Grass Is Singing* "an astonishingly accomplished debut, though perhaps too wedded to romantic stereotypes of the African for present-day tastes." He refers to the predictably potent, Lawrencian figure of Moses, and it is hard to read the book without sensing the haunting of *Lady Chatterley's Lover.* It opens with a news report: a white woman has been murdered by a black servant. How does the white community respond? "The newspaper did not say much. People all over the country must have glanced at the paragraph with its sensational heading and felt a little spurt of anger mingled with what was almost satisfaction, as if some belief had been confirmed, as if something had happened which could only have been expected. When natives steal, murder or rape, that is the feeling white people have." And then? "And then they turned the page to something else."

Lessing stressed, in *The Grass Is Singing,* the isolation of the white farming families, thinly scattered on the landscape, "hungry" for the infrequent social intercourse the seasons afforded. They would all talk at once, then return "to their farms where they saw only their own faces and the faces of their black servants for weeks on end." The report of this murder was an occasion for silence rather than gossip because of the unspeakable elements in it. Lessing organizes the narrative into "us" and an alien "them" structure, an instinctive division whose violation is the mute central theme of the book. The farming district of Ngesi stands for the whole of white-in-black Rhodesia, the borders of the novel, and by extension Africa.

Mary Turner, her protagonist, is a town person. She marries a farmer and moves into an isolated world. The change in her vision of things is realized through detail and symbol. First she half sees, arriving at night, with insistent light-and-dark symbolic language, and gradually subsides into her environment and her relationship with her husband, Dick Turner. The incongruities of her arrival at the dark farmhouse, her tact, Dick's unease, establish roles and provide a gothic frisson. Then tea is brewed, the English sacrament. When day breaks the symbolism evolves because the narrative elements are slow.

Mary never loses her initial fear, but she changes and in that change becomes more vulnerably herself. Lessing uses third-person narrative with the close-focus precision of Joyce in *A Portrait of the Artist:* we observe an individual sensibility evolving, and its emblematic fate. The language is sensual, images of animal instinct and unrehearsed action draw her toward a border she has never before faced, much less crossed. She learns first to hate the collective otherness of the blacks, their presence, their language and smell. She manages them, she is provoked by a trivial misunderstanding to use the whip. She becomes one of "us," terrified, triumphant with power exercised. He—Moses—wipes the blood from his face and turns back to work with his people, who have witnessed her action. It singles him out, her quarry, her nemesis. Her interest in him intensifies. She cannot help watching him. "The powerful, broad-built body fascinated her." He becomes her creature: "She had given him white shorts and shirts to wear in the house, that had been used by her former servants. They were too small for him; as he swept or scrubbed or bent to the stove, his muscles bulged and filled out the thin material of the sleeves until it seemed they would split." She eroticizes him. "He appeared even taller and broader than he was because of the littleness of the house." Her fate, which is his also, advances upon them. He is bathing and senses her eyes upon him; the erotic and political tensions ratchet up. She is at last awake, and so is he, in a different way. They pass through the ordeal of touch, and the balance of power shifts so that after the intense subjectivity of Mary's response we have other takes on the inexorable action. In terms of the culture in which Mary lives, the transgression that gradually surfaces is almost unspeakable in moral and political consequences.

The first page of the novel has told us what the end will be. This is a novel not of suspense but of process, a revenger's tragedy as the concluding sentences, which do not presume to understand, make clear: "Though what thoughts of regret, or pity, or perhaps even wounded human affection were compounded with the satisfaction of his completed revenge, it is impossible to say." He begins to escape, but then stops and allows himself to be apprehended. Why? Who was he? What were his motives? The integrity of the book is in the phrase, "it is impossible to say."

When *The Golden Notebook* appeared, Lessing seemed to betray her declared commitment. She said in 1977, "For me the highest point of literature was the novel of the nineteenth century, the work of Tolstoy, Stendhal, Dostoevsky, Balzac, Turgenev, Chekhov; the work of the great realists"—and she added that the realist novel was "the highest form of prose writing; higher than and out of the reach of any comparison with expressionism, impressionism, symbolism, naturalism, or any other ism." The writers of the nineteenth century had in common "a climate of ethical judgment": she moves away from naive, Marxizing realism but never out of that climate.

The protagonist of *The Golden Notebook,* a writer, suffers writer's block. She keeps the Notebook, and through it runs a harsh feminist streak, at times an androphobia. Lessing was hostile to mainstream 1960s feminism because of what she took to be a facile politicization: "It all ended in a great frazzle of back-biting." Lessing's resistance to the sisterhood alienated key figures, including the poet Adrienne Rich. Yet the South African example of Olive Schreiner remained her point of reference as she avoided formulating and thus arresting an argument. The English notion of realism was not for her a permanent abode. *The Golden Notebook* and *The Four-Gated City* (1969, the last of the Children of Violence group) move into unstable territory, with various points of view, different voices. Anna Wulf in *The Golden Notebook* is clear: Stories and the truth are not on the same plane, and "now what interests me is precisely this—why did I not write an account of what had happened, instead of shaping a 'story' which had nothing to do with the material that fuelled it." As soon as the writer shapes an experience into a coherent story, truth is violated. Rules of syntax and proportion impose themselves on experience and displace it. This sense of the relativity of style accounts for changes in her attitudes to the real and her movement into invented worlds where the language was the reality rather than an attempt to encompass the real.

Her most inventive fiction, not her best, is to be found in the five-volume *Canopus in Argos: Archives* series that opens with *Shikasta* (1979). Gore Vidal was wide-eyed: "I have followed her into the realms of science fiction where she is making a continuum all her own somewhere between John Milton and L. Ron Hubbard." She has not made the other worlds real: for Vidal, Shikasta is not habitable. "I didn't think of that as science fiction at all when I was doing it, not really," she said. But some readers regard it as revelation, as though it proclaimed a new religious reality. Yet "the reincarnation stuff was an attractive metaphor, really, or a literary idea . . . It was a way of telling a story—incorporating ideas that are in our great religions." It grew out of the theory that Judaism, Christianity, and Islam are the same religion but arrested at different times, the setting down of scripture (Old Testament, New Testament, Quran) at different historical moments codifying and ossifying, each scripture claiming to be timeless. Another treachery of language, its arrests.

In *The Four-Gated City* Lessing contrasted the characters of Iris and Martha, who move through the same place. Iris "knew everything about this area, half a dozen streets for about half a mile or a mile of their length; and she knew it all in such detail that when with her, Martha walked in a double vision, as if she were two people: herself and Iris, one eye stating, denying, warding off the total hideousness of the whole area, the other, with Iris, knowing it in love. With Iris, one moved here, in state of love, if love is the delicate but total acknowledgement of what is." In this beautiful passage Lessing suggests that things become real through love. She has moved from a relatively conventional realist position continuous with her early Marxism, into a nuanced, postmodern place where fantasy can sometimes tell the clearest truths. She belongs in much of her later work with Angela Carter.

Angela Olive Stalker, known as Angela Carter (1940–1992), reshapes English fiction in ways that remain provocative for contemporary writers. She is less in the line of Manning, Iris Murdoch, and A. S. Byatt, more a contemporary of Firbank, Spark, and Ballard. Byatt recalls her first meeting with Carter, which entailed attending a reading by Stevie Smith (Florence Margaret Smith, 1902–1971). The hilarious and heart-stopping poet laureate of failed relationships was something of a novelist, especially in the first of her three ventures into fiction, the autobiographical *Novel on Yellow Paper* (1936), written on her long-suffering employer's time. She was a secretary, and her protagonist is a secretary in a world in which her own anti-Semitism is put to the test of an emerging Nazi Germany, and her heart undergoes two failed romances.

Byatt recalled that as she left the reading, "a very disagreeable woman stomped up to me, and she said, My name's Angela Carter. I recognized you and I wanted to stop and tell you that the sort of thing you're doing is no good at all, no good at all. There's nothing in it—that's not where literature is going." When they became friends, Carter talked about the centrality of fairy tales to her writing. Indeed, "she had realized that she was a writer because of fairy tales, because she was hooked on narrative as a child, not by realist novels about social behavior or how to be a good girl, but by these very primitive stories that go I think a lot deeper." This gave Byatt a kind of license.

Other novelists, Elaine Feinstein for example, speak of the ways in which Carter's use of dream material empowered them in writing their own fiction. Carter was a catalyst at the time when British women writers experienced the pressure of reinvention—when they were rattling the bars of social and intellectual cages, finding the latch, and stepping out into their own daylight. What a feminist critic harshly described as "male-identified female writers" had to be left behind, along with restraining genres and conventions. Parody and reinvention were Carter's means to clear a space. Margaret Atwood on Carter's death wrote, "Her vocabulary was a mix of finely-tuned phrase, luscious adjective, witty aphorism, and hearty, up-theirs vulgarity, so evident in her novels *Wise Children* and *Nights at the Circus*." Crucially, "She had an instinctive feeling for the other side."

Carter studied English at the University of Bristol, avoiding the then sexually segregated worlds of Oxford and Cambridge, and married at the age of twenty, acquiring her surname and a relationship that lasted a decade. In that time she wrote two books of poetry and her first four novels, one a year from 1966, among them *The Magic Toyshop* (1967), a kind of declaration of intent in both theme and form for what was to follow. In 1969 she received a Somerset Maugham

Award and on the relatively modest proceeds from that award and her royalties moved to Tokyo. Once separated from England, she found her feet on foreign soil. These experiences inform *The Infernal Desire Machines of Doctor Hoffman* (1972), published as *The War of Dreams* in the United States. Here, after the distractions of magic, genre, and the formal problems raised by contemporary literary theory and philosophy, "reality" is restored. Written necessarily from the outside, it is analytical in its procedures, anti-organic, reverting to a "real" world only when language (of the tyrannical media, of traditional fiction and intimate discourse) has been rendered harmless by a thorough alienation.

Carter wrote only three novels in the last twenty years of her life, concentrating instead on shorter fiction, stage, film and radio drama and adaptations, translations, and editorial projects, notably her Virago anthologies of "subversive stories." The subversions started with language and form: she insisted that reinvention must take place root and branch. The act of writing is collaborative, between two writers, or a living writer and the dead (in her case, the Brothers Grimm, Charlotte Brontë, and others). The writer intervenes in the reader's memory as well, recasting stories, the fairy stories that shape our sense of narrative and of the potential roles of the heroes and villains that conventionally inhabit them. There is also a dialogue between dream and waking, one that must be listened to and expressed.

After her years in Japan she traveled across Asia, North America, and Europe. She was employed as a writer in residence in various institutions and her influence on other writers and on theoretical discourse grew. Her last three novels in different ways explore her themes: *The Passion of New Eve* (1977), published in the year of her second marriage, *Nights at the Circus* (1984), and *Wise Children* (1991). These books, like Italo Calvino's, appear to be shaped out of smaller units harmonized by recurrent pattern rather than plotted into a conventional unity.

In 1979 she published her most celebrated book of short stories, *The Bloody Chamber,* and *The Sadeian Woman and the Ideology of Pornography,* the critical book that defines the transformative processes in thought, style, and attitude she put herself through in order to ensure her independence: "A free woman in an unfree society will be a monster." About *The Bloody Chamber,* she said, "My intention was not to do a 'version' or, as the American edition of the book said, horribly, adult fairy tales, but to extract the latent content from the traditional stories and to use it as the beginnings of new stories." Her one opera libretto is an adaptation of Virginia Woolf's *Orlando.*

Marina Warner, Carter's lucid expositor and heir, describes the ways in which she took the compromised popular romance mode and, in a book like *Wise Children,* "exuberantly mines all the conventions of the genre in a tremendous act of homage to the Shakespeare of comic mischief and enchanted reconcilia-tions," of *A Midsummer Night's Dream* and *The Comedy of Errors*. Carter works within the diminished space of modern English fiction with a formal and radical inventiveness that makes the area unpredictable and challenging. Her Gothic imagination unsettles the conventions of her day as Walpole's did his. In her case the radical project is a sustained body of creative, interpretative, and theoretical work. Her interest in women is not limited to the creative sisterhood. She speaks of the sisterhood ironically as an informal freemasonry with its own concerns, handshakes, winks, and nods.

It would be hard to counter Carter's forceful impressionistic rhetoric. "It is the private quality of this kind of women's language that allows its high degree of unspecificity, just because this subjective privacy is, in fact, what is common to our experience as women. We live in a shared privacy of oblique references, perhaps originally designed to keep whatever is going on from the masters." Those masters were losing their grip not only on women writers but on a num-ber of new male writers, too.

Elaine Feinstein (b. 1930) is part of the challenge, approaching language from her own direction. She is now best known as a poet, but her reputation was formed as a fiction writer with European orientation, and she has pub-lished fifteen novels. Three of them will stand for the larger oeuvre. *The Circle* (1970), her debut novel, was long-listed for the "lost" Man Booker Prize in 2010. It was described at the time by the novelist and poet Robert Nye as "a poet's novel, a tag usually used with a faint sneer of disapproval, but in this case I can-not do otherwise than direct attention to Miss Feinstein's accurate and acute feeling for language and pauses and silence." This sense of pausing she had in-troduced into her classic translations of the poems of the Russian Marina Tsve-taeva, a spacing to indicate the movement of the voice of feeling in counter-point with the natural movement of the prosody and syntax. The subject matter was, like Tsvetaeva's, personal, the family described not unlike her own. The editor, poet, and memoirist Alan Ross commented, "She is able to make dia-logue reveal character and do most of the work," praising her "narrative flair and genuine insight into people's failings and alienation."

*The Border* (1984) Fay Weldon called "a stunning novel, ruthlessly brilliant. It has the pace of a thriller and the passion of a love story." It is a short book, com-bining the diaries of a Jewish couple living in Vienna—Inga is a scientist, her husband, Hans, a poet (reversing the vocations in Feinstein's own marriage)—and the letters Hans sends to Hilde, a woman with whom he had an affair who has since relocated to Moscow. Inga and Hans have sent their son abroad to get away from the danger, which to them seems somehow unreal. It is a story of "too late," moving from Vienna to Paris to the French-Spanish border as, at last, they seek an elusive safety. Inga, in the closing section, become an old lady, tells the story in all its perished complexities to her grandson. The same tensions that informed *The Circle* are again explored, in part confessionally, against a larger backdrop that adds seriousness and, crucially, the vanished Middle Europe to the basic structure.

Europe, the Second World War, and its aftermath also inform *Loving Brecht* (1992), the story of Frieda Bloom and her love for the philandering dramatist, set first in Weimar Germany in its decline, then Moscow (Feinstein's work has gravitated from central Europe toward Russia as a result of her biography and translation work), and then the United States just in time to catch the McCarthy trials. It is a love story and, again, a profound lesson in history as it registers on the living body and spirit. A. S. Byatt noted that "Brecht's presence—dirty, sexy, obsessive, charming, exploiting—is brilliantly constructed from Frieda's mixture of sexual passion and shrewd observation." There is also the matter of politics.

Colm Tóibín (b. 1955) is as well known as a generous, demanding literary journalist of Edwardian energy and scope, as he is as a novelist. He writes about books ancient and modern, from many languages; he writes about music and modern art, landscape, and politics. He publishes in all the right places and is always worth reading, giving belle-lettrism a good name once more. His most celebrated novel, *The Master* (2004), itself grows out of the life and work of Henry James, and he supplemented it with *All a Novelist Needs: Essays on Henry James* (2010). James is for him an American who chooses another nationality, becoming two people, and a homosexual who chooses to keep his secret, becoming two people in a different sense, with consequences for his life and art. "Fiction about actual historical persons, so intrinsically conflicted and impure," said Updike, "feels to be part of postmodernism's rampant eclecticism." In Tóibín James is, Updike remarks, "a triumphantly inert protagonist," silent and blank because he does not acknowledge his homosexuality. Yet surely, we want to say, even as we read this compelling novel, he *does* acknowledge it, in each denial and detour. The historical novel, said James, and this one would be no exception, is "tainted by a fatal cheapness." Historical fiction is "humbug." For Updike, Tóibín's bust of James is made not of marble but soapstone. So it should be, we are tempted to reply: it is not striving to be a classical bust but to reveal a complex living, self-camouflaging being.

Born in County Wexford, Ireland, Colm Tóibín took early bearings from John McGahern, following in his footsteps to University College, Dublin, and then into exile, where he earned his keep by teaching. His initial exile was in Barcelona, the inspiration to go there coming from Hemingway's fiction, which helped to shape his own early writing. He wrote his first novel, *The South* (1990), in which a woman leaves Ireland for Spain, finding there a story unsettlingly similar to the one she left behind. *Brooklyn* (2009) complements *The South*: another tale of emigration, this time the female protagonist goes from Enniscorthy to America. Comparing the two books reveals the considerable advance in technique and understanding in Tóibín's fiction in a mere two decades.

He returned from Spain to work as a journalist and magazine editor in Dublin. It was only a matter of time before he grew impatient with his increasingly settled life in Ireland and set off again in 1985, traveling to Africa, to Latin America, writing on politics and cultural issues, his eye always cast back to Ireland, its troubles, its flickering religious faith. Journalism was better preparation than a course in creative writing for the young writer; his own creative writing students in Texas, he observed later, would benefit from a baton charge, the noise, the smell, the pain, the adrenalin. He had witnessed some of the brutal riots in Oaxaca, Mexico.

*The Heather Blazing* (1992), his second novel, has the political, topographical, and some of the sexual power of John McGahern's *Amongst Women*. This first of his Wexford novels, set in his native Enniscorthy, established Tóibín as a kind of aberrant heir to McGahern, deeply Irish in feelings and connections but differently alienated. The nature of that alienation is explored in *The Story of the Night* (1996), an account of coming out set in Argentina at a time when the retreat and judicial defeat of the generals and the assault on a hypocritical and punitive moral order make the risk of personal disclosure urgent, necessary. The theme of AIDs and its impact on the sufferer and those around him is explored in *The Blackwater Lightship* (1999), his second Wexford novel. The book can be read alongside his most compelling nonfiction book, *Love in a Dark Time: Gay Lives from Wilde to Almodovar* (2002).

Writing about Wendy Moffat's *E. M. Forster: A New Life,* Tóibín notes "a strange moment" in which "she refers to *Maurice* as Forster's 'only truly honest novel.' But *Maurice* is, while fascinating in its own way, also his worst. Perhaps there is a connection between its badness and its 'honesty,' because novels should not be honest." He delivers a judgment that casts a shadow back on *The Master*. Novels, he says, "are a pack of lies that are also a set of metaphors; because the lies and metaphors are chosen and offered shape and structure, they may indeed represent the self, or the play between the unconscious mind and the conscious will, but they are not forms of self-expression, or true confession."

Alan Hollinghurst (b. 1954) has written steadily, producing five lapidary, formally ambitious novels, distinguished essay-reviews, and other occasional writing. He studied at Oxford, then taught there, then taught at University College, London, before becoming a deputy editor of the *Times Literary Supplement,* where he worked until 1990, when his first novel had become a marked success. He is today a classic English man of letters, an anachronism who, like his contemporaries Adam Mars-Jones and Colm Tóibín, makes no bones and not much fuss about being gay. When *The Swimming Pool Library,* his first novel, appeared in 1988, the sexual element was all that the media cared about, the bold portrayal of sexual relations, casual and close, including one vivid, prolonged interracial intimacy, a theme his novels revisit. Edmund White placed it generically between "pastoral romance" and "sulphurous confession," calling it "the best book about gay life yet written by an English author." Hollinghurst has had to resist the enthusiastic expectation of that judgment, which typecasts and anticipates his future moves. A seemingly liberalizing and affirmative tone projects a disabling identity as constraining as censorship, and part of Hollinghurst's caution is his avoidance of ideological expectation while, at the same time, finding his own way with his own material. Gay life is a context of action, but the novel is not only about it; if it were, it would stick with the intense, informative, and strangely pornographic scenes that precede subtler intimacies.

Hollinghurst defended *The Stranger's Child* (2011) against the charge of inadvertent cultural anti-Semitism, discovering how hemmed-in modern writers can be when they venture into zones mined by rival ideologies. The gay themes are unavoidable, and in his first book they are dominant, but much else is going on even there. Hollinghurst's realism is ambitious and the culture he represents is deep-rooted, with long pasts. At Oxford he wrote on Forster and L. P. Hartley, learning some of their obliquities, and on Ronald Firbank, whose outrageousness colors his plots and sometimes his turn of phrase, though Firbank's excesses inoculated him against campness. His 1913 is far removed from the landed, pastoral world of Ian McEwan's *Atonement*. It is a suburban, Forsterian neighborhood, and "never such innocence again" is a point of departure for *The Stranger's Child*. The First World War is around the corner, his England still continuous with that of Victorian and Edwardian novels. He begins with families, war, its effects and aftermaths. The thematic hinge of the novel is not a metafictional plot twist but a poem whose meaning grows and changes as time and history take hold. Each novel has a symbolic core, a point of quest or focus, rather too Murdochian an aspect. In a sense, it is all in the title.

Hollinghurst is a sentence-by-sentence, scene-by-scene writer, never seeming in a hurry even when he has generated impatience in the reader. He is too fond, in his early work, of the passive voice, and sentences begin "There were" and "There was" with a distancing frequency. He writes steadily, revising, between 300 and 400 words a day when a novel is in train. It takes meditative time, sometimes a year or two, before there is enough to begin writing. The measured pace of his books, their careful gravity, makes the climaxes slow and complex. Pace can seem at odds with the element of social comedy, a pervasive Murdochian eroticism, harsh echoes of Waugh and Maugham, plangencies of Angus Wilson.

There is something elegiac about the pre-AIDs world of *The Swimming Pool Library.* An innocence in discovery, a courage in making life choices. Hollinghurst is good at elegy: a rueful sense of time passing also marks the Booker Prize–winning *The Line of Beauty* (2004), an elegy for the 1980s, a decade it had not before seemed necessary to regret, except that this is where the characters' youth passed, and this book like the others includes autobiographical material. Desire, its fulfillment and unfulfillment equally unsatisfactory in time, yet its pursuit wired in to most of his characters and readers, make the book sweet and bitter, comic and dramatic in equal measure.

The pursuit of a transforming love that leads his characters into promiscuity and disappointment is something more he shares with Iris Murdoch. A defining difference between them is Hollinghurst's scrupulousness, stylistically and in terms of plot and character, and his rich lacings of culture. The gramophone, the gallery, and the library are never far away. One of the agreeable things about the rich is that they own their own pictures, and Hollinghurst lingers, listens, sees. After the careful construction of her early novels, in particular *The Bell,* her most Hollinghurstian production, Murdoch was increasingly in a hurry to get on to the next novel, to explore the next idea: ideas come to weigh more than characters and the fiction becomes an extension of another kind of argument. Hollinghurst lives in his fictional worlds one at a time, and though there are plot and thematic and structural overlaps, the worlds of his books are fully differentiated, especially by time and the place they occupy in relation to the AIDs epidemic, which, in *The Line of Beauty,* is spreading. *The Folding Star* (1994) is brittle; Edward Manners, the gay beauty-loving protagonist, needs a dose of irony, which the author is not inclined to administer, though the writing is alert and witty. The book masquerades as a comedy but the author intends the protagonist's needs and disappointments to weigh more heavily than they do for most readers. The intensity of Edward's hunger, disappointment, and loss, his human inadequacy, rob the novel of the intended impact of its climax. *The Spell* (1998) marked a transition to the larger scale of his later novels. This is the world of his first novel, thronging with named and differentiated male characters, its culture darkened and redefined by AIDs and drugs. The eponymous spell is broken just in time.

# 39

# *Propaganda*

Christopher Isherwood, Edward Upward, Paul Bowles, Jane Bowles, Edmund White,

Henry Green, Evelyn Waugh, William Boyd, Graham Greene, R. K. Narayan,

Mulk Raj Anand, Rohinton Mistry, V. S. Naipaul, Caryl Phillips, Timothy Mo

Christopher Isherwood (1904–1986) the Englishman, the European, the radical, before he emigrated to the United States and became a Vedantist, contributed to the development of the novel. He noted the impact of Woolf, Forster, and Lawrence on his own formation (the Hogarth Press published three of his books); he regretted the influence of Joyce, ill-assimilated in his early novels. Drawn to modernism, in struggle with it he produced his most suggestive work. As a Marxist, like his contemporary John Dos Passos, he thought he wanted to achieve an "objective" style and escape the "bourgeois" first-person narrator. *His* eye/I strove for a neutral perspective from which to record a "reality" that was *really* there. The problem was less how language related to the world than how it related to the subject.

When Isherwood declared, "I am a camera," did he have in mind a cine camera? What he, or the character "Christopher" in *Goodbye to Berlin* (1939), said is, "I am a camera with its shutter open, quite passive, recording, not thinking. Recording the man shaving at the window opposite and the woman in the kimono washing her hair. Some day, all this will have to be developed, carefully printed, fixed." This declaration of artistic intent comes in a fiction he was writing about a writer living in Berlin and trying to write. Outside the context of the plot it is a conceit: Isherwood is charmingly indulgent in the sense that, novel after novel, he concentrates upon, even as he pretends to erase, the self, like a magician pushing a rabbit into a hat. The letters and journals prove how autobiographical the whole project is, an apotheosis of the "I."

The cine camera did have a role to play, as he recalls, but it had less to do with emptying out the narrator, more to do with observation. "Film had an over-all effect on my style. I think that an absolute sort of change took place at the time I was writing *Mr. Norris* [*Changes Trains* (1935)], because I'd done a film just before that, the first time I'd worked on a film, and it certainly meant that I visualized much more strongly from then on." When he emigrated to the United States, he earned much of his living writing for the movies, first with *Little Friend*, done for the director Berthold Viertel, whom he later fictionalized as Friedrich Bergmann, a character in *Prater Violet* (1945). He had a habit of thinly fictionalizing relations, friends, and acquaintances, usually without malice. He observed people (again the lens) "like insects under a microscope." Cyril Connolly was unsettled by his cool, "scientific" regard. In the 1930s what mattered was faithful accuracy of construction, he said, not subjective response. This statement is not quite in keeping with his actual practice.

In his early fiction the attempt to say no more than is true, to presume nothing that is not verifiable, leads to a process of statement and erasure. Nothing is verifiable beyond the visible, and the visible itself suggests a range of narrative possibilities. The narrator in *Mr. Norris* figures and refigures. He wants to ask the other person in the train compartment for a match, and he hopes to start a conversation because the journey ahead is a long one. From a chance incident Isherwood draws a range of half-impressions, comic, satirical, erotic. There are oxymorons, qualifying adverbs, a string of negative constructions, an insistence on seemings, reminiscences that blur, a refusal to affirm until there is a collision that, to balance indefinition, results in an equally blank hyperbole, "exactly as though." Unmediated description, in which the meaning is not in question, comes later in the book when the narrator is better acquainted with his strange, powdered, and bewigged subject.

> My first impression was that the stranger's eyes were of an unusually light blue. They met mine for several blank seconds, vacant, unmistakably scared. Startled and innocently naughty, they half reminded me of an incident I couldn't quite place; something which had happened a long time ago, to do with the upper fourth form classroom. They were the eyes of a schoolboy surprised in the act of breaking one of the rules. Not that I had caught him, apparently, at anything except his own thoughts: perhaps he imagined I could read them. At any rate, he seemed not to have heard or seen me cross the compartment from my corner to his own, for he started violently at the sound of my voice; so violently, indeed, that his nervous recoil hit me like repercussion. Instinctively I took a pace backwards.
>
> It was *exactly as though* we had collided with each other bodily in the street. We were both confused, both ready to be apologetic. Smiling, anxious to reassure him, I repeated my question:
>
> "I wonder, sir, if you could let me have a match?"

The stranger reflects, and we see how "his fingers, nervously active, sketched a number of flurried gestures round his waistcoat. For all they conveyed, he might equally have been going to undress, to draw a revolver, or merely to make sure that I hadn't stolen his money." The three possibilities point in different story directions. The interlocutor is engaged and, through engagement, defined. And the scene, increasingly intimate, develops an erotic charge by means of an image that is also a symbol. "The tiny flame of the lighter flickered between us, as perishable as the atmosphere which our exaggerated politeness had created. The merest breath would have extinguished the one, the least incautious gesture or word would have destroyed the other." Their cigarettes are lighted. "The stranger was still doubtful of me. He was wondering whether he hadn't gone too far." In a later chapter the sexually charged Helen Pratt meets Mr. Norris and tells the narrator, "If you take my advice, Bill . . . you won't trust that man an inch." She does not believe his disclaimer. "Oh, I know you. You're soft, like most men. You make up romances about people instead of seeing them as they are."

Though he is harder in *All the Conspirators* (1928) and *The Memorial* (1932), his first two novels, he has found his stride in the Berlin writings and Helen Pratt has got his number. *Mr. Norris* and *Goodbye to Berlin* are soft in the sweet vagueness and longing of the narrator, his biddability, which occasionally rises to an emphasis or a gesture but is generally even, measured. Edmund Wilson admires his steady sense of restraint and proportion. "His real field is social observation," Wilson says, and Isherwood refuses to exaggerate or sentimentalize in 1939, at the same time exploring the decay of the upper classes (Mr. Norris and others), working-class failure of nerve (the Nowaks), Jewish experience (the Landauers), and the unique self-invention that is Sally Bowles.

In "The Nowaks," the narrator, who is a writer, is having trouble with the novel he is writing, set in a country house full of the class issues and anxieties that go with the territory. The narrator has published a novel entitled *All the Conspirators,* and Isherwood confessed in interview that this narrator, who was not Christopher Isherwood, but was, was trying to write *The Memorial.* He disliked, he said, the rather coy deflected self-referentiality of this, as though he was judging his earliest work. He remembers how puritanical he became in his Marxist period, telling himself that "all the exquisiteness of literature should go, one should only deal with the real 'nitty-gritty' of experience." But then, "Why the devil the experiences of people in slums should be any more real than any other kind of experience I can't now see." The irony was that he was actually writing, and he finished *The Memorial.* Another irony, he contributed an article on the German youth movement to Sir Oswald Mosley's fascist paper *Action.* His crucial activity was keeping a diary from which he drew the Berlin stories. The diary was destroyed.

The great liberty he takes in *Goodbye to Berlin* is to abandon the elaborate overall plot he devised for a hefty book to be called *The Lost.* He left only the achieved parts to stand for the whole, resolved in a cycle of seasons and a passage of time but not bound together in a tidy plot parcel. "I realized that in the effort of getting it inter-involved I would throw away the thing which was really precious to me, which was dealing with the experience itself," the very thing that in his view had marred *Mr. Norris.* He hands "the stuff" to us "in a *slab,* and you don't have to fuss with some wretched plotting." There was a moment of illumination: "God! I'll write a book of bits and pieces!"

The most memorable character is also the most "created," Sally Bowles. She is not conventionally attractive or original; she is not very bright. But she is vulnerable and, like Holly Golightly in Truman Capote's *Breakfast at Tiffany's,* she is a spirit of natural innocence at the heart of corruption. Her pretensions are endearing, so unreal are they in the sinister twilight of Weimar Berlin. She is rooted in people he knew. Her surname is taken from the handsome young writer Paul Bowles, whose acquaintance Isherwood made in Berlin, a Platonic appropriation.

After Isherwood's Marxist phase, he went somewhere else. In the United States he threw himself into the arms of another faith, from which he never entirely emerged. Writing by self-declared homosexuals was inevitably a form of propaganda, he said, not setting out to make converts but always suing for inclusion ("acceptance" implies a suppliant posture anathema to him). For the first sixty years of his life his homosexuality was proscribed. Indeed, in some states and countries it is proscribed today. He was increasingly open about it in fiction as in his autobiographies.

The Berlin Isherwood, a homosexual writer addressing a general, not a specialized, readership, practices a kind of "double talk," what the story tells and what it is actually saying. This "double talk," an aspect of irony itself, is not peculiar to homosexual and gay writing: writers with causes (political, religious) approach narrative obliquely and speak with a similarly forked tongue. In gay writing, however, especially from the first half of the twentieth century, what is peculiar is its awareness, and ours as readers, that something transgressing moral codes is present. Reading registers the doubleness of the talk.

The writer may set out, as William Burroughs does, to shock, or as Isherwood does, subversively to normalize. Characters and actions are not justified by argument but given context and made real, admitted into acknowledged experience. Isherwood's thematic radicalism has formal and stylistic corollaries. As he made his way west, eventually to California, and spiritually east, to India, his concern turns from homosexuality to homophobia. Gay writing is often most vigorous where themes of sexuality combine with themes of race, as in James Baldwin, or of class and national difference, as with Isherwood.

He passed through a series of clarifications, comings out. As Cambridge undergraduates, he and his close friend Edward Upward (1903–2009), who had been at school with him at Repton and became the most neglected and long-lived novelist of the age, found "boring and vile" the very politics that soon propelled their fiction, in Isherwood's case through its first decades, in Upward's right through to the end. At the beginning of his novel *In the Thirties* (1962, first of the immensely slow and effortful trilogy of autobiographical novels, *The Spiral Ascent,* which also included in 1969 *The Rotten Elements* and in 1977 *No Home but the Struggle*) Upward says, "The hero comes to communism as a kind of religious conversion, and this represents my own attitude. I came to it not so much through consciousness of the political situation as through despair." The despair was philosophical rather than psychological. Isherwood and Upward were not navel-gazing glum undergraduates; together they created the surreal, Mervyn-Peakean world of the Mortmere stories (published as a book in 1994, the earliest and most naive of Isherwood's collaborations, which later included the famous works with Auden, and those he did with his Vedantic swami Prabhavananda, the Hindu monk, with his "life partner" the portrait artist Don Bachardy, and with Aldous Huxley). Marxism claimed Upward at the end of the Cambridge experience. It was in his case a mystical possession. It puzzled his contemporaries. Upward did not question events in the Soviet Union, turning a blind eye to the show trials. His first novel, *Journey to the Border* (1938), tells of the protagonist's conversion as the fruit of revelation rather than analysis.

Upward shook Isherwood ideologically awake. Isherwood, supported by erratic handouts from his homosexual uncle Henry, had gone to Berlin and was able to prolong his stay there (supplementing his income by teaching and writing) for three and a half years, until it seemed wise to seek new pastures, given the rise of the Nazis. In his Berlin years he was seeing "a great deal of the other half" close up. He liked slumming it among others less fortunate, imprisoned by political and economic circumstances. A natural nonconformist, he was soon repelled by the conformities demanded by the Communist Party, but for a time he followed the route Upward indicated: the Party explained things and suggested that change might be possible, though the Party's attitude to homosexuals—labeling them "fascists" and attacking them on those grounds— angered him. He denied ever using the novel as a political tool. Political action might be the subject of a novel but not its object. The novel ought not to be instrumental, though he noted, "I would always try to root the characters in a kind of dialectical way, and I would always be concerned with the question of where their money came from."

Homosexuals were a group to which he could not help belonging, and he was glad of it. He became impatient with the attention paid to his early work at the expense of the later, which he regarded as more interesting in terms of technique and subject matter. Of his novels, the one he valued most was *A Single Man* (1969), about growing old and mortality that catches the protagonist, George, and topples him on the last page. He spoke of it as "the only book of mine where I did more or less what I wanted to do. It didn't get out of control." It resisted cinematic treatment because he had rendered it so precisely in visual terms that a producer could only repeat, not invent. He visualized it as he did due to the influence of film: The very sequence in which events are recorded, the pace, the transitions, the fades in and out, owe much to the medium. Here "I am a camera" takes on a different value. And so does Isherwood, a prophetic autobiographer. Yet Peter Ackroyd rightly says that after reading the autobiographical *Christopher and His Kind* (1976) we know less, not more, about him. He qualifies, requalifies; each requalification entails erasure. He is artfulness itself masquerading as candor.

Isherwood's third defining clarification was his spiritual conversion. "Vedanta made a very great difference, but I couldn't exactly describe to you what the difference is. I could say what, so to speak, I've got out of it. I simply became convinced, after a long period of knowing Swami Prabhavananda, that there is such a thing as mystic union or the knowledge—we get into terrible semantics here—that there is such a thing as mystical experience." Asked about the charge of sentimentality leveled against some of his writing, he concedes the point and adds, what he would not have said in his formative years, "We're not afraid of what's called pornography, but we are terribly afraid of what we call sentimentality—the rash, incautious expression of feeling." He sees it as necessary in life and forgivable in literature. His feelings for Bowles were decidedly sentimental and proved to be transsexually creative.

When he was in Berlin, Paul (Frederic) Bowles (1910–1999) was single and an experienced homosexual. He spent four months sharing the excitements Isherwood evokes, though at the time, Bowles insists, he was not writing but living. He and Jane (née Auer) Bowles (1917–1973) had an unlikely marriage that should not have lasted, but it did. It began in 1938 and ended thirty-five years later with her death. Jane too was homosexual, each gave the other space, rather too much it might seem from their disordered lives, Paul producing an abundance of sometimes indifferent literary material, Jane writing a few brilliant, careful works and succumbing to alcoholism. Jane directed Paul's interests back to fiction from music in the 1940s, and he gave her credit for his success. She might have given him credit for her own exiguous progress. Their exile in Morocco did not suit her and her last decade there, marred by illness, was miserable. "From the first day, Morocco seemed more dreamlike than real. I felt cut off from what I knew. In the twenty years I've lived here, I've written two short stories and nothing else. It's good for Paul, but not for me."

By the time Paul Bowles came to publish *The Sheltering Sky* (1949), his first novel, set in French North Africa, he had already dazzled Aaron Copland, with whom he studied music and traveled, and impressed Isherwood into his transgendering tribute. Doubleday commissioned *The Sheltering Sky* and then rejected it. John Lehmann published it in London. It is a North African road novel, full of colorful minor characters, ending in two dramas that fall short of tragedy. It is not Kerouac, or rather, it is not *even* Kerouac. Bowles's second novel, *Let It Come Down* (1952), is set in Tangier, where by then he had settled. He showed every page to his wife, just as she had showed him every page of *Two Serious Ladies* (1943), her brilliant comedy. His ill-defined protagonist Nelson Dyar commits a motiveless murder to establish identity through action. Bowles is not Genet, he is certainly not Dostoyevsky. Perhaps he is Paul Auster *avant la lettre*. Bowles lent the manuscript of *The Sheltering Sky* to Charles Henri Ford, who had published Bowles's first short stories in *Blues*. "What a letdown after the stories," Ford declared. Late in life Bowles remarked to one of the steady stream of interviewers that pestered him, "Of course, I've never been a thinking person. A lot seems to happen without my conscious knowledge." T. S. Eliot notes how the mind in fever or near sleep forges, or experiences, unexpected connections. Bowles wrote in bed in a kind of anticipation. "Ninety-five percent of everything I've written has been done in bed." He claims to have been influenced by Poe.

He is readable because of his context, his period, his relations with Stein (he published verse in the journal *transition* at a very young age) and Isherwood, and his wife. Vidal draws attention to his musical talents; as well as working with Aaron Copland, he wrote incidental pieces for Broadway plays, including Tennessee Williams's *The Glass Menagerie*. But none of this makes him a better writer. Stein suggested that he leave the writing to Jane; he could do the music. But he returned to writing. The couple's travels took them for spells to Mexico, Brooklyn at the creative heart of things, Ceylon, Paris, Tangier. During Bowles's half century in Morocco he worked with local storytellers, translating and popularizing their work. His bookcase included inscribed volumes by Kerouac, Burroughs, and Ginsberg. He is an honorary Beat. His themes of violence, movement, and travel have much in common with theirs, and his rejection of deliberation and reflection puts him in their company. In Tangier the Bowleses' visitors included not only the Beats, but Truman Capote, who elegantly introduced Jane's collected writings, Tennessee Williams, and a temporarily dazzled Vidal.

Paul Bowles claimed not to care what critics said. Jane was more sensitive. Anaïs Nin wrote her a "careful, gentle, warm letter" about *Two Serious Ladies*. She was "distressed by the tightness, the involuted quality, the constricted, coiling inward (not into an infinite interior but a tight one)." She was concerned about her possible "constriction as a writer." Jane took the note to heart, it stopped her in her tracks. Given the wit and mystery of *Two Serious Ladies,* it is sad that her tenuous confidence was dealt such a blow. She was wakeful, clearheaded, her control tense and edgy. "I love *Two Serious Ladies,*" Paul Bowles said. "The action is often like the unfolding of a dream, and the background, with its realistic details, somehow emphasizes the sensation of dreaming." She was not a dreamy person, but "she did have a way of making herself absent suddenly, when one could see that she was a thousand miles away. If you addressed her sharply, she returned with a start. And if you asked her about it, she would simply say: 'I don't know. I was somewhere else.'"

---

Edmund (Valentine) White (III) (b. 1940) found in Isherwood's novels and André Gide's *Journals* "the only serious, non-pornographic accounts of gay experience I came across back then." Even their obliquities struck him as mysteriously erotic. And later, in the 1970s, Isherwood's distinction and acceptance encouraged gay and lesbian writers. He seemed to carry the authority of his early publisher, Virginia Woolf, across the divides of an ocean and a world war: "That he should be on our side made us take ourselves more seriously," White said.

White is a writer who from the outset has had a dominant theme. He has explored it through fiction, autobiographical novels (*A Boy's Own Story,* his 1977 breakthrough novel, followed by *The Beautiful Room Is Empty* in 1988 and *The Farewell Symphony* in 1997), memoirs, biographies (of Jean Genet, Arthur Rimbaud, Marcel Proust), essays, and anthologies (*Another Part of the Forest: Gay Short Fiction* in 1994 and earlier the radical and challenging *The Darker Proof: Stories from a Crisis,* the 1987 anthology of gay fiction he edited with the novelist and critic Adam Mars-Jones).

When he writes about his childhood, it is a story of incest—his mother was attracted to him, his handsome and (he confesses) sexually compelling and even desirable father slept with his sister—a world of aberration and instability. He wrote to make sense of his experience, completing his first novel at the age of fifteen, before he was aware of other gay novels. He grew up largely in Chicago and attended the University of Michigan, where he studied Chinese. Then he went to New York and became a writer and journalist. He positioned himself at the center of cultural activity. Some saw him as a latter-day Truman Capote, especially when in memoirs and fiction he began to include the private lives, thinly veiled or not at all, of friends and acquaintances. His first novel, *Forgetting Elena* (1973), is still codedly homosexual, but he gathered candor for a bolder fiction that encompasses the truth without quite telling it, and makes room for actual historical incidents, such as the Stonewall Uprising in Greenwich Village in 1969. Between his second and third volume of autobiographical fiction he had researched and written (it took seven years) his life of the French radical homosexual writer Genet. His essay "Writing Gay" is a telling account of the difficulty of negotiating one's most urgent themes into prose. Being affirmative and authentic is hardest of all. The disciplines of biography were vital to his fiction.

———•———

Isherwood prefaced an interview in the mid-1970s by celebrating Henry Green, reciting from memory a short lyrical passage from *Living* (1929). There is nothing sentimental about Green. Isherwood regarded *Living* as the best proletarian novel in English, a verdict that Anthony Burgess and David Lodge echo. Green demurs. A writer "must be disengaged or else he is writing politics . . . I just wrote what I heard and saw, and . . . the workers in my factory thought it rotten." His "very good friend Christopher Isherwood," he speculates, may never have worked in a factory.

Henry Green is the pen name of Eton-educated Henry Vincent Yorke (1905–1973), a school friend of Anthony Powell. At school he wrote his first published novel, *Blindness* (1926). At Oxford (which he left without benefit of degree) he was a friend of Evelyn Waugh. He came from a wealthy Midland family and began his career at shop-floor level among his father's workers, producing bottling machines. This experience is at the core of *Living,* his first mature novel. David Lodge notes the irony of an Eton-educated novelist producing it. He avoided the gulf between his language and that of his characters by, Lodge notes, "deliberately deforming the narrative discourse—giving it, as he said himself, something of the compactness of Midland dialect and avoiding 'easy elegance.'" This deliberate distancing is an effective, very English exercise in modernism.

By 1952 he had produced nine novels and a memoir entitled *Pack My Bag* (1940), which begins, "I was born a mouthbreather with a silver spoon in 1905." Then he stopped writing and got on with other pastimes, including philandering and alcoholism.

The pseudonym (at school he tried out "Henry Michaels" and "Henry Browne" before settling on "Green") was a way of eluding the snares of a Burke's Peerage background. His maternal grandfather, a Baron, owned one of the great houses of Sussex. His mother was quite *appallingly* refined. His father may have been an industrialist but he was old money, too, and old property, and well into rural pastimes. For Henry style was also a way of neutralizing the class elements that disfigured him in his own eyes. Even in his early prose he does away with the mannerly trappings and writes with almost uninflected directness. His relationship with his characters he wants to make one of trust, so he can remain mute. Cecil Beaton's portrait shows the back of his head.

Among his several female intimates, none of whom felt they understood him any better than his male friends did, one declared, "He didn't really exist . . . There was a hole there. He only really existed in other people. He was living off the fat of other people and once the fat was gone, he would go." This is an interesting recipe for a novelist but not for a lover. He was a serious gin drinker, too, day and night. "He drank because he couldn't write," a friend declared, "and he couldn't write because he drank." There is no sense that he really *wanted* to write any more after *Doting* (1952). He had no more to say—or do, because his writing was about being rather than meaning.

*Doting*, like *Nothing* (1950), is a dialogue novel: He abdicates to his characters, who disclose their inadequacy, paralyzing selfishness, and folly. This is not the steady, accreting dialogue of Ivy Compton-Burnett. It is less about family and money, more about class, desire, concealment, and a love that lays waste to itself. In middle age Diana and Arthur Middleton, prosperous middle-class representatives of a generation spent by the war, seek fulfillment outside their marriage. There is humor, but of a harsh kind. "Laughter relaxes the characters in a novel. And if you can make the reader laugh, he is apt to get careless and go on reading. So you as the writer get a chance to get something into him." The writer is not the narrator; the narrator attends and tonelessly records, he does not affect the action. Yet one suspects the action is closer to home for Henry Vincent Yorke than Henry Green lets on. The novel ends with Green's last words as a novelist: "The next day they all went on very much the same."

In 1958, six years after these final words, the *Paris Review* interviewed him. He maintained the illusion that he was still writing, indeed that he had a commission to write about London during the war, a book to be called *London and Fire, 1940*. The interviewer quotes from Green's *Pack My Bag*: "Prose is not to be read aloud but to oneself alone at night, and it is not quick as poetry but rather a gathering web of insinuations which go further than names however shared can ever go." He brings it close, too close: "Prose should be a long intimacy between strangers with no direct appeal to what both may have known. It should slowly appeal to feelings unexpressed, it should in the end draw tears out of the stone." He notes how Chinese classical painters depict the foreground and the far background but leave out the middle distance, using this as an analogy for the kinds of economy he comes to practice in his later work: "If you are trying to write something which has a life of its own, which is alive, of course the author must keep completely out of the picture."

Anthony Burgess admires the economy that begins in titles *(Living, Caught, Loving, Concluding, Nothing)* and carries into the writing. He speaks of the "closeness of texture" as poetic, and this may have something to do with Green's choice of characteristic detail. In *Living,* the workers are "as real as their pigeons whose sounds and flight weave the novel together." *Party Going* (1939) is full of the approach of war. Fog delays the boat train: Downstairs the working folk, upstairs the moneyed young. An old woman wraps a dead pigeon in paper. The action is not explored. The narrator has handed the novel over to the characters and, as a result, to the reader: as in all modernist works, the reader must actively engage.

"I can never understand these fellows like Evelyn Waugh who did not always have the idea of being a writer. I always wanted to be a writer," said P. G. Wodehouse. Arthur Evelyn St. John Waugh (1903–1966) wanted to be a painter. Writing was a second-best vocation. He remembered in his early old age (he assumed a dufferish identity early and seemed much older than he need have done), the "lean dark, singular man named Henry Yorke" he knew at Oxford, who went on (he said) to "dazzle" with his writings. The more various dazzle of Waugh obscured Green from the start.

Unlike his friend, Waugh finished at Oxford, but with a third-class degree and a chronic hostility to his well-meaning tutor called Cruttwell whom he vilified in fiction, dubbing several bizarre minor characters Cruttwell and ragging and punishing them. At Oxford Waugh insinuated himself into a group that styled itself "the Hypocrites"—aristocratic, homosexual, and resolute aesthetes against a dominant "jock" culture, apolitical cousins of the Cambridge Apostles. After Oxford he tried to set up as a painter, his father Arthur Waugh (1866–1943), a significant critic and publisher, having paid off his substantial university debts. Extravagant living at university helped him move successfully in circles beyond his own, experimenting sexually and socially. The investment paid off in *Brideshead Revisited: The Sacred and Profane Memories of Captain Charles Ryder* (1945). Young Waugh, like Ryder, did not have it in him to be a painter. He was reduced to writing. In 1925 he burned the manuscript of his first novel, *The Temple at Thatch,* and, overwhelmed with failure, attempted to drown himself in the sea. A jellyfish sting sent him clambering back up the beach. Literature owes a debt to that jellyfish. Also to Waugh's father, who humored and supported his son, and to Waugh's Oxford friend Anthony Powell, then working at the publishers Duckworth, who helped obtain a commission for Waugh's *Rossetti: His Life and Works* (1928), a headlong and not very good account of the Pre-Raphaelite poet and painter Dante Gabriel Rossetti.

Already the Waugh style is formed: summary and plausible aesthetic judgments are elegantly delivered. "In Rossetti's own day, no doubt, not a little of the adulation he aroused came from this romance of decay—a sort of spiritual coprophily characteristic of the age." Later: "The sort of unhappiness that beset him was not the sort of unhappiness that does beset a great artist; all his brooding about magic and suicide are symptomatic not so much of genius as of mediocrity. There is a spiritual inadequacy, a sense of ill-organization about all that he did." Waugh's sense of the picturesque, isolated detail and its analogies to sporadic genius also ring true: "Just as the broken arch at Glastonbury Abbey is, in its ruin, so much more moving than it can ever have been when it stood whole and part of a great building, so Rossetti's art, at fitful moments, flames into the exquisite beauty of *Beata Beatrix*." Modern aesthetics, he remarks, find it hard to cope with the complicity of accident and creative intention.

His debut novel, *Decline and Fall*, appeared in the same year as his book on Rossetti. It was the year of Isherwood's *All the Conspirators*, the year before Green's *Living*. *Decline and Fall*, with its needling allusion to Gibbon's great work on the end of the Roman Empire, is also about the final decadence of a once-great empire; but taking Gibbon's title for a work on so small and provincial a scale is only the first of his ironies. The "Prelude," where the names themselves promise a Peacockian romp, contains a whole little world: "Mr. Sniggs, the Junior Dean, and Mr. Postlethwaite, the Domestic Bursar, sat alone in Mr. Sniggs' room overlooking the garden quad at Scone college." He has evoked privilege, hierarchy, class, complicity, surveillance, an air of conspiracy. When the first chapter, "Vocation," opens, the ironies lie deeply layered. Readers know much more than the characters because of the narrator's manner, providing excess by way of omission and suggestive understatement. " 'Sent down for indecent behavior, eh?' said Paul Pennyfeather's guardian."

The proportions throughout are mannerly and all wrong; a child dies of an infection without much fuss, not even a pause for tears, while the arrival for a sports day visit to the school of Mrs. Beste-Chatwynd with her formidable black lover is on an epic scale. Her totally modern world is brittle, and after the principles of permanence that characterized the landed classes, her world is provisional. The architect Otto Silenus (only previous work "the décor for a cinema-film of great length") has transformed the noble pile that was King's Thursday with steel and concrete, displacing what was shady, settled, merely traditional. The rural world has been violated by the Bauhaus and urban modernity, another victim of international modernism. Mrs. Beste-Chatwynd's too-precocious son Peter brews unusual cocktails.

The fact that bibulous, increasingly sardonic Paul Pennyfeather is actually drawn into the headmaster's world of illusions, even if only for a few pages, is proof of the seductive power of prejudice. Waugh's satire subsumes within its caustic scope subjects that generally evoke nostalgia and elegy—Oxford, its dons, undergraduate years, the public school—and finds in them instead cruel and savage humor. The class system and its snobbery and bullying are exemplified in the life of a minor public school, the English church, and the hallowed traditions that "made England what it is": what it is provides the butt. Arnold Bennett gave the book the thumbs up in the *Evening Standard,* noting its palpable malice. It had an impact on Kingsley Amis's first novel, *Lucky Jim* (1954), which resembles it in structural and thematic features—though by the time Amis wrote, the institutions Waugh satirized were held in general contempt by half-radicalized reading classes. Amis was pushing at an open door.

Waugh once wrote that satire can only flourish "in a stable society and presupposes homogeneous moral standards." Against those presuppositions he tilts, and yet the clean, sharp blade of his style and the satisfaction he derives from wielding it suggest that even at this early stage in his writing there is a mismatch between his moral sense and his sense of style. We cannot take our eyes off the author, he is too riveting an ironist. He becomes, in contrast to the almost absent Henry Green narrator or Isherwood's would-be self-effacing Christopher, a point of focus, not that he directs our response but that he refines and distorts, we come to anticipate his techniques of subterfuge. At this level he shares qualities with Wodehouse (the first chapter of *A Handful of Dust* is entitled "Hard Cheese on Tony," but while Wodehouse beguiles and seems at home in the world he draws, Waugh brings into fiction the bullying tactics he brought to the playground and to social relations. Crucially, the occasion for his book, as for Amis's and many first books, is autobiographical. There are scores to settle, humiliations to expiate, and much of the detail, even at its most absurd, can be traced to the author's life. His protagonist is not, of course, himself: he has a tongue in his head. Paul Pennyfeather finds his voice only after he has been debagged, decanted into the college fountain, and expelled for indecent behavior. Aloud, he speaks politely and with restraint. To himself "meekly" he says, "God damn and blast them all to hell." Those who bully and keep him down are articulate.

*Decline and Fall* was an immediate success, seeing its third printing in as many months, and on the strength of the income it generated (including a $500 advance from the United States), the twenty-five-year-old writer moved up the date for his wedding and shifted, as F. Scott Fitzgerald did, into overspend. His bride-to-be was Evelyn Gardner and their set, prosperous and celebrity-struck, referred to them as He-Evelyn and She-Evelyn, an ideal couple. They went on a sponsored honeymoon cruise, He-Evelyn commissioned to write a series of travel articles about it and hoping to come back with sufficient sketches to mount an exhibition (writing still being decidedly a second suit). She-Evelyn fell seriously ill and was hospitalized in Port Said, and when they returned they were again in financial straits. Waugh stayed at an inn in Beckley near Oxford, composing *Vile Bodies*. His wife remained in London, where she fell in love with one of their close friends, and the first flush of romance was busted. This fundamental failure affected the rest of his life and his fiction. Had she died on the ship, sorrow might have turned him into an elegist or romantic writer, but infidelity, like that wake-up-call jellyfish, changed him. He became self-defensive, misogynistic (with exceptions), merciless. His female characters, Martin Amis comments, generally embody "philistinism, will and appetite."

*Vile Bodies,* his second novel, its title drawn from Philippians 3:20–21 ("We await a saviour . . . who shall change our vile body, that it may be fashioned like unto his glorious body, according to the working whereby he is able even to subdue all things unto himself"), appeared in 1930. It was an immediate commercial success, its pessimism and savage satire in keeping with a darkening decade. Originally it was to be called *Bright Young Things,* the subject being young people of the 1920s, including the author himself, their illusions and disillusion. It is formally his most inventive novel. Waugh had many of the instincts of a modernist; he admired the poems of T. S. Eliot with their juxtapositions, voices, fragmentation, and collaring. He was fascinated by cinema and its narrative sleights of hand. He shared with Eliot an interest in the telephone and the ambiguous freedoms it provided in the context of narrative. The novel represents a road not taken: Here Waugh experimented in ways that bring his themes alive with an immediacy that the more conventional, mediated fiction he wrote later did not. The tonal shift from comedy to the intensities of the final battlefield (the chapter titled "Happy Ending") would not have been possible by purely conventional means. Again an autobiographical occasion may lurk behind the novel's change of key (as behind T. S. Eliot's *The Waste Land* and *Ash Wednesday*). As he was writing it he discovered She-Evelyn's infidelity and was negotiating the end of their marriage. This blew a chill through the projected light romantic comedy. The scene in which the protagonist, Adam Fenwyck-Symes, sees the book he has written seized by a customs officer is brutal. Angela Runcible says, "Adam, angel, don't fuss or we shall miss the train." The consequences are hilarious, but the reality of Adam's anxieties gives the experience of reading it a double effect: there is a real toad in this imaginary garden and things that happen in the imagination actually affect the toad in dreadful ways, though not quite so dreadful as the ways Tony Last is affected in the even more frightful world of *A Handful of Dust.*

Before that comes a light, hilariously distasteful comedy, *Black Mischief* (1932). Does it relate to Nabokov's *Pale Fire,* with fictional Zembla and equally fictional Azania being not-remote cousins, and the intrigue, ambivalence, decadence, and comedy having elements in common? The Oxford-educated Emperor Seth (based on Haile Selassie, whose coronation Waugh attended on his first journey to Abyssinia) wants to modernize his country and sets up a Ministry. He employs his old (white) Oxford contemporary Basil Seal to be the Minister. European values and structures are imposed on an alien landscape and culture. Waugh does not provide a happy ending.

In *A Handful of Dust* (1934), with its direct acknowledgment of Eliot in the title, Waugh's narrative originality is clearest. However abundant the description, however complex the plot (here extremely complex in terms of knowledge possessed and withheld and ironic misunderstanding), an economy of means intensifies the dramatic shocks of character and action. William Boyd described the book as *"Madame Bovary* rewritten by Noël Coward." The mention of Coward reminds us of analogies with Firbank, too. The book includes in-jokes for those in the know. It is an insider's book whose ironies deflect attention from the fresh personal wound at the heart of it.

Henry Green was unconvinced by the cruel ending. It is in a different register from the rest of the book. Waugh had written a short story ("The Man Who Liked Dickens") that he thought concluded the book quite well. He made a few adjustments so the bolt-on would work: we move from a satirized social world into a realm of transcendent justice, or injustice. Was this creative short-cut evidence of authorial laziness, or was it right? Odd that a protagonist could so easily be transferable between story and novel. But there is a single *kind* of protagonist in Waugh's early novels, a "he" who bears the sins of the "I," not to expiation but to definition and fixity. The fatalism is overwhelming, transferring responsibility to Fortune when, as a Roman Catholic (he converted after his marriage failed, in 1930), he might have been concerned with will. The ending of *A Handful of Dust* was different in the British and American editions: the story Waugh used in Britain was separately copyrighted in the United States and he had to invent another ending, which entails Toni's revenge on a dreadful but penitent wife, with whom he reconciles only to plan affairs of his own.

Waugh's sense of England and Englishness derives from the culture itself, to which by his adoption of Roman Catholicism he puts himself at an oblique angle, that of a Johnsonian English conservative straitened by religion. For Forster as for Orwell, fictional characters, like people in the street, possess a "given," an "authentic" nature that they can locate and develop. For Waugh, on the other hand, fictional and living characters derive their nature from external "accidentals": family, community, school, church, army—from institutions, their histories, and language. Tony Last's attachment to his ancestral pile, to the countryside and its ways, are evidence of this, and ultimate punishment is to be eternally cut off from them. Waugh's conservatism increased as he began to appreciate, often in other people, the privileged lives of his hosts and aristocratic friends, what was entailed in a society that devalues them, and an aesthetic, like that of some of the modernists, that takes their depredation as a given. The enemy appears in the guise of the Beevers, mother and son, and of those who are attached only to their own pleasure and interest, like She-Evelyn. In time he becomes, in his writing and life, complicit with them, locked in rigid reaction. Waugh and

Orwell, however, share an anxiety about England in decline. Their novels are *topical*. Waugh lasts better because of his style and the negative clarity of his vision.

*Scoop* (1938) is his most entertaining novel, brutally light. He said that journalism was detrimental to novelists, they ought to get out of it as soon as they could. *Scoop* satirizes prewar Fleet Street with an insouciance that the Second World War seems to have driven out of him. Here, not in *Black Mischief* or his journalistic book *Waugh in Abyssinia* (1936), we experience the impact on his imagination of the forces of the institutional-irrational. William Boot's is a fate Kafka would have shuddered at and understood.

During that year his first marriage was annulled. The following year he married again, comfortably, starting a new life. *Scoop* was the first novel to appear in the new life. It belongs decidedly to the first phase, a bitterly productive decade of loss, political and spiritual adjustment that began with *Decline and Fall*.

*Put Out More Flags* (1942) responds directly to its period, the halfway point of the Second World War with its uncertainties, fears, and deprivations. Waugh joined the armed forces promptly and was moved from duty to duty, in 1940 being sent to train with a commando unit that, the following year, was involved in a failed mission to recapture Bardia in Libya, and then to help evacuate Crete. On his way home he wrote this novel, oppressed with a sense of disorganization and waste. He was transferred to the Royal Horse Guards, proving as usual an anarchic and heavy-drinking comrade-in-arms. He decided to train as a parachutist, broke a fibula, and took unpaid leave to write. The fruit of his labors was *Brideshead*. Not only was the war over but much else in this elegiac novel: despite its spiritually and morally questionable ending, it captivated readers in the United States and Britain.

Not all readers. Anthony Burgess, also a Roman Catholic, relished the 1960 revision, at once shorter and less self-indulgent than the 1945 original. One either succumbs to its seduction, he says, or loathes its overblownness. Saul Bellow, disenchanted with England and all the "pansies" he found in the literary garden there, said in a letter, "I loathe snobs and Waugh is one of the worst sort . . . But snobbery *and* piousness? I have an Old Testament eye for abominations, a little reddened by this one." His eye might also have discerned here and in Waugh's earlier work evidence of a reflex anti-Semitism deep-rooted in his acquired class. Martin Amis shares Bellow's revulsion. He starts by anatomizing *Brideshead*'s clichés, then cuts deeper into it. "Equally enthralling and distasteful, it is Waugh's problem comedy," he says, likening it to *Mansfield Park* as "worrying, inordinate, self-conscious, a book that steps out of genre and never really looks at home with its putative author." Amis locates the effects of Waugh's snobbery on the writing: "There is something barefaced, even aggressive, in the programmatic way the novel arranges for its three most unregenerate characters—Sebastian, Lord Marchmain and Julia—to claim the highest spiritual honors." Charles Ryder's first conversion is social and sexual; at Brideshead he is drawn into the baroque. Amis speaks of the disjunction between the novel's heartlessness and its elaborate and elaborated style: But is the baroque not gesture and effect in lieu of actual content? The pillars sustain nothing, an architecture of show without substance, to which the current heirs have nothing but the accidental claim of birthright.

How slowly term-time passes in the novel. Readers who have attended an ancient university in which the terms last eight weeks may wonder how so much can be packed into so short a span. Could a term contain—when colleges were sexually segregated—a whole adolescence two or three times over? Is this the same Oxford of *Decline and Fall?* What magic transformed that sour nest into the place that Sebastian Flight now inhabits, admired, unironized, though he touches with languid irony all that surrounds him? *Brideshead* came to Waugh fast; he wrote without hesitation, confident that what he set down was true to a feeling and came from a source he would not question. "Lasting schlock, the really good bad book," says Amis, "cannot be written otherwise." It needs cliché, shorthand, plangency. It stands a few rungs below a novel of the previous generation, Fitzgerald's differently elegiac *The Great Gatsby.*

Fitzgerald was not pushing a message. Frederic Raphael reminds us that, from his conversion in 1930, Waugh "had employed language both to amuse and, if slyly, to write advertisements for his Faith." He was as acutely sensitive to Roman Catholic criticism as any socialist realist was of the Party's censure; projects were undertaken (biographies of Campion and Knox, the historical novel *Helena* of 1950) in a spirit of expiation and propaganda, writing of a committed and persuasive nature with designs on the reader that, being insidious, can get overlooked, though the conclusion of *Brideshead* is as cruel to the nonbeliever and, I imagine, to some believers, as it is repugnant. Raphael notes, "In fabricating *Brideshead,* Waugh's new, incantatory style becomes almost pagan with restrictive earnestness."

Charles Ryder's conversion put off many admirers, Edmund Wilson among them. Surely it was reactionary just after the war, with new liberal nostrums all about. Could such appalling characters be saved? Raphael says, "One may guess that he is in the grip of art's archest enemy, sincerity." Henry Green, Graham Greene, and Waugh's old sparring partner and friend from Oxford days Harold Acton were persuaded by it.

Had Waugh not been a spendthrift, income from *Brideshead* and his earlier books would have made life comfortable, but he was fitful, acquisitive. He made several trips to the United States, the first in 1947 to discuss a film version of

*Brideshead* that did not come off. Fortunately he visited Forest Lawn Cemetery while in California and the result was the little satirical masterpiece *The Loved One: An Anglo-American Tragedy* (1948), about the American way of death. We encounter in particular the beaming Mr. Joyboy, a schemer vile and fascinating as Uriah Heap. With the dystopian *Love among the Ruins* (1953), in which the arsonist Miles Plastic works at the local euthanasia clinic and death is again hilariously on the cards, this marks the end of Waugh's satirical trajectory.

With *Men at Arms* (1952) Waugh began the trilogy of books—with *Officers and Gentlemen* (1955) and *Unconditional Surrender* (1961)—that, revised as a single work in 1965, constitute *Sword of Honor,* based on his experience of the Second World War. His protagonist Guy Crouchback is Roman Catholic and a gentleman, closely attached to Italy by ties of feeling and real estate. Anthony Burgess compares Crouchback with "the hero of Ford Madox Ford's *Parade's End*" and describes the trilogy as modeled on Ford's tetralogy. It is, he declares, "the whole history of the European struggle itself." Waugh distorts his experiences rather less than in earlier works, his aim being not satire but fidelity. Cyril Connolly dismissed the first volume but revised his opinion and became a cheerleader, "the finest novel to come out of the war." Its staunch contemporary advocate is William Boyd, who (minus the snobbery) identifies as closely with Waugh as Raphael does with Maugham. He suffered a frustration similar to Waugh's: he wanted to be an artist and Fortune, as Waugh called the willful goddess, took him elsewhere. With *Nat Tate: An American Artist, 1928–1960* (1998) Boyd in fiction revisited his dream, as Charles Ryder does. Boyd adapted *Sword of Honor* for television and came to understand the quality of Waugh's economy.

Of all Waugh's books the most vulnerable and engaging is *The Ordeal of Gilbert Pinfold* (1957), the fruit of a mental breakdown partly exacerbated by medication. By 1953 his popularity was not what it had been. The public persona was getting in the way of the work. He felt besieged, he started hearing voices, imagining conspiracies. He was unable to write. Out of this experience, from which, thanks to a change in medication, he enjoyed an almost miraculous recovery, came *The Ordeal,* his "barmy book." He was proud to have come so close to madness. The loneliness he inflicted on Paul Pennyfeather, William Boot, and Tony Last here visits him, and he observes with astonishment what the world can do to its innocents. He was able to mimic and make fun of himself with a degree of affection, as if here he at last obeyed Christ's second commandment, "Thou shalt love thy neighbor as thyself," which entails loving oneself, for many Christians the most difficult obligation.

William Boyd (b. 1952) brings many of the stylistic qualities of Waugh into a less psychologically vexed fictional world. In *Brazzaville Beach* (1990) the protagonist Hope Clearwater declares, "I never really warmed to Clovis—he was far too stupid to inspire real affection—but he always claimed a corner of my heart, largely, I suppose, because of the way he instinctively and unconsciously cupped his genitals whenever he was alarmed or nervous." Clovis is not a tennis champion but a chimp, and Hope is in Africa escaping from the more complex primates, including her husband, to study our extended family, or rather our extended order. Boyd is a gifted storyteller, drawing effortlessly on a broad background—born in Ghana, educated in Scotland, then in France and England. He does belong: "I'm solidly, immutably Scottish but I don't talk about my Scottishness or refer to it very much at all. Very few of the characters in my novels are Scottish, for example." He belongs, but his art does not. Africa provides the setting for three of his best-known novels—his first, *A Good Man in Africa* (1981), dealing with the conflict between decolonization and the discovery of oil, among other contemporary issues; *An Ice-Cream War* (1982), set in North Africa and the First World War, a favorite quarry for the author; and *Brazzaville Beach*.

His most mischievous novel is the fictional biography *Nat Tate*. The Tate and the National Galleries in London provided the artist's name. Tate's short life ended when he plunged off the Staten Island ferry. Like Hart Crane's his body has never been recovered. He was an abstract expressionist and his death an abstract expression. Gore Vidal, leading figures in the art world, and Picasso's biographer John Richardson played along with Boyd in a hoax that persuaded many that it was time to reevaluate this tragic figure. The book was launched on March 31 and published on April 1. At the launch party, though no one claimed intimacy with Tate, no one admitted that they had not heard of him. The book keeps a straight face and tells a convincing and quite moving story, plausible in detail, illuminating in what it has to say about the trajectory of a minor artist aware of his limitations, reaching for the lenitive bottle and so self-critical that he destroys the bulk of his work before killing himself. One surviving Nat Tate painting, "Bridge no. 114," was auctioned at Sotheby's (London) and fetched £7,250, well above the reserve price. Proceeds of the sale (to one W. Boyd) benefited the Artists' General Benevolent Institution.

(Henry) Graham Greene (1904–1991) might have been Henry Greene. What would have happened to Henry Vincent Yorke had that been the case? At Balliol College, Oxford, where he read history and achieved a second-class degree, Greene looked sourly at his louche contemporaries. Waugh marked him absent from the revelries of the in every sense gay group he hung out with.

When he became a Roman Catholic, converting in 1926 in order to marry a Catholic the following year, Greene found loving his neighbor and himself a challenge. In *The Power and the Glory* his whisky priest says, "When you visualized a man or a woman carefully, you could always begin to feel pity . . . That was a quality God's image carried with it." Pity is not love, but it is on the way to a kind of love. And what is hate but "a failure of the imagination"? Greene's imagination often failed, and some of his failures were predictable. Saul Bellow despised his knee-jerk anti-Americanism and his anti-Zionism. They were of a piece with the casual anti-Semitism of Waugh, but Greene knew better what he was up to.

Greene's childhood, by his own report, was unhappy. His father was a housemaster and then headmaster of Berkhamsted School in Hertfordshire, and his fourth son Henry Graham attended first as a boarder and then, after something like a breakdown due in part to bullying, and after six months of psychoanalysis, as a day boy. At the end of his school career Greene became briefly a member of the Communist Party of Great Britain. This was well before the Great Depression, so his conscience, unlike Isherwood's, was stirred less by crisis, more by reflection on social justice and rebellion against the privilege that surrounded him. From an early age he sought a cause to which he might lend, or in which he might lose, himself. The Party was not for him, though in later years he was drawn to Latin American communists, in particular Fidel Castro, whose Stalinist policies he overlooked and whose hostility to the United States he endorsed.

Although he died in his eighties, in his own bed, of a blood disorder, Greene was haunted all his adult life by the conviction that he would be murdered. He did his best to preempt fate. During his troubled school career he swallowed hyposulfate, hay-fever drops, eye drops, deadly nightshade, and a whole tin of hair pomade, but he survived. By his twentieth birthday he was playing Russian roulette, and not for political reasons. He became a Catholic with a severe Protestant temperament. Religion stopped further suicide attempts, but he actively courted danger: that was theologically tolerable. He adopted as his motto lines from Browning's "Bishop Blougram's Apology," which he enjoyed reciting from memory: "Our interest's on the dangerous edge of things, / The honest thief, the tender murderer, / The superstitious atheist, demi-rep / That loves and saves her soul in new French books." A recording of him reciting this survives. He effaces *r*'s and flattens vowels. His inflection is not unlike Eliot's, and *The Waste Land* weighed with him as with Waugh, as did the poems of spiritual acceptance and growth.

The criminal underworld, first in London and then in Brighton, attracted him. *Brighton Rock* (1938), the first novel that is wholly his, dramatizes through the character of Pinkie his self-destructive preoccupations. The themes of damnation and redemption receive more explicitly Catholic treatment in *The Power and the Glory* (1940, called *Labyrinthine Ways* in its original American edition). God's power and glory, if not his kingdom, are (more than sacramentally) embodied in his anonymous protagonist, the whisky priest, who offended the Holy Office in Rome. Greene was advised in 1953 that the book should be proscribed, though later Pope Paul VI changed his mind. In the book Greene presents what Anthony Burgess calls "the torrid decay of tropical townships, where the carious ruins are metaphors for a world without God." The outlawing of wine entails the outlawing of the sacrament itself. Greene's non-English settings tend to be hot, humid, and decayed.

He spent much of the Second World War in Sierra Leone, working under double agent Kim Philby at the Foreign Office as an MI6 agent himself. Parting from his wife soon after the war, though as "good Catholics" they never divorced, he embarked on a series of affairs, two of which provided inspiration for his major postwar novels *The Heart of the Matter* (1948) and *The End of the Affair* (1951). His inability to keep the vow of chastity, he said, kept him from a priest's vocation. He refused a private audience with Padre Pio, who had received the stigmata, for fear that it would change his life. "If you are a saint it's not so difficult to be a saint," says Sarah in *The End of the Affair*. He was not. He insisted on the need for doubt. For his baptismal name Greene chose Thomas.

Burgess recognizes a link between Greene's different settings and his developing spiritual concerns, something he and Greene have in common, which added bitterness to their public estrangement: "Unlike Evelyn Waugh," writes Burgess, "who fictionally identified himself with the fortunes of English Catholics tied, by land or family bonds, to England, Greene is concerned with the Catholic soul working out its salvation or damnation in isolation: the furniture of England is a distraction and an irrelevance." "The furniture of England": the phrase is telling. Waugh loved the material English past, avidly collecting provincial antiques. Greene is not attached to England in those terms, there is no sugar in his retrospect. Waugh regarded it as "improper to speculate on another's damnation," while Greene could not resist creating, then probing, the circumstances of damnation. His writing is not autobiographical in the way that Waugh's is, but it is confessional. Isherwood remarked, "Graham Greene himself would seem the perfect casting for one of the wry tormented skeptics who inhabit the Jansenistic darkness of his novels."

The theologies of Waugh and Greene are hardly complementary, and the books they wrote about Mexico illustrate their difference. Waugh writes from the perspective and with the interests and prejudices of an unreflecting Englishman of a certain class in *Robbery under Law: The Mexican Object-Lesson* (1939). His monarchist, Roman Catholic, capitalist, and racist opinions are delivered with uncontestable finality. Worst of all the inventoried crimes was the nationalization of the oil industry by President Lázaro Cárdenas in 1938. Waugh was bankrolled by the Cowdray Estate, which lost heavily in the expropriation: there is nothing disinterested about his book. *The Lawless Roads: A Mexican Journey* (also 1939), Greene's polemic, was sponsored by British Catholic publishing interests. At the time Greene was accused of having libeled Shirley Temple in a film review: his friends feared prosecution and even imprisonment had he stayed in England. Thus, Shirley Temple catalyzed both *The Lawless Roads* and *The Power and the Glory*.

Cardinal Newman provides its third epigraph. Reflecting on some bleak words of the Apostle, "having no hope, and without God in the world," he remarks, "I can only answer, that there is no Creator, or this living society of men is in a true sense discarded from his Presence . . . *if* there be a God, *since* there is a God, the human race is implicated in some terrible aboriginal calamity." The oil expropriation is displaced, for Greene, by the persecution of the Roman Catholics in the states of Chiapas and Tabasco. The book his most resembles in asperity of vision is *Heart of Darkness*. Conrad is one of the writers Greene is made of. The book is also about England. In the prologue Greene hyperbolizes, without fear of correction from his English Catholic sponsors, "President Calles had begun the fiercest persecution of religion anywhere since the reign of Elizabeth."

Whereas Waugh's trip had no direct issue in his fiction, Greene's led to *The Power and the Glory*. He gave himself over to the otherness of Mexico, his manner being analogous to the self-effacing anthropologist's. What remains solid in every setting, whether Indochina, Liberia, the Congo, Haiti, Cuba, or Mexico, is his vexed Catholicism; his sense of English belonging resolves itself in style.

Before he became enemies with Greene, Burgess most admired *The Heart of the Matter*. His fascination, like Waugh's, was theological. The adulterer Scobie takes sacrilegious communion, and the story seems to condone his act. Waugh found this distasteful, though he admired the novel's structure. Pope Paul VI told Greene he had read it but did not offer an opinion. Raymond Chandler wrote to his publisher, "It has everything in it that makes literature except verve, wit, gusto, music and magic; a cool and elegant set-piece, embalmed by Whispering Glades . . . There is more life in the worst chapter Dickens or Thackeray ever wrote, and they wrote some pretty awful chapters." But he added later, "The end of the Greene book is great. It atones for a lack I had felt before."

When Greene travels, he knows what he is after. His themes dictate, not where he goes, but what he chooses to remember and work into fiction. Edmund Wilson praises in *The Power and the Glory* his "palette of sour colors, a repertory of sickening suggestions, a talent for selecting and rubbing in unpleasant details of modern civilization, such as cheap panes of stained glass, inferior dental drills, insipid correspondence courses, that make good writing and are entirely his own." In this book, however, Wilson finds "too little to set against" the negatives. The priest himself lacks not so much fire as even a spark to make his faith and motive real to us (as they must surely be to him). Wilson speaks of

Greene's "fidelity to the mood of [his] society": the stiffening corpse of England is expressed obliquely in a Mexico stylized and intensified for the purpose.

Lampedusa, whose Sicilian Catholicism is less punishing than Greene's variety, admires the way he is "attracted, without repugnance, to everything that is repulsive and putrid." "A Christian *must* be attracted to fetid carcasses, as hyenas are, or Baudelaire, or the Angel of the Resurrection." There is horror and decomposition in the unsettled nineteenth century of Lampedusa's Sicily in *The Leopard,* but "in Greene horror for the filthiness of the brutish, unredeemed human being is mitigated by the insuppressible resemblance to God which he finds in the most wretched delinquent; his repulsion is transformed, as he has magnificently put it, into 'a forward flight' to try to wash the mud and gore from features which are essentially divine." Lampedusa hears differently from the Anglophone reader, something is added by his generosity. "Out of the most abject ambience imaginable, an ambience of vice, squalor, decay and fear, Greene has managed to create—with his drunken, lustful and yet saintly 'whisky priest'— one of the most powerful figures in English literature." He quotes the priest: "When you saw the lines at the corners of the eyes, the shape of the mouth, how the hair grew, it was impossible to hate." And he admired the way Greene's novels belong together. Greene claimed to be "dominated" by his themes. If a novelist is not dominated, he says, "he has to rely on his talent, and talent, even of a very high order, cannot sustain an achievement, whereas a ruling passion gives . . . to a shelf of novels the unity of a system." Greene divided his work into "novels" and "entertainments," but both kinds, while they might differ in tone, are clearly from the same imagination. In the collected edition he did away with the misleading classification.

Greene has a dozen landscapes but one procedure. Like some Victorian, Edwardian, and modernist precursors, he saw British social institutions as obstacles to the development of identity. His protagonists strive to escape constraint. The motif of exile is everywhere. Exile begins in his own choice of Roman Catholicism. It ends in his decisive rejection of a stable English setting. In a 1968 interview he describes "a restlessness that I've always had to move around and perhaps to see English characters in *a setting which is not protective to them* [my italics], where perhaps they speak a little differently, a little more openly." By contrast, exile seals Waugh's characters into their Englishness.

What matters most to Greene is character and its development under stress, his debt to Conrad being deep. The novel form excites him as a means of exploring and penetrating, not as an end. Form can take care of itself if a story is told faithfully, including its political, religious, and historical contexts. The world is various and its many trials impose different challenges. He looks for transparency of language. His wife alerted him to excessive metaphor: "Tiger, darling," and the tiger would be shot. Burgess said Greene would never permit style "to become a character in its own right." On occasion he would parody modernism. In *The Confidential Agent* (1939), his protagonist walks to a Blooms-bury untouched by the Bloomsbury group, gathering impressions along Oxford Street that make fun of Clarissa Dalloway's exquisite stream of consciousness. He was impatient with Woolf and with Forster. Their lack of underlying faith made their work unserious. His main French enthusiasm was for François Mauriac, with whose spiritual as well as formal concerns Greene felt at home. He wrote about him in the teeth of Sartre, who despised him.

Greene was nervous about analytical criticism of his own work, fearing it might dry up the creative spring, that if he understood what he was doing he might no longer be able to do it. He did not like to be told, time after time, what he knew well, that he was a Roman Catholic writer. To him certain constitutive truths were nonnegotiable. This is part of what it meant to be a Christian writer.

*Stamboul Train* (1932) was his first commercial success: it gave him confidence to abandon his job at the *Times* and devote himself to fiction. But his reputation rests most securely on the novels he published between 1938 and 1951, in particular *Brighton Rock, The Power and the Glory, The Heart of the Matter,* and *The End of the Affair*. It is his period of greatest artistic and spiritual confidence: he understood the risks he was taking and religious doubts had yet to take political shapes. A less spiritual, more journalistic period follows with *The Quiet American* (1955), which brings alive in a prophetic way the growing crisis in Indochina with the French departure and the deepening engagement of the United States in what would become the Vietnam War; *Our Man in Havana* (1958), where Batista'a Cuba and its exotic corruptions can be relived; *A Burnt-Out Case* (1960), set in a leper colony in the Congo where Querry, a protagonist into whom Greene writes many of his own anxieties and concerns, finds spiritual fulfillment and martyrdom; and *The Comedians* (1966), set in Papa Doc Duvalier's Haiti, where ritual and superstition give to politics an authority underwritten by magic and the three foreign protagonists are sucked into the country's speedy and calamitous vortex. Each of these books is rooted in Greene's travels and his experiences in the British Secret Service. All are studies in resignation and a failure that expresses integrity and can be read as a spiritual triumph.

David Lodge affectionately parodied Greene in *The British Museum Is Falling Down* (1965), unburdening himself of an influence he could no longer bear. His Catholicism was not sun-bleached and decadent like Greene's. It was lower-middle-class English Catholicism of the cradle variety. But Greene liked the book and urged Lodge to post it off to Cardinal Heenan. If he read it he might understand the English Catholic rather better than he seemed to do. Fiction remained instrumental, as far as he was concerned.

Early in the 1930s, while he was working on *It's a Battlefield* (1934), Graham Greene addressed a letter to "Dear Mr. Narayan Swami," his full name being Rasipuram Krishnaswami Iyer Narayanaswami (1906–2001), soon to become—at Greene's suggestion—plain R. K. Narayan. "My friend Kit Purna sent me your novel the other day to read, and I should like to tell you as a fellow novelist how much I admired it. I took the liberty of sending it with a covering letter to a publisher, Hamish Hamilton, and I have heard from him today that he wishes to publish it. You couldn't I think have a better publisher. His is a young firm with a very good literary reputation and his connexion with the American publishers, Harper's, may make it possible to find a publisher for it too in the U.S.A."

It was, he said with enthusiasm that never flagged, "a real joy to be of use to a new writer of your quality." What Greene was to Narayan, Forster was to Mulk Raj Anand (1905–2004) and Raja Rao (1908–2006); these were the first Indian English novelists to find a substantial Anglophone readership. All three lived to be grand old men of English fiction. What Greene found in Narayan was also characteristic of other Indian writers who grew up with Gandhi, as it were. Their characters exist only in social relationship, their sense of self depends upon how they are perceived and can take dramatic plunges when a wrong action or a general misperception occurs. In such a world comedy and tragedy are closely aligned. This sense of *subject* subjectivity is new in English fiction accustomed to class but not to caste.

Narayan, whose native language was Tamil but whose family insisted on developing and sharpening his speaking, reading, and writing skills in English, had written stories before, but *Swami and Friends* (1935) was his first novel, and it had been widely rejected before Greene made it his cause. He loved the town of Malgudi that Narayan created, an invented and rather flexible space within which most of his novels occur, a Barchester (he is India's most Trollopian writer), a smaller Wessex, a gentler Yoknapatawpha County, or—as Anthony Burgess suggests—a Sarsaparilla, Patrick White's dramatic but controllable fictional space. It is a thoroughly Indian world. The few British characters who appear are casually observed and do not take center stage. At the age of twelve little Rasipuram had gone on a political march. His family, Brahmin, generally apolitical, was not pleased. The town of Malgudi developed in time and politics as India did, reflecting rather than rhetoricizing the changes. The writer's Anglophone upbringing included the development of an ironic tone that recommended him to the English in particular. This was not Rao's nationalism or Anand's rather earnest radicalism. The reality of these Indians seemed at first assimilable, quaint, beguiling, comic. Today they read differently. At his death, V. S. Naipaul, a beneficiary of Narayan's work, remembered being "enchanted" by the fiction but, writing in *Time,* noted that Narayan was not interested in the politics and problems of modern India, that "wounded civilization." Naipaul may have read him too quickly. It is true, Narayan refused to put his fiction at the service of analysis or cause. And Naipaul graciously forgave him, comparing Narayan's vision of India to Gandhi's (Gandhi does pay a visit to Malgudi). Gandhi, says Naipaul, "had in a heightened way Narayan's mystical idea of an eternal India; and look what happened to him. Narayan, with his glories and limitations, is the Gandhi of modern Indian literature." The novelist Pankaj Mishra, an heir of Narayan's, is closer to the mark when he insists on Narayan's "pragmatic realism" and "refusal to regard good and evil as unmixed."

Narayan's early novels, like Anand's, consider central themes, such as education in India and its negative impact on children. Dickens, whose books he read with fascination, had been agitated by the same theme in the English context. There was also the matter of arranged marriages—less their arrangement than the ways in which the matchmakers brought couples together—and then the situation of women snared in intolerable, binding relationships. His fiction changes key with his fourth and most autobiographical novel, *The English Teacher* (1945), which draws its extraordinary power from the death of Rajam, his own wife, whom he had met in 1933 when she was fifteen years old; he wooed and won her, and her death in 1939 left him desolate and colored the rest of his days.

He wrote fourteen novels, all of them readable, though in some of the later ones the imagination has become too comfortable with its subject matter, settings, and readership. Among the best are *The Financial Expert* (1951), Greene's favorite; *Waiting for the Mahatma* (1955), which, written twenty years after *Untouchable* by Anand, should be read alongside it; *The Guide* (1958); *The Man-Eater of Malgudi* (1961); *The Vendor of Sweets* (1967), which includes among its principal characters a half-American, Grace, who refocuses the generational tensions between her husband and his father, the redoubtable Jagan; *The Painter of Signs* (1977); and *A Tiger for Malgudi* (1983).

Maugham tried to meet Narayan in Mysore in 1938 and subsequently wrote him a letter of admiration. Forster liked his work. Anthony Burgess admired *The Vendor of Sweets,* characteristic of his approach, generally "realistic but drawn to fantasy," and indeed there are elements of effortless, undeliberated "magical realism" in some of the inconsequentialities and coincidences in the novels, and the way the descriptions seem to open out beyond the language itself into those photographic and cinematic images readers carry in their heads like memories. In this novel worlds collide. Here is a schoolboy at his homework: "He opened the political map of Europe and sat gazing at it. It puzzled him how people managed to live in such a crooked country as Europe." The boy continues. "He wondered what the shape of the people might be who lived in places where the outline narrowed as in a cape, and how they managed to escape being strangled by the contour of their land." And how do the mapmakers see the shape of the land, from high towers? Europe is a camel's head. And what might India look like from such perspectives?

For Greene the streets of Malgudi are real, and because they recur novel by novel they become a stable, habitable setting, a place where our own memories are active among the snuff-stalls, canals and ditches, roadworks, the colonial buildings and temples. Comedy, Green remarks, "needs a strong framework of social convention with which the author sympathizes but which he does not share." He muses, "Whom next shall I meet in Malgudi?" He is not waiting for another novel but for an extension of a familiar world. "I am waiting to go out of my door into those loved and shabby streets and see with excitement and the certainty of pleasure a stranger approaching, past the bank, the cinema, the hair-cutting saloon, a stranger who will greet me, I know, with some unexpected and revealing phrase that will open a door on to yet another human existence." The scale and pace of Vikram Seth's *A Suitable Boy* (1993) owes much to the sense of a complete world, visited rather than created by fiction. Narayan's places are spacious but include culs-de-sac, alleyways, dark corners. The novels are relatively brief, as Monica Ali reminds us, but their brevity is not the artistic measure of them. Some readers have problems with his writing because it seems pitched to the English reader, or because he did not write in Tamil. Such critics insist that, English being his second language, his oddnesses of style, in-cluding anachronisms, vestiges of Victorian phrasing, shortcuts, and clichés, demand a different kind of reading, the sort we would bring to translation. Otherwise his English will be disenfranchised, left as it were caught in customs with no passport at all.

Mulk Raj Anand's first notable English novel appeared in London in the same year as Narayan's. Born in Peshawar, Anand studied in Lahore, then as an undergraduate at University College London and as a graduate at Cambridge. While Narayan, a less accomplished taker of exams, remained in India, Anand was able to get the longer perspective not only from London but from Blooms-bury. The focus of his early novels remains on India, where he was affected by a tragedy his family itself created. An aunt was ostracized for having a meal with a Muslim. She went on to commit suicide. Such commonplace dogma-rooted tragedies, irrational-traditional, needed exposing, as did the larger cus-toms that framed them, not least the system of caste.

His first successful book, *Untouchable* (1935), he began in Simla, continued aboard the *Viceroy of India,* and finished in Bloomsbury. The protagonist is a young Indian "sweeper," Bakha, an untouchable resident of a real city, a hand-some, healthy youth, a remote cousin of Kim. Anand owes an equal debt to Kipling and to his friend E. M. Forster, who writes in his preface that the book "has gone straight to the heart of its subject and purified it." The removers of human waste are identified with the human product they dispose of. Unclean, unclean, they warn like lepers as they advance along the street, preparing us to avoid them. If touched by one of these, we must elaborately purify ourselves. *Untouchable* tells of a single day in a neighborhood. Untouchable Bakha accidentally gets above his station: curious, intelligent, he sees into a temple; he discovers corruption and hypocrisy in the priestly class, is found out, and suffers the consequences. Not Christ but the flushing toilet is proposed as the solution to his situation. Still, Bakha goes home from his eventful day resolved to tell his father about Gandhi, and the flushing machine of which he has learned, incidentally, from a poet.

The novel opens in an English mode, descriptive, ironic, presenting the community of "the scavengers, the leather-workers, the watermen, the barbers, the water-carriers, the grass-cutters and other outcasts from Hindu society," who lived among the smells of latrines and the rotting corpses from which the tanners harvested their hides, the middens from which fuel-cakes were made: a place decidedly "uncongenial." To have published such a book in 1935! It is political, of course, in relation not only to caste but also to colonial structures and the opiates of religion. It is a book of abundant adjectives, some of them choice: Bakha's father has a "clumsy, asthmatic cough," at the temple we hear (because we cannot see, being within Bakha's perspective) "a thumping crowd of worshippers."

Most memorable is the scene of the crowd rushing to see and hear Gandhi speak, crushing everything in their way. "The beautiful garden bowers planted by the ancient Hindu kings and since then neglected were thoroughly damaged as the mob followed behind Bakha." (He has found a shortcut.) "It was as if the crowd had determined to crush everything, however ancient or beautiful, that lay in the way of their achievement of all that Gandhi stood for. It was as if they knew, by an instinct surer than that of conscious knowledge, that the things of the old civilization must be destroyed in order to make room for those of the new." The style, remote from Malgudi, recalls Forster's gently polemical manner in *A Passage to India*. Gandhi appears, "the great little man," the white blanket, the shaved head, the protruding ears: we have seen it before, but the man's smile is the challenge, and Anand gropes for words: "There was a Quixotic smile on his thin lips, something Mephistophelian in the determined little chin immediately under his mouth and the long toothless jaws resting on his small neck. But withal there was something beautiful and saintly in the face." And then Gandhi speaks.

"Withal"—Anand has continual recourse to English phrases that are deliberately out of place, ironic in their distance from the subject. He compares handsome young Bakha to a stag. He makes India familiar to a specifically English reader and Indian readers reared on Victorian and Edwardian writing. The descriptive language of *Coolie* (1926) similarly wears gloves. The protagonist here, Munoo, is a boy subject to the injustices of caste and the inherent exploitation of the poor.

Of Anand's many novels, the first two are most read. The trilogy *The Village* (1939), *Across the Black Waters* (1940), and *The Sword and the Sickle* (1942) might have had a bigger readership had the war not deflected them. Anand moves out of the city but not to Malgudi. Lal Singh is a peasant in the Punjab, instinctively a radical, who goes into the army, stirs things up, survives, and returns to his village. The word *Sickle* in the title of the third of these books hints at the direction Anand's politics were taking. *The Private Life of an Indian Prince* (1953) marked the end of the system of historic privileges and acts as a kind of counter-echo to the themes of *Untouchable*. It was followed by a series of autobiographical novels, but as the Montserrat novelist and poet E. A. Markham said, Anand is best at "arresting portraits of poverty in the Punjab"—"portrait" because there is limited character development in the books.

The Indian English novelist and critic Tabish Khair excludes Anand from the list of witty Indian writers. He names "the brilliant, novel length jokes of Salman Rushdie, the Eurocentric humor of V. S. Naipaul," whom he reclaims for the Subcontinent, "the delicious 'irony' of R. K. Narayan," and he builds his list forward to include "Vikram Seth, I. Allan Sealy, Farrakhan Dhondy, Rohinton Mistry, in fact almost anyone except the philosophical Raja Rao and the reality-struck Mulk Raj Anand." There is Forsterian wit, however, in the early novels, and the politics are argued through examples, the fiction attaches the themes and develops them. Bloomsbury claimed him, then released him to the independence movement. He is in his beginnings the most English of the Indian novelists, but his themes were always Indian as were his politics. Orwell, who worked with him at the BBC during the war and was a friend, regarded him as a "cultural curiosity"—the oddness of reading an Indian writing fiction in English, Anglophone Indian literature being "a strange phenomenon." A good deal of the colonial survived in Orwell.

Rohinton Mistry (b. 1952), the Bombay-born Canadian, might have become as exotic as Michael Ondaatje, but his understated approach delivers the world of Mumbai with what Mistry calls a "Tolstoyan realism." The fantastic imagination of Rushdie, the complex metafictionality of Ondaatje, are not for him. *Such a Long Journey* (1991), *A Fine Balance* (1995), and particularly *Family Matters* (2002) contribute more to Indian than to Canadian literature. The autobiographical content is candid: a Parsi family, moderately prosperous, enduring a crisis and trying to contain it while the outer world crowds in. His portrayal of the sick and failing patriarch who turns more tyrannical as he grows weaker, and his heirs and minders, is unpartisan, funny, and finally tragic. The world of Mistry's books is not remote, except in space and time, from that of Balzac. Old Nariman hobbles out on his evening walks and sees the city with the heightened vision of a man released from confinement and nearing death. It has become vivid and magical in ways that, when he was healthy and busy, he never saw. He has a tragedy, too, which comes to light as death approaches. The tragedy of the novel is the impact of his decline on his family, how it sours and changes them.

V. S. Naipaul's self-regard is unwittingly comical. Asked in 1998 whether he is "drained" after writing a book, he begins in his favored, regal third person: "Yes, one is drained. These careers are so slow—" and he lapses into the first person, "I write a book, and at the end of it I am so tired. Something is wrong with my eyes; I feel I'm going blind. My fingers are so sore that I wrap them in tape. There are all these physical manifestations of a great labor." The spiritual manifestations are a Hindu aspect. "Then there is a process of just being nothing— utterly vacant. For the past nine months, really, I've been vacant." Such self-indulgence in *expression,* self-importance, self-pity, hubris, expressed even before he was awarded the Nobel Prize in Literature in 2001, put readers off: he is severe and peremptory with others yet emollient and overly attentive to himself. In 1980 Joan Didion registered that "hint of taint," when Naipaul's name was mentioned. "One catches the construction 'brilliant but': brilliant but obsessive, brilliant but reductive, brilliant but so dazzled by the glare off his particular circumstance—the Indian not an Indian, the Trinidadian not a Trinidadian, the Englishman never an Englishman—that he stays blind to the exigencies of history." Yet those exigencies he most clearly appreciates. It is, after all, only the outsider who sees without sentiment. He sees more of the world than any of his contemporaries, even if, like Proust fussing over little Marcel, his inescapable subject is "I." No matter, the books exist in spite of this peculiar self to which we credit them.

Part of his strategy is to neutralize the reader's sense of his otherness—for example, in the author's note to his books. He was born in Chaguanas, Trinidad, in 1932 and named Vidiadhar Surajprasad Naipaul (there it is, with the Hindu and Brahmin given names: not Victor Sawdon, as in Pritchett, whom he greatly admired). He condensed it to initials because in the past that had been the British fashion; because of the difficulty British readers would have in pronouncing and spelling his original name; and also because he wanted to seem as naturalized, as assimilated, as possible. He omits his early education, and the first place name we are given is intended to inspire confidence. He was educated—at Oxford, then went to London in 1954 to become a writer. He married Patricia Ann Hale. Then he lists his publications. He is, he declares, a writer. "He has followed no other profession."

Selective evidence, intended to seal his privacy, or to elude the condescension of critics who patronize writers from the old colonies? Might it not have been to his credit, if only for the sake of others coming in his wake out of "the colonial abyss" and the exotic confusion from which a scholarship had extracted him, to be a little less self-effacing? Did he expect anyone to follow him? When Naipaul's father died in 1953, the full panorama of his past was available to him. In the eight years that followed he was able to make it real, to make it clear that it was his father's past, not his.

In "Prologue to an Autobiography" he reflected on the difficulty of finding a voice. He remembers where he came from, all the "upheavals and moves: from grandmother's Hindu house in the country, still close to the rituals and social ways of village India; to Port of Spain, the negro, and G.I. life of its streets, the other, ordered life of my colonial English school," followed by "Oxford, London and the freelances' room at the BBC." Already his first major novel is waiting there in his past, though he is not its subject. He started writing at the BBC. He remembered a neighbor in Port of Spain. The memory provided the first sentence of *Miguel Street,* which poured forth in six weeks in 1955. The book was not published until 1959. First came *The Mystic Masseur* (1957), for which he won the John Llewellyn Rhys Memorial Prize, and *The Suffrage of Elvira* (1958), which received a Somerset Maugham Award, an appropriate accolade. For *In a Free State* (1971) he was awarded the Booker Prize.

My sense of the West Indies, and that of many contemporaries of mine, was originally sketched and colored in by *A House for Mr. Biswas* (1961) and *The Middle Passage* (1962). Naipaul was dubbed "Old Misery" by some fellow Caribbean writers. He is of East Indian rather than African extraction, which set him at a periphery and created complex resistances in his attitudes to "them" as in "theirs" to him. *The Middle Passage,* which he insists is a novel because it has a narrator who, if not invented, is an "I" made consistent and continuous in ways the author himself is not. He speaks of the representative inhabitant of Coronie in Surinam: "A derelict man in a derelict land; a man discovering himself, with surprise and resignation, lost in a landscape which had never ceased to be unreal because the scene of an enforced and always temporary residence; the slaves kidnapped from one continent and abandoned on the unprofitable plantations of another, from which there could never more be escape: I was glad to leave Coronie, for, more than lazy Negroes, it held the full desolation that came to those who made the middle passage." And later: "The history of the islands can never be satisfactorily told. Brutality is not the only difficulty. History is built around achievement and creation; and nothing was created in the West Indies." Naipaul's critics take issue with this: "Creation" can begin in resistance and struggle. Eleven years later the poet St. Lucian Derek Walcott responded,

"Nothing will always be created in the West Indies for quite a long time, because whatever will come out of there is like nothing one has ever seen before." What are the images to be, however? Borrowed images or images generated at home? If borrowed, the authentication is borrowed. If forged at home, what will legitimize them?

Naipaul is sure of himself. He has become increasingly confident with the passage of time. The truths he tells, he insists, may have their origins in his own past, but are true in spite of it. "Have you read my book *The Middle Passage?* That book tells black people they can't be white people, which caused immense offense." Well, yes. What chance that he will hear George Lamming, who quotes Djuna Barnes: "Too great a sense of identity makes a man feel he can do no wrong. And too little does the same." Lamming rejects those who are merely in what he calls "the skin trade": The wealth of black experience is not in a return to some long-lost place of origin, but in combining to make a new place. There is a double-edged quality, inward at once with "difference" and with perspectives on "difference," a paradox, a contained dialectic, an irony.

The many cultural and political peripheries that Naipaul traces in fiction, essays, meditations, and travel writings define a center of the first importance for readers of Anglophone fiction and for those who belong to Anglophone cultures. Naipaul is a lucid and provocative literary enigma, a great novelist even as he leaves the conventional novel form behind. He takes no hostages. He refuses to engage or acknowledge the Caribbean writers who used to seek dialogue with him. They now affect to find him an irrelevance, though they keep returning to him. Caryl Phillips rescinded his generous assessment of 1994 in 2000, seeing the later Naipaul as sour, bigoted, having "stifled" the young Vido who wrote vulnerably to his sister and father.

His fellow Nobel Prize laureate Nadine Gordimer praises the scale and range of his novels, seeing them as continuing the great nineteenth-century tradition. *A House for Mr. Biswas* depicts a whole complex society of histories and races and defines one man's hunger in a culture cross-gartered by traditions, superstitions, rules. Half-conscious cultural facts outweigh the facts—for example, that Mister Biswas, though for much of the book the lowest, poorest, and most delinquent of creatures, remains among those of Hindu extraction a recognizable Brahmin, and caste distinction ensures his survival among, and his begrudged protection by, his caste inferiors. That Brahmin recreates Naipaul's father, Seepersad, whose one book of linked short stories, *The Adventures of Gurudeva* (Trinidad, 1943), had meant as much to Biswas as the eponymous house he built. In 1967, after his father's death, Naipaul published the stories in London, with a long introduction. The stories became a footnote to Naipaul's great novel, though their origin and composition were its original subject. In 1999

Naipaul allowed *Between Father and Son: Family Letters* to be published. His father's unbridled affection and ambition for his son become clear.

The place Seepersad wrote from is peripheral to the world we occupy and that V. S. Naipaul chose, but it is in its creation so real as to constitute itself into a center: our sense of the world reconfigures around it and the characters it introduces. He is himself the most real figure. "My father remained unwilling to look at his own life," Naipaul reported. "All that material, which might have committed him to longer work and a longer view, remained locked up and unused. Certain things can never become material. My father never in his life reached that point of rest from which he could look back at the past" and so he became "part of the dereliction he wrote about." *A House for Mr. Biswas* is "very much my father's book. It was written out of his journalism and stories, out of his knowledge, knowledge he had got from the way of looking MacGowan"— his editorial superior—"had trained him in. It was written out of his writing." This collaboration is Naipaul's favorite among his books. It is also, as a novel, his most achieved, one of the great novels of the century.

Naipaul creates the illusion of realism, the sense that nothing has been omitted that constitutes or helps constitute the world he is creating in language and, by extension, in space and time. It is the tradition of *Middlemarch* and *Madame Bovary,* along with that of Dickens and, especially, Conrad. This deliberately *too* attentive realism produces a kind of surrealism. Naipaul is interested in what he calls "hinge" periods and experiences, when a culture is passing from one state into another. He as a young man in his mid-twenties was trying to create "the remote, instinctive life of a peasant community that has very little idea of where it is or where it has been transported. The chapter heading 'Pastoral' is both perfectly true and ironical. Knowledge gradually comes in the course of the book." The coming of knowledge, which is the coming of complex language, is the slow, hard theme.

Behind Naipaul as a stylist and historical intelligence stands, he tells us, Edward Gibbon (1737–1794), whose *The History of the Decline and Fall of the Roman Empire* is the great antireligious analysis of the end of another empire, out of whose wreck Naipaul himself was freed. *A House for Mister Biswas* occupies in Naipaul's work a place analogous to that of Gibbon's autobiography in his own: Gibbon, like Naipaul, asks where and why he began as a writer. Naipaul watches Biswas, fascinated with patterns, becoming a sign writer genuinely in love with the forms of letters, then with single words, then with scraps of sentences snatched from torn newspapers, like a sweeper who gathers a bigger and bigger heap of debris until all of a sudden he has made an actual hill. Mister Biswas was prefigurative as Gibbon insists ancestors are.

The narrative voice is not Mister Biswas's. It assumes an ironic distance from him early on, the stance of a scientist watching a specimen develop, engage, and change in time. The use of specifics—twelve numbers, for example, in the first seventeen lines of narrative—creates an overparticularity that becomes satirical in its literalizing effect. Early in the first chapter Naipaul makes clear what a house represents for Mister Biswas: It is the imagination rather than the actual crumbly facts of it that matter. It is visited again and again: the symbolic erasure of Mister Biswas's birthplace, representing the loss of cultural memory, then marriage and coming "home" to his wife Shama's family, the unwelcome-mat at the door, the nightmare house, the dream house, and most painfully in relation to his own daughter Savi the doll's house that expresses his love, an illusion whose destruction is a measure of his frustration. The wry style of the opening gives way to the circumstantial and matter of fact, the comical, and then the dramatic, especially in the Christmas scenes, with their cruel family dramas, and the lyricism of the conclusion. Mister Biswas has his dream, and his son Anand his escape.

J. M. Coetzee finds convincing evidence of the impact of Somerset Maugham on the formation of Naipaul: Maugham the displaced person, the avid traveler, the insider-outsider, the writer who effaces himself as a man yet discloses himself with almost excessive candor in his fiction. Maugham's impact is most palpable in *Half a Life* (2001). There is no remorse in Naipaul's move away from his past, his no-nonsense take on what it was, his knowledge of what would have happened had it kept its hold on him. Naipaul's gift to English letters Coetzee regards as the "mixed mode" of social analysis, autobiography, fiction, and travel memoir. It is a gift many of his contemporaries also bring to the party, Bellow and Roth for instance. But Naipaul does it differently: the essayist is less a character, and the ideas explored develop as ideas from book to book. "Whenever I have had to write fiction," he says, "I've always had to invent a character who roughly has my background. I thought for many years how to deal with this problem. The answer was to face it boldly—not to create a bogus character but to create, as it were, stages in one's evolution."

Anthony Burgess, no stranger himself to novels that integrate essay material, called Naipaul's *The Enigma of Arrival* (1987) autobiographical. Naipaul describes it as fiction. *A Way in the World* (1994) is likewise generically ambivalent, allowing itself to exploit the freedoms of fiction, the constraints of essay, and personal writing. Naipaul is forthright about his intentions. "*The Enigma* has an autobiographical crust. (So do the fictional writings of Proust and Maugham and most writers: you always know who the writer is.)" He is bold in putting down markers, which are also intended as measuring sticks. "*The Enigma* themes—of flux and movement, the gardens that men grow, constant creation, constant decay—that are contained within this crust, belong to fiction." He insists that the people who "illustrate some of his own philosophical feelings" (he has drifted into the formal third person again) are fictional. It would be an impertinence to harness "real" characters to this plow. "The autobiographical crust defines the writer, the eye that sees, makes it clear that the eye that is looking at this much-written-about English countryside is not English. The crust links imperial England (present in the countryside) to the writer's colonial background. Its further value is that it makes the fiction seem complete and real." This "crust" can be observed in other novels, too—for example, in his other masterpiece, *A Bend in the River* (1979). Here Salim from the east coast of Africa, with Indian antecedents, moves to the heart of an undeveloped country as a merchant and sets up a business in the town on the river bend. The town was Arab, then colonial, and now it is coming to express the culture of a majority, a culture denatured by colonial years and a legacy of greed and the failure of civic values. We meet Metty, the ex-slave, and the other immigrant merchants with material ambitions and their belonging elsewhere; there is the dictator, his creatures and minions, the mistresses. The river flows between banks that endure their changing histories, carrying off indifferently the corpses slain in uprisings, the effluent of small factories, and whatever else man or nature spills.

Naipaul's country of ancestral origin, India, attracts him, and he strives in several books to come to terms with its strange charm and its captivating and exasperating culture. It too was colonized; his own forebears were taken as an instrument of colonization to another colonial world, some of them imported initially (Naipaul's maternal grandfather, for instance) as indentured servants, to administer a Caribbean population whose ancestors had themselves for the most part been imported, as slaves. A strange and dangerous situation, to be an inadvertent colonial, like the Asians in Africa, or the Chinese in Malaysia: When the colonial years end, they are targetable, with decayed rights and privileges, not belonging any more than the once-African population but, being in a minority materially more prosperous, feeling they belong even less.

Kamau Brathwaite, the Jamaican poet, declares, "It was in language that the slave was perhaps most successfully imprisoned by his master, and it was in his (mis-)use of it that he most effectively rebelled." Naipaul stands on the edge of this, dissenting. One rebels, one transcends bondage by taking the imposed language, learning its dynamics, and using it. His is, nonetheless, a vision of disorder and decline, especially disorder and decline at the fringes of the empire.

There is another rhetoric at work, which Joan Didion, reviewing *The Return of Eva Perón, with The Killings in Trinidad* in 1980, sees hardening. She quotes Edward Said's harsh review of *A Bend in the River,* a novel he links with John

Updike's *The Coup*. These books continue "a long tradition of 'hostility to Islam, to the Arabs and the Orient in general [to be found in] grade-school textbooks, comic strips, television, or films, the iconography of Islam is uniformly the same: oil suppliers, terrorists, mobs.'" The polarization between Said and Naipaul "suggests that we have entered another of those eras in which all writing is seen to exist as 'a public relations exercise, a form of applauded lie, fantasy.'" The phrase is Naipaul's, from his essay on the writing of Michael X. Joan Didion adds, "In what looks to be a long season of hardening abstractions, of fixed hallucinations right and left, a season in which a figure like Said himself strikes the new note, Naipaul dwells obdurately (obsessively, reductively) on a landscape that is presumed to comfort the forces of reaction." She is herself in a middle ground and cannot abide the harshness, or the justice, of Naipaul's vision. It is not quite so harsh a vision as she thinks. He is drawn to those "students in Mobutu's Zaire," themselves prey to what he describes as "borrowed ideas—about colonialism and alienation, the consumer society and the decline of the West." They have only just "come from the bush, but already they can talk of Stendhal and Fanon; they have the enthusiasm of people to whom everything is new; and they feel, too, that with the economic collapse of the West (of which the newspapers talk every day) the tide is running Africa's way." He feels for their optimism, recognizing in it something he could not help believing when "everything was new."

Didion celebrates, as it is hard not to do, Naipaul's resistance to theories and his dependence on fact. Theory and ideology are "no more than a scaffolding, something to be 'erected' or 'demolished'; something 'imposed' (a word Naipaul often uses in relation to ideas) on the glitter of the sea, the Congo clogged with hyacinth, the actual world." She looks at the opening of *Guerrillas* (1975) and notes, "The pink haze of the bauxite dust on the first page . . . tells us what we need to know about the history and social organization of the unnamed island on which the action takes place, tells us in one image." A luminous, billowing image, with color, smell, peril in it, tells us "who runs the island and for whose profit the island is run and at what cost to the life of the island this profit has historically been obtained, but all of this implicit information pales in the presence of the physical fact, the dust itself." Naipaul traffics in facts. He sees and feels them with a Homeric impartiality and clarity. He is not a comforting writer any more than Gibbon or Conrad is.

Caryl Phillips (b. 1958) is a significant essayist and interpreter with new news to report as well. *A New World Order: Selected Essays* (2001) is as important as his fiction in the ways it readjusts perspectives on contemporary fiction with his takes on Achebe and Baldwin, Richard Wright, Marvin Gaye, Wole Soyinka, Jamaica Kincaid, and others. Phillips was born in St. Kitts in the Caribbean but brought up in Leeds from the age of four months. St. Kitts is not a memory but an absence he must probe, repossess, and create by means of his fiction. He acknowledges two writers who helped position him as a reader and critic: the Barbadian George Lamming (b. 1927), author of, among other books, *Natives of My Person* (1972); and the Trinidadian Samuel Selvon (1923–1994), author of *The Lonely Londoners* (1956). Both writers arrived in England in 1950, aboard the same ship.

It may be that Phillips's novels, from *The Final Passage* (1985), which grew out of his first visit to St. Kitts when he was twenty-two, to *In the Falling Snow* (2009), his most English novel, develop related themes, suggested in that word "passage," the middle passage, the passage back. Identity is an insistent issue, related to race as, in Tóibín, it relates to sexuality. Critics say his books appeal to those juries that assess political correctness before they open the pages of a novel. His themes, however, are compelling to him, and an author should not be condemned for writing about experiences that are now temporarily as privileged as they have been suppressed in the past.

J. M. Coetzee is impressed less by the sameness of theme in Phillips's novels than by his steep technical development as a writer. His second novel, with *Crossing the River* (1995) his most celebrated, is *A State of Independence* (1986), a clear account of a failed return to the Caribbean. The protagonist's mother is hostile to him, his friends are in a hurry, his girlfriend strange, still available but not understood. The story is told without much nuance, depending on situation rather than style to produce the effects intended. By contrast, *Cambridge* (1991) is set in the first half of the nineteenth century on his native island; a woman, somewhat in the mold of Aphra Behn, goes out to St. Kitts to assess slave life, enjoys a turbulent romance, and goes to pieces psychologically. Then, in *The Nature of Blood* (1997), Phillips gives us four parallel stories of persecution. "In the course of little more than a decade," says Coetzee, "Phillips has progressed from straightforward linear narration and uncomplicated realism to the complex shuttling of voices and intercutting of narrative lines, and even the forays into postmodern alienation effects, which we encounter in *The Nature of Blood*." These novellas, he says, are in effect novels.

*In the Falling Snow,* written largely in his new exile in New York, and at Yale where he is a professor, examines his parents, his own and the current black British generations, against a white background of snow. The book is close up, but the lives examined represent the Anglophone Caribbean diaspora, the experiences of each generation being differently lived and told, "three different ideas of Britain trying to grapple with each other and occupy the same space." The alienated Laurie, the teenager who finds himself involved in a stabbing, is, or would be, redeemable. Phillips retains some of his parents' and some of his own optimism, theirs based on a pioneering hope of betterment, his on personal success.

Timothy Mo (b. 1950), son of an English mother and a Hong Kong Chinese father, was born in Hong Kong and emigrated to Britain at the age of ten. Peter Ackroyd regards him as the most vivid chronicler of the colony before the handback to China. His first novel, *The Monkey King* (1978), which won the Geoffrey Faber Memorial Prize, was set in Hong Kong. In his account it is a place of intense materialism; and it has long been so. In *An Insular Possession* (1986, shortlisted for the Booker Prize) he recreates the colony during the time of the Opium Wars in 1830. His two young American protagonists set out to write the truth about it, believing in the power of written language. For his part, Mo trusts the power of the present tense. This reflects Chinese verb forms; more importantly it avoids, in his words, any "sense of distance from the past, or superiority to it." It leaves the novel wide open to interpretation, the way early Isherwood wished his fiction to be. Mo has been theorized—postcolonial, postmodern—but he resists the glamour and the constraint of the labels applied to his work. "What one wants to do is leave the novel different from how one found it," Mo says, "and yet to contribute to the canon as well, so that it would be difficult to imagine literature without that particular book."

# 40

# The Blues

Richard Wright, Claude McKay, Jean Toomer, Langston Hughes, James Baldwin, William Styron

All the black American writers of the 1920s through to the 1960s owed a debt to W. E. B. Du Bois (1868–1963). He was an awakener, and his book *The Souls of Black Folk* (1903) both foregrounded and set an agenda for black culture. From 1910 he edited *The Crisis,* the magazine of the NAACP, and he kept it alive for years as a focus for black thinking. He published many of the best writers of the day, including Zora Neale Hurston. In 1961 Du Bois "returned" to Africa, to Ghana, and though he did not renounce his American citizenship, he became Ghanaian. He had come "home," and he died there. His life spanned those of several key players in his campaign to make black culture visible, among them Claude McKay (1889–1948), Hurston (1891–1960), and the young writer who took most serious issue with him, Richard Wright (1908–1960). Being a man of great persuasive powers, it was appropriate that his writers should resist him. Hurston called him "Dr. Dubious."

In *The Souls of Black Folk,* at the "dawning of the Twentieth Century," Du Bois addresses the "gentle reader" beloved of novelists and writers of the eighteenth and nineteenth centuries, here with almost parodic intent. The problem of the new century, he tells us in "The Forethought," is "the problem of the color line." "I pray you, then, receive my little book in all charity." With what modesty it comes before us, deferential and polite: the reader is "studying my words with me," as though writer and reader stand at the same distance from the text and enjoy a kind of complicity. It negotiates the reader into a nonoppositional state of mind. Jamaican-born Claude McKay says that when he first read the book, it "shook me like an earthquake."

Richard Wright had *The Souls of Black Folk* in mind when he wrote of books by black authors that were "decorous ambassadors who go a-begging to white America," that "entered the Court of American Public Opinion dressed in the knee-pants of servility, curtsying to show that the Negro was not inferior, that he was human, and that he had a life comparable to that of other people. These were received as poodle dogs who have learned clever tricks." Wright disagreed with Du Bois: black writers had a responsibility to link with the mass of black people, not as Du Bois suggested to develop a personal career and draw the worthy after. Yet when Hurston—using some of the languages of black people, and the folklore that Wright stressed was a primary resource for the black writer—addressed her work to black people, it was her language that embarrassed Wright. His essay "Blueprint for Negro Literature" (1937) has little to do with the ways writers actually work. It begins with Lenin and generalizes in categorical ways: "Two separate cultures sprang up: one for the Negro masses, crude, instinctive, unwritten, and unrecognized; and the other for the sons and daughters of a rising Negro bourgeoisie, bloodless, petulant, mannered and neurotic." It barks orders like a commissar: "Every short story, novel, poem, and play should carry within its lines, implied or explicit, a sense of the oppression of the Negro people, the danger of war, of fascism, of the threatened destruction of culture and civilization; and, too, the faith and necessity to build a new world."

Du Bois knew that culture was the most permeable area of the white hegemony and set great store by the intellectuals and artists of the Harlem Renaissance. Developing the cultural classes was his aim, and he argued controversially for the "talented tenth" of the race who would achieve great things in their careers and pull "all those who were worthy of saving" up after them. His Calvinistic language takes up where the preachers leave off. He admired Stalin and was certain that right ends justify means.

His was a patient and effective campaign. At the beginning of the 1920s American black writing had no real presence. In 1920 the great exodus of black people from South to North and West (two and a half million in twenty-five years) began. Claude McKay remembered, after two years of wandering in the United States experiencing the degradations of racism and menial labor, that arriving in Harlem was like reaching a promised land, his dreams of writing suddenly less far-fetched than they had seemed. Harlem had grown into the center of a culture not new but here intensified, gathered close like a comradely encampment in a hostile world. Jazz was the great emollient. In Harlem, black culture became manifest to liberals who took an interest in a neglected otherness, writers and impresarios keen to understand or make amends. Prominent white patrons of black writers included the heiress and poet Nancy Cunard, with her ambitious collaborative Negritude project; wealthy Charlotte Mason, who for a time turned her demanding patronage from Native Americans to blacks; and Carl Van Vechten, the novelist, photographer, and friend of Gertrude Stein and of the Sitwells. Well-to-do white people flocked to Harlem for the music, dance, and excitement. Du Bois's theory that culture was the thin end of a wedge was tenable. This "First Renaissance" benefited and suffered from becoming fashionable. Fashion as much as merit raised Langston Hughes from elevator attendant to writer. Fashion is fickle, as the fate of Zora Neale Hurston proved: she rose high and fell far. The 1920s wrought a transformation, but a partial one.

That first Harlem flowering ended with the onset of the Great Depression. The second, harsher and less welcoming—partly as a result of the Depression and its disproportionate effect on black citizens, and the arrival of new waves of immigrants from the Caribbean and elsewhere—began in earnest in the mid-1950s when the literary culture had come of age not only in the United States but internationally, with a sense of comradeship and rivalry, the divisions of the 1960s and 1970s already clear. The harbinger of the second flowering was Richard Wright's *Native Son* (1940), with its new self-awareness and confidence.

Wright's name is associated with the Federal Writers' Project, a government relief program launched in 1935 that hired more than 6,000 people (over half of them women) to write state guidebooks and collect folklore and oral histories, including slave narratives. Authors from all disciplines were employed in what was deemed to be socially significant research, documentation, and writing. Conrad Aiken, Nelson Algren, Saul Bellow, John Cheever, Ralph Ellison, Zora Neale Hurston, and John Steinbeck were among the fiction writers involved. For many it was a creative catalyst, a kind of dispersed university. Given its collaborative nature, stylistic experimentation and indulgent individualism were not encouraged. At the heart of the FWP's concerns was anthropological research, an attempt to get an "objective" hold on a complex reality. The age of the documentary had arrived, and for four years, up to 1939, the FWP survived with federal funding. It limped on in some states for another four years with state funding, then fizzled out. For conservative Americans it was another New Deal waste of resources; it also had an inherent political coloring that they saw as communist red even when it was not.

By the time it was over the FWP had set the agenda for a generation of writers. Not all states included black writers in the FWP, but the Illinois Writers' Project did, and the Chicago program was unusual for being racially integrated. The poet and novelist Arna Bontemps (Arnaud "Arna" Wendell Bontemps, 1902–1973), already a figure in the first Harlem Renaissance, was involved in it, along with the poet Margaret (Abigail) Walker (Alexander) (1915–1998), whose novel *Jubilee* (1966) she believed had rather too directly inspired the writing of *Roots: The Saga of an American Family* by Alex Hayley, whom she sued in 1988 for copyright infringement; and Frank (Garvin) Yerby (1916–1991), the historical novelist who went on to become the first millionaire black author. Yerby's *The Dahomean* (later *The Man from Dahomey,* 1971) made amends for his years of writing primarily for a white readership. It tells the story of a captured African prince, enslaved and transported, following in the widening wake of Aphra Behn's *Oroonoko.* Here too Jamaican-born Claude McKay found not uncongenial work. The FWP paid writers around eighty dollars a month for a short twenty- to thirty-hour work week.

Its achievement can in part be measured by the international profile that American black writing had developed less than two decades later. In Paris on September 19, 1956, *Le Congrès des écrivains et artistes noirs* was opened by Alioune Diop, the editor of *Présence africaine*. It lasted for four sweltering days, the formal meetings staged at the Sorbonne in the Amphitéâtre Descartes. Delegations from the nations of Africa and the African diaspora, gathered for the first time, set out to find common ground beyond the variety of their colonial histories, and to reach a resonant conclusion. The Nigerian writer Wole Soyinka spoke in Paris in September 2006 at a gathering to mark the fiftieth anniversary of the *Congrès*. His theme was the civil war then raging in Darfur, Sudan, whose tragedy he viewed from the perspective of that optimistic original conference in which writers appeared as acknowledged legislators and Du Bois's experiment appeared to be paying off internationally. Among high-table spokespersons at the first congress, chief among the writers were Léopold Sédar Senghor, the Senegalese statesman (who called the delegates "cultural militants"), Aimé Césaire from Martinique, and Richard Wright from the United States. One luxury of hindsight is to be able to anatomize the failure of foresight.

James Baldwin reported on the 1956 conference for the magazine *Encounter* in a long article entitled "Princes and Powers" (reprinted in *Nobody Knows My Name*). He translated the word *Noir* in the congress's title as "Negro-African," which roots his article in its period. His was an uneasy take on the event. As an American journalist (not part of the American delegation, which W. E. B. Du Bois, prevented by the U.S. State Department from attending, discredited by means of an open letter), Baldwin commented but did not participate. He chronicled the attempts of delegates to reach general conclusions about the cultural nature of the "Negro-African." He liked Senghor's argument: "Art itself is taken to be perishable, to be made again each time it disappears or is destroyed. What is clung to is the spirit which makes art possible . . . African art is concerned with reaching beyond and beneath nature, to contact, and itself become a part of *la force vitale*." That phrase "and itself become" is persuasive. Is it specific to African art? "He was speaking out of his past," Baldwin says, "which had been lived where art was naturally and spontaneously social, where artistic creation did not presuppose divorce. (Yet [Senghor] was not there. Here he was, in Paris, speaking the adopted language in which he also wrote his poetry.)"

In retrospect, the 1956 *Congrès* in its sweltering hall, with all the disagreements Baldwin witnessed, is remote, its questions left hanging in the air: "Is it possible to describe as a culture what may simply be, after all, a history of oppression?" asks Baldwin, sounding momentarily like V. S. Naipaul, and like Naipaul requiring that we formulate, if not an answer, then a counterquestion. Most pressing for Baldwin is the reality inherent in the languages of the *Congrès*:

"They [he did not say "We"] are all, now, whether they like it or not, related to Europe, stained by European visions and standards, and their relation to themselves, and to each other, and to their past had changed."

The Colombian novelist Gabriel García Márquez said in 1981, "Sooner or later people believe writers rather than the government." He knows the power of witness enhanced by the force of fiction and regards himself as the writer of "true socialist realism," writing that honors the senses and popular ways of storytelling, which have literary value to the degree that they are informed by the spirit of older, deep-rooted customs of telling. *One Hundred Years of Solitude* (1967), he said, "was based on the way my grandmother used to tell her stories. She told things that sounded supernatural and fantastic, but she told them with complete naturalness." It puts one in mind of the lively self-effacing expression of Zora Neale Hurston.

There was for García Márquez, as for emerging black writers in the United States, a continual dialogue and trade-off between journalism and fiction: "Fiction has helped my journalism because it has given it literary value. Journalism has helped my fiction because it has kept me in a close relationship with reality." He speaks of John Hersey's *Hiroshima* as great journalism because it uses the formal resources of fiction to make real what Hersey experienced when he visited Japan in the immediate aftermath of the American bombing. As a writer, the Colombian says, each line he sets down must have a clear basis in reality, whether the literalizing reality of the journalist or the inventive reality of his grandmother. If he is praised for imagination or invention, he feels uneasy. He quotes the Chilean poet Pablo Neruda: "God help me from inventing what I sing."

The most successful child of Du Bois's revolution was Langston Hughes, better remembered, and better, as a poet than a novelist. It was from Hughes's legacy that Wright wanted to free his successors, urging writers to reject the kinds of individualism that for Hughes was a sure prophylactic against American conformism. By the time Wright composed his essay "Blueprint," the huge various "bourgeois" success of Fitzgerald, West, and early Hemingway, which witnessed and participated in the collapse of innocent idealism, community, and economy, was in place, and opposed to it was a largely theoretical analytical "positive" art of social commitment. Meanwhile the facts of life reflected in bruising narratives sold well to American readers hungry for the "real." Black art of the sort Wright advocated set out to analyze, realize, and then, after stark witness, affirm the possibility of a change, whatever the complexity of its themes.

A Marxist writer insisted on "community." The Communist Party placed the writer at center stage—not as a self-revealing star performing for liberal white intellectuals and social establishments, but instead as a person addressing black people en masse. None of the black writers quite fits the Party's job description. Rudolph Fisher and Wallace Thurman, both original in different ways, died tragically young, having done enough to suggest what they might have been, each using given genres to explore black experience. Jean Toomer (1894–1967), the palest black writer of his time, published *Cane* (1923), an unusually strong novel mixing verse, drama, and intense vignettes, in the heyday of modernism; this achievement was followed by forty-four years in which, following his parents' example, he denied that he was black, like Faulkner's Joe Christmas or Philip Roth's Coleman Silk struggling against the "single drop" of black blood that tried to define him. He ended up a disciple of the popular Armenian "mystic" Gurdjieff, who picked off a number of talented and vulnerable individuals, including Katherine Mansfield; less vulnerable, the sulfury occultist Aleister Crowley, the Great Beast, also visited Gurdjieff's Institute.

Nella Larsen's 1928 novel *Quicksand,* about the situation of a woman who is part Danish and part black, and the negotiations she must make in Europe and in the disunited North and South of the United States, is another of the few Harlem Renaissance books that take on the formal challenges of modernism and find in them a means toward subtle political and psychological expression. Her novel *Passing* (1929), set largely in Harlem, is less successful, but her withdrawal from the literary scene was not simply an attempt to *pass* for white. Nellallitea "Nella" Larsen (née Nellie Walker, 1891–1964) dropped out of literary life and was thought to have tried, like Toomer, to "cross the color bar." In fact, what she did was simply to—disappear, back into her first vocation, that of nurse.

Claude (Festus Claudius) McKay (1889–1948) discovered his complex cultural identity in a series of transitions and conversions. He was born in Jamaica, the youngest of eleven children of prosperous peasant farmers. His father was a raconteur with a rich repertoire. McKay's earliest writing was in the "correct" conventional English he learned at school, but in his late teens he was encouraged by Walter Jekyll to develop a Jamaican patois for his stories and especially his verse of rural life. Introducing *Songs of Jamaica* (1912), his first collection, Jekyll declared, "What Italian is to Latin, that in regard to English is the negro variant thereof. It shortens, softens, rejects the harder sounds alike of consonants and vowels; I might almost say, refines." He calls it "a feminine version of masculine English; pre-eminently a language of love, as all will feel who, setting prejudice aside, will allow the charmingly naïve love-songs of this volume to make their due impression upon them." The term *feminine* was ill chosen in relation to McKay, but Jekyll's insistence that the verse be read aloud is valuable. Much of the writing of the Harlem Renaissance and its aftermaths, in standard or variant English from Hurston on, comes fully alive when voice lifts it off the page.

In 1912, with his poems tenuously in print, McKay went to study agronomy in the United States at the Tuskegee Institute, but he dropped out, went on to Kansas State University, and encountered Du Bois's writings. He dropped out a second time, made his way to New York via a series of miscellaneous jobs, menial work and portering on the trains. He came to Harlem at the very beginning of the Renaissance. *Harlem Shadows* (1922), a collection of his poems, was one of the Renaissance's founding texts. But his fiction most clearly expresses his originality of subject matter and political theme.

Though he did not join the Communist Party, he spent twelve years in Europe. First he went to London in 1919, at a time when Anglo-American modernism was finding its way, but where there were also radical groupings into which McKay fit more comfortably. He went on to the Continent, in particular to the Soviet Union, where he was welcomed and met some of the great men of the day, including Trotsky. He wrote essays about the experience of black people in America, and these were translated and published in Russia.

McKay's novel *Home to Harlem* (1928) was a critical and commercial success, "scandalous" in its portrayal of seamy, credible Harlem life in which the struggle for survival in a white-mastered world is developed with Lawrencian intensity but without the support of Lawrencian form and its resolutions. His characters are psychologically complex; they exist in relation to one another in realized environments, one hostile and the other, Harlem, habitable. Du Bois might have been expected to admire the quality of imagination and the success of the writer, but he objected to the ways in which the sexual lives of Harlem were evoked, proving himself, however modern his mission, a man of Victorian values. After reading the book he felt "distinctly like taking a bath." His objections, like Richard Wright's to Zora Neale Hurston's use of dialect, were anxious: white readers might take the book as evidence supporting stereotypes—in this case, of Harlem licentiousness.

McKay's second novel, *Banjo: A Story without a Plot* (1929), seems at first to promise a formal experiment, but there is more plot, more convention, in the structure than the author intended, a picaresque narrative following the experiences of an expatriate black American musician in France, in particular in Marseilles. McKay lived in France and knew the scenes he described. This book and his presence in the country are said to have influenced Senghor, Aimé Césaire (who spoke warmly of *Banjo*), and other writers in a movement taking hold in Francophone Africa and the Caribbean. The book sold badly, and his collection of stories entitled *Gingertown* (1932) was also a disappointment. His final—and some say his finest—novel, *Banana Bottom* (1933), was a fictional return to Jamaica, the story of Bita Plant, who comes home after study in England and tries to find a place and reconcile her learning with a past she understands in a new way. McKay did not go back to Jamaica. He converted to Roman Catholicism in his later years and died at fifty-nine, in the Church, rejecting rather than transfiguring the struggle of his political and artistic life.

Zora Neale Hurston met Langston Hughes (1902–1967) at a party to celebrate a Harlem literary magazine, *Opportunity;* both had won awards, Hughes for his first book of verse, *The Weary Blues,* Hurston for fiction, her story "Spunk." They became for a time friends and collaborators under the supervision of Carl Van Vechten, who also arranged white patronage for them. In 1926 Van Vechten's own novel *Nigger Heaven* appeared, dividing his black friends and acquaintances, some of whom regarded it as a presumptuous affront. Hughes praised it. Wallace Thurman laughed at it and exonerated the author: "Superficiality does not necessarily denote a lack of sincerity, and even superficiality may occasionally delve into deep pots of raw life. What matter if they be flesh pots?" Other white champions of the Harlem Renaissance took an interest in Hughes, some for political and literary, some for other, reasons.

Hurston and Hughes both had roots in rural traditions, and in their fiction, poetry, and dramatic writing they were interested in authentic voice and place. To their critics they would say that the best way to affirm the black experience is by being true to it. Hurston's version of truth was less dependent than Hughes's on the black/white dialectic: there was a sufficiency in the black community. Both of them respected and resisted Du Bois, whose writing and editing helped frame the radical culture in which Missouri-born Hughes grew up. Hughes was raised partly in Lawrence, Kansas, a place like the little town he writes about in his first novel, *Not without Laughter* (1930), set in the period of his childhood and adolescence. Lawrence was where his grandmother lived. She subscribed to Du Bois's *The Crisis,* to which, at the age of nineteen, in 1921, Hughes would contribute one of his most famous poems, "The Negro Speaks of Rivers." His grandfather had joined with John Brown at Harpers Ferry: the Hughes family had a history. He lived some of the time with his mother, who encouraged his writing, and with other relations in Detroit and Cleveland. He completed high school and began writing verse. His father, tired of racism, had set up shop in Mexico. The poet visited him there unhappily and infrequently.

Hughes attended Columbia University for a year, dropped out, traveled, and did various jobs: merchant seaman, Paris nightclub worker, busboy in Washington. He finished his studies at Lincoln University in Pennsylvania. It was there that he wrote *Not without Laughter.* Much of his most durable work was from this first phase of his life, before he was radicalized. He settled in New York and became the "bard of Harlem," a public figure helping to develop black theater there and in Los Angeles and Chicago. He traveled with other black writers in 1932 to the Soviet Union and was allowed to move quite freely in the Asian republics. He remained an advocate of the Soviet experiment right up to the Second World War. In 1937 he signed a petition supporting Stalin's show trials and purges, "An Open Letter to American Liberals." The "liberals" were spineless people unwilling to entertain the consequences of revolution. Lillian Hellman was one of the petition's sponsors. Like many writers of his generation, Hughes disowned his 1930s politics and lost some readers. Invited to testify at Senator McCarthy's show trials, he was traumatized by the experience. He denied that he had ever been a member of the Communist Party, which was factually correct.

Hughes learned from the music of the Harlem Renaissance, its formal, thematic, and commercial strategies. He based poems on the blues, picking up on idioms and on the dialects from which those idioms flowed. The strongest elements in his fiction, as in his dramatic writing, are those that register the speech of characters and communities, a speech not as phonetically rendered as Hurston's, but alive like hers with place and history. He uses dialect and its metaphors as primary material in verse, in fiction, and (less insistently) in his popular weekly Jesse B. Semple tales, which he began in 1943 in the *Chicago Defender* and continued in the *New York Post*. Jesse's is a Harlem voice that muses on his life and times.

*Not without Laughter* is a bittersweet novel, though not a mild one. Hughes does not mask the racism his characters suffer as a condition of their existence. "Some white folks were nice, though," his protagonist Sandy Rogers observes. The book appealed to a wide readership. Its satire is moderate, not scathing, the tone nostalgic. Du Bois and Booker T. Washington are patriarchal rather than revolutionary presences. The *New York Times* reviewer played down Hughes's generic originality. Earlier books of this kind were by white authors. "In the last five years, for example, two Pulitzer prize works, Paul Green's *In Abraham's Bosom* and Julia Peterkin's *Scarlet Sister Mary,* have dealt with the same aspects of Negro life that are to be found in this novel." But Hughes is the first black writer "to treat successfully with the life of the lower class Negro in town as well as city." McKay "dealt with bottom-rung Negro life in its urban forms," but here the rural experience is evoked and Hughes "has come to closer grips with this material than have his white contemporaries." It is less a work of imagination and artifice than testimony, a play of characters rather than plot, which is why the pace at the outset seems so slow. The chief protagonist, in a hurry to grow up, is less compelling than the ancillary characters, old and young. The tension between characters who find the blues "too Negro" and want to move away from black experience and those whose very identity is rooted in it provides a political charge, but the politics are those of the black community.

The *Ways of White Folk* (1934), a collection of stories, expresses its rueful polemic in the title. The stories evoke awkward relationships between white and black people, the problem being laid, as by James Baldwin, at the white door. *Tambourines to Glory* (1958), Hughes's second proper novel, pits rural purity of purpose against urban attenuation and corruption. Hughes described it as "about the goings on of gospel churches," and it has the qualities and actual vestiges in dialogue and stage direction description of his theater writing. From the outset it is dialogue and debate centered on Essie and Laura, who represent sharply contrasted black experiences. Here too Hughes is more interested in character than in plot.

If we read Hughes's fiction in the wake of McKay's and before Richard Wright's, despite its clarity and truthfulness it has an attenuated quality. The Jesse B. Semple tales, too, are invitations into dialogue, shy of confrontation. The reader is let off the hook, perhaps because the writer is letting himself off a hook, too.

Caryl Phillips declares, "It was the novel *Native Son* [1940] which led me to my vocation." That is a large claim, even for an introduction, yet Phillips justifies it in giving an account not only of the book but also of its impact on a particular reader. Wright "more than most writers, sat down at his desk with a clear political and social agenda in mind." The political writer does not let readers off the hook by allowing them to feel sympathy or pity. *Huis clos,* as his friend the philosopher, novelist, and dramatist Jean-Paul Sartre, using the jargon of the law courts, put it.

Richard Wright (1908–1960), whom Hemingway described as "forged in injustice as a sword is forged," grew up in Mississippi and Tennessee. He was drawn to the city, to be with the crowd of people, living with and for it. At nineteen he moved to Chicago. It was the Great Depression, the best and worst of times for a would-be writer to explore the restless and hungry metropolis. He worked with the Chicago South Side Boys Club and the Federal Writers' Project. And he never made any bones about it: He did join the Communist Party and wrote his one great novel while a member, though he parted company with it, as the Party, like later political and ideological systems, failed the needs of an emerging black literary culture. As a young man in 1934 Wright submitted the poem "I Have Seen Black Hands" to *New Masses:* "I am black and have seen black hands / Raised in fists of revolt, side by side with the white fists of white workers . . ."—not a masterpiece, but even at this time he was affirming that black experience produced a distinctive black culture, emerging in the work of black writers who were at last establishing appropriate forms.

Fifteen years later Wright was one of six contributors to *The God That Failed* (1949), a collection of essays by former communists confessing their ideological errors. He keeps company with André Gide, Arthur Koestler, and Ignazio Silone.

By then he had become a permanent expatriate. In 1947, with his white wife and his daughter, he settled in France. He became a focus for the shifting black expatriate community in Paris, the second American literary exile in that city, though he did not aspire to contest Stein's eccentric magnetism.

*Native Son* was the first book by a black author to be a Book-of-the-Month Club choice. In the five months after its publication, sales exceeded half a million copies, a sensational success for a writer still in his early thirties. *Black Boy* (1945), his autobiography, which had its genesis in Joyce's *A Portrait of the Artist* and more pertinently in the blues, was also selected and did well, but it made less of a splash. None of his later books equaled the commercial or literary success of *Native Son*. It has first-person intensity as it focuses on Bigger Thomas, but it is written in the third person, which enables Wright to use a more nuanced narrative voice than his subject would have possessed. We walk, wait, think, and act with Thomas. The book is in three sections, the first two moving fast and painfully to their climaxes, the third, with Bigger Thomas apprehended, slower, less compelling, and less credible.

James Baldwin paid Wright, the father figure he so needed when he was starting out in Greenwich Village and later in Paris, the compliment of titling his first essay collection *Notes of a Native Son* (1955). The compliment is rescinded by the first full essay, in which he links *Native Son* with *Uncle Tom's Cabin* as a book that falls into stereotype, the case Wright made against Zora Neale Hurston's rural dialogue. But just as *Uncle Tom's Cabin* by its success creates a type rather than commits a stereotype, so *Native Son* in its Zolaesque harshness of portrayal creates an American type. That was Wright's intention. Franz Fanon in "L'expérience vécue du noir" ("The Fact of Blackness," 1951, an essay that became the fifth chapter of *Peau noire, masques blancs* [*Black Faces, White Masks*, 1952]) explains Bigger Thomas's actions: "He responds to the world's anticipation." The stereotype to which he conforms is the one to which racism has reduced him.

Saul Bellow sponsored James Baldwin (1924–1987) for a Guggenheim Fellowship, reflecting in his reference that tokenism is at once enabling and degrading. In 1963 he wrote to a friend what he actually thought about Baldwin and his kind, starting with their "stridency . . . and their tone of personal injury, at times nothing but an infant cry." For Bellow the despair of the musician Rufus Scott, the protagonist of *Another Country* who dies at the end of the first section, is sentimental: "He seems to be asking for a nice comfy layette just like the white chilluns have." This is what Baldwin was up against even from a major *soi dissant* liberal writer, a close friend of Ralph Ellison. Bellow confined such language to personal letters, but racism survives between consenting adults. Flannery O'Connor claims Baldwin would have gone unread and untolerated if he had not been black. Gore Vidal knows better: "If Baldwin hadn't been black, and gay, he would not have had to behave as he did." That sense of compulsion: he too "responds to the world's anticipation" and has no choice but to do so.

The author was black. He was also illegitimate and the eldest of his mother's six children. He endured a difficult relationship with his stepfather, the grandson of a slave with a chronic phobia of white people. The boy avoided and at the same time longed to pacify his explosive surrogate. Baldwin said, "His hatred was suppressed and turned against himself. He couldn't let it out—he could only let it out in the house with rage, and I found it happening to myself as well." The day of his stepfather's death there were race riots in Detroit, and by the day of the funeral the riots had spread to Harlem. "As we drove him to the graveyard, the spoils of injustice, anarchy, discontent and hatred were all around us." He never learned the name of his real father. The Nigerian novelist Chinua Achebe connects closely with Baldwin in this respect. Baldwin read *Things Fall Apart* (1958) in Paris. The people in it were familiar: "That book was about my father."

To add to his difficulties, Baldwin was left-handed; because his teachers wanted to correct this "defect," the writing room was, he said, his "torture chamber." He wrote at night, after the day's work, after supper, acclimatized to this from his boyhood when he waited until his brothers and sisters were asleep and within a crowded living space earned a kind of privacy. He never forgot poverty, the challenge of finding where to live, how to survive and write. "You begin to doubt your judgment, you begin to doubt everything. You become imprecise." That is a point of great peril for a writer, "when you're beginning to go under. You've been beaten, and it's been deliberate. The whole society has decided to make you *nothing*." One either drowns or learns, as he did, to resist.

He remembered the painter Beauford Delaney teaching him to look at things, to see, and then to make them visible. "Painters have often taught writers how to see." Delaney's subjects were open, not socially or ethnically circumscribed, and Baldwin shared this ambitious inclusiveness. "All I know is that you have to make the reader *see it*. This I learned from Dostoyevsky"; he also, when he arrived in France, learned it "from Balzac."

His first sense of culture and formal language derived from religion, into which he threw himself soul, if not body, first (body found itself separately, and later). He became a child preacher, plying his gospel at storefronts. Later in life, in Tallahassee, two old ladies heard him speak. "He's little, but he's loud!" By then he was thirty-four and had broken with the church he grew up in when he was seventeen. In the beginning, however, church was a place where he felt safe and was noticed. He liked being noticed. Caryl Phillips speaks of how "through the public window of his life" he "espied a man who positively adored the attention of the media." Even after he had been photographed a thousand times and his face had appeared on the cover of *Time* magazine, he longed for the celebrity of the movie star. After all, as he grew up the movies played almost as big a role as God in his escape from the reality of home life.

Despite this evangelical background, the mature Baldwin did not regard man as fallen or evil by nature, needing to drive out the "old Adam." Humans become evil only if they refuse the call of love, which is the call of life itself. Of all American writers, Baldwin is in this, as in other respects, closest to Walt Whitman. As long as he believed in the Fall he could preach; and when he became unfallen, he could yet sing. He became aware of the impact these experiences had on his style as essayist and novelist, how he built argument or scene toward release, a climax of sense *and* emotion. Prose clarifies not only by reason but by an adjustment of feeling.

He left home, moved to Greenwich Village, and worked at odd jobs while he pursued his writing. During his time in Paris, before he became engaged in the civil rights movement, Henry James's portrayal of the conflicts of Americans in Europe resonated with him, as did his elaborate sentences that refused to simplify. The American was different, irreducible; the black American's experience demanded a nuanced, experimental style. Baldwin was fascinated with James's sense, especially in *The Ambassadors,* of "the failure of Americans to see through to the reality of others." There are the revelations that Europe provides, but there is also a fundamental American element that exists independently of race. "One hears, it seems to me, in the work of all American novelists, even including the mighty Henry James, songs of the plains, the memory of a virgin continent, mysteriously despoiled, though all dreams were to have become possible here." We remember the last paragraph of *The Great Gatsby.* "This did not happen," says Baldwin. "And the panic, then, to which I have referred comes out of the fact that we are now confronting the awful question of whether or not all our dreams have failed. How have we managed to become what we have, in fact, become?" An impossible question, it prompts another, still less answerable except in the action of writing. "And if we are, as indeed we seem to be, so empty and so desperate, what are we to do about it? How shall we put ourselves in touch with reality?"

Baldwin took his bearings from his great predecessors. He felt deeply the elegiac strains of Fitzgerald, lamented the falling off of Hemingway's genius from "about the time of *For Whom the Bell Tolls*"; and he believed that the American innocence of which Dos Passos wrote needed to be violated if moral development was to occur. "As the homeless wanderers of the twentieth century prove, the question of nationality no longer necessarily involves the question of allegiance. Allegiance, after all, has to work two ways; and one can grow weary of an allegiance which is not reciprocal." He liked the way Norman Mailer committed to his characters and let them lead: Despite his often overweening presence, Mailer could follow the reality of the imagined. He was attracted by otherness and achieved, not so much by travel as by imagination, a mode of escape that entailed self-effacement, investment, habitation. Mailer insisted on the stabilizing influence of Tolstoy, who saved him from solipsism even as he delivered him up to the large-scale work. The Beat writers, on the other hand, left Baldwin impatient. Their reality was fluid, malleable, not transformative because always rooted in a deliberately destabilized self. Of other contemporaries he had mixed views. Updike was self-indulgent and irrelevant: "In the main, the concerns of most white Americans—to use *that* phrase—are boring, and terribly, terribly self centered. In the worst sense. Everything is contingent, of course, on what you take yourself to be." These are the strains Bellow claims to hear in Baldwin. It is true that Baldwin, with the pressures and violence surrounding desegregation and the rise of Black Power, himself became blacker in his concerns, more impatient with the culture to which he initially gave himself, most fully in his second novel, *Giovanni's Room* (1956), the year after Rosa Parks and the year before Little Rock. It would have been impossible for him to write *Another Country* even a year after he did—1963 was the year of the murder of the NAACP organizer Medgar Evers, and of the March on Washington of 200,000 people to hear Martin Luther King's "I Have a Dream" speech; and the bombing and riots in Birmingham, Alabama, made the issues unignorable. The moral and artistic distance between *Another Country* (1962) and *Tell Me How Long the Train's Been Gone* (1968) is vast. Baldwin is a kind of seismograph, acutely attuned to his time and his society. History for the artist awake cannot but have artistic consequences inseparable from moral ones. In *The Fire Next Time* (1963), the two relatively brief monitory essays that are now widely celebrated and anthologized, Baldwin the critic becomes Baldwin the prophet and falls foul of his own warning; he becomes imprecise.

His first novel, *Go Tell It on the Mountain,* appeared in 1953. It is ambitious, autobiographical, vulnerable, and virtually all black. "Everyone had always said that John would be a preacher when he grew up, just like his father." John, the boy protagonist, is tyrannized by his father. The book depicts a holiday in the life of the members of a Harlem church community, at the core of which are the boy, his father, his mother, and his father's sister, Aunt Florence, who intercedes on his behalf when the father oversteps the mark. The book is in three sections, the second containing "prayers" by the father, mother, and aunt, in effect dramatic monologues addressing God, which impart the main tensions in lives divided between a rural South and an urban North and spanning two generations, with slavery a memory still open like a wound. The novel established Baldwin as the natural heir of Richard Wright, though some black writers resisted the lyrical thoughts that were, Langston Hughes remarked, "way over the heads of the folks supposedly thinking them."

His second novel is all white. *Giovanni's Room* tells the story of Giovanni, a handsome young Italian waiter, and David, an American in flight from his father. Though engaged to an American girl, David falls in love with Giovanni. An affair ensues. When David's fiancée returns, he goes with her; Giovanni is left behind and commits a capital crime. David hears of it, his fiancée discovers his sexual nature and leaves him, and, just like at the end of a Puccini opera, all hearts are broken by the thwarting of true love. There was a history of black writers writing "raceless" novels; there were even novels on homosexual themes; but a raceless homosexual novel was audacious. It is a powerful book, Baldwin at his most Jamesian in every sense. It went down badly with some critics. Amiri Baraka and Eldridge Cleaver found the homosexual theme totally anathema. Baldwin raises a permanent bulwark against their bigotry: he changed publishers and agents so that the book would be published as intended, refusing to tone it down or change Giovanni's sex, which would have made the romance acceptable. With Gore Vidal's *The City and the Pillar,* this is an act of literary courage that possesses durable literary merit, unlike E. M. Forster's *Maurice,* for example, more a Greenwood parable than a novel. Forster's great homosexual novel is *A Passage to India.*

*Another Country* (1962) divides readers. I regard it as Baldwin's most complete achievement. Anthony Burgess describes it as "a kind of underworld of the afflicted," but I doubt that he could have written *Earthly Powers* without its example. Colm Tóibín, a strong advocate, is disappointed with its form: "This work bears all the marks of a book written sporadically over a long period of time in many different places." The three parts of the novel do stand at a distance from one another with a kind of illusory completeness. There is dependence between them, their juxtaposition tightly planned. In his own account of writing the novel, Baldwin is clear that the arrival of Rufus, the universally attractive but doomed jazz musician, helps make sense of all the other characters' relationships. Here, centering the action in New York, but embracing America, and Europe, more widely, Baldwin writes about races and nations, about North and South, different classes, sexual variety, and about the American dream as it is experienced and as, in the case of the young Frenchman Yves, it is anticipated. Baldwin uses his own experiences and transforms them into representative biography; he creates characters who transgress types and stereotypes. This is parable and novel in the same breath, discovery and self-discovery through the transgressing of arbitrary sexual codes and customs. In the *Paris Review* Baldwin remarked, "The principal action in the book, for me, is the journey of Ida and Vivaldo toward some kind of coherence." Vivaldo, an Italian American, has been in love with Ida's brother Rufus. He is struggling to write and struggling to understand (his writing is an attempt to find and tell the truth). His foil is Richard, the successful writer whose success has been bought with compromise, whose potboilers bring in the money that should make him happy but does not. Richard is an Emersonian innocent, unable to understand "evil," untouched by Rufus's death, blind to his wife's unhappiness.

In tension with Vivaldo, Ida is trying for another kind of understanding. If they can love one another, however volatile the relationship, there is a larger hope, another possible country in which the aggression of the one they currently live in might at last be creatively harnessed or resolved. Vivaldo says, "If you can accept the pain you can use it, you can become better." This is the message of the blues. What the white man has to do is lose his innocence, to see what has been done, and in what he is complicit. It is necessary to ground life in truth (a felt, lived truth) rather than in innocence. Innocence in the context of racial and sexual relations is a manifestation of selfishness and self-deception.

The only characters in the novel who have not chosen to be in New York are Rufus, who chooses to leave by jumping off a bridge to his death, and Ida, who intends to stay and find herself. They are the black characters. White people come and go at will, but must register, one way or another, the blacks. Rufus, who appears and disappears in a little over eighty pages in part one, is deeply wounded by the realities of racism, not least his own: he is (literally after his suicide) "the black corpse floating in the national psyche." His inability to love means that his relationships are marred by distrust, hatred, incompleteness, the raging frustration of thwarted communication, the inability to find words that answer the deep needs and feelings he has. Those with whom he has had relations, all white, are marred by the culture that privileges them.

What is the effect of being made nameless and expendable? But in a sense Rufus's death proves he is neither of those things. He remains, in his absence, at the heart of all the relationships in the book. Rufus is based on Eugene Worth, a close friend of Baldwin's who threw himself off the George Washington Bridge. The suicide scene was almost impossibly painful to write, and he put it off as long as he could. The challenge of retelling it is part of the radical self-questioning a writer must exercise. "The questions which one asks oneself begin, at last, to illuminate the world, and become one's key to the experience of others. One can only face in others what one can face in oneself." The race questions and questions of sexuality intertwine. "On this confrontation depends the measure of our wisdom and compassion. This energy is all that one finds in the rubble of vanished civilizations, and the only hope for ours."

*Tell Me How Long the Train's Been Gone* centers on a black actor remembering his Harlem youth and his career. His life mirrors the changing situation of the

American black man. Baldwin's characters search for self-knowledge and the self-esteem that is inseparable from identity and without which love is impossible. What in terms of fiction is *self-knowledge?* What is the impact of *self-esteem?* Christ's second commandment, "Thou shalt love thy neighbor as thyself," obsesses Baldwin. It can be obeyed only with self-acceptance: one does not need to forgive but to accept oneself. Without it, real and fictional characters see human beings through labels, categories, prejudices.

In *If Beale Street Could Talk* (1974) a young woman fights to free her wrongly imprisoned fiancé. The world of specific social issues became more real for Baldwin in his later fiction. *Just Above My Head* (1979) follows the life of a Harlem gospel singer and his family looking for salvation. Baldwin described his novels (especially the later ones) as shapeless, that "shapelessness" reflecting the "shapelessness" of America. He undersells himself as an artist: his novels are carefully planned and formed, whatever the disproportions.

What did he achieve? As a black writer he created white lives; as a man he wrote credible women; as a gay man he made sense of straight men and women; he brought into credible sexual encounters straight and gay characters, heterosexual women and homosexual men, and most difficult of all, black men and black men. He preaches against artificially stable categories that reduce and ensnare. Rigid sexual categories go with rigid racial categories. If one deconstructs one, it becomes less difficult to deconstruct the other.

While he was writing *Another Country* Baldwin lived for five months in the guesthouse of William (Clark) Styron (Jr.) (1925–2006). "Jimmy was a social animal of nearly manic gusto," Styron said. Styron was himself depressive: one of his best-selling books is *Darkness Visible* (1999), Milton's oxymoron figuring his situation. Styron and Baldwin were experienced writers when Baldwin came to stay. While he created his white characters, Styron was at work on his fourth novel, *The Confessions of Nat Turner* (1967), creating the story of the black leader of the one recorded slave revolt in American history, in Virginia in 1831. Turner "confessed" to Thomas Gray, a white lawyer, before his execution, and it is on this account that Styron based his narrative. Turner, according to Gray, believed he had been enjoined by God to do what he did and to destroy the white race. It is impossible to know what part of the Gray document is in Turner's voice: the document may be an invention. It is short, and Turner is allowed to speak only after the court and others have spoken, warned, and conducted the formalities. Less than a quarter of the document, only 1,648 words, are "his," and their style is not very different from that of the rest of the document. Gray interrupts and takes over the narrative: Turner's voice, if it was his, is sunk in paraphrase. But he has had time to declare that from infancy he had the gift of second sight and was a prophet born. Styron becomes the medium for Turner's stopped voice, writing in his first person. Though Styron knew the settings and landscapes at the remove of a century and a half, given the lack of documentation he had to invent facts.

Both Ellison and Baldwin supported Styron when the protests began, getting louder when the book was awarded a Pulitzer Prize in 1968, a period of intercommunity tension that the book inadvertently fueled. A white man appropriated a black voice; a white jury rewarded him. In Baldwin's words, the book "brought in the whole enormity of the issue of history versus fiction, fiction versus history, and which is which." Baldwin identified with Styron's project: "He writes out of reasons similar to mine—about something that hurt him and frightened him." He was proud, as the descendant of slave owners, to have attempted to voice the circumstances his ancestors colluded in sustaining.

Apart from the issue of appropriation, some critics objected to the stereotypes Styron imported into his characterization of Nat Turner, making him a sexually overcharged and morbidly disturbed character. There were petitions against the book and a black boycott. His intention had been to portray the effects of slavery on black and white people, the ways in which it tried and twisted the tenets of Christian belief. Toni Morrison's reasoned, calm critique is the most telling. Styron's Turner is "a very self-conscious character who says things like, I looked at my black hand. Or, I woke up and I felt black. It is very much on Bill Styron's mind. He feels charged in Nat Turner's skin." Clearly, "he has a right to write about whatever he wants. To suggest otherwise is outrageous. What they should have criticized, and some of them did, was Styron's suggestion that Nat Turner hated black people." The crucial issue is, then, "Why would anybody follow him? What kind of leader is this who has a fundamentally racist contempt that seems unreal to any black person reading it? Any white leader would have some interest and identification with the people he was asking to die. That was what these critics meant when they said Nat Turner speaks like a white man. That racial distance is strong and clear in that book."

Because of depression, Styron was a slow writer. In 1980 he won the American Book Award for *Sophie's Choice,* a book in which, again, but this time more loudly, he heard the voice of his protagonist and took part of the book down from her dictation, as it were. His southern novelist-protagonist Stingo arrives in New York in 1947, where he meets Nathan Landau, a Jew, and his Roman Catholic Polish immigrant girlfriend, Sophie, a survivor of Auschwitz. The narrator's circumstances parallel Styron's own early life—a graduate of Duke University, a reader for a publishing house that dismisses him, then a threadbare flat in Brooklyn where he tries to write his first novel and meets Nathan and Sophie, neighbors already engaged in their vexed affair. For his part, he would like to have been one of Gertrude Stein's lost-generation writers but he could not rise to that. "I had the syrup but it wouldn't pour."

The novel is intense and again controversial, drawing a Catholic out of Auschwitz, exploring themes of Nazism and anti-Semitism in the context of the South's history of slavery and repression, and containing some vivid sexual scenes. The storms it caused were less vehement than those *Nat Turner* stirred up, but they were similar in kind. Anthony Burgess was not persuaded by the parallels Styron drew between Nazism and the American South. Stingo's attempt to find common ground with Sophie leads to strange historical conflations. Her choice is dramatic, brutal, yet because of the complexity of the surrounding plot, incidental. Nathan and Sophie die. Stingo is left reflecting, and morphing into the William Styron who will write *Nat Turner*. This is a kind of self-justifying prequel. It further complicates the political and ideological issues stirred up by *Nat Turner*.

Reflecting on D. M. Thomas's *The White Hotel* (1981), whose enormous success started in the United States and reached Britain on the rebound, Martin Amis writes, "In a country so obsessed with the Holocaust that even a flapping, gobbling, squawking turkey like William Styron's *Sophie's Choice* (that thesaurus of florid commonplaces) enjoyed universal acclaim, *The White Hotel* had a lot going for it. Styron offered sex and the Final Solution; Thomas had all this and psychoanalysis too—the full triumvirate of national fixations." Less unkind, Katherine Ann Porter registered the biblical cadences, the Faulknerish excesses of "an extremely gifted man" who was "very ripe and lush and with a kind of Niagara Falls of energy, and a kind of power" whose dependence on violent incident generated "a kind of exaggerated heat."

The heat of Styron's third novel, *Set This House on Fire* (1960), despite the title is not exaggerated: It exists on this side of distracting controversy and follows a maturing "I," fresh from military service, through a season of discovery in a new Europe, the lost generation supplanted by a new generation of writers and periodicals. The negative reviews the book received in the United States, where it was seen as trying to revive an exhausted expatriate genre, hurt him and may have urged him toward the ambitious risk of *Nat Turner*. The divisive politics of the 1960s were already narrowing the creative space for James Baldwin. Styron need not have been so surprised. In 1968 he signed the "Writers and Editors War Tax Protest" and was regarded as "sound" on Vietnam. Baldwin had been attacked for *Another Country*. A prophet was not needed to predict Styron's difficult trajectory.

# 41

# Displacement and Expropriation

Chinua Achebe, Ngũgĩ wa Thiong'o, George Lamming, Wilson Harris, Ben Okri,

Wole Soyinka, Nadine Gordimer, Olive Schreiner, Bessie Head, Alice Walker

"The African project at present employs my whole time," declares earnest, feck-less Mrs. Jellybee in *Bleak House*. "I am happy to say it is advancing. We hope by this time next year to have from a hundred and fifty to two hundred healthy families cultivating coffee and educating the natives of Borrioboola-Gha, on the left bank of the Niger." To this satire on colonial displacement, Mrs. Jel-lybee neglecting her own family and community in charitable engagement with the benighted races, Chinua Achebe responds with a beautiful sentence: "By the time the River Niger gets to Onitsha it has answered many names, seen a multi-tude of sights; it is now big, experienced and unhurried. Its name is simply *Orimili* or 'plenitude of waters.'" Later on, sure enough, Mrs. Jellybee is "disappointed in Borrioboola-Gha, which turned out a failure in consequence of the king of Bor-rioboola wanting to sell everybody—who survived the climate—for rum." She abandons one lost cause in favor of another, the rights of women to sit in Parlia-ment. In the end, of course, neither cause was lost. History has transformed Mrs. Jellybee into a social visionary. Meanwhile her ragged children tumble over the railings and wipe their runny noses on the upholstery and drapes.

The children of Nigeria in the first half of the twentieth century were better looked after than the young Jellybees. (Albert) Chinua(lumogo) Achebe (1930–2013), born in Ogidi, was educated at a government secondary school in Umua-hia. He began to study medicine but changed to literary studies at the Univer-sity of Ibadan. He went on to become Director of External Broadcasting at the Nigerian Broadcasting Corporation, but with the bloody Biafran war (1967–1970), in which he sided with the Biafran cause, he stepped down. He founded the journal *Okike* and taught for a time in the United States, returning there in 1990 after he suffered disabling injuries in a car accident. He remained resident in the United States until his death.

In *The Education of a British-Protected Child* (2009) Achebe made clear his position in the sometimes acrimoniously politicized realm of African and Anglophone African writing. He describes the space he seeks to occupy as a writer. "What I have attempted to suggest in this rambling essay is the potency of the unpredict-able in human affairs. I could have dwelt on the harsh humiliations of colonial rule or the more dramatic protests against it. But I am also fascinated by that middle ground I spoke about, where the human spirit resists an abridgement of its humanity. And this was to be found in the camp of the colonized, but now and again in the ranks of the colonizers too." There are people he admires from "the other side" who actually respect the colonized and accommodate the cause without distorting or translating it. And there are, by extension, people on his side who do not respect, and whose polemical or dialectical responses lead to the "abridgement" he at all costs wishes to avoid. He distrusts the word *universal*: there is no such thing as a general truth when it comes to literature. Like James Baldwin, with whom he spent memorable days in Florida and whose essay *The Fire Next Time,* especially the first section, impressed him with its restraint and clarity, he is a particularist and resists the tendency to engage in generalized categories such as "African fiction." One of the abiding images from his own culture is that of the Mbari ceremony, in which the new—even sinister colonial novelties like the missionary's bicycle—are included in the making of little figures arranged in scenarios, secondary worlds where people see represented their own changing realities. A novel is, in a sense, an Mbari ceremony in words.

And where do his characters come from? "If I am going to explore a certain kind of character, I must *listen* to this character. Before I can understand how his or her mind operates I must also know how he or she uses words. This is part less of verisimilitude than a wider integrity, knowing the subject as well as addressing the reader." In a nation with such an abundance of languages, accents, and oral traditions, his instinct, which is also that of George Eliot and of Alastair Gray, is sound. But what language to listen in, to listen to, and what language to write?

Much has been made of the language in Achebe's first and most celebrated novel, *Things Fall Apart* (1958). The originality seems to the contemporary reader to be more in plot and subject matter than in language. Many idioms and cadences are close to those of the Victorian and Edwardian writers he read at school. The reader's ear detects something of the archetypal legend-writing style of the Leatherstocking books, combining primeval landscapes and tribal communities, and lacking conventional characters. There is too Achebe's effective use of phrases and fragments of Igbo, which come with the force of refrain. At no point does the reader relax into a conventional posture of reading, and the characters in their otherness, even when they convert to Christianity, keep a distance, like figures in epic.

What is familiar is the tension between fathers and sons, the great Okonkwo having to restore his name after his lazy, flute-playing, good-natured father Unoka has squandered it. Okonkwo collects three wives and feeds them, makes eight children for whom he provides, and with Ezinma, the only surviving daughter of his second wife, he forges an undemonstrative but intense friendship. His father was weak, he proves unbendingly strong, the one feeling he can express being rage, with consequences for his family and others. His own first son, Nwoye, converts to Christianity, becoming Isaac, a further knot in the family theme. The most alarming relationship in the book is that between Okonkwo and Ikemefuna, a delightful boy given to him in payment by a neighboring village to settle a score. Ikemefuna is loved by all, even his guardian, whom he addresses as "father," but to prove his unswerving resolve, when egged on by clansmen he kills the boy. At this point the things so laboriously gathered together by Okonkwo begin to fall apart. Their disintegration is accelerated by the arrival of the missionaries and the beginning of the tribe's conversion.

Achebe was raised as a Christian and rebelled, but he remains remarkably evenhanded in the book. Okonkwo's culture is made complexly real; the Christian incursion locates that culture's points of strength and weakness. Anthony Burgess suggests that Achebe's theme is "the threat of Western modes of corruption to native civilisations which the great world may call primitive but are in fact vital and happy." This sentimentalizes a project that was to record not a threat but a series of facts. The issue of a conflict between the "great world" and "primitive" does not arise because Achebe does not sentimentalize the culture that is being destroyed, any more than he softens the blows with which the colonial program is implemented.

The South African novelist Nadine Gordimer (b. 1923) describes *Things Fall Apart* as "a presentiment: Achebe is going to create *what was complete* before the situation in the title is to come about." The book is less memory than re-creation, hence the feeling that the characters have an archetypal rather than a subjective nature. Gordimer establishes a rule that Achebe seems preemptively to have obeyed: he has "the master story-teller's knowledge that the present—what is happening to his characters now—can be totally meaningful only if (the way it is in our own lives) the past that has formed these people is shown as still within them, directing their lives." The ways in which African writers escape the constraints and projections of the colonial period and elude the artistic constructions of the colonial languages in which they compose entails, it would seem, a filling in of blanks, reinventing stories that colonialism erased or wrote over. An additional duty that Achebe with singular clarity has undertaken is to draw attention to colonialist and imperialist attitudes inherent in writing that we have long taken as liberal. As we have seen, Conrad is a writer whom Achebe reveres and reviles in equal measure.

At a memorial evening held to celebrate the work of James Baldwin, Achebe spoke of the connections between their works, which Baldwin acknowledged. Colm Tóibín reported on the occasion that in *Things Fall Apart,* "the portrait of the father's anger and powerlessness is very close to the portrait of the father in Baldwin's essays and fiction." Not Baldwin's *real* father of course, whose name he never learned. Nor Achebe's *real* father, either—in any case more a grandfather, the story mediated to him by a not wholly acquiescent son, now father.

Achebe's later novels, *No Longer at Ease* (1960), *Arrow of God* (1964), *A Man of the People* (1966), and *Anthills of the Savannah* (1987), especially *Arrow* and *Anthills,* extend the missing narrative. The alienating Biafran experience absolved Achebe from the kinds of political affirmation that can constrain his contemporaries and successors. The first three novels constitute what critics call the "African trilogy" and develop themes of community and colonial consequences. The last two engage with the reality of modern Africa in more emblematic ways, and Achebe moves toward the larger, abstracting forms that he had resisted, his particularism giving way to satirical allegory. Anthony Burgess admires *A Man of the People,* a satire on the cult of personality and the corruption and waste it conceals. V. S. Naipaul treats the theme more comprehensively and "universally" in *A Bend in the River,* but he has had the benefit of Achebe. Burgess acknowledges other Nigerian writers who "fertilized" what he calls "standard literary English with the rhythms and idioms of native dialects," among them Amos Tutuola *(The Palm-Wine Drinkard),* Cyprian Ekwensi *(Jagua Nana),* and Onuora Nzekwu *(Blade among the Boys).* In 1968 Achebe published the Ghanaian writer Ayi Kwei Armah's best-known novel, *The Beautyful Ones Are Not Yet Born,* about how briskly the newly independent states of Africa, despite their noble dreams, turned to embrace corruption and replace the veils they had ripped down.

Achebe and other African writers are troubled by the question of what language to write in: Should they use the language of their education, the colonial language, the enforced lingua franca of a substantial portion of the world, or should they choose instead to write in their birth language? Achebe came to blows with his one-time protégé Ngũgĩ wa Thiong'o (b. 1938), whose first novel, written in English, *Weep Not, Child* (1964), he published in the Heinemann African Writers Series, for which he was general editor in the decade after the appearance of *Things Fall Apart,* the first book to be published in the series. He also published *The River Between* (1965), *The Grain of Wheat* (1967), and *The Black Hermit* (1968) during his tenure. In those years the young Kenyan was known as James Ngũgĩ. His name and his approach to language were to change. In 1986 he published a short book, *Decolonising the Mind: The Politics of Language in African Literature* (1986), informed by Marx and by his near contemporary the Barbados-born novelist George Lamming (b. 1927) and instilled with something of the fiery spirit of Frantz Fanon. It is a serious caution to critical historians such as myself, and a challenge to writers like francophone Leopold Senghor of Senegal and Anglophone Achebe. "Ngũgĩ's book argues passionately and dramatically," Achebe says, "that to speak of African literature in European languages is not only an absurdity but also part of the scheme of Western imperialism to hold Africa in perpetual bondage." Ngũgĩ chastises himself for having written in English. Achebe's defense is complex and subtle. In the first place, he exonerates the British colonial educational policy, which Ngũgĩ portrays as deliberately suppressing native language. That argument is ahistorical and simplistic. Achebe believes in readership, and the best way of delivering the experiences he wishes to explore to the widest audience while remaining true to those experiences is to work elements of the native language in with English, not only at the level of naming and diction but also cadence and narrative structure. By subjecting English to the native language, alteration and expropriation occur. This is Lamming's argument in *Natives of My Person,* a book Caryl Phillips describes as being as "densely textured as Faulkner, and possessing formal ambitions of Joycean proportions." Lamming lays stress on the effect of the Caribbean writers (and he might have included the Anglophone African writers) on *English reading:* the language is after all fundamentally the same, English being a West Indian language. George Lamming wrote in 1960: "An important question for the English critic, is not what the West Indian novel has brought to English writing. It would be more correct to ask what the West Indian novelists have contributed to English reading."

Ngũgĩ is theoretically persuasive, but like Gordimer he generalizes too broadly when he translates the essential conflict in African literature as one between perpetuating colonial languages and liberating African languages. He produces a political schema of use to cultural polemicists rather than to artists. When he came to write in his native language, Gikuyu, he found he had to reacquire it, and having reacquired it he had then to shape it with prose narrative structures that were as alien to it as the colonial language had grown alien to his ear. He has chosen to radicalize part, and in terms of wider readership the wrong part, of the process.

A few ideas recur in Ngũgĩ's work, ideas that grow smooth and slippery with repetition. The issue of language is the most insistent. Achebe corrects his historical account of the colonial imposition of English, and he resents being corrected, digging himself in deeper. Joyce's *A Portrait of the Artist* is a book in which the protagonist decides, by stages, not to be the subject of the colonial language but to make that language subject. Joyce's alternative would have been to learn Irish, a language over which he would never have achieved the mastery he has of English, a language whose resource for his kind of genius would have been sparse. Stage by stage English determines Stephen Dedalus's world, and stage by stage like Proteus he struggles, each battle more demanding and violent than the one before, until he is free in and with language, can use the first-person singular and leave home knowing what home is. Ngũgĩ decides to write in Gikuyu: well and good; but whatever its narrative resources may be, there is no developed tradition of the novel in Gikuyu. To throw off colonial constraint he should discard the novel form itself. Tyranny inheres not only in a language but in its forms.

In the 1996 Clarendon Lectures Ngũgĩ spoke of "Oral Power and Europhone Glory," in particular "Orature, Literature, and Stolen Legacies." "Orature" is a term first used by Ugandan linguist Pio Zirimu and defined as "the use of utterance as an aesthetic means of expression" and, one assumes, the sufficiency of unwritten utterance. The insistence on a return to African language was not an individual decision. Ngũgĩ came together with writers from other African nations at the University of Leeds (Wole Soyinka was an illustrious predecessor there), the voluntary exile in which he wrote *Weep Not, Child,* the first novel to be published by an East African. The movement to return to African languages began there. In 1968 (Ngũgĩ was writing in English at the time) a campaign began to close the university's English Department in Nairobi. This was intended to privilege Kenyan languages and to deprivilege English, to open out reading to the German, French, Italian, and other European classics. A great deal of what Achebe recognized as partial history fed into the movement, which sometimes preferred to forget that many of the African languages survived and had written literatures thanks to the activities of the missionaries and the translations of the Bible into even the smallest languages. Orature, thanks to scripture, survived as literature. Ngũgĩ began as a Christian and in his independent Gikuyu school he read, as Achebe had done, Dickens, Stevenson, Haggard, and Buchan. In 1969 he decided to abandon "James" and to Gikuyuize his name.

He suffered for his language. In 1977 Ngũgĩ was arrested and detained without trial in part for writing theater work in Gikuyu. In his theatrical pieces he abandoned the proscenium arch, encouraged improvisation, and engaged audiences in performance. Theater writing was his "homecoming." His first Gikuyu novel, he says, was written on toilet paper in prison. (In *The Man Died: Prison Notes,* published in 1971, Wole Soyinka works his recollections, in some respects similar to Ngũgĩ's, into a narrative with the dynamic of a novel more compelling than that of his two actual novels. "I'm not really a keen novelist," he confessed. "And I don't consider myself a novelist." He pickpockets the prison doctor to get a pen to write with. The refusal to provide imprisoned writers with the tools of their trade is a primary cruelty of repressive regimes, Soynika suggests.) In 1978 Ngũgĩ's last English novel, *Petals of Blood,* was published. Ironically, his Gikuyu fiction has for the most part been composed in the United States, where he has been a teacher for many decades.

The Gikuyu novels, especially *Wizard of the Crow* (2006), which he translated himself, are marked by the exaggeration and caricature of the oral tradition: distortion is for emphasis and underlines the basic themes. Facial distortion, for example: characters emphasize qualities of terror or alertness. The novel is both "performance" and conventional novelistic realism; human exchanges are not important. He ostensibly addresses two markets, Gikuyu and wider Kenyan, and the international Anglophone readership. To put these readerships on a more equal footing he sets the book in an imagined world called Aburiria, thus freeing his symbolic language from specific referents. Aburiria at one level represents Kenya, but it is not Kenya and the story does not depend on a verifiable geography or politics. John Updike is disappointed with *Wizard,* vast and rich more in indignation than analysis. It is "too aggrieved and grim to be called satire." There is a sense of excess rather than abundance about it.

In the twenty-five novels of the Guianian writer (Sir Theodore) Wilson Harris (b. 1921) there is also excess. Being a mainland writer, not Caribbean, he occupies a curious place between Latin American and Caribbean and between African and American. His background includes Amerindian, Scottish, African, and possibly East Indian elements, a walking melting pot, and he regards his art as licensed by all these attenuated histories. He speaks of "cross-culturality," a phrase that reeks of the classroom and has an oversimplifying political and aesthetic meaning. His own approach to expropriating the novel form (the phrase is García Márquez's, when he won the 1982 Nobel Prize in Literature) has to do less with Ngũgĩ's ideological concerns, more with loading in new content (as a land surveyor in the 1940s, Harris knew the mysteries of the South American interior as few others have done) and through content forcing open conventional form. He described how "the interior of Guyana came alive to me, and seemed like another planet," enchanting and terrifying. "The great waterfalls and trees—so different from the coast where I was born." He was haunted both by a landscape that "seemed alive" and by mysterious signs of pre-Columbian civilizations that had imploded even before the Spanish conquest. Guinean novelist and essayist David Dabydeen (b. 1955) notes, "The whole of Latin America resonates with a sense of loss. Harris is very conscious of pre-Columbian catastrophes, and ties that into conquest and colonial history."

As with early Achebe there is something, in the context of the weary novel form, of the primevalist about Harris. As a South American, he lays claim to magical realism. He is more abundant in output than Achebe or Ngũgĩ. In his work logic confronts magic, the European and the intuitive, shamanistic approach to nature and society are in tension. Columbus arrived an ignorant man. "He kissed the soil purely in terms of his own values. He never considered the values of the Arawaks—a gifted and gentle people. Europe gained nothing except material things—tomatoes, potatoes, above all gold." Europe's gains are different now and entail the voice of these novels dictated, he says, by "a voice in myself" that is at once personal and cultural, a voice that remembers things that the author himself has never known, a voice that restores erasures. Writing entails surrendering to this voice with its unexpected eloquence and knowledge. Both the European and the aboriginal and intuitive imply disciplines, but those disciplines are at odds with one another. The imperialist comes to exploit and is fascinated by what he cannot understand and so must destroy. The jungle becomes inevitably a metaphor for the human unconscious, its latent energies and rages. Imperiling the unconscious places the conscious mind at risk. In one novel the protagonist succumbs to a "poetry" of greater and greater volatility, staccato annotations, without prosody, careering back and forth between bathos and prose. For almost five decades Harris has pursued his visionary way, tracing "the myths that hold us together." That "us" is intended to include the remote European, Australian, African, and Indian reader. *The Ghost of Memory* (2006) was, he declared, his final novel. Ten years earlier he explored community massacre in *Jonestown* (1996). Generally his plots are framed in ways that hold them distant. However vividly detailed, they tend toward abstraction.

Getting started was hard: Three attempts were discarded, and on the fourth Harris managed *The Palace of the Peacock* (1960), in which the protagonist like a conqueror carves a way through, up the river, to bring back cheap native workers. The journey changes him and becomes an odyssey of redemption. Harris had settled in Britain in 1959, and fiction was a way of going home, though his sense of home and the actuality of his developing homeland diverged until he returned and lived through its upheavals. He went on to write three more novels in the series. At Faber T. S. Eliot approved the first and later books for publication. Harris stayed with Faber for all his novels, a remarkable fidelity on both sides. Derek Walcott, Anthony Burgess, C. L. R. James, Caryl Phillips, and Fred D'Aguiar have admired the books. No advocacy has so far drawn to him the wide audience he intends to address.

There is thickness about Harris's fiction, an overload of symbols as in the visions of William Blake, a poet who marked him as his own, though Blake was not foregrounded at Cambridge when Harris studied there, nor was his other guiding star, Herman Melville. Fantasy and dream destabilize the narrative. This wearies readers who are hungry for character, story, a less unstable exoticism. It is writing that will engage future generations of academic interpreters. And Harris can already be seen as having helped to inaugurate a distinct South American extension of the Caribbean traditions in English fiction. Books like *The Mask of the Beggar* (2003), an Odyssean exploration that belongs, in a different key, with *Omeros,* Derek Walcott's verse epic, deserve attention. His own books he regards as chapters in an epic, and the novel form retraces its steps toward that remote origin. "It was always a question of pushing on and probing further, so one could link ancient Homeric myth to pre-Columbian catastrophes, and in linking them discover oneself more deeply and more truly." Dream does overtime for him.

And it does overtime for the Nigerian novelist Ben Okri (b. 1959), too. Dreams and the spirit world are "a part of reality," and good fiction "has the effect on you that dreams do"—to which we are inclined to reply yes, and no. Yes is a response to his best-known protagonist, Azaro, who appears in *The Famished Road* (1991), Okri's Booker Prize–winning novel. Azaro is an *abiku* who keeps contact with the spirit world and brings it to bear on the daily world of his city. The city is generic, not specific, and Azaro is less an individual than a Bunyan-like embodiment of Nigerian spiritualism. He owes as much to Toni Morrison's *Beloved* and to American novelists as he does to his African predecessors and contemporaries. He is often likened to the magical realists of Latin America. Azaro's world is animated, there are voices and emanations from everything. Wilson Harris was a temporary exile from his country; Okri is an exile in earnest from Nigeria, long resident in London, yet he insists on African perspectives. He is not Joyce pinning Dublin down to its very cobbles from far off Trieste: Okri's London-dreamt Nigeria is miasmic, its very geography fluid.

Okri traveled to Britain first as a boy, brought by his father, who came on a scholarship to study law. The family returned to Nigeria when the writer-to-be was seven, his father setting up a practice in Lagos, where he was generous in giving his services pro bono. The son learned from watching his father, who is at the heart of some of his narratives. His mother was a natural storyteller. He composed poems and stories and placed a few of them in local magazines. He failed to get into university in Nigeria. Despite this, he managed to write his first novel, *Flowers and Shadows* (1980). Studying at the University of Essex, he was a published novelist before his twenty-first birthday. "I didn't discover my main story till after I'd written it twice," he said about his first book. He has gone through the same creative process in later books, finding what he has to say rather than having something to say before he sets out. *The Landscapes Within* (1981) was more autobiographical than his debut volume in terms of geography, but the internal landscape was imagined: "I've come to realize that you can't write about Nigeria truthfully without a sense of violence. To be serene is to lie. Relations in Nigeria are violent relations." Nigeria became more real the more he imagined it. He described the perfect artist (which he aspired to be) as a seer of things as they are rather than a teacher of how things ought to be. He has some way to go to achieve objectivity. He suggests that the short story is a more natural and potentially a more fruitful form for African writing than the novel.

*The Famished Road* had a less successful "sequel" in *Songs of Enchantment* (1993). Soon after it was published he found it hard to discuss *The Famished Road,* to detach a prose account from the integrated whole that is a book "not meant to be coherent. It's against the perception of the world as being coherent and therefore readable as a text." He is not attuned to Borges's brilliantly unfolding analytics. He chooses the musical analogy and uses it repeatedly; but what kind of music does he have in mind?

He and his contemporaries break rank with Achebe. Theirs is a later generation, another geography; and Okri is from a different part of Nigeria, with a postcolonial history at odds with Achebe's. Thus, he argues that the effects of colonialism on the African imagination, specifically on his own, may have been exaggerated. It is an interesting revision of the accepted argument, standing back from colonial and postcolonial discourses. He stresses the resilience of Africa: "I'd like to propose that we stop making so narrow what constitutes the African aesthetic. It is not something that is bound only to place, it's bound at a way of looking at the world . . . It's the aesthetic of possibilities, of labyrinths, of riddles—we love riddles—of paradoxes." His own primary sources, he declares, are not earlier texts but "those invisible books of the spirit." No one will pin him down here or in Nigeria. Azaro has grown up into a Protean novelist.

Though she resists, the South African novelist Nadine Gordimer (b. 1923) is either pinned down or pins herself down with each one of her fourteen novels, her twenty volumes of stories that add weight to Okri's contention about the African short narrative, her four books of essays, and the numerous interviews she has given. To her abundant fiction, the counterpoint of her reflective writing, personal, polemical, critical, evolves and changes inflection as the politics of her country do.

When on April 27, 1994, South African elections marked the end of apartheid, it seemed that writers committed to the struggle to end the system of separation and privilege could breathe easy at last. Nadine Gordimer, who received the Nobel Prize in Literature in 1991 for her writing and for her resistance, was seventy-one when she went to vote. From her always elevated perspective she had witnessed the rigidification of a system and had protested. She felt the release and vertigo that anyone devoted to a cause feels when that cause is won and the effort, so real, bloody, and life-consuming at the time, becomes history and the poetry of idealistic expectation is translated into the slow prose of daily life. The impact of resistance on her imagination, as a white woman, was irresistible. Everything related to it. In reacting against a repressive system with its religious fervor she was not alone in developing a counter-rhetoric with its thou shalts and shalt nots. She spoke and understood the awkwardness of her speech as one who had benefited from the disparities of race, education and access, privilege and freedom of movement.

Her presence and success inspired women writers, as she in turn had been inspired by Olive (Emilie Albertina) Schreiner (1855–1920), a pioneer campaigner and a declared opponent of the Boer War. Schreiner's parents were missionaries; her humanism replaced their orthodox faith. The freshness and necessity of *The Story of an African Farm* (1883), written at speed and without sentimentality and published under the pseudonym Ralph Iron, is not matched by her later work but need not be. This one volume, despite structural and technical flaws, is remarkable for its candor, laying themes open for the reader. Schreiner's preface to a later edition discriminates two methods of writing.

> There is the stage method. According to that each character is duly marshaled at first, and ticketed; we know with an immutable certainty that at the right crises each one will reappear and act his part, and, when the curtain falls, all will stand before it bowing . . . But there is another method—the method of the life we all lead. Here nothing can be prophesied. There is a strange coming and going of feet. Men appear, act and re-act upon each other, and pass away. When the crisis comes the man who would fit it does not return. When the curtain falls no one is ready. When the footlights are brightest they are blown out; and what the name of the play is no one knows. If there sits a spectator who knows, he sits so high that the players in the gaslight cannot hear his breathing. Life may be painted according to either method; but the methods are different. The canons of criticism that bear upon the one cut cruelly upon the other.

Alan Paton (1903–1988), too, despite quite an extensive bibliography, has one book that lives, *Cry, the Beloved Country* (1948), an example of Schreiner's first method.

Gordimer quotes approvingly from a jointly authored biography of Olive Schreiner: "We see Olive Schreiner's life writing as a product of a specific social history. We are not only looking at what she experiences but at how she, and others, have perceived that experience; at the concept with which her contemporaries understood their world," and they continue to spin out and out: "and, again, at the consciousness that was possible for her time—after Darwin, before Freud, and during the period when Marx's *Capital* was written." Gordimer in her critical writing and fiction participates in this fatal intellectual expansion from clear particulars to nebulous generalities.

In her essays she referred to the writer as "he," until the turn of the millennium. The white writer, she says—with the neutralizing vocabulary she draws from journalism, verbiage that masks thinness of thought—"has to see the concomitant necessity to find a different way, from that open to the black artist, to reconnect his art through his life to the total reality of the disintegrating present, and to attempt, by rethinking his own attitudes and conceptions, the same position the black man aims for: to be seen as relevant by and become committed to commonly understood, commonly created cultural entities corresponding to a common reality—an indigenous culture." Many of the terms are problematic here. Most treacherous is the notion of a common reality, common understanding, common culture—ideological imperatives with no equivalent in the living cultures of which her struggling society is constituted. She goes on: "The nature of contemporary art here, in the aspect of subject matter, is didactic, apocalyptic, self-pitying, self-accusatory as much as indicting." If apartheid imposed these things, its impact on the artist was tyrannical and appropriative. This is how she tended to experience it, too. "When interviewed abroad, there is often disappointment that you are there, and not in jail in your own country." Exile is no longer an option; personal speech can be an indulgence. Instead of Joyce's synthesizing vision, we are left with fragmentary narratives of a collective creation. "I want to consider what is expected of us by the dynamic collective conscience." And earlier she asks, "If art is freedom of the spirit, how can it exist within the oppressors?" This conformist notion of "art" requires more reflection than it is given.

In troubled times the writer must be "more than a writer." The essential gesture can be an individual's giving the finger to repressive powers or a clenched fist of solidarity with a radical mob. With Rushdie, she says, the issue was not *The Satanic Verses* itself but the censorship and the modes that censorship takes. The novel was pretext, best understood in terms of its effects. One of her most famous essays, "A Writer's Freedom," belongs to the 1960s and 1970s, direct, cajoling, self-righteous, angry—louder than it needs to be. J. M. Coetzee anatomizes Gordimer's habits of indulgent self-righteousness in this essay. Her weakest speech, presuming on the audience's unreflecting complicity, is her Nobel Prize acceptance in which she calculates impact not by means of argument but by touching the strings of cliché.

Gordimer was not educated in Britain, Europe, or the United States. She has received honors and held chairs and residencies, but her take on the issues of South Africa is close-up and developing. She spent one year at university. "This was the first time in my life I'd mixed with blacks, and was more or less the beginning of my political consciousness. Perhaps the good thing about being carted around with my parents was that they would sit playing gin rummy or something while I wandered around the host's house seeing what I could find to read." She read "everybody from Henry Miller to Upton Sinclair." At university she mixed with artists and writers: "I got to know black people as equals. In a general and inclusive, nonracial way, I met people who lived in the world of ideas, in the world that interested me passionately." At this stage her interest in politics was limited. "I felt that all I needed, in my own behavior, was to ignore and defy the color bar. In other words, my own attitude toward blacks seemed to be sufficient action. I didn't see that it was pretty meaningless until much later."

Her points of cultural reference, however, are predominantly European and American. She adjusts to African writers with effort: her literary examples are drawn from a narrow band of those whose work she values, in particular the poet Mongane Wally Serote, whom she quotes frequently. "Blacks must learn to talk; whites must learn to listen" (1981). Her infrequent detailed praise for black novelists comes rather late in her critical writing and usually in response to a commission.

She was tasked with composing a kind of doublespeak, addressing her world readership on the one hand and a local constituency of fellow South African writers and readers on the other, speaking into the ear of her troubled country in its transition without forfeiting respect for her integrity. Coetzee, with whom she had difficult relations because he is an awkward fellow traveler, quotes her declaration, "For the black artist at this stage of his development relevance is the supreme criterion. It is that by which his work will be judged by his own people, and they are the supreme authority." Even at the height of apartheid this would not do. But her position is difficult as a white woman talking for male black writers. "Whites must learn to listen."

Reflecting on her beginnings as a novelist, she speaks of treacherous influences of other writers, all of whom she learned from, but not at the very start. Woolf is important to her once she is started, though "she can be a very dangerous influence on a young writer. It's easy to fall into the cadence. But the content isn't there." She found the same perils in Dos Passos and in Hemingway, an important shaper of her stories against whom she rebelled. She described herself as "starting out with an acute sensibility and a poor narrative gift," a situation of vulnerability against which she struggled. "My narrative gift was weak in my early novels—they tend to fall into beautiful set pieces. It was only with *The Late Bourgeois World* [1966] . . . that I began to develop narrative muscle." Once established, the "acute sensibility" is at risk and needs protecting.

Her second novel, *A World of Strangers* (1958), was banned for twelve years in South Africa, and her fourth, *The Late Bourgeois World*, for a decade. Both circulated widely in private. Burgess singled out the second as "a brief, taut masterpiece" about the fatal consequences of apartheid on an individual's sensibility.

*Guest of Honor* (1970) was deliberately political, the narrative approach "objective" in being conventional: what needed to be foregrounded were the plot and the argument it entailed. Of her books it comes closest to drama and would be the easiest to script into a film. The transition to her sixth novel, *The Conservationist* (1974), joint winner of the Booker Prize with Stanley Middleton's *Holiday,* was ambitious. The narrator here does not elucidate or direct the reader: she leaves more space for readers and makes greater demands on them. Narrative is internalized in the characters: "The novel was full of private references between the characters. Of course, you take a tremendous risk with such a narrative style, and when you do succeed, I think it's the ideal. When you don't, of course, you irritate the reader or you leave him puzzled."

*Burger's Daughter* (1979), her most engaging novel, grew in its historical moment, with independence of conception. "In my writing, politics comes through in a didactic fashion very rarely," she says. "The kind of conversations and polemical arguments you get in *Burger's Daughter,* and in some of my other books—these really play a very minor part. For various reasons to do with the story, they had to be there. But the real influence of politics on my writing is the influence of politics on people." She insists, too loudly because she is also dealing with abstract ideas, "I am dealing with people; here are people who are shaped and changed by politics. In that way my material is profoundly influenced by politics." She did not predetermine this novel but made scrappy notes and began. The snatches of note and dialogue are a germ from which a whole world grows. This book too was banned three weeks after publication, and the ban held for several months. Breaking that ban was a crucial moment for writers in South Africa at the time: when the ban was removed, said Gordimer, "I was pleased, as you can imagine. Not only for myself, but because it established something of a precedent for other writers, since there are in that book blatant contraventions of certain acts."

She incorporated in the book an actual document from the 1976 student riots in Soweto, retaining the students' curious spelling and grammar precisely: one cause of the riots was the students' perception of the poor quality of their education. The book is political, but it has other themes, in particular, Gordimer insists, "commitment. Commitment is not merely a political thing. It's part of the whole ontological problem in life. It's part of my feeling that what a writer does is to try to make sense of life." Writing seeks "that thread of order and logic in the disorder, and the incredible waste and marvelous profligate character of life. What all artists are trying to do is to make sense of life." The book took her four years to write, not because she was busy redrafting it but because it came to her relatively slowly, grew with her and out of her own youth, with its social and religious commitments, which gradually redefined themselves.

Colm Tóibín's first novel, *The South* (1990), owes a debt to *Burger's Daughter*. Gordimer's protagonist comes from South Africa to southern France and is surprised to find how people there live beyond all the issues that beset the South African. A misreading, of course, because as the landscape becomes familiar it grows clear that it is as much a place of histories and conflicts as the one left behind, only different ones, and different time scales. Tóibín was stimulated by Gordimer's portrayal of the intense and illusory sense of liberation. He may have found the seeming ease with which Gordimer wrote inspiriting: there is little evidence in the writing of the struggle she had to get the book out.

Few of her later novels have the universality of *Burger's Daughter*. Yet her eleventh novel, which was her twenty-third book, *None to Accompany Me* (1994), marks a brave transition. Apartheid was over, it was the year of the elections. She wrote two books in one, and neither quite works. Caryl Phillips suggests that events have been too fast for her. The problems of the broken form may illustrate the problems of living in a divided society. In her book of essays *The Essential Gesture: Writing, Politics, and Places* (1988), she recorded her anger as a South African writer at being restricted to one subject. Now that restriction was removed, she had to find a way forward beyond constraint. Her short stories are more resourceful at this time, their completeness limited and particular. She is a writer with something to say and the extended form can go on beyond the end of her statements. A short story can "happen," a novel has to be made. Her weakest suit, Phillips says, is when she talks most directly about the occasions behind her writing. In *None to Accompany Me,* "the demands of fiction become submerged beneath the author's desire to act as reporter from the front line of change." She has news to deliver, but being a fiction writer she must deliver it obliquely. And, he adds ruefully, this seeming radical has become a liberal, and not a very liberal liberal at that: "All too often her narrative capitulates to the lure of rhetoric." Her prose marches "to the beat of history," a martial music treacherous after the war is over.

*The Pickup* (2001) is remarkable for a writer on the brink of her eighties, looking obliquely at a society whose values she cannot in conscience share. Early in her career she was fascinated by Egypt and the Muslim world at large. Here she explores that fascination through character. It is, Coetzee says, "not just an interesting book, in fact, but an astonishing one." A white South African woman picks up a young Muslim "illegal" for sex. She falls in love, and when he is deported she goes with him, they marry, she settles in with his family and finds happiness in a traditional Muslim society with its strict values and sexual customs while he continues his quest for material success. Gordimer does not advocate or condemn: she explores confluences, and what differently cultured lives and loves spark out of and off of one another in their hard separateness.

Coetzee notes how Gordimer, a Jew, portrays sympathetically a world of "ordinary" Muslim women. The girl with a weak heart, born in a mining town in the Transvaal to a comfortable world from which she escaped by means of books, achieves the artistic freedom she has variously struggled for.

In *No Time like the Present* (2012) Gordimer's protagonists are survivors of the anti-apartheid campaigns in South Africa. Steve and Jabulile married when it was illegal for black and white to mix. This is a story of their subsequent lives in the nation they helped to create. Paradoxically, it was easier to know what to do during the years of struggle. Against the institutional and ordered indignity of the past are pitted the gratuitous, anarchic crimes of the present. Reviewing the book in the *New York Times,* the novelist Francine Prose struggles with Gordimer's language. The roughness is sometimes that of an early draft or a literal translation: "This young comrade parent or that was in detention, who knew when she, he, would be released, this one had fathered only in the biological sense, he was somewhere in another country learning the tactics of guerrilla war or in the strange covert use of that elegantly conventional department of relations between countries, diplomacy to gain support for the overthrow of the regime by means of sanctions if not arms." It goes nowhere. Francine Prose finds the story sufficiently compelling to override the language, but it should not be necessary for a reader to make fundamental allowances in reading Gordimer's novel. She is still skilled at "pulling back for a panoramic vista of a time and place, then narrowing her focus to remind us of the highly specific ways that politics shape the private lives of unique individuals, people not unlike ourselves." An editor might have helped.

It hurts Gordimer in the new South Africa to see how black writers "have to submit to an absolute orthodoxy within black consciousness. The poem or the story or the novel must follow a certain line—it's a kind of party line even though what is in question is not a political party, but it is, in the true sense of the word, a party line." She gives examples: "Nobleness of character in blacks must be shown. It's pretty much frowned upon if there's a white character who is human." Such clichés are "fine as a weapon of propaganda in the struggle, which is what such writing is, primarily. But the real writers are victims of this, because as soon as they stray from one or two clearly defined story lines, they're regarded as—"; her interviewer supplies the word *traitors,* and she does not object. Still, she adds aloofly, "Most white writers feel a strong sense of responsibility to promote, defend, and help black writers where possible." In her generation she acknowledges a number of them—poets, essayists, and activists—but among novelists she singles out the South African–born Botswanan Bessie Head (1937–1986).

Wole Soyinka finds Head's novels "very, very gripping, fascinating, challenging, really intellectually intriguing." She could not be more different from Gordimer in background, class, or idiom. In her indeterminate racial identity she is like a character set adrift by history, one who does not belong yet wants to find a place. She was born in South Africa, in the mental hospital to which her mother had been confined, in Pietermaritzburg, and was brought up in a colored family in Natal. By her early teens she knew these were not her people. Because she fictionalized her life, we cannot entirely trust her testimony, but her mother was a white, well-to-do South African whose relationship with a black servant produced this literary issue. The birth was concealed and the child grew up under the 1950 Immorality Act, which condemned her very existence as a mixed-race person. She studied, became a teacher and a magazine writer. In 1964 she was given permission to leave South Africa if she promised never to return (she had been politically active). She went to what was to become Botswana and made her home in Serowe, the parched setting of her best fiction, and was gaining recognition when she contracted hepatitis and died at the age of forty-eight.

*When Rain Clouds Gather* (1968) is her best-known novel, but *Maru* (1971) is also powerful. In these two books together the word *rain* appears 115 times with an unstaunchable thirst. The autobiographically rooted novel *A Question of Power* (1974) Alice Walker writes about with the conviction of one who owes it a particular debt. Head's characters, like her mother and father, whose love she respects and in her own life celebrates, are alive to one another as physical and spiritual beings. Her men have a developed feminine side, her women are strong and imaginative. Head at times resembles in her clarity of characterization the young James Baldwin, seeing through difference and stereotype. The first novel is based on her experience. The hero is Makhaya, who chooses political exile (he has been an activist) in a village in Botswana rather than stay in South Africa, his birthplace. The village, like Achebe's evolving community in *Things Fall Apart,* is at a point of transition, still tyrannized by a chieftain but beginning to open to new ideas, in this case about agriculture. He is brought to the village by a British volunteer, Gilbert, who is white. The story is of Makhaya's struggle, and his partner Paulina's, the challenges they face. Her little boy is a woodcarver, an artist by instinct and vocation, left to tend the cattle and meet a dreadful fate in the parched pastureland. Issues of asphyxiating custom, of power and color, pursue Gilbert into his new life; so do passion and grief. The carrion-eating jackal is observed with such clarity that it becomes pathetic and beautiful. Head is the accomplished chronicler of an ordinary world more credible than the ones Achebe makes, more lived in, less deliberately political. Though her style lacks the larger gestures of Zora Neale Hurston, there is a comparable integrity, a respect for the world. Even her melodrama is convincing. She, like Hurston, was troubled, an outsider who spent time in a mental hospital, an experience that in part informs *A Question of Power.* South Africa has endeavored to reclaim its prodigal daughter with posthumous honors, but she goes her own way, an intractable witness to common lives.

Her British publishers asked her, as a sequel to her first novel, to do something along the lines of *The Catcher in the Rye*. *Maru,* with its powerful protagonist, its heartbreak and serene conclusion, was not what they had in mind. Her writing reinvents realism, delivering in clear, neutral prose a world that fiction had not accommodated before. She avoids blurring the picture with sentiment or anger. Rain does come, but often too late. In *A Question of Power* the natural and social reality she has explored in the earlier novels is unsettled by psychological uncertainty as the protagonist, Elizabeth, a South African refugee, is victimized (or feels victimized) by the very person, the mission principal, who should be her protector. The novel is not only an account of one woman's isolation: Bessie Head entails a more general experience of alienation, into which flow images and states of mind readers might associate with an unstable world of common archetypes, magic, and illusion.

Alice (Malsenior) Walker (b. 1944) was born into a large Georgia family. Her father was a sharecropper and an unlucky dairy farmer, her mother worked on the land and in domestic service. Her grandfather was a storyteller. As a girl she was injured by a brother in a BB gun accident and lost an eye, not only because the family was poor but also because the injury was not treated with urgency. This altered her life and her attitudes: a cheerful child (who began writing secretly at the age of eight) became self-conscious and introverted and recovered self-confidence only as a young adult, away from the world she grew up in, and through her writing.

She was a natural student and attended Spelman College in Atlanta, where one of her professors was Howard Zinn, the author of *A People's History of the United States,* first published in 1980. Zinn she lists as one of the key influences on her life: he alerted her to the treachery of official history and showed her where corrective voices might be found by a careful study of erasures, by listening to dialects. She went on to Sarah Lawrence College in Bronxville, New York, then returned to the South and was active in the civil rights movement, in Mississippi particularly, where she lived with her Jewish civil rights lawyer husband (the first open mixed-race marriage in Mississippi) and where her now-estranged daughter, the writer and activist Rebecca Walker, was born. Her second novel is based in her own experience as an activist.

She wrote her first book of poems while still a student and started writing fiction. Early on she realized, she says, that she could not write except in locations congenial or appropriate to her characters, so real do they become in imagination. Characters, she insists, can dictate the books. Her sense of lending herself to her characters is anathema to writers with more formal intentions. Nadine Gordimer has "always thought bunkum the coy romantic claim of some writers that their characters take over, write themselves, etcetera."

There is little bunkum about her third novel *The Color Purple* (1982), awarded the 1983 Pulitzer Prize and the National Book Award for fiction. Indebted to the apparently artless slave narrative, the orality is translated into a one-way conversation, conducted through letters with a strong candor and address. In her protagonist Celie's experience, men, occasionally redeemable, threaten; women prove sisterly, motherly, nurturing. Celie is a black girl, uneducated but articulate in her own language, whose letters to "Dear God" are prayers, confessions, lyrical narratives. The correspondence from her sister, long withheld from her by a brutal husband, is conducted with an undefended trust. Her sister's style, correct and full of detail of the African world to which she has traveled, provides a stylistic and thematic counterpoint to Celie's narrow world, of which she gradually gains control.

The letters to God begin when Celie is fourteen and build the story of her life to the age of twenty. Suffering and abuse (by her stepfather, who removes her two children when they are born, and by her husband) are reported to God in the hope of some sign, reply, or deliverance. And deliverance comes: she finds a friend and love of an unexpected kind in her husband's abused mistress. There are tangents, Celie's story includes a wider social testimony. Shug Avery is a richly ambiguous figure, a source of energy and emotional and sexual liberation, with theological overtones, since she urges Celie to imagine God in a new way, to color Him or Her in differently. Revisiting the novel a decade after its first publication Walker speaks of its theology. The title relates to the color of morning glory (bindweed) flowers, of bruises, and of Celie's own sex, the site of her violation and liberation. Feisty, large, and assertive Sofia and aunt-in-law Kate are strong figures in a different sense. They enhance Celie's resolve to survive. And there is Nettie, her pretty younger sister who escapes into the wide world with a vocation that gives her faith and confidence. Celie's two children by her stepfather, whom she had assumed were dead, were adopted and Nettie by coincidence finds them. The book ends in a conflagration of coincidences and happiness that readers find either absurd or deeply moving.

Literary critics relate *The Color Purple* to the epistolary tradition of which—in English—Richardson's *Pamela* and *Clarissa* are the prime foremothers. Though Walker is highly literary, Richardson had no direct impact on her book. Celie engages in a one-sided correspondence with the Almighty to start with: her epistle is not a socializing instrument but a means of exploring isolation. When she begins to write to her sister, language and motive change, but the device remains confessional. Her novel belongs in the epistolary genre, but it hardly engages it *as* a genre. It has more in common with slave narratives. Walker is forthright about her debts, to Hurston, to Bessie Head, to Zinn. Richardson is not on the roster.

A year after *The Color Purple* Walker collected her personal, political, and literary essays into a book. The novel's success turned up its volume. *In Search of Our Mother's Gardens: Womanist Prose* (1984) helped restore Zora Neale Hurston to the map of modern fiction. The book's subtitle announced a polemic that builds and widens, as Adrienne Rich's *On Lies, Secrets and Silence* (1979) had done, a freed space for female action and art. When she was a child, Walker says, her own mother's garden was a place apart, a gendered space. From the symbolic memory of it she derives courage and an affirmative rhetoric. The first essay, "Saving the Life That Is Your Own," insists on the importance of role models (Kate Chopin, Hurston). They freed her from the directions she claims to have been pointed in, "toward a plethora of books by mainly white male writers who thought most women worthless if they didn't enjoy bullfighting or hadn't volunteered for the trenches in World War I."

The book's extended epigraph defines "womanist." It has a different inflection from "feminist," being at once less systematic, more cheerful, and racially specific. Walker, in a spoof act of lexicography teases out several meanings.

> 1. From *womanish*. (Opp. Of "girlish," i.e., frivolous, irresponsible, not serious.) A black feminist or feminist of color. From the black folk expression of mothers to female children, "You acting womanish," i.e., like a woman. Usually referring to outrageous, audacious, courageous or *willful* behavior. Wanting to know more and in greater depth than is considered "good" for one. Interested in grown-up doings. Acting grown up. Being grown up . . . Responsible. In charge. *Serious.*
>
> 2. *Also:* A woman who loves other women, sexually and/or non-sexually. Appreciates and prefers women's culture, women's emotional flexibility (values tears as natural counterbalance of laughter), and women's strength. Sometimes loves individual men, sexually and/or nonsexually. Committed to survival and wholeness of entire people, male *and* female. Not a separatist, except periodically, for health.

A womanist "loves music. Loves dance" and "is to feminist as purple to lavender." Her novel as a prime instance of womanism. This rhetoric marks a fruitful division within the American women's movement. Feminism had taken a form that excluded the social group from which Walker came. Her mother and grandmother "waited for a day when the unknown thing that was in them would be made known; but guessed, somehow in their darkness, that on the day of their revelation they would be long dead." As a result, "they walked, and even ran, in slow motion. For they were going nowhere immediate, and the future was not yet within their grasp." The book includes valuable assessments of Flannery O'Conner ("Beyond the Peacock"), of Jean Toomer's "divided life," and of Hurston, the subject of two essays, her spirit being the one Walker most eagerly conjures. There is a section on the civil rights movement, its importance and its legacy in the creative lives of people.

Walker returns to something like the epistolary form in *The Chicken Chronicles* (2011), built out of her website blog in which she recounts the development, in California where she now lives, of her community of chickens. Her most memorable bird is called Gertrude Stein. The human Stein seems to be behind the language of the *Chronicles,* though the earnestness is Walker's own: she is empowering "all the creatures and beings of the planet who have no voice." Gertrude is not alone: Rufus, Hortensia, Agnes of God, Babe, and the Gladyses all find a place in this sunlit coop.

# 42

# Making Space

Henry Handel Richardson, Patrick White, David Malouf, Peter Carey, Christina Stead,

Robertson Davies, Margaret Atwood, Michael Ondaatje, Maurice Shadbolt,

Janet Frame, Keri Hulme, Anita Desai, Salman Rushdie, Earl Lovelace

Judith Wright, the Australian poet, wrote in 1965 of the situation of the writer of European extraction among a citizenry, unlike Nadine Gordimer's, that consists of other displaced Europeans, colonists, frontiersmen, the descendants of transported felons and murderers, the indigenous people so reduced by illness and massacre that they are a minority, whatever their claims. At first the displaced Europeans' culture is one of nostalgia; things are named and colonies founded in fond retrospect, as if to conjure the world that was left behind—"the European mind in contact with a raw, bleak and alien life and landscape, struggling with it in a suffering whose only consummation and reconciliation is found in death." This is the recurring theme of the first Australian writers, of Henry Handel Richardson and Patrick White, founding fathers of Australian fiction.

Except that Henry Handel Richardson was in fact Ethel Florence Lindesay Richardson (1870–1946). In her own person, she was a champion tennis player. Her choice of an unambiguously male pseudonym suggests that she was writing in a conservative culture, even though in Britain, where she ultimately settled and was published, many successful women authors published under their real names. It may have been that she wanted to explore themes improper for a woman. Richardson was born into a once well-to-do family in East Melbourne and enjoyed a peripatetic childhood. As a teenager she was sent to boarding school, the subject of her second novel, the first significant one, *The Getting of Wisdom* (1910), with its unsettling and intense understanding of adolescent sexual ambivalence and desire. For H. G. Wells and for Doris Lessing it is her most accessible book. Lessing placed it "on the shelf with the classic school novels."

She proved a talented musician, and in 1888 she and her sister traveled with their widowed mother to Europe for musical education. Her first novel, *Maurice Guest* (1908), "was a bold book then for man or woman writer," Doris Lessing says. "It is about erotic obsession . . . if it is a good read no one could say it is an easy one, for it is too painful." It is set in Leipzig, where Richardson attended the conservatory. Richardson married a Scottish student of literature who made a distinguished career as the first chair of German at University College, London. Shortly before the First World War she returned to Australia to investigate her family history for the novel trilogy *The Fortunes of Richard Mahony* (1930), consisting of *Australia Felix* (1917), *The Way Home* (1925), and *Ultima Thule* (1929). The protagonist, a doctor based on her father, who died of syphilis when she was nine, slowly succumbs to an unspecified nervous disorder. He is an unwilling exile, and his death and its consequences for his family—which is like her own family, in an Australian setting—make for a powerful work, indebted to some extent to Zola and applauded by Sinclair Lewis. Doris Lessing reads it as unconventional tragedy, the hero "stands in for England, Europe, the Old Country's values," the book is "dense as a plum pudding, nineteenth-century in feel, slow-moving, contemplative, while we watch fates and destinies reveal themselves. People who enjoy Trollope would find themselves at home here: the same sense of quiet and patient irony, the same understanding of weakness."

No wonder. The language is visceral, unsentimental, and credible. *Australia Felix* begins with a local disaster. "In a shaft on the Gravel Pits, a man had been buried alive. At work in a deep wet hole, he had recklessly omitted to slab the walls of a drive; uprights and tailors yielded under the lateral pressure, and the rotten earth collapsed, bringing down the roof in its train. The digger fell forward on his face, his ribs jammed across his pick, his arms pinned to his sides, nose and mouth pressed into the sticky mud as into a mask; and over his defenseless body, with a roar that burst his ear-drums, broke stupendous masses of earth." Each character has a distinctive language of memory; many long to be elsewhere. Her imagination stayed in Australia and retained its alienation after she returned to England and remained there.

Richardson and her sister were suffragettes. Perhaps because of her sexual equivocations she retained her pseudonym. Like Verdi's librettist Boito, the poet and dramatist Gabriele d'Annunzio, and the dancer Isadora Duncan, she fell in love with the actress Eleonora Duse, one of the great performers of her time. After her husband's death Richardson lived with a female intimate, and at her death her personal archive was purged and many papers burned. She is an enigmatic, absent founder for an emerging literature.

Judd, the deserter, murderer, and survivor, declares at the end of Patrick White's *Voss*, "You see, if you live and suffer long enough in a place, you do not leave it altogether. Your spirit is still there." That presence will become legend and the legend "will be written down, eventually, by those who have been troubled by it." He is like Nostromo: even before we meet him, Edmund Bonner, playing with a paper knife, repeats hearsay about Judd's "physical strength and moral integrity." He arrived in Australia a transported convict, and is therefore "an improviser," a talent necessary for survival. Stories that are shaped in and by a place, however alien, eventually find language and a mouth to speak them. White reflected on his "struggle to create completely fresh forms out of the rocks and sticks of words." He takes dictation from the landscape.

Patrick (Victor Martindale) White (1912–1990), Australia's first winner of the Nobel Prize in Literature (1973), is enigmatic, but not in the ways Richardson was. He traveled in the opposite direction, a hard, harsh journey "home." Australia was not eager to welcome him. White's parents were Australian as undoubtedly as anyone of their class and background could be. But Patrick was born in Knightsbridge, London; his parents moved with him to Australia when he was six months old. In Australia as a boy he started writing. Asthmatic, he became a solitary child, reading and writing poetry and plays. At his mother's whim, he was returned to school in England. Between school and university his father allowed him to return home and work on a great sheep estate as a "macaroon." He spent two years there, and although the work was hard and the landscape open and empty, he started writing "behind a closed door" in the evenings, apart from his fellow jackeroos. He went up to Kings College, Cambridge. His first novel was published in 1939, and the following year he joined the Royal Air Force, serving all over the Middle East in World War II. He returned to Australia in 1948, urged by his Greek lifemate Manoly Lascaris, "this small Greek of immense moral strength who became the central mandala in my life's hitherto messy design." They met at a tea party in July 1941, when the Baron Charles de Menasce introduced Lascaris to Flight-Lieutenant Patrick White. The baron was a canny matchmaker. White and Lascaris made an unconventional pair, the Australian tall, gaunt, arrogant, remote, the Greek congenial, welcoming, industrious, and apologetic. Lascaris organized White's life and time and made the books possible, a fact that at times the novelist acknowledged with resentment and gratitude.

When White returned home, he could not understand the Australian accent, nor could the Australians understand him: he talked English and posh. His first three books were published and began to make a mark in Britain and the United States. His reputation grew abroad but at home he was resisted. A quiet, difficult man, he was not liked, but his books inscribe the Australian landscapes in modern fiction. With his fourth book he began to be grudgingly accepted as an odd variety of native.

His 1981 autobiographical meditation *Flaws in the Glass: A Self-Portrait* is a key that "fits the lock of the creative process," Nadine Gordimer says. It recounts his formative odyssey. "I was most myself," he says, "in the neo-Gothic house my parents had rented for the holidays: no connection with any other part of my life, yet in it life seemed to be forming." In this house he experienced the instability of the "I," expressing it in a scene that essentializes his style at its hallucinatory best: the readers are so close that the reflection is their own, then suddenly the author reclaims it. "There was the Long Room, at one end of the garden, at the other the great gilded mirror, all blotches and dimples and ripples. I fluctuated in the watery glass; according to the light I retreated into the depths of the aquarium, or trembled in the foreground like a thread of pale-green samphire. Those who thought they knew me were ignorant of the creature I scarcely knew myself." Walking through London he watched people askance: "I devoured the arrogance of those who had nothing to fear, insolent, tailored men, and their long lean women bleeding under cloche hats, furs thrown open on saltcellars and meager breasts." A brutally eroticized evocation of the English civilized *sauvage:* from these figures he teased out his own snobberies.

Though he was not close to his mother, he said that "he inhabited her" from time to time, like a room in a lodging house, again with that sense of intimacy and emptiness. He took his values from a middle-class background that was hostile to everything he was himself; he knew, with a violent negative capability, what it is to be an evildoer, and also one to whom evil is done. He liked Scandinavia's bleaker literature, Ibsen and Strindberg.

His first novel, *Happy Valley* (1939), made small impact, did not find an American publisher, and was lost sight of with the beginning of the war. In the African landscape where he served, he grew homesick for the Australian. In "the graveyard of postwar London" and in his travels he was writing *The Aunt's Story* (1948). Whatever its successes abroad, in Australia it was unread or misread and he felt more foreign and out of place than he had before. His and Manoly's efforts at farming were not unsuccessful, but they learned on the job, breeding Schnauzers, and there was little time for writing. It was not until 1955 that *The Tree of Man,* originally entitled *A Life Sentence on Earth,* was published. In an intellectually conservative Australia his breach with conventional naturalism was ridiculed. It was harder for Australians to resist *Voss* (1957), the book that made his originality and stature clear, though a newspaper review was headlined "Australia's most Unreadable Novelist."

Many Australian novels follow the *Voss* pattern, starting with transported characters whose guilt is a given, their redemption the theme. Voss himself is an explorer keen to cross Australia and make some kind of sense of it. His patron is Mr. Bonner, uncle of Laura Trevelyan, a newcomer and an orphan. They forge a complex relationship and communicate through visions, a kind of telepathic Skype. The complementary themes of external and internal discovery are set in motion. The unforgiving landscapes through which Voss and his party move are literal, mappable spaces that recall the wild, heightened landscapes of Cormac

McCarthy's *Blood Meridian* in scale, without the ugly human element, scalps and massacres. There are, however, divisions and deaths. The expedition divides into two groups, one led by Voss and one by Judd. The sole survivor is Judd.

In *Voss* Anthony Burgess sees White allied with the great Russian novelists. The scale of the narrative, its moral seriousness and risky deviations from naturalism put it in a category apart from the Anglophone literature of the day: "In *Voss* the grumbling big dog of that continent has been tamed into a highly individual artistic vision." And there is universality, he adds, about the very provincialism of the New South Wales setting of *Riders in the Chariot* (1961). What draws the poet and novelist Patricia Beer is the gap between the order and elegance of the writing and the formal and thematic scale of the enterprise. The writing is a delicate vehicle for its heavy matter. She risks calling *The Fringe of Leaves* (1976) epic and considers the skill with which White deploys minor characters, using them here to set the scene and provide a prologue, in such a way as to give, with great thrift, a sense of the larger world the action will move through. The minor character scenes are perfect, but undetachable, short stories embedded in the larger narrative. Each of them "implies the world" from whatever periphery it speaks.

Of his books his own favorites were *The Aunt's Story,* which Australian readers came to like when it was reissued; *The Solid Mandala* (1966), which was more or less immediately accepted and is his most obliquely personal book; and *The Twyborn Affair* (1979), in which the landscapes of the jackeroo years that drew him back to Australia are most clearly inscribed. When *The Solid Mandala* appeared, he said, "it was realized I might be something they had to put up with." "Pigeon-colored" Mrs. Poulter and Mrs. Dun are on a bus bouncing through dusty countryside. They have different accents, different speech, they speak leisurely. Their theme is verandas, exposure, and privacy. Suddenly Mrs. Poulter declares, "The Mister Browns have got a veranda," and the protagonists are introduced: Waldo, competent, reasonable, with a strong sense of superiority, and Arthur, an innocent, a seeming half-wit, with more to him than the women reckon with. Then, there in the road, the bus passes them, these complementary figures, hand in hand, mutually dependent, White's most Faulknerian creations. *The Sound and the Fury* informs this book, with its changing points of views and voices in the four sections, just as *Nostromo* informs *Voss.* This is not to say the books are imitative, but they do exist on a similar scale and explore some of the same psychological territory.

*The Twyborn Affair,* with great seriousness and at greater length, takes the kinds of risk Woolf took in *Orlando.* The three sections have different settings, and the same soul passes through three characters. In a pre–First World War villa on the French Riviera, Eudoxia is presented; at the sheep station at the foot of the

Snowy Mountains, the scene of White's jackeroo experience, Eudoxia turns into Eddie; and then we are in London in the period when White was there, just before World War II, and our transmigrating soul has moved into the body of Eadith. The structure allows White to evoke a series of binaries, those of sex, of power, rural versus urban, practical as against imaginative. It is his most amusing novel and one of the cruelest. When it was shortlisted for the Booker Prize, he asked for it to be withdrawn to give younger writers the opportunity.

Almost a quarter of a century after his death, White's work still sparks debate. The old curmudgeon is spoken of familiarly as "Patrick." Gay writers revel in the fact that the founding fathers of Australian literature were both homosexual. White is a patron saint, his legacy enabling because he was himself, in his life, his culture, and in the scale of his art, inimitable. His dominance did not stifle, though he may have set the bar too high for most. David Malouf and his contemporaries found it hard to pull free of his gravitational field. The huge empty continent in which Voss perishes requires expansive imaginations to explore and contain. White clears a path for Malouf and Peter Carey, for Rodney Hall and Randolph Stow, thanks not to a confining style but to a liberating, unsentimental individualism. What they have not approached is the sense of a transcendence that underwrites the compelling breaks with naturalism, so that things that are true yet impossible happen and are believed.

Once a national literature is confidently established and the issues of language and identity have been broached (they can never be settled), writers may resist the pressure to continue arguing corners that are no longer corners and fighting battles where the enemy has vanished. The writers for whom White made space were empowered by his work. White will, in another fifty years, become a classic. At present his work resists veneration. He has become a writers' writer. David (George Joseph) Malouf (b. 1934) and Peter (Philip) Carey (b. 1943) are among his principal and very different beneficiaries. Both are immensely prolific across a range of genres.

Malouf, of Lebanese-Christian and Portuguese-Sephardic ancestry, was born and grew up in Brisbane, the setting of his first novel, *Johnno* (1975), about coming of age during the Second World War when Brisbane was a critical international naval port. His second novel explored First World War themes, and his third, *The Great World* (1990), touched on both, tracing the relations of two Australians who meet after the fall of Singapore and are detained by the Japanese in a labor camp. This novel is a major achievement, on a Patrick White scale, though the history he reports is not remote, indeed part of it has been lived through by the narrator. Digger Kean and Vic Curran are complementary, the one calm, thoughtful, and contented, the other fiery, pushy, in flight from a meager childhood, and professionally a player in the money markets of Sydney. They survive the Great Depression only to face the war. Malouf navigates back and forth in time, counterpointing plot and story. The descriptions of war are compelling, but the book's strongest element is its understanding of character and the relations between men and women. He has understood from Lawrence how energies flow within relationships. He likes "that play between movement and stillness in the novel." The scene in which Vic bathes Digger's diseased legs in a Thai river is charged with love; the celebration of common life, its value recognized from the abyss of war, is democratic and visionary. He has a sense of people living in space, a sense of distances and their effects on action, on reflection.

Such narrative assurance, insight, and tact result from a protracted immersion in fiction. Malouf was a precocious child, tackling on the threshold of his teens the complicated narrative structure of *Bleak House*. Part of the joy of reading, even when he was little, was the libidinal excitement he got from relationships and passions evoked. He went to university and taught briefly in Australia but in 1955 began a diasporic life, in England, Tuscany, and back in Australia. In Tuscany he could be private, living as a gay man and writing without the prying of the media or the social interruptions endemic in a cosmopolitan literary life.

*Remembering Babylon* (1993) drew on nineteenth-century Australian history and built on the tradition of White's historical novels, exploring in particular the theme of enforced exile. He prepared the libretto for the operatic adaptation of Patrick White's *Voss*. Like White he is irreducible to type, he will not represent any party or ideology. He admires White's resistances, his abandoning the action plot in favor of a style that teases out of inarticulate characters what they actually mean in a language subtle enough not to entrap them, that "gives the language of feeling to people who don't have it themselves."

That language is in danger of being lost as White's books become harder to find. "I took it for granted that Patrick White was known internationally to be a great writer," said Peter Carey. "I never would have imagined that in 2006 I could walk around bookstores in New York and be unable to find a copy of his work." Carey's own reputation rides high. He (with *Oscar and Lucinda* in 1988 and *True History of the Kelly Gang* in 2001), J. M. Coetzee, and Hilary Mantel have won the Booker Prize twice. He has won the major Australian Miles Franklin Award three times (White would have equaled or exceeded that record had he not bowed out of the prize stakes to make space for newcomers).

Carey as a child was solemn and overly industrious. He did not have Malouf's early sense of vocation. His hardworking parents, who did not read his fiction or know what to make of the direction his erratic life took, had the General Motors dealership in Bacchus Marsh, Victoria, Australia. He spent six years as a boarder at a prestigious private school they struggled to afford. He was sent away at the age of eleven, and this, he half jokes, is responsible for the "string of orphan characters" in his work. "I have the good fortune that my own personal trauma matches my country's great historical trauma. Our first fleet was cast out from 'home.' Nobody really wanted to be there. Convicts, soldiers were all going to starve or survive together." Then the state orphaned the aboriginal population, "through racial policies, stealing indigenous kids from their communities and trying to breed out their blackness . . . Then there were all these kids sent from England to Dr. Barnardo's Homes . . . institutions for homeless and destitute children, some of them run in the most abusive, horrible circumstances."

He started a science degree at Monash University, Melbourne, but an accident and general boredom brought this intellectual adventure to an end. At university he had to dissimulate because he did not take the trouble to understand the lectures. "I was faking my physics experiments, which is very exhausting." Just as boarding school made orphans imaginable, university taught him about fraud and dissimulation. It was a valuable education. *True History of the Kelly Gang* (2000), which has sold 2 million copies worldwide, took the form of a letter from the Australian outlaw-cum-hero Ned Kelly, a horse thief and bank robber who was hanged at the age of twenty-six. Then there was the novel on the Ern Malley literary hoax, *My Life as a Fake* (2003), and *Theft: A Love Story* (2006), in which (echoes of *The Solid Mandala*) the voices of Michael "Butcher" Boone, painter and forger, and his mentally disabled brother Hugh, are plaited into a narrative about the corrupt international art market. Such novels require research and negative capability, but also, obliquely, a good deal of authorial self. Updike admired the accomplishment of Carey's impersonation, its idiomatic and cadential credibility.

Carey and his first wife, married at university, became dropouts, and he went into advertising for five years. He met other writers and developed an interest in fiction. He read modern classics: Joyce and Beckett, Kafka, Faulkner and Greene, Márquez. By 1969 he had written five unpublished novels and left Australia in a state of euphoric confusion. When he returned it was to reenter advertising, divorce, and join the Starlight Community, an alternative-lifestyle group.

Carey had now become a widely published storywriter. His first published novel, *Bliss,* for which he received his first Miles Franklin Award, appeared in 1981. Unlike in his earlier attempts, in this book he adopted a simple form, something starting novelists find it hard to risk. Written from life, heightened by comedy, it is about an advertising executive who has a near-death experience when he suffers a heart attack and after being resuscitated comes to see the world, his marriage, his children, and his work colleagues, for what they are, treacherous and self-serving. He is redeemed by the kind of woman who often redeems men in heterosexual comic novels, an ample, generous woman who, as a *fille de joie* with a heart of honey (her name is Honey), understands sex and, crucially, transcendence. In 1985 his first international success, the Booker-shortlisted novel *Illywhacker,* was published, a comic "life story" of a con man told in bite-sized, staccato chapters because he is old and engagingly, exhaustingly deceitful. "My name is Herbert Badgery. I am a hundred and thirty-nine years old and something of a celebrity. They come and look at me and wonder how I do it." Ten novels followed, each quite different from the one before.

Carey returned to New York, taught creative writing, and wrote. His novels travel widely but Australia remains his chief focus. Asked if his fiction had a single mission, he said, "There was a stage where I might have said, 'the invention of my country,' but I think that as time goes on it's a much looser bundle. Those things are for other people to see, not for me." As the work progresses, Carey confronts increasingly difficult subjects, writing and rewriting his stories until they come out right. In *Jack Maggs* (1997) he sets himself an impossible challenge, squaring up to Dickens and the nineteenth century. He had not read Dickens but was inspired by the critic Edward Said writing about Magwitch, the *Great Expectations* convict, Pip's unexpected benefactor. Carey, no lover of nineteenth-century fiction, found his way to Dickens via *Pickwick* and arrived at *Great Expectations* and Magwitch, "a classic Australian figure. There he is, transported to Australia, a free man after serving his seven-year sentence. He is an Englishman, but only as long as he doesn't go to England." And yet he risks all to return to his fiction, his young gentleman Pip, his life's work and his disappointment.

If it is a historical novel, the history it addresses is the present through the past. It is not pastiche or retrospect. "To label it historical fiction is to risk misunderstanding its context," Carey says. That context is Australia, the penal colony that launches a nation at the expense of its aboriginal people. "We grew up denying it, of course. Certainly it never occurred to us that the land was stolen, or that we had anything to do with the agony of the transported convicts. When we imagined who we were, we somehow imagined ourselves on the soldier's end of the whip." This "false consciousness" was his subject, one that besets postcolonial writers in particular ways.

Patrick White inscribed the Australian landscape; Carey has inscribed versions of "the Australian character" that emerge in history and legend. There is hero in chief Ned Kelly, hanged by the neck for killing a police officer. Among others, he lists "Burke and Wills, the explorers who got lost and died" (shades of *Voss*). Then, "Phar Lap, who was really a New Zealand horse but we think of him as Australian, came to this country and was nobbled and died. Gallipoli, our great national story, is completely about loss." He adds, "Landscape forms character, of course, and ours is a killer. In America the narrative is, Go west.

You might eat a few people on the way, but basically it will be wealth and success. We just get lost and we die." He is one with his folk: "We have an affection for outcasts and oddballs. My stories and novels tend to fit into that tradition." He says his novels are not rooted in autobiography, much as journalists wish they were. "They'll be looking at Ned Kelly—what's the real story? *My Life as a Fake*—they want the historical story, the poetry hoax. They'll want to look at what's personal." He creates templates for readers, not personal confessions.

A year after White's first novel appeared, Christina Stead (1902–1983) published *The Man Who Loved Children* (1940). The American poet Randall Jarrell reintroduced it to American readers in 1965. She is among the most internationally popular twentieth-century Australian writers. Here she tells the story of the dysfunctional Samuel Clemens Pollit family. Sam, the title's "man" and the *paterfamilias,* is an idealist so emphatic and so detached from reality as to be comic and monstrous in equal degrees. He is based on Stead's own father. Henny, Sam's wife, a crusty snob unable to handle money, resembles her mother. The parents' lives are complex, unstable, unhappy.

Doris Lessing spoke of Stead's "most special gift: there has never been a writer who can take you so strongly into a room, or a house, or a street that you are immediately a part of it." The lost world of *The Man Who Loved Children* is real without nostalgia, because the author did not long to return. It can be read, says Lessing, "for its evocation of a lost world as much as for its great virtues. For it is a great novel, one that is always being rediscovered and then for some reason slips away out of sight, and then is found again." While Stead is, Lessing insists, "a great writer," with a list of unique novels to her name, "each one unlike the work of any other writer and unlike each other," it is her variety and eccentricity that keep her from being "finally accepted into the company of great writers."

Stead married and emigrated from Australia. Originally her fifth novel was set in Australia, but her American publisher was unwilling to risk such exoticism, and it was reset in America. Mary McCarthy reviewed it severely, noting anachronisms and a tenuous sense of American life. But family, not American life, was Stead's true subject and the treachery of sentimentalism her theme. An unintended theme might be the delicate connection between narrative intention and setting.

Born and buried in Sidney, Stead spent much of her life abroad, in Britain and the United States, until 1968 when her Marxist businessman husband, with whom she left Australia in 1928, died, and she returned to whatever roots were left. She wrote fifteen novels, some opaque, others highly readable. The occasions for some of her satire have faded, but her characterization is acute and the satire does not resort to caricature or off-the-peg psychology. As a Marxist— her first novel was entitled *Seven Poor Men of Sydney* (1934)—she sees characters embodying the socially formative and transformative characteristics. Already in 1943 she was running a novel-writing workshop at New York University. She also wrote scripts for Hollywood.

Angela Carter admired *The Man Who Loved Children*. She was also fond of *Cotter's England* (1967), Stead's one novel with an English setting. The book, in the United States titled *Dark Places of the Heart*, is set partly in Gateshead (the "Bridgehead" of the novel). She had trouble with the local language but a native friend with an effective transliterative ear helped her. This friend was Anne Dooley, a model for Nellie Cotter, the book's heroine. Carter also admired *A Little Tea, a Little Chat* (1948) and *For Love Alone* (1945), which she said were as good as *The Man Who Loved Children*. *Letty Fox: Her Luck* (1946) found a wide readership in the Anglophone world.

Jonathan Franzen lists some of the hurdles the reader of *The Man Who Loved Children* encounters. It is a long book (Jarrell compares Stead to Tolstoy). But readers soon learn the language of the Samuel Clemens Pollit family. And they laugh at wrong things, the old models of discipline, when children and not parents were punished. "The book intrudes on our better-regulated world like a bad dream from the grandparental past. Its idea of a happy ending is like no other novel's, and probably not at all like yours." Sam Pollit is a monster of projective permissiveness: he demands that his children acknowledge him day and night and in all their actions. They are lights he switches on and shines through. In time Sam Pollit will become the subject of Donald Barthelme's *The Dead Father*. The sooner the better, one cannot help saying: he is the apotheosis of New World optimism and innocence. The "Man" in *The Man Who Loved Children* does not love his wife, nor she him. They speak different languages to the children, planting the confusions and polarities for which parents are generally responsible. Things go bad, then worse, between them. Stead wanted to write with the breadth and authority of a man. This novel is close to life-writing, and the narrator and author cannot be pried apart without damage to both. The daughter Louie gains strength, breaks taboos, finds her feet. In 1940 it was possible to write with the nerves exposed, with laughter, experimenting with voice.

—·—

Although each year Margaret Atwood is named as a contender, the emergence of Canadian literature was marked in 2013 by the award of a Nobel Prize to the short story writer Alice Munroe. The Canadian novel still lives in hope. Canada's proximity to the United States and its colonial British legacies, complicated by the French, make the postcolonial situation exasperating for Canadian writers keen to assert and theorize their otherness. The desire not to be rolled into American literature and at the same time to affirm the distance of an ocean from the colonial grandmother survives. Canada possesses distinctive novelists, born and adoptive, and a literary scene as savage and political as any in the world.

(William) Robertson Davies (1913–1995), in ambition and the scale of his work, is a substantial Canadian writer. He came from a newspaper family, studied in Canada and at Balliol College, Oxford, and built a Canadian media business, with newspapers and radio stations; he was an editor, a journalist, a comic journalist under the pseudonym Samuel Marchbanks, a playwright, an innovative academic, and a novelist with almost a dozen novels to his credit. His novels are grouped into trilogies: the Salterton trilogy (1951–1958), about the challenge of making and maintaining a cultural life in provincial Canada and centers on the survival of a newspaper: he was writing from the life; the Deptford trilogy (1970–1975), into which his Jungian concerns are decanted, and where the provincial Canadian world comes alive in books that can stand alone but work best together; and the Cornish trilogy (1981–1988), written after his academic years were over, and tracing the life and legacy of Francis Cornish in a kind of modern allegory deep-rooted in medieval forms. Two further novels were published, and for symmetry they are referred to as the Toronto Trilogy: he was working on the third at the time of his death.

In his later years, with a flowing mane, a profuse white beard, and a quizzical smile, he looked a wise man and was given Sir Walter Scott's sobriquet, "the wizard of the North." His wizardry was of the Merlin variety. In *The Rebel Angels* (1981), first of the Cornish trilogy, he writes: "What really shapes and conditions and makes us is somebody only a few of us ever have the courage to face: and that is the child you once were, long before formal education ever got its claws into you—that patient, all-demanding child who wants love and power and can't get enough of either and who goes on raging and weeping in your spirit till at last your eyes are closed and all the fools say, 'Doesn't he look peaceful?' It is those pent-up, craving children who make all the wars and all the horrors and all the art and all the beauty and discovery in life, because they are trying to achieve what lay beyond their grasp before they were five years old." This unacknowledged child judges man from a removed plane. Davies is impatient with reason and common sense: there was more in heaven and earth than such children could dream of. He explored and expressed feelings, artistic risk excited him, but he fell short of achieving formal originality because, though tragedy shadows it, his is a comic instinct. "The thing about comedy that I greatly value is that it is infinitely harder to fake than tragedy. I have not often pulled out the *vox humana* and the *voix céleste* stops, but I know I have made quite a few people laugh, and that is not the easiest thing to do." By contrast, "it is extremely easy to be gloomy." He was a performer as a lecturer, a public reciter of his work, solicitous of his readers as of his audiences. Margaret Atwood quotes him: "Give me a copper coin and I will tell you a golden tale."

Anthony Burgess admired *The Rebel Angels*. As a Canadian campus novel it is literally Rabelaisian, in that it includes a lost manuscript by Rabelais, which is found and then stolen. John Parlabane bequeaths "my arsehole, and all necessary integuments thereto appertaining, to the Faculty of Philosophy," for the senior professor to blow through each New Year's Day, issuing "a rich fruity note," his farewell to the world as he sets off in search of the Great Perhaps, which we encountered in *Gargantua and Pantagruel*. The book is written in a spirit of wildly playful hyperbole. The body and its functions are celebrated. Davies advocates—though that word smacks of deliberation, of system, and he is not a systematic writer—feeling over reason, risk over the promptings of common sense.

Among Davies's favorite writers was Victor Hugo, "enviably self-indulgent." His digressiveness, his enthusiasms please him, as does the flow of the story, the reluctance to turn back and revise, or cut. Unlike Carey, he loves the nineteenth-century novel, Balzac especially, the abundance, the whole world of it; and Dickens, Thackeray, and Trollope. He turns to Nabokov who, Davies says, "thought that the most important element in a novelist's armory was what he called by a Russian word, *shamanstvo*. It means the enchanter-quality. The word *shaman* is familiar to everyone." The enchanter may have "what critics call a 'bad literary style'" and still enchant.

His way of writing was straightforward. "I know that many writers—Joyce Cary for instance—compose the principal scenes of a novel before putting the connective work around it; other people work backward and do all sorts of interesting things, but I don't. I just go from start to finish, and that's the first draft." He was a newspaperman and wrote fast, blotting only when necessary—the furriness of his prose is as much an aspect of style as of haste. His sense of character is realistic, even if his sense of reality sometimes isn't. In him Canada has its "great nineteenth century novelist."

With Margaret Eleanor Atwood (b. 1939) the century has decisively turned. "Around the age of seven I wrote a play. The protagonist was a giant; the theme was crime and punishment; the crime was lying, as befits a future novelist; the punishment was being squashed to death by the moon." She became zealous in making the case for Canadian writing as a definable and viable entity among Anglophone literatures. She started out with the disadvantages of her gender and nationality. In her teens she resolved, "As soon as I could, I was going to hit Paris and become incomprehensible." Then she read the contemporary Parisians. In Alain Robbe-Grillet she was prepared to applaud the abandonment of moral implications, but that seemed to entail abandoning plot and character too. She read him in the late 1950s: "It was sort of like reading a cafeteria tray before you've put anything on it." She liked his essays but gave up on the novels: "Nothing happens, and there aren't any jokes." Authors may avoid judging characters but readers will not, perhaps cannot.

Atwood brought her imagination home and built up her authority by writing noticeable fiction, accompanying it with essays and lectures addressing a general literate reader. It is partly thanks to her work as advocate and polemicist that not only the names but the nationality and the connections among Alice Munro, Carol Shields, Michael Ondaatje, and Jay Macpherson are known. She wrote *Survival: A Thematic Guide to Canadian Literature* (1972), a foundation text in Canadian Studies, though schematic and now out of date, and *Strange Things: The Malevolent North in Canadian Literature* (1995).

Substantial writers of a Canadian persuasion are omitted from her canon. That may be because they did not fight what she saw as a necessary battle. What makes her criticism distinctly Canadian is the debt to her mentor Northrop Frye (1912–1991), with whom she studied at the University of Toronto's Victoria College at about the time he was working on *Anatomy of Criticism* (1957). Atwood took it upon herself to instrumentalize and politicize his theories. He was himself an advocate and regular critic of Canadian writing, which in the end he believed (as she was to believe also) could be characterized in general terms by its themes: a fear of nature, the history of colonization and settlement, and a sense of community. For him these themes might develop.

"As long as you continue to write," Atwood says, "you continue to explore the work of writers who have preceded you." Crucially she seeks to create a distance between the literary concerns of Canada and those of the United States, and secondarily those of Canada and those of the United Kingdom. Her fiction does this in setting, theme, and political angle and in its growing ecological insistence. Born in Ottawa, Atwood was the daughter of a distinguished entomologist. Her interest in the human organism and its habitats began early, her father taking her on excursions in the backwoods. She began her formal schooling at eighth-grade level. She was already up to speed, and was writing. At Victoria College she majored in English, with minors in French and philosophy, then went to Harvard to do graduate work in American literature. She collected her MA and completed two additional years of study toward a PhD.

The overwhelming sense of the United States as a political, economic, and above all cultural power unsettled her. Many close friends were American, and the United States provided her main readership. She began by defining the difference of Canada and ended, in April 2003, by writing "A Letter to America," defining instead, at the start of the Iraq War, the difference of the United States. It felt to her to be rolling down the incline toward the dystopian Republic of

Gilead she had created in her Booker Prize–shortlisted novel *The Handmaid's Tale* (1985). So she begins, "Dear America: This is a difficult letter to write, because I'm no longer sure who you are." That "you" had almost become her "me," so much culture was shared; "You were the amazing trio, Hemingway, Fitzgerald, and Faulkner, who traced the dark labyrinths of your hidden heart. You were Sinclair Lewis and Arthur Miller, who, with their own American idealism, went after the sham in you, because they thought you could do better."

But a difference emerges. "You put God on the money, though, even then. You had a way of thinking that the things of Caesar were the same as the things of God: that gave you self-confidence. You have always wanted to be a city upon a hill, a light to all nations, and for a while you were." The Canadians are the Romanized Gaels, looking over the wall at the real Romans. And what do they see? Apart from the invasion of Iraq, "You're gutting the Constitution . . . You're running up a record level of debt . . . You're torching the American economy." Each fact is demonstrated, the consequences are enumerated. She enjoins them to summon their sleeping patriots: "Summon them now, to stand with you, to inspire you, to defend the best in you. You need them." It was a boldly polemical sermon-letter. An oblique and decisive declaration of independence.

Independence entails realignment. When she first read Virginia Woolf, specifically *To the Lighthouse,* she did not get it at all. She felt an adolescent impatience with the content, the social tones, the pace. Rereading it, she experienced a series of epiphanies. "How could I have missed the resonance of Mr. Ramsay's Tennyson quotation, coming as it does like a prophecy of the First World War?" And Lily and Virginia were one, and time dissolves the solidest things, and much else. Here was a crucial foremother. In her turn, over time Atwood has become, if not Virginia Woolf, at least a kind of Canadian Mrs. Ramsay with her own floppy hat and her own recalcitrant garden, missing the children.

Every one of her novels, she says, "begins with a *what if,* and then sets forth its axioms." She knows her work well, she knows where she wants it to fit generically. Referring to *Oryx and Crake* (2003) as, like *The Blind Assassin* (2000), "speculative fiction," not science fiction, she tries to protect her books from the taint of "science fiction," a genre she despises. Later she relents and allows them to be described as "social science fiction."

Orwell's fiction, as much as his essays, marked her: the major novels had arguments that they dramatized and worked out, and *The Handmaid's Tale* was Orwellian in consistency, though her dystopia is from the female point of view. The enemy to the powers that be is "ordinary human decency." Ends do not justify means: the means inevitably define the ends. She also felt the impact of *Darkness at Noon* and of *Brave New World* in the late 1940s, early 1950s. Here too was speculative fiction, though it was not exploratory. The stories she tells come out of the dark, she does not know what she will find as she draws them out. Or they are darkness and she travels through. Not knowing in advance is crucial to the process, which is of finding out, and the surprise of discovery. It puts one in mind of trips to the underworld to bring back, say, Eurydice. Less classically, she likens writing a novel to "wrestling a greased pig in the dark."

Her first successful wrestling match was *The Edible Woman* (1969), which she described as proto-feminist. Her protagonist Marian begins to imbue the food she eats with human attributes and, unable to cannibalize, starts falling apart, even as she feels her fiancée is eating her alive. Atwood makes much play with stereotypes and symbolism. Her first major international novel, however, was *The Handmaid's Tale*. Given her hatred of science fiction, she must have been troubled when she received the Arthur C. Clarke Award for that novel. Offred ("Of Fred," her master's chattel) finds herself in a bleak adult fairy-tale in the Republic of Gilead, where feminism is no longer even a memory and the pro-tagonist's helpless fertility means that she is farmed out, a handmaid in a sterile household, who exists to produce a baby. In this "speculative fiction," nothing is impossible. Offred's starched blinkers keep her looking forward only on a dystopian, totalitarian world. This is a story not of action but of inaction; its drama lies in intensification, wrought through isolation and reflection. There is release in Offred's submission to feeling and to its narrative consequences. A complex futuristic narrative, it is close enough to the present (the coup against the American government and constitution is well within living memory) for the contrivance to work at once as science-fiction fantasy and as satire.

Atwood's most important novel to date is *The Blind Assassin* (2000), which won the Booker Prize. It has the narrative complexity of allegory in places, ask-ing to be read on different levels. John Updike found the book far too long and too self-conscious: "A nagging sense of gimmickry, amid all those spinning wheels of plot, accompanies our awed and often delighted awareness of Atwood's mas-tery of period detail, of costume and setting, of landscape and sky . . . etc." There is no denying the local pleasure of the book, but the overall form is a problem. The animation of some of her characters is her exuberance, not theirs. They are stock figures vigorously drawn, not figures with their own vigor. In *The Penelo-piad* (2005) there is a similar problem. Atwood retells the story of Penelope and Odysseus, largely from Penelope's point of view. The world of women is fore-grounded. Penelope tells her story from the afterlife, and her perceptions are privileged, as with the narrator in Joyce Carol Oates's *Blonde*. Being dead means she is free of social pressures and determinations. She can also see, and tell, all the things her husband got up to on his louche slow boat home. The hero emerges more human than when he was a hero. The tale is told not only in nar-rative prose but also in song, script, transcript, and verse.

Michael Ondaatje's *The Collected Works of Billy the Kid: Left-Handed Poems* (1970) also mixes media, and like Atwood he starts in verse and his prose carries a poetic burden, lush or dense, depending on how one responds to abundant allusive language, as depth or thickness. John Updike is fascinated by the images and symbols in the prose but ventures to suggest that sometimes the medium slows the narrative and works against cohesion. Throughout his writing Ondaatje refers to maps, an instinct to localize rather than to serialize events. There is something stiff in the time sequences of his fiction. Maugham speaks of the "wide liberty of the novel"; Ondaatje takes that as a license not only for narrative but for metaphorical structures, juxtapositions, suspensions.

As with other poets who burst into fiction (D. M. Thomas, for example, with *The White Hotel*), Ondaatje's language can be overcharged, the story "overchoreographed." *The Collected Works of Billy the Kid* consists of runs of verse, short narrative and stream of consciousness, "archival" photographs, and "transcripts" of conversations. Although it is not a novel, it is on its way to becoming one, a kind of pattern-book of forms woven together to animate a popular legend in which Billy and Pat Garrett, his smart, cool antagonist, struggle.

Born in Sri Lanka in 1943, (Philip) Michael Ondaatje was taken to England in 1954 and attended Dulwich College, where he wore socks for the first time, and a tie. He settled in Canada in 1962, studied at the University of Toronto and then at Queen's University, Kingston, Ontario, meeting other writers and beginning his own projects in earnest. He put Sri Lanka out of mind until he was thirty-five.

His first novel, *Coming Through Slaughter,* was published in 1976. In short, insistent, but not always sequential paragraphs it evokes Buddy Bolden, the New Orleans cornettist, ragtime and jazz pioneer, as he enters into the schizophrenia that destroyed his career and resulted in his being institutionalized in 1907. Another historical character, the photographer E. J. Bellocq, is part of the harsh narrative. The form enacts the subjects in their fragmentation, introducing photographs among the snatches of language. The book was a *succès d'estime,* representing an ambitious new departure in Canadian fiction. Ondaatje is also associated with the magazine *Brick,* which Annie Proulx describes as "the best literary publication in North America."

Ondaatje is a slow writer, working and reworking the surface of his prose. *In the Skin of a Lion* (1987) represents his major fictional encounter with Canada, voicing the lives of immigrants who, in the first half of the twentieth century, built Toronto, in particular its bridges and tunnels, but whose contribution to the fabric of the city and, with jazz, to its culture, had been overlooked. As an immigrant himself, he felt their thwarted belonging.

When she was an apprentice writer at the University of East Anglia, Anne Enright read *In the Skin of a Lion*. It provided her with a creative challenge. "A

nun is blown off an unfinished bridge in Toronto, one night in the early twentieth century. She is caught by a construction worker who brings her to safety."
She returned to the passage creatively in her first novel, *The Wig My Father Wore*
(1995), and she lingers over the way Ondaatje achieves his effects, the bridge
worker who "walks to the edge of the bridge and 'steps into the clear air' leaving
nothing to see but 'the fizzing rope, a quick slither.' He dangles below the top
level, working with equal ease in darkness or in fog. 'For night work he is paid
$1.25, swinging up into the rafters of a trestle holding a flare, freefalling like a
dead star.' " She concludes that the manipulation of verb tenses and the disparate
narratives—the worker's history, the nun's, the bridge's, each of which "functions as a single note in the major chord that is the 'worker-hero' "—make the
magic happen. "The scene has some of the hypnagogic strangeness of all false
falls: the stair we miss as we fall asleep. It is terribly moving. Like Gloucester
flinging himself off a cliff that isn't there, on his way to Dover, the effect of it is
hard to describe, although the mechanics seem quite clear." His decentered or
many-voiced technique owes something to John Dos Passos. Nearer at hand he
owes a debt to John Berger, a fact that the Irish novelist Anne Enright underlines. He found direction as he researched and wrote, studying bridge and via-
duct building and the specific history of Toronto as he went; his discoveries
register in the invention of plot. The effort of the writing is in revision, when he
assigns motives and makes connections of which he was unaware in the first
draft. "I think the uncertainty sharpens the focus."

The English Patient (1992), for which he won the Booker Prize and which was
made into an Academy Award–winning film, engages the complex past of Europe. Readers hear in the book echoes of Kipling's *Kim,* not least in his inwardness with a variety of characters, cultures, and histories. The authorial character advises Hana: "You must read Kipling slowly. Watch carefully where the
commas fall so you can discover the natural pauses. He is a writer who used
pen and ink. He looked up from the page a lot." Ondaatje tends toward cliché
and self-parody, William Boyd demonstrates, particularly in the heady romantic zones. Boyd likens the story to *A Farewell to Arms*—a patient, a nurse in an
Italian war—but overlooks the implausibility of Ondaatje's basic plot premise:
it would be "pedantic" to question it, he claims the license of a "poetic" writer.

In *Anil's Ghost* (2000), a dead man returns as a ghost to confront what he lost
in leaving Sri Lanka as a boy, resolving the many voices he heard to two, which
now dissent, now harmonize. Memory, Ondaatje insists, is invention, and "people
who lose their childhood eventually have to retrieve it." He describes himself
as "a mongrel of place. Of race. Of cultures. Of many genres." This is his larger
license. He remembers how when he was young, the second time he heard a
story something had always been added to retain the audience's interest; the

third time, further additions, improvements. What mattered in narrative was less fidelity than the engaging truth. Truth remains true in narrative by change and growth.

*The Cat's Table* (2011) is a boy's return journey, from Sri Lanka to England, on a ship of fools, an autobiography insisting that it is not autobiography at all. Annie Proulx reads it as allegory: "The novel tells of a journey from childhood to the adult world, as well as a passage from the homeland to another country, something of a Dantean experience." The comparison with Dante is off the mark. For all its circumstantial charm, the book is not very well written. Adam Mars Jones cares about style and balks at the generic indecision (what purpose is served by the continual prevarication about autobiographical content?) and at the ways in which the prose is lax and predictive, with "if only we'd known then" and other rueful ingratiations. Generically, given Henty and Hardy Boy characters—a make-believe aristocrat who's a thief, a dog with rabies, a prisoner, a secret policeman, some acrobats, and so on—it is *Boy's Own* fiction. And, sure enough, two more boys (from different backgrounds and of contrasting temperament) companion the protagonist, whose name is Michael. At mealtime the three occupy the Cat's Table, farthest away from the Captain's table, almost out of the range of authority.

---

Janet (Paterson) Frame (1924–2004) and Maurice Shadbolt (1932–2004) are points of departure for New Zealand fiction. Shadbolt, using conventional tools, addresses the history and landscape and, on a smaller scale, does for New Zealand writing what Patrick White did for Australian. *Strangers and Journeys* (1972) traces two families' interconnected lives over three generations. The book is a saga, not an epic: Shadbolt is by instinct a historian. His later work, in particular the New Zealand War trilogy *Season of the Jew* (1987), *Monday's Warriors* (1990), and *The House of Strife* (1993), explores the country's divided heritage and the interaction of colonial and Maori history. The characterization of the emerging Te Kooti (1832–1893), the Maori religious and resistance leader, is unsentimental in its depiction of an irreducible cultural otherness seen first as a threat and then as a defining resource. In 1883 Te Kooti was pardoned and a new spirit began to emerge.

In 1980 Janet Frame wondered aloud whether there are "'pockets' of poetry in the world as there are 'pockets' of depression and wealth, areas breeding poetry like a rare plant which the nation eats to satisfy an extra appetite, enjoying the pleasant taste without thinking too much of the dangers of the 'insane root'?" Her imagination seems to be already engaged on her final novel, *The Carpathians* (1989), where this theme is fully embodied. Frame was a poet as well as a fiction writer. The first of her eleven novels, *Owls Do Cry* (1957), emerges from a polite, confident, sunny 1950s culture, normal in a good way, normative in a bad. It is a world into which history, and her personal story of psychiatric trouble and detention, had broken.

She came from Dunedin in the South Island. Her father was a railway man, her mother had worked as a maid at the Beauchamps's—Katherine Mansfield's family. Her childhood was peripatetic until the Frames settled in Oamaru, the Waimaru of some of her fiction. Her life was marred by the traumatic loss of two older sisters, her brother's epilepsy, a tense and unbearable home. She trained to be a teacher, attempted suicide, then fell in love with her therapist. She was hospitalized in various institutions and in 1951 narrowly avoided a lobotomy.

A collection of her stories was awarded the main New Zealand literary award of the day. In style and approach they are not unlike Mansfield's open-ended vignettes of childhood. They suggest the themes of her extended fiction, the mismatch between the subjective and the common world, and the paradoxes and polarities that follow from it. The stories are from the points of view of children or characters who cannot see a whole scene. Conformity she avoids, and she resists the pressures that go with it.

The stories' success helped Frame recover from eight years of residential care. She found her own way in writing and developed an early kind of magical realism. In 1955, released from hospital, she went to live in an army hut in the garden of Norris Frank Davey (1903–1982), better known as Frank Sargeson, one of the outstanding New Zealand story writers, regarded by some as Katherine Mansfield's equal. His fiction is more decisively rooted in New Zealand than Mansfield's. Sargeson introduced Frame to other writers and encouraged her to organize her writing life. Here, in relative isolation, finding her way back into the social world, she composed *Owls Do Cry*.

Her stylistic experiments and Shadbolt's efforts to synthesize New Zealand and colonial history prepared a space in which Keri Hulme (b. 1947), a living synthesis of cultural elements, could write her one awkward, violent, and memorable Maori-gothic romance, *The Bone People* (1984), which was awarded the Booker Prize in 1985, the first New Zealand novel to have received that award.

In 1956 Janet Frame left New Zealand for London. She did not leave her mental problems behind; intermittently she subjected herself to psychoanalysis. Her psychiatrist encouraged her in her writing, and seven of her novels were dedicated to him. In 1963 she returned from exile, but she traveled to the United States and developed close friendships there. Her autobiographies, which were adapted for television and then into the highly successful feature film *An Angel at My Table,* helped popularize her work.

*The Carpathians* (1988) was awarded the Commonwealth Writers Prize at a time when Frame's name was mentioned in connection with the Nobel Prize.

In Frame's last novel, Mattina Brecon's husband is a novelist trying to repeat a great success. Mattina learns about the astonishing properties of the Memory Flower and travels from New York to New Zealand in quest of it. There the worlds of memory and imposture mingle: the longer she stays, watching her eerie neighbors, the more she loses control, then self-control. This being a world of suspended realism, metafictional elements intrude: Mattina forfeits her narrative to another and is subsumed in the story she came to tell. The book was a tremendous labor to write, given the consistent levels upon which it moves and its central, paradoxical theme of fiction, its nature and its limitations.

Anita (Mazumdar) Desai (b. 1937) avoids the reflex, exotic, symbolic profusion of some contemporary Indian writing, the lush excess of Arundhati Roy, for example, the limber overextension of Vikram Seth. We do not get closer to an experience by overexpressing it. And of course words mean differently in Indian English than in English English or in American English. *Sun, rain, moon, cow,* mean differently in Mussoorie, India, where Desai was born; in London, where three of her novels have been shortlisted for the Booker Prize; and in Cambridge, Massachusetts, where she has taught for many years at MIT. Anita Desai is a restrained writer, and a consistent one; for half a century she has written not only India (which she first left at the age of fourteen, traveling to London, then to the United States) but the world at large. Her characters are generally going somewhere else, the grass being greener, and she follows them into their disappointments. *Clear Light of Day* (1980), her first Booker Prize–shortlisted book, is her most autobiographical, set in the Old Delhi where she grew up.

Her daughter Kiran Desai (b. 1971) did receive the Booker Prize in 2006 for *The Inheritance of Loss,* and the dialogue between mother and daughter contrasts, a generation after and a culture away, with the emblematic British father-son relationship of Kingsley and Martin Amis. A natural generosity and a bond of admiration connects the two women, both exiles from their core subject matter, both open to a world of cultures. The mother builds on her father's memories: "He told me stories that I can't even imagine. The mailman would walk through the forest, ringing a bell to frighten away the tigers, and he would shout, 'In the name of Queen Victoria, make way for the mail!'" The daughter's fiction builds on her mother's memories, and she then generates her own past and present worlds.

Anita Desai's mother was German, her father Bengali. At home German was spoken, at school English, and among the servants and in the street she experienced Bengali, Urdu, Hindi. Her father occasionally recited Byron but did not bring Bengali music into the house. The writings of Rabindranath Tagore, as well as her father's stories, informed her Bengali world—those, and Bengali films she saw, sometimes with her father. Her mother talked incessantly about her German past, and Berlin was as real to Desai as the world she inhabited. Her past is a city of lost languages and lost families, forced at partition to leave Old Delhi, her mother's family destroyed in the war. Only in *Baumgartner's Bombay* (1988), where the action occurs over a single day, the last day of Baumgartner's life, did she create the Indian world as the Germans might have experienced it, her English there taking on the accent and diction they might have used, her mother's past revived. *Under the Volcano* rather than *Ulysses* is its cousin. She did, after all, spend a substantial period in Mexico, reading and researching in San Miguel de Allende—much as an Englishman might have traveled to India during the Raj to conduct research, trying to find a way into life there, even to belong. She claims to see India through her mother's German eyes, always as an outsider, and in Mexico she was perhaps closer than anywhere else to her mother's perspectives. *The Zigzag Way* (2004) is the uneasy product of her Mexican studies, a novel that embraces Cornwall (the mining tradition), Vienna, Mexico (where the mines were), and Harvard, where her bespectacled, scholarly protagonist and his assertive girlfriend come from. An excess of plot and an effortful grappling together of histories make this relatively brief novel seem more a blueprint for a greater work than a finished work.

Her experience of Partition and then of exile made her a writer. Had she remained in India, she has said, "perhaps I would not have found the necessity of putting all the bits together." Her imagination turned west, she read Virginia Woolf over and over: "I was using her as a kind of tuning fork, I wanted to catch that exact note she would strike. Then I became quite frightened that I was trying to replicate her manner of voice, her tone, and that was holding me back from discovering my own." Desai introduced into Anglophone Indian women's fiction elements of stream of consciousness as Woolf practiced it, and feminist themes. Her many stepping-stones have been literary, and many of them poets: Germans, Greeks (Cavafy is behind *Journey to Ithaca* [1995]), Russians, exiles. Exile is an overwhelming theme in her fiction. "Your subject is elsewhere," she says, "and your fear is you may not be able to recover it. When we first came to America and I started teaching, I had an awful feeling that I would never write another thing. I was so far removed from India, the past, family, and what was around me was absolutely not mine." But she wrote *Fasting Feasting* (1999), her third Booker-shortlisted novel, "going right back into the past, and the only way I can write is to keep recovering that past." The past set for her a formal challenge, "like having two different jigsaw puzzles and trying to make one from it." In a sense that is the formal challenge she sets for herself in several of her best books. In an early essay for the *New York Review of Books* she characterized the incommensurate visions of the great Indian leader Jawaharlal Nehru, who was at once "a Cambridge-educated Socialist of the early Fabian school, who worshipped the rivers, forests, and mountains of India with an Aryan passion," and also a man with "a vision of India as a self-supporting industrial power." Her vision is equally irreconcilable, the difference being that she recognizes the fact and records it without seeking to distort or compel. She watched India with detachment. "The web so intricately woven by political and religious threads, by the sacred and the secular, has no seemly pattern, no orderly design: it is tattered and frayed by assault and agitation."

Already, with his Booker Prize–winning novel *Midnight's Children* (1981), Salman Rushdie (Sir Ahmed Salman Rushdie, b. 1947) had rent the web and been in trouble with the Indian authorities; *Shame* (1983) riled the Pakistani civil authorities. These were minor preludes to the firestorm caused by *The Satanic Verses* (1988) that rendered Rushdie toxic and heroic in equal degrees. It is possible once more to talk about him as an author rather than as a political and cultural football. The heat generated by the affair of the fatwa could not last forever. The matter seemed insoluble: no action could be taken to reverse the "sentence of death" Ayatollah Khomeini had proclaimed. No action was precisely the action required. Despite the rhetoric and the efforts of writers, readers, publishers, newspapers, diplomats, and governments, the occasion passed, leaving scars of cultural definition that are instructive and the less sinister for being visible and potentially negotiable. Rushdie remarked in 2005, "After all this fuss, at last that book is beginning to have a literary life—particularly in the academy." The comic elements are registering, the techniques of combination and of deliberate alienation that made the book offensive to those it offended: it had fun with and made fun of sacred-seeming things. It is his most *English* novel, the one that looks closely at the lives of immigrants in London during Mrs. Thatcher's years in office.

Those who attacked the book and its author, and many who supported them, had one thing in common: most contested the issues on principle, not having read the text. Even Michael Foot, the Labor leader, declared that he was a member of the Page 15 club, readers who could not get beyond the fifteenth page. It is a challenging opening, but if we pick up the language, which is in large part a texture of metaphor, the book becomes negotiable.

If it was Rushdie who first coined the phrase "the empire writes back to the centre," the writing back was as much a matter of form as of content. Rushdie challenges conventional realism with magical realism, heightened images and situations, impossible, luminous turns of plot, emblematic coincidences. He introduces elements of fairy tale, legend, Eastern story, layering narratives, into a modern world of gadgets, speed, weapons, the literalizing materialism of the day. Metaphors are layered, too: an airplane in flight breaks open like a seedpod releasing its seeds, like an egg spilling its contents; the falling people are like fragments of tobacco from a broken cigar. The metaphors are cumulative but do not *build*: each one partly erases the one before. Djinns and magic appear in a daily world to transform our sense of the possibilities of fiction and of life. Memory itself becomes open to change.

Rushdie is a man of four nations at least. Born and raised in Bombay, he is an Indian, though his Muslim family is of Kashmiri extraction. Educated in Britain, at Rugby School and then at King's College, Cambridge, where he read history, and resident in the United Kingdom for many years, he is British. His family left Bombay for Pakistan when he was seventeen, and he has spent time there as well. Since 2000 he has lived for the most part in the United States. This various belonging might have been alienating; for him it has been enabling. He began writing as an insider, though with *The Satanic Verses* he conceded that he had become part of "the Indian Diaspora."

Having trained as an actor, he found that discipline helpful in reconciling his backgrounds as he wrote, composing to the read-aloud quality of the words, their accents and inflections. Pace, especially rapid pace, contributes to comedy, and comedy is a mode natural to him: not the broad, irresistible comedy of Amis but a formally zany variety, which it is possible to misread.

His first novel, *Grimus* (1975), was not a success. A creative writing course would have knocked it on the head and probably stopped the author in his tracks. The central problem is generic: It wants to be science fiction, it calls itself science fiction because it wants to win a sci-fi award. But there is little science in it, though there is magic and paired characters. Here begins Rushdie's insistence on pairings of contrast and complementarity, of characters, or of faiths—for example, Hinduism and Sufism, especially the Sufi idea that the divine is not outside creation but contained in the whole of it.

It was a giant step from *Grimus* to *Midnight's Children* (1981), which J. M. Coetzee describes as "the book which revolutionized the Indian English novel." It follows the life of a child born at the stroke of midnight when India's independence is declared, and possessing unusual powers, including a connection to other children born with India in a similar way. Saleem Sinai, whom we are tempted to read as a voice for Rushdie himself, introduces himself: "I have been a swallower of selves; and to know me, just the one of me, you'll have to swallow the lot as well. Consumed multitudes are jostling and shoving inside me." His embodied multiplicity means that as we listen to his life story we are listening to a chorus as well. Thus, his task is not a simple one: "There are so many stories to tell, too many, such an excess of intertwined lives events miracles places rumors." In the opening paragraphs the time sequence is difficult because the narrator has begun his multiple telling. His own story is inseparable from the stories of his ancestors, he will "try and bring the past back as if it had not gone away"—a Proustian purpose—with memory continually contradicted by facts, so that the narrator must incorporate "the battle between memory and fact." The personal and the historical are now inseparable: "Human history hasn't in the past been quite as interconnected as for various reasons it now is."

The self who is inseparable from history is also divided. Rushdie noted how in *Midnight's Children* "there's the narrator and the baby he's exchanged for and they in a way become alter egos—one is like the dark side of the other." Pairings again, and they recur in his later novels. "In *Shame* also, in the two main political protagonists, the civilian and the military despot, they're in a way also defined by each other, and exist locked together." The climactic pairings occur in *The Satanic Verses. Shame* is directly political, about Pakistan and with real characters familiar to his readers from the newspapers, Zia-ul-Haq and Zulfikar Ali Bhutto. No wonder he ran afoul of the authorities, especially when the book received major European attention. The magical-realist devices heightened the caricature and intensified the ridicule of the sinister small-mindedness of men bent on and by power.

After *The Satanic Verses* Rushdie undertook one of his most difficult tasks, especially because he composed it while the fatwa still hung over his head (as perhaps, even though it was rescinded, it still does). The isolated and threatened narrator of *The Moor's Last Sigh* (1995) one is tempted to read as a correlative for the writer. Set in Bombay, Rushdie's hometown, and Cochin, it draws its title from the Moorish retreat from Spain, when the last Moorish king of Granada, to save the Alhambra, abandons it, looking back on the city and heaving the eponymous sigh. Rushdie's book is a saga-epic about four generations of a family, narrated by Moraes Zogoiby, an articulate, highly sexed, curiously deformed late scion of the family. Coetzee resists the fitful narrative discontinuities. They can seem willful and they confuse. For Coetzee the problem with the book is in the historical element, the tying of the narrative to factual history, which means that whatever a character says itself becomes historical in relation to the time of the book's publication and its temporal setting. The secular reader of this book, as of *The Satanic Verses,* loses much, Coetzee says, because both are pitched against a lived religious and historical background and, unlike other Indian saga-writers, Rushdie does not busk to British or American readers but addresses his subject directly, as if to create Indian and Pakistani readers. Coetzee describes the overlays of allusion, the succession of alternatives, the care not to erase what comes before, as palimpsesting.

*The Ground Beneath Her Feet* (1999) and *Fury* (2001) do not extend Rushdie the way his earlier novels did. In *Shalimar the Clown* (2005), however, he breaks new ground. The book began "as a murder story which reveals itself to be a love story which turns into a story of revenge which turns into a story of hatred which turns into a murder story"—which suggests a form out of Calvino, with its spiral of irresolutions. It is a novel of return, to Kashmir, and to Alsace, beautiful, once-idyllic places harshly contested. "Of all my books this was the book that was most completely written by its characters," he says.

Reviewing it, John Updike defined "Rushdian overflow": "His novels pour by in a sparkling voracious onrush, each wave topped with foam, each paragraph luxurious and delicious, but the net effect perilously close to stultification. His prose hops with dropped names, compulsive puns, learned allusions, winks at the reader, and repeated bows to popular culture." This defines in negative terms what James Wood refers to as "hysterical fiction" with its fear of silence, of being misunderstood, its overkill. Sometimes in *Shalimar* a lax associationism comes into play. Los Angeles inevitably conjures—angels. Updike is impatient with the tinsel, with Rushdie's fascination, pre- and post-fatwa, with celebrity. Rushdie writes in *Shalimar,* "The shadow planets actually existed without actually existing," having and eating his cake. "Rushdie in his Manhattan retreat," says Updike, "is no longer a third-world writer but a bard of the grim one world we all, in a state of some dread, inhabit."

"One of the things that has become, to me, more evidently my subject," he told the *Paris Review,* "is the way in which the stories of anywhere are also the stories of everywhere else." That lesson was implicit in Bombay, "a city in which the West was totally mixed up with the East. The accidents of my life have given me the ability to make stories in which different parts of the world are brought together, sometimes harmoniously, sometimes in conflict, and sometimes both— usually both."

---

Earl Lovelace (b. 1935) is one of a generation of writers that set a new agenda for Caribbean writing, active across genres (as an award-winning playwright and a journalist as well as a writer of fiction), and transforming his medium by reflecting the way people, he among them, spoke. He was working on the *Trinidad Guardian* as a proofreader when he was seventeen: he knew the rules and over time he learned to make them accommodating. In his later teens he worked for the Department of Forestry, progressing to agricultural assistant at the Department of Agriculture, work in which he experienced rural Trinidad, its landscapes and people, cultivating his imagination for the fiction he would write. He went abroad to study in Washington, D.C., then earned a masters degree at Johns Hopkins University in Baltimore, where he was declared Visiting Novelist. He had two books to his credit, both published in London, *While Gods Are Falling* (1965) and *The Schoolmaster* (1968), the latter an evocative novel about a new schoolteacher arriving in a remote community and the mark he makes as against the mark it makes on him. He published *The Dragon Can't Dance* (1979), about the impact of a carnival on the slum-dwellers who live on the fringes of Port of Spain, the *Dragon* being of the carnival ilk, but referring also to the man playing the part. He participated in the University of Iowa International Writing Program. In 1982 he returned to teach literature and writing at the University of the West Indies, helping to nurture an emerging generation of Caribbean writers.

Soon after his return he published *The Wine of Astonishment* (1983) in the Heinemann Caribbean Writers Series, which ran parallel to the celebrated African Writers Series and did not represent editorial relegation to a "regionalized" imprint. It chronicles how members of Bonasse, an independent Trinidadian community, retain their identity in the face of corruption and other forms of "progress" that go hand in hand with it. Bolo, a champion stick fighter, strong, brave, sees friends and neighbors humbled and shamed by American troops. He takes a stand. Eva, one of the narrating voices, is a member of the Baptist congregation, responding in her own language to the community and its faith. She is a natural narrator, engaged but with sufficient distance to see things more or less whole.

Lovelace received civic and academic distinctions in Britain, the United States, and at home. *Salt* (1996) was awarded the Commonwealth Writers Prize in 1997. In terms less original than in his earlier books, because more deliberately focused, it explores the aftermath of slavery and colonialism and the difficulties the country continues to live with because of them. The story focuses through Alford George, a schoolteacher who has become a politician. His next novel, *Is Just a Movie* (2011), in its title affirms his language. The process of making a film reveals the nature of the society in which the film is shot, where "extras" are herded together, each one trying to be distinctly visible. "Unfortunately the society has never come to grips with who we are, how we arrived here, and give some kind of good understanding to say, 'This is where we are; let we see what we could do about it!'"

# 43

# Win, Place, and Show

William Golding, Angus Wilson, Margaret Drabble, Malcolm Bradbury,
David Lodge, Iris Murdoch, A. S. Byatt, Hilary Mantel, John Braine,
Alan Sillitoe, Kingsley Amis, John Fowles, Ian McEwan,
Peter Ackroyd, Graham Swift, J. G. Ballard

Most novelists who care about reputation and get out of the starting gate become also-rans. They prosper, win cups and handicaps, and are put out to grass. Once upon a time they went out of print; now they pass into the undiscriminating eternity of print-on-demand and e-book. The publishing industry feeds on also-rans. When publishers and critics quote sales figures in support of literary judgment, they say more about the industry and the state of readership than about the quality of books. Literary and commercial merit do not necessarily concur.

"If I have any insights to offer they may well be those a teacher, a critic, an academic would think too obvious to need stressing," (Sir) William (Gerald) Golding (1911–1994) says, insisting that he and the common reader are on the same side, opposite the specialists. Yet he was made by specialists who, after the initially sluggish sales of *Lord of the Flies* (1954), got to work interpreting and reinterpreting, making it a set text in schools throughout the Anglophone world. Other contemporary authors have suffered a similar fate at the hands of syllabus-setters, among them Doris Lessing, J. D. Salinger, Harper Lee, and John Fowles (who applauds Golding's noncompliance with what readers and critics expect).

Golding, who lectured widely, reading from *Lord of the Flies* as it made its way into the educational system, refused to be drawn out on its meaning. Interpreters were safe from correction. In becoming fodder for schoolchildren and academics, his book was "a moving target" (the title he gave to a collection of occasional writings and lectures in 1982). He came to dislike *Lord of the Flies,* his decisive success, published twenty years after the failure of his first book, a collection of poems. He is described as a "late starter." For a modern writer, perhaps he is.

Nadine Gordimer regarded him as a "novelist-philosopher" and in 1964 called him "the most exciting and interesting of contemporary British writers." His difficulty as an artist of ideas or intuitions, the critic Frank Kermode wrote, was "the difficulty that attends the expression of what is profoundly simple." He was in love with serious meanings and themes, and his mode is allegorical, increasingly so as his work develops. Readers sense equivalences, though they cannot always identify them. William Boyd finds the effect of his intentionality enervating. When the connection between plot and allegory breaks, the fiction labors, as in *Free Fall* (1959), *The Spire* (1964), and even *Darkness Visible* (1979).

Golding recognized the problem. "Men are prisoners of their metaphors," he said, conceding in this phrase his natural propensity to allegorize. Plots are allegorical, images are allegorical, trusting in the adequacy of their logic once the counters are in place. Sometimes in a detail we see how allegory comes to him. In the essay "Egypt from My Outside" he reinvents his momentous pilgrimage. He visits a tomb in which the wall paintings can be seen only if three Egyptian guides with mirrors transmit the sunlight from the opening to the remote internal surface. "That long, angular arm of light, quivering with nerves and the beating of hearts, was a service I had never found the trick of accepting without a kind of shame." The shame is in being served, assisted to vision. Shame is how things come into focus in his books. Guilt must be experienced and acknowledged in the process of getting to the truth, which is more complex, more insoluble, than a character, or a narrator, first imagines. At last the darkness is visible.

He drafted and redrafted his novels by hand. The early versions can be remote from the eventual book, as though he learned what he intended as he wrote, the process of invention being a gradual clarification of sense. Other writers were like him, he believed, surprising themselves. In his lecture "Belief and Creativity," he says he arranged and rearranged into new patterns what he already knew until something he did not know took shape, "the new thing" that rose out of language asking to be recognized. The process must not be analyzed lest analysis explain it away. What was *Lord of the Flies* but "grief, sheer grief, grief, grief, grief."

When *Poems* appeared he had just graduated from Brasenose College, Oxford, the one grammar school boy (from a modest, modestly radical home) among public school boys, a social circumstance that aggravated him. He resented others' privilege. When the university career advisers interviewed him, the notes record "Not Quite" and "NTS," which translate as, "Not Quite a Gentleman" and "Not Top Shelf." He coveted the bona fides that a privileging establishment imparts, in particular the knighthood he actively sought, and received in 1988, more agreeable to him than the Nobel Prize of 1983. He was the first British novelist to be so honored since—Galsworthy.

With *Lord of the Flies* he emerged from the pupa of a not very successful, glum, bearded schoolmaster into a butterfly—a Dingy or Grizzled Skipper. It was not an easy emergence into the light. The manuscript of *Lord of the Flies* had been widely rejected. At Faber and Faber it was about to go back as an "absurd & uninteresting fantasy" when a new editor, Charles Monteith, picked it up and realized something might be done with it, but the author would need to accept severe editing. In its original incarnation the book was substantially longer and, in Gordimer's terms, philosophical. Monteith did for Golding what Maxwell Perkins did for Thomas Wolfe and, more controversially, Gordon Lish for the story writer Raymond Carver. He exercised a meticulous scalpel. The book that emerged from their editorial sessions was spare and clear. Burgess found the end result "a little too systematized and allegorical to be regarded as a true novel." Looking back on it from a distance of two decades, Golding found it "boring and crude. The language is O-level stuff." He regretted having allowed Monteith to effect so complete a transformation, so that the book felt not quite his. Still, Monteith extruded a real novel from the mass and paid the author a £60 advance. The book went on to sell over 10 million copies. Montieth remained Golding's editor and encouraged him on his allegorical way. *The Inheritors* (1955) and *Pincher Martin: The Two Deaths of Christopher Martin* (1956), the novels that immediately followed *Lord of the Flies,* similarly explore theme at the expense of character. *Free Fall's* middlingly hostile reception in 1959 he felt had set him back. After a five-year delay came *The Spire* (1964), restoring his reputation. Here character pulls harder than theme, but his theme is, as usual, the inherence of human evil.

In *The Spire* Golding singled out the character of Jocelin, the dean, who dreams the 400-foot spire, *ad majorem gloriam Dei;* but to build it, a series of evil acts is required. Vidal admires how "you see the church that is being built, smell the dust. You are present at an event that exists only in his imagination. Very few writers have ever had this power. When the priest reveals his sores, you see them, feel the pain." In fact, the material world possesses greater presence than the figures that move in it, who are more tourists than characters, their faces reflected from time-polished surfaces and new-minted symbols.

Golding drank too much for his own good—more even than Kingsley Amis, it is said—and in his cups he could turn contrary and would suffer intense remorse the following day. In public he expressed emphatic opinions that also appear, more guardedly, on paper. "I have always understood the Nazis because I am of that sort by nature," he said, describing himself also as a monster. He disliked Joyce's *Ulysses,* as he disliked "highbrow" and modernist writing. He regarded Jilly Cooper's *Polo,* the 1991 installment of her multivolume Rutshire Chronicles, as "not half bad . . . like Leonardo da Vinci's drawings—anatomically exact." He meant these judgments, their disproportion being an aspect of his man-in-the-street populist posturing. His own art makes demands, at times the modernist demands he is impatient of in other writers. "The strength, profundity, truth of a novel lies not in a plausible likeness and rearrangement of the phenomenal world but in a fitness with itself like the dissonances and consonances of harmony." It is not Nabokov's language, but it is his view. Golding's antinaturalism is demanding. He did not suffer from irony. A small dose might have done his critical judgment some good but would have made his novels more narrowly English.

*Rites of Passage,* the first volume in what turned into the trilogy *To the Ends of the Earth,* which also includes *Close Quarters* (1987) and *Fire Down Below* (1989), won the Booker Prize in 1980. Burgess's *Earthly Powers* was the favorite to win, and the more conventional but highly readable *A Month in the Country* by J. L. (Joseph Lloyd) Carr (1912–1994) was also in the running. All three books invested in the "larger themes" of English fiction, claiming a place in the great tradition. Burgess and Golding are formally innovative, and at this period the Booker Prize judges were interested in such things. Burgess's and Golding's books share a belief that fiction on a large scale can still be written in a diminished society. Both feature homosexuals. Golding's protagonist Edmund Talbot, a young English man about town, is presented with a notebook diary by his godfather, who has secured him an official post with the governor of New South Wales. The nineteenth century has begun. Edmund makes his way to Australia and describes in his journal fellow passengers on a British warship. He is astonished by their bad manners, and his account is witty. Soon the focal drama emerges. Golding drafted the book in a gap in the erratic composition of *Darkness Visible,* and the finished product reads like a diary penned rapidly, the informal nineteenth-century language entirely credible. At one level the book is comic, exploring a theme that obsessed him: the proper conduct of a gentleman; at another level it is somber and unsettling. The Reverend Colley becomes the focus of Talbot's story. At first he seems a silly, unctuous man, anything but a gentleman. When he is drunk he strips off his clothes and tries to bless his fellow passengers, with the hilarious, sad refrain, "joy, joy, joy" on his lips. He ends up starving himself to death out of a sense of guilt, for he has remembered another drunken spree in which he committed an unpardonable act. The comic figure Talbot has joined in ridiculing becomes a victim, our victim, because we have been drawn into complicity by laughter. Colley, too, has kept a journal, and here the actual man emerges. The elements that made for laughter are explained in ways that turn them to pathos. Colley concludes, "With lack of sleep and too much understanding I grow a little crazy, I think, like all men at sea who live too close to each other and too close thereby to all that is monstrous under the sun and moon."

Golding seemed to be a metaphysician of fiction, his numinous themes laced with implausibilities. Though hostile to privilege, he was seldom political in any contemporary sense. He established himself as an original modern writer though his imagination is rooted in a medieval, allegorical zone. *Darkness Visible* is his most ambitious novel; its composition was more demanding on his time and energy than *To the Ends of the Earth,* with the period diary formula and recurring characters. His problem is Miltonic: how to express and explore Good and Evil. Like *Rites of Passage,* the book has a double structure. It begins with Matty, a child who emerges naked and dreadfully disfigured in the Blitz. As with the fallen angels in book 1 of *Paradise Lost,* flames leap, this is a post-lapsarian world. Matty is sent by the state to a Roman Catholic boarding school, where pupils are repelled by him and Mr. Pedigree, a schoolmaster, abuses him sexually. (The exploration of Pedigree's obsession is itself alarmingly sympathetic.) As an adult Matty attracts a following of people who regard him as a saint. A. S. Byatt saw the enigmatic Matty as "the incarnate Second Coming." She also thought he was Horus, the Egyptian god. The book was, in a good sense, she insisted, "spattered with clues and signs, clotted with symbols and puns." But such faux allegory is unstable, insoluble. The latter part of the book relates to two of Matty's followers, the beautiful twins Toni and Sophy; their story begins when they are ten, and is told from Sophy's point of view. Toni is a political activist not averse to violence; Sophy exerts control using her sexuality. The book builds on dualities and concludes in apocalypse.

(Sir) Angus (Frank Johnston) Wilson (1913–1991), like Golding, started late. In *The Wild Garden: Or Speaking of Writing* (1963), a volume of lectures, he says he did not become a writer until he was thirty-five. Various crises contributed to his vocation: it was not "pure" accident. He uses "pure," as in "pure criticism," with irony, because it is never pure, never entirely divorced from biography, intention, or history. Addicted to the great nineteenth-century novelists, Dickens and Balzac especially, he understood their powerful drama as being of a piece with their melodrama and accepted the melodrama. The novels can make more sense "on the symbolic under-level than on the surface story level," and possess "a cosmic significance that is often denied them by critics."

The theme of his own novels he describes as "self-realization." He started writing in the wake of his "nervous crisis" suffered during and just after the Second World War when, leaving a library job at the British Museum, he served in the Naval section at Bletchley Park as a code breaker, translating the Italian naval codes. His work colleagues included several writers, among them Christine Brooke-Rose and the poets F. T. Prince, Henry Reed, and Vernon Watkins. Along with the legendary Alan Turing, he was one of the "known" homosexuals there, and he was accepted. It was less the stress of his work than the return to a homophobic postwar world that precipitated his breakdown. That, and the death of his father, a gambling man with a diminishing private income who had provided him with a childhood of boardinghouses and hotels: "He belonged to the eighteenth-century stream that ran under the Victorian world and emerged as Edwardian." Wilson is himself something of an Edwardian.

He published a book of stories in 1949, another in 1950, and in 1952 *Hemlock and After,* the first of his eight novels, appeared. It was an immediate success. He became a familiar lecturer and public speaker and a book reviewer, and in 1955 began life as a freelance writer.

Anthony Burgess reads his first three novels, including *Anglo-Saxon Attitudes* (1956) and *The Middle Age of Mrs. Eliot* (1958), as realist, in the tradition of George Eliot and, less plausibly, of Zola. He plays down what are Wilson's strongest suits, satirist and ironist. Wilson has a mission: to defend what in 1974 he called "the decaying humanist world of which L. P. Hartley (and, indeed, a great many of us) is trying to make sense under the realistic events of [our] novels." That world was increasingly under attack from political and ideological quarters. *The Old Men at the Zoo* (1961) breaks with "realism." It is his fantasy book, set in what is now the past but was when he was writing it the future, a United Europe hostile to a separate Britain. In the zoo, conflicts of leadership represent larger conflicts. This was the last of his novels to be received with critical respect. His later work received shorter and shorter shrift from critics and readers. The decline began with *Late Call* (1964), which considers the cultural rootlessness of a new town. Sylvia Calvert retires to the New Town where her son is a headmaster. Nothing is "real" there, only in the surrounding countryside. This is Mrs. Moore in *A Passage to India* transported from Chandrapore to Milton Keynes.

The novelist Christopher Bigsby, a member of the East Anglia program, and Rose Tremain, remembering Angus Wilson's brilliant, oversubscribed Dickens lectures (Wilson's *The World of Charles Dickens* was published in 1970), wondered how it was that Wilson had so completely vanished. His books exist today as print-on-demand paperbacks. He had been gregarious, entertaining, a dedicated word-spinner on the page and in the lecture hall. Something happened to the culture of reception. His gentle, liberal perspectives and pointed satire had come to seem conservative in a decade of student demonstrations, strikes, Vietnam, impending revolution. Sensitive to reviews, Wilson was harmed by the increasingly hostile receptions his books attracted. Martin Amis did a thorough job on *As If by Magic* (1973), instilling a slow poison in Wilson's mind. Amis was not his only critic, though he spoke for a smart new set and his criticisms struck home, not least that Wilson's "modern" language, especially that given to his younger characters, was fatally off key. He found carelessness in the writing, as though the author had not bothered to read it out loud to hear repetitions, bad rhymes, and double entendres, faults of emphasis. Amis, like other critics, found Wilson's "sexual tastes," as he acidly puts it, uncongenial. Having spoken of Wilson's falling into the "Biographical Fallacy" as a critic, he falls into it himself. Wilson was drawn to an overrefined superannuated Bloomsbury and, says Amis, to Woolf's "feminine hypersensitivity." In Amis's *The War against Cliché,* this is one of the few clichés that survives. Other readers are less oblique. Raymond Chandler tried *Anglo-Saxon Attitudes.* "I simply could not read Angus Wilson's novel, because it seemed to me he described his characters and did not create them. People of his kind," homosexuals, "have no real emotional life."

Wilson knew what he was up against, a combination of father-killing new writers and a homophobia as unanalyzed as the anti-Semitism of an earlier generation. He suggested to Edmund Wilson that he read John Wain, Kingsley Amis, and that newer generation, commenting, "Though teachers of English in red brick universities, they had done very little reading—knew little but the metaphysical poets and Eliot; knew nothing of continental culture." Edmund Wilson, for his part, welcomed Angus Wilson as the natural heir to Waugh.

*Anglo-Saxon Attitudes* remains Wilson's freshest novel, though all his fiction rewards attention in its clear evocation of a world and time. *Anglo-Saxon Attitudes,* with its title debt to the White King in Lewis Carroll's *Through the Looking-Glass,* is distinctively English, the Englishness colored more by Balzac than by Dickens. He developed what was for him a new technique, building Gerald Middleton on "flashbacks and word echoes which would show how self-realization and the purging of guilt (or the acceptance of it) are inevitably a long process of re-living traumatic experiences in memory." In this he is not far from Golding, though the large world he creates, on something like the scale of a nineteenth-century novel, is more complete and deliberately "answerable" than any Golding built. The central drama extends beyond the confines of the novel. The plot does not delimit but releases a larger sense of that world. As if against Golding the allegorist, he remarks, "Everyone says as a commonplace that a novel is an extended metaphor, but too few, perhaps, insist that the metaphor is everything, the extension only the means of expression." Margaret Drabble (b. 1949) has written, along with her many and often controversial novels, two excellent biographies, one of Arnold Bennett and the other of Angus Wilson. Juxtaposing the lives, one can appreciate to what extent Bennett, with single-minded dedication, played the literary slot machine while Wilson, writing in a diminished Bennett tradition, retains a nostalgic faith in the reader and the vocation. It is not likely, but not impossible, that his time will come again.

In 1970, his reputation already unstable, Wilson joined (Sir) Malcolm (Stanley) Bradbury (1932–2000) in setting up the University of East Anglia's writing program. Bradbury, a significant literary critic, wrote *The History Man* (1975), a satirical campus novel. Howard Kirk, the unprincipled protagonist, professor of sociology at the "University of Watermouth," bites off the hand that fed and continued to feed him. The novel is in the present tense and will remain relevant for another generation because universities increasingly fulfill the role Bradbury anticipated. The Bradbury-Wilson creative writing masters course at the University of East Anglia was among the first such operations in Great Britain. Successful alumni include Ian McEwan, Kazuo Ishiguro, Anne Enright, Tracy Chevalier, Rose Tremain, and Toby Litt.

Bradbury in particular appreciated the paradox of his enterprise, the gap between novelist and critic, academic or otherwise. "Who cooks and who sews?" he asks: there is something like a gender difference between the roles, possible marriage, eventual divorce. Critics are, like his own Howard Kirk, rule makers, acknowledged but not always just, informed or provident legislators of the arts. He is a critic and an inventive novelist, the roles existing in a kind of symbiotic relationship, a standoff necessary so that neither speaks in bad faith, though there is more critic in the novelist than novelist in the critic. The academic is the more rigorous party, the novelist the more amused and forgiving, even in satire. Apart from *The History Man*, Bradbury's books too have fallen into neglect even in the academy, which was their natural habitat. Sefton Goldberg, the academic protagonist of Howard Jacobson's first novel, *Coming from Behind* (1983), teaches in a third-rate polytechnic and in his reveries imagines Bradbury Lodge in Hampstead where successful, envied, and resented writers get together to laugh at the likes of him. "Lodge" is of course David of that ilk, a more considerable and original academic critic and a more ambitious writer than Bradbury.

David Lodge (b. 1935) shares Roman Catholicism with Graham Greene and Evelyn Waugh. He was not, however, a convert; his Catholicism was a matter of conformity rather than rebellion, but conformity to a beleaguered minority. It was a belonging apart from the main liberal streams. His father, an amateur musician, played gigs "in the nightclub where Evelyn Waugh and all the 'Bright Young Things' used to go." He started reading Waugh and later encouraged David, in his mid-teens, to do so. The boy found that the novels made another world, with bright lights, a real and witty place. His father encouraged him to read Dickens, too, but here he resisted all but *Pickwick*.

Lodge is often described as a Catholic and a campus novelist, as though this combination were a limitation, but the modern Church and university provide for an imagination such as his, caught in this "binary pattern," a various and challenging space for activity, and even for a satirical writer an underlying seriousness. At university he was much engaged by Henry James and Joyce, in particular *Ulysses*. He liked the idea of a "precursor text" and some of his novels exploit it, though his later books—*Author, Author* (2004) about Henry James and *A Man of Parts* (2011) about H. G. Wells—draw on "precursor authors," in the case of James and Wells two writers so bound together and so contrasted that the novels function in an illuminating tension, a "binary pattern" entailing literary, moral, and historical themes.

His second novel, *The British Museum Is Falling Down* (1965), was playfully written, spoofing Graham Greene, with whose work his own is intimately bound up. It responded to his personal and collegial friendship with Bradbury when they taught at the University of Birmingham: both had one novel behind them (Lodge's was *The Picturegoers* of 1960). Here the unassimilated influence of Joyce is clearest in the Molly Bloom pastiche of the last chapter. We encounter the usual irony of the modern campus novel: an academic despises the texts he is required to teach. Thus in *Changing Places: A Tale of Two Campuses* (1975), contrasting revolutionary Berkeley, California, with the mild-mannered student troubles at Birmingham in the late 1960s, the American protagonist Morris Zapp of Euphoria State University is a scholar of Jane Austen who confesses he regards her as "a pain in the ass." The distance in language and value between a modern teacher and a classic text reveals the treachery of an ever-expanding, ever-degrading academic establishment in which and against which Lodge, with precise and committed intelligence, worked. *Small World: An Academic Romance* (1984) is an inadvertent sequel to *Changing Places*.

Writing about Lodge's *How Far Can You Go?* (1980), a novel that in the wake of Vatican II broached the issues of Roman Catholic sexual morality, Anthony Burgess contrasts Lodge and Bradbury as campus novelists. Lodge writes history into the novel. A pope dies while he is writing; another pope is selected and promptly dies, and John Paul emerges, popular and conservative. The book proved theologically and historically prescient: living as a character in the novel, the narrator writes it before our eyes. Bradbury does not engage with the wider world in the same way and belongs more narrowly to his time.

———

(Dame) (Jean) Iris Murdoch (1919–1999) was not a late starter. Eight years Golding's junior, she published her first novel, *Under the Net* (1954), in the same year as *Lord of the Flies* appeared. A year earlier she had published *Sartre: Romantic Rationalist,* the first book in English devoted to the soon-to-be-fashionable existential philosopher. She was known well beyond Oxford as a sharp, ambitious intellectual planning a career and, as it were, diligently working the literary and philosophical room.

She was born in Dublin into a middle-class Protestant family, and Ireland did not weigh much with her later in life. She came to regret the way in which she had seemed to celebrate Irish nationalism in *The Red and the Green* (1965), published the year before the Ulster Volunteer Force was formed and four years before "The Troubles" began in earnest.

As a child she moved with her family to London and enjoyed a progressive education. At Somerville College, Oxford, she read classics, philosophy, and ancient history, then at Newnham College, Cambridge, did postgraduate work. At the age of nineteen she joined the Communist Party, remaining a member until it was inexpedient for reasons of employment, but staying on an increasingly vague left of the political spectrum. Wittgenstein was in Cambridge when she studied there, and their paths crossed. Her devotion was "slavish" according to Elias Canetti (1905–1994)—an exile, a Bulgarian-born, German-writing novelist, essayist, and memoirist who received the Nobel Prize in Literature in 1981. He fell in love with the intense quality of Murdoch's listening and conceded that she achieved that rare thing, "loyalty to *many people*." They were lovers, then they were no longer lovers. She was, he decided, an "illegitimate writer" who never had to suffer, a duck's back always immersing itself and shaking off, schoolgirl and schoolmarm rolled into one. His memoir *Party in the Blitz* (published posthumously in German, 2003, in English, 2005) cruelly evokes young Iris on the prowl. He received a copy of her philosophical writings and declared, "My antipathy against her has grown so strong that I must say something about her here." Through her he formulated his harshest judgments of English culture. "The worst of England is its desiccation, the life as a remote-controlled mummy. It isn't, as people say, the Victorian (the mask of hypocrisy can be torn away, and there is something behind it), it is the prescribed desiccation, that begins with moderation and fairness, and ends up in emotional impotence." Those who ended as exiles or temporary residents in England, after the initial relief of moving unhindered through streets made familiar by Dickens, discovered the closed habits that paralyzed the place. Few express themselves so forcefully as Canetti.

Murdoch became a fellow of St. Anne's College, Oxford. Her novels were all moral or problem novels. She was exercised by the struggle between good and evil in politics, society, and relationships, where it is fruitfully complicated by Eros with his unequal distribution of passion. She wrote in the end twenty-six novels, as well as essays, philosophy books, and poems, which variously approached her theme. Her essays that touch on literary subjects generalize; she was not a close reader. Asked by John Banville why she wrote so many books, she said she kept imagining the next one would exonerate her for the errors of the one before.

What she did have, with an instinct as sure as Dickens's, was a sense of how to end chapters in such a way as to compel the reader on. She could orchestrate a narrative. Frederic Raphael, to whom fell the task of writing the movie script of *A Severed Head* (1961, movie 1970), noted, "Her great strength lay in the clever edginess of her conversations." Scripting was easy: "Unlike most writers', much of her dialogue sounded good out loud. I remember, for instance, an unfaithful wife saying, 'It's all or nothing' and the husband's answer: 'Let me recommend nothing.' Facile? You do it." J. B. Priestley had much the same experience when, working with Murdoch, he adapted the book for a stage production in 1963.

Murdoch took her bearings from the Russian novelists, she said, Tolstoy and Dostoyevsky in particular, whom she read in English translation. Proust and George Eliot figured in her pantheon, too. Her imagination was most at home with her male characters, especially university dons and teachers, with male homosexuals and displaced people. There is, too, the magus who compels other characters, the vulnerable and the strong, to do his dark bidding.

*Under the Net,* her point of departure as a novelist, suggests a writer rather different from the one who wrote her Booker Prize–winning *The Sea, the Sea* (1978), a detailed examination of the continuing, emptying power of love, its protagonist a retired theater director whose jealousy is piqued when he encounters an ex-lover after a long period of separation. *Under the Net* is dedicated to Raymond Queneau and owes formal and thematic debts to his *Pierrot mon ami* (1942) and to Samuel Beckett, whose *Murphy* (1938) receives a name check. The book is picaresque, flirts with the experimental, and is funny. In the complexity of plot and the size of the cast it prefigures her approach in her early maturity, those novels analyzed in A. S. Byatt's monograph *Degrees of Freedom: The Early Novels of Iris Murdoch* (1965), still a key to Murdoch and instrumental in the formation of Byatt's own fictional world.

Jake Donaghue, protagonist of *Under the Net,* wants to become a writer. The "net" of the title is what Robert Graves calls "the cool web of language." The development in Murdoch's art and ambition in the four years between her first novel and *The Bell* (1958) is remarkable. She has moved from the picaresque to a realm in which fiction and essay overlap, where exploration of character is sometimes displaced by the requirements of theme. Moral questions take on a life of their own. The plot is elaborated, incidents and clauses in argument striving to harmonize. Throughout the novel there is a kind of libidinal charge, a slow-burning sexual light, fueled by innuendo and ambivalence. One is reminded of John Cowper Powys.

Kingsley Amis found *The Bell* "very *unreal*": in it, "the characters are all abnormal, somehow. Any moment I expect to come across one of them singing the only song he knows. Or turning out to have been a dwarf all along . . . The decade's most over-rated writer?" She was certainly rated. Her characters are abnormal because they come trailing clouds of philosophical intentionality, they have to advance not only plot but argument. James Wood notes that she "so wanted to create free characters and so often failed, her failure is not one of psychological attention or metaphysical shallowness—quite the opposite—but a Fielding-like devotion to excessive plot-making." When one sets out to summarize her plots, they prove "improbable, melodramatic, feeble stories, still highly indebted to eighteenth- and nineteenth-century theatrics"; they are "not adult enough to take the strain of her complex moral analysis." Not *adult* enough: they will do for comedy where excessive plotting contributes to the carnival, but when themes are serious, plotting must be effortless, the characters must move in a stable element.

Martin Amis is Murdoch's most affectionate addict, coming back to her novel by novel, tetchy, and then, even as he resists and ridicules and pushes her off, at last, reluctantly, yielding to the—what are to some of her readers—resistible intoxications and excesses of the synthetic perfumes she unstoppers. He compares *The Black Prince* (1973) to her two previous novels, "an attempt to synthesize her earlier styles, the hang-dog existential shrugs of her work before *The Bell* and the somewhat contrived allegorizing of the work that followed it." Bradley Pearson, another of her writer-protagonists, endeavors to "escape into life" through love but also, as a slave of language, to pull the net through with him; yet words trammel him. The book has Nabokovian elements, flirting with experiment. Here we are given a "true" story and a fiction, an Editor who concludes it with a postscript, many voices and metafictional conceits. It is, in its final twists and turns, as disingenuous and dissatisfying as Ian McEwan's plot-hobbled *Atonement* (2001).

In reviewing Murdoch's *Nuns and Soldiers* (1980), Amis lists things Murdoch believes in, above all *love*. There is an element of the romantic novelist, not only in the class and titles of the characters but in the covert lubriciousness of the writing. Eros is allowed, even urged, to call the shots and the reader to frisk along behind. It is hard to take, but Amis takes it. Until, finally, he can take no more. *The Philosopher's Pupil* (1983) cures him. He anatomizes a style overexcited, wordy, imprecise. "It is non-writing, unwriting, anti-writing." This "long course of methadone" breaks the addiction.

"The greatest art is impersonal," Murdoch declared, much given to comparatives and superlatives. Also to imperatives, categorical statements: There is nothing tentative about her philosophical engagement, she takes on Plato without demur. *Good* art, she says, "is about the pilgrimage from appearance to reality (the subject of every good play and novel) and exemplifies in spite of Plato what his philosophy teaches concerning the therapy of the soul." The reason she cannot commit to any of the experimental teases she provides in her novels is that for her, fiction, like the other arts, is instrumental. This is one element of Englishness against which Canetti rebelled.

She is said to have devised flowcharts so that at any time she would know precisely where her characters were, and in whose company: the action that took place offstage (there is something staged about all the novels) was necessary to the narrative. Overly complex plotting in the earlier novels gives way to complications of theme and tone in the later work. Her work is at once abundant and variable. Some of the novels are indifferent, a few extraordinary, none of the later ones dwelt upon sufficiently by a writer who, having had her vision, was keen to finish and move on. Once concept and plot were known, all that was left was a labor of composition, not the excitement of discovery. In 2001 John Updike called her "the pre-eminent English novelist of the second half of the twentieth century." One hopes this is not the case. A bemused Rebecca West, in the *Paris Review,* may be closer to the mark in her enthusiastic confusion. "But then Iris Murdoch I like enormously except when she begins to clown and be funny, because I don't think she ever is very funny. She writes curious books on goodness. Have you read her philosophic works? I can't make head or tail of them." The male characters, West says, get the best deal. "As for women, goodness is rarely found in women except in the inarticulate mothers of large families, which is just such an idiotic remark, you can't believe it. Is she pulling one's leg? One hopes so. But even so, why?" A. S. Byatt knew and loved a different but still a problematic Iris Murdoch who "learned a great deal from the French surrealists, and then somehow went and sat in Oxford and became a slightly less interesting novelist than she would have been if she had stayed in contact with the world of Beckett and Queneau"; she adds, "I think she developed a theory about the virtues of Jane Austen that wasn't all that good for her."

Antonia Susan Drabble, later Duffy, is better known as A. S. Byatt (b. 1936). She too has theories, most of them rejections of prescriptive rules, and she welcomes those sudden formal surprises—such as those found in Calvino, Borges, and the Latin American magical realists—that challenge her own always-evolving positions. But she is as categorical and didactic as Murdoch, taking bearings from her even as she tries to keep a safe distance from her. Byatt's father was a Queen's Counsel, her mother a scholar. She was comfortably raised and well educated, attending excellent private schools, Cambridge, Bryn Mawr, and Oxford. One of her sisters is the novelist Margaret Drabble, toward whom she maintains a public *froideur* said to have originated in a dispute over a family tea set. When Byatt started publishing novels, they were invariably compared with Drabble's (Drabble published her first novel a year before Byatt, and her rate of production outstripped her sister's by a ratio of three to one). Byatt's *The Game* (1967) is partly about sisterly competition and creative complementarity, more Brontë than Drabble: "I find the Brontës' joint imagination absolutely appalling," Byatt remarked.

She worked in academia, most prominently at University College, London. With Martin Amis and Julian Barnes she feels a certain affinity: they staged their escape from academia early, choosing to forego salary and exist in the less specialized world of journalism, with its assignments, untrammeled by lectures, tutoring, grading, and the enervating administrative tasks that paralyze modern lecturers. By the time she stepped down from university teaching she had internalized academic disciplines and values. She retains in her critical and creative work some of the generous curiosity and reserve of the old-fashioned academic.

Her first novel, *Shadow of the Sun* (1964, reissued as *The Shadow of the Sun*), drafted while she was still an undergraduate, is about a novelist. The writing is careful to the point of stiffness, but the book contains the germ of what was to follow. Anna Severell goes up to Cambridge as Byatt did and as, a decade later, her heroine Frederica Potter in *Still Life* (1985) would do. Byatt entrusts her own experience to her characters, not in a spirit of autobiography but as an experiment in alternative fates and destinies. Her novels are variations on core themes, having to do with restraint and freedom and the situation of women— daughters, wives, and independent figures—in a changing world. Contemporary readers may question the premises of class and its values and tonalities in this and some of the later novels, as they do in Angus Wilson and Iris Murdoch. Anna's father, Henry, is a successful novelist, the sun from whose brilliance Anna strives to escape, running into the arms of marriage and its aftermaths. Further escapes will be required. As in Murdoch's novels there is much staging; set-piece scenes bring the book to a series of halts. The pressure of content, the head of steam, has yet to build.

*The Game* is a more necessary book, and by the time of *The Virgin in the Garden* (1978) Byatt had developed the family theme with authority. "What it is trying to do," she said later, "is to see what you could do if you wrote *Middlemarch* now." But *now* Frederica Potter cannot be Dorothea. She was, like Byatt, born in 1936. Affinities with the writer's own life are many. She shares her objectives, to find a new way in the world for her body and spirit: sex and grace are what she is after. She is fascinated by and alienated from D. H. Lawrence. Ursula and Gudrun teach her something about her own nature and her relations with her sister. The spirit of *The Rainbow* and *Women in Love* hangs over it. *Still Life* continues the story; Frederica goes through Cambridge, and the discursive encounters that slowed up *The Shadow of the Sun* work better here, the pacing being part of the larger rhythm of the novel and the arguments tying in to the characters' fictional lives. Frederica's education (like Byatt's) includes a number of disruptive texts; they affect her consciousness but do not do much to break open Byatt's own sense of style and form, governed still by a lucid correctness. The narrative concludes in 1958. Frederica has found passion with Nigel Reiver. There is still a long way for her to go in her development into an independent adult. Four novels were originally planned, a kind of evolutionary sequence. In *Babel Tower* (1995) Frederica recognizes the awful aftermath of Lawrence in the lives of women of her generation. The book takes up again Frederica's *agon* in 1964, the center of another low, dishonest decade. Relations with Nigel have passed their sell-by date and what has become an abusively possessive relationship is unraveling. J. M. Coetzee speaks of the book's "tepid satire." Satire is not Byatt's main suit, she is no Spark in matters of wit or economy. The ghosting Lawrence text here is *Lady Chatterley's Lover,* and we wonder whether the sun whose dazzle diminished her first protagonist, Anna, was not her father, Henry, but Lawrence. There are connections, too, between Byatt's palimpsestic *Babel* notebooks, Coetzee suggests, and Doris Lessing's *The Golden Notebook* (1962).

Amid the demands of Frederica's story Byatt found time to write what is her best-known novel, the Booker Prize–winning *Possession: A Romance* (1990). Like Alan Hollinghurst's *The Stranger's Child* (2011), it entails fictional biography, invented poems, and research, what Philip Hensher calls "the romance of the archive." Coetzee calls Byatt a "gifted literary ventriloquist," the voice thrown in such a way as to evoke bodies appropriately costumed, their mouths speaking in the correct key for their period and class. Coetzee admired the labor that went to creating Randolph Henry Ash and Christabel LeMotte by making a literary oeuvre to underwrite their romance. To say, as Coetzee does, that "the realism of *Possession* . . . was purely textual," that it resided only in what Updike calls the "marvelous literary pastiche," undervalues the book. Byatt is by inclination a persuasive critical and creative apologist for the idea that books come out of books, writers nourish their imaginations and their forms from the past.

She also raises, through her considerations of Bunyan and George Eliot and her debates with Iris Murdoch, a theme pertinent to writers of fiction in a frayed "realist" tradition. John Updike, with the nineteenth-century novelists at his back, puts it this way: "Without souls to save, are mundane lives worth writing about? The historical novel steals strength and drama from the era of disturbed but pervasive faith in which the genre's model classics were born." Theology ghosts the novels, too. "Byatt is a writer," says Updike, "actively searching for sources of energy outside the comfort zone of British social fiction," yet "she makes books from books, she writes because she reads. Her own recent works of fiction are furiously bookish." He half admires this. She champions the Jamesian "humbug" of the historical novel, what Margaret Drabble refers to as "nostalgia/heritage/fancy dress/costume drama," a commonplace of modern British fiction from Ackroyd to Graham Swift, from Fowles and Julian Barnes to Ishiguro. Why? Byatt suggests motives that explain other novelists' practice, but do they answer her own? Hers is not a "political desire to write the histories of the marginalized" nor, in a period when the sense of self is attenuated, to attach her writing to "historical persons because they are unknowable, only partly available to the imagination, and we find this occluded quality attractive." It *is* a desire, "to write in a more elaborate, more complex way, in longer sentences, and with more figurative language." This she does, at the expense of narrative urgency and pace. In her writing, Updike says, the texture "has the seraglio opulence, the feeling of a flat design luxuriantly filled, to be found at the opposite end of Europe, in the work of the Turkish Orhan Pamuk." She remains susceptible to further stimuli from books. In another writer this could seem the epitome of postmodern process, but because her reading is "directed," in her case it is more like a posture of assent with aesthetic, not metaphysical, expectations. "Her creative method—saturating herself in texts, counting on a flood of information to bring her what she needs—seems a hypertrophied form of normal authorial procedure," Updike concludes, redeemed by "an Iris Murdochian belief in the momentousness of sexual attraction (usually described from the male point of view), and by a fine eye and ear for natural detail as well as for footnotes."

Byatt dislikes some of Murdoch's contemporaries in the so-called Movement, among them the sneering Kingsley Amis of *Lucky Jim* and Philip Larkin as poet. Their treachery is to her in the closed intolerance of their wit. "People of my generation at Cambridge thought Amis was wonderful. They kept saying he stood for qualities of decency. It seems to me it's the one thing he didn't stand for at all." As her writing career began, she was surrounded by "angry young men" and the claim, parroted by journalists, that no one ever spoke for the provinces. What of George Eliot, she asks, of Bennett and Lawrence?

Hilary (Mary) Mantel (b. 1952), though she belongs to the generation of Julian Barnes, Ian McEwan, and Martin Amis, and is a writer of more substance than most, seems an emanation of an earlier period. She has not been a figure "on the scene," keeping apart by disposition, for reasons of health, and by the demands her fiction makes. She has a habit of starting from scratch with each new novel, so the critics have not known what to expect. This creative strategy has obscured other significant novelists, too. They reject the familiar when they embark on a new project. They start from scratch, permitting the critics no expectation to disappoint. Mantel was awarded her first Booker Prize in 2009 for *Wolf Hall*. Set in the time of Henry VIII, the novel reviewed his reign through the sensibility of Thomas Cromwell, who is usually presented as a villain but here is a relatively warm, pragmatic, and intelligent man. With the Booker Prize, Mantel became unignorable. The "humbug" of historical fiction comes good here, as it does in the first sequel, *Bring Up the Bodies* (2012), which also won the Booker Prize. Even James Wood, writing in the *New Yorker*, overruled Henry James: "What gives fiction its vitality is not the accurate detail but the animate one," he said, and Mantel has an eye for those. She advises, "Don't re-arrange history to suit your plot," and, "Make a virtue of the constraints of the facts, or write some other form of fiction." She understands the importance of difference: "Learn to tolerate strange worldviews. Don't pervert the values of the past."

Mantel set one earlier novel in Saudi Arabia and another in South Africa; there is the gothic world of her two Muriel Axon books, about a psychopath and murderer. *A Place of Greater Safety* (1992), her first major historical novel, is set in the French Revolution. In *Fludd* (1989) the new curate of a Roman Catholic parish is the Devil incarnate. *Beyond Black* (2005) creates a conjuror more credible than Byatt's, more broadly and humanly drawn: Alison Hart, the protagonist, is herself haunted, she knows rather too much about the afterlife, and the story is of her exorcism.

What unites these disparate books is Mantel's sense of a dynamic underlying evil of which the world is not always aware. The Devil is busy in the parish, the saint is possessed by demons. At times she puts us in mind of Muriel Spark, but whereas Spark's metaphysics lead toward abstraction, the plot as paradigm, Mantel's lead us into motive and consequence; the human worlds writ small in the lives of Alison Hart or Muriel Axon, or large in the life of Thomas Cromwell, are at once individual struggles and indicative stories. They are always real-seeming and use the whole orchestra of language. Ironies inhere in the story and are not aspects of authorial self-projection or self-protection.

(Sir) Kingsley (William) Amis (1922–1995) provided—together with John (Barrington) Wain (1925–1994), whose *Hurry on Down* (1953), starring Charles Lumley as *picaro*, was a harbinger—the novel branch of that initially anemic and regularly disowned movement called The Movement. It emerged in the early 1950s and stood for a renewal of conventional form and common sense in verse and prose, a reaction to the literary excesses of the 1940s. It was bent on returning English literature to the rails it had gone off with modernism and its aftermaths. In Amis its base note is irony, its tone a variously disguised resentment of all sorts and conditions of things. Were he not an ironist he would be Malvolio. His Jim Dixon and Murdoch's Jake Donoghue are cut from similar cloth. The debut novels *Lucky Jim* and *Under the Net* appeared in the same year, 1954. Both writers are rebellious, not revolutionary, in their relations with received culture and custom. Where Murdoch's Jake speaks in his own person, *Lucky Jim* is third person, the satire more classical, the humor bolder, more "objective." Though Jim is at center stage, the ensemble stays in sight. It may seem that in *Lucky Jim* the end is overplotted, too conveniently contrived, but then Amis is in the tradition of Fielding, and just rewards, even if eccentrically determined and doled out, are the order of the day.

In 1986 J. M. Cohen, the poet and translator of, among many others, Rabelais and Pasternak, expressed a view that blighted his reputation. What threatened literature, he said, was "the trivialization of literary teaching exemplified in David Lodge's *Small World: An Academic Romance* (1984) and the new *trahison des clercs* evident in such writers as Kingsley Amis." Their work can be used "to show that culture's only a racket." In 1998 Frederic Raphael wrote a major essay entitled "Towards a Definition of Culturelessness," describing the narrowing, provincializing forces at work in English culture, the retreat into what it regarded as itself, a retreat from the larger self it might claim to be. "I like it here," says Amis, and uses this as the title for his 1958 novel. His "here" excludes the wider worlds of Forster and Maugham. His is, *pace* Browning, too little with us. "Lucky" Jim Dixon remarks, of a scholarly article he has written, "You don't think I take that sort of thing seriously, do you?"

Kingsley Amis creates convincing vile characters: Irving Macher, the young novelist in *One Fat Englishman* (1963), and Roger Micheldene, the book's protagonist; Bertrand Welch in *Lucky Jim,* the pacifist painter with the unevenly cropped beard, son of unlucky Professor Welch; and the frightening proleptic likeness of himself, in *Ending Up* (1974), as Bernard Bastable, a man with a malicious manner who has failed signally in all conventional human relations. That novel and Larkin's chilling poem "The Old Fools" (1973) breathe the same stale air of unfulfillment, and fear of the approaching yet unknowable fact of death.

In his 2001 essay "The Singer on the Shore" Gabriel Josipovici reminds us that Amis was noted for his ability to mimic people and sounds: "One of my party pieces is FDR as heard by the British over shortwave radio in 1940. This perhaps has something to do with writing fiction; a novelist is a sort of mimic by definition." Amis amused his solitude with mimicry as well. "What both Larkin and Amis couldn't stomach," writes Josipovici, "was pretentiousness in any form, and pretentiousness here means being unaware that you are a walking bundle of clichés. Both Professor Welch and Margaret in *Lucky Jim* are just such bundles, Welch in a comic, Margaret in a tragic mode." Jim, with whom we are expected to sympathize, is adaptable, "full of contradictory impulses," with "a different face for every occasion." He was so successful as a character, so imitated by later writers, that he has become the composite cliché.

As Amis grew older the young chameleon became stable in his coloring, defensive, reactionary. His "hatred of the English pretending to like and understand foreignness turned into a hatred of foreignness" and his "hatred of people like themselves pretending to like modern art turned into a hatred of modern art." This is the Waugh syndrome, but Waugh had passed the way of modernism and retained a wider social world. Hatred of cliché translated Amis into as much a cliché as Waugh became, but on a diminished scale; "the temptations of the higher emotions were constantly exploded in bursts of entirely puerile profanity" in his letters to Larkin. Profanity, Josipovici adds, was a "control mechanism when larger or higher emotions threatened."

The humor of *Lucky Jim* is English and specific to its period. Later contributors to this genre, the British campus novel, include Malcolm Bradbury, David

Lodge, Tom Sharpe, and Howard Jacobson. Its Englishness is not like Wode-house's, parodic and universal: Amis's satire and the value system it endorses—bumptious, pragmatic, chauvinist, specifically male—require complicity. Class above all, then sex and drink (he was, for a time, "drink correspondent for *Pent-house*"), provide themes. Beyond the comic and entertaining the book has a de-bunking mission that, were its quarries not Aunt Sallies, might have proven durable. The book was popular in the United States, where by 1972 it had sold over 1.25 million copies. In one of life's ironies, Amis became a well-paid teacher and lecturer in the United States, notably at Princeton, where as writing fellow he gave the Christian Gauss Lectures on science fiction. Much later he said, "Science fiction is more ambitious than the novel we're used to, because these great abstractions can be discussed: immortality, how we feel about the future, what the future means to us, and how much even we're at the mercy of what's happened in the past." His lectures were published as *New Maps of Hell: A Survey of Science Fiction* (1960). In 1968 he published an emphatic book of essays, *What Became of Jane Austen?,* in which he recycled enthusiasms and aversions, wel-coming Iris Murdoch's first novel (by then a safe bet) and giving the thumbs-down to Colin Wilson's *The Outsider,* which was in vogue.

*Lucky Jim* continues to find readers in ways that, for example, Wain's *Hurry on Down* does not, because its prejudices have become ingrained. It permitted an easy cultural dismissiveness. It let narrow readers feel adequate, even superior. Is the book funny *enough?* Waugh's Paul Pennyfeather survives better than Jim, at home and abroad. Amis has not found a new tone but curdled an old one.

Maugham was impressed with *Lucky Jim* and "the white-collar proletariat" it revealed. "They have no manners, and are woefully unable to deal with any social predicament. Their idea of a celebration is to go to a public house and drink six beers. They are mean, malicious and envious . . . Charity, kindness, generosity, are qualities which they hold in contempt. They are scum." It won the Somerset Maugham Award. "Scum" is a term Amis and Wain themselves applied, from the eminence of Oxford, to working-class parvenus, the "angry young men" with whom they were confused.

John (Gerard) Braine (1922–1986) in his first novel, *Room at the Top* (1957), cre-ated Joe Lampson, a working-class protagonist who is more "real," more com-plex, and much less entertaining than Jim Dixon, closer to the embittered char-acters of Alan Sillitoe (1928–2010). Joe seduces the daughter of a rich man, longing in his heart for the woman he genuinely loved, who dies. The Top is not quite what it was cracked up to be. Alan Sillitoe had much to be angry about, given his harsh background. In *Saturday Night and Sunday Morning* (1958) his protagonist Arthur Seaton breathes bitter working-class air, and Colin, the borstal boy in *The Loneliness of the Long Distance Runner* (1959), has a greater struggle to endure. Anthony Burgess refers to Braine and Sillitoe as "provincial." Murdoch and Amis and Wain of course are not "provincial." After all, they went to Oxford, whereas Braine left school at sixteen and Sillitoe at fourteen, the best he could do being to pull down two honorary degrees from his native Nottingham, rather late in the day.

Burgess, who shares some of Jim Dixon's mannerisms but none of his values, sees Amis's protagonist as "a radical, but radicalism is in his blood rather than in his head. He tests privilege and phony upper-class values, and he finds these extravagantly personified in Bertrand Welch, the son of his professor." Bertrand has the girl Jim wants as well, that timeless theme of "hypergamy" where a man lusts above his station. Burgess concludes: "The author, like his antiheroes, is against culture because culture has the wrong associations." Jim proves more inept than superior, an anarchist not because he has too much imagination but because he has too little. He is not able to be politic, and too set in counterprejudice to free himself. Many of Kingsley Amis's protagonists, like Iris Murdoch's, are teachers or purveyors of a culture they don't wholly credit. One character apologizes for mentioning Elgar, and Byron. In Amis's *That Uncertain Feeling* (1955) the librarian protagonist reads science fiction only. Donald Davie noted Amis's "shocked repudiation of both Philip Roth and Vladimir Nabokov." Amis had his own métier, he was "a master of comic caprice—a perfectly legitimate and entertaining garment for the moralist to appear in." Julian Symons, champion of crime writers, demurred at Amis's claim that John Dickson Carr or Ian Fleming were better novelists than Saul Bellow. Amis was a James Bond fan, publishing *The James Bond Dossier* (1965) under his own name and *The Book of Bond: Or Every Man His Own 007* (also 1965) and *Colonel Sun: A James Bond Adventure* (1968).

Readers, book by book, expected more of Amis, as of Murdoch and Wilson, than they got. Each time he brings the novel off, he always entertains, his plot surprises, there is scant repetition. But the larger surprise, the change of key we experience when, for example, Saul Bellow produces *The Adventures of Augie March* (1953) the year before *Lucky Jim* appeared, never comes. He remains compliant, serving his themes and readers, occasionally scrambling the genres. He earned (and spent) good money. He became a knight, he joylessly won the Booker Prize in 1986 for *The Old Devils*. There was an affinity with Golding's in his sour climbing. His own father was clerk to a manufacturer of mustard.

Mustard or not, Amis was "given every opportunity" and generally took what was given. He attended the City of London School and went to St. John's College, Oxford, where he befriended Larkin (the librarian protagonist of his 1955 novel *That Uncertain Feeling* calls Larkin to mind) and joined the Communist Party. He did National Service, returned to Oxford, let his Party membership lapse, worked hard for a First Class degree, and began a metamorphosis into the curmudgeon he became. Already in *I Like It Here* it is possible to confuse narrator and author and assume that the hostility to "abroad" is Amis's own.

*The Anti-Death League* (1966) is inventive. Burgess called it "a masque of ultimate bitterness—not against human institutions but against God—in the form of a secret-weapon-and-spy story." It is set in 1960s England, and God distributes nastinesses and *is* death, so that the league against death is a league against God. Liberated by the example of science fiction, the book distorts reality and explores ideas in a lightly allegorical and conjectural spirit. Amis stepped away from the social comedy readers expected of him. He told an interviewer, "My feeling when thinking of *The Anti-Death League* was, to some extent, I'm going to show them that I can be overtly serious. And this did mystify some of the critics." Many of his favorite characters come alive here: "James Churchill, Brian Leonard, Max Hunter, Ayscue, and Moti Naidu, the favorite of all of them . . . he is as near to being the author's voice as anybody usually is in one of my novels."

Some of Amis's not strictly genre-based novels draw on other formal constraints. In *The Alteration* (1976) he invents a parallel English history in which the Reformation did not occur and the Roman Church and its musical traditions, including that of the *castrato,* continued in a disconcertingly refocused and defamiliarized world. He wrote lighter, satirical, and comic fiction, never abandoning, though always recasting, the themes introduced in *Lucky Jim.* His later years are marked by disappointment, partly personal, partly social, a bitterness that seems to observe the world but is actually directed at the self. Irony that seasons and intensifies the earlier fiction takes over. The casual, "very mild" anti-Semitism (not so mild if you are a Jew), the stereotyping of Americans, and the intensifying distaste for modernism and innovation render him less and less tolerable. Gore Vidal diagnoses him as suffering from "American cleverness: the fear of being thought stupid, or dull, or behind the times." This may be a misreading: he seems to revel in being behind the times. His *Memoirs* (1991) abound in gossip and hubristic modesty: "Until the age of twenty-four, I was in all departments of writing *abnormally unpromising,*" suffering "bad influences, like Dylan Thomas and Yeats." His first novel, "which will never see the light of day" (one wonders if he preserved it, because if he did, it probably will), "was really affectation from beginning to end—well, it did have a few jokes which I lifted for later stuff, and some bits of background from the town I was living in at the time, Berkhamsted, that were usable in *Take a Girl Like You* many years later."

It is a British irony that the "angry" writers who shook up postwar British fiction were so conventional in approach to form and style. "We were trying to get back, let's say, to the pre-Joyce tradition, really—but not very consciously." Amis hates experimental prose and refuses to believe that anyone can enjoy it.

"I dislike, as I think most readers dislike, being in the slightest doubt about what is taking place, what is meant." Among his influences he numbers "early Joyce," by which he means *Dubliners* and not *A Portrait of the Artist,* as well as the more predictable galaxy of Wodehouse, Waugh, Powell, Elizabeth Taylor, "early Angus Wilson." For him, the successful inventiveness of fiction is, closely observed, merely "following up the implications of your original idea." Wodehouse taught him a crucial lesson: "You must never offer the reader anything simply as funny and nothing more. Make it acceptable as information, comment, narrative, etc, so that if the joke flops the reader has still got *something.*"

John (Robert) Fowles (1926–2005) noted in his diary for March 24, 1983, about *Granta's Best of Young British Novelists,* that Martin Amis was "vogueishly bitter (if not actually sick)"; he "makes his father seem like a warm-hearted humanist by comparison." In October of the prior year in the *Observer,* Martin Amis had reviewed Fowles's novel *Mantissa* (not the healthiest of his books, a take on the excesses of deconstruction whose earnest intention is satirical). After summarizing the ambitious, tangled subject matter of the book, Amis changes key. "But never mind about all that for now. Let us swim back to the surface and inspect the quality of the performance on offer. Seldom in his fiction has Fowles played host to humor, gaiety or brio. Here, alas, he lets his hair down." He adds, "Fowles's success, particularly in America, has something to do with making culture palatable—with giving people the impression that culture is what they are getting." They are not: after a devastating analysis, Amis concludes, "Few writers have ever blown the whistle on themselves so piercingly."

Malcolm Bradbury needs Fowles in constructing his map of postmodern British fiction and dubs him "the tricky impresario." One gets a feeling for the kinds of pretension that irritated Kingsley Amis. Fowles takes the "nostalgic modes," the conventions of the novel that are still serviceable for Murdoch, Amis, and in another sense Golding (for whom he entertained a "quasi-fraternal, quasi-nepotal affection"), and incorporates into them elements of experimental fiction. He writes books that appeal to the general fiction market and to the academic theorist at home and abroad. The experimental novel need not, it seems, entail experimental *writing.* (In *Mantissa* the main experiment, apart from the protracted dialogue between man and woman, life and art, and all the other polarities he can muster, has to do with the present tense.) Gore Vidal wrote in 1980, "Fowles is regarded as a sort of Daphne du Maurier with grammar," an inadequate judgment, we might infer from Vidal's tone, but not one he sets out to correct. Remarking that even though "he is not in Golding's class," Vidal says he admires the variety of approach: "Each book is quite different from the one before it. This confuses critics and readers, but delights me."

His most famous novel is *The French Lieutenant's Woman* (1969). It bears the same kind of relation to Thomas Hardy's *Tess of the D'Urbervilles* as Paul Scott's *The Jewel in the Crown* does to *A Passage to India*. Fowles's book entertains ideas and attempts to embody them. The basic narrative is engaging in a reminiscent style, but littered with narrative anachronisms. Hardy and modern history are uneasily at his elbow, the literary and theoretical discussions are suggestive. He entertains ideas and we are entertained. Ideas about narrative are proposed, but remain inconsequential. This is how to be safely modern, retaining readers and gaining the ear of the academy.

Charles is engaged to Ernestina but falls in love with "the French lieutenant's woman," Sarah, mysterious and perhaps tragic. Fowles provides three separate endings. It is a conventional Victorian novel that plays with the convention of the more or less happy and more or less moral ending. The conceit is that the characters to some extent learn to exercise free will in spite of the author's control. And there in the corner of the railway carriage is the flummoxed author, old and out of control, looking for his characters like a latter-day Pirandello. Sometimes he is a studious anthropologist. Sometimes he turns the hands of his watch back and reruns the story in a different direction. Sometimes we believe, because he has told us, that he has left the scene, only to reappear at the edge of vision. This author is not dead, and his pretense of having lost control opens up a host of variations on convention. The form is not reinvented but becomes porous and the reader's experience is one not of enjoying a tale but of enjoying, in a different spirit, a telling.

Fowles's first novel to appear, *The Collector* (1963), was a sinister narrative, gothic, highly successful in the marketplace. He wrote *The Magus* first, but it was published three years later, in 1966. He had been a schoolmaster in Greece, and *The Magus* draws on autobiography not only for settings but for elements of plot. As a successful writer he chose to move to a remote Dorset farm where he partly based and wrote *The French Lieutenant's Woman*. Wearying of isolation, he moved to Lyme Regis and spent much of his remaining creative life at Belmont House. There he wrote his later books, none on a par with the first three.

He read French and German at Oxford, and stayed with French. His translations are important in defining the slightly unusual space in which his imagination works—English and Gallic and on easy terms with the Continent. His excellent afterword to Alain-Fournier's *The Lost Domain* takes its epigraph from an Alain-Fournier letter of 1911: "I like the marvelous only when it is strictly enveloped in reality; not when it upsets or exceeds it." Sartre and Camus, says Fowles, "came to us after the war as strange and exciting. I always liked Camus best. Sartre I often found hard to understand. I can remember giving up *L'être et le néant* in a mixture of despair and disgust." It surprised him that he was re-garded as a paid-up existentialist and that his work was studied closely for its links to French thought. Like Golding's, his "depths" were often inadvertent; he was not Rodin's thinker but a man with instinctive preferences and suffi-ciently English to be at heart a pragmatist.

The writer whose name recurs in Fowles's essays and whose mark is every-where seen is Hardy. In Hardy the erotic gains potency because it remains un-stated, even when a perfunctory description, or indication, of its acts is most needed, as in *Tess*. Fowles describes himself as "both ravished and tormented" by the erotic, and it is the mainspring of his fiction. He claims to have com-posed, over a year, and then entirely destroyed, a pornographic novel. "It was not prudishness that made me burn it, but much more a feeling of blasphemy, an error of bad taste. It broke that secret, bared the hidden part." He compares the punishing "erotic succubus" that some writers carry to the "money succu-bus" that rides them, two jockeys riding a single nag.

*Atonement* (2001) is "a beautiful and majestic fictional panorama," Updike says, adding, with part of his tongue in his cheek, "about star-crossed literature majors." Ian (Russell) McEwan (b. 1948) has said that novels come to him ini-tially as a particular scene, indelibly vivid. Then he has to figure out where in the novel-to-be that scene will go. The task is to coordinate his spots of time into a continuous narrative, so that the envisioned scenes and later connecting scenes cohere. He began as a short-story writer. *First Love, Last Rites* (1975) re-ceived a Somerset Maugham Award, followed by *In Between the Sheets* (1978). The condensed dynamic of the short story extends into his longer fiction with its sense of heightened points of time.

Raymond Carver's stories give the impression of contained pressures, human intensities; in McEwan's the investment is more in circumstance, "gothic" ele-ments of plot, elaborated literary contrivances, as if Hemingway has not dark-ened their door. But in one way he resembles Hemingway: his material always needs stretching to make a novel. The same challenge confronts Julian Barnes, but Barnes turns it to account. McEwan and Barnes make patterns and struc-tures: plot is hard. Pieces fit into structure like story elements in a coherent col-lection. Calculation can stand in for dramatic necessity. Jonathan Franzen finds McEwan's early novels irresistible and unbearable at the same time: *The Comfort of Strangers* (1981) and *The Innocent* (1990) "were so powerfully *icky* that I'd wanted to take a hot shower after reading them."

McEwan follows Nabokov, writing key scenes on *fiches Bristol* then filling in the spaces between. "In *Enduring Love*," says Frederic Raphael, disappointed by

McEwan's writing and puzzled by its celebrity, "the only good scene is the first, in which a hot-air balloon plays its buoyant part. What, in the rest of the book, remains in the mind?" The title of this 1997 novel takes some explaining. "The result, again and again, of McEwan's method is that overheated fancy kills imagination. In the true art of fiction . . . plot is character, character is plot, as Heracleitus might say."

Born in Aldershot, McEwan spent a peripatetic childhood in the wake of his father's military postings in Asia, then in Germany, and in Libya. He uses the time spent in Libya in his polemical writings after the Salman Rushdie fatwa and 9/11, to stress that he had lived in a humane and civilized Muslim society (as a child, in a British compound), and how his hostility to Islam has to do with extremist "Islamism." When he was twelve his family was back in England. He went on to read English literature at the relatively new University of Sussex, then took a masters in creative writing at Malcolm Bradbury's new program at the University of East Anglia. He became one of Bradbury's first graduates. When, years later, he was accused of plagiarism for a passage in *Atonement,* an army of supporters marshaled in his defense—Martin Amis, Margaret Atwood, Kazuo Ishiguro, Thomas Pynchon, Zadie Smith, and John Updike among them. Much seems to rest upon McEwan, his integrity is not to be impugned.

Rebecca West reported, "Somebody told me I ought to read a wonderful thing about how a family of children buried Mum in a cellar under concrete and she began to smell. But that's the sole point of the story. Mum just smells. That's all that happens. It is not enough." The interviewer recognized "the new McEwan." As for "his sense of unmovable evil in human life": perhaps, West concedes, but so what? "He doesn't really do very much with it, does he?" As a result of his stories and the first two novels, *The Cement Garden* (1978) and *The Comfort of Strangers,* he was nicknamed Ian Macabre.

He varied his palette from all black and grey, adding other shades. In *The Child in Time* (1987) and *The Innocent* the moral world is the same but there is more resistance. *Black Dogs* (1992) marks the end of the initial phase in his work. When, five years later, he is back in action with *Enduring Love* (1997), he has become more conventional in plot and theme, an adjustment the critics welcomed. The following year *Amsterdam* was awarded the Booker Prize and in 2001 *Atonement,* his most popular and conventionally English novel, with an implausible concluding device, was published. Here is Fowles's formal heir, McEwan's manipulation of the narrative less forthright but no more subtle.

Like many of his books, *Atonement* was translated to the big screen and earned the apotheosis of an Oscar. His fiction is translatable to that more popular and remunerative medium. *On Chesil Beach* (2007) on a smaller scale shares themes with *Atonement*. *Saturday* (2005) enters a topical, modern world, and global warming is the concern of *Solar* (2010). After the neurosurgeon in *Saturday* Mc-Ewan risks another scientist, Nobel Prize–winner Michael Beard, whose ambition to "save the planet" has been negatively affected by the prize. It is a huge step away from the theme of virginity and frigidity in *On Chesil Beach,* with its *dos-y-dos* dialogue, characters snared in a theme-driven plot that will not release them, its stifling and finally stifled English tone. "They were young, educated, and both virgins on this, their wedding night, and they lived in a time when a conversation about sexual difficulties was plainly impossible. But it is never easy." The die is cast. "McEwan's method makes him the fancy-fingered Gepetto of his lay figures," says Raphael. "A writer who never surprises himself is rarely surprising." Forsterian cadences and constructions are arch beyond the period requirements (the book is set in 1962). Forster ghosts the couple arriving at their honeymoon hotel in Dorset, "in weather that was not perfect for mid July or the circumstances, but entirely adequate; it was not raining, but nor was it quite warm enough, according to Florence, to eat outside on the terrace as they had hoped." The intense politeness of the novel, which in more expansive times would have been called a novella, not only on the grounds of its extent but of its action and themes, give it a fable quality. The characters do not breathe sea air or any air at all.

Peter Ackroyd (b. 1949) shares with Vidal a penchant for hyperbolic judgments, sometimes partly true. And like Vidal he is more compelling as a critic than as a novelist. In a lecture he reprinted, delivered in 1981, he announced "the collapse, or the evident decay, of American culture in its modernist and internationalist guise, a collapse which will provide certain clues to the renewal of our native culture here in Britain." Bellow, Updike, Roth, and Heller are spent forces. Once upon a time they seemed free, with a larger language than British writers dared access; like "new Elizabethans, they employed the language as a melodic instrument, creating elaborate structures out of the air." This metaphor could hardly be less choice: "melodic instrument"? "out of the air"? "It was as if they had a more comprehensive and more humane vision of life than our narrow, domestic sagas allowed us." But no longer! The redcoats are coming. American writers lived "off the fat of society—a society they looked to not as observers or as critics, but only as clients seeking financial support." After complaining about American novelists' false, facile generalizations, he adds, "The prose of contemporary American novelists is like a veneer upon a painting, so thick that the human figures are distorted and unrecognizable beneath."

Against these decayed dragons he sets the plucky English Beowulfs: Alan Sillitoe, Beryl Bainbridge, Francis King, and Angus Wilson. He talks of "the new realism" and "paranoid realism"; the latter a term that has not caught on, though James Wood's "hysterical realism" has. The approved English writers "have made a compact with smaller truths, but their truths are human truths and they evoke *our society* [my italics] with a rare clarity, as if it were being seen for the first time. Their fiction is an exploration. Characteristically, American fiction is a statement."

Ackroyd's book *Albion: The Origins of the English Imagination* (2002) is an essay in cultural anthropology. When he stalks about his ghosted island, he must continually burr and vibrate like a metal detector. He wants to track down the elements that distinguish the English imagination from all others. He beards it in its den, finding in dark recesses Caedmon's Hymn, biographies beginning in the Anglo-Saxon lives of saints, travel books starting with *The Voyage of St. Brendan,* an artistic tradition in Anglo-Saxon stone carving and marginalia. Now Dowland, now Vaughan Williams, provide sweet Muzac. His vision is conservative and optimistic: there is persistence in traditions, they survive even when a Roman road has become a modern street. Ackroyd's sense of tradition is full of latencies that writers access whether or not they are familiar with the "originals." The anxiety of influence becomes a viral anxiety; an abiding culture informs even when it is mute: atavism at work. He uses the phrase "ethnic unity" without irony. "It has often been suggested that understatement is a national characteristic," he says.

On the subjects of biography and history, he concedes that the line dividing them from fiction is uncertain, and his own fiction grows out of history, plotting with facts but filling with imagination. His fiction begins with *The Great Fire of London* (1982), a recasting of Dickens's *Little Dorrit,* followed by a make-believe autobiography of Oscar Wilde (1983), and his *pièce de résistance* the vast novel *Hawksmoor* (1985), which investigates an eighteenth-century string of sacrificial murders and familiarizes the reader with the architects Nicholas Hawksmoor, Sir Christopher Wren, and Sir John Vanbrugh. Then Chatterton and George Meredith, Doctor Dee, Milton, Karl Marx, George Gissing and Thomas de Quincey, Charles Lamb, William Blake, Dickens, and other biographical sources feed his voracious fiction. The links between the novels and his biographical and historical works, and his television series on Dickens, London, the Romantics, the Thames, are close.

Under the editorship of the American Bill Buford, *Granta* magazine published in 1983 its list of twenty "best of young British novelists," an exercise it repeated in 1993 and 2003. It subsequently provided American lists (1996 and 2007) and Spanish (2010). Much was expected of the writers chosen for the first list and much was delivered, though writers excluded and those from the "generation" preceding suffered eclipse.

Graham (Colin) Swift (b. 1949) is the most conventionally subtle and English novelist on the first *Granta* list. The characters he creates in his nine novels have their ancestry in early Wells and in Bennett. *Waterland* (1983), which was made into a successful film, was his first substantial achievement, demonstrating the scale on which a British novel could still be written, a novel of place different in form and texture from the American writing of the period. Swift includes the stuff of comedy, a marriage; and of adventure and intrigue, a kidnapping; along with saga, three centuries of the history of the Cricks and Atkinsons and of the Fens; and in a Melvillean spirit, an account of the lore of the eel. Fragments gather into a whole. What he calls magic is present, and it works. "For writer and reader, fiction should always have that flicker of the magical."

It should also hold to the real. *Last Orders* (1996) was awarded the Booker Prize, not without some controversy because the unspoken connections within a group of World War II veterans bore structural affinities with Faulkner's *As I Lay Dying,* and the last orders of the title are both alcoholic and funereal. Swift's use of the present tense is effective, the elements of common speech are convincing and are a crucial part of the book's attraction—the casual, traditional richness of the banter of a generation connected by history and class, and even in decline comforted by this shared dialect.

*Wish You Were Here* (2011) is also about funeral arrangements and demonstrates once more Swift's stable, penetrating humanism, his grasp of how we lived and how we live, how they qualify and rewrite one another. It also takes modern history as its context, and the plot unfolds within a familiar world of fading daily news. It is 2006. Jack Luxton and his wife, Ellie, taciturn, middle-aged, run a caravan park on the Isle of Wight. The family dairy farm, worked for generations, has failed after the outbreak of foot-and-mouth disease and Jack's father's cancer and suicide. Jack's brother Tom joined the army and was posted to Iraq. As the novel opens, Jack receives news of his brother's death. It falls to him to collect the remains on "repatriation" and organize the burial. There is a trip to an Oxfordshire airbase for the ceremonial retrieval, then a private burial in the family plot in Devon. Jack's and Ellie's pasts are ploughed up by these events, and Tom's death takes Jack to an abyss of his own. Swift chooses an epigraph from William Blake: "Are these things done on Albion's shore?" The deaths at home and abroad, the pyres of livestock, the inquests, revelations, broken hearts, are non-negotiable. Swift sees events from varied points of view, suggesting the Hardyesque isolation of people drawn together by events yet driven apart by their consequences.

———•———

From 1975 to 1979 twenty-five issues of a tabloid literary magazine called *Bananas* appeared, edited first by the novelist Emma Tennant and later by Abigail Mozley, with guest editors including Elaine Feinstein (Russia) and Martin Feinstein (Latin America). Contributors included J. G. Ballard, Angela Carter, Beryl Bainbridge, Bruce Chatwin, and even Philip Roth. It was given over to what was to be called "speculative fiction." It set itself against the stale fare provided by the established writers of the day. In its third issue it carefully collated statements by Kingsley Amis, Margaret Drabble, Pamela Hansford Johnson, John Wain, and other figures. The homogeneity amounted to a new decorum. Attitudes, values, the same insouciant, commonsensical tones sounded—ironic, forthright, a negation of individualism but comfortably bourgeois, leveling away from modernism and experiment.

*Bananas* was after a different quarry at home and abroad. Salman Rushdie speaking in 1988 shared its impatience with "the kind of Anita Brookner, A. N. Wilson, Piers Paul Reid kind of writing." Something new is afoot, a group of writers apart from, even at odds with, the measured, predictable mainstream tradition. Rushdie names Timothy Mo, Martin Amis, Ian McEwan, Julian Barnes, and Angela Carter. What interests him is that it was "beginning to look like . . . a literary generation of some quality, and then that it's so very unEnglish a generation. It's horizons are broader, it's experience of life is perhaps not so relentlessly white middle class."

Rushdie might have included, as a harbinger, what Martin Amis describes as the "distempered talent" of J. G. (James Graham) Ballard (1930–2009). He is not a conventional English ironist: we read him without that protective visor. His directness and rigor give him rather a Continental aspect. He practices a Kafkaesque discipline: what can he omit, not what can he add. He despises the modern world, not out of nostalgia for the past, but out of existential clarity. For fifty years he punished it in various ways, by water, fire, wind, sandstorm. Having flayed Marsyas, he restored his skin and flayed him a second time. His characters are sodomized, driven crazy, hurt, reduced, but they live to suffer another, and another, day.

His novels, like his stories, are developed metaphors. Martin Amis says his prose rhythms "control everything: the crowds, the weather, the motion sculpture of the highways." He moves well away from realism: "The more superbly an author throws away the crutches of verisimilitude," says Amis, and he should know, being the bravest modern British crutch-thrower, "the more heavily he must lean on his own style and wit." The real contemporary world is always there but now no longer subordinated to plot and character. The highway cloverleaf, the towering trunks of council flats, the huge pods of sports stadia: this is nature now, and in it, in the thing man has created, wanders man, its subject. *The Atrocity Exhibition* (1970) marks Ballard's transition from his science-fiction phase to a harsh post-sci-fi world, his focus turning on the environment in which we actually live, yet retaining the formal logic of the science fiction he read in his formative years. In *Concrete Island* (1974) it is impossible not to recognize a made-over Robinson Crusoe. The problems of continuity are similar to those in Defoe's novel—but for remoteness, substitute alienating and unbreachable inhuman and mechanical proximity.

*Crash* (1973) is a short novel rooted in Ballard's political, imaginative, and chemical excesses, with its notorious car-sex scenarios. He writes to his subject with intimate attention and in disregard of the reader, who looks on and is neither directed nor consoled. Characters matter less than conditions and circumstances, as in a scientific experiment unfolding, its consequences recorded without sentiment. Such dreams as there are, are dreams of separation, as in *The Unlimited Dream Company* (1979), where the alienated protagonist, called Blake after the visionary poet and artist of Innocence and Experience, crashes a plane in the Thames, is rescued and recognized as the long-awaited Messiah by a community of religious zealots, and transforms Shepperton (where Ballard lived) into an unassailable Eden, fortified by a miraculously recrudescing nature against the incursions of civic man, a place of libidinal freedom. It is worth remembering that Ballard trained as a pilot in the Canadian Air Force, though he was expelled from the RCAF, as he had been from King's College, London. In *Hello America* (1981) it is the year 2114 and an expedition sets out for America in a steamship, the SS *Apollo*, named after the *Apollo* spacecraft, to discover the no longer habitable, ecologically ravaged continent. It is largely a shipboard novel, each character working out psychological issues. The science is as intriguing as that in Wells's *The Invisible Man*, though the topicality of many of the references requires extensive footnoting for new readers unfamiliar with Jerry Brown, the Manson murders, the Soviet Union (so rapidly remote). Wells's West Coast liberalism and credulity are reduced to unredeemable rubble. Nuclear weapons get a good press.

His "breakthrough" book was *Empire of the Sun* (1984), his least typical creation and a contender for the Booker Prize. It draws on his life. Jim Graham (J.G.) and his parents live in Shanghai, which, after Pearl Harbor, suffers Japanese occupation. The boy and his parents are separated; he surrenders to the Japanese and develops ambivalent relations with them, their organization and machines of war. The book, with its engaging narrative and psychology, is more conventional and assimilable than the earlier bitter pills Ballard provides, but it shares the theme of collusion between victim and victimizer, Stockholm syndrome anatomized in a historical context. His protagonist sees the great flashes in the sky that were Hiroshima and Nagasaki. Ballard had seen them through his characters, burned on the mind's retina. That light illuminated his fiction.

Three years later, with *The Day of Creation* (1987), we are back with the familiar Ballard, whose destiny, Amis says, is to remain "a cult writer, the genuine article: extreme, exclusive, almost a one-man genre." This is his *Heart of Dark-*

*ness,* and he is "our leading investigator of the effects of technology, pornography and television." His later novels often take the form of mysteries, though without the resolutions of a Christie or P. D. James. There is nostalgia for the days before shopping malls: "We had a real community, not just a population of cash tills. Now it's gone, vanished overnight when that money factory opened. We're swamped by outsiders, thousands of them with nothing larger on their minds than the next bargain sale." And later: "Consumerism is a collective enterprise. People here want to share and celebrate, they want to come together. When we go shopping we take part in a collective ritual of affirmation." This fiction is too rueful to work as satire, a world enervated, running down. Even its entropic mysteries are without solution. People flicker on the screens of memory or imagination, tuned in to conflict and political extremism with a sallow nostalgia. Cataclysm is his theme, in a dozen forms, intensified, unresolved. "Think of the future as a cable TV program going on forever."

# | 44 |

## Truths in Fiction, the Metamorphosis of Journalism

E. L. Doctorow, John Gardner, Norman Mailer, Kurt Vonnegut, Louis-Ferdinand Céline,

Joseph Heller, Joan Didion, Tom Wolfe, Hunter S. Thompson, Cormac McCarthy,

Michael Chabon, Richard Ford, Bret Easton Ellis

E. L. (Edgar Lawrence) Doctorow (b. 1931), born and raised in the Bronx, was the grandson of Russian-Jewish immigrants and named, he says, after Edgar Allan Poe. His first published story was written when he was a schoolboy under the spell of Franz Kafka. At Kenyon College, in Ohio, he experienced the New Criticism, which was in part responsible for his attention to detail, his trust in the power of the well-made sentence, and (a quality not to be taken for granted in a modern writer) his faith in the possible intelligence of the reader. It was excellent training for an editor-to-be. Theodore Dreiser, who filled in every blank space with lived detail and wrote "the literature of the everything said," had an impact on him. The New York in which "Carrie and Hurstwood play out their love affair," says Doctorow, is "one you may trust down to the last streetlamp." From Kenyon he went to Columbia University and studied drama, then responded to the draft, serving in the American army in Germany.

His first novel is a short, intense moral parable, *Welcome to Hard Times* (1960), an anti-western made into a film starring Henry Fonda. The author called it "the second worst movie ever made." About undercutting familiar genres he said, "You are playing against the music already in the reader's head, and you can always get some nice effects that way." Hard Times is a hamlet in the Dakota Territory into which an evil man strays and does his disruptive worst. How is evil to be resisted without descending to its level? Updike spoke of the young author's "puckish truculence."

Doctorow worked as a mass-market paperback editor at New American Library, where he inherited Ayn Rand and Ian Fleming. He went on to the Dial Press, editing James Baldwin, Ernest J. Gaines, Norman Mailer, and others. He learned "how to break books down and put them back together," disclosing "the value of tension, of keeping tension on the page," how to "spot self-indulgence" and edit it out. The editor is Dr. Frankenstein's cousin: "You're at ease in the book the way a surgeon is at ease in a human chest, with all the blood and the guts and everything."

His second novel, *Big as Life* (1966), played against the genre of science fiction. Mailer told him it did not go far enough. It lacked the courage of its convictions. Much later, he said in an interview, "One of the things I had to learn as a writer was to trust the act of writing. To put myself in the position of writing to find out what I was writing." He continued as a part-time novelist until, in 1969, he left the relative safety of editorial employment to write full time.

His first major novel was *The Book of Daniel* (1971), based on the lives and deaths in 1953 of Julius and Ethel Rosenberg, convicted of passing nuclear weapon secrets to Soviet agents. It began as a dogged, consecutive narrative of facts. He gave up. In a state of agitation he started again. "I began to type something. I didn't even know what it was. What it was of course was the book I had been looking for, struggling for. I was writing in a voice that I subsequently realized was the voice of Daniel, the couple's son." And it worked, stepping away from his perspective and into that of the boy. "Not I, but Daniel, would write this book. And the act of writing would become part of the story."

*Ragtime* (1975) began, Doctorow says, in "a deep moment of personal desperation." He wanted to write and had no subject. "I was facing the wall of my study in my house in New Rochelle and so I started to write about the wall . . . Then I wrote about the house that was attached to the wall." As it happens, the history of the United States adhered to it: "I thought about the era and what Broadview Avenue looked like then: trolley cars ran along the avenue down at the bottom of the hill; people wore white clothes in the summer to stay cool. Teddy Roosevelt was President." His imagination spiraled out into that time. The book is about a number of famous Americans bound together by common people, about the American Dream, about America itself, its connections and disconnections with Europe and with landscape, its infatuation with celebrity and success, its greed, injustice, sentimentalism, idealism. *Ragtime* is the closest thing to that chimera "the great American novel" that I have encountered.

Historical characters coexist naturally with fictional; the drama of connections is breathtaking. Doctorow took Mailer's advice and saw the thing through, America at the turn of the century in all its obduracy and promise. He renders radical politics clearheadedly, the argument of ends versus means having to include, among expendable means, characters the author has made real. Key figures go from rags to riches. That's part of *Ragtime;* the music is another key part, race a third. The core conflict of the book, between the uncompromising principles of a black musician and a brutish redneck community, is harrowing. What begins in romance passes through tragedy and reaches a radical climax that defines not the time in which the book was set so much as the time in which it was published. We experience a world riven by ideologies and prejudices. Updike warms to Doctorow's "information-rich prose" and notes that his "impertinent imagination holds fast to the reality of history even as he paints it in heightened colors."

Those heightened colors offended his prolific fellow-novelist John Gardner (1933–1982), author of *Grendel* (a novelization of *Beowulf,* told from the monster's point of view) and other fiction. His novels have some of the play, if not playfulness, of John Barth, and a realism displaced by the gothic. "I've never been terribly fond of realism because of certain things that realism seems to commit me to," he said. The laborious devising of settings and establishing "true" detail seem to him a waste in fiction: "the value systems of the people involved is [sic] the important thing" rather than where they live, as though setting cannot reveal character. "The point is realism of imagination, convincingness of imagination," he insists.

Gardner's *On Moral Fiction* (1978) is a score-settling book-length essay on his contemporaries, and it achieved greater celebrity than his novels about alienated, solitary figures seeking redemption. The media took him up as champion of common readers against the demands made on the intelligence by Bellow, Pynchon, Barthelme, and, in a particularly charged passage, Doctorow. He chooses the *Ragtime* scene in which Emma Goldman massages Evelyn Nesbit, a famous beauty who instinctively makes common cause with the poor. From the closet Younger Brother watches and has a spectacular orgasm. The scene, taken out of context and displayed as pornography, becomes pornographic, and Gardner can call Tolstoy to the witness box and ventriloquize his objection to Maupassant who at times fails to retain "a correct moral relation" to the thing described. The verdict: "Doctorow's writing is meretricious, or at the very least frigid in Longinus' sense: the writer is not deeply involved in his characters' lives." This is precisely wrong, the scene in question being erotic, joyful, and exuberant, intensely human in a fiction that has hitherto abounded in harshness. Gardner tries to clear a space for his kind of novel, focused, classicizing, the non-Jewish American *agon,* but his "moral fiction" is a reductive, provincial category.

Doctorow avoids establishing a "style." *The Book of Daniel* taught him that each novel needs "to invent itself. I think that the minute a writer knows what his style is, he's finished. Because then you see your own limits, and you hear your own voice in your head." When a writer can hear his or her own voice, self-imitation begins. "I have books that work themselves out and find their own voice—their voice, not mine." Generally he works slowly, writing and rewriting. His later novels, notably *Loon Lake* (1980) with its wonderfully kinetic imagery (Doctorow, after Dreiser, is the master of the American train, its rush and turn, its rhythms), the rapidly written *World's Fair* (1985), *Billy Bathgate* (1989), and *The*

*March* (2005), start from scratch, each proposes a separate world. Themes and motifs recur, but the books do not add up to a single oeuvre as Bellow's, Roth's, or Mailer's do: serial originality, each novel a first.

Doctorow's essays define an American dimension that his novels, especially *Ragtime*, belie in scope and inclusiveness. In *Poets and Presidents* (1993) he organizes the essays (written over two decades) not chronologically but in the "order of a thought process that goes: from the lives of some classic American authors, to the place of their work in the *composition of our national character* [my italics], to the ideas we can take from them as applicable to ourselves and our times, to our times as they're constructed by our politics, to the states of mind we live in that we call our culture." This use of "we" and "our," this sense of shared culture, is bracing and exclusive. His "underlying presumption" is: "The writers I speak of (white male) made of themselves repositories of American myth." This is the American voice that—despite its note of leavening irony— non-American, and nonmale or nonwhite American, readers can find presumptuous, chilling.

Doctorow sets the scene with Camus, Sartre, Tolstoy. American writers, he declares, "have tended to be less fervent about the social value of art and therefore less vulnerable to crises of conscience." A suggestive generalization—is it sustainable, if one is not in league with John Gardner? Doctorow evokes wilderness, isolation, and vulnerability in nature, themes of suicide, alcoholism, but not revolution: "some inconsolability of rugged individualism formulated entirely as a private faith." The thwarting of revolution is a theme of *Ragtime,* and as we look for exceptions across the spectrum of modern American fiction, we begin to take his point. "We see the public value of our work as an accident of its private diction." He quotes W. H. Auden, a naturalized American, who declares that a writer's politics endanger him more than his natural cupidity. We are "independent entrepreneurs of ourselves."

Of *Ragtime* he declares, "Everything . . . is true. It is as true as I could make it. I think my vision of J. P. Morgan, for instance, is more accurate to the soul of that man than his authorized biography." He concedes that "the main research for Morgan was looking at the great photograph of him by Edward Steichen." He has a sure grasp of history and setting, as of character, but he confesses, not altogether credibly, "Morgan, Emma Goldman, Henry Ford, Evelyn Nesbit: all of them are made up. The historical characters in the book are Mother, Father, Tateh, The Little Boy, The Little Girl." He deflects the question, but it stays there: the historical elements are too vivid and contextualized to have been simply invented, though the relationships he imagines, the dialogues he orchestrates, are hypothetical. He wants it both ways. He has not stretched facts, he says: "The appropriate word is *discovered* or *revealed*. Everything in that book is absolutely true." Readers content themselves with this casuistry.

———•———

The poet and editor Phyllis Hartnoll, a British publisher's reader, reported on the submission of a young American's first novel. She praised the energy and promise, but the overwriting repelled her. "Judging it as I would the book of a young English writer, and putting aside considerations of American crudity, vanity, under-development, and protracted adolescence—all of which play their part in the American judgment of books—I would say that his publishers have done him a disservice by publishing the book as it stands." She advised against acquiring it.

*The Naked and the Dead* (1948) *was* published in Britain in 1949, the year *1984* appeared. The narrative follows an infantry platoon fighting the Japanese in the Philippines in World War II. The author was Norman [Kingsley] Mailer (1923–2007). Hartnoll's report underlines the gulf between British and American editing in the late 1940s, and the specific prejudices against a bold, abundant American imagination. Some Americans side with Phyllis Hartnoll. Few readers dispute the fact that *The Naked and the Dead* is long, wordy, a charge leveled at the later Mailer also.

Gore Vidal remembers his first reaction to *The Naked and the Dead:* "It's a fake." On subsequent visits it remained a fake, derivative of André Malraux, and of Dos Passos in its attempts at direct presentation, use of flashback, and other devices. The tyranny of linear time is a given. Tyranny is central to Mailer's book, the boot in the face, the war against fascism generating unresisted fascism in the ranks. Sergeant Croft and Lieutenant Hearn are human, but they work under General Cummings, a lackluster Ahab. Mailer tries to be all-inclusive in terms of class, ethnicity: he wanted to write a comprehensive American novel. The absence of female characters and the relentlessly macho prose prove a Melvillean limitation.

Mailer wanted to write a great war novel. He lacked the experience and sincerity for the job. The son of a prosperous family, raised in Brooklyn, he attended Harvard and published his first story at the age of eighteen. In 1943 he was drafted into the American army and served in the Philippines, experiencing little combat (he ended the war as a cook) but gathering material for his book. It was published while he was studying at the Sorbonne in Paris, and it spent sixty-two weeks on the *New York Times* best-sellers list. Gore Vidal, a highly sensitized critic repelled by Mailer's egotism and homophobia, disliked the faux-religious tone and manner. Mailer in his abundance was kin to Thomas Woolf, but with a historical and human subject he could not get a purchase on. Vidal points to what he considers Mailer's specific failure. "What matters finally is not the world's judgment of oneself but one's own judgment of the world. Any writer who lacks this final arrogance will not survive very long in America." Mailer had all the other arrogances, but in his first novel not this one. In 1971 Mailer head-butted Vidal just before a recording of the Dick Cavett Show because Vidal gave a bad review to *The Prisoner of Love* (1971), and the on-screen exchange is a classic of television invective. In the end, Vidal exercised the survivor's prerogative and forgave his adversary: "Yet of all my contemporaries I retain the greatest affection for Norman as a force and as an artist. He is a man whose faults, though many, add to rather than subtract from the sum of his natural achievements."

Martin Amis initially described Mailer as "this pampered super-brat." But it is hard to resist his energy and directness. As he goes, he adjusts, not erasing but incorporating what comes before. Mailer stalks a subject and is not always quite sure when he has caught it, sometimes going beyond the point. His life is of a piece with his readjusting writing lens: he makes mistakes, acknowledges them, moves on. So he stabbed one of his six wives (so he ran through *six* wives); so he helped a lifer obtain parole and the lifer reoffended within six weeks, murdering a restaurant employee in the East Village; so he silenced debates when he was president of PEN yet maintained an often absurd libertarian position, not least in his campaign for mayor of New York City, with a program that included secession from the state and the devising of an idealistic, devolved civic anarchism. Some writers, Amis says, possess a "psychic thesaurus." Mailer's includes the words: *ego, bitch, blood, obscenity, psyche, hip, soul, tears, risk, dare, danger, death.* "When *The Naked and the Dead* appeared," Amis remembers, "I thought someone the size of Dickens was among us"—not a bad comparison in terms of scope, copiousness, and diverse focus.

James Baldwin prophesied that Mailer's destiny would be "to help excavate the buried consciousness of this country," recalling Stephen Dedalus: "to forge in the smithy of my soul the uncreated conscience of my race." But Mailer got distracted, the claims of history filtered by an overbearing ego. His humor is deadpan, the kind that divides understanders from misunderstanders. Of *Tough Guys Don't Dance* (1984) Martin Amis says, "Laughs in Mailer derive from close observation of things that are, so to speak, funny already"; here "the humor arises from the humorlessness."

The novelist and essayist Jonathan Lethem as a teenager was enthralled by Mailer's *Advertisements for Myself* (1959), its crudity, vanity, its fight-picking verve. Among writers Mailer was unusually plucky even for an American, and Lethem, who is intellectual and frilly by comparison, projects himself into the hairy-chested avatar. Mailer was for some of his immediate successors what Hemingway had been to him, a force and a model. To the pugilistic "Hemingway tradition" into which he writes, Amis says, Mailer brings "the element of paranoia." He differs fundamentally from Hemingway, who recognizes what he's up against. Mailer is unsure, thrashing about, a lot of language is involved. Economy and limitation of effect are not on his agenda. Philip Roth calls *Advertisements* "a chronicle for the most part of why I did it and what it was like—and who I have it in for: his life as a substitute for his fiction."

Joyce Carol Oates in *The Faith of a Writer* notes that *The Naked and the Dead* was the fruit of all Mailer had learned up to the age of twenty-five. He invented the characters from life, he made notes and studied them, then put them away and started writing. The book took shape a certain distance from the preparation: "The novel itself seemed merely the end of a long active assembly line." His second novel, by contrast, was the fruit of inspiration. *Barbary Shore* (1951) surprised him. *Why Are We in Vietnam?* (1967) he regarded as the fruit of "dictation" by the voice of Ranald ("D.J.") Jethroe, the "highly improbable sixteen year old genius—I did not even know if he was black or white," his Texan Holden Caulfield.

"Who but an American," asks Nadine Gordimer with something of Hartnoll's distaste, "could have written *Advertisements for Myself*? Or, having written it, would have given it that title? Even Norman Mailer begins to show that the fatal flaw in his strong but flawed talent may be this obsessive turning in on himself, a rending apart if not a contemplation of the navel." Does he ever sit still enough to do that? Are his energies not invested in a whole body in movement? "If he is in fact attempting to be America's first existentialist writer, this tendency points to the unlikelihood that he will succeed. Self-obsession rules out the explicit moral clarity demanded by an existential approach." It is not conventional egotism, the romantic privileging of self, but rather an awareness of the uncontainable, wayward body, with its functions and thoughts, that he partly is. In the great anti-Vietnam protests in Washington he found himself in the company of the poet Robert Lowell, who becomes a character in *The Armies of the Night* (1968), as Mailer does in Lowell's poems. Though the powerful, high-pitched poet and Mailer are so different, their temperaments are similar. Lowell's "confessionalism" is in fact a clinical engagement with who and what one is but cannot control or fully know.

In *Armies* Mailer perfected his self-fictionalization. Bernard Malamud says, "After he had invented 'Norman Mailer' he produced *The Armies of the Night,* a beautiful feat of prestidigitation, if not fiction." Already the gap between fact and fiction, narrator and writer, is blurring. Vidal refers to *Armies* and *The Executioner's Song* (1979) as "non-fiction novels." Classification of *Oswald's Tale: An American Mystery* (1996), is difficult, too. Is it a biography or a "biography" of John Kennedy's murderer, Lee Harvey Oswald? Don DeLillo's 1988 *Libra* explores the same subject with more invention and supposition. For DeLillo the exhaustive Warren Report presented to President Johnson in September 1964 was a Joycean text, a "megaton novel" supporting the view of Oswald as sole agent. Mailer had the same original texts and additional fictional and speculative material that had accumulated in the eight years following the assassination. This made his task more complex.

*Armies* is in two parts, "History as a Novel" and "The Novel as History." The symmetry is false: the omission of the indefinite article from "History" in the second half suggests History's authoritative singularity, the Novel's multiplicity and relativity. Mailer follows early Dos Passos, still popular when he wrote, in assembling and documenting his account, and Dreiser in detailing it. He is experimental and realist in equal degrees. Tolstoy he declares is his master: thanks to him, he escapes the solipsism of which he finds the Beats guilty, and dares to approach major themes. The present or near-present tense is where he is most at home. As a writer he fully inhabits the world in which he lives. *Barbary Shore* may be a parable with surreal elements, but it focuses on the Cold War by means of a Brooklyn boarding house and has something in common with Conrad's *Under Western Eyes*. *The Deer Park* (1955) is based in his experience as a Hollywood screenwriter. Because of its sexual content it was slow to find a publisher but became a best seller.

From 1960, for two decades, every four years Mailer attended and described the Republican and Democratic Party conventions. John Kennedy, alive and dead, fascinated him. In "Superman Comes to the Supermarket," written for *Esquire* in 1960, we have one of the first exemplary texts of the New Journalism, followed up in later convention reports including the celebrated "Miami and the Siege of Chicago." The 1960 text steps, via sustained metaphor, beyond the realm of reportage and essay. The disclosure is invasive, it is about ourselves, as readers. "Since the First World War Americans have been leading a double life, and our history has moved on two rivers, one visible, the other underground; there has been the history of politics which is concrete, factual, practical and unbelievably dull if not for the consequences of the actions of some of these men; and there is a subterranean river of untapped, ferocious, lonely and romantic desires, that concentration of ecstasy and violence which is the dream life of the nation." The underground river surfaced during the Second World War and "the life of the nation was intense, of the present, electric; as a lady said, 'That was the time when we gave parties which changed people's lives.'" Then it subsided again, but its memory and current were felt, and it broke through with the surprise of Truman's victory, the Korean war, the Bomb. The nation summoned Ike, replacing Uncle with Father, and the treason trials began. We were back to two divided rivers. We were back to a world of "rhetoric without life." Then along came Kennedy with new promise. Tom Wolfe recalled his eureka moment when journalism and fiction were emancipated: "It was the discovery that it was possible in nonfiction, in journalism, to use any literary device, from the traditional dialogisms of the essay to stream-of-consciousness."

*An American Dream* (1965) was serialized, and written, as Dickens wrote, while the serialization was in progress. When it was "brought to book," Mailer's editor was E. L. Doctorow. *Ragtime* was a decade away. Mailer enjoyed the pressure and immediacy of serial writing and journalism. *The Executioner's Song* is a novelized account of the death and life of the murderer Gary Gilmour, based largely on interviews with the victim's and the murderer's friends and family. Gilmore demanded execution: the appeals process had gone on long enough. The book was awarded one of Mailer's two Pulitzer Prizes. The enormous *Harlot's Ghost* (1991) weighs in at 1,310 pages and is based on extensive research into two postwar decades of the CIA.

*Why Are We in Vietnam?* may prove his most enduring novel. It takes place in Alaska, where a rich Texan father and his adolescent son go hunting. The father is obsessed with killing a grizzly bear, a latter-day capitalist Ahab, only Ahab with a helicopter and a gun so powerful that when he hits his prey, he destroys it. The hunting techniques and the disparity of the quest are easily emblematic. Political allegory haunts the novel, from the title to the boy's announcement that he will go as a soldier to Vietnam. The focus is on nature and man, what place an armed American man can occupy in the world. There is something like hope in the decisive rebellion of the son, his declaration of independence. When he encounters the bear, he expresses his integrity, approaching it in a spirit of humility and wonder. His father deprives him of the moment. He is initiated not into the sacredness of nature but into generational and familial alienation.

Mailer's least accomplished novel was his hardest won. Begun in 1972, *Ancient Evenings* was not published until 1983. It proves Henry James right about historical fiction. Set 3,000 years ago in the court of Ramses IX, on the Night of the Pig, it is, Anthony Burgess insists, "taboo-breaking," with fecal imagery, the sodomizing of the foe and other unsettling details, including direct contact between the living and the dead, reincarnation, and gods with hyperbolic libidos. It was not quite so radical-seeming in 1983 as it would have been in 1948. Controversy made it another best seller. William Burroughs acknowledged that *The Western Lands* (1987) was inspired by it.

Mailer's place can be plotted on the jagged line that runs from Miller through Burroughs. But he is a documentary artist, too busy with the city and the age to permit himself a pastoral afternoon, even in Central Park. The nonfiction novel is his natural métier, he is most answerable when his writing imitates fact. He is not a fragmenting futurist but a romantic without an answering landscape. His aesthetics project a lurid sexual, philosophical, and spiritual politics. He is a deep journalist, the depth measured by his performative arrogance and his corrective sense of justice, to which he subjects his own aberrations. If we set his nonfiction novels alongside Capote's, we contrast Capote's artfulness, insisting on his sources, his gathering of evidence, and covering over lacunae and lies, with Mailer's less devious approach. *The Castle in the Forest* (2007) was the first of a projected trilogy and deals with Hitler's childhood. But Mailer died at eighty-four, shortly after it was published to relatively friendly reviews.

The same year, also at age eighty-four, another Second World War veteran died, a writer less controversial and more universally loved, Kurt Vonnegut Jr. (1922–2007). For a time Mailer and Vonnegut were friends because their wives were. When they went out, "Kurt and I would sit there like bookends. We would be terribly careful with one another; we both knew the huge cost of a literary feud, so we certainly didn't want to argue." They never discussed one another's books, or writing, except once, when Vonnegut, Mailer reports, "looked up and sighed: 'Well, I finished my novel today and it like to killed me.' When Kurt is feeling heartfelt, he tends to speak in an old Indiana accent." Vonnegut's wife re-sisted. She said, "'Oh, Kurt, you always say that whenever you finish a book,' and he replied, 'Well, whenever I finish a book I do say it, and it is always true, and it gets more true, and this last one like to killed me more than any.'"

Mailer's documentary and descriptive concentration on his subjects means he mines deep and wide. After the war experience, after his time at the Sorbonne, he had a perspective, and in this he resembled Gore Vidal. Peter Ackroyd writes in a review, "Vidal came to Europe and discovered America; Vonnegut stayed in America and seems to have found himself with increasingly little to write about." Note the phrase "increasingly little," the dream of any Flaubertian writer.

"So it goes." Vonnegut's Billy Pilgrim is a peculiar individual, not just a pro-jection. With Vidal we hear tones, styles, litheness; we come away more with a sense of the narrator than of his characters. However deliciously, they drown in style, sometimes parodic, sometimes "period," sometimes efficiently contempo-rary. Between us and the screen, there he is, now shadow, now a body interposed. His narratives seem to occur within the rectangle of a large or little screen, the bites he feeds us are of a preconsidered length. The magician remains in the act. Billy Pilgrim, on the other hand: he stands apart from his author, you can hold a conversation with him. Maybe that's the problem. At a certain point Vonnegut realized the critics were out to get him, they wanted him "squashed like a bug," not just because he was rich. "The hidden complaint was that I was barbarous, that I wrote without having made a systematic study of great literature, that I was no gentleman, since I had done hack writing so cheerfully for vulgar magazines—that I had not paid my academic dues." Billy Pilgrim, "c'est moi," just as Bunyan's Christian carried the burden of the author's own soul.

Billy was, like Vonnegut, born in 1922, on the fourth of July, a totemic American as well as an alter ego. He is a mess of contradictions, a scrawny giant, gaunt like a camp victim. He studies optometry and he communicates with the inhabitants of "the Planet Tralfamadore, Where the Flying Saucers Come From. Peace." They kidnap him, exhibit him as a zoo creature, and nobody on earth believes him when he returns. Billy, drafted in 1943 (the same year as Mailer, and Vonnegut), becomes a chaplain's assistant and is packed off to the front line. He is taken prisoner (like the author) by earthmen at the Battle of the Bulge. He is shunted unpredictably in time as in space by captors who, after adventures, deposit him in Dresden, where as conscripted labor he is made to live in a cool meat-cellar (Slaughterhouse-Five), well under ground, with carcasses for company. He survives the firebombing of Dresden, gathering human and other remains with the cleanup teams. Arriving home, he is sent to a sanatorium to recover. Here he reads the books of one of Vonnegut's recurrent, mysterious alter-egos, the sci-fi writer Kilgore Trout who plays a prominent role in Vonnegut's best-selling *Breakfast of Champions* (1973). He lives and relives the separate moments of his life and is finally killed by the man who promised to track him down and murder him for a deed he did not commit.

Vonnegut remarked to his friend Saul Steinberg, "I'm a novelist, and many of my friends are novelists and good ones, but when we talk I keep feeling we are in two very different businesses. What makes me feel that way?" The silence between them is timed at six seconds. Steinberg replies, "It's very simple. There are two sorts of artists, one not being in the least superior to the other. But one responds to the history of his or her art so far, and the other responds to life itself." So it goes. There is distance between "autobiographical collage," Vonnegut's description of the method of *Slaughterhouse-Five* (1969), in which form comes with content, and the conventionally shaped Vidal construction, even when Vidal's subject matter is unexpected and challenging, whether in *The City and the Pillar* or in his fanciful futurology. The past of *Slaughterhouse-Five* was written and published within the present that was the Vietnam War: part of its impact was its untimely timeliness. Much of its force is in its immediacy: simple sentences, illustrations, urgency, and clarity. "The point is to write as much as you know as quickly as possible." The speed of the journalist, a style unaffected, plain as Defoe's.

Doris Lessing calls him "moral in an old-fashioned way . . . he has made nonsense of the little categories, the unnatural divisions into 'real' literature and the rest, because he is comic and sad at once, because his painful seriousness is never solemn." His acknowledgment and expression of the nuanced nature of experience makes him "unique among us; and these same qualities account for the way a few academics still try to patronize him." As though what he does is easier than the resolved plotting of more derivatively artful novelists. *Slaughterhouse-Five* declares itself a failure in its closing lines, David Lodge remarks; in fact, it is Vonnegut's best book, "and one of the most memorable novels of the postwar period in English." Vonnegut told John Barth's writing students that, "like all writers," he wrote fiction "in the secret utopian hope of changing the world." That's how real his art is, inhabiting its reality.

After Vonnegut was liberated by the Soviet Army, the war was over and he returned to the United States. He went to the University of Chicago to study anthropology and returned to journalism as a reporter, chasing ambulances. His research plans were rejected, but in 1971 his fourth—and his first successful—novel, *Cat's Cradle* (1963), was accepted for the master's program: it had sufficient "anthropological content." When he was teaching at Iowa, *Cat's Cradle* became a best seller. He began on *Slaughterhouse-Five*. Because it stays close to his own memories, yet retains precision and humour, *Slaughterhouse-Five, or The Children's Crusade: A Duty-Dance with Death* (the full title, like an eighteenth-century blurb-title, goes on for forty-five words) surpasses *Cat's Cradle* as a novel. It engages memory at its most extreme; it risks direct address ("All this happened, more or less") before establishing the indirection of the narrative.

But *Cat's Cradle* is essential Vonnegut. Felix Hoenikker, a fictional inventor of the A-bomb, plays cat's cradle at the moment the bomb is dropping through the air on Hiroshima. One of Vonnegut's jobs entailed interviewing scientists about their research. He came to believe that the scientists lacked a moral understanding of the consequences of their wilder findings: their intellectual freedom imperiled the human species. Hoenikker discovered the formula for "ice-nine," a fatal transformer of water into a solid substance. The story takes us to an impoverished fictional island in the Caribbean where a hybrid dialect of English is spoken and Papa Monzano (not unlike Papa Doc Duvalier of Haiti) tyrannizes. Vonnegut the anthropologist created a weird, consistent, and coherent society, its suppressed religion of Bokononism, its extreme Christianity. The science is as plausible as in a novel by Wells, and the climax almost credible. Apocalypse comes when by accident the waters of the world solidify, and John (or Jonah; the book opens on a parodic note, "Call me Jonah") the narrator-protagonist—living in a cave with a handful of survivors—commits his account to paper, a testament to human stupidity. The invention of a religion, a language, and a political system, as well as the invention of the water-science necessary for the plot, combine elements that on the face of it are incompatible: a primitive social order and specialized scientific work. Incompatibility is the theme: the world is not ready for the extreme discoveries of science and is at risk when entertaining them. The story is satirical, comic, exciting; the fates of the too-numerous and stylized characters rather matter.

In his "autobiographical collage" *Palm Sunday,* Vonnegut graded his works to date, giving his first novel, *Player Piano* (1952) a B, his second and third books both A's, and so on. His two A+ novels are *Cat's Cradle* and *Slaughterhouse-Five.* His later work he grades more harshly, with a couple of D's and C's. The highest marks are reserved for books in which the science elements, such as time travel, are developed as crucial parts of the plot, leaving the narrator free to get out of painful spaces long enough to establish an ironic purchase on them. *Breakfast of Champions* merits only a C despite its popularity; he used felt-tip sketches, long paradoxes, leaps in time, to foreground the process of composition, metafiction taking control, though the author's identity is not in doubt. The I who debates with I shares Vonnegut's life experience. Some characters and themes weave through the novels—familiarly, if not reassuringly, suggesting that the number and variety of books belong to a single project. With *Timequake* (1997) he called it a day: the millennium was before him, he had issued warnings and told the story of his time obliquely, luminously, setting formal challenges that distracted him and us from the explosive material that was his subject, and then delivered it in full.

Vonnegut the voice of conscience, the Trotskyite, the devotee of homegrown socialist leaders, was also Vonnegut the rich investor. His portfolio of shares included Dow Chemical, manufacturers of napalm, despite the reek of charred flesh in Dresden and his stated opposition to the Vietnam War. He spoke up for green causes yet invested in strip-mining companies. Having signed the anti-Vietnam pledge by writers and editors to withhold taxes in protest against the war, he would not bestir himself to campaign for the antiwar presidential candidate. In his eighties he spoke out unguardedly of suicide bombers who go to death for their "self-respect." In the second Bush administration, he reports a sardonic nostalgia for the Nixon years.

There are no realized women characters in Vonnegut, though he claims his ideal reader, the one he wrote for, was his beloved sister, three of whose children he adopted at her death. Her warmth, her tones, her close silence, elicited from him jokes and hard truths. He does not regret the absence of love themes and women. "I have other things I want to talk about." He compares his experience with Ralph Ellison's. If the hero of *Invisible Man* "had found somebody worth loving, somebody who was crazy about him, that would have been the end of the story."

Don DeLillo dedicated his thirteenth novel, *Cosmopolis* (2003), to Vonnegut and to Paul Auster. It is his traffic jam novel: the young billionaire protagonist despite all his money cannot get the jam to break. The president is in town, the town is New York. With Eric Packer go fiction and metafiction. Updike describes the book as one of "extravagant wealth and electronic mysticism." What

DeLillo seems to have learned from Vonnegut is a lesson about the open plot: "The trouble with a tale where anything can happen is that somehow nothing happens." Vonnegut escapes this peril because however metafictional and science-fictional he becomes, there is historical incident, and slowly it yields its truths to imagination and memory. The reality of Dresden he lived, but it took time for him to register the magnitude of the event: "It was a secret, burning down cities—boiling pisspots and flaming prams." To tell the truth, he had to avoid heroisms. A friend's wife remarked to him that, as soldiers, he and his comrades "were just children then. It's not fair to pretend that you were men like Wayne and Sinatra, and it's not fair to future generations, because you're going to make war look good." He needed this "very important clue": "She freed me to write about what infants we really were: seventeen, eighteen, nine-teen, twenty, twenty-one. We were baby-faced, and as a prisoner of war I don't think I had to shave very often. I don't recall that that was a problem."

Kurt Vonnegut and Joseph Heller (1923–1999) are cut from similar motley. Dark humorists, veterans of the Second World War at its most extreme (Heller had sixty bombing missions in six months of 1944), they had their big success relatively early, and then a long, troubled aftermath. Neither was ever quite made welcome at the top table of American literature. The unconventionality of their success was held against them. "Oh God," said Vonnegut when he learned of Heller's death, "this is a calamity for American literature." John Updike took it in his stride. The "sweet man" had produced his "important" novel first. "Too many homines unius libri like Heller," said Anthony Burgess, with Vonnegut in mind, too—one-book men. One book can be enough. And one-book writers generally have a substantial bibliography underfloating the tip of the iceberg.

Like Vonnegut's, Heller's writing was affected by Louis-Ferdinand Céline (1894–1961), an "important" novelist with a decisive first book, whose anti-Semitism (an insistent aspect of a wider misanthropy) has affected his legacy. Some of his books cannot be legally reprinted in France. Céline developed a gappy, epi-sodic, colloquial style. His best work absorbs the picaresque spirit into the style itself. The discontinuities, the diverse vernacularity, the Rabelaisian hyperbo-les and abrupt transitions disclose a protagonist in transit through a world of disparities. There was nothing new in the constituent parts, but the ensemble was appropriate to the extreme experience of modern men. In English his best-known book is his first, *Journey to the End of Night* (*Voyage au bout de la nuit*, 1932) with its antiheroic protagonist, Ferdinand Bardamu, his experiences drawing on Celine's own picaresque life. It involves the First World War, French colonial Africa, and the United States in the postwar period, and then Bardamu (like Céline) becomes a physician among the Paris poor. Modern medicine and sci-ence are satirized, along with modern industrial practice (he spent time at the

Ford Motor Company) and other aspects of a world distorted by the will of money, machines, and untried ideas.

His misanthropy is expressed in hollow, nihilistic laughter as the tumbril bears us to a place of execution. Bardamu in the end works at an asylum not far from the "normal" world he has created. Henry Miller channeled Céline's writing to American readers. Charles Bukowski called him "the greatest writer of 2000 years," a verdict worthy of Céline himself. He became a defining port of call for many would-be moderns. Kerouac and Burroughs are in his debt as well.

Joseph Heller, son of Russian-Jewish immigrants, was born in Brooklyn. He started writing early, in an earnest spirit. When he left school, he wandered among jobs for a year, as an apprentice blacksmith, delivery boy, clerk, and then enlisted in 1942 in the Army Air Corps. On the Italian Front in 1944 he flew the combat missions that the jinxed protagonist Captain John Yossarian in *Catch-22* flies, though Heller's missions were less perilous than Yossarian's, mainly milk runs with limited flak. After the war, he studied English at the University of Southern California and New York University under the Servicemen's Readjustment Act of 1944, better known as the G.I. Bill. The arts benefited from the Bill, which assisted writers, including Lawrence Ferlinghetti, Norman Mailer, Frank McCourt, and James Wright. Heller told Vonnegut that but for the war, he would have been in dry-cleaning. He took his MA in English from Columbia University and went to Oxford on a Fulbright for a year. At Pennsylvania State University he taught "composition" for two years, and then creative writing— fiction and script—at Yale. Then he went into advertising and began publishing his not very distinguished stories.

What turned Heller into the author of *Catch-22*? He is not a "literary" writer but in his culture an everyman, which is one reason he speaks directly to an enormous range of readers. Howard Jacobson contrasts novelists "who mind their words" in the manner of Flaubert, "and novelists who don't—those who inherit the line of interminable telling, of inexhaustibility and seeming garrulousness, that begins with Rabelais and gets a second wind with Dickens." Though Heller is of the latter kind, Kafka's *The Trial* stayed with him as a grim comic nightmare, and the popular Jewish iconoclastic tradition of downbeat humor affected both of them. It is a kind of humor that has come to draw on and feed back into cinema and television. Kafka was a keen filmgoer, influenced by early European cinema; Heller for his part relished the 1940s and 1950s comedy of Abbott and Costello and the Phil Silvers Show featuring Sergeant Bilko (1955–1959). He in turn had an impact on the film *MASH* (1970) and *M\*A\*S\*H* the television series (1972–1983). Vietnam becomes a frame through which we read the novel's action, the blunders and attrition of that slow, unambiguous defeat. Over 10 million copies of *Catch-22* have sold since it was first published to mixed reviews.

*Catch-22* (1961) was originally to be entitled *Catch-18* but Leon Uris (1924–2003) published *Mila 18*—about the Jewish experience under the Nazis in the Warsaw ghetto—earlier that year and Uris was famous already with *Battle Cry* (1953) and *Exodus* (1958), both with successful film versions. *Catch-22* as a phrase has become part of the language. It describes those lose-lose situations in which the outcome will be negative whatever choice is made. "Yossarian was in the hospital with a pain in his liver that fell just short of being jaundice. The doctors were puzzled by the fact that it wasn't quite jaundice. If it became jaundice they could treat it. If it didn't become jaundice and went away they could discharge him. But this just being short of jaundice all the time confused them." The catch here is that either way the illness turns he will be returned to active service. During these respites, these "betweens," the terror of the situation is exacerbated. Everything entails and then includes its opposite. Heller's humor ("he catches us out with comedy," Jacobson says) and his anger are contiguous. He does not preach and yet radically instructs.

Heller had written some lackluster stories. One day in 1953, two lines came to him.

> It was love at first sight.
> The first time he saw the chaplain, [name] fell madly in love with him.

The narrative began to take shape, he wrote twenty pages out by hand, he was on his way. When the book was published in 1961, after years of index cards (shades of Nabokov) and breathless narrative runs, the first two lines had become,

> It was love at first sight.
> The first time Yossarian saw the chaplain he fell madly in love with him.

Robert Gottlieb, his Simon and Schuster editor, worked closely with the author and tried to deflect some of the critics. Waugh repaid Heller's admiration by a tart letter to Gottlieb: "You are mistaken in calling it a novel. It is a collection of sketches—often repetitious—totally without structure." Waugh was familiar with Céline's *Voyage,* which he had read in John Marks's English translation (1934), and Céline may have read Waugh's *Black Mischief* and *A Handful of Dust* when they appeared in French. Heller was American, and a Jew, writing in vernaculars that offended Waugh.

Heller's novel begins in high comedy, but in the second half the humor continues in a minor key, bleak and relentless. The Army Air Corps captain, inventing dozens of excuses to get out of combat missions, is thwarted and launched into a hostile sky. It's everyone's fault, it's no one's fault, blame can never be assigned or responsibility affixed. The world is mad, and Yossarian must navigate that madness on its terms or become its victim.

Nadine Gordimer speaks of *Catch-22* in the same breath with the German novelist Günter Grass's *The Tin Drum*. "Like Grass's Oscar, Heller's Captain Yossarian is a kind of Last Man—a sum total of humanness . . . in a world where men have imprisoned themselves. The law of supply and demand grills and drills them. God is a searchlight turned on now and then by the jailers in the observation tower." Yossarian decides to "live forever, or die in the attempt." In the preface Heller wrote for a new edition of *Catch-22* in 1994, he declares his hero still alive. One day he will pass away: "But it won't be by my hand." And *Closing Time* (1994) revisits some *Catch-22* survivors in their later years.

Many characters do survive, they even prosper within paradox: Milo Minderbinder the entrepreneur, for example, turns everything to credit and sells out to the Germans on reasonable terms; the women we meet prey on the men, the world remains impervious to the feminizing effect that the end of hostilities (will it ever be called peace?) might be expected to bring. The main ideological conflict underlying the war is ignored: what matters is the conflict within a single culture, a single organization, not the enemy without but the one within. The abstractions of ideology are as nothing to human nature, playing with the overextended structures of hierarchy and restraint.

Of his remaining six novels, only the second, *Something Happened* (1974), rivals *Catch-22*. Its arresting first sentence, Joyce Carol Oates suggests, more or less *dictates* what is to follow. Heller's false starts on novels begin with just such sentences; they begin to germinate but then stop growing. If growth continues for a hundred or more pages, there will be a book. "I get the willies when I see closed doors. Even at work, where I am doing so well now, the sight of a closed door is sometimes enough to make me dread that something horrible is happening behind it, something that is going to affect me adversely; if I am tired and dejected from a night of lies or booze or sex or just nerves and insomnia, I can almost smell the disaster mounting invisibly and flooding out toward me through the frosted glass panes. My hands may perspire, and my voice may come out strange. I wonder why. Something must have happened to me sometime." The writing continues in the present tense, with its limitations and shortenings, and its immediacy. Here, Vonnegut says, in a description that fits *Catch-22* as well, though it is a more hectic production, "Mr. Heller is a first-rate humorist who cripples his own jokes intentionally—with the unhappiness of the characters who perceive them." His estranged daughter, Erica Heller, in an evenhanded memoir calls it her father's best, "569 pages of hilarious but mordant, caustically wrapped, smoldering rage." The book takes revenges on the protagonist's family, and Bob Slocum shares as much with the older Heller as Yossarian does with the younger. His wife drinks too much and has been bleached by time (and neglect). The daughter is drab and hostile. Some of the dialogue, she remembers, actually occurred, including the line, "What makes you think you're interesting enough to write about?" in the chapter entitled "My Daughter is Unhappy."

Mailer begat the "New Journalism." Fact validates fiction, between journalism and fiction the line blurs; fiction aspires to the kind of truth it pretended to tell in Defoe. Throughout Mailer there is a pull in directions we recognize as New Journalistic: autobiography, social commentary, and history exist alongside invented autobiography, invented history. Joan Didion praised *An American Dream* for its direct truthfulness, including in its depiction of women. In *Sexual Politics* Kate Millett took a contrary view, and Mailer responded indirectly with his polemic *The Prisoner of Sex* (1971), a defense of Lawrence and Henry Miller. There is no brave virtue in political incorrectness for its own sake. One aspect of the New Journalism, however, is its redneck instincts.

Mailer's co-conspirators include the Truman Capote of *In Cold Blood*, Joan Didion herself, Hunter S. Thompson, and Tom Wolfe. In the background are ranged Kerouac and Burroughs, Vonnegut and Heller. Something big was brewing in response to the curdling historical moment. For fiction to be of service, it had to look unblinking at the world as it is.

Joan Didion (b. 1934) has written five novels, and essays and journalism that shade into fiction. Some of her work is in effect a collaboration with her husband, John Gregory Dunne (1932–2003): teamwork in which she took the lead, but the two made common cause. Were it not for the collaborative element Tom Wolfe might have described her work, as he did that of others, as intimate journalism or literary nonfiction, the adjective "literary" suggesting "fact plus"—not plus interpretation but plus atmosphere, dialogue, color, smell, texture, a bringing-alive licensed to body forth the merely factual. There is in collaborative fiction, of course, a formal intimacy that might from one angle seem like a greater objectivity. New Journalistic writing can be read "like a novel" though never conventionally *as* a novel. The true elements impose a different discipline on the reader who may judge the quality of the prose but must also enter into a moral engagement with the writing, too. The author tends to be present, sometimes as filter, sometimes standing in the light and overshadowing the subject. The author's, or the narrator's, subjectivity is exposed, and the reader's also, as a result.

Borrowing Orwell's title, Didion contributed "Why I Write" to the *New York Times* in 1976. It is the text of a talk she gave; its informal "voice" is an aspect of its theme. One reason she stole the title, she says, is the sound it made, the three repeated vowels, I I I. "In many ways writing is the act of saying I, of imposing oneself upon other people, of saying listen to me, see it my way, change your mind. It's an aggressive, even a hostile act." She describes herself as incapable of understanding abstract terms and themes. "I write entirely to find out what I'm thinking, what I'm looking at, what I see and what it means. What I want and what I fear. Why did the oil refineries around Carquinez Straits seem sinister to me in the summer of 1956? Why have the night lights in the bevatron burned in my mind for twenty years?" So she began *Play It as It Lays* (1970) "just as I have begun each of my novels, with no notion of 'character' or 'plot' or even 'incident.' I had only two pictures in my mind . . . and a technical intention, which was to write a novel so elliptical and fast that it would be over before you noticed it, a novel so fast that it would scarcely exist on the page at all." The thrift in her writing entails stopping when she has no more to say, leaving the white silence. "The arrangement of the words matters," but that mattering entails the disposition of spaces in which they hang.

(Thomas) Tom (Kennerly) Wolfe (b. 1931) cofathered with Norman Mailer the New Journalism. Wolfe nurtured and promoted it, its apotheosis coming in 1973 with the anthology *The New Journalism,* which he co-edited with E. W. Johnson. He and Hunter S. Thompson accelerated its decline in the 1980s. Elements survive, the elements that antedated it. For a decade a creative locus of controversy and reinvention, it produces posthumously considerable smoke and critical controversy.

Wolfe was a good baseball pitcher, playing semiprofessionally while a student and even auditioning in 1952 for the New York Giants. He did not make it. He went to Yale to do a doctorate in American studies, looking at how the Communist Party had worked with American writers from 1929 through 1942. In the course of his research he interviewed Malcolm Cowley, Archibald MacLeish, and others. He moved into journalism, reporting for leading papers, and during the newspaper strike of 1962 he got work at *Esquire.* His first published feature was originally an exasperated letter to his editor explaining what he intended to say, rather than a formal article saying it. The editor removed the greeting and ran the letter with its manic immediacy, the writing urgent with deadline, spattered with exclamation marks, hot voiced. This was the undesigned infancy and innocence of New Journalism, a state it passed through briskly. Having discovered the Tom Wolfe style, he began to impersonate himself.

To fiction the New Journalism restored the authority of fact and the kinds of subject matter to which the widest range of readers could relate. From fiction it borrowed episodic techniques, parceling the story into visualized scenes, each from the point of view of a more or less differentiated observer, with the kinds of transition one might expect in a story or on screen. Dialogue was "heard" rather than reported. There was abundant detail not necessarily relevant to the main "story" but illuminating character, context, relationship. When Wolfe encountered in *Esquire* (the epicenter of New Journalism) the writing of Gay Talese, he had come home. It was the early 1960s. Other magazines, notably *New York,* for which Wolfe did some controversial writing, joined in.

By the mid-1960s Mailer and Capote were inadvertent contributors to the movement. *In Cold Blood* brought fame to Capote and (for a time, until the probing into his veracity began) legitimacy to the form, the "nonfiction novel," as he called it, insisting on the truth of the adduced facts and exchanges. Capote wrote as though unaware of New Journalism, as though he had invented the reportage novel. In 1965 Wolfe published his essays *The Kandy-Kolored Tangerine-Flake Streamline Baby.* They embody, as essays and as stories, the new discipline he was advocating, and they availed themselves of the then relatively new drug culture as subject matter and linguistic and formal resource. Vietnam was a recurrent theme. Vonnegut noted in a review how eager Wolfe was to get attention, how hectic the writing. He got attention, gathering in his wake the larger figures of Mailer and Capote, both represented in Wolfe's anthology, along with Didion, Talese, and Hunter S. Thompson. In 1972 in two *Esquire* essays Wolfe described the New Journalism. Definition and the 1973 anthology led to a kind of closure: New Journalism made itself vulnerable and was attacked. Wolfe satirized the *New Yorker* and its culture in two pieces in *New York,* mixing fiction with satire to such an extent that it was impossible to tease out what was fact. The principle of New Journalism—factual authenticity—was betrayed. Dwight MacDonald attacked Wolfe for bastardizing the form. This "Parajournalism" discredited the author, whose defense was spirited but unconvincing.

When the debates were over, Wolfe turned to novel writing. In 1987 he published his most celebrated book, *The Bonfire of the Vanities,* the title borrowed from the great scourge of moral and material excess in fifteenth-century Renaissance Florence. The Dominican friar Girolamo Savonarola ignited literal bonfires into which were cast the vanities of the age—puffs, powders, patches, billet-doux, books. Wolfe's novel, set in New York, is on a substantial scale, an example of what Barth called "the literature of exhaustion," while Wolfe regarded Barth as a specimen of postmodern decadentism, the literature-out-of-literature syndrome he purported to despise.

Wolfe, journalist to the core, with the instincts of a PR man, since 1962, summer and winter, has worn white suits as a kind of trademark. We knew in 2011 that his *next* novel would be entitled *Back to Blood*. We knew what it would be about. No Stendhalian reticence and few surprises. When it would come, the reviewers would know what to say, and the first thing would be whether it was worth the $7 million his new publishers allegedly paid for it. For *I Am Charlotte Simmons* (2004) he received the *Literary Review*'s Bad Sex in Fiction Award and said in self-defense that the sex scenes were *intended* to be bad. *A Man in Full* (1998) was well received, but his fellow novelists, among them Mailer, Updike, and John Irving, were not wholehearted. Wolfe responded in an essay, "My Three Stooges." Updike had written that the book "amounts to entertainment, not literature, even literature in a modest aspirant form. Like a movie desperate to recoup its backers' investment, the novel tries too hard to please us." Then in the *New York Review of Books* Mailer dubbed Wolfe "the most gifted best-seller writer to come along since Margaret Mitchell." Wolfe is talented, he said, but incapable of the liftoff required for the Graf Zeppelin novel he aspires to write.

John Irving joined the attack in a radio interview: reading Wolfe, he said, is "like reading a bad newspaper or a bad piece in a magazine. It makes you wince." If, as Wolfe claims, in the 1960s New Journalism routed the novel "as literature's main event," the fact that he turned to fiction in *Bonfire* suggests the triumph was short-lived, even *journalistic*. He justifies his fiction by invoking Thackeray, whose *Vanity Fair* is one of his rhetorical touchstones. Dickens, Dostoyevsky, Balzac, and Zola are also called as witnesses in his defense. They had been reporters in their time. "At this weak, pale, tabescent moment in the history of American literature," he says, taxing our memory of Latin verbs (*tabescere,* to waste away), "we need a battalion, a brigade, of Zolas to head out into this wild, bizarre, unpredictable, hog-stomping Baroque country of ours and reclaim its literary property."

To get *The Bonfire* written he asked the editor of *Rolling Stone* to commission it as a serial and, in imitation of Dickens, in response to the pressure of delivering thirty installments (the first three were published together, removing Wolfe's intended cushion), work began. It finds in 1980s New York conditions and corruptions (remotely, he concedes) analogous to those of Renaissance Florence. He researched it on the ground, shadowing the police, interviewing, investigating. Greed, corruption, class, racism, and the politics that go with them are his subjects, essentialized from journalism. Sherman McCoy is the real McCoy—white, gentile, rich. The assistant district attorney is a Jew called Larry Kramer, and there's the unkosher Reverend Reginald Bacon, a Harlem black activist. The journalist is an alcoholic British interloper called Peter Fallow (the Dickensian tick of symbolic naming). Each character resembles a real person, as in a roman à clef, but we are reminded that this is fiction and that any similarity to, say, the Reverend Jesse Jackson, or to Christopher Hitchens, is fortuitous.

*The Bonfire* was an immediate best seller. If mobile phones had been in vogue in the 1980s, it would be the novel for the moment. His rich, vain, vulnerable, bond-trading protagonist is a prototype for the twenty-first century villain; his wife and daughter, his mistress, his fall, seem to leap from the pages of timeless newspapers: the training Wolfe got in the no-longer-new New Journalism made him prescient and took him close to the bone. The action is catalyzed by a hit-and-run accident where the victim is a black youth, the perpetrator alleg-edly McCoy in the company of his mistress. The journalist is assigned to cover the story in a series of articles: all the elements are in place for an acrimonious, laddish modern story. It should have made an excellent movie, but it did not.

It is not surprising to learn that Wolfe supported George W. Bush in the 2004 presidential election, or that so much of his work contributes to the conservative and libertarian right. To this he attributes his unpopularity among American writers. It certainly is an element. His negative characters verge on stereotype, and the politics that flow from stereotypes can be treacherous. He says "you can" and means "you should": "You can dramatize reality in fiction so easily and with such economy, bring so many strands of a society onto one plotline. You can have a real impact with fiction provided that you deal with reality, provided you want to show how society works, how it fits together." He points to *The Grapes of Wrath* and the effect it had. His *Bonfire,* by contrast, though he would never say so, was entertainment. It is not surprising that he is at home in the company of neoconservatives, though they should be a little uneasy in his.

Hunter S. (Stockton) Thompson (1937–2005) started his working life as a jour-nalist, first as a copy boy at *Time* magazine on $51 a week (he was fired), then at other papers. His pieces for the *Herald Tribune* written while he was in Puerto Rico show how competent he became in conventional journalism. In *Hell's An-gels: The Strange and Terrible Saga of the Outlaw Motorcycle Gangs* (1966) he revealed where he would go. He spent eighteen months researching the book, traveling with the bikers; he learned their language, and through it his own. He was independent-minded and refused to separate himself from a story—true, imag-ined, or hallucinated. He took the New Journalism over the edge, into gonzo journalism, before, incapacitated with health problems, he pushed himself over the edge. His suicide was in character, an act of choice, of positive will, in the circumstances. He had long before traveled to Ketchum, Idaho, to research Hemingway's suicide. Hemingway was almost sixty-two when he shot himself. Thompson was sixty-seven, and in a wheelchair.

Tom Wolfe included two Thompson contributions in the anthology *The New Journalism,* an extract from *Hell's Angels* and his 1970 feature essay "The Ken-tucky Derby is Decadent and Depraved," in which while the racecourse watches the race he (and his co-conspirator, the cartoonist Ralph Steadman) watch the course and anatomize the people with their alliterative confusion of disorders and depravities. Steadman's vision cannily complements Thompson's. Gonzo journalism is a heightening of New Journalism, outdoing the haystacks of exclamation marks with a first person who is a raving, sometimes deranged individual to whom people respond. The news story becomes the story of the interference narrative introduces into events if a narrator refuses to efface himself. Steadman and Thompson fueled one another.

Photographs show Thompson in trademark dark glasses, as distinctive as Wolfe's white suit, often smoking, leaner than his friend Johnny Depp, who plays him in *Fear and Loathing in Las Vegas: A Savage Journey to the Heart of the American Dream* (novel 1971, film 1998). The myth of the man with the gun (he loved weapons, spent a short time in prison as an accessory in an armed robbery, and joined the Air Force soon after, partly out of a fascination with weaponry), the writer with his pen dipped in vitriol, alcohol, mescaline, and cocaine, and laced with LSD, the figure of Raoul Duke: whenever he came into a story or an article, it had to expand to accommodate him and his sense of the world. He had brutal things to say about America. He frightened "official" people, he was always unpredictable to them, though with garden-variety Americans he was, Wolfe said, a "real southern gentleman," referring to his Kentucky background and courtesy. He was naturally insubordinate. His anger with America is rooted in deep love and a betrayed patriotism. He attended the Democratic Party Convention in Chicago in 1968 and saw the end of the American dream take shape in that traumatic week.

Parody, homage, and imitation are ways of learning. He copied and retyped the great works he admired, letting the language pass in at the eye, be processed, and then out through the pen on to the page. He completed, among other self-assignments, *The Great Gatsby* and *A Farewell to Arms*. This form of acquisition, or possession, was a way of learning and hearing. Behind Tom Jones and Partridge, behind Mr. Pickwick and Sam Weller, so behind Raoul Drake and his attorney Dr. Gonzo (the 300-pound Samoan attorney with the amazing shirts) loom the tall bent and the squat tubby figures of Don Quixote and Sancho Panza. Thompson's novel, five years in the making, originally ran in *Rolling Stone* magazine. The two men, their car, and a trunk full of drugs provide the picaresque road-novel basis for the narrative—though their road bends back upon itself, and the world through which they miasmically move is relatively stable. Las Vegas would have made a more natural setting than New York for Savonarola, given the range of vanities on offer. But Duke and Gonzo are there to participate, to push buttons, pull handles, and break rules. Duke retains a purchase on the action, however addled he is in the story. There is no loss of narratorial control, and this is an element in the humor and acid nostalgia. After all, the 1960s were over. However immediate the book feels, it is an elegy.

Thompson went to the Mint 400 races outside Las Vegas as a reporter. His piece was never published, the "research" folded into his novel instead. The accuracy with which Duke, his senses heightened by drugs, describes the races— not the action, which is start, dust clouds, and stop, but the waiting, drinking, and distraction—is New Journalism at its most precise, engaged in the teeth of the narrator's disengagement. Fiction and nonfiction are at creative odds.

Thompson's independent-mindedness suggests that he is at heart a libertarian. He would have been part of the gun lobby, but he would not have kept company with the neoconservatives Wolfe entertains. His hatred for Richard Nixon was a driving force in his satire, yet when in 2004 George W. Bush and Dick Cheney were lining themselves up, he said he would support even Nixon against this axis of candidates.

---

If we configured the stars rather differently from the way we have done so far in this book, drawing a line from Fenimore Cooper through the Melville of *Moby-Dick,* down to Crane, Wolfe, Faulkner, with a bend to Burroughs, we might have an appropriate star chart for Cormac McCarthy (born Charles McCarthy, 1933). He is American, solitary, apocalyptic. He is learned and skeptical. He cannot understand Henry James or Proust, they seem too passive, fanciful, unmasculine, and he is a macho writer, of the kind who has written few women characters and is fascinated by homosexual violation. He does not much like foreign films. He is hostile to Latin American magical realism, though his own writing shares imaginative space with it. Women, Indians, Mexicans, black people, and white people all get bad press in *Blood Meridian.*

Each of his novels engages big themes. He is also in pursuit of his characters' psychologies, epic histories, and panoramas, Homerically impartial, which is to say, merciless. No one is let off, least of all the reader. There is a daunting abundance in his writing. In some of the books the description is so full that the landscape changes with each reading, different details foreground themselves, and different themes.

Howard Erskine of Random House, who had been Faulkner's editor, accepted *The Orchard Keeper,* the first of McCarthy's ten novels, in 1965. He saw McCarthy through his first two decades of authorship. Most notable of McCarthy's novels is *Blood Meridian or the Evening Redness in the West* (1985); the Border Trilogy, comprising *All the Pretty Horses* (1992), *The Crossing* (1994), and *Cities of the Plain* (1998); *No Country for Old Men* (2005); and *The Road* (2006).

*Blood Meridian* took some time to be recognized. Early reviews were unenthusiastic. First was the issue of genre. It is a western. It is cowboys and Indians, cowboys and cowboys, cowboys and Mexicans. It is man against nature and

nature against man. It plays with all the adventure genres of children's literature, which makes the desecrations of character and social vision the more terrible. It takes elements deeply rooted in readers' imaginations and memories,
narratives of survival and ultimate justice, and turns them toward darker ends,
without the consolation of closed narrative and happily ever after. In the final
scene we are not allowed to see what has happened to the one character we followed through thick and thick, and cared about despite his brutalities. Three
men look into the outhouse and see what the Judge has done to him. Unspeakable. We are left imagining the worst, and the worst we can imagine by that
stage is worse than anything we might have been able to imagine before.

The character we care about is "the kid," nameless, who becomes, still nameless, "the man," and survives the worst violence of the novel only to meet his unspecified fate three pages from the end. As "the kid" he is a runaway from
Tennessee (which is where McCarthy, born in Rhode Island, grew up, attended
but did not finish university, and lived during his first marriage). His mother has
died and he flees his father, going to Texas where there are few constraints and
many dangers. McCarthy himself after his divorce moved to El Paso, Texas, and
began to remake his world. The kid courts danger.

The character most dreaded is a fascinating, inhuman, or superhuman giant
of a man, Judge Holden, white as bone, hairless, given to sitting on promontories and walking about naked, collecting fossils, experiences, a man who dances
as though he were weightless, who knows all the languages of the world, and
who is contrary to all rules and laws. A child-killer, he is sexually indeterminate. He is Ahab, Kurtz, and other figures of European and American fiction
who, freighted with the best that culture can offer, have lost their values. "War
is God," he tells the kid, and he is wedded to two things: destruction and his
own survival. He has a kind of transcendent existence, living impossibly on.
"Whatever in creation exists without my knowledge," he declares, "exists without my consent." He has a right to destroy it. "The man who believes that the
secrets of the world are forever hidden lives in mystery and fear. Superstition
will drag him down. The rain will erode the deeds of his life. But the man who
sets himself the task of singling out the thread of order from the tapestry will
by the decision alone have taken charge of the world and it is only by such taking charge that he will effect a way to dictate the terms of his own fate."

*Blood Meridian* accompanies the Glanton gang, a historical band of scalp hunters, each member with his own psychosis, scores to settle, things to escape.
Their mission is to clear out the natives, and they are paid by the number of
scalps they collect. McCarthy describes the atrocities in such lurid detail as to
suggest complicity. His reservation of judgment amounts to acceptance as he
hyperbolizes beyond the historical facts: the scale of the landscape, of the armies

and tribes, the number of scalps and ears collected. The perpetrators become victims and vice versa as the gang descends into the moral morass it has made.

McCarthy refuses to use exclamation marks. Emphasis should inhere in language precisely deployed. He builds long sentences and heavy emphases by piling up clauses, linking sentences by conjunctions in a breathless, uninterrupted aria followed by runs of dialogue, sometimes meditative, often staccato for contrast. He dislikes semicolons, probably because they hover between comma and colon, not sure which way to swing. The description of landscape is gorgeous; of human habitation, apart from the few idyllic communities the gang destroys, sordid; yet the technique of gorgeous writing carries over and is applied indifferently to the sordid. Any living thing, however innocent, is in for it. The style aestheticizes destruction, rendering it cumulatively neutral. Otherwise we might say the theme is power and its abuses, and the difficulty of establishing order when property cannot be safely or legitimately owned.

McCarthy's excess breaks with modernism, a break that modernism itself facilitated. In Australia the Tasmanian writer Richard Flanagan (b. 1961) finds an analogous escape from modernism and its aesthetic restraints in *Death of a River Guide* (1994) and *The Sound of One Hand Clapping* (1997). Writers who celebrate the margins thrive best in these abundant, exuberant, generically unfixed forms, from Lowry and Burroughs to the lavish writers of today, in some of whom the impulse is lyrical-political, as in Arundhati Roy (b. 1961) in *The God of Small Things* (1997), in others apocalyptic, as in writers older and younger, Doris Lessing in her Mara and Dann novels, Kurt Vonnegut in *Galápagos* (1985), Russell Hoban in *Riddley Walker* (1980).

Michael Chabon (b. 1963) builds on genres whose literary merits continue to be debated—comic books, fantasy, sci-fi, horror, detective, pulp, and apocalyptic fiction. He came to the defense of McCarthy's *The Road* (2006), in part fascinated by the fact that McCarthy, after his highbrow allegorical and epic-historical fiction, should commit an apocalyptic sci-fi novel marked by a strict economy of style. There have been many books like it in the last century. As Chabon read and reread *The Road*, its genre wavered, it seemed to him as much horror as sci-fi. Or prophecy. In any case, it was in some sense generically slumming, the way Doris Lessing, Gore Vidal, and Margaret Atwood do. Whatever genre, if any, it ultimately belongs to, "the intensity with which it's been imagined and been brought into language" justifies it.

Chabon's virtues are found in generic experiment, as in *The Yiddish Policemen's Union* (2007), which combines mystery and historical elements, and as in his most celebrated book, *The Amazing Adventures of Kavalier & Clay* (2000), plays on and away from comic book and children's genres even in the moment of the title. Chabon spent five and a half years writing a novel he would abandon: *Fountain*

*City* stands as a warning to other writers and a testament to his integrity: it was, Chabon said, "erasing me, breaking me down, burying me alive, drowning me, kicking me down the stairs." In self-defense he put it out of his misery. A versatile and resourceful writer, he learned a lesson, not in what he could not do so much as in what was not worth doing.

———•———

Mississippi-born Richard Ford (b. 1944) admired the southern writer Walker Percy (1916–1990), in particular *The Moviegoer,* his present-tense debut novel, whose protagonist, Percy, said that he "feels himself quite alienated from . . . the old South and the new America." He edited the stories of another Mississippian, Eudora Welty.

Getting started was an effort. "When I was nineteen," said Ford, "I began to read *Absalom, Absalom!* slowly, slowly, page by patient page, since I was slightly dyslexic. I was working on the railroad, the Missouri-Pacific in Little Rock. I hadn't been doing well in school, but I started reading." At the University of California, Irvine, Ford studied with E. L. Doctorow and Oakley Hall, who also numbered Michael Chabon among his students and whose 1958 novel *Warlock* made a mark on the young Thomas Pynchon. Ford's first two novels, *A Piece of My Heart* (1976) and *The Ultimate Good Luck* (1981), were well received but did not sell. He taught creative writing and then in 1982 went to work as a sportswriter for *Inside Sports.* The magazine folded, and when *Sports Illustrated* did not offer him a job he fell back on fiction and wrote a novel rooted in his failure. *The Sportswriter* (1986) is the first book in the Frank Bascombe trilogy, which also includes his Pulitzer Prize–winning *Independence Day* (1995) and *The Lay of the Land* (2006).

After the success of *The Sportswriter* Ford published *Rock Springs* (1987), a collection of stories set mainly in Montana, the setting too for *Wildlife,* his unsuccessful 1990 novel about a professional golfer who becomes a fireman. The *Rock Springs* stories were seen as part of a movement dubbed "dirty realism." The chief purveyor was Raymond Carver (1938–1988), a writer who began in Faulknerian vein, was edited down to his celebrated minimalism by Gordon Lish at Knopf, and was posthumously reinflated in editions based on his original manuscripts and prepared by his widow, Tess Gallagher. Salman Rushdie admired Lish's Carver, "a very ambitious writer, and his books are incredibly original because they push the boundaries of how to say things, how to suggest things," the downside being his influence: "A lot of the school of Carver became an excuse for saying banal things in banal ways. As if that was all you had to do—have two people sitting down across the table with a bottle of whiskey talking to each other in clichés." The subject matter of Carver's own fiction, the crises in the lives of

"regular people" in isolating and intense situations, certainly influenced his contemporaries, but not all of them in negative or minimalizing ways. Ford, with
whom he taught for a period, and the storywriter and memoirist Tobias Wolff
(b. 1945), owe him more than clichés.

Ford's Frank Bascombe is too socially elevated to count as a dirty realist protagonist. The extended novel is not a natural form for dirty realism, if it exists at
all: Wolff and others see it as no more than a promotional, journalistic category.
Bascombe has, however, fallen below where he feels he should be: the novelist
becomes a sportswriter, the sportswriter is further reduced and diminished in
his ambitions in life and living, his relationships, his resilience and endurance.
There is a moment, after one of his crises of trust with his girlfriend, Vicki,
when he has something like a vision of secular redemption:

> In fact, I would like it as well as it's possible to like any life: a life of
> small flourishes and clean napkins. A life where sex plays an ever-
> important nightly role—better than with any of the eighteen or so
> women I knew before and "loved." A life appreciative of history and
> its generations. A life of possible fidelity, of going fishing with some
> best friend, of having a little Sheila or a little Matthew of our own,
> of buying a fifth-wheel travel trailer—a cruising brute—and from
> its tiny portholes seeing the country. Paul and Clarissa could come
> along and join our gang. I could sell my house and move not to
> Pheasant Run but to an old Quakerstone in Bucks County. Possibly
> when our work is done, a tour in the Peace Corps or Vista—of "do-
> ing something with our lives." I wouldn't need to sleep in my clothes
> or wake up on the floor. I could forget about being *in* my emotions
> and not be bothered by such things.

The fact that it cannot be, given the way he's made, does not diminish its
objective possibility. It is not entirely illusion, but it is inaccessible to him. If he
could stop saying maybe and perhaps and make it happen! But he is laced tight
into a habit of disappointment. Frank is not Rabbit Angstrom. His immersion in
an indulgent self-scrutiny confines the reader. Characters of the kind he distrusts
when he encounters them in Forster and James emerge, clearly drawn, comical,
sad, alarming; there is laughter and exasperation, plausible suburban neighbors
of the kind not even good fences make good. The narrator, Ford insists, is a man
with a history, but also a man who surprises his author and himself. Things
happen to him, and they happen in him. Auden, Ford remarks in an interview,
is "always trying to find good uses for his neuroses. He said that neurosis represented not necessarily a debility but an opportunity; that neurosis is a gift,

something whose effects we can make use of in some inventive way." Ford and Bascombe agree with Auden. But the climax of the trilogy is more dramatic than credible, well in excess of the events that lead up to it. The in fact highly successful "failed novelist" who is the sportswriter lets himself down at the end, an artistic failure that is *thematically* appropriate. Failure at the end of an odyssey is ephemeral. What continues mattering is the journey.

———————

For Bret Easton Ellis (b. 1964), artifice does not live so close to the surface. On the surface are elements designed, it would seem, to upset women in the way *The Satanic Verses* upset the Muslim in the street. In an interview, speaking of himself in the second person, Ellis asks, "So you're a misogynist, a racist—so what? Does it make your art less interesting?" Posed in this way, he expects the reply to begin with a *yes* and then end, with a David Foster Wallace elision, in *no*, the "y-no" response to the New Journalism and to the Brat Pack. Part of the deliberate affront is his insistent insouciance. "If you're writing about a misogynist, does that then make a book misogynist? I don't think I'm a misogynist. But even if I was, so what? . . . So you're a homophobe, or a racist—so what? Does that make your art less interesting? I don't think so." Ellis refuses to define his own sexuality: he does not like biographical readings, and besides, he does not seem sure: definition in such areas is of little creative value.

Ellis was eleven years old when P. G. Wodehouse died. Patrick Bateman, the Wall Street executive and protagonist of his notorious and popular *American Psycho* (1991), has been likened to Bertie Wooster, a Wooster whose blood-splattered apartment and chaotic diary urgently need a Jeeves to tidy them up, to suggest new and more nuanced ways of disposal, to provide hangover remedies and attend to skin blemishes and smooth over bad hair mornings. Ellis, like Wodehouse, has the courage of his convictions: he does not blink, he carries things to their logical conclusion. Bertie ends up at the Drones' club, or back under Aunt Agatha's thumb. Patrick ends up in one of the fashionable restaurants or drinking destinations, or in bed with assorted steaming female body parts, desires still unfulfilled. Each sexual and murderous encounter with the hot hardbodies he brings home is more extreme than the last, reaching a nadir in the scene with a corpse, a starved rat, and a cleaver. Sometimes an anticipated murder-date ends in exhaustive anatomically explicit sex, without mace, blades, drills, or staple guns. Occasionally Patrick kills people in the street, the "slanty-eyed" oriental delivery boy, the beggar, the "faggot" with his little dog. There is a drizzle of blood on his clothes, and he has trouble with his dry-cleaner, who survives only by accident. His more or less steady girlfriend Evelyn is safe from all his aberrations, in love with his gym-fit body, his unrivaled understanding of modern etiquette, the hierarchy of restaurant fashion, and the revealing se-miotics of brands and styles. He is exhaustively knowledgeable about popular music, delivering full essays on musicians and records. "In many ways Patrick Bateman was me," Ellis declared, "his rage, his disgust and to a degree his pas-sivity stem from what I was feeling at the time. And boredom."

At first the plethora of brand names, each stitch of clothing on every charac-ter getting a name check, irritates. Then it amuses, not least in the variations Ellis plays, and the abundance of labels he reads. Tom Wolfe commented: "Brand names, tastes in clothes and furniture, manners, the way people treat children, servants, or their superiors, are important clues to an individual's expectations. This is something else that I am criticized for, mocked for, ridiculed for." It is not new. "I take some solace in the fact that the leading critic of Balzac's day, Sainte-Beuve, used to say the same thing about Balzac's fixation on furniture. You can learn the names of more arcane pieces of furniture reading Balzac than you can reading a Sotheby's catalogue."

We are "in a brand name culture." Brand names, and violence: How is it that the violence, so stomach-turning, so nauseating, becomes tolerable, an aspect of the humor? How is it that Ellis generates in the reader concern for, even sympa-thy with, so extreme a figure? Much depends on a deadpan tone, the circumstan-tial style, its insistent dwelling only on the surface, the cutting open of victims to create new surfaces. The society he creates is materialized, dehumanized, and as he anatomizes it in every sense he treats the reader as a confidant. He has no one else to confide in, and it is hard to resist his confidences, delivered almost always in a matter-of-fact, uninflected voice. As he descends deeper into his world of unfulfillable desires, the words *murder* and *merger, execution* and *acquisition,* dovetail. This psychological thriller is a satire on the Wall Street boom-culture of the 1980s (which, *mutatis mutandis,* persists), and a work of sadistic pornography. He told the *Paris Review* that the book is "about lifestyle being sold as life, a lifestyle that never seemed to include passion, creativity, curiosity, ro-mance, pain."

Ellis was born in Los Angeles, the setting for *Less Than Zero* (1985), his first novel, and its sequel, *Imperial Bedrooms* (2010). In *Less Than Zero* his protagonist Clay returns from his university in the east to spend Christmas at home and reenter the rich, amoral yuppie, druggy society in which he grew up. Ellis started writing the book when he was nineteen (he started *American Psycho* three years later), and it appeared to controversial acclaim when he was twenty-one. In *Im-perial Bedrooms* Clay returns from the east, this time to make a film, and redis-covers his friends and their circles reconfigured by middle age. Blair, with whom he had an affair, has married bisexual and promiscuous Trent. They throw Gats-byesque parties at their home in Beverly Hills. Clay has a more conventional psychology than Patrick Bateman; the novels he moves through are brutal but less compelling than Bateman's.

Like Clay, Ellis went east to university, attending Bennington in Vermont. His contemporaries and friends included the southern writer Donna Tartt and the critic and novelist-to-be Jonathan Lethem. The early, instant success of *Less Than Zero* surprised them. Fame brought him into different company, the "Brat Pack" (or "Bret Pack") that included Jay McInerney (b. 1955), whose second-person novel *Bright Lights, Big City* (1984), set in the cocaine culture of the time, appeared the year before Ellis's book. A third Brat Packer was California-born Tama Janow-itz (b. 1957). *American Dad* (1981) and *Slaves of New York* (1986) are her Brat Pack bona fides. Chuck Palahniuk (b. 1962) is a kind of junior member. Ellis suggests that his *Fight Club* (1996) comes from the same zone as *American Psycho*.

*The Rules of Attraction* (1987) is Ellis's "college novel," a brutal dry run in a New Hampshire college, preparing the kinds of characters that thrive in the Wall Street environment of *American Psycho*. His later work has been more metafictional. *Glamorama* (1998) is set in the world of high fashion and features a terrorist conspiracy consisting entirely of models. *Lunar Park* (2005), the spoof celebrity autobiography, tells the ghost story of a "Bret Easton Ellis" who shares with Bret Easton Ellis experiences and attitudes, and whose house, which he occupies with his wife and son, is haunted. If the name of the character being the same as the name of the novelist confuses readers, "So what. So what? Confusion is interesting. It's not such a bad thing. And I don't care. I know that sounds awfully cocky and brutal and snotty. I don't care if someone is confused, and why should I care?"

At first Ellis resisted Norman Mailer's criticism that he followed the narrator's every thought and kept himself out of it. "And yes, when I wrote *American Psycho*," he says, "I had a huge note on my desk saying 'NO METAPHORS!,' because Patrick Bateman can't see something as being like anything else. There were so many beautiful metaphors I couldn't use, because I realized Patrick Bateman would never use them in a million years." He understands Mailer's point, that the novelist establishes the narrator and then keeps a distance. "I do admire certain novels where that occurs. But most of the time, these novels are about people who are not college professors, and yet they're thinking and speaking as if they were college professors, and I find that completely distracting."

# *Pariahs*

Franz Kafka, Saul Bellow, Bernard Malamud, Mordecai Richler,

J. D. Salinger, Philip Roth, Jeffrey Eugenides, Paul Auster, Martin Amis

In *Testaments Betrayed* the Czech novelist Milan Kundera considers how certain authors know just how their texts should look on the page: the physical aspect of the writing is part of its meaning. "You can *see* the long, intoxicating flight of [Franz] Kafka's prose in the text's typographical appearance, which is often a single 'endless' paragraph, over pages, enfolding even long passages of dialogue." The Israeli novelist Aharon Appelfeld described Kafka as a "melodic writer." The intended melody is disrupted if the visual aspect is obscured. The two long paragraphs that make up the second chapter of Kafka's *The Castle* are broken into four in the edition his friend Max Brod prepared, Kundera says; in one French translation there are ninety, in another ninety-five. "French editions of Kafka's novels have been subjected to an articulation that is not their own: paragraphs much more numerous, and therefore much shorter, which simulate a more logical, more rational organization of the text and which dramatize it, sharply separating all the dialogue exchanges." Editors and translators try to make the original "comprehensible," even when that kind of comprehensibility runs counter to Kafka's intentions. And not even a footnote signals the change. "The Pleiade edition of Kafka's novels contains over five hundred pages of notes. Yet I find not a single sentence there giving such a reason."

The books of stories Kafka saw published in his lifetime he wanted printed with wide margins in large type, a wish that "was justified, logical, serious, related to his aesthetic, or, more specifically, to his way of articulating prose." Any serious writer or reader will understand: "An author who divides his text into many short paragraphs will not insist so on large type: a lavishly articulated page can be read easily"; but "a text that flows out in an endless paragraph is very much less legible. The eye finds no place to stop or rest, the lines are easily 'lost track of.'" Kundera writes, "I look through the German paperback edition of *The Castle:* on a small page, thirty-nine appallingly cramped lines of an 'endless paragraph': it's illegible; or it's legible only as *information;* or as a *document;* in any case not as a text meant for aesthetic perception." It feeds the modern habit of reading as consumption. Kundera finds a forty-page appendix including "all the passages Kafka deleted from his manuscript." He concludes, "In that indifference to the author's aesthetic wishes is reflected all the sadness of the posthumous fate of Kafka's work."

Kafka sent the text of *Die Verwandlung (The Metamorphosis),* written in 1915, to a magazine edited by the great Austrian novelist Robert Musil, author of *The Man without Qualities.* Musil agreed to print it if Kafka would shorten it. Kafka preferred it to remain unpublished. He knew what he wanted his page to look like, and he knew *why* he wanted it to look like that. The act of reading is the completion of the act of writing, and the size, pace, and forms the eye encounters are part of the text's meaning.

Contemporary novelists are generally less scrupulous about visual aspects of their work. Yet the visual can be crucial in composition and reception. Writers with a sense of aesthetic wholeness make their own demands on publishers and readers. Kafka was a short-story writer whose novellas and novels make the reading demands of the short story, as though a lyric writer composed an epic and required readers to construe the large work in lyric terms. It is less a matter of textual density than of a concentrated attention, the process of reading slows, the book cannot be devoured. The process is built into the aesthetic intention of the writing. At twenty-one in a letter Kafka prophesied the kind of work he would create: "We need the books that affect us like a disaster, that grieve us deeply, like the death of someone we loved more than ourselves, like being banished into forests far from everyone, like a suicide. A book must be the axe for the frozen sea inside us. That is my belief." The forest is from fairy tale, banishment is from his love of Russian literature.

Franz Kafka (1883–1924) was born in Prague into a German-speaking family. He celebrated his bar mitzvah and reluctantly attended synagogue four times a year with his father, a Jew more by identity than by faith, though later the Yiddish theater exercised a cultural claim on him. His father was severe, vain, and ready to misunderstand the excessively lean and unconventional boy. At eighteen Martin Amis took the father's side: "Kafka is a fucking fool."

Kafka wrote in German though he spoke and read Czech and conducted his romance with Milena Jesenská in that language, and he acquired French and a passion for French literature, Flaubert in particular. At university in Prague he began as a chemist but became a law student, which proved useful to his fiction. He worked for two insurance companies and saw numerous small claims cases, and then in management of an asbestos factory. For five years, from 1912, when he contracted tuberculosis, he had a relationship and correspondence with Felice Bauer, his equivalent (though not in sensual terms) to Flaubert's Louise Colet. Elias Canetti suggests that "in the course of seven months he got used to this correspondence, and one has the feeling he didn't particularly want to see her." His intense romance with Dora Diamant was different in kind. It thrived on presence and took him to Berlin, where they were lovers. But illness took him back to Prague, then to a sanatorium near Vienna. His throat was so painful that in the end he died of starvation. He left his few published and all his unpublished works to his friend Max Brod—according to Brod himself—to destroy. Brod disregarded his instructions, hence the survival of the writer. (Some twenty notebooks remained in Dora Diamant's possession, but in 1933 they were confiscated from her apartment by the Nazis and disappeared.)

Kafka was a scrupulous editor of the work he saw into print. But publication of the three novels was posthumous: *Der Prozess (The Trial)* appeared in 1925, followed by *Das Schloss (The Castle)* in 1926 and *Amerika* or *Der Verschollene* (1927). The books have been translated and retranslated, each version different because Kafka never produced a definitive text for any of them, and a kind of indefinition at once constrains and licenses the German editor and the translator. It is as though Kafka had provided templates; translators make choices and confine the sense to their understanding.

In his copy of Edwin and Willa Muir's translation of the novella *The Metamorphosis,* or more accurately *The Transformation,* Nabokov impatiently retranslated much of the work between the lines. Gregor wakes up transmorphed into "einem ungeheuren Ungeziefer." This is rendered variously as "a gigantic insect," "an enormous bug," and "a monstrous vermin." Whatever term we choose, here and elsewhere in Kafka metaphor is entertained as fact; metaphor, the "incommensurable" itself, "irrupts" into the real world and is accommodated by its logic. The language is matter-of-fact, flat, which makes it believable. In his lecture notes Nabokov the entomologist draws the transformed Gregor Samsa from the details Kafka provides: the creature combines so many elements, and is so large in scale, as to be fantastic, yet he is planted in the midst of a drab, daily world. Kafka elicits from each reader a different metamorphosis, based on our deepest aversions. There are hundreds of "interpretations" of *The Metamorphosis.* Readers tire of theoretical approaches. Biography can "explain" the relations in the story between father, mother, sister, and the transformed son. But Gustav Janouch reports him saying, "Samsa is not merely Kafka and nothing else. *Metamorphosis* is not a confession, although it is—in a certain sense—an indiscretion." He warns us off and draws us in. Indiscretion as against confession: we may find the contrasted pairing useful in reading not only Kafka but those who have learned from him, even those who least seem to resemble him. He says of Strindberg: "We are his contemporaries and successors; one has only to close one's eyes and one's own blood delivers lectures on Strindberg." One might say that of Kafka himself and note the importance of drama to Kafka's work: economy, precision, succinct setting, disregard of inessential context, speech. In reading Herzen's memoirs Kafka says, "the whole of the unconscious man emerges, purposeful, self-tormenting, having himself firmly in hand and then going to pieces again."

The Italian fiction writer Primo Levi is an heir to Kafka. The Holocaust changed and confirmed Kafka's vision. "With *The Trial*," Levi said, "Kafka predicted the time when it was a crime simply to be a Jew. I was in fact commissioned by Einaudi to translate the book into Italian. Looking back, I wish I hadn't: the undertaking disturbed me badly. I went into a deep, deep depression . . . And so I haven't read any Kafka since: he involves me too much." The life with its three broken engagements, the tedium of what his father called "bread jobs," the asphyxiating relationship with his family, his insomnia, his tuberculosis: he was a catalog of insoluble problems, and as against his father's vanity he suffered a chronic self-disgust. He dies, as K. dies in *The Trial*, painfully, pointlessly. All this intolerable circumstance makes for the clean thrift of his style, the toneless report on incomprehensible experience. Flaubert mattered so to him because of his single-mindedness, his ambition to write with and of as little as he humanly could. "There is infinite hope," he said elsewhere, "but not for us."

Whitman was for Kafka a supreme formal innovator, an elixir he could not quite take. Kafka's *Amerika*, with San Francisco on the East Coast and a bridge joining Boston and New York, was an illusory solace, a contrary illusion to the nightmare of *The Castle*. Canetti describes the difference Kafka makes, his "almost Chinese way of reacting to the world as a whole. I don't believe it's the usual European way, which we know from the course of European philosophy, of seeing a separate, ruling, divine, transcendent power behind everything." For him, "things are still one. He doesn't separate concepts from concrete or sensuous details." He kept his distance from the -isms of the day, expressionism (which might have been a natural destination) above all. "Though when he was not writing Kafka felt that the only salvation for him was to write," says Gabriel Josipovici, "once he was writing he felt that what he was doing was meaningless, without relation to the world or the truth, worse even than meaningless, the perpetuation of a downright lie. His writing is the description of the failure of writing; were his writing to succeed, he would have failed; failing, he perhaps succeeded." It is a philosophically sterile, creatively fruitful paradox.

———•———

Those North American novelists who intend to throw off Europe never altogether manage it. They hold onto a thread or two, not Anatole France but Proust, not Thomas Mann but Kafka and the haunting, vanished culture of Mitteleuropa, its extinguished multilingual multiculturalism. Americans who respond most readily to Kafka are, like him, secular Jews or half-Jews, accidental heirs to the Old Testament, to the eastern heart of Europe that produced so much, including the Holocaust. They are singled out by history and race, and then by choice. Some want to find a way back, but the highway is blocked by rubble and the desuetude of spent traditions. Saul Bellow notes, ruefully, Kafka's dislike of Balzac: too many characters, when what really interests him are symbols. And this is Bellow's own legacy from Kafka. The Philip Roth who wrote in *The Counterlife* (1986), "I've got Jew on the Brain. Jews are my Tahiti, my Giverny, my Dada, my String Theory, my Lost Horizon," is equally Kafka's heir.

After the Second World War, Middle Europe survives in Canada and the United States, in the immigration and its first and second generations of offspring—in Saul (born Solomon) Bellow (1915–2005), for example. It provides a living, alternative, polyglot modernism to the cultural hunger Pound and Eliot fed with a deliberated amalgam constructed out of safely dead cultures. In Paris, Bellow, who was impatient with modernism, called on the last of the great modernists, Samuel Beckett. The meeting was brief and uneventful.

Speaking at the 1986 memorial service for the novelist and storywriter Bernard Malamud (1914–1986), Bellow said, "We were cats of the same breed. The sons of Eastern European immigrant Jews, we had gone early into the streets of our respective cities," Malamud's being Brooklyn, Bellow's not the Lachine of his birth but the Chicago of his formative years; both "were Americanized by schools, newspapers, subways, streetcars, sandlots. Melting Pot children, we had assumed the American program to be the real thing: no barriers to the freest and fullest American choices." They found or made their own barriers in due course. They came to terms with other thing they were, Jews, displaced Europeans, tangential to the intellectual establishment and yet, or therefore, necessary interpreters. Malamud at times, as in his apocalyptic final novel *God's Grace* (1982) with its articulate chimps and God's Voice, is a fabulist; in *The Fixer* (1966) he includes all the elements of a nineteenth-century Russian novel; the book has a translated feel. Both are works of flawless construction and do not invite rereading. *The Assistant* (1957), his second novel, is his most natural, set in a modern New York ghetto where a goy beats up a grocer, experiences remorse, and becomes an orthodox Jew. It is an unexpected turn of plot, yet convincing in the world of Malamudic transformations and supernatural interventions.

To Cynthia Ozick, Bellow wrote about the "unspeakable evasion" of the Holocaust in his own work. It was a palpable chasm, existing beyond the imaginable, yet real. Writers mature, he told an interviewer, as they force themselves to confront hard experiences. They must identify them first—for James Baldwin, sexuality and race; for Virginia Woolf, gender and a complex erotic; for Solomon Bellow, Jewishness, the Holocaust, Europe's and America's relations to facts that, while peculiarly and profoundly his, are also universal. Real also were his Yiddish roots: in 1952 he translated Isaac Bashevis Singer's "Gimpel the Fool" for the *Partisan Review,* the first time Singer was published in English.

Americans too meekly adopted the standards of British English, the "correct" *New Yorker* style. In commending Malamud for a Guggenheim Fellowship, Bellow stressed, "It is upon writers like Mr. Malamud that the future of literature in America depends, writers who have not sought to protect themselves by joining schools or by identification with prevailing tastes and tendencies. The greatest threat to writing today is the threat of conformism." He grew impatient with Malamud, though his public endorsements and tributes continued. He is grateful for the injection of radicalism he had received from Malamud in his twenties. It had purged him (though not so decisively as he thought) of illusion and sentimentality. At the time he was, mercilessly, writing *Herzog.* He is merciless about the culture he has chosen, almost against its will. "It was made clear to me when I studied literature in the university that as a Jew and the son of Russian Jews I would probably never have the right *feeling* for Anglo-Saxon traditions, for English words." He had to fight free of such projected constraints and prejudices. His response to Henry James is like Achebe's to Conrad when it came to racial stereotyping. James's presentation of Jewish and black characters in, for example, *What Maisie Knew,* is disgustingly forthright.

From experiences of teachers and of the canon they taught he developed an aversion to the academic world and the way it ingested literature, how "the educated people of modern countries" make it their vocation to "reduce masterpieces to discourse." This derived from modernism itself, which was "dominated by a tone of elegy from the twenties to the fifties, the atmosphere of Eliot in *The Waste Land* and that of Joyce in *A Portrait of the Artist as a Young Man.*" Their tone became second nature. "Sensibility absorbed this sadness, this view of the artist as the only contemporary link with an age of gold, forced to watch the sewage flowing in the Thames, every aspect of modern civilization doing violence to his (artist-patrician) feelings. This went much farther than it should have been allowed to go." By the time he wrote his third novel, *The Adventures of Augie March* (1953), it had become his vocation to redirect the current.

The concise but very slow-to-read journal-form novel *Dangling Man* (1944) and the American-Dostoyevskian *The Victim* (1947) are formative work: Bellow's themes are there, but language has not found voice. In *Dangling Man* the protagonist expects to be drafted for military service. He quits his job but does not enlist; he waits to be called up. He spends a listless, frustrated year dangling, dependent on his wife, meditating in a self-induced and then enforced passivity. At last he stops waiting and, in desperation, enlists. He cannot find a way to make use of his freedom and so it is not freedom, and he surrenders. Philosophical questions are posed at every turn, but they are not embodied in plot and character. Argument runs alongside action, or inaction, in a not quite harmonious counterpoint. Bellow accuses a critic of too close a reading of *Dangling Man,* of being so interested in meaning, in symbol rather than detail, in intention rather than enactment, that she loses a sense of its literary quality. But the novelist too is in the wrong: "I think this is a fault of all American books, including my own. They pant so after meaning . . . A work of art should rest on perception."

*The Victim,* drawing on Dostoyevsky's *The Eternal Husband,* deals with more than anti-Semitism: the balance between the Jew-hating loafer, Kirby Allbee, and the considerate and intelligent Jew, Leventhal, is subtle, their interdependence symbiotic. "Oh, I think that realistic literature from the first has been a victim literature," Bellow remarked, a literature of "ordinary individuals" up against "the external world" that "will conquer them." *The Victim* is realistic only in its trappings. In fact it is schematic like a parable, like Kafka's *The Trial,* and as harsh as the Parable of the Talents. Coetzee says it is "within inches of joining *Billy Budd* in the first rank of American novellas," failing because Leventhal is in some way held back by the author, so the intolerable situation can be developed.

A complete revolution in his writing occurs with *The Adventures of Augie March.* When he found the style, "I was turned on like a hydrant in summer," he was writing "in a jail-breaking spirit." It was not unlike sexual excitement. Roth noted that the style "combines literary complexity with conversational ease, joins the idiom of the academy with the idiom of the streets (not all streets—certain streets); the style is special, private, energetic, and though it can at times be unwieldy, it generally serves Bellow brilliantly." It is in similar terms that Roth described his own objectives—that his language might have "the turns, vibrations, intonations, and cadences, the spontaneity and ease, of spoken language" but at the same time be anchored to the page by "irony, precision, and ambiguity."

Looking back on it in 1995, in a letter to Martin Amis, Bellow flinched when he reread the book: "It seems to me now one of those stormy, formless American phenomena—like Action Painting." By then he had progressed to what Amis calls the "sparer utterance" of his later style and looked askance at his real, messy coming into being. Part of the miracle is how fully he incorporated his own experiences without committing autobiography: this is a version of Kafka's "indiscretion," the use of individual experience to create a universal template comparable to Dickens's in *David Copperfield.*

He began the book in Paris on a Guggenheim grant. "You leave the U.S.A. and from abroad you think of nothing else," he said later. "What I found was the relief of turning away from mandarin English and putting my own accents into the language. My earlier books had been straight and respectable . . . But in *Augie March* I wanted to invent a new sort of American sentence. Something like a fusion between colloquialism and elegance." This mixed register breaks with the discriminated dictions of British fiction and the decorums of the *New Yorker*: "I was driven by a passion to *invent*." J. M. Coetzee notes, "Not since Mark Twain had an American writer handled the demotic with such verve." Bellow describes the book as "a widening spiral that begins in the parish, ghetto, slum and spreads into the greater world, and there Augie comes to the fore because of the multiplication of people around him and the greater difficulty of experience." Augie begins as an observer, developing toward engagement. Bellow defends the "low seriousness" of *Augie*: it goes with the mixed register, the rich geographical and cultural panorama, the humor and, most of all, the character. One is put in mind of Dreiser, who went a long way down this path, in a style that can verge on camp, given the inventiveness of his metaphors and the unsettling force of his ironies. Bellow worried about the density of his writing, the hyperabundance of detail and observation, yet his antagonism to his British editor John Lehmann strengthened his resolve. Lehmann was not enthusiastic enough, and he was homosexual. Bellow was not keen on English homosexuals, who seemed to him affected and pathologically ironic. Though Augie washed up nicely, for much of the novel he is battered, filthy, and bleary.

*Augie March* has abundant "literary qualities," but as Amis insists, it needs to be read for its plenitude: to isolate elements, to foreground themes, to systematize the picaresque flow, is to kill it. It is alive, a process, the writer shrugging off the rigidity of his earlier work, finding voices and a voice, not his, not unlike his, to make the narrative. It also attempts to encompass a series of adjacent worlds; variety of incident and geography give it epic qualities, more Fielding or Smollett than classic Dickens (the Dickens it *does* resemble is his last picaresque effort, *The Life and Adventures of Martin Chuzzlewit*). Augie is so acted *upon* that we focus on what is doing the actions. For much of the novel he is a punching bag, though he speaks and he takes solid shape, having started a dozen careers, warmed a dozen susceptible hearts, and eluded capture even when he wants to be captured. He's the sort of fellow who always lavishly disappoints, even himself. Amis notes that here for the first time in Bellow, style and content are inseparable. "And style is morality. Style judges. No other writer and no other novel"—how categorical Amis is when he has the bit between his teeth—"makes you feel surer about this."

Coetzee begs to differ, not about the literary qualities but about the success of the novel. "Once it becomes clear that the hero is to lead a charmed life, *Augie March* begins to pay for its lack of dramatic structure and indeed of intellectual organization. The book becomes steadily less engaging as it proceeds." He sees the book progressing by a series of brilliantly executed set pieces, these *tours de force* coming to seem mechanical in construction and in the ways in which they comment on one another. He singles out for particular criticism the scenes in Mexico where Augie, with one of his most emotionally brutal lovers, tries to train a cowardly eagle to hunt iguanas. Here *in ovo* is Cormac McCarthy, his tremendous geographies, his weirdly misshapen characters, and the places rendered with an accuracy closer and more luminous than Lowry's in the same general area at roughly the same period. In the end Coetzee's objections are moral, a morality that for him is inseparable from the aesthetic qualities of the book. If this is the story of "the coming to maturity of Bellow's generation," "how good a representative of that generation is Augie?" Was this in fact Bellow's intention? Was he here, or anywhere, saying "a great *Yes!* to America?"

Neither *Seize the Day* (1956) nor *Henderson the Rain King* (1959), with its "truculent and unsqueamish honesty" (the phrase is Nadine Gordimer's), for all their invention, risks the scope or achieves the narrative authority of *Augie March*. Bellow had to dig into himself, and again into the incidents of his own life, in this case his emotionally and financially costly second divorce, for his second great novel, *Herzog* (1964). He was writing, again, against the grain of experience, discovering how radical, when his personal anger and outrage were at their most intense, is the power of moderation, of the measured tone. He speaks of it as a kind of musical form, an unachievable desire within the character. Moses Herzog (the name borrowed from the Jewish funeral in Joyce's *Ulysses*, "M. Shulomowitz, Joseph Goldwater, Moses Herzog, Harris Rosenberg . . .") "wants very much to have effective virtues. But that's a source of comedy in the book." To Bellow, one of the themes is "the imprisonment of the individual in a shameful and impotent privacy." It is shameful because it entails his intellectual and sexual prowess, and impotent because no matter how hard he tries, how many letters he writes and to whom among the living and the dead, it is irreversible. Here his protagonist, mired in old habits of mind, clichéd expectations of self, experiences the collapse not only of his life but of the emotional, moral, and intellectual foundations upon which it depended. One by one his garments of self-respect and self-belief are removed. And he remains responsible for his own decline. Bellow portrays the forces ranged against him, yet Herzog, though he can be reduced and reduced, exiled and re-exiled, cannot be extinguished. He gathers himself together and overcomes his obsession with letter writing. He decides to put his house in order, literally and metaphorically. The book is not without self-pity, but so caustic that self-pity itself is comical.

*Mr. Sammler's Planet* (1970), Bellow says, "isn't even a novel. It's a dramatic essay of some sort, wrung from me by the crazy sixties." *Humboldt's Gift* (1975) is also a dramatic essay, but a novel, too, the third of his major ones, for which he received a Pulitzer Prize and which propelled him toward the Nobel Prize in Literature he was awarded the following year. It began as a short story rooted in his difficult relationship with the poet Delmore Schwartz. Power, material values, and art are brought into a telling collision in the reported unraveling of the older, visionary, and alcoholic protagonist Von Humboldt Fleisher, who has died impecunious, and Charlie Citrine (the name adapted from J. Citron in the list of Jews in *Ulysses* also), the first-person narrator, another "indiscretion" of the novelist. Against the backdrop of Humboldt's dogged self-destructive version of integrity, Citrine's Hollywood success thanks to Humboldt's gift of a copyright is vast and ironic. It is a voluble novel, the central relationships painfully lived, its garrulity that of a speaking voice with the natural, almost erotic, charm of *Augie March.* Chicago is nowhere more real in Bellow, and its petty criminal world represented by the minor crook Rinaldo Cantabile, seemingly fresh from *The Sopranos,* is sinisterly funny. The theme of expensive divorce is never far away in Bellow's novels of this period. Citrine is alive and successful. Humboldt in death lives on, like Finnegan in *Finnegans Wake,* controlling the moral action.

In *The Dean's December* (1982) Bellow's impatience with the modern world and what he came to see as its absurdities began to alter his fiction. Modern intellectual revolutions had "rearranged our souls"; there was no way back, elegy and satire were the only resources left to "us," that "us" itself becoming less inclusive than it had seemed before. In *Mr. Sammler's Planet* he suggests that the horror of the Holocaust, poverty, and the intellectual tyrannies, political and otherwise, that constrain individuals were endemic in the twentieth century as never before. "This *is* Lenin's age of wars and revolutions. The idea has gotten around by now." He distinguishes between "cleans" and "dirties" in American fiction. Much contemporary radicalism is without content: "A genuine radicalism, which truly challenges authority, we need desperately. But a radicalism of posture is easy and banal. Radical criticism requires knowledge, not posture, not slogans, not rant." The dirties are the inadequate radicals. The cleans, by contrast, are drab and dated. Yet, "There may be truths on the side of life." As against all those writers who nihilistically see the world as hostile, he suggests that truth is not invariably "so punitive."

After *More Die of Heartbreak* (1987) a stylistic change begins, the language sheds its excess, plot comes to the fore in *A Theft* (1989). Bellow was feeling his age, writing had become effortful and his sense of readership tenuous, as though, for all his celebrity, he had passed, still living, into the category of "literature." *Ravelstein* (2000), his last novel, published five years before his death, builds upon a story he had written and draws in earlier work. Amis declares it "a masterpiece with no analogues. The world has never heard this prose before" (indeed, it had never heard the prose of *Augie March* before either), "prose of such tremulous and crystallized beauty." In *It All Adds Up: From the Dim Past to the Uncertain Future,* Bellow wrote, "Disappointment with its human material is built into the contemporary novel. It is assumed that society cannot give the novelist 'suitable' themes and characters. Therefore the important humanity of the novel must be the writer's own."

Anthony Burgess compares Bellow to another Canadian Jew, Mordecai Richler (1931–2001). Though his maternal grandfather was a rabbi, Richler was born in a poor neighborhood of Montreal, son of a scrap yard dealer. He claims to be the child of a double ghetto, Jewish *and* Canadian. His community fueled his discontent and provided key material for his fiction. "He didn't write about 'Canada'—whatever that is—only the particular and isolated corner of the Jewish quarter of Anglo Montreal in francophone Quebec in the Canadian section of North America; a ghetto in a ghetto in a ghetto in a ghetto," Burgess said. Unlike the Bellows', the Richlers' emigration stopped in Canada. At nineteen, resolved to be a writer, Mordecai made his way to Paris, hoping to find the lost generation. He came home disappointed. He made his way to London. Again he came home with a different disappointment, and married.

He could never keep his counsel on Canadian politics, especially on issues of language and independence in his native province of Quebec. Skeptical of the large claims made in Canada for Canadian literature, he made fun of writers who were "world famous in Canada." Like Bellow he rejected political correctness, and in Italy, where his books were acclaimed, the adjective "Richleriano" was devised to mean "politically incorrect." He despised "identity politics," the proscribed types and stereotypes that could not be uttered for fear of giving offense, and the consequent weakening of the satirical impulse. He offended Jews, English-Canadian nationalists, and the Quebecois.

In his fourth novel, *The Apprenticeship of Duddy Kravitz* (1959), Richler "found a voice." Into a hitherto stable world of Canadian fiction comes Duddy as a Huck Finn figure, or a minor-key Augie March from Montreal backstreets like the ones in which Richler grew up, who develops material ambitions, romances, and in his attempts to get rich reveals the dark, hard, human, and absurd character of his society. Burgess was drawn to his sixth novel, *Cocksure* (1968), set in a 1960s London variously "swinging." The unlikely protagonist is a Canadian publisher, a veteran of World War II. In a corrupt age he is the gullible victim of various venalities. Overemphatic satire produces, Burgess says, not humor and a desire for moral resolution but rather sourness of spirit: the believable, not unsympathetic protagonist is a vulnerable outsider in a world of caricatures. Two imaginations, one realist, one satirical, are unreconciled.

*Solomon Gursky Was Here* (1989) was "the first South American North American novel," devising a Magical Realism rooted less in Márquez than in Chagall. For this he received the 1990 Commonwealth Writers' Prize. The wandering Jew starts circulating in a new picaresque, and stereotypes of Canadian character and writing drop away. This magic is leavened with jokes. It also recycles paragraphs from Richler's journalism. This ecology of self says something about the open texture of the fiction.

In *Barney's Vision* (1997), the autobiography of Barney Panofsky, the protagonist suffers (we learn toward the end) from advancing Alzheimer's. This accounts for the narrative and memory gaps and the strange pace and order of the material. A mystery underpins the story, told from a variety of points of view. Here for the last time Duddy Kravitz appears. He manages to inveigle himself into several Richler novels.

———•———

Now, an adjustment in scale. From the voluminous writing and public face of Bellow and (on a smaller scale) of Richler, attention turns to what at first looks like a pale square in an album from which the photograph has been removed. Twice in *Franny and Zooey* (1961) J. D. (Jerome David) Salinger (1919–2010) invokes the spirit of Kafka. Salinger's reputation rests primarily on a single novel, *The Catcher in the Rye* (1951), buttressed by a book of nine stories and two skinny books about the Glass family. Updike regretted the narrowing they represented. "Their invention has become a hermitage for him. He loves them to the detriment of artistic moderation." Nadine Gordimer described his prose as "a very clean window-pane, yet to get into the room beyond needs quite a sustained effort to suspend one's consciousness of all terms of reference other than those that direct the life of the Glasses." The door into their world was not locked but stiff on its hinges.

His "spurning of the world" (Roth's phrase: he compares Salinger's with Malamud's more calculating withdrawal) adds a frisson to the mention of his name. He was a powerful magnet for author molesters, journalists, and would-be biographers. Obituary headlines played to the recluse more than the writer, the *New York Times* dubbing him "the Garbo of letters."

In the Glass family stories and in *Catcher,* Salinger presents his natural-seeming but existentially challenged protagonists in a "real" world that regards them with unease. As in Kafka's *The Metamorphosis,* the world is real, characters are real, but they step out of a different kind of reality, their being in the fiction incongruous and illuminating. In *Franny and Zooey,* the Kafka quotations are in sharp contrast to one another. "'Don't you want to join us?' I was recently asked by an acquaintance when he ran across me alone after midnight in a coffeehouse that was already almost deserted. 'No, I don't,' I said." This Kafka is afraid of being alone.

Then, fraught with ambiguity: "The happiness of being with people." In Kafka Gregor Samsa is physically transformed; Salinger's misfits *seem* to fit, are normal-looking, even beautiful, but out of place.

Salinger's troubled teenager Holden Caulfield, the progenitor of Roth's Alexander Portnoy, Sylvia Plath's Esther Greenwood, Martin Amis's Charles Highway, David Malouf's Dante, William Gaddis's *J R*, Jonathan Safran Foer's Oskar Schell, and other unsettled young protagonists and narrators, is as famous as Huckleberry Finn. Like Twain's, Salinger's readership has become younger with the passage of time. *Catcher* is now assigned to children rounding the corner into their teens, a curriculum decision that strikes some parents as ill judged. The book opens with a sentence that pays tribute to the opening of Twain's greater book and defines the voice and character of Holden. He refuses to give us "all that David Copperfield kind of crap" about himself. The "goddam" world he's experienced is "phony." He is a boy who knows a bit about Dickens and has a smart, world-weary swagger borrowed from boys older than himself. Like Huck he's a truant, in Lodge's words "a youthful runaway from a world of adult hypocrisy, venality and, to use one of his own favorite words, phoniness."

When *Nine Stories* appeared in 1953, it was part of the education of Philip Roth, John Updike, and Harold Brodkey. Updike liked the way "they don't snap shut" but remain open and continue developing in the reader's head. Salinger's dialogue is perfectly gauged. Lodge defines "skaz" through looking at Huck's and then at Holden's dialogue: "In longer sentences, clauses are strung together as they seem to occur to the speaker, rather than being subordinated to each other in complex structures." This democratic syntax, this phrase-equalizing parataxis, imitates the ways in which actual speech makes its way to the ear. It is crucial to the liberation of American dialogue from the hypotactic patterns of English fiction. Salinger modeled his writing on Fitzgerald's, *Gatsby* being his favorite modern novel, an enthusiasm he shares with Holden, who says, "I was crazy about *The Great Gatsby*," adding fondly, "Old Gatsby. Old sport. That killed me." Salinger corresponded with and even met Hemingway, who made a mark, but not so deep or intimate as Fitzgerald.

Salinger was immediately received as the most talented of his contemporaries. He resisted the personalization of his work, demanding that his Cary Grantish face be removed from dust jackets, rejecting fan mail, and retiring to New Hampshire. His last publication, in the *New Yorker* in 1965, was a long story or novella entitled "Hapworth 16, 1924," a further installment in the Glass series. A poor film was made of one of his stories and he never licensed another for big or little screen. Forty-five years of vigorously protected privacy and silence, with the occasional treacherous breach, ended with in 2010 with his death and a flood of rumors about a stockpile of unpublished writings. As rumor gradually turns to fact, his could prove to be a long and sensational posthumous literary career, but in his case the death of the author has not been exaggerated.

From what is known of his boyhood, it is possible to say that Holden's and his life coincided in several respects. Son of an assimilated, prosperous European Jewish merchant and an Irish mother, Salinger failed out of one school; his parents sent him to Valley Forge Military Academy in Pennsylvania, the model for Pencey Prep. He rather enjoyed it. He was a lackluster university student. More successful was the evening class he took at Columbia where he wrote a story that got published. By 1941 he was contributing to the *New Yorker*. The first story, "Slight Rebellion Off Madison," was a sketch for a scene in *Catcher,* which itself has the loose structural feel of a series of connected stories rather than a flow of chapters. The *New Yorker* took six years to print it.

Drafted, he served in counterintelligence and lived in Devon, England. In 1944 he was with the landing at Utah Beach and saw action in the Battle of the Bulge (where Kurt Vonnegut was taken prisoner). The fighting he survived was gruesome. At the war's end, exhausted, he was hospitalized with something like a breakdown, writing to Hemingway that he was "in an almost constant state of despondency." He stayed in Europe long enough to marry a German doctor. It did not last. He returned to his parents' Manhattan home and continued writing, getting to know the great William Shawn, "my editor, mentor and (heaven help him) closest friend," with whom he shared his famous neuroses. Burgess suggested that in *Catcher* Salinger had "learned something from the Beats." If so, it was a proleptic learning: the Beats were forming but had yet to emerge in solid print, something that occurred around 1956–1958. Learning may have been the other way around.

Faulkner, not an avid reader of new fiction, spoke of *Catcher* as "the best one" of the new books he had read. There were vocal detractors. *Franny and Zooey* (1961), says Mary McCarthy, "suffers from this terrible sort of metropolitan sentimentality and it's *so* narcissistic. And to me, also, it seemed so false, so calculated. Combining the plain man with an absolutely megalomaniac egoism." The *New Yorker* turned down *Catcher,* having published six of Salinger's stories. Holden's precocity was not credible; the writing too showy. But the book is not "about" adolescent disquiet; it is not "about" in that sense at all. It creates a character trying to come to terms with the death of his little brother. He is as specific in culture and nature as Alexander Portnoy or Oskar Schelling, and to make of his a universal experience is to use the work in ways that betray it. It *is* "about" the 1940s, about a world going wrong, witnessed by a boy whose life has taken an incomprehensible turn. Holden, capable of sarcasm and anger, is still developing a protective knack of irony. Here is an infant Gatsby, before Daisy, without the illusions that will lure him into life's deep end.

"Mailerism" is one pole, "Salingerism" the other, says Philip (Milton) Roth (b. 1933). The one, dramatizing the writer, continually plays with and defies "fame," construed as media attention, critical engagement, and controversy; the other plays against "fame" and acquires it by that means, growing larger the less it publishes. Roth, a Mailerist in output and thematic risk, if not personal projection, dedicated *Reading Myself and Others* (1976) to Saul Bellow, "the 'other' I have read from the beginning with the deepest pleasure and admiration." Bellow reads Roth with almost the same expectations and disappointments with which he reads himself, remarking in a letter on "that ingenuous, possibly childish love of literature you and I have." The childishness has to do with taking literature directly to heart. In 1998 Bellow, having read *I Married a Communist* in typescript, thought he might be just in time to make a difference. "I was particularly aware of the absence of distance," he said, hence the failure of irony, and hence the failure of a humorous grasp on the material. The main fault is the character of Ira: "this cast-iron klutz," he calls him. And he cautions against a fiction that emerges out of ideas rather than characters and situations. "I have a thing about *Ideas* in stories. Camus's *The Plague* was an *IDEA*. Good or bad? Not so hot, in my opinion." Such candor between writers is not to be presumed.

Roth reflects on "the relationship between the written and the unwritten world," a coupling he prefers to "imagination and reality, or art and life." The suggestion is that the written can be *true*. That truth will depend on style, and he is concerned with language as having "the turns, vibrations, intonations, and cadences, the spontaneity and ease, of spoken language" but at the same time a print quality, a page-ness, anchored by "irony, precision, and ambiguity." He has a habit of falling into italics for the *clinching* phrase. There are books in which style weighs more than content. Self-regard is in play. *My Life as a Man* (1974) is about the thrills, vertigo, and final satisfaction of writing from and of the self. Though the self is fictionalized, the fiction is thin, like the convenient shadow-fancies that facilitate onanism. Style over content, a solipsistic spider, decidedly male, stirs its guts and lets out a shimmering thread.

Though his protagonists in their circumstances and concerns can resemble him, he will not have it that his work is autobiography or confession, even in those instances where a character is called Philip Roth, because the effect would violate the fact of fiction, "not only to falsify their suppositional nature but . . . to slight whatever artfulness leads some readers to think that they must be autobiographical." Amis notes "the longing to escape inherited identities" but at the same time to honor them, as a history, a faith, a root that goes deep in time, language, and space. It is an attempt through fiction to square the actual "me" with the world. He understands his characters' circumstances. He has been there.

Roth was born in Newark, New Jersey, and spent his childhood there, the son of first-generation Galician Jews. He studied English at Bucknell University, then went to the University of Chicago for graduate work. There he got to know Bellow. He taught writing briefly, then at Iowa and Princeton, becoming a long-term academic at the University of Pennsylvania and retiring in 1991. He is aware how much of his fiction stems from the geography and social structures of his childhood. He recalls too the intense male friendships of his adolescence, "the opportunity they provided for uncensored talk" on every subject, especially sex, and full of joking. It was here that the gendered social tones of his narrators have their origin. He also experienced what he saw as the warfare between parents and children, a painful theme in many of his books. In *American Pastoral* he describes "the daughter who transports him out of the longed-for American pastoral and into everything that is its antithesis and its enemy, into the fury, the violence, and the desperation of the counter-pastoral—into the indigenous American berserk." *American Pastoral* is his most powerful and painful book, invested with his geographies, his history, a helpless elegy for a place, a family, a culture, a country. In its elaborate and sometimes implausible contrivance it brings to a climax the parent-child theme: we corrupt our children even when, especially when, with the greatest care and affection, we believe we are protecting and preparing them for life.

His first book, *Goodbye, Columbus* (1959), consisted of the title novella and five stories. It is set in New Jersey, claiming the landscape of much of his fiction and marking out his themes. Here he evokes the values and expectations of middle-class American Jews and sends them up. The novella is about assimilation ("Jewish men and their Gentile women") and, crucially, about a man and a woman finding they are not in love. It was published on the brink of the 1960s, what Roth called "the demythologizing decade," and contains some of his most provocative, if not his most controversial, writing.

*Portnoy's Complaint* (1969) was also a literary scandal, on two grounds. Masturbation is a subject "so difficult to talk about and yet so near at hand," Roth remarked. After his earlier work, Martin Amis sat back "asking for more, and he gave us less." The style is brilliant and mature, full of surprise, but the themes are narrow. Alex Portnoy, a Jewish boy, lives in New Jersey. He masturbates a lot because of his mother. This commonplace predicament generates the comedy. Burgess draws attention to the second controversial element. Roth embeds his sexual theme firmly in the Jewish community and comments on Jewish mothers in a less than affirmative spirit.

*Portnoy* Roth describes as "a novel cast in the form of an analytic monologue by a lust-ridden, mother-addicted young Jewish bachelor"—the analyst eliciting the narrative. The book is "farcical," assembling "blocks of consciousness" or "chunks of material of varying shapes and sizes piled atop one another and held together by association rather than chronology"—a modernism that wants to seem open, even accidental, but with design and intent, the sequence clear. Asked if he was influenced by stand-up comics, he declared the principal influence was a "sit-down comic named Franz Kafka," *The Metamorphosis* in particular. Not that the novel is "Kafkaesque," but Kafka was a yeast, he "giggled to himself while he worked. Of course! It was all so *funny,* this morbid preoccupation with punishment and guilt."

More directly indebted to Kafka, too indebted perhaps, is *The Breast* (1972), the first of Roth's three Kepesh novels. David Alan Kepesh, a.k.a. *The Professor of Desire* (1977) and finally *The Dying Animal* (2001), irrepressible seducer of students and self-serving libertine, wakes up one morning after an "endocrinopathic catastrophe" to discover that he has been transformed into an enormous breast. Everything else is the same, real, but feels different to this dilated, hypersensitive erogenous zone with a five-inch nipple and a troubled consciousness. John Gardner gives this book the thumbs-up. The allegory pleases him because it is contained and sufficiently comical not to threaten our morality with its evocation of (Kepesh's phrase in a solipsistic monologue in a later book) "the delightful imbecility of lust."

Eight years after Kepesh was created, Roth's great alter ego, Nathan Zuckerman, narrator of nine (roughly one-third) of Roth's novels, including the greatest ones, was born. His first foray into the world was in *The Ghost Writer* (1979). Here young Zuckerman is a writer inflamed with early success, setting off with arrogant trepidation to visit the remote house of the writer E. I. Lonoff (based perhaps on Malamud) to meet him for the first time. A snowstorm detains him and he spends the night. Nathan's backstory is close to Roth's own. He is a graduate of the University of Chicago, he has published some stories, he wants a writer-guru. The book is a first-person meditation on the vocation of writing, Jewishness, isolation, sex, and fathers. His own father objects to some of his stories, which, he fears, might feed anti-Semitic feeling. The case against Portnoy is not far away. Zuckerman had hoped to find Lonoff admirable. He is in fact human, with more failings than most, licensed and forgiven by art. For Lonoff, writing stands in for the complexities of living. Roth's themes are in this book as in a well-organized primer, an excellent way in to Roth and Zuckerman, like and unlike as they insist on being.

The exhaustive, hilarious, and penetrating exploration of Oedipal themes becomes, in the later novels, an exploration of Laius's and Jocasta's anxieties: for the older man, the offspring (son or daughter) becomes a promise, a challenge, and a threat. Swede Levov in *American Pastoral* (1997) and Coleman Silk in *The Human Stain* (2000) are confronted by their offspring, who, culturally, represent a whole generation, sons and daughters, students, employees, who feel deceived, suckered by their predecessors. The protagonists are hyperliterary, their vulnerable self-scrutiny the product of irreducible, frustrated egotism. There is a Bellovian fullness to these narratives, a nineteenth-century amplitude at once realistic and nostalgic. Milan Kundera noted that in Roth's later work this nostalgia for the simpler, more wholesome-seeming world of the author's parents and grandparents—when the struggle to survive and prosper was ennobling (at least for those who survived and prospered)—fuels a fiction formally and thematically conservative. From that earlier world Roth has drawn "an entire novelistic background," then moved it into the foreground.

The three great Zuckerman novels are preceded by *Sabbath's Theater* (1995), a book of Shakespearean dimensions. Roth set himself to write "a realistic novel about imagined events." Amis describes it as "an upheaval novel, a crisis novel, a howl novel." It is all those things, but it is also a kind of overture in which the themes of the later books are introduced by the orchestra.

Both *American Pastoral* and *The Human Stain* question the nostrums of American liberal and progressive thought. Multiculturalism has led to cultural Balkanization, exacerbating conflicts between groups and individual alienation. As J. M. Coetzee notes, Faulkner is not far from the style and the themes of *The Human Stain,* in which Coleman Silk shares a fateful genetic heritage with Joe Christmas, only more so because he also contains American Indian and other bloods: a melting pot in himself, which adds to the irony of his fate. More than Joe Christmas, in his refusal to use the first line of defense, he resembles the resolutely taciturn Lucas Beauchamp in Faulkner's *Intruder in the Dust.*

Time has not dealt kindly with the Zuckerman of *The Ghost Writer.* Now he is alone in a place worse than Lonoff ever reached. He's in the Berkshires, where, ironically, he had gone to visit Lonoff. He has lost his prostate, his bladder control, his sexual potency. He has no human or animal companion. Silk seeks him out as—a ghost writer for his tragic story. Ironically, this is what Zuckerman (again, we are tempted to say) becomes, a witness of others' lives, a sleuth into mysteries that exclude him. But his style gets close in to its subjects: the diction is varied in response to the different characters' language. There are so many varieties of colloquial English in America, and Roth masters them. It seems effortless, at once learned and street-savvy, multicultural in another, older sense. As he discovers, again, "there really is no bottom to what is not known. The truth about us is endless. As are the lies." The novelist can imagine ends, uncover lies, touch bottom momentarily with an unblinkered narrative. His approach is straightforward: he introduces the cast of characters, misreads them, and one by one goes into their lives, so that in the end we understand where everyone is coming from—bigots, bullies, victims. The procedure becomes predictable. Longueurs occur when we embark on another of those "chunks of material of varying shapes and sizes," each one a novella in itself. Boxing, crows, cancer, common-room politics, Vietnam veteran events—they grow together, intersect, and a complex, comprehensible world emerges that cannot be reduced to a pattern or judged with clarity. Its existence in time is what Roth sets out to achieve. Past and present are entailed, everything from the world of Doctorow's *Ragtime* to the Vietnam War and the wild Continental radicalisms of 1968. If the novel succeeds, it will continue to resonate, it will have a future, like those big novels of the nineteenth century that we read even after school is out.

There is also the Roth of *Our Gang* (1971), a novel that expresses his hostility to Nixon. *Our Gang* belongs in the line of Nasby and Ward, and of Mencken, who hated President Harding with equal vehemence. And there are the short novels. *Everyman* (2006) Nadine Gordimer singles out as evidence that Roth belongs to a triumvirate—including the Mexican Carlos Fuentes and the Colombian Gabriel García Márquez—of old men in whom "the violent upsurge of sexual desire in the face of old age is the opposition of man to his own creation, death." There is nothing sudden in the upsurge of sexual desire in *Everyman:* it has marked every book Roth has written.

Of the short later novels, *Indignation* (2008) summarizes Roth's recurrent anxieties. A campus novel set in the early 1950s, it centers on a young male student of intelligence and principle who does not want to go to the Korean War. It is hilarious, and tragic, not only in its conclusion but incident by incident, the sequence of misunderstandings that condemn a character whose omniscience has a metaphysical dimension. The title is taken from the Chinese National Anthem. Here most purely we experience Roth's "daily awareness of government *as a coercive force.*" Hence, the question that recurs in his consideration of family, business, love, and other relationships: "Who or what shall have influence and jurisdiction over one's own life has been a concern in much of my work."

For Jonathan Franzen in his apprentice years Roth was a bitter enemy. Over time he has come to value him. "I still campaign against *American Pastoral,* but when I finally got around to reading *Sabbath's Theater* its fearlessness and ferocity became an inspiration. It had been a long time since I'd felt as grateful to a writer as I did when reading the bit where Mickey Sabbath's best friend catches him in the bathtub holding a picture of the friend's adolescent daughter and a pair of her underpants, or the scene in which Sabbath finds a paper coffee cup in the pocket of his army jacket and decides to abase himself by begging for money in the subway." He sees Roth almost as a charm, "a correction and reproach to the sentimentality of certain young American writers and not-so-young critics who seem to believe, in defiance of Kafka, that literature is about being nice."

He may have in mind the work of his friend Jeffrey (Kent) Eugenides (b. 1960), whose novels, on a substantial scale and full of dramatic promise, resolve in pools of sweetness. He was awarded the Pulitzer Prize for his second novel, *Middlesex* (2002), the title referring not to the English shire but to the sexual peculiarity of Calliope Stephanides, a boy by nature, a girl by nurture. S/he is also Greek-American, a further destabilizing situation for the narrative to play with. His first novel, *The Virgin Suicides* (1993), and *The Marriage Plot* (2011) attracted considerable attention. He is a crowned prince of the "abundant realist" school of long novels packed with detail and slow-motion reflection on short- and long-term issues affecting the lives of characters, some of whom are interesting. An account of his own life opens a number of biographical windows in his novels. He was born and reared in suburban Detroit, a city he loves and whose decline he laments, though he has not yet begun to paint it in the ways that Roth anatomized the decline of Newark in *American Pastoral* and elsewhere. *The Virgin Suicides* is informed by its culture. He studied at Brown University. In a gap year he went to Europe and volunteered in Calcutta with Mother Teresa's hospice movement. Scenes from *The Marriage Plot* and the earlier novels are memory vignettes given a new context. He moved to Manhattan, befriended a number of his contemporaries, notably Jonathan Franzen, then on to Berlin where he lived for five years on a grant, returning to a professorship in the creative writing program at Princeton.

What mars his fiction, often compelling in narrative, is the self-satisfaction of some of his protagonists and by extension of the narrator, so mired in his culture and its attitudes that the surrounding realities, domestic and foreign, are real only "in relation." The characters are sincere and self-aware; it is the larger supporting fictional frame, those parts of it that have to do less with detail and more with the kinds of construction that move a novel beyond the author's controlling reach, that have yet to be acknowledged and mastered. In particular *The Marriage Plot,* which visits the fictional territory of Bellow and Roth, of Fitzgerald and Hemingway, is technically resourceful but cloying. Only one, solipsistic zone of experience is real to each point of view. In Puritan writing with overbearing hubris the subject sees himself as the focus of severe divine attention ("I am the greatest sinner"): everything relates to his own *agon*. Eugenides's moral worlds are culture- and class-bound. His fiction is real for the credulous elect. It is not proof against a reader's own irony or foreignness, which can in certain circumstances, as in a literature narrowly partisan, amount to the same thing.

Like Philip Roth, Paul (Benjamin) Auster (b. 1947) was born in Newark, New Jersey. It is hard not to think of Roth when we read Auster, who tries to play some of the same games. One of his stronger creations is Nathan Glass, the protagonist of *The Brooklyn Follies* (2005), who calls to mind Roth's Nathan Zuckerman. Glass proclaims, "All men contain several men inside them, and most of us bounce from one self to another without ever knowing who we are." His nephew concludes, "When a person is lucky enough to live inside a story . . . the pains of this world disappear. For as long as the story goes on, reality no longer exists." This is the principle of Auster's fiction: the sufficiency, for its duration, of a narrated reality. "The closer I come to the end of what I am able to say, the more reluctant I am to say anything. I want to postpone the moment of ending, and in this way delude myself into thinking that I have only just begun, that the better part of my story still lies ahead."

Roth's writer-characters write well, like Roth himself; Auster's writer-characters write like Auster, and this is a different kind of blessing for the reader. "One reads Auster's novels very fast," writes James Wood, "because they are lucidly written, because the grammar of the prose is the grammar of the most familiar realism (the kind that is, in fact, comfortingly artificial), and because the plots, full of sneaky turns and surprises and violent irruptions, have what the *Times* once called 'all the suspense and pace of a bestselling thriller.' There are no semantic obstacles, lexical difficulties, or syntactical challenges." Often he is writing in a version or parody of detective and crime fiction: one might say the language is fit for that purpose, though taken over the extent of his fictional production, including eighteen novels, more variation might have been hoped for. One quality the writing has: translatability. Auster's fame in Europe and elsewhere has much to do with this. His work is also eminently malleable and responsive to modern literary theory, a serviceable pretext.

I interviewed Auster when the *New York Trilogy* (1987), consisting of three short novels—*City of Glass* (1985), *Ghosts* (1986), and *The Locked Room* (1986)—was published in Britain. He seemed to write *without style*. There were clichés in plotting and in language, and they reached us with the highest critical accolades. The incursion in the novels of characters from Melville and Hawthorne puzzled: Were they doing anything beyond tying him into an American tradition? It was not an enjoyable encounter: the interviewer could not mask his incredulity. "Where do we look for the depths? On the surface," Hugo von Hofmannsthal said. The surface is all we have as readers. Here were surfaces covered in intended depths, turned-out pockets, the loam of excavations, but was there depth in all the deliberate effort at depth? Year after year big and little novels pile up, the accolades continue. In *The Music of Chance* (1990) the narrator tautologizes, "It was one of those random, accidental encounters that seem to materialize out of thin air." Hemingway would have said it once, Roth at most twice. Auster says it three times, the third time with a cliché so it is sure to sink in.

The narrator of *Leviathan* (1992) is an American novelist called Peter Aaron. The initials are no accident. Russian dolls: a writer is writing about a writer writing about a writer, the last of these being Benjamin Sachs. With so many writers around, one waits in vain for the writing to reach a certain expressive level. Efficiently, briskly, with a string of cliché firecrackers, it does the business. *The Book of Illusions* (2002) almost convinces as a novel. There is literature professor David Zimmer, deep in mourning for his wife and sons who have died in a plane crash. He pulls away from grief by working on a book about a silent film actor, Hector Mann, whose film consoled him. Auster does some research and starts to make Mann's film world real, but he is not Doctorow and his book is not about Mann. It is about aftermaths and false starts. Professor Zimmer's book gets published; then Mann's widow writes to summon the writer to the bedside of the moribund actor in New Mexico. He does not go voluntarily: a woman takes him at gunpoint, all the way from Maine. The extended but fast-moving denouement, with mystery, murder, mayhem, and escape, itself has a denouement: we discover that the story was probably the sorrowing professor's escapist fantasy. He felt better after: Do we? This is not the first, second, or third time Auster has destabilized a fast, improbable narrative compounded of conventional elements and acknowledged that it is made up by a character. We are in an unsubtle, even a banal, version of the postmodern world.

---

When Martin (Louis) Amis (b. 1949) more or less emigrated to the United States, it marked the symbolic final removal of the center of Anglophone fiction to the New World. It also brought his strong, acid elixir to bear in a place that has need of it. New York has long been the capital of the fiction industry de facto, and from 1891, when the United States ceased to sanction piracy of non-American works, British and other Anglophone writers collected their fattest fees and royalty checks in dollars. But the departure of England's (not to mince words) outstanding contemporary novelist will be as decisive in its way for fiction as W. H. Auden's departure on the brink of the Second World War was for poetry. Amis's imagination already has dual nationality; his politics might currently seem more at home in Manhattan than Hampstead. To receive money from abroad is one thing, to move there lock, stock, and barrel something else, not a sell-out but a buy-out. There are overriding reasons. Frederic Raphael, reviewing Amis's 2000 memoir in which he comes to terms with his father, Kingsley, writes, "*Experience* is at once artful and artless: Holden Caulfield meets Herzog, and it is good.

Saul Bellow has anointed Martin a *goyish* Jew (and, since Kingsley's demise, taken him on as his adopted son)."

Despite his recurrent theme—Britain in irreversible decline as represented by modern London, and west London in particular—Martin Amis as a writer belongs less with his British contemporaries and friends, the group with which he emerged in the 1970s as his father had in the Movement of the 1950s, than with his revered Bellow and with Roth. He belongs with the great muralists of modern fiction, male, generically promiscuous, all reluctant modernists, careless of political correctness, assertive, making novels some of which resemble those of the nineteenth century in that they successfully create large, coherent, fully inhabited worlds.

And in his fascinated love of language and his avid response to the *abstract* challenges of form he belongs with Nabokov, the exception to every rule. In *Visiting Mrs. Nabokov* (1993) Amis writes the touching, diffident title essay, as though he were writing of the mother he somehow missed; her death, her air-blue gown, the memory of her courtesy and her real curiosity, reveal an aspect of Amis that is unexpected because exposed. I found my way into Amis, whose fiction I resisted for years, through his essays and reviews. He is less a critic than a reader, remaining close to the page, engaging words and the different ways writers use them, what they can and cannot do, and how their works connect with one another. Thomas Harris of the Hannibal books "has become a serial murderer of English sentences, and *Hannibal* is a necropolis of prose," he says, indignant when a writer lets him- or herself down; he is forgiving as soon as they get it right. Wide awake, he makes new connections and generally hopes for, even if he is not expecting, the best.

Faulkner does not feature much in Amis's world; Beckett is dealt with reductively, Kafka is more an idea, a paradigm, than a writer. These are not limitations but indications of a range. Most of his essays are about male writers, Iris Murdoch being a key exception. The early essays have an anti-American bias one is tempted to say he inherits from his father, a junior triumphalism of which the fact of American literature would cure him. Anthony Burgess, he notes in 1980, writes "short novels that go on for a long time," a phenomenon he lays at the American door. In America "writers routinely devastate acres of woodland for their spy thrillers, space operas, family sagas, and so on." And John Fowles's success in, "giving people the impression that culture is what they are getting."

Reviewing Cyril Connolly's *The Rock Pool,* Amis praises the lack of pretension, as though this were a serious virtue in a writer. Certainly among his English contemporaries it seems to be a meager "touchstone," like praising a chef's food for being "not too tasty." Here he began, in attitudes, sometimes bumptiously expressed, agreeable to his seniors: "A novelist needs to be unsophisticated, childish, even rather obtuse and naïve." We may agree, and reflect that Martin Amis's struggle to remain a novelist is an attempt to keep that freshness. He is capable of unexpected enthusiasm, as we have seen. He is ready to be surprised by what he reads, and ready to be surprised also by what he writes.

His novels can be as specific and cruel as anything by Bret Easton Ellis, more affecting in the sense that his characters are three-dimensional, their world also. The laughter they occasion comes from an existential source; underlying the caricatures and hyperboles of his narrators' language are characters as solid and nuanced as Ford Madox Ford's or Saul Bellow's, with inferable motives for action. Incidents are generally not gratuitous and at the same time not predictable. He avoids clichés of plot as of language. A narrator who believes he is in control can turn out to be a victim, as in *Money*, or find the plot for which he thought he was responsible wrested from him, as in *London Fields*. "You can't stop people, once they *start*. You can't stop people, once they *start creating*."

Readers of Amis's generation know how precisely he captures aspects of their world, how he belongs to its advancing present tense and registers it in the changing pulses of the prose, starting with that period after the political dreams of the 1960s soured and he and his close contemporaries came alarmingly awake. The contemporary who meant most to him as a friend, confidant, and *semblable*, and who no doubt helped keep him on course when the media were at their most hostile, was the commentator and journalist Christopher Hitchens (1949–2011).

Charles Highway with his "big-cocked name" narrates Amis's first novel, *The Rachel Papers* (1973), the prototypical Amis protagonist and not far (he admits) from the young Amis himself: smart, articulate, deploying wide-ranging, generally canonical literary allusions, oversexed, keen to pop his cherry before he reaches twenty. Rachel, the object of his desires, is otherwise engaged. He schemes to separate her from her American boyfriend. Amis knows from the start how language registers differentiate characters as eloquently as accents do, and Highway is eager to mask and then escape the limitations of class, and of a personality shaped by forces of nurture that override the givens of his nature. He introduces himself: "I wear glasses for a start, have done since I was nine. And my medium-length, arseless, waistless figure, corrugated ribcage and bandy legs gang up to dispel any hint of aplomb . . . I remember I used to have to fold the bands of my trousers almost double, and bulk out the seats with shirts intended for grown men. I dress more thoughtfully now, though not so much with taste as with insight." What really matters is "that I am nineteen years of age, and twenty tomorrow." What *really* really matters is that the novel is about the novelist. As in *London Fields, The Information,* and elsewhere, birthdays play a symbolic role, this time marking an urgent transition (and fictional time-span) in a kind of *bildungsroman.* In *London Fields* the birthday is the anticipated day of the climactic "murder," and in *The Information* it marks the beginning of middle age, a confrontation with the protagonist's failure and with his friend's unendurable success.

The first three novels—*The Rachel Papers,* the Murdochian *Dead Babies* (1975: issued in paperback as *Dark Secrets,* 1977), and *Success* (1978), with its stepbrother rivalry, its sexual and social satire—center on protagonists distorted by disappointment, disillusion, thwarted vanity, who survive even as "the beautiful and damned" go under. In *Success* he introduces his first paired characters, a plot strategy of complementarities (male/male and male/female) he repeats in later books. What for Fitzgerald was subject for elegy Amis observes from a point of view analogous to that of the servant or improbable secondary character in Victorian fiction, here promoted to a focal role. This formula recurs, there is a sameness in the kinds of laughter Amis elicits in these and some of the later books, but the comedy deepens, darkens. Like every disillusioned child of the false dawn of 1968, Amis is concerned with deception, especially self-deception. The emptiness of the success of his conventionally agreeable characters, such as Quentin in *Dead Babies,* or Gregory in *Success,* is made clear when they are hoisted on their own petards, and Amis's narrators (and Amis) assist where they can and record the nemesis with gusto. These are not satires *as such,* to borrow Keith Talent's phrase from *London Fields.* No just order is restored, something is destroyed, a minor key is sustained.

The early novels are apparently conventional in terms of plot. Amis does not plug into postcolonialism, neo-modernism, or experimentalism; he does not introduce new subject matter or disrupt form to draw attention to anything but the writing, with its startling clarity, sentence by cliché-less sentence, and its humor. He knows precisely how speech works in dialogue and in the narrative core, where he manages the first-person narrator not as a surrogate for himself but as an actual character in relation to the plot. This is true even of *The Rachel Papers.* The aesthetic integrity of the novels is admirable, even if, compared with the later work, a little effortful. As Diana Parry, despairing of Appleseed Rectory in *Dead Babies,* remarks, in the form of a question that sets the agenda for Amis's sinking England, "Don't you think we must have made a mistake a long time ago to end up like this. That something went wrong and that's why we're all so dead now?" The three Americans, Marvell Buzhardt, Skip Marshall, and Roxeanne Smith, are sinister, not dead themselves but accelerators in the process of brutalization. "But pity the dead babies. Now, before it starts. They couldn't know what was behind them, nor what was to come. The past? They had none. Like children after a long day's journey, their lives arranged themselves in a patchwork of vanished mornings, lost afternoons and probable yesterdays." Amis strikes this heart-stopping note when he registers, as we do along with him, what is.

*Other People: A Mystery Story* (1981) is described as a "transitional novel," which is to say it is a deliberate attempt, not in itself successful, to change gear. A young woman emerges from a coma with no memory and no ability to relate. The narrator is not the protagonist but a voice from which the girl (now calling herself Mary Lamb) flees into the corrupt and corrupting world. She finds her way, rises, and has her comeuppance, as Amis's protagonists do. In her case, having in a sense *made herself,* the mystery of who she "really is" is resolved. There is smoke and mirrors of a metafictional kind, which Amis handles uneasily, but he is learning the skills necessary for *London Fields.*

The next "phase" is the remarkable flowering in the "London trilogy" consisting of *Money: A Suicide Note* (1984), *London Fields* (1989), and *The Information* (1995), which together trace a characteristic world that incorporates Amis's London and his New York, places his prose redefines. Composition of the suite was interrupted by his experimental masterpiece *Time's Arrow: Or the Nature of the Offence* (1991), told "bassackward." He set himself a challenge that had been attempted by other writers—Fitzgerald in "The Life of Benjamin Button," Philip K. Dick in *Blade Runner,* C. H. Sisson in *Christopher Homm.* What is new is the way in which Amis incorporates the reverse narrative principle into the narrative style itself, and applies it to the Holocaust. "I saw the old Jew float to the surface of the deep latrine, how he splashed and struggled into life, and was hoisted out by the jubilant guards, his clothes cleansed by the mire. Then they put his beard back on."

Dr. Mengele, the narrator's boss, works miracles of healing in this reverse world, poignant, agonizingly so, because of the merciless irony of reversal. The destroyed world is reconstituted in its pulse and color. Out of the death trenches thousands emerge, as at a day of resurrection. Amis set himself the rule of not inventing, "you have such a horror of adding to what you are describing." The arrow of the title is many things, most memorably the static, painted hands on the Treblinka tower clock. Amis did the dreadful research, his narrator a kind of innocent incubus, a "passenger or parasite" living within the head of a doctor from a Nazi death camp. Our journey traces his life from its sour deathbed in the United States, where we know "him" as Tod Friendly (the given name is German for "death"), and he flickers on like a faulty neon, to his birth in Germany where he is roughly planted in conception and christened Odilo Unverdorben (the surname translates as "Undepraved," he returns to "innocence"). The narrator is paradoxically innocent, sentimental; the book builds to the appalling, astonishing reverse reading of Auschwitz. Amis acknowledges a debt to Robert Jay Lifton's *The Nazi Doctors,* the stimulus for his novel not only in the story it tells but in the psychology of Tod Friendly with his detachable incubus, always moving away from consequences and guilt.

Reflecting on *The Information,* Margaret Atwood sets Amis alongside David Foster Wallace: "Why this self-loathing?" she asks. Is *that* what underpins the London trilogy? Are the narrators inseparable from the writer's "self," and do we as readers trace John Self, Samson Young (the American writer with a two-decade writer's block), and Richard Toll, sour, middle-aged narrators, back to Amis, and to Amis's point of view? When "Martin Amis" becomes a consoling, patient character in *Money,* trying to buck up the flailing protagonist, does this not let the author off that facile identity hook? Is the ridiculously successful and always mysteriously present, though absent, Mark Asprey, one of whose pen names is Marius Appleby, not a more likely Amis surrogate (the initials, reiterated, are an obvious clue) than dying Samson Young, who is occupying his flat in *London Fields?* Attempts at biographical readings of Amis are limiting, even those that relate to *The Rachel Papers* and *The Pregnant Widow* (2010). The books can be grouped in tonally related batches, and there is an inevitable Amis inflection, but each novel untangles different illusions with a different narrative outlook. The murder mystery of *London Fields,* in which a victim plans and colludes in her own murder, is remote from Muriel Spark's pure, abstract plotting in *The Driver's Seat,* not only in scale (it is Amis's longest and most formally elaborated performance) but in techniques of control and projections that, with their brilliant handling of chronology, point in the direction of *Time's Arrow.*

The world of *Money* is Rabelaisian in its extremes of debauchery, the writer going along with each hyperbole and the language it proposes, English and American, as he shunts back and forth across the Atlantic. The book grows deeper and stormier with the sexual, psychological, and financial intrigues against him. Subsequent novels are more controlled and intense. His most Falstaffian villain is the gross, belching, eloquent, resourceful, low-life darts enthusiast Keith Talent (Amis's most complete monster, cheat, porno-addict, rapist, his savory misnomer) with his long-suffering wife and his sweet, abused, slowly corrupted daughter, Kim, the Little Nell of *London Fields,* and his deathless dog, Clive. Nicola Six is a sexy nemesis, Nabokovian, her fictionality established early, who begins to act in ways the narrator cannot anticipate or control. And there are Guy Clinch, the cheatable innocent, the novel's paymaster, English in his values and vulnerabilities, his son Marmaduke, titanic toddler, and his American wife, Hope, with a mind of her own.

Amis always seems to offend. *London Fields* failed to make the cut for the Booker Prize shortlist in 1989 because two of the panel did not like the ways in which it treated women. That year the prize went to Kazuo Ishiguro for *The*

*Remains of the Day.* The novelist Maggie Gee and Helen McNeil, according to the prize director, Martyn Goff, "simply felt that the author should make it clear he didn't favor or bless that sort of treatment. Really, there was only two of them and they should have been outnumbered as the other three were in agreement." The chairman of the judges, David Lodge, regretted caving in. The secret discussions of a judging panel have seldom been more public. Amis's *Night Train* (1997) might answer his female critics. It is narrated by Mike Hoolihan, an American detective, a recovering alcoholic, looking into a suicide. Mike is a woman. The language is—*pace* Updike, who disparaged it—convincingly American. Having envisaged an almost apocalyptic United States, one wonders why Amis considered emigrating; revisiting the London trilogy, the motives grow clearer.

Amis is a great essayist. Since the turn of the millennium his nonfiction has come into its own. His indignant writing against the *trahison des clercs* of our own time has made him few friends. Journalistic hostility to his success in drawing down large publisher's advances has told against him. He became the media whipping boy of British fiction, and the reception of *Yellow Dog* (2003), with its tabloid hack Clint Smoker, and *House of Meetings* (2006) was ugly. Amis did not need to defend them, but he did so anyway. Keeping counsel has never been his strong suit, and this is one reason for admiring him. The literary challenge of the style of *Yellow Dog,* he said, made contemporary readers aware of "how thick they are," and they did not much like it. He saw the book's reception as further evidence of resentment of "a higher voice" in fiction, by which he meant not a socially superior voice but one that is able to move in the higher registers. *The Pregnant Widow* he revised and added to until it was a definitive return to the 1970s as he experienced them, but the view taken is from "the present," another reverse chronology, as it were, a making (tragic) sense of the upheavals of the last forty years, seen in comic and appalling germination. The book is a companion piece to *Lionel Asbo: State of England* (2012), in which the title character wins £90 million on the lottery. Lionel is extreme, certainly, and entertaining, though he lacks the solid necessity, the epic girth, of Keith Talent.

One constant in Amis's prose is its unostentatious allusiveness. Philip Larkin's poetry, for example, feeds in as phrase and cadence: This is how a reader's language is colonized, in a good way, by a memorable writer. The "black sailed unfamiliar" of "Next Please" is clearly the vehicle Amis has in view much of the time. And when a narrator suddenly suffers an irruption of Larkin, or Shakespeare, or Auden, you glimpse the novelist through the fictional voice. In the end, it is the novels' intelligence and the integrity of their conception, the completeness of their fictionality, the *necessity* of all they tell and do, that sets them apart as unillusioned takes on a world that spins faster and faster.

*Timeline*

*Index*

# Timeline

1203?–1272 **Bartholomeus Anglicus,** author of *De proprietatibus rerum,* ca. 1240; English translation *On the Properties of Things* by John of Trevisa completed in 1398.

1280?–1364 **Ranulf Higden,** author of *Polychronicon,* translation into English by John of Trevisa completed in 1387, updated and printed by Caxton in 1482.

1405?–1471 **Thomas Malory,** compiler of *Le Morte d'Arthur,* completed ca. 1470; Caxton edition 1485.

1410–1420 *The Travels of Sir John Mandeville,* composed in French between 1350 and 1371, appeared in English translations (the first printed version in 1499).

1415?–1492? **William Caxton,** the first English printer, produced editions of many key narratives, including Chaucer's *Canterbury Tales, The Golden Legend,* Virgil's *Eneydos* (1490), Higden.

1480?–1545 **Fray Antonio de Guevara,** author of *Relox* (1529), *Epistolas familiares* (1539–1541).

1494?–1553 **François Rabelais,** author of *Gargantua and Pantagruel* (1532–1552); English translation by Thomas Urquhart and Peter Motteaux (1653, 1693–1694).

1516–1587 **John Foxe,** author of *Actes and Monuments,* known as *Foxe's Book of Martyrs* (1563, and three further editions before Foxe died, with numerous expanded editions and abridgments after his death).

1547–1616 **Miguel de Cervantes Saavedra,** author of *Don Quixote,* parts I and II (1605, 1615); first English translation by Thomas Shelton of part I in 1612, part II in 1620; other notable early translations include those by Charles Jervas and Tobias Smollett; the outstanding contemporary translation is by Edith Grossman.

1553?–1606 **John Lyly,** author of *Euphues: The Anatomy of Wit* (1579), *Euphues and His England* (1580).

1554–1586 **Sir Philip Sidney,** author of *The Countess of Pembroke's Arcadia* (1590, 1593).

1554 *Lazarillo de Tormes,* the first picaresque novel, published anonymously in Spain; English translation by David Rowland in 1576.

1567–1601? **Thomas Nashe,** author of *Pierce Penniless* (1592), *The Unfortunate Traveller* (1594).

1611–1660? **Sir Thomas Urquhart,** translator of Rabelais, author of *Pantochronachanon* (1652), *The Jewel* (1652).

1628–1688 **John Bunyan,** author of *Grace Abounding to the Chief of Sinners* (1666), *The Pilgrim's Progress* (1678), *The Life and Death of Mr. Badman* (1680).

1640–1689 **Aphra Behn,** author of *Love-Letters between a Nobleman and His Sister* (1684), *Oroonoko* (1688).

1660–1731 **Daniel Defoe,** author of *The Consolidator; or, Memoirs of Sundry Transactions from the World in the Moon* (1705), *Robinson Crusoe* (1719), *The Farther Adventures of Robinson Crusoe* (1719), *Memoirs of a Cavalier* (1720), *The Life, Adventures and Piracies of the Famous Captain Singleton* (1720), *A Journal of the Plague Year* (1722), *Moll Flanders* (1722), *Colonel Jack* (1722), *Roxana* (1724).

1667–1745 **Jonathan Swift,** author of *Gulliver's Travels* (1726, 1735).

1668–1747 **Alain-René Lesage,** author of *Gil Blas* (1715–1735), translated anonymously, then by Tobias Smollett in 1748.

1689–1761 **Samuel Richardson,** author of *Pamela; or, Virtue Rewarded* (1740), *Clarissa; or, The History of a Young Lady* (1748), *The History of Sir Charles Grandison* (1753).

1693?–1756 **Eliza Haywood,** author of *Anti-Pamela; or, Feign'd Innocence Detected* (1741), *The History of Betsy Thoughtless* (1751), *The History of Jemmy and Jenny Jetsam* (1753).

1694–1778 **Voltaire** (François-Marie Arouet), author of *Candide* (1759), epistolary essays *Letters on the English Nation* (1733).

1707–1754 **Henry Fielding,** author of *An Apology for the Life of Mrs. Shamela
Andrews* (1741), *Joseph Andrews* (1742), *Jonathan Wild* (1743), *The History of Tom
Jones: A Foundling* (1749), *A Journey from This World to the Next* (1749), *Amelia*
(1751).

1709–1789 **John Cleland,** author of *Fanny Hill: Memoirs of a Woman of Pleasure*
(1748, 1749), *Memoirs of a Coxcomb* (1751).

1709–1784 **Samuel Johnson,** author of *The History of Rasselas, Prince of Abissinia*
(1759).

1713–1784 **Denis Diderot,** author of *Le neveu de Rameau* (*Rameau's Nephew,* 1761,
1772).

1713–1768 **Laurence Sterne,** author of *Tristram Shandy* (1759–1765), *A Sentimental Journey* (1768).

1717–1797 **Horace Walpole,** author of *The Castle of Otranto* (1764).

1721–1771 **Tobias Smollett,** translator of *Gil Blas, Don Quixote,* and the works of
Voltaire; author of *The Adventures of Roderick Random* (1748), *Peregrine Pickle*
(1751), *Ferdinand Count Fathom* (1753), *The Expedition of Humphry Clinker* (1771).

1729–1807 **Clara Reeve,** author of *The Old English Baron* (1778), *The Progress of
Romance* (1785).

1730?–1774 **Oliver Goldsmith,** author of *The Vicar of Wakefield* (1776).

1736–1794 **Rudolf Raspe,** author of *The Surprising Adventures of Baron Munchausen*
(1785).

1743–1825 **Anna Laetitia Barbauld,** novelist, critic, and editor of *The British
Novelists* in fifty volumes (1810).

1752–1840 **Frances (Fanny) Burney,** author of *Evelina* (1778), *Cecilia* (1782),
*Camilla* (1796), *The Wanderer* (1814).

1756–1836 **William Godwin,** author of *Caleb Williams* (1794).

1759–1844 **William Beckford,** author of *Vathek: An Arabian Tale* (1786).

1764–1823 **Ann Radcliffe,** author of *A Sicilian Romance* (1790), *Romance of the Forest* (1791), *The Mysteries of Udolpho* (1794), *The Italian* (1797).

1768–1849 **Maria Edgeworth,** author of *Castle Rackrent* (1800), *Belinda* (1801), *The Absentee* (1812), *Ormond* (1817).

1770–1835 **James Hogg,** author of *The Private Memoirs and Confessions of a Justified Sinner* (1824).

1771–1810 **Charles Brockden Brown,** author of *Wieland* (1798).

1771–1832 **Sir Walter Scott,** author of *Waverley* (1814), *Guy Mannering* (1815), *The Antiquary* (1816), *Old Mortality* (1816), *Rob Roy* (1817), *The Heart of Midlothian* (1818), *Ivanhoe* (1819), *The Bride of Lammermoor* (1819), *The Abbot* (1820), *Kenilworth* (1821), *The Fortunes of Nigel* (1822), *Peveril of the Peak* (1823); critical writings include *Lives of the Novelists* (1821–1824).

1775–1817 **Jane Austen,** author of *Sense and Sensibility* (1811), *Pride and Prejudice* (1813), *Mansfield Park* (1814), *Emma* (1815), *Persuasion* (1818), *Northanger Abbey* (1818).

1775–1818 **Matthew Gregory Lewis,** author of *The Monk* (1796).

1779–1839 **John Galt,** author of *The Ayrshire Legatee* (1820), *The Annals of the Parish* (1821).

1779–1863 **Frances Trollope,** author of *The Life and Adventures of Jonathan Jefferson Whitlaw* (1836), *Michael Armstrong, the Factory Boy* (1840), *The Vicar of Wrexhill* (1837), *The Widow Barnaby* (1838), *The Widow Married* (1839).

1780–1824 **Charles Robert Maturin,** author of *Melmoth the Wanderer* (1820).

1782–1854 **Susan Ferrier,** author of *Marriage* (1818), *The Inheritance* (1824), *Destiny; or, The Chief's Daughter* (1831).

1783–1859 **Washington Irving,** author of *A History of New York by Diedrich Knickerbocker* (1809), *The Sketch Book of Geoffrey Crayon, Gent.* (1819).

1783–1842 **Stendhal** (Marie-Henri Beyle), author of *Le rouge et le noir* (1830), *La Chartreuse de Parme* (1839).

1785–1866 **Thomas Love Peacock,** author of *Headlong Hall* (1815), *Melincourt* (1817), *Nightmare Abbey* (1818), *Crotchet Castle* (1831), *Gryll Grange* (1861).

1789–1851 **James Fenimore Cooper,** author of *The Pioneers* (1823), *The Pilot* (1824), *The Last of the Mohicans* (1826), *The Prairie* (1827), *The Red Rover* (1828), *The Pathfinder* (1840), *The Deerslayer* (1841).

1792–1848 **Frederick Marryat,** author of *Peter Simple* (1834), *Mr. Midshipman Easy* (1836), *Poor Jack* (1840), The *Children of the New Forest* (1847).

1795–1881 **Thomas Carlyle,** author of *Sartor Resartus* (1831); historical writings include *The French Revolution: A History* (1837).

1797–1851 **Mary Shelley,** author of *Frankenstein; or, The Modern Prometheus* (1818), *The Last Man* (1826), *The Fortunes of Perkin Warbeck: A Romance* (1830).

1799–1850 **Honoré de Balzac,** author of *La comédie humaine* (1829–1847).

1802–1885 **Victor Hugo,** author of *Le dernier jour d'un condamné* (1829), *Notre-Dame de Paris* (1831), *Les misérables* (1862).

1803–1873 **Edward Bulwer-Lytton,** author of *Falkland* (1827), *Pelham* (1828), *Paul Clifford* (1830), *The Last Days of Pompeii* (1834).

1804–1881 **Benjamin Disraeli,** author of *Vivian Gray* (1826), *Coningsby; or, The New Generation* (1844), *Sybil; or, The Two Nations* (1845), *Tancred; or, The New Crusade* (1847), *Lothair* (1870).

1804–1864 **Nathaniel Hawthorne,** author of *Fanshawe* (1828), *The Scarlet Letter* (1850), *The House of the Seven Gables* (1851), *The Blithedale Romance* (1852), *The Marble Faun* (1860).

1805–1882 **Harrison Ainsworth,** author of *Rookwood* (1834), *Crichton* (1837), *Jack Sheppard* (1839).

1809–1852 **Nikolai Gogol,** author of *Taras Bulba* (1835), *Dead Souls* (1842), "The Overcoat" (1842).

1809–1849 **Edgar Allan Poe,** author of *The Narrative of Arthur Gordon Pym of Nantucket* (1838); critical writings include "The Philosophy of Composition" (1846), *Essays and Reviews* (1984).

1810–1865 **Elizabeth Gaskell,** author of *Mary Barton* (1848), *Cranford* (1853), *Ruth* (1853), *North and South* (1855), *Wives and Daughters* (unfinished, 1866); and the biography *Life of Charlotte Brontë* (1857).

1811–1896 **Harriet Beecher Stowe,** author of *Uncle Tom's Cabin* (1852).

1811–1863 **William Makepeace Thackeray,** author of *The Yellowplush Papers* (1837), *The Luck of Barry Lyndon* (1844), *Vanity Fair: A Novel without a Hero* (1848), *The History of Pendennis* (1850), *The History of Henry Esmond* (1852), *The Newcomes* (1855), *The Virginians* (1859), *Dennis Duval* (1864); critical writings include *English Humorists of the Eighteenth Century* (1867).

1812–1870 **Charles Dickens,** author of *The Pickwick Papers* (1837), *Oliver Twist* (1839), *Nicholas Nickleby* (1839), *The Old Curiosity Shop* (1841), *Barnaby Rudge* (1841), *Martin Chuzzlewit* (1844), *Dombey and Son* (1848), *David Copperfield* (1850), *Bleak House* (1853), *Hard Times* (1854), *Little Dorrit* (1857), *A Tale of Two Cities* (1859), *Great Expectations* (1861), *Our Mutual Friend* (1865), *The Mystery of Edwin Drood* (unfinished, 1870); other writings include *The Letters of Charles Dickens: Edited by His Sister-in-Law and His Eldest Daughter* (1880).

1815–1882 **Richard Henry Dana Jr.,** author of *Two Years Before the Mast* (1840, revised 1869).

1815–1882 **Anthony Trollope,** author of *The Macdermots of Ballycloran* (1847), *The Warden* (1855), *Barchester Towers* (1857), *Doctor Thorne* (1858), *Framley Parsonage* (1861), *Orley Farm* (1862), *The Small House at Allington* (1864), *Can You Forgive Her?* (1864), *The Last Chronicle of Barset* (1867), *Phineas Finn* (1869), *He Knew He Was Right* (1869), *The Eustace Diamonds* (1873), *The Way We Live Now* (1875); *An Autobiography* (1883); critical writings include *Thackeray* (1879).

1816–1855 **Charlotte Brontë** writing as Currer Bell, author of *Jane Eyre* (1847), *Shirley* (1849), *Villette* (1853), *The Professor* (1857).

1818–1848 **Emily Brontë** writing as Ellis Bell, author of *Wuthering Heights* (1847).

1818–1883 **Ivan Sergeyevich Turgenev,** author of *Rudin* (1857), *A House of Gentlefolk* (1859), *On the Eve* (1860), *Fathers and Sons* (1862).

1819–1861 **Arthur Hugh Clough,** author of *Amours de Voyage* (1849).

1819–1880 **George Eliot** (Mary Anne Evans), author of *Adam Bede* (1859), *The Mill on the Floss* (1860), *Silas Marner* (1861), *Romola* (1863), *Felix Holt* (1866), *Middlemarch* (1872), *Daniel Deronda* (1876).

1819–1875 **Charles Kingsley,** author of *Hypatia* (1853), *Westward Ho!* (1855), *The Water Babies* (1863).

1819–1891 **Herman Melville,** author of *Typee* (1846), *Omoo* (1847), *Mardi* (1849), *Redburn* (1849), *White-Jacket* (1850), *Moby-Dick; or, The Whale* (1851), *Pierre* (1852), *The Confidence-Man* (1857), *Billy Budd, Sailor* (unfinished, 1924).

1820–1849 **Anne Brontë** writing as Acton Bell, author of *Agnes Grey* (1847), *The Tenant of Wildfell Hall* (1848).

1821–1881 **Fyodor Dostoyevsky,** author of *The House of the Dead* (1862), *Notes from Underground* (1864), *Crime and Punishment* (1866), *The Idiot* (1869), *Demons* (1872), *The Brothers Karamazov* (1880); critical and autobiographical writing in *A Writer's Diary* (1873–1881).

1821–1880 **Gustave Flaubert,** author of *Madame Bovary* (1857), *Salammbô* (1862), *L'éducation sentimentale* (1869), *Trois contes* (1877), *Bouvard et Pécuchet* (1881).

1824–1889 **Wilkie Collins,** author of *The Woman in White* (1860), *No Name* (1862), *The Moonstone* (1868).

1825–1900 **Richard Doddridge Blackmore,** author of *Lorna Doone* (1869).

1828–1909 **George Meredith,** author of *The Shaving of Shagpat* (1856), *The Ordeal of Richard Feverel* (1859), *Rhoda Fleming* (1865), *The Adventures of Harry Richmond* (1871), *The Egoist* (1879), *Diana of the Crossways* (1885).

1828–1910 **Leo Tolstoy,** author of *War and Peace* (1869), *Anna Karenina* (1877), *The Death of Ivan Ilyich* (1886), *The Kreutzer Sonata* (1889), *Resurrection* (1899); critical writings include *What Is Art?* (1897).

1832–1888 **Louisa May Alcott,** author of *Little Women; or, Meg, Jo, Beth and Amy* (1868), *Good Wives* (1869), *Little Men: Life at Plumfield with Jo's Boys* (1871).

1832–1898 **Lewis Carroll** (Charles Lutwidge Dodgson), author of *Alice's Adventures in Wonderland* (1865), *Through the Looking-Glass and What Alice Found There* (1871).

1834–1896 **George du Maurier,** author of *Peter Ibbetson* (1891), *Trilby* (1894).

1834–1896 **William Morris,** author of *News from Nowhere* (1890), *The Well at the World's End* (1896).

1834–1867 **Artemus Ward** (Charles Farrar Browne), author of *Artemus Ward, His Book* (1862).

1835–1902 **Samuel Butler,** author of *Erewhon* (1872), *The Fair Haven* (1973), *The Way of All Flesh* (posthumous, 1903).

1835–1910 **Mark Twain** (Samuel Langhorne Clemens), author of *The Adventures of Tom Sawyer* (1876), *The Prince and the Pauper* (1881), *Adventures of Huckleberry Finn* (1884), *A Connecticut Yankee in King Arthur's Court* (1889), *Pudd'nhead Wilson* (1894); critical writings include *How to Tell a Story and Other Essays* (1897).

1836–1902 **Bret Harte,** author of *Condensed Novels: New Burlesques* (1867).

1837–1920 **William Dean Howells,** author of *The Lady of the Aroostook* (1879), *A Modern Instance* (1882), *The Rise of Silas Lapham* (1885), *Indian Summer* (1886), *Annie Kilburn* (1888), *A Hazard of New Fortunes* (1890); critical and journalistic writings include *Literary Friends and Acquaintances* (1890), *Criticism and Fiction* (1891), *My Literary Passions* (1895), *Literature and Life* (1902).

1839–1908 **Ouida** (Maria Louise Ramé), author of *Under Two Flags* (1867).

1839–1894 **Walter Pater,** author of *Marius the Epicurean* (1885).

1840–1928 **Thomas Hardy,** author of *Under the Greenwood Tree* (1872), *Far from the Madding Crowd* (1874), *The Return of the Native* (1878), *The Mayor of Casterbridge* (1886), *The Woodlanders* (1887), *Tess of the d'Urbervilles* (1891), *Jude the Obscure* (1895); autobiographical, *The Early Life of Thomas Hardy* (1928), *The Later Years of Thomas Hardy* (1930).

1840–1902 **Émile François Zola,** author of *Thérèse Raquin* (1867), Les Rougon-Macquart series (1871–1893), *Fécondité* (1899).

1841–1922 **William Henry Hudson,** author of *Green Mansions* (1904), *Far Away and Long Ago* (1918).

1843–1916 **Henry James,** author of *Watch and Ward* (1871), *Roderick Hudson* (1875), *The American* (1877), *The Europeans* (1878), *Washington Square* (1880), *The Portrait of a Lady* (1881), *The Bostonians* (1886), *The Princess Casamassima* (1886), *The Tragic Muse* (1890), *The Spoils of Poynton* (1897), *What Maisie Knew* (1897), *The Awkward Age* (1899), *The Wings of the Dove* (1902), *The Ambassadors* (1903), *The Golden Bowl* (1904); critical writings include *French Poets and Novelists* (1878), *Hawthorne* (1879), *Views and Reviews* (1908), *Notes on Novelists* (1914), *The Art of the Novel: Critical Prefaces* (posthumous, 1934).

1844–1925 **George Washington Cable,** author of *The Grandissimes* (1880), *Madame Delphine* (1881).

1847–1912 **Bram Stoker,** author of *Dracula* (1897).

1848–1887 **Richard Jefferies,** author of *Bevis* (1882), *The Story of My Heart* (1883), *After London; or, Wild England* (1885).

1849–1928 **Edmund Gosse,** author of *Father and Son* (1907).

1849–1909 **Sarah Orne Jewett,** author of *A Country Doctor* (1884), *The Country of the Pointed Firs* (1896).

1850–1904 **Kate Chopin,** author of *At Fault* (1890), *The Awakening* (1899).

1850–1894 **Robert Louis Stevenson,** author of *Treasure Island* (1883), *Strange Case of Dr. Jekyll and Mr. Hyde* (1886), *Kidnapped* (1886), *The Black Arrow* (1888), *The Master of Ballantrae* (1889), *Catriona* (1893), *Weir of Hermiston* (1896); critical and memoir writings include *Familiar Studies of Men and Books* (1882), *Memories and Portraits* (1887), *Valima Letters* (1895).

1851–1920 **Mrs. Humphry Ward,** author of *Miss Bretherton* (1884), *Robert Elsmere* (1888), *The History of David Grieve* (1892), *Lady Rose's Daughter* (1903), *The Marriage of William Ashe* (1905), *The Testing of Diana Mallory* (1908), *Delia Blanchflower* (1914); critical writings include *A Writer's Recollections* (1918).

1852–1933 **George Moore,** author of *A Modern Lover* (1883), *Esther Waters* (1894); memoirs, *Confessions of a Young Man* (1886), *Conversations in Ebury Street* (1924).

1854–1900 **Oscar Wilde,** author of *The Picture of Dorian Gray* (1891).

1855–1924 **Marie Corelli** (Mary Mackay), author of *A Romance of Two Worlds* (1886), *The Soul of Lilith* (1892), *The Sorrows of Satan* (1895), *God's Good Man* (1904), *Innocent: Her Fancy and His Fact* (1914).

1855–1920 **Olive Schreiner,** author of *The Story of an African Farm* (1883).

1856–1925 **Henry Rider Haggard,** author of *King Solomon's Mines* (1885), *Allan Quatermain* (1887), *She* (1887), *The People of the Mist* (1894).

1857–1924 **Joseph Conrad,** author of *Almayer's Folly* (1895), *An Outcast of the Islands* (1896), *The Nigger of the "Narcissus"* (1897), *Heart of Darkness* (1899), *Lord Jim* (1900), *The Inheritors* (with Ford Madox Ford, 1901), *Typhoon* (1902), *Nostromo* (1904), *The Secret Agent* (1907), *Under Western Eyes* (1911), *Chance* (1913), *Victory* (1915), *The Shadow Line* (1917), *The Arrow of Gold* (1919), *The Rescue* (1920), *The Nature of a Crime* (with Ford Madox Ford, 1923), *The Rover* (1923); critical and memoir writings include *A Personal Record* (1912), *Notes on Life and Letters* (1921), *Notes on My Books* (1921), *Last Essays* (1926).

1857–1903 **George Gissing,** author of *Workers in the Dawn* (1880), *New Grub Street* (1891), *The Private Papers of Henry Ryecroft* (1903).

1859–1930 **Arthur Conan Doyle,** author of *The Hound of the Baskervilles* (1901), *The Lost World* (1912).

1859–1932 **Kenneth Grahame,** author of *The Wind in the Willows* (1908).

1859–1927 **Jerome K. Jerome,** author of *Three Men in a Boat* (1889).

1860–1937 **J. M. Barrie,** author of *Auld Licht Idylls* (1888), *A Window in Thrums* (1889), *The Little Minister* (1891), *Peter and Wendy* (1911).

1862–1937 **Edith Wharton,** author of *The House of Mirth* (1905), *Madame de Treymes* (1907), *Ethan Frome* (1911), *The Custom of the Country* (1913), *The Age of Innocence* (1920); critical writings include *The Writing of Fiction* (1925); autobiography includes *A Backward Glance* (1934).

1863–1945 **Arthur Morrison,** author of *Tales of Mean Streets* (1894), *A Child of the Jago* (1896).

1865–1936 **Rudyard Kipling,** author of *The Light That Failed* (1890), *Captains Courageous* (1897), *Kim* (1901).

1866–1946 **H. G. Wells,** author of *The Time Machine* (1895), *The Island of Doctor Moreau* (1896), *The Invisible Man* (1897), *The War of the Worlds* (1898), *Love and Mr. Lewisham* (1900), *The First Men on the Moon* (1901), *Kipps* (1905), *A Modern Utopia* (1905), *The War in the Air* (1908), *Tono-Bungay* (1909), *The History of Mr. Polly* (1910), *The New Machiavelli* (1911), *Marriage* (1912), *Men Like Gods* (1923), *The Shape of Things to Come* (1933).

1867–1931 **Arnold Bennett,** author of *A Man from the North* (1898), *Anna of the Five Towns* (1902), *Leonora* (1903), *Teresa of Watling Street* (1904), *The Old Wives' Tale* (1908), *Clayhanger* (1910), *Hilda Lessways* (1911), *These Twain* (1916), *The Pretty Lady* (1918), *Riceyman Steps* (1923), *Venus Rising from the Sea* (1931); critical writings include *The Author's Craft* (1914), *Books and Persons: Being Comments on a Past Epoch, 1908–1911* (1917), *The Journal of Arnold Bennett* (1932).

1867–1933 **John Galsworthy,** author of *The Forsyte Saga* (1906–1921), *A Modern Comedy* (1924–1928), *End of the Chapter* (1931–1933).

1868–1952 **Norman Douglas,** author of *South Wind* (1917), *They Went* (1920); travel writings include *Siren Land* (1911), *Fountains in the Sand* (1912), *Old Calabria* (1915).

1870–1902 **Frank Norris,** author of *McTeague: A Story of San Francisco* (1899), *The Octopus: A Story of California* (1901), *The Pit* (1903).

1870–1946 **Henry Handel Richardson** (Ethel Florence Lindesay Richardson), author of *Maurice Guest* (1908), *The Getting of Wisdom* (1910), *The Fortunes of Richard Mahony* (1930: *Australia Felix,* 1917; *The Way Home,* 1925; and *Ultima Thule,* 1929).

1871–1900 **Stephen Crane,** author of *Maggie: A Girl of the Streets* (1893), *The Red Badge of Courage* (1895).

1871–1945 **Theodore Dreiser,** author of *Sister Carrie* (1900), *Jennie Gerhardt* (1911), *An American Tragedy* (1925), *Trilogy of Desire* (1912–1947).

1871–1922 **Marcel Proust,** author of *À la recherche du temps perdu* (1913–1925), *Le temps retrouvé* (1927).

1872–1956 **Max Beerbohm,** author of *Zuleika Dobson* (1911), *A Christmas Garland* (1912).

1872–1939 **Zane Grey,** author of *Riders of the Purple Sage* (1912).

1872–1963 **John Cowper Powys,** author of *Wood and Stone* (1915), *Wolf Solent* (1929), *A Glastonbury Romance* (1932), *Weymouth Sands* (1934), *Maiden Castle* (1936), *Owen Glendower* (1940), *Porius* (1951); critical writings include *Suspended Judgments* (1916).

1873–1947 **Willa Cather,** author of *Alexander's Bridge* (1912), *O Pioneers!* (1913), *The Song of the Lark* (1915), *One of Ours* (1922), *The Professor's House* (1925), *My Mortal Enemy* (1926), *Death Comes for the Archbishop* (1927); critical writings include *On Writing: Critical Studies on Writing as an Art* (1949).

1873–1939 **Ford Madox Ford,** author of *The Queen Who Flew* (1894), Fifth Queen trilogy (1906–1908), *A Call* (1910), *Ladies Whose Bright Eyes: A Romance* (1911), *The Young Lovell* (1913), *The Good Soldier* (1915), *Parade's End* (*Some Do Not . . .* , 1924; *No More Parades,* 1925; *A Man Could Stand Up,* 1926; *Last Post,* 1928), *No Enemy* (1929), *The Rash Act* (1933), *It Was the Nightingale* (1933); critical and other writings include *The Soul of London* (1905), *The Heart of the Country* (1906), *The Spirit of the People* (1907), *The Critical Attitude* (1911), *Joseph Conrad: A Personal Remembrance* (1924), *The English Novel: From the Earliest Days to the Death of Joseph Conrad* (1929), *Return to Yesterday* (1932), *Portraits from Life* (1937), *The March of Literature* (1938).

1873–1945 **Ellen Glasgow,** author of *Barren Ground* (1925), *The Romantic Comedians* (1926).

1873–1957 **Dorothy Richardson,** author of *Pilgrimage* (thirteen novels, published 1915–1935).

1874–1936 **G. K. Chesterton,** author of *The Napoleon of Notting Hill* (1904), *The Man Who Was Thursday: A Nightmare* (1908), *Manalive* (1912), *The Flying Inn* (1914); memoir, *The Autobiography* (1936).

1874–1965 **Somerset Maugham,** author of *Liza of Lambeth* (1897), *Mrs. Craddock* (1902), *The Magician* (1907), *Of Human Bondage* (1915), *The Moon and Sixpence*

(1919), *The Painted Veil* (1925), *Cakes and Ale: Or the Skeleton in the Cupboard* (1930), *The Narrow Corner* (1932), *Up at the Villa* (1941), *The Razor's Edge* (1944); critical and other writings include *The Summing Up* (1938), *A Writer's Notebook* (1949), *Ten Novels and Their Authors* (1954).

1874–1946 **Gertrude Stein,** author of *Three Lives* (1909), *The Making of Americans: Being the History of a Family's Progress* (1925), *The Autobiography of Alice B. Toklas* (1933), *Ida: A Novel* (1941).

1875–1953 **T. F. Powys,** author of *Mr. Weston's Good Wine* (1927).

1876–1941 **Sherwood Anderson,** author of *Windy McPherson's Son* (1916), *Marching Men* (1917), *Winesburg, Ohio: Stories* (1919), *Poor White* (1920), *Many Marriages* (1923), *Dark Laughter* (1925); critical and other writings include *A Story Teller's Story* (memoir, 1924), *The Modern Writer* (1925), *Perhaps Women* (1931), *Puzzled America* (1935), *A Writer's Conception of Realism* (1939).

1876–1916 **Jack London,** author of *The Call of the Wild* (1903), *White Fang* (1906), *The Iron Heel* (1908).

1878–1968 **Upton Sinclair,** author of *The Jungle* (1906), *Sylvia* (1913), *King Coal* (1917), *Oil* (1927), *Dragon's Teeth* (1942), *Another Pamela* (1952).

1879–1970 **E. M. Forster,** author of *Where Angels Fear to Tread* (1905), *The Longest Journey* (1907), *A Room with a View* (1908), *Howards End* (1910), *A Passage to India* (1924), *Maurice* (1913–1914, publication 1971); critical writings include *Aspects of the Novel* (1927), *Abinger Harvest* (1936).

1880–1964 **Carl Van Vechten,** author of *Nigger Heaven* (1926).

1881–1927 **Mary Webb,** author of *The Golden Arrow* (1916), *Precious Bane* (1924).

1881–1975 **P. G. Wodehouse,** author of *Love among the Chickens* (1908), *Psmith in the City* (1910), *The Man with Two Left Feet* (1917), *My Man Jeeves* (1919).

1882–1941 **James Joyce,** author of *Dubliners* (1914), *A Portrait of the Artist as a Young Man* (1916), *Ulysses* (1922), *Finnegans Wake* (1939).

1882–1957 **Wyndham Lewis,** author of *Tarr* (1918), *The Wild Body: A Soldier of Humor and Other Stories* (1927), *The Human Age* (1928–1955), *The Apes of God*

(1930), *Self-Condemned* (1954); critical and polemical writings include *The Art of Being Ruled* (1926), *Time and Western Man* (1927), *Paleface: The Philosophy of the Melting Pot* (1929), *Men without Art* (1934), *The Writer and the Absolute* (1952).

1882–1935 **Frederic Manning,** author of *Her Privates, We* (1930).

1882–1941 **Virginia Woolf,** author of *The Voyage Out* (1915), *Night and Day* (1919), *Jacob's Room* (1922), *Mrs. Dalloway* (1925), *To the Lighthouse* (1927), *Orlando* (1928), *The Waves* (1931), *Flush: A Biography* (1933), *The Years* (1937), *Between the Acts* (1941); critical writings include *The Common Reader: First Series* (1925), *A Room of One's Own* (1929), *The Common Reader: Second Series* (1932), *Three Guineas* (1938), and *Essays of Virginia Woolf,* edited by Andrew McNeillie et al. (several volumes, 1987–2012).

1883–1924 **Franz Kafka,** author of *Die Verwandlung* (*The Metamorphosis,* 1915), *Der Process* (*The Trial,* 1925), *Der Schloss* (*The Castle,* 1926), *Amerika* (1927).

1883–1972 **Compton Mackenzie,** author of *Sinister Street* (1914), *Extraordinary Women* (1928), *The Four Winds of Love* (1937–1945), *The Monarch of the Glen* (1941), *Whisky Galore* (1947).

1884–1969 **Ivy Compton-Burnett,** author of *Dolores* (1911), *Pastors and Masters* (1925), *Brothers and Sisters* (1929), *A House and Its Head* (1935), *Manservant and Maidservant* (1947), *The Present and the Past* (1953), *A Heritage and Its History* (1959), *The Mighty and Their Fall* (1961), *A God and His Gifts* (1963).

1884–1941 **Hugh Walpole,** author of *The Duchess of Wrexe: Her Decline and Death* (1914), *Farthing Hall* (with J. B. Priestley, 1929); critical writings include *Joseph Conrad* (1916), *The English Novel: Some Notes on Its Evolution* (1924), *Reading: An Essay* (1926), *Anthony Trollope* (1928), *A Letter to a Modern Novelist* (1932).

1885–1930 **D. H. Lawrence,** author of *The White Peacock* (1911), *The Trespasser* (1912), *Sons and Lovers* (1913), *The Rainbow* (1915), *Women in Love* (1920), *The Lost Girl* (1920), *Aaron's Rod* (1922), *Kangaroo* (1923), *The Plumed Serpent* (1926), *Lady Chatterley's Lover* (1928); critical writings include *Studies in Classic American Literature* (1923), *À Propos of Lady Chatterley's Lover* (1929).

1885–1951 **Sinclair Lewis,** author of *Main Street* (1920), *Babbitt* (1922), *Arrowsmith* (1925), *Elmer Gantry* (1927).

1886–1926 **Ronald Firbank,** author of *Vainglory* (1915), *Inclinations* (1916), *Caprice* (1917), *Valmouth* (1919), *Sorrow in Sunlight* (*Prancing Nigger,* 1924), *Concerning the Eccentricities of Cardinal Pirelli* (1926).

1886–1943 **Radclyffe Hall,** author of *The Well of Loneliness* (1928).

1888–1957 **Joyce Cary,** author of *Mister Johnson* (1939), *Herself Surprised* (1941), *To Be a Pilgrim* (1942), *The Horse's Mouth* (1944).

1888–1959 **Raymond Chandler,** author of *The Big Sleep* (1939), *Farewell, My Lovely* (1940), *The High Window* (1942), *The Lady in the Lake* (1943), *The Long Goodbye* (1953); other writings include *Raymond Chandler Speaking* (1977).

1888–1981 **Anita Loos,** author of *Gentlemen Prefer Blonds: The Intimate Diary of a Professional Lady* (1928).

1889–1948 **Claude McKay,** author of *Home to Harlem* (1928), *Banjo: A Story without a Plot* (1929), *Banana Bottom* (1933).

1890–1937 **Mary Butts,** author of *Ashe of Rings* (1925), *Death of Felicity Taverner* (1932).

1890–1976 **Agatha Christie,** author of *The Mysterious Affair at Styles* (1920).

1890–1937 **H. P. Lovecraft,** author of *The Case of Charles Dexter Ward* (1943).

1890–1980 **Katherine Anne Porter,** author of *Pale Horse, Pale Rider* (1939), *Ship of Fools* (1962); critical writings include *Collected Essays and Occasional Writings* (1970).

1890–1979 **Jean Rhys** (Ella Gwendolen Rees Williams), author of *Quartet* (1928), *After Leaving Mr. Mackenzie* (1930), *Voyage in the Dark* (1934), *Good Morning, Midnight* (1939), *Wide Sargasso Sea* (1966).

1891–1960 **Zora Neale Hurston,** author of *Jonah's Gourd Vine* (1934), *Their Eyes Were Watching God* (1937), *Moses, Man of the Mountain* (1939), *Dust Tracks on a Road* (1942).

1891–1988 **Storm Jameson,** author of *Love in Winter* (1926), *The Lovely Ship* (1927), *The Voyage Home* (1930), *A Richer Dust* (1931), *In the Second Year* (1936).

1891–1964 **Nella Larsen,** author of *Quicksand* (1928).

1891–1980 **Henry Miller,** author of *Tropic of Cancer* (1934), *Black Spring* (1936), *Tropic of Capricorn* (1939), *The Colossus of Maroussi* (1941), *The Rosy Crucifixion* (*Sexus, Plexus,* and *Nexus,* 1949–1960).

1892–1962 **Richard Aldington,** author of *Death of a Hero* (1929).

1892–1982 **Djuna Barnes,** author of *Ryder* (1928), *Ladies Almanack* (1928), *Nightwood* (1936).

1892–1977 **James Cain,** author of *The Postman Always Rings Twice* (1934), *Mildred Pierce* (1941), *Double Indemnity* (1943).

1892–1981 **David Garnett,** author of *Dope-Darling: A Story of Cocaine* (1919), *Lady into Fox* (1920), *A Man in the Zoo* (1924), *Aspects of Love* (1955).

1892–1983 **Rebecca West** (Cicely Isabel Fairfield), author of *The Return of the Soldier* (1918), *The Judge* (1922), *The Thinking Reed* (1936), The *Fountain Overflows* (1956); critical writings include *Henry James* (1916), *The Strange Necessity: Essays and Reviews* (1928), *Ending in Earnest: A Literary Log* (1931), *The Court and the Castle: Some Treatments of a Recurring Theme* (1958).

1893–1970 **Vera Brittain,** author of *Testament of Youth* (1933).

1893–1957 **Dorothy L. Sayers,** author of *Whose Body?* (1923).

1893–1978 **Sylvia Townsend Warner,** author of *Mr. Fortune's Maggot* (1927), *The True Heart* (1929), *The Corner That Held Them* (1948).

1894–1961 **Louis-Ferdinand Céline,** author of *Voyage au bout de la nuit* (1932).

1894–1962 **E. E. Cummings,** author of *The Enormous Room* (1922).

1894–1961 **Dashiell Hammett,** author of *Red Harvest* (1929), *The Maltese Falcon* (1930), *The Glass Key* (1931), *The Thin Man* (1934).

1894–1963 **Aldous Huxley,** author of *Crome Yellow* (1921), *Antic Hay* (1923), *Point Counter Point* (1928), *Brave New World* (1932), *Eyeless in Gaza* (1936), *After Many* *a Summer* (1939), *Island* (1962); critical writings include *Collected Essays* (1958), *Literature and Science* (1963).

1894–1984 **J. B. Priestley,** author of *The Good Companions* (1929), *Angel Pavement* (1930).

1894–1967 **Jean Toomer,** author of *Cane* (1923).

1895–1985 **Robert Graves,** author of *My Head! My Head!* (1925), *The Real David Copperfield* (1933), *I, Claudius* (1934), *Claudius the God and His Wife Messalina* (1935), *Count Belisarius* (1938), *Sergeant Lamb of the Ninth* (1940), *Proceed, Sergeant Lamb* (1941), *The Story of Marie Powell: Wife to Mr. Milton* (1943), *The Golden Fleece* (1944), *King Jesus* (1946), *Homer's Daughter* (1955).

1895–1982 **Ngaio Marsh,** author of *A Man Lay Dead* (1934).

1895–1972 **L. P. Hartley,** author of *The Shrimp and the Anemone* (1944), *The Sixth Heaven* (1946), *Eustace and Hilda* (1947), *The Go-Between* (1953), *The Hireling* (1957), *Facial Justice* (1960).

1895–1977 **Henry Williamson,** author of *The Flax of Dreams* (four volumes, 1921–1928), *Tarka the Otter* (1927), *A Chronicle of Ancient Sunlight* (fifteen volumes, 1951–1969).

1895–1972 **Edmund Wilson,** author of *I Thought of Daisy* (1929), *Memoirs of Hecate County* (stories, 1946); critical and other writings include *Axel's Castle: A Study of the Imaginative Literature of 1870–1930* (1931), *The American Jitters* (1932), *The Triple Thinkers: Ten Essays on Literature* (1938, revised to *Twelve Essays* in 1948), *To the Finland Station* (1940), *The Wound and the Bow* (1941), *The Shores of Light: A Literary Chronicle of the Twenties and Thirties* (1952), *A Piece of My Mind: Reflections at Sixty* (1956), *The American Earthquake: A Documentary of the Twenties and Thirties* (1958), *Patriotic Gore: Studies in the Literature of the American Civil War* (1962), *The Bit between My Teeth: A Literary Chronicle of 1950–1965* (1966), *The Twenties: From Notebooks and Diaries of the Period* (1975), *The Thirties* (1980), *The Forties* (1983), *The Fifties* (1986), *The Sixties* (1993).

1896–1963 **Katherine Burdekin,** author of *Swastika Night* (1937).

1896–1981 **A. J. Cronin,** author of *Hatter's Castle* (1931), *The Citadel* (1937).

1896–1970 **John Dos Passos,** author of *Three Soldiers* (1920), *Rosinante to the Road Again* (1922), *Manhattan Transfer* (1925), *U.S.A.* (1938: *The 42nd Parallel,* 1930; *Nineteen Nineteen,* 1932; *The Big Money,* 1936), *District of Columbia* (1952: *Adventures of a Young Man,* 1939; *Number One,* 1943; *The Grand Design,* 1949), *Midcentury* (1961); other writings include *State of the Nation* (1944).

1896–1940 **F. Scott Fitzgerald,** author of *This Side of Paradise* (1920), *The Beautiful and Damned* (1922), *The Great Gatsby* (1925), *Tender Is the Night* (1934), *The Last Tycoon* (1941); other writings include *The Crack-Up* (1945).

1896–1957 **Giuseppe Tomasi di Lampedusa,** author of *Il gattopardo* (*The Leopard,* 1958).

1896–1952 **Josephine Tey** (Elizabeth Mackintosh), author of *The Man in the Queue* (1929), *The Daughter of Time* (1951).

1897–1962 **William Faulkner,** author of *Soldier's Pay* (1926), *Sartoris* (1929), *The Sound and the Fury* (1929), *As I Lay Dying* (1930), *Sanctuary* (1931), *Light in August* (1932), *Absalom, Absalom!* (1936), *The Wild Palms* (1939), *The Hamlet* (1940), *Intruder in the Dust* (1948), *Requiem for a Nun* (1951), *A Fable* (1954), *The Town* (1957), *The Mansion* (1959), *The Reivers* (1962).

1897–1999 **Naomi Mitchison,** author of *The Conquered* (1923).

1897–1975 **Thornton Wilder,** author of *The Cabala* (1926), *The Bridge of San Luis Rey* (1927), *Heaven's My Destination* (1935), *Ides of March* (1948), *The Eighth Day* (1967).

1898–1935 **Winifred Holtby,** author of *South Riding* (1936).

1899–1973 **Elizabeth Bowen,** author of *The Hotel* (1927), *The Last September* (1929), *The House in Paris* (1935), *The Death of the Heart* (1938), *The Heat of the Day* (1948), *Eva Trout: Or Changing Scenes* (1968).

1899–1966 **C. S. Forester,** author of the twelve Horatio Hornblower novels (1937–1967).

1899–1961 **Ernest Hemingway,** author of *The Sun Also Rises* (1926), *A Farewell to Arms* (1929), *To Have and Have Not* (1937), *For Whom the Bell Tolls* (1940), *Across the River and into the Trees* (1950), *The Old Man and the Sea* (1951); critical and memoir writings include *A Moveable Feast* (1964).

**1899–1998 Janet Lewis,** author of *The Invasion: A Narrative of Events concerning the Johnson Family of St. Mary's* (1932), *The Wife of Martin Guerre* (1941), *Against a Darkening Sky* (1943), *The Trial of Sören Qvist* (1947), *The Ghost of Monsieur Scarron* (1959).

**1899–1977 Vladimir Nabokov,** author of several Russian novels translated into English (second date is that of the approved translation), including *Mary* (1926, 1970), *King, Queen, Knave* (1928, 1968), *Luzhin's Defense* (1930, 1964), *The Eye* (1930, 1971), *Glory* (1932, 1971), *Laughter in the Dark* (1933, 1938), *Despair* (1934, 1965), *Invitation to a Beheading* (1936, 1959), *The Gift* (1938, 1963); English novels include *The Real Life of Sebastian Knight* (1941), *Bend Sinister* (1947), *Lolita* (1955), *Pnin* (1957), *Pale Fire* (1962), *Ada, or Ardor* (1969), *Transparent Things* (1972), *Look at the Harlequins!* (1974); critical and other writings include *Speak, Memory* (1967), *Strong Opinions* (1973), *Lectures on Literature* (1980), *Lectures on Russian Literature* (1981), *Lectures on Don Quixote* (1983).

**1900–1945 Zelda Fitzgerald** (Zelda Sayre), author of *Save Me the Waltz* (1932).

**1900–1976 Richard Hughes,** author of *A High Wind in Jamaica* (1929), *The Fox in the Attic* (1961), *The Wooden Shepherdess* (1973).

**1900–1984 Ethel Mannin,** author of *Martha* (1922), *Children of the Earth* (1930), *Ragged Banner: A Novel with an Index* (1931), *All Experience* (1932), *Love's Winnowing* (1932), *Venetian Blinds* (1933), *Men Are Unwise* (1934), *Cactus* (1935), *The Pure Flame* (1936), *South to Samarkand* (1936), *Red Rose* (1941), *The Late Miss Guthrie* (1976).

**1900–1949 Margaret Mitchell,** author of *Gone with the Wind* (1936).

**1900–1997 V. S. Pritchett,** author of *Clare Drummer* (1929), *Nothing Like Leather* (1935), *Dead Man Leading* (1937), *Mr. Beluncle* (1951); critical and autobiographical writings include *In My Good Books* (1943), *The Living Novel* (1946), *Books in General* (1953), *A Cab at the Door* (1968), *George Meredith and English Comedy* (1970), *Midnight Oil* (1971), *The Myth Makers: Essays on European, Russian and South American Novelists* (1979), *The Tale Bearers: Essays on English, American and Other Writers* (1980), *The Complete Essays* (1991), *The Pritchett Century* (1999, edited by Oliver Pritchett), *The Essential Pritchett* (2004).

**1900–1938 Thomas Wolfe,** author of *Look Homeward, Angel: A Story of the Buried Life* (1929), *Of Time and the River* (1935).

1901–2000 **Barbara Cartland,** author of *Jigsaw* (1923).

1901–1991 **Laura Riding,** author of *Four Unposted Letters to Catherine* (1930), *Everybody's Letters* (1933), *A Trojan Ending* (1937).

1902–1973 **Arna Bontemps,** author of *God Sends Sunday* (1931), *Black Thunder* (1936).

1902–1989 **Stella Gibbons,** author of *Cold Comfort Farm* (1932).

1902–1974 **Georgette Heyer,** author of *The Black Moth* (1921).

1902–1967 **Langston Hughes,** author of *Not without Laughter* (1930), *Tambourines to Glory* (1958).

1902–1971 **Stevie Smith,** author of *Novel on Yellow Paper* (1936).

1902–1983 **Christina Stead,** author of *Seven Poor Men of Sydney* (1934), *The Man Who Loved Children* (1940), *For Love Alone* (1945), *Letty Fox: Her Luck* (1946), *A Little Tea, a Little Chat* (1948), *Cotter's England* (1967).

1902–1968 **John Steinbeck,** author of *Cup of Gold* (1929), *To a God Unknown* (1933), *Tortilla Flat* (1935), *In Dubious Battle* (1936), *Of Mice and Men* (1937), *The Grapes of Wrath* (1939), *Cannery Row* (1945), *The Pearl* (1947), *East of Eden* (1952), *Sweet Thursday* (1954), *The Short Reign of Pippin IV: A Fabrication* (1957), *The Winter of Our Discontent* (1961), *Travels with Charley: In Search of America* (1962), *The Acts of King Arthur and His Noble Knights* (1976).

1903–1987 **Erskine Caldwell,** author of *Tobacco Road* (1932), *God's Little Acre* (1933).

1903–1974 **Walter Greenwood,** author of *Love on the Dole* (1932).

1903–1977 **Anaïs Nin,** author of *Cities of the Interior* (1959), *Delta of Venus* (1977); other writings include *D. H. Lawrence: An Unprofessional Study* (1932).

1903–1950 **George Orwell** (Eric Arthur Blair), author of *Burmese Days* (1934), *A Clergyman's Daughter* (1935), *Keep the Aspidistra Flying* (1936), *Coming Up for Air* (1939), *Animal Farm: A Fairy Story* (1945), *Nineteen Eighty-Four* (1949); critical writings include *Inside the Whale and Other Essays* (1946).

1903–1988 **Alan Paton,** author of *Cry, the Beloved Country* (1948).

1903–2009 **Edward Upward,** author of *The Spiral Ascent* (1962–1977: *In the Thirties,* 1962; *The Rotten Elements,* 1969; *No Home but the Struggle,* 1977).

1903–1966 **Evelyn Waugh,** author of *Decline and Fall* (1928), *Vile Bodies* (1930), *Black Mischief* (1932), *A Handful of Dust* (1934), *Scoop* (1938), *Put Out More Flags* (1942), *Brideshead Revisited: The Sacred and Profane Memories of Captain Charles Ryder* (1945), *The Loved One: An Anglo-American Tragedy* (1948), *Helena* (1950), *Men at Arms* (1952), *Love among the Ruins* (1953), *Officers and Gentlemen* (1955), *The Ordeal of Gilbert Pinfold* (1957), *Unconditional Surrender* (1961).

1903–1940 **Nathanael West** (Nathan Wallenstein Weinstock), author of *The Dream Life of Balso Snell* (1931), *Miss Lonelyhearts* (1933), *A Cool Million: The Dismantling of Lemuel Pitkin* (1934), *The Day of the Locust* (1939).

1904–1966 **Margery Allingham,** author of *Blackkerchief Dick* (1923).

1904–1979 **James T. Farrell,** author of the Studs Lonigan trilogy: *Young Lonigan* (1932), *The Young Manhood of Studs Lonigan* (1934), *Judgment Day* (1935).

1904–1991 **Graham Greene,** author of *The Man Within* (1929), *Stamboul Train* (1932), *It's a Battlefield* (1934), *Brighton Rock* (1938), *The Confidential Agent* (1939), *The Power and the Glory* (1940), *The Heart of the Matter* (1948), *The End of the Affair* (1951), *The Quiet American* (1955), *Our Man in Havana* (1958), *A Burnt-Out Case* (1960), *The Comedians* (1966), *Monsignor Quixote* (1982); other writings include *The Lawless Roads: A Mexican Journey* (1939).

1904–1986 **Christopher Isherwood,** author of *All the Conspirators* (1928), *The Memorial* (1932), *Mr. Norris Changes Trains* (1935), *Goodbye to Berlin* (1939), *Prater Violet* (1945), *The World in the Evening* (1954), *Down There on a Visit* (1962), *A Single Man* (1969); other writings include *Christopher and His Kind* (1976), *Diaries: 1939–1960*.

1905–2004 **Mulk Raj Anand,** author of *Untouchable* (1935), *Coolie* (1936), *The Village* (1939), *Across the Black Waters* (1939), *The Sword and the Sickle* (1942), *The Private Life of an Indian Prince* (1953).

1905–1974 **H. E. Bates,** author of *The Two Sisters* (1926), *How Sleep the Brave* (1943), *Fair Stood the Wind for France* (1944), *The Darling Buds of May* (1958), *The Triple Echo* (1971).

1905–1973 **Henry Green** (Henry Vincent Yorke), author of *Blindness* (1926), *Living* (1929), *Party Going* (1939), *Caught* (1943), *Loving* (1945), *Back* (1946), *Concluding* (1948), *Nothing* (1950), *Doting* (1952); other writings include the memoir *Pack My Bag* (1940).

1905–1983 **Arthur Koestler,** author of *Darkness at Noon* (1940).

1905–1970 **John O'Hara,** author of *Appointment in Samara* (1934), *BUtterfield 8* (1935), *Pal Joey* (1940), *The Lockwood Concern* (1965).

1905–2000 **Anthony Powell,** author of *A Dance to the Music of Time* (twelve volumes, 1951–1975).

1905–1982 **Ayn Rand** (Alissa Zinovyevna Rosenbaum), author of *We the Living* (1936), *The Fountainhead* (1943), *Atlas Shrugged* (1957).

1905–1980 **C. P. Snow,** author of *Strangers and Brothers* (eleven novels, 1940–1970); critical and other writings include *The Two Cultures and the Scientific Revolution* (1959), *Trollope: His Life and Art* (1975), *The Realists* (1978).

1906–1989 **Samuel Beckett,** author of *Murphy* (1938), *Molloy* (1951), *Malone Dies* (1951), *The Unnamable* (1953), *Watt* (1945, publication 1953), *How It Is* (1961), *Dream of Fair to Middling Women* (1932, publication 1993); stories include *More Pricks Than Kicks* (1934); critical writings include *Proust* (1931).

1906–1998 **Catherine Cookson,** author of *Kate Hannigan* (1950).

1906–1994 **Michael Innes** (James Innes Mackintosh Stewart), author of *Death at the President's Lodging* (1936).

1906–2001 **R. K. Narayan,** author of *Swami and Friends* (1935), *The English Teacher* (1945), *The Financial Expert* (1951), *Waiting for the Mahatma* (1955), *The Guide* (1958), *The Man-Eater of Malgudi* (1961), *The Vendor of Sweets* (1967), *The Painter of Signs* (1977), *A Tiger for Malgudi* (1983).

1907–1988 **Robert A. Heinlein,** author of *Rocket Ship Galileo* (1947), *Red Planet* (1949), *Starship Trooper* (1959), *Stranger in a Strange Land* (1961), *Time Enough for Love* (1973).

1907–1989 **Daphne du Maurier,** author of *The Loving Spirit* (1931), *Jamaica Inn* (1936), *Rebecca* (1938), *Frenchman's Creek* (1941), *Hungry Hill* (1943), *My Cousin Rachel* (1951), *The Scapegoat* (1957).

1908–1980 **Olivia Manning,** author of *Fortunes of War: The Balkan Trilogy* (1981, separate volumes 1960, 1962, 1965), *Fortunes of War: The Levant Trilogy* (1982, separate volumes 1977, 1978, 1980).

1908–2006 **Raja Rao,** author of *Kanthapure* (1938), *The Serpent and the Rope* (1960).

1908–1960 **Richard Wright,** author of *Native Son* (1940), *The Outsider* (1953), *The Long Dream* (1958); other writings include *Black Boy* (1945), *American Hunger* (1977).

1909–1957 **Malcolm Lowry,** author of *Ultramarine* (1933), *Under the Volcano* (1947).

1909–2001 **Eudora Welty,** author of *Delta Wedding* (1946).

1910–1999 **Paul Bowles,** author of *The Sheltering Sky* (1949), *Let It Come Down* (1952).

1911–1994 **William Golding,** author of *Lord of the Flies* (1954), *The Inheritors* (1955), *Pincher Martin: The Two Deaths of Christopher Martin* (1956), *Free Fall* (1959), *The Spire* (1964), *Darkness Visible* (1979), *Rites of Passage* (1980), *Close Quarters* (1987), *Fire Down Below* (1989); other writings include *A Moving Target* (1982).

1911–1996 **Flann O'Brien** (Brian O'Nolan, Brian Ó Nualláin, Myles na gCopaleen), author of *At Swim-Two-Birds* (1939), *The Hard Life* (1962), *The Dalkey Archive* (1964), *The Third Policeman* (1967).

1912–1994 **J. L. Carr,** author of *A Month in the Country* (1980).

1912–1990 **Lawrence Durrell,** author of *The Black Book* (1938), *The Alexandria Quartet* (*Justine*, 1957; *Balthazar*, 1958; *Mountolive*, 1958; *Clea*, 1960).

1912–1989 **Mary McCarthy,** author of *The Company She Keeps* (1942), *The Groves of Academe* (1952), *A Charmed Life* (1955), *The Group* (1962); other writings include *Ideas and the Novel* (1980), *Intellectual Memoirs* (1992), *A Bolt from the Blue and Other Essays* (2002).

1912–1975 **Elizabeth Taylor,** author of *At Mrs. Lippincote's* (1945), *A Game of Hide and Seek* (1951), *The Real Life of Angel Deverell* (1957).

1912–1990 **Patrick White,** author of *Happy Valley* (1939), *The Aunt's Story* (1948), *The Tree of Man* (1955), *Voss* (1957), *Riders in the Chariot* (1961), *The Solid Mandala* (1966), *The Fringe of Leaves* (1976), *The Twyborn Affair* (1979); other writings include *Flaws in the Glass: A Self-Portrait* (1981).

1913–1995 **Robertson Davies,** author of the Salterton trilogy (1951–1958), the Deptford trilogy (1970–1975), the Cornish trilogy (1981–1988).

1913–1991 **Angus Wilson,** author of *Hemlock and After* (1952), *Anglo-Saxon Attitudes* (1956), *The Middle Age of Mrs. Eliot* (1958), *The Old Men at the Zoo* (1961), *Late Call* (1964), *As If by Magic* (1973); other writings include *The Wild Garden: Or Speaking of Writing* (1963), *The World of Charles Dickens* (1970), *Diversity and Depth in Fiction: Selected Critical Writings* (1983).

1914–1997 **William S. Burroughs,** author of *And the Hippos Were Boiled in Their Tanks* (1945, with Jack Kerouac, published 2008), *Queer* (1952, published 1985), *Junkie: Confessions of an Unredeemed Drug Addict* (1953), *Naked Lunch* (1959), *The Wild Boys* (1971), *Cities of the Red Night* (1981), *Place of Dead Roads* (1983), *The Western Lands* (1987).

1914–1994 **Ralph Ellison,** author of *Invisible Man* (1952), *Three Days before the Shooting* (2010).

1914–1965 **Randall Jarrell,** author of *Pictures from an Institution* (1954).

1914–1986 **Bernard Malamud,** author of *The Assistant* (1957), *The Fixer* (1966), *Dubin's Lives* (1979), *God's Grace* (1982).

1914–2000 **Patrick O'Brian,** author of the Aubrey-Maturin novels.

1915–2005 **Saul Bellow,** author of *Dangling Man* (1944), *The Victim* (1947), *The Adventures of Augie March* (1953), *Seize the Day* (1956), *Henderson the Rain King* (1959), *Herzog* (1964), *Mr. Sammler's Planet* (1970), *Humboldt's Gift* (1975), *The Dean's December* (1982), *More Die of Heartbreak* (1987), *A Theft* (1989), *Ravelstein* (2000); other writings include *It All Adds Up* (1994), *Saul Bellow: Letters* (2010).

1915–1998 **Margaret Walker,** author of *Jubilee* (1966).

1915–1948 **Denton Welch,** author of *Maiden Voyage* (1943), *In Youth Is Pleasure* (1944), *Brave and Cruel* (1949), *A Voice through a Cloud* (unfinished, 1950).

1916–1990 **Walker Percy,** author of *The Moviegoer* (1961), *The Thanatos Syndrome* (1987).

1916– **Mary Stewart,** author of *Madam, Will You Talk?* (1955).

1916–1991 **Frank Yerby,** author of *The Man from Dahomey* (1971).

1917–1973 **Jane Bowles,** author of *Two Serious Ladies* (1943).

1917–1993 **Anthony Burgess** (John Anthony Burgess Wilson), author of *The Malayan Trilogy* (1956–1959), *A Clockwork Orange* (1962), *The Enderby Quartet* (1963–1984), *Nothing Like the Sun* (1964), *Napoleon Symphony* (1974), *Abba Abba* (1977), *1985* (1978), *Earthly Powers* (1980), *The End of the World: An Entertainment* (1982), *Any Old Iron* (1988), *A Dead Man in Deptford* (1993); critical writings include *The Novel Today* (1963), *Here Comes Everybody: An Introduction to James Joyce for the Ordinary Reader* (1965), *Ninety-Nine Novels: The Best in English since 1939* (1984).

1917–2008 **Arthur C. Clarke,** author of *Childhood's End* (1953), *The City and the Stars* (1958), *Glide Path* (1963), *2001: A Space Odyssey* (1968), *Rendezvous with Rama* (1972), *The Fountains of Paradise* (1979).

1917–1967 **Carson McCullers** (Lula Carson Smith), author of *The Heart Is a Lonely Hunter* (1940), *Reflections in a Golden Eye* (1941), *The Member of the Wedding* (1946), *The Ballad of the Sad Café* (1951), *Clock without Hands* (1961).

1918–2006 **Muriel Spark,** author of *The Comforters* (1957), *Robinson* (1958), *Memento Mori* (1959), *The Ballad of Peckham Rye* (1960), *The Bachelors* (1960), *The Prime of Miss Jean Brodie* (1961), *Girls of Slender Means* (1963), *The Mandelbaum Gate* (1965), *The Driver's Seat* (1970), *The Abbess of Crewe* (1974), *Territorial Rights* (1979), *Loitering with Intent* (1981), *A Far Cry from Kensington* (1988), *Reality and Dreams* (1996), *Aiding and Abetting* (2000), *The Finishing School* (2004).

1919–2013 **Doris Lessing,** author of *The Grass Is Singing* (1950), *The Golden Notebook* (1962), *The Four-Gated City* (1969), *Briefing for a Descent into Hell* (1971), *Shikasta* (1979), *The Good Terrorist* (1985).

1919–1999 **Iris Murdoch,** author of *Under the Net* (1954), *The Sandcastle* (1957), *The Bell* (1958), *A Severed Head* (1961), *The Red and the Green* (1965), *Bruno's Dream* (1969), *The Black Prince* (1973), *The Sea, the Sea* (1978), *Nuns and Soldiers* (1980), *The Philosopher's Pupil* (1983); other writings include *Existentialists and Mystics: Writings on Philosophy and Literature* (1997).

1919–2010 **J. D. Salinger,** author of *The Catcher in the Rye* (1951), *Franny and Zooey* (1961).

1920–1992 **Isaac Asimov,** author of the Foundation series (1950–1993), Lucky Starr series (1952–1958); other writings include *It's Been a Good Life* (2002).

1920–2012 **Ray Bradbury,** author of *The Martian Chronicles* (1950), *Fahrenheit 451* (1953), *Something Wicked This Way Comes* (1962), *The Halloween Tree* (1972).

1920– **P. D. James,** author of *Cover Her Face* (1962).

1920–1978 **Paul Scott,** author of *The Raj Quartet* (1968–1974), *Staying On* (1977).

1920–1997 **Amos Tutuola,** author of *The Palm-Wine Drinkard* (1952).

1921–2007 **Cyprian Ekwensi,** author of *The Drummer Boy* (1960), *Jagua Nana* (1961).

1921–1992 **Alex Haley,** author of *Roots: The Saga of an American Family* (1976).

1921– **Wilson Harris,** author of *The Palace of the Peacock* (1960), *Jonestown* (1996), *The Mask of the Beggar* (2003), *The Ghost of Memory* (2006).

1921–1995 **Patricia Highsmith,** author of *Strangers on a Train* (1950).

1922–1995 **Kingsley Amis,** author of *Lucky Jim* (1954), *That Uncertain Feeling* (1955), *I Like It Here* (1958), *Take a Girl Like You* (1960), *One Fat Englishman* (1963), *The Anti-Death League* (1966), *Ending Up* (1974), *The Alteration* (1976), *Jake's Thing* (1978), *The Old Devils* (1986); other writings include *New Maps of Hell: A Survey of Science Fiction* (1960), *The James Bond Dossier* (1965), *Memoirs* (1991).

1922–1986 **John Braine,** author of *Room at the Top* (1957).

1922–1998 **William Gaddis,** author of *The Recognitions* (1955), *J R* (1975), *Carpenter's Gothic* (1985), *A Frolic of His Own* (1994), *Agapē Agape* (2002); critical and other writings include *The Rush for Second Place* (2002).

1922–1969 **Jack Kerouac,** author of *On the Road* (1957), *The Dharma Bums* (1958), *Visions of Gerard* (1963), *Desolation Angels* (1965).

1922–2007 **Kurt Vonnegut,** author of *Player Piano* (1952), *Cat's Cradle* (1963), *Slaughterhouse-Five* (1969), *Breakfast of Champions* (1973), *Deadeye Dick* (1982), *Galápagos* (1985), *Timequake* (1997); other writings include *Palm Sunday* (1981).

1923–2012 **Christine Brooke-Rose,** author of *The Language of Love* (1957), *The Dear Deceit* (1960), *Out* (1964), *Such* (1966), *Between* (1968), *Thru* (1975), *Amalgamemnon* (1984), *Xorandor* (1966), *Verbivore* (1990) *Textermination* (1991), *Remake* (1996), *Next* (1998), *Subscript* (1999), *Life, End of* (2006).

1923– **Nadine Gordimer,** author of *A World of Strangers* (1958), *The Late Bourgeois World* (1966), *A Guest of Honor* (1970), *The Conservationist* (1974), *Burger's Daughter* (1979), *None to Accompany Me* (1994), *The Pickup* (2001), *No Time like the Present* (2012); other writings include *Telling Times: Writing and Living, 1950–2008* (2010).

1923–1999 **Joseph Heller,** author of *Catch-22* (1961), *Something Happened* (1974), *Closing Time* (1994).

1923–2007 **Norman Mailer,** author of *The Naked and the Dead* (1948), *Barbary Shore* (1951), *An American Dream* (1965), *Why Are We in Vietnam?* (1967), *The Armies of the Night* (1968), *The Prisoner of Sex* (1971), *The Executioner's Song* (1979), *Ancient Evenings* (1983), *Tough Guys Don't Dance* (1984), *Harlot's Ghost* (1991), *The Castle in the Forest* (2007); other writings include *Advertisements for Myself* (1959), *Cannibals and Christians* (1966), *Pieces and Pontifications* (1982), *Oswald's Tale: An American Mystery* (1996).

1923–1994 **Samuel Selvon,** author of *The Lonely Londoners* (1956).

1924–1987 **James Baldwin,** author of *Go Tell It on the Mountain* (1953), *Giovanni's Room* (1956), *Another Country* (1962), *Tell Me How Long the Train's Been Gone* (1968), *If Beale Street Could Talk* (1974), *Just Above My Head* (1979); other writings include *Notes of a Native Son* (1955), *Nobody Knows My Name: More Notes of a Native Son* (1961), *The Fire Next Time* (1963).

1924–1984 **Truman Capote,** author of *Other Voices, Other Rooms* (1948), *The Grass Harp* (1951), *Breakfast at Tiffany's* (1958), *In Cold Blood* (1966).

1924–2004 **Janet Frame,** author of *Owls Do Cry* (1957), *The Carpathians* (1989).

1924– **William Gass,** author of *Omensetter's Luck* (1966), *In the Heart of the Heart of the Country* (1968), *Willie Master's Lonesome Wife* (1968), *The Tunnel* (1995), *Cartesian Sonata and Other Novellas* (1998).

1924–2003 **Leon Uris,** author of *Battle Cry* (1953), *Exodus* (1958), *Mila 18* (1961).

1925–1964 **Flannery O'Connor,** author of *Wise Blood* (1952), *The Violent Bear It Away* (1960).

1925–1994 **John Wain,** author of *Hurry on Down* (1953).

1925–2011 **Russell Hoban,** author of *Turtle Diary* (1975), *Riddley Walker* (1980), *Pilgermann* (1983).

1925–2012 **Gore Vidal,** author of *Williwaw* (1946), *The City and the Pillar* (1948), *The Judgment of Paris* (1952), *Julian* (1964), *Washington, D.C.* (1967), *Myra Breckenridge* (1968), *Burr* (1973), *Myron* (1974), *1876* (1976), *Kalki* (1978), *Creation* (1981), *Duluth* (1983), *Lincoln* (1984), *Empire* (1987), *The Golden Age* (2000); critical and other writings include *United States: Essays, 1952–1992* (1993), *Palimpsest: A Memoir* (1995), *The Last Empire: Essays, 1992–2000* (2001), *Point to Point Navigation: A Memoir* (2006), *The Selected Essays of Gore Vidal* (2008).

1925–2013 **Elmore Leonard,** author of *The Bounty Hunters* (1953), *Get Shorty* (1990), *Rum Punch* (1992), *Tishomingo Blues* (2002), *Djibouti* (2010), *Raylan* (2011).

1925–2006 **William Styron,** author of *Set This House on Fire* (1960), *The Confessions of Nat Turner* (1967), *Sophie's Choice* (1980), *Darkness Visible* (1999).

1926– **Harper Lee,** author of *To Kill a Mockingbird* (1960).

1926–1988 **John Clellon Holmes,** author of *Go* (1952).

1926–2005 **John Fowles,** author of *The Collector* (1963), *The Magus* (1966), *The French Lieutenant's Woman* (1969), *Daniel Martin* (1977), *Mantissa* (1982); other writings include *Wormholes: Essays and Occasional Writings* (1998).

1927– **George Lamming,** author of *In the Castle of My Skin* (1953), *Natives of My Person* (1972).

1928–1982 **Philip K. Dick,** author of *The Man in the High Castle* (1962), *The Three Stigmata of Palmer Eldritch* (1965), *Do Androids Dream of Electric Sheep?* (1968), *A Scanner Darkly* (1977).

1928–2004 **Hubert Selby Jr.,** author of *Last Exit to Brooklyn* (1964).

1928–2010 **Alan Sillitoe,** author of *Saturday Night and Sunday Morning* (1958), *The Loneliness of the Long Distance Runner* (1959).

1928– **Cynthia Ozick,** author of *Trust* (1966), *The Puttermesser Papers* (1997), *Foreign Bodies* (2010); critical writings include *Art and Ardor* (1983), *Metaphor & Memory* (1989), *What Henry James Knew and Other Essays on Writers* (1993), *Fame & Folly: Essays* (1996), *Quarrel & Quandary* (2000).

1928– **Onuora Nzekwu,** author of *Blade among the Boys* (1962).

1929– **Ursula K. Le Guin,** author of *Roscannon's World* (1966), *The Left Hand of Darkness* (1969), *The Telling* (2000).

1930–2009 **J. G. Ballard,** author of *The Atrocity Exhibition* (1970), *Crash* (1973), *Concrete Island* (1974), *The Unlimited Dream Company* (1979), *Hello America* (1981), *Empire of the Sun* (1984), *The Day of Creation* (1987).

1930– **Ruth Rendell,** author of *From Doon with Death* (1964).

1930– **Edna O'Brien,** author of *The Country Girls* (1960), *The Lonely Girl* (retitled *Girl with Green Eyes,* 1962), *Girls in Their Married Bliss* (1964), *A Pagan Place* (1970), *House of Splendid Isolation* (1994), *Down by the River* (1996), *Byron in Love* (2009).

1930– **John Barth,** author of *The Sot-Weed Factor* (1960), *Giles Goat-Boy* (1966), *Once upon a Time: A Floating Opera* (1996), *Coming Soon!!!* (2001).

1930– **Harry Mathews,** author of *The Conversions* (1962), *Tlooth* (1966), *The Sinking of the Odradek Stadium* (1975), *Cigarettes* (1987).

1930– **Elaine Feinstein,** author of *The Circle* (1970), *The Border* (1984), *Loving Brecht* (1992).

1930–2013 **Chinua Achebe,** author of *Things Fall Apart* (1958), *No Longer at Ease* (1960), *Arrow of God* (1964), *A Man of the People* (1966), *Anthills of the Savannah* (1987); other writings include *Hopes and Impediments: Selected Essays, 1965– 1987* (1988), *The Education of a British-Protected Child* (2009).

1931– **Walter Abish,** author of *Alphabetical Africa* (1974), *How German Is It / Wie deutsch ist es* (1980).

1931– **Toni Morrison** (Chloe Ardelia Wofford), author of *The Bluest Eye* (1970), *Song of Solomon* (1977), *Beloved* (1987), *Jazz* (1992), *Home* (2012).

1931–1989 **Donald Barthelme,** author of *Snow White* (1967), *The Dead Father* (1975), *Paradise* (1986), *The King* (1990); critical writings include *Guilty Pleasures* (1974).

1931–2001 **Mordecai Richler,** author of *The Apprenticeship of Duddy Kravitz* (1959), *Cocksure* (1968), *Solomon Gursky Was Here* (1989), *Barney's Vision* (1997).

1931– **E. L. Doctorow,** author of *Welcome to Hard Times* (1960), *Big as Life* (1966), *The Book of Daniel* (1971), *Ragtime* (1975), *Loon Lake* (1980), *World's Fair* (1985), *Billy Bathgate* (1989), *The March* (2005); other writings include *Poets and Presidents: Selected Essays, 1977–1992* (1995).

1931– **Tom Wolfe,** author of *The Bonfire of the Vanities* (1987), *A Man in Full* (1998), *I Am Charlotte Simmons* (2004); other writings include *The Kandy-Kolored Tangerine-Flake Streamline Baby* (1965), and *The New Journalism,* edited with E. W. Johnson (1973).

1931– **Cormac McCarthy,** author of *The Orchard Keeper* (1965), *Blood Meridian or the Evening Redness in the West* (1985), *All the Pretty Horses* (1992), *The Crossing* (1994), *Cities of the Plain* (1998), *No Country for Old Men* (2005), *The Road* (2006).

1931– **Frederic Michael Raphael,** author of *Lindmann* (1963), *Like Men Betrayed* (1970), *The Glittering Prizes* (1976), *A Double Life* (1993), *Fame and Fortune* (2007), *Final Demands* (2010); critical writings include *Somerset Maugham and His World* (1976), *The Necessity of Anti-Semitism* (1998).

1932–2000 **Malcolm Bradbury,** author of *The History Man* (1975); other writings include *The Social Context of Modern English Literature* (1971), *The Modern American Novel* (1983), *The Modern British Novel* (1993).

1932–2004 **Maurice Shadbolt,** author of *Strangers and Journeys* (1972), *Season of the Jew* (1987), *Monday's Warriors* (1990), *The House of Strife* (1993).

1932–2009 **John Updike,** author of *The Poorhouse Fair* (1959), *Rabbit, Run* (1960), *The Centaur* (1963), *Couples* (1968), *Bech: A Book* (1970), *Rabbit Redux* (1971), *Rabbit Is Rich* (1981), *Bech Is Back* (1982), *The Witches of Eastwick* (1984), *Rabbit at Rest* (1990), *Memories of the Ford Administration* (1992), *Bech at Bay* (1998), *Rabbit Remembered* (2001), *Terrorist* (2006); critical and other writings include *Self-Consciousness* (1989), *Due Considerations: Essays and Criticism* (2007).

1932– **V. S. Naipaul,** author of *The Mystic Masseur* (1957), *The Suffrage of Elvira* (1958), *Miguel Street* (1959), *A House for Mr. Biswas* (1961), *In a Free State* (1971), *Guerrillas* (1975), *A Bend in the River* (1979), *The Enigma of Arrival* (1987), *A Way in the World* (1994), *Half a Life* (2001); other writings include *The Middle Passage* (1962), *Reading & Writing: A Personal Account* (2000), *The Writer and the World* (2002), *Literary Occasions: Essays* (2003).

1933– **Philip Roth,** author of *Goodbye, Columbus* (1959), *Portnoy's Complaint* (1969), *Our Gang* (1971), *The Breast* (1972), *My Life as a Man* (1974), *The Professor of Desire* (1977), *The Ghost Writer* (1979), *Sabbath's Theater* (1995), *American Pastoral* (1997), *I Married a Communist* (1998), *The Human Stain* (2000), *The Dying Animal* (2001), *Everyman* (2006), *Indignation* (2008); other writings include *Reading Myself and Others* (1976).

1933–1973 **B. S. Johnson,** author of *Travelling People* (1963), *Albert Angelo* (1964), *The Unfortunates* (1969), *House Mother Normal* (1971), *Christie Malry's Own Double-Entry* (1973).

1933–1982 **John Gardner,** author of *Grendel* (1971); other writings include *The Forms of Fiction* (1962), *On Moral Fiction* (1978).

1933– **Barbara Taylor Bradford,** author of *A Woman of Substance* (1979).

1934– **Alasdair Gray,** author of *Lanark: A Life in Four Books* (1981), *Janine* (1984), *Something Leather* (1990), *Poor Things* (1992).

1934– **Wole Soyinka,** author of *The Interpreters* (1964), *Season of Anomy* (1972).

1934– **Joan Didion,** author of *Run River* (1963), *Play It as It Lays* (1970).

1934–2006 **John McGahern,** author of *The Barracks* (1963), *The Dark* (1965), *The Leavetaking* (1975), *The Pornographer* (1980), *Amongst Women* (1990), *That They May Face the Rising Sun* (2001).

1934– **David Malouf,** author of *Johnno* (1975), *An Imaginary Life* (1978), *Fly Away Peter* (1982), *The Great World* (1990), *Remembering Babylon* (1993), *The Conversation at Curlow Creek* (1996), *Ransom* (2009).

1935–1979 **J. G. Farrell,** author of *Troubles* (1970), *The Siege of Krishnapur* (1973), *The Singapore Grip* (1978).

1935– **Thomas Keneally,** author of *Schindler's Ark* (1982).

1935– **D. M. Thomas,** author of *The White Hotel* (1981).

1935– **Earl Lovelace,** author of *While Gods Are Falling* (1965), *The Schoolmaster* (1968), *The Dragon Can't Dance* (1979), *The Wine of Astonishment* (1983), *Salt* (1996), *Is Just a Movie* (2011).

1935– **David Lodge,** author of *The Picturegoers* (1960), *The British Museum Is Falling Down* (1965), *Changing Places: A Tale of Two Campuses* (1975), *How Far Can You Go?* (1980), *Small World: An Academic Romance* (1984), *Paradise News* (1991), *Author, Author* (2004), *A Man of Parts* (2011); other writings include *Language of Fiction* (1966), *The Novelist at the Crossroads* (1971), *The Modes of Modern Writing* (1977), *The Art of Fiction* (1992), *Consciousness and the Novel* (2003).

1935– **Annie Proulx,** author of *The Shipping News* (1993).

1936– **Don DeLillo,** author of *Americana* (1971), *Ratner's Star* (1976), *Players* (1977), *Amazons* (1980), *White Noise* (1985), *Libra* (1988), *Mao II* (1991), *Underworld* (1997), *The Body Artist* (2001), *Cosmopolis* (2003), *Falling Man* (2007).

1936– **A. S. Byatt,** author of *Shadow of the Sun* (1964), *The Game* (1967), *The Virgin in the Garden* (1978), *Still Life* (1985), *Possession: A Romance* (1990), *The Biographer's Tale* (2001); other writings include *Degrees of Freedom: The Early Novels of Iris Murdoch* (1965).

1936– **Larry McMurtry,** author of *The Last Picture Show* (1966), *Lonesome Dove* (1985).

1937– **Thomas Pynchon,** author of *V.* (1963), *The Crying of Lot 49* (1966), *Gravity's Rainbow* (1973), *Vineland* (1990), *Mason & Dixon* (1997), *Against the Day* (2006).

1937– **Jilly Cooper,** author of *Emily* (1975), *Polo* (1991).

1937– **Anita Desai,** author of *Clear Light of Day* (1980), *Baumgartner's Bombay* (1988), *Journey to Ithaca* (1995), *Fasting Feasting* (1999), *The Zigzag Way* (2004).

1937–1986 **Bessie Head,** author of *When Rain Clouds Gather* (1968), *Maru* (1971), *A Question of Power* (1974).

1937–2005 **Hunter S. Thompson,** author of *Hell's Angels: The Strange and Terrible Saga of the Outlaw Motorcycle Gangs* (1966), *Fear and Loathing in Las Vegas: A Savage Journey to the Heart of the American Dream* (1971).

1938– **Joyce Carol Oates,** author of *With Shuddering Fall* (1964), *them* (1969), *Wonderland* (1971), *Do with Me What You Will* (1973), *The Assassins* (1975), *Childwold* (1976), *Because It Is Bitter, and Because It Is My Heart* (1990), *Black Water* (1992), *Zombie* (1995), *Blonde* (2000); critical writings include *Contraries: Essays* (1981), *The Faith of a Writer* (2003).

1938– **Ngũgĩ wa Thiong'o,** author of *Weep Not, Child* (1964), *The River Between* (1965), *The Grain of Wheat* (1967), *The Black Hermit* (1968), *Petals of Blood* (1978), *Wizard of the Crow* (2006); other writings include *Decolonising the Mind: The Politics of Language in African Literature* (1986).

1939– **Ayi Kwei Armah,** author of *The Beautyful Ones Are Not Yet Born* (1968).

1939– **Margaret Atwood,** author of *The Edible Woman* (1969), *Surfacing* (1972), *The Handmaid's Tale* (1985), *The Robber Bride* (1993), *The Blind Assassin* (2000), *Oryx and Crake* (2003); other writings include *Survival: A Thematic Guide to Canadian Literature* (1972), *Strange Things: The Malevolent North in Canadian Literature* (1995); *Negotiating with the Dead: A Writer on Writing* (2002), *In Other Worlds: SF and the Human Imagination* (2012).

1940– **Edmund White,** author of *Forgetting Elena* (1973), *A Boy's Own Story* (1977), *The Beautiful Room Is Empty* (1988), *The Farewell Symphony* (1997).

1940– **J. M. Coetzee,** author of *Dusklands* (1974), *In the Heart of the Country* (1977), *Waiting for the Barbarians* (1980), *Life & Times of Michael K* (1983), *Foe* (1986), *Age* *of Iron* (1990), *The Master of Petersburg* (1994), *The Lives of Animals* (1999), *Disgrace* (1999), *Elizabeth Costello* (2003); critical writings include *Stranger Shores: Literary Essays, 1986–1999* (2001), *Inner Workings: Literary Essays, 2000–2005* (2007).

1940–1989 **Bruce Chatwin,** author of *In Patagonia* (1977), *The Viceroy of Ouidah* (1980), *On the Black Hill* (1982), *The Songlines* (1987), *Utz* (1988).

1940–1992 **Angela Carter,** author of *The Magic Toyshop* (1967), *The Infernal Desire Machines of Doctor Hoffman* (1972), *The Passion of New Eve* (1977), *Nights at the Circus* (1984), *Wise Children* (1991).

1940– **Gabriel Josipovici,** author of *Mobius the Stripper* (1974), *Contre-Jour: A Triptych after Pierre Bonnard* (1986), *The Big Glass* (1991), *In a Hotel Garden* (1993), *Moo Pak* (1995), *Goldberg: Variations* (2001), *Infinity* (2012); critical and other writings include *A Life* (2001), *Whatever Happened to Modernism* (2011).

1941– **Anne Tyler,** author of *If Morning Ever Comes* (1964), *Celestial Navigation* (1974), *Earthly Possessions* (1977), *Dinner at the Homesick Restaurant* (1982), *The Accidental Tourist* (1985), *Breathing Lessons* (1988), *Back When We Were Grownups* (2001).

1942– **Howard Jacobson,** author of *Coming from Behind* (1983), *The Finkler Question* (2010).

1943– **Marilynne Robinson,** author of *Housekeeping* (1980), *Gilead* (2004), *Home* (2008); critical writings include *Absence of Mind: The Dispelling of Inwardness from the Modern Myth of the Self* (2010), *When I Was a Child I Read Books: Essays* (2012).

1943– **Peter Carey,** author of *Bliss* (1981), *Illywhacker* (1985), *Oscar and Lucinda* (1988), *Jack Maggs* (1997), *True History of the Kelly Gang* (2000), *My Life as a Fake* (2003), *Theft: A Love Story* (2006).

1943– **Michael Ondaatje,** author of *The Collected Works of Billy the Kid: Left-Handed Poems* (1970), *Coming Through Slaughter* (1976), *In the Skin of a Lion* (1987), *The English Patient* (1992), *Anil's Ghost* (2000), *The Cat's Table* (2011).

1944– **Alice Walker,** author of *The Color Purple* (1982); other writings include *In Search of Our Mother's Gardens: Womanist Prose* (1984), *The Chicken Chronicles* (2011).

1944– **Richard Ford,** author of *A Piece of My Heart* (1976), *The Ultimate Good Luck* (1981), *The Sportswriter* (1986), *Independence Day* (1995), *The Lay of the Land* (2006).

1946– **Julian Barnes,** author of *Metroland* (1980), *Before She Met Me* (1982), *Flaubert's Parrot* (1984), *A History of the World in 10 1/2 Chapters* (1989), *Talking It Over* (1991), *The Porcupine* (1992), *England, England* (1998), *Love, Etc.* (2000), *Arthur and George* (2005), *The Sense of an Ending* (2011).

1947– **Danielle Steel,** author of *Going Home* (1973).

1947– **Keri Hulme,** author of *The Bone People* (1984).

1947– **Salman Rushdie,** author of *Grimus* (1975), *Midnight's Children* (1981), *Shame* (1983), *The Satanic Verses* (1988), *The Moor's Last Sigh* (1995), *The Ground Beneath Her Feet* (1999), *Fury* (2001), *Shalimar the Clown* (2005).

1947– **Stephen King,** author of *Carrie* (1974), *The Shining* (1977), *It* (1986), *Duma Key* (2008); other writings include *On Writing: A Memoir of the Craft* (2000).

1947– **Paul Auster,** author of *City of Glass* (1985), *Ghosts* (1986), *The Locked Room* (1986), *The Music of Chance* (1990), *Leviathan* (1992), *The Book of Illusions* (2002), *The Brooklyn Follies* (2005).

1948– **Ian McEwan,** author of *The Cement Garden* (1978), *The Comfort of Strangers* (1981), *The Child in Time* (1987), *The Innocent* (1990), *Black Dogs* (1992), *Enduring Love* (1997), *Amsterdam* (1998), *Atonement* (2001), *Saturday* (2005), *On Chesil Beach* (2007), *Solar* (2010).

1949– **Margaret Drabble,** author of *The Millstone* (1965); other writings include *Arnold Bennett: A Biography* (1974), *A Writer's Britain: Landscapes in Literature* (1979), *Angus Wilson: A Biography* (1995).

1949– **Peter Ackroyd,** author of *The Great Fire of London* (1982), *The Last Testament of Oscar Wilde* (1983), *Hawksmoor* (1985); other writings include *The Collection* (2001), *Albion: The Origins of the English Imagination* (2002).

1949– **Graham Swift,** author of *Shuttlecock* (1981), *Waterland* (1983), *Last Orders* (1996), *Wish You Were Here* (2011); other writings include *Making an Elephant* (2009).

1949– **Martin Amis,** author of *The Rachel Papers* (1973), *Dead Babies* (1975), *Success* (1978), *Other People: A Mystery Story* (1981), *Money: A Suicide Note* (1984), *London Fields* (1989), *Time's Arrow: Or the Nature of the Offence* (1991), *The Information* (1995), *Night Train* (1997), *Yellow Dog* (2003), *House of Meetings* (2006), *The Pregnant Widow* (2010), *Lionel Asbo: State of England* (2012); other writings include *Visiting Mrs. Nabokov, and Other Excursions* (1993), *The War against Cliché: Essays and Reviews, 1971–2000* (2001).

1950– **Timothy Mo,** author of *The Monkey King* (1978), *An Insular Possession* (1986).

1952– **Rohinton Mistry,** author of *Such a Long Journey* (1991), *A Fine Balance* (1995), *Family Matters* (2002).

1952– **William Boyd,** author of *A Good Man in Africa* (1981), *An Ice-Cream War* (1982), *Brazzaville Beach* (1990), *Nat Tate: An American Artist, 1928–1960* (1998).

1952– **Vikram Seth,** author of *The Golden Gate* (verse novel, 1986), *A Suitable Boy* (1993), *An Equal Music* (1999).

1952– **Hilary Mantel,** author of *Fludd* (1989), *A Place of Greater Safety* (1992), *Beyond Black* (2005), *Wolf Hall* (2009), *Bring Up the Bodies* (2012).

1954– **Kazuo Ishiguro,** author of *A Pale View of Hills* (1982), *An Artist of the Floating World* (1986), *The Remains of the Day* (1989), *The Unconsoled* (1995), *When We Were Orphans* (2000), *Never Let Me Go* (2005).

1954– **Alan Hollinghurst,** author of *The Swimming Pool Library* (1988), *The Folding Star* (1994), *The Spell* (1998), *The Line of Beauty* (2004), *The Stranger's Child* (2011).

1955– **Colm Tóibín,** author of *The South* (1990), *The Heather Blazing* (1992), *The Story of the Night* (1996), *The Blackwater Lightship* (1999), *The Master* (2004), *Brooklyn* (2009); critical writings include *Love in a Dark Time: Gay Lives from Wilde to Almodovar* (2002), *All a Novelist Needs: Essays on Henry James* (2010).

1955– **Jay McInerney,** author of *Bright Lights, Big City* (1984).

1957– **Tama Janowitz,** author of *American Dad* (1981), *Slaves of New York* (1986).

1958– **Caryl Phillips,** author of *The Final Passage* (1985), *A State of Independence* (1986), *Cambridge* (1991), *Crossing the River* (1993), *The Nature of Blood* (1997), *In* *the Falling Snow* (2009); other writings include *A New World Order: Selected Essays* (2001).

1958– **Helen Fielding,** author of *Bridget Jones's Diary* (1996), *Bridget Jones: The Edge of Reason* (1999).

1959– **Ben Okri,** author of *Flowers and Shadows* (1980), *The Landscapes Within* (1981), *The Famished Road* (1991), *Songs of Enchantment* (1993).

1959– **Jeanette Winterson,** author of *Oranges Are Not the Only Fruit* (1985), *The Passion* (1987), *Sexing the Cherry* (1989), *Written on the Body* (1992), *Gut Symmetries* (1997), *The PowerBook* (2000); critical and autobiographical writings include *Why Be Happy When You Could Be Normal?* (2012).

1959– **Jonathan Franzen,** author of *The Twenty-Seventh City* (1988), *Strong Motion* (1992), *The Corrections* (2001), *Freedom* (2010); other writings include *How to Be Alone* (2002), *The Discomfort Zone* (2006).

1960– **Jeffrey Eugenides,** author of *The Virgin Suicides* (1993), *Middlesex* (2002), *The Marriage Plot* (2011).

1961– **Richard Flanagan,** author of *Death of a River Guide* (1994), *The Sound of One Hand Clapping* (1997).

1961– **Arundhati Roy,** author of *The God of Small Things* (1997).

1962– **Anne Enright,** author of *The Wig My Father Wore* (1995), *The Gathering* (2007).

1962– **Chuck Palahniuk,** author of *Fight Club* (1996).

1962–2008 **David Foster Wallace,** author of *The Broom of the System* (1987), *Infinite Jest* (1996), *The Pale King: An Unfinished Novel* (2011).

1963– **Michael Chabon,** author of *The Amazing Adventures of Kavalier & Clay* (2000), *The Yiddish Policemen's Union* (2007).

1964– **Bret Easton Ellis,** author of *Less Than Zero* (1985), *The Rules of Attraction* (1987), *American Psycho* (1991), *Glamorama* (1998), *Lunar Park* (2005), *Imperial Bedrooms* (2010).

# Index

Page numbers in **bold** indicate the information is found in the Timeline.